# LEARNSMART ADVANTAGE WORKS

**LEARNSMART**

| A | B | C | D | |
|---|---|---|---|---|
| 30.5% | 33.5% | 22.6% | 8.7% | 4.7% |

| A | B | C | D | |
|---|---|---|---|---|
| 19.3% | 38.6% | 28.0% | 9.6% | 4.5% |

Without LearnSmart

## More C students
## earn B's

*Study: 690 students / 6 institutions

## Over 20%
more students
pass the class
with LearnSmart

*A&P Research Study

**LEARNSMART** Pass Rate - 70%

Without LearnSmart Pass Rate - 57%

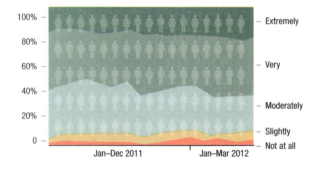

100%
80%
60%
40%
20%
0

— Extremely

— Very

— Moderately

— Slightly
— Not at all

Jan–Dec 2011          Jan–Mar 2012

## More than 60%
of all students agreed
LearnSmart was a
very or extremely
helpful learning tool

*Based on 750,000 student survey responses

 **> AVAILABLE** *ON-THE-GO*

http://bit.ly/LS4Apple

http://bit.ly/LS4Droid

How do you rank against your peers?

What you know (green) and what you still need to review (yellow), based on your answers.

Let's see how confident you are on the questions.

# COMPARE AND CHOOSE WHAT'S RIGHT FOR YOU

| | BOOK | LEARNSMART | ASSIGNMENTS | |
|---|:---:|:---:|:---:|---|
| **connect** | ✓ | ✓ | ✓ | LearnSmart, assignments, and SmartBook—all in one digital product for maximum savings! |
| **connect** Looseleaf | ✓ | ✓ | ✓ | Pop the pages into your own binder or carry just the pages you need. |
| **connect** Bound Book | ✓ | ✓ | ✓ | The #1 Student Choice! |
| **SMARTBOOK** Access Code | ✓ | ✓ | | The first and only book that adapts to you! |
| **LEARNSMART** ADVANTAGE Access Code | | ✓ | | The smartest way to get from a B to an A. |
| **Course**Smart eBook | ✓ | | | Save some green and some trees! |
| **create** | ✓ | ✓ | ✓ | Check with your instructor about a custom option for your course. |

> Buy directly from the source at http://shop.mheducation.com.

# Crafting and Executing Strategy

## THE QUEST FOR COMPETITIVE ADVANTAGE

Concepts and Cases

# Crafting and Executing Strategy

## THE QUEST FOR COMPETITIVE ADVANTAGE

Concepts and Cases   |   TWENTIETH EDITION

**Arthur A. Thompson**
*The University of Alabama*

**Margaret A. Peteraf**
*Dartmouth College*

**John E. Gamble**
*Texas A&M University–Corpus Christi*

**A. J. Strickland III**
*The University of Alabama*

CRAFTING AND EXECUTING STRATEGY: THE QUEST FOR COMPETITIVE ADVANTAGE, CONCEPTS AND CASES, TWENTIETH EDITION

Published by McGraw-Hill Education, 2 Penn Plaza, New York, NY 10121. Copyright © 2016 by McGraw-Hill Education. All rights reserved. Printed in the United States of America. Previous editions © 2014, 2012, 2010, and 2008. No part of this publication may be reproduced or distributed in any form or by any means, or stored in a database or retrieval system, without the prior written consent of McGraw-Hill Education, including, but not limited to, in any network or other electronic storage or transmission, or broadcast for distance learning.

Some ancillaries, including electronic and print components, may not be available to customers outside the United States.

This book is printed on acid-free paper.

1 2 3 4 5 6 7 8 9 0 DOW/DOW 1 0 9 8 7 6 5

ISBN 978-0-07-772059-9
MHID 0-07-772059-8

Senior Vice President, Products & Markets: Kurt L. Strand
Vice President, General Manager, Products & Markets: Michael Ryan
Vice President, Content Design & Delivery: Kimberly Meriwether David
Managing Director: Susan Gouijnstook
Director: Michael Ablassmeir
Director, Product Development: Meghan Campbell
Product Developer: Trina Hauger
Marketing Manager: Elizabeth Trepkowski

Director, Content Design & Delivery: Terri Schiesl
Program Manager: Mary Conzachi
Content Project Managers: Mary E. Powers, Daryl Bruflodt
Buyer: Michael McCormick
Design: Srdjan Savanovic
Content Licensing Specialists: Keri Johnson
Cover Image: © D-BASE/iStock, Getty Images
Compositor: Laserwords Private Limited
Printer: R. R. Donnelley

All credits appearing on page or at the end of the book are considered to be an extension of the copyright page.

### Library of Congress Cataloging-in-Publication Data

Thompson, Arthur A., 1940-
    Crafting and executing strategy : the quest for competitive advantage : concepts and cases/ Arthur A. Thompson, Margaret A. Peteraf, John E. Gamble, A. J. Strickland III. -- Twentieth edition.
        pages cm
    ISBN 978-0-07-772059-9 (alk. paper)
    1. Strategic planning. 2. Strategic planning–Case studies. I. Title.
HD30.28.T53 2015
658.4′012–dc23                                                                        2014033211

The Internet addresses listed in the text were accurate at the time of publication. The inclusion of a website does not indicate an endorsement by the authors or McGraw-Hill Education, and McGraw-Hill Education does not guarantee the accuracy of the information presented at these sites.

To our families and especially our spouses:
Hasseline, Paul, and Kitty.

**Arthur A. Thompson, Jr.,** earned his B.S. and Ph.D. degrees in economics from The University of Tennessee, spent three years on the economics faculty at Virginia Tech, and served on the faculty of The University of Alabama's College of Commerce and Business Administration for 24 years. In 1974 and again in 1982, Dr. Thompson spent semester-long sabbaticals as a visiting scholar at the Harvard Business School.

His areas of specialization are business strategy, competition and market analysis, and the economics of business enterprises. In addition to publishing over 30 articles in some 25 different professional and trade publications, he has authored or co-authored five textbooks and six computer-based simulation exercises. His textbooks and strategy simulations have been used at well over 1,000 college and university campuses worldwide.

Dr. Thompson spends much of his off-campus time giving presentations, putting on management development programs, working with companies, and helping operate a business simulation enterprise in which he is a major partner.

Dr. Thompson and his wife of 53 years have two daughters, two grandchildren, and a Yorkshire Terrier.

**Margaret A. Peteraf** is the Leon E. Williams Professor of Management at the Tuck School of Business at Dartmouth College. She is an internationally recognized scholar of strategic management, with a long list of publications in top management journals. She has earned myriad honors and prizes for her contributions, including the 1999 Strategic Management Society Best Paper Award recognizing the deep influence of her work on the field of Strategic Management. Professor Peteraf is a fellow of the Strategic Management Society and the Academy of Management. She served previously as a member of the Board of Governors of both the Society and the Academy of Management and as Chair of the Business Policy and Strategy Division of the Academy. She has also served in various editorial roles and on numerous editorial boards, including the *Strategic Management Journal,* the *Academy of Management Review,* and *Organization Science.* She has taught in Executive Education programs in various programs around the world and has won teaching awards at the MBA and Executive level.

Professor Peteraf earned her Ph.D., M.A., and M.Phil. at Yale University and held previous faculty appointments at Northwestern University's Kellogg Graduate School of Management and at the University of Minnesota's Carlson School of Management.

**John E. Gamble** is a Professor of Management and Dean of the College of Business at Texas A&M University–Corpus Christi. His teaching and research for nearly 20 years has focused on strategic management at the undergraduate and graduate levels. He has conducted courses in strategic management in Germany since 2001, which have been sponsored by the University of Applied Sciences in Worms.

Dr. Gamble's research has been published in various scholarly journals and he is the author or co-author of more than 75 case studies published in an assortment of strategic management and strategic marketing texts. He has done consulting on industry and market analysis for clients in a diverse mix of industries.

Professor Gamble received his Ph.D., Master of Arts, and Bachelor of Science degrees from The University of Alabama and was a faculty member in the Mitchell College of Business at the University of South Alabama before his appointment to the faculty at Texas A&M University–Corpus Christi.

**Dr. A. J. (Lonnie) Strickland** is the Thomas R. Miller Professor of Strategic Management at the Culverhouse School of Business at The University of Alabama. He is a native of north Georgia, and attended the University of Georgia, where he received a Bachelor of Science degree in math and physics; Georgia Institute of Technology, where he received a Master of Science in industrial management; and Georgia State University, where he received his Ph.D. in business administration.

Lonnie's experience in consulting and executive development is in the strategic management arena, with a concentration in industry and competitive analysis. He has developed strategic planning systems for numerous firms all over the world. He served as Director of Marketing and Strategy at BellSouth, has taken two companies to the New York Stock Exchange, is one of the founders and directors of American Equity Investment Life Holding (AEL), and serves on numerous boards of directors. He is a very popular speaker in the area of strategic management.

Lonnie and his wife, Kitty, have been married for 48 years. They have two children and two grandchildren. Each summer, Lonnie and his wife live on their private game reserve in South Africa where they enjoy taking their friends on safaris.

# PREFACE

**B**y offering the most engaging, clearly articulated, and conceptually sound text on strategic management, *Crafting and Executing Strategy* has been able to maintain its position as the leading textbook in strategic management for 30 years. With this latest edition, we build on this strong foundation, maintaining the attributes of the book that have long made it the most teachable text on the market, while updating the content, sharpening its presentation, and providing enlightening new illustrations and examples.

The distinguishing mark of the 20th edition is its enriched and enlivened presentation of the material in each of the 12 chapters, providing an as up-to-date and engrossing discussion of the core concepts and analytical tools as you will find anywhere. As with each of our new editions, there is an accompanying lineup of exciting new cases that bring the content to life and are sure to provoke interesting classroom discussions, deepening students' understanding of the material in the process.

While this 20th edition retains the 12-chapter structure of the prior edition, every chapter—indeed every paragraph and every line—has been reexamined, refined, and refreshed. New content has been added to keep the material in line with the latest developments in the theory and practice of strategic management. In other areas, coverage has been trimmed to keep the book at a more manageable size. Scores of new examples have been added, along with 15 new Illustration Capsules, to enrich understanding of the content and to provide students with a ringside view of strategy in action. The result is a text that cuts straight to the chase in terms of what students really need to know and gives instructors a leg up on teaching that material effectively. It remains, as always, solidly mainstream and balanced, mirroring *both* the penetrating insight of academic thought and the pragmatism of real-world strategic management.

A standout feature of this text has always been the tight linkage between the content of the chapters and the cases. The lineup of cases that accompany the 20th edition is outstanding in this respect—a truly appealing mix of strategically relevant and thoughtfully crafted cases, certain to engage students and sharpen their skills in applying the concepts and tools of strategic analysis. Many involve high-profile companies that the students will immediately recognize and relate to; all are framed around key strategic issues and serve to add depth and context to the topical content of the chapters. We are confident you will be impressed with how well these cases work in the classroom and the amount of student interest they will spark.

For some years now, growing numbers of strategy instructors at business schools worldwide have been transitioning from a purely text-case course structure to a more robust and energizing text-case-simulation course structure. Incorporating a competition-based strategy simulation has the strong appeal of providing class members with *an immediate and engaging opportunity to apply the concepts and analytical tools covered in the chapters and to become personally involved in crafting and executing a strategy for a virtual company that they have been assigned to manage and that competes head-to-head with companies run by other class members.* Two widely used and pedagogically effective online strategy simulations, *The Business Strategy Game* and *GLO-BUS,* are optional companions for this text. Both simulations were created by Arthur Thompson, one of the text authors, and, like the cases, are closely linked to the content of each chapter in the text. The Exercises for Simulation Participants, found at the end of each chapter, provide clear guidance to class members in applying the concepts and analytical tools covered in the chapters to the issues and decisions that they have to wrestle with in managing their simulation company.

To assist instructors in assessing student achievement of program learning objectives, in line with AACSB requirements, the 20th edition includes a set of Assurance of Learning Exercises at the end of each chapter that link to the specific learning objectives appearing at the beginning of each chapter and highlighted throughout the text. An important instructional feature of the 20th edition is its more closely *integrated* linkage of selected chapter-end Assurance of Learning Exercises and cases to the publisher's web-based assignment and assessment platform called Connect™. Your students will be able to use the online Connect™ supplement to (1) complete two of the Assurance of Learning Exercises appearing at the end of each of the 12 chapters, (2) complete chapter-end quizzes, and (3) enter their answers to a select number of the suggested assignment questions for 7 of the 31 cases in this edition. Many of the Connect™ exercises are automatically graded, thereby enabling you to easily assess the learning that has occurred.

In addition, both of the companion strategy simulations have a built-in Learning Assurance Report that quantifies how well each member of your class performed on nine skills/learning measures *versus tens of thousands of other students worldwide* who completed the simulation in the past 12 months. We believe the chapter-end Assurance of Learning Exercises, the all-new online and automatically graded Connect™ exercises, and the Learning Assurance Report generated at the conclusion of *The Business Strategy Game* and *GLO-BUS* simulations provide you with easy-to-use, empirical measures of student learning in your course. All can be used in conjunction with other instructor-developed or school-developed scoring rubrics and assessment tools to comprehensively evaluate course or program learning outcomes and measure compliance with AACSB accreditation standards.

Taken together, the various components of the 20th-edition package and the supporting set of instructor resources provide you with enormous course design flexibility and a powerful kit of teaching/learning tools. We've done our very best to ensure that the elements constituting the 20th edition will work well for you in the classroom, help you economize on the time needed to be well prepared for each class, and cause students to conclude that your course is one of the very best they have ever taken—from the standpoint of both enjoyment and learning.

## DIFFERENTIATING FEATURES OF THE 20TH EDITION

Six standout features strongly differentiate this text and the accompanying instructional package from others in the field:

1. *Our integrated coverage of the two most popular perspectives on strategic management—positioning theory and resource-based theory—is unsurpassed by any other leading strategy text.* Principles and concepts from both the positioning perspective and the resource-based perspective are prominently and comprehensively integrated into our coverage of crafting both single-business and multibusiness strategies. By highlighting the relationship between a firm's resources and

capabilities to the activities it conducts along its value chain, we show explicitly how these two perspectives relate to one another. Moreover, in Chapters 3 through 8 it is emphasized repeatedly that a company's strategy must be matched *not only* to its external market circumstances *but also* to its internal resources and competitive capabilities.

2. *Our coverage of cooperative strategies and the role that interorganizational activity can play in the pursuit of competitive advantage, is similarly distinguished.* The topics of the value net (newly added), strategic alliances, licensing, joint ventures, and other types of collaborative relationships are featured prominently in a number of chapters and are integrated into other material throughout the text. We show how strategies of this nature can contribute to the success of single-business companies as well as multibusiness enterprises, whether with respect to firms operating in domestic markets or those operating in the international realm.

3. *With a stand-alone chapter devoted to this topic, our coverage of business ethics, corporate social responsibility, and environmental sustainability goes well beyond that offered by any other leading strategy text.* Chapter 9, "Ethics, Corporate Social Responsibility, Environmental Sustainability, and Strategy," fulfills the important functions of (1) alerting students to the role and importance of ethical and socially responsible decision making and (2) addressing the accreditation requirement of the AACSB International that business ethics be visibly and thoroughly embedded in the core curriculum. Moreover, discussions of the roles of values and ethics are integrated into portions of other chapters to further reinforce why and how considerations relating to ethics, values, social responsibility, and sustainability should figure prominently into the managerial task of crafting and executing company strategies.

4. *Long known as an important differentiator of this text, the case collection in the 20th edition is truly unrivaled* from the standpoints of student appeal, teachability, and suitability for drilling students in the use of the concepts and analytical treatments in Chapters 1 through 12. The 31 cases included in this edition are the very latest, the best, and the most on target that we could find. The ample information about the cases in the Instructor's Manual makes it effortless to select a set of cases each term that will capture the interest of students from start to finish.

5. *The text is now more tightly linked to the publisher's trailblazing web-based assignment and assessment platform called Connect™.* This will enable professors to gauge class members' prowess in accurately completing (a) selected chapter-end exercises, (b) chapter-end quizzes, and (c) the creative author-developed exercises for seven of the cases in this edition.

6. *Two cutting-edge and widely used strategy simulations*—The Business Strategy Game *and* GLO-BUS—*are optional companions to the 20th edition.* These give you an unmatched capability to employ a text-case-simulation model of course delivery.

## ORGANIZATION, CONTENT, AND FEATURES OF THE 20TH-EDITION TEXT CHAPTERS

- Chapter 1 serves as a brief, general introduction to the topic of strategy, focusing on the central questions of *"What is strategy?"* and *"Why is it important?"* As such, it serves as the perfect accompaniment for your opening-day lecture on what the course is all about and why it matters. Using the newly added example of Starbucks to drive home the concepts in this chapter, we introduce students to what we mean by "competitive advantage" and the key features of business-level strategy. Describing strategy making as a process, we explain why a company's strategy is partly planned and partly reactive and why a strategy tends to co-evolve with its environment over time. We show that a viable business model must provide both an attractive value proposition for the company's customers and a formula for making profits for the company. New to this chapter is a depiction of how the Value-Price-Cost Framework can be used to frame this discussion. We show how the mark of a winning strategy is its ability to pass three tests: (1) the *fit test* (for internal and external fit), (2) the *competitive advantage test,* and (3) the *performance test.* And we explain why good company performance depends not only upon a sound strategy but upon solid strategy execution as well.

- Chapter 2 presents a more complete overview of the strategic management process, covering topics ranging from the role of vision, mission, and values to what constitutes good corporate governance. It makes a great assignment for the second day of class and provides a smooth transition into the heart of the course. It introduces students to such core concepts as strategic versus financial objectives, the balanced scorecard, strategic intent, and business-level versus corporate-level strategies. It explains why *all managers are on a company's strategy-making, strategy-executing team* and why a company's strategic plan is a collection of strategies devised by different managers at different levels in the organizational hierarchy. The chapter concludes with a section on the role of the board of directors in the strategy-making, strategy-executing process and examines the conditions that led to recent high-profile corporate governance failures.

- The next two chapters introduce students to the two most fundamental perspectives on strategy making: the positioning view, exemplified by Michael Porter's "five forces model of competition"; and the resource-based view. Chapter 3 provides *what has long been the clearest, most straightforward discussion of the five forces framework to be found in any text on strategic management.* It also offers a set of complementary analytical tools for conducting competitive analysis and demonstrates the importance of tailoring strategy to fit the circumstances of a company's industry and competitive environment. What's new in this edition is the inclusion of the value net framework for conducting analysis of how cooperative as well as competitive moves by various parties contribute to the creation and capture of value in an industry.

- Chapter 4 presents the resource-based view of the firm, showing why resource and capability analysis is such a powerful tool for sizing up a company's competitive assets. It offers a simple framework for identifying a company's resources and capabilities and explains how the VRIN framework can be used to determine whether they can provide the company with a sustainable competitive advantage over its competitors. Other topics covered in this chapter include dynamic capabilities, SWOT analysis, value chain analysis, benchmarking, and competitive strength assessments, thus enabling a solid appraisal of a company's relative cost position and customer value proposition vis-á-vis its rivals. *An important feature of this chapter is a table showing how key financial and operating ratios are calculated and how to interpret them.* Students will find this table handy in doing the number crunching needed to evaluate whether a company's strategy is delivering good financial performance.

- Chapter 5 sets forth the basic approaches available for competing and winning in the marketplace in terms of the five generic competitive strategies—low-cost leadership, differentiation, best-cost provider, focused differentiation, and focused low cost. It describes when each of these approaches works best and what pitfalls to avoid. It explains the role of *cost drivers* and *uniqueness drivers* in reducing a company's costs and enhancing its differentiation, respectively.

- Chapter 6 focuses on *other strategic actions* a company can take to complement its competitive approach and maximize the power of its overall strategy. These include a variety of offensive or defensive competitive moves, and their timing, such as blue-ocean strategies and first-mover advantages and disadvantages. It also includes choices concerning the breadth of a company's activities (or its *scope* of operations along an industry's entire value chain), ranging from horizontal mergers and acquisitions, to vertical integration, outsourcing, and strategic alliances. This material serves to segue into the scope issues covered in the next two chapters on international and diversification strategies.

- Chapter 7 takes up the topic of how to compete in international markets. It begins with a discussion of why differing market conditions across countries must necessarily influence a company's strategic choices about how to enter and compete in foreign markets. It presents five major strategic options for expanding a company's geographic scope and competing in foreign markets: export strategies, licensing, franchising, establishing a wholly owned subsidiary via acquisition or "greenfield" venture, and alliance strategies. It includes coverage of topics such as Porter's Diamond of National Competitive Advantage, profit sanctuaries, and the choice between multidomestic, global, and transnational strategies. This chapter explains the impetus for sharing, transferring, or accessing valuable resources and capabilities across national borders in the quest for competitive advantage, connecting the material to that on the resource-based view from Chapter 4. The chapter concludes with a discussion of the unique characteristics of competing in developing-country markets.

- Chapter 8 concerns strategy making in the multibusiness company, introducing the topic of corporate-level strategy with its special focus on diversification. The first portion of this chapter describes when and why diversification makes good strategic sense, the different means of diversifying a company's business lineup, and the pros and cons of related versus unrelated diversification strategies. The second part of the chapter looks at how to evaluate the attractiveness of a diversified company's business lineup, how to decide whether it has a good diversification strategy, and what the strategic options are for improving a diversified company's future performance. The evaluative technique integrates material concerning both industry analysis and the resource-based view, in that it considers the relative attractiveness of the various industries the company has diversified into, the company's competitive strength in each of its lines of business, and the extent to which its different businesses exhibit both *strategic fit* and *resource fit*.

- Although the topic of ethics and values comes up at various points in this textbook, Chapter 9 brings more direct attention to such issues and may be used as a stand-alone assignment in either the early, middle, or late part of a course. It concerns the themes of ethical standards in business, approaches to ensuring consistent ethical standards for companies with international operations, corporate social responsibility, and environmental sustainability. The contents of this chapter are sure to give students some things to ponder, rouse lively discussion, and help to make students more *ethically aware* and conscious of *why all companies should conduct their business in a socially responsible and sustainable manner.*

- The next three chapters (Chapters 10, 11, and 12) comprise a module on strategy execution that is presented in terms of a 10-step framework. Chapter 10 provides an overview of this framework and then explores the first three of these tasks: (1) staffing the organization with people capable of executing the strategy well, (2) building the organizational capabilities needed for successful strategy execution, and (3) creating an organizational structure supportive of the strategy execution process.

- Chapter 11 discusses five additional managerial actions that advance the cause of good strategy execution: (1) *allocating resources* to enable the strategy execution process, (2) ensuring that *policies and procedures* facilitate rather than impede strategy execution, (3) using *process management tools* and *best practices* to drive continuous improvement in the performance of value chain activities, (4) installing *information and operating systems* that help company personnel carry out their strategic roles, and (5) using *rewards and incentives* to encourage good strategy execution and the achievement of performance targets.

- Chapter 12 completes the framework with a consideration of the roles of corporate culture and leadership in promoting good strategy execution. The recurring theme throughout the final three chapters is that executing strategy involves deciding on the specific actions, behaviors, and conditions needed for a smooth strategy-supportive operation and then following through to get things done and deliver results. The goal here is to ensure that students understand that the strategy-executing phase is a *make-things-happen and make-them-happen-right* kind of managerial exercise—one that is critical for achieving operating excellence and reaching the goal of strong company performance.

In this latest edition, we have put our utmost effort into ensuring that the 12 chapters are consistent with the latest and best thinking of academics and practitioners in the field of strategic management and provide the topical coverage required for both undergraduate and MBA-level strategy courses. The ultimate test of the text, of course, is the positive pedagogical impact it has in the classroom. If this edition sets a more effective stage for your lectures and does a better job of helping you persuade students that the discipline of strategy merits their rapt attention, then it will have fulfilled its purpose.

## THE CASE COLLECTION

The 31-case lineup in this edition is flush with interesting companies and valuable lessons for students in the art and science of crafting and executing strategy. There's a good blend of cases from a length perspective—21 of the 31 cases are under 15 pages yet offer plenty for students to chew on; 5 are medium-length cases; and the remainder are detail-rich cases that call for more sweeping analysis.

At least 28 of the 31 cases involve companies, products, people, or activities that students will have heard of, know about from personal experience, or can easily identify with. The lineup includes at least 15 cases that will deepen student understanding of the special demands of competing in industry environments where product life cycles are short and competitive maneuvering among rivals is quite active. Twenty-four of the cases involve situations in which company resources and competitive capabilities play as large a role in the strategy-making, strategy executing scheme of things as industry and competitive conditions do. Scattered throughout the lineup are 12 cases concerning non-U.S. companies, globally competitive industries, and/or cross-cultural situations. These cases, in conjunction with the globalized content of the text chapters, provide abundant material for linking the study of strategic management tightly to the ongoing globalization of the world economy. You'll also find 5 cases dealing with the strategic problems of family-owned or relatively small entrepreneurial businesses and 25 cases involving public companies and situations where students can do further research on the Internet.

The "Guide to Case Analysis" follows the last case. It contains sections on what a case is, why cases are a standard part of courses in strategy, preparing a case for class discussion, doing a written case analysis, doing an oral presentation, and using financial ratio analysis to assess a company's financial condition. We suggest having students read this guide before the first class discussion of a case.

A number of cases have accompanying videotape segments on the DVD.

# THE TWO STRATEGY SIMULATION SUPPLEMENTS: *THE BUSINESS STRATEGY GAME* AND *GLO-BUS*

*The Business Strategy Game* and *GLO-BUS: Developing Winning Competitive Strategies*—two competition-based strategy simulations that are delivered online and that feature automated processing and grading of performance—are being marketed by the publisher as companion supplements for use with the 20th edition (and other texts in the field).

- *The Business Strategy Game* is the world's most popular strategy simulation, having been used by over 2,500 instructors in courses involving approximately 750,000 students on 1,050 university campuses in 66+ countries.
- *GLO-BUS,* a somewhat simpler strategy simulation introduced in 2004, has been used by more than 1,450+ instructors in courses involving over 180,000 students at 640+ university campuses in 48+ countries.

## How the Strategy Simulations Work

In both *The Business Strategy Game (BSG)* and *GLO-BUS,* class members are divided into teams of one to five persons and assigned to run a company that competes head-to-head against companies run by other class members.

- In *BSG,* team members run an athletic footwear company, producing and marketing both branded and private-label footwear.
- In *GLO-BUS,* team members operate a digital camera company that designs, assembles, and markets entry-level digital cameras and upscale, multifeatured cameras.

In both simulations, companies compete in a global market arena, selling their products in four geographic regions—Europe-Africa, North America, Asia-Pacific, and Latin America. Each management team is called upon to craft a strategy for their company and make decisions relating to plant operations, workforce compensation, pricing and marketing, social responsibility/citizenship, and finance.

Company co-managers are held accountable for their decision making. Each company's performance is scored on the basis of earnings per share, return-on-equity investment, stock price, credit rating, and image rating. Rankings of company performance, along with a wealth of industry and company statistics, are available to company co-managers after each decision round to use in making strategy adjustments and operating decisions for the next competitive round. You can be certain that the market environment, strategic issues, and operating challenges that company co-managers must contend with are *very tightly linked* to what your class members will be reading about in the text chapters. The circumstances that co-managers face in running their simulation company embrace the very concepts, analytical tools, and strategy options they encounter in the text chapters (this is something you can quickly confirm by skimming through some of the Exercises for Simulation Participants that appear at the end of each chapter).

We suggest that you schedule 1 or 2 practice rounds and anywhere from 4 to 10 regular (scored) decision rounds (more rounds are better than fewer rounds). Each decision round represents a year of company operations and will entail roughly two hours of time for company co-managers to complete. In traditional 13-week, semester-long courses, there is merit in scheduling one decision round per week. In courses that run 5 to 10 weeks, it is wise to schedule two decision rounds per week for the last several weeks of the term (sample course schedules are provided for courses of varying length and varying numbers of class meetings).

When the instructor-specified deadline for a decision round arrives, the simulation server automatically accesses the saved decision entries of each company, determines the competitiveness and buyer appeal of each company's product offering relative to the other companies being run by students in your class, and then awards sales and market shares to the competing companies, geographic region by geographic region. The unit sales volumes awarded to each company *are totally governed by:*

- How its prices compare against the prices of rival brands.
- How its product quality compares against the quality of rival brands.
- How its product line breadth and selection compare.
- How its advertising effort compares.
- And so on, for a total of 11 competitive factors that determine unit sales and market shares.

The competitiveness and overall buyer appeal of each company's product offering *in comparison to the product offerings of rival companies* is all-decisive—this algorithmic feature is what makes *BSG* and *GLO-BUS* "competition-based" strategy simulations. Once each company's sales and market shares are awarded based on the competitiveness of its respective overall product offering, the various company and industry reports detailing the outcomes of the decision round are then generated. Company co-managers can access the results of the decision round 15 to 20 minutes after the decision deadline.

## The Compelling Case for Incorporating Use of a Strategy Simulation

There are *three exceptionally important benefits* associated with using a competition-based simulation in strategy courses taken by seniors and MBA students:

- *A three-pronged text-case-simulation course model delivers significantly more teaching-learning power than the traditional text-case model.* Using *both* cases and a strategy simulation to drill students in thinking strategically and applying what they read in the text chapters is a stronger, more effective means of helping them connect theory with practice and develop better business judgment. What cases do that a simulation cannot is give class members broad exposure to a variety of companies and industry situations and insight into the kinds of strategy-related problems managers face. But what a competition-based strategy simulation does far better than case analysis is thrust class members squarely into *an active, hands-on managerial role* where they are totally responsible for assessing market conditions, determining how to respond to the actions of competitors, forging a long-term direction and strategy for their company, and making all kinds of operating decisions. Because they are held fully account-able for their decisions and their company's performance, *co-managers are strongly motivated* to dig deeply into company operations, probe for ways to be more cost-efficient and competitive, and ferret out strategic moves and deci-sions calculated to boost company performance. *Consequently, incorporating both case assignments and a strategy simulation to develop the skills of class members in thinking strategically and applying the concepts and tools of strate-gic analysis turns out to be more pedagogically powerful than relying solely on case assignments—there's stronger retention of the lessons learned and better achievement of course learning objectives.*

To provide you with quantitative evidence of the learning that occurs with using *The Business Strategy Game* or *GLO-BUS,* there is a built-in Learning Assurance Report showing how well each class member performs on nine skills/learning measures versus tens of thousands of students worldwide who have completed the simulation in the past 12 months.

- *The competitive nature of a strategy simulation arouses positive energy and steps up the whole tempo of the course by a notch or two.* Nothing sparks class excite-ment quicker or better than the concerted efforts on the part of class members at each decision round to achieve a high industry ranking and avoid the perilous con-sequences of being outcompeted by other class members. Students really enjoy taking on the role of a manager, running their own company, crafting strategies, making all kinds of operating decisions, trying to outcompete rival companies, and getting immediate feedback on the resulting company performance. Lots of back-and-forth chatter occurs when the results of the latest simulation round become available and co-managers renew their quest for strategic moves and actions that will strengthen company performance. Co-managers become *emotionally invested* in running their company and figuring out what strategic moves to make to boost their company's performance. Interest levels climb. All this stimulates learning and causes students to see the practical relevance of the subject matter and the benefits of taking your course.

  As soon as your students start to say "Wow! Not only is this fun but I am learn-ing a lot," *which they will,* you have won the battle of engaging students in the subject matter and moved the value of taking your course to a much higher plateau in the business school curriculum. This translates into *a livelier, richer learning experience from a student perspective and better instructor-course evaluations.*

- *Use of a fully automated online simulation reduces the time instructors spend on course preparation, course administration, and grading.* Since the simulation exercise involves a 20- to 30-hour workload for student teams (roughly 2 hours per decision round times 10 to 12 rounds, plus optional assignments), simulation adopters often compensate by trimming the number of assigned cases from, say, 10 to 12 to perhaps 4 to 6. This significantly reduces the time instructors spend reading cases, studying teaching notes, and otherwise getting ready to lead class discussion of a case or grade oral team presentations. Course preparation time is further cut because you can use several class days to have students meet in the computer lab to work on upcoming decision rounds or a three-year strategic plan (in lieu of lecturing on a chapter or covering an additional assigned case). Not only does use of a simulation permit assigning fewer cases, but it also permits you to eliminate at least one assignment that entails considerable grading on your part. Grading one less written case or essay exam or other written assignment saves enormous time. With *BSG* and *GLO-BUS,* grading is effortless and takes only minutes; once you enter percentage weights for each assignment in your online grade book, a suggested overall grade is calculated for you. You'll be pleasantly surprised—and quite pleased—at how little time it takes to gear up for and administer *The Business Strategy Game* or *GLO-BUS.*

In sum, incorporating use of a strategy simulation turns out to be *a win–win proposition for both students and instructors.* Moreover, a very convincing argument can be made that a competition-based strategy simulation is *the single most effective teaching/learning tool that instructors can employ to teach the discipline of business and competitive strategy, to make learning more enjoyable, and to promote better achievement of course learning objectives.*

## A Bird's-Eye View of *The Business Strategy Game*

The setting for *The Business Strategy Game (BSG)* is the global athletic footwear industry (there can be little doubt in today's world that a globally competitive strategy simulation is *vastly superior* to a simulation with a domestic-only setting). Global market demand for footwear grows at the rate of 7 to 9 percent annually for the first five years and 5 to 7 percent annually for the second five years. However, market growth rates vary by geographic region—North America, Latin America, Europe-Africa, and Asia-Pacific.

Companies begin the simulation producing branded and private-label footwear in two plants, one in North America and one in Asia. They have the option to establish production facilities in Latin America and Europe-Africa, either by constructing new plants or by buying previously constructed plants that have been sold by competing companies. Company co-managers exercise control over production costs on the basis of the styling and quality they opt to manufacture, plant location (wages and incentive compensation vary from region to region), the use of best practices and Six Sigma programs to reduce the production of defective footwear and to boost worker productivity, and compensation practices.

All newly produced footwear is shipped in bulk containers to one of four geographic distribution centers. All sales in a geographic region are made from footwear inventories in that region's distribution center. Costs at the four regional distribution centers are a function of inventory storage costs, packing and shipping fees, import tariffs paid on incoming pairs shipped from foreign plants, and exchange rate impacts. At the start of the simulation, import tariffs average $4 per pair in Europe-Africa, $6 per pair in Latin America, and $8 in the Asia-Pacific region. However, the Free Trade Treaty of the Americas allows tariff-free movement of footwear between North America and Latin America. Instructors have the option to alter tariffs as the game progresses.

Companies market their brand of athletic footwear to footwear retailers worldwide and to individuals buying online at the company's website. Each company's sales and market share in the branded footwear segments hinge on its competitiveness on 11 factors: attractive pricing, footwear styling and quality, product line breadth, advertising, use of mail-in rebates, appeal of celebrities endorsing a company's brand, success in convincing footwear retailers to carry its brand, number of weeks it takes to fill retailer orders, effectiveness of a company's online sales effort at its website, and customer loyalty. Sales of private-label footwear hinge solely on being the low-price bidder.

All told, company co-managers make as many as 53 types of decisions each period that cut across production operations (up to 10 decisions per plant, with a maximum of four plants), plant capacity additions/sales/upgrades (up to 6 decisions per plant), worker compensation and training (3 decisions per plant), shipping (up to 8 decisions per plant), pricing and marketing (up to 10 decisions in four geographic regions), bids to sign celebrities (2 decision entries per bid), financing of company operations (up to 8 decisions), and corporate social responsibility and environmental sustainability (up to 6 decisions).

Each time company co-managers make a decision entry, an assortment of on-screen calculations instantly shows the projected effects on unit sales, revenues, market shares, unit costs, profit, earnings per share, ROE, and other operating statistics. The on-screen calculations help team members evaluate the relative merits of one decision entry versus another and put together a promising strategy.

Companies can employ any of the five generic competitive strategy options in selling branded footwear—low-cost leadership, differentiation, best-cost provider, focused low cost, and focused differentiation. They can pursue essentially the same strategy worldwide or craft slightly or very different strategies for the Europe-Africa, Asia-Pacific, Latin America, and North America markets. They can strive for competitive advantage based on more advertising, a wider selection of models, more appealing styling/quality, bigger rebates, and so on.

*Any well-conceived, well-executed competitive approach is capable of succeeding, provided it is not overpowered by the strategies of competitors or defeated by the presence of too many copycat strategies that dilute its effectiveness.* The challenge for each company's management team is to craft and execute a competitive strategy that produces good performance on five measures: earnings per share, return on equity investment, stock price appreciation, credit rating, and brand image.

All activity for *The Business Strategy Game* takes place at **www.bsg-online.com**.

## A Bird's-Eye View of *GLO-BUS*

The industry setting for *GLO-BUS* is the digital camera industry. Global market demand grows at the rate of 8 to 10 percent annually for the first five years and 4 to 6 percent annually for the second five years. Retail sales of digital cameras are seasonal, with about 20 percent of consumer demand coming in each of the first three quarters of each calendar year and 40 percent coming during the big fourth-quarter retailing season.

Companies produce entry-level and upscale, multifeatured cameras of varying designs and quality in a Taiwan assembly facility and ship assembled cameras directly to retailers in North America, Asia-Pacific, Europe-Africa, and Latin America. All cameras are assembled as retail orders come in and are shipped immediately upon completion of the assembly process—companies maintain no finished-goods inventories, and all parts and components are delivered on a just-in-time basis (which eliminates the need to track inventories and simplifies the accounting for plant operations and costs). Company co-managers exercise control over production costs on the basis of the designs and components they specify for their cameras, workforce compensation and training, the length of warranties offered (which affects warranty costs), the amount spent for technical support provided to buyers of the company's cameras, and their management of the assembly process.

Competition in each of the two product market segments (entry-level and multifeatured digital cameras) is based on 10 factors: price, camera performance and quality, number of quarterly sales promotions, length of promotions in weeks, size of the promotional discounts offered, advertising, number of camera models, size of the retail dealer network, warranty period, and amount/caliber of technical support provided to camera buyers. Low-cost leadership, differentiation strategies, best-cost provider strategies, and focus strategies are all viable competitive options. Rival companies can strive to be the clear market leader in either entry-level cameras or upscale multifeatured cameras or both. They can focus on one or two geographic regions or strive for geographic balance. They can pursue essentially the same strategy worldwide or craft slightly or very different strategies for the Europe-Africa, Asia-Pacific, Latin America, and North America markets. Just as with *The Business Strategy Game,* almost any well-conceived, well-executed competitive approach is capable of succeeding, *provided it is not overpowered by the strategies of competitors or defeated by the presence of too many copycat strategies that dilute its effectiveness.*

Company co-managers make 49 types of decisions each period, ranging from R&D, camera components, and camera performance (10 decisions) to production operations and worker compensation (15 decisions) to pricing and marketing (15 decisions) to the financing of company operations (4 decisions) to corporate social responsibility (5 decisions). *Each time participants make a decision entry, an assortment of on-screen calculations instantly shows the projected effects on unit sales, revenues, market shares, unit costs, profit, earnings per share, ROE, and other operating statistics. These on-screen calculations help team members evaluate the relative merits of one decision entry versus another and stitch the separate decisions into a cohesive and promising strategy.* Company performance is judged on five criteria: earnings per share, return on equity investment, stock price, credit rating, and brand image.

All activity for *GLO-BUS* occurs at **www.glo-bus.com**.

## Administration and Operating Features of the Two Simulations

The Internet delivery and user-friendly designs of both *BSG* and *GLO-BUS* make them incredibly easy to administer, even for first-time users. And the menus and controls are so similar that you can readily switch between the two simulations or use one in your undergraduate class and the other in a graduate class. If you have not yet used either of the two simulations, you may find the following of particular interest:

- Setting up the simulation for your course is done online and takes about 10 to 15 minutes. Once setup is completed, no other administrative actions are required beyond those of moving participants to a different team (should the need arise) and monitoring the progress of the simulation (to whatever extent desired).

- Participant's Guides are delivered electronically to class members at the website—students can read the guide on their monitors or print out a copy, as they prefer.

- There are 2- to 4-minute Video Tutorials scattered throughout the software (including each decision screen and each page of each report) that provide on-demand guidance to class members who may be uncertain about how to proceed.

- Complementing the Video Tutorials are detailed and clearly written Help sections explaining "all there is to know" about (a) each decision entry and the relevant cause-effect relationships, (b) the information on each page of the Industry Reports, and (c) the numbers presented in the Company Reports. *The Video Tutorials and the Help screens allow company co-managers to figure things out for themselves, thereby curbing the need for students to ask the instructor "how things work."*

- Team members running the same company who are logged in simultaneously on different computers at different locations can click a button to enter Collaboration Mode, enabling them to work collaboratively from the same screen in viewing reports and making decision entries, and click a second button to enter Audio Mode, letting them talk to one another.

  ○ When in "Collaboration Mode," each team member sees the same screen at the same time as all other team members who are logged in and have joined Collaboration Mode. If one team member chooses to view a particular decision screen, that same screen appears on the monitors for all team members in Collaboration Mode.

  ○ Each team member controls their own color-coded mouse pointer (with their first-name appearing in a color-coded box linked to their mouse pointer) and can make a decision entry or move the mouse to point to particular on-screen items.

  ○ A decision entry change made by one team member is seen by all, in real time, and all team members can immediately view the on-screen calculations that result from the new decision entry.

  ○ If one team member wishes to view a report page and clicks on the menu link to the desired report, that same report page will immediately appear for the other team members engaged in collaboration.

  ○ Use of Audio Mode capability requires that each team member work from a computer with a built-in microphone (if they want to be heard by their team members) and speakers (so they may hear their teammates) or else have a headset with a microphone that they can plug into their desktop or laptop. A headset is recommended for best results, but most laptops now are equipped with a built-in microphone and speakers that will support use of our new voice chat feature.

  ○ Real-time VoIP audio chat capability among team members who have entered both the Audio Mode and the Collaboration Mode is a tremendous boost in functionality that enables team members to go online simultaneously on computers at different locations and conveniently and effectively collaborate in running their simulation company.

  ○ In addition, instructors have the capability to join the online session of any company and speak with team members, thus circumventing the need for team members to arrange for and attend a meeting in the instructor's office. Using the standard menu for administering a particular industry, instructors can connect with the company desirous of assistance. Instructors who wish not only to talk but also to enter Collaboration (highly recommended because all attendees are then viewing the same screen) have a red-colored mouse pointer linked to a red box labeled Instructor.

      Without a doubt, the Collaboration and Voice-Chat capabilities are hugely valuable for students enrolled in online and distance-learning courses where meeting face-to-face is impractical or time-consuming. Likewise, the instructors of online and distance-learning courses will appreciate having the capability to join the online meetings of particular company teams when their advice or assistance is requested.

- Both simulations are quite suitable for use in distance-learning or online courses (and are currently being used in such courses on numerous campuses).

- Participants and instructors are notified via e-mail when the results are ready (usually about 15 to 20 minutes after the decision round deadline specified by the instructor/game administrator).

- Following each decision round, participants are provided with a complete set of reports—a six-page Industry Report, a one-page Competitive Intelligence report for each geographic region that includes strategic group maps and bulleted lists of competitive strengths and weaknesses, and a set of Company Reports (income statement, balance sheet, cash flow statement, and assorted production, marketing, and cost statistics).

- Two "open-book" multiple-choice tests of 20 questions are built into each simulation. The quizzes, which you can require or not as you see fit, are taken online and automatically graded, with scores reported instantaneously to participants and automatically recorded in the instructor's electronic grade book. Students are automatically provided with three sample questions for each test.

- Both simulations contain a three-year strategic plan option that you can assign. Scores on the plan are automatically recorded in the instructor's online grade book.

- At the end of the simulation, you can have students complete online peer evaluations (again, the scores are automatically recorded in your online grade book).

- Both simulations have a Company Presentation feature that enables each team of company co-managers to easily prepare PowerPoint slides for use in describing their strategy and summarizing their company's performance in a presentation to either the class, the instructor, or an "outside" board of directors.

- *A Learning Assurance Report provides you with hard data concerning how well your students performed vis-à-vis students playing the simulation worldwide over the past 12 months.* The report is based on nine measures of student proficiency, business know-how, and decision-making skill and can also be used in evaluating the extent to which your school's academic curriculum produces the desired degree of student learning insofar as accreditation standards are concerned.

For more details on either simulation, please consult Section 2 of the Instructor's Manual accompanying this text or register as an instructor at the simulation websites (**www.bsg-online.com** and **www.glo-bus.com**) to access even more comprehensive information. You should also consider signing up for one of the webinars that the simulation authors conduct several times each month (sometimes several times weekly) to demonstrate how the software works, walk you through the various features and menu options, and answer any questions. You have an open invitation to call the senior author of this text at (205) 722-9145 to arrange a personal demonstration or talk about how one of the simulations might work in one of your courses. We think you'll be quite impressed with the cutting-edge capabilities that have been programmed into *The Business Strategy Game* and *GLO-BUS,* the simplicity with which both simulations can be administered, and their exceptionally tight connection to the text chapters, core concepts, and standard analytical tools.

# RESOURCES AND SUPPORT MATERIALS FOR THE 20TH EDITION

## For Students

**Key Points Summaries**   At the end of each chapter is a synopsis of the core concepts, analytical tools, and other key points discussed in the chapter. These chapter-end synopses, along with the core concept definitions and margin notes scattered throughout each chapter, help students focus on basic strategy principles, digest the messages of each chapter, and prepare for tests.

**Two Sets of Chapter-End Exercises**   Each chapter concludes with two sets of exercises. The *Assurance of Learning Exercises* can be used as the basis for class discussion, oral presentation assignments, short written reports, and substitutes for case assignments. The *Exercises for Simulation Participants* are designed expressly for use by adopters who have incorporated use of a simulation and want to go a step further in tightly and explicitly connecting the chapter content to the simulation company their students are running. The questions in both sets of exercises (along with those Illustration Capsules that qualify as "mini-cases") can be used to round out the rest of a 75-minute class period should your lecture on a chapter last for only 50 minutes.

**The Connect™ Management Web-Based Assignment and Assessment Platform**   Beginning with the 18th edition, we began taking advantage of the publisher's innovative Connect™ assignment and assessment platform and created several features that simplify the task of assigning and grading three types of exercises for students:

- There are self-scoring chapter tests consisting of 20 to 25 multiple-choice questions that students can take to measure their grasp of the material presented in each of the 12 chapters.
- There are two author-developed Interactive Application exercises for each of the 12 chapters that drill students in the use and application of the concepts and tools of strategic analysis.
- The Connect™ platform also includes author-developed Interactive Application exercises for 14 of the 31 cases in this edition that require students to work through answers to a select number of the assignment questions for the case. These exercises have multiple components and can include calculating assorted financial ratios to assess a company's financial performance and balance sheet strength, identifying a company's strategy, doing five-forces and driving-forces analysis, doing a SWOT analysis, and recommending actions to improve company performance. The content of these case exercises is tailored to match the circumstances presented in each case, calling upon students to do whatever strategic thinking and strategic analysis are called for to arrive at pragmatic, analysis-based action recommendations for improving company performance.

All of the Connect™ exercises are automatically graded (with the exception of those exercise components that entail student entry of short-answer and/or essay answers), thereby simplifying the task of evaluating each class member's performance and monitoring the learning outcomes. The progress-tracking function built into the Connect™ Management system enables you to:

- View scored work immediately and track individual or group performance with assignment and grade reports.
- Access an instant view of student or class performance relative to learning objectives.
- Collect data and generate reports required by many accreditation organizations, such as AACSB.

**LearnSmart and SmartBook TM**   LearnSmart is an adaptive study tool proven to strengthen memory recall, increase class retention, and boost grades. Students are able to study more efficiently because they are made aware of what they know and don't know. Real-time reports quickly identify the concepts that require more attention from individual students—or the entire class. SmartBook is the first and only adaptive reading experience designed to change the way students read and learn. It creates a personalized reading experience by highlighting the most impactful concepts a student needs to learn at that moment in time. As a student engages with SmartBook, the reading experience continuously adapts by highlighting content based on what the student knows and doesn't know. This ensures that the focus is on the content he or she needs to learn, while simultaneously promoting long-term retention of material. Use SmartBook's real-time reports to quickly identify the concepts that require more attention from individual students–or the entire class. The end result? Students are more engaged with course content, can better prioritize their time, and come to class ready to participate.

## For Instructors

**Instructor Library**   The Connect Management Instructor Library is your repository for additional resources to improve student engagement in and out of class. You can select and use any asset that enhances your lecture.

**Instructor's Manual**   The accompanying IM contains:

- A section on suggestions for organizing and structuring your course.
- Sample syllabi and course outlines.
- A set of lecture notes on each chapter.
- Answers to the chapter-end Assurance of Learning Exercises.
- A copy of the test bank.
- A comprehensive case teaching note for each of the 31 cases. These teaching notes are filled with suggestions for using the case effectively, have very thorough, analysis-based answers to the suggested assignment questions for the case, and contain an epilogue detailing any important developments since the case was written.

**Test Bank and EZ Test Online**   There is a test bank containing over 900 multiple-choice questions and short-answer/essay questions. It has been tagged with AACSB and Bloom's Taxonomy criteria. All of the test bank questions are also accessible within a computerized test bank powered by McGraw-Hill's flexible electronic testing program, EZ Test Online (www.eztestonline.com). Using EZ Test Online allows you to create paper and online tests or quizzes. With EZ Test Online, instructors can select questions from multiple McGraw-Hill test banks or author their own and then either print the test for paper distribution or give it online.

**PowerPoint Slides**   To facilitate delivery preparation of your lectures and to serve as chapter outlines, you'll have access to approximately 500 colorful and professional-looking slides displaying core concepts, analytical procedures, key points, and all the figures in the text chapters.

***The Business Strategy Game* and *GLO-BUS* Online Simulations**   Using one of the two companion simulations is a powerful and constructive way of emotionally connecting students to the subject matter of the course. We know of no more effective way to arouse the competitive energy of students and prepare them for the challenges of real-world business decision making than to have them match strategic wits with classmates in running a company in head-to-head competition for global market leadership.

# ACKNOWLEDGMENTS

We heartily acknowledge the contributions of the case researchers whose case-writing efforts appear herein and the companies whose cooperation made the cases possible. To each one goes a very special thank-you. We cannot overstate the importance of timely, carefully researched cases in contributing to a substantive study of strategic management issues and practices.

A great number of colleagues and students at various universities, business acquaintances, and people at McGraw-Hill provided inspiration, encouragement, and counsel during the course of this project. Like all text authors in the strategy field, we are intellectually indebted to the many academics whose research and writing have blazed new trails and advanced the discipline of strategic management. In addition, we'd like to thank the following reviewers who provided seasoned advice and splendid suggestions over the years for improving the chapters:

Robert B. Baden, Edward Desmarais, Stephen F. Hallam, Joy Karriker, Wendell Seaborne, Joan H. Bailar, David Blair, Jane Boyland, William J. Donoher, Stephen A. Drew, Jo Anne Duffy, Alan Ellstrand, Susan Fox-Wolfgramm, Rebecca M. Guidice, Mark Hoelscher, Sean D. Jasso, Xin Liang, Paul Mallette, Dan Marlin, Raza Mir, Mansour Moussavi, James D. Spina, Monica A. Zimmerman, Dennis R. Balch, Jeffrey R. Bruehl, Edith C. Busija, Donald A. Drost, Randall Harris, Mark Lewis Hoelscher, Phyllis Holland, James W. Kroeger, Sal Kukalis, Brian W. Kulik, Paul Mallette, Anthony U. Martinez, Lee Pickler, Sabine Reddy, Thomas D. Schramko, V. Seshan, Charles Strain, Sabine Turnley, S. Stephen Vitucci, Andrew Ward, Sibin Wu, Lynne Patten, Nancy E. Landrum, Jim Goes, Jon Kalinowski, Rodney M. Walter, Judith D. Powell, Seyda Deligonul, David Flanagan, Esmerlda Garbi, Mohsin Habib, Kim Hester, Jeffrey E. McGee, Diana J. Wong, F. William Brown, Anthony F. Chelte, Gregory G. Dess, Alan B. Eisner, John George, Carle M. Hunt, Theresa Marron-Grodsky, Sarah Marsh, Joshua D. Martin, William L. Moore, Donald Neubaum, George M. Puia, Amit Shah, Lois M. Shelton, Mark Weber, Steve Barndt, J. Michael Geringer, Ming-Fang Li, Richard Stackman, Stephen Tallman, Gerardo R. Ungson, James Boulgarides, Betty Diener, Daniel F. Jennings, David Kuhn, Kathryn Martell, Wilbur Mouton, Bobby Vaught, Tuck Bounds, Lee Burk, Ralph Catalanello, William Crittenden, Vince Luchsinger, Stan Mendenhall, John Moore, Will Mulvaney, Sandra Richard, Ralph Roberts, Thomas Turk, Gordon Von Stroh, Fred Zimmerman, S. A. Billion, Charles Byles, Gerald L. Geisler, Rose Knotts, Joseph Rosenstein, James B. Thurman, Ivan Able, W. Harvey Hegarty, Roger Evered, Charles B. Saunders, Rhae M. Swisher, Claude I. Shell, R. Thomas Lenz, Michael C. White, Dennis Callahan, R. Duane Ireland, William E. Burr II, C. W. Millard, Richard Mann, Kurt Christensen, Neil W. Jacobs, Louis W. Fry, D. Robley Wood, George J. Gore, and William R. Soukup.

We owe a debt of gratitude to Professors Catherine A. Maritan, Jeffrey A. Martin, Richard S. Shreve, and Anant K. Sundaram for their helpful comments on various chapters. We'd also like to thank the following students of the Tuck School of Business for their assistance with the revisions: Sarah Boole, Kenneth P. Fraser, John L. Gardner, Dennis L. Huggins, Peter Jacobson, Jacob Adam Johnson, Heather Levy, Judith H. Lin, Brian R. McKenzie, Andrew J. Miller, Kiera O'Brien, Sara Paccamonti, Avni V. Patel, Maximilian A. Pinto, Christopher C. Sukenik, Ross M. Templeton, and Nicholas J. Ziemba. And we'd like to acknowledge the help of Dartmouth students

Mathieu A. Bertrand, Meghan L. Cooney, Harold W. Greenstone, Campbell Haynes, Alexander P. Judson, Sarah E. Knapp, Amy Li, Roger L. Melick, Alexander C. Olesen, Mahala S. Pagan, Jenna Pfeffer, Jordan M. West, and Sean Zhang, as well as Tuck staff member Mary Biathrow.

As always, we value your recommendations and thoughts about the book. Your comments regarding coverage and contents will be taken to heart, and we always are grateful for the time you take to call our attention to printing errors, deficiencies, and other shortcomings. Please e-mail us at **athompso@cba.ua.edu**, **margaret.a.peteraf@tuck.dartmouth.edu**, **john.gamble@tamucc.edu**, or **astrickl@cba.ua.edu**.

Arthur A. Thompson

Margaret A. Peteraf

John E. Gamble

A. J. Strickland

# Crafting and Executing Strategy

## THE QUEST FOR COMPETITIVE ADVANTAGE

Concepts and Cases

## Chapter Structure and Organization

**Part I:** Concepts and Techniques for Crafting and Executing Strategy

| **Section A:** Introduction and Overview | **Section B:** Core Concepts and Analytical Tools | **Section C:** Crafting a Strategy | **Section D:** Executing the Strategy |

What Is Strategy and Why Does It Matter?

The Managerial Process of Crafting and Executing Company Strategies

Concepts and Analytical Tools for Evaluating a Company's Situation

Tailoring Strategy to Various Company Situations

The Links between Ethics, Corporate Social Responsibility, Sustainability, and Strategy

Managerial Keys to Successfully Executing the Chosen Strategy

**Chapter 1**

**Chapter 2**

**Chapters 3 and 4**

**Chapter 9**

**Chapters 10, 11, and 12**

Single-Business Companies

**Chapters 5, 6, and 7**

Multibusiness or Diversified Companies

**Chapter 8**

**Part II: Cases in Crafting and Executing Strategy**

Section A: Crafting Strategy in Single-Business Companies (20 cases)
Section B: Crafting Strategy in Diversified Companies (2 cases)
Section C: Implementing and Executing Strategy (6 cases)
Section D: Strategy, Ethics, and Social Responsibility (3 cases)

**CHAPTER 1**

## What Is Strategy and Why Is It Important?

### Learning Objectives

THIS CHAPTER WILL HELP YOU UNDERSTAND:

**LO 1** What we mean by a company's *strategy*.

**LO 2** The concept of a *sustainable competitive advantage.*

**LO 3** The five most basic strategic approaches for setting a company apart from rivals and winning a sustainable competitive advantage.

**LO 4** That a company's strategy tends to evolve because of changing circumstances and ongoing efforts by management to improve the strategy.

**LO 5** Why it is important for a company to have a viable business model that outlines the company's customer value proposition and its profit formula.

**LO 6** The three tests of a winning strategy.

**Learning Objectives** are listed at the beginning of each chapter; corresponding numbered indicators in the margins show where learning objectives are covered in the text.

**Illustration Capsules** appear in boxes throughout each chapter to provide in-depth examples, connect the text presentation to real-world companies, and convincingly demonstrate "strategy in action." Some are appropriate for use as mini-cases.

**ILLUSTRATION CAPSULE 9.4**

### TOMS's Well-Balanced Triple Bottom Line

Having sold over 2 million pairs of shoes worldwide, self-designated "Chief Shoe Giver" Blake Mycoskie founded TOMS on the principle of "One for One." Operating under the belief that "the way you shop can change the world," TOMS donates a pair of shoes to a child in need in over 50 different countries for every pair purchased. Each pair is made with sustainable materials that include organic canvas and recycled materials that minimize TOMS's ecological footprint. TOMS has been recognized with the Award for Corporate Excellence by the Office of the Secretary of State, while *Fortune* magazine has named Mycoskie to its "40 under 40" list.

Mycoskie credits much of TOMS's growth not to success in traditional avenues of advertising but, rather, to the story behind the TOMS shoe as told by TOMS's customers. By focusing on the story behind its product and the importance of sustainable giving, TOMS generates brand awareness through motivated customers who share their feel-good purchases with friends and family. By utilizing user marketing rather than corporate marketing, TOMS successfully pitches a grassroots company-image and bundles a lifestyle with its product.

TOMS's environmental sustainability approach includes offering a line of vegan shoes, which contain no animal by-products, and maintaining its commitment to use earth and animal-friendly materials whenever possible. Its shoeboxes are made with 80 percent recycled waste and are printed with soy ink. Through these production considerations, TOMS caters to an environmentally conscious demographic with few established competitors and with loyal consumers who have helped TOMS experience sustained growth despite the global recession.

From Shoe Giving Trips to employee training on the importance of environmental sustainability, TOMS aspires to offer its employees "more than a 9-to-5" job. This commitment to a worthwhile cause creates not only happier employees but also more autonomous and creative global citizens who work together to inspire change. By attaining economic growth through an emphasis on *social justice* and environmental *sustainability*, TOMS has maintained a well-balanced triple bottom line.

*Note: Developed with Sean Zhang.*

*Source: Keynote statements by Blake Mycoskie and other information posted at www.toms.com.*

**Margin Notes** define core concepts and call attention to important ideas and principles.

LO 4

The concepts of corporate social responsibility and environmental sustainability and how companies balance these duties with economic responsibilities to shareholders.

CORE CONCEPT

**Corporate social responsibility (CSR)** refers to a company's *duty* to operate in an honorable manner, provide good working conditions for employees, encourage workforce diversity, be a good steward of the environment, and actively work to better the quality of life in the local communities where it operates and in society at large.

The idea that businesses have an obligation to foster social betterment, a much-debated topic over the past 50 years, took root in the 19th century when progressive companies in the aftermath of the industrial revolution began to provide workers with housing and other amenities. The notion that corporate executives should balance the interests of all stakeholders—shareholders, employees, customers, suppliers, the communities in which they operate, and society at large—began to blossom in the 1960s. Some years later, a group of chief executives of America's 200 largest corporations, calling themselves the Business Roundtable, came out in strong support of the concept of **corporate social responsibility (CSR):**

> Balancing the shareholder's expectations of maximum return against other priorities is one of the fundamental problems confronting corporate management. The shareholder must receive a good return but the legitimate concerns of other constituencies (customers, employees, communities, suppliers and society at large) also must have the appropriate attention. . . . [Leading managers] believe that by giving enlightened consideration to balancing the legitimate claims of all its constituents, a corporation will best serve the interest of its shareholders.

Today, corporate social responsibility is a concept that resonates in western Europe, the United States, Canada, and such developing nations as Brazil and India.

## The Concepts of Corporate Social Responsibility and Good Corporate Citizenship

The essence of socially responsible business behavior is that a company should balance strategic actions to benefit shareholders against the *duty* to be a good corporate citizen. The underlying thesis is that company managers should display a *social conscience* in operating the business and specifically take into account how management decisions and company actions affect the well-being of employees, local communities, the environment, and society at large.[20] Acting in a socially responsible manner thus encompasses more than just participating in community service projects and donating money to charities and other worthy causes. Demonstrating

**FIGURE 5.2** Cost Drivers: The Keys to Driving Down Company Costs

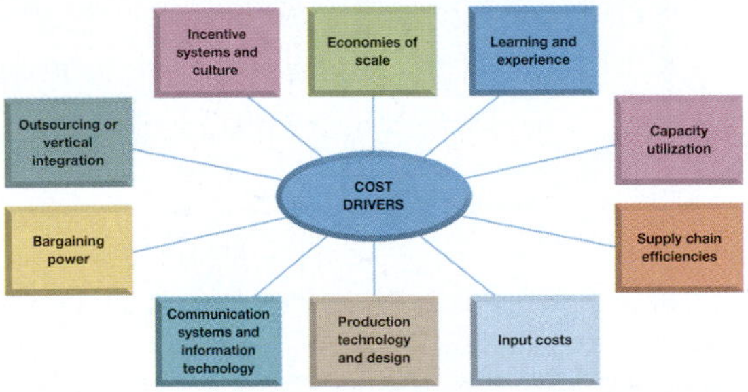


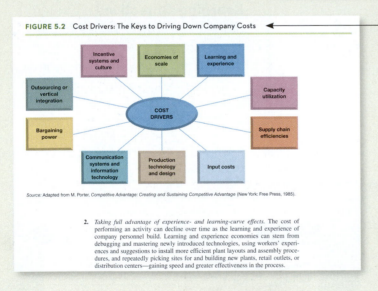

*Source:* Adapted from M. Porter, *Competitive Advantage: Creating and Sustaining Competitive Advantage* (New York: Free Press, 1985).

2. *Taking full advantage of experience- and learning-curve effects.* The cost of performing an activity can decline over time as the learning and experience of company personnel build. Learning and experience economies can stem from debugging and mastering newly introduced technologies, using workers' experiences and suggestions to install more efficient plant layouts and assembly procedures, and repeatedly picking sites for and building new plants, retail outlets, or distribution centers—gaining speed and greater effectiveness in the process.

**Figures** scattered throughout the chapters provide conceptual and analytical frameworks.

**Key Points** at the end of each chapter provide a handy summary of essential ideas and things to remember.

KEY POINTS

1. Deciding which of the five generic competitive strategies to employ—overall low cost, broad differentiation, focused low cost, focused differentiation, or best cost—is perhaps the most important strategic commitment a company makes. It tends to drive the remaining strategic actions a company undertakes and sets the whole tone for pursuing a competitive advantage over rivals.
2. In employing a low-cost provider strategy and trying to achieve a low-cost advantage over rivals, a company must do a better job than rivals of cost-effectively managing value chain activities and/or it must find innovative ways to eliminate cost-producing activities. An effective use of cost drivers is key. Low-cost provider strategies work particularly well when price competition is strong and the products of rival sellers are virtually identical, when there are not many ways to differentiate, when buyers are price-sensitive or have the power to bargain down prices, when buyer switching costs are low, and when industry newcomers are likely to use a low introductory price to build market share.
3. Broad differentiation strategies seek to produce a competitive edge by incorporating attributes that set a company's product or service offering apart from rivals in ways that buyers consider valuable and worth paying for. This depends on the appropriate use of value drivers. Successful differentiation allows a firm to (1) command a premium price for its product, (2) increase unit sales (if additional buyers are won over by the differentiating features), and/or (3) gain buyer loyalty to its brand (because some buyers are strongly attracted to the differentiating

## EXERCISE FOR SIMULATION PARTICIPANTS

1. Is your company's strategy ethical? Why or why not? Is there anything that your company has done or is now doing that could legitimately be considered "shady" by your competitors? — **LO 1**

2. In what ways, if any, is your company exercising corporate social responsibility? What are the elements of your company's CSR strategy? Are there any changes to this strategy that you would suggest? — **LO 4**

3. If some shareholders complained that you and your co-managers have been spending too little or too much on corporate social responsibility, what would you tell them? — **LO 3, LO 4**

4. Is your company striving to conduct its business in an environmentally sustainable manner? What specific *additional* actions could your company take that would make an even greater contribution to environmental sustainability? — **LO 4**

5. In what ways is your company's environmental sustainability strategy in the best long-term interest of shareholders? Does it contribute to your company's competitive advantage or profitability? — **LO 4**

**Exercises** at the end of each chapter, linked to learning objectives, provide a basis for class discussion, oral presentations, and written assignments. Several chapters have exercises that qualify as mini-cases.

## ENDNOTES

[1] James E. Post, Anne T. Lawrence, and James Weber, *Business and Society: Corporate Strategy, Public Policy, Ethics*, 10th ed. (New York: McGraw-Hill, 2002).
[2] Mark S. Schwartz, "Universal Moral Values for Corporate Codes of Ethics," *Journal of Business Ethics* 59, no. 1 (June 2005), pp. 27–44.
[3] Mark S. Schwartz, "A Code of Ethics for Corporate Codes of Ethics," *Journal of Business Ethics* 41, no. 1–2 (November–December 2002), pp. 27–43.
[4] T. L. Beauchamp and N. E. Bowie, *Ethical Theory and Business* (Upper Saddle River, NJ: Prentice-Hall, 2001).
[5] www.cnn.com/2012/10/15/world/child-labor-index-2014/ (accessed February 6, 2014).
[6] U.S. Department of Labor, "The Department of Labor's 2012 Findings on the Worst Forms of Child Labor," www.dol.gov/ilab/programs/ocft/PDF/2012OCFTreport.pdf.
[7] W. M. Greenfield, "In the Name of Corporate Social Responsibility," *Business Horizons* 47, no. 1 (January–February 2004), p. 22.
[8] Rajib Sanyal, "Determinants of Bribery in

[12] Thomas Donaldson and Thomas W. Dunfee, "Towards a Unified Conception of Business Ethics: Integrative Social Contracts Theory," *Academy of Management Review* 19, no. 2 (April 1994), pp. 252–284; Andrew Spicer, Thomas W. Dunfee, and Wendy J. Bailey, "Does National Context Matter in Ethical Decision Making? An Empirical Test of Integrative Social Contracts Theory," *Academy of Management Journal* 47, no. 4 (August 2004), p. 610.
[13] Lynn Paine, Rohit Deshpande, Joshua D. Margolis, and Kim Eric Bettcher, "Up to Code: Does Your Company's Conduct Meet World-Class Standards?" *Harvard Business Review* 83, no. 12 (December 2005), pp. 122–133.
[14] John F. Veiga, Timothy D. Golden, and Kathleen Dechant, "Why Managers Bend Company Rules," *Academy of Management Executive* 18, no. 2 (May 2004).
[15] www.reuters.com/article/2014/03/06/us-sac-martoma-idUSBREA23TL20140306.
[16] Lorin Berlin and Emily Peck, "National Mortgage Settlement: States, Big Banks Reach $25 Billion Deal," *Huff Post Business*, February 9, 2012, www.huffingtonpost.

[20] Timothy M. Devinney, "Is the Socially Responsible Corporation a Myth? The Good, the Bad, and the Ugly of Corporate Social Responsibility," *Academy of Management Perspectives* 23, no. 2 (May 2009), pp. 44–56.
[21] Information posted at www.generalmills.com (accessed March 13, 2013).
[22] Adrian Henriques, "ISO 26000: A New Standard for Human Rights?" *Institute for Human Rights and Business*, March 23, 2010, www.institutehrb.org/blogs/guest/iso_26000_a_new_standard_for_human_rights.html?gclid=CJih7HJN2aICFv65Q0drVOdyQ (accessed July 7, 2010).
[23] Gerald I.J.M. Zetsloot and Marcel N. A. van Marrewijk, "From Quality to Sustainability," *Journal of Business Ethics* 55 (2004), pp. 79–82.
[24] Tilde Herrera, "PG&E Claims Industry First with Supply Chain Footprint Project," *GreenBiz.com*, June 30, 2010, www.greenbiz.com/news/2010/06/30/pge-claims-industry-first-supply-chain-carbon-footprint-project.
[25] J. G. Speth, *The Bridge at the End of the World: Capitalism, the Environment, and*

**Thirty-one cases** detail the strategic circumstances of actual companies and provide practice in applying the concepts and tools of strategic analysis.

---

## CASE 03

### Whole Foods Market in 2014: Vision, Core Values, and Strategy

Arthur A. Thompson
The University of Alabama

Founded in 1980, Whole Foods Market had evolved from a local supermarket for natural and health foods in Austin, Texas, into the most visible and best-known leader of the natural and organic food movement across the United States, helping the industry gain acceptance among growing numbers of consumers concerned about the food they ate. The company had 2013 sales revenues of $12.9 billion and in spring 2014 had 379 stores in the United States, Canada, and Great Britain. Over the past 22 years, sales had grown at a compound annual rate of 25.2 percent, and profits had grown at a compound average rate of 30.4 percent. In 2013, Whole Foods was the 8th-largest food and drug retailer in the United States (up from 21st in 2009) and ranked 232nd on *Fortune* magazine's 2013 list of the 500 largest companies in the United States. Over 7 million customers visited Whole Foods stores in 41 U.S. states, Canada, and the United Kingdom each week, and Whole Foods was the number-two retail brand on Twitter, with 4 million followers.

Whole Foods' mission was "to promote the vitality and well-being of all individuals by supplying the highest quality, most wholesome foods available." The core of the mission involved promoting organically grown foods, healthy eating, and the sustainability of the world's entire ecosystem. For many years, the company used the slogan "Whole Foods, Whole People, Whole Planet" to capture the essence of its mission. John Mackey, the company's cofounder and co-CEO, was convinced that Whole Foods' rapid growth and market success had much to do with its having "remained a uniquely mission-driven company—highly selective about what we sell, dedicated to our core values and

stringent quality standards, and committed to sustainable agriculture."

Mackey's vision was for Whole Foods to become an international brand synonymous with carrying the highest-quality natural and organic foods available and being the best food retailer in every community in which a Whole Foods store was located. The company sought to offer the highest-quality, least processed, most flavorful and naturally preserved foods available, and it marketed them in appealing store environments that made shopping at Whole Foods interesting and enjoyable. Mackey believed that marketing high-quality natural and organic foods to more and more customers in more and more communities would, over time, gradually transform the diets of individuals in a manner that would help them live longer, healthier, more pleasurable lives.

### THE NATURAL AND ORGANIC FOODS INDUSTRY

The retail grocery industry in the United States—which included conventional supermarkets, supercenters, and limited-assortment and natural/gourmet-positioned supermarkets—had sales of approximately $603 billion in 2012, up 3 percent over 2011.[1] Within this broader category, retail sales of food products labeled "natural" were approximately $81 billion, a 10 percent increase over the prior year.[2]

Foods labeled "organic" generated estimated retail sales across North America approaching $35 billion in 2013, up from $9 billion in 2002. *Natural*

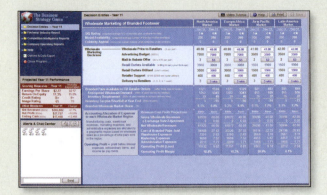

***The Business Strategy Game* or *GLO-BUS* Simulation Exercises** Either one of these text supplements involves teams of students managing companies in a head-to-head contest for global market leadership. Company co-managers have to make decisions relating to product quality, production, workforce compensation and training, pricing and marketing, and financing of company operations. The challenge is to craft and execute a strategy that is powerful enough to deliver good financial performance despite the competitive efforts of rival companies. Each company competes in America, Latin America, Europe-Africa, and Asia-Pacific.

# Crafting and Executing Strategy

**THE QUEST FOR COMPETITIVE ADVANTAGE**

Concepts and Cases

# BRIEF CONTENTS

# CONTENTS

## 8  Corporate Strategy  210

**PART 2**  Cases in Crafting and Executing Strategy

*Section A: Crafting Strategy in Single-Business Companies*

# PART 1

## Concepts and Techniques for Crafting and Executing Strategy

# What Is Strategy and Why Is It Important?

## Learning Objectives

THIS CHAPTER WILL HELP YOU UNDERSTAND:

**LO 1**   What we mean by a company's *strategy*.

**LO 2**   The concept of a *sustainable competitive advantage.*

**LO 3**   The ~~five~~ *three* most basic strategic approaches for setting a company apart from rivals and winning a sustainable competitive advantage.

**LO 4**   That a company's strategy tends to evolve because of changing circumstances and ongoing efforts by management to improve the strategy.

**LO 5**   Why it is important for a company to have a viable business model that outlines the company's customer value proposition and its profit formula.

**LO 6**   The three tests of a winning strategy.

> Strategy is about making choices, trade-offs; it's about deliberately choosing to be different.
>
> Michael Porter – *Professor and Consultant*

> If you don't have a competitive advantage, don't compete.
>
> Jack Welch – *Former CEO of General Electric*

> If your firm's strategy can be applied to any other firm, you don't have a very good one.
>
> David J. Collis and Michael G. Rukstad
> – *Consultants and Professors*

According to *The Economist,* a leading publication on business, economics, and international affairs, "In business, strategy is king. Leadership and hard work are all very well and luck is mighty useful, but it is strategy that makes or breaks a firm."[1] Luck and circumstance can explain why some companies are blessed with initial, short-lived success. But only a well-crafted, well-executed, constantly evolving strategy can explain why an elite set of companies somehow manages to rise to the top and stay there, year after year, pleasing their customers, shareholders, and other stakeholders alike in the process. Companies such as ExxonMobil, IBM, Southwest Airlines, FedEx, Google, Apple, Coca-Cola, Procter & Gamble, McDonald's, and Berkshire Hathaway come to mind—but long-lived success is not just the province of U.S. companies. Diverse kinds of companies, both large and small, from many different countries have been able to sustain strong performance records, including Russia's Gazprom (in energy), Korea's Samsung (in electronics), Singapore Airlines, Sweden's IKEA (in home furnishings), Mexico's America Movil (in telecommunications), and Japan's Toyota Motor.

In this opening chapter, we define the concept of strategy and describe its many facets. We explain what is meant by a competitive advantage, discuss the relationship between a company's strategy and its business model, and introduce you to the kinds of competitive strategies that can give a company an advantage over rivals in attracting customers and earning above-average profits. We look at what sets a winning strategy apart from others and why the caliber of a company's strategy determines whether the company will enjoy a competitive advantage over other firms. By the end of this chapter, you will have a clear idea of why the tasks of crafting and executing strategy are core management functions and why excellent execution of an excellent strategy is the most reliable recipe for turning a company into a standout performer over the long term.

## WHAT DO WE MEAN BY *STRATEGY*?

A company's **strategy** is the set of actions that its managers take to outperform the company's competitors and achieve superior profitability. The objective of a well-crafted strategy is not merely temporary competitive success and profits in the short run, but rather the sort of lasting success that can support growth and secure the company's future over the long term. Achieving this entails making a managerial commitment to a coherent array of well-considered choices about how to compete.[2] These include choices about:

- *How* to attract and please customers.
- *How* to compete against rivals.
- *How* to position the company in the marketplace and capitalize on attractive opportunities to grow the business.
- *How* to respond to changing economic and market conditions.
- *How* to manage each functional piece of the business (R&D, supply chain activities, production, sales and marketing, distribution, finance, and human resources).
- *How* to achieve the company's performance targets.

In most industries, companies have considerable freedom in choosing the *hows* of strategy.[3] Thus some companies strive to achieve lower costs than rivals, while others aim for product superiority or more personalized customer service or enhanced quality dimensions that rivals cannot match. Some companies opt for wide product lines, while others concentrate their energies on a narrow product lineup. Some competitors deliberately confine their operations to local or regional markets; others opt to compete nationally, internationally (several countries), or globally (all or most of the major country markets worldwide).

## Strategy Is about Competing Differently

Mimicking the strategies of successful industry rivals—with either copycat product offerings or maneuvers to stake out the same market position—rarely works. Rather, every company's strategy needs to have some distinctive element that draws in customers and produces a competitive edge. Strategy, at its essence, is about competing differently—doing what rival firms *don't* do or what rival firms *can't* do.[4] This does not mean that the key elements of a company's strategy have to be 100 percent different, but rather that they must differ in at least *some important respects*. A strategy stands a better chance of succeeding when it is predicated on actions, business approaches, and competitive moves aimed at (1) appealing to buyers in ways that *set a company apart from its rivals* and (2) staking out a market position that is not crowded with strong competitors.

A company's strategy provides direction and guidance, in terms of not only what the company *should* do but also what it *should not* do. Knowing what not to do can be as important as knowing what to do, strategically. At best, making the wrong strategic moves will prove a distraction and a waste of company resources. At worst, it can bring about unintended long-term consequences that put the company's very survival at risk.

Figure 1.1 illustrates the broad types of actions and approaches that often characterize a company's strategy in a particular business or industry. For a more concrete example of the specific actions constituting a firm's strategy, see Illustration Capsule 1.1, describing Starbucks's strategy in the specialty coffee market.

## Strategy and the Quest for Competitive Advantage

The heart and soul of any strategy are the actions and moves in the marketplace that managers are taking to gain a competitive advantage over rivals. A company achieves a competitive advantage whenever it has some type of edge over rivals in attracting buyers and coping with competitive forces. There are many routes to competitive advantage, but they all involve either giving buyers what they perceive as superior value

**FIGURE 1.1   Identifying a Company's Strategy—What to Look For**

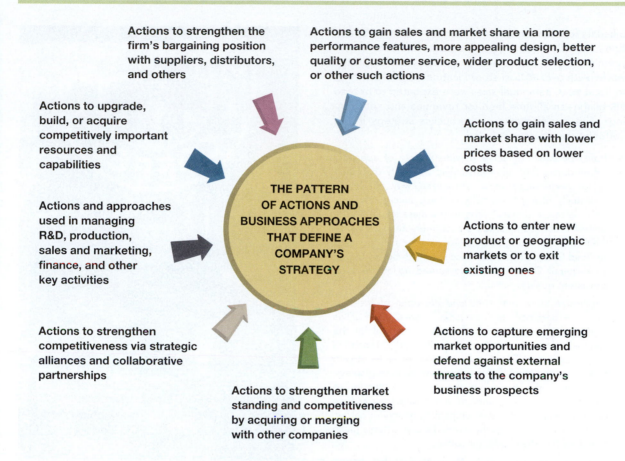

Actions to strengthen the firm's bargaining position with suppliers, distributors, and others

Actions to gain sales and market share via more performance features, more appealing design, better quality or customer service, wider product selection, or other such actions

Actions to upgrade, build, or acquire competitively important resources and capabilities

Actions to gain sales and market share with lower prices based on lower costs

Actions and approaches used in managing R&D, production, sales and marketing, finance, and other key activities

THE PATTERN OF ACTIONS AND BUSINESS APPROACHES THAT DEFINE A COMPANY'S STRATEGY

Actions to enter new product or geographic markets or to exit existing ones

Actions to strengthen competitiveness via strategic alliances and collaborative partnerships

Actions to strengthen market standing and competitiveness by acquiring or merging with other companies

Actions to capture emerging market opportunities and defend against external threats to the company's business prospects

compared to the offerings of rival sellers or giving buyers the same value as others at a lower cost to the firm. Superior value can mean a good product at a lower price, a superior product that is worth paying more for, or a best-value offering that represents an attractive combination of price, features, quality, service, and other attributes. Delivering superior value or delivering value more efficiently—whatever form it takes—nearly always requires performing value chain activities differently than rivals do and building competencies and resource capabilities that are not readily matched. In Illustration Capsule 1.1, it's evident that Starbucks has gained a competitive advantage over its rivals in the coffee shop industry through its efforts to create an upscale experience for coffee drinkers by catering to individualized tastes, enhancing the atmosphere and comfort of the shops, and delivering a premium product produced under environmentally sound, Fair Trade practices. By differentiating itself in this manner from other coffee purveyors, Starbucks has been able to charge prices for its coffee that are well above those of its rivals and far exceed the low cost of its inputs. Its expansion policies have allowed the company to make it easy for customers to find a Starbucks shop almost anywhere, further enhancing the brand and cementing customer loyalty. A creative *distinctive* strategy such as that used by Starbucks is a company's most reliable ticket for developing a competitive advantage over its rivals. If a strategy is not distinctive, then there can be no competitive advantage, since no firm would be meeting customer needs better or operating more efficiently than any other.

# Starbucks's Strategy in the Coffeehouse Market

Since its founding in 1985 as a modest nine-store operation in Seattle, Washington, Starbucks had become the premier roaster and retailer of specialty coffees in the world, with over 18,800 store locations as of April 2013. In fiscal 2013, its annual sales were expected to exceed $15 billion—an all-time high for revenues and net earnings. The key elements of Starbucks's strategy in the coffeehouse industry included:

- *Train "baristas" to serve a wide variety of specialty coffee drinks that allow customers to satisfy their individual preferences in a customized way.* Starbucks essentially brought specialty coffees, such as cappuccinos, lattes, and macchiatos, to the mass market in the United States, encouraging customers to personalize their coffee-drinking habits. Requests for such items as an "Iced Grande Hazelnut Macchiato with Soy Milk, and no Hazelnut Drizzle" could be served up quickly with consistent quality.

- *Emphasize store ambience and elevation of the customer experience at Starbucks stores.* Starbucks's management viewed each store as a billboard for the company and as a contributor to building the company's brand and image. The company went to great lengths to make sure the store fixtures, the merchandise displays, the artwork, the music, and the aromas all blended to create an inviting environment that evoked the romance of coffee and signaled the company's passion for coffee. Free Wi-Fi drew those who needed a comfortable place to work while they had their coffee.

- *Purchase and roast only top-quality coffee beans.* The company purchased only the highest-quality arabica beans and carefully roasted coffee to exacting standards of quality and flavor. Starbucks did not use chemicals or artificial flavors when preparing its roasted coffees.

- *Foster commitment to corporate responsibility.* Starbucks was protective of the environment and contributed positively to the communities where Starbucks stores were located. In addition, Starbucks promoted Fair Trade practices and paid above-market prices for coffee beans to provide its growers and suppliers with sufficient funding to sustain their operations and provide for their families.

- *Expand the number of Starbucks stores domestically and internationally.* Starbucks operated stores in high-traffic, high-visibility locations in the United States and abroad. The company's ability to vary store size and

format made it possible to locate stores in settings such as downtown and suburban shopping areas, office buildings, and university campuses. The company also focused on making Starbucks a global brand, expanding its reach to more than 60 countries in 2013.

- *Broaden and periodically refresh in-store product offerings.* Noncoffee products by Starbucks included teas, fresh pastries and other food items, candy, juice drinks, music CDs, and coffee mugs and coffee accessories.

- *Fully exploit the growing power of the Starbucks name and brand image with out-of-store sales.* Starbucks's Consumer Packaged Goods division included domestic and international sales of Frappuccino, coffee ice creams, and Starbucks coffees.

*Source:* Company documents, 10-Ks, and information posted on Starbucks's website.

If a company's competitive edge holds promise for being *sustainable* (as opposed to just temporary), then so much the better for both the strategy and the company's future profitability. What makes a competitive advantage **sustainable** (or durable), as opposed to temporary, are elements of the strategy that give buyers lasting reasons to prefer a company's products or services over those of competitors—*reasons that competitors are unable to nullify or overcome despite their best efforts*. In the case of Starbucks, the company's unparalleled name recognition, its reputation for high-quality specialty coffees served in a comfortable, inviting atmosphere, and the accessibility of the shops make it difficult for competitors to weaken or overcome Starbucks's competitive advantage. Not only has Starbucks's strategy provided the company with a sustainable competitive advantage, but it has made Starbucks one of the most admired companies on the planet.

Five of the most frequently used and dependable strategic approaches to setting a company apart from rivals, building strong customer loyalty, and winning a competitive advantage are:

1. *A low-cost provider strategy*—achieving a cost-based advantage over rivals. Walmart and Southwest Airlines have earned strong market positions because of the low-cost advantages they have achieved over their rivals. Low-cost provider strategies can produce a durable competitive edge when rivals find it hard to match the low-cost leader's approach to driving costs out of the business.

2. *A broad differentiation strategy*—seeking to differentiate the company's product or service from that of rivals in ways that will appeal to a broad spectrum of buyers. Successful adopters of differentiation strategies include Apple (innovative products), Johnson & Johnson in baby products (product reliability), LVMH (luxury and prestige), and BMW (engineering design and performance). One way to sustain this type of competitive advantage is to be sufficiently innovative to thwart the efforts of clever rivals to copy or closely imitate the product offering.

3. *A focused low-cost strategy*—concentrating on a narrow buyer segment (or market niche) and outcompeting rivals by having lower costs and thus being able to serve niche members at a lower price. Private-label manufacturers of food, health and beauty products, and nutritional supplements use their low-cost advantage to offer supermarket buyers lower prices than those demanded by producers of branded products.

4. *A focused differentiation strategy*—concentrating on a narrow buyer segment and outcompeting rivals by offering buyers customized attributes that meet their specialized needs and tastes better than rivals' products. Lululemon, for example, specializes in high-quality yoga clothing and the like, attracting a devoted set of buyers in the process. Jiffy Lube International in quick oil changes, McAfee in virus protection software, and The Weather Channel in cable TV provide some other examples of this strategy.

5. *A best-cost provider strategy*—giving customers more value for the money by satisfying their expectations on key quality features, performance, and/or service attributes while beating their price expectations. This approach is a hybrid strategy that blends elements of low-cost provider and differentiation strategies; the aim is to have lower costs than rivals while simultaneously offering better differentiating attributes. Target is an example of a company that is known for its hip product design (a reputation it built by featuring cheap-chic designers such as Isaac Mizrahi), as well as a more appealing shopping ambience for discount store shoppers. Its dual focus on low costs as well as differentiation shows how a best-cost provider strategy can offer customers great value for the money.

Winning a *sustainable* competitive edge over rivals with any of the preceding five strategies generally hinges as much on building competitively valuable expertise and capabilities that rivals cannot readily match as it does on having a distinctive product offering. Clever rivals can nearly always copy the attributes of a popular product or service, but for rivals to match the experience, know-how, and specialized capabilities that a company has developed and perfected over a long period of time is substantially harder to do and takes much longer. FedEx, for example, has superior capabilities in next-day delivery of small packages, while Google is known for its Internet search capabilities. Apple has demonstrated impressive product innovation capabilities in digital music players, smartphones, and e-readers. Hyundai has become the world's fastest-growing automaker as a result of its advanced manufacturing processes and unparalleled quality control system. Each of these capabilities has proved hard for competitors to imitate or best.

## Why a Company's Strategy Evolves over Time

**LO 4**

A company's strategy tends to evolve because of changing circumstances and ongoing efforts by management to improve the strategy.

The appeal of a strategy that yields a sustainable competitive advantage is that it offers the potential for an enduring edge over rivals. However, managers of every company must be willing and ready to modify the strategy in response to changing market conditions, advancing technology, unexpected moves by competitors, shifting buyer needs, emerging market opportunities, and new ideas for improving the strategy. Most of the time, a company's strategy evolves incrementally as management fine-tunes various pieces of the strategy and adjusts the strategy in response to unfolding events.[5] However, on occasion, major strategy shifts are called for, such as when the strategy is clearly failing or when industry conditions change in dramatic ways. Industry environments characterized by high-velocity change require companies to repeatedly adapt their strategies.[6] For example, companies in industries with rapid-fire advances in technology like medical equipment, electronics, and wireless devices often find it essential to adjust key elements of their strategies several times a year, sometimes even finding it necessary to "reinvent" their approach to providing value to their customers.

Regardless of whether a company's strategy changes gradually or swiftly, the important point is that the task of crafting strategy is not a one-time event but always a work in progress. Adapting to new conditions and constantly evaluating what is working well enough to continue and what needs to be improved are normal parts of the strategy-making process, resulting in an *evolving strategy.*[7]

*Changing circumstances and ongoing management efforts to improve the strategy cause a company's strategy to evolve over time—a condition that makes the task of crafting strategy a work in progress, not a one-time event.*

## A Company's Strategy Is Partly Proactive and Partly Reactive

*A company's strategy is shaped partly by management analysis and choice and partly by the necessity of adapting and learning by doing.*

The evolving nature of a company's strategy means that the typical company strategy is a blend of (1) *proactive,* planned initiatives to improve the company's financial performance and secure a competitive edge and (2) *reactive* responses to unanticipated developments and fresh market conditions. The biggest portion of a company's current strategy flows from previously initiated actions that have proven themselves in the marketplace and newly launched initiatives aimed at edging out rivals and boosting financial performance. This part of management's action plan for running the company is its **deliberate strategy,** consisting of proactive strategy

**FIGURE 1.2**   A Company's Strategy Is a Blend of Proactive Initiatives and Reactive Adjustments

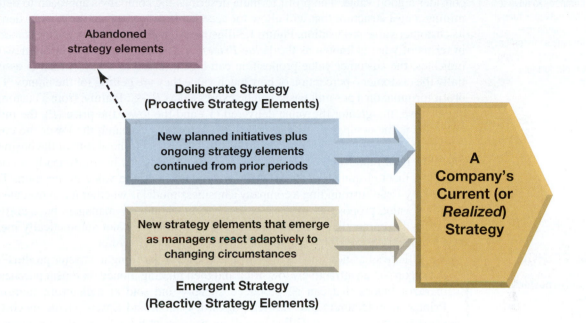

elements that are both planned and realized as planned (while other planned strategy elements may not work out and are abandoned in consequence)—see Figure 1.2.[8]

But managers must always be willing to supplement or modify the proactive strategy elements with as-needed reactions to unanticipated conditions. Inevitably, there will be occasions when market and competitive conditions take an unexpected turn that calls for some kind of strategic reaction. Hence, *a portion of a company's strategy is always developed on the fly,* coming as a response to fresh strategic maneuvers on the part of rival firms, unexpected shifts in customer requirements, fast-changing technological developments, newly appearing market opportunities, a changing political or economic climate, or other unanticipated happenings in the surrounding environment. These adaptive strategy adjustments make up the firm's **emergent strategy.** A company's strategy *in toto* (its **realized strategy**) thus tends to be a *combination* of proactive and reactive elements, with certain strategy elements being *abandoned* because they have become obsolete or ineffective. A company's realized strategy can be observed in the pattern of its actions over time, which is a far better indicator than any of its strategic plans on paper or any public pronouncements about its strategy.

> **CORE CONCEPT**
>
> A company's **deliberate strategy** consists of *proactive* strategy elements that are planned; its **emergent strategy** consists of *reactive* strategy elements that emerge as changing conditions warrant.

## A COMPANY'S STRATEGY AND ITS BUSINESS MODEL

At the core of every sound strategy is the company's **business model.** A business model is management's blueprint for delivering a valuable product or service to customers in a manner that will generate revenues sufficient to cover costs and yield an attractive profit.[9] The two elements of a company's business model are (1) its *customer value proposition* and (2) its *profit formula*. The customer value proposition lays out the company's approach to satisfying buyer wants and needs at a price customers will consider a good value. The profit formula describes the company's approach to determining a cost structure that will allow for acceptable profits, given the pricing tied to its customer value proposition. Figure 1.3 illustrates the elements of the business model in terms of what is known as the *Value-Price-Cost Framework*.[10] As the framework indicates, the customer value proposition can be expressed as $V - P$, which is essentially the customers' perception of how much value they are getting for the money. The profit formula, on a per-unit basis, can be expressed as $P - C$. Plainly, from a customer perspective, the greater the value delivered ($V$) and the lower the price ($P$), the more attractive is the company's value proposition. On the other hand, the lower the costs ($C$), given the customer value proposition ($V - P$), the greater the ability of the business model to be a moneymaker. Thus the profit formula reveals how efficiently a company can meet customer wants and needs and deliver on the value proposition. The nitty-gritty issue surrounding a company's business model is whether it can execute its customer value proposition profitably. Just because company managers have crafted a strategy for competing and running the business, this does not automatically mean that the strategy will lead to profitability—it may or it may not.

Gillette's business model in razor blades involves selling a "master product"—the razor—at an attractively low price and then making money on repeat purchases of razor blades that can be produced cheaply and sold at high profit margins. Printer manufacturers like Hewlett-Packard, Canon, and Epson pursue much the same business model as Gillette—selling printers at a low (virtually break-even) price and making large profit margins on the repeat purchases of printer supplies, especially ink cartridges. McDonald's invented the business model for fast food—providing value to customers in the form of economical quick-service meals at clean, convenient locations. Its profit formula involves such elements as standardized cost-efficient store design, stringent specifications for ingredients, operating procedures specified in detail for each unit, and heavy reliance on advertising and in-store promotions to drive volume. Illustration Capsule 1.2 describes three contrasting business models in radio broadcasting.

**FIGURE 1.3**   The Business Model and the Value-Price-Cost Framework

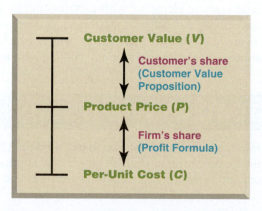

# Pandora, Sirius XM, and Over-the-Air Broadcast Radio: Three Contrasting Business Models

| | Pandora | Sirius XM | Over-the-Air Radio Broadcasters |
|---|---|---|---|
| **Customer value proposition** | • Through free-of-charge Internet radio service, allowed PC, tablet computer, and smartphone users to create up to 100 personalized music and comedy stations.<br><br>• Utilized algorithms to generate playlists based on users' predicted music preferences.<br><br>• Offered programming interrupted by brief, occasional ads; eliminated advertising for Pandora One subscribers. | • For a monthly subscription fee, provided Satellite-based music, news, sports, national and regional weather, traffic reports in limited areas, and talk radio programming.<br><br>• Also offered subscribers streaming Internet channels and the ability to create personalized commercial-free stations for online and mobile listening.<br><br>• Offered programming interrupted only by brief, occasional ads. | • Provided free-of-charge music, national and local news, local traffic reports, national and local weather, and talk radio programming.<br><br>• Included frequent programming interruption for ads. |
| **Profit formula** | *Revenue generation:* Display, audio, and video ads targeted to different audiences and sold to local and national buyers; subscription revenues generated from an advertising-free option called Pandora One.<br>*Cost structure:* Fixed costs associated with developing software for computers, tablets, and smartphones. Fixed and variable costs related to operating data centers to support streaming network, content royalties, marketing, and support activities. | *Revenue generation:* Monthly subscription fees, sales of satellite radio equipment, and advertising revenues.<br>*Cost structure:* Fixed costs associated with operating a satellite-based music delivery service and streaming Internet service. Fixed and variable costs related to programming and content royalties, marketing, and support activities. | *Revenue generation:* Advertising sales to national and local businesses.<br>*Cost structure:* Fixed costs associated with terrestrial broadcasting operations. Fixed and variable costs related to local news reporting, advertising sales operations, network affiliate fees, programming and content royalties, commercial production activities, and support activities. |
| | *Profit margin:* Profitability dependent on generating sufficient advertising revenues and subscription revenues to cover costs and provide attractive profits. | *Profit margin:* Profitability dependent on attracting a sufficiently large number of subscribers to cover costs and provide attractive profits. | *Profit margin:* Profitability dependent on generating sufficient advertising revenues to cover costs and provide attractive profits. |

# WHAT MAKES A STRATEGY A WINNER?

A **winning strategy** must pass three tests:
1. The Fit Test
2. The Competitive Advantage Test
3. The Performance Test

Three tests can be applied to determine whether a strategy is a *winning strategy:*

1. ***The Fit Test:*** *How well does the strategy fit the company's situation?* To qualify as a winner, a strategy has to be well matched to industry and competitive conditions, a company's best market opportunities, and other pertinent aspects of the business environment in which the company operates. No strategy can work well unless it exhibits good *external fit* and is in sync with prevailing market conditions. At the same time, a winning strategy must be tailored to the company's resources and competitive capabilities and be supported by a complementary set of functional activities (i.e., activities in the realms of supply chain management, operations, sales and marketing, and so on). That is, it must also exhibit *internal fit* and be compatible with a company's ability to execute the strategy in a competent manner. Unless a strategy exhibits good fit with both the external and internal aspects of a company's overall situation, it is likely to be an underperformer and fall short of producing winning results. Winning strategies also exhibit *dynamic fit* in the sense that they evolve over time in a manner that maintains close and effective alignment with the company's situation even as external and internal conditions change.[11]

2. ***The Competitive Advantage Test:*** *Is the strategy helping the company achieve a sustainable competitive advantage?* Strategies that fail to achieve a durable competitive advantage over rivals are unlikely to produce superior performance for more than a brief period of time. Winning strategies enable a company to achieve a competitive advantage over key rivals that is long-lasting. The bigger and more durable the competitive advantage, the more powerful it is.

3. ***The Performance Test:*** *Is the strategy producing good company performance?* The mark of a winning strategy is strong company performance. Two kinds of performance indicators tell the most about the caliber of a company's strategy: (1) competitive strength and market standing and (2) profitability and financial strength. Above-average financial performance or gains in market share, competitive position, or profitability are signs of a winning strategy.

Strategies that come up short on one or more of the preceding tests are plainly less appealing than strategies passing all three tests with flying colors. Managers should use the same questions when evaluating either proposed or existing strategies. New initiatives that don't seem to match the company's internal and external situations should be scrapped before they come to fruition, while existing strategies must be scrutinized on a regular basis to ensure they have good fit, offer a competitive advantage, and are contributing to above-average performance or performance improvements.

# WHY CRAFTING AND EXECUTING STRATEGY ARE IMPORTANT TASKS

Crafting and executing strategy are top-priority managerial tasks for two big reasons. First, a clear and reasoned strategy is management's prescription for doing business, its road map to competitive advantage, its game plan for pleasing customers, and its formula for improving performance. High-achieving enterprises are nearly always the product of astute, creative, and proactive strategy making. Companies don't get to the top of the industry rankings or stay there with illogical strategies, copycat strategies, or timid attempts to try to do better. Only a handful of companies can boast of hitting home runs in the marketplace due to lucky breaks or the good fortune of having stumbled into the right market at the right time with the right product. Even if this is the case, success will not be lasting unless the companies subsequently craft a strategy that capitalizes on their luck, builds on what is working, and discards the rest. So there can be little argument that the process of crafting a company's strategy matters—and matters a lot.

Second, even the best of strategies will lead to failure if it is not executed proficiently. The processes of crafting and executing strategies must go hand in hand if a company is to be successful in the long term. The chief executive officer of one successful company put it well when he said:

> In the main, our competitors are acquainted with the same fundamental concepts and techniques and approaches that we follow, and they are as free to pursue them as we are. More often than not, the difference between their level of success and ours lies in the relative thoroughness and self-discipline with which we and they develop and execute our strategies for the future.

## Good Strategy + Good Strategy Execution = Good Management

Crafting and executing strategy are thus core management functions. Among all the things managers do, nothing affects a company's ultimate success or failure more fundamentally than how well its management team charts the company's direction, develops competitively effective strategic moves and business approaches, and pursues what needs to be done internally to produce good day-in, day-out strategy execution and operating excellence. Indeed, *good strategy and good strategy execution are the most telling signs of good management.* The rationale for using the twin standards of good strategy making and good strategy execution to determine whether a company is well managed is therefore compelling: *The better conceived a company's strategy and the more competently it is executed, the more likely the company will be a standout performer in the marketplace.* In stark contrast, a company that lacks clear-cut direction, has a flawed strategy, or can't execute its strategy competently is a company whose financial performance is probably suffering, whose business is at long-term risk, and whose management is sorely lacking.

## THE ROAD AHEAD

Throughout the chapters to come and in Part 2 of this text, the spotlight is trained on the foremost question in running a business enterprise: *What must managers do, and do well, to make a company a winner in the marketplace?* The answer that emerges is that doing a good job of managing inherently requires good strategic thinking and good management of the strategy-making, strategy-executing process.

The mission of this book is to provide a solid overview of what every business student and aspiring manager needs to know about crafting and executing strategy. We will explore what good strategic thinking entails, describe the core concepts and tools of strategic analysis, and examine the ins and outs of crafting and executing strategy. The accompanying cases will help build your skills in

How well a company performs is directly attributable to the caliber of its strategy and the proficiency with which the strategy is executed.

both diagnosing how well the strategy-making, strategy-executing task is being performed and prescribing actions for how the strategy in question or its execution can be improved. The strategic management course that you are enrolled in may also include a strategy simulation exercise in which you will run a company in head-to-head competition with companies run by your classmates. Your mastery of the strategic management concepts presented in the following chapters will put you in a strong position to craft a winning strategy for your company and figure out how to execute it in a cost-effective and profitable manner. As you progress through the chapters of the text and the activities assigned during the term, we hope to convince you that first-rate capabilities in crafting and executing strategy are essential to good management.

As you tackle the content and accompanying activities of this book, ponder the following observation by the essayist and poet Ralph Waldo Emerson: "Commerce is a game of skill which many people play, but which few play well." If your efforts help you become a savvy player and better equip you to succeed in business, the time and energy you spend here will indeed prove worthwhile.

## KEY POINTS

1. A company's strategy is its game plan to attract and please customers, outperform its competitors, and achieve superior profitability.

2. The central thrust of a company's strategy is undertaking moves to build and strengthen the company's long-term competitive position and financial performance by *competing differently* from rivals and gaining a sustainable competitive advantage over them.

3. A company achieves a *competitive advantage* when it provides buyers with superior value compared to rival sellers or offers the same value at a lower cost to the firm. The advantage is *sustainable* if it persists despite the best efforts of competitors to match or surpass this advantage.

4. A company's strategy typically evolves over time, emerging from a blend of (1) proactive deliberate actions on the part of company managers to improve the strategy and (2) reactive emergent responses to unanticipated developments and fresh market conditions.

5. A company's business model sets forth the logic for how its strategy will create value for customers and at the same time generate revenues sufficient to cover costs and realize a profit. Thus, it contains two crucial elements: (1) the *customer value proposition*—a plan for satisfying customer wants and needs at a price customers will consider good value, and (2) the *profit formula*—a plan for a cost structure that will enable the company to deliver the customer value proposition profitably. These elements are illustrated by the Value-Price-Cost Framework.

6. A winning strategy will pass three tests: (1) *Fit* (external, internal, and dynamic consistency), (2) *Competitive Advantage* (durable competitive advantage), and (3) *Performance* (outstanding financial and market performance).

7. Crafting and executing strategy are core management functions. How well a company performs and the degree of market success it enjoys are directly attributable to the caliber of its strategy and the proficiency with which the strategy is executed.

## ASSURANCE OF LEARNING EXERCISES

1. Based on your experiences as a coffee consumer, does Starbucks's strategy (as described in Illustration Capsule 1.1) seem to set it apart from rivals? Does the strategy seem to be keyed to a cost-based advantage, differentiating features, serving the unique needs of a niche, or some combination of these? What is there about Starbucks's strategy that can lead to sustainable competitive advantage?

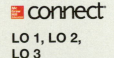

LO 1, LO 2, LO 3

2. Elements of eBay's strategy have evolved in meaningful ways since the company's founding in 1995. After reviewing all of the links at the company's investor relations site, which can be found at **investor.ebayinc.com**, prepare a one- to two-page report that discusses how its strategy has evolved. Your report should also assess how well eBay's strategy passes the three tests of a winning strategy.

LO 4, LO 6

3. Go to **www.nytco.com/investors** and check whether *The New York Times*' recent financial reports indicate that its business model is working. Does the company's business model remain sound as more consumers go to the Internet to find general information and stay abreast of current events and news stories? Is its revenue stream from advertisements growing or declining? Are its subscription fees and circulation increasing or declining?

LO 5

## EXERCISE FOR SIMULATION PARTICIPANTS

Three basic questions must be answered by managers of organizations of all sizes as they begin the process of crafting strategy:

- What is our present situation?
- Where do we want to go from here?
- How are we going to get there?

After you have read the Participant's Guide or Player's Manual for the strategy simulation exercise that you will participate in during this academic term, you and your co-managers should come up with brief one- or two-paragraph answers to these three questions *prior* to entering your first set of decisions. While your answer to the first of the three questions can be developed from your reading of the manual, the second and third questions will require a collaborative discussion among the members of your company's management team about how you intend to manage the company you have been assigned to run.

1. *What is our company's current situation?* A substantive answer to this question should cover the following issues:
   - Is your company in a good, average, or weak competitive position vis-à-vis rival companies?
   - Does your company appear to be in a sound financial condition?
   - Does it appear to have a competitive advantage, and is it likely to be sustainable?
   - What problems does your company have that need to be addressed?

LO 1, LO 2, LO 3

15

**LO 4, LO 6**

2. *Where do we want to take the company during the time we are in charge?* A complete answer to this question should say something about each of the following:
   - What goals or aspirations do you have for your company?
   - What do you want the company to be known for?
   - What market share would you like your company to have after the first five decision rounds?
   - By what amount or percentage would you like to increase total profits of the company by the end of the final decision round?
   - What kinds of performance outcomes will signal that you and your co-managers are managing the company in a successful manner?

**LO 4, LO 5**

3. *How are we going to get there?* Your answer should cover these issues:
   - Which of the basic strategic and competitive approaches discussed in this chapter do you think makes the most sense to pursue?
   - What kind of competitive advantage over rivals will you try to achieve?
   - How would you describe the company's business model?
   - What kind of actions will support these objectives?

# ENDNOTES

[1] B. R, "Strategy," *The Economist,* October 19, 2012, www.economist.com/blogs/schumpeter/2012/10/z-business-quotations-1 (accessed January 4, 2014).

[2] Jan Rivkin, "An Alternative Approach to Making Strategic Choices," Harvard Business School case 9-702-433, 2001.

[3] Michael E. Porter, "What Is Strategy?" *Harvard Business Review* 74, no. 6 (November–December 1996), pp. 65–67.

[4] Ibid.

[5] Eric T. Anderson and Duncan Simester, "A Step-by-Step Guide to Smart Business Experiments," *Harvard Business Review* 89, no. 3 (March 2011).

[6] Shona L. Brown and Kathleen M. Eisenhardt, *Competing on the Edge: Strategy as Structured Chaos* (Boston, MA: Harvard Business School Press, 1998).

[7] Cynthia A. Montgomery, "Putting Leadership Back into Strategy," *Harvard Business Review* 86, no. 1 (January 2008).

[8] Henry Mintzberg and J. A. Waters, "Of Strategies, Deliberate and Emergent," *Strategic Management Journal* 6 (1985); Costas Markides, "Strategy as Balance: From 'Either-Or' to 'And,'" *Business Strategy Review* 12, no. 3 (September 2001).

[9] Mark W. Johnson, Clayton M. Christensen, and Henning Kagermann, "Reinventing Your Business Model," *Harvard Business Review* 86, no. 12 (December 2008); Joan Magretta, "Why Business Models Matter," *Harvard Business Review* 80, no. 5 (May 2002).

[10] A. Brandenburger and H. Stuart, "Value-Based Strategy," *Journal of Economics and Management Strategy* 5 (1996), pp. 5–24; D. Hoopes, T. Madsen, and G. Walker, "Guest Editors' Introduction to the Special Issue: Why Is There a Resource-Based View? Toward a Theory of Competitive Heterogeneity," *Strategic Management Journal* 24 (2003), pp. 889–992; and M. Peteraf and J. Barney, "Unravelling the Resource-Based Tangle," *Managerial and Decision Economics* 24 (2003), pp. 309–323.

[11] Rivkin, "An Alternative Approach to Making Strategic Choices."

### CHAPTER 2

# Charting a Company's Direction

## Its Vision, Mission, Objectives, and Strategy

## Learning Objectives

**LO 1**  Why it is critical for company managers to have a clear strategic vision of where a company needs to head and why.

**LO 2**  The importance of setting both strategic and financial objectives.

**LO 3**  Why the strategic initiatives taken at various organizational levels must be tightly coordinated to achieve companywide performance targets.

**LO 4**  What a company must do to achieve operating excellence and to execute its strategy proficiently.

**LO 5**  The role and responsibility of a company's board of directors in overseeing the strategic management process.

Vision without action is merely a dream. . . .Vision with action can change the world.

Joel A. Barker – *Consultant and Author*

To succeed in your mission, you must have single-minded devotion to your goal.

Abdul Kalam – *Former President of India*

A good goal is like a strenuous exercise—it makes you stretch.

Mary Kay Ash – *Founder of Mary Kay Cosmetics*

If crafting and executing strategy are critically important managerial tasks, then it is essential to know exactly what is involved in developing a strategy and executing it proficiently. Is any analysis required? What goes into charting a company's strategic course and long-term direction? Does a company need a strategic plan? What are the various components of the strategy-making, strategy-executing process and to what extent are company personnel—aside from senior management—involved in the process?

This chapter presents an overview of the ins and outs of crafting and executing company strategies.

Special attention is given to management's direction-setting responsibilities—charting a strategic course, setting performance targets, and choosing a strategy capable of producing the desired outcomes. We also explain why strategy making is a task for a company's entire management team and discuss which kinds of strategic decisions tend to be made at which levels of management. The chapter concludes with a look at the roles and responsibilities of a company's board of directors and how good corporate governance protects shareholder interests and promotes good management.

## WHAT DOES THE STRATEGY-MAKING, STRATEGY-EXECUTING PROCESS ENTAIL?

The process of crafting and executing a company's strategy is an ongoing, continuous process consisting of five interrelated stages:

1. *Developing a strategic vision* that charts the company's long-term direction, a *mission statement* that describes the company's purpose, and a set of *core values* to guide the pursuit of the vision and mission.
2. *Setting objectives* for measuring the company's performance and tracking its progress in moving in the intended long-term direction.
3. *Crafting a strategy* for advancing the company along the path management has charted and achieving its performance objectives.
4. *Executing the chosen strategy* efficiently and effectively.

## FIGURE 2.1    The Strategy-Making, Strategy-Executing Process

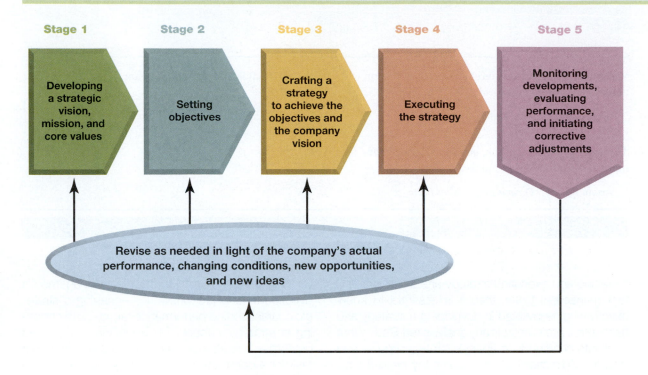

5. *Monitoring developments, evaluating performance, and initiating corrective adjustments* in the company's vision and mission statement, objectives, strategy, or approach to strategy execution in light of actual experience, changing conditions, new ideas, and new opportunities.

Figure 2.1 displays this five-stage process, which we examine next in some detail. The first three stages of the strategic management process involve making a strategic plan. A **strategic plan** maps out where a company is headed, establishes strategic and financial targets, and outlines the competitive moves and approaches to be used in achieving the desired business results.[1]

A company's **strategic plan** lays out its future direction, performance targets, and strategy.

# STAGE 1: DEVELOPING A STRATEGIC VISION, MISSION STATEMENT, AND SET OF CORE VALUES

**LO 1**

Why it is critical for company managers to have a clear strategic vision of where a company needs to head and why.

Very early in the strategy-making process, a company's senior managers must wrestle with the issue of what directional path the company should take. Can the company's prospects be improved by changing its product offerings, or the markets in which it participates, or the customers it aims to serve? Deciding to commit the company to one path versus another pushes managers to draw some carefully reasoned conclusions about whether the company's present strategic course offers attractive opportunities for growth and profitability or whether changes of one kind or another in the company's strategy and long-term direction are needed.

# Developing a Strategic Vision

Top management's views and conclusions about the company's long-term direction and what product-market-customer business mix seems optimal for the road ahead constitute a **strategic vision** for the company. A strategic vision delineates management's aspirations for the business, providing a panoramic view of "where we are going" and a convincing rationale for why this makes good business sense for the company. A strategic vision thus points an organization in a particular direction, charts a strategic path for it to follow, builds commitment to the future course of action, and molds organizational identity. A clearly articulated strategic vision communicates management's aspirations to stakeholders (customers, employees, stockholders, suppliers, etc.) and helps steer the energies of company personnel in a common direction. For instance, Henry Ford's vision of a car in every garage had power because it captured the imagination of others, aided internal efforts to mobilize the Ford Motor Company's resources, and served as a reference point for gauging the merits of the company's strategic actions.

> ### CORE CONCEPT
>
> A **strategic vision** describes "where we are going"—management's aspirations for the company and the course and direction charted to achieve them.
>
> Exam

Well-conceived visions are *distinctive* and *specific* to a particular organization; they avoid generic, feel-good statements like "We will become a global leader and the first choice of customers in every market we serve."[2] Likewise, a strategic vision proclaiming management's quest "to be the market leader" or "to be the most innovative" or "to be recognized as the best company in the industry" offers scant guidance about a company's direction or the kind of company that management is striving to build.

A surprising number of the vision statements found on company websites and in annual reports are vague and unrevealing, saying very little about the company's future direction. Some could apply to almost any company in any industry. Many read like a public relations statement—high-sounding words that someone came up with because it is fashionable for companies to have an official vision statement.[3] But the real purpose of a vision statement is to serve as a management tool for giving the organization a sense of direction.

For a strategic vision to function as a valuable management tool, it must convey what top executives want the business to look like and provide managers at all organizational levels with a reference point in making strategic decisions and preparing the company for the future. It must say something definitive about how the company's leaders intend to position the company beyond where it is today. Table 2.1 provides some dos and don'ts in composing an effectively worded vision statement. Illustration Capsule 2.1 provides a critique of the strategic visions of several prominent companies.

> An effectively communicated vision is a valuable management tool for enlisting the commitment of company personnel to actions that move the company in the intended direction.

# Communicating the Strategic Vision

A strategic vision has little value to the organization unless it's effectively communicated down the line to lower-level managers and employees. A vision cannot provide direction for middle managers or inspire and energize employees unless everyone in the company is familiar with it and can observe management's commitment to the vision. It is particularly important for executives to provide a compelling rationale for a dramatically *new* strategic vision and company direction. When company personnel don't understand or accept the need for redirecting organizational efforts, they are prone to resist change. Hence, explaining the basis for the new direction, addressing employee concerns head-on, calming fears, lifting spirits, and providing updates and progress reports as events unfold all become part of the task in mobilizing support for the vision and winning commitment to needed actions.

Winning the support of organization members for the vision nearly always means putting "where we are going and why" in writing, distributing the statement

**TABLE 2.1    Wording a Vision Statement—the Dos and Don'ts**

| The Dos | The Don'ts |
|---|---|
| **Be graphic.** Paint a clear picture of where the company is headed and the market position(s) the company is striving to stake out. | **Don't be vague or incomplete.** Never skimp on specifics about where the company is headed or how the company intends to prepare for the future. |
| **Be forward-looking and directional.** Describe the strategic course that will help the company prepare for the future. | **Don't dwell on the present.** A vision is not about what a company once did or does now; it's about "where we are going." |
| **Keep it focused.** Focus on providing managers with guidance in making decisions and allocating resources. | **Don't use overly broad language.** Avoid all-inclusive language that gives the company license to pursue any opportunity. |
| **Have some wiggle room.** Language that allows some flexibility allows the directional course to be adjusted as market, customer, and technology circumstances change. | **Don't state the vision in bland or uninspiring terms.** The best vision statements have the power to motivate company personnel and inspire shareholder confidence about the company's future. |
| **Be sure the journey is feasible.** The path and direction should be within the realm of what the company can accomplish; over time, a company should be able to demonstrate measurable progress in achieving the vision. | **Don't be generic.** A vision statement that could apply to companies in any of several industries (or to any of several companies in the same industry) is not specific enough to provide any guidance. |
| **Indicate why the directional path makes good business sense.** The directional path should be in the long-term interests of stakeholders (especially shareholders, employees, and suppliers). | **Don't rely on superlatives.** Visions that claim the company's strategic course is the "best" or "most successful" usually lack specifics about the path the company is taking to get there. |
| **Make it memorable.** To give the organization a sense of direction and purpose, the vision needs to be easily communicated. Ideally, it should be reducible to a few choice lines or a memorable slogan. | **Don't run on and on.** A vision statement that is not short and to the point will tend to lose its audience. |

*Sources:* John P. Kotter, *Leading Change* (Boston: Harvard Business School Press, 1996); Hugh Davidson, *The Committed Enterprise* (Oxford: Butterworth Heinemann, 2002); and Michel Robert, *Strategy Pure and Simple II* (New York: McGraw-Hill, 1992).

organizationwide, and having top executives personally explain the vision and its rationale to as many people as feasible. Ideally, executives should present their vision for the company in a manner that reaches out and grabs people. An engaging and convincing strategic vision has enormous motivational value—for the same reason that a stonemason is more inspired by the opportunity to build a great cathedral for the ages than a house. Thus, executive ability to paint a convincing and inspiring picture of a company's journey to a future destination is an important element of effective strategic leadership.

**Expressing the Essence of the Vision in a Slogan**    The task of effectively conveying the vision to company personnel is assisted when management can capture the vision of where to head in a catchy or easily remembered slogan. A number of organizations have summed up their vision in a brief phrase. Nike's slogan is "to bring

# Examples of Strategic Visions— How Well Do They Measure Up?

| Vision Statement | Effective Elements | Shortcomings |
|---|---|---|
| **Coca-Cola**<br><br>Our vision serves as the framework for our Roadmap and guides every aspect of our business by describing what we need to accomplish in order to continue achieving sustainable, quality growth.<br>• People: Be a great place to work where people are inspired to be the best they can be.<br>• Portfolio: Bring to the world a portfolio of quality beverage brands that anticipate and satisfy people's desires and needs.<br>• Partners: Nurture a winning network of customers and suppliers; together we create mutual, enduring value.<br>• Planet: Be a responsible citizen that makes a difference by helping build and support sustainable communities.<br>• Profit: Maximize long-term return to shareowners while being mindful of our overall responsibilities.<br>• Productivity: Be a highly effective, lean, and fast-moving organization. | • Graphic<br>• Focused<br>• Flexible<br>• Makes good business sense | • Long<br>• Not forward-looking |
| **Procter & Gamble**<br><br>We will provide branded products and services of superior quality and value that improve the lives of the world's consumers, now and for generations to come. As a result, consumers will reward us with leadership sales, profit and value creation, allowing our people, our shareholders and the communities in which we live and work to prosper. | • Forward-looking<br>• Flexible<br>• Feasible<br>• Makes good business sense | • Not graphic<br>• Not focused<br>• Not memorable |
| **Heinz**<br>We define a compelling, sustainable future and create the path to achieve it. | • Forward-looking<br>• Flexible | • Not graphic<br>• Not focused<br>• Confusing<br>• Not memorable<br>• Not necessarily feasible |

*Note:* Developed with Jenna P. Pfeffer.

*Source:* Company documents and websites (accessed February 12, 2012).

innovation and inspiration to every athlete in the world." The Mayo Clinic's vision is to provide "the best care to every patient every day," while Greenpeace's aspires "to halt environmental abuse and promote environmental solutions." Even Scotland Yard has a catchy vision, which is "to make London the safest major city in the world." Creating a short slogan to illuminate an organization's direction and purpose and using it repeatedly as a reminder of "where we are headed and why" helps rally organization members to hurdle whatever obstacles lie in the company's path and maintain their focus.

## Why a Sound, Well-Communicated Strategic Vision Matters

A well-thought-out, forcefully communicated strategic vision pays off in several respects: (1) It crystallizes senior executives' own views about the firm's long-term direction; (2) it reduces the risk of rudderless decision making; (3) it is a tool for winning the support of organization members to help make the vision a reality; (4) it provides a beacon for lower-level managers in setting departmental objectives and crafting departmental strategies that are in sync with the company's overall strategy; and (5) it helps an organization prepare for the future. When top executives are able to demonstrate significant progress in achieving these five benefits, the first step in organizational direction setting has been successfully completed.

> The distinction between a strategic vision and a mission statement is fairly clear-cut: A **strategic vision** portrays a company's aspirations for its *future* ("where we are going"), whereas a company's **mission** describes the scope and purpose of its *present* business ("who we are, what we do, and why we are here").
>
> *Evan*

# Developing a Company Mission Statement

The defining characteristic of a strategic vision is what it says about the company's *future strategic course*—"the direction we are headed and the shape of our business in the future." It is aspirational. In contrast, a **mission statement** describes the enterprise's *present business and purpose*—"who we are, what we do, and why we are here." It is purely descriptive. Ideally, a company mission statement (1) identifies the company's products and/or services, (2) specifies the buyer needs that the company seeks to satisfy and the customer groups or markets that it serves, and (3) gives the company its own identity. The mission statements that one finds in company annual reports or posted on company websites are typically quite brief; some do a better job than others of conveying what the enterprise is all about.

Consider, for example, the mission statement of Trader Joe's (a specialty grocery chain):

> The mission of Trader Joe's is to give our customers the best food and beverage values that they can find anywhere and to provide them with the information required for informed buying decisions. We provide these with a dedication to the highest quality of customer satisfaction delivered with a sense of warmth, friendliness, fun, individual pride, and company spirit.

Note that Trader Joe's mission statement does a good job of conveying "who we are, what we do, and why we are here" but it provides no sense of "where we are headed."

An example of a well-stated mission statement with ample specifics about what the organization does is that of the Occupational Safety and Health Administration (OSHA): "to assure the safety and health of America's workers by setting and enforcing standards; providing training, outreach, and education; establishing partnerships; and encouraging continual improvement in workplace safety and health." YouTube's mission statement, while short, still captures the essence of what the company is about: "to provide fast and easy video access and the ability to share videos frequently." An example of a not-so-revealing mission statement is that of Microsoft. "To help people and businesses throughout the world realize their full potential" says nothing about its products or business makeup and could apply to many companies in many different industries. A person unfamiliar with Microsoft could not discern from its mission statement that it is a globally known provider of PC software and a leading maker of video game consoles (the popular Xbox 360). Coca-Cola, which markets nearly 400 beverage brands in over 200 countries, also has an uninformative mission statement: "to refresh the world; to inspire moments of optimism and happiness; to create value and make a difference." The usefulness of a mission statement that cannot convey the essence of a company's business activities and purpose is unclear.

> To be well worded, a company mission statement must employ language specific enough to distinguish its business makeup and purpose from those of other enterprises and give the company its own identity.

Occasionally, companies couch their mission in terms of making a profit. This, too, is flawed. Profit is more correctly an *objective* and a *result* of what a company does. Moreover, earning a profit is the obvious intent of every commercial enterprise. Such companies as Volkswagen, Wegmans, Edward Jones, The Boston Consulting Group, DreamWorks Animation, and Intuit are each striving to earn a profit for shareholders; but plainly the fundamentals of their businesses are substantially different when it comes to "who we are and what we do." It is management's answer to "make a profit doing what and for whom?" that reveals the substance of a company's true mission and business purpose.

## Linking the Vision and Mission with Company Values

Many companies have developed a set of values to guide the actions and behavior of company personnel in conducting the company's business and pursuing its strategic vision and mission. By **values** (or **core values,** as they are often called), we mean certain designated beliefs, traits, and behavioral norms that management has determined should guide the pursuit of its vision and mission. Values relate to such things as fair treatment, honor and integrity, ethical behavior, innovativeness, teamwork, a passion for top-notch quality or superior customer service, social responsibility, and community citizenship.

> **CORE CONCEPT**
>
> A company's **values** are the beliefs, traits, and behavioral norms that company personnel are expected to display in conducting the company's business and pursuing its strategic vision and mission.

Most companies have articulated four to eight core values that company personnel are expected to display and that are supposed to be mirrored in how the company conducts its business. At Kodak, the core values are respect for the dignity of the individual, uncompromising integrity, unquestioned trust, constant credibility, continual improvement and personal renewal, and open celebration of individual and team achievements. At Foster Wheeler, a global engineering and construction firm, the five core values are integrity, accountability, high performance, valuing people, and teamwork. In its quest to be the world's leading home-improvement retailer, Home Depot embraces eight values—entrepreneurial spirit, excellent customer service, giving back to the community, respect for all people, doing the right thing, taking care of people, building strong relationships, and creating shareholder value.

Do companies practice what they preach when it comes to their professed values? Sometimes no, sometimes yes—it runs the gamut. At one extreme are companies with window-dressing values; the values are given lip service by top executives but have little discernible impact on either how company personnel behave or how the company operates. Such companies have value statements because they are in vogue and make the company look good. At the other extreme are companies whose executives are committed to grounding company operations on sound values and principled ways of doing business. Executives at these companies deliberately seek to ingrain the designated core values into the corporate culture—the core values thus become an integral part of the company's DNA and what makes the company tick. At such values-driven companies, executives "walk the talk" and company personnel are held accountable for embodying the stated values in their behavior.

At companies where the stated values are real rather than cosmetic, managers connect values to the pursuit of the strategic vision and mission in one of two ways. In companies with values that are deeply entrenched in the corporate culture, senior managers are careful to craft a vision, mission, strategy, and set of operating practices that match established values; moreover, they repeatedly emphasize how the value-based behavioral norms contribute to the company's business success. If the company changes to a different vision or strategy, executives take care to explain how and why the core values continue to be relevant. Few companies with sincere commitment to established core values ever undertake strategic moves that conflict with ingrained values. In new

# Patagonia, Inc.:
# A Values-Driven Company

## PATAGONIA'S MISSION STATEMENT

Build the best product, cause no unnecessary harm, use business to inspire and implement solutions to the environmental crisis.

## PATAGONIA'S CORE VALUES

**Quality:** Pursuit of ever-greater quality in everything we do.

**Integrity:** Relationships built on integrity and respect.

**Environmentalism:** Serve as a catalyst for personal and corporate action.

**Not Bound by Convention:** Our success—and much of the fun—lies in developing innovative ways to do things.

Patagonia, Inc., is an American outdoor clothing and gear company that clearly "walks the talk" with respect to its mission and values. While its mission is relatively vague about the types of products Patagonia offers, it clearly states the foundational "how" and "why" of the company. The four core values individually reinforce the mission in distinct ways, charting a defined path for employees to follow. At the same time, each value is reliant on the others for maximum effect. The values' combined impact on internal operations and public perception has made Patagonia a strong leader in the outdoor gear world.

While many companies espouse the pursuit of **quality** as part of their strategy, at Patagonia quality must come through honorable practices or not at all. Routinely, the company opts for more expensive materials and labor to maintain internal consistency with the mission. Patagonia learned early on that it could not make good products in bad factories, so it holds its manufacturers accountable through a variety of auditing partnerships and alliances. In this way, the company maintains relationships built on **integrity** and respect. In addition to keeping faith with those who make its products, Patagonia relentlessly pursues integrity in sourcing production inputs. Central to its **environmental** mission and core values, it targets for use sustainable and recyclable materials, ethically procured. Demonstrating leadership in environmentalism, Patagonia established foundations to support ecological causes, even **defying convention** by giving 1 percent of profits to conservation causes. These are but a few examples of the ways in which Patagonia's core values fortify each other and support the mission.

For Patagonia, quality would not be possible without integrity, unflinching environmentalism, and the company's unconventional approach. Since its founding in 1973 by rock climber Yvon Chouinard, Patagonia has remained remarkably consistent to the spirit of these values. This has endeared the company to legions of loyal customers while leading other businesses in protecting the environment. More than an apparel and gear company, Patagonia inspires everyone it touches to do their best for the planet and each other, in line with its mission and core values.

*Note:* Developed with Nicholas J. Ziemba.

*Sources:* Patagonia, Inc., "Corporate Social Responsibility," *The Footprint Chronicles,* 2007, and "Becoming a Responsible Company," www.patagonia.com/us/patagonia.go?assetid=2329 (accessed February 28, 2014).

companies, top management has to consider what values and business conduct should characterize the company and then draft a value statement that is circulated among managers and employees for discussion and possible modification. A final value statement that incorporates the desired behaviors and that connects to the vision and mission is then officially adopted. Some companies combine their vision, mission, and values into a single statement or document, circulate it to all organization members, and in many instances post the vision, mission, and value statement on the company's website. Illustration Capsule 2.2 describes how core values underlie the company's mission at Patagonia, Inc., a widely known and quite successful outdoor clothing and gear company.

# STAGE 2: SETTING OBJECTIVES

The managerial purpose of setting **objectives** is to convert the vision and mission into specific performance targets. Objectives reflect management's aspirations for company performance in light of the industry's prevailing economic and competitive conditions and the company's internal capabilities. Well-stated objectives must be *specific, quantifiable* or *measurable,* and *challenging* and must contain a *deadline for achievement.* As Bill Hewlett, cofounder of Hewlett-Packard, shrewdly observed, "You cannot manage what you cannot measure. . . . And what gets measured gets done."[4] Concrete, measurable objectives are managerially valuable for three reasons: (1) They focus organizational attention and align actions throughout the organization, (2) they serve as *yardsticks* for tracking a company's performance and progress, and (3) they motivate employees to expend greater effort and perform at a high level.

**LO 2**

The importance of setting both strategic and financial objectives.

**CORE CONCEPT**

**Objectives** are an organization's performance targets—the specific results management wants to achieve.

## The Imperative of Setting Stretch Objectives

The experiences of countless companies teach that one of the best ways to promote outstanding company performance is for managers to deliberately set performance targets high enough to *stretch an organization to perform at its full potential and deliver the best possible results.* Challenging company personnel to go all out and deliver "stretch" gains in performance pushes an enterprise to be more inventive, to exhibit more urgency in improving both its financial performance and its business position, and to be more intentional and focused in its actions. Stretch objectives spur exceptional performance and help build a firewall against contentment with modest gains in organizational performance.

Manning Selvage & Lee (MS&L), a U.S. public relations firm, used ambitious stretch objectives to triple its revenues in three years. A company exhibits *strategic intent* when it relentlessly pursues an ambitious strategic objective, concentrating the full force of its resources and competitive actions on achieving that objective. MS&L's strategic intent was to become one of the leading global PR firms, which it achieved with the help of its stretch objectives. Honda's long-standing strategic intent of producing an ultra-light jet was finally realized in 2012 when the five-passenger plane dubbed the "Honda Civic of the sky" went into production. Google has the strategic intent of developing drones for the delivery of online orders through Amazon and has been making good progress toward meeting that stretch goal.

**CORE CONCEPT**

**Stretch objectives** set performance targets high enough to *stretch* an organization to perform at its full potential and deliver the best possible results.

**CORE CONCEPT**

A company exhibits **strategic intent** when it relentlessly pursues an ambitious strategic objective, concentrating the full force of its resources and competitive actions on achieving that objective.

## What Kinds of Objectives to Set

Two distinct types of performance targets are required: those relating to financial performance and those relating to strategic performance. **Financial objectives** communicate management's goals for financial performance. **Strategic objectives** are goals concerning a company's marketing standing and competitive position. A company's set of financial and strategic objectives should include both near-term and longer-term performance targets. Short-term (quarterly or annual) objectives focus attention on delivering performance improvements in the current period and satisfy shareholder expectations for near-term progress. Longer-term targets (three to five years off) force managers to consider what to do *now* to put the company in position to perform better later. Long-term objectives are critical for achieving optimal long-term performance and stand as a barrier to a nearsighted management philosophy and an undue focus on short-term results. When trade-offs have to be made between achieving long-term objectives and achieving short-term objectives, long-term objectives should take precedence (unless the achievement of one or more short-term performance targets has unique importance). Examples of commonly used financial and strategic objectives are listed in Table 2.2.

# The Need for a Balanced Approach to Objective Setting

The importance of setting and attaining financial objectives is obvious. Without adequate profitability and financial strength, a company's long-term health and ultimate survival are jeopardized. Furthermore, subpar earnings and a weak balance sheet alarm shareholders and creditors and put the jobs of senior executives at risk. However, good financial performance, by itself, is not enough. Of equal or greater importance is a company's strategic performance—outcomes that indicate whether a company's market position and competitiveness are deteriorating, holding steady, or improving. *A stronger market standing and greater competitive vitality—especially when accompanied by competitive advantage—is what enables a company to improve its financial performance.*

Moreover, a company's financial performance measures are really *lagging indicators* that reflect the results of past decisions and organizational activities.[5] But a company's past or current financial performance is not a reliable indicator of its future prospects—poor financial performers often turn things around and do better, while good financial performers can fall upon hard times. The best and most reliable *leading indicators* of a company's future financial performance and business prospects are strategic outcomes that indicate whether the company's competitiveness and market position are stronger or weaker. The accomplishment of strategic objectives signals that the company is well positioned to sustain or improve its performance. For instance, if a

## TABLE 2.2    Common Financial and Strategic Objectives

| Financial Objectives | Strategic Objectives |
|---|---|
| • An *x* percent increase in annual revenues | • Winning an *x* percent market share |
| • Annual increases in after-tax profits *of x* percent | • Achieving lower overall costs than rivals |
| • Annual increases in earnings per share of *x* percent | • Overtaking key competitors on product performance, quality, or customer service |
| • Annual dividend increases of *x* percent | • Deriving *x* percent of revenues from the sale of new products introduced within the past five years |
| • Profit margins of *x* percent | |
| • An *x* percent return on capital employed (ROCE) or return on shareholders' equity (ROE) investment | • Having broader or deeper technological capabilities than rivals |
| | • Having a wider product line than rivals |
| • Increased shareholder value in the form of an upward-trending stock price | • Having a better-known or more powerful brand name than rivals |
| • Bond and credit ratings of *x* | • Having stronger national or global sales and distribution capabilities than rivals |
| • Internal cash flows of *x* dollars to fund new capital investment | • Consistently getting new or improved products to market ahead of rivals |

# Examples of Company Objectives

## WALGREENS

Increase revenues from $72 billion in 2012 to more than $130 billion in 2016; increase operating income from $3.5 billion in 2012 to $8.5 billion to $9.0 billion by 2016; increase operating cash flow from $4.4 billion in 2012 to approximately $8 billion in 2016; generate $1 billion in cost savings from combined pharmacy and general merchandise purchasing synergies by 2016.

## PEPSICO

Accelerate top-line growth; build and expand our better-for-you snacks and beverages and nutrition businesses; improve our water use efficiency by 20 percent per unit of production by 2015; reduce packaging weight by 350 million pounds; improve our electricity use efficiency by 20 percent per unit of production by 2015; maintain appropriate financial flexibility with ready access to global capital and credit markets at favorable interest rates.

## YUM! BRANDS (KFC, PIZZA HUT, TACO BELL, WINGSTREET)

Increase operating profit derived from operations in emerging markets from 48 percent in 2010 to

57 percent in 2015; increase number of KFC units in Africa from 655 in 2010 to 2,100 in 2020; increase KFC revenues in Africa from $865 million in 2010 to $1.94 billion in 2014; increase number of KFC units in India from 101 in 2010 to 1,250 in 2020; increase number of KFC units in Vietnam from 87 in 2010 to 500 in 2020; increase number of KFC units in Russia from 150 in 2010 to 500 in 2020; open 100 new Taco Bell units in international markets in 2015; increase annual cash flows from operations from $1.5 billion in 2010 to $2.1 billion in 2015.

*Source:* Information posted on company websites.

---

company is achieving ambitious strategic objectives such that its competitive strength and market position are on the rise, then there's reason to expect that its *future* financial performance will be better than its current or past performance. If a company is losing ground to competitors and its market position is slipping—outcomes that reflect weak strategic performance (and, very likely, failure to achieve its strategic objectives)—then its ability to maintain its present profitability is highly suspect.

Consequently, it is important to use a performance measurement system that strikes a *balance* between financial objectives and strategic objectives.[6] The most widely used framework of this sort is known as the **Balanced Scorecard.**[7] This is a method for linking financial performance objectives to specific strategic objectives that derive from a company's business model. It provides a company's employees with clear guidelines about how their jobs are linked to the overall objectives of the organization, so they can contribute most productively and collaboratively to the achievement of these goals. In 2010, nearly 50 percent of global companies used a balanced-scorecard approach to measuring strategic and financial performance.[8] Organizations that have adopted the balanced-scorecard approach include 7-Eleven, Allianz Italy, Wells Fargo, Ford Motor, Verizon, SAS Institute, Exxon-Mobil, Caterpillar, Pfizer, and DuPont.[9] Illustration Capsule 2.3 provides selected strategic and financial objectives of three prominent companies.

### CORE CONCEPT

The **Balanced Scorecard** is a widely used method for combining the use of both strategic and financial objectives, tracking their achievement, and giving management a more complete and balanced view of how well an organization is performing.

## Setting Objectives for Every Organizational Level

Objective setting should not stop with top management's establishing of companywide performance targets. Company objectives need to be broken down into performance targets for each of the organization's separate businesses, product lines, functional departments, and individual work units. Employees within various functional areas and operating levels will be guided much better by specific objectives relating directly to their departmental activities than broad organizational-level goals. Objective setting is thus a *top-down process* that must extend to the lowest organizational levels. This means that each organizational unit must take care to set performance targets that support—rather than conflict with or negate—the achievement of companywide strategic and financial objectives.

The ideal situation is a team effort in which each organizational unit strives to produce results that contribute to the achievement of the company's performance targets and strategic vision. Such consistency signals that organizational units know their strategic role and are on board in helping the company move down the chosen strategic path and produce the desired results.

## STAGE 3: CRAFTING A STRATEGY

**LO 3**

Why the strategic initiatives taken at various organizational levels must be tightly coordinated to achieve companywide performance targets.

As indicated in Chapter 1, the task of stitching a strategy together entails addressing a series of "hows": *how* to attract and please customers, *how* to compete against rivals, *how* to position the company in the marketplace, *how* to respond to changing market conditions, *how* to capitalize on attractive opportunities to grow the business, and *how* to achieve strategic and financial objectives. Astute entrepreneurship is called for in choosing among the various strategic alternatives and in proactively searching for opportunities to do new things or to do existing things in new or better ways.[10] The faster a company's business environment is changing, the more critical it becomes for its managers to be good entrepreneurs in diagnosing the direction and force of the changes under way and in responding with timely adjustments in strategy. Strategy makers have to pay attention to early warnings of future change and be willing to experiment with dare-to-be-different ways to establish a market position in that future. When obstacles appear unexpectedly in a company's path, it is up to management to adapt rapidly and innovatively. *Masterful strategies come from doing things differently from competitors where it counts—out-innovating them, being more efficient, being more imaginative, adapting faster—rather than running with the herd.* Good strategy making is therefore inseparable from good business entrepreneurship. One cannot exist without the other.

## Strategy Making Involves Managers at All Organizational Levels

A company's senior executives obviously have lead strategy-making roles and responsibilities. The chief executive officer (CEO), as captain of the ship, carries the mantles of chief direction setter, chief objective setter, chief strategy maker, and chief strategy implementer for the total enterprise. Ultimate responsibility for *leading* the strategy-making, strategy-executing process rests with the CEO. And the CEO is always fully accountable for the results the strategy produces, whether good or bad. In some enterprises, the CEO or owner functions as chief architect of the strategy, personally deciding what the key elements of the company's strategy will be, although he or she may seek the advice of key subordinates and board members. A CEO-centered approach to strategy development is characteristic of small owner-managed companies and some large corporations that were founded by the present CEO or that have a CEO with strong strategic leadership skills. Steve Jobs at Apple, Reed Hastings at Netflix, Meg Whitman at eBay and now at Hewlett-Packard, Warren Buffet at Berkshire Hathaway, and Howard Schultz at Starbucks are prominent examples of corporate CEOs who have wielded a heavy hand in shaping their company's strategy.

In most corporations, however, strategy is the product of more than just the CEO's handiwork. Typically, other senior executives—business unit heads, the chief financial officer, and vice presidents for production, marketing, and other functional departments have influential strategy-making roles and help fashion the chief strategy components. Normally, a company's chief financial officer is in charge of devising and implementing an appropriate financial strategy; the production vice president takes the lead in developing the company's production strategy; the marketing vice president orchestrates sales and marketing strategy; a brand manager is in charge of the strategy for a particular brand in the company's product lineup; and so on. Moreover, the strategy-making efforts of top managers are complemented by advice and counsel from the company's board of directors; normally, all major strategic decisions are submitted to the board of directors for review, discussion, and official approval.

But strategy making is by no means solely a *top* management function, the exclusive province of owner-entrepreneurs, CEOs, high-ranking executives, and board members. The more a company's operations cut across different products, industries, and geographic areas, the more that headquarters executives have little option but to delegate considerable strategy-making authority to down-the-line managers in charge of particular subsidiaries, divisions, product lines, geographic sales offices, distribution centers, and plants. On-the-scene managers who oversee specific operating units can be reliably counted on to have more detailed command of the strategic issues and choices for the particular operating unit under their supervision—knowing the prevailing market and competitive conditions, customer requirements and expectations, and all the other relevant aspects affecting the several strategic options available. Managers with day-to-day familiarity of, and authority over, a specific operating unit thus have a big edge over headquarters executives in making wise strategic choices for their operating unit. The result is that, in most of today's companies, crafting and executing strategy is a *collaborative team effort* in which *every company manager plays a strategy-making role*—ranging from minor to major—for the area he or she heads.

> In most companies, crafting and executing strategy is a *collaborative team effort* in which every manager has a role for the area he or she heads; it is rarely something that only high-level managers do.

Take, for example, a company like General Electric, a global corporation with more than $220 billion in revenues, more than 300,000 employees, operations in some 160 countries, and businesses that include jet engines, lighting, power generation, electric transmission and distribution equipment, housewares and appliances, medical equipment, media and entertainment, locomotives, security devices, water purification, and financial services. While top-level headquarters executives may well be personally involved in shaping GE's *overall* strategy and fashioning *important* strategic moves, they simply cannot know enough about the situation in every GE organizational unit to direct every strategic move made in GE's worldwide organization. Rather, it takes involvement on the part of GE's whole management team—top executives, business group heads, the heads of specific business units and product categories, and key managers in plants, sales offices, and distribution centers—to craft the thousands of strategic initiatives that end up composing the whole of GE's strategy.

# A Company's Strategy-Making Hierarchy

In diversified companies like GE, where multiple and sometimes strikingly different businesses have to be managed, crafting a full-fledged strategy involves four distinct types of strategic actions and initiatives. Each of these involves different facets of the company's overall strategy and calls for the participation of different types of managers, as shown in Figure 2.2.

As shown in Figure 2.2, **corporate strategy** is orchestrated by the CEO and other senior executives and establishes an overall strategy for managing a *set of businesses* in a diversified, multibusiness company. Corporate strategy concerns how to improve the combined performance of the set of businesses the company has diversified into by capturing cross-business synergies and turning them into competitive advantage. It addresses the questions of what businesses to hold or divest, which new markets to enter, and how to best enter new markets (by acquisition, creation of a strategic alliance, or through internal development, for example). Corporate strategy and business diversification are the subjects of Chapter 8, in which they are discussed in detail.

**Business strategy** is concerned with strengthening the market position, building competitive advantage, and improving the performance of a single line of business unit. Business strategy is primarily the responsibility of business unit heads, although corporate-level executives may well exert strong influence; in diversified companies it is not unusual for corporate officers to insist that business-level objectives and strategy conform to corporate-level objectives and strategy themes. The business head has at least two other strategy-related roles: (1) seeing that lower-level strategies are well conceived, consistent, and adequately matched to the over-all business strategy, and (2) keeping corporate-level officers (and sometimes the board of directors) informed of emerging strategic issues.

**Functional-area strategies** concern the approaches employed in managing particular functions within a business—like research and development (R&D), production, procurement of inputs, sales and marketing, distribution, customer service, and finance. A company's marketing strategy, for example, represents the managerial game plan for running the sales and marketing part of the business. A company's product development strategy represents the game plan for keeping the company's product lineup in tune with what buyers are looking for.

Functional strategies flesh out the details of a company's business strategy. Lead responsibility for functional strategies within a business is normally delegated to the heads of the respective functions, with the general manager of the business having final approval. Since the different functional-level strategies must be compatible with the overall business strategy and with one another to have beneficial impact, the general business manager may at times exert stronger influence on the content of the functional strategies.

**Operating strategies** concern the relatively narrow approaches for managing key operating units (e.g., plants, distribution centers, purchasing centers) and specific operating activities with strategic significance (e.g., quality control, materials purchasing, brand management, Internet sales). A plant manager needs a strategy for accomplishing the plant's objectives, carrying out the plant's part of the company's overall manufacturing game plan, and dealing with any strategy-related problems that exist at the plant. A company's advertising manager needs a strategy for getting maximum audience exposure and sales impact from the ad budget. Operating strategies, while of limited scope, add further detail and completeness to functional strategies and to

---

**CORE CONCEPT**

**Corporate strategy** establishes an overall game plan for managing a *set of businesses* in a diversified, multibusiness company.
**Business strategy** is primarily concerned with strengthening the company's market position and building competitive advantage in a *single-business company* or in a *single business unit* of a diversified multibusiness corporation.

---

**CORE CONCEPT**

**Business strategy** is strategy at the *single-business level,* concerning how to improve performance or gain a competitive advantage in a particular line of business.

## FIGURE 2.2    A Company's Strategy-Making Hierarchy

Orchestrated by the CEO and other senior executives.

**Corporate Strategy**
**(for the set of businesses as a whole)**
• How to gain advantage from managing a set of businesses

In the case of a single-business company, these two levels of the strategy-making hierarchy merge into one level—*Business Strategy*—that is orchestrated by the company's CEO and other top executives.

**Two-Way Influence**

Orchestrated by the senior executives of each line of business, often with advice from the heads of functional areas within the business and other key people.

**Business Strategy**
**(one for each business the company has diversified into)**
• How to gain and sustain a competitive advantage for a single line of business

**Two-Way Influence**

Orchestrated by the heads of major functional activities within a particular business, often in collaboration with other key people.

**Functional Area Strategies**
**(within each business)**
• How to manage a particular activity within a business in ways that support the business strategy

**Two-Way Influence**

Orchestrated by brand managers, plant managers, and the heads of other strategically important activities, such as distribution, purchasing, and website operations, often with input from other key people.

**Operating Strategies**
**(within each functional area)**
• How to manage activities of strategic significance within each functional area, adding detail and completeness

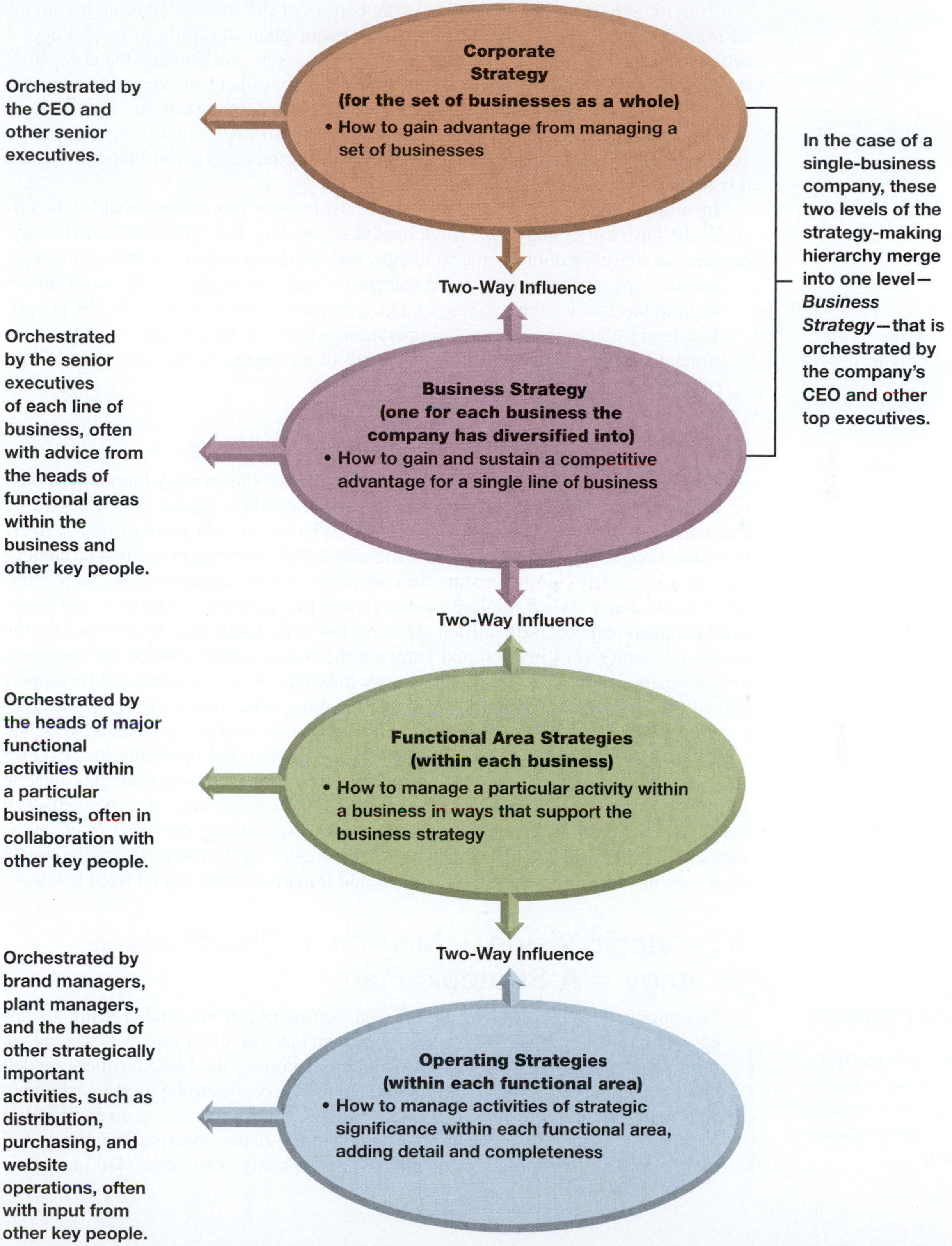

the overall business strategy. Lead responsibility for operating strategies is usually delegated to frontline managers, subject to the review and approval of higher-ranking managers.

Even though operating strategy is at the bottom of the strategy-making hierarchy, its importance should not be downplayed. A major plant that fails in its strategy to achieve production volume, unit cost, and quality targets can damage the company's reputation for quality products and undercut the achievement of company sales and profit objectives. Frontline managers are thus an important part of an organization's strategy-making team. One cannot reliably judge the strategic importance of a given action simply by the strategy level or location within the managerial hierarchy where it is initiated.

In single-business companies, the uppermost level of the strategy-making hierarchy is the business strategy, so a single-business company has three levels of strategy: business strategy, functional-area strategies, and operating strategies. Proprietorships, partnerships, and owner-managed enterprises may have only one or two strategy-making levels since their strategy-making process requires only a few key people. The larger and more diverse the operations of an enterprise, the more points of strategic initiative it has and the more levels of management that have a significant strategy-making role.

> A company's strategy is at full power only when its many pieces are united.

## Uniting the Strategy-Making Hierarchy

Ideally, the pieces of a company's strategy up and down the strategy hierarchy should be cohesive and mutually reinforcing, fitting together like a jigsaw puzzle. *Anything less than a unified collection of strategies weakens the overall strategy and is likely to impair company performance.*[11] It is the responsibility of top executives to achieve this unity by clearly communicating the company's vision, objectives, and major strategy components to down-the-line managers and key personnel. Midlevel and front-line managers cannot craft unified strategic moves without first understanding the company's long-term direction and knowing the major components of the corporate and/or business strategies that their strategy-making efforts are supposed to support and enhance. Thus, as a general rule, strategy making must start at the top of the organization and then proceed downward from the corporate level to the business level and then from the business level to the associated functional and operating levels. Once strategies up and down the hierarchy have been created, lower-level strategies must be scrutinized for consistency with and support of higher-level strategies. Any strategy conflicts must be addressed and resolved, either by modifying the lower-level strategies with conflicting elements or by adapting the higher-level strategy to accommodate what may be more appealing strategy ideas and initiatives bubbling up from below.

## A Strategic Vision + Mission + Objectives + Strategy = A Strategic Plan

**CORE CONCEPT**

> A company's **strategic plan** lays out its future direction, business purpose, performance targets, and strategy.

Developing a strategic vision and mission, setting objectives, and crafting a strategy are basic direction-setting tasks. They map out where a company is headed, its purpose, the targeted strategic and financial outcomes, the basic business model, and the competitive moves and internal action approaches to be used in achieving the desired business results. Together, these elements constitute a **strategic plan** for coping with industry conditions, outcompeting rivals, meeting objectives, and making progress toward aspirational goals.[12] Typically, a strategic plan includes a commitment to allocate resources to the plan and specifies a time period for achieving goals (usually three to five years).

In companies that do regular strategy reviews and develop explicit strategic plans, the strategic plan usually ends up as a written document that is circulated to most managers. Near-term performance targets are the part of the strategic plan most often communicated to employees more generally and spelled out explicitly. A number of companies summarize key elements of their strategic plans in the company's annual report to shareholders, in postings on their websites, or in statements provided to the business media; others, perhaps for reasons of competitive sensitivity, make only vague, general statements about their strategic plans.[13] In small, privately owned companies, it is rare for strategic plans to exist in written form. Small-company strategic plans tend to reside in the thinking and directives of owner-executives; aspects of the plan are revealed in conversations with company personnel about where to head, what to accomplish, and how to proceed.

## STAGE 4: EXECUTING THE STRATEGY

Managing the implementation of a strategy is easily the most demanding and time-consuming part of the strategy management process. Converting strategic plans into actions and results tests a manager's ability to direct organizational change, motivate employees, build and strengthen competitive capabilities, create and nurture a strategy-supportive work climate, and meet or beat performance targets. Initiatives to put the strategy in place and execute it proficiently must be launched and managed on many organizational fronts.

Management's action agenda for executing the chosen strategy emerges from assessing what the company will have to do to achieve the targeted financial and strategic performance. Each company manager has to think through the answer to the question "What needs to be done in my area to execute my piece of the strategic plan, and what actions should I take to get the process under way?" How much internal change is needed depends on how much of the strategy is new, how far internal practices and competencies deviate from what the strategy requires, and how well the present work culture supports good strategy execution. Depending on the amount of internal change involved, full implementation and proficient execution of the company strategy (or important new pieces thereof) can take several months to several years.

In most situations, managing the strategy execution process includes the following principal aspects:

- Creating a strategy-supporting structure.
- Staffing the organization to obtain needed skills and expertise.
- Developing and strengthening strategy-supporting resources and capabilities.
- Allocating ample resources to the activities critical to strategic success.
- Ensuring that policies and procedures facilitate effective strategy execution.
- Organizing the work effort along the lines of best practice.
- Installing information and operating systems that enable company personnel to perform essential activities.
- Motivating people and tying rewards directly to the achievement of performance objectives.
- Creating a company culture conducive to successful strategy execution.
- Exerting the internal leadership needed to propel implementation forward.

Good strategy execution requires diligent pursuit of operating excellence. It is a job for a company's whole management team. Success hinges on the skills and cooperation of operating managers who can push for needed changes in their organizational units and consistently deliver good results. Management's handling of the strategy implementation process can be considered successful if things go smoothly enough that the company meets or beats its strategic and financial performance targets and shows good progress in achieving management's strategic vision.

# STAGE 5: EVALUATING PERFORMANCE AND INITIATING CORRECTIVE ADJUSTMENTS

The fifth component of the strategy management process—monitoring new external developments, evaluating the company's progress, and making corrective adjustments—is the trigger point for deciding whether to continue or change the company's vision and mission, objectives, strategy, and/or strategy execution methods.[14] As long as the company's strategy continues to pass the three tests of a winning strategy discussed in Chapter 1 (good fit, competitive advantage, strong performance), company executives may decide to stay the course. Simply fine-tuning the strategic plan and continuing with efforts to improve strategy execution are sufficient.

But whenever a company encounters disruptive changes in its environment, questions need to be raised about the appropriateness of its direction and strategy. If a company experiences a downturn in its market position or persistent shortfalls in performance, then company managers are obligated to ferret out the causes—do they relate to poor strategy, poor strategy execution, or both?—and take timely corrective action. A company's direction, objectives, and strategy have to be revisited anytime external or internal conditions warrant.

Likewise, managers are obligated to assess which of the company's operating methods and approaches to strategy execution merit continuation and which need improvement. Proficient strategy execution is always the product of much organizational learning. It is achieved unevenly—coming quickly in some areas and proving troublesome in others. Consequently, top-notch strategy execution entails vigilantly searching for ways to improve and then making corrective adjustments whenever and wherever it is useful to do so.

> A company's vision, mission, objectives, strategy, and approach to strategy execution are never final; managing strategy is an ongoing process.

# CORPORATE GOVERNANCE: THE ROLE OF THE BOARD OF DIRECTORS IN THE STRATEGY-CRAFTING, STRATEGY-EXECUTING PROCESS

**LO 5**

The role and responsibility of a company's board of directors in overseeing the strategic management process.

Although senior managers have the *lead responsibility* for crafting and executing a company's strategy, it is the duty of a company's board of directors to exercise strong oversight and see that management performs the various tasks involved in each of the five stages of the strategy-making, strategy-executing process in a manner that best serves the interests of shareholders and other stakeholders.[15] A company's board of directors has four important obligations to fulfill:

1. *Oversee the company's financial accounting and financial reporting practices.* While top executives, particularly the company's CEO and CFO (chief financial

officer), are primarily responsible for seeing that the company's financial statements fairly and accurately report the results of the company's operations, board members have a *legal obligation* to warrant the accuracy of the company's financial reports and protect shareholders. It is their job to ensure that generally accepted accounting principles (GAAP) are used properly in preparing the company's financial statements and that proper financial controls are in place to prevent fraud and misuse of funds. Virtually all boards of directors have an audit committee, always composed entirely of *outside directors* (*inside directors* hold management positions in the company and either directly or indirectly report to the CEO). The members of the audit committee have the lead responsibility for overseeing the decisions of the company's financial officers and consulting with both internal and external auditors to ensure accurate financial reporting and adequate financial controls.

2. *Critically appraise the company's direction, strategy, and business approaches.* Board members are also expected to guide management in choosing a strategic direction and to make independent judgments about the validity and wisdom of management's proposed strategic actions. This aspect of their duties takes on heightened importance when the company's strategy is failing or is plagued with faulty execution, and certainly when there is a precipitous collapse in profitability. But under more normal circumstances, many boards have found that meeting agendas become consumed by compliance matters with little time left to discuss matters of strategic importance. The board of directors and management at Philips Electronics hold annual two- to three-day retreats devoted exclusively to evaluating the company's long-term direction and various strategic proposals. The company's exit from the semiconductor business and its increased focus on medical technology and home health care resulted from management-board discussions during such retreats.[16]

3. *Evaluate the caliber of senior executives' strategic leadership skills.* The board is always responsible for determining whether the current CEO is doing a good job of strategic leadership (as a basis for awarding salary increases and bonuses and deciding on retention or removal).[17] Boards must also exercise due diligence in evaluating the strategic leadership skills of other senior executives in line to succeed the CEO. When the incumbent CEO steps down or leaves for a position elsewhere, the board must elect a successor, either going with an insider or deciding that an outsider is needed to perhaps radically change the company's strategic course. Often, the outside directors on a board visit company facilities and talk with company personnel personally to evaluate whether the strategy is on track, how well the strategy is being executed, and how well issues and problems are being addressed by various managers. For example, independent board members at GE visit operating executives at each major business unit once a year to assess the company's talent pool and stay abreast of emerging strategic and operating issues affecting the company's divisions. Home Depot board members visit a store once per quarter to determine the health of the company's operations.[18]

4. *Institute a compensation plan for top executives that rewards them for actions and results that serve shareholder interests.* A basic principle of corporate governance is that the owners of a corporation (the shareholders) delegate operating authority and managerial control to top management in return for compensation. In their role as *agents* of shareholders, top executives have a clear and

unequivocal duty to make decisions and operate the company in accord with shareholder interests. (This does not mean disregarding the interests of other stakeholders—employees, suppliers, the communities in which the company operates, and society at large.) Most boards of directors have a compensation committee, composed entirely of directors from *outside* the company, to develop a salary and incentive compensation plan that rewards senior executives for boosting the company's *long-term* performance on behalf of shareholders. The compensation committee's recommendations are presented to the full board for approval. But during the past 10 to 15 years, many boards of directors have done a poor job of ensuring that executive salary increases, bonuses, and stock option awards are tied tightly to performance measures that are truly in the long-term interests of shareholders. Rather, compensation packages at many companies have increasingly rewarded executives for short-term performance improvements—most notably, for achieving quarterly and annual earnings targets and boosting the stock price by specified percentages. This has had the perverse effect of causing company managers to become preoccupied with actions to improve a company's near-term performance, often motivating them to take unwise business risks to boost short-term earnings by amounts sufficient to qualify for multimillion-dollar compensation packages (that many see as obscenely large). The focus on short-term performance has proved damaging to long-term company performance and shareholder interests— witness the huge loss of shareholder wealth that occurred at many financial institutions in 2008–2009 because of executive risk taking in subprime loans, credit default swaps, and collateralized mortgage securities. As a consequence, the need to overhaul and reform executive compensation has become a hot topic in both public circles and corporate boardrooms. Illustration Capsule 2.4 discusses how weak governance at the mortgage companies Fannie Mae and Freddie Mac allowed opportunistic senior managers to secure exorbitant bonuses while making decisions that imperiled the futures of the companies they managed.

Effective corporate governance requires the board of directors to oversee the company's strategic direction, evaluate its senior executives, handle executive compensation, and oversee financial reporting practices.

Every corporation should have a strong independent board of directors that (1) is well informed about the company's performance, (2) guides and judges the CEO and other top executives, (3) has the courage to curb management actions the board believes are inappropriate or unduly risky, (4) certifies to shareholders that the CEO is doing what the board expects, (5) provides insight and advice to management, and (6) is intensely involved in debating the pros and cons of key decisions and actions.[19] Boards of directors that lack the backbone to challenge a strong-willed or "imperial" CEO or that rubber-stamp almost anything the CEO recommends without probing inquiry and debate abdicate their fiduciary duty to represent and protect shareholder interests.

# Corporate Governance Failures at Fannie Mae and Freddie Mac

Excessive executive compensation in the financial services industry ranks high among examples of failed corporate governance. Corporate governance at the government-sponsored mortgage giants Fannie Mae and Freddie Mac was particularly weak. The politically appointed boards at both enterprises failed to understand the risks of the subprime loan strategies being employed, did not adequately monitor the decisions of the CEO, did not exercise effective oversight of the accounting principles being employed (which led to inflated earnings), and approved executive compensation systems that allowed management to manipulate earnings to receive lucrative performance bonuses. The audit and compensation committees at Fannie Mae were particularly ineffective in protecting shareholder interests, with the audit committee allowing the company's financial officers to audit reports prepared under their direction and used to determine performance bonuses. Fannie Mae's audit committee also was aware of management's use of questionable accounting practices that reduced losses and recorded one-time gains to achieve financial targets linked to bonuses. In addition, the audit committee failed to investigate formal charges of accounting improprieties filed by a manager in the Office of the Controller.

Fannie Mae's compensation committee was equally ineffective. The committee allowed the company's CEO, Franklin Raines, to select the consultant employed to design the mortgage firm's executive compensation plan and agreed to a tiered bonus plan that would permit Raines and other senior managers to receive maximum bonuses without great difficulty. The compensation plan allowed Raines to earn performance-based bonuses of $52 million and a total compensation of $90 million between 1999 and 2004. Raines was forced to resign in December 2004 when the Office of Federal Housing Enterprise Oversight found that Fannie Mae executives had fraudulently inflated earnings to receive bonuses linked to financial performance. Securities and Exchange Commission investigators also found evidence of improper accounting at Fannie Mae and required the company to restate its earnings between 2002 and 2004 by $6.3 billion.

Poor governance at Freddie Mac allowed its CEO and senior management to manipulate financial data to receive performance-based compensation as well. Freddie Mac CEO Richard Syron received 2007 compensation of $19.8 million while the mortgage company's share price

declined from a high of $70 in 2005 to $25 at year-end 2007. During Syron's tenure as CEO, the company became embroiled in a multibillion-dollar accounting scandal, and Syron personally disregarded internal reports dating to 2004 that cautioned of an impending financial crisis at the company. Forewarnings within Freddie Mac and by federal regulators and outside industry observers proved to be correct, with loan underwriting policies at Freddie Mac and Fannie Mae leading to combined losses at the two firms in 2008 of more than $100 billion. The price of Freddie Mac's shares had fallen to below $1 by the time of Syron's resignation in September 2008.

Both organizations were placed into a conservatorship under the direction of the U.S. government in September 2008 and were provided bailout funds of more than $180 billion by mid-2012. At that point, the U.S. Treasury amended the organizations' bailout terms to require that all profits be transferred to the government while downsizing the firms. By early 2014, the bailout had finally been fully repaid.

*Sources:* Chris Isidore, "Mortgage Bailout Now Profitable for Taxpayers," *CNNMoney,* February 21, 2014; Alan Zibel and Nick Timiraos "Fannie, Freddie Bailout Receives Revamp," *The Wall Street Journal Online,* August 17, 2012; Eric Dash, "Fannie Mae to Restate Results by $6.3 Billion because of Accounting," *The New York Times Online,* December 7, 2006; Annys Shin, "Fannie Mae Sets Executive Salaries," *The Washington Post,* February 9, 2006, p. D4; and Scott DeCarlo, Eric Weiss, Mark Jickling, and James R. Cristie, *Fannie Mae and Freddie Mac: Scandal in U.S. Housing* (Nova, 2006), pp. 266–286.

# KEY POINTS

The strategic management process consists of five interrelated and integrated stages:

1. *Developing a strategic vision* of the company's future, a *mission statement* that defines the company's current purpose, and a set of *core values* to guide the pursuit of the vision and mission. This stage of strategy making provides direction for the company, motivates and inspires company personnel, aligns and guides actions throughout the organization, and communicates to stakeholders management's aspirations for the company's future.

2. *Setting objectives* to convert the vision and mission into performance targets that can be used as yardsticks for measuring the company's performance. Objectives need to spell out *how much* of *what kind* of performance *by when*. Two broad types of objectives are required: *financial objectives* and *strategic objectives*. A *balanced-scorecard* approach for measuring company performance entails setting both *financial objectives and strategic objectives*.

3. *Crafting a strategy* to achieve the objectives and move the company along the strategic course that management has charted. Masterful strategies come from doing things differently from competitors where it counts—out-innovating them, being more efficient, being more imaginative, adapting faster—rather than running with the herd. In large diversified companies, the strategy-making hierarchy consists of four levels, each of which involves a corresponding level of management: corporate strategy (multibusiness strategy), business strategy (strategy for individual businesses that compete in a single industry), functional-area strategies within each business (e.g., marketing, R&D, logistics), and operating strategies (for key operating units, such as manufacturing plants). Thus, strategy making is an inclusive collaborative activity involving not only senior company executives but also the heads of major business divisions, functional-area managers, and operating managers on the frontlines.

4. *Executing the chosen strategy* and converting the strategic plan into action. Management's agenda for executing the chosen strategy emerges from assessing what the company will have to do to achieve the targeted financial and strategic performance. Management's handling of the strategy implementation process can be considered successful if things go smoothly enough that the company meets or beats its strategic and financial performance targets and shows good progress in achieving management's strategic vision.

5. *Monitoring developments, evaluating performance, and initiating corrective adjustments* in light of actual experience, changing conditions, new ideas, and new opportunities. This stage of the strategy management process is the trigger point for deciding whether to continue or change the company's vision and mission, objectives, strategy, and/or strategy execution methods.

The sum of a company's strategic vision, mission, objectives, and strategy constitutes a *strategic plan* for coping with industry conditions, outcompeting rivals, meeting objectives, and making progress toward aspirational goals. *Stretch objectives* spur exceptional performance and help build a firewall against contentment with modest gains in organizational performance. A company exhibits *strategic intent* when it relentlessly pursues an ambitious strategic objective, concentrating the full force of its resources and competitive actions on achieving that objective.

Boards of directors have a duty to shareholders to play a vigilant role in overseeing management's handling of a company's strategy-making, strategy-executing process. This entails four important obligations: (1) Ensure that the company issues accurate financial reports and has adequate financial controls, (2) critically appraise the company's direction, strategy, and strategy execution, (3) evaluate the caliber of senior executives' strategic leadership skills, and (4) institute a compensation plan for top executives that rewards them for actions and results that serve shareholder interests.

# ASSURANCE OF LEARNING EXERCISES

1. Using the information in Table 2.1, critique the adequacy and merit of the following vision statements, listing effective elements and shortcomings. Rank the vision statements from best to worst once you complete your evaluation.

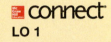

**LO 1**

| Vision Statement | Effective Elements | Shortcomings |
|---|---|---|
| **Amazon** <br> Our vision is to be earth's most customer centric company; to build a place where people can come to find and discover anything they might want to buy online. | | |
| **BASF** <br> We are "The Chemical Company" successfully operating in all major markets. <br> • Our customers view BASF as their partner of choice. <br> • Our innovative products, intelligent solutions and services make us the most competent worldwide supplier in the chemical industry. <br> • We generate a high return on assets. <br> • We strive for sustainable development. <br> • We welcome change as an opportunity. <br> • We, the employees of BASF, together ensure our success. | | |
| **MasterCard** <br> • A world beyond cash. | | |
| **Hilton Hotels Corporation** <br> Our vision is to be the first choice of the world's travelers. Hilton intends to build on the rich heritage and strength of our brands by: <br> • Consistently delighting our customers <br> • Investing in our team members <br> • Delivering innovative products and services <br> • Continuously improving performance <br> • Increasing shareholder value <br> • Creating a culture of pride <br> • Strengthening the loyalty of our constituents | | |

*Source:* Company websites and annual reports.

**LO 2** 2. Go to the company websites for ExxonMobil (**ir.exxonmobil.com**), Pfizer (**www.pfizer.com/investors**), and Intel (**www.intc.com**) to find some examples of strategic and financial objectives. Make a list of four objectives for each company, and indicate which of these are strategic and which are financial.

**LO 3** 3. American Airlines' Chapter 11 reorganization plan filed in 2012 involved the company reducing operating expenses by $2 billion while increasing revenues by $1 billion. The company's strategy to increase revenues included expanding the number of international flights and destinations and increasing daily departures for its five largest markets by 20 percent. The company also intended to upgrade its fleet by spending $2 billion to purchase new aircraft and refurbish the first-class cabins for planes not replaced. A final component of the restructuring plan included a merger with US Airways to create a global airline with more than 56,700 daily flights to 336 destinations in 56 countries. The merger was expected to produce cost savings from synergies of more than $1 billion and result in a stronger airline capable of paying creditors and rewarding employees and shareholders. Explain why the strategic initiatives at various organizational levels and functions require tight coordination to achieve the results desired by American Airlines.

**LO 4** 4. Go to the investor relations website for Walmart (**investors.walmartstores.com**) and review past presentations Walmart has made during various investor conferences by clicking on the Events option in the navigation bar. Prepare a one- to two-page report that outlines what Walmart has said to investors about its approach to strategy execution. Specifically, what has management discussed concerning staffing, resource allocation, policies and procedures, information and operating systems, continuous improvement, rewards and incentives, corporate culture, and internal leadership at the company?

**LO 5** 5. Based on the information provided in Illustration Capsule 2.4, explain how corporate governance at Freddie Mac failed the enterprise's shareholders and other stakeholders. Which important obligations to shareholders were fulfilled by Fannie Mae's board of directors? What is your assessment of how well Fannie Mae's compensation committee handled executive compensation at the government-sponsored mortgage giant?

# EXERCISE FOR SIMULATION PARTICIPANTS

**LO 1** 1. Meet with your co-managers and prepare a strategic vision statement for your company. It should be at least one sentence long and no longer than a brief paragraph. When you are finished, check to see if your vision statement meets the conditions for an effectively worded strategic vision set forth in Table 2.1. If not, then revise it accordingly. What would be a good slogan that captures the essence of your strategic vision and that could be used to help communicate the vision to company personnel, shareholders, and other stakeholders?

**LO 2** 2. What are your company's financial objectives? What are your company's strategic objectives?

**LO 3** 3. What are the three to four key elements of your company's strategy?

# ENDNOTES

[1] Gordon Shaw, Robert Brown, and Philip Bromiley, "Strategic Stories: How 3M Is Rewriting Business Planning," *Harvard Business Review* 76, no. 3 (May–June 1998); David J. Collis and Michael G. Rukstad, "Can You Say What Your Strategy Is?" *Harvard Business Review* 86, no. 4 (April 2008).

[2] Hugh Davidson, *The Committed Enterprise: How to Make Vision and Values Work* (Oxford: Butterworth Heinemann, 2002); W. Chan Kim and Renée Mauborgne, "Charting Your Company's Future," *Harvard Business Review* 80, no. 6 (June 2002), pp. 77–83; James C. Collins and Jerry I. Porras, "Building Your Company's Vision," *Harvard Business Review* 74, no. 5 (September–October 1996), pp. 65–77; Jim Collins and Jerry Porras, *Built to Last: Successful Habits of Visionary Companies* (New York: HarperCollins, 1994); Michel Robert, *Strategy Pure and Simple II: How Winning Companies Dominate Their Competitors* (New York: McGraw-Hill, 1998).

[3] Davidson, *The Committed Enterprise,* pp. 20 and 54.

[4] As quoted in Charles H. House and Raymond L. Price, "The Return Map: Tracking Product Teams," *Harvard Business Review* 60, no. 1 (January–February 1991), p. 93.

[5] Robert S. Kaplan and David P. Norton, *The Strategy-Focused Organization* (Boston: Harvard Business School Press, 2001); Robert S. Kaplan and David P. Norton, *The Balanced Scorecard: Translating Strategy into Action* (Boston: Harvard Business School Press, 1996).

[6] Ibid.; Kevin B. Hendricks, Larry Menor, and Christine Wiedman, "The Balanced Scorecard: To Adopt or Not to Adopt," *Ivey Business Journal* 69, no. 2 (November–December 2004), pp. 1–7; Sandy Richardson, "The Key Elements of Balanced Scorecard Success," *Ivey Business Journal* 69, no. 2 (November–December 2004), pp. 7–9.

[7] Kaplan and Norton, *The Balanced Scorecard.*

[8] Information posted on the website of Bain and Company, www.bain.com (accessed May 27, 2011).

[9] Information posted on the website of the Balanced Scorecard Institute, balancedscorecard.org (accessed May 27, 2011).

[10] Henry Mintzberg, Bruce Ahlstrand, and Joseph Lampel, *Strategy Safari: A Guided Tour through the Wilds of Strategic Management* (New York: Free Press, 1998); Bruce Barringer and Allen C. Bluedorn, "The Relationship between Corporate Entrepreneurship and Strategic Management," *Strategic Management Journal* 20 (1999), pp. 421–444; Jeffrey G. Covin and Morgan P. Miles, "Corporate Entrepreneurship and the Pursuit of Competitive Advantage," *Entrepreneurship: Theory and Practice* 23, no. 3 (Spring 1999), pp. 47–63; David A. Garvin and Lynne C. Levesque, "Meeting the Challenge of Corporate Entrepreneurship," *Harvard Business Review* 84, no. 10 (October 2006), pp. 102–112.

[11] Joseph L. Bower and Clark G. Gilbert, "How Managers' Everyday Decisions Create or Destroy Your Company's Strategy," *Harvard Business Review* 85, no. 2 (February 2007), pp. 72–79.

[12] Gordon Shaw, Robert Brown, and Philip Bromiley, "Strategic Stories: How 3M Is Rewriting Business Planning," *Harvard Business Review* 76, no. 3 (May–June 1998), pp. 41–50.

[13] David J. Collis and Michael G. Rukstad, "Can You Say What Your Strategy Is?" *Harvard Business Review* 86, no. 4 (April 2008), pp. 82–90.

[14] Cynthia A. Montgomery, "Putting Leadership Back into Strategy," *Harvard Business Review* 86, no. 1 (January 2008), pp. 54–60.

[15] Jay W. Lorsch and Robert C. Clark, "Leading from the Boardroom," *Harvard Business Review* 86, no. 4 (April 2008), pp. 105–111.

[16] Ibid.

[17] Stephen P. Kaufman, "Evaluating the CEO," *Harvard Business Review* 86, no. 10 (October 2008), pp. 53–57.

[18] Ibid.

[19] David A. Nadler, "Building Better Boards," *Harvard Business Review* 82, no. 5 (May 2004), pp. 102–105; Cynthia A. Montgomery and Rhonda Kaufman, "The Board's Missing Link," *Harvard Business Review* 81, no. 3 (March 2003), pp. 86–93; John Carver, "What Continues to Be Wrong with Corporate Governance and How to Fix It," *Ivey Business Journal* 68, no. 1 (September–October 2003), pp. 1–5. See also Gordon Donaldson, "A New Tool for Boards: The Strategic Audit," *Harvard Business Review* 73, no. 4 (July–August 1995), pp. 99–107.

### CHAPTER 3

# Evaluating a Company's External Environment

## Learning Objectives

THIS CHAPTER WILL HELP YOU UNDERSTAND:

**LO 1**  How to recognize the factors in a company's broad macro-environment that may have strategic significance.

**LO 2**  How to use analytic tools to diagnose the competitive conditions in a company's industry.

**LO 3**  How to map the market positions of key groups of industry rivals.

**LO 4**  How to use multiple frameworks to determine whether an industry's outlook presents a company with sufficiently attractive opportunities for growth and profitability.

> Without competitors, there would be no need for strategy.
>
> Kenichi Ohmae – *Consultant and Author*

> It is nice to have valid competition; it pushes you to do better.
>
> Gianni Versace – *Entrepreneur and Founder of Gianni Versace S.p.A.*

> In essence, the job of a strategist is to understand and cope with competition.
>
> Michael Porter – *Harvard Business School Professor and Cofounder of Monitor Consulting*

In order to chart a company's strategic course wisely, managers must first develop a deep understanding of the company's present situation. Two facets of a company's situation are especially pertinent: (1) its external environment—most notably, the competitive conditions of the industry in which the company operates; and (2) its internal environment—particularly the company's resources and organizational capabilities.

Insightful diagnosis of a company's external and internal environments is a prerequisite for managers to succeed in crafting a strategy that is an excellent *fit* with the company's situation—the first test of a winning strategy. As depicted in Figure 3.1, strategic thinking begins with an appraisal of the company's external and internal environments (as a basis for deciding on a long-term direction and developing a strategic vision), moves toward an evaluation of the most promising alternative strategies and business models, and culminates in choosing a specific strategy.

This chapter presents the concepts and analytic tools for zeroing in on those aspects of a company's external environment that should be considered in making strategic choices. Attention centers on the broad environmental context, the specific market arena in which a company operates, the drivers of change, the positions and likely actions of rival companies, and the factors that determine competitive success. In Chapter 4, we explore the methods of evaluating a company's internal circumstances and competitive capabilities.

## THE STRATEGICALLY RELEVANT FACTORS IN THE COMPANY'S MACRO-ENVIRONMENT

Every company operates in a broad **"macro-environment"** that comprises six principal components: political factors, economic conditions in the firm's general environment (local, country, regional, worldwide), sociocultural forces, technological factors, environmental factors (concerning the natural environment), and legal/regulatory conditions. Each of these components has the potential to affect the firm's more immediate industry and competitive environment, although some are likely to have a more important effect than others (see Figure 3.2). An analysis of the impact of these factors is often referred to as **PESTEL analysis,** an acronym that serves as a reminder of the six components

## FIGURE 3.1   From Thinking Strategically about the Company's Situation to Choosing a Strategy

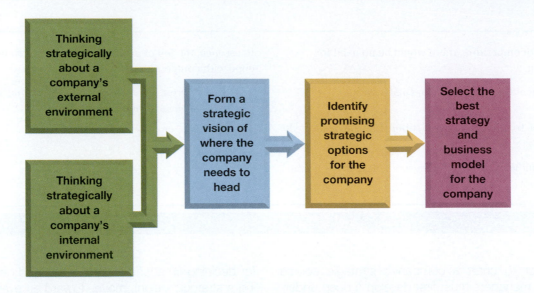

involved (political, economic, sociocultural, technological, environmental, legal/regulatory).

Since macro-economic factors affect different industries in different ways and to different degrees, it is important for managers to determine which of these represent the most *strategically relevant factors* outside the firm's industry boundaries. By *strategically relevant,* we mean important enough to have a bearing on the decisions the company ultimately makes about its long-term direction, objectives, strategy, and business model. The impact of the outer-ring factors depicted in Figure 3.2 on a company's choice of strategy can range from big to small. But even if those factors change slowly or are likely to have a low impact on the company's business situation, they still merit a watchful eye.

For example, the strategic opportunities of cigarette producers to grow their businesses are greatly reduced by antismoking ordinances, the decisions of governments to impose higher cigarette taxes, and the growing cultural stigma attached to smoking. Motor vehicle companies must adapt their strategies to customer concerns about high gasoline prices and to environmental concerns about carbon emissions. Companies in the food processing, restaurant, sports, and fitness industries have to pay special attention to changes in lifestyles, eating habits, leisure-time preferences, and attitudes toward nutrition and fitness in fashioning their strategies. Table 3.1 provides a brief description of the components of the macro-environment and some examples of the industries or business situations that they might affect.

As company managers scan the external environment, they must be alert for potentially important outer-ring developments, assess their impact and influence, and adapt the company's direction and strategy as needed. However, the factors in a company's environment having the *biggest* strategy-shaping impact typically pertain to the company's immediate industry and competitive environment. Consequently, it is on a company's industry and competitive environment that we concentrate the bulk of our attention in this chapter.

**FIGURE 3.2   The Components of a Company's Macro-Environment**

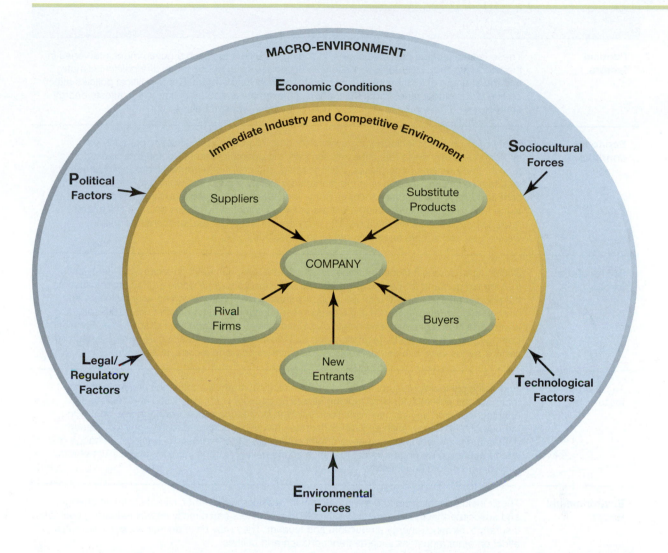

## ASSESSING THE COMPANY'S INDUSTRY AND COMPETITIVE ENVIRONMENT

Thinking strategically about a company's industry and competitive environment entails using some well-validated concepts and analytic tools. These include the five forces framework, the value net, driving forces, strategic groups, competitor analysis, and key success factors. Proper use of these analytic tools can provide managers with the understanding needed to craft a strategy that fits the company's situation within their industry environment. The remainder of this chapter is devoted to describing how managers can use these tools to inform and improve their strategic choices.

**LO 2**

How to use analytic tools to diagnose the competitive conditions in a company's industry.

**TABLE 3.1    The Six Components of the Macro-Environment**

| Component | Description |
|---|---|
| **Political factors** | These factors include political policies, including the extent to which a government intervenes in the economy. They include such matters as tax policy, fiscal policy, tariffs, the political climate, and the strength of institutions such as the federal banking system. Some political policies affect certain types of industries more than others. An example is energy policy, which affects energy producers and heavy users of energy more than other types of businesses. |
| **Economic conditions** | Economic conditions include the general economic climate and specific factors such as interest rates, exchange rates, the inflation rate, the unemployment rate, the rate of economic growth, trade deficits or surpluses, savings rates, and per-capita domestic product. Economic factors also include conditions in the markets for stocks and bonds, which can affect consumer confidence and discretionary income. Some industries, such as construction, are particularly vulnerable to economic downturns but are positively affected by factors such as low interest rates. Others, such as discount retailing, may benefit when general economic conditions weaken, as consumers become more price-conscious. |
| **Sociocultural forces** | Sociocultural forces include the societal values, attitudes, cultural influences, and lifestyles that impact demand for particular goods and services, as well as demographic factors such as the population size, growth rate, and age distribution. Sociocultural forces vary by locale and change over time. An example is the trend toward healthier lifestyles, which can shift spending toward exercise equipment and health clubs and away from alcohol and snack foods. Population demographics can have large implications for industries such as health care, where costs and service needs vary with demographic factors such as age and income distribution. |
| **Technological factors** | Technological factors include the pace of technological change and technical developments that have the potential for wide-ranging effects on society, such as genetic engineering and nanotechnology. They include institutions involved in creating new knowledge and controlling the use of technology, such as R&D consortia, university-sponsored technology incubators, patent and copyright laws, and government control over the Internet. Technological change can encourage the birth of new industries, such as the delivery drone industry, and disrupt others, such as the recording industry. |
| **Environmental forces** | These include ecological and environmental forces such as weather, climate, climate change, and associated factors like water shortages. These factors can directly impact industries such as insurance, farming, energy production, and tourism. They may have an indirect but substantial effect on other industries such as transportation and utilities. |
| **Legal and regulatory factors** | These factors include the regulations and laws with which companies must comply, such as consumer laws, labor laws, antitrust laws, and occupational health and safety regulation. Some factors, such as banking deregulation, are industry-specific. Others, such as minimum wage legislation, affect certain types of industries (low-wage, labor-intensive industries) more than others. |

# THE FIVE FORCES FRAMEWORK

The character and strength of the competitive forces operating in an industry are never the same from one industry to another. The most powerful and widely used tool for diagnosing the principal competitive pressures in a market is the *five forces framework*.[1] This framework, depicted in Figure 3.3, holds that competitive pressures on

**FIGURE 3.3    The Five Forces Model of Competition: A Key Analytic Tool**

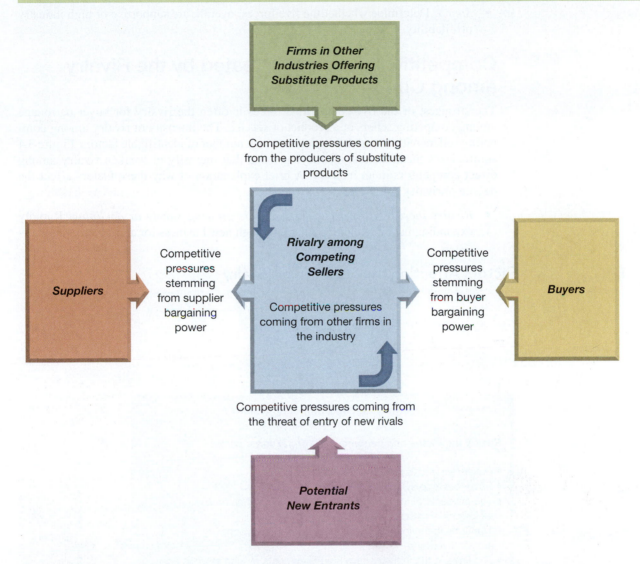

*Sources:* Adapted from M. E. Porter, "How Competitive Forces Shape Strategy," *Harvard Business Review* 57, no. 2 (1979), pp. 137–145; and M. E. Porter, "The Five Competitive Forces That Shape Strategy," *Harvard Business Review* 86, no. 1 (2008), pp. 80–86.

companies within an industry come from five sources. These include (1) competition from *rival sellers,* (2) competition from *potential new entrants* to the industry, (3) competition from producers of *substitute products,* (4) *supplier* bargaining power, and (5) *customer* bargaining power.

Using the five forces model to determine the nature and strength of competitive pressures in a given industry involves three steps:

- *Step 1:* For each of the five forces, identify the different parties involved, along with the specific factors that bring about competitive pressures.

- *Step 2:* Evaluate how strong the pressures stemming from each of the five forces are (strong, moderate, or weak).
- *Step 3:* Determine whether the five forces, overall, are supportive of high industry profitability.

## Competitive Pressures Created by the Rivalry among Competing Sellers

The strongest of the five competitive forces is often the rivalry for buyer patronage among competing sellers of a product or service. The intensity of rivalry among competing sellers within an industry depends on a number of identifiable factors. Figure 3.4 summarizes these factors, identifying those that intensify or weaken rivalry among direct competitors in an industry. A brief explanation of why these factors affect the degree of rivalry is in order:

- *Rivalry increases when buyer demand is growing slowly or declining.* Rapidly expanding buyer demand produces enough new business for all industry members

**FIGURE 3.4    Factors Affecting the Strength of Rivalry**

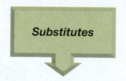

**Rivalry among Competing Sellers**

*Rivalry increases and becomes a stronger force when:*

- Buyer demand is growing slowly.
- Buyer costs to switch brands are low.
- The products of industry members are commodities or else weakly differentiated.
- The firms in the industry have excess production capacity and/or inventory.
- The firms in the industry have high fixed costs or high storage costs.
- Competitors are numerous or are of roughly equal size and competitive strength.
- Rivals have diverse objectives, strategies, and/or countries of origin.
- Rivals have emotional stakes in the business or face high exit barriers.

*Rivalry decreases and becomes a weaker force under the opposite conditions.*

to grow without having to draw customers away from rival enterprises. But in markets where buyer demand is slow-growing or shrinking, companies desperate to gain more business typically employ price discounts, sales promotions, and other tactics to increase their sales volumes at the expense of rivals, sometimes to the point of igniting a fierce battle for market share.

- *Rivalry increases as it becomes less costly for buyers to switch brands.* The less costly it is for buyers to switch their purchases from one seller to another, the easier it is for sellers to steal customers away from rivals. When the cost of switching brands is higher, buyers are less prone to brand switching and sellers have protection from rivalrous moves. Switching costs include not only monetary costs but also the time, inconvenience, and psychological costs involved in switching brands. For example, retailers may not switch to the brands of rival manufacturers because they are hesitant to sever long-standing supplier relationships or incur any technical support costs or retraining expenses in making the switchover.

- *Rivalry increases as the products of rival sellers become less strongly differentiated.* When rivals' offerings are identical or weakly differentiated, buyers have less reason to be brand-loyal—a condition that makes it easier for rivals to convince buyers to switch to their offerings. Moreover, when the products of different sellers are virtually identical, shoppers will choose on the basis of price, which can result in fierce price competition among sellers. On the other hand, strongly differentiated product offerings among rivals breed high brand loyalty on the part of buyers who view the attributes of certain brands as more appealing or better suited to their needs.

- *Rivalry is more intense when there is excess supply or unused production capacity, especially if the industry's product has high fixed costs or high storage costs.* Whenever a market has excess supply (overproduction relative to demand), rivalry intensifies as sellers cut prices in a desperate effort to cope with the unsold inventory. A similar effect occurs when a product is perishable or seasonal, since firms often engage in aggressive price cutting to ensure that everything is sold. Likewise, whenever fixed costs account for a large fraction of total cost so that unit costs are significantly lower at full capacity, firms come under significant pressure to cut prices whenever they are operating below full capacity. Unused capacity imposes a significant cost-increasing penalty because there are fewer units over which to spread fixed costs. The pressure of high fixed or high storage costs can push rival firms into price concessions, special discounts, rebates, and other volume-boosting competitive tactics.

- *Rivalry intensifies as the number of competitors increases and they become more equal in size and capability.* When there are many competitors in a market, companies eager to increase their meager market share often engage in price-cutting activities to drive sales, leading to intense rivalry. When there are only a few competitors, companies are more wary of how their rivals may react to their attempts to take market share away from them. Fear of retaliation and a descent into a damaging price war leads to restrained competitive moves. Moreover, when rivals are of comparable size and competitive strength, they can usually compete on a fairly equal footing—an evenly matched contest tends to be fiercer than a contest in which one or more industry members have commanding market shares and substantially greater resources than their much smaller rivals.

- *Rivalry becomes more intense as the diversity of competitors increases in terms of long-term directions, objectives, strategies, and countries of origin.* A diverse group of sellers often contains one or more mavericks willing to try novel or rule-breaking market approaches, thus generating a more volatile and less predictable competitive environment. Globally competitive markets are often more rivalrous, especially when aggressors have lower costs and are intent on gaining a strong foothold in new country markets.

- *Rivalry is stronger when high exit barriers keep unprofitable firms from leaving the industry.* In industries where the assets cannot easily be sold or transferred to other uses, where workers are entitled to job protection, or where owners are committed to remaining in business for personal reasons, failing firms tend to hold on longer than they might otherwise—even when they are bleeding red ink. Deep price discounting of this sort can destabilize an otherwise attractive industry.

Evaluating the strength of rivalry in an industry is a matter of determining whether the factors stated here, taken as a whole, indicate that the rivalry is relatively strong, moderate, or weak. When rivalry is *strong,* the battle for market share is generally so vigorous that the profit margins of most industry members are squeezed to bare-bones levels. When rivalry is *moderate,* a more normal state, the maneuvering among industry members, while lively and healthy, still allows most industry members to earn acceptable profits. When rivalry is *weak,* most companies in the industry are relatively well satisfied with their sales growth and market shares and rarely undertake offensives to steal customers away from one another. Weak rivalry means that there is no downward pressure on industry profitability due to this particular competitive force.

## The Choice of Competitive Weapons

Competitive battles among rival sellers can assume many forms that extend well beyond lively price competition. For example, competitors may resort to such marketing tactics as special sales promotions, heavy advertising, rebates, or low-interest-rate financing to drum up additional sales. Rivals may race one another to differentiate their products by offering better performance features or higher quality or improved customer service or a wider product selection. They may also compete through the rapid introduction of next-generation products, the frequent introduction of new or improved products, and efforts to build stronger dealer networks, establish positions in foreign markets, or otherwise expand distribution capabilities and market presence. Table 3.2 provides a sampling of the types of competitive weapons available to rivals, along with their primary effects with respect to price ($P$), cost ($C$), and value ($V$)—the elements of an effective business model and the value-price-cost framework, as discussed in Chapter 1.

## Competitive Pressures Associated with the Threat of New Entrants

New entrants into an industry threaten the position of rival firms since they usually compete fiercely for market share and add to the production capacity and number of rivals in the process. But even the *threat* of new entry increases the competitive pressures in an industry. This is because incumbent firms typically lower prices and increase defensive actions in an attempt to deter new entry when the threat of entry is high. Just how serious the threat of entry is in a particular market depends on two classes of factors: the *expected reaction of incumbent firms to new entry* and what are known as *barriers to entry.* The threat of entry is low when incumbent firms are

**TABLE 3.2**  Common "Weapons" for Competing with Rivals

| Types of Competitive Weapons | Primary Effects |
| --- | --- |
| Discounting prices, holding clearance sales | Lowers price ($P$), increases total sales volume and market share, lowers profits if price cuts are not offset by large increases in sales volume |
| Offering coupons, advertising items on sale | Increases sales volume and total revenues, lowers price ($P$), increases unit costs ($C$), may lower profit margins per unit sold ($P - C$) |
| Advertising product or service characteristics, using ads to enhance a company's image | Boosts buyer demand, increases product differentiation and perceived value ($V$), increases total sales volume and market share, but may increase unit costs ($C$) and lower profit margins per unit sold |
| Innovating to improve product performance and quality | Increases product differentiation and value ($V$), boosts buyer demand, boosts total sales volume, likely to increase unit costs ($C$) |
| Introducing new or improved features, increasing the number of styles to provide greater product selection | Increases product differentiation and value ($V$), strengthens buyer demand, boosts total sales volume and market share, likely to increase unit costs ($C$) |
| Increasing customization of product or service | Increases product differentiation and value ($V$), increases buyer switching costs, boosts total sales volume, often increases unit costs ($C$) |
| Building a bigger, better dealer network | Broadens access to buyers, boosts total sales volume and market share, may increase unit costs ($C$) |
| Improving warranties, offering low-interest financing | Increases product differentiation and value ($V$), increases unit costs ($C$), increases buyer switching costs, boosts total sales volume and market share |

likely to retaliate against new entrants with sharp price discounting and other moves designed to make entry unprofitable and when entry barriers are high. Entry barriers are high under the following conditions:[2]

- *Industry incumbents enjoy large cost advantages over potential entrants.* Existing industry members frequently have costs that are hard for a newcomer to replicate. The cost advantages of industry incumbents can stem from (1) scale economies in production, distribution, advertising, or other activities, (2) the learning-based cost savings that accrue from experience in performing certain activities such as manufacturing or new product development or inventory management, (3) cost-savings accruing from patents or proprietary technology, (4) exclusive partnerships with the best and cheapest suppliers of raw materials and components, (5) favorable locations, and (6) low fixed costs (because incumbents have older facilities that have been mostly depreciated). The bigger the cost advantages of industry incumbents, the riskier it becomes for outsiders to attempt entry (since they will have to accept thinner profit margins or even losses until the cost disadvantages can be overcome).

- *Customers have strong brand preferences and high degrees of loyalty to seller.* The stronger buyers' attachment to established brands, the harder it is for a newcomer to break into the marketplace. In such cases, a new entrant must have the financial resources to spend enough on advertising and sales promotion to overcome customer loyalties and build its own clientele. Establishing brand recognition and building customer loyalty can be a slow and costly process. In addition, if it is difficult or costly for a customer to switch to a new brand, a new entrant may have to offer a discounted price or otherwise persuade buyers that its brand is worth the switching costs. Such barriers discourage new entry because they act to boost financial requirements and lower expected profit margins for new entrants.

- *Patents and other forms of intellectual property protection are in place.* In a number of industries, entry is prevented due to the existence of intellectual property protection laws that remain in place for a given number of years. Often, companies have a "wall of patents" in place to prevent other companies from entering with a "me too" strategy that replicates a key piece of technology.

- *There are strong "network effects" in customer demand.* In industries where buyers are more attracted to a product when there are many other users of the product, there are said to be "network effects," since demand is higher the larger the network of users. Video game systems are an example, since users prefer to have the same systems as their friends so that they can play together on systems they all know and can share games. When incumbents have a large existing base of users, new entrants with otherwise comparable products face a serious disadvantage in attracting buyers.

- *Capital requirements are high.* The larger the total dollar investment needed to enter the market successfully, the more limited the pool of potential entrants. The most obvious capital requirements for new entrants relate to manufacturing facilities and equipment, introductory advertising and sales promotion campaigns, working capital to finance inventories and customer credit, and sufficient cash to cover startup costs.

- *There are difficulties in building a network of distributors/dealers or in securing adequate space on retailers' shelves.* A potential entrant can face numerous distribution-channel challenges. Wholesale distributors may be reluctant to take on a product that lacks buyer recognition. Retailers must be recruited and convinced to give a new brand ample display space and an adequate trial period. When existing sellers have strong, well-functioning distributor–dealer networks, a newcomer has an uphill struggle in squeezing its way into existing distribution channels. Potential entrants sometimes have to "buy" their way into wholesale or retail channels by cutting their prices to provide dealers and distributors with higher markups and profit margins or by giving them big advertising and promotional allowances. As a consequence, a potential entrant's own profits may be squeezed unless and until its product gains enough consumer acceptance that distributors and retailers are anxious to carry it.

- *There are restrictive regulatory policies.* Regulated industries like cable TV, telecommunications, electric and gas utilities, radio and television broadcasting, liquor retailing, and railroads entail government-controlled entry. Government agencies can also limit or even bar entry by requiring licenses and permits, such as the medallion required to drive a taxicab in New York City. Government-mandated safety regulations and environmental pollution standards also create entry barriers because they raise entry costs.

- *There are restrictive trade policies.* In international markets, host governments commonly limit foreign entry and must approve all foreign investment applications. National governments commonly use tariffs and trade restrictions (antidumping rules, local content requirements, quotas, etc.) to raise entry barriers for foreign firms and protect domestic producers from outside competition.

Figure 3.5 summarizes the factors that cause the overall competitive pressure from potential entrants to be strong or weak. An analysis of these factors can help managers determine whether the threat of entry into their industry is high or low, *in general*. But certain kinds of companies—those with sizable financial resources, proven competitive capabilities, and a respected brand name—may be able to hurdle an industry's entry barriers even when they are high.[3] For example, when Honda opted to enter the U.S. lawn-mower market in competition against Toro, Snapper, Craftsman,

Whether an industry's entry barriers ought to be considered high or low depends on the resources and capabilities possessed by the pool of potential entrants.

## FIGURE 3.5   Factors Affecting the Threat of Entry

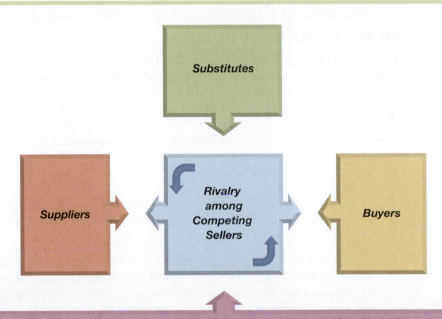

**Competitive Pressures from Potential Entrants**

*Threat of entry is a stronger force when incumbents are unlikely to make retaliatory moves against new entrants and entry barriers are low. Entry barriers are high (and threat of entry is low) when:*
- Incumbents have large cost advantages over potential entrants due to:
  - High economies of scale
  - Significant experience-based cost advantages or learning curve effects
  - Other cost advantages (e.g., favorable access to inputs, technology, location, or low fixed costs)
- Customers have strong brand preferences and/or loyalty to incumbent sellers.
- Patents and other forms of intellectual property protection are in place.
- There are strong network effects.
- Capital requirements are high.
- There is limited new access to distribution channels and shelf space.
- Government policies are restrictive.
- There are restrictive trade policies.

High entry barriers and weak entry threats today do not always translate into high entry barriers and weak entry threats tomorrow.

John Deere, and others, it was easily able to hurdle entry barriers that would have been formidable to other newcomers because it had long-standing expertise in gasoline engines and a reputation for quality and durability in automobiles that gave it instant credibility with homeowners. As a result, Honda had to spend relatively little on inducing dealers to handle the Honda lawn-mower line or attracting customers.

It is also important to recognize that the threat of entry changes as the industry's prospects grow brighter or dimmer and as entry barriers rise or fall. For example, key patents that have prevented new entry in the market for functional 3-D printers expired in February 2014, opening the way for new competition in this industry. Use of the Internet for shopping has made it much easier for e-tailers to enter into competition against some of the best-known retail chains. On the other hand, new strategic actions by incumbent firms to increase advertising, strengthen distributor–dealer relations, step up R&D, or improve product quality can erect higher roadblocks to entry.

## Competitive Pressures from the Sellers of Substitute Products

Companies in one industry are vulnerable to competitive pressure from the actions of companies in a closely adjoining industry whenever buyers view the products of the two industries as good substitutes. For instance, the producers of sugar experience competitive pressures from the sales and marketing efforts of the makers of Equal, Splenda, Sweet 'N Low, and Truvia. Newspapers are struggling to maintain their relevance to subscribers who can watch the news on numerous TV channels and use the Internet to read blogs or other online news sources. Similarly, the producers of eyeglasses and contact lenses face competitive pressures from doctors who do corrective laser surgery.

As depicted in Figure 3.6, three factors determine whether the competitive pressures from substitute products are strong or weak. Competitive pressures are stronger when:

1. *Good substitutes are readily available and attractively priced.* The presence of readily available and attractively priced substitutes creates competitive pressure by placing a ceiling on the prices industry members can charge without risking sales erosion. This price ceiling, at the same time, puts a lid on the profits that industry members can earn unless they find ways to cut costs.

2. *Buyers view the substitutes as comparable or better in terms of quality, performance, and other relevant attributes.* The availability of substitutes inevitably invites customers to compare performance, features, ease of use, and other attributes as well as price. The users of paper cartons constantly weigh the price-performance trade-offs with plastic containers and metal cans, for example.

3. *The costs that buyers incur in switching to the substitutes are low.* Low switching costs make it easier for the sellers of attractive substitutes to lure buyers to their offerings; high switching costs deter buyers from purchasing substitute products.

Before assessing the competitive pressures coming from substitutes, company managers must identify the substitutes, which is less easy than it sounds since it involves (1) determining where the industry boundaries lie and (2) figuring out which other products or services can address the same basic customer needs as those produced by industry members. Deciding on the industry boundaries is necessary for

**FIGURE 3.6    Factors Affecting Competition from Substitute Products**

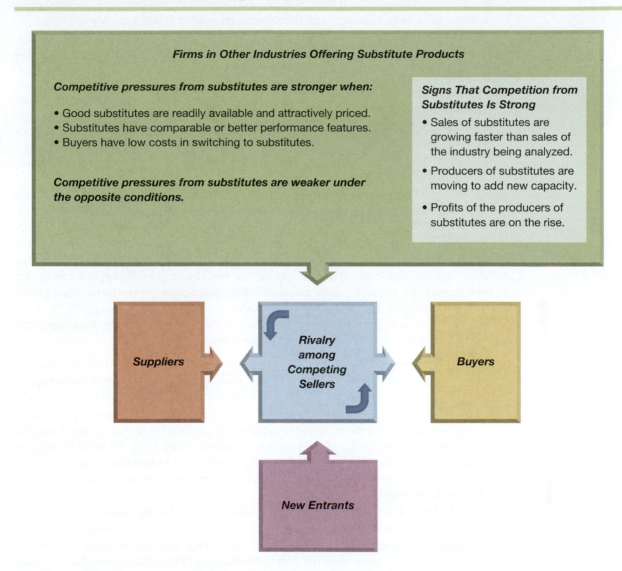

determining which firms are direct rivals and which produce substitutes. This is a matter of perspective—there are no hard-and-fast rules, other than to say that other brands of the same basic product constitute rival products and not substitutes.

## Competitive Pressures Stemming from Supplier Bargaining Power

Whether the suppliers of industry members represent a weak or strong competitive force depends on the degree to which suppliers have sufficient *bargaining power* to influence the terms and conditions of supply in their favor. Suppliers with strong bargaining power can erode industry profitability by charging industry members higher prices, passing costs on to them, and limiting their opportunities to find better deals. For instance, Microsoft and Intel, both of which supply PC makers with essential components, have been known to use their dominant market status not only to charge PC makers premium prices but also to leverage their power over PC makers in other ways. The bargaining power of these two companies over their customers is so great that both companies have faced antitrust charges on numerous occasions. Prior to a legal agreement ending the practice, Microsoft pressured PC makers to load only Microsoft products on the PCs they shipped. Intel has defended itself against similar antitrust charges, but in filling orders for newly introduced Intel chips, it continues to give top priority to PC makers that use the biggest percentages of Intel chips in their PC models. Being on Intel's list of preferred customers helps a PC maker get an early allocation of Intel's latest chips and thus allows the PC maker to get new models to market ahead of rivals.

Small-scale retailers often must contend with the power of manufacturers whose products enjoy well-known brand names, since consumers expect to find these products on the shelves of the retail stores where they shop. This provides the manufacturer with a degree of pricing power and often the ability to push hard for favorable shelf displays. Supplier bargaining power is also a competitive factor in industries where unions have been able to organize the workforce (which supplies labor). Air pilot unions, for example, have employed their bargaining power to increase pilots' wages and benefits in the air transport industry.

As shown in Figure 3.7, a variety of factors determine the strength of suppliers' bargaining power. Supplier power is stronger when:

- *Demand for suppliers' products is high and the products are in short supply.* A surge in the demand for particular items shifts the bargaining power to the suppliers of those products; suppliers of items in short supply have pricing power.

- *Suppliers provide differentiated inputs that enhance the performance of the industry's product.* The more valuable a particular input is in terms of enhancing the performance or quality of the products of industry members, the more bargaining leverage suppliers have. In contrast, the suppliers of commodities are in a weak bargaining position, since industry members have no reason other than price to prefer one supplier over another.

- *It is difficult or costly for industry members to switch their purchases from one supplier to another.* Low switching costs limit supplier bargaining power by enabling industry members to change suppliers if any one supplier attempts to raise prices by more than the costs of switching. Thus, the higher the switching costs of industry members, the stronger the bargaining power of their suppliers.

- *The supplier industry is dominated by a few large companies and it is more concentrated than the industry it sells to.* Suppliers with sizable market shares and strong demand for the items they supply generally have sufficient bargaining power to charge high prices and deny requests from industry members for lower prices or other concessions.

- *Industry members are incapable of integrating backward to self-manufacture items they have been buying from suppliers.* As a rule, suppliers are safe from the threat of self-manufacture by their customers until the volume of parts a customer needs becomes large enough for the customer to justify backward integration into self-manufacture of the component. When industry members can threaten credibly to self-manufacture suppliers' goods, their bargaining power over suppliers increases proportionately.

**FIGURE 3.7   Factors Affecting the Bargaining Power of Suppliers**

**Suppliers**

**Supplier bargaining power is stronger when:**
- Suppliers' products and/or services are in short supply.
- Suppliers' products and/or services are differentiated.
- Industry members incur high costs in switching their purchases to alternative suppliers.
- The supplier industry is more concentrated than the industry it sells to and is dominated by a few large companies.
- Industry members do not have the potential to integrate backward in order to self-manufacture their own inputs.
- Suppliers' products do not account for more than a small fraction of the total costs of the industry's products.
- There are no good substitutes for what the suppliers provide.
- Industry members do not account for a big fraction of suppliers' sales.

**Supplier bargaining power is weaker under the opposite conditions.**

*Substitutes*

*Rivalry among Competing Sellers*

*Buyers*

*New Entrants*

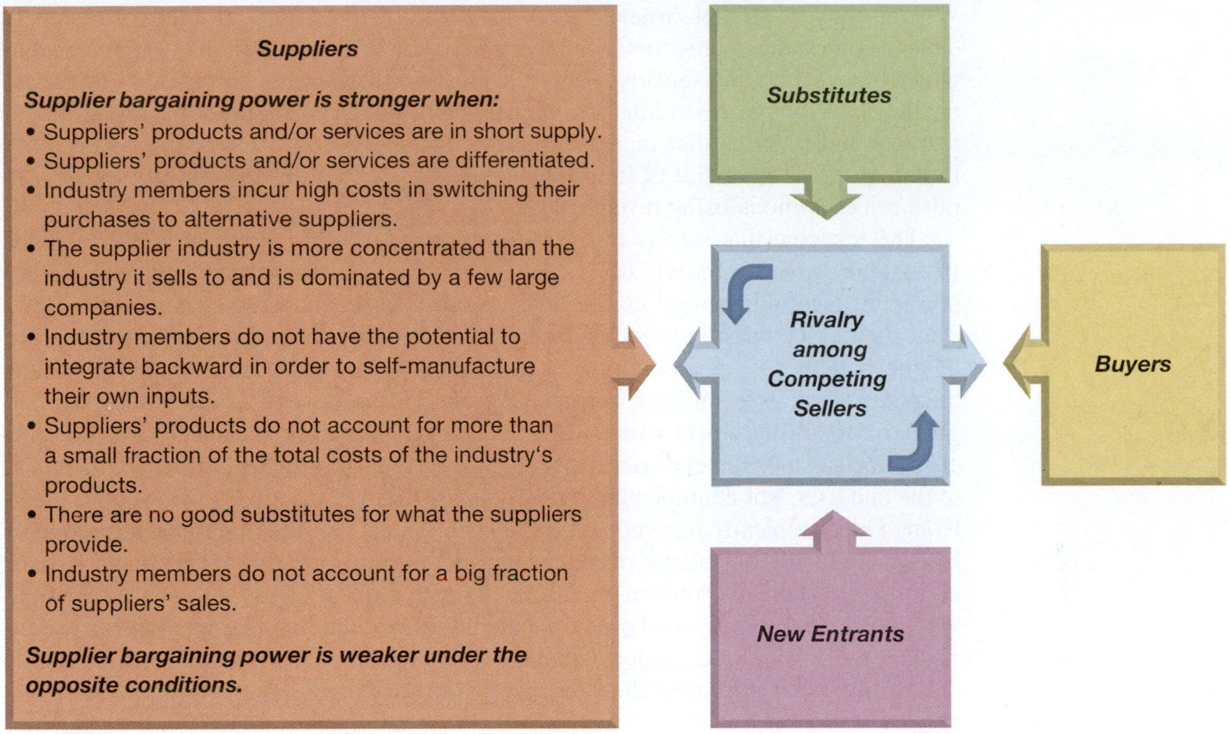

- *Suppliers provide an item that accounts for no more than a small fraction of the costs of the industry's product.* The more that the cost of a particular part or component affects the final product's cost, the more that industry members will be sensitive to the actions of suppliers to raise or lower their prices. When an input accounts for only a small proportion of total input costs, buyers will be less sensitive to price increases. Thus, suppliers' power increases when the inputs they provide do *not* make up a large proportion of the cost of the final product

- *Good substitutes are not available for the suppliers' products.* The lack of readily available substitute inputs increases the bargaining power of suppliers by increasing the dependence of industry members on the suppliers.

- *Industry members are not major customers of suppliers.* As a rule, suppliers have less bargaining leverage when their sales to members of the industry constitute a big percentage of their total sales. In such cases, the well-being of suppliers is closely tied to the well-being of their major customers, and their dependence upon them increases. The bargaining power of suppliers is stronger, then, when they are *not* bargaining with major customers.

In identifying the degree of supplier power in an industry, it is important to recognize that different types of suppliers are likely to have different amounts of bargaining power. Thus, the first step is for managers to identify the different types of suppliers, paying particular attention to those that provide the industry with important inputs. The next step is to assess the bargaining power of each type of supplier separately.

# Competitive Pressures Stemming from Buyer Bargaining Power and Price Sensitivity

Whether buyers are able to exert strong competitive pressures on industry members depends on (1) the degree to which buyers have bargaining power and (2) the extent to which buyers are price-sensitive. Buyers with strong bargaining power can limit industry profitability by demanding price concessions, better payment terms, or additional features and services that increase industry members' costs. Buyer price sensitivity limits the profit potential of industry members by restricting the ability of sellers to raise prices without losing revenue due to lost sales.

The leverage that buyers have in negotiating favorable terms of sale can range from weak to strong. Individual consumers, for example, rarely have much bargaining power in negotiating price concessions or other favorable terms with sellers. However, their price sensitivity varies by individual and by the type of product they are buying (whether it's a necessity or a discretionary purchase, for example). Business buyers, in contrast, can have considerable bargaining power. Retailers tend to have greater bargaining power over industry sellers if they have influence over the purchase decisions of the end user or if they are critical in providing sellers with access to the end user. For example, large retail chains like Walmart, Best Buy, Staples, and Home Depot typically have considerable negotiating leverage in purchasing products from manufacturers because of manufacturers' need for access to their broad base of customers. Major supermarket chains like Kroger, Safeway, and Publix have sufficient bargaining power to demand promotional allowances and lump-sum payments (called *slotting fees*) from food products manufacturers in return for stocking certain brands or putting them in the best shelf locations. Motor vehicle manufacturers have strong bargaining power in negotiating to buy original-equipment tires from tire makers not only because they buy in large quantities but also because consumers are more likely to buy replacement tires that match the tire brand on their vehicle at the time of its purchase.

Figure 3.8 summarizes the factors determining the strength of buyer power in an industry. Note that the first five factors are the mirror image of those determining the bargaining power of suppliers, as described next.

Buyer bargaining power is stronger when:

- *Buyer demand is weak in relation to industry supply.* Weak or declining demand and the resulting excess supply create a "buyers' market," in which bargain-hunting buyers are able to press for better deals and special treatment.

- *Industry goods are standardized or differentiation is weak.* In such circumstances, buyers make their selections on the basis of price, which increases price competition among vendors.

- *Buyers' costs of switching to competing brands or substitutes are relatively low.* Switching costs put a cap on how much industry producers can raise prices or reduce quality before they will lose the buyer's business.

- *Buyers are large and few in number relative to the number of sellers.* The larger the buyers, the more important their business is to the seller and the more sellers will be willing to grant concessions.

- *Buyers pose a credible threat of integrating backward into the business of sellers.* Companies like Anheuser-Busch, Coors, and Heinz have partially integrated backward into metal-can manufacturing to gain bargaining power in obtaining the balance of their can requirements from otherwise powerful metal-can manufacturers.

## FIGURE 3.8    Factors Affecting the Bargaining Power of Buyers

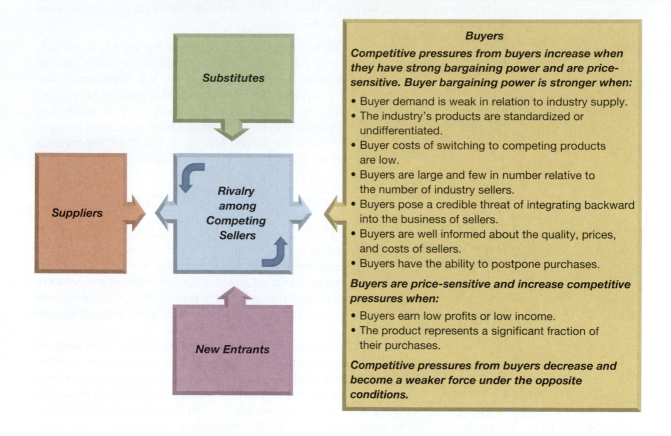

**Buyers**

***Competitive pressures from buyers increase when they have strong bargaining power and are price-sensitive. Buyer bargaining power is stronger when:***

- Buyer demand is weak in relation to industry supply.
- The industry's products are standardized or undifferentiated.
- Buyer costs of switching to competing products are low.
- Buyers are large and few in number relative to the number of industry sellers.
- Buyers pose a credible threat of integrating backward into the business of sellers.
- Buyers are well informed about the quality, prices, and costs of sellers.
- Buyers have the ability to postpone purchases.

***Buyers are price-sensitive and increase competitive pressures when:***

- Buyers earn low profits or low income.
- The product represents a significant fraction of their purchases.

***Competitive pressures from buyers decrease and become a weaker force under the opposite conditions.***

- *Buyers are well informed about sellers' products, prices, and costs.* The more information buyers have, the better bargaining position they are in. The mushrooming availability of product information on the Internet (and its ready access on smartphones) is giving added bargaining power to consumers, since they can use this to find or negotiate better deals.

- *Buyers have discretion to delay their purchases or perhaps even not make a purchase at all.* Consumers often have the option to delay purchases of durable goods, such as major appliances, or discretionary goods, such as hot tubs and home entertainment centers, if they are not happy with the prices offered. Business customers may also be able to defer their purchases of certain items, such as plant equipment or maintenance services. This puts pressure on sellers to provide concessions to buyers so that the sellers can keep their sales numbers from dropping off.

The following factors increase buyer price sensitivity and result in greater competitive pressures on the industry as a result:

- *Buyer price sensitivity increases when buyers are earning low profits or have low income.* Price is a critical factor in the purchase decisions of low-income consumers and companies that are barely scraping by. In such cases, their high price sensitivity limits the ability of sellers to charge high prices.

- *Buyers are more price-sensitive if the product represents a large fraction of their total purchases.* When a purchase eats up a large portion of a buyer's budget or represents a significant part of his or her cost structure, the buyer cares more about price than might otherwise be the case.

The starting point for the analysis of buyers as a competitive force is to identify the different types of buyers along the value chain—then proceed to analyzing the bargaining power and price sensitivity of each type separately. It is important to recognize that *not all buyers of an industry's product have equal degrees of bargaining power with sellers, and some may be less sensitive than others to price, quality, or service differences.* For example, apparel manufacturers confront significant bargaining power when selling to big retailers like Target, Macy's, or L.L.Bean, but they can command much better prices selling to small owner-managed apparel boutiques.

## Is the Collective Strength of the Five Competitive Forces Conducive to Good Profitability?

Assessing whether each of the five competitive forces gives rise to strong, moderate, or weak competitive pressures sets the stage for evaluating whether, overall, the strength of the five forces is conducive to good profitability. Are some of the competitive forces sufficiently powerful to undermine industry profitability? Can companies in this industry reasonably expect to earn decent profits in light of the prevailing competitive forces?

The most extreme case of a "competitively unattractive" industry occurs when all five forces are producing strong competitive pressures: Rivalry among sellers is vigorous, low entry barriers allow new rivals to gain a market foothold, competition from substitutes is intense, and both suppliers and buyers are able to exercise considerable

> **CORE CONCEPT**
>
> The strongest of the five forces determines the extent of the downward pressure on an industry's profitability.

leverage. Strong competitive pressures coming from all five directions drive industry profitability to unacceptably low levels, frequently producing losses for many industry members and forcing some out of business. But an industry can be competitively unattractive without all five competitive forces being strong. In fact, *intense competitive pressures from just one of the five forces may suffice to destroy the conditions for good profitability and prompt some companies to exit the business.*

As a rule, *the strongest competitive forces determine the extent of the competitive pressure on industry profitability.* Thus, in evaluating the strength of the five forces overall and their effect on industry profitability, managers should look to the strongest forces. Having more than one strong force will not worsen the effect on industry profitability, but it does mean that the industry has multiple competitive challenges with which to cope. In that sense, an industry with three to five strong forces is even more "unattractive" as a place to compete. Especially intense competitive conditions seem to be the norm in tire manufacturing, apparel, and commercial airlines, three industries where profit margins have historically been thin.

In contrast, when the overall impact of the five competitive forces is moderate to weak, an industry is "attractive" in the sense that the *average* industry member can reasonably expect to earn good profits and a nice return on investment. The ideal competitive environment for earning superior profits is one in which both suppliers and customers are in weak bargaining positions, there are no good substitutes, high barriers block further entry, and rivalry among present sellers is muted. Weak competition is the best of all possible worlds for also-ran companies because even they can usually eke out a decent profit—if a company can't make a decent profit when competition is weak, then its business outlook is indeed grim.

# Matching Company Strategy to Competitive Conditions

Working through the five forces model step by step not only aids strategy makers in assessing whether the intensity of competition allows good profitability but also promotes sound strategic thinking about how to better match company strategy to the specific competitive character of the marketplace. Effectively matching a company's business strategy to prevailing competitive conditions has two aspects:

1. Pursuing avenues that shield the firm from as many of the different competitive pressures as possible.
2. Initiating actions calculated to shift the competitive forces in the company's favor by altering the underlying factors driving the five forces.

But making headway on these two fronts first requires identifying competitive pressures, gauging the relative strength of each of the five competitive forces, and gaining a deep enough understanding of the state of competition in the industry to know which strategy buttons to push.

> A company's strategy is increasingly effective the more it provides some insulation from competitive pressures, shifts the competitive battle in the company's favor, and positions the firm to take advantage of attractive growth opportunities.

# COMPLEMENTORS AND THE VALUE NET

Not all interactions among industry participants are necessarily competitive in nature. Some have the potential to be cooperative, as the value net framework demonstrates. Like the five forces framework, the value net includes an analysis of buyers, suppliers, and substitutors (see Figure 3.9). But it differs from the five forces framework in several important ways.

First, the analysis focuses on the interactions of industry participants with a particular company. Thus it places that firm in the center of the framework, as Figure 3.9 shows. Second, the category of "competitors" is defined to include not only the focal firm's direct competitors or industry rivals but also the sellers of substitute products and potential entrants. Third, the value net framework introduces a new category of industry participant that is not found in the five forces framework—that of "complementors." **Complementors** are the producers of complementary products, which are products that enhance the value of the focal firm's products when they are used together. Some examples include snorkels and swim fins or shoes and shoelaces.

The inclusion of complementors draws particular attention to the fact that success in the marketplace need not come at the expense of other industry participants. Interactions among industry participants may be cooperative in nature rather than competitive. In the case of complementors, an increase in sales for them is likely to increase the sales of the focal firm as well. But the value net framework also encourages managers to consider other forms of cooperative interactions and realize that value is created jointly by all industry participants. For example, a company's success in the marketplace depends on establishing a reliable supply chain for its inputs, which implies the need for cooperative relations with its suppliers. Often a firm works hand in hand with its suppliers to ensure a smoother, more efficient operation for both parties. Newell-Rubbermaid, for example, works cooperatively as a supplier to companies such as Kmart and Kohl's. Even direct rivals may work cooperatively if they participate in industry trade associations or engage in joint lobbying efforts. Value net analysis can help managers discover the potential to improve their position through cooperative as well as competitive interactions.

> **CORE CONCEPT**
>
> **Complementors** are the producers of complementary products, which are products that enhance the value of the focal firm's products when they are used together.

## FIGURE 3.9    The Value Net

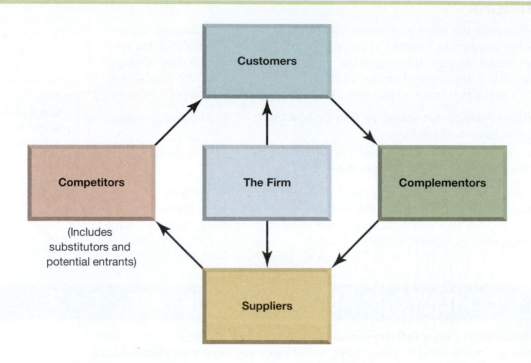

# INDUSTRY DYNAMICS AND THE FORCES DRIVING CHANGE

While it is critical to understand the nature and intensity of competitive and cooperative forces in an industry, it is equally critical to understand that the intensity of these forces is fluid and subject to change. All industries are affected by new developments and ongoing trends that alter industry conditions, some more speedily than others. Any strategies devised by management will therefore play out in a dynamic industry environment, so it's imperative that managers consider the factors driving industry change and how they might affect the industry environment. Moreover, with early notice, managers may be able to influence the direction or scope of environmental change and improve the outlook.

Industry and competitive conditions change because forces are enticing or pressuring certain industry participants (competitors, customers, suppliers, complementors) to alter their actions in important ways. The most powerful of the change agents are called **driving forces** because they have the biggest influences in reshaping the industry landscape and altering competitive conditions. Some driving forces originate in the outer ring of the company's macro-environment (see Figure 3.2), but most originate in the company's more immediate industry and competitive environment.

Driving-forces analysis has three steps: (1) identifying what the driving forces are, (2) assessing whether the drivers of change are, on the whole, acting to make

### CORE CONCEPT

**Driving forces** are the major underlying causes of change in industry and competitive conditions.

the industry more or less attractive, and (3) determining what strategy changes are needed to prepare for the impact of the driving forces. All three steps merit further discussion.

# Identifying the Forces Driving Industry Change

Many developments can affect an industry powerfully enough to qualify as driving forces. Some drivers of change are unique and specific to a particular industry situation, but most drivers of industry and competitive change fall into one of the following categories:

- *Changes in an industry's long-term growth rate.* Shifts in industry growth up or down have the potential to affect the balance between industry supply and buyer demand, entry and exit, and the character and strength of competition. Whether demand is growing or declining is one of the key factors influencing the intensity of rivalry in an industry, as explained earlier. But the strength of this effect will depend on how changes in the industry growth rate affect entry and exit in the industry. If entry barriers are low, then growth in demand will attract new entrants, increasing the number of industry rivals and changing the competitive landscape.

- *Increasing globalization.* Globalization can be precipitated by such factors as the blossoming of consumer demand in developing countries, the availability of lower-cost foreign inputs, and the reduction of trade barriers, as has occurred recently in many parts of Latin America and Asia. The forces of globalization are sometimes such a strong driver that companies find it highly advantageous, if not necessary, to spread their operating reach into more and more country markets.

- *Emerging new Internet capabilities and applications.* The Internet of the future will feature faster speeds, dazzling applications, and over a billion connected gadgets performing an array of functions, thus driving a host of industry and competitive changes. But Internet-related impacts vary from industry to industry. The challenges are to assess precisely how emerging Internet developments are altering a particular industry's landscape and to factor these impacts into the strategy-making equation.

- *Shifts in buyer demographics.* Shifts in buyer demographics and the ways products are used can greatly alter industry and competitive conditions. Longer life expectancies and growing percentages of relatively well-to-do retirees, for example, are driving demand growth in such industries as health care, prescription drugs, recreational living, and vacation travel.

- *Technological change and manufacturing process innovation.* Advances in technology can cause disruptive change in an industry by introducing substitutes or can alter the industry landscape by opening up whole new industry frontiers. For instance, advances in battery technology are beginning to change how motor vehicles are powered.

- *Product innovation.* An ongoing stream of product innovations tends to alter the pattern of competition in an industry by attracting more first-time buyers, rejuvenating industry growth, and/or increasing product differentiation, with concomitant effects on rivalry, entry threat, and buyer power. Product innovation has been a key driving force in industries such as smartphones, video games, and prescription drugs.

- *Entry or exit of major firms.* Entry by a major firm thus often produces a new ball game, not only with new key players but also with new rules for competing. Similarly, exit of a major firm changes the competitive structure by reducing the number of market leaders and increasing the dominance of the leaders who remain.

- *Diffusion of technical know-how across companies and countries.* As knowledge about how to perform a particular activity or execute a particular manufacturing technology spreads, products tend to become more commodity-like. Knowledge diffusion can occur through scientific journals, trade publications, onsite plant tours, word of mouth among suppliers and customers, employee migration, and Internet sources.

- *Changes in cost and efficiency.* Widening or shrinking differences in the costs among key competitors tend to dramatically alter the state of competition. Declining costs of producing PCs have enabled price cuts and spurred PC sales (especially lower-priced models) by making them more affordable to lower-income households worldwide.

- *Reductions in uncertainty and business risk.* Many companies are hesitant to enter industries with uncertain futures or high levels of business risk because it is unclear how much time and money it will take to overcome various technological hurdles and achieve acceptable production costs (as is the case in the infant solar power industry). Over time, however, diminishing risk levels and uncertainty tend to stimulate new entry and capital investments on the part of growth-minded companies seeking new opportunities, thus dramatically altering industry and competitive conditions.

- *Regulatory influences and government policy changes.* Government regulatory actions can often mandate significant changes in industry practices and strategic approaches—as has recently occurred in the world's banking industry. New rules and regulations pertaining to government-sponsored health insurance programs are driving changes in the health care industry. In international markets, host governments can drive competitive changes by opening their domestic markets to foreign participation or closing them to protect domestic companies.

- *Changing societal concerns, attitudes, and lifestyles.* Emerging social issues as well as changing attitudes and lifestyles can be powerful instigators of industry change. Mounting consumer concerns about the use of chemical additives and the nutritional content of food products are driving changes in the restaurant and food industries. Shifting societal concerns, attitudes, and lifestyles alter the pattern of competition, favoring those players that respond with products targeted to the new trends and conditions.

While many forces of change may be at work in a given industry, *no more than three or four* are likely to be true driving forces powerful enough to qualify as the *major determinants* of why and how the industry is changing. Thus, company strategists must resist the temptation to label every change they see as a driving force. Table 3.3 lists the most common driving forces

## Assessing the Impact of the Forces Driving Industry Change

The second step in driving-forces analysis is to determine whether the prevailing change drivers, on the whole, are acting to make the industry environment more or less attractive. Getting a handle on the collective impact of the driving forces requires looking at the likely effects of each factor separately, since the driving forces may not all be pushing change in the same direction. For example, one driving force may be acting to spur demand for the industry's product while another is working to curtail demand. Whether the net effect on industry demand is up or down hinges on which driver of change is the more powerful.

The most important part of driving-forces analysis is to determine whether the collective impact of the driving forces will increase or decrease market demand, make competition more or less intense, and lead to higher or lower industry profitability.

The real payoff of driving-forces analysis is to help managers understand what strategy changes are needed to prepare for the impacts of the driving forces.

**TABLE 3.3   The Most Common Drivers of Industry Change**

- Changes in the long-term industry growth rate
- Increasing globalization
- Emerging new Internet capabilities and applications
- Shifts in buyer demographics
- Technological change and manufacturing process innovation
- Product and marketing innovation
- Entry or exit of major firms
- Diffusion of technical know-how across companies and countries
- Changes in cost and efficiency
- Reductions in uncertainty and business risk
- Regulatory influences and government policy changes
- Changing societal concerns, attitudes, and lifestyles

## Adjusting the Strategy to Prepare for the Impacts of Driving Forces

The third step in the strategic analysis of industry dynamics—where the real payoff for strategy making comes—is for managers to draw some conclusions about *what strategy adjustments will be needed to deal with the impacts of the driving forces.* But taking the "right" kinds of actions to prepare for the industry and competitive changes being wrought by the driving forces first requires accurate diagnosis of the forces driving industry change and the impacts these forces will have on both the industry environment and the company's business. To the extent that managers are unclear about the drivers of industry change and their impacts, or if their views are off-base, the chances of making astute and timely strategy adjustments are slim. So driving-forces analysis is not something to take lightly; it has practical value and is basic to the task of thinking strategically about where the industry is headed and how to prepare for the changes ahead.

**LO 3**

How to map the market positions of key groups of industry rivals.

## STRATEGIC GROUP ANALYSIS

Within an industry, companies commonly sell in different price/quality ranges, appeal to different types of buyers, have different geographic coverage, and so on. Some are more attractively positioned than others. Understanding which companies are strongly positioned and which are weakly positioned is an integral part of analyzing an industry's competitive structure. The best technique for revealing the market positions of industry competitors is **strategic group mapping.**

**CORE CONCEPT**

**Strategic group mapping** is a technique for displaying the different market or competitive positions that rival firms occupy in the industry.

# Using Strategic Group Maps to Assess the Market Positions of Key Competitors

A **strategic group** consists of those industry members with similar competitive approaches and positions in the market. Companies in the same strategic group can resemble one another in a variety of ways. For example, they may have comparable product-line breadth, emphasize the same distribution channels, depend on identical technological approaches, or offer buyers essentially the same product attributes or similar services and technical assistance.[4] Evaluating strategy options entails examining what strategic groups exist, identifying the companies within each group, and determining if a competitive "white space" exists where industry competitors are able to create and capture altogether new demand. As part of this process, the number of strategic groups in an industry and their respective market positions can be displayed on a strategic group map.

The procedure for constructing a *strategic group map* is straightforward:

- Identify the competitive characteristics that delineate strategic approaches used in the industry. Typical variables used in creating strategic group maps are price/quality range (high, medium, low), geographic coverage (local, regional, national, global), product-line breadth (wide, narrow), degree of service offered (no frills, limited, full), use of distribution channels (retail, wholesale, Internet, multiple), degree of vertical integration (none, partial, full), and degree of diversification into other industries (none, some, considerable).
- Plot the firms on a two-variable map using pairs of these variables.
- Assign firms occupying about the same map location to the same strategic group.
- Draw circles around each strategic group, making the circles proportional to the size of the group's share of total industry sales revenues.

This produces a two-dimensional diagram like the one for the U.S. beer industry in Illustration Capsule 3.1.

Several guidelines need to be observed in creating strategic group maps. First, the two variables selected as axes for the map should *not* be highly correlated; if they are, the circles on the map will fall along a diagonal and reveal nothing more about the relative positions of competitors than would be revealed by comparing the rivals on just one of the variables. For instance, if companies with broad product lines use multiple distribution channels while companies with narrow lines use a single distribution channel, then looking at the differences in distribution-channel approaches adds no new information about positioning.

Second, the variables chosen as axes for the map should reflect important differences among rival approaches—when rivals differ on both variables, the locations of the rivals will be scattered, thus showing how they are positioned differently. Third, the variables used as axes don't have to be either quantitative or continuous; rather, they can be discrete variables, defined in terms of distinct classes and combinations. Fourth, drawing the sizes of the circles on the map proportional to the combined sales of the firms in each strategic group allows the map to reflect the relative sizes of each strategic group. Fifth, if more than two good variables can be used as axes for the map, then it is wise to draw several maps to give different exposures to the competitive positioning relationships present in the industry's structure—there is not necessarily one best map for portraying how competing firms are positioned.

# Comparative Market Positions of Producers in the U.S. Beer Industry: A Strategic Group Map Example

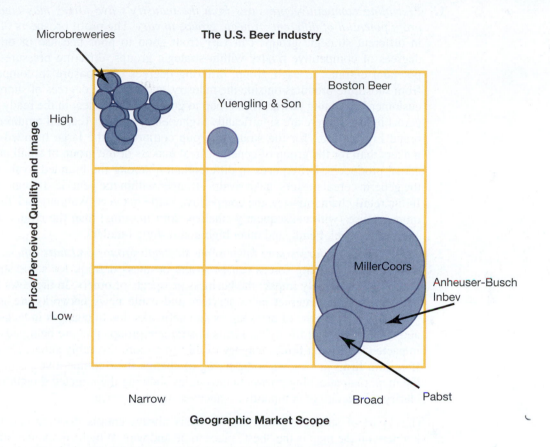

**The U.S. Beer Industry**

Microbreweries

Yuengling & Son

Boston Beer

High

Low

MillerCoors

Anheuser-Busch Inbev

Pabst

Narrow

Broad

**Price/Perceived Quality and Image**

**Geographic Market Scope**

*Note:* Circles are drawn roughly proportional to the sizes of the chains, based on revenues.

# The Value of Strategic Group Maps

Strategic group maps are revealing in several respects. The most important has to do with identifying which industry members are close rivals and which are distant rivals. Firms in the same strategic group are the closest rivals; the next closest rivals are in the immediately adjacent groups. Often, firms in strategic groups that are far apart on the map hardly compete at all. For instance, Walmart's clientele, merchandise selection, and pricing points are much too different to justify calling Walmart a close competitor of Neiman Marcus or Saks Fifth Avenue. For the same reason, the beers produced by Yuengling & Son are really not in competition with the beers produced by Pabst.

> Strategic group maps reveal which companies are close competitors and which are distant competitors.

The second thing to be gleaned from strategic group mapping is that *not all positions on the map are equally attractive.*[5] Two reasons account for why some positions can be more attractive than others:

1. *Prevailing competitive pressures from the industry's five forces may cause the profit potential of different strategic groups to vary.* The profit prospects of firms in different strategic groups can vary from good to poor because of differing degrees of competitive rivalry within strategic groups, differing pressures from potential entrants to each group, differing degrees of exposure to competition from substitute products outside the industry, and differing degrees of supplier or customer bargaining power from group to group. For instance, in the ready-to-eat cereal industry, there are significantly higher entry barriers (capital requirements, brand loyalty, etc.) for the strategic group comprising the large branded-cereal makers than for the group of generic-cereal makers or the group of small natural-cereal producers. Differences in differentiation among the branded rivals versus the generic cereal makers make rivalry stronger within the generic strategic group. In the retail chain industry, the competitive battle between Walmart and Target is more intense (with consequently smaller profit margins) than the rivalry among Versace, Chanel, Fendi, and other high-end fashion retailers.

2. *Industry driving forces may favor some strategic groups and hurt others.* Likewise, industry driving forces can boost the business outlook for some strategic groups and adversely impact the business prospects of others. In the news industry, for example, Internet news services and cable news networks are gaining ground at the expense of newspapers and networks due to changes in technology and changing social lifestyles. Firms in strategic groups that are being adversely impacted by driving forces may try to shift to a more favorably situated position. If certain firms are known to be trying to change their competitive positions on the map, then attaching arrows to the circles showing the targeted direction helps clarify the picture of competitive maneuvering among rivals.

> Some strategic groups are more favorably positioned than others because they confront weaker competitive forces and/or because they are more favorably impacted by industry driving forces.

Thus, part of strategic group map analysis always entails drawing conclusions about where on the map is the "best" place to be and why. Which companies/strategic groups are destined to prosper because of their positions? Which companies/strategic groups seem destined to struggle? What accounts for why some parts of the map are better than others?

## COMPETITOR ANALYSIS

Unless a company pays attention to the strategies and situations of competitors and has some inkling of what moves they will be making, it ends up flying blind into competitive battle. As in sports, scouting the opposition is an essential part of game plan development. Having good information about the strategic direction and likely moves of key competitors allows a company to prepare defensive countermoves, to craft its own strategic moves with some confidence about what market maneuvers to expect from rivals in response, and to exploit any openings that arise from competitors' missteps. The question is where to look for such information, since rivals rarely reveal their strategic intentions openly. If information is not directly available, what are the best indicators?

> Studying competitors' past behavior and preferences provides a valuable assist in anticipating what moves rivals are likely to make next and outmaneuvering them in the marketplace.

Michael Porter's **Framework for Competitor Analysis** points to four indicators of a rival's likely strategic moves and countermoves. These include a rival's *current* *strategy, objectives, resources and capabilities,* and *assumptions* about itself and the industry, as shown in Figure 3.10. A strategic profile of a rival that provides good clues to its behavioral proclivities can be constructed by characterizing the rival along these four dimensions.

**Current Strategy**    To succeed in predicting a competitor's next moves, company strategists need to have a good understanding of each rival's current strategy, as an indicator of its pattern of behavior and best strategic options. Questions to consider include: How is the competitor positioned in the market? What is the basis for its competitive advantage (if any)? What kinds of investments is it making (as an indicator of its growth trajectory)?

**Objectives**    An appraisal of a rival's objectives should include not only its financial performance objectives but strategic ones as well (such as those concerning market share). What is even more important is to consider the extent to which the rival is meeting these objectives and whether it is under pressure to improve. Rivals with good financial performance are likely to continue their present strategy with only minor fine-tuning. Poorly performing rivals are virtually certain to make fresh strategic moves.

**Resources and Capabilities**    A rival's strategic moves and countermoves are both enabled and constrained by the set of resources and capabilities the rival has at hand. Thus a rival's resources and capabilities (and efforts to acquire new resources and capabilities) serve as a strong signal of future strategic actions (and reactions to your company's moves). Assessing a rival's resources and capabilities involves sizing up not only its strengths in this respect but its weaknesses as well.

## FIGURE 3.10    A Framework for Competitor Analysis

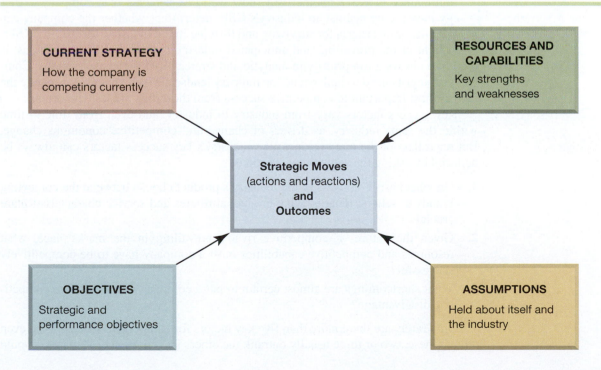

**Assumptions**   How a rival's top managers think about their strategic situation can have a big impact on how the rival behaves. Banks that believe they are "too big to fail," for example, may take on more risk than is financially prudent. Assessing a rival's assumptions entails considering its assumptions about itself as well as about the industry it participates in.

Information regarding these four analytic components can often be gleaned from company press releases, information posted on the company's website (especially the presentations management has recently made to securities analysts), and such public documents as annual reports and 10-K filings. Many companies also have a competitive intelligence unit that sifts through the available information to construct up-to-date strategic profiles of rivals. Doing the necessary detective work can be time-consuming, but scouting competitors well enough to anticipate their next moves allows managers to prepare effective countermoves (perhaps even beat a rival to the punch) and to take rivals' probable actions into account in crafting their own best course of action.

# KEY SUCCESS FACTORS

An industry's **key success factors (KSFs)** are those competitive factors that most affect industry members' ability to survive and prosper in the marketplace: the particular strategy elements, product attributes, operational approaches, resources, and competitive capabilities that spell the difference between being a strong competitor and a weak competitor—and between profit and loss. KSFs by their very nature are so important to competitive success that *all firms* in the industry must pay close attention to them or risk becoming an industry laggard or failure. To indicate the significance of KSFs another way, how well the elements of a company's strategy measure up against an industry's KSFs determines whether the company can meet the basic criteria for surviving and thriving in the industry. Identifying KSFs, in light of the prevailing and anticipated industry and competitive conditions, is therefore always a top priority in analytic and strategy-making considerations. Company strategists need to understand the industry landscape well enough to separate the factors most important to competitive success from those that are less important.

Key success factors vary from industry to industry, and even from time to time within the same industry, as drivers of change and competitive conditions change. But regardless of the circumstances, an industry's key success factors can always be deduced by asking the same three questions:

1.  On what basis do buyers of the industry's product choose between the competing brands of sellers? That is, what product attributes and service characteristics are crucial?

2.  Given the nature of competitive rivalry prevailing in the marketplace, what resources and competitive capabilities must a company have to be competitively successful?

3.  What shortcomings are almost certain to put a company at a significant competitive disadvantage?

Only rarely are there more than five key factors for competitive success. And even among these, two or three usually outrank the others in importance. Managers should therefore bear in mind the purpose of identifying key success factors—to determine which factors are most important to competitive success—and resist the temptation to label a factor that has only minor importance as a KSF.

In the beer industry, for example, although there are many types of buyers (wholesale, retail, end consumer), it is most important to understand the preferences and buying behavior of the beer drinkers. Their purchase decisions are driven by price, taste, convenient access, and marketing. Thus the KSFs include a *strong network of wholesale distributors* (to get the company's brand stocked and favorably displayed in retail outlets, bars, restaurants, and stadiums, where beer is sold) and *clever advertising* (to induce beer drinkers to buy the company's brand and thereby pull beer sales through the established wholesale and retail channels). Because there is a potential for strong buyer power on the part of large distributors and retail chains, competitive success depends on some mechanism to offset that power, of which advertising (to create demand pull) is one. Thus the KSFs also include *superior product differentiation* (as in microbrews) or *superior firm size and branding capabilities* (as in national brands). The KSFs also include *full utilization of brewing capacity* (to keep manufacturing costs low and offset the high advertising, branding, and product differentiation costs).

Correctly diagnosing an industry's KSFs raises a company's chances of crafting a sound strategy. The key success factors of an industry point to those things that every firm in the industry needs to attend to in order to retain customers and weather the competition. If the company's strategy cannot deliver on the key success factors of its industry, it is unlikely to earn enough profits to remain a viable business.

# THE INDUSTRY OUTLOOK FOR PROFITABILITY

Each of the frameworks presented in this chapter—PESTEL, five forces analysis, driving forces, strategy groups, competitor analysis, and key success factors—provides a useful perspective on an industry's outlook for future profitability. Putting them all together provides an even richer and more nuanced picture. Thus, the final step in evaluating the industry and competitive environment is to use the results of each of the analyses performed to determine whether the industry presents the company with strong prospects for competitive success and attractive profits. The important factors on which to base a conclusion include:

**LO 4**

How to use multiple frameworks to determine whether an industry's outlook presents a company with sufficiently attractive opportunities for growth and profitability.

- How the company is being impacted by the state of the macro-environment.
- Whether strong competitive forces are squeezing industry profitability to subpar levels.
- Whether the presence of complementors and the possibility of cooperative actions improve the company's prospects.
- Whether industry profitability will be favorably or unfavorably affected by the prevailing driving forces.
- Whether the company occupies a stronger market position than rivals.
- Whether this is likely to change in the course of competitive interactions.
- How well the company's strategy delivers on the industry key success factors.

As a general proposition, *the anticipated industry environment is fundamentally attractive if it presents a company with good opportunity for above-average profitability; the industry outlook is fundamentally unattractive if a company's profit prospects are unappealingly low.*

However, it is a mistake to think of a particular industry as being equally attractive or unattractive to all industry participants and all potential entrants.[6] Attractiveness is relative, not absolute, and conclusions one way or the other have to be drawn from the perspective of a particular company. For instance, a favorably positioned competitor may see ample opportunity to capitalize on the vulnerabilities of weaker rivals even though industry conditions are otherwise somewhat dismal. At the same time, industries attractive to insiders may be unattractive to outsiders because of the difficulty of challenging current market leaders or because they have more attractive opportunities elsewhere.

When a company decides an industry is fundamentally attractive and presents good opportunities, a strong case can be made that it should invest aggressively to capture the opportunities it sees and to improve its long-term competitive position in the business. When a strong competitor concludes an industry is becoming less attractive, it may elect to simply protect its present position, investing cautiously—if at all—and looking for opportunities in other industries. A competitively weak company in an unattractive industry may see its best option as finding a buyer, perhaps a rival, to acquire its business.

## KEY POINTS

Thinking strategically about a company's external situation involves probing for answers to the following questions:

1.  *What are the strategically relevant factors in the macro-environment, and how do they impact an industry and its members?* Industries differ significantly as to how they are affected by conditions in the broad macro-environment. Using PESTEL analysis to identify which of these factors is strategically relevant is the first step to understanding how a company is situated in its external environment.

2.  *What kinds of competitive forces are industry members facing, and how strong is each force?* The strength of competition is a composite of five forces: (1) rivalry within the industry, (2) the threat of new entry into the market, (3) inroads being made by the sellers of substitutes, (4) supplier bargaining power, and (5) buyer bargaining power. All five must be examined force by force, and their collective strength evaluated. One strong force, however, can be sufficient to keep average industry profitability low. Working through the five forces model aids strategy makers in assessing how to insulate the company from the strongest forces, identify attractive arenas for expansion, or alter the competitive conditions so that they offer more favorable prospects for profitability.

3.  *What cooperative forces are present in the industry, and how can a company harness them to its advantage?* Interactions among industry participants are not only competitive in nature but cooperative as well. This is particularly the case when complements to the products or services of an industry are important. The value net framework assists managers in sizing up the impact of cooperative as well as competitive interactions on their firm.

4. *What factors are driving changes in the industry, and what impact will they have on competitive intensity and industry profitability?* Industry and competitive conditions change because certain forces are acting to create incentives or pressures for change. The first step is to identify the three or four most important drivers of change affecting the industry being analyzed (out of a much longer list of potential drivers). Once an industry's change drivers have been identified, the analytic task becomes one of determining whether they are acting, individually and collectively, to make the industry environment more or less attractive.

5. *What market positions do industry rivals occupy—who is strongly positioned and who is not?* Strategic group mapping is a valuable tool for understanding the similarities, differences, strengths, and weaknesses inherent in the market positions of rival companies. Rivals in the same or nearby strategic groups are close competitors, whereas companies in distant strategic groups usually pose little or no immediate threat. The lesson of strategic group mapping is that some positions on the map are more favorable than others. The profit potential of different strategic groups may not be the same because industry driving forces and competitive forces likely have varying effects on the industry's distinct strategic groups.

6. *What strategic moves are rivals likely to make next?* Anticipating the actions of rivals can help a company prepare effective countermoves. Using the Framework for Competitor Analysis is helpful in this regard.

7. *What are the key factors for competitive success?* An industry's key success factors (KSFs) are the particular strategy elements, product attributes, operational approaches, resources, and competitive capabilities that all industry members must have in order to survive and prosper in the industry. For any industry, they can be deduced by answering three basic questions: (1) On what basis do buyers of the industry's product choose between the competing brands of sellers, (2) what resources and competitive capabilities must a company have to be competitively successful, and (3) what shortcomings are almost certain to put a company at a significant competitive disadvantage?

8. *Is the industry outlook conducive to good profitability?* The last step in industry analysis is summing up the results from applying each of the frameworks employed in answering questions 1 to 6: PESTEL, five forces analysis, driving forces, strategic group mapping, competitor analysis, and key success factors. Applying multiple lenses to the question of what the industry outlook looks like offers a more robust and nuanced answer. If the answers from each framework, seen as a whole, reveal that a company's profit prospects in that industry are above-average, then the industry environment is basically attractive *for that company.* What may look like an attractive environment for one company may appear to be unattractive from the perspective of a different company.

Clear, insightful diagnosis of a company's external situation is an essential first step in crafting strategies that are well matched to industry and competitive conditions. To do cutting-edge strategic thinking about the external environment, managers must know what questions to pose and what analytic tools to use in answering these questions. This is why this chapter has concentrated on suggesting the right questions to ask, explaining concepts and analytic approaches, and indicating the kinds of things to look for.

## ASSURANCE OF LEARNING EXERCISES

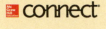 **LO 2**

1. Prepare a brief analysis of the coffee industry using the information provided on the industry trade association websites. Based upon the information provided on these websites, draw a five forces diagram for the coffee industry and briefly discuss the nature and strength of each of the five competitive forces.

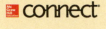 **LO 3**

2. Based on the strategic group map in Illustration Capsule 3.1, which producers are Yuengling & Son's closest competitors? Between which two strategic groups is competition the strongest? Why do you think no beer producers are positioned in the lower left corner of the map? Which company/strategic group faces the weakest competition from the members of other strategic groups?

**LO 1, LO 4**

3. The National Restaurant Association publishes an annual industry fact book that can be found at **www.restaurant.org**. Based on information in the latest report, does it appear that macro-environmental factors and the economic characteristics of the industry will present industry participants with attractive opportunities for growth and profitability? Explain.

## EXERCISE FOR SIMULATION PARTICIPANTS

**LO 1, LO 2, LO 3, LO 4**

1. Which of the factors listed in Table 3.1 might have the most strategic relevance for your industry?

2. Which of the five competitive forces is creating the strongest competitive pressures for your company?

3. What are the "weapons of competition" that rival companies in your industry can use to gain sales and market share? See Table 3.2 to help you identify the various competitive factors.

4. What are the factors affecting the intensity of rivalry in the industry in which your company is competing? Use Figure 3.4 and the accompanying discussion to help you in pinpointing the specific factors most affecting competitive intensity. Would you characterize the rivalry and jockeying for better market position, increased sales, and market share among the companies in your industry as fierce, very strong, strong, moderate, or relatively weak? Why?

5. Are there any driving forces in the industry in which your company is competing? If so, what impact will these driving forces have? Will they cause competition to be more or less intense? Will they act to boost or squeeze profit margins? List at least two actions your company should consider taking in order to combat any negative impacts of the driving forces.

6. Draw a strategic group map showing the market positions of the companies in your industry. Which companies do you believe are in the most attractive position on the map? Which companies are the most weakly positioned? Which companies

do you believe are likely to try to move to a different position on the strategic group map?

7. What do you see as the key factors for being a successful competitor in your industry? List at least three.

8. Does your overall assessment of the industry suggest that industry rivals have sufficiently attractive opportunities for growth and profitability? Explain.

## ENDNOTES

[1] Michael E. Porter, *Competitive Strategy* (New York: Free Press, 1980); Michael E. Porter, "The Five Competitive Forces That Shape Strategy," *Harvard Business Review* 86, no. 1 (January 2008), pp. 78–93.
[2] J. S. Bain, *Barriers to New Competition* (Cambridge, MA: Harvard University Press, 1956); F. M. Scherer, *Industrial Market Structure and Economic Performance* (Chicago: Rand McNally, 1971).
[3] C. A. Montgomery and S. Hariharan, "Diversified Expansion by Large Established Firms,"

*Journal of Economic Behavior & Organization* 15, no. 1 (January 1991).
[4] Mary Ellen Gordon and George R. Milne, "Selecting the Dimensions That Define Strategic Groups: A Novel Market-Driven Approach," *Journal of Managerial Issues* 11, no. 2 (Summer 1999), pp. 213–233.
[5] Avi Fiegenbaum and Howard Thomas, "Strategic Groups as Reference Groups: Theory, Modeling and Empirical Examination of Industry and Competitive Strategy," *Strategic Management Journal* 16 (1995), pp. 461–476;

S. Ade Olusoga, Michael P. Mokwa, and Charles H. Noble, "Strategic Groups, Mobility Barriers, and Competitive Advantage," *Journal of Business Research* 33 (1995), pp. 153–164.
[6] B. Wernerfelt and C. Montgomery, "What Is an Attractive Industry?" *Management Science* 32, no. 10 (October 1986), pp. 1223–1230.

### CHAPTER 4

# Evaluating a Company's Resources, Capabilities, and Competitiveness

## Learning Objectives

**LO 1**   How to take stock of how well a company's strategy is working.

**LO 2**   Why a company's resources and capabilities are centrally important in giving the company a competitive edge over rivals.

**LO 3**   How to assess the company's strengths and weaknesses in light of market opportunities and external threats.

**LO 4**   How a company's value chain activities can affect the company's cost structure and customer value proposition.

**LO 5**   How a comprehensive evaluation of a company's competitive situation can assist managers in making critical decisions about their next strategic moves.

A new strategy nearly always involves acquiring new resources and capabilities.

**Laurence Capron and Will Mitchell** – *INSEAD and University of Toronto Professors and Consultants*

Only firms who are able to continually build new strategic assets faster and cheaper than their competitors will earn superior returns over the long term.

**C. C. Markides and P. J. Williamson** – *London Business School Professors and Consultants*

The greatest achievement of the human spirit is to live up to one's opportunities and make the most of one's resources.

**Luc de Clapiers** – *Writer and Moralist*

Chapter 3 described how to use the tools of industry and competitor analysis to assess a company's external environment and lay the groundwork for matching a company's strategy to its external situation. This chapter discusses techniques for evaluating a company's internal situation, including its collection of resources and capabilities and the activities it performs along its value chain. Internal analysis enables managers to determine whether their strategy is likely to give the company a significant competitive edge over rival firms. Combined with external analysis, it facilitates an understanding of how to reposition a firm to take advantage of new opportunities and to cope with emerging competitive threats. The analytic spotlight will be trained on six questions:

1. How well is the company's present strategy working?
2. What are the company's most important resources and capabilities, and will they give the

company a lasting competitive advantage over rival companies?
3. What are the company's strengths and weaknesses in relation to the market opportunities and external threats?
4. How do a company's value chain activities impact its cost structure and customer value proposition?
5. Is the company competitively stronger or weaker than key rivals?
6. What strategic issues and problems merit front-burner managerial attention?

In probing for answers to these questions, five analytic tools—resource and capability analysis, SWOT analysis, value chain analysis, benchmarking, and competitive strength assessment—will be used. All five are valuable techniques for revealing a company's competitiveness and for helping company managers match their strategy to the company's own particular circumstances.

## QUESTION 1: HOW WELL IS THE COMPANY'S PRESENT STRATEGY WORKING?

In evaluating how well a company's present strategy is working, the best way to start is with a clear view of what the strategy entails. Figure 4.1 shows the key components of a single-business company's strategy. The first thing to examine is the company's

**LO 1**

How to take stock of how well a company's strategy is working.

competitive approach. What moves has the company made recently to attract customers and improve its market position—for instance, has it cut prices, improved the design of its product, added new features, stepped up advertising, entered a new geographic market, or merged with a competitor? Is it striving for a competitive advantage based on low costs or a better product offering? Is it concentrating on serving a broad spectrum of customers or a narrow market niche? The company's functional strategies in R&D, production, marketing, finance, human resources, information technology, and so on further characterize company strategy, as do any efforts to establish alliances with other enterprises.

The three best indicators of how well a company's strategy is working are (1) whether the company is achieving its stated financial and strategic objectives, (2) whether its financial performance is above the industry average, and (3) whether it is gaining customers and increasing its market share. Persistent shortfalls in meeting company performance targets and weak marketplace performance relative to rivals are reliable warning signs that the company has a weak strategy, suffers from poor strategy execution, or both. Specific indicators of how well a company's strategy is working include:

- Trends in the company's sales and earnings growth.
- Trends in the company's stock price.
- The company's overall financial strength.

## FIGURE 4.1 Identifying the Components of a Single-Business Company's Strategy

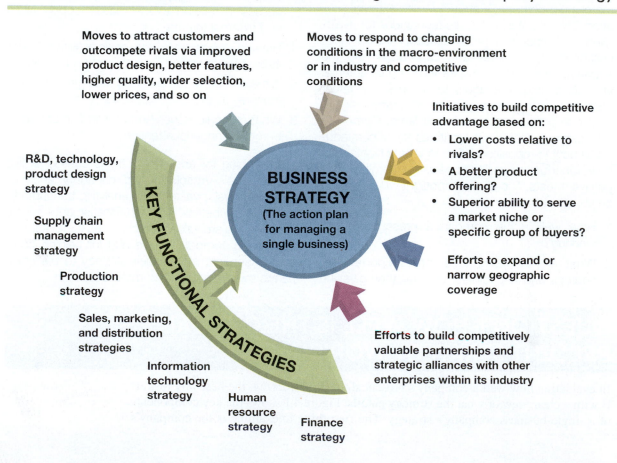

- The company's customer retention rate.
- The rate at which new customers are acquired.
- Evidence of improvement in internal processes such as defect rate, order fulfillment, delivery times, days of inventory, and employee productivity.

The stronger a company's current overall performance, the more likely it has a well-conceived, well-executed strategy. The weaker a company's financial performance and market standing, the more its current strategy must be questioned and the more likely the need for radical changes. Table 4.1 provides a compilation of the financial ratios most commonly used to evaluate a company's financial performance and balance sheet strength.

> Sluggish financial performance and second-rate market accomplishments almost always signal weak strategy, weak execution, or both.

## TABLE 4.1   Key Financial Ratios: How to Calculate Them and What They Mean

| Ratio | How Calculated | What It Shows |
|---|---|---|
| **Profitability ratios** | | |
| 1. Gross profit margin | $\dfrac{\text{Sales revenues} - \text{Cost of goods sold}}{\text{Sales revenues}}$ | Shows the percentage of revenues available to cover operating expenses and yield a profit. |
| 2. Operating profit margin (or return on sales) | $\dfrac{\text{Sales revenues} - \text{Operating expenses}}{\text{Sales revenues}}$ *or* $\dfrac{\text{Operating income}}{\text{Sales revenues}}$ | Shows the profitability of current operations without regard to interest charges and income taxes. Earnings before interest and taxes is known as *EBIT* in financial and business accounting. |
| 3. Net profit margin (or net return on sales) | $\dfrac{\text{Profits after taxes}}{\text{Sales revenues}}$ | Shows after-tax profits per dollar of sales. |
| 4. Total return on assets | $\dfrac{\text{Profits after taxes} + \text{Interest}}{\text{Total assets}}$ | A measure of the return on total investment in the enterprise. Interest is added to after-tax profits to form the numerator, since total assets are financed by creditors as well as by stockholders. |
| 5. Net return on total assets (ROA) | $\dfrac{\text{Profits after taxes}}{\text{Total assets}}$ | A measure of the return earned by stockholders on the firm's total assets. |
| 6. Return on stockholders' equity (ROE) | $\dfrac{\text{Profits after taxes}}{\text{Total stockholders' equity}}$ | The return stockholders are earning on their capital investment in the enterprise. A return in the 12%–15% range is average. |
| 7. Return on invested capital (ROIC)—sometimes referred to as return on capital employed (ROCE) | $\dfrac{\text{Profits after taxes}}{\text{Long-term debt} + \text{Total stockholders' equity}}$ | A measure of the return that shareholders are earning on the monetary capital invested in the enterprise. A higher return reflects greater bottom-line effectiveness in the use of long-term capital. |
| **Liquidity ratios** | | |
| 1. Current ratio | $\dfrac{\text{Current assets}}{\text{Current liabilities}}$ | Shows a firm's ability to pay current liabilities using assets that can be converted to cash in the near term. Ratio should be higher than 1.0. |

*(continued)*

**TABLE 4.1**    *(continued)*

| Ratio | How Calculated | What It Shows |
|---|---|---|
| 2. Working capital | Current assets − Current liabilities | The cash available for a firm's day-to-day operations. Larger amounts mean the company has more internal funds to (1) pay its current liabilities on a timely basis and (2) finance inventory expansion, additional accounts receivable, and a larger base of operations without resorting to borrowing or raising more equity capital. |
| **Leverage ratios** | | |
| 1. Total debt-to-assets ratio | $$\frac{\text{Total debt}}{\text{Total assets}}$$ | Measures the extent to which borrowed funds (both short-term loans and long-term debt) have been used to finance the firm's operations. A low ratio is better—a high fraction indicates overuse of debt and greater risk of bankruptcy. |
| 2. Long-term debt-to-capital ratio | $$\frac{\text{Long-term debt}}{\text{Long-term debt} + \text{Total stockholders' equity}}$$ | A measure of creditworthiness and balance sheet strength. It indicates the percentage of capital investment that has been financed by both long-term lenders and stockholders. A ratio below 0.25 is preferable since the lower the ratio, the greater the capacity to borrow additional funds. Debt-to-capital ratios above 0.50 indicate an excessive reliance on long-term borrowing, lower creditworthiness, and weak balance sheet strength. |
| 3. Debt-to-equity ratio | $$\frac{\text{Total debt}}{\text{Total stockholders' equity}}$$ | Shows the balance between debt (funds borrowed both short term and long term) and the amount that stockholders have invested in the enterprise. The further the ratio is below 1.0, the greater the firm's ability to borrow additional funds. Ratios above 1.0 put creditors at greater risk, signal weaker balance sheet strength, and often result in lower credit ratings. |
| 4. Long-term debt-to-equity ratio | $$\frac{\text{Long-term debt}}{\text{Total stockholders' equity}}$$ | Shows the balance between long-term debt and stockholders' equity in the firm's *long-term* capital structure. Low ratios indicate a greater capacity to borrow additional funds if needed. |
| 5. Times-interest-earned (or coverage) ratio | $$\frac{\text{Operating income}}{\text{Interest expenses}}$$ | Measures the ability to pay annual interest charges. Lenders usually insist on a minimum ratio of 2.0, but ratios above 3.0 signal progressively better creditworthiness. |
| **Activity ratios** | | |
| 1. Days of inventory | $$\frac{\text{Inventory}}{\text{Cost of goods sold} \div 365}$$ | Measures inventory management efficiency. Fewer days of inventory are better. |
| 2. Inventory turnover | $$\frac{\text{Cost of goods sold}}{\text{Inventory}}$$ | Measures the number of inventory turns per year. Higher is better. |
| 3. Average collection period | $$\frac{\text{Accounts receivable}}{\text{Total sales} \div 365}$$ *or* $$\frac{\text{Accounts receivable}}{\text{Average daily sales}}$$ | Indicates the average length of time the firm must wait after making a sale to receive cash payment. A shorter collection time is better. |

*(continued)*

**TABLE 4.1** *(concluded)*

| Ratio | How Calculated | What It Shows |
|---|---|---|
| **Other important measures of financial performance** | | |
| 1. Dividend yield on common stock | $\dfrac{\text{Annual dividends per share}}{\text{Current market price per share}}$ | A measure of the return that shareholders receive in the form of dividends. A "typical" dividend yield is 2%–3%. The dividend yield for fast-growth companies is often below 1%; the dividend yield for slow-growth companies can run 4%–5%. |
| 2. Price-to-earnings (P/E) ratio | $\dfrac{\text{Current market price per share}}{\text{Earnings per share}}$ | P/E ratios above 20 indicate strong investor confidence in a firm's outlook and earnings growth; firms whose future earnings are at risk or likely to grow slowly typically have ratios below 12. |
| 3. Dividend payout ratio | $\dfrac{\text{Annual dividends per share}}{\text{Earnings per share}}$ | Indicates the percentage of after-tax profits paid out as dividends. |
| 4. Internal cash flow | After-tax profits + Depreciation | A rough estimate of the cash a company's business is generating after payment of operating expenses, interest, and taxes. Such amounts can be used for dividend payments or funding capital expenditures. |
| 5. Free cash flow | After-tax profits + Depreciation − Capital expenditures − Dividends | A rough estimate of the cash a company's business is generating after payment of operating expenses, interest, taxes, dividends, and desirable reinvestments in the business. The larger a company's free cash flow, the greater its ability to internally fund new strategic initiatives, repay debt, make new acquisitions, repurchase shares of stock, or increase dividend payments. |

## QUESTION 2: WHAT ARE THE COMPANY'S MOST IMPORTANT RESOURCES AND CAPABILITIES, AND WILL THEY GIVE THE COMPANY A LASTING COMPETITIVE ADVANTAGE OVER RIVAL COMPANIES?

An essential element of deciding whether a company's overall situation is fundamentally healthy or unhealthy entails examining the attractiveness of its resources and capabilities. A company's resources and capabilities are its **competitive assets** and determine whether its competitive power in the marketplace will be impressively strong or disappointingly weak. Companies with second-rate competitive assets nearly always are relegated to a trailing position in the industry.

**Resource and capability analysis** provides managers with a powerful tool for sizing up the company's competitive assets and determining whether they can provide the foundation necessary for competitive success in the marketplace. This is a two-step process. The first step is to identify the company's resources and

**CORE CONCEPT**

A company's resources and capabilities represent its **competitive assets** and are determinants of its competitiveness and ability to succeed in the marketplace.

**LO 2**

Why a company's resources and capabilities are centrally important in giving the company a competitive edge over rivals.

**CORE CONCEPT**

A **resource** is a competitive asset that is owned or controlled by a company; a **capability** or **competence** is the capacity of a firm to perform some internal activity competently. Capabilities are developed and enabled through the deployment of a company's resources.

capabilities. The second step is to examine them more closely to ascertain which are the most competitively important and whether they can support a sustainable competitive advantage over rival firms.[1] This second step involves applying the *four tests of a resource's competitive power.*

# Identifying the Company's Resources and Capabilities

A firm's resources and capabilities are the fundamental building blocks of its competitive strategy. In crafting strategy, it is essential for managers to know how to take stock of the company's full complement of resources and capabilities. But before they can do so, managers and strategists need a more precise definition of these terms.

In brief, a **resource** is a productive input or competitive asset that is owned or controlled by the firm. Firms have many different types of resources at their disposal that vary not only in kind but in quality as well. Some are of a higher quality than others, and some are more competitively valuable, having greater potential to give a firm a competitive advantage over its rivals. For example, a company's brand is a resource, as is an R&D team—yet some brands such as Coca-Cola and Kleenex are well known, with enduring value, while others have little more name recognition than generic products. In similar fashion, some R&D teams are far more innovative and productive than others due to the outstanding talents of the individual team members, the team's composition, its experience, and its chemistry.

A **capability** is the capacity of a firm to perform some internal activity competently. Like resources, capabilities vary in form, quality, and competitive importance, with some being more competitively valuable than others. Apple's product innovation capabilities are widely recognized as being far superior to those of its competitors; Nordstrom is known for its superior incentive management capabilities; PepsiCo is admired for its marketing and brand management capabilities. *Organizational capabilities are developed and enabled through the deployment of a company's resources.*[2]

**Types of Company Resources**  A useful way to identify a company's resources is to look for them within categories, as shown in Table 4.2. Broadly speaking, resources can be divided into two main categories: **tangible** and **intangible** resources. Although *human resources* make up one of the most important parts of a company's resource base, we include them in the intangible category to emphasize the role played by the skills, talents, and knowledge of a company's human resources.

Tangible resources are the most easily identified, since tangible resources are those that can be *touched* or *quantified* readily. Obviously, they include various types of *physical resources* such as manufacturing facilities and mineral resources, but they also include a company's *financial resources, technological resources,* and *organizational resources* such as the company's communication and control systems. Note that technological resources are included among tangible resources, *by convention,* even though some types, such as copyrights and trade secrets, might be more logically categorized as intangible.

Intangible resources are harder to discern, but they are often among the most important of a firm's competitive assets. They include various sorts of *human assets and intellectual capital,* as well as a company's *brands, image, and reputational assets.* While intangible resources have no material existence on their own, they are often embodied in something material. Thus, the skills and knowledge resources of a firm

## TABLE 4.2   Types of Company Resources

**Tangible resources**

- *Physical resources:* land and real estate; manufacturing plants, equipment, and/or distribution facilities; the locations of stores, plants, or distribution centers, including the overall pattern of their physical locations; ownership of or access rights to natural resources (such as mineral deposits)

- *Financial resources:* cash and cash equivalents; marketable securities; other financial assets such as a company's credit rating and borrowing capacity

- *Technological assets:* patents, copyrights, production technology, innovation technologies, technological processes

- *Organizational resources:* IT and communication systems (satellites, servers, workstations, etc.); other planning, coordination, and control systems; the company's organizational design and reporting structure

**Intangible resources**

- *Human assets and intellectual capital:* the education, experience, knowledge, and talent of the workforce, cumulative learning, and tacit knowledge of employees; collective learning embedded in the organization, the intellectual capital and know-how of specialized teams and work groups; the knowledge of key personnel concerning important business functions; managerial talent and leadership skill; the creativity and innovativeness of certain personnel

- *Brands, company image, and reputational assets:* brand names, trademarks, product or company image, buyer loyalty and goodwill; company reputation for quality, service, and reliability; reputation with suppliers and partners for fair dealing

- *Relationships:* alliances, joint ventures, or partnerships that provide access to technologies, specialized know-how, or geographic markets; networks of dealers or distributors; the trust established with various partners

- *Company culture and incentive system:* the norms of behavior, business principles, and ingrained beliefs within the company; the attachment of personnel to the company's ideals; the compensation system and the motivation level of company personnel

are embodied in its managers and employees; a company's brand name is embodied in the company logo or product labels. Other important kinds of intangible resources include a company's *relationships* with suppliers, buyers, or partners of various sorts, and the *company's culture and incentive system.* A more detailed listing of the various types of tangible and intangible resources is provided in Table 4.2.

Listing a company's resources category by category can prevent managers from inadvertently overlooking some company resources that might be competitively important. At times, it can be difficult to decide exactly how to categorize certain types of resources. For example, resources such as a work group's specialized expertise in developing innovative products can be considered to be technological assets or human assets or intellectual capital and knowledge assets; the work ethic and drive of a company's workforce could be included under the company's human assets or its culture and incentive system. In this regard, it is important to remember that *it is not exactly how a resource is categorized that matters but, rather, that all of the company's different types of resources are included in the inventory.* The real purpose of using categories in identifying a company's resources is *to ensure that none of a company's resources go unnoticed when sizing up the company's competitive assets.*

**Identifying Capabilities**   Organizational capabilities are more complex entities than resources; indeed, they are built up through the use of resources and draw on some combination of the firm's resources as they are exercised. Virtually all organizational capabilities are *knowledge-based, residing in people and in a company's intellectual capital, or in organizational processes and systems, which embody tacit knowledge.* For example, Procter & Gamble's brand management capabilities draw on the knowledge of the company's brand managers, the expertise of its marketing department, and the company's relationships with retailers, since brand building is a cooperative activity requiring retailer support. The video game design capabilities for which Electronic Arts is known derive from the creative talents and technological expertise of its highly talented game developers, the company's culture of creativity, and a compensation system that generously rewards talented developers for creating best-selling video games.

Because of their complexity, capabilities are harder to categorize than resources and more challenging to search for as a result. There are, however, two approaches that can make the process of uncovering and identifying a firm's capabilities more systematic. The first method takes the completed listing of a firm's resources as its starting point. Since capabilities are built from resources and utilize resources as they are exercised, a firm's resources can provide a strong set of clues about the types of capabilities the firm is likely to have accumulated. This approach simply involves looking over the firm's resources and considering whether (and to what extent) the firm has built up any related capabilities. So, for example, a fleet of trucks, the latest RFID tracking technology, and a set of large automated distribution centers may be indicative of sophisticated capabilities in logistics and distribution. R&D teams composed of top scientists with expertise in genomics may suggest organizational capabilities in developing new gene therapies or in biotechnology more generally.

The second method of identifying a firm's capabilities takes a functional approach. Many capabilities relate to fairly specific functions; these draw on a limited set of resources and typically involve a single department or organizational unit. Capabilities in injection molding or continuous casting or metal stamping are manufacturing-related; capabilities in direct selling, promotional pricing, or database marketing all connect to the sales and marketing functions; capabilities in basic research, strategic innovation, or new product development link to a company's R&D function. This approach requires managers to survey the various functions a firm performs to find the different capabilities associated with each function.

A problem with this second method is that many of the most important capabilities of firms are inherently *cross-functional*. Cross-functional capabilities draw on a number of different kinds of resources and are multidimensional in nature—they spring from the effective collaboration among people with different types of expertise working in different organizational units. An example is Nike's cross-functional design process, spanning R&D activities, marketing research efforts, styling expertise, and manufacturing. Cross-functional capabilities and other complex capabilities involving numerous linked and closely integrated competitive assets are sometimes referred to as **resource bundles.**

It is important not to miss identifying a company's resource bundles, since they can be the most competitively important of a firm's competitive assets. Resource bundles can sometimes pass the four tests of a resource's competitive power (described below) even when the individual components of the resource bundle cannot. For example, although Callaway Golf Company's engineering capabilities and market research capabilities are matched relatively well by rivals Cobra Golf and Ping Golf, the company's bundling of resources used in its product development process (including cross-functional development systems, technological

## CORE CONCEPT

A **resource bundle** is a linked and closely integrated set of competitive assets centered around one or more cross-functional capabilities.

capabilities, knowledge of consumer preferences, and a collaborative organizational culture) gives it a competitive advantage that has allowed it to remain the largest seller of golf equipment for more than a decade.

# Assessing the Competitive Power of a Company's Resources and Capabilities

To assess their competitive power, one must go beyond merely identifying a company's resources and capabilities to probe their *caliber*.[3] Thus, the second step in resource and capability analysis is designed to ascertain which of a company's resources and capabilities are competitively superior and to what extent they can support a company's quest for a sustainable competitive advantage over market rivals. When a company has competitive assets that are central to its strategy and superior to those of rival firms, they can support a competitive advantage, as defined in Chapter 1. If this advantage proves durable *despite the best efforts of competitors to overcome it*, then the company is said to have a *sustainable* **competitive advantage.** While it may be difficult for a company to achieve a sustainable competitive advantage, it is an important strategic objective because it imparts a potential for attractive and long-lived profitability.

### The Four Tests of a Resource's Competitive Power
The competitive power of a resource or capability is measured by how many of four specific tests it can pass.[4] These tests are referred to as the **VRIN tests for sustainable competitive advantage**—*VRIN* is a shorthand reminder standing for *Valuable, Rare, Inimitable,* and *Nonsubstitutable.* The first two tests determine whether a resource or capability can support a competitive advantage. The last two determine whether the competitive advantage can be sustained.

**CORE CONCEPT**

The **VRIN tests for sustainable competitive advantage** ask whether a resource is Valuable, Rare, Inimitable, and Nonsubstitutable.

1. *Is the resource or capability competitively **Valuable?*** To be competitively valuable, a resource or capability must be directly relevant to the company's strategy, making the company a more effective competitor. Unless the resource or capability contributes to the effectiveness of the company's strategy, it cannot pass this first test. An indicator of its effectiveness is whether the resource enables the company to strengthen its business model by improving its customer value proposition and/or profit formula (see Chapter 1). Companies have to guard against contending that something they do well is necessarily competitively valuable. Apple's operating system for its personal computers by some accounts is superior to Microsoft's Windows 8, but Apple has failed in converting its resources devoted to operating system design into anything more than moderate competitive success in the global PC market.

2. *Is the resource or capability **Rare**—is it something rivals lack?* Resources and capabilities that are common among firms and widely available cannot be a source of competitive advantage. All makers of branded cereals have valuable marketing capabilities and brands, since the key success factors in the ready-to-eat cereal industry demand this. They are not rare. However, the brand strength of Oreo cookies is uncommon and has provided Kraft Foods with greater market share as well as the opportunity to benefit from brand extensions such as Double Stuf Oreos and Mini Oreos. A resource or capability is considered rare if it is held by only a small number of firms in an industry or specific competitive domain. Thus, while general management capabilities are not rare in an absolute sense, they are relatively rare in some of the less developed regions of the world and in some business domains.

3.  *Is the resource or capability **Inimitable**—is it hard to copy?* The more difficult and more costly it is for competitors to imitate a company's resource or capability, the more likely that it can also provide a *sustainable* competitive advantage. Resources and capabilities tend to be difficult to copy when they are unique (a fantastic real estate location, patent-protected technology, an unusually talented and motivated labor force), when they must be built over time in ways that are difficult to imitate (a well-known brand name, mastery of a complex process technology, years of cumulative experience and learning), and when they entail financial outlays or large-scale operations that few industry members can undertake (a global network of dealers and distributors). Imitation is also difficult for resources and capabilities that reflect a high level of *social complexity* (company culture, interpersonal relationships among the managers or R&D teams, trust-based relations with customers or suppliers) and *causal ambiguity,* a term that signifies the hard-to-disentangle nature of the complex resources, such as a web of intricate processes enabling new drug discovery. Hard-to-copy resources and capabilities are important competitive assets, contributing to the longevity of a company's market position and offering the potential for sustained profitability.

4.  *Is the resource or capability **Nonsubstitutable**—is it invulnerable to the threat of substitution from different types of resources and capabilities?* Even resources that are competitively valuable, rare, and costly to imitate may lose much of their ability to offer competitive advantage if rivals possess equivalent substitute resources. For example, manufacturers relying on automation to gain a cost-based advantage in production activities may find their technology-based advantage nullified by rivals' use of low-wage offshore manufacturing. Resources can contribute to a sustainable competitive advantage only when resource substitutes aren't on the horizon.

> ## CORE CONCEPT
>
> **Social complexity** and **causal ambiguity** are two factors that inhibit the ability of rivals to imitate a firm's most valuable resources and capabilities. Causal ambiguity makes it very hard to figure out how a complex resource contributes to competitive advantage and therefore exactly what to imitate.

The vast majority of companies are not well endowed with standout resources or capabilities, capable of passing all four tests with high marks. Most firms have a mixed bag of resources—one or two quite valuable, some good, many satisfactory to mediocre. Resources and capabilities that are valuable pass the first of the four tests. As key contributors to the effectiveness of the strategy, they are relevant to the firm's competitiveness but are no guarantee of competitive advantage. They may offer no more than competitive parity with competing firms.

Passing both of the first two tests requires more—it requires resources and capabilities that are not only valuable but also rare. This is a much higher hurdle that can be cleared only by resources and capabilities that are *competitively superior.* Resources and capabilities that are competitively superior are the company's true strategic assets. They provide the company with a competitive advantage over its competitors, if only in the short run.

To pass the last two tests, a resource must be able to maintain its competitive superiority in the face of competition. It must be resistant to imitative attempts and efforts by competitors to find equally valuable substitute resources. Assessing the availability of substitutes is the most difficult of all the tests since substitutes are harder to recognize, but the key is to look for resources or capabilities held by other firms or being developed that *can serve the same function* as the company's core resources and capabilities.[5]

Very few firms have resources and capabilities that can pass all four tests, but those that do enjoy a sustainable competitive advantage with far greater profit potential. Walmart is a notable example, with capabilities in logistics and supply chain management that have surpassed those of its competitors for over 40 years. Lincoln Electric Company, less well known but no less notable in its achievements, has been the world leader in welding products for over 100 years as a result of its unique piecework incentive system for compensating production workers and the unsurpassed worker productivity and product quality that this system has fostered.

### A Company's Resources and Capabilities Must Be Managed Dynamically

Even companies like Walmart and Lincoln Electric cannot afford to rest on their laurels. Rivals that are initially unable to replicate a key resource may develop better and better substitutes over time. Resources and capabilities can depreciate like other assets if they are managed with benign neglect. Disruptive changes in technology, customer preferences, distribution channels, or other competitive factors can also destroy the value of key strategic assets, turning resources and capabilities "from diamonds to rust."[6]

Resources and capabilities must be continually strengthened and nurtured to sustain their competitive power and, at times, may need to be broadened and deepened to allow the company to position itself to pursue emerging market opportunities.[7] Organizational resources and capabilities that grow stale can impair competitiveness unless they are refreshed, modified, or even phased out and replaced in response to ongoing market changes and shifts in company strategy. Management's challenge in managing the firm's resources and capabilities dynamically has two elements: (1) attending to the ongoing modification of existing competitive assets, and (2) casting a watchful eye for opportunities to develop totally new kinds of capabilities.

> A company requires a dynamically evolving portfolio of resources and capabilities to sustain its competitiveness and help drive improvements in its performance.

### The Role of Dynamic Capabilities

Companies that know the importance of recalibrating and upgrading their most valuable resources and capabilities ensure that these activities are done on a continual basis. By incorporating these activities into their routine managerial functions, they gain the experience necessary to be able to do them consistently well. At that point, their ability to freshen and renew their competitive assets becomes a capability in itself—a **dynamic capability.** A dynamic capability is the ability to modify, deepen, or augment the company's existing resources and capabilities.[8] This includes the capacity to improve existing resources and capabilities incrementally, in the way that Toyota aggressively upgrades the company's capabilities in fuel-efficient hybrid engine technology and constantly fine-tunes its famed Toyota production system. A dynamic capability also includes the capacity to add new resources and capabilities to the company's competitive asset portfolio. An example is Pfizer's acquisition capabilities, which have enabled it to replace degraded resources such as expiring patents with newly acquired capabilities in biotechnology.

> **CORE CONCEPT**
>
> A **dynamic capability** is an ongoing capacity of a company to modify its existing resources and capabilities or create new ones.

## QUESTION 3: WHAT ARE THE COMPANY'S STRENGTHS AND WEAKNESSES IN RELATION TO THE MARKET OPPORTUNITIES AND EXTERNAL THREATS?

In evaluating a company's overall situation, a key question is whether the company is in a position to pursue attractive market opportunities and defend against external threats to its future well-being. The simplest and most easily applied tool for conducting this examination is widely known as *SWOT analysis,* so named because it zeros in on a company's internal **S**trengths and **W**eaknesses, market **O**pportunities, and external **T**hreats. A first-rate SWOT analysis provides the basis for crafting a strategy that capitalizes on the company's strengths, overcomes its weaknesses, aims squarely at

> **LO 3**
>
> How to assess the company's strengths and weaknesses in light of market opportunities and external threats.

capturing the company's best opportunities, and defends against competitive and macro-environmental threats.

## Identifying a Company's Internal Strengths

A **strength** is something a company is good at doing or an attribute that enhances its competitiveness in the marketplace. A company's strengths depend on the quality of its resources and capabilities. Resource and capability analysis provides a way for managers to assess the quality objectively. While resources and capabilities that pass the VRIN tests of sustainable competitive advantage are among the company's greatest strengths, other types can be counted among the company's strengths as well. A capability that is not potent enough to produce a sustainable advantage over rivals may yet enable a series of temporary advantages if used as a basis for entry into a new market or market segment. A resource bundle that fails to match those of top-tier competitors may still allow a company to compete successfully against the second tier.

### Assessing a Company's Competencies—What Activities Does It Perform Well?
One way to appraise the degree of a company's strengths has to do with the company's skill level in performing key pieces of its business—such as supply chain management, R&D, production, distribution, sales and marketing, and customer service. A company's skill or proficiency in performing different facets of its operations can range from the extreme of having minimal ability to perform an activity (perhaps having just struggled to do it the first time) to the other extreme of being able to perform the activity better than any other company in the industry.

When a company's proficiency rises from that of mere ability to perform an activity to the point of being able to perform it consistently well and at acceptable cost, it is said to have a **competence**—a true *capability,* in other words. A **core competence** is a proficiently performed internal activity that is *central* to a company's strategy and competitiveness. A core competence is a more competitively valuable strength than a competence because of the activity's key role in the company's strategy and the contribution it makes to the company's market success and profitability. Often, core competencies can be leveraged to create new markets or new product demand, as the engine behind a company's growth. 3M Corporation has a core competence in product innovation—its record of introducing new products goes back several decades and new product introduction is central to 3M's strategy of growing its business.

A **distinctive competence** is a competitively valuable activity that a company *performs better than its rivals.* A distinctive competence thus signifies greater proficiency than a core competence. Because a distinctive competence represents a level of proficiency that rivals do not have, it qualifies as a *competitively superior strength* with competitive advantage potential. This is particularly true when the distinctive competence enables a company to deliver standout value to customers (in the form of lower prices, better product performance, or superior service). For instance, Walt Disney has a distinctive competence in feature film animation.

The conceptual differences between a competence, a core competence, and a distinctive competence draw attention to the fact that a company's strengths and competitive assets are not all equal.[9] All competencies have some value. But mere ability to perform an activity well does not necessarily give a company competitive clout. Some competencies merely enable market survival because most rivals also have them—indeed, not having a competence that rivals have can result in competitive *disadvantage*. An apparel manufacturer cannot survive without the capability to produce its apparel items very cost-efficiently, given the intensely price-competitive nature of the apparel industry. A maker of cell phones cannot survive without good product design and product innovation capabilities.

## Identifying Company Weaknesses and Competitive Deficiencies

A **weakness,** or *competitive deficiency,* is something a company lacks or does poorly (in comparison to others) or a condition that puts it at a disadvantage in the marketplace. A company's internal weaknesses can relate to (1) inferior or unproven skills, expertise, or intellectual capital in competitively important areas of the business; (2) deficiencies in competitively important physical, organizational, or intangible assets; or (3) missing or competitively inferior capabilities in key areas. *Company weaknesses are thus internal shortcomings that constitute competitive liabilities.* Nearly all companies have competitive liabilities of one kind or another. Whether a company's internal weaknesses make it competitively vulnerable depends on how much they matter in the marketplace and whether they are offset by the company's strengths.

> ### CORE CONCEPT
>
> A company's **strengths** represent its competitive assets; its **weaknesses** are shortcomings that constitute competitive liabilities.

Table 4.3 lists many of the things to consider in compiling a company's strengths and weaknesses. Sizing up a company's complement of strengths and deficiencies is akin to constructing a *strategic balance sheet,* where strengths represent *competitive assets* and weaknesses represent *competitive liabilities.* Obviously, the ideal condition is for the company's competitive assets to outweigh its competitive liabilities by an ample margin—a 50-50 balance is definitely not the desired condition!

## Identifying a Company's Market Opportunities

Market opportunity is a big factor in shaping a company's strategy. Indeed, managers can't properly tailor strategy to the company's situation without first identifying its market opportunities and appraising the growth and profit potential each one holds. Depending on the prevailing circumstances, a company's opportunities can be plentiful or scarce, fleeting or lasting, and can range from wildly attractive to marginally interesting to unsuitable. Table 4.3 displays a sampling of potential market opportunities.

Newly emerging and fast-changing markets sometimes present stunningly big or "golden" opportunities, but it is typically hard for managers at one company to peer into "the fog of the future" and spot them far ahead of managers at other companies.[10] But as the fog begins to clear, golden opportunities are nearly always seized rapidly—and the companies that seize them are usually those that have been actively waiting, staying alert with diligent market reconnaissance, and preparing themselves to capitalize on shifting market conditions by patiently assembling an arsenal of resources to enable aggressive action when the time comes. In mature markets, unusually attractive market opportunities emerge sporadically, often after long periods of relative calm—but future market conditions may be more predictable, making emerging opportunities easier for industry members to detect.

> A company is well advised to pass on a particular market opportunity unless it has or can acquire the resources and capabilities needed to capture it.

In evaluating a company's market opportunities and ranking their attractiveness, managers have to guard against viewing every *industry* opportunity as a *company* opportunity. Rarely does a company have the resource depth to pursue all available market opportunities simultaneously without spreading itself too thin. Some

**TABLE 4.3**   **What to Look for in Identifying a Company's Strengths, Weaknesses, Opportunities, and Threats**

| Potential Strengths and Competitive Assets | Potential Weaknesses and Competitive Deficiencies |
| --- | --- |
| • Competencies that are well matched to industry key success factors<br>• Ample financial resources to grow the business<br>• Strong brand-name image and/or company reputation<br>• Economies of scale and/or learning- and experience-curve advantages over rivals<br>• Other cost advantages over rivals<br>• Attractive customer base<br>• Proprietary technology, superior technological skills, important patents<br>• Strong bargaining power over suppliers or buyers<br>• Resources and capabilities that are valuable and rare<br>• Resources and capabilities that are hard to copy and for which there are no good substitutes<br>• Superior product quality<br>• Wide geographic coverage and/or strong global distribution capability<br>• Alliances and/or joint ventures that provide access to valuable technology, competencies, and/or attractive geographic markets | • No clear strategic vision<br>• No well-developed or proven core competencies<br>• No distinctive competencies or competitively superior resources<br>• Lack of attention to customer needs<br>• A product or service with features and attributes that are inferior to those of rivals<br>• Weak balance sheet, short on financial resources to grow the firm, too much debt<br>• Higher overall unit costs relative to those of key competitors<br>• Too narrow a product line relative to rivals<br>• Weak brand image or reputation<br>• Weaker dealer network than key rivals and/or lack of adequate distribution capability<br>• Lack of management depth<br>• A plague of internal operating problems or obsolete facilities<br>• Too much underutilized plant capacity<br>• Resources that are readily copied or for which there are good substitutes |
| **Potential Market Opportunities** | **Potential External Threats to a Company's Future Profitability** |
| • Sharply rising buyer demand for the industry's product<br>• Serving additional customer groups or market segments<br>• Expanding into new geographic markets<br>• Expanding the company's product line to meet a broader range of customer needs<br>• Utilizing existing company skills or technological know-how to enter new product lines or new businesses<br>• Falling trade barriers in attractive foreign markets<br>• Acquiring rival firms or companies with attractive technological expertise or capabilities<br>• Entering into alliances or joint ventures to expand the firm's market coverage or boost its competitive capability | • Increasing intensity of competition among industry rivals—may squeeze profit margins<br>• Slowdowns in market growth<br>• Likely entry of potent new competitors<br>• Growing bargaining power of customers or suppliers<br>• A shift in buyer needs and tastes away from the industry's product<br>• Adverse demographic changes that threaten to curtail demand for the industry's product<br>• Adverse economic conditions that threaten critical suppliers or distributors<br>• Changes in technology—particularly disruptive technology that can undermine the company's distinctive competencies<br>• Restrictive foreign trade policies<br>• Costly new regulatory requirements<br>• Tight credit conditions<br>• Rising prices on energy or other key inputs |

companies have resources and capabilities better-suited for pursuing some opportunities, and a few companies may be hopelessly outclassed in competing for any of an industry's attractive opportunities. *The market opportunities most relevant to a company are those that match up well with the company's competitive assets, offer the best prospects for growth and profitability, and present the most potential for competitive advantage.*

## Identifying the Threats to a Company's Future Profitability

Often, certain factors in a company's external environment pose *threats* to its profitability and competitive well-being. Threats can stem from such factors as the emergence of cheaper or better technologies, the entry of lower-cost foreign competitors into a company's market stronghold, new regulations that are more burdensome to a company than to its competitors, unfavorable demographic shifts, and political upheaval in a foreign country where the company has facilities. Table 4.3 shows a representative list of potential threats.

External threats may pose no more than a moderate degree of adversity (all companies confront some threatening elements in the course of doing business), or they may be imposing enough to make a company's situation look tenuous. On rare occasions, market shocks can give birth to a *sudden-death* threat that throws a company into an immediate crisis and a battle to survive. Many of the world's major financial institutions were plunged into unprecedented crisis in 2008–2009 by the aftereffects of high-risk mortgage lending, inflated credit ratings on subprime mortgage securities, the collapse of housing prices, and a market flooded with mortgage-related investments (collateralized debt obligations) whose values suddenly evaporated. It is management's job to identify the threats to the company's future prospects and to evaluate what strategic actions can be taken to neutralize or lessen their impact.

## What Do the SWOT Listings Reveal?

SWOT analysis involves more than making four lists. The two most important parts of SWOT analysis are *drawing conclusions* from the SWOT listings about the company's overall situation and *translating these conclusions into strategic actions* to better match the company's strategy to its internal strengths and market opportunities, to correct important weaknesses, and to defend against external threats. Figure 4.2 shows the steps involved in gleaning insights from SWOT analysis.

The final piece of SWOT analysis is to translate the diagnosis of the company's situation into actions for improving the company's strategy and business prospects. *A company's internal strengths should always serve as the basis of its strategy—placing heavy reliance on a company's best competitive assets is the soundest route to attracting customers and competing successfully against rivals.*[11] As a rule, strategies that place heavy demands on areas where the company is weakest or has unproven competencies should be avoided. Plainly, managers must look toward correcting competitive weaknesses that make the company vulnerable, hold down profitability, or disqualify it from pursuing an attractive opportunity. Furthermore, a company's strategy should be aimed squarely at capturing attractive market opportunities that are suited to the company's collection of capabilities. How much attention to devote to defending against external threats to the company's future performance hinges on how vulnerable the company is, whether defensive moves can be taken to lessen their impact, and whether the costs of undertaking such moves represent the best use of company resources.

Simply making lists of a company's strengths, weaknesses, opportunities, and threats is not enough; the payoff from SWOT analysis comes from the conclusions about a company's situation and the implications for strategy improvement that flow from the four lists.

**FIGURE 4.2**    The Steps Involved in SWOT Analysis: Identify the Four Components of SWOT, Draw Conclusions, Translate Implications into Strategic Actions

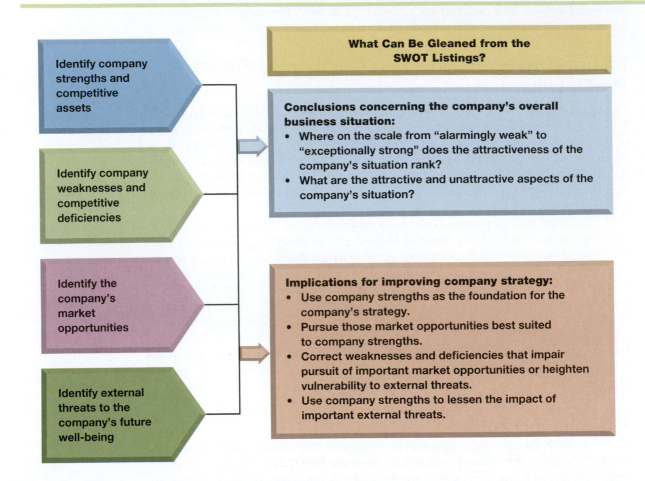

# QUESTION 4: HOW DO A COMPANY'S VALUE CHAIN ACTIVITIES IMPACT ITS COST STRUCTURE AND CUSTOMER VALUE PROPOSITION?

**LO 4**

How a company's value chain activities can affect the company's cost structure and customer value proposition.

Company managers are often stunned when a competitor cuts its prices to "unbelievably low" levels or when a new market entrant introduces a great new product at a surprisingly low price. While less common, new entrants can also storm the market with a product that ratchets the quality level up so high that customers will abandon competing sellers even if they have to pay more for the new product. This is what seems to be happening with Apple's iPad in the market for e-readers and tablet PCs.

Regardless of where on the quality spectrum a company competes, it must remain competitive in terms of its customer value proposition in order to stay in the game.

Tiffany's value proposition, for example, remains attractive to customers who want customer service, the assurance of quality, and a high-status brand despite the availability of cut-rate diamond jewelry online. Target's customer value proposition has withstood the Walmart low-price juggernaut by attention to product design, image, and attractive store layouts in addition to efficiency.

The value provided to the customer depends on how well a customer's needs are met for the price paid. How well customer needs are met depends on the perceived quality of a product or service as well as on other, more tangible attributes. The greater the amount of customer value that the company can offer profitably compared to its rivals, the less vulnerable it will be to competitive attack. For managers, the key is to keep close track of how *cost effectively* the company can deliver value to customers relative to its competitors. If it can deliver the same amount of value with lower expenditures (or more value at the same cost), it will maintain a competitive edge.

Two analytic tools are particularly useful in determining whether a company's costs and customer value proposition are competitive: value chain analysis and benchmarking.

## The Concept of a Company Value Chain

Every company's business consists of a collection of activities undertaken in the course of producing, marketing, delivering, and supporting its product or service. All the various activities that a company performs internally combine to form a **value chain**—so called because the underlying intent of a company's activities is ultimately to *create value for buyers*.

As shown in Figure 4.3, a company's value chain consists of two broad categories of activities: the *primary activities* foremost in creating value for customers and the requisite *support activities* that facilitate and enhance the performance of the primary activities.[12] The exact natures of the primary and secondary activities that make up a company's value chain vary according to the specifics of a company's business; hence, the listing of the primary and support activities in Figure 4.3 is illustrative rather than definitive. For example, the primary activities at a hotel operator like Starwood Hotels and Resorts mainly consist of site selection and construction, reservations, and hotel operations (check-in and check-out, maintenance and housekeeping, dining and room service, and conventions and meetings); principal support activities that drive costs and impact customer value include hiring and training hotel staff and handling general administration. Supply chain management is a crucial activity for Nissan and Amazon.com but is not a value chain component of Facebook or Twitter. Sales and marketing are dominant activities at Procter & Gamble and Sony but have only minor roles at CBS and Bain Capital.

With its focus on value-creating activities, the value chain is an ideal tool for examining the workings of a company's customer value proposition and business model. It permits a deep look at the company's cost structure and ability to offer low prices. It reveals the emphasis that a company places on activities that enhance differentiation and support higher prices, such as service and marketing. It also includes a profit margin component, since profits are necessary to compensate the company's owners and investors, who bear risks and provide capital. Tracking the profit margin along with the value-creating activities is critical because unless an enterprise succeeds in delivering customer value profitably (with a sufficient return on invested capital), it can't survive for long. Attention to a company's profit formula

The higher a company's costs are above those of close rivals, the more competitively vulnerable the company becomes.

The greater the amount of customer value that a company can offer profitably relative to close rivals, the less competitively vulnerable the company becomes.

**CORE CONCEPT**

A company's **value chain** identifies the primary activities and related support activities that create customer value.

**FIGURE 4.3    A Representative Company Value Chain**

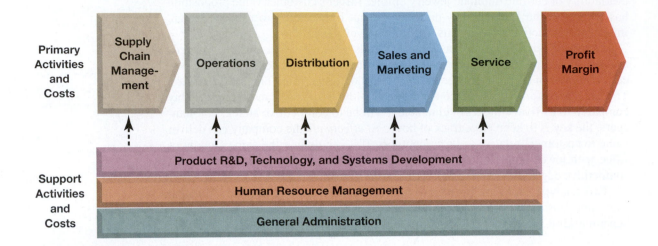

**PRIMARY ACTIVITIES**

- **Supply Chain Management**—Activities, costs, and assets associated with purchasing fuel, energy, raw materials, parts and components, merchandise, and consumable items from vendors; receiving, storing, and disseminating inputs from suppliers; inspection; and inventory management.

- **Operations**—Activities, costs, and assets associated with converting inputs into final product form (production, assembly, packaging, equipment maintenance, facilities, operations, quality assurance, environmental protection).

- **Distribution**—Activities, costs, and assets dealing with physically distributing the product to buyers (finished goods warehousing, order processing, order picking and packing, shipping, delivery vehicle operations, establishing and maintaining a network of dealers and distributors).

- **Sales and Marketing**—Activities, costs, and assets related to sales force efforts, advertising and promotion, market research and planning, and dealer/distributor support.

- **Service**—Activities, costs, and assets associated with providing assistance to buyers, such as installation, spare parts delivery, maintenance and repair, technical assistance, buyer inquiries, and complaints.

**SUPPORT ACTIVITIES**

- **Product R&D, Technology, and Systems Development**—Activities, costs, and assets relating to product R&D, process R&D, process design improvement, equipment design, computer software development, telecommunications systems, computer-assisted design and  engineering, database capabilities, and development of computerized support systems.

- **Human Resource Management**—Activities, costs, and assets associated with the recruitment, hiring, training, development, and compensation of all types of personnel; labor relations activities; and development of knowledge-based skills and core competencies.

- **General Administration**—Activities, costs, and assets relating to general management, accounting and finance, legal and regulatory affairs, safety and security, management information systems, forming strategic alliances and collaborating with strategic partners, and other "overhead" functions.

*Source:* Based on the discussion in Michael E. Porter, *Competitive Advantage* (New York: Free Press, 1985), pp. 37–43.

# American Giant: Using the Value Chain to Compare Costs of Producing a Hoodie in the U.S. and Asia

American Giant Clothing Company claims to make the world's best hooded sweatshirt, and it makes them in American plants, despite the higher cost of U.S production, as shown below. Why is this a good choice for the company? Because costs are not the only thing that matters. American Giant's proximity to its factories allows for better communication and control, better quality monitoring, and faster production cycles. This in turn has led to a much higher-quality product—so much higher that the company is selling far more hoodies than it could if it produced lower-cost, lower-quality products overseas. Demand has soared for its hoodies, and American Giant's reputation has soared along with it, giving the company a strong competitive advantage in the hoodie market.

## American Giant's Value Chain Activities and Costs in Producing and Selling a Hoodie Sweatshirt: U.S. versus Asian production

| | U.S. | Asia |
|---|---|---|
| 1. Fabric (Highly automated plants make the spinning, knitting, and dyeing of cotton cheaper for American Giant's U.S. suppliers.) | $17.40 | $18.40 |
| 2. Trim and hardware | 3.20 | 2.30 |
| 3. Labor (Without highly automated sweatshirt manufacture, U.S. labor costs would be even higher.) | 17.00 | 5.50 |
| 4. Duty | 0.00 | 3.50 |
| 5. Shipping (Shipping from overseas is more expensive and takes longer.) | 0.50 | 1.70 |
| 6. Total company costs | $38.10 | $31.40 |
| 7. Wholesale markup over company costs (company operating profit) | 41.90 | 48.60 |
| 8. Retail price (American Giant sells online to keep the price lower by avoiding middlemen and their markups.) | $80.00 | $80.00 |

*Source:* Stephanie Clifford, "U.S. Textile Plants Return, with Floors Largely Empty of People," *The New York Times,* Business Day, September 19, 2013, www.nytimes.com/2013/09/20/business/us-textile-factories-return.html?emc=eta1&_r=0 (accessed February 14, 2014).

in addition to its customer value proposition is the essence of a sound business model, as described in Chapter 1.

Illustration Capsule 4.1 shows representative costs for various activities performed by American Giant, a maker of high-quality sweatshirts, in producing at either U.S. or Asian plants.

## Comparing the Value Chains of Rival Companies

Value chain analysis facilitates a comparison of how rivals, activity by activity, deliver value to customers. Even rivals in the same industry may differ significantly in terms of the activities they perform. For instance, the "operations" component of the value chain for a manufacturer that makes all of its own parts and components and assembles them into a finished product differs from the "operations" of a rival producer that buys the needed parts and components from outside suppliers and performs only assembly operations. How each activity is performed may affect a company's relative cost position as well as its capacity for differentiation. Thus, even a simple comparison of how the activities of rivals' value chains differ can reveal competitive differences.

**A Company's Primary and Secondary Activities Identify the Major Components of Its Internal Cost Structure**    The combined costs of all the various primary and support activities constituting a company's value chain define its internal cost structure. Further, the cost of each activity contributes to whether the company's overall cost position relative to rivals is favorable or unfavorable. Key purposes of value chain analysis and benchmarking are to develop the data for comparing a company's costs activity by activity against the costs of key rivals and to learn which internal activities are a source of cost advantage or disadvantage.

Evaluating a company's cost competitiveness involves using what accountants call *activity-based costing* to determine the costs of performing each value chain activity.[13] The degree to which a company's total costs should be broken down into costs for specific activities depends on how valuable it is to know the costs of specific activities versus broadly defined activities. At the very least, cost estimates are needed for each broad category of primary and support activities, but cost estimates for more specific activities within each broad category may be needed if a company discovers that it has a cost disadvantage vis-à-vis rivals and wants to pin down the exact source or activity causing the cost disadvantage. However, a company's own *internal costs* may be insufficient to assess whether its product offering and customer value proposition are competitive with those of rivals. Cost and price differences among competing companies can have their origins in activities suppliers perform or through distribution allies involved in getting the product to the final customer or end user, in which case the company's entire *value chain system* becomes relevant.

> A company's cost competitiveness depends not only on the costs of internally performed activities (its own value chain) but also on costs in the value chains of its suppliers and distribution-channel allies.

## The Value Chain System

A company's value chain is embedded in a larger system of activities that includes the suppliers' value chains and the value chains of whatever wholesale distributors and retailers it uses in getting its product or service to end users. This *value chain system* has implications that extend far beyond the company's costs. It can affect attributes like product quality that enhance differentiation and have importance for the company's customer value proposition, as well as its profitability.[14] Suppliers' value chains are relevant because suppliers perform activities and incur costs in creating and delivering the purchased inputs utilized in a company's own value-creating activities. The costs, performance features, and quality of these inputs influence a company's own costs and product differentiation capabilities. Anything a company can do to help its suppliers drive down the costs of their value chain activities or improve the quality and performance of the items being supplied can enhance its own competitiveness—a powerful reason for working collaboratively with suppliers in managing supply chain activities.[15]

Similarly, the value chains of a company's distribution-channel partners are relevant because (1) the costs and margins of a company's distributors and retail dealers are part of the price the ultimate consumer pays and (2) the activities that distribution allies perform affect sales volumes and customer satisfaction. For these reasons, companies normally work closely with their distribution allies (who are their direct customers) to perform value chain activities in mutually beneficial ways. For instance, motor vehicle manufacturers have a competitive interest in working closely with their automobile dealers to promote higher sales volumes and better customer satisfaction with dealers' repair and maintenance services. Producers of kitchen cabinets are heavily dependent on the sales and promotional activities of their distributors and building supply retailers and on whether distributors and retailers operate cost-effectively enough to be able to sell at prices that lead to attractive sales volumes.

As a consequence, *accurately assessing a company's competitiveness entails scrutinizing the nature and costs of value chain activities throughout the entire value chain system for delivering its products or services to end-use customers.* A typical value chain system that incorporates the value chains of suppliers and forward-channel allies (if any) is shown in Figure 4.4. As was the case with company value chains, the specific activities constituting value chain systems vary significantly from industry to industry. The primary value chain system activities in the pulp and paper industry (timber farming, logging, pulp mills, and papermaking) differ from the primary value chain system activities in the home appliance industry (parts and components manufacture, assembly, wholesale distribution, retail sales) and yet again from the computer software industry (programming, disk loading, marketing, distribution).

## Benchmarking: A Tool for Assessing Whether the Costs and Effectiveness of a Company's Value Chain Activities Are in Line

**Benchmarking** entails comparing how different companies (and *different types* of companies) perform various value chain activities—how materials are purchased, how inventories are managed, how products are assembled, how fast the company can get new products to market, how customer orders are filled and shipped—and then making cross-company comparisons of the costs and effectiveness of these

> **CORE CONCEPT**
>
> **Benchmarking** is a potent tool for improving a company's own internal activities that is based on learning how other companies perform them and borrowing their "best practices."

## FIGURE 4.4   A Representative Value Chain System

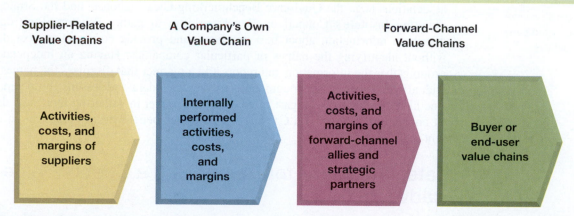

*Source:* Based in part on the single-industry value chain displayed in Michael E. Porter, *Competitive Advantage* (New York: Free Press, 1985), p. 35.

activities.[16] The objectives of benchmarking are to identify the best practices in performing an activity and to emulate those best practices.

A **best practice** is a method of performing an activity or business process that consistently delivers superior results compared to other approaches.[17] To qualify as a legitimate best practice, the method must have been employed by at least one enterprise and shown to be *unusually effective* in lowering costs, improving quality or performance, shortening time requirements, enhancing safety, or achieving some other highly positive operating outcome. Best practices thus identify a path to operating excellence with respect to value chain activities.

Xerox led the way in the use of benchmarking to become more cost-competitive, quickly deciding not to restrict its benchmarking efforts to its office equipment rivals but to extend them to *any company regarded as "world class"* in performing *any activity* relevant to Xerox's business. Other companies quickly picked up on Xerox's approach. Toyota managers got their idea for just-in-time inventory deliveries by studying how U.S. supermarkets replenished their shelves. Southwest Airlines reduced the turnaround time of its aircraft at each scheduled stop by studying pit crews on the auto racing circuit. More than 80 percent of Fortune 500 companies reportedly use benchmarking for comparing themselves against rivals on cost and other competitively important measures.

The tough part of benchmarking is not whether to do it but, rather, how to gain access to information about other companies' practices and costs. Sometimes benchmarking can be accomplished by collecting information from published reports, trade groups, and industry research firms or by talking to knowledgeable industry analysts, customers, and suppliers. Sometimes field trips to the facilities of competing or noncompeting companies can be arranged to observe how things are done, compare practices and processes, and perhaps exchange data on productivity and other cost components. However, such companies, even if they agree to host facilities tours and answer questions, are unlikely to share competitively sensitive cost information. Furthermore, comparing two companies' costs may not involve comparing apples to apples if the two companies employ different cost accounting principles to calculate the costs of particular activities.

Benchmarking the costs of company activities against those of rivals provides hard evidence of whether a company is cost-competitive.

However, a third and fairly reliable source of benchmarking information has emerged. The explosive interest in benchmarking costs and identifying best practices has prompted consulting organizations (e.g., Accenture, A. T. Kearney, Benchnet—The Benchmarking Exchange, and Best Practices, LLC) and several associations (e.g., the Qualserve Benchmarking Clearinghouse, and the Strategic Planning Institute's Council on Benchmarking) to gather benchmarking data, distribute information about best practices, and provide comparative cost data without identifying the names of particular companies. Having an independent group gather the information and report it in a manner that disguises the names of individual companies protects competitively sensitive data and lessens the potential for unethical behavior on the part of company personnel in gathering their own data about competitors. Illustration Capsule 4.2 describes benchmarking practices in the cement industry.

# Strategic Options for Remedying a Cost or Value Disadvantage

The results of value chain analysis and benchmarking may disclose cost or value disadvantages relative to key rivals. Such information is vital in crafting strategic actions

# Delivered-Cost Benchmarking in the Cement Industry

Cement is a dry powder that creates concrete when mixed with water and sand. People interact with concrete every day. It is often the building material of choice for sidewalks, curbs, basements, bridges, and municipal pipes. Cement is manufactured at billion-dollar continuous-process plants by mining limestone, crushing it, scorching it in a kiln, and then milling it again.

About 24 companies (CEMEX, Holcim, and Lafarge are some of the biggest) manufacture cement at 90 U.S. plants with the capacity to produce 110 million tons per year. Plants serve tens of markets distributed across multiple states. Companies regularly benchmark "delivered costs" to understand whether their plants are cost leaders or laggards.

Delivered-cost benchmarking studies typically subdivide manufacturing and logistics costs into five parts: fixed-bin, variable-bin, freight-to-terminal, terminal operating, and freight-to-customer costs. These cost components are estimated using different sources.

Fixed- and variable-bin costs represent the cost of making a ton of cement and moving it to the plant's storage silos. They are the hardest to estimate. Fortunately, the cement industry association PCA publishes key data for every plant that features plant location, age, capacity, technology, and fuel. Companies combine the industry data, satellite imagery revealing quarry characteristics, and news reports with the company's proprietary plant-level financial data to develop their estimates of competitors' costs. The basic assumption is that plants of similar size utilizing similar technologies and raw-material inputs will have similar cost performance.

Logistics costs (including freight-to-terminal, terminal operating, and freight-to-customer costs) are much easier to accurately estimate. Cement companies use common carriers to move their product by barge, train, and truck transit modes. Freight pricing is competitive on a per-mile basis by mode, meaning that the company's per-ton-mile barge cost applies to the competition. By combining the per-ton-mile cost with origin-destination distances, freight costs are easily calculated. Terminal operating costs, the costs of operating barge or rail terminals that store cement and transfer it to trucks for local delivery, represent the smallest fraction of total supply chain cost and typically vary little within mode type. For example, most barge terminals cost $10 per ton to run, whereas rail terminals are less expensive and cost $5 per ton.

By combining all five estimated cost elements, the company benchmarks its estimated relative cost position by market. Using this data, strategists can identify which of the company's plants are most exposed to volume fluctuations, which are in greatest need of investment or closure, which markets the company should enter or exit, and which competitors are the most likely candidates for product or asset swaps.

*Note:* Developed with Peter Jacobson.

*Source:* www.cement.org (accessed January 25, 2014).

---

to eliminate any such disadvantages and improve profitability. Information of this nature can also help a company to find new avenues for enhancing its competitiveness through lower costs or a more attractive customer value proposition. There are three main areas in a company's total value chain system where company managers can try to improve its efficiency and effectiveness in delivering customer value: (1) a company's own internal activities, (2) suppliers' part of the value chain system, and (3) the forward-channel portion of the value chain system.

# Improving Internally Performed Value Chain Activities

Managers can pursue any of several strategic approaches to reduce the costs of internally performed value chain activities and improve a company's cost competitiveness. They can *implement best practices* throughout the company, particularly for high-cost activities. They can *redesign the product and/or some of its components* to eliminate high-cost components or facilitate speedier and more economical manufacture or assembly. They can *relocate high-cost activities* (such as manufacturing) to geographic areas where they can be performed more cheaply or *outsource activities* to lower-cost vendors or contractors.

To improve the effectiveness of the company's customer value proposition and enhance differentiation, managers can take several approaches. They can *adopt best practices for quality, marketing, and customer service.* They can *reallocate resources to activities that address buyers' most important purchase criteria,* which will have the biggest impact on the value delivered to the customer. They can *adopt new technologies that spur innovation, improve design, and enhance creativity.* Additional approaches to managing value chain activities to lower costs and/or enhance customer value are discussed in Chapter 5.

### Improving Supplier-Related Value Chain Activities

Supplier-related cost disadvantages can be attacked by pressuring suppliers for lower prices, switching to lower-priced substitute inputs, and collaborating closely with suppliers to identify mutual cost-saving opportunities.[18] For example, just-in-time deliveries from suppliers can lower a company's inventory and internal logistics costs and may also allow suppliers to economize on their warehousing, shipping, and production scheduling costs—a win-win outcome for both. In a few instances, companies may find that it is cheaper to integrate backward into the business of high-cost suppliers and make the item in-house instead of buying it from outsiders.

Similarly, a company can enhance its customer value proposition through its supplier relationships. Some approaches include selecting and retaining suppliers that meet higher-quality standards, providing quality-based incentives to suppliers, and integrating suppliers into the design process. Fewer defects in parts from suppliers not only improve quality throughout the value chain system but can lower costs as well since less waste and disruption occur in the production processes.

### Improving Value Chain Activities of Distribution Partners

Any of three means can be used to achieve better cost competitiveness in the forward portion of the industry value chain:

1. Pressure distributors, dealers, and other forward-channel allies to reduce their costs and markups.
2. Collaborate with them to identify win-win opportunities to reduce costs—for example, a chocolate manufacturer learned that by shipping its bulk chocolate in liquid form in tank cars instead of as 10-pound molded bars, it could not only save its candy bar manufacturing customers the costs associated with unpacking and melting but also eliminate its own costs of molding bars and packing them.
3. Change to a more economical distribution strategy, including switching to cheaper distribution channels (selling direct via the Internet) or integrating forward into company-owned retail outlets.

The means to enhancing differentiation through activities at the forward end of the value chain system include (1) engaging in cooperative advertising and promotions with forward allies (dealers, distributors, retailers, etc.), (2) creating exclusive arrangements with downstream sellers or utilizing other mechanisms that increase their incentives to enhance delivered customer value, and (3) creating and enforcing standards for downstream activities and assisting in training channel partners in business practices. Harley-Davidson, for example, enhances the shopping experience and perceptions of buyers by selling through retailers that sell Harley-Davidson motorcycles exclusively and meet Harley-Davidson standards.

## Translating Proficient Performance of Value Chain Activities into Competitive Advantage

A company that does a *first-rate job* of managing its value chain activities *relative to competitors* stands a good chance of profiting from its competitive advantage. A company's value-creating activities can offer a competitive advantage in one of two ways (or both):

1. They can contribute to greater efficiency and lower costs relative to competitors.
2. They can provide a basis for differentiation, so customers are willing to pay relatively more for the company's goods and services.

Achieving a cost-based competitive advantage requires determined management efforts to be cost-efficient in performing value chain activities. Such efforts have to be ongoing and persistent, and they have to involve each and every value chain activity. The goal must be continuous cost reduction, not a one-time or on-again–off-again effort. Companies like Dollar General, Nucor Steel, Irish airline Ryanair, Greyhound Lines, and French discount retailer Carrefour have been highly successful in managing their value chains in a low-cost manner.

Ongoing and persistent efforts are also required for a competitive advantage based on differentiation. Superior reputations and brands are built up slowly over time, through continuous investment and activities that deliver consistent, reinforcing messages. Differentiation based on quality requires vigilant management of activities for quality assurance throughout the value chain. While the basis for differentiation (e.g., status, design, innovation, customer service, reliability, image) may vary widely among companies pursuing a differentiation advantage, companies that succeed do so on the basis of a commitment to coordinated value chain activities aimed purposefully at this objective. Examples include Grey Goose Vodka (status), IKEA (design), FedEx (reliability), 3M (innovation), and Nordstrom (customer service).

### How Value Chain Activities Relate to Resources and Capabilities

There is a close relationship between the value-creating activities that a company performs and its resources and capabilities. An organizational capability or competence implies a *capacity* for action; in contrast, a value-creating activity *initiates* the action. With respect to resources and capabilities, activities are "where the rubber hits the road." When companies engage in a value-creating activity, they do so by drawing on specific company resources and capabilities that underlie and enable the activity. For example, brand-building activities depend on human resources, such as experienced brand managers (including their knowledge and expertise in this arena), as well as organizational capabilities in advertising and marketing. Cost-cutting activities may derive from organizational capabilities in inventory management, for example, and resources such as inventory tracking systems.

Because of this correspondence between activities and supporting resources and capabilities, value chain analysis can complement resource and capability analysis as another tool for assessing a company's competitive advantage. Resources and capabilities that are *both valuable and rare* provide a company with *what it takes* for competitive advantage. For a company with competitive assets of this sort, the potential is there. When these assets are deployed in the form of a value-creating activity, that potential is realized due to their competitive superiority. Resource analysis is one tool for identifying competitively superior resources and capabilities. But their value and the competitive superiority of that value can be assessed objectively only *after* they are deployed. Value chain analysis and benchmarking provide the type of data needed to make that objective assessment.

> Performing value chain activities with capabilities that permit the company to either outmatch rivals on differentiation or beat them on costs will give the company a competitive advantage.

There is also a dynamic relationship between a company's activities and its resources and capabilities. Value-creating activities are more than just the embodiment of a resource's or capability's potential. They also contribute to the formation and development of capabilities. The road to competitive advantage begins with management efforts to build organizational expertise in performing certain competitively important value chain activities. With consistent practice and continuous investment of company resources, these activities rise to the level of a reliable organizational capability or a competence. To the extent that top management makes the growing capability a cornerstone of the company's strategy, this capability becomes a core competence for the company. Later, with further organizational learning and gains in proficiency, the core competence may evolve into a distinctive competence, giving the company superiority over rivals in performing an important value chain activity. Such superiority, if it gives the company significant competitive clout in the marketplace, can produce an attractive competitive edge over rivals. Whether the resulting competitive advantage is on the cost side or on the differentiation side (or both) will depend on the company's choice of which types of competence-building activities to engage in over this time period.

# QUESTION 5: IS THE COMPANY COMPETITIVELY STRONGER OR WEAKER THAN KEY RIVALS?

**LO 5**

How a comprehensive evaluation of a company's competitive situation can assist managers in making critical decisions about their next strategic moves.

Using resource analysis, value chain analysis, and benchmarking to determine a company's competitiveness on value and cost is necessary but not sufficient. A more comprehensive assessment needs to be made of the company's *overall* competitive strength. The answers to two questions are of particular interest: First, how does the company rank relative to competitors on each of the important factors that determine market success? Second, all things considered, does the company have a *net* competitive advantage or disadvantage versus major competitors?

An easy-to-use method for answering these two questions involves developing quantitative strength ratings for the company and its key competitors on each industry key success factor and each competitively pivotal resource, capability, and value chain activity. Much of the information needed for doing a competitive strength assessment comes from previous analyses. Industry and competitive analyses reveal the key success factors and competitive forces that separate industry winners from losers. Benchmarking data and scouting key competitors provide a basis for judging rivals' competitive strength on such factors as cost, key product attributes, customer service, image and reputation, financial strength, technological skills, distribution capability, and other factors. Resource and capability analysis reveals which of these are competitively important, given the external situation, and whether the company's competitive advantages are sustainable. SWOT analysis provides a more comprehensive and forward-looking picture of the company's overall situation.

Step 1 in doing a competitive strength assessment is to make a list of the industry's key success factors and other telling measures of competitive strength or weakness (6 to 10 measures usually suffice). Step 2 is to assign weights to each of the measures of competitive strength based on their perceived importance. (The sum of the weights for each measure must add up to 1.) Step 3 is to calculate weighted strength ratings by scoring each competitor on each strength measure (using a 1-to-10 rating scale, where 1 is very weak and 10 is very strong) and multiplying the assigned rating by the assigned weight. Step 4 is to sum the weighted strength ratings on each factor to get an overall measure of competitive strength for each company being rated. Step 5 is to use the overall strength ratings to draw conclusions about the size and extent of the company's net competitive advantage or disadvantage and to take specific note of areas of strength and weakness.

Table 4.4 provides an example of competitive strength assessment in which a hypothetical company (ABC Company) competes against two rivals. In the example, relative cost is the most telling measure of competitive strength, and the other strength measures are of lesser importance. The company with the highest rating on a given measure has an implied competitive edge on that measure, with the size of its edge reflected in the difference between its weighted rating and rivals' weighted ratings. For instance, Rival 1's 3.00 weighted strength rating on relative cost signals a considerable cost advantage over ABC Company (with a 1.50 weighted score on relative cost) and an even bigger cost advantage over Rival 2 (with a weighted score of 0.30). The measure-by-measure ratings reveal the competitive areas in which a company is strongest and weakest, and against whom.

The overall competitive strength scores indicate how all the different strength measures add up—whether the company is at a net overall competitive advantage or disadvantage against each rival. The higher a company's *overall weighted strength rating,* the stronger its *overall competitiveness* versus rivals. The bigger the difference between a company's overall weighted rating and the scores of *lower-rated* rivals, the greater is its implied *net competitive advantage.* Thus, Rival 1's overall weighted score of 7.70 indicates a greater net competitive advantage over Rival 2 (with a score of 2.10) than over ABC Company (with a score of 5.95). Conversely, the bigger the difference between a company's overall rating and the scores of *higher-rated* rivals, the greater its implied *net competitive disadvantage.* Rival 2's score of 2.10 gives it a smaller net competitive disadvantage against ABC Company (with an overall score of 5.95) than against Rival 1 (with an overall score of 7.70).

High-weighted competitive strength ratings signal a strong competitive position and possession of competitive advantage; low ratings signal a weak position and competitive disadvantage.

## Strategic Implications of Competitive Strength Assessments

In addition to showing how competitively strong or weak a company is relative to rivals, the strength ratings provide guidelines for designing wise offensive and

**TABLE 4.4**    A Representative Weighted Competitive Strength Assessment

| Key Success Factor/Strength Measure | Importance Weight | Competitive Strength Assessment (rating scale: 1 = very weak, 10 = very strong) | | | | | |
|---|---|---|---|---|---|---|---|
| | | ABC Co. | | Rival 1 | | Rival 2 | |
| | | Strength Rating | Weighted Score | Strength Rating | Weighted Score | Strength Rating | Weighted Score |
| Quality/product performance | 0.10 | 8 | 0.80 | 5 | 0.50 | 1 | 0.10 |
| Reputation/image | 0.10 | 8 | 0.80 | 7 | 0.70 | 1 | 0.10 |
| Manufacturing capability | 0.10 | 2 | 0.20 | 10 | 1.00 | 5 | 0.50 |
| Technological skills | 0.05 | 10 | 0.50 | 1 | 0.05 | 3 | 0.15 |
| Dealer network/ distribution capability | 0.05 | 9 | 0.45 | 4 | 0.20 | 5 | 0.25 |
| New product innovation capability | 0.05 | 9 | 0.45 | 4 | 0.20 | 5 | 0.25 |
| Financial resources | 0.10 | 5 | 0.50 | 10 | 1.00 | 3 | 0.30 |
| Relative cost position | 0.30 | 5 | 1.50 | 10 | 3.00 | 1 | 0.30 |
| Customer service capabilities | 0.15 | 5 | 0.75 | 7 | 1.05 | 1 | 0.15 |
| Sum of importance weights | **1.00** | | | | | | |
| **Overall weighted competitive strength rating** | | | **5.95** | | **7.70** | | **2.10** |

defensive strategies. For example, if ABC Company wants to go on the offensive to win additional sales and market share, such an offensive probably needs to be aimed directly at winning customers away from Rival 2 (which has a lower overall strength score) rather than Rival 1 (which has a higher overall strength score). Moreover, while ABC has high ratings for technological skills (a 10 rating), dealer network/distribution capability (a 9 rating), new product innovation capability (a 9 rating), quality/product performance (an 8 rating), and reputation/image (an 8 rating), these strength measures have low importance weights—meaning that ABC has strengths in areas that don't translate into much competitive clout in the marketplace. Even so, it outclasses Rival 2 in all five areas, plus it enjoys substantially lower costs than Rival 2 (ABC has a 5 rating on relative cost position versus a 1 rating for Rival 2)—and relative cost position carries the highest importance weight of all the strength measures. ABC also has greater competitive strength than Rival 3 regarding customer service capabilities (which carries the second-highest importance weight). Hence, because ABC's strengths are in the very areas where Rival 2 is weak, ABC is in a good position to attack Rival 2. Indeed, ABC may well be able to persuade a number of Rival 2's customers to switch their purchases over to its product.

But ABC should be cautious about cutting price aggressively to win customers away from Rival 2, because Rival 1 could interpret that as an attack by ABC to win away Rival 1's customers as well. And Rival 1 is in far and away the best position to compete on the basis of low price, given its high rating on relative cost in an industry where low costs are competitively important (relative cost carries an importance weight of 0.30). Rival 1's strong relative cost position vis-à-vis both ABC and Rival 2 arms it with the ability to use its lower-cost advantage to thwart any price cutting on ABC's part. Clearly ABC is vulnerable to any retaliatory price cuts by Rival 1—Rival 1 can easily defeat both ABC and Rival 2 in a price-based battle for sales and market share. If ABC wants to defend against its vulnerability to potential price cutting by Rival 1, then it needs to aim a portion of its strategy at lowering its costs.

The point here is that a competitively astute company should utilize the strength scores in deciding what strategic moves to make. When a company has important competitive strengths in areas where one or more rivals are weak, it makes sense to consider offensive moves to exploit rivals' competitive weaknesses. When a company has important competitive weaknesses in areas where one or more rivals are strong, it makes sense to consider defensive moves to curtail its vulnerability.

> A company's competitive strength scores pinpoint its strengths and weaknesses against rivals and point directly to the kinds of offensive and defensive actions it can use to exploit its competitive strengths and reduce its competitive vulnerabilities.

## QUESTION 6: WHAT STRATEGIC ISSUES AND PROBLEMS MERIT FRONT-BURNER MANAGERIAL ATTENTION?

The final and most important analytic step is to zero in on exactly what strategic issues company managers need to address—and resolve—for the company to be more financially and competitively successful in the years ahead. This step involves drawing on the results of both industry analysis and the evaluations of the company's internal situation. The task here is to get a clear fix on exactly what strategic and competitive challenges confront the company, which of the company's competitive shortcomings need fixing, and what specific problems merit company managers' front-burner attention. *Pinpointing the precise things that management needs to worry about sets the agenda for deciding what actions to take next to improve the company's performance and business outlook.*

The "worry list" of issues and problems that have to be wrestled with can include such things as *how* to stave off market challenges from new foreign competitors, *how* to combat the price discounting of rivals, *how* to reduce the company's high costs, *how* to sustain the company's present rate of growth in light of slowing buyer demand, *whether* to correct the company's competitive deficiencies by acquiring a rival company with the missing strengths, *whether* to expand into foreign markets, *whether* to reposition the company and move to a different strategic group, *what to do* about growing buyer interest in substitute products, and *what to do* to combat the aging demographics of the company's customer base. The worry list

> Compiling a "worry list" of problems creates an agenda of strategic issues that merit prompt managerial attention.

A good strategy must contain ways to deal with all the strategic issues and obstacles that stand in the way of the company's financial and competitive success in the years ahead.

thus always centers on such concerns as "how to . . . ," "what to do about . . . ," and "whether to . . ."—the purpose of the worry list is to identify the specific issues and problems that management needs to address, not to figure out what specific actions to take. Deciding what to do—which strategic actions to take and which strategic moves to make—comes later (when it is time to craft the strategy and choose among the various strategic alternatives).

If the items on the worry list are relatively minor—which suggests that the company's strategy is mostly on track and reasonably well matched to the company's overall situation—company managers seldom need to go much beyond fine-tuning the present strategy. If, however, the problems confronting the company are serious and indicate the present strategy is not well suited for the road ahead, the task of crafting a better strategy needs to be at the top of management's action agenda.

## KEY POINTS

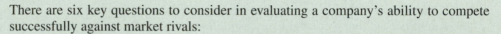

There are six key questions to consider in evaluating a company's ability to compete successfully against market rivals:

1. *How well is the present strategy working?* This involves evaluating the strategy in terms of the company's financial performance and market standing. The stronger a company's current overall performance, the less likely the need for radical strategy changes. The weaker a company's performance and/or the faster the changes in its external situation (which can be gleaned from PESTEL and industry analysis), the more its current strategy must be questioned.

2. *Do the company's resources and capabilities have sufficient competitive power to give it a sustainable advantage over competitors?* The answer to this question comes from conducting the four tests of a resource's competitive power—the VRIN tests. If a company has resources and capabilities that are competitively *valuable* and *rare,* the firm will have a competitive advantage over market rivals. If its resources and capabilities are also hard to copy *(inimitable),* with no good substitutes *(nonsubstitutable),* then the firm may be able to sustain this advantage even in the face of active efforts by rivals to overcome it.

3. *Is the company able to seize market opportunities and overcome external threats to its future well-being?* The answer to this question comes from performing a SWOT analysis. The two most important parts of SWOT analysis are (1) drawing conclusions about what strengths, weaknesses, opportunities, and threats tell about the company's overall situation and (2) acting on the conclusions to better match the company's strategy to its internal strengths and market opportunities, to correct the important internal weaknesses, and to defend against external threats. A company's strengths and competitive assets are strategically relevant because they are the most logical and appealing building blocks for strategy; internal weaknesses are important because they may represent vulnerabilities that need correction. External opportunities and threats come into play because a good strategy necessarily aims at capturing a company's most attractive opportunities and at defending against threats to its well-being.

4. *Are the company's cost structure and value proposition competitive?* One telling sign of whether a company's situation is strong or precarious is whether its costs

are competitive with those of industry rivals. Another sign is how the company compares with rivals in terms of differentiation—how effectively it delivers on its customer value proposition. Value chain analysis and benchmarking are essential tools in determining whether the company is performing particular functions and activities well, whether its costs are in line with those of competitors, whether it is differentiating in ways that really enhance customer value, and whether particular internal activities and business processes need improvement. They complement resource and capability analysis by providing data at the level of individual activities that provides more objective evidence of whether individual resources and capabilities, or bundles of resources and linked activity sets, are competitively superior.

5. *On an overall basis, is the company competitively stronger or weaker than key rivals?* The key appraisals here involve how the company matches up against key rivals on industry key success factors and other chief determinants of competitive success and whether and why the company has a *net* competitive advantage or disadvantage. Quantitative competitive strength assessments, using the method presented in Table 4.4, indicate where a company is competitively strong and weak and provide insight into the company's ability to defend or enhance its market position. As a rule, a company's competitive strategy should be built around its competitive strengths and should aim at shoring up areas where it is competitively vulnerable. When a company has important competitive strengths in areas where one or more rivals are weak, it makes sense to consider offensive moves to exploit rivals' competitive weaknesses. When a company has important competitive weaknesses in areas where one or more rivals are strong, it makes sense to consider defensive moves to curtail its vulnerability.

6. *What strategic issues and problems merit front-burner managerial attention?* This analytic step zeros in on the strategic issues and problems that stand in the way of the company's success. It involves using the results of industry analysis as well as resource and value chain analysis of the company's competitive situation to identify a "worry list" of issues to be resolved for the company to be financially and competitively successful in the years ahead. Actually deciding on a strategy and what specific actions to take is what comes after the list of strategic issues and problems that merit front-burner management attention is developed.

*Like good industry analysis, solid analysis of the company's competitive situation vis-à-vis its key rivals is a valuable precondition for good strategy making.*

## ASSURANCE OF LEARNING EXERCISES

1. Using the financial ratios provided in Table 4.1 and the financial statement information presented on pp. 110–112 for Costco Wholesale Corporation, calculate the following ratios for Costco for both 2012 and 2013:

   **LO 1**

   a. Gross profit margin

   b. Operating profit margin

   c. Net profit margin

   d. Times-interest-earned (or coverage) ratio

e. Return on stockholders' equity

f. Return on assets

g. Debt-to-equity ratio

h. Days of inventory

i. Inventory turnover ratio

j. Average collection period

Based on these ratios, did Costco's financial performance improve, weaken, or remain about the same from 2012 to 2013?

## Consolidated Statements of Income for Costco Wholesale Corporation, 2012–2013 (in millions, except per share data)

| | 2013 | 2012 |
|---|---|---|
| **Revenue** | | |
| Net sales | $102,870 | $97,062 |
| Membership fees | 2,286 | 2,075 |
| Total revenue | 105,156 | 99,137 |
| **Operating Expenses** | | |
| Merchandise costs | $ 91,948 | $86,823 |
| Selling, general, and administrative | 10,104 | 9,518 |
| Preopening expenses | 51 | 37 |
| Operating income | 3,053 | 2,759 |
| Other income (expense) | | |
| Interest expense | (99) | (95) |
| Interest income and other, net | 97 | 103 |
| Income before income taxes | 3,051 | 2,767 |
| Provision for income taxes | 990 | 1,000 |
| Net income including noncontrolling interests | 2,061 | 1,767 |
| Net income attributable to noncontrolling interests | (22) | (58) |
| Net income attributable to Costco | $ 2,039 | $ 1,709 |
| Net income per common share attributable to Costco: | | |
| Basic | $ 4.68 | $ 3.94 |
| Diluted | $ 4.63 | $ 3.89 |
| Shares used in calculation (000's) | | |
| Basic | 435,741 | 433,620 |
| Diluted | 440,512 | 439,373 |

# Consolidated Balance Sheets for Costco Wholesale Corporation, 2012–2013 (in millions, except per share data)

| | September 1, 2013 | September 2, 2012 |
|---|---|---|
| **Assets** | | |
| Current Assets | | |
| Cash and cash equivalents ......................................... | $ 4,644 | $ 3,528 |
| Short-term investments ............................................. | 1,480 | 1,326 |
| Receivables, net ...................................................... | 1,201 | 1,026 |
| Merchandise inventories ........................................... | 7,894 | 7,096 |
| Deferred income taxes and other current assets ........ | 621 | 550 |
| Total current assets ................................................. | $15,840 | $13,526 |
| Property and Equipment | | |
| Land ....................................................................... | $ 4,409 | $ 4,032 |
| Buildings and improvements ..................................... | 11,556 | 10,879 |
| Equipment and fixtures ............................................. | 4,472 | 4,261 |
| Construction in progress ........................................... | 585 | 374 |
| | 21,022 | 19,546 |
| Less accumulated depreciation and amortization ....... | (7,141) | (6,585) |
| Net property and equipment ..................................... | 13,881 | 12,961 |
| Other assets ............................................................ | 562 | 653 |
| Total assets ............................................................. | $30,283 | $ 27,140 |
| **Liabilities and Equity** | | |
| Current Liabilities | | |
| Accounts payable ..................................................... | $ 7,872 | $ 7,303 |
| Accrued salaries and benefits ................................... | 2,037 | 1,832 |
| Accrued member rewards .......................................... | 710 | 661 |
| Accrued sales and other taxes .................................. | 382 | 397 |
| Deferred membership fees ........................................ | 1,167 | 1,101 |
| Other current liabilities ............................................. | 1,089 | 966 |
| Total current liabilities ............................................. | 13,257 | 12,260 |
| Long-term debt, excluding current portion ................. | 4,998 | 1,381 |
| Deferred income taxes and other liabilities ................ | 1,016 | 981 |

*(continued)*

| | | |
|---|---|---|
| Total liabilities ........................................................ | $19,271 | $14,622 |
| Commitments and Contingencies | | |
| Equity | | |
| Preferred stock $.005 par value; 100,000,000 shares authorized; no shares issued and outstanding | 0 | 0 |
| Common stock $.005 par value; 900,000,000 shares authorized; 436,839,000 and 432,350,000 shares issued and outstanding | 2 | 2 |
| Additional paid-in capital ......................................... | $ 4,670 | $ 4,369 |
| Accumulated other comprehensive (loss) income ... | (122) | 156 |
| Retained earnings ................................................... | 6,283 | 7,834 |
| Total Costco stockholders' equity ............................ | 10,833 | 12,361 |
| Noncontrolling interests .......................................... | 179 | 157 |
| Total equity ............................................................ | 11,012 | 12,518 |
| **Total Liabilities and Equity** .................................. | $30,283 | $27,140 |

*Source:* Costco Wholesale Corporation 2013 10-K.

**LO 2, LO 3**  **2.** Panera Bread operates more than 1,600 bakery-cafés in more than 44 states and Canada. How many of the four tests of the competitive power of a resource does the store network pass? Using your general knowledge of this industry, perform a SWOT analysis. Explain your answers.

**connect**

**LO 4**  **3.** Review the information in Illustration Capsule 4.1 concerning American Giant's average costs of producing and selling a hoodie sweatshirt, and compare this with the representative value chain depicted in Figure 4.3. Then answer the following questions:

    **a.** Which of the company's costs correspond to the primary value chain activities depicted in Figure 4.3?

    **b.** Which of the company's costs correspond to the support activities described in Figure 4.3?

    **c.** How would its various costs and activities differ if the company chose to produce its hoodies in Asia?

    **d.** What value chain activities might be important in securing or maintaining American Giant's competitive advantage? Explain your answer.

**LO 5**  **4.** Using the methodology illustrated in Table 4.3 and your knowledge as an automobile owner, prepare a competitive strength assessment for General Motors and its rivals Ford, Chrysler, Toyota, and Honda. Each of the five automobile manufacturers should be evaluated on the key success factors and strength measures of cost competitiveness, product-line breadth, product quality and reliability, financial resources and profitability, and customer service. What does your competitive strength assessment disclose about the overall competitiveness of each automobile manufacturer? What factors account most for Toyota's competitive success? Does Toyota have competitive weaknesses that were disclosed by your analysis? Explain.

# EXERCISE FOR SIMULATION PARTICIPANTS

1. Using the formulas in Table 4.1 and the data in your company's latest financial statements, calculate the following measures of financial performance for your company: **LO 1**
   a. Operating profit margin
   b. Total return on total assets
   c. Current ratio
   d. Working capital
   e. Long-term debt-to-capital ratio
   f. Price-to-earnings ratio

2. On the basis of your company's latest financial statements and all the other available data regarding your company's performance that appear in the industry report, list the three measures of financial performance on which your company did best and the three measures on which your company's financial performance was worst. **LO 1**

3. What hard evidence can you cite that indicates your company's strategy is working fairly well (or perhaps not working so well, if your company's performance is lagging that of rival companies)? **LO 1**

4. What internal strengths and weaknesses does your company have? What external market opportunities for growth and increased profitability exist for your company? What external threats to your company's future well-being and profitability do you and your co-managers see? What does the preceding SWOT analysis indicate about your company's present situation and future prospects—where on the scale from "exceptionally strong" to "alarmingly weak" does the attractiveness of your company's situation rank? **LO 2, LO 3**

5. Does your company have any core competencies? If so, what are they? **LO 2, LO 3**

6. What are the key elements of your company's value chain? Refer to Figure 4.3 in developing your answer. **LO 4**

7. Using the methodology presented in Table 4.4, do a weighted competitive strength assessment for your company and two other companies that you and your co-managers consider to be very close competitors. **LO 5**

# ENDNOTES

[1] Birger Wernerfelt, "A Resource-Based View of the Firm," *Strategic Management Journal* 5, no. 5 (September–October 1984), pp. 171–180; Jay Barney, "Firm Resources and Sustained Competitive Advantage," *Journal of Management* 17, no. 1 (1991), pp. 99–120.

[2] R. Amit and P. Schoemaker, "Strategic Assets and Organizational Rent," *Strategic Management Journal* 14 (1993).

[3] Jay B. Barney, "Looking Inside for Competitive Advantage," *Academy of Management Executive* 9, no. 4 (November 1995), pp. 49–61; Christopher A. Bartlett and Sumantra Ghoshal, "Building Competitive Advantage through People," *MIT Sloan Management Review* 43, no. 2 (Winter 2002), pp. 34–41; Danny Miller, Russell Eisenstat, and Nathaniel Foote, "Strategy from the Inside Out: Building Capability-Creating Organizations," *California Management Review* 44, no. 3 (Spring 2002), pp. 37–54.

[4] M. Peteraf and J. Barney, "Unraveling the Resource-Based Tangle," *Managerial and Decision Economics* 24, no. 4 (June–July 2003), pp. 309–323.

[5] Margaret A. Peteraf and Mark E. Bergen, "Scanning Dynamic Competitive Landscapes: A Market-Based and Resource-Based Framework," *Strategic Management Journal* 24 (2003), pp. 1027–1042.

[6] C. Montgomery, "Of Diamonds and Rust: A New Look at Resources," in C. Montgomery (ed.), *Resource-Based and Evolutionary Theories of the Firm* (Boston: Kluwer Academic, 1995), pp. 251–268.

[7] Constance E. Helfat and Margaret A. Peteraf, "The Dynamic Resource-Based View: Capability Lifecycles," *Strategic Management Journal* 24, no. 10 (2003).

[8] D. Teece, G. Pisano, and A. Shuen, "Dynamic Capabilities and Strategic Management," *Strategic Management Journal* 18, no. 7 (1997),

pp. 509–533; K. Eisenhardt and J. Martin, "Dynamic Capabilities: What Are They?" *Strategic Management Journal* 21, no. 10–11 (2000), pp. 1105–1121; M. Zollo and S. Winter, "Deliberate Learning and the Evolution of Dynamic Capabilities," *Organization Science* 13 (2002), pp. 339–351; C. Helfat et al., *Dynamic Capabilities: Understanding Strategic Change in Organizations* (Malden, MA: Blackwell, 2007).

[9] David W. Birchall and George Tovstiga, "The Strategic Potential of a Firm's Knowledge Portfolio," *Journal of General Management* 25, no. 1 (Autumn 1999), pp. 1–16; Nick Bontis, Nicola C. Dragonetti, Kristine Jacobsen, and Goran Roos, "The Knowledge Toolbox: A Review of the Tools Available to Measure and Manage Intangible Resources," *European Management Journal* 17, no. 4 (August 1999), pp. 391–401; David Teece, "Capturing Value from Knowledge Assets: The New Economy, Markets for Know-How, and Intangible Assets," *California Management Review* 40, no. 3 (Spring 1998), pp. 55–79.

[10] Donald Sull, "Strategy as Active Waiting," *Harvard Business Review* 83, no. 9 (September 2005), pp. 121–126.

[11] M. Peteraf, "The Cornerstones of Competitive Advantage: A Resource-Based View," *Strategic Management Journal,* March 1993, pp. 179–191.

[12] Michael Porter in his 1985 best seller, *Competitive Advantage* (New York: Free Press).

[13] John K. Shank and Vijay Govindarajan, *Strategic Cost Management* (New York: Free Press, 1993), especially chaps. 2–6, 10, and 11; Robin Cooper and Robert S. Kaplan, "Measure Costs Right: Make the Right Decisions," *Harvard Business Review* 66, no. 5 (September–October, 1988), pp. 96–103; Joseph A. Ness and Thomas G. Cucuzza, "Tapping the Full Potential of ABC," *Harvard Business Review* 73, no. 4 (July–August 1995), pp. 130–138.

[14] Porter, *Competitive Advantage,* p. 34.

[15] Hau L. Lee, "The Triple-A Supply Chain," *Harvard Business Review* 82, no. 10 (October 2004), pp. 102–112.

[16] Gregory H. Watson, *Strategic Benchmarking: How to Rate Your Company's Performance against the World's Best* (New York: Wiley, 1993); Robert C. Camp, *Benchmarking: The Search for Industry Best Practices That Lead to Superior Performance* (Milwaukee: ASQC Quality Press, 1989); Dawn Iacobucci and Christie Nordhielm, "Creative Benchmarking," *Harvard Business Review* 78 no. 6 (November–December 2000), pp. 24–25.

[17] www.businessdictionary.com/definition/best-practice.html (accessed December 2, 2009).

[18] Reuben E. Stone, "Leading a Supply Chain Turnaround," *Harvard Business Review* 82, no. 10 (October 2004), pp. 114–121.

### CHAPTER 5

# The Five Generic Competitive Strategies

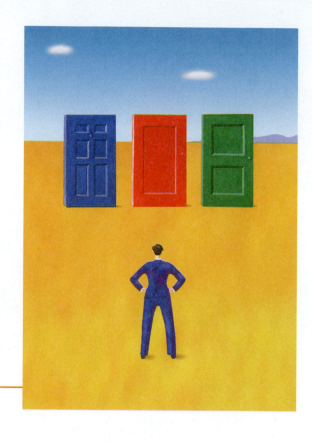

## Learning Objectives

**LO 1**  What distinguishes each of the five generic strategies and why some of these strategies work better in certain kinds of competitive conditions than in others.

**LO 2**  The major avenues for achieving a competitive advantage based on lower costs.

**LO 3**  The major avenues to a competitive advantage based on differentiating a company's product or service offering from the offerings of rivals.

**LO 4**  The attributes of a best-cost provider strategy—a hybrid of low-cost provider and differentiation strategies.

> A strategy delineates a territory in which a company seeks to be unique.
>
> **Michael E. Porter** – *Professor and Cofounder of Monitor Consulting*

> I learnt the hard way about positioning in business, about catering to the right segments.
>
> **Shaffi Mather** –*Social Entrepreneur*

> I'm spending my time trying to understand our competitive position and how we're serving customers.
>
> **Lou Gerstner** – *Former CEO Credited with IBM's Turnaround*

A company can employ any of several basic approaches to competing successfully and gaining a competitive advantage over rivals, but they all involve *delivering more value* to the customer than rivals or *delivering value more efficiently* than rivals (or both). More value for the customer can mean a good product at a lower price, a superior product worth paying more for, or a best-value offering that represents an attractive combination of price, features, service, and other appealing attributes. Greater efficiency means delivering a given level of value to customers at a lower cost to the company. But whatever approach to delivering value the company takes, it nearly always requires performing value chain activities differently than rivals and building competitively valuable resources and capabilities that rivals cannot readily match or trump.

This chapter describes the five *generic competitive strategy options.* Which of the five to employ is a company's foremost choice in crafting an overall strategy and beginning its quest for competitive advantage.

## TYPES OF GENERIC COMPETITIVE STRATEGIES

A company's competitive strategy *deals exclusively with the specifics of management's game plan for competing successfully*—its specific efforts to position itself in the marketplace, please customers, ward off competitive threats, and achieve a particular kind of competitive advantage. The chances are remote that any two companies—even companies in the same industry—will employ competitive strategies that are exactly alike in every detail. However, when one strips away the details to get at the real substance, the two biggest factors that distinguish one competitive strategy from another boil down to (1) whether a company's market target is broad or narrow and (2) whether the company is pursuing a competitive advantage linked to lower costs or differentiation. These two factors give rise to five competitive strategy options, as shown in Figure 5.1 and listed next.[1]

**LO1**

What distinguishes each of the five generic strategies and why some of these strategies work better in certain kinds of competitive conditions than in others.

1. *A low-cost provider strategy*—striving to achieve lower overall costs than rivals on comparable products that attract a broad spectrum of buyers, usually by underpricing rivals.

## FIGURE 5.1    The Five Generic Competitive Strategies

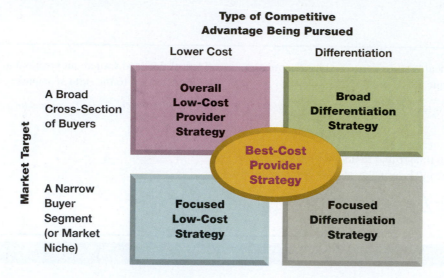

*Source:* This is an expanded version of a three-strategy classification discussed in Michael E. Porter, *Competitive Strategy* (New York: Free Press, 1980).

2.  *A broad differentiation strategy*—seeking to differentiate the company's product offering from rivals' products by offering superior attributes that will appeal to a broad spectrum of buyers.

3.  *A focused low-cost strategy*—concentrating on a narrow buyer segment (or market niche) and outcompeting rivals on costs, thus being able to serve niche members at a lower price.

4.  *A focused differentiation strategy*—concentrating on a narrow buyer segment (or market niche) and outcompeting rivals by offering niche members customized attributes that meet their tastes and requirements better than rivals' products.

5.  *A best-cost provider strategy*—giving customers *more value for their money* by satisfying buyers' expectations on key quality, features, performance, and/or service attributes while beating their price expectations. This option is a *hybrid* strategy that blends elements of low-cost provider and differentiation strategies; the aim is to have the lowest (best) costs and prices among sellers offering products with comparable differentiating attributes.

The remainder of this chapter explores the ins and outs of these five generic competitive strategies and how they differ.

# LOW-COST PROVIDER STRATEGIES

Striving to be the industry's overall low-cost provider is a powerful competitive approach in markets with many price-sensitive buyers. A company achieves **low-cost leadership** when it becomes the industry's lowest-cost provider rather than just being one of perhaps several competitors with comparatively low costs. Successful low-cost providers boast lower costs than rivals—but not necessarily the absolutely lowest possible cost. In striving for a cost advantage over rivals, company managers must incorporate features and services that buyers consider essential. A product offering that is too frills-free can be viewed by consumers as offering little value regardless of its pricing.

A company has two options for translating a low-cost advantage over rivals into attractive profit performance. Option 1 is to use the lower-cost edge to underprice competitors and attract price-sensitive buyers in great enough numbers to increase total profits. Option 2 is to maintain the present price, be content with the present market share, and use the lower-cost edge to earn a higher profit margin on each unit sold, thereby raising the firm's total profits and overall return on investment.

While many companies are inclined to exploit a low-cost advantage by using option 1 (attacking rivals with lower prices), this strategy can backfire if rivals respond with their own retaliatory price cuts (in order to protect their customer base). A rush to cut prices can often trigger a price war that lowers the profits of all price discounters. The bigger the risk that rivals will respond with matching price cuts, the more appealing it becomes to employ the second option for using a low-cost advantage to achieve higher profitability.

## The Two Major Avenues for Achieving a Cost Advantage

To achieve a low-cost edge over rivals, a firm's cumulative costs across its overall value chain must be lower than competitors' cumulative costs. There are two major avenues for accomplishing this:[2]

1. Perform value chain activities more cost-effectively than rivals.
2. Revamp the firm's overall value chain to eliminate or bypass some cost-producing activities.

**Cost-Efficient Management of Value Chain Activities**   For a company to do a more cost-efficient job of managing its value chain than rivals, managers must diligently search out cost-saving opportunities in every part of the value chain. No activity can escape cost-saving scrutiny, and all company personnel must be expected to use their talents and ingenuity to come up with innovative and effective ways to keep costs down. Particular attention must be paid to a set of factors known as **cost drivers** that have a strong effect on a company's costs and can be used as levers to lower costs. Figure 5.2 shows the most important cost drivers. Cost-cutting approaches that demonstrate an effective use of the cost drivers include:

1. *Capturing all available economies of scale.* Economies of scale stem from an ability to lower unit costs by increasing the scale of operation. Often a large plant or distribution center is more economical to operate than a small one. In global industries, selling a mostly standard product worldwide tends to lower unit costs as opposed to making separate products for each country market, an approach in which costs are typically higher due to an inability to reach the most economic scale of production for each country. There are economies of scale in advertising as well. For example, Anheuser-Busch could afford to pay the $4 million cost of a 30-second Super Bowl ad in 2014 because the cost could be spread out over the hundreds of millions of units of Budweiser that the company sells.

**LO 2**

The major avenues for achieving a competitive advantage based on lower costs.

**CORE CONCEPT**

A **low-cost provider's** basis for competitive advantage is lower overall costs than competitors. Successful **low-cost leaders,** who have the lowest industry costs, are exceptionally good at finding ways to drive costs out of their businesses and still provide a product or service that buyers find acceptable.

A low-cost advantage over rivals can translate into better profitability than rivals attain.

**CORE CONCEPT**

A **cost driver** is a factor that has a strong influence on a company's costs.

**FIGURE 5.2   Cost Drivers: The Keys to Driving Down Company Costs**

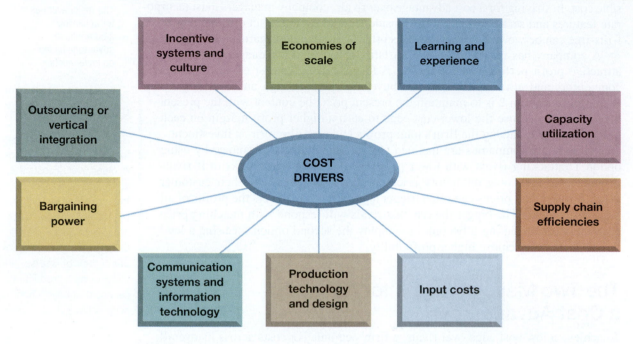

*Source:* Adapted from M. Porter, *Competitive Advantage: Creating and Sustaining Competitive Advantage* (New York: Free Press, 1985).

2. *Taking full advantage of experience- and learning-curve effects.* The cost of performing an activity can decline over time as the learning and experience of company personnel build. Learning and experience economies can stem from debugging and mastering newly introduced technologies, using workers' experiences and suggestions to install more efficient plant layouts and assembly procedures, and repeatedly picking sites for and building new plants, retail outlets, or distribution centers—gaining speed and greater effectiveness in the process.

3. *Operating facilities at full capacity.* Whether a company is able to operate at or near full capacity has a big impact on unit costs when its value chain contains activities associated with substantial fixed costs. Higher rates of capacity utilization allow depreciation and other fixed costs to be spread over a larger unit volume, thereby lowering fixed costs per unit. The more capital-intensive the business and the higher the fixed costs as a percentage of total costs, the greater the unit-cost penalty for operating at less than full capacity.

4. *Improving supply chain efficiency.* Partnering with suppliers to streamline the ordering and purchasing process, to reduce inventory carrying costs via just-in-time inventory practices, to economize on shipping and materials handling, and to ferret out other cost-saving opportunities is a much-used approach to cost reduction. A company with a distinctive competence in cost-efficient supply chain management, such as BASF (the world's leading chemical company), can sometimes achieve a sizable cost advantage over less adept rivals.

5. *Substituting lower-cost inputs wherever there is little or no sacrifice in product quality or performance.* If the costs of certain raw materials and parts are "too

high," a company can switch to using lower-cost items or maybe even design the high-cost components out of the product altogether.

6. *Using the company's bargaining power vis-à-vis suppliers or others in the value chain system to gain concessions.* Home Depot, for example, has sufficient bargaining clout with suppliers to win price discounts on large-volume purchases.

7. *Using online systems and sophisticated software to achieve operating efficiencies.* For example, sharing data and production schedules with suppliers, coupled with the use of enterprise resource planning (ERP) and manufacturing execution system (MES) software, can reduce parts inventories, trim production times, and lower labor requirements.

8. *Improving process design and employing advanced production technology.* Often production costs can be cut by (1) using design for manufacture (DFM) procedures and computer-assisted design (CAD) techniques that enable more integrated and efficient production methods, (2) investing in highly automated robotic production technology, and (3) shifting to a mass-customization production process. Dell's highly automated PC assembly plant in Austin, Texas, is a prime example of the use of advanced product and process technologies. Many companies are ardent users of total quality management (TQM) systems, business process reengineering, six sigma methodology, and other business process management techniques that aim at boosting efficiency and reducing costs.

9. *Being alert to the cost advantages of outsourcing or vertical integration.* Outsourcing the performance of certain value chain activities can be more economical than performing them in-house if outside specialists, by virtue of their expertise and volume, can perform the activities at lower cost. On the other hand, there can be times when integrating into the activities of either suppliers or distribution-channel allies can lower costs through greater production efficiencies, reduced transaction costs, or a better bargaining position.

10. *Motivating employees through incentives and company culture.* A company's incentive system can encourage not only greater worker productivity but also cost-saving innovations that come from worker suggestions. The culture of a company can also spur worker pride in productivity and continuous improvement. Companies that are well known for their cost-reducing incentive systems and culture include Nucor Steel, which characterizes itself as a company of "20,000 teammates," Southwest Airlines, and Walmart.

**Revamping the Value Chain System to Lower Costs**    Dramatic cost advantages can often emerge from redesigning the company's value chain system in ways that eliminate costly work steps and entirely bypass certain cost-producing value chain activities. Such value chain revamping can include:

• *Selling direct to consumers and bypassing the activities and costs of distributors and dealers.* To circumvent the need for distributors and dealers, a company can (1) create its own direct sales force (which adds the costs of maintaining and supporting a sales force but which may well be cheaper than using independent distributors and dealers to access buyers) and/or (2) conduct sales operations at the company's website (incurring costs for website operations and shipping may be a substantially cheaper way to make sales than going through distributor–dealer channels). Costs in the wholesale and retail portions of the value chain frequently represent 35 to 50 percent of the final price consumers pay, so establishing a direct sales force or selling online may offer big cost savings.

- *Streamlining operations by eliminating low-value-added or unnecessary work steps and activities.* At Walmart, some items supplied by manufacturers are delivered directly to retail stores rather than being routed through Walmart's distribution centers and delivered by Walmart trucks. In other instances, Walmart unloads incoming shipments from manufacturers' trucks arriving at its distribution centers and loads them directly onto outgoing Walmart trucks headed to particular stores without ever moving the goods into the distribution center. Many supermarket chains have greatly reduced in-store meat butchering and cutting activities by shifting to meats that are cut and packaged at the meatpacking plant and then delivered to their stores in ready-to-sell form.

- *Reducing materials handling and shipping costs by having suppliers locate their plants or warehouses close to the company's own facilities.* Having suppliers locate their plants or warehouses close to a company's own plant facilitates just-in-time deliveries of parts and components to the exact workstation where they will be used in assembling the company's product. This not only lowers incoming shipping costs but also curbs or eliminates the company's need to build and operate storerooms for incoming parts and components and to have plant personnel move the inventories to the workstations as needed for assembly.

Illustration Capsule 5.1 describes how Walmart has managed its value chain in the retail grocery portion of its business to achieve a dramatic cost advantage over rival supermarket chains and become the world's biggest grocery retailer.

### Examples of Companies That Revamped Their Value Chains to Reduce Costs

Nucor Corporation, the most profitable steel producer in the United States and one of the largest steel producers worldwide, drastically revamped the value chain process for manufacturing steel products by using relatively inexpensive electric arc furnaces and continuous casting processes. Using electric arc furnaces to melt recycled scrap steel eliminated many of the steps used by traditional steel mills that made their steel products from iron ore, coke, limestone, and other ingredients using costly coke ovens, basic oxygen blast furnaces, ingot casters, and multiple types of finishing facilities—plus Nucor's value chain system required far fewer employees. As a consequence, Nucor produces steel with a far lower capital investment, a far smaller workforce, and far lower operating costs than traditional steel mills. Nucor's strategy to replace the traditional steelmaking value chain with its simpler, quicker value chain approach has made it one of the world's lowest-cost producers of steel, allowing it to take a huge amount of market share away from traditional steel companies and earn attractive profits. (Nucor reported a profit in 180 out of 184 quarters during 1966–2012—a remarkable feat in a mature and cyclical industry notorious for roller-coaster bottom-line performance.)

Southwest Airlines has achieved considerable cost savings by reconfiguring the traditional value chain of commercial airlines, thereby permitting it to offer travelers dramatically lower fares. Its mastery of fast turnarounds at the gates (about 25 minutes versus 45 minutes for rivals) allows its planes to fly more hours per day. This translates into being able to schedule more flights per day with fewer aircraft, allowing Southwest to generate more revenue per plane on average than rivals. Southwest does not offer assigned seating, baggage transfer to connecting airlines, or first-class seating and service, thereby eliminating all the cost-producing activities associated with these features. The company's fast and user-friendly online reservation system facilitates e-ticketing and reduces staffing requirements at telephone reservation

Success in achieving a low-cost edge over rivals comes from outmanaging rivals in finding ways to perform value chain activities faster, more accurately, and more cost-effectively.

# How Walmart Managed Its Value Chain to Achieve a Huge Low-Cost Advantage over Rival Supermarket Chains

Walmart has achieved a very substantial cost and pricing advantage over rival supermarket chains both by revamping portions of the grocery retailing value chain and by outmanaging its rivals in efficiently performing various value chain activities. Its cost advantage stems from a series of initiatives and practices:

- Instituting extensive information sharing with vendors via online systems that relay sales at its checkout counters directly to suppliers of the items, thereby providing suppliers with real-time information on customer demand and preferences (creating an estimated 6 percent cost advantage). It is standard practice at Walmart to collaborate extensively with vendors on all aspects of the purchasing and store delivery process to squeeze out mutually beneficial cost savings. Procter & Gamble, Walmart's biggest supplier, went so far as to integrate its enterprise resource planning (ERP) system with Walmart's.

- Pursuing global procurement of some items and centralizing most purchasing activities so as to leverage the company's buying power (creating an estimated 2.5 percent cost advantage).

- Investing in state-of-the-art automation at its distribution centers; operating a truck fleet that makes 24-hour-a-day deliveries to Walmart stores while minimizing the mileage that trucks travel empty, thereby reducing costs and environmental impact; and putting other assorted cost-saving practices into place at its headquarters, distribution centers, and stores (resulting in an estimated 4 percent cost advantage).

- Striving to optimize the product mix and achieve greater sales turnover (resulting in about a 2 percent cost advantage).

- Installing security systems and store operating procedures that lower shrinkage rates (producing a cost advantage of about 0.5 percent).

- Negotiating preferred real estate rental and leasing rates with real estate developers and owners of its store sites (yielding a cost advantage of 2 percent).

- Managing and compensating its workforce in a manner that produces lower labor costs (yielding an estimated 5 percent cost advantage).

Together, these value chain initiatives give Walmart an approximately 22 percent cost advantage over Kroger, Safeway, and other leading supermarket chains. With such a sizable cost advantage, Walmart has been able to underprice its rivals and rapidly become the world's leading supermarket retailer.

In order to maintain its cost advantages, which are very much tied to scale and growth, Walmart has adapted to more broadly reach a changing and growing customer base. Walmart stores range from giant, 24-hour Supercenters to Neighborhood Markets and Express stores that better fit the needs of customers in urban or fast-moving locales, and in the same way the company has tailored its international expansion by country. With further innovation in online and fresh delivery sales, Walmart is well poised to continue its growth and low-cost leadership.

*Sources:* Information at **www.walmart.com**; Marco Iansiti and Roy Levien, "Strategy as Ecology," *Harvard Business Review* 82, no. 3 (March 2004), p. 70; and Clare O'Connor, "Wal-Mart vs. Amazon: World's Biggest E-Commerce Battle Could Boil Down to Vegetables," *Forbes* Online, March 2014.

centers and airport counters. Its use of automated check-in equipment reduces staffing requirements for terminal check-in. The company's carefully designed point-to-point route system minimizes connections, delays, and total trip time for passengers, allowing about 75 percent of Southwest passengers to fly nonstop to their destinations and at the same time reducing Southwest's costs for flight operations.

## The Keys to Being a Successful Low-Cost Provider

While low-cost providers are champions of frugality, they seldom hesitate to spend aggressively on resources and capabilities *that promise to drive costs out of the business.* Indeed, having competitive assets of this type and ensuring that they remain competitively superior is essential for achieving competitive advantage as a low-cost provider. Walmart has been an early adopter of state-of-the-art technology throughout its operations, as Illustration Capsule 5.1 suggests; *however, Walmart carefully estimates the cost savings of new technologies before it rushes to invest in them.* By continuously investing in complex, cost-saving technologies that are hard for rivals to match, Walmart has sustained its low-cost advantage for over 30 years.

Other companies noted for their successful use of low-cost provider strategies include Vizio in big-screen TVs, Briggs & Stratton in small gasoline engines, Bic in ballpoint pens, Stride Rite in footwear, Poulan in chain saws, and General Electric and Whirlpool in major home appliances.

## When a Low-Cost Provider Strategy Works Best

A low-cost provider strategy becomes increasingly appealing and competitively powerful when:

1. *Price competition among rival sellers is vigorous.* Low-cost providers are in the best position to compete offensively on the basis of price, to gain market share at the expense of rivals, to win the business of price-sensitive buyers, to remain profitable despite strong price competition, and to survive price wars.

2. *The products of rival sellers are essentially identical and readily available from many eager sellers.* Look-alike products and/or overabundant product supply set the stage for lively price competition; in such markets, it is the less efficient, higher-cost companies whose profits get squeezed the most.

3. *It is difficult to achieve product differentiation in ways that have value to buyers.* When the differences between product attributes or brands do not matter much to buyers, buyers are nearly always sensitive to price differences, and industry-leading companies tend to be those with the lowest-priced brands.

4. *Most buyers use the product in the same ways.* With common user requirements, a standardized product can satisfy buyers' needs, in which case low price, not features or quality, becomes the dominant factor in causing buyers to choose one seller's product over another's.

5. *Buyers incur low costs in switching their purchases from one seller to another.* Low switching costs give buyers the flexibility to shift purchases to lower-priced sellers having equally good products or to attractively priced substitute products. A low-cost leader is well positioned to use low price to induce potential customers to switch to its brand.

# Pitfalls to Avoid in Pursuing a Low-Cost Provider Strategy

Perhaps the biggest mistake a low-cost provider can make is getting carried away with overly aggressive price cutting. *Higher unit sales and market shares do not automatically translate into higher profits.* A lower price improves profitability only if the lower price increases unit sales enough to offset the loss in revenues due to a lower margin on each unit sold.

A second pitfall is *relying on an approach to reduce costs that can be easily copied by rivals.* If rivals find it relatively easy or inexpensive to imitate the leader's low-cost methods, then the leader's advantage will be too short-lived to yield a valuable edge in the marketplace.

A third pitfall is *becoming too fixated on cost reduction.* Low costs cannot be pursued so zealously that a firm's offering ends up being too feature-poor to generate buyer appeal. Furthermore, a company driving hard to push down its costs has to guard against ignoring declining buyer sensitivity to price, increased buyer interest in added features or service, or new developments that alter how buyers use the product. Otherwise, it risks losing market ground if buyers start opting for more upscale or feature-rich products.

Even if these mistakes are avoided, a low-cost provider strategy still entails risk. An innovative rival may discover an even lower-cost value chain approach. Important cost-saving technological breakthroughs may suddenly emerge. And if a low-cost provider has heavy investments in its present means of operating, then it can prove costly to quickly shift to the new value chain approach or a new technology.

> A low-cost provider is in the best position to win the business of price-sensitive buyers, set the floor on market price, and still earn a profit.

> Reducing price does not lead to higher total profits unless the added gains in unit sales are large enough to offset the loss in revenues due to lower margins per unit sold.

> A low-cost provider's product offering must always contain enough attributes to be attractive to prospective buyers—low price, by itself, is not always appealing to buyers.

# BROAD DIFFERENTIATION STRATEGIES

Differentiation strategies are attractive whenever buyers' needs and preferences are too diverse to be fully satisfied by a standardized product offering. Successful product differentiation requires careful study to determine what attributes buyers find appealing, valuable, and worth paying for.[3] Then the company must incorporate these desirable features into its product or service to clearly set itself apart from rivals lacking attributes. A differentiation strategy calls for a customer value proposition that is *unique.* The strategy achieves its aim when an attractively large number of buyers find the customer value proposition appealing and become strongly attached to a company's differentiated attributes.

Successful differentiation allows a firm to do one or more of the following:

- Command a premium price for its product.
- Increase unit sales (because additional buyers are won over by the differentiating features).
- Gain buyer loyalty to its brand (because some buyers are strongly attracted to the differentiating features and bond with the company and its products).

Differentiation enhances profitability whenever a company's product can command a sufficiently higher price or produce sufficiently bigger unit sales *to more than cover the added costs of achieving the differentiation.* Company differentiation strategies fail when buyers don't value the brand's uniqueness sufficiently and/or when a company's approach to differentiation is easily matched by its rivals.

> **LO 3**
>
> The major avenues to a competitive advantage based on differentiating a company's product or service offering from the offerings of rivals.

> **CORE CONCEPT**
>
> The essence of a **broad differentiation strategy** is to offer unique product attributes that a wide range of buyers find appealing and worth paying for.

Companies can pursue differentiation from many angles: a unique taste (Red Bull, Listerine); multiple features (Microsoft Office, Apple iPad); wide selection and one-stop shopping (Home Depot, Amazon.com); superior service (Ritz-Carlton, Nordstrom); spare parts availability (Caterpillar in machines); engineering design and performance (Mercedes, BMW); luxury and prestige (Rolex, Gucci); product reliability (Whirlpool and Bosch in large home appliances); quality manufacture (Michelin in tires); technological leadership (3M Corporation in bonding and coating products); a full range of services (Charles Schwab in stock brokerage); and wide product selection (Campbell's soups).

## Managing the Value Chain to Create the Differentiating Attributes

Differentiation is not something hatched in marketing and advertising departments, nor is it limited to the catchalls of quality and service. Differentiation opportunities can exist in activities all along an industry's value chain. The most systematic approach that managers can take, however, involves focusing on the **value drivers,** a set of factors—analogous to cost drivers—that are particularly effective in creating differentiation. Figure 5.3 contains a list of important value drivers. Ways that managers can enhance differentiation based on value drivers include the following:

1. *Create product features and performance attributes that appeal to a wide range of buyers.* This applies to the physical as well as functional attributes of a product, including features such as added user safety or enhanced environmental protection. Styling and appearance are big differentiating factors in the apparel and motor vehicle industries. Size and weight matter in binoculars and smartphones. Most companies employing broad differentiation strategies make a point of incorporating innovative and novel features in their product or service offering, especially those that improve performance.

2. *Improve customer service or add extra services.* Better customer services, in areas such as delivery, returns, and repair, can be as important in creating differentiation as superior product features. Examples include superior technical assistance to buyers, higher-quality maintenance services, more and better product information provided to customers, more and better training materials for end users, better credit terms, quicker order processing, and greater customer convenience.

3. *Invest in production-related R&D activities.* Engaging in production R&D may permit custom-order manufacture at an efficient cost, provide wider product variety and selection through product "versioning," or improve product quality. Many manufacturers have developed flexible manufacturing systems that allow different models and product versions to be made on the same assembly line. Being able to provide buyers with made-to-order products can be a potent differentiating capability.

4. *Strive for innovation and technological advances.* Successful innovation is the route to more frequent first-on-the-market victories and is a powerful differentiator. If the innovation proves hard to replicate, through patent protection or other means, it can provide a company with a first mover advantage that is sustainable.

5. *Pursue continuous quality improvement.* Quality control processes reduce product defects, prevent premature product failure, extend product life, make it economical to offer longer warranty coverage, improve economy of use, result in

### CORE CONCEPT

A **value driver** is a factor that can have a strong differentiating effect.

**FIGURE 5.3**   **Value Drivers: The Keys to Creating a Differentiation Advantage**

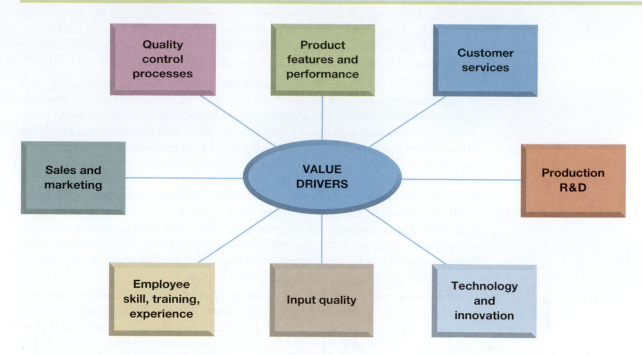

*Source:* Adapted from M. Porter, *Competitive Advantage: Creating and Sustaining Competitive Advantage* (New York: Free Press, 1985).

more end-user convenience, or enhance product appearance. Companies whose quality management systems meet certification standards, such as the ISO 9001 standards, can enhance their reputation for quality with customers.

6. *Increase marketing and brand-building activities.* Marketing and advertising can have a tremendous effect on the value perceived by buyers and therefore their willingness to pay more for the company's offerings. They can create differentiation even when little tangible differentiation exists otherwise. For example, blind taste tests show that even the most loyal Pepsi or Coke drinkers have trouble telling one cola drink from another.[4] Brands create customer loyalty, which increases the perceived "cost" of switching to another product.

7. *Seek out high-quality inputs.* Input quality can ultimately spill over to affect the performance or quality of the company's end product. Starbucks, for example, gets high ratings on its coffees partly because it has very strict specifications on the coffee beans purchased from suppliers.

8. *Emphasize human resource management activities that improve the skills, expertise, and knowledge of company personnel.* A company with high-caliber intellectual capital often has the capacity to generate the kinds of ideas that drive product innovation, technological advances, better product design and product performance, improved production techniques, and higher product quality. Well-designed incentive compensation systems can often unleash the efforts of talented personnel to develop and implement new and effective differentiating attributes.

### Revamping the Value Chain System to Increase Differentiation

Just as pursuing a cost advantage can involve the entire value chain system, the same is true for a differentiation advantage. Activities performed upstream by suppliers or downstream by distributors and retailers can have a meaningful effect on customers' perceptions of a company's offerings and its value proposition. Approaches to enhancing differentiation through changes in the value chain system include:

- *Coordinating with channel allies to enhance customer value.* Coordinating with downstream partners such as distributors, dealers, brokers, and retailers can contribute to differentiation in a variety of ways. Methods that companies use to influence the value chain activities of their channel allies include setting standards for downstream partners to follow, providing them with templates to standardize the selling environment or practices, training channel personnel, or cosponsoring promotions and advertising campaigns. Coordinating with retailers is important for enhancing the buying experience and building a company's image. Coordinating with distributors or shippers can mean quicker delivery to customers, more accurate order filling, and/or lower shipping costs. The Coca-Cola Company considers coordination with its bottler-distributors so important that it has at times taken over a troubled bottler for the purpose of improving its management and upgrading its plant and equipment before releasing it again.[5]

- *Coordinating with suppliers to better address customer needs.* Collaborating with suppliers can also be a powerful route to a more effective differentiation strategy. Coordinating and collaborating with suppliers can improve many dimensions affecting product features and quality. This is particularly true for companies that engage only in assembly operations, such as Dell in PCs and Ducati in motorcycles. Close coordination with suppliers can also enhance differentiation by speeding up new product development cycles or speeding delivery to end customers. Strong relationships with suppliers can also mean that the company's supply requirements are prioritized when industry supply is insufficient to meet overall demand.

## Delivering Superior Value via a Broad Differentiation Strategy

Differentiation strategies depend on meeting customer needs in unique ways or creating new needs through activities such as innovation or persuasive advertising. The objective is to offer customers something that rivals can't—at least in terms of the level of satisfaction. There are four basic routes to achieving this aim.

The first route is to incorporate product attributes and user features that *lower the buyer's overall costs* of using the company's product. This is the least obvious and most overlooked route to a differentiation advantage. It is a differentiating factor since it can help business buyers be more competitive in their markets and more profitable. Producers of materials and components often win orders for their products by reducing a buyer's raw-material waste (providing cut-to-size components), reducing a buyer's inventory requirements (providing just-in-time deliveries), using online systems to reduce a buyer's procurement and order processing costs, and providing free technical support. This route to differentiation can also appeal to individual consumers who are looking to economize on their overall costs of consumption. Making a company's product more economical for a buyer to use can be done by incorporating energy-efficient features (energy-saving appliances and lightbulbs help cut buyers' utility bills; fuel-efficient vehicles cut buyer costs for gasoline) and/or by increasing maintenance intervals and product reliability so as to lower buyer costs for maintenance and repairs.

A second route is to incorporate *tangible* features that increase customer satisfaction with the product, such as product specifications, functions, and styling. This can be accomplished by including attributes that add functionality, enhance the design, save time for the user, are more reliable, or make the product cleaner, safer, quieter, simpler to use, more portable, more convenient, or longer-lasting than rival brands. Smartphone manufacturers are in a race to introduce next-generation devices capable of being used for more purposes and having simpler menu functionality.

A third route to a differentiation-based competitive advantage is to incorporate *intangible* features that enhance buyer satisfaction in noneconomic ways. Toyota's Prius appeals to environmentally conscious motorists not only because these drivers want to help reduce global carbon dioxide emissions but also because they identify with the image conveyed. Bentley, Ralph Lauren, Louis Vuitton, Burberry, Cartier, and Coach have differentiation-based competitive advantages linked to buyer desires for status, image, prestige, upscale fashion, superior craftsmanship, and the finer things in life. Intangibles that contribute to differentiation can extend beyond product attributes to the reputation of the company and to customer relations or trust.

> Differentiation can be based on *tangible* or *intangible* attributes.

The fourth route is to *signal the value* of the company's product offering to buyers. Typical signals of value include a high price (in instances where high price implies high quality and performance), more appealing or fancier packaging than competing products, ad content that emphasizes a product's standout attributes, the quality of brochures and sales presentations, and the luxuriousness and ambience of a seller's facilities (important for high-end retailers and for offices or other facilities frequented by customers). They make potential buyers aware of the professionalism, appearance, and personalities of the seller's employees and/or make potential buyers realize that a company has prestigious customers. Signaling value is particularly important (1) when the nature of differentiation is based on intangible features and is therefore subjective or hard to quantify, (2) when buyers are making a first-time purchase and are unsure what their experience with the product will be, (3) when repurchase is infrequent, and (4) when buyers are unsophisticated.

Regardless of the approach taken, achieving a successful differentiation strategy requires, first, that the company have capabilities in areas such as customer service, marketing, brand management, and technology that can create and support differentiation. That is, the resources, competencies, and value chain activities of the company must be well matched to the requirements of the strategy. For the strategy to result in competitive advantage, the company's competencies must also be sufficiently unique in delivering value to buyers that they help set its product offering apart from those of rivals. They must be competitively superior. There are numerous examples of companies that have differentiated themselves on the basis of distinctive capabilities. When a major news event occurs, many people turn to Fox News and CNN because they have the capability to devote more airtime to breaking news stories and get reporters on the scene very quickly. Avon and Mary Kay Cosmetics have differentiated themselves from other cosmetics and personal care companies by assembling a sales force numbering in the hundreds of thousands that gives them a direct sales capability— their sales associates personally demonstrate products to interested buyers, take their orders on the spot, and deliver the items to buyers' homes.

The most successful approaches to differentiation are those that are difficult for rivals to duplicate. Indeed, this is the route to a sustainable differentiation advantage. While resourceful competitors can, in time, clone almost any tangible product attribute, socially complex intangible attributes, such as company reputation, long-standing relationships with buyers, and image are much harder to imitate. Differentiation that creates switching costs that lock in buyers also provides a route to sustainable advantage. For example, if a buyer makes a substantial investment in learning to use one type of system, that buyer is less likely to switch to a competitor's system. (This has kept many users from switching away from Microsoft Office products, despite the fact that there are other applications with superior features.) As a rule, differentiation yields a longer-lasting and more profitable competitive edge when it is based on a well-established brand image, patent-protected product innovation, complex technical superiority, a reputation for superior product quality and reliability, relationship-based customer service, and unique competitive capabilities.

## When a Differentiation Strategy Works Best

Differentiation strategies tend to work best in market circumstances where:

- *Buyer needs and uses of the product are diverse.* Diverse buyer preferences allow industry rivals to set themselves apart with product attributes that appeal to particular buyers. For instance, the diversity of consumer preferences for menu selection, ambience, pricing, and customer service gives restaurants exceptionally wide latitude in creating a differentiated product offering. Other industries with diverse buyer needs include magazine publishing, automobile manufacturing, footwear, and kitchen appliances.

- *There are many ways to differentiate the product or service that have value to buyers.* Industries in which competitors have opportunities to add features to products and services are well suited to differentiation strategies. For example, hotel chains can differentiate on such features as location, size of room, range of guest services, in-hotel dining, and the quality and luxuriousness of bedding and furnishings. Similarly, cosmetics producers are able to differentiate based upon prestige and image, formulations that fight the signs of aging, UV light protection, exclusivity of retail locations, the inclusion of antioxidants and natural ingredients, or prohibitions against animal testing. Basic commodities, such as chemicals, mineral deposits, and agricultural products, provide few opportunities for differentiation.

- *Few rival firms are following a similar differentiation approach.* The best differentiation approaches involve trying to appeal to buyers on the basis of attributes that rivals are not emphasizing. A differentiator encounters less head-to-head rivalry when it goes its own separate way in creating value and does not try to outdifferentiate rivals on the very same attributes. When many rivals base their differentiation efforts on the same attributes, the most likely result is weak brand differentiation and "strategy overcrowding"—competitors end up chasing much the same buyers with much the same product offerings.

- *Technological change is fast-paced and competition revolves around rapidly evolving product features.* Rapid product innovation and frequent introductions of next-version products heighten buyer interest and provide space for companies to pursue distinct differentiating paths. In video game hardware and video games, golf equipment, mobile phones, and automobile navigation systems, competitors are locked into an ongoing battle to set themselves apart by introducing the best next-generation products. Companies that fail to come up with new and improved products and distinctive performance features quickly lose out in the marketplace.

# Pitfalls to Avoid in Pursuing a Differentiation Strategy

Differentiation strategies can fail for any of several reasons. *A differentiation strategy keyed to product or service attributes that are easily and quickly copied is always suspect.* Rapid imitation means that no rival achieves differentiation, since whenever one firm introduces some value-creating aspect that strikes the fancy of buyers, fast-following copycats quickly reestablish parity. This is why a firm must seek out sources of value creation that are time-consuming or burdensome for rivals to match if it hopes to use differentiation to win a sustainable competitive edge.

*Differentiation strategies can also falter when buyers see little value in the unique attributes of a company's product.* Thus, even if a company succeeds in setting its product apart from those of rivals, its strategy can result in disappointing sales and profits if the product does not deliver adequate value to buyers. Any time many potential buyers look at a company's differentiated product offering with indifference, the company's differentiation strategy is in deep trouble.

*The third big pitfall is overspending on efforts to differentiate the company's product offering, thus eroding profitability.* Company efforts to achieve differentiation nearly always raise costs—often substantially, since marketing and R&D are expensive undertakings. The key to profitable differentiation is either to keep the unit cost of achieving differentiation below the price premium that the differentiating attributes can command (thus increasing the profit margin per unit sold) or to offset thinner profit margins per unit by selling enough additional units to increase total profits. If a company goes overboard in pursuing costly differentiation, it could be saddled with unacceptably low profits or even losses.

Other common mistakes in crafting a differentiation strategy include:

- *Offering only trivial improvements in quality, service, or performance features vis-à-vis rivals' products.* Trivial differences between rivals' product offerings may not be visible or important to buyers. If a company wants to generate the fiercely loyal customer following needed to earn superior profits and open up a differentiation-based competitive advantage over rivals, then its strategy must result in *strong rather than weak product differentiation.* In markets where differentiators do no better than achieve weak product differentiation, customer loyalty is weak, the costs of brand switching are low, and no one company has enough of a market edge to command a price premium over rival brands.

- *Over-differentiating so that product quality, features, or service levels exceed the needs of most buyers.* A dazzling array of features and options not only drives up product price but also runs the risk that many buyers will conclude that a less deluxe and lower-priced brand is a better value since they have little occasion to use the deluxe attributes.

- *Charging too high a price premium.* While buyers may be intrigued by a product's deluxe features, they may nonetheless see it as being overpriced relative to the value delivered by the differentiating attributes. A company must guard against turning off would-be buyers with what is perceived as "price gouging." Normally, the bigger the price premium for the differentiating extras, the harder it is to keep buyers from switching to competitors' lower-priced offerings.

Over-differentiating and overcharging are fatal differentiation strategy mistakes.

*A low-cost provider strategy can defeat a differentiation strategy when buyers are satisfied with a basic product and don't think "extra" attributes are worth a higher price.*

# FOCUSED (OR MARKET NICHE) STRATEGIES

What sets focused strategies apart from low-cost provider and broad differentiation strategies is concentrated attention on a narrow piece of the total market. The target segment, or niche, can be in the form of a geographic segment (such as New England), or a customer segment (such as urban hipsters), or a product segment (such as a class of models or some version of the overall product type). Community Coffee, the largest family-owned specialty coffee retailer in the United States, has a geographic focus on the state of Louisiana and communities across the Gulf of Mexico. Community holds only a small share of the national coffee market but has recorded sales in excess of $100 million and has won a strong following in the 20-state region where its coffee is distributed. Examples of firms that concentrate on a well-defined market niche keyed to a particular product or buyer segment include Zipcar (car rental in urban areas), Comedy Central (cable TV), Blue Nile (online jewelry), Tesla Motors (electric cars), and CGA, Inc. (a specialist in providing insurance to cover the cost of lucrative hole-in-one prizes at golf tournaments). Microbreweries, local bakeries, bed-and-breakfast inns, and retail boutiques have also scaled their operations to serve narrow or local customer segments.

## A Focused Low-Cost Strategy

A focused strategy based on low cost aims at securing a competitive advantage by serving buyers in the target market niche at a lower cost and lower price than those of rival competitors. This strategy has considerable attraction when a firm can lower costs significantly by limiting its customer base to a well-defined buyer segment. The avenues to achieving a cost advantage over rivals also serving the target market niche are the same as those for low-cost leadership—use the cost drivers to keep the costs of value chain activities to a bare minimum and search for innovative ways to bypass nonessential activities. The only real difference between a low-cost provider strategy and a focused low-cost strategy is the size of the buyer group to which a company is appealing—the former involves a product offering that appeals broadly to almost all buyer groups and market segments, whereas the latter aims at just meeting the needs of buyers in a narrow market segment.

Focused low-cost strategies are fairly common. Producers of private-label goods are able to achieve low costs in product development, marketing, distribution, and advertising by concentrating on making generic items imitative of name-brand merchandise and selling directly to retail chains wanting a low-priced store brand. The Perrigo Company has become a leading manufacturer of over-the-counter health care products, with 2013 sales of more than $3.5 billion, by focusing on producing private-label brands for retailers such as Walmart, CVS, Walgreens, Rite-Aid, and Safeway. Budget motel chains, like Motel 6, Sleep Inn, and Super 8, cater to price-conscious travelers who just want to pay for a clean, no-frills place to spend the night. Illustration Capsule 5.2 describes how Aravind's focus on lowering the costs of cataract removal allowed it to address the needs of the "bottom of the pyramid" in India's population, where blindness due to cataracts is an endemic problem.

## A Focused Differentiation Strategy

Focused differentiation strategies involve offering superior products or services designed to appeal to the unique preferences and needs of a narrow, well-defined group of buyers. Successful use of a focused differentiation strategy depends on (1) the existence of a buyer segment that is looking for special product attributes or seller capabilities and (2) a firm's ability to stand apart from rivals competing in the same target market niche.

# Aravind Eye Care System's Focused Low-Cost Strategy

Cataracts, the largest cause of preventable blindness, can be treated with a quick surgical procedure that restores sight; however, poverty and limited access to care prevent millions worldwide from obtaining surgery. The Aravind Eye Care System has found a way to address this problem, with a *focused low-cost strategy* that has made cataract surgery not only affordable for more people in India but free for the very poorest. On the basis of this strategy, Aravind has achieved world renown and become the largest provider of eye care in the world.

High volume and high efficiency are at the cornerstone of Aravind's strategy. The Aravind network, with its nine eye hospitals in India, has become one of the most productive systems in the world, conducting about 350,000 surgeries a year in addition to seeing over 2.8 million outpatients each year. Using the unique model of screening eye camps all over the country, Aravind reaches a broader cross-section of the market for surgical treatment. Additionally, Aravind attains very high staff productivity, with each surgeon performing more than 2,500 surgeries annually compared to 125 for a comparable American surgeon.

What enabled this level of productivity (with no loss in quality of care) was the development of a standardized system of surgical treatment, capitalizing on the fact that cataract removal was already a fairly routine process. Aravind streamlined as much of the process as possible, reducing discretionary elements to a minimum, and tracking outcomes to ensure continuous process improvement. At Aravind's hospitals, there is no wasted

time between surgeries, as different teams of support staff prepare patients for surgery and bring them to the operating theater so that surgeons simply need to turn from one table to another to perform surgery on the next prepared patient. Aravind also drove costs down through the creation of its own manufacturing division, Aurolab, to produce intraocular lenses, suture needles, pharmaceuticals, and surgical blades in India.

Aravind's low costs allow it to keep its prices for cataract surgery very low, at 500 rupees ($10) per patient compared to an average cost of $1,500 for surgery in the United States. Nevertheless, the system provides surgical outcomes and quality comparable to clinics in the United States. As a result of its unique fee system and effective management, Aravind is also able to provide free eye care to 60 percent of its patients from the revenue generated from the paying patients.

*Note:* Developed with Avni V. Patel.

*Sources:* G. Natchiar, A. L. Robin, R. Thulasiraj, et al., "Attacking the Backlog of India's Curable Blind; The Aravind Eye Hospital Model," *Archives of Ophthalmology* 112 (1994), pp. 987–993; D. F. Chang, "Tackling the Greatest Challenge in Cataract Surgery," *British Journal of Ophthalmology* 89 (2005), pp. 1073–1077; "Driving Down the Cost of High Quality Care," *McKinsey Health International,* December 2011; and S. Kandavel, "Aravind Eye Care to Set Up Next Hospital in Chennai," *The Economic Times* Online, December 25, 2012.

Companies like L. A. Burdick's (gourmet chocolates), Rolls-Royce, and Four Seasons Hotels and Resorts employ successful differentiation-based focused strategies targeted at upscale buyers wanting products and services with world-class attributes. Indeed, most markets contain a buyer segment willing to pay a big price premium for the very finest items available, thus opening the strategic window for some competitors to pursue differentiation-based focused strategies aimed at the very top of the market pyramid. Another successful focused differentiator is "fashion food retailer" Trader Joe's, a 418-store, 39-state chain that is a combination gourmet deli and food warehouse. Customers shop Trader Joe's as much for entertainment as for conventional grocery items—the store stocks out-of-the-ordinary culinary treats like raspberry salsa, salmon burgers, and jasmine fried rice, as well as the standard goods normally found in supermarkets. What sets Trader Joe's apart is not just its unique combination of food novelties and competitively priced grocery items but also its capability to turn an otherwise mundane grocery excursion into a whimsical treasure hunt that is just plain fun. Illustration Capsule 5.3 describes how Popchips has been gaining attention with a focused differentiation strategy.

## When a Focused Low-Cost or Focused Differentiation Strategy Is Attractive

A focused strategy aimed at securing a competitive edge based on either low costs or differentiation becomes increasingly attractive as more of the following conditions are met:

- The target market niche is big enough to be profitable and offers good growth potential.
- Industry leaders have chosen not to compete in the niche—in which case focusers can avoid battling head to head against the industry's biggest and strongest competitors.
- It is costly or difficult for multisegment competitors to meet the specialized needs of niche buyers and at the same time satisfy the expectations of their mainstream customers.
- The industry has many different niches and segments, thereby allowing a focuser to pick the niche best suited to its resources and capabilities. Also, with more niches there is more room for focusers to avoid competing for the same customers.
- Few if any rivals are attempting to specialize in the same target segment—a condition that reduces the risk of segment overcrowding.

The advantages of focusing a company's entire competitive effort on a single market niche are considerable, especially for smaller and medium-sized companies that may lack the breadth and depth of resources to tackle going after a broader customer base with a more complex set of needs. YouTube has become a household name by concentrating on short video clips posted online. Papa John's and Domino's Pizza have created impressive businesses by focusing on the home delivery segment.

## The Risks of a Focused Low-Cost or Focused Differentiation Strategy

Focusing carries several risks. One is the chance that competitors will find effective ways to match the focused firm's capabilities in serving the target niche—perhaps by coming up with products or brands specifically designed to appeal to buyers in the target niche or by developing expertise and capabilities that offset the focuser's strengths. In the lodging business, large chains like Marriott have launched multibrand strategies that allow them to compete effectively in several lodging segments simultaneously. Marriott has flagship JW Marriott and Ritz-Carlton hotels with deluxe accommodations for business travelers and resort vacationers. Its Courtyard by Marriott and SpringHill Suites brands cater to business travelers looking for moderately priced lodging, while Marriott Residence Inns and TownePlace Suites are designed as a "home away from home" for travelers staying five or more nights, and Fairfield Inn & Suites is intended to appeal to travelers looking for quality lodging at an "affordable" price. Multibrand strategies are attractive to large companies like Marriott precisely because they enable a company to enter a market niche and siphon business away from companies that employ a focused strategy.

# Popchips' Focused Differentiation Strategy

Potato chips are big business: Americans consume $7 billion worth annually. But the industry is a hard one to break into since it's a mature, slow-growth industry, dominated by a few large competitors. Frito-Lay alone (maker of Lays and Ruffles) has a commanding 60 percent market share. These characteristics are enough to dissuade most potential entrants, but not Popchips, a small potato chip startup. Despite difficult odds, Popchips has made impressive inroads into the industry over the last seven years, with the help of a *focused differentiation strategy.*

Popchips was founded in 2007 by Keith Belling, a serial entrepreneur, and Pat Turpin, a former Costco snack executive. Their idea was simple: Take advantage of high-income purchasers' growing desire for tasty, low-fat snacks. Using an innovative cooking method, they found a way to halve the fat content in potato chips while preserving flavor. Popchips has a differentiated product. But its real point of differentiation is its brand and distribution strategy. Most potato chips have mass distribution and a broad buyer base. Belling and Turpin decided from the outset to narrow their distribution and narrow their targeted buyers. They hoped that focusing on a market niche would allow their product to stand out from the bags of Lays and cans of Pringles in aisles all over America. Popchips' target: upper-income, health-conscious urban and suburban consumers.

To that end, the firm has signed distribution deals with Whole Foods, Target, and, reflecting Turpin's roots, Costco. Popchips' marketing emphasizes social marketing and word-of-mouth recommendations. The company sends out samples to key tastemakers who tweet, blog, or recommend the product in traditional media. Ashton Kutcher, MTV's former *Punk'd* host, was so impressed with the chips that he volunteered to promote them. As with *Punk'd,* Popchips' advertising is similarly irreverent, with taglines like "love. without the handles."

Popchips' differentiation strategy is succeeding. Since 2009, the company's sales have accounted for

nearly all potato chip sales growth at natural supermarket stores, like Whole Foods, giving it a 15 percent market share in this niche distribution channel. The company's 2012 sales were $93 million, nearly doubling since 2010. That's particularly impressive given that the industry growth rate has been a paltry 4 percent. In 2013, *Forbes* put Popchips at number 5 on its list of America's Most Promising Companies.

*Note:* Developed with Dennis L. Huggins.

*Sources:* Molly Maier, "Chips, Pretzels and Corn Snacks—US—January 2012," *Mintel,* January 2012, www.oxygen.mintel.com (accessed February 1, 2012); Lindsay Blakely and Caitlin Elsaesser, "One Snacker at a Time: How Popchips Grew without Losing Its Character," *CBS News,* January 2011, www.cbsnews.com (accessed February 1, 2012); Laura Petrecca, "Popchips CEO Keith Belling Is 'Poptimist' on Healthy Snacks," *USA Today,* March 2010, www.usatoday.com (accessed February 13, 2012); www.forbes.com (accessed March 28, 2013); and Popchips' website.

A second risk of employing a focused strategy is the potential for the preferences and needs of niche members to shift over time toward the product attributes desired by the majority of buyers. An erosion of the differences across buyer segments lowers entry barriers into a focuser's market niche and provides an open invitation for rivals in adjacent segments to begin competing for the focuser's customers. A third risk is that the segment may become so attractive that it is soon inundated with competitors, intensifying rivalry and splintering segment profits. And there is always the risk for segment growth to slow to such a small rate that a focuser's prospects for future sales and profit gains become unacceptably dim.

# BEST-COST PROVIDER STRATEGIES

As Figure 5.1 indicates, **best-cost provider strategies** stake out a middle ground between pursuing a low-cost advantage and a differentiation advantage and between appealing to the broad market as a whole and a narrow market niche. This permits companies to aim squarely at the sometimes great mass of value-conscious buyers looking for a better product or service at an economical price. Value-conscious buyers frequently shy away from both cheap low-end products and expensive high-end products, but they are quite willing to pay a "fair" price for extra features and functionality they find appealing and useful. The essence of a best-cost provider strategy is giving customers *more value for the money* by satisfying buyer desires for appealing features and charging a lower price for these attributes compared to rivals with similar-caliber product offerings.[6] From a competitive-positioning standpoint, best-cost strategies are thus a *hybrid,* balancing a strategic emphasis on low cost against a strategic emphasis on differentiation (desirable features delivered at a relatively low price).

To profitably employ a best-cost provider strategy, a company *must have the capability to incorporate upscale attributes into its product offering at a lower cost than rivals.* When a company can incorporate more appealing features, good to excellent product performance or quality, or more satisfying customer service into its product offering *at a lower cost than rivals,* then it enjoys "best-cost" status—it is the low-cost provider of a product or service with *upscale attributes.* A best-cost provider can use its low-cost advantage to underprice rivals whose products or services have similarly upscale attributes and it still earns attractive profits.

*Being a best-cost provider is different from being a low-cost provider* because the additional attractive attributes entail additional costs (which a low-cost provider can avoid by offering buyers a basic product with few frills). Moreover, the two strategies aim at a distinguishably different market target. *The target market for a best-cost provider is value-conscious buyers*—buyers who are looking for appealing extras and functionality at a comparatively low price. Value-hunting buyers (as distinct from *price-conscious buyers* looking for a basic product at a bargain-basement price) often constitute a very sizable part of the overall market for a product or service.

## When a Best-Cost Provider Strategy Works Best

A best-cost provider strategy works best in markets where product differentiation is the norm and an attractively large number of value-conscious buyers can be induced to purchase midrange products rather than cheap, basic products or expensive, top-of-the-line products. A best-cost provider needs to position itself *near the middle of the market*

# American Giant's Best-Cost Provider Strategy

Bayard Winthrop, founder and owner of American Giant, set out to make a hoodie like the soft, ultra-thick Navy sweatshirts his dad used to wear in the 1950s. But he also had two other aims: He wanted it to have a more updated look with a tailored fit, and he wanted it produced cost-effectively so that it could be sold at a great price. To accomplish these aims, he designed the sweatshirt with the help of a former industrial engineer from Apple and an internationally renowned pattern maker, rethinking every aspect of sweatshirt design and production along the way. The result was a hoodie differentiated from others on the basis of extreme attention to fabric, fit, construction, and durability. The hoodie is made from heavy-duty cotton that is run through a machine that carefully picks loops of thread out of the fabric to create a thick, combed, ring-spun fleece fabric that feels three times thicker than most sweatshirts. A small amount of spandex paneling along the shoulders and sides creates the fitted look and maintains the shape, keeping the sweatshirt from looking slouchy or sloppy. It has double stitching with strong thread on critical seams to avoid deterioration and boost durability. The zippers and draw cord are customized to match the sweatshirt's color—an uncommon practice in the business.

American Giant sources yarn from Parkdale, South Carolina, and turns it into cloth at the nearby Carolina Cotton Works. This reduces transport costs, creates a more dependable, durable product that American Giant can easily quality-check, and shortens product turnaround to about a month, lowering inventory costs. This process also enables the company to use a genuine "Made in the U.S.A" label, a perceived quality driver.

American Giant disrupts the traditional, expensive distribution models by having no stores or resellers. Instead, it sells directly to customers from its website, with free two-day shipping and returns. Much of the company's growth comes from word of mouth and a strong public relations effort that promotes the brand in magazines, newspapers, and key business-oriented television programs. American Giant has a robust refer-a-friend program that offers a discount to friends of, and a credit to, current owners. Articles in popular media proclaiming its product "the greatest hoodie ever made" have made demand for its sweatshirts skyrocket.

At $79 for the original men's hoodie, American Giant is not cheap but offers customers value in terms of both price and quality. The price is higher than what one would pay at The Gap or American Apparel and comparable to Levi's, J.Crew, or Banana Republic. But its quality is more on par with high-priced designer brands, while its price is far more affordable.

*Note:* Developed with Sarah Boole.

*Sources:* www.nytimes.com/2013/09/20/business/us-textile-factories-return.html?emc=eta1&_r=0; www.american-giant.com; www.slate.com/articles/technology/technology/2012/12/american_giant_hoodie_this_is_the_greatest_sweatshirt_known_to_man.html; www.businessinsider.com/this-hoodie-is-so-insanely-popular-you-have-to-wait-months-to-get-it-2013-12.

with either a medium-quality product at a below-average price or a high-quality product at an average or slightly higher price. Best-cost provider strategies also work well in recessionary times, when masses of buyers become value-conscious and are attracted to economically priced products and services with more appealing attributes. But unless a company has the resources, know-how, and capabilities to incorporate upscale product or service attributes at a lower cost than rivals, adopting a best-cost strategy is ill-advised. Illustration Capsule 5.4 describes how American Giant has applied the principles of the best-cost provider strategy in producing and marketing its hoodie sweatshirts.

## The Risk of a Best-Cost Provider Strategy

A company's biggest vulnerability in employing a best-cost provider strategy is getting squeezed between the strategies of firms using low-cost and high-end differentiation strategies. Low-cost providers may be able to siphon customers away with the appeal of a lower price (despite less appealing product attributes). High-end differentiators may be able to steal customers away with the appeal of better product attributes (even though their products carry a higher price tag). Thus, to be successful, a best-cost provider must achieve significantly lower costs in providing upscale features so that it can outcompete high-end differentiators on the basis of a *significantly* lower price. Likewise, it must offer buyers *significantly* better product attributes to justify a price above what low-cost leaders are charging. In other words, it must offer buyers a more attractive customer value proposition.

# THE CONTRASTING FEATURES OF THE FIVE GENERIC COMPETITIVE STRATEGIES: A SUMMARY

A company's competitive strategy should be well matched to its internal situation and predicated on leveraging its collection of competitively valuable resources and capabilities.

Deciding which generic competitive strategy should serve as the framework on which to hang the rest of the company's strategy is not a trivial matter. Each of the five generic competitive strategies *positions* the company differently in its market and competitive environment. Each establishes a *central theme* for how the company will endeavor to outcompete rivals. Each creates some boundaries or guidelines for maneuvering as market circumstances unfold and as ideas for improving the strategy are debated. Each entails differences in terms of product line, production emphasis, marketing emphasis, and means of maintaining the strategy, as shown in Table 5.1.

Thus a choice of which generic strategy to employ spills over to affect many aspects of how the business will be operated and the manner in which value chain activities must be managed. Deciding which generic strategy to employ is perhaps the most important strategic commitment a company makes—it tends to drive the rest of the strategic actions a company decides to undertake.

## Successful Competitive Strategies Are Resource-Based

For a company's competitive strategy to succeed in delivering good performance and gain a competitive edge over rivals, it has to be well matched to a company's internal situation and underpinned by an appropriate set of resources, know-how, and competitive capabilities. To succeed in employing a low-cost provider strategy, a company must have the resources and capabilities to keep its costs below those of its competitors. This means having the expertise to cost-effectively manage value chain activities better than rivals, leveraging the cost drivers effectively, and/or having the innovative capability to bypass certain value chain activities being performed by rivals. To succeed in a differentiation strategy, a company must have the resources and capabilities to leverage value drivers effectively and incorporate attributes into its product offering that a broad range of buyers will find appealing. Successful focused strategies (both low cost and differentiation) require the capability to do an outstanding job of

**TABLE 5.1** Distinguishing Features of the Five Generic Competitive Strategies

| | Low-Cost Provider | Broad Differentiation | Focused Low-Cost Provider | Focused Differentiation | Best-Cost Provider |
|---|---|---|---|---|---|
| **Strategic target** | • A broad cross-section of the market. | • A broad cross-section of the market. | • A narrow market niche where buyer needs and preferences are distinctively different. | • A narrow market niche where buyer needs and preferences are distinctively different. | • Value-conscious buyers.<br>• A middle-market range. |
| **Basis of competitive strategy** | • Lower overall costs than competitors. | • Ability to offer buyers something attractively different from competitors' offerings. | • Lower overall cost than rivals in serving niche members. | • Attributes that appeal specifically to niche members. | • Ability to offer better goods at attractive prices. |
| **Product line** | • A good basic product with few frills (acceptable quality and limited selection). | • Many product variations, wide selection; emphasis on differentiating features. | • Features and attributes tailored to the tastes and requirements of niche members. | • Features and attributes tailored to the tastes and requirements of niche members. | • Items with appealing attributes and assorted features; better quality, not best. |
| **Production emphasis** | • A continuous search for cost reduction without sacrificing acceptable quality and essential features. | • Build in whatever differentiating features buyers are willing to pay for; strive for product superiority. | • A continuous search for cost reduction for products that meet basic needs of niche members. | • Small-scale production or custom-made products that match the tastes and requirements of niche members. | • Build in appealing features and better quality at lower cost than rivals. |
| **Marketing emphasis** | • Low prices, good value.<br>• Try to make a virtue out of product features that lead to low cost. | • Tout differentiating features.<br>• Charge a premium price to cover the extra costs of differentiating features. | • Communicate attractive features of a budget-priced product offering that fits niche buyers' expectations. | • Communicate how product offering does the best job of meeting niche buyers' expectations. | • Emphasize delivery of *best value for the money.* |
| **Keys to maintaining the strategy** | • Economical prices, good value.<br>• Strive to manage costs down, year after year, in every area of the business. | • Stress constant innovation to stay ahead of imitative competitors.<br>• Concentrate on a few key differentiating features. | • Stay committed to serving the niche at the lowest overall cost; don't blur the firm's image by entering other market segments or adding other products to widen market appeal. | • Stay committed to serving the niche better than rivals; don't blur the firm's image by entering other market segments or adding other products to widen market appeal. | • Unique expertise in simultaneously managing costs down while incorporating upscale features and attributes. |
| **Resources and capabilities required** | • Capabilities for driving costs out of the value chain system.<br>• *Examples:* large-scale automated plants, an efficiency-oriented culture, bargaining power. | • Capabilities concerning quality, design, intangibles, and innovation.<br>• *Examples:* marketing capabilities, R&D teams, technology. | • Capabilities to lower costs on niche goods.<br>• *Examples:* lower input costs for the specific product desired by the niche, batch production capabilities. | • Capabilities to meet the highly specific needs of niche members.<br>• *Examples:* custom production, close customer relations. | • Capabilities to simultaneously deliver lower cost and higher-quality/ differentiated features.<br>• *Examples:* TQM practices, mass customization. |

satisfying the needs and expectations of niche buyers. Success in employing a best-cost strategy requires the resources and capabilities to incorporate upscale product or service attributes at a lower cost than rivals. *For all types of generic strategies, success in sustaining the competitive edge depends on having resources and capabilities that rivals have trouble duplicating and for which there are no good substitutes.*

# KEY POINTS

1.  Deciding which of the five generic competitive strategies to employ—overall low cost, broad differentiation, focused low cost, focused differentiation, or best cost—is perhaps the most important strategic commitment a company makes. It tends to drive the remaining strategic actions a company undertakes and sets the whole tone for pursuing a competitive advantage over rivals.

2.  In employing a low-cost provider strategy and trying to achieve a low-cost advantage over rivals, a company must do a better job than rivals of cost-effectively managing value chain activities and/or it must find innovative ways to eliminate cost-producing activities. An effective use of cost drivers is key. Low-cost provider strategies work particularly well when price competition is strong and the products of rival sellers are virtually identical, when there are not many ways to differentiate, when buyers are price-sensitive or have the power to bargain down prices, when buyer switching costs are low, and when industry newcomers are likely to use a low introductory price to build market share.

3.  Broad differentiation strategies seek to produce a competitive edge by incorporating attributes that set a company's product or service offering apart from rivals in ways that buyers consider valuable and worth paying for. This depends on the appropriate use of value drivers. Successful differentiation allows a firm to (1) command a premium price for its product, (2) increase unit sales (if additional buyers are won over by the differentiating features), and/or (3) gain buyer loyalty to its brand (because some buyers are strongly attracted to the differentiating features and bond with the company and its products). Differentiation strategies work best when buyers have diverse product preferences, when few other rivals are pursuing a similar differentiation approach, and when technological change is fast-paced and competition centers on rapidly evolving product features. A differentiation strategy is doomed when competitors are able to quickly copy the appealing product attributes, when a company's differentiation efforts fail to interest many buyers, and when a company overspends on efforts to differentiate its product offering or tries to overcharge for its differentiating extras.

4.  A focused strategy delivers competitive advantage either by achieving lower costs than rivals in serving buyers constituting the target market niche or by developing a specialized ability to offer niche buyers an appealingly differentiated offering that meets their needs better than rival brands do. A focused strategy based on either low cost or differentiation becomes increasingly attractive when the target market niche is big enough to be profitable and offers good growth potential, when it is costly or difficult for multisegment competitors to meet the specialized

needs of the target market niche and at the same time satisfy their mainstream customers' expectations, when there are one or more niches that present a good match for a focuser's resources and capabilities, and when few other rivals are attempting to specialize in the same target segment.

5. Best-cost strategies create competitive advantage by giving buyers *more value for the money*—delivering superior quality, features, performance, and/or service attributes while also beating customer expectations on price. To profitably employ a best-cost provider strategy, a company *must have the capability to incorporate attractive or upscale attributes at a lower cost than rivals*. A best-cost provider strategy works best in markets with large numbers of value-conscious buyers desirous of purchasing better products and services for less money.

6. In all cases, competitive advantage depends on having competitively superior resources and capabilities that are a good fit for the chosen generic strategy. A sustainable advantage depends on maintaining that competitive superiority with resources, capabilities, and value chain activities that rivals have trouble matching and for which there are no good substitutes.

## ASSURANCE OF LEARNING EXERCISES

1. Best Buy is the largest consumer electronics retailer in the United States, with 2013 sales of almost $50 billion. The company competes aggressively on price with such rivals as Costco, Sam's Club, Walmart, and Target, but it is also known by consumers for its first-rate customer service. Best Buy customers have commented that the retailer's sales staff is exceptionally knowledgeable about the company's products and can direct them to the exact location of difficult-to-find items. Best Buy customers also appreciate that demonstration models of PC monitors, digital media players, and other electronics are fully powered and ready for in-store use. Best Buy's Geek Squad tech support and installation services are additional customer service features that are valued by many customers.

   **LO 1, LO 2, LO 3, LO 4**

   How would you characterize Best Buy's competitive strategy? Should it be classified as a low-cost provider strategy? A differentiation strategy? A best-cost strategy? Explain your answer.

2. Illustration Capsule 5.1 discusses Walmart's low-cost position in the supermarket industry. Based on information provided in the capsule, explain how Walmart has built its low-cost advantage in the industry and why a low-cost provider strategy is well suited to the industry.

   **connect**

   **LO 2**

3. Stihl is the world's leading manufacturer and marketer of chain saws, with annual sales exceeding $3.7 billion. With innovations dating to its 1929 invention of the gasoline-powered chain saw, the company holds over 1,000 patents related to chain saws and outdoor power tools. The company's chain saws, leaf blowers, and hedge trimmers sell at price points well above competing brands and are sold only by its network of over 40,000 independent dealers in more than 160 countries.

   **LO 1, LO 2, LO 3, LO 4**

How would you characterize Stihl's competitive strategy? Should it be classified as a low-cost provider strategy? A differentiation strategy? A best-cost strategy? Also, has the company chosen to focus on a narrow piece of the market, or does it appear to pursue a broad market approach? Explain your answer.

**LO 3**

4. Explore BMW's website at **www.bmwgroup.com** and see if you can identify at least three ways in which the company seeks to differentiate itself from rival automakers. Is there reason to believe that BMW's differentiation strategy has been successful in producing a competitive advantage? Why or why not?

## EXERCISE FOR SIMULATION PARTICIPANTS

**LO 1, LO 2,**
**LO 3, LO 4**

1. Which one of the five generic competitive strategies best characterizes your company's strategic approach to competing successfully?

2. Which rival companies appear to be employing a low-cost provider strategy?

3. Which rival companies appear to be employing a broad differentiation strategy?

4. Which rival companies appear to be employing a best-cost provider strategy?

5. Which rival companies appear to be employing some type of focused strategy?

6. What is your company's action plan to achieve a sustainable competitive advantage over rival companies? List at least three (preferably more than three) specific kinds of decision entries on specific decision screens that your company has made or intends to make to win this kind of competitive edge over rivals.

## ENDNOTES

[1] Michael E. Porter, *Competitive Strategy: Techniques for Analyzing Industries and Competitors* (New York: Free Press, 1980), chap. 2; Michael E. Porter, "What Is Strategy?" *Harvard Business Review* 74, no. 6 (November–December 1996).

[2] M. Porter, *Competitive Advantage: Creating and Sustaining Superior Performance* (New York: Free Press, 1985).

[3] Richard L. Priem, "A Consumer Perspective on Value Creation," *Academy of Management Review* 32, no. 1 (2007), pp. 219–235.

[4] jrscience.wcp.muohio.edu/nsfall01/FinalArticles/Final-IsitWorthitBrandsan.html

[5] D. Yoffie, "Cola Wars Continue: Coke and Pepsi in 2006," Harvard Business School case 9-706-447.

[6] Peter J. Williamson and Ming Zeng, "Value-for-Money Strategies for Recessionary Times," *Harvard Business Review* 87, no. 3 (March 2009), pp. 66–74.

### CHAPTER 6

# Strengthening a Company's Competitive Position

## Strategic Moves, Timing, and Scope of Operations

## Learning Objectives

**LO 1**  Whether and when to pursue offensive or defensive strategic moves to improve a company's market position.

**LO 2**  When being a first mover or a fast follower or a late mover is most advantageous.

**LO 3**  The strategic benefits and risks of expanding a company's horizontal scope through mergers and acquisitions.

**LO 4**  The advantages and disadvantages of extending the company's scope of operations via vertical integration.

**LO 5**  The conditions that favor farming out certain value chain activities to outside parties.

**LO 6**  When and how strategic alliances can substitute for horizontal mergers and acquisitions or vertical integration and how they can facilitate outsourcing.

> The objective is to enlarge the scope of your advantage which can only happen at someone else's expense.
>
> Bruce Henderson – *Founder and Former CEO of the Boston Consulting Group*

> Think of your priorities not in terms of what activities you do, but when you do them. Timing is everything.
>
> Dan Millman – *Author and Lecturer*

> In the virtual economy, collaboration is a new competitive imperative.
>
> Michael Dell – *Founder and CEO of Dell Inc.*

Once a company has settled on which of the five generic competitive strategies to employ, attention turns to what *other strategic actions* it can take to complement its competitive approach and maximize the power of its overall strategy. The first set of decisions concerns whether to undertake offensive or defensive competitive moves, and the timing of such moves. The second set concerns the breadth of a company's activities (or its *scope* of operations along an industry's entire value chain). All in all, the following measures to strengthen a company's competitive position must be considered:

- Whether to go on the offensive and initiate aggressive strategic moves to improve the company's market position.
- Whether to employ defensive strategies to protect the company's market position.
- When to undertake strategic moves—whether advantage or disadvantage lies in being a first mover, a fast follower, or a late mover.
- Whether to bolster the company's market position by merging with or acquiring another company in the same industry.
- Whether to integrate backward or forward into more stages of the industry value chain system.
- Which value chain activities, if any, should be outsourced.
- Whether to enter into strategic alliances or partnership arrangements with other enterprises.

This chapter presents the pros and cons of each of these strategy-enhancing measures.

## LAUNCHING STRATEGIC OFFENSIVES TO IMPROVE A COMPANY'S MARKET POSITION

No matter which of the five generic competitive strategies a firm employs, there are times when a company should *go on the offensive* to improve its market position and performance. **Strategic offensives** are called for when a company spots opportunities to gain profitable market share at its rivals' expense or when a company has no choice but to try to whittle away at a strong rival's competitive advantage. Companies like Samsung, Amazon, Facebook, and Google play hardball, aggressively pursuing competitive advantage and trying to reap the benefits a competitive

**LO 1**

Whether and when to pursue offensive or defensive strategic moves to improve a company's market position.

edge offers—a leading market share, excellent profit margins, and rapid growth.[1] The best offensives tend to incorporate several principles: (1) focusing relentlessly on building competitive advantage and then striving to convert it into a sustainable advantage, (2) applying resources where rivals are least able to defend themselves, (3) employing the element of surprise as opposed to doing what rivals expect and are prepared for, and (4) displaying a capacity for swift and decisive actions to overwhelm rivals.[2]

> Sometimes a company's best strategic option is to seize the initiative, go on the attack, and launch a strategic offensive to improve its market position.

## Choosing the Basis for Competitive Attack

As a rule, challenging rivals on competitive grounds where they are strong is an uphill struggle.[3] Offensive initiatives that exploit competitor weaknesses stand a better chance of succeeding than do those that challenge competitor strengths, especially if the weaknesses represent important vulnerabilities and weak rivals can be caught by surprise with no ready defense.

*Strategic offensives should exploit the power of a company's strongest competitive assets*—its most valuable resources and capabilities such as a better-known brand name, a more efficient production or distribution system, greater technological capability, or a superior reputation for quality. But a consideration of the company's strengths should not be made without also considering the rival's strengths and weaknesses. A strategic offensive should be based on those areas of strength where the company has its greatest competitive advantage over the targeted rivals. If a company has especially good customer service capabilities, it can make special sales pitches to the customers of those rivals that provide subpar customer service. Likewise, it may be beneficial to pay special attention to buyer segments that a rival is neglecting or is weakly equipped to serve.

> The best offensives use a company's most powerful resources and capabilities to attack rivals in the areas where they are weakest.

Ignoring the need to tie a strategic offensive to a company's competitive strengths and what it does best is like going to war with a popgun—the prospects for success are dim. For instance, it is foolish for a company with relatively high costs to employ a price-cutting offensive. Likewise, it is ill advised to pursue a product innovation offensive without having proven expertise in R&D and new product development.

The principal offensive strategy options include the following:

1. *Offering an equally good or better product at a lower price.* Lower prices can produce market share gains if competitors don't respond with price cuts of their own and if the challenger convinces buyers that its product is just as good or better. However, such a strategy increases total profits only if the gains in additional unit sales are enough to offset the impact of lower prices and thinner margins per unit sold. Price-cutting offensives should be initiated only by companies that have *first achieved a cost advantage.*[4] British airline EasyJet used this strategy successfully against rivals such as British Air, Alitalia, and Air France by first cutting costs to the bone and then targeting leisure passengers who care more about low price than in-flight amenities and service.[5]

2. *Leapfrogging competitors by being first to market with next-generation products.* In technology-based industries, the opportune time to overtake an entrenched competitor is when there is a shift to the next generation of the technology. Microsoft got its next-generation Xbox 360 to market a full 12 months ahead of Sony's PlayStation 3 and Nintendo's Wii, helping it build a sizable market share and develop a reputation for cutting-edge innovation in the video game industry. Sony was careful to avoid a repeat, releasing its PlayStation 4 in November 2013 just as Microsoft released its Xbox One.

3. *Pursuing continuous product innovation to draw sales and market share away from less innovative rivals.* Ongoing introductions of new and improved products can put rivals under tremendous competitive pressure, especially when rivals' new product development capabilities are weak. But such offensives can be sustained only if a company can keep its pipeline full and maintain buyer enthusiasm for its new and better product offerings.

4. *Pursuing disruptive product innovations to create new markets.* While this strategy can be riskier and more costly than a strategy of continuous innovation, it can be a game changer if successful. Disruptive innovation involves perfecting new products with a few trial users and then quickly rolling them out to the whole market in an attempt to get the vast majority of buyers to embrace an altogether new and better value proposition quickly. Examples include online universities, Facebook, Tumblr, Twitter, Priceline.com, CampusBookRentals, Square (mobile credit card processing), and Amazon's Kindle.

5. *Adopting and improving on the good ideas of other companies (rivals or otherwise).* The idea of warehouse-type home improvement centers did not originate with Home Depot cofounders Arthur Blank and Bernie Marcus; they got the "big-box" concept from their former employer, Handy Dan Home Improvement. But they were quick to improve on Handy Dan's business model and take Home Depot to the next plateau in terms of product-line breadth and customer service. Offensive-minded companies are often quick to adopt any good idea (not nailed down by a patent or other legal protection) and build upon it to create competitive advantage for themselves.

6. *Using hit-and-run or guerrilla warfare tactics to grab market share from complacent or distracted rivals.* Options for "guerrilla offensives" include occasionally lowballing on price (to win a big order or steal a key account from a rival), surprising rivals with sporadic but intense bursts of promotional activity (offering a discounted trial offer to draw customers away from rival brands), or undertaking special campaigns to attract the customers of rivals plagued with a strike or problems in meeting buyer demand.[6] Guerrilla offensives are particularly well suited to small challengers that have neither the resources nor the market visibility to mount a full-fledged attack on industry leaders.

7. *Launching a preemptive strike to secure an industry's limited resources or capture a rare opportunity.*[7] What makes a move preemptive is its one-of-a-kind nature—whoever strikes first stands to acquire competitive assets that rivals can't readily match. Examples of preemptive moves include (1) securing the best distributors in a particular geographic region or country, (2) obtaining the most favorable site at a new interchange or intersection, in a new shopping mall, and so on, (3) tying up the most reliable, high-quality suppliers via exclusive partnerships, long-term contracts, or acquisition, and (4) moving swiftly to acquire the assets of distressed rivals at bargain prices. To be successful, a preemptive move doesn't have to totally block rivals from following; it merely needs to give a firm a prime position that is not easily circumvented.

How long it takes for an offensive to yield good results varies with the competitive circumstances.[8] It can be short if buyers respond immediately (as can occur with a dramatic cost-based price cut, an imaginative ad campaign, or a disruptive innovation). Securing a competitive edge can take much longer if winning consumer acceptance of an innovative product will take some time or if the firm may need several years to debug a new technology or put a new production capacity in place. But how long it takes for an offensive move to improve a company's market standing (and whether it can do so) also depends on whether market rivals recognize the threat and begin a counterresponse. And whether rivals will respond depends on whether they are capable of making an effective response and if they believe that a counterattack is worth the expense and the distraction.[9]

## Choosing Which Rivals to Attack

Offensive-minded firms need to analyze which of their rivals to challenge as well as how to mount the challenge. The following are the best targets for offensive attacks:[10]

- *Market leaders that are vulnerable.* Offensive attacks make good sense when a company that leads in terms of market share is not a true leader in terms of serving the market well. Signs of leader vulnerability include unhappy buyers, an inferior product line, aging technology or outdated plants and equipment, a preoccupation with diversification into other industries, and financial problems. Caution is well advised in challenging strong market leaders—there's a significant risk of squandering valuable resources in a futile effort or precipitating a fierce and profitless industrywide battle for market share.

- *Runner-up firms with weaknesses in areas where the challenger is strong.* Runner-up firms are an especially attractive target when a challenger's resources and capabilities are well suited to exploiting their weaknesses.

- *Struggling enterprises that are on the verge of going under.* Challenging a hard-pressed rival in ways that further sap its financial strength and competitive position can weaken its resolve and hasten its exit from the market. In this type of situation, it makes sense to attack the rival in the market segments where it makes the most profits, since this will threaten its survival the most.

- *Small local and regional firms with limited capabilities.* Because small firms typically have limited expertise and resources, a challenger with broader and/or deeper capabilities is well positioned to raid their biggest and best customers—particularly those that are growing rapidly, have increasingly sophisticated requirements, and may already be thinking about switching to a supplier with a more full-service capability.

## Blue-Ocean Strategy—A Special Kind of Offensive

A **blue-ocean strategy** seeks to gain a dramatic and durable competitive advantage by abandoning efforts to beat out competitors in existing markets and, instead, *inventing a new market segment that renders existing competitors irrelevant and allows a company to create and capture altogether new demand.*[11] This strategy views the business universe as consisting of two distinct types of market space. One is where industry boundaries are well defined, the competitive rules of the game are understood, and companies try to outperform rivals by capturing a bigger share of existing demand. In such markets, intense competition constrains a company's prospects for rapid growth and superior profitability since rivals move quickly to either imitate or counter the successes of competitors. The second type of market space is a "blue ocean," where the industry does not really exist yet, is untainted by competition, and offers wide-open opportunity for profitable and rapid growth if a company can create new demand with a new type of product offering.

A terrific example of such blue-ocean market space is the online auction industry that eBay created and now dominates. Other companies that have created blue-ocean market spaces include NetJets in fractional jet ownership, Drybar in hair blowouts, Tune Hotels in limited service "backpacker" hotels, and Cirque du Soleil in live entertainment. Cirque du Soleil "reinvented the circus" by pulling in a whole new group of customers—adults and corporate clients—who not only were noncustomers of traditional circuses (like Ringling Brothers) but also were willing to pay several times more than the price of a conventional circus ticket to have a "sophisticated entertainment experience" featuring stunning visuals and star-quality acrobatic acts. Zipcar Inc. is presently using a blue-ocean strategy to compete against entrenched rivals in the rental-car industry. It rents cars by the hour or day (rather than by the week) to members who pay a yearly fee for access to cars parked in designated spaces located conveniently throughout large cities. By allowing drivers under 25 years of age to rent cars and by targeting city dwellers who need to supplement their use of public transportation with short-term car rentals, Zipcar entered uncharted waters in the rental-car industry, growing rapidly in the process.

> Good defensive strategies can help protect a competitive advantage but rarely are the basis for creating one.

Blue-ocean strategies provide a company with a great opportunity in the short run. But they don't guarantee a company's long-term success, which depends more on whether a company can protect the market position it opened up and sustain its early advantage. See Illustration Capsule 6.1 for an example of a company that opened up new competitive space in online luxury retailing only to see its blue-ocean waters ultimately turn red.

## DEFENSIVE STRATEGIES—PROTECTING MARKET POSITION AND COMPETITIVE ADVANTAGE

In a competitive market, all firms are subject to offensive challenges from rivals. The purposes of defensive strategies are to lower the risk of being attacked, weaken the impact of any attack that occurs, and induce challengers to aim their efforts at other rivals. While defensive strategies usually don't enhance a firm's competitive advantage, they can definitely help fortify the firm's competitive position, protect its most valuable resources and capabilities from imitation, and defend whatever competitive advantage it might have. Defensive strategies can take either of two forms: actions to block challengers or actions to signal the likelihood of strong retaliation.

### Blocking the Avenues Open to Challengers

The most frequently employed approach to defending a company's present position involves actions that restrict a challenger's options for initiating a competitive attack. There are any number of obstacles that can be put in the path of would-be challengers. A defender can introduce new features, add new models, or broaden its product line to close off gaps and vacant niches to opportunity-seeking challengers. It can thwart rivals' efforts to attack with a lower price by maintaining its own lineup of economy-priced options. It can discourage buyers from trying competitors' brands by lengthening warranties, making early announcements about impending new products or price changes, offering free training and support services, or providing coupons and sample giveaways to buyers most prone to experiment. It can induce potential buyers to reconsider switching. It can challenge the quality or safety of rivals' products.

# Gilt Groupe's Blue-Ocean Strategy in the U.S. Flash-Sale Industry

Luxury-fashion flash sales exploded onto the U.S. e-commerce scene when Gilt Groupe launched its business in 2007. Flash sales offer limited quantities of high-end designer brands at steep discounts to site members over a very narrow timeframe: The opportunity to snap up an incredible bargain is over in a "flash." The concept of online, time-limited, designer-brand sale events, available to members only, had been invented six years earlier by the French company Vente Privée. But since Vente Privée operated in Europe, the U.S. market represented a wide-open blue ocean of uncontested opportunity. Gilt Groupe's only rival was Ideeli, another U.S. startup that had launched in the same year.

Gilt Groupe thrived and grew rapidly in the calm waters of the early days of the U.S. industry. Its tremendous growth stemmed from its recognition of an underserved segment of the population—the web-savvy, value-conscious fashionista—and also from fortuitous timing. The Great Recession hit the United States in December 2007, causing a sharp decline in consumer buying and leaving designers with unforeseen quantities of luxury items they could not sell. The fledgling flash-sale industry was the perfect channel to offload some of the excess inventory since it still maintained the cachet of exclusivity, with members-only sales and limited-time availability.

Gilt's revenue grew exponentially from $25 million in 2008 to upward of $550 million by 2012. But the company's success prompted an influx of fast followers into the luxury flash-sale industry, including HauteLook, RueLaLa, Lot18, and Vente-Privee.com, which entered the market at around the same time as Gilt. The new rivals not only competed for online customers, who could switch costlessly from site to site (since memberships were free), but also competed for unsold designer inventory. As the U.S. economy came out of the recession, much less of this type of inventory was available. Larger players had also begun to enter the flash-sale market in the United States, with Nordstrom's acquisition of HauteLook, eBay's purchase of RueLaLa, and Amazon.com's 2011 acquisition of MyHabit.com. In

late 2011, Vente Privée announced the launch of its U.S. online site, a joint venture with American Express.

As the competitive waters have begun to roil and turn increasingly red, Gilt Groupe has been looking for new ways to compete, expanding into a variety of online luxury product and service niches and venturing overseas. While the company is not yet profitable in traditional terms, under new management at Gilt Groupe, internal measures of operating profits have become positive and the company is more serious than ever about an IPO in 2014 or 2015. Some of Gilt's competitors have successfully gone public in recent years, showing that there may still be plenty of room to survive and prosper in a more crowded competitive space. But only time will tell.

*Note:* Developed with Judith H. Lin.

*Sources:* Matthew Carroll, "The Rise of Gilt Groupe," *Forbes.com,* January 2012; Mark Brohan, "The Top 500 Guide," *Internet Retailer,* June 2011; Colleen Debaise, "Launching Gilt Groupe, a Fashionable Enterprise," *The Wall Street Journal,* October 2010, www.wsj.com (accessed February 26, 2012); about.americanexpress.com/news/pr/2011/vente_usa.aspx (accessed March 3, 2012); and J. Del Ray, "Gilt Groupe Eyes Late 2014 IPO—For Real, This Time," *AllThingsD* Online, November 21, 2013 (accessed March 29, 2014).

Finally, a defender can grant volume discounts or better financing terms to dealers and distributors to discourage them from experimenting with other suppliers, or it can convince them to handle its product line *exclusively* and force competitors to use other distribution outlets.

There are many ways to throw obstacles in the path of would-be challengers.

## Signaling Challengers That Retaliation Is Likely

The goal of signaling challengers that strong retaliation is likely in the event of an attack is either to dissuade challengers from attacking at all or to divert them to less threatening options. Either goal can be achieved by letting challengers know the battle will cost more than it is worth. Signals to would-be challengers can be given by:

- Publicly announcing management's commitment to maintaining the firm's present market share.
- Publicly committing the company to a policy of matching competitors' terms or prices.
- Maintaining a war chest of cash and marketable securities.
- Making an occasional strong counterresponse to the moves of weak competitors to enhance the firm's image as a tough defender.

To be an effective defensive strategy, signaling needs to be accompanied by a *credible commitment* to follow through.

To be an effective defensive strategy, however, signaling needs to be accompanied by a *credible commitment* to follow through.

## TIMING A COMPANY'S OFFENSIVE AND DEFENSIVE STRATEGIC MOVES

*When* to make a strategic move is often as crucial as *what* move to make. Timing is especially important when **first-mover advantages** or **disadvantages** exist. Under certain conditions, being first to initiate a strategic move can have a high payoff in the form of a competitive advantage that later movers can't dislodge. Moving first is no guarantee of success, however, since first movers also face some significant disadvantages. Indeed, there are circumstances in which it is more advantageous to be a fast follower or even a late mover. Because the timing of strategic moves can be consequential, it is important for company strategists to be aware of the nature of first-mover advantages and disadvantages and the conditions favoring each type of move.[12]

**CORE CONCEPT**

Because of **first-mover advantages** and **disadvantages,** competitive advantage can spring from *when* a move is made as well as from *what* move is made.

## The Potential for First-Mover Advantages

Market pioneers and other types of first movers typically bear greater risks and greater development costs than firms that move later. If the market responds well to its initial move, the pioneer will benefit from a monopoly position (by virtue of being first to market) that enables it to recover its investment costs and make an attractive profit. If the firm's pioneering move gives it a competitive advantage that can be sustained even after other firms enter the market space, its first-mover advantage will be greater still. The extent of this type of advantage, however, will depend on whether and how fast follower firms can piggyback on the pioneer's success and either imitate or improve on its move.

**LO 2**

When being a first mover or a fast follower or a late mover is most advantageous.

There are five such conditions in which first-mover advantages are most likely to arise:

1.  *When pioneering helps build a firm's reputation and creates strong brand loyalty.* Customer loyalty to an early mover's brand can create a tie that binds, limiting the success of later entrants' attempts to poach from the early mover's customer base and steal market share.

2.  *When a first mover's customers will thereafter face significant switching costs.* Switching costs can protect first movers when consumers make large investments in learning how to use a specific company's product or in purchasing complementary products that are also brand-specific. Switching costs can also arise from loyalty programs or long-term contracts that give customers incentives to remain with an initial provider.

3.  *When property rights protections thwart rapid imitation of the initial move.* In certain types of industries, property rights protections in the form of patents, copyrights, and trademarks prevent the ready imitation of an early mover's initial moves. First-mover advantages in pharmaceuticals, for example, are heavily dependent on patent protections, and patent races in this industry are common. In other industries, however, patents provide limited protection and can frequently be circumvented. Property rights protections also vary among nations, since they are dependent on a country's legal institutions and enforcement mechanisms.

4.  *When an early lead enables the first mover to move down the learning curve ahead of rivals.* When there is a steep learning curve and when learning can be kept *proprietary,* a first mover can benefit from volume-based cost advantages that grow ever larger as its experience accumulates and its scale of operations increases. This type of first-mover advantage is self-reinforcing and, as such, can preserve a first mover's competitive advantage over long periods of time. Honda's advantage in small multiuse motorcycles has been attributed to such an effect.

5.  *When a first mover can set the technical standard for the industry.* In many technology-based industries, the market will converge around a single technical standard. By establishing the industry standard, a first mover can gain a powerful advantage that, like experience-based advantages, builds over time. The lure of such an advantage, however, can result in standard wars among early movers, as each strives to set the industry standard. The key to winning such wars is to enter early on the basis of strong fast-cycle product development capabilities, gain the support of key customers and suppliers, employ penetration pricing, and make allies of the producers of complementary products.

Illustration Capsule 6.2 describes how Amazon.com achieved a first-mover advantage in online retailing.

## The Potential for Late-Mover Advantages or First-Mover Disadvantages

In some instances there are advantages *to being an adept follower* rather than a first mover. Late-mover advantages (or *first-mover disadvantages*) arise in four instances:

-   When the costs of pioneering are high relative to the benefits accrued and imitative followers can achieve similar benefits with far lower costs. This is often the case when second movers can learn from a pioneer's experience and avoid making the same costly mistakes as the pioneer.

# Amazon.com's First-Mover Advantage in Online Retailing

Amazon.com's path to becoming the world's largest online retailer began in 1994 when Jeff Bezos, a Manhattan hedge fund analyst at the time, noticed that the number of Internet users was increasing by 2,300 percent annually. Bezos saw the tremendous growth as an opportunity to sell products online that would be demanded by a large number of Internet users and could be easily shipped. Bezos launched the online bookseller Amazon.com in 1995. The startup's revenues soared to $148 million in 1997, $610 million in 1998, and $1.6 billion in 1999. Bezos's business plan—hatched while on a cross-country trip with his wife in 1994—made him *Time* magazine's Person of the Year in 1999.

The volume-based and reputational benefits of Amazon.com's early entry into online retailing had delivered a first-mover advantage, but between 2000 and 2013 Bezos undertook a series of additional strategic initiatives to solidify the company's number-one ranking in the industry. Bezos undertook a massive building program in the late-1990s that added five new warehouses and fulfillment centers at a total cost of $300 million. The additional warehouse capacity was added years before it was needed, but Bezos wanted to move preemptively against potential rivals and ensure that, as demand continued to grow, the company could continue to offer its customers the best selection, the lowest prices, and the cheapest and most convenient delivery. The company also expanded its product line to include sporting goods, tools, toys, grocery items, electronics, and digital music downloads, giving it another means of maintaining its experience and scale-based advantages. Amazon.com's 2013 revenues of $74.5 billion not only made it the world's leading Internet retailer but made it larger than its 12 biggest competitors combined. As a result, Jeff Bezos's shares in Amazon.com made him the 12th wealthiest person in the United States, with an estimated net worth of $27.2 billion.

Moving down the learning curve in Internet retailing was not an entirely straightforward process for Amazon.com. Bezos commented in a *Fortune* article profiling the company, "We were investors in every bankrupt, 1999-vintage e-commerce startup. Pets.com, living.com, kozmo.com. We invested in a lot of high-profile flameouts." He went on to specify that although the ventures were a "waste of money," they "didn't take us off our own mission." Bezos also suggested that gaining advantage as a first mover is "taking a million tiny steps—and learning quickly from your missteps."

*Sources:* Mark Brohan, "The Top 500 Guide," *Internet Retailer,* June 2009, www.internetretailer.com (accessed June 17, 2009); Josh Quittner, "How Jeff Bezos Rules the Retail Space," *Fortune,* May 5, 2008, pp. 126–134; S. Banjo and P. Ziobro, "After Decades of Toil, Web Sales Remain Small for Many Retailers," *The Wall Street Journal* Online, August 27, 2013 (accessed March 2014); Company Snapshot, *Bloomberg Businessweek* Online (accessed March 28, 2014); Forbes.com; and company website.

- When an innovator's products are somewhat primitive and do not live up to buyer expectations, thus allowing a follower with better-performing products to win disenchanted buyers away from the leader.
- When rapid market evolution (due to fast-paced changes in either technology or buyer needs) gives second movers the opening to leapfrog a first mover's products with more attractive next-version products.
- When market uncertainties make it difficult to ascertain what will eventually succeed, allowing late movers to wait until these needs are clarified.
- When customer loyalty to the pioneer is low and a first mover's skills, know-how, and actions are easily copied or even surpassed

## To Be a First Mover or Not

In weighing the pros and cons of being a first mover versus a fast follower versus a late mover, it matters whether the race to market leadership in a particular industry is a marathon or a sprint. In marathons, a slow mover is not unduly penalized—first-mover advantages can be fleeting, and there's ample time for fast followers and sometimes even late movers to catch up.[13] Thus the speed at which the pioneering innovation is likely to catch on matters considerably as companies struggle with whether to pursue an emerging market opportunity aggressively (as a first mover) or cautiously (as a late mover). For instance, it took 5.5 years for worldwide mobile phone use to grow from 10 million to 100 million, and it took close to 10 years for the number of at-home broadband subscribers to grow to 100 million worldwide. The lesson here is that there is a market penetration curve for every emerging opportunity. Typically, the curve has an inflection point at which all the pieces of the business model fall into place, buyer demand explodes, and the market takes off. The inflection point can come early on a fast-rising curve (like the use of e-mail) or farther up on a slow-rising curve (like the use of broadband). Any company that seeks competitive advantage by being a first mover thus needs to ask some hard questions:

- Does market takeoff depend on the development of complementary products or services that currently are not available?
- Is new infrastructure required before buyer demand can surge?
- Will buyers need to learn new skills or adopt new behaviors?
- Will buyers encounter high switching costs in moving to the newly introduced product or service?
- Are there influential competitors in a position to delay or derail the efforts of a first mover?

When the answers to any of these questions are yes, then a company must be careful not to pour too many resources into getting ahead of the market opportunity—the race is likely going to be closer to a 10-year marathon than a 2-year sprint.[14] On the other hand, if the market is a winner-take-all type of market, where powerful first-mover advantages insulate early entrants from competition and prevent later movers from making any headway, then it may be best to move quickly despite the risks.

# STRENGTHENING A COMPANY'S MARKET POSITION VIA ITS SCOPE OF OPERATIONS

**CORE CONCEPT**

The **scope of the firm** refers to the range of activities that the firm performs internally, the breadth of its product and service offerings, the extent of its geographic market presence, and its mix of businesses.

Apart from considerations of competitive moves and their timing, there is another set of managerial decisions that can affect the strength of a company's market position. These decisions concern the scope of a company's operations—the breadth of its activities and the extent of its market reach. Decisions regarding the **scope of the firm** focus on which activities a firm will perform internally and which it will not.

Consider, for example, Ralph Lauren Corporation. In contrast to Rare Essentials, a boutique clothing store that sells apparel at a single retail store, Ralph Lauren designs, markets, and distributes fashionable apparel and other merchandise to more than 10,000 major department stores and specialty retailers throughout the world. In addition, it operates nearly 400 Ralph Lauren retail stores, more than

200 factory stores, and 7 e-commerce sites. Scope decisions also concern which segments of the market to serve—decisions that can include geographic market segments as well as product and service segments. Almost 40 percent of Ralph Lauren's sales are made outside the United States, and its product line includes apparel, fragrances, home furnishings, eyewear, watches and jewelry, and handbags and other leather goods. The company has also expanded its brand lineup through the acquisitions of Chaps menswear and casual retailer Club Monaco.

Decisions such as these, in essence, determine where the boundaries of a firm lie and the degree to which the operations within those boundaries cohere. They also have much to do with the direction and extent of a business's growth. In this chapter, we introduce the topic of company scope and discuss different types of scope decisions in relation to a company's business-level strategy. In the next two chapters, we develop two additional dimensions of a firm's scope. Chapter 7 focuses on international expansion— a matter of extending the company's geographic scope into foreign markets. Chapter 8 takes up the topic of corporate strategy, which concerns diversifying into a mix of different businesses. *Scope issues are at the very heart of corporate-level strategy.*

Several dimensions of firm scope have relevance for business-level strategy in terms of their capacity to strengthen a company's position in a given market. These include the firm's **horizontal scope,** which is the range of product and service segments that the firm serves within its product or service market. Mergers and acquisitions involving other market participants provide a means for a company to expand its horizontal scope. Expanding the firm's vertical scope by means of vertical integration can also affect the success of its market strategy. **Vertical scope** is the extent to which the firm engages in the various activities that make up the industry's entire value chain system, from initial activities such as raw-material production all the way to retailing and after-sale service activities. *Outsourcing decisions* concern another dimension of scope since they involve narrowing the firm's boundaries with respect to its participation in value chain activities. We discuss the pros and cons of each of these options in the sections that follow. Since *strategic alliances and partnerships* provide an alternative to vertical integration and acquisition strategies and are sometimes used to facilitate outsourcing, we conclude this chapter with a discussion of the benefits and challenges associated with *cooperative arrangements* of this nature.

> **CORE CONCEPT**
>
> **Horizontal scope** is the range of product and service segments that a firm serves within its focal market.

> **CORE CONCEPT**
>
> **Vertical scope** is the extent to which a firm's internal activities encompass the range of activities that make up an industry's entire value chain system, from raw-material production to final sales and service activities.

# HORIZONTAL MERGER AND ACQUISITION STRATEGIES

Mergers and acquisitions are much-used strategic options to strengthen a company's market position. A *merger* is the combining of two or more companies into a single corporate entity, with the newly created company often taking on a new name. An *acquisition* is a combination in which one company, the acquirer, purchases and absorbs the operations of another, the acquired. The difference between a merger and an acquisition relates more to the details of ownership, management control, and financial arrangements than to strategy and competitive advantage. The resources and competitive capabilities of the newly created enterprise end up much the same whether the combination is the result of an acquisition or a merger.

Horizontal mergers and acquisitions, which involve combining the operations of firms *within the same product or service market,* provide an effective means for firms to rapidly increase the scale and horizontal scope of their core business. For example,

> **LO 3**
>
> The strategic benefits and risks of expanding a company's horizontal scope through mergers and acquisitions.

the merger of AMR Corporation (parent of American Airlines) with US Airways has increased the airlines' scale of operations and extended their reach geographically to create the world's largest airline.

Merger and acquisition strategies typically set sights on achieving any of five objectives:[15]

1. *Creating a more cost-efficient operation out of the combined companies.* When a company acquires another company in the same industry, there's usually enough overlap in operations that less efficient plants can be closed or distribution and sales activities partly combined and downsized. Likewise, it is usually feasible to squeeze out cost savings in administrative activities, again by combining and downsizing such administrative activities as finance and accounting, information technology, human resources, and so on. The combined companies may also be able to reduce supply chain costs because of greater bargaining power over common suppliers and closer collaboration with supply chain partners. By helping to consolidate the industry and remove excess capacity, such combinations can also reduce industry rivalry and improve industry profitability.

2. *Expanding a company's geographic coverage.* One of the best and quickest ways to expand a company's geographic coverage is to acquire rivals with operations in the desired locations. Since a company's size increases with its geographic scope, another benefit is increased bargaining power with the company's suppliers or buyers. Greater geographic coverage can also contribute to product differentiation by enhancing a company's name recognition and brand awareness. Banks like JPMorgan Chase, Wells Fargo, and Bank of America have used acquisition strategies to establish a market presence and gain name recognition in an ever-growing number of states and localities. Food products companies like Nestlé, Kraft, Unilever, and Procter & Gamble have made acquisitions an integral part of their strategies to expand internationally.

3. *Extending the company's business into new product categories.* Many times a company has gaps in its product line that need to be filled in order to offer customers a more effective product bundle or the benefits of one-stop shopping. For example, customers might prefer to acquire a suite of software applications from a single vendor that can offer more integrated solutions to the company's problems. Acquisition can be a quicker and more potent way to broaden a company's product line than going through the exercise of introducing a company's own new product to fill the gap. Coca-Cola has increased the effectiveness of the product bundle it provides to retailers by acquiring beverage makers Minute Maid, Odwalla, Hi-C, and Glacéau Vitaminwater.

4. *Gaining quick access to new technologies or other resources and capabilities.* Making acquisitions to bolster a company's technological know-how or to expand its skills and capabilities allows a company to bypass a time-consuming and expensive internal effort to build desirable new resources and capabilities. From 2000 through May 2013, Cisco Systems purchased 106 companies to give it more technological reach and product breadth, thereby enhancing its standing as the world's largest provider of hardware, software, and services for creating and operating Internet networks.

5. *Leading the convergence of industries whose boundaries are being blurred by changing technologies and new market opportunities.* In fast-cycle industries or industries whose boundaries are changing, companies can use acquisition strategies to hedge their bets about the direction that an industry will take, to increase

their capacity to meet changing demands, and to respond flexibly to changing buyer needs and technological demands. News Corporation has prepared for the convergence of media services with the purchase of satellite TV companies to complement its media holdings in TV broadcasting (the Fox network and TV stations in various countries), cable TV (Fox News, Fox Sports, and FX), filmed entertainment (Twentieth Century Fox and Fox studios), newspapers, magazines, and book publishing.

Horizontal mergers and acquisitions can strengthen a firm's competitiveness in five ways: (1) by improving the efficiency of its operations, (2) by heightening its product differentiation, (3) by reducing market rivalry, (4) by increasing the company's bargaining power over suppliers and buyers, and (5) by enhancing its flexibility and dynamic capabilities.

Illustration Capsule 6.3 describes how Bristol-Myers Squibb developed its "string-of-pearls" horizontal acquisition strategy to fill in its pharmaceutical product development gaps.

## Why Mergers and Acquisitions Sometimes Fail to Produce Anticipated Results

Despite many successes, mergers and acquisitions do not always produce the hoped-for outcomes.[16] Cost savings may prove smaller than expected. Gains in competitive capabilities may take substantially longer to realize or, worse, may never materialize at all. Efforts to mesh the corporate cultures can stall due to formidable resistance from organization members. Key employees at the acquired company can quickly become disenchanted and leave; the morale of company personnel who remain can drop to disturbingly low levels because they disagree with newly instituted changes. Differences in management styles and operating procedures can prove hard to resolve. In addition, the managers appointed to oversee the integration of a newly acquired company can make mistakes in deciding which activities to leave alone and which activities to meld into their own operations and systems.

A number of mergers and acquisitions have been notably unsuccessful. The 2008 merger of Arby's and Wendy's is a prime example. After only three years, Wendy's decided to sell Arby's due to the roast beef sandwich chain's continued poor profit performance. The jury is still out on whether Microsoft's 2011 acquisition of Skype for $8.5 billion, the United-Continental airlines merger, and Google's $12.5 billion acquisition of cell phone manufacturer Motorola Mobility will prove to be moneymakers or money losers.

# VERTICAL INTEGRATION STRATEGIES

Expanding the firm's vertical scope by means of a vertical integration strategy provides another possible way to strengthen the company's position in its core market. A **vertically integrated firm** is one that participates in multiple stages of an industry's value chain system. Thus, if a manufacturer invests in facilities to produce component parts that it had formerly purchased from suppliers, or if it opens its own chain of retail stores to bypass its former distributors, it is engaging in vertical integration. A good example of a vertically integrated firm is Maple Leaf Foods, a major Canadian producer of fresh and processed meats whose best-selling brands include Maple Leaf

**LO 4**

The advantages and disadvantages of extending the company's scope of operations via vertical integration.

# Bristol-Myers Squibb's "String-of-Pearls" Horizontal Acquisition Strategy

Back in 2007, the pharmaceutical company Bristol-Myers Squibb had a problem: Its top-selling drugs, Plavix and Abilify, would go off patent by 2012 and its drug pipeline was nearly empty. Together these drugs (the first for heart attacks, the second for depression) accounted for nearly half of the company's sales. Not surprisingly, the company's stock price had stagnated and was underperforming that of its peers.

Developing new drugs is difficult: New drugs must be identified, tested in increasingly sophisticated trials, and approved by the Food and Drug Administration. On average, this process takes 13 years and costs $2 billion. The success rate is low: Only one drug in eight manages to pass through clinical testing. In 2007, Bristol-Myers Squibb had only six new drugs at the clinical testing stage.

At the time, many drug companies were diversifying into new markets like over-the-counter drugs to better manage drug development risk. Bristol-Myers Squibb's management pursued a different strategy: product diversification through horizontal acquisitions. Bristol-Myers Squibb targeted small companies in new treatment areas, with the objective of reducing new product development risk by betting on preidentified drugs. The small companies it targeted, with one or two drugs in development, needed cash; Bristol-Myers Squibb needed new drugs. The firm's management called this its "string-of-pearls" strategy.

To implement its approach and obtain the cash it needed, Bristol-Myers Squibb sold its stake in Mead Johnson, a nutritional supplement manufacturer. Then it went on a shopping spree. Starting in 2007, the

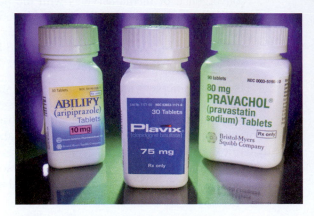

company spent over $8 billion on 18 transactions, including 12 horizontal acquisitions. In the process, the company acquired many promising new drug candidates for common diseases such as cancer, cardiovascular disease, rheumatoid arthritis, and hepatitis C.

By early 2012, the company's string-of-pearls acquisitions were estimated to have added over $4 billion of new revenue to the company's coffers. Despite management changes over the subsequent year leading to the loss of two of the visionaries of the "string-of-pearls" concept, the new R&D chief remained committed to continuing the strategy. Analysts reported that Bristol-Myers Squibb had one of the best pipelines among drug makers. Investors agreed: The company's stock price has climbed consistently since 2007, outperforming its competitors and experiencing annual growth of over 20 percent in early 2013.

*Note:* Developed with Dennis L. Huggins.

*Sources:* D. Armstrong and M. Tirrell, "Bristol's Buy of Inhibitex for Hepatitis Drug Won't Be Last," *Bloomberg Businessweek,* January 2012, **www.bloomberg.com** (accessed January 30, 2012); S. M. Paul et al., "How to Improve R&D Productivity: The Pharmaceutical Industry's Grand Challenge," *Nature Reviews,* March 2010, pp. 203–214; Bristol-Myers Squibb 2007 and 2011 annual reports; and D. Armstrong, "Bristol-Myers New R&D Chief Plans to Keep Focus on Cancer," *Bloomberg* Online, April 8, 2013.

---

and Schneiders. Maple Leaf Foods participates in hog and poultry production, with company-owned hog and poultry farms; it has its own meat-processing and rendering facilities; it packages its products and distributes them from company-owned distribution centers; and it conducts marketing, sales, and customer service activities for its wholesale and retail buyers but does not otherwise participate in the final stage of the meat-processing vertical chain—the retailing stage.

A vertical integration strategy can expand the firm's range of activities *backward* into sources of supply and/or *forward* toward end users. When Tiffany & Co., a manufacturer and retailer of fine jewelry, began sourcing, cutting, and polishing its own diamonds, it integrated backward along the diamond supply chain. Mining giant De Beers Group and Canadian miner Aber Diamond integrated forward when they entered the diamond retailing business.

A firm can pursue vertical integration by starting its own operations in other stages of the vertical activity chain or by acquiring a company already performing the activities it wants to bring in-house. Vertical integration strategies can aim at *full integration* (participating in all stages of the vertical chain) or *partial integration* (building positions in selected stages of the vertical chain). Firms can also engage in *tapered integration* strategies, which involve a mix of in-house and outsourced activity in any given stage of the vertical chain. Oil companies, for instance, supply their refineries with oil from their own wells as well as with oil that they purchase from other producers—they engage in tapered backward integration. Boston Beer Company, the maker of Samuel Adams, engages in tapered forward integration, since it operates brew-pubs but sells the majority of its products through third-party distributors.

## The Advantages of a Vertical Integration Strategy

Under the right conditions, a vertical integration strategy can add materially to a company's technological capabilities, strengthen the firm's competitive position, and boost its profitability.[17] But it is important to keep in mind that vertical integration has no real payoff strategy-wise or profit-wise unless the extra investment can be justified by compensating improvements in company costs, differentiation, or competitive strength.

**Integrating Backward to Achieve Greater Competitiveness**   It is harder than one might think to generate cost savings or improve profitability by integrating backward into activities such as the manufacture of parts and components (which could otherwise be purchased from suppliers with specialized expertise in making the parts and components). For **backward integration** to be a cost-saving and profitable strategy, a company must be able to (1) achieve the same scale economies as outside suppliers and (2) match or beat suppliers' production efficiency with no drop-off in quality. Neither outcome is easily achieved. To begin with, a company's in-house requirements are often too small to reach the optimum size for low-cost operation. For instance, if it takes a minimum production volume of 1 million units to achieve scale economies and a company's in-house requirements are just 250,000 units, then it falls far short of being able to match the costs of outside suppliers (which may readily find buyers for 1 million or more units). Furthermore, matching the production efficiency of suppliers is fraught with problems when suppliers have considerable production experience, when the technology they employ has elements that are hard to master, and/or when substantial R&D expertise is required to develop next-version components or keep pace with advancing technology in components production.

That said, occasions still arise when a company can improve its cost position and competitiveness by performing a broader range of industry value chain activities in-house rather than having such activities performed by outside suppliers. When there are few suppliers and when the item being supplied is a major component, vertical integration can lower costs by limiting supplier power. Vertical integration can also lower costs by facilitating the coordination of production flows and avoiding bottleneck problems. Furthermore, when a company has proprietary know-how that it wants to keep from rivals, then in-house performance of value-adding activities related to this know-how is beneficial even if such activities could otherwise be performed by outsiders.

**CORE CONCEPT**

**Backward integration** involves entry into activities previously performed by suppliers or other enterprises positioned along earlier stages of the industry value chain system; **forward integration** involves entry into value chain system activities closer to the end user.

Apple decided to integrate backward into producing its own chips for iPhones, chiefly because chips are a major cost component, suppliers have bargaining power, and in-house production would help coordinate design tasks and protect Apple's proprietary iPhone technology. International Paper Company backward integrates into pulp mills that it sets up near its paper mills and reaps the benefits of coordinated production flows, energy savings, and transportation economies. It does this, in part, because outside suppliers are generally unwilling to make a site-specific investment for a buyer.

Backward vertical integration can produce a differentiation-based competitive advantage when performing activities internally contributes to a better-quality product or service offering, improves the caliber of customer service, or in other ways enhances the performance of the final product. On occasion, integrating into more stages along the industry value chain system can add to a company's differentiation capabilities by allowing it to strengthen its core competencies, better master key skills or strategy-critical technologies, or add features that deliver greater customer value. Spanish clothing maker Inditex has backward integrated into fabric making, as well as garment design and manufacture, for its successful Zara brand. By tightly controlling the process and postponing dyeing until later stages, Zara can respond quickly to changes in fashion trends and supply its customers with the hottest items. NewsCorp backward integrated into film studios (Twentieth Century Fox) and TV program production to ensure access to high-quality content for its TV stations (and to limit supplier power).

### Integrating Forward to Enhance Competitiveness

Like backward integration, **forward integration** can lower costs by increasing efficiency and bargaining power. In addition, it can allow manufacturers to gain better access to end users, improve market visibility, and include the end user's purchasing experience as a differentiating feature. For example, Harley's company-owned retail stores are essentially little museums, filled with iconography, that provide an environment conducive to selling not only motorcycles and gear but also memorabilia, clothing, and other items featuring the brand. Insurance companies and brokerages like Allstate and Edward Jones have the ability to make consumers' interactions with local agents and office personnel a differentiating feature by focusing on building relationships.

In many industries, independent sales agents, wholesalers, and retailers handle competing brands of the same product and have no allegiance to any one company's brand—they tend to push whatever offers the biggest profits. To avoid dependence on distributors and dealers with divided loyalties, Goodyear has integrated forward into company-owned and franchised retail tire stores. Consumer-goods companies like Under Armour, Pepperidge Farm, Bath & Body Works, Nike, and Ann Taylor's have integrated forward into retailing and operate their own branded stores in factory outlet malls, enabling them to move overstocked items, slow-selling items, and seconds.

Some producers have opted to integrate forward by selling directly to customers at the company's website. Bypassing regular wholesale and retail channels in favor of direct sales and Internet retailing can have appeal if it reinforces the brand and enhances consumer satisfaction or if it lowers distribution costs, produces a relative cost advantage over certain rivals, and results in lower selling prices to end users. In addition, sellers are compelled to include the Internet as a retail channel when a sufficiently large number of buyers in an industry prefer to make purchases online. However, a company that is vigorously pursuing online sales to consumers at the same time that it is also heavily promoting sales to consumers through its network of wholesalers and retailers is *competing directly against its distribution allies.* Such actions constitute *channel conflict* and create a tricky route to negotiate. A company that is actively trying to expand online sales to consumers is signaling a weak strategic commitment to its dealers *and* a willingness to cannibalize dealers' sales and growth potential. The likely result is angry dealers and loss of dealer goodwill. Quite possibly, a company may stand to lose more sales by offending its dealers than it gains from its own online sales effort. Consequently, in industries where the strong support and goodwill of dealer networks is essential, companies may conclude that it is important to avoid channel conflict and that *their websites should be designed to partner with dealers rather than compete against them.*

## The Disadvantages of a Vertical Integration Strategy

Vertical integration has some substantial drawbacks beyond the potential for channel conflict.[18] The most serious drawbacks to vertical integration include the following concerns:

- Vertical integration raises a firm's capital investment in the industry, thereby *increasing business risk.*
- Vertically integrated companies are often *slow to embrace technological advances* or more efficient production methods when they are saddled with older technology or facilities. A company that obtains parts and components from outside suppliers can always shop the market for the newest, best, and cheapest parts, whereas a vertically integrated firm with older plants and technology may choose to continue making suboptimal parts rather than face the high costs of premature abandonment.
- Vertical integration can result in *less flexibility in accommodating shifting buyer preferences.* It is one thing to design out a component made by a supplier and another to design out a component being made in-house (which can mean laying off employees and writing off the associated investment in equipment and facilities). Integrating forward or backward locks a firm into relying on its own in-house activities and sources of supply.
- Vertical integration *may not enable a company to realize economies of scale* if its production levels are below the minimum efficient scale. Small companies in particular are likely to suffer a cost disadvantage by producing in-house.
- Vertical integration poses all kinds of *capacity-matching problems.* In motor vehicle manufacturing, for example, the most efficient scale of operation for making axles is different from the most economic volume for radiators, and different yet again for both engines and transmissions. Consequently, integrating across several production stages in ways that achieve the lowest feasible costs can be a monumental challenge.
- Integration forward or backward often *calls for developing new types of resources and capabilities.* Parts and components manufacturing, assembly operations, wholesale distribution and retailing, and direct sales via the Internet represent different kinds of businesses, operating in different types of industries, with different key success factors. Many manufacturers learn the hard way that company-owned wholesale and retail networks require skills that they lack, fit poorly with what they do best, and detract from their overall profit performance. Similarly, a company that tries to produce many components in-house is likely to find itself very hard-pressed to keep up with technological advances and cutting-edge production practices for each component used in making its product.

## Weighing the Pros and Cons of Vertical Integration

All in all, therefore, a strategy of vertical integration can have both strengths and weaknesses. The tip of the scales depends on (1) whether vertical integration can enhance the performance of strategy-critical activities in ways that lower cost, build expertise, protect proprietary know-how, or increase differentiation, (2) what impact vertical integration will have on investment costs, flexibility, and response times, (3) what administrative costs will be incurred by coordinating operations across more vertical chain activities, and (4) how difficult it will be for the company to acquire the set of skills and capabilities needed to operate in another stage of the vertical chain. *Vertical integration strategies have merit according to which capabilities and value-adding activities truly need to be performed in-house and which can be performed better or cheaper by outsiders.* Absent solid benefits, integrating forward or backward is not likely to be an attractive strategy option.

Kaiser Permanente, the largest managed care organization in the United States, has made vertical integration a central part of its strategy, as described in Illustration Capsule 6.4.

## OUTSOURCING STRATEGIES: NARROWING THE SCOPE OF OPERATIONS

**LO 5**

The conditions that favor farming out certain value chain activities to outside parties.

**CORE CONCEPT**

**Outsourcing** involves contracting out certain value chain activities that are normally performed in-house to outside vendors.

In contrast to vertical integration strategies, outsourcing strategies narrow the scope of a business's operations, in terms of what activities are performed internally. **Outsourcing** involves contracting out certain value chain activities that are normally performed in-house to outside vendors.[19] Many PC makers, for example, have shifted from assembling units in-house to outsourcing the entire assembly process to manufacturing specialists, which can operate more efficiently due to their greater scale, experience, and bargaining power over components makers. Nike has outsourced most of its manufacturing-related value chain activities, so it can concentrate on marketing and managing its brand.

Outsourcing certain value chain activities makes strategic sense whenever:

- *An activity can be performed better or more cheaply by outside specialists.* A company should generally *not* perform any value chain activity internally that can be performed more efficiently or effectively by outsiders—the chief exception occurs when a particular activity is strategically crucial and internal control over that activity is deemed essential. Dolce & Gabbana, for example, contracts out the production of sunglasses under its label to Luxottica—the world's best sunglass manufacturing company, known for its Oakley and Ray-Ban brands.

- *The activity is not crucial to the firm's ability to achieve sustainable competitive advantage.* Outsourcing of support activities such as maintenance services, data processing, data storage, fringe-benefit management, and website operations has become commonplace. Colgate-Palmolive, for instance, has been able to reduce its information technology operational costs by more than 10 percent per year through an outsourcing agreement with IBM.

- *The outsourcing improves organizational flexibility and speeds time to market.* Outsourcing gives a company the flexibility to switch suppliers in the event that its present supplier falls behind competing suppliers. Moreover, seeking out new suppliers with the needed capabilities already in place is frequently quicker, easier,

# Kaiser Permanente's Vertical Integration Strategy

Kaiser Permanente's unique business model features a vertical integration strategy that enables it to deliver higher-quality care to patients at a lower cost. Kaiser Permanente is the largest vertically integrated health care delivery system in the United States, with $53.1 billion in revenues and $2.7 billion in net income in 2013. It functions as a health insurance company with over 9 million members and a provider of health care services with 37 hospitals, 618 medical offices, and more than 17,000 physicians. As a result of its vertical integration, Kaiser Permanente is better able to efficiently match demand for services by health plan members to capacity of its delivery infrastructure, including physicians and hospitals. Moreover, its prepaid financial model helps to incentivize the appropriate delivery of health care services.

Unlike Kaiser Permanente, the majority of physicians and hospitals in the United States provide care on a fee-for-service revenue model or per-procedure basis. Consequently, most physicians and hospitals earn higher revenues by providing more services, which limits investments in preventive care. In contrast, Kaiser Permanente providers are incentivized to focus on health promotion, disease prevention, and chronic disease management. Kaiser Permanente pays primary care physicians more than local averages to attract top talent, and surgeons are salaried rather than paid by procedure to encourage the optimal level of care. Physicians from multiple specialties work collaboratively to coordinate care and treat the overall health of patients rather than individual health issues.

One result of this strategy is enhanced efficiency, enabling Kaiser Permanente to provide health insurance that is, on average, 10 percent cheaper than that of its competitors. Further, the care provided is of higher quality based on national standards of care. For the sixth year in a row, Kaiser Permanente health plans received the highest overall quality-of-care rating of any

health plan in California, which accounts for 7 million of its 9 million members. Kaiser Permanente is also consistently praised for member satisfaction. Four of Kaiser's health plan regions, accounting for 90 percent of its membership, were ranked highest in member satisfaction by J.D. Power and Associates. The success of Kaiser Permanente's vertical integration strategy is the primary reason why many health care organizations are seeking to replicate its model as they transition from a fee-for-service revenue model to an accountable care model.

*Note:* Developed with Christopher C. Sukenik.

*Sources:* "Kaiser Foundation Hospitals and Health Plan Report Fiscal Year 2013 and Fourth Quarter Financial Results," *PRNewswire*, February 14, 2014, www.prnewswire.com; Kaiser Permanente website and 2012 annual report; and J. O'Donnell, "Kaiser Permanente CEO on Saving Lives, Money," *USA Today,* October 23, 2012.

less risky, and cheaper than hurriedly retooling internal operations to replace obsolete capabilities or trying to install and master new technologies.

- *It reduces the company's risk exposure to changing technology and buyer preferences.* When a company outsources certain parts, components, and services, its suppliers must bear the burden of incorporating state-of-the-art technologies and/or undertaking redesigns and upgrades to accommodate a company's plans to introduce next-generation products. If what a supplier provides falls out of favor with buyers, or is rendered unnecessary by technological change, it is the supplier's business that suffers rather than the company's.

- *It allows a company to concentrate on its core business, leverage its key resources, and do even better what it already does best.* A company is better able to enhance its own capabilities when it concentrates its full resources and energies on performing only those activities. United Colors of Benetton and Sisley, for example, outsource the production of handbags and other leather goods while devoting their energies to the clothing lines for which they are known. Apple outsources production of its iPod, iPhone, and iPad models to Chinese contract manufacturer Foxconn and concentrates in-house on design, marketing, and innovation.

### The Risk of Outsourcing Value Chain Activities

*The biggest danger of outsourcing is that a company will farm out the wrong types of activities and thereby hollow out its own capabilities.*[20] For example, in recent years, companies anxious to reduce operating costs have opted to outsource such strategically important activities as product development, engineering design, and sophisticated manufacturing tasks—the very capabilities that underpin a company's ability to lead sustained product innovation. While these companies have apparently been able to lower their operating costs by outsourcing these functions to outsiders, *their ability to lead the development of innovative new products is weakened because so many of the cutting-edge ideas and technologies for next-generation products come from outsiders.*

A company must guard against outsourcing activities that hollow out the resources and capabilities that it needs to be a master of its own destiny.

Another risk of outsourcing comes from the lack of direct control. It may be difficult to monitor, control, and coordinate the activities of outside parties via contracts and arm's-length transactions alone. Unanticipated problems may arise that cause delays or cost overruns and become hard to resolve amicably. Moreover, contract-based outsourcing can be problematic because outside parties lack incentives to make investments specific to the needs of the outsourcing company's internal value chain.

Companies like Cisco Systems are alert to these dangers. Cisco guards against loss of control and protects its manufacturing expertise by designing the production methods that its contract manufacturers must use. Cisco keeps the source code for its designs proprietary, thereby controlling the initiation of all improvements and safeguarding its innovations from imitation. Further, Cisco uses the Internet to monitor the factory operations of contract manufacturers around the clock so that it knows immediately when problems arise and can decide whether to get involved.

## STRATEGIC ALLIANCES AND PARTNERSHIPS

Strategic alliances and cooperative partnerships provide one way to gain some of the benefits offered by vertical integration, outsourcing, and horizontal mergers and acquisitions while minimizing the associated problems. Companies frequently engage in cooperative strategies as an alternative to vertical integration or horizontal mergers and acquisitions. Increasingly, companies are also employing strategic alliances and partnerships to extend their scope of operations via international expansion and diversification strategies, as we describe in Chapters 7 and 8. Strategic alliances and cooperative arrangements are now a common means of narrowing a company's scope of operations as well, serving as a useful way to manage outsourcing (in lieu of traditional, purely price-oriented contracts).

For example, oil and gas companies engage in considerable vertical integration—but Shell Oil Company and Pemex (Mexico's state-owned petroleum company) have found that joint ownership of their Deer Park Refinery in Texas lowers their investment costs and risks in comparison to going it alone. The colossal failure of the Daimler-Chrysler merger formed an expensive lesson for Daimler AG about what can go wrong with horizontal mergers and acquisitions; its 2010 strategic alliance with Renault-Nissan is allowing the two companies to achieve jointly the global scale required for cost competitiveness in cars and trucks while avoiding the type of problems that so plagued Daimler-Chrysler. In 2013, Ford Motor Company joined Daimler and Renault-Nissan in an effort to develop affordable, mass-market hydrogen fuel cell vehicles by 2017.

Many companies employ strategic alliances to manage the problems that might otherwise occur with outsourcing—Cisco's system of alliances guards against loss of control, protects its proprietary manufacturing expertise, and enables the company to monitor closely the assembly operations of its partners while devoting its energy to designing new generations of the switches, routers, and other Internet-related equipment for which it is known.

A **strategic alliance** is a formal agreement between two or more separate companies in which they agree to work collaboratively toward some strategically relevant objective. Typically, they involve shared financial responsibility, joint contribution of resources and capabilities, shared risk, shared control, and mutual dependence. They may be characterized by cooperative marketing, sales, or distribution; joint production; design collaboration; or projects to jointly develop new technologies or products. They can vary in terms of their duration and the extent of the collaboration; some are intended as long-term arrangements, involving an extensive set of cooperative activities, while others are designed to accomplish more limited, short-term objectives.

Collaborative arrangements may entail a contractual agreement, but they commonly stop short of formal ownership ties between the partners (although sometimes an alliance member will secure minority ownership of another member). A special type of strategic alliance involving ownership ties is the **joint venture**. A joint venture entails forming a *new corporate entity that is jointly owned* by two or more companies that agree to share in the revenues, expenses, and control of the newly formed entity. Since joint ventures involve setting up a mutually owned business, they tend to be more durable but also riskier than other arrangements. In other types of strategic alliances, the collaboration between the partners involves a much less rigid structure in which the partners retain their independence from one another. If a strategic alliance is not working out, a partner can choose to simply walk away or reduce its commitment to collaborating at any time.

An alliance becomes "strategic," as opposed to just a convenient business arrangement, when it serves any of the following purposes:[21]

1. It facilitates achievement of an important business objective (like lowering costs or delivering more value to customers in the form of better quality, added features, and greater durability).

2. It helps build, strengthen, or sustain a core competence or competitive advantage.

**LO 6**

When and how strategic alliances can substitute for horizontal mergers and acquisitions or vertical integration and how they can facilitate outsourcing.

**CORE CONCEPT**

A **strategic alliance** is a formal agreement between two or more separate companies in which they agree to work cooperatively toward some common objective.

**CORE CONCEPT**

A **joint venture** is a partnership involving the establishment of an independent corporate entity that the partners own and control jointly, sharing in its revenues and expenses.

3. It helps remedy an important resource deficiency or competitive weakness.

4. It helps defend against a competitive threat, or mitigates a significant risk to a company's business.

5. It increases bargaining power over suppliers or buyers.

6. It helps open up important new market opportunities.

7. It speeds the development of new technologies and/or product innovations.

Strategic cooperation is a much-favored approach in industries where new technological developments are occurring at a furious pace along many different paths and where advances in one technology spill over to affect others (often blurring industry boundaries). Whenever industries are experiencing high-velocity technological advances in many areas simultaneously, firms find it virtually essential to have cooperative relationships with other enterprises to stay on the leading edge of technology, even in their own area of specialization. In industries like these, alliances are all about fast cycles of learning, gaining quick access to the latest round of technological know-how, and developing dynamic capabilities. In bringing together firms with different skills and knowledge bases, alliances open up learning opportunities that help partner firms better leverage their own resources and capabilities.[22]

It took a $3.2 billion joint venture involving the likes of Sprint-Nextel, Clearwire, Intel, Time Warner Cable, Google, Comcast, and Bright House Networks to roll out next-generation 4G wireless services based on Sprint's and Clearwire's WiMax mobile networks. WiMax was an advanced Wi-Fi technology that allowed people to browse the Internet at speeds as great as 10 times faster than other cellular Wi-Fi technologies. The venture was a necessity for Sprint-Nextel and Clearwire since they lacked the financial resources to handle the rollout on their own. The appeal of the partnership for Time Warner, Comcast, and Bright House was the ability to bundle the sale of wireless services to their cable customers, while Intel had the chip sets for WiMax and

hoped that WiMax would become the dominant wireless Internet format. Google's interest in the alliance was its desire to strengthen its lead in desktop searches on wireless devices.

Clear Channel Communications has entered into a series of partnerships to provide a multiplatform launchpad for artists like Taylor Swift, Phoenix, and Sara Bareilles. In 2010, Clear Channel partnered with MySpace, Hulu, and the artist management company 19 Entertainment for *If I Can Dream,* an original reality series in which unsigned musicians and actors share a "real world"–style house in Los Angeles and document their attempts at stardom. Clear Channel helped promote the show by conducting exclusive radio interviews and performances with the talent, which in turn helped the show become a top-30 weekly program on Hulu.[23]

Because of the varied benefits of strategic alliances, many large corporations have become involved in 30 to 50 alliances, and a number have formed hundreds of alliances. Genentech, a leader in biotechnology and human genetics, has formed R&D alliances with over 30 companies to boost its prospects for developing new cures for various diseases and ailments. Companies that have formed a host of alliances need to manage their alliances like a portfolio—terminating those that no longer serve a useful purpose or that have produced meager results, forming promising new alliances, and restructuring existing alliances to correct performance problems and/or redirect the collaborative effort.

# Capturing the Benefits of Strategic Alliances

The extent to which companies benefit from entering into alliances and partnerships seems to be a function of six factors:[24]

1. *Picking a good partner.* A good partner must bring complementary strengths to the relationship. To the extent that alliance members have nonoverlapping strengths, there is greater potential for synergy and less potential for coordination problems and conflict. In addition, a good partner needs to share the company's vision about the overall purpose of the alliance and to have specific goals that either match or complement those of the company. Strong partnerships also depend on good chemistry among key personnel and compatible views about how the alliance should be structured and managed.

2. *Being sensitive to cultural differences.* Cultural differences among companies can make it difficult for their personnel to work together effectively. Cultural differences can be problematic among companies from the same country, but when the partners have different national origins, the problems are often magnified. Unless there is respect among all the parties for cultural differences, including those stemming from different local cultures and local business practices, productive working relationships are unlikely to emerge.

3. *Recognizing that the alliance must benefit both sides.* Information must be shared as well as gained, and the relationship must remain forthright and trustful. If either partner plays games with information or tries to take advantage of the other, the resulting friction can quickly erode the value of further collaboration. Open, trustworthy behavior on both sides is essential for fruitful collaboration.

4. *Ensuring that both parties live up to their commitments.* Both parties have to deliver on their commitments for the alliance to produce the intended benefits. The division of work has to be perceived as fairly apportioned, and the caliber of the benefits received on both sides has to be perceived as adequate.

5. *Structuring the decision-making process so that actions can be taken swiftly when needed.* In many instances, the fast pace of technological and competitive changes dictates an equally fast decision-making process. If the parties get bogged down in discussions or in gaining internal approval from higher-ups, the alliance can turn into an anchor of delay and inaction.

6. *Managing the learning process and then adjusting the alliance agreement over time to fit new circumstances.* One of the keys to long-lasting success is adapting the nature and structure of the alliance to be responsive to shifting market conditions, emerging technologies, and changing customer requirements. Wise allies are quick to recognize the merit of an evolving collaborative arrangement, where adjustments are made to accommodate changing conditions and to overcome whatever problems arise in establishing an effective working relationship.

Most alliances that aim at sharing technology or providing market access turn out to be temporary, lasting only a few years. This is not necessarily an indicator of failure, however. Strategic alliances can be terminated after a few years simply because they have fulfilled their purpose; indeed, many alliances are intended to be of limited duration, set up to accomplish specific short-term objectives. Longer-lasting collaborative arrangements, however, may provide even greater strategic benefits. Alliances are more likely to be long-lasting when (1) they involve collaboration with partners that do not compete directly, such as suppliers or distribution allies, (2) a trusting relationship has been established, and (3) both parties conclude that continued collaboration is in their mutual interest, perhaps because new opportunities for learning are emerging.

## The Drawbacks of Strategic Alliances and Partnerships

While strategic alliances provide a way of obtaining the benefits of vertical integration, mergers and acquisitions, and outsourcing, they also suffer from some of the same drawbacks. Anticipated gains may fail to materialize due to an overly optimistic view of the synergies or a poor fit in terms of the combination of resources and capabilities. When outsourcing is conducted via alliances, there is no less risk of becoming dependent on other companies for essential expertise and capabilities—indeed, this may be the Achilles' heel of such alliances. Moreover, there are additional pitfalls to collaborative arrangements. The greatest danger is that a partner will gain access to a company's proprietary knowledge base, technologies, or trade secrets, enabling the partner to match the company's core strengths and costing the company its hard-won competitive advantage. This risk is greatest when the alliance is among industry rivals or when the alliance is for the purpose of collaborative R&D, since this type of partnership requires an extensive exchange of closely held information.

The question for managers is when to engage in a strategic alliance and when to choose an alternative means of meeting their objectives. The answer to this question depends on the relative advantages of each method and the circumstances under which each type of organizational arrangement is favored.

The principal advantages of strategic alliances over vertical integration or horizontal mergers and acquisitions are threefold:

1. They lower investment costs and risks for each partner by facilitating resource pooling and risk sharing. This can be particularly important when investment needs and uncertainty are high, such as when a dominant technology standard has not yet emerged.

2. They are more flexible organizational forms and allow for a more adaptive response to changing conditions. Flexibility is essential when environmental conditions or technologies are changing rapidly. Moreover, strategic alliances under such circumstances may enable the development of each partner's dynamic capabilities.

3. They are more rapidly deployed—a critical factor when speed is of the essence. Speed is of the essence when there is a winner-take-all type of competitive situation, such as the race for a dominant technological design or a race down a steep experience curve, where there is a large first-mover advantage.

The key advantages of using strategic alliances rather than arm's-length transactions to manage outsourcing are (1) the increased ability to exercise control over the partners' activities and (2) a greater willingness for the partners to make relationship-specific investments. Arm's-length transactions discourage such investments since they imply less commitment and do not build trust.

On the other hand, there are circumstances when other organizational mechanisms are preferable to alliances and partnering. Mergers and acquisitions are especially suited for situations in which strategic alliances or partnerships do not go far enough in providing a company with access to needed resources and capabilities. Ownership ties are more permanent than partnership ties, allowing the operations of the merger or acquisition participants to be tightly integrated and creating more in-house control and autonomy. Other organizational mechanisms are also preferable to alliances when there is limited property rights protection for valuable know-how and when companies fear being taken advantage of by opportunistic partners.

While it is important for managers to understand when strategic alliances and partnerships are most likely (and least likely) to prove useful, it is also important to know how to manage them.

## How to Make Strategic Alliances Work

A surprisingly large number of alliances never live up to expectations. Even though the number of strategic alliances increases by about 25 percent annually, about 60 to 70 percent of alliances continue to fail each year.[25] The success of an alliance depends on how well the partners work together, their capacity to respond and adapt to changing internal and external conditions, and their willingness to renegotiate the bargain if circumstances so warrant. A successful alliance requires real in-the-trenches collaboration, not merely an arm's-length exchange of ideas. Unless partners place a high value on the contribution each brings to the alliance and the cooperative arrangement results in valuable win-win outcomes, it is doomed to fail.

While the track record for strategic alliances is poor on average, many companies have learned how to manage strategic alliances successfully and routinely defy this average. Samsung Group, which includes Samsung Electronics, successfully manages an ecosystem of over 1,300 partnerships that enable productive activities from global procurement to local marketing to collaborative R&D. Companies that have greater success in managing their strategic alliances and partnerships often credit the following factors:

- *They create a system for managing their alliances.* Companies need to manage their alliances in a systematic fashion, just as they manage other functions. This means setting up a process for managing the different aspects of alliance management from partner selection to alliance termination procedures. To ensure that the system is followed on a routine basis by all company managers, many companies create a set of explicit procedures, process templates, manuals, or the like.

- *They build relationships with their partners and establish trust.* Establishing strong interpersonal relationships is a critical factor in making strategic alliances work since such relationships facilitate opening up channels of communication, coordinating activity, aligning interests, and building trust.

- *They protect themselves from the threat of opportunism by setting up safeguards.* There are a number of means for preventing a company from being taken advantage of by an untrustworthy partner or unwittingly losing control over key assets. Contractual safeguards, including noncompete clauses, can provide other forms of protection.

- *They make commitments to their partners and see that their partners do the same.* When partners make credible commitments to a joint enterprise, they have stronger incentives for making it work and are less likely to "free-ride" on the efforts of other partners. Because of this, equity-based alliances tend to be more successful than nonequity alliances.[26]

- *They make learning a routine part of the management process.* There are always opportunities for learning from a partner, but organizational learning does not take place automatically. Whatever learning occurs cannot add to a company's knowledge base unless the learning is incorporated systematically into the company's routines and practices.

Finally, managers should realize that alliance management is an organizational capability, much like any other. It develops over time, out of effort, experience, and learning. For this reason, it is wise to begin slowly, with simple alliances designed to meet limited, short-term objectives. Short-term partnerships that are successful often become the basis for much more extensive collaborative arrangements. Even when strategic alliances are set up with the hope that they will become long-term engagements, they have a better chance of succeeding if they are phased in so that the partners can learn how they can work together most fruitfully.

## KEY POINTS

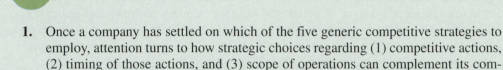

1. Once a company has settled on which of the five generic competitive strategies to employ, attention turns to how strategic choices regarding (1) competitive actions, (2) timing of those actions, and (3) scope of operations can complement its competitive approach and maximize the power of its overall strategy.

2. Strategic offensives should, as a general rule, be grounded in a company's strategic assets and employ a company's strengths to attack rivals in the competitive areas where they are weakest.

3. Companies have a number of offensive strategy options for improving their market positions: using a cost-based advantage to attack competitors on the basis of price or value, leapfrogging competitors with next-generation technologies, pursuing continuous product innovation, adopting and improving the best ideas of others, using hit-and-run tactics to steal sales away from unsuspecting rivals, and launching preemptive strikes. A blue-ocean type of offensive strategy seeks to gain a dramatic new competitive advantage by inventing a new industry or distinctive market segment that renders existing competitors largely irrelevant and allows a company to create and capture altogether new demand.

4. The purposes of defensive strategies are to lower the risk of being attacked, weaken the impact of any attack that occurs, and influence challengers to aim their efforts at other rivals. Defensive strategies to protect a company's position usually take one of two forms: (1) actions to block challengers or (2) actions to signal the likelihood of strong retaliation.

5. The timing of strategic moves also has relevance in the quest for competitive advantage. Company managers are obligated to carefully consider the advantages or disadvantages that attach to being a first mover versus a fast follower versus a late mover.

6. Decisions concerning the scope of a company's operations—which activities a firm will perform internally and which it will not—can also affect the strength of a company's market position. The *scope of the firm* refers to the range of its activities, the breadth of its product and service offerings, the extent of its geographic market presence, and its mix of businesses. Companies can expand their scope horizontally (more broadly within their focal market) or vertically (up or down the industry value chain system that starts with raw-material production and ends with sales and service to the end consumer). Horizontal mergers and acquisitions (combinations of market rivals) provide a means for a company to expand its horizontal scope. Vertical integration expands a firm's vertical scope.

7. Horizontal mergers and acquisitions typically have any of five objectives: lowering costs, expanding geographic coverage, adding product categories, gaining new technologies or other resources and capabilities, and preparing for the convergence of industries. They can strengthen a firm's competitiveness in five ways: (1) by improving the efficiency of its operations, (2) by heightening its product differentiation, (3) by reducing market rivalry, (4) by increasing the company's bargaining power over suppliers and buyers, and (5) by enhancing its flexibility and dynamic capabilities.

8. Vertical integration, forward or backward, makes most strategic sense if it strengthens a company's position via either cost reduction or creation of a differentiation-based advantage. Otherwise, the drawbacks of vertical integration (increased investment, greater business risk, increased vulnerability to technological changes, less flexibility in making product changes, and the potential for channel conflict) are likely to outweigh any advantages.

9. Outsourcing involves contracting out pieces of the value chain formerly performed in-house to outside vendors, thereby narrowing the scope of the firm. Outsourcing can enhance a company's competitiveness whenever (1) an activity can be performed better or more cheaply by outside specialists; (2) the activity is not crucial to the firm's ability to achieve sustainable competitive advantage; (3) the outsourcing improves organizational flexibility, speeds decision making, and cuts cycle time; (4) it reduces the company's risk exposure; and (5) it permits a company to concentrate on its core business and focus on what it does best.

10. Strategic alliances and cooperative partnerships provide one way to gain some of the benefits offered by vertical integration, outsourcing, and horizontal mergers and acquisitions while minimizing the associated problems. They serve as an alternative to vertical integration and mergers and acquisitions; they serve as a supplement to outsourcing, allowing more control relative to outsourcing via arm's-length transactions.

11. Companies that manage their alliances well generally (1) create a system for managing their alliances, (2) build relationships with their partners and establish trust, (3) protect themselves from the threat of opportunism by setting up safeguards, (4) make commitments to their partners and see that their partners do the same, and (5) make learning a routine part of the management process.

## ASSURANCE OF LEARNING EXERCISES

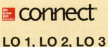

1. Live Nation operates music venues, provides management services to music artists, and promotes more than 22,000 live music events annually. The company merged with Ticketmaster and acquired concert and festival promoters in the United States, Australia, and Great Britain. How has the company used horizontal mergers and acquisitions to strengthen its competitive position? Are these moves primarily offensive or defensive? Has either Live Nation or Ticketmaster achieved any type of advantage based on the timing of its strategic moves?

**LO 1, LO 2, LO 3**

**connect**

**LO 4**
2. Kaiser Permanente, a standout among managed health care systems, has become a model of how to deliver good health care cost-effectively. Illustration Capsule 6.4 describes how Kaiser Permanente has made vertical integration a central part of its strategy. What value chain segments has Kaiser Permanente chosen to enter and perform internally? How has vertical integration aided the organization in building competitive advantage? Has vertical integration strengthened its market position? Explain why or why not.

**LO 5**
3. Perform an Internet search to identify at least two companies in different industries that have entered into outsourcing agreements with firms with specialized services. In addition, describe what value chain activities the companies have chosen to outsource. Do any of these outsourcing agreements seem likely to threaten any of the companies' competitive capabilities?

**LO 6**
4. Using your university library's subscription to LexisNexis, EBSCO, or a similar database, find two examples of how companies have relied on strategic alliances or joint ventures to substitute for horizontal or vertical integration.

# EXERCISE FOR SIMULATION PARTICIPANTS

**LO 1, LO 2**
1. Has your company relied more on offensive or defensive strategies to achieve your rank in the industry? What options for being a first mover does your company have? Do any of these first-mover options hold competitive advantage potential?

**LO 3**
2. Does your company have the option to merge with or acquire other companies? If so, which rival companies would you like to acquire or merge with?

**LO 4**
3. Is your company vertically integrated? Explain.

**LO 5, LO 6**
4. Is your company able to engage in outsourcing? If so, what do you see as the pros and cons of outsourcing? Are strategic alliances involved? Explain.

# ENDNOTES

[1] George Stalk, Jr., and Rob Lachenauer, "Hardball: Five Killer Strategies for Trouncing the Competition," *Harvard Business Review* 82, no. 4 (April 2004); Richard D'Aveni, "The Empire Strikes Back: Counterrevolutionary Strategies for Industry Leaders," *Harvard Business Review* 80, no. 11 (November 2002); David J. Bryce and Jeffrey H. Dyer, "Strategies to Crack Well-Guarded Markets," *Harvard Business Review* 85, no. 5 (May 2007).

[2] George Stalk, "Playing Hardball: Why Strategy Still Matters," *Ivey Business Journal* 69, no.2 (November–December 2004), pp. 1–2; W. J. Ferrier, K. G. Smith, and C. M. Grimm, "The Role of Competitive Action in Market Share Erosion and Industry Dethronement: A Study

of Industry Leaders and Challengers," *Academy of Management Journal* 42, no. 4 (August 1999), pp. 372–388.

[3] David B. Yoffie and Mary Kwak, "Mastering Balance: How to Meet and Beat a Stronger Opponent," *California Management Review* 44, no. 2 (Winter 2002), pp. 8–24.

[4] Ian C. MacMillan, Alexander B. van Putten, and Rita Gunther McGrath, "Global Gamesmanship," *Harvard Business Review* 81, no. 5 (May 2003); Ashkay R. Rao, Mark E. Bergen, and Scott Davis, "How to Fight a Price War," *Harvard Business Review* 78, no. 2 (March–April 2000).

[5] D. B. Yoffie and M. A. Cusumano, "Judo Strategy— the Competitive Dynamics of

Internet Time," *Harvard Business Review* 77, no. 1 (January–February 1999), pp. 70–81.

[6] Ming-Jer Chen and Donald C. Hambrick, "Speed, Stealth, and Selective Attack: How Small Firms Differ from Large Firms in Competitive Behavior," *Academy of Management Journal* 38, no. 2 (April 1995), pp. 453–482; William E. Rothschild, "Surprise and the Competitive Advantage," *Journal of Business Strategy* 4, no. 3 (Winter 1984), pp. 10–18.

[7] Ian MacMillan, "Preemptive Strategies," *Journal of Business Strategy* 14, no. 2 (Fall 1983), pp. 16–26.

[8] Ian C. MacMillan, "How Long Can You Sustain a Competitive Advantage?" in Liam Fahey (ed.), *The Strategic Planning Management*

*Reader* (Englewood Cliffs, NJ: Prentice Hall, 1989), pp. 23–24.

[9] Kevin P. Coyne and John Horn, "Predicting Your Competitor's Reactions," *Harvard Business Review* 87, no. 4 (April 2009), pp. 90–97.

[10] Philip Kotler, *Marketing Management,* 5th ed. (Englewood Cliffs, NJ: Prentice Hall, 1984).

[11] W. Chan Kim and Renée Mauborgne, "Blue Ocean Strategy," *Harvard Business Review* 82, no. 10 (October 2004), pp. 76–84.

[12] Jeffrey G. Covin, Dennis P. Slevin, and Michael B. Heeley, "Pioneers and Followers: Competitive Tactics, Environment, and Growth," *Journal of Business Venturing* 15, no. 2 (March 1999), pp. 175–210; Christopher A. Bartlett and Sumantra Ghoshal, "Going Global: Lessons from Late-Movers," *Harvard Business Review* 78, no. 2 (March–April 2000), pp. 132–145.

[13] Costas Markides and Paul A. Geroski, "Racing to Be 2nd: Conquering the Industries of the Future," *Business Strategy Review* 15, no. 4 (Winter 2004), pp. 25–31.

[14] Fernando Suarez and Gianvito Lanzolla, "The Half-Truth of First-Mover Advantage," *Harvard Business Review* 83, no. 4 (April 2005), pp. 121–127.

[15] Joseph L. Bower, "Not All M&As Are Alike—and That Matters," *Harvard Business Review* 79, no. 3 (March 2001); O. Chatain and P. Zemsky, "The Horizontal Scope of the Firm: Organizational Tradeoffs vs. Buyer-Supplier Relationships," *Management Science* 53, no. 4 (April 2007), pp. 550–565.

[16] Jeffrey H. Dyer, Prashant Kale, and Harbir Singh, "When to Ally and When to Acquire," *Harvard Business Review* 82, no. 4 (July–August 2004), pp. 109–110.

[17] John Stuckey and David White, "When and When Not to Vertically Integrate," *Sloan Management Review* (Spring 1993), pp. 71–83.

[18] Thomas Osegowitsch and Anoop Madhok, "Vertical Integration Is Dead, or Is It?" *Business Horizons* 46, no. 2 (March–April 2003), pp. 25–35.

[19] Ronan McIvor, "What Is the Right Outsourcing Strategy for Your Process?" *European Management Journal* 26, no. 1 (February 2008), pp. 24–34.

[20] Gary P. Pisano and Willy C. Shih, "Restoring American Competitiveness," *Harvard Business Review* 87, no. 7–8 (July–August 2009), pp. 114–125; Jérôme Barthélemy, "The Seven Deadly Sins of Outsourcing," *Academy of Management Executive* 17, no. 2 (May 2003), pp. 87–100.

[21] Jason Wakeam, "The Five Factors of a Strategic Alliance," *Ivey Business Journal* 68, no. 3 (May–June 2003), pp. 1–4.

[22] A. Inkpen, "Learning, Knowledge Acquisition, and Strategic Alliances," *European Management Journal* 16, no. 2 (April 1998), pp. 223–229.

[23] *Advertising Age,* May 24, 2010, p. 14.

[24] Patricia Anslinger and Justin Jenk, "Creating Successful Alliances," *Journal of Business Strategy* 25, no. 2 (2004), pp. 18–23; Rosabeth Moss Kanter, "Collaborative Advantage: The Art of the Alliance," *Harvard Business Review* 72, no. 4 (July–August 1994), pp. 96–108; Gary Hamel, Yves L. Doz, and C. K. Prahalad, "Collaborate with Your Competitors—and Win," *Harvard Business Review* 67, no. 1 (January–February 1989), pp. 133–139.

[25] Jonathan Hughes and Jeff Weiss, "Simple Rules for Making Alliances Work," *Harvard Business Review* 85, no. 11 (November 2007), pp. 122–131.

[26] Y. G. Pan and D. K. Tse, "The Hierarchical Model of Market Entry Modes," *Journal of International Business Studies* 31, no. 4 (2000), pp. 535–554.

# CHAPTER 7

# Strategies for Competing in International Markets

## Learning Objectives

THIS CHAPTER WILL HELP YOU UNDERSTAND:

**LO 1** The primary reasons companies choose to compete in international markets.

**LO 2** How and why differing market conditions across countries influence a company's strategy choices in international markets.

**LO 3** The five major strategic options for entering foreign markets.

**LO 4** The three main strategic approaches for competing internationally.

**LO 5** How companies are able to use international operations to improve overall competitiveness.

**LO 6** The unique characteristics of competing in developing-country markets.

> Profit is the most global aspect of a business, and it is cross-functional.
>
> Carlos Ghosn – *Chairman and CEO of Both Renault and Nissan*

> The response to the Starbucks brand has been phenomenal in our international markets.
>
> Howard Schultz – *Chairman and CEO of Starbucks*

> Globalization has changed us into a company that searches the world, not just to sell or to source, but to find intellectual capital—the world's best talents and greatest ideas.
>
> Jack Welch – *Former Chairman and CEO of GE*

Any company that aspires to industry leadership in the 21st century must think in terms of global, not domestic, market leadership. The world economy is globalizing at an accelerating pace as ambitious, growth-minded companies race to build stronger competitive positions in the markets of more and more countries, as countries previously closed to foreign companies open up their markets, and as information technology shrinks the importance of geographic distance. The forces of globalization are changing the competitive landscape in many industries, offering companies attractive new opportunities and at the same time introducing new competitive threats. Companies in industries where these forces are greatest are therefore under considerable pressure to come up with a strategy for competing successfully in international markets.

This chapter focuses on strategy options for expanding beyond domestic boundaries and competing in the markets of either a few or a great many countries. In the process of exploring these options, we introduce such concepts as multidomestic, transnational, and global strategies; the Porter diamond of national competitive advantage; and profit sanctuaries. The chapter also includes sections on cross-country differences in cultural, demographic, and market conditions; strategy options for entering foreign markets; the importance of locating value chain operations in the most advantageous countries; and the special circumstances of competing in developing markets such as those in China, India, Brazil, Russia, and eastern Europe.

## WHY COMPANIES DECIDE TO ENTER FOREIGN MARKETS

A company may opt to expand outside its domestic market for any of five major reasons:

**LO 1**

The primary reasons companies choose to compete in international markets.

1. *To gain access to new customers.* Expanding into foreign markets offers potential for increased revenues, profits, and long-term growth; it becomes an especially attractive option when a company encounters dwindling growth opportunities in

its home market. Companies often expand internationally to extend the life cycle of their products, as Honda has done with its classic 50-cc motorcycle, the Honda cub (which is still selling well in developing markets, more than 50 years after it was first introduced in Japan). A larger target market also offers companies the opportunity to earn a return on large investments more rapidly. This can be particularly important in R&D-intensive industries, where development is fast-paced or competitors imitate innovations rapidly.

2. *To achieve lower costs through economies of scale, experience, and increased purchasing power.* Many companies are driven to sell in more than one country because domestic sales volume alone is not large enough to capture fully economies of scale in product development, manufacturing, or marketing. Similarly, firms expand internationally to increase the rate at which they accumulate experience and move down the learning curve. International expansion can also lower a company's input costs through greater pooled purchasing power. The relatively small size of country markets in Europe and limited domestic volume explains why companies like Michelin, BMW, and Nestlé long ago began selling their products all across Europe and then moved into markets in North America and Latin America.

3. *To gain access to low-cost inputs of production.* Companies in industries based on natural resources (e.g., oil and gas, minerals, rubber, and lumber) often find it necessary to operate in the international arena since raw-material supplies are located in different parts of the world and can be accessed more cost-effectively at the source. Other companies enter foreign markets to access low-cost human resources; this is particularly true of industries in which labor costs make up a high proportion of total production costs.

4. *To further exploit its core competencies.* A company may be able to extend a market-leading position in its domestic market into a position of regional or global market leadership by leveraging its core competencies further. Walmart is capitalizing on its considerable expertise in discount retailing to expand into the United Kingdom, Japan, China, and Latin America. Walmart executives believe the company has tremendous growth opportunities in China. Companies can often leverage their resources internationally by replicating a successful business model, using it as a basic blueprint for international operations, as Starbucks and McDonald's have done.[1]

5. *To gain access to resources and capabilities located in foreign markets.* An increasingly important motive for entering foreign markets is to acquire resources and capabilities that may be unavailable in a company's home market. Companies often make acquisitions abroad or enter into cross-border alliances to gain access to capabilities that complement their own or to learn from their partners.[2] In other cases, companies choose to establish operations in other countries to utilize local distribution networks, gain local managerial or marketing expertise, or acquire technical knowledge.

In addition, companies that are the suppliers of other companies often expand internationally when their major customers do so, to meet their customers' needs abroad and retain their position as a key supply chain partner. Automotive parts suppliers, for example, have followed automobile manufacturers abroad, and retail-goods suppliers, such as Newell-Rubbermaid, have followed their discount retailer customers, such as Walmart, into foreign markets.

# WHY COMPETING ACROSS NATIONAL BORDERS MAKES STRATEGY MAKING MORE COMPLEX

Crafting a strategy to compete in one or more countries of the world is inherently more complex for five reasons. First, different countries have different home-country advantages in different industries; competing effectively requires an understanding of these differences. Second, there are location-based advantages to conducting particular value chain activities in different parts of the world. Third, different political and economic conditions make the general business climate more favorable in some countries than in others. Fourth, companies face risk due to adverse shifts in currency exchange rates when operating in foreign markets. And fifth, differences in buyer tastes and preferences present a challenge for companies concerning customizing versus standardizing their products and services.

## Home-Country Industry Advantages and the Diamond Model

Certain countries are known for their strengths in particular industries. For example, Chile has competitive strengths in industries such as copper, fruit, fish products, paper and pulp, chemicals, and wine. Japan is known for competitive strength in consumer electronics, automobiles, semiconductors, steel products, and specialty steel. Where industries are more likely to develop competitive strength depends on a set of factors that describe the nature of each country's business environment and vary from country to country. Because strong industries are made up of strong firms, the strategies of firms that expand internationally are usually grounded in one or more of these factors. The four major factors are summarized in a framework developed by Michael Porter and known as the *Diamond of National Competitive Advantage* (see Figure 7.1).[3]

**Demand Conditions**   The demand conditions in an industry's home market include the relative size of the market, its growth potential, and the nature of domestic buyers' needs and wants. Differing population sizes, income levels, and other demographic factors give rise to considerable differences in market size and growth rates from country to country. Industry sectors that are larger and more important in their home market tend to attract more resources and grow faster than others. For example, owing to widely differing population demographics and income levels, there is a far bigger market for luxury automobiles in the United States and Germany than in Argentina, India, Mexico, and China. At the same time, in developing markets like India, China, Brazil, and Malaysia, market growth potential is far higher than it is in the more mature economies of Britain, Denmark, Canada, and Japan. The potential for market growth in automobiles is explosive in China, where 2013 sales of new vehicles amounted to 18 million, surpassing U.S. sales of 15.6 million and making China the world's largest market for the fourth year in a row.[4] Demanding domestic buyers for an industry's products spur greater innovativeness and improvements in quality. Such conditions foster the development of stronger industries, with firms that are capable of translating a home-market advantage into a competitive advantage in the international arena.

## FIGURE 7.1    The Diamond of National Competitive Advantage

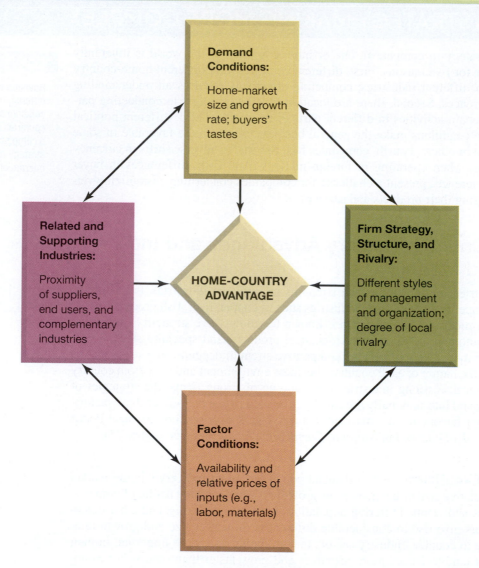

*Source:* Adapted from M. Porter, "The Competitive Advantage of Nations," *Harvard Business Review,* March–April 1990, pp. 73–93.

**Factor Conditions**    Factor conditions describe the availability, quality, and cost of raw materials and other inputs (called *factors of production*) that firms in an industry require for producing their products and services. The relevant factors of production vary from industry to industry but can include different types of labor, technical or managerial knowledge, land, financial capital, and natural resources. Elements of a country's infrastructure may be included as well, such as its transportation, communication, and banking systems. For instance, in India there are efficient, well-developed national channels for distributing groceries, personal care items, and other packaged products to the country's 3 million retailers, whereas in China distribution is primarily local and there is a limited national network for distributing most products. Competitively strong industries and firms develop where relevant factor conditions are favorable.

**Related and Supporting Industries**   Robust industries often develop in locales where there is a cluster of related industries, including others within the same value chain system (e.g., suppliers of components and equipment, distributors) and the makers of complementary products or those that are technologically related. The sports car makers Ferrari and Maserati, for example, are located in an area of Italy known as the "engine technological district," which includes other firms involved in racing, such as Ducati Motorcycles, along with hundreds of small suppliers. The advantage to firms that develop as part of a related-industry cluster comes from the close collaboration with key suppliers and the greater knowledge sharing throughout the cluster, resulting in greater efficiency and innovativeness.

**Firm Strategy, Structure, and Rivalry**   Different country environments foster the development of different styles of management, organization, and strategy. For example, strategic alliances are a more common strategy for firms from Asian or Latin American countries, which emphasize trust and cooperation in their organizations, than for firms from North America, where individualism is more influential. In addition, countries vary in terms of the competitive rivalry of their industries. Fierce rivalry in home markets tends to hone domestic firms' competitive capabilities and ready them for competing internationally.

For an industry in a particular country to become competitively strong, all four factors must be favorable for that industry. When they are, the industry is likely to contain firms that are capable of competing successfully in the international arena. Thus the diamond framework can be used to reveal the answers to several questions that are important for competing on an international basis. First, it can help predict *where foreign entrants into an industry are most likely to come from*. This can help managers prepare to cope with new foreign competitors, since the framework also reveals something about the basis of the new rivals' strengths. Second, it can reveal the countries in which foreign rivals are likely to be weakest and thus can help managers decide *which foreign markets to enter first*. And third, because it focuses on the attributes of a country's business environment that allow firms to flourish, it reveals something about the advantages of conducting particular business activities in that country. Thus the diamond framework is an aid to deciding *where to locate different value chain activities most beneficially*—a topic that we address next.

# Opportunities for Location-Based Advantages

Increasingly, companies are locating different value chain activities in different parts of the world to exploit location-based advantages that vary from country to country. This is particularly evident with respect to the location of manufacturing activities. Differences in wage rates, worker productivity, energy costs, and the like, create sizable variations in manufacturing costs from country to country. By locating its plants in certain countries, firms in some industries can reap major manufacturing cost advantages because of lower input costs (especially labor), relaxed government regulations, the proximity of suppliers and technologically related industries, or unique natural resources. In such cases, the low-cost countries become principal production sites, with most of the output being exported to markets in other parts of the world. Companies that build production facilities in low-cost countries (or that source their products from contract manufacturers in these countries) gain a competitive advantage over rivals with plants in countries where costs are higher. The competitive role of low manufacturing costs is most evident in low-wage countries like China, India,

Pakistan, Cambodia, Vietnam, Mexico, Brazil, Guatemala, the Philippines, and several countries in Africa and eastern Europe that have become production havens for manufactured goods with high labor content (especially textiles and apparel). Hourly compensation for manufacturing workers in 2012 averaged about $1.46 in India, $1.74 in China, $2.10 in the Philippines, $6.36 in Mexico, $8.95 in Hungary, $9.46 in Taiwan, $11.20 in Brazil, $12.10 in Portugal, $20.72 in South Korea, $24.77 in New Zealand, $35.71 in Japan, $35.34 in the United States, $35.67 in Canada, $45.79 in Germany, and $63.36 in Norway.[5] Not surprisingly, China has emerged as the manufacturing capital of the world—virtually all of the world's major manufacturing companies now have facilities in China.

For other types of value chain activities, input quality or availability are more important considerations. Tiffany entered the mining industry in Canada to access diamonds that could be certified as "conflict free" and not associated with either the funding of African wars or unethical mining conditions. Many U.S. companies locate call centers in countries such as India and Ireland, where English is spoken and the workforce is well educated. Other companies locate R&D activities in countries where there are prestigious research institutions and well-trained scientists and engineers. Likewise, concerns about short delivery times and low shipping costs make some countries better locations than others for establishing distribution centers.

## The Impact of Government Policies and Economic Conditions in Host Countries

Cross-country variations in government policies and economic conditions affect both the opportunities available to a foreign entrant and the risks of operating within the host country. The governments of some countries are anxious to attract foreign investments, and thus they go all out to create a business climate that outsiders will view as favorable. Governments anxious to spur economic growth, create more jobs, and raise living standards for their citizens usually enact policies aimed at stimulating business innovation and capital investment; Ireland is a good example. They may provide such incentives as reduced taxes, low-cost loans, site location and site development assistance, and government-sponsored training for workers to encourage companies to construct production and distribution facilities. When new business-related issues or developments arise, "pro-business" governments make a practice of seeking advice and counsel from business leaders. When tougher business-related regulations are deemed appropriate, they endeavor to make the transition to more costly and stringent regulations somewhat business-friendly rather than adversarial.

On the other hand, governments sometimes enact policies that, from a business perspective, make locating facilities within a country's borders less attractive. For example, the nature of a company's operations may make it particularly costly to achieve compliance with a country's environmental regulations. Some governments provide subsidies and low-interest loans to domestic companies to enable them to better compete against foreign companies. To discourage foreign imports, governments may enact deliberately burdensome procedures and requirements regarding customs inspection for foreign goods and may impose tariffs or quotas on imports. Additionally, they may specify that a certain percentage of the parts and components used in manufacturing a product be obtained from local suppliers, require prior approval of capital spending projects, limit withdrawal of funds from the country, and require partial ownership of foreign company operations by local companies or investors. There are times when a government may place restrictions on exports to ensure adequate local supplies and regulate the prices of imported and locally produced goods. Such government actions make a country's business climate less attractive and in some cases may be sufficiently onerous as to discourage a company from locating facilities in that country or even selling its products there.

A country's business climate is also a function of the political and economic risks associated with operating within its borders. **Political risks** have to do with the instability of weak governments, growing possibilities that a country's citizenry will revolt against dictatorial government leaders, the likelihood of new onerous legislation or regulations on foreign-owned businesses, and the potential for future elections to produce corrupt or tyrannical government leaders. In industries that a government deems critical to the national welfare, there is sometimes a risk that the government will nationalize the industry and expropriate the assets of foreign companies. In 2012, for example, Argentina nationalized the country's top oil producer, YPF, which was owned by Spanish oil major Repsol. Other political risks include the loss of investments due to war or political unrest, regulatory changes that create operating uncertainties, security risks due to terrorism, and corruption. **Economic risks** have to do with the stability of a country's economy and monetary system—whether inflation rates might skyrocket or whether uncontrolled deficit spending on the part of government or risky bank lending practices could lead to a breakdown of the country's monetary system and prolonged economic distress. In some countries, the threat of piracy and lack of protection for intellectual property are also sources of economic risk. Another is fluctuations in the value of different currencies—a factor that we discuss in more detail next.

> **CORE CONCEPT**
>
> **Political risks** stem from instability or weakness in national governments and hostility to foreign business. **Economic risks** stem from the stability of a country's monetary system, economic and regulatory policies, and the lack of property rights protections.

## The Risks of Adverse Exchange Rate Shifts

When companies produce and market their products and services in many different countries, they are subject to the impacts of sometimes favorable and sometimes unfavorable changes in currency exchange rates. The rates of exchange between different currencies can vary by as much as 20 to 40 percent annually, with the changes occurring sometimes gradually and sometimes swiftly. *Sizable shifts in exchange rates pose significant risks for two reasons:*

1. They are hard to predict because of the variety of factors involved and the uncertainties surrounding when and by how much these factors will change.
2. They shuffle the cards of which countries represent the low-cost manufacturing locations and which rivals have the upper hand in the marketplace.

To illustrate the economic risks associated with fluctuating exchange rates, consider the case of a U.S. company that has located manufacturing facilities in Brazil (where the currency is *reals*—pronounced "ray-alls") and that exports most of the Brazilian-made goods to markets in the European Union (where the currency is euros). To keep the numbers simple, assume that the exchange rate is 4 Brazilian reals for 1 euro and that the product being made in Brazil has a manufacturing cost of 4 Brazilian reals (or 1 euro). Now suppose that the exchange rate shifts from 4 reals per euro to 5 reals per euro (meaning that the real has declined in value and that the euro is stronger). Making the product in Brazil is now more cost-competitive because a Brazilian good costing 4 reals to produce has fallen to only 0.8 euro at the new exchange rate (4 reals divided by 5 reals per euro = 0.8 euro). This clearly puts the producer of the

Brazilian-made good *in a better position to compete* against the European makers of the same good. On the other hand, should the value of the Brazilian real grow stronger in relation to the euro—resulting in an exchange rate of 3 reals to 1 euro—the same Brazilian-made good formerly costing 4 reals (or 1 euro) to produce now has a cost of 1.33 euros (4 reals divided by 3 reals per euro = 1.33 euros), putting the producer of the Brazilian-made good in a weaker competitive position vis-à-vis the European producers. Clearly, the attraction of manufacturing a good in Brazil and selling it in Europe is far greater when the euro is strong (an exchange rate of 1 euro for 5 Brazilian reals) than when the euro is weak and exchanges for only 3 Brazilian reals.

But there is one more piece to the story. When the exchange rate changes from 4 reals per euro to 5 reals per euro, not only is the cost competitiveness of the Brazilian manufacturer stronger relative to European manufacturers of the same item but the Brazilian-made good that formerly cost 1 euro and now costs only 0.8 euro can also be sold to consumers in the European Union for a lower euro price than before. In other words, the combination of a stronger euro and a weaker real acts to *lower the price of Brazilian-made goods* in all the countries that are members of the European Union, which is likely to *spur sales of the Brazilian-made good in Europe and boost Brazilian exports to Europe.* Conversely, should the exchange rate shift from 4 reals per euro to 3 reals per euro—which makes the Brazilian manufacturer less cost-competitive with European manufacturers of the same item—the Brazilian-made good that formerly cost 1 euro and now costs 1.33 euros will sell for a higher price in euros than before, thus weakening the demand of European consumers for Brazilian-made goods and acting to reduce Brazilian exports to Europe. Thus Brazilian exporters are likely to experience (1) rising demand for their goods in Europe whenever the Brazilian real grows weaker relative to the euro and (2) falling demand for their goods in Europe whenever the real grows stronger relative to the euro. Consequently, from the standpoint of a company with Brazilian manufacturing plants, *a weaker Brazilian real is a favorable exchange rate shift* and *a stronger Brazilian real is an unfavorable exchange rate shift.*

It follows from the previous discussion that shifting exchange rates have a big impact on the ability of domestic manufacturers to compete with foreign rivals. For example, U.S.-based manufacturers locked in a fierce competitive battle with low-cost foreign imports benefit from a *weaker* U.S. dollar. There are several reasons why this is so:

- Declines in the value of the U.S. dollar against foreign currencies raise the U.S. dollar costs of goods manufactured by foreign rivals at plants located in the countries whose currencies have grown stronger relative to the U.S. dollar. A *weaker* dollar acts to reduce or eliminate whatever cost advantage foreign manufacturers may have had over U.S. manufacturers (and helps protect the manufacturing jobs of U.S. workers).

- A *weaker* dollar makes foreign-made goods more expensive in dollar terms to U.S. consumers—this curtails U.S. buyer demand for foreign-made goods, stimulates greater demand on the part of U.S. consumers for U.S.-made goods, and reduces U.S. imports of foreign-made goods.

- A *weaker* U.S. dollar enables the U.S.-made goods to be sold at lower prices to consumers in countries whose currencies have grown stronger relative to the U.S. dollar—such lower prices boost foreign buyer demand for the now relatively cheaper U.S.-made goods, thereby stimulating exports of U.S.-made goods to foreign countries and creating more jobs in U.S.-based manufacturing plants.

- A *weaker* dollar has the effect of increasing the dollar value of profits a company earns in foreign-country markets where the local currency is stronger relative to the dollar. For example, if a U.S.-based manufacturer earns a profit of €10 million on its sales in Europe, those €10 million convert to a larger number of dollars when the dollar grows weaker against the euro.

*A weaker U.S. dollar is therefore an economically favorable exchange rate shift for manufacturing plants based in the United States.* A decline in the value of the U.S. dollar strengthens the cost competitiveness of U.S.-based manufacturing plants and boosts buyer demand for U.S.-made goods. When the value of the U.S. dollar is expected to remain weak for some time to come, foreign companies have an incentive to build manufacturing facilities in the United States to make goods for U.S. consumers rather than export the same goods to the United States from foreign plants where production costs in dollar terms have been driven up by the decline in the value of the dollar. Conversely, a *stronger* U.S. dollar is an *unfavorable exchange rate shift* for U.S.-based manufacturing plants because it makes such plants less cost-competitive with foreign plants and weakens foreign demand for U.S.-made goods. A strong dollar also weakens the incentive of foreign companies to locate manufacturing facilities in the United States to make goods for U.S. consumers. The same reasoning applies to companies that have plants in countries in the European Union where euros are the local currency. A weak euro versus other currencies enhances the cost competitiveness of companies manufacturing goods in Europe vis-à-vis foreign rivals with plants in countries whose currencies have grown stronger relative to the euro; a strong euro versus other currencies weakens the cost competitiveness of companies with plants in the European Union.

Fluctuating exchange rates pose significant economic risks to a company's competitiveness in foreign markets. Exporters are disadvantaged when the currency of the country where goods are being manufactured grows stronger relative to the currency of the importing country.

Domestic companies facing competitive pressure from lower-cost imports benefit when their government's currency grows *weaker* in relation to the currencies of the countries where the lower-cost imports are being made.

## Cross-Country Differences in Demographic, Cultural, and Market Conditions

Buyer tastes for a particular product or service sometimes differ substantially from country to country. In France, consumers prefer top-loading washing machines, while in most other European countries consumers prefer front-loading machines. People in Hong Kong prefer compact appliances, but in Taiwan large appliances are more popular. Ice cream flavors like eel, shark fin, and dried shrimp appeal to Japanese customers, whereas fruit-based flavors have more appeal in the United States and in Europe. Sometimes, product designs suitable in one country are inappropriate in another because of differing local standards—for example, in the United States electrical devices run on 110-volt electric systems, but in some European countries the standard is a 240-volt electric system, necessitating the use of different electrical designs and components. Cultural influences can also affect consumer demand for a product. For instance, in South Korea, many parents are reluctant to purchase PCs even when they can afford them because of concerns that their children will be distracted from their schoolwork by surfing the Web, playing PC-based video games, and becoming Internet "addicts."[6]

Consequently, companies operating in an international marketplace have to wrestle with *whether and how much to customize their offerings in each country market to match local buyers' tastes and preferences or whether to pursue a strategy of offering a mostly standardized product worldwide.* While making products that are closely matched to local tastes makes them more appealing to local buyers, customizing a company's products country by country may raise production and distribution costs due to the greater variety of designs and components, shorter production runs, and the complications of added inventory handling and distribution logistics. Greater standardization of a global company's product offering, on the other hand, can lead to scale economies and learning-curve effects, thus contributing to the achievement of a low-cost advantage. *The tension between the market pressures to localize a company's product offerings country by country and the competitive pressures to lower costs is one of the big strategic issues that participants in foreign markets have to resolve.*

# STRATEGIC OPTIONS FOR ENTERING INTERNATIONAL MARKETS

**LO 3**

The five major strategic options for entering foreign markets.

Once a company decides to expand beyond its domestic borders, it must consider the question of how to enter foreign markets. There are five primary strategic options for doing so:

1. Maintain a home-country production base and *export* goods to foreign markets.
2. *License* foreign firms to produce and distribute the company's products abroad.
3. Employ a *franchising* strategy in foreign markets.
4. Establish a *subsidiary* in a foreign market via acquisition or internal development.
5. Rely on *strategic alliances* or joint ventures with foreign companies.

Which option to employ depends on a variety of factors, including the nature of the firm's strategic objectives, the firm's position in terms of whether it has the full range of resources and capabilities needed to operate abroad, country-specific factors such as trade barriers, and the transaction costs involved (the costs of contracting with a partner and monitoring its compliance with the terms of the contract, for example). The options vary considerably regarding the level of investment required and the associated risks—but higher levels of investment and risk generally provide the firm with the benefits of greater ownership and control.

## Export Strategies

Using domestic plants as a production base for exporting goods to foreign markets is an excellent initial strategy for pursuing international sales. It is a conservative way to test the international waters. The amount of capital needed to begin exporting is often minimal; existing production capacity may well be sufficient to make goods for export. With an export-based entry strategy, a manufacturer can limit its involvement in foreign markets by contracting with foreign wholesalers experienced in importing to handle the entire distribution and marketing function in their countries or regions of the world. If it is more advantageous to maintain control over these functions, however, a manufacturer can establish its own distribution and sales organizations in some or all of the target foreign markets. Either way, a home-based production and export strategy helps the firm minimize its direct investments in foreign countries. Such strategies are commonly favored by Chinese, Korean, and Italian companies— products are designed and manufactured at home and then distributed through local channels in the importing countries. The primary functions performed abroad relate chiefly to establishing a network of distributors and perhaps conducting sales promotion and brand-awareness activities.

Whether an export strategy can be pursued successfully over the long run depends on the relative cost competitiveness of the home-country production base. In some industries, firms gain additional scale economies and learning-curve benefits from centralizing production in plants whose output capability exceeds demand in any one country market; exporting enables a firm to capture such economies. However, an export strategy is vulnerable when (1) manufacturing costs in the home country are substantially higher than in foreign countries where rivals have plants, (2) the costs of shipping the product to distant foreign markets are relatively high, (3) adverse shifts occur in currency exchange rates, and (4) importing countries impose tariffs or erect other trade barriers. Unless an exporter can keep its production and shipping costs competitive with rivals' costs, secure adequate local distribution and marketing support of its products, and hedge against unfavorable changes in currency exchange rates, its success will be limited.

## Licensing Strategies

Licensing as an entry strategy makes sense when a firm with valuable technical know-how, an appealing brand, or a unique patented product has neither the internal organizational capability nor the resources to enter foreign markets. Licensing also has the advantage of avoiding the risks of committing resources to country markets that are unfamiliar, politically volatile, economically unstable, or otherwise risky. By licensing the technology, trademark, or production rights to foreign-based firms, the firm can generate income from royalties while shifting the costs and risks of entering foreign markets to the licensee. The big disadvantage of licensing is the risk of providing valuable technological know-how to foreign companies and thereby losing some degree of control over its use; monitoring licensees and safeguarding the company's proprietary know-how can prove quite difficult in some circumstances. But if the royalty potential is considerable and the companies to which the licenses are being granted are trustworthy and reputable, then licensing can be a very attractive option. Many software and pharmaceutical companies use licensing strategies to compete in foreign markets.

## Franchising Strategies

While licensing works well for manufacturers and owners of proprietary technology, franchising is often better suited to the international expansion efforts of service and retailing enterprises. McDonald's, Yum! Brands (the parent of Pizza Hut, KFC, Taco Bell, and WingStreet), the UPS Store, Roto-Rooter, 7-Eleven, and Hilton Hotels have all used franchising to build a presence in foreign markets. Franchising has many of the same advantages as licensing. The franchisee bears most of the costs and risks of establishing foreign locations; a franchisor has to expend only the resources to recruit, train, support, and monitor franchisees. The problem a franchisor faces is maintaining quality control; foreign franchisees do not always exhibit strong commitment to consistency and standardization, especially when the local culture does not stress the same kinds of quality concerns. A question that can arise is whether to allow foreign franchisees to make modifications in the franchisor's product offering so as to better satisfy the tastes and expectations of local buyers. Should McDonald's give franchisees in each nation some leeway in what products they put on their menus? Should the franchised KFC units in China be permitted to substitute spices that appeal to Chinese consumers? Or should the same menu offerings be rigorously and unvaryingly required of all franchisees worldwide?

# Foreign Subsidiary Strategies

While exporting, licensing, and franchising rely upon the resources and capabilities of allies to deliver goods or services to buyers in international markets, companies pursuing international expansion may elect to take responsibility for the performance of all essential value chain activities. Companies that prefer direct control over all aspects of operating in a foreign market can establish a wholly owned subsidiary, either by acquiring a foreign company or by establishing operations from the ground up via internal development. A subsidiary business that is established by setting up the entire operation from the ground up is called a **greenfield venture.**

Acquisition is the quicker of the two options, and it may be the least risky and most cost-efficient means of hurdling such entry barriers as gaining access to local distribution channels, building supplier relationships, and establishing working relationships with government officials and other key constituencies. Buying an ongoing operation allows the acquirer to move directly to the task of transferring resources and personnel to the newly acquired business, redirecting and integrating the activities of the acquired business into its own operation, putting its own strategy into place, and accelerating efforts to build a strong market position.

One thing an acquisition-minded firm must consider is whether to pay a premium price for a successful local company or to buy a struggling competitor at a bargain price. If the buying firm has little knowledge of the local market but ample capital, it is often better off purchasing a capable, strongly positioned firm. However, when the acquirer sees promising ways to transform a weak firm into a strong one and has the resources and managerial know-how to do so, a struggling company can be the better long-term investment.

Entering a new foreign country via a greenfield venture makes sense when a company already operates in a number of countries, has experience in establishing new subsidiaries and overseeing their operations, and has a sufficiently large pool of resources and capabilities to rapidly equip a new subsidiary with the personnel and competencies it needs to compete successfully and profitably. Four other conditions make a greenfield venture strategy appealing:

- When creating an internal startup is cheaper than making an acquisition.
- When adding new production capacity will not adversely impact the supply–demand balance in the local market.
- When a startup subsidiary has the ability to gain good distribution access (perhaps because of the company's recognized brand name).
- When a startup subsidiary will have the size, cost structure, and capabilities to compete head-to-head against local rivals.

Greenfield ventures in foreign markets can also pose problems, just as other entry strategies do. They represent a costly capital investment, subject to a high level of risk. They require numerous other company resources as well, diverting them from other uses. They do not work well in countries without strong, well-functioning markets and institutions that protect the rights of foreign investors and provide other legal protections. Moreover, an important disadvantage of greenfield ventures relative to other means of international expansion is that they are the slowest entry route—particularly if the objective is to achieve a sizable market share. On the other hand, successful greenfield ventures may offer higher returns to compensate for their high risk and slower path.

## Alliance and Joint Venture Strategies

Strategic alliances, joint ventures, and other cooperative agreements with foreign companies are a widely used means of entering foreign markets.[7] A company can benefit immensely from a foreign partner's familiarity with local government regulations, its knowledge of the buying habits and product preferences of consumers, its distribution-channel relationships, and so on.[8] Both Japanese and American companies are actively forming alliances with European companies to better compete in the 28-nation European Union and to capitalize on the opening of eastern European markets. Many U.S. and European companies are allying with Asian companies in their efforts to enter markets in China, India, Thailand, Indonesia, and other Asian countries.

Another reason for cross-border alliances is to capture economies of scale in production and/or marketing. By joining forces in producing components, assembling models, and marketing their products, companies can realize cost savings not achievable with their own small volumes. A third reason to employ a collaborative strategy is to share distribution facilities and dealer networks, thus mutually strengthening each partner's access to buyers. A fourth benefit of a collaborative strategy is the learning and added expertise that comes from performing joint research, sharing technological know-how, studying one another's manufacturing methods, and understanding how to tailor sales and marketing approaches to fit local cultures and traditions. A fifth benefit is that cross-border allies can direct their competitive energies more toward mutual rivals and less toward one another; teaming up may help them close the gap on leading companies. And, finally, alliances can be a particularly useful way for companies across the world to gain agreement on important technical standards—they have been used to arrive at standards for assorted PC devices, Internet-related technologies, high-definition televisions, and mobile phones.

Cross-border alliances are an attractive means of gaining the aforementioned types of benefits (as compared to merging with or acquiring foreign-based companies) because they allow a company to preserve its independence (which is not the case with a merger) and avoid using scarce financial resources to fund acquisitions. Furthermore, an alliance offers the flexibility to readily disengage once its purpose has been served or if the benefits prove elusive, whereas mergers and acquisitions are more permanent arrangements.[9]

Illustration Capsule 7.1 shows how California-based Solazyme, a maker of biofuels and other green products, has used cross-border strategic alliances to fuel its growth.

### The Risks of Strategic Alliances with Foreign Partners
Alliances and joint ventures with foreign partners have their pitfalls, however. Sometimes a local partner's knowledge and expertise turns out to be less valuable than expected (because its knowledge is rendered obsolete by fast-changing market conditions or because its operating practices are archaic). Cross-border allies typically must overcome language and cultural barriers and figure out how to deal with diverse (or conflicting) operating practices. The transaction costs of working out a mutually agreeable

Collaborative strategies involving alliances or joint ventures with foreign partners are a popular way for companies to edge their way into the markets of foreign countries.

Cross-border alliances enable a growth-minded company to widen its geographic coverage and strengthen its competitiveness in foreign markets; at the same time, they offer flexibility and allow a company to retain some degree of autonomy and operating control.

# Solazyme's Cross-Border Alliances with Unilever, Sephora, Qantas, and Roquette

Solazyme, a California-based company that produces oils for nutritional, cosmetic, and biofuel products from algae, was named "America's Fastest-Growing Manufacturing Company" by *Inc. Magazine* in 2011. The company has fueled its rapid growth through a variety of cross-border strategic alliances with much larger partners. These partnerships not only have facilitated Solazyme's entry into new markets but have also created value through resource sharing and risk spreading.

Its partnership with Unilever, a giant British-Dutch consumer-goods company, initially focused on collaborative R&D. Projects were aimed at meeting the growing demand for completely renewable, natural, and sustainable personal care products through the use of algal oils. By further developing Solazyme's technology platform, the partnership has taken off; with the ability to produce Solazyme's oils and other biomaterials efficiently and at large scale, Unilever is now taking the next step of marketing and selling those products as part of

its ambitious goal to use only sustainable agricultural raw materials by 2020.

Solazyme has entered into a variety of marketing and distribution agreements with French cosmetics company Sephora (now part of LVMH). In March 2011, Solazyme launched its luxury skin care brand, Algenist, with Sephora's help. Sephora has also agreed to distribute Solazyme's antiaging skin care line, making it available in Sephora stores and at Sephora.com.

In 2011, Solazyme also signed a contract with Australian airline Qantas to supply, test, and refine Solazyme's jet fuel product, SolaJet. Solazyme stands to gain valuable input on how to design and distribute its product while receiving media attention and the marketing advantage of a well-known customer. Likewise, Qantas hopes to better understand how it will achieve its sustainability goals while building its reputation as a sustainability leader in the airline industry.

However, not every partnership ends successfully, regardless of the strength of the initial motivations and relationship. Because its algae require sugar to produce oil, Solazyme developed an interest in securing a stable supply of this feedstock. For this purpose, Solazyme created a 50-50 joint venture with French starch processor Roquette to develop, produce, and market food products globally. By working with Roquette, Solazyme hoped to lower its exposure to sugar price fluctuations, trading the use of its innovative technological resources in return for Roquette's manufacturing infrastructure and expertise. But in 2013, the joint venture dissolved—both parties felt that after the exchange of ideas, technologies, and goals, they would be better off going it alone on the algal food product frontier.

*Note:* Developed with John L. Gardner and Harold W. Greenstone.

*Sources:* Company website; **gigaom.com/**, **www.businessgreen.com/**, **www.reuters.com/**, and **www.foodnavigator-usa.com/** (all accessed March 4, 2012); S. Daniels, "Solazyme & Roquette to Each Go It Alone on Microalgae-Sourced Ingredients," **www.foodnavigator-usa.com** (accessed April 1, 2014); and D. Cardwell, "Unilever to Buy Oil Derived from Algae from Solazyme," *The New York Times* Online, September 25, 2013 (accessed April 1, 2014).

arrangement and monitoring partner compliance with the terms of the arrangement can be high. The communication, trust building, and coordination costs are not trivial in terms of management time.[10] Often, partners soon discover they have conflicting objectives and strategies, deep differences of opinion about how to proceed, or important differences in corporate values and ethical standards. Tensions build up, working relationships cool, and the hoped-for benefits never materialize.[11] It is not unusual for there to be little personal chemistry among some of the key people on whom the success or failure of the alliance depends—the rapport such personnel need to work well together may never emerge. And even if allies are able to develop productive personal relationships, they can still have trouble reaching mutually agreeable ways to deal with key issues or launching new initiatives fast enough to stay abreast of rapid advances in technology or shifting market conditions.

One worrisome problem with alliances or joint ventures is that a firm may risk losing some of its competitive advantage if an alliance partner is given full access to its proprietary technological expertise or other competitively valuable capabilities. There is a natural tendency for allies to struggle to collaborate effectively in competitively sensitive areas, thus spawning suspicions on both sides about forthright exchanges of information and expertise. It requires many meetings of many people working in good faith over a period of time to iron out what is to be shared, what is to remain proprietary, and how the cooperative arrangements will work.

Even if the alliance proves to be a win-win proposition for both parties, there is the danger of becoming overly dependent on foreign partners for essential expertise and competitive capabilities. Companies aiming for global market leadership need to develop their own resource capabilities in order to be masters of their destiny. Frequently, experienced international companies operating in 50 or more countries across the world find less need for entering into cross-border alliances than do companies in the early stages of globalizing their operations.[12] Companies with global operations make it a point to develop senior managers who understand how "the system" works in different countries, plus they can avail themselves of local managerial talent and know-how by simply hiring experienced local managers and thereby detouring the hazards of collaborative alliances with local companies. One of the lessons about cross-border partnerships is that they are more effective in helping a company establish a beachhead of new opportunity in world markets than they are in enabling a company to achieve and sustain global market leadership.

# INTERNATIONAL STRATEGY: THE THREE MAIN APPROACHES

Broadly speaking, a firm's **international strategy** is simply its strategy for competing in two or more countries simultaneously. Typically, a company will start to compete internationally by entering one or perhaps a select few foreign markets—selling its products or services in countries where there is a ready market for them. But as it expands further internationally, it will have to confront head-on two conflicting pressures: the demand for responsiveness to local needs versus the prospect of efficiency gains from offering a standardized product globally. Deciding upon the degree to vary its competitive approach to fit the specific market conditions and buyer preferences in each host country is perhaps the foremost strategic issue that must be addressed when a company is operating in two or more foreign markets.[13] Figure 7.2 shows a company's three options for resolving this issue: choosing a *multidomestic, global,* or *transnational* strategy.

**LO 4**

The three main strategic approaches for competing internationally.

**CORE CONCEPT**

An **international strategy** is a strategy for competing in two or more countries simultaneously.

## FIGURE 7.2   Three Approaches for Competing Internationally

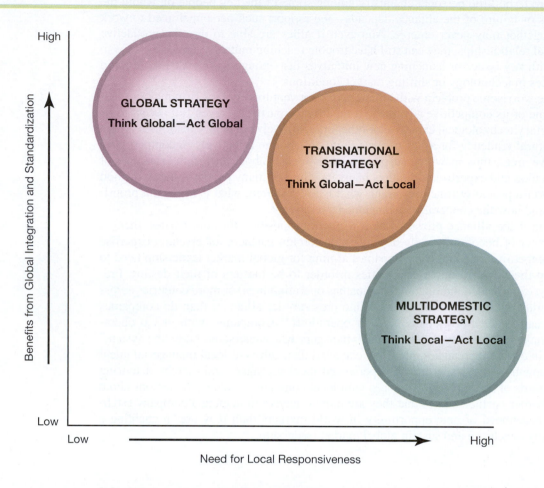

## Multidomestic Strategies—A "Think-Local, Act-Local" Approach

A **multidomestic strategy** is one in which a company varies its product offering and competitive approach from country to country in an effort to meet differing buyer needs and to address divergent local-market conditions. It involves having plants produce different product versions for different local markets and adapting marketing and distribution to fit local customs, cultures, regulations, and market requirements. Castrol, a specialist in oil lubricants, produces over 3,000 different formulas of lubricants to meet the requirements of different climates, vehicle types and uses, and equipment applications that characterize different country markets. In the food products industry, it is common for companies to vary the ingredients in their products and sell the localized versions under local brand names to cater to country-specific tastes and eating preferences. Motor vehicle manufacturers routinely produce smaller, more fuel-efficient vehicles for European markets, where roads are narrower and gasoline prices are two to three times higher than in the North American market (where many consumers prefer larger vehicles). The models they manufacture for the Asian market are different yet again—and local managers tailor the sales and marketing of these vehicles to local cultures, buyer tastes, and competitive conditions.

In essence, a multidomestic strategy represents a **think-local, act-local** approach to international strategy. A think-local, act-local approach to strategy making is most appropriate when the need for local responsiveness is high due to significant cross-country differences in demographic, cultural, and market conditions and when the potential for efficiency gains from standardization is limited, as depicted in Figure 7.2. A think-local, act-local approach is possible only when decision making is decentralized, giving local managers considerable latitude for crafting and executing strategies for the country markets they are responsible for. Giving local managers decision-making authority allows them to address specific market needs and respond swiftly to local changes in demand. It also enables them to focus their competitive efforts, stake out attractive market positions vis-à-vis local competitors, react to rivals' moves in a timely fashion, and target new opportunities as they emerge.[14]

Despite their obvious benefits, think-local, act-local strategies have three big drawbacks:

1. They hinder transfer of a company's capabilities, knowledge, and other resources across country boundaries, since the company's efforts are not integrated or coordinated across country boundaries. This can make the company less innovative overall.

2. They raise production and distribution costs due to the greater variety of designs and components, shorter production runs for each product version, and complications of added inventory handling and distribution logistics.

3. They are not conducive to building a single, worldwide competitive advantage. When a company's competitive approach and product offering vary from country to country, the nature and size of any resulting competitive edge also tends to vary. At the most, multidomestic strategies are capable of producing a group of local competitive advantages of varying types and degrees of strength.

## Global Strategies—A "Think-Global, Act-Global" Approach

A **global strategy** contrasts sharply with a multidomestic strategy in that it takes a standardized, globally integrated approach to producing, packaging, selling, and delivering the company's products and services worldwide. Companies employing a global strategy sell the same products under the same brand names everywhere, utilize much the same distribution channels in all countries, and compete on the basis of the same capabilities and marketing approaches worldwide. Although the company's strategy or product offering may be adapted in minor ways to accommodate specific situations in a few host countries, the company's fundamental competitive approach (low cost, differentiation, best cost, or focused) remains very much intact worldwide and local managers stick close to the global strategy.

A **think-global, act-global** approach prompts company managers to integrate and coordinate the company's strategic moves worldwide and to expand into most, if not all, nations where there is significant buyer demand. It puts considerable strategic emphasis on building a *global* brand name and aggressively pursuing opportunities to transfer ideas, new products, and capabilities from one country to another. Global strategies are characterized by relatively centralized value chain activities, such as production and distribution. While there may be more than one manufacturing plant and distribution center to minimize transportation costs, for example, they tend to be few in number. Achieving the efficiency potential of a global strategy requires that resources and best practices be shared, value chain

---

**CORE CONCEPT**

A **global strategy** is one in which a company employs the same basic competitive approach in all countries where it operates, sells standardized products globally, strives to build global brands, and coordinates its actions worldwide with strong headquarters control. It represents a **think-global, act-global** approach.

activities be integrated, and capabilities be transferred from one location to another as they are developed. These objectives are best facilitated through centralized decision making and strong headquarters control.

Because a global strategy cannot accommodate varying local needs, it is an appropriate strategic choice when there are pronounced efficiency benefits from standardization and when buyer needs are relatively homogeneous across countries and regions. A globally standardized and integrated approach is especially beneficial when high volumes significantly lower costs due to economies of scale or added experience (moving the company further down a learning curve). It can also be advantageous if it allows the firm to replicate a successful business model on a global basis efficiently or engage in higher levels of R&D by spreading the fixed costs and risks over a higher-volume output. It is a fitting response to industry conditions marked by global competition.

Ford's global design strategy is a move toward a think-global, act-global strategy, involving the development and production of standardized models with country-specific modifications limited to what is required to meet local country emission and safety standards. The 2010 Ford Fiesta and 2011 Ford Focus were the company's first global design models to be marketed in Europe, North America, Asia, and Australia. Whenever country-to-country differences are small enough to be accommodated within the framework of a global strategy, a global strategy is preferable because a company can more readily unify its operations and focus on establishing a brand image and reputation that are uniform from country to country. Moreover, with a global strategy a company is better able to focus its full resources on securing a sustainable low-cost or differentiation-based competitive advantage over both domestic rivals and global rivals.

There are, however, several drawbacks to global strategies: (1) They do not enable firms to address local needs as precisely as locally based rivals can, (2) they are less responsive to changes in local market conditions, in the form of either new opportunities or competitive threats, (3) they raise transportation costs and may involve higher tariffs, and (4) they involve higher coordination costs due to the more complex task of managing a globally integrated enterprise.

## Transnational Strategies—A "Think-Global, Act-Local" Approach

**CORE CONCEPT**

A **transnational strategy** is a **think-global, act-local** approach that incorporates elements of both multidomestic and global strategies.

A **transnational strategy** (sometimes called *glocalization*) incorporates elements of both a globalized and a localized approach to strategy making. This type of middle-ground strategy is called for when there are relatively high needs for local responsiveness as well as appreciable benefits to be realized from standardization, as Figure 7.2 suggests. A transnational strategy encourages a company to **think global, act local** to balance these competing objectives.

Often, companies implement a transnational strategy with mass-customization techniques that enable them to address local preferences in an efficient, semistandardized manner. McDonald's, KFC, and Starbucks have discovered ways to customize their menu offerings in various countries without compromising costs, product quality, and operating effectiveness. Unilever is responsive to local market needs regarding its consumer products, while realizing global economies of scale in certain functions. Otis Elevator found that a transnational strategy delivers better results than a global strategy when it is competing in countries like China, where local needs are highly differentiated. By switching from its customary single-brand approach to a multibrand strategy aimed at serving different segments of the market, Otis was able to double its market share in China and increased its revenues sixfold over a nine-year period.[15]

As a rule, most companies that operate internationally endeavor to employ as global a strategy as customer needs and market conditions permit. Electronic Arts (EA) has two major design studios—one in Vancouver, British Columbia, and one in Los Angeles—and smaller design studios in San Francisco, Orlando, London, and Tokyo. This dispersion of design studios helps EA to design games that are specific to different cultures—for example, the London studio took the lead in designing the popular FIFA Soccer game to suit European tastes and to replicate the stadiums, signage, and team rosters; the U.S. studio took the lead in designing games involving NFL football, NBA basketball, and NASCAR racing.

A transnational strategy is far more conducive than other strategies to transferring and leveraging subsidiary skills and capabilities. But, like other approaches to competing internationally, transnational strategies also have significant drawbacks:

1. They are the most difficult of all international strategies to implement due to the added complexity of varying the elements of the strategy to situational conditions.

2. They place large demands on the organization due to the need to pursue conflicting objectives simultaneously.

3. Implementing the strategy is likely to be a costly and time-consuming enterprise, with an uncertain outcome.

Illustration Capsule 7.2 explains how Four Seasons Hotels has been able to compete successfully on the basis of a transnational strategy.

Table 7.1 provides a summary of the pluses and minuses of the three approaches to competing internationally.

**TABLE 7.1**  **Advantages and Disadvantages of Multidomestic, Global, and Transnational Strategies**

|  | Advantages | Disadvantages |
|---|---|---|
| **Multidomestic** (think local, act local) | • Can meet the specific needs of each market more precisely<br>• Can respond more swiftly to localized changes in demand<br>• Can target reactions to the moves of local rivals<br>• Can respond more quickly to local opportunities and threats | • Hinders resource and capability sharing or cross-market transfers<br>• Has higher production and distribution costs<br>• Is not conducive to a worldwide competitive advantage |
| **Global** (think global, act global) | • Has lower costs due to scale and scope economies<br>• Can lead to greater efficiencies due to the ability to transfer best practices across markets<br>• Increases innovation from knowledge sharing and capability transfer<br>• Offers the benefit of a global brand and reputation | • Cannot address local needs precisely<br>• Is less responsive to changes in local market conditions<br>• Involves higher transportation costs and tariffs<br>• Has higher coordination and integration costs |
| **Transnational** (think global, act local) | • Offers the benefits of both local responsiveness and global integration<br>• Enables the transfer and sharing of resources and capabilities across borders<br>• Provides the benefits of flexible coordination | • Is more complex and harder to implement<br>• Entails conflicting goals, which may be difficult to reconcile and require trade-offs<br>• Involves more costly and time-consuming implementation |

# Four Seasons Hotels: Local Character, Global Service

Four Seasons Hotels is a Toronto, Canada–based manager of luxury hotel properties. With 92 properties located in many of the world's most popular tourist destinations and business centers, Four Seasons commands a following of many of the world's most discerning travelers. In contrast to its key competitor, Ritz-Carlton, which strives to create one uniform experience globally, Four Seasons Hotels has gained market share by deftly combining local architectural and cultural experiences with globally consistent luxury service.

When moving into a new market, Four Seasons always seeks out a local capital partner. The understanding of local custom and business relationships this financier brings is critical to the process of developing a new Four Seasons hotel. Four Seasons also insists on hiring a local architect and design consultant for each property, as opposed to using architects or designers it's worked with in other locations. While this can be a challenge, particularly in emerging markets, Four Seasons has found it is worth it in the long run to have a truly local team.

The specific layout and programming of each hotel is also unique. For instance, when Four Seasons opened its hotel in Mumbai, India, it prioritized space for large banquet halls to target the Indian wedding market. In India, weddings often draw guests numbering in the thousands. When moving into the Middle East, Four Seasons designed its hotels with separate prayer rooms for men and women. In Bali, where destination weddings are common, the hotel employs a "weather shaman" who, for some guests, provides reassurance that the weather will cooperate for their special day. In all cases, the objective is to provide a truly local experience.

When staffing its hotels, Four Seasons seeks to strike a fine balance between employing locals who have an innate understanding of the local culture alongside expatriate staff or "culture carriers" who understand the DNA of Four Seasons. It also uses global systems to track customer preferences and employs globally consistent service standards. Four Seasons claims that its guests experience the same high level of service globally but that no two experiences are the same.

While it is much more expensive and time-consuming to design unique architectural and programming experiences, doing so is a strategic trade-off Four Seasons has made to achieve the local experience demanded by its high-level clientele. Likewise, it has recognized that maintaining globally consistent operation processes and service standards is important too. Four Seasons has struck the right balance between thinking globally and acting locally—the marker of a truly transnational strategy. As a result, the company has been rewarded with an international reputation for superior service and a leading market share in the luxury hospitality segment.

*Note:* Developed with Brian R. McKenzie.

*Sources:* Four Seasons annual report and corporate website; and interview with Scott Woroch, Executive Vice President of Development, Four Seasons Hotels, February 22, 2014.

# INTERNATIONAL OPERATIONS AND THE QUEST FOR COMPETITIVE ADVANTAGE

There are three important ways in which a firm can gain competitive advantage (or offset domestic disadvantages) by expanding outside its domestic market. First, it can use location to lower costs or achieve greater product differentiation. Second, it can transfer competitively valuable resources and capabilities from one country to another or share them across international borders to extend its competitive advantages. And third, it can benefit from cross-border coordination opportunities that are not open to domestic-only competitors.

## Using Location to Build Competitive Advantage

To use location to build competitive advantage, a company must consider two issues: (1) whether to concentrate each activity it performs in a few select countries or to disperse performance of the activity to many nations, and (2) in which countries to locate particular activities.

### When to Concentrate Activities in a Few Locations
It is advantageous for a company to concentrate its activities in a limited number of locations when:

- *The costs of manufacturing or other activities are significantly lower in some geographic locations than in others.* For example, much of the world's athletic footwear is manufactured in Asia (Vietnam, China, and Korea) because of low labor costs; much of the production of circuit boards for PCs is located in Taiwan because of both low costs and the high-caliber technical skills of the Taiwanese labor force.

- *Significant scale economies exist in production or distribution.* The presence of significant economies of scale in components production or final assembly means that a company can gain major cost savings from operating a few super-efficient plants as opposed to a host of small plants scattered across the world. Makers of digital cameras and LED TVs located in Japan, South Korea, and Taiwan have used their scale economies to establish a low-cost advantage in this way. Achieving low-cost provider status often requires a company to have the largest worldwide manufacturing share (as distinct from brand share or market share), with production centralized in one or a few giant plants. Some companies even use such plants to manufacture units sold under the brand names of rivals to further boost production-related scale economies. Likewise, a company may be able to reduce its distribution costs by establishing large-scale distribution centers to serve major geographic regions of the world market (e.g., North America, Latin America, Europe and the Middle East, and the Asia-Pacific region).

- *Sizable learning and experience benefits are associated with performing an activity.* In some industries, learning-curve effects can allow a manufacturer to lower unit costs, boost quality, or master a new technology *more quickly* by concentrating production in a few locations. The key to riding down the learning curve is to concentrate production in a few locations to increase the cumulative volume at a plant (and thus the experience of the plant's workforce) as rapidly as possible.

- *Certain locations have superior resources, allow better coordination of related activities, or offer other valuable advantages.* Companies often locate a research unit or a sophisticated production facility in a particular country to take advantage of its pool of technically trained personnel. Samsung became a leader in memory chip technology by establishing a major R&D facility in Silicon Valley and transferring the know-how it gained back to its operations in South Korea. Where just-in-time inventory practices yield big cost savings and/or where an assembly firm has long-term partnering arrangements with its key suppliers, parts manufacturing plants may be clustered around final-assembly plants. A customer service center or sales office may be opened in a particular country to help cultivate strong relationships with pivotal customers located nearby.

**LO 5**

How companies are able to use international operations to improve overall competitiveness.

Companies that compete internationally can pursue competitive advantage in world markets by locating their value chain activities in whatever nations prove most advantageous.

**When to Disperse Activities across Many Locations**    In some instances, dispersing activities across locations is more advantageous than concentrating them. Buyer-related activities—such as distribution, marketing, and after-sale service—usually must take place close to buyers. This means physically locating the capability to perform such activities in every country or region where a firm has major customers. For example, firms that make mining and oil-drilling equipment maintain operations in many locations around the world to support customers' needs for speedy equipment repair and technical assistance. Large public accounting firms have offices in numerous countries to serve the foreign operations of their international corporate clients. Dispersing activities to many locations is also competitively important when high transportation costs, diseconomies of large size, and trade barriers make it too expensive to operate from a central location. Many companies distribute their products from multiple locations to shorten delivery times to customers. In addition, dispersing activities helps hedge against the risks of fluctuating exchange rates, supply interruptions (due to strikes, natural disasters, or transportation delays), and adverse political developments. Such risks are usually greater when activities are concentrated in a single location.

Even though global firms have strong reason to disperse buyer-related activities to many international locations, such activities as materials procurement, parts manufacture, finished-goods assembly, technology research, and new product development can frequently be decoupled from buyer locations and performed wherever advantage lies. Components can be made in Mexico; technology research done in Frankfurt; new products developed and tested in Phoenix; and assembly plants located in Spain, Brazil, Taiwan, or South Carolina, for example. Capital can be raised wherever it is available on the best terms.

## Sharing and Transferring Resources and Capabilities across Borders to Build Competitive Advantage

When a company has competitively valuable resources and capabilities, it may be able to leverage them further by expanding internationally. If its resources retain their value in foreign contexts, then entering new foreign markets can extend the company's resource-based competitive advantage over a broader domain. For example, companies like Hermes, Prada, and Gucci have utilized their powerful brand names to extend their differentiation-based competitive advantages into markets far beyond their home-country origins. In each of these cases, the luxury brand name represents a valuable competitive asset that can readily be *shared* by all of the company's international stores, enabling them to attract buyers and gain a higher degree of market penetration over a wider geographic area than would otherwise be possible.

Another way for a company to extend its competitive advantage internationally is to *transfer* technological know-how or other important resources and capabilities from its operations in one country to its operations in other countries. For instance, if a company discovers ways to assemble a product faster and more cost-effectively at one plant, then that know-how can be transferred to its assembly plants in other countries. Whirlpool, the leading global manufacturer of home appliances, with 65 manufacturing and technology research centers around the world, uses an online global information technology platform to quickly and effectively transfer key product innovations and improved production techniques both across national borders and across various appliance brands. Walmart is expanding its international operations with a strategy that involves transferring its considerable resource capabilities in distribution and dis-count retailing to its retail units in 26 foreign countries.

Cross-border sharing or transferring resources and capabilities provides a cost-effective way for a company to leverage its core competencies more fully and extend its competitive advantages into a wider array of geographic markets. The cost of shar-ing or transferring already developed resources and capabilities across country bor-ders is low in comparison to the time and considerable expense it takes to create them. Moreover, deploying them abroad spreads the fixed development costs over a greater volume of unit sales, thus contributing to low unit costs and a potential cost-based competitive advantage in recently entered geographic markets. Even if the shared or transferred resources or capabilities have to be adapted to local-market conditions, this can usually be done at low additional cost.

Consider the case of Walt Disney's theme parks as an example. The success of the theme parks in the United States derives in part from core resources such as the Disney brand name and characters like Mickey Mouse that have universal appeal and world-wide recognition. These resources can be freely shared with new theme parks as Dis-ney expands internationally. Disney can also replicate its theme parks in new countries cost-effectively since it has already borne the costs of developing its core resources, park attractions, basic park design, and operating capabilities. The cost of replicating its theme parks abroad should be relatively low, even if the parks need to be adapted to a variety of local country conditions. By expanding internationally, Disney is able to enhance its competitive advantage over local theme park rivals. It does so by leverag-ing the differentiation advantage conferred by resources such as the Disney name and the park attractions. And by moving into new foreign markets, it augments its competi-tive advantage worldwide through the efficiency gains that come from cross-border resource sharing and low-cost capability transfer and business model replication.

Sharing and transferring resources and capabilities across country borders may also contribute to the development of broader or deeper competencies and capabilities—helping a company achieve *dominating depth* in some competitively valuable area. For example, the reputation for quality that Honda established worldwide began in motor-cycles but enabled the company to command a position in both automobiles and outdoor power equipment in multiple-country markets. A one-country customer base is often too small to support the resource buildup needed to achieve such depth; this is particu-larly true in a developing or protected market, where competitively powerful resources are not required. By deploying capabilities across a larger international domain, a company can gain the experience needed to upgrade them to a higher performance standard. And by facing a more challenging set of international competitors, a com-pany may be spurred to develop a stronger set of competitive capabilities. Moreover, by entering international markets, firms may be able to augment their capability set by learning from international rivals, cooperative partners, or acquisition targets.

However, cross-border resource sharing and transfers of capabilities are not guar-anteed recipes for competitive success. For example, whether a resource or capability can confer a competitive advantage abroad depends on the conditions of rivalry in each particular market. If the rivals in a foreign-country market have superior resources and capabilities, then an entering firm may find itself at a competitive disadvantage even if it has a resource-based advantage domestically and can transfer the resources at low cost. In addition, since lifestyles and buying habits differ internationally, resources and capabilities that are valuable in one country may not have value in another. Some-times a popular or well-regarded brand in one country turns out to have little competi-tive clout against local brands in other countries.

For example, Netherlands-based Royal Philips Electronics, with 2012 sales of about €25 billion in more than 60 countries, is a leading seller of electric shavers, lighting products, small appliances, televisions, DVD players, and health care products. It has proven competitive capabilities in a number of businesses and countries and has been consistently profitable on a global basis. But the company's Philips and Magnavox brand names and the resources it has invested in its North American organization have proved inadequate in changing its image as a provider of low-end TVs and DVD players, recruiting retailers that can effectively merchandise its Magnavox and Philips products, and exciting consumers with the quality and features of its products. It has lost money in North America every year since 1988.

## Benefiting from Cross-Border Coordination

Companies that compete on an international basis have another source of competitive advantage relative to their purely domestic rivals: They are able to benefit from coordinating activities across different countries' domains.[16] For example, an international manufacturer can shift production from a plant in one country to a plant in another to take advantage of exchange rate fluctuations, to cope with components shortages, or to profit from changing wage rates or energy costs. Production schedules can be coordinated worldwide; shipments can be diverted from one distribution center to another if sales rise unexpectedly in one place and fall in another. By coordinating their activities, international companies may also be able to enhance their leverage with host-country governments or respond adaptively to changes in tariffs and quotas. Efficiencies can also be achieved by shifting workloads from where they are unusually heavy to locations where personnel are underutilized.

# CROSS-BORDER STRATEGIC MOVES

While international competitors can employ any of the offensive and defensive moves discussed in Chapter 6, there are two types of strategic moves that are particularly suited for companies competing internationally. Both involve the use of "profit sanctuaries."

**Profit sanctuaries** are country markets (or geographic regions) in which a company derives substantial profits because of a strong or protected market position. In most cases, a company's biggest and most strategically crucial profit sanctuary is its home market, but international and global companies may also enjoy profit sanctuary status in other nations where they have a strong position based on some type of competitive advantage. Companies that compete globally are likely to have more profit sanctuaries than companies that compete in just a few country markets; a domestic-only competitor, of course, can have only one profit sanctuary. Nike, which markets its products in 190 countries, has two major profit sanctuaries: North America and Greater China (where it earned $2.5 billion and $809 million respectively in operating profits in 2013).

## Using Profit Sanctuaries to Wage a Strategic Offensive

Profit sanctuaries are valuable competitive assets, providing the financial strength to support strategic offensives in selected country markets and fuel a company's race for world-market leadership. The added financial capability afforded by multiple profit sanctuaries gives an international competitor the financial strength to wage a market offensive against a domestic competitor whose only profit sanctuary is its home market. The international company has the flexibility of lowballing its prices or launching high-cost marketing campaigns in the domestic company's home market and grabbing market share at the domestic company's expense. Razor-thin margins or even losses in these markets can be subsidized with the healthy profits earned in its profit sanctuaries—a practice called **cross-market subsidization.** The international company can adjust the depth of its price cutting to move in and capture market share quickly, or it can shave prices slightly to make gradual market inroads (perhaps over a decade or more) so as not to threaten domestic firms precipitously and trigger protectionist government actions. If the domestic company retaliates with matching price cuts or increased marketing expenses, it thereby exposes its entire revenue stream and profit base to erosion; its profits can be squeezed substantially and its competitive strength sapped, even if it is the domestic market leader.

When taken to the extreme, cut-rate pricing attacks by international competitors may draw charges of unfair "dumping." A company is said to be *dumping* when it sells its goods in foreign markets at prices that are (1) well below the prices at which it normally sells them in its home market or (2) well below its full costs per unit. Almost all governments can be expected to retaliate against perceived dumping practices by imposing special tariffs on goods being imported from the countries of the guilty companies. Indeed, as the trade among nations has mushroomed over the past 10 years, most governments have joined the World Trade Organization (WTO), which promotes fair trade practices among nations and actively polices dumping. Companies deemed guilty of dumping frequently come under pressure from their own government to cease and desist, especially if the tariffs adversely affect innocent companies based in the same country or if the advent of special tariffs raises the specter of an international trade war.

> **CORE CONCEPT**
>
> **Cross-market subsidization**—supporting competitive offensives in one market with resources and profits diverted from operations in another market—can be a powerful competitive weapon.

## Using Profit Sanctuaries to Defend against International Rivals

Cross-border tactics involving profit sanctuaries can also be used as a means of defending against the strategic moves of rivals with multiple profit sanctuaries of their own. If a company finds itself under competitive attack by an international rival in one country market, one way to respond is to conduct a counterattack against the rival in one of its key markets in a different country—preferably where the rival is least protected and has the most to lose. This is a possible option when rivals compete against one another in much the same markets around the world.

For companies with at least one profit sanctuary, having a presence in a rival's key markets can be enough to deter the rival from making aggressive attacks. The reason for this is that the combination of market presence in the rival's key markets and a profit sanctuary elsewhere can send a signal to the rival that the company could quickly ramp up production (funded by the profit sanctuary) to mount a competitive counterattack if the rival attacks one of the company's key markets.

When international rivals compete against one another in multiple-country markets, this type of deterrence effect can restrain them from taking aggressive action against one another, due to the fear of a retaliatory response that might escalate the battle into a cross-border competitive war. **Mutual restraint** of this sort tends to stabilize the competitive position of multimarket rivals against one another. And while it may prevent each firm from making any

> **CORE CONCEPT**
>
> When the same companies compete against one another in multiple geographic markets, the threat of cross-border counterattacks may be enough to deter aggressive competitive moves and encourage **mutual restraint** among international rivals.

major market share gains at the expense of its rival, it also protects against costly competitive battles that would be likely to erode the profitability of both companies without any compensating gain.

# STRATEGIES FOR COMPETING IN THE MARKETS OF DEVELOPING COUNTRIES

**LO 6**

The unique characteristics of competing in developing-country markets.

Companies racing for global leadership have to consider competing in developing-economy markets like China, India, Brazil, Indonesia, Thailand, and Russia—countries where the business risks are considerable but where the opportunities for growth are huge, especially as their economies develop and living standards climb toward levels in the industrialized world.[17] In today's world, a company that aspires to international market leadership (or to sustained rapid growth) cannot ignore the market opportunities or the base of technical and managerial talent such countries offer. For example, in 2013 China was the world's second-largest economy (behind the United States), based on purchasing power and its population of 1.3 billion people. Due to the rapid growth of a wealthy class, it may soon become the world's largest consumer of luxury products. China is already the world's largest consumer of many commodities. Thus, no company that aspires to global market leadership can afford to ignore the strategic importance of establishing competitive market positions in the so-called BRIC countries (Brazil, Russia, India, and China), as well as in other parts of the Asia-Pacific region, Latin America, and eastern Europe.

Tailoring products to fit market conditions in developing countries, however, often involves more than making minor product changes and becoming more familiar with local cultures. McDonald's has had to offer vegetable burgers in parts of Asia and to rethink its prices, which are often high by local standards and affordable only by the well-to-do. Kellogg has struggled to introduce its cereals successfully because consumers in many less developed countries do not eat cereal for breakfast. Single-serving packages of detergents, shampoos, pickles, cough syrup, and cooking oils are very popular in India because they allow buyers to conserve cash by purchasing only what they need immediately. Thus, many companies find that trying to employ a strategy akin to that used in the markets of developed countries is hazardous.[18] Experimenting with some, perhaps many, local twists is usually necessary to find a strategy combination that works.

## Strategy Options for Competing in Developing-Country Markets

There are several options for tailoring a company's strategy to fit the sometimes unusual or challenging circumstances presented in developing-country markets:

- *Prepare to compete on the basis of low price.* Consumers in developing markets are often highly focused on price, which can give low-cost local competitors the edge unless a company can find ways to attract buyers with bargain prices as well as better products. For example, in order to enter the market for laundry detergents in India, Unilever had to develop a low-cost detergent (named Wheel), construct new low-cost production facilities, package the detergent in single-use amounts so that it could be sold at a very low unit price, distribute the product to local merchants by handcarts, and craft an economical marketing campaign that included painted signs on buildings and demonstrations near stores. The new brand quickly captured $100 million in sales and was the top detergent brand in India based on 2011 dollar sales. Unilever later replicated the strategy in India with low-priced packets of shampoos and deodorants and in South America with a detergent brand-named Ala.

- *Modify aspects of the company's business model to accommodate the unique local circumstances of developing countries.* For instance, when Dell entered China, it discovered that individuals and businesses were not accustomed to placing orders through the Internet. To adapt, Dell modified its direct sales model to rely more heavily on phone and fax orders while waiting for a greater acceptance of online ordering. Further, because numerous Chinese government departments and state-owned enterprises insisted that hardware vendors make their bids through distributors and systems integrators (as opposed to dealing directly with Dell salespeople as did large enterprises in other countries), Dell opted to use third parties in marketing its products to this buyer segment. But Dell was careful not to abandon the parts of its business model that gave it a competitive edge over rivals.

- *Try to change the local market to better match the way the company does business elsewhere.* An international company often has enough market clout to drive major changes in the way a local country market operates. When Japan's Suzuki entered India, it triggered a quality revolution among Indian auto parts manufacturers. Local component suppliers teamed up with Suzuki's vendors in Japan and worked with Japanese experts to produce higher-quality products. Over the next two decades, Indian companies became proficient in making top-notch components for vehicles, won more prizes for quality than companies in any country other than Japan, and broke into the global market as suppliers to many automakers in Asia and other parts of the world. Mahindra and Mahindra, one of India's premier automobile manufacturers, has been recognized by a number of organizations for its product quality. Among its most noteworthy awards was its number-one ranking by J.D. Power Asia Pacific for new-vehicle overall quality.

- *Stay away from developing markets where it is impractical or uneconomical to modify the company's business model to accommodate local circumstances.* Home Depot's CFO, Carol Tomé, argues that there are few developing countries where Home Depot can operate successfully.[19] The company expanded successfully into Mexico, but it has avoided entry into other developing countries because its value proposition of good quality, low prices, and attentive customer service relies on (1) good highways and logistical systems to minimize store inventory costs, (2) employee stock ownership to help motivate store personnel to provide good customer service, and (3) high labor costs for housing construction and home repairs that encourage homeowners to engage in do-it-yourself projects. Relying on these factors in North American markets has worked spectacularly for Home Depot, but the company found that it could not count on these factors in China, from which it withdrew in 2012.

Company experiences in entering developing markets like Argentina, Vietnam, Malaysia, and Brazil indicate that profitability seldom comes quickly or easily. Building a market for the company's products can often turn into a long-term process that involves reeducation of consumers, sizable investments in advertising to alter tastes and buying habits, and upgrades of the local infrastructure

> Profitability in developing markets rarely comes quickly or easily—new entrants have to adapt their business models to local conditions, which may not always be possible.

(transportation systems, distribution channels, etc.). In such cases, a company must be patient, work within the system to improve the infrastructure, and lay the foundation for generating sizable revenues and profits once conditions are ripe for market takeoff.

## DEFENDING AGAINST GLOBAL GIANTS: STRATEGIES FOR LOCAL COMPANIES IN DEVELOPING COUNTRIES

If opportunity-seeking, resource-rich international companies are looking to enter developing-country markets, what strategy options can local companies use to survive? As it turns out, the prospects for local companies facing global giants are by no means grim. Studies of local companies in developing markets have disclosed five strategies that have proved themselves in defending against globally competitive companies.[20]

1.  *Develop business models that exploit shortcomings in local distribution networks or infrastructure.* In many instances, the extensive collection of resources possessed by the global giants is of little help in building a presence in developing markets. The lack of well-established local wholesaler and distributor networks, telecommunication systems, consumer banking, or media necessary for advertising makes it difficult for large internationals to migrate business models proved in developed markets to emerging markets. Emerging markets sometimes favor local companies whose managers are familiar with the local language and culture and are skilled in selecting large numbers of conscientious employees to carry out labor-intensive tasks. Shanda, a Chinese producer of massively multiplayer online role-playing games (MMORPG), overcame China's lack of an established credit card network by selling prepaid access cards through local merchants. The company's focus on online games also protects it from shortcomings in China's software piracy laws. An India-based electronics company carved out a market niche for itself by developing an all-in-one business machine, designed especially for India's millions of small shopkeepers, that tolerates the country's frequent power outages.

2.  *Utilize keen understanding of local customer needs and preferences to create customized products or services.* When developing-country markets are largely made up of customers with strong local needs, a good strategy option is to concentrate on customers who prefer a local touch and to accept the loss of the customers attracted to global brands.[21] A local company may be able to astutely exploit its local orientation—its familiarity with local preferences, its expertise in traditional products, its long-standing customer relationships. A small Middle Eastern cell phone manufacturer competes successfully against industry giants Samsung, Apple, Nokia, and Motorola by selling a model designed especially for Muslims— it is loaded with the Koran, alerts people at prayer times, and is equipped with a compass that points them toward Mecca. Shenzhen-based Tencent has become the leader in instant messaging in China through its unique understanding of Chinese behavior and culture.

3.  *Take advantage of aspects of the local workforce with which large international companies may be unfamiliar.* Local companies that lack the technological capabilities of foreign entrants may be able to rely on their better understanding of the local labor force to offset any disadvantage. Focus Media is China's largest outdoor advertising firm and has relied on low-cost labor to update its 130,000 LCD displays and billboards in 90 cities in a low-tech manner, while

international companies operating in China use electronically networked screens that allow messages to be changed remotely. Focus uses an army of employees who ride to each display by bicycle to change advertisements with programming contained on a USB flash drive or DVD. Indian information technology firms such as Infosys Technologies and Satyam Computer Services have been able to keep their personnel costs lower than those of international competitors EDS and Accenture because of their familiarity with local labor markets. While the large internationals have focused recruiting efforts in urban centers like Bangalore and Delhi, driving up engineering and computer science salaries in such cities, local companies have shifted recruiting efforts to second-tier cities that are unfamiliar to foreign firms.

4. *Use acquisition and rapid-growth strategies to better defend against expansion-minded internationals.* With the growth potential of developing markets such as China, Indonesia, and Brazil obvious to the world, local companies must attempt to develop scale and upgrade their competitive capabilities as quickly as possible to defend against the stronger international's arsenal of resources. Most successful companies in developing markets have pursued mergers and acquisitions at a rapid-fire pace to build first a nationwide and then an international presence. Hindalco, India's largest aluminum producer, has followed just such a path to achieve its ambitions for global dominance. By acquiring companies in India first, it gained enough experience and confidence to eventually acquire much larger foreign companies with world-class capabilities.[22] When China began to liberalize its foreign trade policies, Lenovo (the Chinese PC maker) realized that its long-held position of market dominance in China could not withstand the onslaught of new international entrants such as Dell and HP. Its acquisition of IBM's PC business allowed Lenovo to gain rapid access to IBM's globally recognized PC brand, its R&D capability, and its existing distribution in developed countries. This has allowed Lenovo not only to hold its own against the incursion of global giants into its home market but to expand into new markets around the world.[23]

5. *Transfer company expertise to cross-border markets and initiate actions to contend on an international level.* When a company from a developing country has resources and capabilities suitable for competing in other country markets, launching initiatives to transfer its expertise to foreign markets becomes a viable strategic option. Televisa, Mexico's largest media company, used its expertise in Spanish culture and linguistics to become the world's most prolific producer of Spanish-language soap operas. By continuing to upgrade its capabilities and learn from its experience in foreign markets, a company can sometimes transform itself into one capable of competing on a worldwide basis, as an emerging global giant. Sundaram Fasteners of India began its foray into foreign markets as a supplier of radiator caps to GM—an opportunity it pursued when GM first decided to outsource the production of this part. As a participant in GM's supplier network, the company learned about emerging technical standards, built its capabilities, and became one of the first Indian companies to achieve QS 9000 quality certification. With the expertise it gained and its recognition for meeting quality standards, Sundaram was then able to pursue opportunities to supply automotive parts in Japan and Europe.

Illustration Capsule 7.3 discusses how a travel agency in China used a combination of these strategies to become that country's largest travel consolidator and online travel agent.

# How Ctrip Successfully Defended against International Rivals to Become China's Largest Online Travel Agency

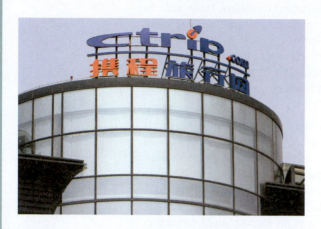

Ctrip has utilized a business model tailored to the Chinese travel market, its access to low-cost labor, and its unique understanding of customer preferences and buying habits to build scale rapidly and defeat foreign rivals such as Expedia and Travelocity in becoming the largest travel agency in China. The company was founded in 1999 with a focus on business travelers, since corporate travel accounts for the majority of China's travel bookings. The company initially placed little emphasis on online transactions, since at the time there was no national ticketing system in China, most hotels did not belong to a national or international chain, and most consumers preferred paper tickets to electronic tickets. To overcome this infrastructure shortcoming and enter the online market, the company established its own central database of 5,600 hotels located throughout China and flight information for all major airlines operating in China. Ctrip set up a call center of 3,000 representatives that could use its proprietary database to provide travel information for up to 100,000 customers per day. Because most of its transactions were not done over the Internet at the start, the company hired couriers in all major cities in China to ride by bicycle or scooter to collect payments and deliver tickets to Ctrip's corporate customers. Ctrip also initiated a loyalty program that provided gifts and incentives to the administrative personnel who arranged travel for business executives, who were more likely to use online services. By 2011, Ctrip.com held 60 percent of China's online travel market, having grown 40 percent every year since 1999, leading to a market cap coming close to those of some major U.S. online travel agencies.

However, the phenomenal growth of the Chinese market for such travel agency services (expected to more than double by 2016), along with changing technological ability and preferences, has led to a new type of competition: online, and more pivotally, mobile travel booking. Dominance in the mobile space has driven a competitor, Qunar, to experience a huge surge in growth. While this competition has been a negative in a traditional financial sense for Ctrip, analysts believe that new technology will ultimately end up benefiting the entire industry. Additionally, Qunar's entry has provided the two companies the opportunity to utilize another important local strategy to grow and remain competitive against global firms—a partnership, which Ctrip and Qunar undertook in 2013, combining their unique advantages to cross-sell travel products. The relative and absolute success of Ctrip and its competitor-partner Qunar will be seen in the coming years, but to date we have already observed the effects of an effective local-market strategy.

*Note:* Developed with Harold W. Greenstone.

*Sources:* Arindam K. Bhattacharya and David C. Michael, "How Local Companies Keep Multinationals at Bay," *Harvard Business Review* 86, no. 3 (March 2008), pp. 85–95; B. Perez, "Ctrip Likely to Gain More Business from Stronger Qunar Platform," *South China Morning Press* Online, October 2, 2013 (accessed April 3, 2014); B. Cao, "Qunar Jumps on Mobile User Growth as Ctrip Tumbles," *Bloomberg* Online, January 5, 2014 (accessed April 3, 2014); www.thatsmags.com/shanghai/article/detail/480/a-journey-with-ctrip; and money.cnn.com/quote/quote.html?symb=EXPE (accessed March 28, 2012).

## KEY POINTS

1. Competing in international markets allows a company to (1) gain access to new customers, (2) achieve lower costs through greater economies of scale, learning, and increased purchasing power, (3) gain access to low-cost inputs of production, (4) further exploit its core competencies, and (5) gain access to resources and capabilities located outside the company's domestic market.

2. Strategy making is more complex for five reasons: (1) Different countries have *home-country advantages* in different industries; (2) there are location-based advantages to performing different value chain activities in different parts of the world; (3) varying political and economic risks make the business climate of some countries more favorable than others; (4) companies face the risk of adverse shifts in exchange rates when operating in foreign countries; and (5) differences in buyer tastes and preferences present a conundrum concerning the trade-off between customizing and standardizing products and services.

3. The strategies of firms that expand internationally are usually grounded in home-country advantages concerning demand conditions, factor conditions, related and supporting industries, and firm strategy, structure, and rivalry, as described by the Diamond of National Competitive Advantage framework.

4. There are five strategic options for entering foreign markets. These include maintaining a home-country production base and *exporting* goods to foreign markets, *licensing* foreign firms to produce and distribute the company's products abroad, employing a *franchising* strategy, establishing a foreign *subsidiary via an acquisition or greenfield venture,* and using *strategic alliances or other collaborative partnerships.*

5. A company must choose among three alternative approaches for competing internationally: (1) a *multidomestic strategy*—a *think-local, act-local* approach to crafting international strategy; (2) a *global strategy*—a *think-global, act-global* approach; and (3) a combination *think-global, act-local* approach, known as a *transnational strategy.* A multidomestic strategy (think local, act local) is appropriate for companies that must vary their product offerings and competitive approaches from country to country in order to accommodate different buyer preferences and market conditions. The global strategy (think global, act global) works best when there are substantial cost benefits to be gained from taking a standardized, globally integrated approach and there is little need for local responsiveness. A transnational strategy (think global, act local) is called for when there is a high need for local responsiveness as well as substantial benefits from taking a globally integrated approach. In this approach, a company strives to employ the same basic competitive strategy in all markets but still customizes its product offering and some aspect of its operations to fit local market circumstances.

6. There are three general ways in which a firm can gain competitive advantage (or offset domestic disadvantages) in international markets. One way involves locating various value chain activities among nations in a manner that lowers costs or achieves greater product differentiation. A second way draws on an international competitor's ability to extend its competitive advantage by cost-effectively sharing, replicating, or transferring its most valuable resources and capabilities across borders. A third looks for benefits from cross-border coordination that are unavailable to domestic-only competitors.

7. Two types of strategic moves are particularly suited for companies competing internationally. Both involve the use of profit sanctuaries—country markets where a company derives substantial profits because of its strong or protected market position. Profit sanctuaries are useful in waging strategic offenses in international markets through *cross-subsidization*—a practice of supporting competitive offensives in

one market with resources and profits diverted from operations in another market (the profit sanctuary). They may be used defensively to encourage *mutual restraint* among competitors when there is international *multimarket competition* by signaling that each company has the financial capability for mounting a strong counterattack if threatened. For companies with at least one profit sanctuary, having a presence in a rival's key markets can be enough to deter the rival from making aggressive attacks.

8. Companies racing for global leadership have to consider competing in developing markets like the BRIC countries—Brazil, Russia, India, and China—countries where the business risks are considerable but the opportunities for growth are huge. To succeed in these markets, companies often have to (1) compete on the basis of low price, (2) modify aspects of the company's business model to accommodate local circumstances, and/or (3) try to change the local market to better match the way the company does business elsewhere. Profitability is unlikely to come quickly or easily in developing markets, typically because of the investments needed to alter buying habits and tastes, the increased political and economic risk, and/or the need for infrastructure upgrades. And there may be times when a company should simply stay away from certain developing markets until conditions for entry are better suited to its business model and strategy.

9. Local companies in developing-country markets can seek to compete against large international companies by (1) developing business models that exploit shortcomings in local distribution networks or infrastructure, (2) utilizing a superior understanding of local customer needs and preferences or local relationships, (3) taking advantage of competitively important qualities of the local workforce with which large international companies may be unfamiliar, (4) using acquisition strategies and rapid-growth strategies to better defend against expansion-minded international companies, or (5) transferring company expertise to cross-border markets and initiating actions to compete on an international level.

## ASSURANCE OF LEARNING EXERCISES

**LO 1, LO 3**

1. Chile's largest producer of wine, Concha y Toro, chooses to compete in Europe, North America, the Caribbean, and Asia using an export strategy. Go to the Investor Relations section of the company's website (www.conchaytoro.com/the-company/investor-relations/) to review the company's press releases, annual reports, and presentations. Why does it seem that the company has avoided developing vineyards and wineries in wine-growing regions outside South America? What reasons does Concha y Toro likely have to pursue exporting rather than stick to a domestic-only sales and distribution strategy?

**connect**

**LO 1, LO 3**

2. Collaborative agreements with foreign companies in the form of strategic alliances or joint ventures are widely used as a means of entering foreign markets. They are also used as a means of acquiring resources and capabilities by learning from foreign partners. And they are used to put together powerful combinations of complementary resources and capabilities by accessing the complementary resources and capabilities of a foreign partner. Illustration Capsule 7.1 provides examples of four cross-border strategic alliances that Solazyme has participated in. What were each of these partnerships (with Unilever, Sephora, Qantas, and Roquette) designed to achieve, and why would they make sense for a company like Solazyme? (Analyze each partnership separately based on the information provided in the capsule.)

3. Assume you are in charge of developing the strategy for an international company selling products in some 50 different countries around the world. One of the issues you face is whether to employ a multidomestic strategy, a global strategy, or a transnational strategy.

   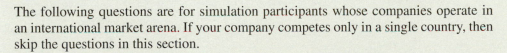

   **LO 2, LO 4**

   a. If your company's product is mobile phones, which of these strategies do you think it would make better strategic sense to employ? Why?

   b. If your company's product is dry soup mixes and canned soups, would a multidomestic strategy seem to be more advisable than a global strategy or a transnational strategy? Why?

   c. If your company's product is large home appliances such as washing machines, ranges, ovens, and refrigerators, would it seem to make more sense to pursue a multidomestic strategy, a global strategy, or a transnational strategy? Why?

4. Your company is an American-based footwear producer. Over the past few years, while demand for your products has been increasing, costs have been rising steadily and your production capabilities are limited. What options might you have to decrease costs and increase production to meet rising demand?   **LO 5**

5. Assume you are the CEO of an online retailer looking to expand your services into developing-country markets. Much of the success of your business model depends on the ability to ship items quickly and without delays as well as provide unrivaled customer service. What concerns might you have entering a developing-country market given your business model? What would be the necessary conditions for your business to succeed?   **LO 2, LO 6**

# EXERCISE FOR SIMULATION PARTICIPANTS

The following questions are for simulation participants whose companies operate in an international market arena. If your company competes only in a single country, then skip the questions in this section.

1. To what extent, if any, have you and your co-managers adapted your company's strategy to take shifting exchange rates into account? In other words, have you undertaken any actions to try to minimize the impact of adverse shifts in exchange rates?   **LO 2**

2. To what extent, if any, have you and your co-managers adapted your company's strategy to take geographic differences in import tariffs or import duties into account?   **LO 2**

3. Which one of the following best describes the strategic approach your company is taking in trying to compete successfully on an international basis?   **LO 4**

   - Multidomestic or think-local, act-local approach.
   - Global or think-global, act-global approach.
   - Transnational or think-global, act-local approach.

Explain your answer and indicate two or three chief elements of your company's strategy for competing in two or more different geographic regions.

# ENDNOTES

[1] Sidney G. Winter and Gabriel Szulanski, "Getting It Right the Second Time," *Harvard Business Review* 80, no. 1 (January 2002), pp. 62–69.

[2] P. Dussauge, B. Garrette, and W. Mitchell, "Learning from Competing Partners: Outcomes and Durations of Scale and Link Alliances in Europe, North America and Asia," *Strategic Management Journal* 21, no. 2 (February 2000), pp. 99–126; K. W. Glaister and P. J. Buckley, "Strategic Motives for International Alliance Formation," *Journal of Management Studies* 33, no. 3 (May 1996), pp. 301–332.

[3] M. Porter, "The Competitive Advantage of Nations," *Harvard Business Review,* March–April 1990, pp. 73–93.

[4] Tom Mitchell and Avantika Chilkoti, "China Car Sales Accelerate Away from US and Brazil in 2013," *Financial Times,* January 9, 2014, www.ft.com/cms/s/0/8c649078-78f8-11e3-b381-00144feabdc0.html#axzz2rpEqjkZO.

[5] U.S. Department of Labor, Bureau of Labor Statistics, "International Comparisons of Hourly Compensation Costs in Manufacturing 2012," August 9, 2013. (The numbers for India and China are estimates.)

[6] Sangwon Yoon, "South Korea Targets Internet Addicts; 2 Million Hooked," *Valley News,* April 25, 2010, p. C2.

[7] Joel Bleeke and David Ernst, "The Way to Win in Cross-Border Alliances," *Harvard Business Review* 69, no. 6 (November–December 1991), pp. 127–133; Gary Hamel, Yves L. Doz, and C. K. Prahalad, "Collaborate with Your Competitors—and Win," *Harvard Business Review* 67, no. 1 (January–February 1989), pp. 134–135.

[8] K. W. Glaister and P. J. Buckley, "Strategic Motives for International Alliance Formation," *Journal of Management Studies* 33, no. 3 (May 1996), pp. 301–332.

[9] Jeffrey H. Dyer, Prashant Kale, and Harbir Singh, "When to Ally and When to Acquire," *Harvard Business Review* 82, no. 7–8 (July–August 2004).

[10] Yves Doz and Gary Hamel, Alliance Advantage: *The Art of Creating Value through Partnering* (Harvard Business School Press, 1998); Rosabeth Moss Kanter, "Collaborative Advantage: The Art of the Alliance," *Harvard Business Review* 72, no. 4 (July–August 1994), pp. 96–108.

[11] Jeremy Main, "Making Global Alliances Work," *Fortune,* December 19, 1990, p. 125.

[12] C. K. Prahalad and Kenneth Lieberthal, "The End of Corporate Imperialism," *Harvard Business Review* 81, no. 8 (August 2003), pp. 109–117.

[13] Pankaj Ghemawat, "Managing Differences: The Central Challenge of Global Strategy," *Harvard Business Review* 85, no. 3 (March 2007).

[14] C. A. Bartlett and S. Ghoshal, *Managing across Borders: The Transnational Solution,* 2nd ed. (Boston: Harvard Business School Press, 1998).

[15] Lynn S. Paine, "The China Rules," *Harvard Business Review* 88, no. 6 (June 2010), pp. 103–108.

[16] C. K. Prahalad and Yves L. Doz, *The Multinational Mission*: *Balancing Local Demands and Global Vision* (New York: Free Press, 1987).

[17] David J. Arnold and John A. Quelch, "New Strategies in Emerging Markets," *Sloan Management Review* 40, no. 1 (Fall 1998), pp. 7–20.

[18] Tarun Khanna, Krishna G. Palepu, and Jayant Sinha, "Strategies That Fit Emerging Markets," *Harvard Business Review* 83, no. 6 (June 2005), p. 63; Arindam K. Bhattacharya and David C. Michael, "How Local Companies Keep Multinationals at Bay," *Harvard Business Review* 86, no. 3 (March 2008), pp. 94–95.

[19] www.ajc.com/news/business/home-depot-eschews-large-scale-international-expan/nSQBh/ (accessed February 2, 2014).

[20] Tarun Khanna and Krishna G. Palepu, "Emerging Giants: Building World-Class Companies in Developing Countries," *Harvard Business Review* 84, no. 10 (October 2006), pp. 60–69.

[21] Niroj Dawar and Tony Frost, "Competing with Giants: Survival Strategies for Local Companies in Emerging Markets," *Harvard Business Review* 77, no. 1 (January–February 1999), p. 122; Guitz Ger, "Localizing in the Global Village: Local Firms Competing in Global Markets," *California Management Review* 41, no. 4 (Summer 1999), pp. 64–84.

[22] N. Kumar, "How Emerging Giants Are Rewriting the Rules of M&A," *Harvard Business Review,* May 2009, pp. 115–121.

[23] H. Rui and G. Yip, "Foreign Acquisitions by Chinese Firms: A Strategic Intent Perspective," *Journal of World Business* 43 (2008), pp. 213–226.

### CHAPTER 8

# Corporate Strategy

## Diversification and the Multibusiness Company

## Learning Objectives

**LO 1**   When and how business diversification can enhance shareholder value.

**LO 2**   How related diversification strategies can produce cross-business strategic fit capable of delivering competitive advantage.

**LO 3**   The merits and risks of unrelated diversification strategies.

**LO 4**   The analytic tools for evaluating a company's diversification strategy.

**LO 5**   What four main corporate strategy options a diversified company can employ for solidifying its strategy and improving company performance.

The desire for reinvention seems to arise most often when companies hear the siren call of synergy and start to expand beyond their core businesses.

> James Surowiecki – *Writer on Business and Finance for* The New Yorker

Diversification and globalization are the keys to the future.

> Fujio Mitarai – *Legendary Chairman and CEO of Canon, Inc.*

How many senior executives discuss the crucial distinction between competitive strategy at the level of a business and competitive strategy at the level of an entire company?

> C. K. Prahalad and Gary Hamel – *Professors, Authors, and Consultants*

In this chapter, we move up one level in the strategy-making hierarchy, from strategy making in a single-business enterprise to strategy making in a diversified enterprise. Because a diversified company is a collection of individual businesses, the strategy-making task is more complicated. In a one-business company, managers have to come up with a plan for competing successfully in only a single industry environment—the result is what Chapter 2 labeled as *business strategy* (or *business-level strategy*). But in a diversified company, the strategy-making challenge involves assessing multiple industry environments and developing a *set of business strategies,* one for each industry arena in which the diversified company operates. And top executives at a diversified company must still go one step further and devise a companywide (or *corporate*) strategy for improving the performance of the company's overall business lineup and for making a rational whole out of its diversified collection of individual businesses.

In the first portion of this chapter, we describe what crafting a diversification strategy entails, when and why diversification makes good strategic sense, the various approaches to diversifying a company's business lineup, and the pros and cons of related versus unrelated diversification strategies. The second part of the chapter looks at how to evaluate the attractiveness of a diversified company's business lineup, how to decide whether it has a good diversification strategy, and the strategic options for improving a diversified company's future performance.

## WHAT DOES CRAFTING A DIVERSIFICATION STRATEGY ENTAIL?

The task of crafting a diversified company's overall *corporate strategy* falls squarely in the lap of top-level executives and involves four distinct facets:

1. *Picking new industries to enter and deciding on the means of entry*. The decision to pursue business diversification requires that management decide which new industries to enter and whether to enter by starting a new business from the ground

up, acquiring a company already in the target industry, or forming a joint venture or strategic alliance with another company.

2. *Pursuing opportunities to leverage cross-business value chain relationships, where there is strategic fit, into competitive advantage.* The task here is to determine whether there are opportunities to strengthen a diversified company's businesses by such means as transferring competitively valuable resources and capabilities from one business to another, combining the related value chain activities of different businesses to achieve lower costs, sharing the use of a powerful and well-respected brand name across multiple businesses, and encouraging knowledge sharing and collaborative activity among the businesses.

3. *Establishing investment priorities and steering corporate resources into the most attractive business units.* Typically, this translates into pursuing rapid-growth strategies in the company's most promising businesses, initiating profit improvement or turnaround strategies in weak-performing businesses that have potential, and divesting businesses that are no longer attractive or that don't fit into management's long-range plans.

4. *Initiating actions to boost the combined performance of the corporation's collection of businesses.* Strategic options for improving the corporation's overall performance include (1) sticking closely with the existing business lineup and pursuing opportunities presented by these businesses, (2) broadening the scope of diversification by entering additional industries, (3) retrenching to a narrower scope of diversification by divesting poorly performing businesses, and (4) broadly restructuring the entire company by divesting some businesses and acquiring others so as to put a whole new face on the company's business lineup.

The demanding and time-consuming nature of these four tasks explains why corporate executives generally refrain from becoming immersed in the details of crafting and executing business-level strategies. Rather, the normal procedure is to delegate lead responsibility for business strategy to the heads of each business, giving them the latitude to develop strategies suited to the particular industry environment in which their business operates and holding them accountable for producing good financial and strategic results.

# WHEN TO CONSIDER DIVERSIFYING

As long as a company has plentiful opportunities for profitable growth in its present industry, there is no urgency to pursue diversification. But growth opportunities are often limited in mature industries and declining markets. In addition, changing industry conditions—new technologies, inroads being made by substitute products, fast-shifting buyer preferences, or intensifying competition—can undermine a company's ability to deliver ongoing gains in revenues and profits. Consider, for example, what the growing use of debit cards and online bill payment has done to the check-printing business and what mobile phone companies and marketers of Voice over Internet Protocol (VoIP) have done to the revenues of long-distance providers such as AT&T, British Telecommunications, and NTT in Japan. Thus, diversifying into new industries always merits strong consideration whenever a single-business company encounters diminishing market opportunities and stagnating sales in its principal business.

The decision to diversify presents wide-ranging possibilities. A company can diversify into closely related businesses or into totally unrelated businesses. It can diversify its present revenue and earnings base to a small or major extent. It can move into one or two large new businesses or a greater number of small ones. It can achieve diversification by acquiring an existing company, starting up a new business from scratch, or forming a joint venture with one or more companies to enter new businesses. In every case, however, the decision to diversify must start with a strong economic justification for doing so.

# BUILDING SHAREHOLDER VALUE: THE ULTIMATE JUSTIFICATION FOR DIVERSIFYING

Diversification must do more for a company than simply spread its business risk across various industries. In principle, diversification cannot be considered a success unless it results in *added long-term economic value for shareholders*—value that shareholders cannot capture on their own by purchasing stock in companies in different industries or investing in mutual funds so as to spread their investments across several industries.

> **LO 1**
>
> When and how business diversification can enhance shareholder value.

Business diversification stands little chance of building shareholder value without passing the following three **Tests of Corporate Advantage.**[1]

1.  *The industry attractiveness test.* The industry to be entered through diversification must be structurally attractive (in terms of the five forces), have resource requirements that match those of the parent company, and offer good prospects for growth, profitability, and return on investment.

2.  *The cost of entry test.* The cost of entering the target industry must not be so high as to exceed the potential for good profitability. A catch-22 can prevail here, however. The more attractive an industry's prospects are for growth and good long-term profitability, the more expensive it can be to enter. Entry barriers for startup companies are likely to be high in attractive industries—if barriers were low, a rush of new entrants would soon erode the potential for high profitability. And buying a well-positioned company in an appealing industry often entails a high acquisition cost that makes passing the cost of entry test less likely. Since the owners of a successful and growing company usually demand a price that reflects their business's profit prospects, it's easy for such an acquisition to fail the cost of entry test.

3.  *The better-off test.* Diversifying into a new business must offer potential for the company's existing businesses and the new business to perform better together under a single corporate umbrella than they would perform operating as independent, stand-alone businesses—an effect known as **synergy.** For example, let's say that company A diversifies by purchasing company B in another industry. If A and B's consolidated profits in the years to come prove no greater than what each could have earned on its own, then A's diversification won't provide its shareholders with any added value. Company A's shareholders could have achieved the same $1 + 1 = 2$ result by merely purchasing stock in company B. Diversification does not result in added long-term value for shareholders unless it produces a $1 + 1 = 3$ effect, whereby the businesses *perform better together as part of the same firm than they could have performed as independent companies.*

> **CORE CONCEPT**
>
> To add shareholder value, a move to diversify into a new business must pass the three **Tests of Corporate Advantage:**
> 1. The Industry Attractiveness Test
> 2. The Cost of Entry Test
> 3. The Better-off Test

> **CORE CONCEPT**
>
> Creating added value for shareholders via diversification requires building a multibusiness company in which the whole is greater than the sum of its parts—such $1 + 1 = 3$ effects are called **synergy.**

Diversification moves must satisfy all three tests to grow shareholder value over the long term. Diversification moves that can pass only one or two tests are suspect.

# APPROACHES TO DIVERSIFYING THE BUSINESS LINEUP

The means of entering new businesses can take any of three forms: acquisition, internal startup, or joint ventures with other companies.

## Diversifying by Acquisition of an Existing Business

Acquisition is a popular means of diversifying into another industry. Not only is it quicker than trying to launch a new operation, but it also offers an effective way to hurdle such entry barriers as acquiring technological know-how, establishing supplier relationships, achieving scale economies, building brand awareness, and securing adequate distribution. Acquisitions are also commonly employed to access resources and capabilities that are complementary to those of the acquiring firm and that cannot be developed readily internally. Buying an ongoing operation allows the acquirer to move directly to the task of building a strong market position in the target industry, rather than getting bogged down in trying to develop the knowledge, experience, scale of operation, and market reputation necessary for a startup entrant to become an effective competitor.

> **CORE CONCEPT**
>
> An **acquisition premium**, or control premium, is the amount by which the price offered exceeds the preacquisition market value of the target company.

However, acquiring an existing business can prove quite expensive. The costs of acquiring another business include not only the acquisition price but also the costs of performing the due diligence to ascertain the worth of the other company, the costs of negotiating the purchase transaction, and the costs of integrating the business into the diversified company's portfolio. If the company to be acquired is a successful company, the acquisition price will include a hefty *premium* over the preacquisition value of the company for the right to control the company. For example, the $28 billion that Berkshire Hathaway and 3G Capital agreed to pay for H. J. Heinz Company in 2014 included a 30 percent premium over its one-year average share price.[2] Premiums are paid in order to convince the shareholders and managers of the target company that it is in their financial interests to approve the deal. The average premium paid by U.S. companies was 19 percent in 2013, but it was more often in the 20 to 25 percent range over the last 10 years.[3]

While acquisitions offer an enticing means for entering a new business, many fail to deliver on their promise.[4] Realizing the potential gains from an acquisition requires a successful integration of the acquired company into the culture, systems, and structure of the acquiring firm. This can be a costly and time-consuming operation. Acquisitions can also fail to deliver long-term shareholder value if the acquirer overestimates the potential gains and pays a premium in excess of the realized gains. High integration costs and excessive price premiums are two reasons that an acquisition might fail the cost of entry test. Firms with significant experience in making acquisitions are better able to avoid these types of problems.[5]

## Entering a New Line of Business through Internal Development

Achieving diversification through *internal development* involves starting a new business subsidiary from scratch. Internal development has become an increasingly important way for companies to diversify and is often referred to as **corporate venturing** or *new venture development*. Although building a new business from the ground up is generally a time-consuming and uncertain process, it avoids the pitfalls associated with entry via acquisition and may allow the firm to realize greater profits in the end. It may offer a viable means of entering a new or emerging industry where there are no good acquisition candidates.

Entering a new business via internal development, however, poses some significant hurdles. An internal new venture not only has to overcome industry entry barriers but also must invest in new production capacity, develop sources of supply, hire and train employees, build channels of distribution, grow a customer base, and so on, unless the new business is quite similar to the company's existing business. The risks associated with internal startups can be substantial, and the likelihood of failure is often high. Moreover, the culture, structures, and organizational systems of some companies may impede innovation and make it difficult for corporate entrepreneurship to flourish.

Generally, internal development of a new business has appeal only when (1) the parent company already has in-house most of the resources and capabilities it needs to piece together a new business and compete effectively; (2) there is ample time to launch the business; (3) the internal cost of entry is lower than the cost of entry via acquisition; (4) adding new production capacity will not adversely impact the supply–demand balance in the industry; and (5) incumbent firms are likely to be slow or ineffective in responding to a new entrant's efforts to crack the market.

> **CORE CONCEPT**
>
> **Corporate venturing** (or *new venture development*) is the process of developing new businesses as an outgrowth of a company's established business operations. It is also referred to as *corporate entrepreneurship* or *intrapreneurship* since it requires entrepreneurial-like qualities within a larger enterprise.

## Using Joint Ventures to Achieve Diversification

Entering a new business via a joint venture can be useful in at least three types of situations.[6] First, a joint venture is a good vehicle for pursuing an opportunity that is too complex, uneconomical, or risky for one company to pursue alone. Second, joint ventures make sense when the opportunities in a new industry require a broader range of competencies and know-how than a company can marshal on its own. Many of the opportunities in satellite-based telecommunications, biotechnology, and network-based systems that blend hardware, software, and services call for the coordinated development of complementary innovations and the tackling of an intricate web of financial, technical, political, and regulatory factors simultaneously. In such cases, pooling the resources and competencies of two or more companies is a wiser and less risky way to proceed. Third, companies sometimes use joint ventures to diversify into a new industry when the diversification move entails having operations in a foreign country. However, as discussed in Chapters 6 and 7, partnering with another company has significant drawbacks due to the potential for conflicting objectives, disagreements over how to best operate the venture, culture clashes, and so on. Joint ventures are generally the least durable of the entry options, usually lasting only until the partners decide to go their own ways.

## Choosing a Mode of Entry

The choice of how best to enter a new business—whether through internal development, acquisition, or joint venture—depends on the answers to four important questions:

- Does the company have all of the resources and capabilities it requires to enter the business through internal development, or is it lacking some critical resources?
- Are there entry barriers to overcome?
- Is speed an important factor in the firm's chances for successful entry?
- Which is the least costly mode of entry, given the company's objectives?

### The Question of Critical Resources and Capabilities

If a firm has all the resources it needs to start up a new business or will be able to easily purchase or lease any missing resources, it may choose to enter the business via internal development. However, if missing critical resources cannot be easily purchased or leased, a firm wishing to enter a new business must obtain these missing resources through either acquisition or joint venture. Bank of America acquired Merrill Lynch to obtain critical investment banking resources and capabilities that it lacked. The acquisition of these additional capabilities complemented Bank of America's strengths in corporate banking and opened up new business opportunities for the company. Firms often acquire other companies as a way to enter foreign markets where they lack local marketing knowledge, distribution capabilities, and relationships with local suppliers or customers. McDonald's acquisition of Burghy, Italy's only national hamburger chain, offers an example.[7] If there are no good acquisition opportunities or if the firm wants to avoid the high cost of acquiring and integrating another firm, it may choose to enter via joint venture. This type of entry mode has the added advantage of spreading the risk of entering a new business, an advantage that is particularly attractive when uncertainty is high. De Beers's joint venture with the luxury goods company LVMH provided De Beers not only with the complementary marketing capabilities it needed to enter the diamond retailing business but also with a partner to share the risk.

### The Question of Entry Barriers

The second question to ask is whether entry barriers would prevent a new entrant from gaining a foothold and succeeding in the industry. If entry barriers are low and the industry is populated by small firms, internal development may be the preferred mode of entry. If entry barriers are high, the company may still be able to enter with ease if it has the requisite resources and capabilities for overcoming high barriers. For example, entry barriers due to reputational advantages may be surmounted by a diversified company with a widely known and trusted corporate name. But if the entry barriers cannot be overcome readily, then the only feasible entry route may be through acquisition of a well-established company. While entry barriers may also be overcome with a strong complementary joint venture, this mode is the more uncertain choice due to the lack of industry experience.

### The Question of Speed

Speed is another determining factor in deciding how to go about entering a new business. Acquisition is a favored mode of entry when speed is of the essence, as is the case in rapidly changing industries where fast movers can secure long-term positioning advantages. Speed is important in industries where early movers gain experience-based advantages that grow ever larger over time as they move down the learning curve. It is also important in technology-based industries where there is a race to establish an industry standard or leading technological platform. But in other cases it can be better to enter a market after the uncertainties about technology or consumer preferences have been resolved and learn from the missteps of early entrants. In these cases, joint venture or internal development may be preferred.

### The Question of Comparative Cost

The question of which mode of entry is most cost-effective is a critical one, given the need for a diversification strategy to pass the cost of entry test. Acquisition can be a high-cost mode of entry due to the need to pay a premium over the share price of the target company. When the premium is high, the price of the deal will exceed the worth of the acquired company as a stand-alone business by a substantial amount. Whether it is worth it to pay that high a price will depend on how much extra value will be created by the new combination of companies in the form of synergies. Moreover, the true cost of an acquisition must include the **transaction costs** of identifying and evaluating potential targets, negotiating a price, and completing other aspects of deal making. In addition, the true cost must take into account the costs of integrating the acquired company into the parent company's portfolio of businesses.

Joint ventures may provide a way to conserve on such entry costs. But even here, there are organizational coordination costs and transaction costs that must be considered, including settling on the terms of the arrangement. If the partnership doesn't proceed smoothly and is not founded on trust, these costs may be significant.

# CHOOSING THE DIVERSIFICATION PATH: RELATED VERSUS UNRELATED BUSINESSES

Once a company decides to diversify, it faces the choice of whether to diversify into **related businesses, unrelated businesses,** or some mix of both. Businesses are said to be *related* when their value chains exhibit competitively important cross-business commonalities. By this, we mean that there is a close correspondence between the businesses in terms of *how they perform* key value chain activities and *the resources and capabilities each needs* to perform those activities. The big appeal of related diversification is the opportunity to build shareholder value by leveraging these cross-business commonalities into competitive advantages, thus allowing the company as a whole to perform better than just the sum of its individual businesses. Businesses are said to be *unrelated* when the resource requirements and key value chain activities are so dissimilar that no competitively important cross-business commonalities exist.

The next two sections explore the ins and outs of related and unrelated diversification.

# DIVERSIFICATION INTO RELATED BUSINESSES

A related diversification strategy involves building the company around businesses where there is good *strategic fit across corresponding value chain activities.* **Strategic fit** exists whenever one or more activities constituting the value chains of different businesses are sufficiently similar to present opportunities for cross-business sharing or transferring of the resources and capabilities that enable these activities.[8] Prime examples of such opportunities include:

**LO 2**

How related diversification strategies can produce cross-business strategic fit capable of delivering competitive advantage.

- *Transferring specialized expertise, technological know-how, or other competitively valuable strategic assets from one business's value chain to another's.* Google's ability to transfer software developers and other information technology specialists from other business applications to the development of its Android mobile operating system and Chrome operating system for PCs aided considerably in the success of these new internal ventures.
- *Sharing costs between businesses by combining their related value chain activities into a single operation.* For instance, it is often feasible to manufacture the products of different businesses in a single plant, use the same warehouses for shipping and distribution, or have a single sales force for the products of different businesses if they are marketed to the same types of customers.

- *Exploiting the common use of a well-known brand name.* For example, Yamaha's name in motorcycles gave the company instant credibility and recognition in entering the personal-watercraft business, allowing it to achieve a significant market share without spending large sums on advertising to establish a brand identity for the WaveRunner. Likewise, Apple's reputation for producing easy-to-operate computers was a competitive asset that facilitated the company's diversification into digital music players and smartphones.

- *Sharing other resources (besides brands) that support corresponding value chain activities across businesses.* When Disney acquired Marvel Comics, management saw to it that Marvel's iconic characters, such as Spiderman, Iron Man, and Captain America, were shared with many of the other Disney businesses, including its theme parks, retail stores, and video game business. (Disney's characters, starting with Mickey Mouse, have always been among the most valuable of its resources.) Automobile companies like Ford share resources such as their relationships with suppliers and dealer networks across their lines of business.

- *Engaging in cross-business collaboration and knowledge sharing to create new competitively valuable resources and capabilities.* Businesses performing closely related value chain activities may seize opportunities to join forces, share knowledge and talents, and collaborate to create altogether new capabilities (such as virtually defect-free assembly methods or increased ability to speed new products to market) that will be mutually beneficial in improving their competitiveness and business performance.

Related diversification is based on value chain matchups with respect to *key* value chain activities—those that play a central role in each business's strategy and that link to its industry's key success factors. Such matchups facilitate the sharing or transfer of the resources and capabilities that enable the performance of these activities and underlie each business's quest for competitive advantage. By facilitating the sharing or transferring of such important competitive assets, related diversification can elevate each business's prospects for competitive success.

The resources and capabilities that are leveraged in related diversification are **specialized resources and capabilities.** By this, we mean that they have very *specific* applications; their use is restricted to a limited range of business contexts in which these applications are competitively relevant. Because they are adapted for particular applications, specialized resources and capabilities must be utilized by particular types of businesses operating in specific kinds of industries to have value; they have limited utility outside this designated range of industry and business applications. This is in contrast to **general resources and capabilities** (such as general management capabilities, human resource management capabilities, and general accounting services), which can be applied usefully across a wide range of industry and business types.

L'Oréal is the world's largest beauty products company, with more than $30 billion in revenues and a successful strategy of related diversification built upon leveraging a highly specialized set of resources and capabilities. These include 22 dermatologic and cosmetic research centers, R&D capabilities and scientific knowledge concerning skin and hair care, patents and secret formulas for hair and skin care products, and robotic applications developed specifically for testing the safety of hair and skin care products. These resources and capabilities are highly valuable for businesses focused on products for human skin and hair—they are *specialized* to such applications, and, in consequence, they are of little or no value beyond this restricted range of applications. To leverage these resources in a way that maximizes their potential value, L'Oréal has diversified into cosmetics, hair care products, skin care products, and fragrances (but not food, transportation, industrial services, or any application area far from the narrow domain in which its specialized resources are competitively relevant). L'Oréal's businesses are related to one another on the basis of its value-generating specialized resources and capabilities and the cross-business linkages among the value chain activities that they enable.

Corning's most competitively valuable resources and capabilities are specialized to applications concerning fiber optics and specialty glass and ceramics. Over the course of its 150-year history, it has developed an unmatched understanding of fundamental glass science and related technologies in the field of optics. Its capabilities now span a variety of sophisticated technologies and include expertise in domains such as custom glass composition, specialty glass melting and forming, precision optics, high-end transmissive coatings, and optomechanical materials. Corning has leveraged these specialized capabilities into a position of global leadership in five related market segments: display technologies based on glass substrates, environmental technologies using ceramic substrates and filters, optical fibers and cables for telecommunications, optical biosensors for drug discovery, and specialty materials employing advanced optics and specialty glass solutions. The market segments into which Corning has diversified are all related by their reliance on Corning's specialized capability set and by the many value chain activities that they have in common as a result.

General Mills has diversified into a closely related set of food businesses on the basis of its capabilities in the realm of "kitchen chemistry" and food production technologies. Its businesses include General Mills cereals, Pillsbury and Betty Crocker baking products, yogurts, organic foods, dinner mixes, canned goods, and snacks. Earlier it had diversified into restaurant businesses on the mistaken notion that all food businesses were related. By exiting these businesses in the mid-1990s, the company was able to improve its overall profitability and strengthen its position in its remaining businesses. The lesson from its experience—and a takeaway for the managers of any diversified company—is that *it is not product relatedness that defines a well-crafted related diversification strategy.* Rather, *the businesses must be related in terms of their key value chain activities and the specialized resources and capabilities that enable these activities.*[9] An example is Citizen Holdings Company, whose products appear to be different (watches, miniature card calculators, handheld televisions) but are related in terms of their common reliance on miniaturization know-how and advanced precision technologies.

While companies pursuing related diversification strategies may also have opportunities to share or transfer their *general* resources and capabilities (e.g., information systems; human resource management practices; accounting and tax services; budgeting, planning, and financial reporting systems; expertise in legal and regulatory affairs; and fringe-benefit management systems), *the most competitively valuable opportunities for resource sharing or transfer always come from leveraging their specialized resources and capabilities.* The reason for this is that specialized resources and capabilities drive the key value-creating activities that both connect the businesses (at points along their value chains where there is strategic fit) and link to the key success factors in the markets where they are competitively relevant. Figure 8.1 illustrates the range of opportunities to share and/or transfer specialized resources and capabilities among the value chain activities of related businesses. It is important to recognize that *even though general resources and capabilities may be shared by multiple business units, such resource sharing alone cannot form the backbone of a strategy keyed to related diversification.*

**FIGURE 8.1**    Related Businesses Provide Opportunities to Benefit from Competitively Valuable Strategic Fit

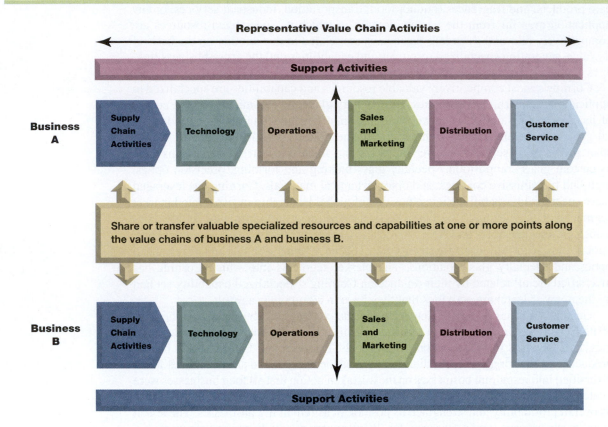

## Identifying Cross-Business Strategic Fit along the Value Chain

Cross-business strategic fit can exist anywhere along the value chain—in R&D and technology activities, in supply chain activities and relationships with suppliers, in manufacturing, in sales and marketing, in distribution activities, or in customer service activities.[10]

**Strategic Fit in Supply Chain Activities**    Businesses with strategic fit with respect to their supply chain activities can perform better together because of the potential for transferring skills in procuring materials, sharing resources and capabilities in logistics, collaborating with common supply chain partners, and/or increasing leverage with shippers in securing volume discounts on incoming parts and components. Dell Computer's strategic partnerships with leading suppliers of microprocessors, circuit boards, disk drives, memory chips, flat-panel displays, wireless capabilities, long-life batteries, and other PC-related components have been an important element of the company's strategy to diversify into servers, data storage devices, networking components, and LED TVs—products that include many components common to PCs and that can be sourced from the same strategic partners that provide Dell with PC components.

**Strategic Fit in R&D and Technology Activities**    Businesses with strategic fit in R&D or technology development perform better together than apart because of potential cost savings in R&D, shorter times in getting new products to market, and more innovative products or processes. Moreover, technological advances in one business can lead to increased sales for both. Technological innovations have been the driver behind the efforts of cable TV companies to diversify into high-speed Internet access (via the use of cable modems) and, further, to explore providing local and long-distance telephone service to residential and commercial customers either through a single wire or by means of Voice over Internet Protocol (VoIP) technology.

**Manufacturing-Related Strategic Fit**  Cross-business strategic fit in manufacturing-related activities can be exploited when a diversifier's expertise in quality control and cost-efficient production methods can be transferred to another business. When Emerson Electric diversified into the chain-saw business, it transferred its expertise in low-cost manufacture to its newly acquired Beaird-Poulan business division. The transfer drove Beaird-Poulan's new strategy—to be the low-cost provider of chain-saw products—and fundamentally changed the way Beaird-Poulan chain saws were designed and manufactured. Another benefit of production-related value chain commonalities is the ability to consolidate production into a smaller number of plants and significantly reduce overall production costs. When snowmobile maker Bombardier diversified into motorcycles, it was able to set up motorcycle assembly lines in the manufacturing facility where it was assembling snowmobiles. When Smucker's acquired Procter & Gamble's Jif peanut butter business, it was able to combine the manufacture of the two brands of peanut butter products while gaining greater leverage with vendors in purchasing its peanut supplies.

**Strategic Fit in Sales and Marketing Activities**  Various cost-saving opportunities spring from diversifying into businesses with closely related sales and marketing activities. When the products are sold directly to the same customers, sales costs can often be reduced by using a single sales force instead of having two different salespeople call on the same customer. The products of related businesses can be promoted at the same website and included in the same media ads and sales brochures. There may be opportunities to reduce costs by consolidating order processing and billing and by using common promotional tie-ins. When global power-tool maker Black & Decker acquired Vector Products, it was able to use its own global sales force to sell the newly acquired Vector power inverters, vehicle battery chargers, and rechargeable spotlights because the types of customers that carried its power tools (discounters like Kmart, home centers, and hardware stores) also stocked the types of products produced by Vector.

A second category of benefits arises when different businesses use similar sales and marketing approaches. In such cases, there may be competitively valuable opportunities to transfer selling, merchandising, advertising, and product differentiation skills from one business to another. Procter & Gamble's product lineup includes Pampers diapers, Olay beauty products, Tide laundry detergent, Crest toothpaste, Charmin toilet tissue, Gillette razors and blades, Duracell batteries, Oral-B toothbrushes, and Head & Shoulders shampoo. All of these have different competitors and different supply chain and production requirements, but they all move through the same wholesale distribution systems, are sold in common retail settings to the same shoppers, and require the same marketing and merchandising skills.

**Distribution-Related Strategic Fit**  Businesses with closely related distribution activities can perform better together than apart because of potential cost savings in sharing the same distribution facilities or using many of the same wholesale distributors and retail dealers. When Conair Corporation acquired Allegro Manufacturing's travel bag and travel accessory business, it was able to consolidate its own distribution centers for hair dryers and curling irons with those of Allegro, thereby generating cost savings for both businesses. Likewise, since Conair products and Allegro's neck rests, ear plugs, luggage tags, and toiletry kits were sold by the same types of retailers (discount stores, supermarket chains, and drugstore chains), Conair was able to convince many of the retailers not carrying Allegro products to take on the line.

**Strategic Fit in Customer Service Activities**    Strategic fit with respect to customer service activities can enable cost savings or differentiation advantages, just as it does along other points of the value chain. For example, cost savings may come from consolidating after-sale service and repair organizations for the products of closely related businesses into a single operation. Likewise, different businesses can often use the same customer service infrastructure. For instance, an electric utility that diversifies into natural gas, water, appliance repair services, and home security services can use the same customer data network, the same call centers and local offices, the same billing and accounting systems, and the same customer service infrastructure to support all of its products and services. Through the transfer of best practices in customer service across a set of related businesses or through the sharing of resources such as proprietary information about customer preferences, a multibusiness company can also create a differentiation advantage through higher-quality customer service.

## Strategic Fit, Economies of Scope, and Competitive Advantage

What makes related diversification an attractive strategy is the opportunity to convert cross-business strategic fit into a competitive advantage over business rivals whose operations do not offer comparable strategic-fit benefits. The greater the relatedness among a diversified company's businesses, the bigger a company's window for converting strategic fit into competitive advantage via (1) transferring skills or knowledge, (2) combining related value chain activities to achieve lower costs, (3) leveraging the use of a well-respected brand name, (4) sharing other valuable resources, and (5) using cross-business collaboration and knowledge sharing to create new resources and capabilities and drive innovation.

**Strategic Fit and Economies of Scope**    Strategic fit in the value chain activities of a diversified corporation's different businesses opens up opportunities for **economies of scope**—a concept distinct from *economies of scale*. Economies of *scale* are cost savings that accrue directly from a larger-sized operation—for example, unit costs may be lower in a large plant than in a small plant. Economies of *scope,* however, *stem directly from strategic fit along the value chains of related businesses,* which in turn enables the businesses to share resources or to transfer them from business to business at low cost. Such economies are open only to firms engaged in related diversification, since they are the result of related businesses performing R&D together, transferring managers from one business to another, using common manufacturing or distribution facilities, sharing a common sales force or dealer network, using the same established brand name, and the like. *The greater the cross-business economies associated with resource* *sharing and transfer, the greater the potential for a related diversification strategy to give a multibusiness enterprise a cost advantage over rivals.*

### From Strategic Fit to Competitive Advantage, Added Profitability, and Gains in Shareholder Value

The cost advantage from economies of scope is due to the fact that resource sharing allows a multibusiness firm to spread resource costs across its businesses and to avoid the expense of having to acquire and maintain duplicate sets of resources—one for each business. But related diversified companies can benefit from strategic fit in other ways as well.

Sharing or transferring valuable specialized assets among the company's businesses can help each business perform its value chain activities more proficiently. This translates into competitive advantage for the businesses in one or two basic ways: (1) The businesses can contribute to greater efficiency and lower costs relative to their competitors, and/or (2) they can provide a basis for differentiation so that customers are willing to pay relatively more for the businesses' goods and services. In either or both of these ways, a firm with a well-executed related diversification strategy can boost the chances of its businesses attaining a competitive advantage.

The competitive advantage potential that flows from the capture of strategic-fit benefits is what enables a company pursuing related diversification to achieve $1 + 1 = 3$ financial performance and the hoped-for gains in shareholder value. The greater the relatedness among a diversified company's businesses, the bigger a company's window for converting strategic fit into competitive advantage. The strategic and business logic is compelling: Capturing the benefits of strategic fit along the value chains of its related businesses gives a diversified company a clear path to achieving competitive advantage over undiversified competitors and competitors whose own diversification efforts don't offer equivalent strategic-fit benefits.[11] Such competitive advantage potential provides a company with a dependable basis for earning profits and a return on investment that exceeds what the company's businesses could earn as stand-alone enterprises. Converting the competitive advantage potential into greater profitability is what fuels $1 + 1 = 3$ gains in shareholder value—the necessary outcome for satisfying the *better-off test* and proving the business merit of a company's diversification effort.

> Diversifying into related businesses where competitively valuable strategic-fit benefits can be captured puts a company's businesses in position to perform better financially as part of the company than they could have performed as independent enterprises, thus providing a clear avenue for increasing shareholder value and satisfying the *better-off test*.

There are five things to bear in mind here:

1. Capturing cross-business strategic-fit benefits via a strategy of related diversification builds shareholder value in ways that shareholders cannot undertake by simply owning a portfolio of stocks of companies in different industries.

2. The capture of cross-business strategic-fit benefits is possible only via a strategy of related diversification.

3. The greater the relatedness among a diversified company's businesses, the bigger the company's window for converting strategic fit into competitive advantage.

4. The benefits of cross-business strategic fit come from the transferring or sharing of competitively valuable resources and capabilities among the businesses—resources and capabilities that are *specialized* to certain applications and have value only in specific types of industries and businesses.

5. The benefits of cross-business strategic fit are not automatically realized when a company diversifies into related businesses; *the benefits materialize only after management has successfully pursued internal actions to capture them.*

Illustration Capsule 8.1 describes Microsoft's acquisition of Skype in pursuit of the strategic-fit benefits of a related diversification strategy.

## Microsoft's Acquisition of Skype: Pursuing the Benefits of Cross-Business Strategic Fit

From humble beginnings in Gates's family garage, Microsoft has grown to exceed $77.85 billion of revenue in 2013 and offer a product line extending from gaming (Xbox) and Internet services (Internet Explorer and Bing) to mobile devices (Windows Phones). In 2011, Microsoft diversified its product line yet again through acquiring Skype Global for $8.5 billion in cash. Although Microsoft had previously ventured into the Internet communications industry with Windows Live Messenger, Skype offered Microsoft broader device support, mobile video calling, and access to over 170 million Skype users, potential new clients for Microsoft's existing products.

Microsoft considered Skype a valuable acquisition due to the strategic fit between the value chain activities of the two companies. Moreover, Skype's communication expertise combined with Microsoft's market reach offered an opportunity to generate new competitively valuable resources and capabilities. With the communications industry gradually shifting toward more face-to-face calling, Skype gave Microsoft an already-established visual communications platform to complement its existing Xbox Live services, Office Suite, and new Windows 8 software. In turn, as the leading operating system (OS) software developer in the world, Microsoft could expand Skype's scope and reach by prepackaging future Windows OS releases with Skype software.

In addition to offering cross-business collaboration and value chain–supporting opportunities, Skype also offered several immediate resources. Skype CEO Tony Bates possessed extensive knowledge of the Internet communications market and could ensure the long-term operational and strategic continuity of Skype.

Recognizing Bates's specialized expertise and experience, Microsoft retained Bates as head of its newly formed Microsoft Skype Division. Additionally, Microsoft gained access to over 50 Skype communications patents and the already-established relationships with many of Skype's previous partners (and Microsoft competitors), including Facebook, Sony, and Verizon. Moreover, by keeping the Skype name and opting to replace its Windows Live Messenger client, Microsoft could exploit the well-known Skype brand for its history of reliability and quality. With such a rich set of opportunities for the cross-business sharing and transferring of resources and capabilities, Microsoft believed that its acquisition of Skype would generate synergies and increase its competitiveness.

Only time will tell, but given Skype's growth and Microsoft's plans to incorporate Skype in its Windows 8 platform and Xbox Live services, the outcome of this related diversification move seems promising.

*Note:* Developed with Sean Zhang.

*Sources:* Company websites; www.cbsnews.com/8301-505124_162-42340380/with-verizon-and-facebook-partnerships-skype-positions-itself-for-app-world-dominance/; dealbook.nytimes.com/2011/05/10/microsoft-to-buy-skype-for-8-5-billion/; and www.nytimes.com/2012/05/29/technology/microsoft-at-work-on-meshing-its-products-with-skype.html?pagewanted=all&_r=1& (accessed February 21, 2013).

# DIVERSIFICATION INTO UNRELATED BUSINESSES

**LO 3**

The merits and risks of unrelated diversification strategies.

Achieving cross-business strategic fit is not a motivation for unrelated diversification. Companies that pursue a strategy of unrelated diversification generally exhibit a willingness to diversify into *any business in any industry* where senior managers see an opportunity to realize consistently good financial results. Such companies are frequently labeled *conglomerates* because their business interests range broadly across diverse industries. Companies engaged in unrelated diversification nearly always enter new businesses by acquiring an established company rather than by forming a startup subsidiary within their own corporate structures or participating in joint ventures.

With a strategy of unrelated diversification, an acquisition is deemed to have potential if it passes the industry-attractiveness and cost of entry tests and if it has good prospects for attractive financial performance. Thus, with an unrelated diversification strategy, company managers spend much time and effort screening acquisition candidates and evaluating the pros and cons of keeping or divesting existing businesses, using such criteria as:

- Whether the business can meet corporate targets for profitability and return on investment.
- Whether the business is in an industry with attractive growth potential.
- Whether the business is big enough to contribute *significantly* to the parent firm's bottom line.

But the key to successful unrelated diversification is to go beyond these considerations and *ensure that the strategy passes the better-off test as well.* This test requires more than just growth in revenues; it requires *growth in profits*—beyond what could be achieved by a mutual fund or a holding company that owns shares of the businesses without adding any value. Unless the combination of businesses is more profitable together under the corporate umbrella than they are apart as independent businesses, *the strategy cannot create economic value for shareholders.* And unless it does so, there is *no real justification for unrelated diversification,* since top executives have a fiduciary responsibility to maximize long-term shareholder value for the company's owners (its shareholders).

# Building Shareholder Value via Unrelated Diversification

Given the absence of cross-business strategic fit with which to create competitive advantages, building shareholder value via unrelated diversification ultimately hinges on the ability of the parent company to improve its businesses (and make the combination *better off* ) via other means. Critical to this endeavor is the role that the parent company plays as a *corporate parent.*[12] To the extent that a company has strong *parenting capabilities*—capabilities that involve nurturing, guiding, grooming, and governing constituent businesses—a corporate parent can propel its businesses forward and help them gain ground over their market rivals. Corporate parents also contribute to the competitiveness of their unrelated businesses by sharing or transferring *general resources and capabilities* across the businesses—competitive assets that have utility in *any type* of industry and that can be leveraged across a wide range of business types as a result. Examples of the kinds of general resources that a corporate parent leverages in unrelated diversification include the corporation's reputation, credit rating, and access to financial markets; governance mechanisms; management training programs; a corporate ethics program; a central data and communications center; shared administrative resources such as public relations and legal services; and common systems for functions such as budgeting, financial reporting, and quality control.

### The Benefits of Astute Corporate Parenting   One of the most important ways that corporate parents contribute to the success of their businesses is

by offering high-level oversight and guidance.[13] The top executives of a large diversified corporation have among them many years of accumulated experience in a variety of business settings and can often contribute expert problem-solving skills, creative strategy suggestions, and first-rate advice and guidance on how to improve competitiveness and financial performance to the heads of the company's various business subsidiaries. This is especially true in the case of newly acquired, smaller businesses. Particularly astute high-level guidance from corporate executives can help the subsidiaries perform better than they would otherwise be able to do through the efforts of the business unit heads alone. The outstanding leadership of Royal Little, the founder of Textron, was a major reason that the company became an exemplar of the unrelated diversification strategy while he was CEO. Little's bold moves transformed the company from its origins as a small textile manufacturer into a global powerhouse known for its Bell helicopters, Cessna aircraft, and host of other strong brands in a wide array of industries. Norm Wesley, a former CEO of the conglomerate Fortune Brands, is similarly credited with driving the sharp rise in the company's stock price while he was at the helm. Under his leadership, Fortune Brands became the $7 billion maker of products ranging from spirits (e.g., Jim Beam bourbon and rye, Gilbey's gin and vodka, Courvoisier cognac) to golf products (e.g., Titleist golf balls and clubs, FootJoy golf shoes and apparel, Scotty Cameron putters) to hardware (e.g., Moen faucets, American Lock security devices). (Fortune Brands has since been converted into two separate entities, Beam Inc. and Fortune Brands Home & Security.)

Corporate parents can also create added value for their businesses by providing them with other types of general resources that lower the operating costs of the individual businesses or that enhance their operating effectiveness. The administrative resources located at a company's corporate headquarters are a prime example. They typically include legal services, accounting expertise and tax services, and other elements of the administrative infrastructure, such as risk management capabilities, information technology resources, and public relations capabilities. Providing individual businesses with general support resources such as these creates value by *lowering companywide overhead costs,* since each business would otherwise have to duplicate the centralized activities.

Corporate brands that do not connote any specific type of product are another type of general corporate resource that can be shared among unrelated businesses. GE's brand is an example, having been applied to businesses as diverse as financial services (GE Capital), medical imaging (GE medical diagnostics), and lighting (GE lightbulbs). Corporate brands that are applied in this fashion are sometimes called **umbrella brands.** Utilizing a well-known corporate name (GE) in a diversified company's individual businesses has the potential not only to lower costs (by spreading the fixed cost of developing and maintaining the brand over many businesses) but also to enhance each business's customer value proposition by linking its products to a name that consumers trust. In similar fashion, a corporation's reputation for well-crafted products, for product reliability, or for trustworthiness can lead to greater customer willingness to purchase the products of a wider range of a diversified company's businesses. Incentive systems, financial control systems, and a company's culture are other types of general corporate resources that may prove useful in enhancing the daily operations of a diverse set of businesses.

We discuss two other commonly employed ways for corporate parents to add value to their unrelated businesses next.

## CORE CONCEPT

**Corporate parenting** refers to the role that a diversified corporation plays in nurturing its component businesses through the provision of top management expertise, disciplined control, financial resources, and other types of *general resources and capabilities* such as long-term planning systems, business development skills, management development processes, and incentive systems.

An **umbrella brand** is a corporate brand name that can be applied to a wide assortment of business types. As such, it is a type of *general resource* that can be leveraged in unrelated diversification.

## Judicious Cross-Business Allocation of Financial Resources

By reallocating surplus cash flows from some businesses to fund the capital requirements of other businesses—in essence, having the company serve as an *internal capital market*—corporate parents may also be able to create value. Such actions can be particularly important in times when credit is unusually tight (such as in the wake of the worldwide banking crisis that began in 2008) or in economies with less well developed capital markets. Under these conditions, with strong financial resources a corporate parent can add value by shifting funds from business units generating excess cash (more than they need to fund their own operating requirements and new capital investment opportunities) to other, cash-short businesses with appealing growth prospects. A parent company's ability to function as its own internal capital market enhances overall corporate performance and increases shareholder value to the extent that (1) its top managers have better access to information about investment opportunities internal to the firm than do external financiers or (2) it can provide funds that would otherwise be unavailable due to poor financial market conditions.

## Acquiring and Restructuring Undervalued Companies

Another way for parent companies to add value to unrelated businesses is by acquiring weakly performing companies at a bargain price and then *restructuring* their operations in ways that produce sometimes dramatic increases in profitability. **Restructuring** refers to overhauling and streamlining the operations of a business—combining plants with excess capacity, selling off underutilized assets, reducing unnecessary expenses, revamping its product offerings, consolidating administrative functions to reduce overhead costs, and otherwise improving the operating efficiency and profitability of a company. Restructuring generally involves transferring seasoned managers to the newly acquired business, either to replace the top layers of management or to step in temporarily until the business is returned to profitability or is well on its way to becoming a major market contender.

> ### CORE CONCEPT
>
> **Restructuring** refers to overhauling and streamlining the activities of a business—combining plants with excess capacity, selling off underutilized assets, reducing unnecessary expenses, and otherwise improving the productivity and profitability of a company.

Restructuring is often undertaken when a diversified company acquires a new business that is performing well below levels that the corporate parent believes are achievable. Diversified companies that have capabilities in restructuring (sometimes called *turnaround capabilities*) are able to significantly boost the performance of weak businesses in a relatively wide range of industries. Newell Rubbermaid (whose diverse product line includes Sharpie pens, Levolor window treatments, Goody hair accessories, Calphalon cookware, and Lenox power and hand tools) developed such a strong set of turnaround capabilities that the company was said to "Newellize" the businesses it acquired.

Successful unrelated diversification strategies based on restructuring require the parent company to have considerable expertise in identifying underperforming target companies and in negotiating attractive acquisition prices so that each acquisition passes the cost of entry test. The capabilities in this regard of Lord James Hanson and Lord Gordon White, who headed up the storied British conglomerate Hanson Trust, played a large part in Hanson Trust's impressive record of profitability.

# The Path to Greater Shareholder Value through Unrelated Diversification

For a strategy of unrelated diversification to produce companywide financial results above and beyond what the businesses could generate operating as stand-alone entities, corporate executives must do three things to pass the three tests of corporate advantage:

**CORE CONCEPT**

A diversified company has a **parenting advantage** when it is more able than other companies to boost the combined performance of its individual businesses through high-level guidance, general oversight, and other corporate-level contributions.

1. Diversify into industries where the businesses can produce consistently good earnings and returns on investment (to satisfy the industry-attractiveness test).
2. Negotiate favorable acquisition prices (to satisfy the cost of entry test).
3. Do a superior job of corporate parenting via high-level managerial oversight and resource sharing, financial resource allocation and portfolio management, and/or the restructuring of underperforming businesses (to satisfy the better-off test).

The best corporate parents understand the nature and value of the kinds of resources at their command and know how to leverage them effectively across their businesses. Those that are able to create more value in their businesses than other diversified companies have what is called a **parenting advantage.** When a corporation has a parenting advantage, its top executives have the best chance of being able to craft and execute an unrelated diversification strategy that can satisfy all three tests of corporate advantage and truly enhance long-term economic shareholder value.

# The Drawbacks of Unrelated Diversification

Unrelated diversification strategies have two important negatives that undercut the pluses: very demanding managerial requirements and limited competitive advantage potential.

**Demanding Managerial Requirements**   Successfully managing a set of fundamentally different businesses operating in fundamentally different industry and competitive environments is a challenging and exceptionally difficult proposition.[14] Consider, for example, that corporations like General Electric, ITT, Mitsubishi, and Bharti Enterprises have dozens of business subsidiaries making hundreds and sometimes thousands of products. While headquarters executives can glean information about an industry from third-party sources, ask lots of questions when making occasional visits to the operations of the different businesses, and do their best to learn about the company's different businesses, they still remain heavily dependent on briefings from business unit heads and on "managing by the numbers"—that is, keeping a close track on the financial and operating results of each subsidiary. Managing by the numbers works well enough when business conditions are normal and the heads of the various business units are capable of consistently meeting their numbers. But problems arise if things start to go awry in a business and corporate management has to get deeply involved in the problems of a business it does not know much about. Because every business tends to encounter rough sledding at some juncture, unrelated diversification is thus a somewhat risky strategy from a managerial perspective.[15] Just one or two unforeseen problems or big strategic mistakes—which are much more likely without close corporate oversight—can cause a precipitous drop in corporate earnings and crash the parent company's stock price.

Hence, competently overseeing a set of widely diverse businesses can turn out to be much harder than it sounds. In practice, comparatively few companies have proved that they have top-management capabilities that are up to the task. There are far more companies whose corporate executives have failed at delivering consistently good financial results with an unrelated diversification strategy than there are companies with corporate executives who have been successful.[16] Unless a company truly has a parenting advantage, the odds are that the result of unrelated diversification will be $1 + 1 = 2$ or even less.

**Limited Competitive Advantage Potential**   The second big negative is that *unrelated diversification offers only a limited potential for competitive advantage beyond what each individual business can generate on its own.* Unlike a related diversification strategy, unrelated diversification provides no cross-business strategic-fit benefits that allow each business to perform its key value chain activities in a more efficient and effective manner. A cash-rich corporate parent pursuing unrelated diversification can provide its subsidiaries with much-needed capital, may achieve economies of scope in activities relying on general corporate resources, and may even offer some managerial know-how to help resolve problems in particular business units, but otherwise it has little to offer in the way of enhancing the competitive strength of its individual business units. In comparison to the highly specialized resources that facilitate related diversification, the general resources that support unrelated diversification tend to be relatively low value, for the simple reason that they are more common. Unless they are of exceptionally high quality (such as GE's world-renowned general management capabilities or Newell Rubbermaid's turnaround capabilities), resources and capabilities that are general in nature are less likely to provide a source of competitive advantage for diversified companies. Without the competitive advantage potential of strategic fit in competitively important value chain activities, consolidated performance of an unrelated group of businesses stands to be little more than the sum of what the individual business units could achieve if they were independent, in most circumstances.

> Relying solely on leveraging general resources and the expertise of corporate executives to wisely manage a set of unrelated businesses is *a much weaker foundation for enhancing shareholder value* than is a strategy of related diversification.

# Misguided Reasons for Pursuing Unrelated Diversification

Companies sometimes pursue unrelated diversification for reasons that are misguided. These include the following:

- *Risk reduction.* Spreading the company's investments over a set of diverse industries to spread risk cannot create long-term shareholder value since the company's shareholders can more flexibly (and more efficiently) reduce their exposure to risk by investing in a diversified portfolio of stocks and bonds.

- *Growth.* While unrelated diversification may enable a company to achieve rapid or continuous growth, firms that pursue growth for growth's sake are unlikely to maximize shareholder value. Only *profitable growth*—the kind that comes from creating added value for shareholders—can justify a strategy of unrelated diversification.

- *Stabilization.* Managers sometimes pursue broad diversification in the hope that market downtrends in some of the company's businesses will be partially offset by cyclical upswings in its other businesses, thus producing somewhat less earnings volatility. In actual practice, however, there's no convincing evidence that the consolidated profits of firms with unrelated diversification strategies are more stable or less subject to reversal in periods of recession and economic stress than the profits of firms with related diversification strategies.

- *Managerial motives.* Unrelated diversification can provide benefits to managers such as higher compensation (which tends to increase with firm size and degree

Only *profitable growth*—the kind that comes from creating added value for shareholders—can justify a strategy of unrelated diversification.

of diversification) and reduced unemployment risk. Pursuing diversification for these reasons will likely reduce shareholder value and violate managers' fiduciary responsibilities.

Because unrelated diversification strategies *at their best* have only a limited potential for creating long-term economic value for shareholders, it is essential that managers not compound this problem by taking a misguided approach toward unrelated diversification, in pursuit of objectives that are more likely to destroy shareholder value than create it.

## COMBINATION RELATED-UNRELATED DIVERSIFICATION STRATEGIES

There's nothing to preclude a company from diversifying into both related and unrelated businesses. Indeed, in actual practice the business makeup of diversified companies varies considerably. Some diversified companies are really *dominant-business enterprises*—one major "core" business accounts for 50 to 80 percent of total revenues and a collection of small related or unrelated businesses accounts for the remainder. Some diversified companies are *narrowly diversified* around a few (two to five) related or unrelated businesses. Others are *broadly diversified* around a wide-ranging collection of related businesses, unrelated businesses, or a mixture of both. A number of multibusiness enterprises have diversified into unrelated areas but have a collection of related businesses within each area—thus giving them a business portfolio consisting of *several unrelated groups of related businesses*. There's ample room for companies to customize their diversification strategies to incorporate elements of both related and unrelated diversification, as may suit their own competitive asset profile and strategic vision. *Combination related-unrelated diversification strategies have particular appeal for companies with a mix of valuable competitive assets, covering the spectrum from general to specialized resources and capabilities.*

Figure 8.2 shows the range of alternatives for companies pursuing diversification.

## EVALUATING THE STRATEGY OF A DIVERSIFIED COMPANY

### LO 4

The analytic tools for evaluating a company's diversification strategy.

Strategic analysis of diversified companies builds on the concepts and methods used for single-business companies. But there are some additional aspects to consider and a couple of new analytic tools to master. The procedure for evaluating the pluses and minuses of a diversified company's strategy and deciding what actions to take to improve the company's performance involves six steps:

1. Assessing the attractiveness of the industries the company has diversified into, both individually and as a group.
2. Assessing the competitive strength of the company's business units and drawing a nine-cell matrix to simultaneously portray industry attractiveness and business unit competitive strength.
3. Evaluating the extent of cross-business strategic fit along the value chains of the company's various business units.

**FIGURE 8.2**   **Three Strategy Options for Pursuing Diversification**

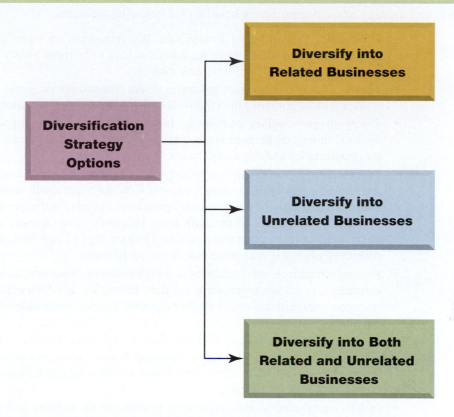

4. Checking whether the firm's resources fit the requirements of its present business lineup.
5. Ranking the performance prospects of the businesses from best to worst and determining what the corporate parent's priorities should be in allocating resources to its various businesses.
6. Crafting new strategic moves to improve overall corporate performance.

The core concepts and analytic techniques underlying each of these steps merit further discussion.

## Step 1: Evaluating Industry Attractiveness

A principal consideration in evaluating the caliber of a diversified company's strategy is the attractiveness of the industries in which it has business operations. Several questions arise:

1. Does each industry the company has diversified into represent a good market for the company to be in—does it pass the industry-attractiveness test?
2. Which of the company's industries are most attractive, and which are least attractive?
3. How appealing is the whole group of industries in which the company has invested?

The more attractive the industries (both individually and as a group) that a diversified company is in, the better its prospects for good long-term performance.

**Calculating Industry-Attractiveness Scores**    A simple and reliable analytic tool for gauging industry attractiveness involves calculating quantitative industry-attractiveness scores based on the following measures:

- *Market size and projected growth rate.* Big industries are more attractive than small industries, and fast-growing industries tend to be more attractive than slow-growing industries, other things being equal.
- *The intensity of competition.* Industries where competitive pressures are relatively weak are more attractive than industries where competitive pressures are strong.
- *Emerging opportunities and threats.* Industries with promising opportunities and minimal threats on the near horizon are more attractive than industries with modest opportunities and imposing threats.
- *The presence of cross-industry strategic fit.* The more one industry's value chain and resource requirements match up well with the value chain activities of other industries in which the company has operations, the more attractive the industry is to a firm pursuing related diversification. However, cross-industry strategic fit is not something that a company committed to a strategy of unrelated diversification considers when it is evaluating industry attractiveness.
- *Resource requirements.* Industries in which resource requirements are within the company's reach are more attractive than industries in which capital and other resource requirements could strain corporate financial resources and organizational capabilities.
- *Social, political, regulatory, and environmental factors.* Industries that have significant problems in such areas as consumer health, safety, or environmental pollution or those subject to intense regulation are less attractive than industries that do not have such problems.
- *Industry profitability.* Industries with healthy profit margins and high rates of return on investment are generally more attractive than industries with historically low or unstable profits.

Each attractiveness measure is then assigned a weight reflecting its relative importance in determining an industry's attractiveness, since not all attractiveness measures are equally important. The intensity of competition in an industry should nearly always carry a high weight (say, 0.20 to 0.30). Strategic-fit considerations should be assigned a high weight in the case of companies with related diversification strategies; but for companies with an unrelated diversification strategy, strategic fit with other industries may be dropped from the list of attractiveness measures altogether. The importance weights must add up to 1.

Finally, each industry is rated on each of the chosen industry-attractiveness measures, using a rating scale of 1 to 10 (where a *high* rating signifies *high* attractiveness, and a *low* rating signifies *low* attractiveness). *Keep in mind here that the more intensely competitive an industry is, the lower the attractiveness rating for that industry.* Likewise, the more the resource requirements associated with being in a particular industry are beyond the parent company's reach, the lower the attractiveness rating. On the other hand, the presence of good cross-industry strategic fit should be given a very high attractiveness rating, since there is good potential for competitive advantage and added shareholder value. Weighted attractiveness scores are then calculated by multiplying the industry's rating on each measure by the corresponding weight. For example, a rating of 8 times a weight of 0.25 gives a weighted attractiveness score of 2. The sum of the weighted scores for all the attractiveness measures provides an overall industry-attractiveness score. This procedure is illustrated in Table 8.1.

**TABLE 8.1**   Calculating Weighted Industry-Attractiveness Scores

| Industry-Attractiveness Measure | Importance Weight | Industry A | | Industry B | | Industry C | |
|---|---|---|---|---|---|---|---|
| | | Attractiveness Rating* | Weighted Score | Attractiveness Rating* | Weighted Score | Attractiveness Rating* | Weighted Score |
| Market size and projected growth rate | 0.10 | 8 | 0.80 | 3 | 0.30 | 5 | 0.50 |
| Intensity of competition | 0.25 | 8 | 2.00 | 2 | 0.50 | 5 | 1.25 |
| Emerging opportunities and threats | 0.10 | 6 | 0.60 | 5 | 0.50 | 4 | 0.40 |
| Cross-industry strategic fit | 0.30 | 8 | 2.40 | 2 | 0.60 | 3 | 0.90 |
| Resource requirements | 0.10 | 5 | 0.50 | 5 | 0.50 | 4 | 0.40 |
| Social, political, regulatory, and environmental factors | 0.05 | 8 | 0.40 | 3 | 0.15 | 7 | 1.05 |
| Industry profitability | 0.10 | 5 | 0.50 | 4 | 0.40 | 6 | 0.60 |
| **Sum of importance weights** | **1.00** | | | | | | |
| **Weighted overall industry-attractiveness scores** | | | 7.20 | | 2.95 | | 5.10 |

*Rating scale:* 1 = very unattractive to company; 10 = very attractive to company.

## Interpreting the Industry-Attractiveness Scores   Industries with

a score much below 5 probably do not pass the attractiveness test. If a company's industry-attractiveness scores are all above 5, it is probably fair to conclude that the group of industries the company operates in is attractive as a whole. But the group of industries takes on a decidedly lower degree of attractiveness as the number of industries with scores below 5 increases, especially if industries with low scores account for a sizable fraction of the company's revenues.

For a diversified company to be a strong performer, a substantial portion of its revenues and profits must come from business units with relatively high attractiveness scores. It is particularly important that a diversified company's principal businesses be in industries with a good outlook for growth and above-average profitability. Having a big fraction of the company's revenues and profits come from industries with slow growth, low profitability, or intense competition tends to drag overall company performance down. Business units in the least attractive industries are potential candidates for divestiture, unless they are positioned strongly enough to overcome the unattractive aspects of their industry environments or they are a strategically important component of the company's business makeup.

## Step 2: Evaluating Business Unit Competitive Strength

The second step in evaluating a diversified company is to appraise the competitive strength of each business unit in its respective industry. Doing an appraisal of each business unit's strength and competitive position in its industry not only reveals its chances for success in its industry but also provides a basis for ranking the units from competitively strongest to competitively weakest and sizing up the competitive strength of all the business units as a group.

### Calculating Competitive-Strength Scores for Each Business Unit

Quantitative measures of each business unit's competitive strength can be calculated using a procedure similar to that for measuring industry attractiveness. The following factors are used in quantifying the competitive strengths of a diversified company's business subsidiaries:

- *Relative market share.* A business unit's *relative market share* is defined as the ratio of its market share to the market share held by the largest rival firm in the industry, with market share measured in unit volume, not dollars. For instance, if business A has a market-leading share of 40 percent and its largest rival has 30 percent, A's relative market share is 1.33. (Note that only business units that are market share leaders in their respective industries can have relative market shares greater than 1.) If business B has a 15 percent market share and B's largest rival has 30 percent, B's relative market share is 0.5. *The further below 1 a business unit's relative market share is, the weaker its competitive strength and market position vis-à-vis rivals.*

- *Costs relative to competitors' costs.* Business units that have low costs relative to those of key competitors tend to be more strongly positioned in their industries than business units struggling to maintain cost parity with major rivals. The only time a business unit's competitive strength may not be undermined by having higher costs than rivals is when it has incurred the higher costs to strongly differentiate its product offering and its customers are willing to pay premium prices for the differentiating features.

- *Ability to match or beat rivals on key product attributes.* A company's competitiveness depends in part on being able to satisfy buyer expectations with regard to features, product performance, reliability, service, and other important attributes.

- *Brand image and reputation.* A widely known and respected brand name is a valuable competitive asset in most industries.

- *Other competitively valuable resources and capabilities.* Valuable resources and capabilities, including those accessed through collaborative partnerships, enhance a company's ability to compete successfully and perhaps contend for industry leadership.

- *Ability to benefit from strategic fit with other business units.* Strategic fit with other businesses within the company enhances a business unit's competitive strength and may provide a competitive edge.

- *Ability to exercise bargaining leverage with key suppliers or customers.* Having bargaining leverage signals competitive strength and can be a source of competitive advantage.
- *Profitability relative to competitors.* Above-average profitability on a consistent basis is a signal of competitive advantage, while consistently below-average profitability usually denotes competitive disadvantage.

After settling on a set of competitive-strength measures that are well matched to the circumstances of the various business units, the company needs to assign weights indicating each measure's importance. As in the assignment of weights to industry-attractiveness measures, the importance weights must add up to 1. Each business unit is then rated on each of the chosen strength measures, using a rating scale of 1 to 10 (where a *high* rating signifies competitive *strength,* and a *low* rating signifies competitive *weakness*). In the event that the available information is too limited to confidently assign a rating value to a business unit on a particular strength measure, it is usually best to use a score of 5—this avoids biasing the overall score either up or down. Weighted strength ratings are calculated by multiplying the business unit's rating on each strength measure by the assigned weight. For example, a strength score of 6 times a weight of 0.15 gives a weighted strength rating of 0.90. The sum of the weighted ratings across all the strength measures provides a quantitative measure of a business unit's overall market strength and competitive standing. Table 8.2 provides sample calculations of competitive-strength ratings for three businesses.

### Interpreting the Competitive-Strength Scores    Business units with competitive-strength ratings above 6.7 (on a scale of 1 to 10) are strong market contenders in their industries. Businesses with ratings in the 3.3-to-6.7 range have moderate competitive strength vis-à-vis rivals. Businesses with ratings below 3.3 are in competitively weak market positions. If a diversified company's business units all have competitive-strength scores above 5, it is fair to conclude that its business units are all fairly strong market contenders in their respective industries. But as the number of business units with scores below 5 increases, there's reason to question whether the company can perform well with so many businesses in relatively weak competitive positions. This concern takes on even more importance when business units with low scores account for a sizable fraction of the company's revenues.

### Using a Nine-Cell Matrix to Simultaneously Portray Industry Attractiveness and Competitive Strength    The industry-attractiveness and business-strength scores can be used to portray the strategic positions of each business in a diversified company. Industry attractiveness is plotted on the vertical axis and competitive strength on the horizontal axis. A nine-cell grid emerges from dividing the vertical axis into three regions (high, medium, and low attractiveness) and the horizontal axis into three regions (strong, average, and weak competitive strength). As shown in Figure 8.3, scores of 6.7 or greater on a rating scale of 1 to 10 denote high industry attractiveness, scores of 3.3 to 6.7 denote medium attractiveness, and scores below 3.3 signal low attractiveness. Likewise, high competitive strength is defined as scores greater than 6.7, average strength as scores of 3.3 to 6.7, and low strength as scores below 3.3. *Each business unit is plotted on the nine-cell matrix according to its overall attractiveness score and strength score, and then it is shown as a "bubble."*

**TABLE 8.2**    Calculating Weighted Competitive-Strength Scores for a Diversified Company's Business Units

| Competitive-Strength Measures | Importance Weight | Competitive-Strength Assessments | | | | | |
| --- | --- | --- | --- | --- | --- | --- | --- |
| | | Business A in Industry A | | Business B in Industry B | | Business C in Industry C | |
| | | Strength Rating* | Weighted Score | Strength Rating* | Weighted Score | Strength Rating* | Weighted Score |
| Relative market share | 0.15 | 10 | 1.50 | 2 | 0.30 | 6 | 0.90 |
| Costs relative to competitors' costs | 0.20 | 7 | 1.40 | 4 | 0.80 | 5 | 1.00 |
| Ability to match or beat rivals on key product attributes | 0.05 | 9 | 0.45 | 5 | 0.25 | 8 | 0.40 |
| Ability to benefit from strategic fit with sister businesses | 0.20 | 8 | 1.60 | 4 | 0.80 | 8 | 0.80 |
| Bargaining leverage with suppliers/customers | 0.05 | 9 | 0.45 | 2 | 0.10 | 6 | 0.30 |
| Brand image and reputation | 0.10 | 9 | 0.90 | 4 | 0.40 | 7 | 0.70 |
| Competitively valuable capabilities | 0.15 | 7 | 1.05 | 2 | 0.30 | 5 | 0.75 |
| Profitability relative to competitors | 0.10 | 5 | 0.50 | 2 | 0.20 | 4 | 0.40 |
| **Sum of importance weights** | **1.00** | | | | | | |
| **Weighted overall competitive strength scores** | | | **7.85** | | **3.15** | | **5.25** |

*Rating scale:* 1 = very weak; 10 = very strong.

The size of each bubble is scaled to the percentage of revenues the business generates relative to total corporate revenues. The bubbles in Figure 8.3 were located on the grid using the three industry-attractiveness scores from Table 8.1 and the strength scores for the three business units in Table 8.2.

The locations of the business units on the attractiveness–strength matrix provide valuable guidance in deploying corporate resources. In general, *a diversified company's best prospects for good overall performance involve concentrating corporate resources on business units having the greatest competitive strength and industry attractiveness.* Businesses plotted in the three cells in the upper left portion of the attractiveness–strength matrix have both favorable industry attractiveness and

**FIGURE 8.3   A Nine-Cell Industry-Attractiveness–Competitive-Strength Matrix**

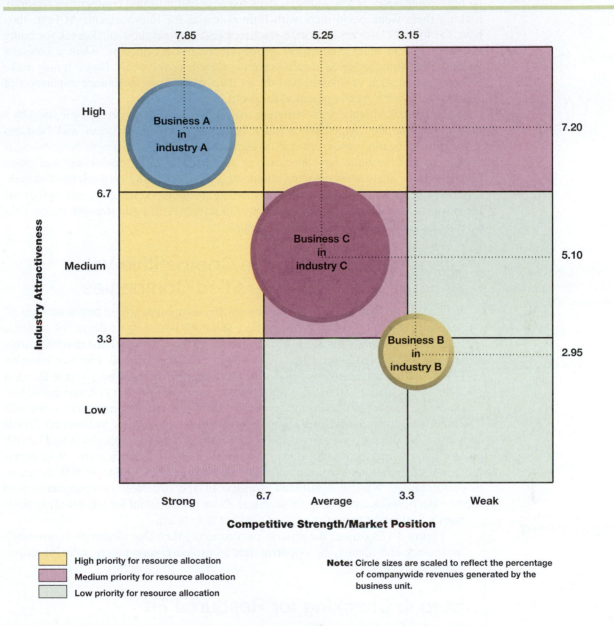

competitive strength and should receive a high investment priority. Business units plotted in these three cells (like business A) are referred to as "grow and build" businesses because of their capability to drive future increases in shareholder value.

Next in priority come businesses positioned in the three diagonal cells stretching from the lower left to the upper right (like business C). Such businesses usually merit intermediate priority in the parent's resource allocation ranking. However, some businesses in the medium-priority diagonal cells may have brighter or dimmer prospects than others. For example, a small business in the upper right cell of the matrix, despite being in a highly attractive industry, may occupy too weak a competitive position in its industry to justify the investment and resources needed to turn it into a strong market contender.

Businesses in the three cells in the lower right corner of the matrix (like business B) have comparatively low industry attractiveness and minimal competitive strength, making them weak performers with little potential for improvement. At best, they have the lowest claim on corporate resources and may be good candidates for being divested (sold to other companies). However, there are occasions when a business located in the three lower-right cells generates sizable positive cash flows. It may make sense to retain such businesses and divert their cash flows to finance expansion of business units with greater potential for profit growth.

The nine-cell attractiveness–strength matrix provides clear, strong logic for why a diversified company needs to consider both industry attractiveness and business strength in allocating resources and investment capital to its different businesses. A good case can be made for concentrating resources in those businesses that enjoy higher degrees of attractiveness and competitive strength, being very selective in making investments in businesses with intermediate positions on the grid, and withdrawing resources from businesses that are lower in attractiveness and strength unless they offer exceptional profit or cash flow potential.

> The greater the value of cross-business strategic fit in enhancing the performance of a diversified company's businesses, the more competitively powerful is the company's related diversification strategy.

## Step 3: Determining the Competitive Value of Strategic Fit in Diversified Companies

While this step can be bypassed for diversified companies whose businesses are all unrelated (since, by design, strategic fit is lacking), assessing the degree of strategic fit across a company's businesses is central to evaluating its related diversification strategy. But more than just strategic-fit identification is needed. *The real question is how much competitive value can be generated from strategic fit.* Are the cost savings associated with economies of scope likely to give one or more individual businesses a cost-based advantage over rivals? How much competitive value will come from the cross-business transfer of skills, technology, or intellectual capital or the sharing of competitive assets? Will leveraging a potent umbrella brand or corporate image strengthen the businesses and increase sales significantly? Will cross-business collaboration to create new competitive capabilities lead to significant gains in performance? Without significant strategic fit and dedicated company efforts to capture the benefits, one has to be skeptical about the potential for a diversified company's businesses to perform better together than apart.

Figure 8.4 illustrates the process of comparing the value chains of a company's businesses and identifying opportunities to exploit competitively valuable cross-business strategic fit.

### CORE CONCEPT

A company pursuing related diversification exhibits **resource fit** when its businesses have matching specialized resource requirements along their value chains; a company pursuing unrelated diversification has resource fit when the parent company has adequate corporate resources (parenting and general resources) to support its businesses' needs and add value.

## Step 4: Checking for Resource Fit

The businesses in a diversified company's lineup need to exhibit good **resource fit.** In firms with a related diversification strategy, resource fit exists *when the firm's businesses have matching specialized resource requirements at points along their value chains* that are critical for the businesses' market success. Matching resource requirements are important in related diversification because they facilitate resource sharing and low-cost resource transfer. In companies pursuing unrelated diversification, resource fit exists when the company has solid *parenting capabilities or resources of a general nature that it can share or transfer to its component businesses.* Firms pursuing related diversification and firms with combination related-unrelated diversification strategies can also benefit from leveraging

## FIGURE 8.4   Identifying the Competitive Advantage Potential of Cross-Business Strategic Fit

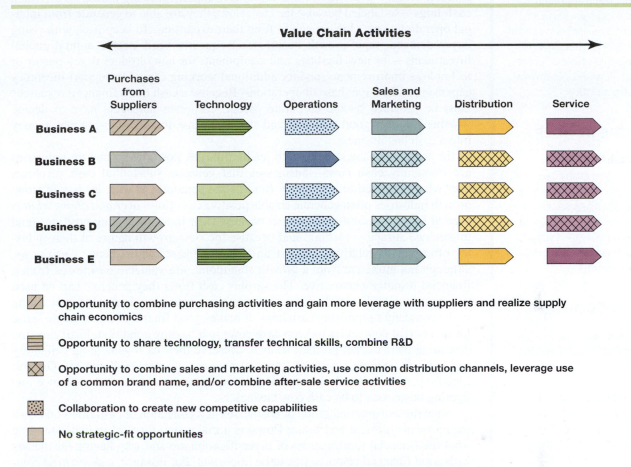

**Value Chain Activities**

|  | Purchases from Suppliers | Technology | Operations | Sales and Marketing | Distribution | Service |

Opportunity to combine purchasing activities and gain more leverage with suppliers and realize supply chain economics

Opportunity to share technology, transfer technical skills, combine R&D

Opportunity to combine sales and marketing activities, use common distribution channels, leverage use of a common brand name, and/or combine after-sale service activities

Collaboration to create new competitive capabilities

No strategic-fit opportunities

corporate parenting capabilities and other general resources. Another dimension of resource fit that concerns all types of multibusiness firms is whether they have resources sufficient to support their group of businesses without being spread too thin.

**Financial Resource Fit**   One dimension of resource fit concerns whether a diversified company can generate the internal cash flows sufficient to fund the capital requirements of its businesses, pay its dividends, meet its debt obligations, and otherwise remain financially healthy. (Financial resources, including the firm's ability to borrow or otherwise raise funds, are a type of general resource.) While additional capital can usually be raised in financial markets, it is important for a diversified firm to have a healthy **internal capital market** that can support the financial requirements of its business lineup. The greater the extent to which a diversified company is able to fund investment in its businesses through internally generated cash flows rather than from equity issues or borrowing, the more powerful its financial resource fit and the less dependent the firm is on external financial resources. This can provide a competitive advantage over single business rivals when credit market conditions are tight, as they have been in the United States and abroad in recent years.

### CORE CONCEPT

A strong **internal capital market** allows a diversified company to add value by shifting capital from business units generating *free cash flow* to those needing additional capital to expand and realize their growth potential.

## CORE CONCEPT

A **portfolio approach** to ensuring financial fit among a firm's businesses is based on the fact that different businesses have different cash flow and investment characteristics.

## CORE CONCEPT

A **cash hog** business generates cash flows that are too small to fully fund its growth; it thereby requires cash infusions to provide additional working capital and finance new capital investment.

## CORE CONCEPT

A **cash cow** business generates cash flows over and above its internal requirements, thus providing a corporate parent with funds for investing in cash hog businesses, financing new acquisitions, or paying dividends.

A **portfolio approach** to ensuring financial fit among a firm's businesses is based on the fact that different businesses have different cash flow and investment characteristics. For example, business units in rapidly growing industries are often **cash hogs**—so labeled because the cash flows they are able to generate from internal operations aren't big enough to fund their expansion. To keep pace with rising buyer demand, rapid-growth businesses frequently need sizable annual capital investments—for new facilities and equipment, for new product development or technology improvements, and for additional working capital to support inventory expansion and a larger base of operations. Because a cash hog's financial resources must be provided by the corporate parent, corporate managers have to decide whether it makes good financial and strategic sense to keep pouring new money into a cash hog business.

In contrast, business units with leading market positions in mature industries are frequently **cash cows**—businesses that generate substantial cash surpluses over what is needed to adequately fund their operations. Market leaders in slow-growth industries often generate sizable positive cash flows *over and above what is needed for growth and reinvestment* because their industry-leading positions tend to generate attractive earnings and because the slow-growth nature of their industry often entails relatively modest annual investment requirements. Cash cows, although not attractive from a growth standpoint, are valuable businesses from a financial resource perspective. The surplus cash flows they generate can be used to pay corporate dividends, finance acquisitions, and provide funds for investing in the company's promising cash hogs. It makes good financial and strategic sense for diversified companies to keep cash cows in a healthy condition, fortifying and defending their market position so as to preserve their cash-generating capability and have an ongoing source of financial resources to deploy elsewhere. General Electric considers its advanced materials, equipment services, and appliance and lighting businesses to be cash cow businesses.

Viewing a diversified group of businesses as a collection of cash flows and cash requirements (present and future flows) is a major step forward in understanding what the financial ramifications of diversification are and why having businesses with good financial resource fit can be important. For instance, *a diversified company's businesses exhibit good financial resource fit when the excess cash generated by its cash cow businesses is sufficient to fund the investment requirements of promising cash hog businesses.* Ideally, investing in promising cash hog businesses over time results in growing the hogs into self-supporting *star businesses* that have strong or market-leading competitive positions in attractive, high-growth markets and high levels of profitability. Star businesses are often the cash cows of the future. When the markets of star businesses begin to mature and their growth slows, their competitive strength should produce self-generated cash flows that are more than sufficient to cover their investment needs. The "success sequence" is thus cash hog to young star (but perhaps still a cash hog) to self-supporting star to cash cow. While the practice of viewing a diversified company in terms of cash cows and cash hogs has declined in popularity, it illustrates one approach to analyzing financial resource fit and allocating financial resources across a portfolio of different businesses.

Aside from cash flow considerations, there are two other factors to consider in assessing whether a diversified company's businesses exhibit good financial fit:

- *Does each of the individual businesses adequately contribute to achieving companywide performance targets?* A business exhibits poor financial fit if it soaks up a disproportionate share of the company's financial resources, while making subpar or insignificant contributions to the bottom line. Too many underperforming businesses reduce the company's overall performance and ultimately limit growth in shareholder value.

- *Does the corporation have adequate financial strength to fund its different businesses and maintain a healthy credit rating?* A diversified company's strategy fails the resource-fit test when the resource needs of its portfolio unduly stretch the company's financial health and threaten to impair its credit rating. Many of the world's largest banks, including Royal Bank of Scotland, Citigroup, and HSBC, recently found themselves so undercapitalized and financially overextended that they were forced to sell off some of their business assets to meet regulatory requirements and restore public confidence in their solvency.

**Nonfinancial Resource Fit**    Just as a diversified company must have adequate financial resources to support its various individual businesses, it must also have a big enough and deep enough pool of managerial, administrative, and competitive capabilities to support all of its different businesses. The following two questions help reveal whether a diversified company has sufficient nonfinancial resources:

- *Does the company have (or can it develop) the specific resources and capabilities needed to be successful in each of its businesses?* Sometimes the resources a company has accumulated in its core business prove to be a poor match with the competitive capabilities needed to succeed in the businesses into which it has diversified. For instance, BTR, a multibusiness company in Great Britain, discovered that the company's resources and managerial skills were quite well suited for parenting its industrial manufacturing businesses but not for parenting its distribution businesses (National Tyre Services and Texas-based Summers Group). As a result, BTR decided to divest its distribution businesses and focus exclusively on diversifying around small industrial manufacturing. For companies pursuing related diversification strategies, a mismatch between the company's competitive assets and the key success factors of an industry can be serious enough to warrant divesting businesses in that industry or not acquiring a new business. In contrast, when a company's resources and capabilities are a good match with the key success factors of industries it is not presently in, it makes sense to take a hard look at acquiring companies in these industries and expanding the company's business lineup.

- *Are the company's resources being stretched too thinly by the resource requirements of one or more of its businesses?* A diversified company must guard against overtaxing its resources and capabilities, a condition that can arise when (1) it goes on an acquisition spree and management is called on to assimilate and oversee many new businesses very quickly or (2) it lacks sufficient resource depth to do a creditable job of transferring skills and competencies from one of its businesses to another. The broader the diversification, the greater the concern about whether corporate executives are overburdened by the demands of competently parenting so many different businesses. Plus, the more a company's diversification strategy is tied to transferring know-how or technologies from existing businesses to newly acquired businesses, the more it has to develop a deep-enough resource pool to supply these businesses with the resources and capabilities they need to be successful.[17] Otherwise, its competitive assets end up being spread too thinly across many businesses, and the opportunity for achieving $1 + 1 = 3$ outcomes slips through the cracks.

# Step 5: Ranking Business Units and Assigning a Priority for Resource Allocation

Once a diversified company's strategy has been evaluated from the perspective of industry attractiveness, competitive strength, strategic fit, and resource fit, the next step is to use this information to rank the performance prospects of the businesses from best to worst. Such ranking helps top-level executives assign each business a priority for resource support and capital investment.

The locations of the different businesses in the nine-cell industry-attractiveness–competitive-strength matrix provide a solid basis for identifying high-opportunity businesses and low-opportunity businesses. Normally, competitively strong businesses in attractive industries have significantly better performance prospects than competitively weak businesses in unattractive industries. Also, the revenue and earnings outlook for businesses in fast-growing industries is normally better than for businesses in slow-growing industries. As a rule, *business subsidiaries with the brightest profit and growth prospects, attractive positions in the nine-cell matrix, and solid strategic and resource fit should receive top priority for allocation of corporate resources.* However, in ranking the prospects of the different businesses from best to worst, it is usually wise to also take into account each business's past performance in regard to sales growth, profit growth, contribution to company earnings, return on capital invested in the business, and cash flow from operations. While past performance is not always a reliable predictor of future performance, it does signal whether a business is already performing well or has problems to overcome.

**Allocating Financial Resources**    Figure 8.5 shows the chief strategic and financial options for allocating a diversified company's financial resources. Divesting businesses with the weakest future prospects and businesses that lack adequate strategic fit and/or resource fit is one of the best ways of generating additional funds for redeployment to businesses with better opportunities and better strategic and resource fit. Free cash flows from cash cow businesses also add to the pool of funds that can be usefully redeployed. *Ideally,* a diversified company will have sufficient financial resources to strengthen or grow its existing businesses, make any new acquisitions that are desirable, fund other promising business opportunities, pay off existing debt, and periodically increase dividend payments to shareholders and/or repurchase shares of stock. But, as a practical matter, a company's financial resources are limited. Thus, to make the best use of the available funds, top executives must steer resources to those businesses with the best prospects and either divest or allocate minimal resources to businesses with marginal prospects—this is why ranking the performance prospects of the various businesses from best to worst is so crucial. Strategic uses of corporate resources should usually take precedence over financial options (see Figure 8.5) unless there is a compelling reason to strengthen the firm's balance sheet or better reward shareholders.

**LO 5**

What four main corporate strategy options a diversified company can employ for solidifying its strategy and improving company performance.

# Step 6: Crafting New Strategic Moves to Improve Overall Corporate Performance

The conclusions flowing from the five preceding analytic steps set the agenda for crafting strategic moves to improve a diversified company's overall performance. The strategic options boil down to four broad categories of actions (see Figure 8.6):

**FIGURE 8.5**    The Chief Strategic and Financial Options for Allocating a Diversified Company's Financial Resources

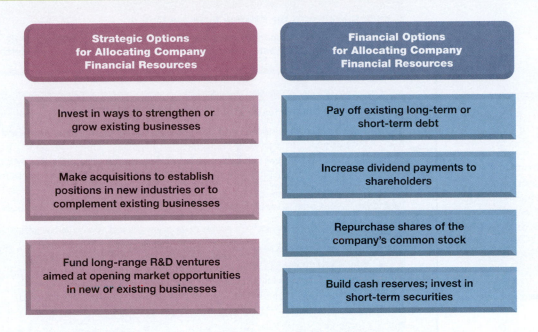

1. Sticking closely with the existing business lineup and pursuing the opportunities these businesses present.
2. Broadening the company's business scope by making new acquisitions in new industries.
3. Divesting certain businesses and retrenching to a narrower base of business operations.
4. Restructuring the company's business lineup and putting a whole new face on the company's business makeup.

**Sticking Closely with the Present Business Lineup**    The option of sticking with the current business lineup makes sense when the company's existing businesses offer attractive growth opportunities and can be counted on to create economic value for shareholders. As long as the company's set of existing businesses have good prospects and are in alignment with the company's diversification strategy, then major changes in the company's business mix are unnecessary. Corporate executives can concentrate their attention on getting the best performance from each of the businesses, steering corporate resources into the areas of greatest potential and profitability. The specifics of "what to do" to wring better performance from the present business lineup have to be dictated by each business's circumstances and the preceding analysis of the corporate parent's diversification strategy.

**Broadening a Diversified Company's Business Base**    Diversified companies sometimes find it desirable to build positions in new industries, whether related or unrelated. Several motivating factors are in play. One is sluggish growth that makes the potential revenue and profit boost of a newly acquired business look

**FIGURE 8.6**   A Company's Four Main Strategic Alternatives after It Diversifies

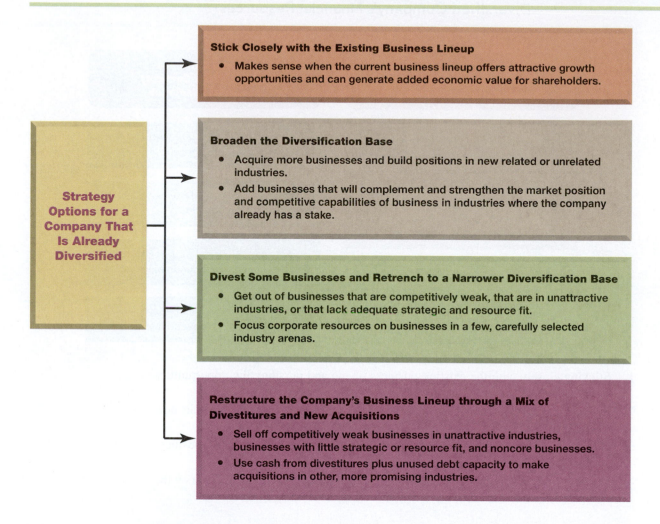

**Strategy Options for a Company That Is Already Diversified**

**Stick Closely with the Existing Business Lineup**
- Makes sense when the current business lineup offers attractive growth opportunities and can generate added economic value for shareholders.

**Broaden the Diversification Base**
- Acquire more businesses and build positions in new related or unrelated industries.
- Add businesses that will complement and strengthen the market position and competitive capabilities of business in industries where the company already has a stake.

**Divest Some Businesses and Retrench to a Narrower Diversification Base**
- Get out of businesses that are competitively weak, that are in unattractive industries, or that lack adequate strategic and resource fit.
- Focus corporate resources on businesses in a few, carefully selected industry arenas.

**Restructure the Company's Business Lineup through a Mix of Divestitures and New Acquisitions**
- Sell off competitively weak businesses in unattractive industries, businesses with little strategic or resource fit, and noncore businesses.
- Use cash from divestitures plus unused debt capacity to make acquisitions in other, more promising industries.

attractive. A second is the potential for transferring resources and capabilities to other related or complementary businesses. A third is rapidly changing conditions in one or more of a company's core businesses, brought on by technological, legislative, or demographic changes. For instance, the passage of legislation in the United States allowing banks, insurance companies, and stock brokerages to enter each other's businesses spurred a raft of acquisitions and mergers to create full-service financial enterprises capable of meeting the multiple financial needs of customers. A fourth, and very important, motivating factor for adding new businesses is to complement and strengthen the market position and competitive capabilities of one or more of the company's present businesses. Procter & Gamble's acquisition of Gillette strengthened and extended P&G's reach into personal care and household products—Gillette's businesses included Oral-B toothbrushes, Gillette razors and razor blades, Duracell batteries, and Braun shavers and small appliances.

Another important avenue for expanding the scope of a diversified company is to grow by extending the operations of existing businesses into additional country markets, as discussed in Chapter 7. Expanding a company's geographic scope may offer an exceptional competitive advantage potential by facilitating the full capture of economies of scale and learning- and experience-curve effects. In some businesses, the volume of sales needed to realize full economies of scale and/or benefit fully from experience-curve effects exceeds the volume that can be achieved by operating within the boundaries of just one or several country markets, especially small ones.

**Retrenching to a Narrower Diversification Base**    A number of diversified firms have had difficulty managing a diverse group of businesses and have elected to exit some of them. Selling a business outright to another company is far and away the most frequently used option for divesting a business. In 2012, Sara Lee Corporation sold its International Coffee and Tea business to J.M. Smucker, while Nike sold its Umbro and Cole Haan brands to focus on brands like Jordan and Converse that are more complementary to the Nike brand. But sometimes a business selected for divestiture has ample resources and capabilities to compete successfully on its own. In such cases, a corporate parent may elect to spin the unwanted business off as a financially and managerially independent company, either by selling shares to the public via an initial public offering or by distributing shares in the new company to shareholders of the corporate parent. Darden Restaurants, owner of the Olive Garden chain, expects to complete a spin-off of its Red Lobster chain in 2015 and distribute the new shares of Red Lobster to Darden shareholders. Kimberly-Clark, a global health and hygiene consumer products company, spun off its health care business, K-C Health Care, in 2014.

Retrenching to a narrower diversification base is usually undertaken when top management concludes that its diversification has ranged too far afield and that the company can improve long-term performance by concentrating on a smaller number of businesses. But there are other important reasons for divesting one or more of a company's present businesses. Sometimes divesting a business has to be considered because market conditions in a once-attractive industry have badly deteriorated. A business can become a prime candidate for divestiture because it lacks adequate strategic or resource fit, because it is a cash hog with questionable long-term potential, or because remedying its competitive weaknesses is too expensive relative to the likely gains in profitability. Sometimes a company acquires businesses that, down the road, just do not work out as expected even though management has tried its best. Subpar performance by some business units is bound to occur, thereby raising questions of whether to divest them or keep them and attempt a turnaround. Other business units, despite adequate financial performance, may not mesh as well with the rest of the firm as was originally thought. For instance, PepsiCo divested its group of fast-food restaurant businesses to focus on its core soft-drink and snack-food businesses, where their specialized resources and capabilities could add more value.

On occasion, a diversification move that seems sensible from a strategic-fit standpoint turns out to be a poor *cultural fit*.[18] When several pharmaceutical companies diversified into cosmetics and perfume, they discovered their personnel had little respect for the "frivolous" nature of such products compared to the far nobler task of developing miracle drugs to cure the ill. The absence of shared values and cultural compatibility between the medical research and chemical-compounding expertise of the pharmaceutical companies and the fashion and marketing orientation of the cosmetics business was the undoing of what otherwise was diversification into businesses with technology-sharing potential, product development fit, and some overlap in distribution channels.

A **spin-off** is an independent company created when a corporate parent divests a business either by selling shares to the public via an initial public offering or by distributing shares in the new company to shareholders of the corporate parent.

Diversified companies need to divest low-performing businesses or businesses that don't fit in order to concentrate on expanding existing businesses and entering new ones where opportunities are more promising.

A useful guide to determine whether or when to divest a business subsidiary is to ask, "If we were not in this business today, would we want to get into it now?" When the answer is no or probably not, divestiture should be considered. Another signal that a business should be divested occurs when it is worth more to another company than to the present parent; in such cases, shareholders would be well served if the company sells the business and collects a premium price from the buyer for whom the business is a valuable fit.

### Restructuring a Diversified Company's Business Lineup

Restructuring a diversified company on a companywide basis *(corporate restructuring)* involves divesting some businesses and/or acquiring others, so as to put a whole new face on the company's business lineup.[19] Performing radical surgery on a company's business lineup is appealing when its financial performance is being squeezed or eroded by:

- A serious mismatch between the company's resources and capabilities and the type of diversification that it has pursued.
- Too many businesses in slow-growth, declining, low-margin, or otherwise unattractive industries.
- Too many competitively weak businesses.
- The emergence of new technologies that threaten the survival of one or more important businesses.
- Ongoing declines in the market shares of one or more major business units that are falling prey to more market-savvy competitors.
- An excessive debt burden with interest costs that eat deeply into profitability.
- Ill-chosen acquisitions that haven't lived up to expectations.

On occasion, corporate restructuring can be prompted by special circumstances—such as when a firm has a unique opportunity to make an acquisition so big and important that it has to sell several existing business units to finance the new acquisition or when a company needs to sell off some businesses in order to raise the cash for entering a potentially big industry with wave-of-the-future technologies or products. As businesses are divested, corporate restructuring generally involves aligning the remaining business units into groups with the best strategic fit and then redeploying the cash flows from the divested businesses to either pay down debt or make new acquisitions to strengthen the parent company's business position in the industries it has chosen to emphasize.

Over the past decade, corporate restructuring has become a popular strategy at many diversified companies, especially those that had diversified broadly into many different industries and lines of business. VF Corporation, maker of North Face and other popular "lifestyle" apparel brands, has used a restructuring strategy to provide its shareholders with returns that are more than five times greater than shareholder returns for competing apparel makers. Since its acquisition and turnaround of North Face in 2000, VF has spent nearly $5 billion to acquire 19 additional businesses, including about $2 billion in 2011 for Timberland. New apparel brands acquired by VF Corporation include 7 For All Mankind sportswear, Vans skateboard shoes, Nautica, John Varvatos, Reef surf wear, and Lucy athletic wear. By 2014, VF Corporation had become an $11 billion powerhouse—one of the largest and most profitable apparel and footwear companies in the world. It was listed as number 250 on *Fortune*'s 2013 list of the 500 largest U.S. companies.

Illustration Capsule 8.2 discusses how Kraft Foods has been pursuing long-term growth and increased shareholder value by restructuring its operations.

## ILLUSTRATION CAPSULE 8.2

# Growth through Restructuring at Kraft Foods

In 2012, Kraft Foods, the 90-year-old darling of the consumer packaged-goods industry, moved to improve its long-term performance by *restructuring* the corporation—the latest move by CEO Irene Rosenfeld, who was brought in to turn around the company's performance. In addition to trimming operations, the restructuring plan called for spinning off the North American grocery unit that included Kraft Macaroni and Cheese, Oscar Meyer, and other nonsnack brands from the $32 billion fast-growing global snacks business that included Oreo and Cadbury (the British confectionary acquired in 2010). While the grocery business would retain the name Kraft, the star of this strategic separation was the core snack business, renamed Mondelez. With this radical new operational structure in place, Kraft hoped to improve its ability to focus on new opportunities and pursue profitable growth.

Managing these two large and very different businesses jointly had made it difficult for Kraft to act nimbly and adapt to changing market conditions. It also inhibited the company from executing new strategies free from significant portfolio-wide considerations. In announcing her intention to split the company in September 2011, CEO Irene Rosenfeld said, "Simply put, we have now reached a point where North American Grocery and Global Snacks will each benefit from standing on its own and focusing on its unique drivers for success." She noted that as separate businesses, "each will have the leadership, resources, and mandate to realize its full potential."

As part of the restructuring effort, Rosenfeld reduced the number of management centers and sold off some underperforming brands. More recently, the new North American grocery business Kraft Foods Group has undertaken further restructuring to streamline its organizational structure and brand identity. Although in refashioning the company, Rosenfeld sacrificed some of the operational benefits the company enjoyed as a single entity, managers and investors have already begun to see some of the positive effects of appropriately scaled focus.

*Note:* Developed with Maximilian A. Pinto and Harold W. Greenstone.

*Sources:* S. Webb, "New Reality Makes Kraft Split Vital," *Food Global News,* September 2011; J. Jannarone, "Mondelez Can Slim Way to Success," *The Wall Street Journal* Online, May 28, 2013 (accessed March 31, 2014); M. J. de la Merced, "Kraft Foods, in Split, Is Keeping Oreos but Not Velveeta," *The New York Times Dealbook* Online, August 4, 2011 (accessed March 31, 2014); E. J. Schultz, "Kraft Restructures as It Eyes More Brand-Building," *Advertising Age* Online, June 14, 2013 (accessed March 31, 2014); E. J. Schultz, "Could Kraft Split Be a Blueprint for Blue Chips?" *Advertising Age,* August 2011; www.nytimes.com/2007/02/21/business/21kraft.html (accessed March 2, 2012); and stocks.investopedia.com/ (accessed March 2, 2012).

## KEY POINTS

**1.** The purpose of diversification is to build shareholder value. Diversification builds shareholder value when a diversified group of businesses can perform better under the auspices of a single corporate parent than they would as independent, stand-alone businesses—the goal is to achieve not just a 1 + 1 = 2 result but, rather, to realize important 1 + 1 = 3 performance benefits. Whether getting into a new business has the potential to enhance shareholder value hinges on whether a company's entry into that business can pass the three tests of corporate advantage: the industry-attractiveness test, the cost of entry test, and the better-off test.

2. Entry into new businesses can take any of three forms: acquisition, internal startup, or joint venture. The choice of which is best depends on the firm's resources and capabilities, the industry's entry barriers, the importance of speed, and relative costs.

3. There are two fundamental approaches to diversification—into related businesses and into unrelated businesses. The rationale for *related* diversification is to benefit from *strategic fit:* Diversify into businesses with commonalities across their respective value chains, and then capitalize on the strategic fit by sharing or transferring the resources and capabilities across matching value chain activities to gain competitive advantages.

4. *Unrelated* diversification strategies surrender the competitive advantage potential of strategic fit at the value chain level in return for the potential that can be realized from superior corporate parenting or the sharing and transfer of general resources and capabilities. An outstanding corporate parent can benefit its businesses through (1) providing high-level oversight and making available other corporate resources, (2) allocating financial resources across the business portfolio, and (3) restructuring underperforming acquisitions.

5. Related diversification provides a stronger foundation for creating shareholder value than does unrelated diversification, since the *specialized resources and capabilities* that are leveraged in related diversification tend to be more valuable competitive assets than the *general resources and capabilities* underlying unrelated diversification, which in most cases are relatively common and easier to imitate.

6. Analyzing how good a company's diversification strategy is consists of a six-step process:

   **Step 1:** *Evaluate the long-term attractiveness of the industries into which the firm has diversified.* Determining industry attractiveness involves developing a list of industry-attractiveness measures, each of which might have a different importance weight.

   **Step 2:** *Evaluate the relative competitive strength of each of the company's business units.* The purpose of rating the competitive strength of each business is to gain a clear understanding of which businesses are strong contenders in their industries, which are weak contenders, and what the underlying reasons are for their strength or weakness. The conclusions about industry attractiveness can be joined with the conclusions about competitive strength by drawing a nine-cell industry-attractiveness–competitive-strength matrix that helps identify the prospects of each business and the level of priority each business should be given in allocating corporate resources and investment capital.

   **Step 3:** *Check for cross-business strategic fit.* A business is more attractive strategically when it has value chain relationships with the other business units that offer the potential to (1) combine operations to realize economies of scope, (2) transfer technology, skills, know-how, or other resource capabilities from one business to another, (3) leverage the use of a trusted brand name or other resources that enhance differentiation, (4) share other competitively valuable resources among the company's businesses, and (5) build new resources and competitive capabilities via cross-business collaboration. Cross-business strategic fit represents a significant avenue for producing competitive advantage beyond what any one business can achieve on its own.

**Step 4:** *Check whether the firm's resources fit the resource requirements of its present business lineup.* In firms with a related diversification strategy, resource fit exists when the firm's businesses have matching resource requirements at points along their value chains that are critical for the businesses' market success. In companies pursuing unrelated diversification, resource fit exists when the company has solid parenting capabilities or resources of a general nature that it can share or transfer to its component businesses. When there is financial resource fit among the businesses of any type of diversified company, the company can generate internal cash flows sufficient to fund the capital requirements of its businesses, pay its dividends, meet its debt obligations, and otherwise remain financially healthy.

**Step 5:** *Rank the performance prospects of the businesses from best to worst, and determine what the corporate parent's priority should be in allocating resources to its various businesses.* The most important considerations in judging business unit performance are sales growth, profit growth, contribution to company earnings, and the return on capital invested in the business. Normally, strong business units in attractive industries should head the list for corporate resource support.

**Step 6:** *Craft new strategic moves to improve overall corporate performance.* This step entails using the results of the preceding analysis as the basis for selecting one of four different strategic paths for improving a diversified company's performance: (1) Stick closely with the existing business lineup and pursue opportunities presented by these businesses, (2) broaden the scope of diversification by entering additional industries, (3) retrench to a narrower scope of diversification by divesting poorly performing businesses, or (4) broadly restructure the business lineup with multiple divestitures and/or acquisitions.

## ASSURANCE OF LEARNING EXERCISES

1. See if you can identify the value chain relationships that make the businesses of the following companies related in competitively relevant ways. In particular, you should consider whether there are cross-business opportunities for (1) transferring skills and technology, (2) combining related value chain activities to achieve economies of scope, and/or (3) leveraging the use of a well-respected brand name or other resources that enhance differentiation.

**connect**

**LO 1, LO 2, LO 3, LO 4**

### Bloomin' Brands

- Outback Steakhouse
- Carrabba's Italian Grill
- Roy's Restaurant (Hawaiian fusion cuisine)
- Bonefish Grill (market-fresh fine seafood)
- Fleming's Prime Steakhouse & Wine Bar

### L'Oréal

- Maybelline, Lancôme, Helena Rubinstein cosmetics
- L'Oréal, Garnier, and SoftSheen-Carson hair care products
- Redken, Matrix, L'Oréal Professional, Kiehl's, and Kérastase professional hair care and skin care products
- Ralph Lauren, Yves Saint Laurent, and Giorgio Armani fragrances
- La Roche-Posay, Vichy Laboratories, Dermablend, and SkinCeuticals dermocosmetics

### Johnson & Johnson

- Baby products (powder, shampoo, oil, lotion)
- Band-Aids and other first-aid products
- Women's health and personal care products
- Neutrogena, Lubriderm, and Aveeno skin care products
- Nonprescription drugs (Tylenol, Motrin, Pepcid AC, Mylanta, Benadryl)
- Prescription drugs
- Oral health care (Listerine, Rembrandt)
- Nutritionals (Splenda, Lactaid)
- Prosthetic and other medical devices
- Surgical and hospital products
- Vision care (Acuvue contact lenses, Visine)

**LO 1, LO 2, LO 3, LO 4**

2. Peruse the business group listings for United Technologies shown below and listed at its website (www.utc.com). How would you characterize the company's corporate strategy—related diversification, unrelated diversification, or a combination related-unrelated diversification strategy? Explain your answer.
   - Carrier—the world's largest provider of air-conditioning, heating, and refrigeration solutions.
   - Hamilton Sundstrand—a provider of technologically advanced aerospace and industrial products.
   - Otis—the world's leading manufacturer, installer, and maintainer of elevators, escalators, and moving walkways.
   - Pratt & Whitney—a global leader in the design, manufacture, service, and support of aircraft engines, industrial gas turbines, and space propulsion systems.
   - Sikorsky—a world leader in helicopter design, manufacture, and service.
   - UTC Fire & Security—a supplier of fire and security systems developed for commercial, industrial, and residential customers.
   - UTC Power—a full-service provider of environmentally advanced power solutions.

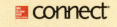

**LO 1, LO 2, LO 3, LO 4, LO 5**

3. ITT is a technology-oriented engineering and manufacturing company with the following business divisions and products:
   - Industrial Process Division—industrial pumps, valves, and monitoring and control systems; aftermarket services for the chemical, oil and gas, mining, pulp and paper, power, and biopharmaceutical markets.

- Motion Technologies Division—durable brake pads, shock absorbers, and damping technologies for the automotive and rail markets.
- Interconnect Solutions—connectors and fittings for the production of automobiles, aircraft, railcars and locomotives, oil field equipment, medical equipment, and industrial equipment.
- Control Technologies—energy absorption and vibration dampening equipment, transducers and regulators, and motion controls used in the production of robotics, medical equipment, automobiles, subsea equipment, industrial equipment, aircraft, and military vehicles.

Based on the above listing, would you say that ITT's business lineup reflects a strategy of related diversification, unrelated diversification, or a combination of related and unrelated diversification? What benefits are generated from any strategic fit existing between ITT's businesses? Also, what types of companies should ITT consider acquiring that might improve shareholder value? Justify your answer.

## EXERCISE FOR SIMULATION PARTICIPANTS

1. In the event that your company has the opportunity to diversify into other products or businesses of your choosing, would you opt to pursue related diversification, unrelated diversification, or a combination of both? Explain why.  **LO 1, LO 2, LO 3**

2. What specific resources and capabilities does your company possess that would make diversifying into related businesses attractive? Indicate what kinds of strategic-fit benefits could be captured by transferring these resources and competitive capabilities to newly acquired related businesses.  **LO 1, LO 2**

3. If your company opted to pursue a strategy of related diversification, what industries or product categories could it diversify into that would allow it to achieve economies of scope? Name at least two or three such industries or product categories, and indicate the specific kinds of cost savings that might accrue from entry into each.  **LO 1, LO 2**

4. If your company opted to pursue a strategy of unrelated diversification, what industries or product categories could it diversify into that would allow it to capitalize on using its present brand name and corporate image to good advantage in the newly entered businesses or product categories? Name at least two or three such industries or product categories, and indicate the *specific benefits* that might be captured by transferring your company's umbrella brand name to each.  **LO 1, LO 3**

## ENDNOTES

[1] Michael E. Porter, "From Competitive Advantage to Corporate Strategy," *Harvard Business Review* 45, no. 3 (May–June 1987), pp. 46–49.
[2] www.zerohedge.com/news/2013-02-14/heinz-confirms-it-will-be-acquired-buffett-28-billion-transaction-7250share (accessed February 2, 2014).
[3] finance.fortune.cnn.com/2012/07/31/companies-are-paying-up-for-deals/;

blogs.wsj.com/cfo/2013/11/26/why-are-takeover-prices-plummeting/ (accessed February 2, 2014).
[4] A. Shleifer and R. Vishny, "Takeovers in the 60s and the 80s—Evidence and Implications," *Strategic Management Journal* 12 (Winter 1991), pp. 51–59; T. Brush, "Predicted Change in Operational Synergy and Post-Acquisition Performance of Acquired

Businesses," *Strategic Management Journal* 17, no. 1 (1996), pp. 1–24; J. P. Walsh, "Top Management Turnover Following Mergers and Acquisitions," *Strategic Management Journal* 9, no. 2 (1988), pp. 173–183; A. Cannella and D. Hambrick, "Effects of Executive Departures on the Performance of Acquired Firms," *Strategic Management Journal* 14 (Summer 1993), pp. 137–152; R. Roll, "The Hubris Hypothesis of

Corporate Takeovers," *Journal of Business* 59, no. 2 (1986), pp. 197–216; P. Haspeslagh and D. Jemison, *Managing Acquisitions* (New York: Free Press, 1991).

[5] M.L.A. Hayward, "When Do Firms Learn from Their Acquisition Experience? Evidence from 1990–1995," *Strategic Management Journal* 23, no. 1 (2002), pp. 21–29; G. Ahuja and R. Katila, "Technological Acquisitions and the Innovation Performance of Acquiring Firms: A Longitudinal Study," *Strategic Management Journal* 22, no. 3 (2001), pp. 197–220; H. Barkema and F. Vermeulen, "International Expansion through Start-Up or Acquisition: A Learning Perspective," *Academy of Management Journal* 41, no. 1 (1998), pp. 7–26.

[6] Yves L. Doz and Gary Hamel, *Alliance Advantage: The Art of Creating Value through Partnering* (Boston: Harvard Business School Press, 1998), chaps. 1 and 2.

[7] J. Glover, "The Guardian," March 23, 1996, www.mcspotlight.org/media/press/guardpizza_23mar96.html.

[8] Michael E. Porter, *Competitive Advantage* (New York: Free Press, 1985), pp. 318–319, 337–353; Porter, "From Competitive Advantage to Corporate Strategy," pp. 53–57;

Constantinos C. Markides and Peter J. Williamson, "Corporate Diversification and Organization Structure: A Resource-Based View," *Academy of Management Journal* 39, no. 2 (April 1996), pp. 340–367.

[9] David J. Collis and Cynthia A. Montgomery, "Creating Corporate Advantage," *Harvard Business Review* 76, no. 3 (May–June 1998), pp. 72–80; Markides and Williamson, "Corporate Diversification and Organization Structure."

[10] Jeanne M. Liedtka, "Collaboration across Lines of Business for Competitive Advantage," *Academy of Management Executive* 10, no. 2 (May 1996), pp. 20–34.

[11] Kathleen M. Eisenhardt and D. Charles Galunic, "Coevolving: At Last, a Way to Make Synergies Work," *Harvard Business Review* 78, no. 1 (January–February 2000), pp. 91–101; Constantinos C. Markides and Peter J. Williamson, "Related Diversification, Core Competences and Corporate Performance," *Strategic Management Journal* 15 (Summer 1994), pp. 149–165.

[12] A. Campbell, M. Goold, and M. Alexander, "Corporate Strategy: The Quest for Parenting Advantage," *Harvard Business Review* 73, no. 2 (March–April 1995), pp. 120–132.

[13] Cynthia A. Montgomery and B. Wernerfelt, "Diversification, Ricardian Rents, and Tobin-Q," *RAND Journal of Economics* 19, no. 4 (1988), pp. 623–632.

[14] Patricia L. Anslinger and Thomas E. Copeland, "Growth through Acquisitions: A Fresh Look," *Harvard Business Review* 74, no. 1 (January–February 1996), pp. 126–135.

[15] M. Lubatkin and S. Chatterjee, "Extending Modern Portfolio Theory," *Academy of Management Journal* 37, no.1 (February 1994), pp. 109–136.

[16] Lawrence G. Franko, "The Death of Diversification? The Focusing of the World's Industrial Firms, 1980–2000," *Business Horizons* 47, no. 4 (July–August 2004), pp. 41–50.

[17] David J. Collis and Cynthia A. Montgomery, "Competing on Resources: Strategy in the 90s," *Harvard Business Review* 73, no. 4 (July–August 1995), pp. 118–128.

[18] Peter F. Drucker, *Management: Tasks, Responsibilities, Practices* (New York: Harper & Row, 1974), p. 709.

[19] Lee Dranikoff, Tim Koller, and Anton Schneider, "Divestiture: Strategy's Missing Link," *Harvard Business Review* 80, no. 5 (May 2002), pp. 74–83.

### CHAPTER 9

# Ethics, Corporate Social Responsibility, Environmental Sustainability, and Strategy

## Learning Objectives

THIS CHAPTER WILL HELP YOU UNDERSTAND:

**LO 1** How the standards of ethical behavior in business are no different from the ethical standards and norms of the larger society and culture in which a company operates.

**LO 2** What drives unethical business strategies and behavior.

**LO 3** The costs of business ethics failures.

**LO 4** The concepts of corporate social responsibility and environmental sustainability and how companies balance these duties with economic responsibilities to shareholders.

Social obligation is much bigger than supporting worthy causes. It includes anything that impacts people and the quality of their lives.

> **William Ford Jr.** – *Chairman of the Ford Motor Company*

The time is always right to do what is right.

> **Martin Luther King, Jr.** – *Civil Rights Activist and Humanitarian*

Since most corporate competitors have the same problems with sustainability and social reputation, it's worth trying to solve them together.

> **Simon Mainwaring** – *Founder and CEO of We First, Inc.*

Clearly, a company has a responsibility to make a profit and grow the business. Just as clearly, a company and its personnel have a duty to obey the law and play by the rules of fair competition. But does a company also have a duty to go beyond legal requirements and conform to the ethical norms of the societies in which it operates? Does it have an obligation to contribute to the betterment of society, independent of the needs and preferences of the customers it serves? Should a company display a social conscience and devote a portion of its resources to bettering society? Should its strategic initiatives be screened for possible negative effects on future generations of the world's population?

This chapter focuses on whether a company, in the course of trying to craft and execute a strategy that delivers value to both customers and shareholders, also has a duty to (1) act in an ethical manner, (2) be a committed corporate citizen and allocate some of its resources to improving the well-being of employees, the communities in which it operates, and society as a whole, and (3) adopt business practices that conserve natural resources, protect the interests of future generations, and preserve the well-being of the planet.

## WHAT DO WE MEAN BY *BUSINESS ETHICS*?

Ethics concerns principles of right or wrong conduct. **Business ethics** is the application of ethical principles and standards to the actions and decisions of business organizations and the conduct of their personnel.[1] *Ethical principles in business are not materially different from ethical principles in general.* Why? Because business actions have to be judged in the context of society's standards of right and wrong, not with respect to a special set of ethical standards applicable only to business situations. If dishonesty is considered unethical and immoral, then dishonest behavior in business—whether it relates to customers, suppliers, employees, shareholders, competitors, or government—qualifies as equally unethical and immoral. If being ethical entails not deliberately harming others, then failing to recall

> **CORE CONCEPT**
>
> **Business ethics** deals with the application of general ethical principles to the actions and decisions of businesses and the conduct of their personnel.

a defective or unsafe product swiftly, regardless of the cost, is likewise unethical. If society deems bribery unethical, then it is unethical for company personnel to make payoffs to government officials to win government contracts or bestow favors to customers to win or retain their business. In short, ethical behavior in business situations requires adhering to generally accepted norms about right or wrong conduct. As a consequence, company managers have an obligation—indeed, a duty—to observe ethical norms when crafting and executing strategy.

# WHERE DO ETHICAL STANDARDS COME FROM—ARE THEY UNIVERSAL OR DEPENDENT ON LOCAL NORMS?

Notions of right and wrong, fair and unfair, moral and immoral are present in all societies and cultures. But there are three distinct schools of thought about the extent to which ethical standards travel across cultures and whether multinational companies can apply the same set of ethical standards in any and all locations where they operate.

## The School of Ethical Universalism

According to the school of **ethical universalism,** the most fundamental conceptions of right and wrong are *universal* and transcend culture, society, and religion.[2] For instance, being truthful (not lying and not being deliberately deceitful) strikes a chord of what's right in the peoples of all nations. Likewise, demonstrating integrity of character, not cheating or harming people, and treating others with decency are concepts that resonate with people of virtually all cultures and religions.

Common moral agreement about right and wrong actions and behaviors across multiple cultures and countries gives rise to universal ethical standards that apply to members of all societies, all companies, and all businesspeople. These universal ethical principles set forth the traits and behaviors that are considered virtuous and that a good person is supposed to believe in and to display. Thus, adherents of the school of ethical universalism maintain that it is entirely appropriate to expect all businesspeople to conform to these universal ethical standards.[3] For example, people in most societies would concur that it is unethical for companies to knowingly expose workers to toxic chemicals and hazardous materials or to sell products known to be unsafe or harmful to the users.

The strength of ethical universalism is that it draws upon the collective views of multiple societies and cultures to put some clear boundaries on what constitutes ethical and unethical business behavior, regardless of the country or culture in which a company's personnel are conducting activities. This means that with respect to basic moral standards that do not vary significantly according to local cultural beliefs, traditions, or religious convictions, a multinational company can develop a code of ethics that it applies more or less evenly across its worldwide operations. It can avoid the slippery slope that comes from having different ethical standards for different company personnel depending on where in the world they are working.

# The School of Ethical Relativism

While undoubtedly there are some universal moral prescriptions (like being truthful and trustworthy), there are also observable variations from one society to another as to what constitutes ethical or unethical behavior. Indeed, differing religious beliefs, social customs, traditions, core values, and behavioral norms frequently give rise to different standards about what is fair or unfair, moral or immoral, and ethically right or wrong. For instance, European and American managers often establish standards of business conduct that protect human rights such as freedom of movement and residence, freedom of speech and political opinion, and the right to privacy. In China, where societal commitment to basic human rights is weak, human rights considerations play a small role in determining what is ethically right or wrong in conducting business activities. In Japan, managers believe that showing respect for the collective good of society is a more important ethical consideration. In Muslim countries, managers typically apply ethical standards compatible with the teachings of Muhammad. Consequently, the school of **ethical relativism** holds that a "one-size-fits-all" template for judging the ethical appropriateness of business actions and the behaviors of company personnel is totally inappropriate. Rather, the underlying thesis of ethical relativism is that whether certain actions or behaviors are ethically right or wrong depends on the ethical norms of the country or culture in which they take place. For businesses, this implies that when there are cross-country or cross-cultural differences in ethical standards, it is appropriate for *local ethical standards to take precedence over what the ethical standards may be in a company's home market.*[4] In a world of ethical relativism, there are few absolutes when it comes to business ethics, and thus few ethical absolutes for consistently judging the ethical correctness of a company's conduct in various countries and markets.

This need to contour local ethical standards to fit local customs, local notions of fair and proper individual treatment, and local business practices gives rise to multiple sets of ethical standards. It also poses some challenging ethical dilemmas. Consider the following two examples.

### The Use of Underage Labor

In industrialized nations, the use of underage workers is considered taboo. Social activists are adamant that child labor is unethical and that companies should neither employ children under the age of 18 as full-time employees nor source any products from foreign suppliers that employ underage workers. Many countries have passed legislation forbidding the use of underage labor or, at a minimum, regulating the employment of people under the age of 18. However, in Ethiopia, Zimbabwe, Pakistan, Afghanistan, Somalia, Burma, North Korea, and more than 50 other countries, it is customary to view children as potential, even necessary, workers. In other countries, like China, India, Russia, and Brazil, child labor laws are often poorly enforced.[5] As of 2012, the International Labor Organization estimated that there were about 215 million child laborers age 5 to 17 and that some 115 million of them were engaged in hazardous work.[6]

While exposing children to hazardous work and long work hours is unquestionably deplorable, the fact remains that poverty-stricken families in many poor countries cannot subsist without the work efforts of young family members; sending their children to school instead of having them work is not a realistic option. If such children are not permitted to work (especially those in the 12-to-17 age group)—due to pressures

**CORE CONCEPT**

The school of **ethical relativism** holds that differing religious beliefs, customs, and behavioral norms across countries and cultures give rise to *multiple sets of standards concerning what is ethically right or wrong.* These differing standards mean that whether business-related actions are right or wrong depends on the prevailing local ethical standards.

Under ethical relativism, there can be no one-size-fits-all set of authentic ethical norms against which to gauge the conduct of company personnel.

imposed by activist groups in industrialized nations—they may be forced to go out on the streets begging or to seek work in parts of the "underground" economy such as drug trafficking and prostitution.[7] So, if all businesses in countries where employing underage workers is common succumb to the pressures to stop employing underage labor, then have they served the best interests of the underage workers, their families, and society in general? Illustration Capsule 9.1 describes IKEA's approach to dealing with this issue regarding its global supplier network.

**The Payment of Bribes and Kickbacks**    A particularly thorny area facing multinational companies is the degree of cross-country variability in paying bribes.[8] In many countries in eastern Europe, Africa, Latin America, and Asia, it is customary to pay bribes to government officials in order to win a government contract, obtain a license or permit, or facilitate an administrative ruling.[9] In some developing nations, it is difficult for any company, foreign or domestic, to move goods through customs without paying off low-level officials. Senior managers in China and Russia often use their power to obtain kickbacks when they purchase materials or other products for their companies.[10] Likewise, in many countries it is normal to make payments to prospective customers in order to win or retain their business. Some people stretch to justify the payment of bribes and kickbacks on grounds that bribing government officials to get goods through customs or giving kickbacks to customers to retain their business or win new orders is simply a payment for services rendered, in the same way that people tip for service at restaurants.[11] But while this is a clever rationalization, it rests on moral quicksand.

Companies that forbid the payment of bribes and kickbacks in their codes of ethical conduct and that are serious about enforcing this prohibition face a particularly vexing problem in countries where bribery and kickback payments are an entrenched local custom. Complying with the company's code of ethical conduct in these countries is very often tantamount to losing business to competitors that have no such scruples—an outcome that penalizes ethical companies and ethical company personnel (who may suffer lost sales commissions or bonuses). On the other hand, the payment of bribes or kickbacks not only undercuts the company's code of ethics but also risks breaking the law. The Foreign Corrupt Practices Act (FCPA) prohibits U.S. companies from paying bribes to government officials, political parties, political candidates, or others in all countries where they do business. The Organization for Economic Cooperation and Development (OECD) has antibribery standards that criminalize the bribery of foreign public officials in international business transactions—all 34 OECD member countries and 6 nonmember countries have adopted these standards.

Despite laws forbidding bribery to secure sales and contracts, the practice persists. As of December 2012, 221 individuals and 90 entities were sanctioned under criminal proceedings for foreign bribery by the OECD. At least 83 of the sanctioned individuals were sentenced to prison. In 2014, Alcoa agreed to pay $384 million to settle charges brought by the Justice Department and the Securities and Exchange Commission (SEC) that it used bribes to lock in lucrative contracts in Bahrain. French oil giant Total settled criminal charges for $398 million the prior year for similar behavior in Iran. Other well-known companies caught up in recent or ongoing bribery cases include Archer Daniels Midland, the global agribusiness trader; Swiss oil-field services firm Weatherford; Avon; and Walmart. In 2013, the Ralph Lauren Corporation struck a nonprosecution agreement with the SEC to forfeit illicit profits made due to bribes paid by a subsidiary in Argentina. When the parent company found the problem, it immediately reported it

# IKEA's Global Supplier Standards: Maintaining Low Costs While Fighting the Root Causes of Child Labor

Known for its stylish ready-to-assemble home furnishings, IKEA has long relied on an extensive supplier network to manufacture its products and support its rapid global expansion. It has worked hard to develop a successful approach to encourage high ethical standards among its suppliers, including standards concerning the notoriously difficult issue of child labor.

IKEA's initial plan to combat the use of child labor by its suppliers involved (1) contracts that threatened immediate cancellation and (2) random audits by a third-party partner. Despite these safeguards, the company discovered that some of its Indian suppliers were still employing children. IKEA realized that this issue would crop up again and again if it continued to use low-cost suppliers in developing countries—a critical element in its cost-containment strategy.

To address this problem, IKEA developed and introduced its new code for suppliers, IWAY, that addresses social, safety, and environmental issues across its purchasing model. When faced with a supplier slip-up, IKEA works with the company to figure out and tackle the root cause of violations. Using child labor, for example, can signal bigger problems: production inefficiencies that require the lowest-cost labor, lack of alternative options for children like school or supervised community centers, family health or income challenges that mean children need to become breadwinners, and so on. IKEA takes action to provide technical expertise to improve working conditions and processes, offer financing help at reasonable

rates, run training programs onsite, and help develop resources and infrastructure in areas where its suppliers are based. The IKEA foundation also began focusing on these issues through partnerships with UNICEF and Save the Children aimed at funding long-term community programs that support access to education, health care, and sustainable family incomes. It expects the programs will reach 15 million children by 2017.

IKEA's proactive approach has reduced some of the risks involved in relying on suppliers in developing countries. Through its approach, IKEA has been able to maintain its core strategic principles even when they seem to be at odds: low costs, great design, adherence to its ethical principles, and a commitment to a better world.

*Note:* Developed with Kiera O'Brien.

*Sources:* IKEA, "About the Company: This is IKEA," www.ikea.com/ms/en_US/this-is-ikea/people-and-planet/people-and-communities/ (accessed January 24, 2014); and Elain Cohen, "Banning Child Labor: The Symptom or the Cause?" *CSR Newswire,* www.csrwire.com/blog/posts/547-banning-child-labor-the-symptom-or-the-cause (accessed January 24, 2014).

---

to the SEC and provided substantial assistance with the investigation. The company paid only $882,000 in penalties (above the forfeited profits) as a result.

## Using the Principle of Ethical Relativism to Create Ethical Standards Is Problematic for Multinational Companies

Relying upon the principle of ethical relativism to determine what is right or wrong poses major problems for multinational companies trying to decide which ethical standards to enforce companywide. It is a slippery slope indeed to resolve such ethical diversity without any kind of higher-order moral compass. Consider,

> Codes of conduct based on ethical relativism can be *ethically problematic* for multinational companies by creating a maze of conflicting ethical standards.

for example, the ethical inconsistency of a multinational company that, in the name of ethical relativism, declares it impermissible to engage in kickbacks unless such payments are customary and generally overlooked by legal authorities. It is likewise problematic for a multinational company to declare it ethically acceptable to use underage labor at its plants in those countries where child labor is allowed but ethically inappropriate to employ underage labor at its plants elsewhere. If a country's culture is accepting of environmental degradation or practices that expose workers to dangerous conditions (toxic chemicals or bodily harm), should a multinational company lower its ethical bar in that country but rule the very same actions to be ethically wrong in other countries?

Business leaders who rely upon the principle of ethical relativism to justify conflicting ethical standards for operating in different countries have little moral basis for establishing or enforcing ethical standards companywide. Rather, when a company's ethical standards vary from country to country, the clear message being sent to employees is that the company has no ethical standards or convictions of its own and prefers to let its standards of ethical right and wrong be governed by the customs and practices of the countries in which it operates. Applying multiple sets of ethical standards without some kind of higher-order moral compass is scarcely a basis for holding company personnel to high standards of ethical behavior. And it can lead to prosecutions of both companies and individuals alike when there are conflicting sets of laws.

## Ethics and Integrative Social Contracts Theory

**CORE CONCEPT**

According to **integrated social contracts theory,** universal ethical principles based on the collective views of multiple societies form a "social contract" that all individuals and organizations have a duty to observe in all situations. *Within the boundaries of this social contract,* local cultures or groups can specify what *additional* actions may or may not be ethically permissible.

According to integrated social contracts theory, adherence to universal or "first-order" ethical norms should always take precedence over local or "second-order" norms.

**Integrative social contracts theory** provides a middle position between the opposing views of ethical universalism and ethical relativism.[12] According to this theory, the ethical standards a company should try to uphold are governed by both (1) a limited number of universal ethical principles that are widely recognized as putting legitimate ethical boundaries on behaviors in *all* situations and (2) the circumstances of local cultures, traditions, and values that further prescribe what constitutes ethically permissible behavior. The universal ethical principles are based on the collective views of multiple cultures and societies and combine to form a "social contract" that all individuals, groups, organizations, and businesses in all situations have a duty to observe. *Within the boundaries of this social contract,* local cultures or groups can specify what *other* actions may or may not be ethically permissible. While this system leaves some "moral free space" for the people in a particular country (or local culture, or profession, or even a company) to make specific interpretations of what other actions may or may not be permissible, *universal ethical norms always take precedence.* Thus, local ethical standards can be *more* stringent than the universal ethical standards but *never less so.* For example, both the legal and medical professions have standards regarding what kinds of advertising are ethically permissible that extend beyond the universal norm that advertising not be false or misleading.

The strength of integrated social contracts theory is that it accommodates the best parts of ethical universalism and ethical relativism. Moreover, integrative social contracts theory offers managers in multinational companies clear guidance in resolving cross-country ethical differences: Those parts of the company's code of ethics that involve universal ethical norms must be enforced worldwide, but within these boundaries there is room for ethical diversity and the opportunity for host-country cultures to exert *some* influence over the moral and ethical standards of business units operating in that country.

A good example of the application of integrative social contracts theory to business involves the payment of bribes and kickbacks. Yes, bribes and kickbacks seem to be common in some countries. But the fact that bribery flourishes in a country does not mean it is an authentic or legitimate ethical norm. Virtually all of the world's major religions (e.g., Buddhism, Christianity, Confucianism, Hinduism, Islam, Judaism, Sikhism, and Taoism) and all moral schools of thought condemn bribery and corruption. Therefore, a multinational company might reasonably conclude that there is a universal ethical principle to be observed in this case—one of refusing to condone bribery and kickbacks on the part of company personnel no matter what the local custom is and no matter what the sales consequences are.

> In instances involving *universally applicable* ethical norms (like paying bribes), there can be *no compromise* on what is ethically permissible and what is not.

## HOW AND WHY ETHICAL STANDARDS IMPACT THE TASKS OF CRAFTING AND EXECUTING STRATEGY

Many companies have acknowledged their ethical obligations in official codes of ethical conduct. In the United States, for example, the Sarbanes–Oxley Act, passed in 2002, requires that companies whose stock is publicly traded have a code of ethics or else explain in writing to the SEC why they do not. But there's a big difference between having a code of ethics because it is mandated and having ethical standards that truly provide guidance for a company's strategy and business conduct.[13] *The litmus test of whether a company's code of ethics is cosmetic is the extent to which it is embraced in crafting strategy and in operating the business day to day.*

It is up to senior executives to lead the way on compliance with the company's ethical code of conduct. They can do so by making it a point to consider three sets of questions whenever a new strategic initiative is under review:

- Is what we are proposing to do fully compliant with our code of ethical conduct? Are there any areas of ambiguity that may be of concern?
- Is it apparent that this proposed action is in harmony with our code? Are any conflicts or potential problems evident?
- Is there anything in the proposed action that could be considered ethically objectionable? Would our customers, employees, suppliers, stockholders, competitors, communities, the SEC, or the media view this action as ethically objectionable?

Unless questions of this nature are posed—either in open discussion or by force of habit in the minds of strategy makers—there's a risk that strategic initiatives will become disconnected from the company's code of ethics. If a company's executives believe strongly in living up to the company's ethical standards, they will unhesitatingly reject strategic initiatives and operating approaches that don't measure up. However, in companies with a cosmetic approach to ethics, any strategy–ethics linkage stems mainly from a desire to avoid the risk of embarrassment and possible disciplinary action for approving a strategic initiative that is deemed by society to be unethical and perhaps illegal.

While most company managers are careful to ensure that a company's strategy is within the bounds of what is *legal,* evidence indicates they are not always so careful to ensure that all elements of their strategies and operating activities are within the bounds of what is considered *ethical.* In recent years, there have been revelations of ethical misconduct on the part of managers at such companies as Koch Industries,

**LO 2**

What drives unethical
business strategies
and behavior.

casino giant Las Vegas Sands, Hewlett-Packard, GlaxoSmithKline, Marathon Oil Corporation, Kraft Foods Inc., Motorola Solutions, Pfizer, Oracle Corporation, several leading investment banking firms, and a host of mortgage lenders. The consequences of crafting strategies that cannot pass the test of moral scrutiny are manifested in sizable fines, devastating public relations hits, sharp drops in stock prices that cost shareholders billions of dollars, criminal indictments, and convictions of company executives. The fallout from all these scandals has resulted in heightened management attention to legal and ethical considerations in crafting strategy.

# DRIVERS OF UNETHICAL BUSINESS STRATEGIES AND BEHAVIOR

Apart from the "business of business is business, not ethics" kind of thinking apparent in recent high-profile business scandals, three other main drivers of unethical business behavior also stand out:[14]

- Faulty oversight, enabling the unscrupulous pursuit of personal gain and self-interest.
- Heavy pressures on company managers to meet or beat short-term performance targets.
- A company culture that puts profitability and business performance ahead of ethical behavior.

### Faulty Oversight, Enabling the Unscrupulous Pursuit of Personal Gain and Self-Interest    People who are obsessed with wealth accumulation, power, status, and their own self-interest often push ethical principles aside in their quest for personal gain. Driven by greed and ambition, they exhibit few qualms in skirting the rules or doing whatever is necessary to achieve their goals. A general disregard for business ethics can prompt all kinds of unethical strategic maneuvers and behaviors at companies.

The U.S. government has been conducting a multiyear investigation of insider trading, the illegal practice of exchanging confidential information to gain an advantage in the stock market. Focusing on the hedge fund industry and nicknamed "Operation Perfect Hedge," the investigation has brought to light scores of violations and led to at least 79 guilty pleas or convictions by early 2014. Among the most prominent of those convicted was Raj Rajaratnam, the former head of Galleon Group, who was sentenced to 11 years in prison and fined $10 million. At SAC Capital, a $14 billion hedge fund, eight hedge fund managers were convicted of insider trading, in what has been called the most lucrative insider trading scheme in U.S. history. The company has agreed to pay $1.8 billion in penalties and has been forced to stop managing money for outside investors.[15] Since Operation Perfect Hedge began, abnormal jumps in the stock price of target firms (a sign of insider trading) have fallen 45 percent.

Responsible corporate governance and oversight by the company's corporate board is necessary to guard against self-dealing and the manipulation of information to disguise such actions by a company's managers. **Self-dealing** occurs when managers take advantage of their position to further their own private interests rather than those of the firm. As discussed in Chapter 2, the duty of the corporate board (and its compensation and audit committees in particular) is to guard against

**CORE CONCEPT**

**Self-dealing** occurs when managers take advantage of their position to further their own private interests rather than those of the firm.

such actions. A strong, independent board is necessary to have proper oversight of the company's financial practices and to hold top managers accountable for their actions.

A particularly egregious example of the lack of proper oversight is the scandal over mortgage lending and banking practices that resulted in a crisis for the U.S. residential real estate market and heartrending consequences for many home buyers. This scandal stemmed from consciously unethical strategies at many banks and mortgage companies to boost the fees they earned on home mortgages by deliberately lowering lending standards to approve so-called subprime loans for home buyers whose incomes were insufficient to make their monthly mortgage payments. Once these lenders earned their fees on these loans, they repackaged the loans to hide their true nature and auctioned them off to unsuspecting investors, who later suffered huge losses when the high-risk borrowers began to default on their loan payments. (Government authorities later forced some of the firms that auctioned off these packaged loans to repurchase them at the auction price and bear the losses themselves.) A lawsuit by the attorneys general of 49 states charging widespread and systematic fraud ultimately resulted in a $26 billion settlement by the five largest U.S. banks (Bank of America, Citigroup, JPMorgan Chase, Wells Fargo, and Ally Financial). Included in the settlement were new rules designed to increase oversight and reform policies and practices among the mortgage companies. The settlement includes what are believed to be a set of robust monitoring and enforcement mechanisms that should help prevent such abuses in the future.[16]

### Heavy Pressures on Company Managers to Meet Short-Term Performance Targets

When key personnel find themselves scrambling to meet the quarterly and annual sales and profit expectations of investors and financial analysts, they often feel enormous pressure to *do whatever it takes* to protect their reputation for delivering good results. Executives at high-performing companies know that investors will see the slightest sign of a slowdown in earnings growth as a red flag and drive down the company's stock price. In addition, slowing growth or declining profits could lead to a downgrade of the company's credit rating if it has used lots of debt to finance its growth. The pressure to "never miss a quarter"—so as not to upset the expectations of analysts, investors, and creditors—prompts nearsighted managers to engage in short-term maneuvers to make the numbers, regardless of whether these moves are really in the best long-term interests of the company. Sometimes the pressure induces company personnel to continue to stretch the rules until the limits of ethical conduct are overlooked.[17] Once ethical boundaries are crossed in efforts to "meet or beat their numbers," the threshold for making more extreme ethical compromises becomes lower.

In 2014, the SEC charged Diamond Foods (maker of Pop Secret and Emerald Nuts) with accounting fraud, alleging that the company falsified costs in order to boost earnings and stock prices. The company has agreed to pay $5 million to settle SEC fraud charges, while its (now ousted) CEO must pay $125,000 to settle a separate charge of negligence and return $4 million in bonuses to the company. Litigation continues against its now former CFO. The real blow for the company was that its pending acquisition of potato chip giant Pringles fell apart as a result of the scandal, thwarting the company's dreams of becoming the second-largest snack company in the world.[18]

Company executives often feel pressured to hit financial performance targets because their compensation depends heavily on the company's performance. Over the last two decades, it has become fashionable for boards of directors to grant lavish bonuses, stock option awards, and other compensation benefits to executives for meeting specified performance targets. So outlandishly large were these rewards that executives had strong personal incentives to bend the rules and engage in behaviors that allowed the targets to be met. Much of the accounting manipulation at the root of recent corporate scandals has entailed situations in which executives benefited enormously from misleading accounting or other shady activities that allowed them to hit the numbers and receive incentive awards ranging from $10 million to more than $1 billion for hedge fund managers.

The fundamental problem with **short-termism**—the tendency for managers to focus excessive attention on short-term performance objectives—is that it doesn't create value for customers or improve the firm's competitiveness in the marketplace; that is, it sacrifices the activities that are the most reliable drivers of higher profits and added shareholder value in the long run. Cutting ethical corners in the name of profits carries exceptionally high risk for shareholders—the steep stock price decline and tarnished brand image that accompany the discovery of scurrilous behavior leave shareholders with a company worth much less than before—and the rebuilding task can be arduous, taking both considerable time and resources.

**A Company Culture That Puts Profitability and Business Performance Ahead of Ethical Behavior**    When a company's culture spawns an ethically corrupt or amoral work climate, people have a company-approved license to ignore "what's right" and engage in any behavior or strategy they think they can get away with. Such cultural norms as "Everyone else does it" and "It is okay to bend the rules to get the job done" permeate the work environment. At such companies, ethically immoral people are certain to play down observance of ethical strategic actions and business conduct. Moreover, cultural pressures to utilize unethical means if circumstances become challenging can prompt otherwise honorable people to behave unethically. A perfect example of a company culture gone awry on ethics is Enron, a now-defunct but infamous company found guilty of one of the most sprawling business frauds in U.S. history.[19]

Enron's leaders encouraged company personnel to focus on the current bottom line and to be innovative and aggressive in figuring out how to grow current earnings—regardless of the methods. Enron's annual "rank and yank" performance evaluation process, in which the lowest-ranking 15 to 20 percent of employees were let go, made it abundantly clear that bottom-line results were what mattered most. The name of the game at Enron became devising clever ways to boost revenues and earnings, even if this sometimes meant operating outside established policies. In fact, outside-the-lines behavior was celebrated if it generated profitable new business.

A high-performance–high-rewards climate came to pervade the Enron culture, as the best workers (determined by who produced the best bottom-line results) received impressively large incentives and bonuses. On Car Day at Enron, an array of luxury sports cars arrived for presentation to the most successful employees. Understandably, employees wanted to be seen as part of Enron's star team and partake in the benefits granted to Enron's best and brightest employees. The high monetary rewards, the ambitious and hard-driving people whom the company hired and promoted, and the competitive, results-oriented culture combined to give Enron a reputation not only for trampling competitors but also for internal ruthlessness. The company's win-at-all-costs mindset nurtured a culture that gradually and then more rapidly fostered the erosion of ethical standards, eventually making a mockery of the company's stated values of integrity and respect. When it became evident in fall 2001 that Enron was a house of cards propped up by deceitful accounting and myriad unsavory practices, the company imploded in a matter of weeks—one of the biggest bankruptcies of all time, costing investors $64 billion in losses.

In contrast, when high ethical principles are deeply ingrained in the corporate culture of a company, culture can function as a powerful mechanism for communicating ethical behavioral norms and gaining employee buy-in to the company's moral standards, business principles, and corporate values. In such cases, the ethical principles embraced in the company's code of ethics and/or in its statement of corporate values are seen as integral to the company's identity, self-image, and ways of operating. The message that ethics matters—and matters a lot—resounds loudly and clearly throughout the organization and in its strategy and decisions. Illustration Capsule 9.2 discusses Novo Nordisk's approach to building an ethical culture and putting its ethical principles into practice.

## WHY SHOULD COMPANY STRATEGIES BE ETHICAL?

There are two reasons why a company's strategy should be ethical: (1) because a strategy that is unethical is morally wrong and reflects badly on the character of the company and its personnel, and (2) because an ethical strategy can be good business and serve the self-interest of shareholders.

### The Moral Case for an Ethical Strategy

Managers do not dispassionately assess what strategic course to steer—how strongly committed they are to observing ethical principles and standards definitely comes into play in making strategic choices. Ethical strategy making is generally the product of managers who are of strong moral character (i.e., who are trustworthy, have integrity, and truly care about conducting the company's business honorably). Managers with high ethical principles are usually advocates of a corporate code of ethics and strong ethics compliance, and they are genuinely committed to upholding corporate values and ethical business principles. They demonstrate their commitment by displaying the company's stated values and living up to its business principles and ethical standards. They understand the difference between merely adopting value statements and codes of ethics and ensuring that they are followed strictly in a company's actual strategy and business conduct. As a consequence, ethically strong managers consciously opt for strategic actions that can pass the strictest moral scrutiny—they display no tolerance for strategies with ethically controversial components.

**LO 3**

The costs of business ethics failures.

### The Business Case for Ethical Strategies

In addition to the moral reasons for adopting ethical strategies, there may be solid business reasons. Pursuing unethical strategies and tolerating unethical conduct not only damages a company's reputation but also may result in a wide-ranging set of other costly consequences. Figure 9.1 shows the kinds of costs a company can incur when unethical behavior on its part is discovered, the wrongdoings of company personnel are headlined in the media, and it is forced to make amends for its behavior. The more egregious are a company's ethical violations, the higher the costs and the bigger the damage to its reputation (and to the reputations of the company personnel involved). In high-profile instances, the costs of ethical misconduct can easily run into

# How Novo Nordisk Puts Its Ethical Principles into Practice

Novo Nordisk is a $13.8 billion global pharmaceutical company, known for its innovation and leadership in diabetes treatments. It is also known for its dedication to ethical business practices. In 2012, the company was listed as the global leader in business ethics by *Corporate Knights,* a corporate social responsibility advisory firm.

Novo Nordisk's company policies are explicit in their attention to both bioethics and business ethics. In the realm of bioethics, the company is committed to conducting its research involving people, animals, and gene technology in accordance with the highest global ethical standards. Moreover, the company requires that all of its suppliers and other external partners also adhere to Novo Nordisk's bioethical standards. In the realm of business ethics, the policies dictate (1) that high ethical standards be applied consistently across the company's value chain, (2) that all ethical dilemmas encountered be addressed transparently, and (3) that company officers and employees be held accountable for complying with all laws, regulations, and company rules.

Novo Nordisk's strong culture of responsibility helps to translate the company's policies into practice. At Novo Nordisk, every employee pledges to conduct himself or herself according to the Novo Nordisk Way, a set of behavioral norms that has come to define the company's culture. It's a culture that promotes teamwork, cooperation, respect for others, and fairness. The commitment to business ethics grew out of those values, which are promoted throughout the company by hiring practices, management leadership, and employee mobility to foster a global one-company culture.

As part of this process, Novo Nordisk has set up a business ethics board, composed of senior management. The board identifies key ethical challenges for the company, drafting guidelines and developing training programs. The training programs are rigorous: All Novo Nordisk employees are trained annually in business ethics. The board is also responsible for ensuring compliance. It has set up an anonymous hotline and conducts ethics audits. During 2012, 48 audits were conducted. The goal of the audits is to maintain a culture that promotes the principles of the Novo Nordisk Way.

Implementing a code of ethics across an organization of 26,000 employees is very difficult and lapses do occur. But such incidents are exceptional and are swiftly addressed by the company. For example, when insider trading allegations came to light against a corporate executive in 2008, the company immediately suspended and subsequently fired the employee.

*Note:* Developed with Dennis L. Huggins.

*Sources:* J. Edwards, "Novo Nordisk Exec Charged with Insider Trading; Cash Stashed in Caribbean," *CBS News,* September 2008, www.cbsnews.com (accessed February 19, 2012); company filings and website (accessed April 1, 2014); and Corporate Knights, "The 8th Annual Global 100," global100.org/ (accessed February 20, 2012).

**FIGURE 9.1**   **The Costs Companies Incur When Ethical Wrongdoing Is Discovered**

| Visible Costs | Internal Administrative Costs | Intangible or Less Visible Costs |
|---|---|---|
| • Government fines and penalties<br><br>• Civil penalties arising from class-action lawsuits and other litigation aimed at punishing the company for its offense and the harm done to others<br><br>• The costs to shareholders in the form of a lower stock price (and possibly lower dividends) | • Legal and investigative costs incurred by the company<br><br>• The costs of providing remedial education and ethics training to company personnel<br><br>• The costs of taking corrective actions<br><br>• Administrative costs associated with ensuring future compliance | • Customer defections<br><br>• Loss of reputation<br><br>• Lost employee morale and higher degrees of employee cynicism<br><br>• Higher employee turnover<br><br>• Higher recruiting costs and difficulty in attracting talented employees<br><br>• Adverse effects on employee productivity<br><br>• The costs of complying with often harsher government regulations |

*Source:* Adapted from Terry Thomas, John R. Schermerhorn, and John W. Dienhart, "Strategic Leadership of Ethical Behavior," *Academy of Management Executive* 18, no. 2 (May 2004), p. 58.

the hundreds of millions and even billions of dollars, especially if they provoke widespread public outrage and many people were harmed. The penalties levied on executives caught in wrongdoing can skyrocket as well, as the 150-year prison term sentence of infamous financier and Ponzi scheme perpetrator Bernie Madoff illustrates.

The fallout of a company's ethical misconduct goes well beyond the costs of making amends for the misdeeds. Customers shun companies caught up in highly publicized ethical scandals. Rehabilitating a company's shattered reputation is time-consuming and costly. Companies known to have engaged in unethical conduct have difficulty in recruiting and retaining talented employees. Most ethically upstanding people are repulsed by a work environment where unethical behavior is condoned; they don't want to get entrapped in a compromising situation, nor do they want their personal reputations tarnished by the actions of an unsavory employer. Creditors are unnerved by the unethical actions of a borrower because of the potential business fallout and subsequent risk of default on loans.

All told, a company's unethical behavior risks doing considerable damage to shareholders in the form of lost revenues, higher costs, lower profits, lower stock prices, and a diminished business reputation. To a significant degree, therefore, ethical strategies and ethical conduct are *good business*. Most companies understand the value of operating in a manner that wins the approval of suppliers, employees, investors, and society at large. Most businesspeople recognize the risks and adverse fallout attached to the discovery of unethical behavior. Hence, companies have an incentive to employ strategies that can pass the test of being ethical. Even if a company's managers

Conducting business in an ethical fashion is not only morally right—it is in a company's enlightened self-interest.

Shareholders suffer major damage when a company's unethical behavior is discovered. Making amends for unethical business conduct is costly, and it takes years to rehabilitate a tarnished company reputation.

are not personally committed to high ethical standards, they have good reason to operate within ethical bounds, if only to (1) avoid the risk of embarrassment, scandal, disciplinary action, fines, and possible jail time for unethical conduct on their part and (2) escape being held accountable for lax enforcement of ethical standards and unethical behavior by personnel under their supervision.

# STRATEGY, CORPORATE SOCIAL RESPONSIBILITY, AND ENVIRONMENTAL SUSTAINABILITY

### LO 4

The concepts of corporate social responsibility and environmental sustainability and how companies balance these duties with economic responsibilities to shareholders.

### CORE CONCEPT

**Corporate social responsibility (CSR)** refers to a company's *duty* to operate in an honorable manner, provide good working conditions for employees, encourage workforce diversity, be a good steward of the environment, and actively work to better the quality of life in the local communities where it operates and in society at large.

The idea that businesses have an obligation to foster social betterment, a much-debated topic over the past 50 years, took root in the 19th century when progressive companies in the aftermath of the industrial revolution began to provide workers with housing and other amenities. The notion that corporate executives should balance the interests of all stakeholders—shareholders, employees, customers, suppliers, the communities in which they operate, and society at large—began to blossom in the 1960s. Some years later, a group of chief executives of America's 200 largest corporations, calling themselves the Business Roundtable, came out in strong support of the concept of **corporate social responsibility (CSR):**

> Balancing the shareholder's expectations of maximum return against other priorities is one of the fundamental problems confronting corporate management. The shareholder must receive a good return but the legitimate concerns of other constituencies (customers, employees, communities, suppliers and society at large) also must have the appropriate attention. . . . [Leading managers] believe that by giving enlightened consideration to balancing the legitimate claims of all its constituents, a corporation will best serve the interest of its shareholders.

Today, corporate social responsibility is a concept that resonates in western Europe, the United States, Canada, and such developing nations as Brazil and India.

## The Concepts of Corporate Social Responsibility and Good Corporate Citizenship

The essence of socially responsible business behavior is that a company should balance strategic actions to benefit shareholders against the *duty* to be a good corporate citizen. The underlying thesis is that company managers should display a *social conscience* in operating the business and specifically take into account how management decisions and company actions affect the well-being of employees, local communities, the environment, and society at large.[20] Acting in a socially responsible manner thus encompasses more than just participating in community service projects and donating money to charities and other worthy causes. Demonstrating social responsibility also entails undertaking actions that earn trust and respect from all stakeholders—operating in an honorable and ethical manner, striving to make the company a great place to work, demonstrating genuine respect for the environment, and trying to make a difference in bettering society. As depicted in Figure 9.2, corporate responsibility programs commonly include the following elements:

- *Striving to employ an ethical strategy and observe ethical principles in operating the business.* A sincere commitment to observing ethical principles is a necessary

**FIGURE 9.2**   The Five Components of a Corporate Social Responsibility Strategy

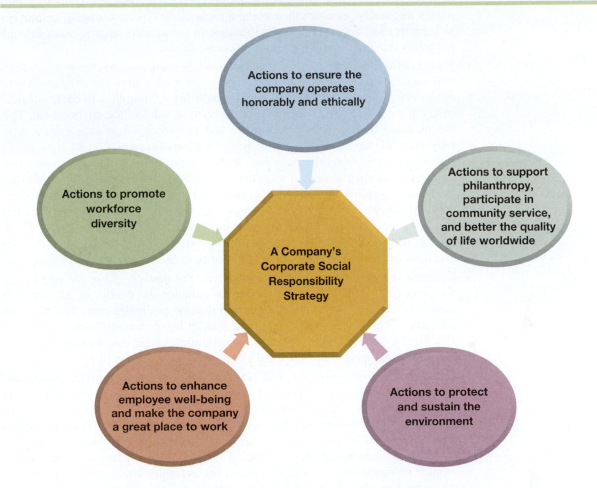

*Source:* Adapted from material in Ronald Paul Hill, Debra Stephens, and Iain Smith, "Corporate Social Responsibility: An Examination of Individual Firm Behavior," *Business and Society Review* 108, no. 3 (September 2003), p. 348.

component of a CSR strategy simply because unethical conduct is incompatible with the concept of good corporate citizenship and socially responsible business behavior.

- *Making charitable contributions, supporting community service endeavors, engaging in broader philanthropic initiatives, and reaching out to make a difference in the lives of the disadvantaged.* Some companies fulfill their philanthropic obligations by spreading their efforts over a multitude of charitable and community activities—for instance, Wells Fargo and Google support a broad variety of community, art, and social welfare programs. Others prefer to focus their energies more narrowly. McDonald's, for example, concentrates on sponsoring the Ronald McDonald House program (which provides a home away from home for the families of seriously ill children receiving treatment at nearby hospitals). British Telecom gives 1 percent of its profits directly to communities, largely for education—teacher training, in-school workshops, and digital technology. Leading prescription drug maker GlaxoSmithKline and other pharmaceutical companies either donate or heavily discount medicines for distribution in the least developed nations. Companies frequently reinforce their philanthropic efforts by encouraging employees to support charitable causes and participate in community affairs, often through programs that match employee contributions.

- *Taking actions to protect the environment and, in particular, to minimize or eliminate any adverse impact on the environment stemming from the company's own business activities.* Corporate social responsibility as it applies to environmental protection entails actively striving to be a good steward of the environment. This means using the best available science and technology to reduce environmentally harmful aspects of the company's operations *below the levels required by prevailing environmental regulations.* It also means putting time and money into improving the environment in ways that extend beyond a company's own industry boundaries—such as participating in recycling projects, adopting energy conservation practices, and supporting efforts to clean up local water supplies. Retailers like Walmart and Home Depot in the United States and B&Q in the United Kingdom have pressured their suppliers to adopt stronger environmental protection practices in order to lower the carbon footprint of their entire supply chains.

- *Creating a work environment that enhances the quality of life for employees.* Numerous companies exert extra effort to enhance the quality of life for their employees at work and at home. This can include onsite day care, flexible work schedules, workplace exercise facilities, special leaves for employees to care for sick family members, work-at-home opportunities, career development programs and education opportunities, special safety programs, and the like.

- *Building a diverse workforce with respect to gender, race, national origin, and other aspects that different people bring to the workplace.* Most large companies in the United States have established workforce diversity programs, and some go the extra mile to ensure that their workplaces are attractive to ethnic minorities and inclusive of all groups and perspectives. At some companies, the diversity initiative extends to suppliers—sourcing items from small businesses owned by women or members of ethnic minorities, for example. The pursuit of workforce diversity can also be good business. At Coca-Cola, where strategic success depends on getting people all over the world to become loyal consumers of the company's beverages, efforts to build a public persona of inclusiveness for people of all races, religions, nationalities, interests, and talents have considerable strategic value.

The particular combination of socially responsible endeavors a company elects to pursue defines its **corporate social responsibility strategy.** Illustration Capsule 9.3 describes Burt's Bees' approach to corporate social responsibility—an approach that ensures that social responsibility is reflected in all of the company's actions and endeavors. As the Burt's Bees example shows, the specific components emphasized in a CSR strategy vary from company to company and are typically linked to a company's core values. General Mills, for example, centers its CSR strategy around three themes: nourishing lives (via healthier and easier-to-prepare foods), nourishing communities (via charitable donations to community causes and volunteerism for community service projects), and nourishing the environment (via efforts to conserve natural resources, reduce energy and water usage, promote recycling, and otherwise support environmental sustainability).[21] Starbucks's CSR strategy includes four main elements (ethical sourcing, community service, environmental

**CORE CONCEPT**

A company's **CSR strategy** is defined by the specific combination of socially beneficial activities the company opts to support with its contributions of time, money, and other resources.

# Burt's Bees: A Strategy Based on Corporate Social Responsibility

Burt's Bees is a leading company in natural personal care, offering nearly 200 products including its popular beeswax lip balms and skin care creams. The brand has enjoyed tremendous success as consumers have begun to embrace all-natural, environmentally friendly products, boosting Burt's Bees' revenues to over $250 million by 2012. Much of Burt's Bees' success can be attributed to its skillful use of corporate social responsibility (CSR) as a strategic tool to engage customers and differentiate itself from competitors.

While many companies have embraced corporate social responsibility, few companies have managed to integrate CSR as fully and seamlessly throughout their organizations as has Burt's Bees. The company's business model is centered on a principle Burt's Bees refers to as "The Greater Good," which specifies that all company practices must be socially responsible. The execution of this strategy is managed by a special committee dedicated to leading the organization to attain its CSR goals with respect to three primary areas: natural well-being, humanitarian responsibility, and environmental sustainability.

Natural well-being is focused on the ingredients used to create Burt's Bees products. Today, the average Burt's Bees product contains over 99 percent natural ingredients; by 2020, the brand expects to produce only 100 percent natural products.

Burt's Bees' humanitarian focus is centered on its relationships with employees and suppliers. A key part of this effort involves a mandatory employee training program that focuses on four key areas: outreach, wellness, world-class leadership, and the environment. Another is the company's Responsible Sourcing Mission, which lays out a carefully prescribed set of guidelines for sourcing responsible suppliers and managing supplier relationships.

A focus on caring for the environment is clearly interwoven into all aspects of Burt's Bees. By focusing on environmentally efficient processes, the company

uses its in-house manufacturing capability as a point of strategic differentiation.

Burt's Bees faced some consumer backlash when it was purchased recently by The Clorox Company, whose traditional image is viewed in sharp contrast to Burt's Bees' values. But while Burt's Bees is still only a small part of Clorox's total revenue, it has become its fastest-growing division.

*Note:* Developed with Ross M. Templeton.

*Sources:* Company websites; Louise Story, "Can Burt's Bees Turn Clorox Green?" *The New York Times,* January 6, 2008; Bill Chameides, "Burt's Bees Are Busy on the Sustainability Front," *Huffington Post,* June 25, 2010; Katie Bird, "Burt's Bees' International Performance Weaker than Expected," *Cosmetics Design,* January 6, 2011, CosmeticsDesign.com; "Burt's Bees, Marks & Spencer Share Staff Engagement Tactics," *Environmental Leader,* May 31, 2011, EnvironmentalLeader.com; and blogs.newsobserver.com/ (accessed March 1, 2012).

stewardship, and farmer support), all of which have touch points with the way that the company procures its coffee—a key aspect of its product differentiation strategy. Some companies use other terms, such as *corporate citizenship, corporate responsibility,* or *sustainable responsible business (SRB)* to characterize their CSR initiatives.

Although there is wide variation in how companies devise and implement a CSR strategy, communities of companies concerned with corporate social responsibility (such as CSR Europe) have emerged to help companies share best CSR practices. Moreover, a number of reporting standards have been developed, including ISO 26000—a new internationally recognized standard for social responsibility set by the International Standards Organization (ISO).[22] Companies that exhibit a strong commitment to corporate social responsibility are often recognized by being included on lists such as *Corporate Responsibility* magazine's "100 Best Corporate Citizens" or *Corporate Knights* magazine's "Global 100 Most Sustainable Corporations."

**Corporate Social Responsibility and the Triple Bottom Line**   CSR initiatives undertaken by companies are frequently directed at improving the company's *triple bottom line (TBL)*—a reference to three types of performance metrics: *economic, social,* and *environmental.* The goal is for a company to succeed simultaneously in all three dimensions, as illustrated in Figure 9.3.[23] The three dimensions of performance are often referred to in terms of the "three pillars" of "people, planet, and profit." The term *people* refers to the various social initiatives that make up CSR strategies, such as corporate giving, community involvement, and company efforts to improve the lives of its internal and external stakeholders. *Planet* refers to a firm's ecological impact and environmental practices. The term *profit* has a broader meaning with respect to the triple bottom line than it does otherwise. It encompasses not only the

**FIGURE 9.3**   The Triple Bottom Line: Excelling on Three Measures of Company Performance

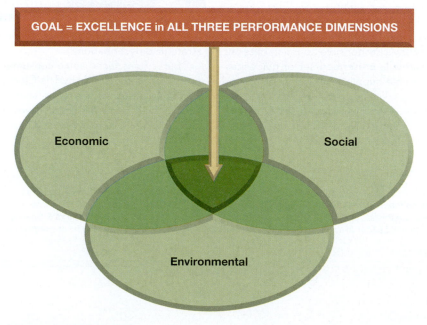

*Source:* Developed with help from Amy E. Florentino.

# TOMS's Well-Balanced Triple Bottom Line

Having sold over 2 million pairs of shoes worldwide, self-designated "Chief Shoe Giver" Blake Mycoskie founded TOMS on the principle of "One for One." Operating under the belief that "the way you shop can change the world," TOMS donates a pair of shoes to a child in need in over 50 different countries for every pair purchased. Each pair is made with sustainable materials that include organic canvas and recycled materials that minimize TOMS's ecological footprint. TOMS has been recognized with the Award for Corporate Excellence by the Office of the Secretary of State, while *Fortune* magazine has named Mycoskie to its "40 under 40" list.

Mycoskie credits much of TOMS's growth not to success in traditional avenues of advertising but, rather, to the story behind the TOMS shoe as told by TOMS's customers. By focusing on the story behind its product and the importance of sustainable giving, TOMS generates brand awareness through motivated customers who share their feel-good purchases with friends and family. By utilizing user marketing rather than corporate marketing, TOMS successfully pitches a grassroots company-image and bundles a lifestyle with its product.

TOMS's environmental sustainability approach includes offering a line of vegan shoes, which contain no animal by-products, and maintaining its commitment to use earth and animal-friendly materials whenever possible. Its shoeboxes are made with 80 percent recycled waste and are printed with soy ink. Through these production considerations, TOMS caters to an environmentally conscious demographic with few established competitors and with loyal consumers who have helped TOMS experience sustained growth despite the global recession.

From Shoe Giving Trips to employee training on the importance of environmental sustainability, TOMS aspires to offer its employees "more than a 9-to-5" job. This commitment to a worthwhile cause creates not only happier employees but also more autonomous and creative global citizens who work together to inspire change. By attaining *economic* growth through an emphasis on *social* justice and *environmental* sustainability, TOMS has maintained a well-balanced triple bottom line.

*Note:* Developed with Sean Zhang.

*Source:* Keynote statements by Blake Mycoskie and other information posted at **www.toms.com**.

---

profit a firm earns for its shareholders but also the economic impact that the company has on society more generally, in terms of the overall value that it creates and the overall costs that it imposes on society. For example, Procter & Gamble's Swiffer cleaning system, one of the company's best-selling products, not only offers an earth-friendly design but also outperforms less ecologically friendly alternatives in terms of its broader economic impact: It reduces demands on municipal water sources, saves electricity that would be needed to heat mop water, and doesn't add to the amount of detergent making its way into waterways and waste treatment facilities. Nike sees itself as bringing people, planet, and profits into balance by producing innovative new products in a more sustainable way, recognizing that sustainability is key to its future profitability. TOMS shoes has built its strategy around maintaining a well-balanced triple bottom line, as explained in Illustration Capsule 9.4.

Many companies now make a point of citing the beneficial outcomes of their CSR strategies in press releases and issue special reports for consumers and investors to review. Staples, the world's largest office products company, makes reporting an important part of its commitment to corporate responsibility; the company posts a "Staples Soul Report" on its website that describes its initiatives and accomplishments in the areas of diversity, environment, community, and ethics. Triple-bottom-line reporting is emerging as an increasingly important way for companies to make the results of their CSR strategies apparent to stakeholders and for stakeholders to hold companies accountable for their impact on society. The use of standard reporting frameworks and metrics, such as those developed by the Global Reporting Initiative, promotes greater transparency and facilitates benchmarking CSR efforts across firms and industries.

Investment firms have created mutual funds consisting of companies that are excelling on the basis of the triple bottom line in order to attract funds from environmentally and socially aware investors. The Dow Jones Sustainability World Index is made up of the top 10 percent of the 2,500 companies listed in the Dow Jones World Index in terms of economic performance, environmental performance, and social performance. Companies are evaluated in these three performance areas, using indicators such as corporate governance, climate change mitigation, and labor practices. Table 9.1 shows a sampling of the companies selected for the Dow Jones Sustainability World Index in 2013.

**TABLE 9.1**   A Selection of Companies Recognized for Their Triple-Bottom-Line Performance in 2013

| Name | Market Sector | Country |
| --- | --- | --- |
| Volkswagen AG | Automobiles & Components | Germany |
| Australia & New Zealand Banking Group Ltd. | Banks | Australia |
| Siemens AG | Capital Goods | Germany |
| Adecco SA | Commercial & Professional Services | Switzerland |
| Panasonic Corp. | Consumer Durables & Apparel | Japan |
| Tabcorp Holdings Ltd. | Consumer Services | Australia |
| Citigroup Inc. | Diversified Financials | United States |
| BG Group PLC | Energy | United Kingdom |
| Woolworths Ltd. | Food & Staples Retailing | Australia |
| Nestlé SA | Food, Beverage, & Tobacco | Switzerland |
| Abbott Laboratories | Health Care Equipment & Services | United States |
| Henkel AG & Co. KGaA | Household & Personal Products | Germany |
| Allianz SE | Insurance | Germany |
| Akzo Nobel NV | Materials | Netherlands |
| Telenet Group Holding NV | Media | Belgium |
| Roche Holding AG | Pharmaceuticals, Biotechnology, & Life Sciences | Switzerland |
| Stockland | Real Estate | Australia |

| Name | Market Sector | Country |
| --- | --- | --- |
| Lotte Shopping Co Ltd. | Retailing | Republic of Korea |
| Taiwan Semiconductor Manufacturing Co. Ltd. | Semiconductors & Semiconductor Equipment | Taiwan |
| SAP AG | Software & Services | Germany |
| Alcatel-Lucent | Technology Hardware & Equipment | France |
| KT Corp. | Telecommunication Services | Republic of Korea |
| Air France-KLM | Transportation | France |
| EDP—Energias de Portugal SA | Utilities | Portugal |

*Source:* Reprinted with permission from RobecoSAM AG. **www.sustainability-indices.com/review/industry-group-leaders-2013.jsp** (accessed February 7, 2014).

## What Do We Mean by *Sustainability* and *Sustainable Business Practices*?

The term *sustainability* is used in a variety of ways. In many firms, it is synonymous with corporate social responsibility; it is seen by some as a term that is gradually replacing CSR in the business lexicon. Indeed, sustainability reporting and TBL reporting are often one and the same, as illustrated by the Dow Jones Sustainability World Index, which tracks the same three types of performance measures that constitute the triple bottom line.

More often, however, the term takes on a more focused meaning, concerned with the relationship of a company to its *environment* and its use of *natural resources,* including land, water, air, plants, animals, minerals, fossil fuels, and biodiversity. It is widely recognized that the world's natural resources are finite and are being consumed and degraded at rates that threaten their capacity for renewal. Since corporations are the biggest users of natural resources, managing and maintaining these resources is critical for the long-term economic interests of corporations.

For some companies, this issue has direct and obvious implications for the continued viability of their business model and strategy. Pacific Gas and Electric has begun measuring the full carbon footprint of its supply chain to become not only a "greener" company but a more efficient energy producer.[24] Beverage companies such as Coca-Cola and PepsiCo are having to rethink their business models because of the prospect of future worldwide water shortages. For other companies, the connection is less direct, but all companies are part of a business ecosystem whose economic health depends on the availability of natural resources. In response, most major companies have begun to change *how* they do business, emphasizing the use of **sustainable business practices,** defined as those capable of meeting the needs of the present without compromising the ability to meet the needs of the future. Many have also begun to incorporate a consideration of environmental sustainability into their strategy-making activities.

**Environmental sustainability strategies** entail deliberate and concerted actions to operate businesses in a manner that protects natural resources and ecological support systems, guards against outcomes that will ultimately endanger the

**CORE CONCEPT**

**Sustainable business practices** are those that meet the needs of the present without compromising the ability to meet the needs of the future.

**CORE CONCEPT**

A company's **environmental sustainability strategy** consists of its deliberate actions to protect the environment, provide for the longevity of natural resources, maintain ecological support systems for future generations, and guard against ultimate endangerment of the planet.

planet, and is therefore sustainable for centuries.[25] One aspect of environmental sustainability is keeping use of the Earth's natural resources within levels that can be replenished via the use of sustainable business practices. In the case of some resources (like crude oil, fresh water, and edible fish from the oceans), scientists say that use levels either are already unsustainable or will be soon, given the world's growing population and propensity to consume additional resources as incomes and living standards rise. Another aspect of sustainability concerns containing the adverse effects of greenhouse gases and other forms of air pollution so as to reduce their impact on undesirable climate and atmospheric changes. Other aspects of sustainability include greater reliance on sustainable energy sources, greater use of recyclable materials, the use of sustainable methods of growing foods (to reduce topsoil depletion and the use of pesticides, herbicides, fertilizers, and other chemicals that may be harmful to human health or ecological systems), habitat protection, environmentally sound waste management practices, and increased attempts to decouple environmental degradation and economic growth (according to scientists, economic growth has historically been accompanied by declines in the well-being of the environment).

Unilever, a diversified producer of processed foods, personal care, and home cleaning products, is among the many committed corporations pursuing sustainable business practices. The company tracks 11 sustainable agricultural indicators in its processed-foods business and has launched a variety of programs to improve the environmental performance of its suppliers. Examples of such programs include special low-rate financing for tomato suppliers choosing to switch to water-conserving irrigation systems and training programs in India that have allowed contract cucumber growers to reduce pesticide use by 90 percent while improving yields by 78 percent. Unilever has also reengineered many internal processes to improve the company's overall performance on sustainability measures. For example, the company's factories have reduced water usage by 63 percent and total waste by 67 percent since 1995 through the implementation of sustainability initiatives. Unilever has also redesigned packaging for many of its products to conserve natural resources and reduce the volume of consumer waste. For example, the company's Suave shampoo bottles were reshaped to save almost 150 tons of plastic resin per year, which is the equivalent of 15 million fewer empty bottles making it to landfills annually. As the producer of Lipton Tea, Unilever is the world's largest purchaser of tea leaves; the company has committed to sourcing all of its tea from Rainforest Alliance Certified farms by 2015, due to their comprehensive triple-bottom-line approach toward sustainable farm management.

## Crafting Corporate Social Responsibility and Sustainability Strategies

While CSR and environmental sustainability strategies take many forms, those that both provide valuable social benefits *and* fulfill customer needs in a superior fashion may also contribute to a company's competitive advantage.[26] For example, while carbon emissions may be a generic social concern for financial institutions such as Wells Fargo, Ford's sustainability strategy for reducing carbon emissions has produced both competitive advantage and environmental benefits. Its Ford Fusion hybrid automobile not only is among the least polluting automobiles but also now ranks 1 out of 22 in hybrid cars, with exceptional fuel economy, a quiet powertrain, and a spacious cabin. It has gained the attention and loyalty of fuel-conscious buyers and given Ford a new green image. Green Mountain Coffee Roasters' commitment to protect the welfare of coffee growers and their families (in particular, making sure they receive a fair price) also meets its customers' wants and needs. In its dealings with suppliers at small farmer cooperatives in Peru, Mexico, and Sumatra, Green Mountain pays fair trade prices for coffee beans. Green Mountain also purchases about 29 percent of its coffee directly from farmers so as to cut out intermediaries and see that farmers realize a higher price for their efforts—coffee is the world's second most heavily traded commodity after oil, requiring the labor of some 20 million people, most of whom live at the poverty level.[27] Its consumers are aware of these efforts and purchase Green Mountain coffee, in part, to encourage such practices.

CSR strategies and environmental sustainability strategies are more likely to contribute to a company's competitive advantage if they are linked to a company's competitively important resources and capabilities or value chain activities. Thus, it is common for companies engaged in natural resource extraction, electric power production, forestry and paper products manufacture, motor vehicles production, and chemical production to place more emphasis on addressing environmental concerns than, say, software and electronics firms or apparel manufacturers. Companies whose business success is heavily dependent on maintaining high employee morale or attracting and retaining the best and brightest employees are somewhat more prone to stress the well-being of their employees and foster a positive, high-energy workplace environment that elicits the dedication and enthusiastic commitment of employees, thus putting real meaning behind the claim "Our people are our greatest asset." Ernst & Young, one of the four largest global accounting firms, stresses its "People First" workforce diversity strategy that is all about respecting differences, fostering individuality, and promoting inclusiveness so that its more than 175,000 employees in over 150 countries can feel valued, engaged, and empowered in developing creative ways to serve the firm's clients. Costco Wholesale, the warehouse club, credits its success to its treatment of its employees, who are paid an average of $20.89 an hour, not including overtime—far above the industry average. Eighty-eight percent of Costco's employees have company-sponsored insurance; CEO Craig Jelinek is committed to ensuring that his people make a living wage and receive health benefits, an approach that he says "also puts more money back into the economy. It's really that simple." Between 2009 and 2014, Costco sales grew 39 percent and stock prices doubled—an anomaly in an industry plagued by turmoil and downsizing.

At Whole Foods Market, a $12.9 billion supermarket chain specializing in organic and natural foods, its environmental sustainability strategy is evident in almost every segment of its company value chain and is a big part of its differentiation strategy. The company's procurement policies encourage stores to purchase fresh fruits and vegetables from local farmers and screen processed-food items for more than 400 common ingredients that the company considers unhealthy or environmentally unsound. Spoiled food items are sent to regional composting centers rather than landfills, and all cleaning products used in its stores are biodegradable. The company also has created the Animal Compassion Foundation to develop natural and humane ways of raising farm animals and has converted all of its vehicles to run on biofuels.

Not all companies choose to link their corporate environmental or social agendas to their value chain, their business model, or their industry. For example, the Clorox Company Foundation supports programs that serve youth, focusing its giving on non-profit civic organizations, schools, and colleges. However, unless a company's social responsibility initiatives become part of the way it operates its business every day, the initiatives are unlikely to catch fire and be fully effective. As an executive at Royal Dutch/Shell put it, corporate social responsibility "is not a cosmetic; it must be rooted

*CSR strategies and environmental sustainability strategies that both provide valuable social benefits and fulfill customer needs in a superior fashion can lead to competitive advantage. Corporate social agendas that address only social issues may help boost a company's reputation for corporate citizenship but are unlikely to improve its competitive strength in the marketplace.*

in our values. It must make a difference to the way we do business."[28] The same is true for environmental sustainability initiatives.

# The Moral Case for Corporate Social Responsibility and Environmentally Sustainable Business Practices

Every action a company takes can be interpreted as a statement of what it stands for.

The moral case for why businesses should act in a manner that benefits all of the company's stakeholders—not just shareholders—boils down to "It's the right thing to do." Ordinary decency, civic-mindedness, and contributions to society's well-being should be expected of any business.[29] In today's social and political climate, most business leaders can be expected to acknowledge that socially responsible actions are important and that businesses have a duty to be good corporate citizens. But there is a complementary school of thought that business operates on the basis of an implied social contract with the members of society. According to this contract, society grants a business the right to conduct its business affairs and agrees not to unreasonably restrain its pursuit of a fair profit for the goods or services it sells. In return for this "license to operate," a business is obligated to act as a responsible citizen, do its fair share to promote the general welfare, and avoid doing any harm. Such a view clearly puts a moral burden on a company to operate honorably, provide good working conditions to employees, be a good environmental steward, and display good corporate citizenship.

# The Business Case for Corporate Social Responsibility and Environmentally Sustainable Business Practices

Whatever the moral arguments for socially responsible business behavior and environmentally sustainable business practices, there are definitely good business reasons why companies should be public-spirited and devote time and resources to social responsibility initiatives, environmental sustainability, and good corporate citizenship:

- *Such actions can lead to increased buyer patronage.* A strong visible social responsibility or environmental sustainability strategy gives a company an edge in appealing to consumers who prefer to do business with companies that are good corporate citizens. Ben & Jerry's, Whole Foods Market, Stonyfield Farm, and The Body Shop have definitely expanded their customer bases because of their visible and well-publicized activities as socially conscious companies. More and more companies are also recognizing the cash register payoff of social responsibility strategies that reach out to people of all cultures and demographics (women, retirees, and ethnic groups).

The higher the public profile of a company or its brand, the greater the scrutiny of its activities and the higher the potential for it to become a target for pressure group action.

- *A strong commitment to socially responsible behavior reduces the risk of reputation-damaging incidents.* Companies that place little importance on operating in a socially responsible manner are more prone to scandal and embarrassment. Consumer, environmental, and human rights activist groups are quick to criticize businesses whose behavior they consider to be out of line, and they are adept at getting their message into the media and onto the Internet. Pressure groups can generate widespread adverse publicity, promote boycotts, and influence like-minded or sympathetic buyers to avoid an offender's products.

Research has shown that product boycott announcements are associated with a decline in a company's stock price.[30] When a major oil company suffered damage to its reputation on environmental and social grounds, the CEO repeatedly said that the most negative impact the company suffered—and the one that made him fear for the future of the company—was that bright young graduates were no longer attracted to working for the company. For many years, Nike received stinging criticism for not policing sweatshop conditions in the Asian factories that produced Nike footwear, a situation that caused Nike cofounder and chairman Phil Knight to observe that "Nike has become synonymous with slave wages, forced overtime, and arbitrary abuse."[31] In response, Nike began an extensive effort to monitor conditions in the 800 factories of the contract manufacturers that produced Nike shoes. As Knight said, "Good shoes come from good factories and good factories have good labor relations." Nonetheless, Nike has continually been plagued by complaints from human rights activists that its monitoring procedures are flawed and that it is not doing enough to correct the plight of factory workers. As this suggests, a damaged reputation is not easily repaired.

- *Socially responsible actions and sustainable business practices can lower costs and enhance employee recruiting and workforce retention.* Companies with deservedly good reputations for social responsibility and sustainable business practices are better able to attract and retain employees, compared to companies with tarnished reputations. Some employees just feel better about working for a company committed to improving society. This can contribute to lower turnover and better worker productivity. Other direct and indirect economic benefits include lower costs for staff recruitment and training. For example, Starbucks is said to enjoy much lower rates of employee turnover because of its full-benefits package for both full-time and part-time employees, management efforts to make Starbucks a great place to work, and the company's socially responsible practices. Sustainable business practices are often concomitant with greater operational efficiencies. For example, when a U.S. manufacturer of recycled paper, taking eco-efficiency to heart, discovered how to increase its fiber recovery rate, it saved the equivalent of 20,000 tons of waste paper—a factor that helped the company become the industry's lowest-cost producer. By helping two-thirds of its employees to stop smoking and by investing in a number of wellness programs for employees, Johnson & Johnson has saved $250 million on its health care costs over the past decade.[32]

- *Opportunities for revenue enhancement may also come from CSR and environmental sustainability strategies.* The drive for sustainability and social responsibility can spur innovative efforts that in turn lead to new products and opportunities for revenue enhancement. Electric cars such as the Chevy Volt and the Nissan Leaf are one example. In many cases, the revenue opportunities are tied to a company's core products. PepsiCo and Coca-Cola, for example, have expanded into the juice business to offer a healthier alternative to their carbonated beverages. General Electric has created a profitable new business in wind turbines. In other cases, revenue enhancement opportunities come from innovative ways to reduce waste and use the by-products of a company's production. Tyson Foods now produces jet fuel for B-52 bombers from the vast amount of animal waste resulting from its meat product business. Staples has become one of the largest nonutility corporate producers of renewable energy in the United States due to its installation of solar power panels in all of its outlets (and the sale of what it does not consume in renewable energy credit markets).

- *Well-conceived CSR strategies and sustainable business practices are in the best long-term interest of shareholders.* When CSR and sustainability strategies increase buyer patronage, offer revenue-enhancing opportunities, lower costs, increase productivity, and reduce the risk of reputation-damaging incidents, they contribute to the economic value created by a company and improve its profitability. A two-year study of leading companies found that improving environmental compliance and developing environmentally friendly products can enhance earnings per share, profitability, and the likelihood of winning contracts. The stock prices of companies that rate high on social and environmental performance criteria have been found to perform 35 to 45 percent better than the average of the 2,500 companies that constitute the Dow Jones Global Index.[33] A review of 135 studies indicated there is a positive, but small, correlation between good corporate behavior and good financial performance; only 2 percent of the studies showed that dedicating corporate resources to social responsibility harmed the interests of shareholders.[34] Furthermore, socially responsible business behavior helps avoid or preempt legal and regulatory actions that could prove costly and otherwise burdensome. In some cases, it is possible to craft corporate social responsibility strategies that contribute to competitive advantage and, at the same time, deliver greater value to society. For instance, Walmart, by working with its suppliers to reduce the use of packaging materials and revamping the routes of its delivery trucks to cut out 100 million miles of travel, saved $200 million in costs (which enhanced its cost competitiveness vis-à-vis rivals) and lowered carbon emissions.[35] Thus, a social responsibility strategy that packs some punch and is more than rhetorical flourish can produce outcomes that are in the best interest of shareholders.

Socially responsible strategies that create value for customers and lower costs can improve company profits and shareholder value at the same time that they address other stakeholder interests.

In sum, companies that take social responsibility and environmental sustainability seriously can improve their business reputations and operational efficiency while also reducing their risk exposure and encouraging loyalty and innovation. Overall, companies that take special pains to protect the environment (beyond what is required by law), are active in community affairs, and are generous supporters of charitable causes and projects that benefit society are more likely to be seen as good investments and as good companies to work for or do business with. Shareholders are likely to view the business case for social responsibility as a strong one, particularly when it results in the creation of more customer value, greater productivity, lower operating costs, and lower business risk—all of which should increase firm profitability and enhance shareholder value even as the company's actions address broader stakeholder interests.

There's little hard evidence indicating shareholders are disadvantaged in any meaningful way by a company's actions to be socially responsible.

Companies are, of course, sometimes rewarded for bad behavior—a company that is able to shift environmental and other social costs associated with its activities onto society as a whole can reap large short-term profits. The major cigarette producers for many years were able to earn greatly inflated profits by shifting the health-related costs of smoking onto others and escaping any responsibility for the harm their products caused to consumers and the general public. Only recently have they been facing the prospect of having to pay high punitive damages for their actions. Unfortunately, the cigarette makers are not alone in trying to evade paying for the social harms of their operations for as long as they can. Calling a halt to such actions usually hinges on (1) the effectiveness of activist social groups in publicizing the adverse consequences of a company's social irresponsibility and marshaling public opinion for something to be done, (2) the enactment of legislation or regulations to correct the inequity, and (3) decisions on the part of socially conscious buyers to take their business elsewhere.

# KEY POINTS

1. Ethics concerns standards of right and wrong. Business ethics concerns the application of ethical principles to the actions and decisions of business organizations and the conduct of their personnel. Ethical principles in business are not materially different from ethical principles in general.

2. There are three schools of thought about ethical standards for companies with international operations:

   - According to the *school of ethical universalism,* common understandings across multiple cultures and countries about what constitutes right and wrong behaviors give rise to universal ethical standards that apply to members of all societies, all companies, and all businesspeople.

   - According to the *school of ethical relativism,* different societal cultures and customs have divergent values and standards of right and wrong. Thus, what is ethical or unethical must be judged in the light of local customs and social mores and can vary from one culture or nation to another.

   - According to the *integrated social contracts theory,* universal ethical principles based on the collective views of multiple cultures and societies combine to form a "social contract" that all individuals in all situations have a duty to observe. Within the boundaries of this social contract, local cultures or groups can specify what additional actions are not ethically permissible. However, universal norms always take precedence over local ethical norms.

3. Apart from the "business of business is business, not ethics" kind of thinking, three other factors contribute to unethical business behavior: (1) faulty oversight that enables the unscrupulous pursuit of personal gain, (2) heavy pressures on company managers to meet or beat short-term earnings targets, and (3) a company culture that puts profitability and good business performance ahead of ethical behavior. In contrast, culture can function as a powerful mechanism for promoting ethical business conduct when high ethical principles are deeply ingrained in the corporate culture of a company.

4. Business ethics failures can result in three types of costs: (1) visible costs, such as fines, penalties, and lower stock prices, (2) internal administrative costs, such as legal costs and costs of taking corrective action, and (3) intangible costs or less visible costs, such as customer defections and damage to the company's reputation.

5. The term *corporate social responsibility* concerns a company's *duty* to operate in an honorable manner, provide good working conditions for employees, encourage workforce diversity, be a good steward of the environment, and support philanthropic endeavors in local communities where it operates and in society at large. The particular combination of socially responsible endeavors a company elects to pursue defines its corporate social responsibility (CSR) strategy.

6. The triple bottom line refers to company performance in three realms: economic, social, and environmental. Increasingly, companies are reporting their performance with respect to all three performance dimensions.

7. *Sustainability* is a term that is used in various ways, but most often it concerns a firm's relationship to the environment and its use of natural resources. Sustainable business practices are those capable of meeting the needs of the present without

compromising the world's ability to meet future needs. A company's environmental sustainability strategy consists of its deliberate actions to protect the environment, provide for the longevity of natural resources, maintain ecological support systems for future generations, and guard against ultimate endangerment of the planet.

8. CSR strategies and environmental sustainability strategies that both provide valuable social benefits *and* fulfill customer needs in a superior fashion can lead to competitive advantage.

9. The moral case for corporate social responsibility and environmental sustainability boils down to a simple concept: It's the right thing to do. There are also solid reasons why CSR and environmental sustainability strategies may be good business—they can be conducive to greater buyer patronage, reduce the risk of reputation-damaging incidents, provide opportunities for revenue enhancement, and lower costs. Well-crafted CSR and environmental sustainability strategies are in the best long-term interest of shareholders, for the reasons just mentioned and because they can avoid or preempt costly legal or regulatory actions.

## ASSURANCE OF LEARNING EXERCISES

**LO 1, LO 4** 1. Widely known as an ethical company, Dell recently committed itself to becoming a more environmentally sustainable business. After reviewing the About Dell section of its website (www.dell.com/learn/us/en/uscorp1/about-dell), prepare a list of 10 specific policies and programs that help the company achieve its vision of driving social and environmental change while still remaining innovative and profitable.

**LO 2, LO 3** 2. Prepare a one- to two-page analysis of a recent ethics scandal using your university library's access to LexisNexis or other Internet resources. Your report should (1) discuss the conditions that gave rise to unethical business strategies and behavior and (2) provide an overview of the costs resulting from the company's business ethics failure.

**connect** 3. Based on information provided in Illustration Capsule 9.3, explain how Burt's Bees' CSR strategy has contributed to its success in the marketplace. How are the company's various stakeholder groups affected by its commitment to social responsibility? How would you evaluate its triple-bottom-line performance?

**LO 4**

**connect** 4. Go to www.google.com/green/ and read about the company's latest initiatives surrounding sustainability. What are Google's key policies and actions that help it reduce its environmental footprint? How does the company integrate the idea of creating a "better web that's better for the environment" with its strategies for creating profit and value. How do these initiatives help build competitive advantage for Google?

**LO 4**

# EXERCISE FOR SIMULATION PARTICIPANTS

1. Is your company's strategy ethical? Why or why not? Is there anything that your company has done or is now doing that could legitimately be considered "shady" by your competitors? **LO 1**

2. In what ways, if any, is your company exercising corporate social responsibility? What are the elements of your company's CSR strategy? Are there any changes to this strategy that you would suggest? **LO 4**

3. If some shareholders complained that you and your co-managers have been spending too little or too much on corporate social responsibility, what would you tell them? **LO 3, LO 4**

4. Is your company striving to conduct its business in an environmentally sustainable manner? What specific *additional* actions could your company take that would make an even greater contribution to environmental sustainability? **LO 4**

5. In what ways is your company's environmental sustainability strategy in the best long-term interest of shareholders? Does it contribute to your company's competitive advantage or profitability? **LO 4**

# ENDNOTES

[1] James E. Post, Anne T. Lawrence, and James Weber, *Business and Society: Corporate Strategy, Public Policy, Ethics,* 10th ed. (New York: McGraw-Hill, 2002).

[2] Mark S. Schwartz, "Universal Moral Values for Corporate Codes of Ethics," *Journal of Business Ethics* 59, no. 1 (June 2005), pp. 27–44.

[3] Mark S. Schwartz, "A Code of Ethics for Corporate Codes of Ethics," *Journal of Business Ethics* 41, no. 1–2 (November–December 2002), pp. 27–43.

[4] T. L. Beauchamp and N. E. Bowie, *Ethical Theory and Business* (Upper Saddle River, NJ: Prentice-Hall, 2001).

[5] www.cnn.com/2013/10/15/world/child-labor-index-2014/ (accessed February 6, 2014).

[6] U.S. Department of Labor, "The Department of Labor's 2012 Findings on the Worst Forms of Child Labor," www.dol.gov/ilab/programs/ocft/PDF/2012OCFTreport.pdf.

[7] W. M. Greenfield, "In the Name of Corporate Social Responsibility," *Business Horizons* 47, no. 1 (January–February 2004), p. 22.

[8] Rajib Sanyal, "Determinants of Bribery in International Business: The Cultural and Economic Factors," *Journal of Business Ethics* 59, no. 1 (June 2005), pp. 139–145.

[9] Transparency International, *Global Corruption Report,* www.globalcorruptionreport.org.

[10] Roger Chen and Chia-Pei Chen, "Chinese Professional Managers and the Issue of Ethical Behavior," *Ivey Business Journal* 69, no. 5 (May–June 2005), p. 1.

[11] Antonio Argandoa, "Corruption and Companies: The Use of Facilitating Payments," *Journal of Business Ethics* 60, no. 3 (September 2005), pp. 251–264.

[12] Thomas Donaldson and Thomas W. Dunfee, "Towards a Unified Conception of Business Ethics: Integrative Social Contracts Theory," *Academy of Management Review* 19, no. 2 (April 1994), pp. 252–284; Andrew Spicer, Thomas W. Dunfee, and Wendy J. Bailey, "Does National Context Matter in Ethical Decision Making? An Empirical Test of Integrative Social Contracts Theory," *Academy of Management Journal* 47, no. 4 (August 2004), p. 610.

[13] Lynn Paine, Rohit Deshpandé, Joshua D. Margolis, and Kim Eric Bettcher, "Up to Code: Does Your Company's Conduct Meet World-Class Standards?" *Harvard Business Review* 83, no. 12 (December 2005), pp. 122–133.

[14] John F. Veiga, Timothy D. Golden, and Kathleen Dechant, "Why Managers Bend Company Rules," *Academy of Management Executive* 18, no. 2 (May 2004).

[15] www.reuters.com/article/2014/02/06/us-sac-martoma-idUSBREA131TL20140206.

[16] Lorin Berlin and Emily Peck, "National Mortgage Settlement: States, Big Banks Reach $25 Billion Deal," *Huff Post Business,* February 9, 2012, www.huffingtonpost.com/2012/02/09/-national-mortgage-settlement_n_1265292.html (accessed February 15, 2012).

[17] Ronald R. Sims and Johannes Brinkmann, "Enron Ethics (Or: Culture Matters More than Codes)," *Journal of Business Ethics* 45, no. 3 (July 2003), pp. 244–246.

[18] www.sfgate.com/business/bottomline/article/SEC-charges-Diamond-Foods-with-accounting-fraud-5129129.php (accessed February 7, 2014).

[19] Kurt Eichenwald, *Conspiracy of Fools: A True Story* (New York: Broadway Books, 2005).

[20] Timothy M. Devinney, "Is the Socially Responsible Corporation a Myth? The Good, the Bad, and the Ugly of Corporate Social Responsibility," *Academy of Management Perspectives* 23, no. 2 (May 2009), pp. 44–56.

[21] Information posted at www.generalmills.com (accessed March 13, 2013).

[22] Adrian Henriques, "ISO 26000: A New Standard for Human Rights?" *Institute for Human Rights and Business,* March 23, 2010, www.institutehrb.org/blogs/guest/iso_26000_a_new_standard_for_human_rights.html?gclid=CJih7NjN2aICFVs65QodrVOdyQ (accessed July 7, 2010).

[23] Gerald I.J.M. Zetsloot and Marcel N. A. van Marrewijk, "From Quality to Sustainability," *Journal of Business Ethics* 55 (2004), pp. 79–82.

[24] Tilde Herrera, "PG&E Claims Industry First with Supply Chain Footprint Project," *GreenBiz.com,* June 30, 2010, www.greenbiz.com/news/2010/06/30/pge—claims-industry-first-supply-chain-carbon-footprint-project.

[25] J. G. Speth, *The Bridge at the End of the World: Capitalism, the Environment, and Crossing from Crisis to Sustainability* (New Haven, CT: Yale University Press, 2008).

[26] Michael E. Porter and Mark R. Kramer, "Strategy & Society: The Link between Competitive Advantage and Corporate Social Responsibility," *Harvard Business Review* 84, no. 12 (December 2006), pp. 78–92.

[27] David Hess, Nikolai Rogovsky, and Thomas W. Dunfee, "The Next Wave of Corporate Community Involvement: Corporate Social Initiatives," *California Management Review* 44, no. 2 (Winter 2002), pp. 110–125; Susan Ariel Aaronson, "Corporate Responsibility in

the Global Village: The British Role Model and the American Laggard," *Business and Society Review* 108, no. 3 (September 2003), p. 323.

[28] N. Craig Smith, "Corporate Responsibility: Whether and How," *California Management Review* 45, no. 4 (Summer 2003), p. 63.

[29] Jeb Brugmann and C. K. Prahalad, "Cocreating Business's New Social Compact," *Harvard Business Review* 85, no. 2 (February 2007), pp. 80–90.

[30] Wallace N. Davidson, Abuzar El-Jelly, and Dan L. Worrell, "Influencing Managers to Change Unpopular Corporate Behavior through Boycotts and Divestitures: A Stock Market Test," *Business and Society* 34, no. 2 (1995), pp. 171–196.

[31] Tom McCawley, "Racing to Improve Its Reputation: Nike Has Fought to Shed Its Image as an Exploiter of Third-World Labor Yet It Is Still a Target of Activists," *Financial Times,* December 2000, p. 14.

[32] Michael E. Porter and Mark Kramer, "Creating Shared Value," *Harvard Business Review* 89, no. 1–2 (January–February 2011).

[33] James C. Collins and Jerry I. Porras, *Built to Last: Successful Habits of Visionary Companies,* 3rd ed. (London: HarperBusiness, 2002).

[34] Joshua D. Margolis and Hillary A. Elfenbein, "Doing Well by Doing Good: Don't Count on It," *Harvard Business Review* 86, no. 1 (January 2008), pp. 19–20; Lee E. Preston, Douglas P. O'Bannon, Ronald M. Roman, Sefa Hayibor, and Bradley R. Agle, "The Relationship between Social and Financial Performance: Repainting a Portrait," *Business and Society* 38, no. 1 (March 1999), pp. 109–125.

[35] Leonard L. Berry, Ann M. Mirobito, and William B. Baun, "What's the Hard Return on Employee Wellness Programs?" *Harvard Business Review* 88, no. 12 (December 2010), p. 105.

### CHAPTER 10

# Building an Organization Capable of Good Strategy Execution

## People, Capabilities, and Structure

## Learning Objectives

**LO 1**  What managers must do to execute strategy successfully.

**LO 2**  Why hiring, training, and retaining the right people constitute a key component of the strategy execution process.

**LO 3**  That good strategy execution requires continuously building and upgrading the organization's resources and capabilities.

**LO 4**  What issues to consider in establishing a strategy-supportive organizational structure and organizing the work effort.

**LO 5**  The pros and cons of centralized and decentralized decision making in implementing the chosen strategy.

Any strategy, however brilliant, needs to be implemented properly if it is to deliver the desired results.

Costas Markides – *London Business School Professor and Consultant*

Teamwork is the ability to direct individual accomplishments toward organizational objectives. It is the fuel that allows common people to attain uncommon results.

Andrew Carnegie – *Steel Industry Magnate and Philanthropist*

Coming together is a beginning. Keeping together is progress. Working together is success.

Henry Ford – *Founder of the Ford Motor Company*

Once managers have decided on a strategy, the emphasis turns to converting it into actions and good results. Putting the strategy into place and getting the organization to execute it well call for different sets of managerial skills. Whereas crafting strategy is largely an analysis-driven activity focused on market conditions and the company's resources and capabilities, executing strategy is primarily operations-driven, revolving around the management of people, business processes, and organizational structure. Successful strategy execution depends on doing a good job of working with and through others; building and strengthening competitive capabilities; creating an appropriate organizational structure; allocating resources; instituting strategy-supportive policies, processes, and systems; and instilling a discipline of getting things done. Executing strategy is an action-oriented, make-things-happen task that tests a manager's ability to direct organizational change, achieve continuous improvement in operations and business processes, create and nurture a strategy-supportive culture, and consistently meet or beat performance targets.

Experienced managers are well aware that it is much easier to develop a sound strategic plan than it is to execute the plan and achieve targeted outcomes. According to one executive, "It's been rather easy for us to decide where we wanted to go. The hard part is to get the organization to act

on the new priorities."[1] It takes adept managerial leadership to convincingly communicate a new strategy and the reasons for it, overcome pockets of doubt, secure the commitment of key personnel, build consensus for how to implement the strategy, and move forward to get all the pieces into place and deliver results. *Just because senior managers announce a new strategy doesn't mean that organization members will embrace it and move forward enthusiastically to implement it.* Company personnel must understand—in their heads and hearts— why a new strategic direction is necessary and where the new strategy is taking them.[2] Instituting change is, of course, easier when the problems with the old strategy have become obvious and/or the company has spiraled into a financial crisis.

But the challenge of successfully implementing new strategic initiatives goes well beyond managerial adeptness in overcoming resistance to change. What really makes executing strategy a tougher, more time-consuming management challenge than crafting strategy are the wide array of managerial activities that must be attended to, the many ways to put new strategic initiatives in place and keep things moving, and the number of bedeviling issues that always crop up and have to be resolved. It takes first-rate "managerial smarts" to zero in on what exactly needs to be done and how to get good results in a timely manner. Excellent people-management skills and perseverance are required to get a variety of initiatives launched and to integrate the efforts of many different work groups into a smoothly functioning whole. Depending on how much consensus building and organizational change is involved, the process of implementing strategy changes can take several months to several years. Achieving *real proficiency* in executing the strategy can take even longer.

Like crafting strategy, *executing strategy is a job for a company's whole management team—not just a few senior managers.* While the chief executive officer and the heads of major units (business divisions, functional departments, and key operating units) are ultimately responsible for seeing that strategy is executed successfully, the process typically affects every part of the firm—all value chain activities and all work groups. Top-level managers must rely on the active support of middle and lower managers to institute whatever new operating practices are needed in the various operating units to achieve proficient strategy execution. Middle and lower-level managers must ensure that frontline employees perform strategy-critical value chain activities well and produce operating results that allow company-wide performance targets to be met. Consequently, *all company personnel are actively involved in the strategy execution process in one way or another.*

# A FRAMEWORK FOR EXECUTING STRATEGY

**CORE CONCEPT**

Good strategy execution requires a *team effort.* All managers have strategy-executing responsibility in their areas of authority, and all employees are active participants in the strategy execution process.

**LO 1**

What managers must do to execute strategy successfully.

The managerial approach to implementing and executing a strategy always has to be customized to fit the particulars of a company's situation. Making minor changes in an existing strategy differs from implementing radical strategy changes. The techniques for successfully executing a low-cost provider strategy are different from those for executing a high-end differentiation strategy. Implementing a new strategy for a struggling company in the midst of a financial crisis is a different job from improving strategy execution in a company that is doing relatively well. Moreover, some managers are more adept than others at using particular approaches to achieving certain kinds of organizational changes. Hence, there's no definitive managerial recipe for successful strategy execution that cuts across all company situations and all strategies or that works for all managers. Rather, the specific actions required to execute a strategy—the "to-do list" that constitutes management's action agenda—always represent management's judgment about how best to proceed in light of prevailing circumstances.

## The Principal Components of the Strategy Execution Process

Despite the need to tailor a company's strategy-executing approaches to the particulars of the situation at hand, certain managerial bases must be covered no matter what the circumstances. These include 10 basic managerial tasks (see Figure 10.1):

1. Staffing the organization with managers and employees capable of executing the strategy well.
2. Developing the resources and organizational capabilities required for successful strategy execution.
3. Creating a strategy-supportive organizational structure.
4. Allocating sufficient resources (budgetary and otherwise) to the strategy execution effort.
5. Instituting policies and procedures that facilitate strategy execution.

6. Adopting best practices and business processes to drive continuous improvement in strategy execution activities.
7. Installing information and operating systems that enable company personnel to carry out their strategic roles proficiently.
8. Tying rewards and incentives directly to the achievement of strategic and financial targets.
9. Instilling a corporate culture that promotes good strategy execution.
10. Exercising the internal leadership needed to propel strategy implementation forward.

How well managers perform these 10 tasks has a decisive impact on whether the outcome of the strategy execution effort is a spectacular success, a colossal failure, or something in between.

In devising an action agenda for executing strategy, managers should start by conducting *a probing assessment of what the organization must do differently to carry out the strategy successfully.* Each manager needs to ask the question "What needs to be done in my area of responsibility to implement our part of the company's strategy, and what should I do to get these things accomplished?" It is then incumbent on every manager to determine *precisely how to make the necessary internal changes.* Successful strategy implementers have a knack for diagnosing what their organizations need to do to execute the chosen strategy well and figuring out how to get these things done efficiently. They are masters in promoting results-oriented behaviors on the part of company personnel and following through on making the right things happen in a timely fashion.[3]

In big organizations with geographically scattered operating units, senior executives' action agenda mostly involves communicating the case for change, building consensus for how to proceed, installing strong managers to move the process forward in key organizational units, directing resources to the right places, establishing deadlines and measures of progress, rewarding those who achieve implementation milestones, and personally leading the strategic change process. Thus, the bigger the organization, the more that successful strategy execution depends on the cooperation and implementation skills of operating managers who can promote needed changes at the lowest organizational levels and deliver results. In small organizations, top managers can deal directly with frontline managers and employees, personally orchestrating the action steps and implementation sequence, observing firsthand how implementation is progressing, and deciding how hard and how fast to push the process along. Whether the organization is large or small and whether strategy implementation involves sweeping or minor changes, effective leadership requires a keen grasp of what to do and how to do it in light of the organization's circumstances. Then it remains for company personnel in strategy-critical areas to step up to the plate and produce the desired results.

**What's Covered in Chapters 10, 11, and 12**   In the remainder of this chapter and in the next two chapters, we discuss what is involved in performing the 10 key managerial tasks that shape the process of executing strategy. This chapter explores the first three of these tasks (highlighted in blue in Figure 10.1): (1) staffing the organization with people capable of executing the strategy well, (2) developing the resources and building the organizational capabilities needed for successful strategy execution, and (3) creating an organizational structure supportive of the strategy execution process. Chapter 11 concerns the tasks of allocating resources, instituting strategy-facilitating policies and procedures, employing business process management

When strategies fail, it is often because of poor execution. Strategy execution is therefore a critical managerial endeavor.

The two best signs of good strategy execution are whether a company is meeting or beating its performance targets and whether it is performing value chain activities in a manner that is conducive to companywide operating excellence.

**FIGURE 10.1    The 10 Basic Tasks of the Strategy Execution Process**

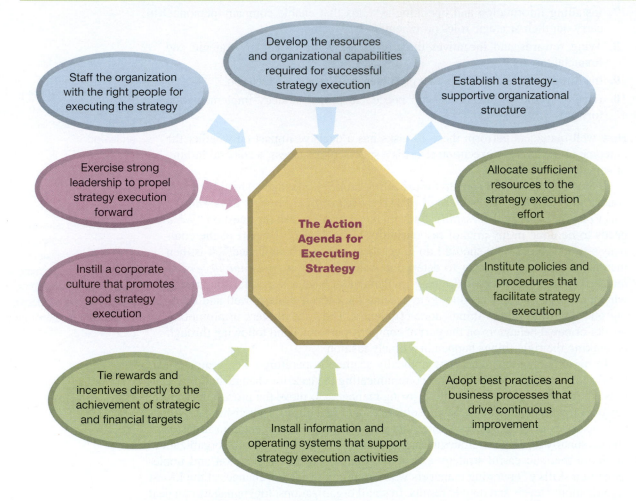

tools and best practices, installing operating and information systems, and tying rewards to the achievement of good results (highlighted in green in Figure 10.1). Chapter 12 deals with the two remaining tasks: creating a strategy-supportive corporate culture and exercising the leadership needed to drive the execution process forward (highlighted in purple).

# BUILDING AN ORGANIZATION CAPABLE OF GOOD STRATEGY EXECUTION: THREE KEY ACTIONS

Proficient strategy execution depends foremost on having in place an organization capable of the tasks demanded of it. Building an execution-capable organization is thus always a top priority. As shown in Figure 10.2, three types of organization-building actions are paramount:

1. *Staffing the organization*—putting together a strong management team, and recruiting and retaining employees with the needed experience, technical skills, and intellectual capital.

**FIGURE 10.2   Building an Organization Capable of Proficient Strategy Execution: Three Key Actions**

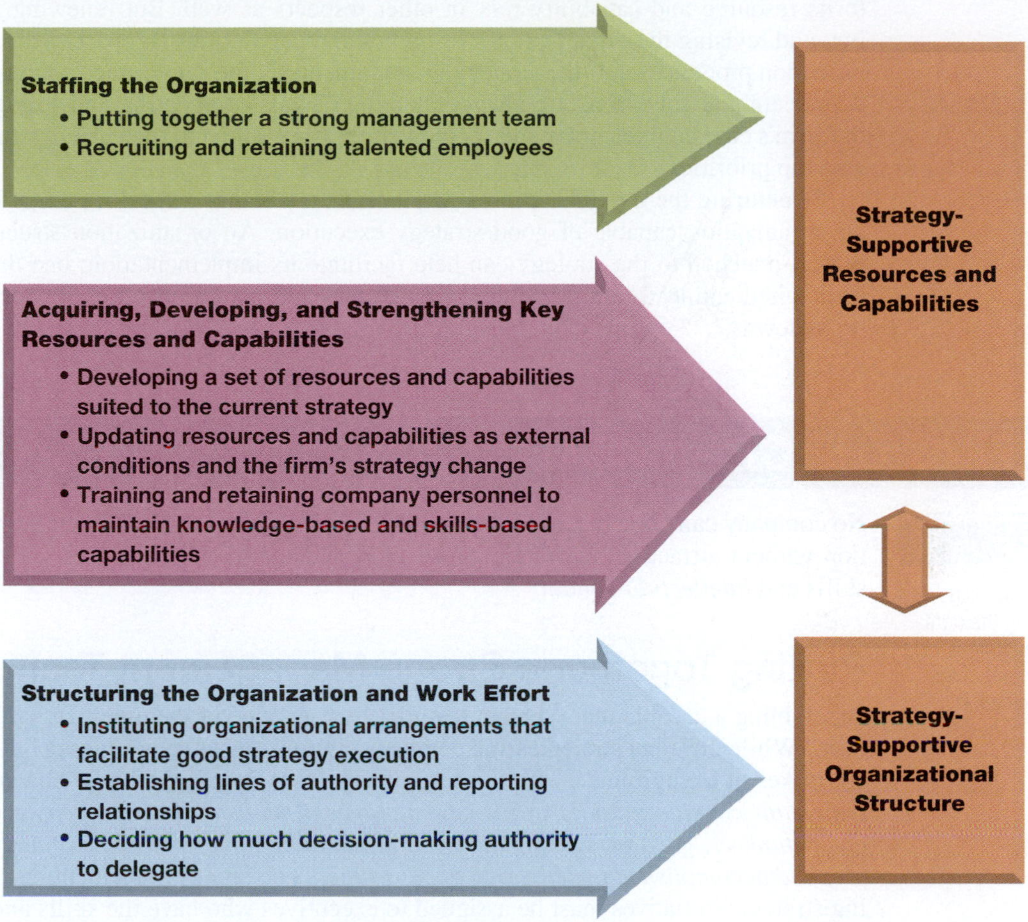

**Staffing the Organization**
- Putting together a strong management team
- Recruiting and retaining talented employees

**Acquiring, Developing, and Strengthening Key Resources and Capabilities**
- Developing a set of resources and capabilities suited to the current strategy
- Updating resources and capabilities as external conditions and the firm's strategy change
- Training and retaining company personnel to maintain knowledge-based and skills-based capabilities

**Structuring the Organization and Work Effort**
- Instituting organizational arrangements that facilitate good strategy execution
- Establishing lines of authority and reporting relationships
- Deciding how much decision-making authority to delegate

**Strategy-Supportive Resources and Capabilities**

**Strategy-Supportive Organizational Structure**

2. *Acquiring, developing, and strengthening the resources and capabilities required for good strategy execution*—accumulating the required resources, developing proficiencies in performing strategy-critical value chain activities, and updating the company's capabilities to match changing market conditions and customer expectations.

3. *Structuring the organization and work effort*—organizing value chain activities and business processes, establishing lines of authority and reporting relationships, and deciding how much decision-making authority to delegate to lower-level managers and frontline employees.

Implementing a strategy depends critically on ensuring that strategy-supportive resources and capabilities are in place, ready to be deployed. These include the skills, talents, experience, and knowledge of the company's human resources (managerial and otherwise)—see Figure 10.2. Proficient strategy execution depends heavily on competent personnel of all types, but because of the many managerial tasks involved and the role of leadership in strategy execution, assembling a strong management team is especially important.

If the strategy being implemented is a new strategy, the company may need to add to its resource and capability mix in other respects as well. But renewing, upgrading, and revising the organization's resources and capabilities is a part of the strategy execution process even if the strategy is fundamentally the same, since strategic assets depreciate and conditions are always changing. Thus, augmenting and strengthening the firm's core competencies and seeing that they are suited to the current strategy are also top priorities.

Structuring the organization and work effort is another critical aspect of building an organization capable of good strategy execution. An organization structure that is well matched to the strategy can help facilitate its implementation; one that is not well suited can lead to higher bureaucratic costs and communication or coordination breakdowns.

# STAFFING THE ORGANIZATION

No company can hope to perform the activities required for successful strategy execution without attracting and retaining talented managers and employees with suitable skills and *intellectual capital*.

## Putting Together a Strong Management Team

Assembling a capable management team is a cornerstone of the organization-building task.[4] While different strategies and company circumstances sometimes call for different mixes of backgrounds, experiences, management styles, and know-how, *the most important consideration is to fill key managerial slots with smart people who are clear thinkers, good at figuring out what needs to be done, skilled in managing people, and accomplished in delivering good results.*[5] The task of implementing challenging strategic initiatives must be assigned to executives who have the skills and talents to handle them and who can be counted on to get the job done well. Without a capable, results-oriented management team, the implementation process is likely to be hampered by missed deadlines, misdirected or wasteful efforts, and managerial ineptness. Weak executives are serious impediments to getting optimal results because they are unable to differentiate between ideas that have merit and those that are misguided—the caliber of work done under their supervision suffers.[6] In contrast, managers with strong strategy implementation capabilities have a talent for asking tough, incisive questions. They know enough about the details of the business to be able to ensure the soundness of the decisions of the people around them, and they can discern whether the resources people are asking for to put the strategy in place make sense. They are good at getting things done through others, partly by making sure they have the right people under them, assigned to the right jobs. They consistently follow through on issues, monitor progress carefully, make adjustments when needed, and keep important details from slipping through the cracks. In short, they understand how to drive organizational change, and they have the managerial discipline requisite for first-rate strategy execution.

Sometimes a company's existing management team is up to the task. At other times it may need to be strengthened by promoting qualified people from within or by bringing in outsiders whose experiences, talents, and leadership styles better suit the situation. In turnaround and rapid-growth situations, and in instances when a company doesn't have insiders with the requisite know-how, filling key management slots from the outside is a standard organization-building approach. In addition, it is important to identify and replace managers who are incapable, for whatever reason, of making the required changes in a timely and cost-effective manner. For a management team to be truly effective at strategy execution, it must be composed of managers who recognize that organizational changes are needed and who are ready to get on with the process.

> Putting together a talented management team with the right mix of experiences, skills, and abilities to get things done is one of the first steps to take in launching the strategy-executing process.

The overriding aim in building a management team should be to assemble a *critical mass* of talented managers who can function as agents of change and oversee top-notch strategy execution. Every manager's success is enhanced (or limited) by the quality of his or her managerial colleagues and the degree to which they freely exchange ideas, debate ways to make operating improvements, and join forces to tackle issues and solve problems. When a first-rate manager enjoys the help and support of other first-rate managers, it's possible to create a managerial whole that is greater than the sum of individual efforts—talented managers who work well together as a team can produce organizational results that are dramatically better than what one or two star managers acting individually can achieve.[7]

Illustration Capsule 10.1 describes Deloitte's highly effective approach to developing employee talent and a top-caliber management team.

## Recruiting, Training, and Retaining Capable Employees

Assembling a capable management team is not enough. Staffing the organization with the right kinds of people must extend to all kinds of company personnel for value chain activities to be performed competently. *The quality of an organization's people is always an essential ingredient of successful strategy execution—knowledgeable, engaged employees are a company's best source of creative ideas for the nuts-and-bolts operating improvements that lead to operating excellence.* Companies like Google, SAS, The Boston Consulting Group, Edward Jones, Quicken Loans, Genentech, Intuit, Salesforce.com, and Goldman Sachs make a concerted effort to recruit the best and brightest people they can find and then retain them with excellent compensation packages, opportunities for rapid advancement and professional growth, and interesting assignments. Having a pool of "A players" with strong skill sets and lots of brainpower is essential to their business.

> In many industries, adding to a company's talent base and building intellectual capital are more important to good strategy execution than are additional investments in capital projects.

Facebook makes a point of hiring the very brightest and most talented programmers it can find and motivating them with both good monetary incentives and the challenge of working on cutting-edge technology projects. McKinsey & Company, one of the world's premier management consulting firms, recruits only cream-of-the-crop MBAs at the nation's top-10 business schools; such talent is essential to McKinsey's strategy of performing high-level consulting for the world's top corporations. The leading global accounting firms screen candidates not only on the basis of their accounting expertise but also on whether they possess the people skills needed to relate well with clients and colleagues. Southwest Airlines goes to considerable lengths to hire people who can have fun and be fun on the job; it uses special interviewing and screening methods to gauge whether applicants for customer-contact jobs have outgoing personality traits that match its strategy of creating a high-spirited, fun-loving in-flight atmosphere for passengers. Southwest Airlines is so selective that only about 3 percent of the people who apply are offered jobs.

# Management Development at Deloitte Touche Tohmatsu Limited

**EXHIBIT 1**

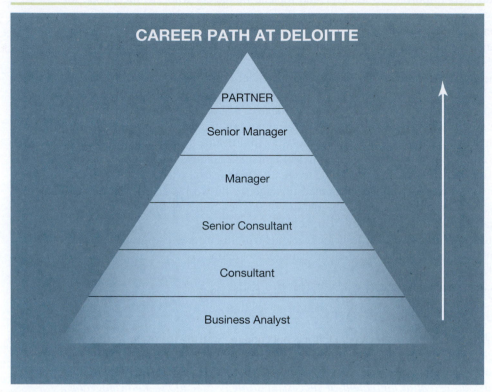

**CAREER PATH AT DELOITTE**

PARTNER

Senior Manager

Manager

Senior Consultant

Consultant

Business Analyst

Hiring, retaining, and cultivating talent are critical activities at Deloitte, the world's largest professional services firm. By offering robust learning and development programs, Deloitte has been able to create a strong talent pipeline to the firm's partnership. Deloitte's emphasis on learning and development, across all stages of the employee life cycle, has led to recognitions such as being ranked number one on *Chief Executives'* list of "Best Private Companies for Leaders" and being listed among *Fortune's* "100 Best Companies to Work For." The following programs contribute to Deloitte's successful execution of its talent strategy:

- *Clear path to partnership.* During the initial recruiting phase and then throughout an employee's tenure at the firm, Deloitte lays out a clear career path. The path indicates the expected timeline for promotion to each of the firm's hierarchy levels, along with the competencies and experience required. Deloitte's transparency on career paths, coupled with its in-depth performance management process, helps employees clearly understand their performance. This serves as a motivational tool for top performers, often leading to career acceleration. (See Exhibit 1.)

- *Formal training programs.* Like other leading organizations, Deloitte has a program to ensure that recent college graduates are equipped with the necessary training and tools for succeeding on the job. Yet Deloitte's commitment to formal training is evident at all levels within the organization. Each time an employee is promoted, he or she attends "milestone" school, a weeklong simulation that replicates true business situations employees would face as they transition to new stages of career development. In addition, Deloitte institutes mandatory training hours for all of its employees to ensure that individuals continue to further their professional development.

- *Special programs for high performers.* Deloitte also offers fellowships and programs to help employees acquire new skills and enhance their leadership development. For example, the Global Fellows program helps top performers work with senior leaders in the organization to focus on the realities of delivering client service across borders. Deloitte has also established the

Emerging Leaders Development program, which utilizes skill building, 360-degree feedback, and one-on-one executive coaching to help top-performing managers and senior managers prepare for partnership.

- *Sponsorship, not mentorship.* To train the next generation of leaders, Deloitte has implemented formal mentorship programs to provide leadership development support. Deloitte, however, uses the term *sponsorship* to describe this initiative. A sponsor is tasked with taking a vested interest in an individual and advocating on his or her behalf. Sponsors help rising leaders navigate the firm, develop new competencies, expand their network, and hone the skills needed to accelerate their career.

*Note:* Developed with Heather Levy.

*Sources:* Company websites; **www.accountingweb.com/article/leadership-development-community-service-integral-deloitte-university/220845** (accessed February 2014).

---

In high-tech companies, the challenge is to staff work groups with gifted, imaginative, and energetic people who can bring life to new ideas quickly and inject into the organization what one Dell executive calls "hum."[8] The saying "People are our most important asset" may seem trite, but it fits high-technology companies precisely. Besides checking closely for functional and technical skills, Dell tests applicants for their tolerance of ambiguity and change, their capacity to work in teams, and their ability to learn on the fly. Companies like Zappos, Amazon.com, Google, and Cisco Systems have broken new ground in recruiting, hiring, cultivating, developing, and retaining talented employees—almost all of whom are in their 20s and 30s. Cisco goes after the top 10 percent, raiding other companies and endeavoring to retain key people at the companies it acquires. Cisco executives believe that a cadre of star engineers, programmers, managers, salespeople, and support personnel is the backbone of the company's efforts to execute its strategy and remain the world's leading provider of Internet infrastructure products and technology.

> The best companies make a point of recruiting and retaining talented employees—the objective is to make the company's entire workforce (managers and rank-and-file employees) a genuine competitive asset.

In recognition of the importance of a talented and energetic workforce, companies have instituted a number of practices aimed at staffing jobs with the best people they can find:

1. Spending considerable effort on screening and evaluating job applicants—selecting only those with suitable skill sets, energy, initiative, judgment, aptitude for learning, and personality traits that mesh well with the company's work environment and culture.

2. Providing employees with training programs that continue throughout their careers.

3. Offering promising employees challenging, interesting, and skill-stretching assignments.

4. Rotating people through jobs that span functional and geographic boundaries. Providing people with opportunities to gain experience in a variety of international settings is increasingly considered an essential part of career development in multinational companies.

5. Making the work environment stimulating and engaging so that employees will consider the company a great place to work.

6. Encouraging employees to challenge existing ways of doing things, to be creative and innovative in proposing better ways of operating, and to push their ideas for new products or businesses. Progressive companies work hard at creating an environment in which employees are made to feel that their views and suggestions count.

7. Striving to retain talented, high-performing employees via promotions, salary increases, performance bonuses, stock options and equity ownership, benefit packages including health insurance and retirement packages, and other perks, such as flexible work hours and onsite day care.

8. Coaching average performers to improve their skills and capabilities, while weeding out underperformers.

# DEVELOPING AND BUILDING CRITICAL RESOURCES AND CAPABILITIES

**LO 3**

That good strategy execution requires continuously building and upgrading the organization's resources and capabilities.

High among the organization-building priorities in the strategy execution process is the need to build and strengthen competitively valuable resources and capabilities. As explained in Chapter 4, a company's ability to perform value-creating activities and realize its strategic objectives depends upon its resources and capabilities. In the course of crafting strategy, it is important for managers to identify the resources and capabilities that will enable the firm's strategy to succeed. Good strategy execution requires putting those resources and capabilities into place, strengthening them as needed, and then modifying them as market conditions evolve.

If the strategy being implemented is new, company managers may have to acquire new resources, significantly broaden or deepen certain capabilities, or even add entirely new competencies in order to put the strategic initiatives in place and execute them proficiently. But even if the strategy has not changed materially, good strategy execution involves refreshing and strengthening the firm's resources and capabilities to keep them in top form.

## Three Approaches to Building and Strengthening Capabilities

Building new competencies and capabilities is a multistage process that occurs over a period of months and years. It is not something that is accomplished overnight.

Building core competencies and competitive capabilities is a time-consuming, managerially challenging exercise. While some assist can be gotten from discovering how best-in-industry or best-in-world companies perform a particular activity, trying to replicate and then improve on the capabilities of others is easier said than done—for the same reasons that one is unlikely to ever become a world-class slopestyle snowboarder just by studying what Olympic gold medalist Jamie Anderson does.

With deliberate effort, well-orchestrated organizational actions, and continued practice, however, it is possible for a firm to become proficient at capability building despite the difficulty. Indeed, by making capability-building activities a *routine* part of their strategy execution endeavors, some firms are able to develop *dynamic capabilities* that assist them in managing resource and capability change, as discussed in Chapter 4. The most common approaches to capability building include (1) developing capabilities internally, (2) acquiring capabilities through mergers and acquisitions, and (3) accessing capabilities via collaborative partnerships.

**Developing Capabilities Internally**    Capabilities develop incrementally along an evolutionary development path as organizations search for solutions to their problems. The process is a complex one, since capabilities are the product of *bundles of skills and know-how that are integrated into organizational routines* and *deployed* *within activity systems* through the combined efforts of teams that are often cross-functional in nature, spanning a variety of departments and locations. For instance, the capability of speeding new products to market involves the *collaborative efforts* of personnel in R&D, engineering and design, purchasing, production, marketing, and distribution. Similarly, the capability to provide superior customer service is a team effort among people in customer call centers (where orders are taken and inquiries are answered), shipping and delivery, billing and accounts receivable, and after-sale support. The process of building a capability begins when managers set an objective of developing a particular capability and organize activity around that objective.[9] Managers can ignite the process by having high aspirations and setting "stretch objectives" for the organization, as described in Chapter 2.[10]

Because the process is incremental, the first step is to develop the *ability* to do something, however imperfectly or inefficiently. This entails selecting people with the requisite skills and experience, upgrading or expanding individual abilities as needed, and then molding the efforts of individuals into a joint effort to create an organizational ability. At this stage, progress can be fitful since it depends on experimenting, actively searching for alternative solutions, and learning through trial and error.[11]

As experience grows and company personnel learn how to perform the activities consistently well and at an acceptable cost, the ability *evolves* into a tried-and-true competence. Getting to this point requires a *continual investment* of resources and *systematic efforts* to improve processes and solve problems creatively as they arise. Improvements in the functioning of a capability come from task repetition and the resulting *learning by doing* of individuals and teams. But the process can be accelerated by making learning a more deliberate endeavor and providing the incentives that will motivate company personnel to achieve the desired ends.[12] This can be critical to successful strategy execution when market conditions are changing rapidly.

It is generally much easier and less time-consuming to update and remodel a company's existing capabilities as external conditions and company strategy change than it is to create them from scratch. Maintaining capabilities in top form may simply require exercising them continually and fine-tuning them as necessary. Refreshing and updating capabilities require only a limited set of modifications to a set of routines that is otherwise in place. Phasing out an existing capability takes significantly less effort than adding a brand new one. Replicating a company capability, while not an easy process, still begins with an *established template*.[13] Even the process of augmenting a capability may require less effort if it involves the recombination of well-established company capabilities and draws on existing company resources.[14] Companies like Cray in large computers and Honda in gasoline engines, for example, have leveraged the expertise of their talent pool by frequently re-forming high-intensity teams and reusing key people on special projects designed to augment their capabilities. Canon combined miniaturization capabilities that it developed in producing calculators with its existing capabilities in precision optics to revolutionize the 35-mm camera market.[15] Toyota, en route to overtaking General Motors as the global leader in motor vehicles, aggressively upgraded its capabilities in fuel-efficient hybrid engine technology and constantly fine-tuned its famed Toyota Production System to enhance its already proficient capabilities in manufacturing top-quality vehicles at relatively low costs.

Managerial actions to develop core competencies and competitive capabilities generally take one of two forms: either strengthening the company's base of skills, knowledge, and experience or coordinating and integrating the efforts of the various work groups and departments. Actions of the first sort can be undertaken at all managerial

> A company's capabilities must be continually refreshed and renewed to remain aligned with changing customer expectations, altered competitive conditions, and new strategic initiatives.

levels, but actions of the second sort are best orchestrated by senior managers who not only appreciate the strategy-executing significance of strong capabilities but also have the clout to enforce the necessary cooperation and coordination among individuals, groups, and departments.[16]

**Acquiring Capabilities through Mergers and Acquisitions**    Sometimes the best way for a company to upgrade its portfolio of capabilities is by acquiring (or merging with) another company with attractive resources and capabilities.[17] An acquisition aimed at building a stronger portfolio of resources and capabilities can be every bit as valuable as an acquisition aimed at adding new products or services to the company's lineup of offerings. The advantage of this mode of acquiring new capabilities is primarily one of speed, since developing new capabilities internally can, at best, take many years of effort and, at worst, come to naught. Capabilities-motivated acquisitions are essential (1) when the company does not have the ability to create the needed capability internally (perhaps because it is too far afield from its existing capabilities) and (2) when industry conditions, technology, or competitors are moving at such a rapid clip that time is of the essence.

At the same time, acquiring capabilities in this way is not without difficulty. Capabilities involve tacit knowledge and complex routines that cannot be transferred readily from one organizational unit to another. This may limit the extent to which the new capability can be utilized. For example, the Newell Company acquired Rubbermaid in part for its famed product innovation capabilities. Transferring these capabilities to other parts of the Newell organization proved easier said than done, however, contributing to a slump in the firm's stock prices that lasted for some time. Integrating the capabilities of two firms involved in a merger or acquisition may pose an additional challenge, particularly if there are underlying incompatibilities in their supporting systems or processes. Moreover, since internal fit is important, there is always the risk that under new management the acquired capabilities may not be as productive as they had been. In a worst-case scenario, the acquisition process may end up damaging or destroying the very capabilities that were the object of the acquisition in the first place.

**Accessing Capabilities through Collaborative Partnerships**
A third way of obtaining valuable resources and capabilities is to form collaborative partnerships with suppliers, competitors, or other companies having the cutting-edge expertise. There are three basic ways to pursue this course of action:

1.  *Outsource the function in which the company's capabilities are deficient to a key supplier or another provider.* Whether this is a wise move depends on what can be safely delegated to outside suppliers or allies and which internal capabilities are key to the company's long-term success. As discussed in Chapter 6, outsourcing has the advantage of conserving resources so that the firm can focus its energies on those activities most central to its strategy. It may be a good choice for firms that are too small and resource-constrained to execute all the parts of their strategy internally.

2.  *Collaborate with a firm that has complementary resources and capabilities in a joint venture, strategic alliance, or other type of partnership established for the purpose of achieving a shared strategic objective.* This requires launching initiatives to identify the most attractive potential partners and to establish collaborative working relationships. Since the success of the venture will depend on how well the partners work together, potential partners should be selected as much for their management style, culture, and goals as for their resources and capabilities.

3. *Engage in a collaborative partnership for the purpose of learning how the partner does things, internalizing its methods and thereby acquiring its capabilities.* This may be a viable method when each partner has something to learn from the other and can achieve an outcome *beneficial to both partners.* For example, firms some-times enter into collaborative marketing arrangements whereby each partner is granted access to the other's dealer network for the purpose of expanding sales in geographic areas where the firms lack dealers. BMW and Continental Tire recently teamed up to develop self-driving car technology and prototype vehicles capable of highly automated driving on freeways. But if the intended gains are only one-sided, the arrangement more likely involves an abuse of trust. In con-sequence, it not only puts the cooperative venture at risk but also encourages the firm's partner to treat the firm similarly or refuse further dealings with the firm.

## The Strategic Role of Employee Training

Training and retraining are important when a company shifts to a strategy requiring different skills, competitive capabilities, and operating methods. Training is also stra-tegically important in organizational efforts to build skill-based competencies. And it is a key activity in businesses where technical know-how is changing so rapidly that a company loses its ability to compete unless its employees have cutting-edge knowl-edge and expertise. Successful strategy implementers see to it that the training func-tion is both adequately funded and effective. If better execution of the chosen strategy calls for new skills, deeper technological capability, or the building and using of new capabilities, training efforts need to be placed near the top of the action agenda.

The strategic importance of training has not gone unnoticed. Over 600 companies have established internal "universities" to lead the training effort, facilitate continuous organizational learning, and upgrade their company's knowledge resources. Many companies conduct orientation sessions for new employees, fund an assortment of competence-building training programs, and reimburse employees for tuition and other expenses associated with obtaining additional college education, attending pro-fessional development courses, and earning professional certification of one kind or another. A number of companies offer online, just-in-time training courses to employees around the clock. Increasingly, employees at all levels are expected to take an active role in their own professional development and assume responsibility for keeping their skills up to date and in sync with the company's needs.

## Strategy Execution Capabilities and Competitive Advantage

As firms get better at executing their strategies, they develop capabilities in the domain of strategy execution much as they build other organizational capabilities. Superior strategy execution capabilities allow companies to get the most from their other orga-nizational resources and competitive capabilities. In this way they contribute to the success of a firm's business model. But excellence in strategy execution can also be a more direct source of competitive advantage, since more efficient and effective strat-egy execution can lower costs and permit firms to deliver more value to customers. Superior strategy execution capabilities may also enable a company to react more quickly to market changes and beat other firms to the market with new products and services. This can allow a company to profit from a period of uncontested market

# Zara's Strategy Execution Capabilities

Zara, a member of Inditex Group, is a "fast fashion" retailer. As soon as designs are seen in high-end fashion houses such as Prada, Zara's design team sets to work altering the clothing designs so that they can produce high fashion at mass-retailing prices. Zara's strategy is clever, but by no means unique. The company's competitive advantage is in strategy execution. Every step of Zara's value chain execution is geared toward putting fashionable clothes in stores quickly, realizing high turnover, and strategically driving traffic.

The first key lever is a quick production process. Zara's design team uses inspiration from high fashion and nearly real-time feedback from stores to create up-to-the-minute pieces. Manufacturing largely occurs in factories close to headquarters in Spain, northern Africa, and Turkey, all areas considered to have a high cost of labor. Placing the factories strategically close allows for more flexibility and greater responsiveness to market needs, thereby outweighing the additional labor costs. The entire production process, from design to arrival at stores, takes only two weeks, while other retailers take six months. While traditional retailers commit up to 80 percent of their lines by the start of the season, Zara commits only 50 to 60 percent, meaning that up to half of the merchandise to hit stores is designed and manufactured during the season. Zara purposefully manufactures in small lot sizes to avoid discounting later on and also to encourage impulse shopping, as a particular item could be gone in a few days. From start to finish, Zara has engineered its production process to maximize turnover and turnaround time, creating a true advantage in this step of strategy execution.

Zara also excels at driving traffic to stores. First, the small lot sizes and frequent shipments (up to twice a week per store) drive customers to visit often and purchase quickly. Zara shoppers average 17 visits per year, versus 4 to 5 for The Gap. On average, items stay in a Zara store only 11 days. Second, Zara spends no money on advertising, but it occupies some of the most expensive retail space in town, always near the high-fashion houses it imitates. Proximity reinforces the high-fashion association, while the busy street drives significant foot traffic. Overall, Zara has managed to create competitive advantage in every level of strategy execution by tightly aligning design, production, advertising, and real estate with the overall strategy of fast fashion: extremely fast and extremely flexible.

*Note:* Developed with Sara Paccamonti.

*Sources:* Suzy Hansen, "How Zara Grew into the World's Largest Fashion Retailer," *The New York Times,* November 9, 2012, www.nytimes.com/2012/11/11/magazine/how-zara-grew-into-the-worlds-largest-fashion-retailer.html?pagewanted=all (accessed February 5, 2014); and Seth Stevenson, "Polka Dots Are In? Polka Dots It Is!" *Slate,* June 21, 2012, www.slate.com/articles/arts/operations/2012/06/zara_s_fast_fashion_how_the_company_gets_new_styles_to_stores_so_quickly_.html (accessed February 5, 2014).

> Superior strategy execution capabilities are the only source of sustainable competitive advantage when strategies are easy for rivals to copy.

dominance. See Illustration Capsule 10.2 for an example of Zara's route to competitive advantage.

Because strategy execution capabilities are socially complex capabilities that develop with experience over long periods of time, they are hard to imitate. And there is no substitute for good strategy execution. (Recall the tests of resource advantage from Chapter 4.) As such, they may be as important a source of sustained competitive advantage as the core competencies that drive a firm's strategy. Indeed, they may be a far more important avenue for securing a competitive edge over rivals in situations where it is relatively easy for rivals to copy promising strategies. In such cases, the only way for firms to achieve lasting competitive advantage is to *out-execute* their competitors.

# MATCHING ORGANIZATIONAL STRUCTURE TO THE STRATEGY

While there are few hard-and-fast rules for organizing the work effort to support good strategy execution, there is one: A firm's organizational structure should be *matched* to the particular requirements of implementing the firm's strategy. Every company's strategy is grounded in its own set of organizational capabilities and value chain activities. Moreover, every firm's organization chart is partly a product of its particular situation, reflecting prior organizational patterns, varying internal circumstances, executive judgments about reporting relationships, and the politics of who gets which assignments. Thus, the determinants of the fine details of each firm's organizational structure are unique. But some considerations in organizing the work effort are common to all companies. These are summarized in Figure 10.3 and discussed in the following sections.

**LO 4**

What issues to consider in establishing a strategy-supportive organizational structure and organizing the work effort.

A company's organizational structure should be matched to the particular requirements of implementing the firm's strategy.

## Deciding Which Value Chain Activities to Perform Internally and Which to Outsource

Aside from the fact that an outsider, because of its expertise and specialized know-how, may be able to perform certain value chain activities better or cheaper than a company can perform them internally (as discussed in Chapter 6), outsourcing can also sometimes make a positive contribution to strategy execution. Outsourcing

**FIGURE 10.3** Structuring the Work Effort to Promote Successful Strategy Execution

Decide which value chain activities to perform internally and which ones to outsource

Align the organizational structure with the strategy

Decide how much authority to centralize at the top and how much to delegate to down-the-line managers and employees

Facilitate collaboration with external partners and strategic allies

An Organizational Structure Matched to the Requirements of Successful Strategy Execution

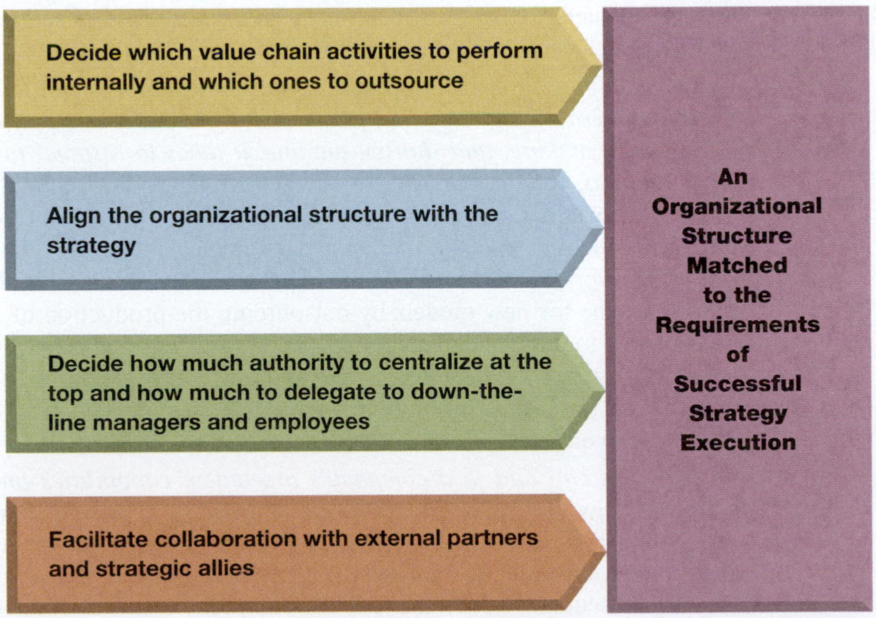

Wisely choosing which activities to perform internally and which to outsource can lead to several strategy-executing advantages—lower costs, heightened strategic focus, less internal bureaucracy, speedier decision making, and a better arsenal of organizational capabilities.

the performance of selected activities to outside vendors enables a company to heighten its strategic focus and *concentrate its full energies on performing those value chain activities that are at the core of its strategy, where it can create unique value*. For example, E. & J. Gallo Winery outsources 95 percent of its grape production, letting farmers take on weather-related and other grape-growing risks while it concentrates its full energies on wine production and sales.[18] Broadcom, a global leader in chips for broadband communication systems, outsources the manufacture of its chips to Taiwan Semiconductor, thus freeing company personnel to focus their full energies on R&D, new chip design, and marketing. Nike concentrates on design, marketing, and distribution to retailers, while outsourcing virtually all production of its shoes and sporting apparel. Illustration Capsule 10.3 describes Apple's decisions about which activities to outsource and which to perform in-house.

Such heightened focus on performing strategy-critical activities can yield three important execution-related benefits:

- *The company improves its chances for outclassing rivals in the performance of strategy-critical activities and turning a competence into a distinctive competence.* At the very least, the heightened focus on performing a select few value chain activities should promote more effective performance of those activities. This could materially enhance competitive capabilities by either lowering costs or improving product or service quality. Whirlpool, ING Insurance, Hugo Boss, Japan Airlines, and Chevron have outsourced their data processing activities to computer service firms, believing that outside specialists can perform the needed services at lower costs and equal or better quality. A relatively large number of companies outsource the operation of their websites to web design and hosting enterprises. Many businesses that get a lot of inquiries from customers or that have to provide 24/7 technical support to users of their products around the world have found that it is considerably less expensive to outsource these functions to specialists (often located in foreign countries where skilled personnel are readily available and worker compensation costs are much lower) than to operate their own call centers. NOVO1 is a company that specializes in call center operation, with five such centers located in the United States.

- *The streamlining of internal operations that flows from outsourcing often acts to decrease internal bureaucracies, flatten the organizational structure, speed internal decision making, and shorten the time it takes to respond to changing market conditions.* In consumer electronics, where advancing technology drives new product innovation, organizing the work effort in a manner that expedites getting next-generation products to market ahead of rivals is a critical competitive capability. The world's motor vehicle manufacturers have found that they can shorten the cycle time for new models by outsourcing the production of many parts and components to independent suppliers. They then work closely with the suppliers to swiftly incorporate new technology and to better integrate individual parts and components to form engine cooling systems, transmission systems, electrical systems, and so on.

- *Partnerships can add to a company's arsenal of capabilities and contribute to better strategy execution.* By building, continually improving, and then leveraging partnerships, a company enhances its overall organizational capabilities and strengthens its competitive assets—assets that deliver more value to customers and consequently pave the way for competitive success. Soft-drink and beer

# Which Value Chain Activities Does Apple Outsource and Why?

Innovation and design are core competencies for Apple and the drivers behind the creation of winning products such as the iPod, iPhone, and iPad. In consequence, all activities directly related to new product development and product design are performed internally. For example, Apple's Industrial Design Group is responsible for creating the look and feel of all Apple products—from the MacBook Air to the iPhone, and beyond to future products.

Producing a continuing stream of great new products and product versions is key to the success of Apple's strategy. But executing this strategy takes more than innovation and design capabilities. Manufacturing flexibility and speed are imperative in the production of Apple products to ensure that the latest ideas are reflected in the products and that the company meets the high demand for its products—especially around launch.

For these capabilities, Apple turns to outsourcing, as do the majority of its competitors in the consumer electronics space. Apple outsources the manufacturing of products like its iPhone to Asia, where contract manufacturing organizations (CMOs) create value through their vast scale, high flexibility, and low cost. Perhaps no company better epitomizes the Asian CMO value proposition than Foxconn, a company that assembles

not only for Apple but for Hewlett-Packard, Motorola, Amazon.com, and Samsung as well. Foxconn's scale is incredible, with its largest facility (Foxconn City in Shenzhen, China) employing over 230,000 workers. Such scale offers companies a significant degree of flexibility, as Foxconn has the ability to hire 3,000 employees on practically a moment's notice. Apple, more so than its competitors, is able to capture CMO value creation by leveraging its immense sales volume and strong cash position to receive preferred treatment.

*Note:* Developed with Margaret W. Macauley.

*Sources:* Company website; and Charles Duhigg and Keith Bradsher, "How the U.S. Lost Out on iPhone Work," *The New York Times,* January 21, 2012, www.nytimes.com/2012/01/22/business/apple-america-and-a-squeezed-middle-class.html?pagewanted=all&_r=0 (accessed March 5, 2012).

---

manufacturers cultivate their relationships with their bottlers and distributors to strengthen access to local markets and build loyalty, support, and commitment for corporate marketing programs, without which their own sales and growth would be weakened. Similarly, fast-food enterprises like Wendy's and Burger King find it essential to work hand in hand with franchisees on outlet cleanliness, consistency of product quality, in-store ambience, courtesy and friendliness of store personnel, and other aspects of store operations. Unless franchisees continuously deliver sufficient customer satisfaction to attract repeat business, a fast-food chain's sales and competitive standing will quickly suffer. Companies like Boeing, Aerospatiale, Verizon Communications, and Dell have learned that their central R&D groups cannot begin to match the innovative capabilities of a well-managed network of supply chain partners.

However, as emphasized in Chapter 6, a company must guard against going overboard on outsourcing and becoming overly dependent on outside suppliers. A company cannot be the master of its own destiny unless it maintains expertise and resource depth in performing those value chain activities that underpin its long-term competitive success.[19] As a general rule, therefore, it is the strategically less important activities for which outsourcing is likely to make the most strategic sense—activities like handling customer inquiries and providing technical support, doing the payroll, administering employee benefit programs, providing corporate security, maintaining fleet vehicles, operating the company's website, conducting employee training, and performing an assortment of information and data processing functions.

# Aligning the Firm's Organizational Structure with Its Strategy

The design of the firm's **organizational structure** is a critical aspect of the strategy execution process. The organizational structure comprises the formal and informal arrangement of tasks, responsibilities, and lines of authority and communication by which the firm is administered.[20] It specifies the linkages among parts of the organization, the reporting relationships, the direction of information flows, and the decision-making processes. It is a key factor in strategy implementation since it exerts a strong influence on how well managers can coordinate and control the complex set of activities involved.[21]

A well-designed organizational structure is one in which the various parts (e.g., decision-making rights, communication patterns) are aligned with one another and also matched to the requirements of the strategy. With the right structure in place, managers can orchestrate the various aspects of the implementation process with an even hand and a light touch. Without a supportive structure, strategy execution is more likely to become bogged down by administrative confusion, political maneuvering, and bureaucratic waste.

*Good organizational design may even contribute to the firm's ability to create value for customers and realize a profit.* By enabling lower bureaucratic costs and facilitating operational efficiency, it can lower a firm's operating costs. By facilitating the coordination of activities within the firm, it can improve the capability-building process, leading to greater differentiation and/or lower costs. Moreover, by improving the speed with which information is communicated and activities are coordinated, it can enable the firm to beat rivals to the market and profit from a period of unrivaled advantage.

## Making Strategy-Critical Activities the Main Building Blocks of the Organizational Structure

In any business, some activities in the value chain are always more critical to successful strategy execution than others. For instance, ski apparel companies like Sport Obermeyer, Arc'teryx, and Spyder must be good at styling and design, low-cost manufacturing, distribution (convincing an attractively large number of dealers to stock and promote the company's brand), and marketing and advertising (building a brand image that generates buzz and appeal among ski enthusiasts). For discount stockbrokers, like Scottrade and TD Ameritrade, the strategy-critical activities are fast access to information, accurate order execution, efficient record keeping and transaction processing, and good customer service. With respect to such core value chain activities, it is important for management to build its organizational structure around proficient performance of these activities, making them the centerpieces or main building blocks in the enterprise's organizational structure.

The rationale is compelling: If activities crucial to strategic success are to have the resources, decision-making influence, and organizational impact they need, they must be centerpieces in the enterprise's organizational scheme. Making them the focus of structuring efforts will also facilitate their coordination and promote good internal fit—an essential attribute of a winning strategy, as summarized in Chapter 1 and elaborated in Chapter 4. To the extent that implementing a new strategy entails new or altered key activities or capabilities, different organizational arrangements may be required.

## Matching Type of Organizational Structure to Strategy Execution Requirements

Organizational structures can be classified into a limited number of standard types. The type that is most suitable for a given firm will depend on the firm's size and complexity as well as its strategy. As firms grow and their needs for structure evolve, their structural form is likely to evolve from one type to another. The four basic types are the *simple structure*, the *functional structure*, the *multidivisional structure*, and the *matrix structure*, as described next.

*1. Simple Structure*   A **simple structure** is one in which a central executive (often the owner-manager) handles all major decisions and oversees the operations of the organization with the help of a small staff.[22] Simple structures are also known as *line-and-staff structures*, since a central administrative staff supervises line employees who conduct the operations of the firm, or *flat structures*, since there are few levels of hierarchy. The simple structure is characterized by limited task specialization; few rules; informal relationships; minimal use of training, planning, and liaison devices; and a lack of sophisticated support systems. It has all the advantages of simplicity, including low administrative costs, ease of coordination, flexibility, quick decision making, adaptability, and responsiveness to change. Its informality and lack of rules may foster creativity and heightened individual responsibility.

Simple organizational structures are typically employed by small firms and entrepreneurial startups. The simple structure is the most common type of organizational structure since small firms are the most prevalent type of business. As an organization grows, however, this structural form becomes inadequate to the demands that come with size and complexity. In response, growing firms tend to alter their organizational structure from a simple structure to a *functional structure*.

*2. Functional Structure*   A **functional structure** is one that is organized along functional lines, where a function represents a major component of the firm's value chain, such as R&D, engineering and design, manufacturing, sales and marketing, logistics, and customer service. Each functional unit is supervised by functional line managers who report to the chief executive officer and a corporate staff. This arrangement allows functional managers to focus on their area of responsibility, leaving it to the CEO and headquarters to provide direction and ensure that the activities of the functional managers are coordinated and integrated. Functional structures are also known as *departmental structures*, since the functional units are commonly called departments, and *unitary structures* or *U-forms*, since a single unit is responsible for each function.

In large organizations, functional structures lighten the load on top management, in comparison to simple structures, and enable more efficient use of managerial resources. Their primary advantage, however, is greater *task specialization*, which promotes learning, enables the realization of scale economies, and offers productivity advantages not otherwise available. Their chief disadvantage is that the departmental boundaries can inhibit the flow of information and limit the opportunities for cross-functional cooperation and coordination.

**CORE CONCEPT**

A **simple structure** consists of a central executive (often the owner-manager) who handles all major decisions and oversees all operations with the help of a small staff. Simple structures are also called *line-and-staff structures* or *flat structures*.

**CORE CONCEPT**

A **functional structure** is organized into functional departments, with departmental managers who report to the CEO and small corporate staff. Functional structures are also called *departmental structures* and *unitary structures* or *U-forms*.

The primary advantage of a functional structure is greater *task specialization*, which promotes learning, enables the realization of scale economies, and offers productivity advantages not otherwise available.

It is generally agreed that a functional structure is the best organizational arrangement when a company is in just one particular business (irrespective of which of the five generic competitive strategies it opts to pursue). For instance, a technical instruments manufacturer may be organized around research and development, engineering, supply chain management, assembly, quality control, marketing, and technical services. A discount retailer, such as Dollar General or Kmart, may organize around such functional units as purchasing, warehousing, distribution logistics, store operations, advertising, merchandising and promotion, and customer service. Functional structures can also be appropriate for firms with high-volume production, products that are closely related, and a limited degree of vertical integration. For example, General Motors now manages all of its brands (Cadillac, GMC, Chevrolet, Buick, etc.) under a common functional structure designed to promote technical transfer and capture economies of scale.

As firms continue to grow, they often become more diversified and complex, placing a greater burden on top management. At some point, the centralized control that characterizes the functional structure becomes a liability, and the advantages of functional specialization begin to break down. To resolve these problems and address a growing need for coordination across functions, firms generally turn to the *multidivisional structure*.

### CORE CONCEPT

A **multidivisional structure** is a decentralized structure consisting of a set of operating divisions organized along business, product, customer group, or geographic lines and a central corporate headquarters that allocates resources, provides support functions, and monitors divisional activities. Multidivisional structures are also called *divisional structures* or *M-forms*.

**3. *Multidivisional Structure***   A **multidivisional structure** is a decentralized structure consisting of a set of operating divisions organized along market, customer, product, or geographic lines, along with a central corporate headquarters, which monitors divisional activities, allocates resources, performs assorted support functions, and exercises overall control. Since each division is essentially a business (often called a *single business unit* or *SBU*), the divisions typically operate as independent profit centers (i.e., with profit and loss responsibility) and are organized internally along functional lines. Division managers oversee day-to-day operations and the development of business-level strategy, while corporate executives attend to overall performance and corporate strategy, the elements of which were described in Chapter 8. Multidivisional structures are also called *divisional structures* or *M-forms,* in contrast with U-form (functional) structures.

Multidivisional structures are common among companies pursuing some form of diversification strategy or international strategy, with operations in a number of businesses or countries. When the strategy is one of unrelated diversification, as in a conglomerate, the divisions generally represent businesses in separate industries. When the strategy is based on related diversification, the divisions may be organized according to industries, customer groups, product lines, geographic regions, or technologies. In this arrangement, the decision about where to draw the divisional lines depends foremost on the nature of the relatedness and the strategy-critical building blocks, in terms of which businesses have key value chain activities in common. For example, a company selling closely related products to business customers as well as two types of end consumers—online buyers and in-store buyers—may organize its divisions according to customer groups since the value chains involved in serving the three groups differ. Another company may organize by product line due to commonalities in product development and production within each product line. Multidivisional structures are also common among vertically integrated firms. There the major building blocks are often divisional units performing one or more of the major processing steps along the value chain (e.g., raw-material production, components manufacture, assembly, wholesale distribution, retail store operations).

Multidivisional structures offer significant advantages over functional structures in terms of facilitating the management of a complex and diverse set of operations.[23] Putting business-level strategy in the hands of division managers while leaving corporate strategy to top executives reduces the potential for information overload and improves the quality of decision making in each domain. This also minimizes the costs of coordinating divisionwide activities while enhancing top management's ability to control a diverse and complex operation. Moreover, multidivisional structures can help align individual incentives with the goals of the corporation and spur productivity by encouraging competition for resources among the different divisions.

But a multidivisional structure can also present some problems to a company pursuing related diversification, because having independent business units—each running its own business in its own way—inhibits cross-business collaboration and the capture of cross-business synergies, which are critical for the success of a related diversification strategy, as Chapter 8 explains. To solve this type of problem, firms turn to more complex structures, such as the matrix structure.

*4. Matrix Structure*   A **matrix structure** is a combination structure in which the organization is organized along two or more dimensions at once (e.g., business, geographic area, value chain function) for the purpose of enhancing cross-unit communication, collaboration, and coordination. In essence, it overlays one type of structure onto another type. Matrix structures are managed through multiple reporting relationships, so a middle manager may report to several bosses. For instance, in a matrix structure based on product line, region, and function, a sales manager for plastic containers in Georgia might report to the manager of the plastics division, the head of the southeast sales region, and the head of marketing.

Matrix organizational structures have evolved from the complex, overformalized structures that were popular in the 1960s, 70s, and 80s but often produced inefficient, unwieldy bureaucracies. The modern incarnation of the matrix structure is generally a more flexible arrangement, with a single primary reporting relationship that can be overlaid with a *temporary* secondary reporting relationship as need arises. For example, a software company that is organized into functional departments (software design, quality control, customer relations) may assign employees from those departments to different projects on a temporary basis, so an employee reports to a project manager as well as to his or her primary boss (the functional department head) for the duration of a project.

Matrix structures are also called *composite structures* or *combination structures*. They are often used for project-based, process-based, or team-based management. Such approaches are common in businesses involving projects of limited duration, such as consulting, architecture, and engineering services. The type of close cross-unit collaboration that a flexible matrix structure supports is also needed to build competitive capabilities in strategically important activities, such as speeding new products to market, that involve employees scattered across several organizational units.[24] Capabilities-based matrix structures that combine process departments (like new product development) with more traditional functional departments provide a solution.

An advantage of matrix structures is that they facilitate the sharing of plant and equipment, specialized knowledge, and other key resources. Thus, they lower costs by enabling the realization of economies of scope. They also have the advantage of flexibility in form and may allow for better oversight since supervision is provided from more than one perspective. A disadvantage is that they add another layer of management, thereby increasing bureaucratic costs and possibly decreasing response time to new situations.[25] In addition, there is a potential for confusion among employees due to dual reporting relationships and divided loyalties. While there is some controversy over the utility of matrix structures, the modern approach to matrix structures does much to minimize their disadvantages.[26]

## CORE CONCEPT

A **matrix structure** is a combination structure that overlays one type of structure onto another type, with multiple reporting relationships. It is used to foster cross-unit collaboration. Matrix structures are also called *composite structures* or *combination structures*.

# Determining How Much Authority to Delegate

Under any organizational structure, there is room for considerable variation in how much authority top managers retain and how much is delegated to down-the-line managers and employees. In executing strategy and conducting daily operations, companies must decide how much authority to delegate to the managers of each organizational unit—especially the heads of divisions, functional departments, plants, and other operating units—and how much decision-making latitude to give individual employees in performing their jobs. The two extremes are to *centralize decision making* at the top or to *decentralize decision making* by giving managers and employees at all levels considerable decision-making latitude in their areas of responsibility. As shown in Table 10.1, the two approaches are based on sharply different underlying principles and beliefs, with each having its pros and cons.

**TABLE 10.1   Advantages and Disadvantages of Centralized versus Decentralized Decision Making**

| Centralized Organizational Structures | Decentralized Organizational Structures |
|---|---|
| **Basic tenets**<br>• Decisions on most matters of importance should be in the hands of top-level managers who have the experience, expertise, and judgment to decide what is the best course of action.<br>• Lower-level personnel have neither the knowledge, time, nor inclination to properly manage the tasks they are performing.<br>• Strong control from the top is a more effective means for coordinating company actions. | **Basic tenets**<br>• Decision-making authority should be put in the hands of the people closest to, and most familiar with, the situation.<br>• Those with decision-making authority should be trained to exercise good judgment.<br>• A company that draws on the combined intellectual capital of all its employees can outperform a command-and-control company. |
| **Chief advantages**<br>• Fixes accountability through tight control from the top.<br>• Eliminates potential for conflicting goals and actions on the part of lower-level managers.<br>• Facilitates quick decision making and strong leadership under crisis situations. | **Chief advantages**<br>• Encourages company employees to exercise initiative and act responsibly.<br>• Promotes greater motivation and involvement in the business on the part of more company personnel.<br>• Spurs new ideas and creative thinking.<br>• Allows for fast response to market change.<br>• Entails fewer layers of management. |
| **Primary disadvantages**<br>• Lengthens response times by those closest to the market conditions because they must seek approval for their actions.<br>• Does not encourage responsibility among lower-level managers and rank-and-file employees.<br>• Discourages lower-level managers and rank-and-file employees from exercising any initiative. | **Primary disadvantages**<br>• May result in higher-level managers being unaware of actions taken by empowered personnel under their supervision.<br>• Can lead to inconsistent or conflicting approaches by different managers and employees.<br>• Can impair cross-unit collaboration. |

**Centralized Decision Making: Pros and Cons**   In a highly centralized organizational structure, *top executives retain authority for most strategic and operating decisions* and keep a tight rein on business unit heads, department heads, and the managers of key operating units. Comparatively little discretionary authority is granted to frontline supervisors and rank-and-file employees. The command-and-control paradigm of centralized structures is based on the underlying assumptions that frontline personnel have neither the time nor the inclination to direct and properly control the work they are performing and that they lack the knowledge and judgment to make wise decisions about how best to do it—hence the need for managerially prescribed policies and procedures, close supervision, and tight control. The thesis underlying centralized structures is that strict enforcement of detailed procedures backed by rigorous managerial oversight is the most reliable way to keep the daily execution of strategy on track.

One advantage of a centralized structure, with tight control by the manager in charge, is that it is easy to know who is accountable when things do not go well. This structure can also reduce the potential for conflicting decisions and actions among lower-level managers who may have differing perspectives and ideas about how to tackle certain tasks or resolve particular issues. For example, a manager in charge of an engineering department may be more interested in pursuing a new technology than is a marketing manager who doubts that customers will value the technology as highly. Another advantage of a command-and-control structure is that it can facilitate strong leadership from the top in a crisis situation that affects the organization as a whole and can enable a more uniform and swift response.

But there are some serious disadvantages as well. Hierarchical command-and-control structures do not encourage responsibility and initiative on the part of lower-level managers and employees. They can make a large organization with a complex structure sluggish in responding to changing market conditions because of the time it takes for the review-and-approval process to run up all the layers of the management bureaucracy. Furthermore, to work well, centralized decision making requires top-level managers to gather and process whatever information is relevant to the decision. When the relevant knowledge resides at lower organizational levels (or is technical, detailed, or hard to express in words), it is difficult and time-consuming to get all the facts in front of a high-level executive located far from the scene of the action—full understanding of the situation cannot be readily copied from one mind to another. Hence, centralized decision making is often impractical—the larger the company and the more scattered its operations, the more that decision-making authority must be delegated to managers closer to the scene of the action.

**Decentralized Decision Making: Pros and Cons**   In a highly decentralized organization, *decision-making authority is pushed down to the lowest organizational level capable of making timely, informed, competent decisions.* The objective is to put adequate decision-making authority in the hands of the people closest to and most familiar with the situation and train them to weigh all the factors and exercise good judgment. At Starbucks, for example, employees are encouraged to exercise initiative in promoting customer satisfaction—there's the oft-repeated story of a store employee who, when the computerized cash register system went offline, offered free coffee to waiting customers, thereby avoiding customer displeasure and damage to Starbucks's reputation.[27]

The case for empowering down-the-line managers and employees to make decisions related to daily operations and strategy execution is based on the belief that a company that draws on the combined intellectual capital of all its employees can

> The ultimate goal of decentralized decision making is to put authority in the hands of those persons closest to and most knowledgeable about the situation.

outperform a command-and-control company.[28] The challenge in a decentralized system is maintaining adequate control. With decentralized decision making, top management maintains control by placing limits on the authority granted to company personnel, installing companywide strategic control systems, holding people accountable for their decisions, instituting compensation incentives that reward people for doing their jobs well, and creating a corporate culture where there's strong peer pressure on individuals to act responsibly.[29]

Decentralized organizational structures have much to recommend them. Delegating authority to subordinate managers and rank-and-file employees encourages them to take responsibility and exercise initiative. It shortens organizational response times to market changes and spurs new ideas, creative thinking, innovation, and greater involvement on the part of all company personnel. In worker-empowered structures, jobs can be defined more broadly, several tasks can be integrated into a single job, and people can direct their own work. Fewer managers are needed because deciding how to do things becomes part of each person's or team's job. Further, today's online communication systems and smartphones make it easy and relatively inexpensive for people at all organizational levels to have direct access to data, other employees, managers, suppliers, and customers. They can access information quickly (via the Internet or company network), readily check with superiors or whomever else as needed, and take responsible action. Typically, there are genuine gains in morale and productivity when people are provided with the tools and information they need to operate in a self-directed way.

But decentralization also has some disadvantages. Top managers lose an element of control over what goes on and may thus be unaware of actions being taken by personnel under their supervision. Such lack of control can be problematic in the event that empowered employees make decisions that conflict with those of others or that serve their unit's interests at the expense of other parts of the company. Moreover, because decentralization gives organizational units the authority to act independently, there is risk of too little collaboration and coordination between different units.

Many companies have concluded that the advantages of decentralization outweigh the disadvantages. Over the past several decades, there's been a decided shift from centralized, hierarchical structures to flatter, more decentralized structures that stress employee empowerment. This shift reflects a strong and growing consensus that authoritarian, hierarchical organizational structures are not well suited to implementing and executing strategies in an era when extensive information and instant communication are the norm and when a big fraction of the organization's most valuable assets consists of intellectual capital that resides in its employees' capabilities.

### Capturing Cross-Business Strategic Fit in a Decentralized Structure

Diversified companies striving to capture the benefits of synergy between separate businesses must beware of giving business unit heads full rein to operate independently. Cross-business strategic fit typically must be captured either by enforcing close cross-business collaboration or by centralizing the performance of functions requiring close coordination at the corporate level.[30] For example, if businesses with overlapping process and product technologies have their own independent R&D departments—each pursuing its own priorities, projects, and strategic agendas—it's hard for the corporate parent to prevent duplication of effort, capture either economies of scale or economies of scope, or encourage more collaborative R&D efforts. Where cross-business strategic fit with respect to R&D is important, the best solution is usually to centralize the R&D function and have a coordinated corporate R&D effort that serves the interests of both the individual businesses and

Efforts to decentralize decision making and give company personnel some leeway in conducting operations must be tempered with the need to maintain adequate control and cross-unit coordination.

the company as a whole. Likewise, centralizing the related activities of separate businesses makes sense when there are opportunities to share a common sales force, use common distribution channels, rely on a common field service organization, use common e-commerce systems, and so on.

# Facilitating Collaboration with External Partners and Strategic Allies

Organizational mechanisms—whether formal or informal—are also required to ensure effective working relationships with each major outside constituency involved in strategy execution. Strategic alliances, outsourcing arrangements, joint ventures, and cooperative partnerships can contribute little of value without active management of the relationship. Unless top management sees that constructive organizational bridge building with external partners occurs and that productive working relationships emerge, the potential value of cooperative relationships is lost and the company's power to execute its strategy is weakened. For example, if close working relationships with suppliers are crucial, then supply chain management must enter into considerations of how to create an effective organizational structure. If distributor, dealer, or franchisee relationships are important, then someone must be assigned the task of nurturing the relationships with such forward-channel allies.

Building organizational bridges with external partners and strategic allies can be accomplished by appointing "relationship managers" with responsibility for making particular strategic partnerships generate the intended benefits. Relationship managers have many roles and functions: getting the right people together, promoting good rapport, facilitating the flow of information, nurturing interpersonal communication and cooperation, and ensuring effective coordination.[31] Multiple cross-organization ties have to be established and kept open to ensure proper communication and coordination. There has to be enough information sharing to make the relationship work and periodic frank discussions of conflicts, trouble spots, and changing situations.

Organizing and managing a network structure provides a mechanism for encouraging more effective collaboration and cooperation among external partners. A **network structure** is the arrangement linking a number of independent organizations involved in some common undertaking. A well-managed network structure typically includes one firm in a more central role, with the responsibility of ensuring that the right partners are included and the activities across the network are coordinated. The high-end Italian motorcycle company Ducati operates in this manner, assembling its motorcycles from parts obtained from a hand-picked integrated network of parts suppliers.

> ## CORE CONCEPT
>
> A **network structure** is the arrangement linking a number of independent organizations involved in some common undertaking, with one firm typically in a more central role.

# Further Perspectives on Structuring the Work Effort

All organizational designs have their strategy-related strengths and weaknesses. To do a good job of matching structure to strategy, strategy implementers first have to pick a basic organizational design and modify it as needed to fit the company's particular business lineup. They must then (1) supplement the design with appropriate coordinating mechanisms (cross-functional task forces, special project teams, self-contained work teams, etc.) and (2) institute whatever networking and communications arrangements are necessary to support effective execution of the firm's strategy. Some companies may avoid setting up "ideal" organizational arrangements because they do not want to disturb existing reporting relationships or because they need to accommodate other situational idiosyncrasies, yet they must still work toward the goal of building a competitively capable organization.

What can be said unequivocally is that building a capable organization entails a process of consciously knitting together the efforts of individuals and groups. Organizational capabilities emerge from establishing and nurturing cooperative working relationships among people and groups to perform activities in a more efficient, value-creating fashion. While an appropriate organizational structure can facilitate this, organization building is a task in which senior management must be deeply involved. Indeed, effectively managing both internal organizational processes and external collaboration to create and develop competitively valuable organizational capabilities remains a top challenge for senior executives in today's companies.

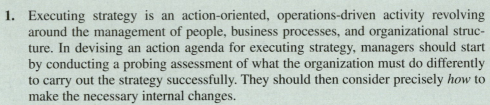

## KEY POINTS

1. Executing strategy is an action-oriented, operations-driven activity revolving around the management of people, business processes, and organizational structure. In devising an action agenda for executing strategy, managers should start by conducting a probing assessment of what the organization must do differently to carry out the strategy successfully. They should then consider precisely *how* to make the necessary internal changes.

2. Good strategy execution requires a *team effort*. All managers have strategy-executing responsibility in their areas of authority, and all employees are active participants in the strategy execution process.

3. Ten managerial tasks are part of every company effort to execute strategy: (1) staffing the organization with the right people, (2) developing the resources and building the necessary organizational capabilities, (3) creating a supportive organizational structure, (4) allocating sufficient resources, (5) instituting supportive policies and procedures, (6) adopting processes for continuous improvement, (7) installing systems that enable proficient company operations, (8) tying incentives to the achievement of desired targets, (9) instilling the right corporate culture, and (10) exercising internal leadership to propel strategy execution forward.

4. The two best signs of good strategy execution are that a company is meeting or beating its performance targets and is performing value chain activities in a manner that is conducive to companywide operating excellence. *Shortfalls in performance signal weak strategy, weak execution, or both.*

5. Building an organization capable of good strategy execution entails three types of actions: (1) *staffing the organization*—assembling a talented management team and recruiting and retaining employees with the needed experience, technical skills, and intellectual capital; (2) *acquiring, developing, and strengthening strategy-supportive resources and capabilities*—accumulating the required resources, developing proficiencies in performing strategy-critical value chain activities, and updating the company's capabilities to match changing market conditions and customer expectations; and (3) *structuring the organization and work effort*—instituting organizational arrangements that facilitate good strategy execution,

deciding how much decision-making authority to delegate, and managing external relationships.

6. Building core competencies and competitive capabilities is a time-consuming, managerially challenging exercise that can be approached in three ways: (1) developing capabilities internally, (2) acquiring capabilities through mergers and acquisitions, and (3) accessing capabilities via collaborative partnerships.

7. In building capabilities internally, the first step is to develop the *ability* to do something, through experimenting, actively searching for alternative solutions, and learning by trial and error. As experience grows and company personnel learn how to perform the activities consistently well and at an acceptable cost, the ability evolves into a tried-and-true capability. The process can be accelerated by making learning a more deliberate endeavor and providing the incentives that will motivate company personnel to achieve the desired ends.

8. As firms get better at executing their strategies, they develop capabilities in the domain of strategy execution. Superior strategy execution capabilities allow companies to get the most from their organizational resources and capabilities. But excellence in strategy execution can also be a more direct source of competitive advantage, since more efficient and effective strategy execution can lower costs and permit firms to deliver more value to customers. Because they are socially complex capabilities, superior strategy execution capabilities are hard to imitate and have no good substitutes. As such, they can be an important source of *sustainable* competitive advantage. Any time rivals can readily duplicate successful strategies, making it impossible to *out-strategize* rivals, the chief way to achieve lasting competitive advantage is to *out-execute* them.

9. Structuring the organization and organizing the work effort in a strategy-supportive fashion has four aspects: (1) deciding which value chain activities to perform internally and which ones to outsource; (2) aligning the firm's organizational structure with its strategy; (3) deciding how much authority to centralize at the top and how much to delegate to down-the-line managers and employees; and (4) facilitating the necessary collaboration and coordination with external partners and strategic allies.

10. To align the firm's organizational structure with its strategy, it is important to make strategy-critical activities the main building blocks. There are four basic types of organizational structures: the simple structure, the functional structure, the multidivisional structure, and the matrix structure. Which is most appropriate depends on the firm's size, complexity, and strategy.

## ASSURANCE OF LEARNING EXERCISES

1. The foundation of Nike's global sports apparel dominance lies in the company's continual ability to outcompete rivals by aligning its superior design, innovation, and marketing capabilities with outsourced manufacturing. Such a strategy necessitates a complex marriage of innovative product designs with fresh marketing techniques and a global chain of suppliers and manufacturers. Explore Nike's most

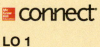

**LO 1**

recent strategic management changes (**nikeinc.com/news/nike-announces-strategic-leadership-changes**). How well do these changes reflect the company's focus on innovative design and marketing strategies? Has the company's relentless focus on apparel innovation affected its supply chain management? Do these changes—or Nike's strategy, more broadly—reflect the company's ubiquitous Swoosh logo and "Just Do It" slogan? Visit Nike's corporate website for more in-depth information: **nikeinc.com/pages/about-nike-inc**.

**LO 2**

2. Search online to read about Jeff Bezos's management of his new executives. Specifically, explore Amazon.com's "S-Team" meetings (**management.fortune.cnn.com/2012/11/16/jeff-bezos-amazon/**). Why does Bezos begin meetings of senior executives with 30 minutes of silent reading? How does this focus the group? Why does Bezos insist new ideas must be written and presented in memo form? How does this reflect the founder's insistence on clear, concise, and innovative thinking in his company? And does this exercise work as a de facto crash course for new Amazon executives? Explain why this small but crucial management strategy reflects Bezos's overriding goal of cohesive and clear idea presentation.

**LO 2, LO 3**

3. Review Facebook's Careers page (**www.Facebook.com/careers/**). The page emphasizes Facebook's core values and explains how potential employees could fit that mold. Bold and decisive thinking and a commitment to transparency and social connectivity drive the page and the company as a whole. Then research Facebook's internal management training programs, called "employee boot camps," using a search engine like Google or Bing. How do these programs integrate the traits and stated goals on the Careers page into specific and tangible construction of employee capabilities? Boot camps are open to all Facebook employees, not just engineers. How does this internal training prepare Facebook employees of all types to "move fast and break things"?

**LO 4**

4. Review Valve Corporation's company handbook online: **www.valvesoftware.com/company/Valve_Handbook_LowRes.pdf**. Specifically, focus on Valve's corporate structure. Valve has hundreds of employees but no managers or bosses at all. Valve's gaming success hinges on innovative and completely original experiences like Portal and Half-Life. Does it seem that Valve's corporate structure uniquely promotes this type of gaming innovation? Why or why not? How would you characterize Valve's organizational structure? Is it completely unique, or could it be characterized as a multidivisional, matrix, or functional structure? Explain your answer.

**LO 5**

5. Keep Valve's unique structure in mind. Using Google Scholar or your university's access to online databases, do a search for recent writings on decentralized decision making and employee empowerment. According to these articles, under which conditions should a company strive for more centralization? Can employee empowerment ever backfire, and, if so, how should companies build and impose a more effective organizational structure?

## EXERCISE FOR SIMULATION PARTICIPANTS

1. How would you describe the organization of your company's top-management team? Is some decision making decentralized and delegated to individual managers? If so, explain how the decentralization works. Or are decisions made more by consensus, with all co-managers having input? What do you see as the advantages and disadvantages of the decision-making approach your company is employing?  **LO 5**

2. What specific actions have you and your co-managers taken to develop core competencies or competitive capabilities that can contribute to good strategy execution and potential competitive advantage? If no actions have been taken, explain your rationale for doing nothing.  **LO 3**

3. What value chain activities are most crucial to good execution of your company's strategy? Does your company have the ability to outsource any value chain activities? If so, have you and your co-managers opted to engage in outsourcing? Why or why not?  **LO 1, LO 4**

## ENDNOTES

[1] Steven W. Floyd and Bill Wooldridge, "Managing Strategic Consensus: The Foundation of Effective Implementation," *Academy of Management Executive* 6, no. 4 (November 1992), p. 27.

[2] Jack Welch with Suzy Welch, *Winning* (New York: HarperBusiness, 2005).

[3] Larry Bossidy and Ram Charan, *Execution: The Discipline of Getting Things Done* (New York: Crown Business, 2002).

[4] Christopher A. Bartlett and Sumantra Ghoshal, "Building Competitive Advantage through People," *MIT Sloan Management Review* 43, no. 2 (Winter 2002), pp. 34–41.

[5] Justin Menkes, "Hiring for Smarts," *Harvard Business Review* 83, no. 11 (November 2005), pp. 100–109; Justin Menkes, *Executive Intelligence* (New York: HarperCollins, 2005).

[6] Menkes, *Executive Intelligence,* pp. 68, 76.

[7] Jim Collins, *Good to Great* (New York: HarperBusiness, 2001).

[8] John Byrne, "The Search for the Young and Gifted," *Businessweek,* October 4, 1999, p. 108.

[9] C. Helfat and M. Peteraf, "The Dynamic Resource-Based View: Capability Lifecycles," *Strategic Management Journal* 24, no. 10 (October 2003), pp. 997–1010.

[10] G. Hamel and C. K. Prahalad, "Strategy as Stretch and Leverage," *Harvard Business Review* 71, no. 2 (March–April 1993), pp. 75–84.

[11] G. Dosi, R. Nelson, and S. Winter (eds.), *The Nature and Dynamics of Organizational Capabilities* (Oxford, England: Oxford University Press, 2001).

[12] S. Winter, "The Satisficing Principle in Capability Learning," *Strategic Management Journal* 21, no. 10–11 (October–November 2000), pp. 981–996; M. Zollo and S. Winter, "Deliberate Learning and the Evolution of Dynamic Capabilities," *Organization Science* 13, no. 3 (May–June 2002), pp. 339–351.

[13] G. Szulanski and S. Winter, "Getting It Right the Second Time," *Harvard Business Review* 80 (January 2002), pp. 62–69.

[14] B. Kogut and U. Zander, "Knowledge of the Firm, Combinative Capabilities, and the Replication of Technology," *Organization Science* 3, no. 3 (August 1992), pp. 383–397.

[15] C. Helfat and R. Raubitschek, "Product Sequencing: Co-evolution of Knowledge, Capabilities and Products," *Strategic Management Journal* 21, no. 10–11 (October–November 2000), pp. 961–980.

[16] Robert H. Hayes, Gary P. Pisano, and David M. Upton, *Strategic Operations: Competing through Capabilities* (New York: Free Press, 1996); Jonas Ridderstrale, "Cashing In on Corporate Competencies," *Business Strategy Review* 14, no. 1 (Spring 2003), pp. 27–38; Danny Miller, Russell Eisenstat, and Nathaniel Foote, "Strategy from the Inside Out: Building Capability-Creating Organizations," *California Management Review* 44, no. 3 (Spring 2002), pp. 37–55.

[17] S. Karim and W. Mitchell, "Path-Dependent and Path-Breaking Change: Reconfiguring Business Resources Following Acquisitions in the US Medical Sector, 1978–1995," *Strategic Management Journal* 21, no. 10–11 (October–November 2000), pp. 1061–1082; L. Capron, P. Dussauge, and W. Mitchell, "Resource Redeployment Following Horizontal Acquisitions in Europe and North America, 1988–1992," *Strategic Management Journal* 19, no. 7 (July 1998), pp. 631–662.

[18] J. B. Quinn, *Intelligent Enterprise* (New York: Free Press, 1992).

[19] Gary P. Pisano and Willy C. Shih, "Restoring American Competitiveness," *Harvard Business Review* 87, no. 7–8 (July–August 2009), pp. 114–125.

[20] A. Chandler, *Strategy and Structure* (Cambridge, MA: MIT Press, 1962).

[21] E. Olsen, S. Slater, and G. Hult, "The Importance of Structure and Process to Strategy Implementation," *Business Horizons* 48, no. 1 (2005), pp. 47–54; H. Barkema, J. Baum, and E. Mannix, "Management Challenges in a

New Time," *Academy of Management Journal* 45, no. 5 (October 2002), pp. 916–930.

[22] H. Mintzberg, *The Structuring of Organizations* (Englewood Cliffs, NJ: Prentice Hall, 1979); C. Levicki, *The Interactive Strategy Workout,* 2nd ed. (London: Prentice Hall, 1999).

[23] O. Williamson, *Market and Hierarchies* (New York: Free Press, 1975); R. M. Burton and B. Obel, "A Computer Simulation Test of the M-Form Hypothesis," *Administrative Science Quarterly* 25 (1980), pp. 457–476.

[24] J. Baum and S. Wally, "Strategic Decision Speed and Firm Performance," *Strategic Management Journal* 24 (2003), pp. 1107–1129.

[25] C. Bartlett and S. Ghoshal, "Matrix Management: Not a Structure, a Frame of Mind," *Harvard Business Review,* July–August 1990, pp. 138–145.

[26] M. Goold and A. Campbell, "Structured Networks: Towards the Well Designed Matrix," *Long Range Planning* 36, no. 5 (2003), pp. 427–439.

[27] Iain Somerville and John Edward Mroz, "New Competencies for a New World," in Frances Hesselbein, Marshall Goldsmith, and Richard Beckard (eds.), *The Organization of the Future* (San Francisco: Jossey-Bass, 1997), p. 70.

[28] Stanley E. Fawcett, Gary K. Rhoads, and Phillip Burnah, "People as the Bridge to Competitiveness: Benchmarking the 'ABCs' of an Empowered Workforce," *Benchmarking: An International Journal* 11, no. 4 (2004), pp. 346–360.

[29] Robert Simons, "Control in an Age of Empowerment," *Harvard Business Review* 73 (March–April 1995), pp. 80–88.

[30] Jeanne M. Liedtka, "Collaboration across Lines of Business for Competitive Advantage," *Academy of Management Executive* 10, no. 2 (May 1996), pp. 20–34.

[31] Rosabeth Moss Kanter, "Collaborative Advantage: The Art of the Alliance," *Harvard Business Review* 72, no. 4 (July–August 1994), pp. 96–108.

### CHAPTER 11

# Managing Internal Operations

## Actions That Promote Good Strategy Execution

## Learning Objectives

THIS CHAPTER WILL HELP YOU UNDERSTAND:

**LO 1**   Why resource allocation should always be based on strategic priorities.

**LO 2**   How well-designed policies and procedures can facilitate good strategy execution.

**LO 3**   How best practices and process management tools drive continuous improvement in the performance of value chain activities and promote superior strategy execution.

**LO 4**   The role of information and operating systems in enabling company personnel to carry out their strategic roles proficiently.

**LO 5**   How and why the use of well-designed incentives and rewards can be management's single most powerful tool for promoting adept strategy execution.

> Adhering to budgeting rules shouldn't trump good decision-making.
>
> Emily Oster – *Economist and Author*

> Pay your people the least possible and you'll get the same from them.
>
> Malcolm Forbes – *Late Publisher of* Forbes *Magazine*

> Apple is a very disciplined company, and we have great processes. But that's not what it's about. Process makes you more efficient.
>
> Steve Jobs – *Cofounder of Apple, Inc.*

In Chapter 10, we emphasized that proficient strategy execution begins with three types of managerial actions: staffing the organization with the right people; acquiring, developing, and strengthening the firm's resources and capabilities; and structuring the organization in a manner supportive of the strategy execution effort.

In this chapter, we discuss five additional managerial actions that advance the cause of good strategy execution:

- Allocating ample resources to execution-critical value chain activities.

- Instituting policies and procedures that facilitate strategy execution.

- Employing process management tools to drive continuous improvement in how value chain activities are performed.

- Installing information and operating systems that enable company personnel to carry out their strategic roles proficiently.

- Using rewards and incentives to promote better strategy execution and the achievement of strategic and financial targets.

# ALLOCATING RESOURCES TO THE STRATEGY EXECUTION EFFORT

Early in the strategy implementation process, managers must determine what resources (in terms of funding, people, and so on) will be required and how they should be distributed across the company's various organizational units. This includes carefully screening requests for more people and new facilities and equipment, approving those that will contribute to the strategy execution effort, and turning down those that don't. Should internal cash flows prove insufficient to fund the planned strategic initiatives, then management must raise additional funds through borrowing or selling additional shares of stock to investors.

A company's ability to marshal the resources needed to support new strategic initiatives has a major impact on the strategy execution process. Too little funding and an insufficiency of other types of resources slow progress and impede the efforts of

**LO 1**

Why resource allocation should always be based on strategic priorities.

organizational units to execute their pieces of the strategic plan proficiently. Too much funding and an overabundance of other resources waste organizational resources and reduce financial performance. Both outcomes argue for managers to be deeply involved in reviewing budget proposals and directing the proper kinds and amounts of resources to strategy-critical organizational units.

A change in strategy nearly always calls for budget reallocations and resource shifting. Previously important units with a lesser role in the new strategy may need downsizing. Units that now have a bigger strategic role may need more people, new equipment, additional facilities, and above-average increases in their operating budgets. Implementing a new strategy requires managers to take an active and sometimes forceful role in shifting resources, not only to amply support activities with a critical role in the new strategy but also to find opportunities to execute the strategy more cost-effectively. This requires putting enough resources behind new strategic initiatives to

> *The funding requirements of good strategy execution must drive how capital allocations are made and the size of each unit's operating budget. Underfunding organizational units and activities pivotal to the strategy impedes successful strategy implementation.*

fuel their success and making the tough decisions to kill projects and activities that are no longer justified. Google's strong support of R&D activities helped it to grow to a $350 billion giant in just 16 years. It was named the world's most innovative company by *Fast Company* magazine in 2014, for innovations such as Google Glass wearable computers, self-driving automobiles, and Shopping Express, an experimental same-day delivery service from stores such as Whole Foods, Target, and Office Depot. In 2013, however, Google decided to kill its 20 percent time policy, which allowed its staff to work on side projects of their choice one day a week. While this program gave rise to many innovations, such as Gmail and AdSense (a big contributor to Google's revenues), it also meant that fewer resources were available to projects that were deemed closer to the core of Google's mission.

> *A company's operating budget must be strategy-driven (in order to amply fund the performance of key value chain activities).*

Visible actions to reallocate operating funds and move people into new organizational units signal a determined commitment to strategic change. Such actions can catalyze the implementation process and give it credibility. Microsoft has made a practice of regularly shifting hundreds of programmers to new high-priority programming initiatives within a matter of weeks or even days. Fast-moving developments in many markets are prompting companies to abandon traditional annual budgeting and resource allocation cycles in favor of resource allocation processes supportive of more rapid adjustments in strategy. In response to rapid technological change in the communications industry, AT&T has prioritized investments and acquisitions that have allowed it to offer its enterprise customers faster, more flexible networks and provide innovative new customer services, such as its Sponsored Data plan.

Merely fine-tuning the execution of a company's existing strategy seldom requires big shifts of resources from one area to another. In contrast, new strategic initiatives generally require not only big shifts in resources but a larger allocation of resources to the effort as well. However, there are times when strategy changes or new execution initiatives need to be made without adding to total company expenses. In such circumstances, managers have to work their way through the existing budget line by line and activity by activity, looking for ways to trim costs and shift resources to activities that are higher-priority in the strategy execution effort. In the event that a company needs to make significant cost cuts during the course of launching new strategic initiatives, managers must be especially creative in finding ways to do more with less. Indeed, it is not unusual for strategy changes and the drive for good strategy execution to be aimed at achieving considerably higher levels of operating efficiency and, at the same time, making sure critical value chain activities are performed as effectively as possible.

# INSTITUTING POLICIES AND PROCEDURES THAT FACILITATE STRATEGY EXECUTION

A company's policies and procedures can either support or hinder good strategy execution. Anytime a company moves to put new strategy elements in place or improve its strategy execution capabilities, some changes in work practices are usually needed. Managers are thus well advised to carefully review existing policies and procedures and to revise or discard those that are out of sync.

As shown in Figure 11.1, well-conceived policies and operating procedures facilitate strategy execution in three ways:

1. *By providing top-down guidance regarding how things need to be done.* Policies and procedures provide company personnel with a set of guidelines for how to perform organizational activities, conduct various aspects of operations, solve problems as they arise, and accomplish particular tasks. In essence, they represent a store of organizational or managerial knowledge about efficient and effective ways of doing things—a set of well-honed *routines* for running the company. They clarify uncertainty about how to proceed in executing strategy and align the actions and behavior of company personnel with the requirements for good strategy execution. Moreover, they place limits on ineffective

> **LO 2**
>
> How well-designed policies and procedures can facilitate good strategy execution.

> A company's policies and procedures provide a set of well-honed *routines* for running the company and executing the strategy.

## FIGURE 11.1   How Policies and Procedures Facilitate Good Strategy Execution

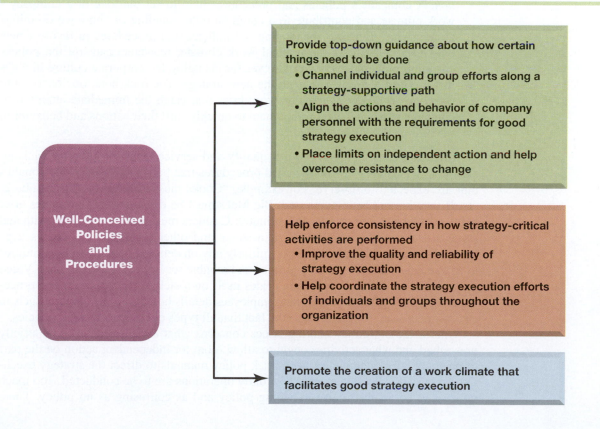

**Well-Conceived Policies and Procedures**

**Provide top-down guidance about how certain things need to be done**
- Channel individual and group efforts along a strategy-supportive path
- Align the actions and behavior of company personnel with the requirements for good strategy execution
- Place limits on independent action and help overcome resistance to change

**Help enforce consistency in how strategy-critical activities are performed**
- Improve the quality and reliability of strategy execution
- Help coordinate the strategy execution efforts of individuals and groups throughout the organization

**Promote the creation of a work climate that facilitates good strategy execution**

independent action. When they are well matched with the requirements of the strategy implementation plan, they channel the efforts of individuals along a path that supports the plan. When existing ways of doing things pose a barrier to strategy execution initiatives, actions and behaviors have to be changed. Under these conditions, the managerial role is to establish and enforce new policies and operating practices that are more conducive to executing the strategy appropriately. Policies are a particularly useful way to counteract tendencies for some people to resist change. People generally refrain from violating company policy or going against recommended practices and procedures without gaining clearance or having strong justification.

2. *By helping ensure consistency in how execution-critical activities are performed.* Policies and procedures serve to standardize the way that activities are performed. This can be important for ensuring the quality and reliability of the strategy execution process. It helps align and coordinate the strategy execution efforts of individuals and groups throughout the organization—a feature that is particularly beneficial when there are geographically scattered operating units. For example, eliminating significant differences in the operating practices of different plants, sales regions, or customer service centers or in the individual outlets in a chain operation helps a company deliver consistent product quality and service to customers. Good strategy execution nearly always entails an ability to replicate product quality and the caliber of customer service at every location where the company does business—anything less blurs the company's image and lowers customer satisfaction.

3. *By promoting the creation of a work climate that facilitates good strategy execution.* A company's policies and procedures help to set the tone of a company's work climate and contribute to a common understanding of "how we do things around here." Because abandoning old policies and procedures in favor of new ones invariably alters the internal work climate, managers can use the policy-changing process as a powerful lever for changing the corporate culture in ways that produce a stronger fit with the new strategy. The trick here, obviously, is to come up with new policies or procedures that catch the immediate attention of company personnel and prompt them to quickly shift their actions and behavior in the desired direction.

To ensure consistency in product quality and service behavior patterns, McDonald's policy manual spells out detailed procedures that personnel in each McDonald's unit are expected to observe. For example, "Cooks must turn, never flip, hamburgers. If they haven't been purchased, Big Macs must be discarded in 10 minutes after being cooked and French fries in 7 minutes. Cashiers must make eye contact with and smile at every customer." Retail chain stores and other organizational chains (e.g., hotels, hospitals, child care centers) similarly rely on detailed policies and procedures to ensure consistency in their operations and reliable service to their customers. Video game developer Valve Corporation prides itself on a lack of rigid policies and procedures; its 37-page handbook for new employees details how things get done in such an environment—an ironic tribute to the fact that all types of companies need policies.

One of the big policy-making issues concerns what activities need to be strictly prescribed and what activities ought to allow room for independent action on the part of personnel. Few companies need thick policy manuals to direct the strategy execution process or prescribe exactly how daily operations are to be conducted. Too much policy can be as obstructive as wrong policy and as confusing as no policy. There is wisdom in a middle approach: *Prescribe enough policies to give organization members clear direction and to place reasonable boundaries on their actions; then empower them to act within these boundaries in pursuit of company goals.* Allowing company personnel to act with some degree of freedom is especially appropriate when individual creativity and initiative are more essential to good strategy execution than are standardization and strict conformity. Instituting policies that facilitate strategy execution can therefore mean policies that require things be done according to a precisely defined standard or policies that give employees substantial leeway to do activities the way they think best.

> There is wisdom in a middle-ground approach: Prescribe enough policies to give organization members clear direction and to place reasonable boundaries on their actions; then empower them to act within these boundaries in pursuit of company goals.

## ADOPTING BEST PRACTICES AND EMPLOYING PROCESS MANAGEMENT TOOLS

Company managers can significantly advance the cause of competent strategy execution by adopting best practices and using process management tools to drive continuous improvement in how internal operations are conducted. One of the most widely used methods for gauging how well a company is executing its strategy entails benchmarking the company's performance of particular activities and business processes against "best-in-industry" and "best-in-world" performers.[1] It can also be useful to look at "best-in-company" performers of an activity if a company has a number of different organizational units performing much the same function at different locations. Identifying, analyzing, and understanding how top-performing companies or organizational units conduct particular value chain activities and business processes provide useful yardsticks for judging the effectiveness and efficiency of internal operations and setting performance standards for organizational units to meet or beat.

**LO 3**

How best practices and process management tools drive continuous improvement in the performance of value chain activities and promote superior strategy execution.

### How the Process of Identifying and Incorporating Best Practices Works

As discussed in Chapter 4, *benchmarking* is the backbone of the process of identifying, studying, and implementing *best practices*. The role of benchmarking is to look outward to find best practices and then to develop the data for measuring how well a company's own performance of an activity stacks up against the best-practice standard. However, benchmarking is more complicated than simply identifying which companies are the best performers of an activity and then trying to imitate their approaches—especially if these companies are in other industries. Normally, the best practices of other organizations must be *adapted* to fit the specific circumstances of a company's own business, strategy, and operating requirements. Since each organization is unique, the telling part of any best-practice initiative is how well the company puts its own version of the best practice into place and makes it work. Indeed, a best practice remains little more than another company's interesting success story unless company personnel buy into the task of translating what can be learned from other companies into real action and results. The agents of change must be frontline employees who are convinced of the need to abandon the old ways of doing things and switch to a best-practice mindset.

Wide-scale use of best practices across a company's entire value chain promotes operating excellence and good strategy execution.

As shown in Figure 11.2, to the extent that a company is able to successfully adapt a best practice pioneered elsewhere to fit its circumstances, it is likely to improve its performance of the activity, perhaps dramatically—an outcome that promotes better strategy execution. It follows that a company can make giant strides toward excellent strategy execution by adopting a best-practice mindset and successfully *implementing the use of best practices across more of its value chain activities.* The more that organizational units use best practices in performing their work, the closer a company moves toward performing its value chain activities more effectively and efficiently. This is what operational excellence is all about. Employing best practices to improve internal operations and strategy execution has powerful appeal—legions of companies across the world are now making concerted efforts to employ best practices in performing many value chain activities, and they regularly benchmark their performance of these activities against best-in-industry or best-in-world performers.

## Business Process Reengineering, Total Quality Management, and Six Sigma Quality Programs: Tools for Promoting Operating Excellence

Three other powerful management tools for promoting operating excellence and better strategy execution are business process reengineering, total quality management (TQM) programs, and Six Sigma quality control programs. Each of these merits discussion since many companies around the world use these tools to help execute strategies tied to cost reduction, defect-free manufacture, superior product quality, superior customer service, and total customer satisfaction.

**Business Process Reengineering**    Companies searching for ways to improve their operations have sometimes discovered that the execution of strategy-critical activities is hampered by a disconnected organizational arrangement whereby pieces of an activity are performed in several different functional departments, with no one manager or group being accountable for optimal performance of the entire activity.

**FIGURE 11.2**    From Benchmarking and Best-Practice Implementation to Operational Excellence in Strategy Execution

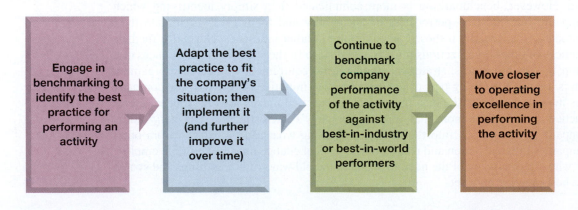

This can easily occur in such inherently cross-functional activities as customer service (which can involve personnel in order filling, warehousing and shipping, invoicing, accounts receivable, after-sale repair, and technical support), particularly for companies with a functional organizational structure.

To address the suboptimal performance problems that can arise from this type of situation, a company can *reengineer the work effort,* pulling the pieces of an activity out of different departments and creating a single department or cross-functional work group to take charge of the whole process. The use of cross-functional teams has been popularized by the practice of **business process reengineering,** which involves radically redesigning and streamlining the workflow (often enabled by cutting-edge use of online technology and information systems), with the goal of achieving quantum gains in performance of the activity.[2]

The reengineering of value chain activities has been undertaken at many companies in many industries all over the world, with excellent results being achieved at some firms.[3] Hallmark reengineered its process for developing new greeting cards, creating teams of mixed-occupation personnel (artists, writers, lithographers, merchandisers, and administrators) to work on a single holiday or greeting card theme. The reengineered process speeded development times for new lines of greeting cards by up to 24 months, was more cost-efficient, and increased customer satisfaction.[4] In the order-processing section of General Electric's circuit breaker division, elapsed time from order receipt to delivery was cut from three weeks to three days by consolidating six production units into one, reducing a variety of former inventory and handling steps, automating the design system to replace a human custom-design process, and cutting the organizational layers between managers and workers from three to one. Productivity rose 20 percent in one year, and unit manufacturing costs dropped 30 percent. Northwest Water, a British utility, used process reengineering to eliminate 45 work depots that served as home bases to crews who installed and repaired water and sewage lines and equipment. Under the reengineered arrangement, crews worked directly from their vehicles, receiving assignments and reporting work completion from computer terminals in their trucks. Crew members became contractors to Northwest Water rather than employees, a move that not only eliminated the need for the work depots but also allowed Northwest Water to eliminate a big percentage of the bureaucratic personnel and supervisory organization that managed the crews.[5]

While business process reengineering has been criticized as an excuse for downsizing, it has nonetheless proved itself a useful tool for streamlining a company's work effort and moving closer to operational excellence. It has also inspired more technologically based approaches to integrating and streamlining business processes, such as *enterprise resource planning,* a software-based system implemented with the help of consulting companies such as SAP (the leading provider of business software).

> **CORE CONCEPT**
>
> **Business process reengineering** involves radically redesigning and streamlining how an activity is performed, with the intent of achieving quantum improvements in performance.

### Total Quality Management Programs

**Total quality management (TQM)** is a comprehensive, structured approach to management that emphasizes continuous improvement in all phases of operations, 100 percent accuracy in performing tasks, involvement and empowerment of employees at all levels, team-based work design, benchmarking, and total customer satisfaction.[6] While TQM concentrates on producing quality goods and fully satisfying customer expectations, it achieves its biggest successes when it is extended to employee efforts in *all departments*—human resources, billing, accounting, and information systems—that may lack pressing, customer-driven incentives to improve. It involves reforming the corporate culture and shifting to a continuous-improvement business

> **CORE CONCEPT**
>
> **Total quality management (TQM)** entails creating a total quality culture, involving managers and employees at all levels, bent on continuously improving the performance of every value chain activity.

philosophy that permeates every facet of the organization.[7] TQM aims at instilling enthusiasm and commitment to doing things right from the top to the bottom of the organization. Management's job is to kindle an organizationwide search for ways to improve that involves all company personnel exercising initiative and using their ingenuity. TQM doctrine preaches that there's no such thing as "good enough" and that everyone has a responsibility to participate in continuous improvement. TQM is thus a race without a finish. Success comes from making little steps forward each day, a process that the Japanese call *kaizen.*

TQM takes a fairly long time to show significant results—very little benefit emerges within the first six months. The long-term payoff of TQM, if it comes, depends heavily on management's success in implanting a culture within which the TQM philosophy and practices can thrive. But it is a management tool that has attracted numerous users and advocates over several decades, and it can deliver good results when used properly.

**CORE CONCEPT**

**Six Sigma programs** utilize advanced statistical methods to improve quality by reducing defects and variability in the performance of business processes.

### Six Sigma Quality Control Programs

**Six Sigma programs** offer another way to drive continuous improvement in quality and strategy execution. This approach entails the use of advanced statistical methods to identify and remove the causes of defects (errors) and undesirable variability in performing an activity or business process. When performance of an activity or process reaches "Six Sigma quality," there are *no more than 3.4 defects per million iterations* (equal to 99.9997 percent accuracy).[8]

There are two important types of Six Sigma programs. The Six Sigma process of define, measure, analyze, improve, and control (DMAIC, pronounced "de-may-ic") is an improvement system for existing processes falling below specification and needing incremental improvement. The Six Sigma process of define, measure, analyze, design, and verify (DMADV, pronounced "de-mad-vee") is used to develop *new* processes or products at Six Sigma quality levels. DMADV is sometimes referred to as Design for Six Sigma, or DFSS. Both Six Sigma programs are overseen by personnel who have completed Six Sigma "master black belt" training, and they are executed by personnel who have earned Six Sigma "green belts" and Six Sigma "black belts." According to the Six Sigma Academy, personnel with black belts can save companies approximately $230,000 per project and can complete four to six projects a year.[9]

The statistical thinking underlying Six Sigma is based on the following three principles: (1) All work is a process, (2) all processes have variability, and (3) all processes create data that explain variability.[10] Six Sigma's DMAIC process is a particularly good vehicle for improving performance when there are *wide variations* in how well an activity is performed. For instance, airlines striving to improve the on-time performance of their flights have more to gain from actions to curtail the number of flights that are late by more than 30 minutes than from actions to reduce the number of flights that are late by less than 5 minutes. Six Sigma quality control programs are of particular interest for large companies, which are better able to shoulder the cost of the large investment required in employee training, organizational infrastructure, and consulting services. For example, to realize a cost savings of $4.4 billion from rolling out its Six Sigma program, GE had to invest $1.6 billion and suffer losses from the program during its first year.[11]

Since the programs were first introduced, thousands of companies and nonprofit organizations around the world have used Six Sigma to promote operating excellence. For companies at the forefront of this movement, such as Motorola, GE, Ford, and Honeywell (Allied Signal), the cost savings as a percentage of revenue varied from

1.2 to 4.5 percent, according to data analysis conducted by iSixSigma (an organization that provides free articles, tools, and resources concerning Six Sigma). More recently, there has been a resurgence of interest in Six Sigma practices, with companies such as Coca-Cola, Ocean Spray, GEICO, and Merrill Lynch turning to Six Sigma as a vehicle to improve their bottom lines. The use of Six Sigma at Bank of America has helped the bank reap about $2 billion in revenue gains and cost savings. The bank holds an annual "Best of Six Sigma Expo" to celebrate the teams that help it succeed.

Six Sigma has also been used to improve processes in health care. A Milwaukee hospital used Six Sigma to improve the accuracy of administering the proper drug doses to patients. DMAIC analysis of the three-stage process by which prescriptions were written by doctors, filled by the hospital pharmacy, and then administered to patients by nurses revealed that most mistakes came from misreading the doctors' handwriting. The hospital implemented a program requiring doctors to enter the prescription on the hospital's computers, which slashed the number of errors dramatically. In recent years, Pfizer embarked on 85 Six Sigma projects to streamline its R&D process and lower the cost of delivering medicines to patients in its pharmaceutical sciences division.

Illustration Capsule 11.1 describes Whirlpool's use of Six Sigma in its appliance business.

Despite its potential benefits, Six Sigma is not without its problems. There is evidence, for example, that Six Sigma techniques can stifle innovation and creativity. The essence of Six Sigma is to reduce variability in processes, but creative processes, by nature, include quite a bit of variability. In many instances, breakthrough innovations occur only after thousands of ideas have been abandoned and promising ideas have gone through multiple iterations and extensive prototyping. Google's chairman, Eric Schmidt, has declared that applying Six Sigma measurement and control principles to creative activities at Google would choke off innovation altogether.[12]

A blended approach to Six Sigma implementation that is gaining in popularity pursues incremental improvements in operating efficiency, while R&D and other processes that allow the company to develop new ways of offering value to customers are given freer rein. Managers of these **ambidextrous organizations** are adept at employing continuous improvement in operating processes but allowing R&D to operate under a set of rules that allows for exploration and the development of breakthrough innovations. However, the two distinctly different approaches to managing employees must be carried out by tightly integrated senior managers to ensure that the separate and diversely oriented units operate with a common purpose. Ciba Vision, a global leader in contact lenses, has dramatically reduced operating expenses through the use of continuous-improvement programs, while simultaneously and harmoniously developing a new series of contact lens products that have allowed its revenues to increase by 300 percent over a 10-year period.[13] An enterprise that systematically and wisely applies Six Sigma methods to its value chain, activity by activity, can make major strides in improving the proficiency with which its strategy is executed without sacrificing innovation. As is the case with TQM, obtaining managerial commitment, establishing a quality culture, and fully involving employees are all of critical importance to the successful implementation of Six Sigma quality programs.[14]

> **Ambidextrous organizations** are adept at employing continuous improvement in operating processes but allowing R&D to operate under a set of rules that allows for exploration and the development of breakthrough innovations.

## The Difference between Business Process Reengineering and Continuous-Improvement Programs like Six Sigma and TQM
Whereas business process reengineering aims at *quantum gains* on the

# Whirlpool's Use of Six Sigma to Promote Operating Excellence

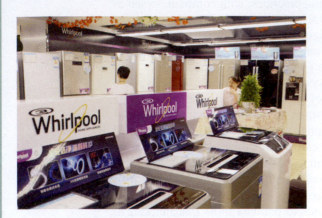

Top management at Whirlpool Corporation (with 59 manufacturing and technology centers around the world and sales in some 170 countries totaling $19 billion in 2013) has a vision of Whirlpool appliances in "Every Home . . . Everywhere with Pride, Passion, and Performance." One of management's chief objectives in pursuing this vision is to build unmatched customer loyalty to the Whirlpool brand. Whirlpool's strategy to win the hearts and minds of appliance buyers the world over has been to produce and market appliances with top-notch quality and innovative features that users will find appealing. In addition, Whirlpool's strategy has been to offer a wide selection of models (recognizing that buyer tastes and needs differ) and to strive for low-cost production efficiency, thereby enabling Whirlpool to price its products very competitively. Executing this strategy at Whirlpool's operations in North America (where it is the market leader), Latin America (where it is also the market leader), Europe (where it ranks third), and Asia (where it is number one in India and has a foothold with huge

growth opportunities elsewhere) has involved a strong focus on continuous improvement, lean manufacturing capabilities, and operating excellence. To marshal the efforts of its 69,000 employees in executing the strategy successfully, management developed a comprehensive Operational Excellence program with Six Sigma as one of the centerpieces.

The Operational Excellence initiative, which began in the 1990s, incorporated Six Sigma techniques to improve the quality of Whirlpool products and, at the same time, lower costs and trim the time it took to get product innovations to the marketplace. The Six Sigma program helped Whirlpool save $175 million in manufacturing costs in its first three years.

To sustain the productivity gains and cost savings, Whirlpool embedded Six Sigma practices within each of its manufacturing facilities worldwide and instilled a culture based on Six Sigma and lean manufacturing skills and capabilities. In 2002, each of Whirlpool's operating units began taking the Six Sigma initiative to a higher level by first placing the needs of the customer at the center of every function—R&D, technology, manufacturing, marketing, and administrative support—and then striving to consistently improve quality levels while eliminating all unnecessary costs. The company systematically went through every aspect of its business with the view that company personnel should perform every activity at every level in a manner that delivers value to the customer and leads to continuous improvement on how things are done.

Whirlpool management believes that the company's Operational Excellence process has been a major contributor in sustaining the company's position as the leading global manufacturer and marketer of home appliances.

*Sources:* **www.whirlpool.com** and LexisNexis-Edgar Online (accessed April 3, 2014).

---

**Business process reengineering aims at one-time quantum improvement, while continuous-improvement programs like TQM and Six Sigma aim at ongoing incremental improvements.**

order of 30 to 50 percent or more, total quality programs like TQM and Six Sigma stress *ongoing incremental progress,* striving for inch-by-inch gains again and again in a never-ending stream. The two approaches to improved performance of value chain activities and operating excellence are not mutually exclusive; it makes sense to use them in tandem. Reengineering can be used first to produce a good basic design that yields quick, dramatic improvements in performing a business process. Total quality or Six Sigma programs can then be used as a follow-on to reengineering and best-practice implementation to deliver continuing improvements over a longer period of time.

# Capturing the Benefits of Initiatives to Improve Operations

The biggest beneficiaries of benchmarking and best-practice initiatives, reengineering, TQM, and Six Sigma are companies that view such programs not as ends in themselves but as tools for implementing company strategy more effectively. The least rewarding payoffs occur when company managers seize on the programs as novel ideas that might be worth a try. In most such instances, they result in strategy-blind efforts to simply manage better.

There's an important lesson here. Business process management tools all need to be linked to a company's strategic priorities to contribute effectively to improving the strategy's execution. Only strategy can point to which value chain activities matter and what performance targets make the most sense. Without a strategic framework, managers lack the context in which to fix things that really matter to business unit performance and competitive success.

To get the most from initiatives to execute strategy more proficiently, managers must have a clear idea of what specific outcomes really matter. Is it high on-time delivery, lower overall costs, fewer customer complaints, shorter cycle times, a higher percentage of revenues coming from recently introduced products, or something else? Benchmarking best-in-industry and best-in-world performance of targeted value chain activities provides a realistic basis for setting internal performance milestones and longer-range targets. Once initiatives to improve operations are linked to the company's strategic priorities, then comes the managerial task of building a total quality culture that is genuinely committed to achieving the performance outcomes that strategic success requires.[15]

Managers can take the following action steps to realize full value from TQM or Six Sigma initiatives and promote a culture of operating excellence:[16]

1. Demonstrating visible, unequivocal, and unyielding commitment to total quality and continuous improvement, including specifying measurable objectives for increasing quality and making continual progress.

2. Nudging people toward quality-supportive behaviors by:

   a. Screening job applicants rigorously and hiring only those with attitudes and aptitudes that are right for quality-based performance.

   b. Providing quality training for employees.

   c. Using teams and team-building exercises to reinforce and nurture individual effort. (The creation of a quality culture is facilitated when teams become more cross-functional, multitask-oriented, and increasingly self-managed.)

   d. Recognizing and rewarding individual and team efforts to improve quality regularly and systematically.

   e. Stressing prevention (doing it right the first time), not correction (instituting ways to undo or overcome mistakes).

3. Empowering employees so that authority for delivering great service or improving products is in the hands of the doers rather than the overseers—*improving quality has to be seen as part of everyone's job.*

4. Using online systems to provide all relevant parties with the latest best practices, thereby speeding the diffusion and adoption of best practices throughout the organization. Online systems can also allow company personnel to exchange data and opinions about how to upgrade the prevailing best-in-company practices.

5. Emphasizing that performance can and must be improved, because competitors are not resting on their laurels and customers are always looking for something better.

In sum, benchmarking, the adoption of best practices, business process reengineering, TQM, and Six Sigma techniques all need to be seen and used as part of a bigger-picture effort to execute strategy proficiently. Used properly, all of these tools are capable of improving the proficiency with which an organization performs its value chain activities. Not only do improvements from such initiatives add up over time and strengthen organizational capabilities, but they also help build a culture of operating excellence. All this lays the groundwork for gaining a competitive advantage.[17] While it is relatively easy for rivals to also implement process management tools, it is much more difficult and time-consuming for them to instill a deeply ingrained culture of operating excellence (as occurs when such techniques are religiously employed and top management exhibits lasting commitment to operational excellence throughout the organization).

# INSTALLING INFORMATION AND OPERATING SYSTEMS

Company strategies can't be executed well without a number of internal systems for business operations. Qantas Airways, JetBlue, Ryanair, British Airways, and other successful airlines cannot hope to provide passenger-pleasing service without a user-friendly online reservation system, an accurate and speedy baggage-handling system, and a strict aircraft maintenance program that minimizes problems requiring at-the-gate service that delay departures. FedEx has internal communication systems that allow it to coordinate its over 90,000 vehicles in handling a daily average of 10 million shipments to 220 countries. Its leading-edge flight operations systems allow a single controller to direct as many as 200 of FedEx's aircraft simultaneously, overriding their flight plans should weather problems or other special circumstances arise. In addition, FedEx has created a series of e-business tools for customers that allow them to ship and track packages online, create address books, review shipping history, generate custom reports, simplify customer billing, reduce internal warehousing and inventory management costs, purchase goods and services from suppliers, and respond to their own quickly changing customer demands. All of FedEx's systems support the company's strategy of providing businesses and individuals with a broad array of package delivery services and enhancing its competitiveness against United Parcel Service, DHL, and the U.S. Postal Service.

Amazon.com ships customer orders of books, CDs, and myriad other items from a global network of some 94 warehouses (in 2014). The warehouses are so technologically sophisticated that they require about as many lines of code to run as Amazon's website does. Using complex picking algorithms, computers initiate the order-picking process by sending signals to workers' wireless receivers, telling them which items to pick off the shelves in which order. Computers also generate data on mix-boxed items, chute backup times, line speed, worker productivity, and shipping weights on orders. Systems are upgraded regularly, and productivity improvements are aggressively pursued. Amazon's warehouse efficiency and cost per order filled are so low that one of the fastest-growing and most profitable parts of Amazon's business is using its warehouses to run the e-commerce operations of large retail chains such as Target.

Otis Elevator, the world's largest manufacturer of elevators, with more than 2.5 million elevators and escalators installed worldwide, has a 24/7 remote electronic monitoring system that can detect when an elevator or escalator installed on a customer's site has any of 325 problems.[18] If the monitoring system detects a problem, it analyzes and diagnoses the cause and location, then makes the service call to an Otis mechanic at the nearest location, and helps the mechanic (who is equipped with a web-enabled cell phone) identify the component causing the problem. The company's maintenance system helps keep outage times under three hours. All trouble-call data are relayed to design and manufacturing personnel, allowing them to quickly alter design specifications or manufacturing procedures when needed to correct recurring problems. All customers have online access to performance data on each of their Otis elevators and escalators.

Well-conceived state-of-the-art operating systems not only enable better strategy execution but also strengthen organizational capabilities—enough at times to provide a competitive edge over rivals. For example, a company with a differentiation strategy based on superior quality has added capability if it has systems for training personnel in quality techniques, tracking product quality at each production step, and ensuring that all goods shipped meet quality standards. If the systems it employs are advanced systems that have not yet been adopted by rivals, the systems may provide the company with a competitive advantage as long as the costs of deploying the systems do not outweigh their benefits. Similarly, a company striving to be a low-cost provider is competitively stronger if it has an unrivaled benchmarking system that identifies opportunities to implement best practices and drive costs out of the business faster than others can. Fast-growing companies get an important assist from having capabilities in place to recruit and train new employees in large numbers and from investing in infrastructure that gives them the capability to handle rapid growth as it occurs, rather than having to scramble to catch up to customer demand.

## Instituting Adequate Information Systems, Performance Tracking, and Controls

Accurate and timely information about daily operations is essential if managers are to gauge how well the strategy execution process is proceeding. Companies everywhere are capitalizing on today's technology to install real-time data-generating capability. Most retail companies now have automated online systems that generate daily sales reports for each store and maintain up-to-the-minute inventory and sales records on each item. Manufacturing plants typically generate daily production reports and track labor productivity on every shift. Transportation companies have elaborate information systems to provide real-time arrival information for buses and trains that is automatically sent to digital message signs and platform audio address systems.

Siemens Healthcare, one of the largest suppliers to the health care industry, uses a cloud-based business activity monitoring (BAM) system to continuously monitor and improve the company's processes across more than 125 countries. Customer satisfaction is one of Siemens's most important business objectives, so the reliability of its order management and services is crucial. Prezi is a presentation software company that uses the business intelligence platform GoodData to access companywide data in a quick, meaningful way. Data dashboards are constantly being updated so that Prezi teams can see how product development and sales strategies are working in real time. Companies that rely on customer-contact personnel to act promptly and creatively in pleasing customers have installed online information systems that make essential customer data accessible to such personnel through a few keystrokes; this enables them to respond more effectively to customer inquiries and to deliver personalized customer service.

Information systems need to cover five broad areas: (1) customer data, (2) operations data, (3) employee data, (4) supplier and/or strategic partner data, and (5) financial performance data. All key strategic performance indicators must be tracked and reported in real time whenever possible. Real-time information systems permit company managers to stay on top of implementation initiatives and daily operations and to intervene if things seem to be drifting off course. Tracking key performance indicators, gathering information from operating personnel, quickly identifying and diagnosing problems, and taking corrective actions are all integral pieces of the process of managing strategy execution and overseeing operations.

*Having state-of-the-art operating systems, information systems, and real-time data is integral to superior strategy execution and operating excellence.*

Statistical information gives managers a feel for the numbers, briefings and meetings provide a feel for the latest developments and emerging issues, and personal contacts add a feel for the people dimension. All are good barometers of how well things are going and what operating aspects need management attention. Managers must identify problem areas and deviations from plans before they can take action to get the organization back on course, by either improving the approaches to strategy execution or fine-tuning the strategy. Jeff Bezos, Amazon.com's CEO, is an ardent proponent of managing by the numbers. As he puts it, "Math-based decisions always trump opinion and judgment. The trouble with most corporations is that they make judgment-based decisions when data-based decisions could be made."[19]

**Monitoring Employee Performance**   Information systems also provide managers with a means for monitoring the performance of empowered workers to see that they are acting within the specified limits.[20] Leaving empowered employees to their own devices in meeting performance standards without appropriate checks and balances can expose an organization to excessive risk.[21] Instances abound of employees' decisions or behavior going awry, sometimes costing a company huge sums or producing lawsuits and reputation-damaging publicity.

Scrutinizing daily and weekly operating statistics is one of the ways in which managers can monitor the results that flow from the actions of subordinates without resorting to constant over-the-shoulder supervision; if the operating results look good, then it is reasonable to assume that empowerment is working. But close monitoring of operating performance is only one of the control tools at management's disposal. Another valuable lever of control in companies that rely on empowered employees, especially in those that use self-managed work groups or other such teams, is peer-based control. Because peer evaluation is such a powerful control device, companies organized into teams can remove some layers of the management hierarchy and rely on strong peer pressure to keep team members operating between the white lines. This is especially true when a company has the information systems capability to monitor team performance daily or in real time.

# USING REWARDS AND INCENTIVES TO PROMOTE BETTER STRATEGY EXECUTION

It is essential that company personnel be enthusiastically committed to executing strategy successfully and achieving performance targets. Enlisting such commitment typically requires use of an assortment of motivational techniques and rewards. Indeed, *an effectively designed reward structure is the single most powerful tool management has for mobilizing employee commitment to successful strategy execution.* But incentives and rewards do more than just strengthen the resolve of company personnel to succeed—they also focus employees' attention on the accomplishment of specific strategy execution objectives. Not only do they spur the efforts of individuals to achieve those aims, but they also help to coordinate the activities of individuals throughout the organization by aligning their personal motives with the goals of the organization. In this manner, reward systems serve as an indirect type of control mechanism that conserves on the more costly control mechanism of supervisory oversight.

To win employees' sustained, energetic commitment to the strategy execution process, management must be resourceful in designing and using motivational incentives—both monetary and nonmonetary. The more a manager understands what motivates subordinates and the more he or she relies on motivational incentives as a tool for achieving the targeted strategic and financial results, the greater will be employees' commitment to good day-in, day-out strategy execution and the achievement of performance targets.[22]

**LO 5**

How and why the use of well-designed incentives and rewards can be management's single most powerful tool for promoting adept strategy execution.

## Incentives and Motivational Practices That Facilitate Good Strategy Execution

Financial incentives generally head the list of motivating tools for gaining wholehearted employee commitment to good strategy execution and focusing attention on strategic priorities. Generous financial rewards always catch employees' attention and produce *high-powered incentives* for individuals to exert their best efforts. A company's package of monetary rewards typically includes some combination of base-pay increases, performance bonuses, profit-sharing plans, stock awards, company contributions to employee 401(k) or retirement plans, and piecework incentives (in the case of production workers). But most successful companies and managers also make extensive use of nonmonetary incentives. Some of the most important nonmonetary approaches companies can use to enhance employee motivation include the following:[23]

- *Providing attractive perks and fringe benefits.* The various options include coverage of health insurance premiums, wellness programs, college tuition reimbursement, generous paid vacation time, onsite child care, onsite fitness centers and massage services, opportunities for getaways at company-owned recreational facilities, personal concierge services, subsidized cafeterias and free lunches, casual dress every day, personal travel services, paid sabbaticals, maternity and paternity leaves, paid leaves to care for ill family members, telecommuting, compressed workweeks (four 10-hour days instead of five 8-hour days), flextime (variable work schedules that accommodate individual needs), college scholarships for children, and relocation services.

- *Giving awards and public recognition to high performers and showcasing company successes.* Many companies hold award ceremonies to honor top-performing individuals, teams, and organizational units and to celebrate important company milestones and achievements. Others make a special point of recognizing the outstanding accomplishments of individuals, teams, and organizational units at informal company gatherings or in the company newsletter. Such actions foster a positive *esprit de corps* within the organization and may also act to spur healthy competition among units and teams within the company.

- *Relying on promotion from within whenever possible.* This practice helps bind workers to their employer, and employers to their workers. Moreover, it provides strong incentives for good performance. Promoting from within also helps ensure that people in positions of responsibility have knowledge specific to the business, technology, and operations they are managing.

A properly designed reward structure is management's single most powerful tool for mobilizing employee commitment to successful strategy execution and aligning efforts throughout the organization with strategic priorities.

**CORE CONCEPT**

Financial rewards provide **high-powered incentives** when rewards are tied to specific outcome objectives.

- *Inviting and acting on ideas and suggestions from employees.* Many companies find that their best ideas for nuts-and-bolts operating improvements come from the suggestions of employees. Moreover, research indicates that giving decision-making power to down-the-line employees increases their motivation and satisfaction as well as their productivity. The use of self-managed teams has much the same effect.

- *Creating a work atmosphere in which there is genuine caring and mutual respect among workers and between management and employees.* A "family" work environment where people are on a first-name basis and there is strong camaraderie promotes teamwork and cross-unit collaboration.

- *Stating the strategic vision in inspirational terms that make employees feel they are a part of something worthwhile in a larger social sense.* There's strong motivating power associated with giving people a chance to be part of something exciting and personally satisfying. Jobs with a noble purpose tend to inspire employees to give their all. As described in Chapter 9, this not only increases productivity but reduces turnover and lowers costs for staff recruitment and training as well.

- *Sharing information with employees about financial performance, strategy, operational measures, market conditions, and competitors' actions.* Broad disclosure and prompt communication send the message that managers trust their workers and regard them as valued partners in the enterprise. Keeping employees in the dark denies them information useful to performing their jobs, prevents them from being intellectually engaged, saps their motivation, and detracts from performance.

- *Providing a comfortable and attractive working environment.* An appealing workplace environment can have decidedly positive effects on employee morale and productivity. Providing a comfortable work environment, designed with ergonomics in mind, is particularly important when workers are expected to spend long hours at work.

For specific examples of the motivational tactics employed by several prominent companies (many of which appear on *Fortune*'s list of the 100 best companies to work for in America), see Illustration Capsule 11.2.

## Striking the Right Balance between Rewards and Punishment

While most approaches to motivation, compensation, and people management accentuate the positive, companies also make it clear that lackadaisical or indifferent effort and subpar performance can result in negative consequences. At General Electric, McKinsey & Company, several global public accounting firms, and other companies that look for and expect top-notch individual performance, there's an "up-or-out" policy—managers and professionals whose performance is not good enough to warrant promotion are first denied bonuses and stock awards and eventually weeded out. At most companies, senior executives and key personnel in underperforming units are pressured to raise performance to acceptable levels and keep it there or risk being replaced.

As a general rule, it is unwise to take off the pressure for good performance or play down the adverse consequences of shortfalls in performance. There is scant evidence that a no-pressure, no-adverse-consequences work environment leads to superior strategy execution or operating excellence. As the CEO of a major bank put it, "There's a deliberate policy here to create a level of anxiety. Winners usually play like

# How the Best Companies to Work for Motivate and Reward Employees

Companies design a variety of motivational and reward practices to create a work environment that energizes employees and promotes better strategy execution. Other benefits of a successful recognition system include high job satisfaction, high retention rates, and increased output. Here's a sampling of what some of the best companies to work for in America are doing to motivate their employees:

- Software developer SAS prioritizes work-life balance and mental health for its workforce of 7,000. The onsite health center it hosts for families of all employees maintains a staff of 53 medical and support personnel, including nurses, registered dietitians, lab technicians, and clinical psychologists. The sprawling headquarters also has a Frisbee golf course, indoor swimming pool, and walking and biking trails decorated with sculptures from the company's 4,000-item art collection. With such an environment, it should come as no surprise that 95 percent of employees report looking forward to heading to the office every day.

- Salesforce.com Inc., a global cloud-computing company based in San Francisco, has been listed by *Forbes* magazine as the most innovative company in America. Doubling its workforce from 5,000 to 10,000 in the past two years, Salesforce.com incentivizes new hires to work cooperatively with existing teams. The company's recognition programs include rewards for achievement both in the office and in the larger community. For example, in 2013, top sellers were awarded two-week trips to Bhutan for their dedication and results.

- DPR Construction is one of the nation's top-50 general contractors, serving clients like Facebook, Pixar, and Genentech. The company fosters teamwork and

equality across levels with features like open-office floor plans, business cards with no titles, and a bonus plan for employees. DPR also prioritizes safety for its employees. In 1999, a craftsperson who reached 30,000 consecutive safe work hours was rewarded with a new Ford F-150 truck. Management created a new safety award in his name that includes a plaque, a $2,000 trip, a 40-hour week off with pay, and a safety jacket with hours printed on it. In 2013, thirteen craftspeople received this generous award for their dedication to safety.

- Hilcorp, an oil and gas exploration company, made headlines in 2011 for its shocking generosity. After reaching its five-year goal to double in size, the company gave every employee a $50,000 dream car voucher (or $35,000 in cash). Building on this success, later that year Hilcorp announced an incentive program called Dream 2015. This plan promises to award every person in the company $100,000 in 2015 if certain goals are met.

*Note:* Developed with Meghan L. Cooney.

*Sources:* "100 Best Companies to Work For, 2014," *Fortune,* **money.cnn.com/magazines/fortune/best-companies/** (accessed February 15, 2014); and company profiles, *GreatRated!* **us.greatrated.com/sas** (accessed February 24, 2014).

they're one touchdown behind."[24] A number of companies deliberately give employees heavy workloads and tight deadlines to test their mettle—personnel are pushed hard to achieve "stretch" objectives and are expected to put in long hours (nights and weekends if need be). High-performing organizations nearly always have a cadre of ambitious people who relish the opportunity to climb the ladder of success, love a challenge, thrive in a performance-oriented environment, and find some competition and pressure useful to satisfy their own drives for personal recognition, accomplishment, and self-satisfaction.

However, if an organization's motivational approaches and reward structure induce too much stress, internal competitiveness, job insecurity, and fear of unpleasant consequences, the impact on workforce morale and strategy execution can be counterproductive. Evidence shows that managerial initiatives to improve strategy execution should incorporate more positive than negative motivational elements because when cooperation is positively enlisted and rewarded, rather than coerced by orders and threats (implicit or explicit), people tend to respond with more enthusiasm, dedication, creativity, and initiative.[25]

## Linking Rewards to Achieving the Right Outcomes

To create a strategy-supportive system of rewards and incentives, a company must reward people for accomplishing results, not for just dutifully performing assigned tasks. Showing up for work and performing assignments do not, by themselves, guarantee results. To make the work environment results-oriented, managers need to focus jobholders' attention and energy on what to *achieve* as opposed to what to *do*.[26] Employee productivity among employees at Best Buy's corporate headquarters rose by 35 percent after the company began to focus on the results of each employee's work rather than on employees' willingness to come to work early and stay late.

> Incentives must be based on accomplishing the right results, not on dutifully performing assigned tasks.

Ideally, every organizational unit, every manager, every team or work group, and perhaps every employee should be held accountable for achieving outcomes that contribute to good strategy execution and business performance. If the company's strategy is to be a low-cost provider, the incentive system must reward actions and achievements that result in lower costs. If the company has a differentiation strategy focused on delivering superior quality and service, the incentive system must reward such outcomes as Six Sigma defect rates, infrequent customer complaints, speedy order processing and delivery, and high levels of customer satisfaction. If a company's growth is predicated on a strategy of new product innovation, incentives should be tied to such factors as the percentages of revenues and profits coming from newly introduced products.

> The key to creating a reward system that promotes good strategy execution is to make measures of good business performance and good strategy execution the *dominating basis* for designing incentives, evaluating individual and group efforts, and handing out rewards.

Incentive compensation for top executives is typically tied to such financial measures as revenue and earnings growth, stock price performance, return on investment, and creditworthiness or to strategic measures such as market share growth. However, incentives for department heads, teams, and individual workers may be tied to performance outcomes more closely related to their strategic area of responsibility. In manufacturing, incentive compensation may be tied to unit manufacturing costs, on-time production and shipping, defect rates, the number and extent of work stoppages due to equipment breakdowns, and so on. In sales and marketing, there may be incentives for achieving dollar sales or unit volume targets, market share, sales penetration of each target customer group, the fate of newly introduced products, the frequency of customer complaints, the number of new accounts acquired, and customer satisfaction. Which performance measures to base incentive compensation on depends on the situation—the priority placed on various financial and strategic objectives, the requirements for strategic and competitive success, and the specific results needed to keep strategy execution on track.

Illustration Capsule 11.3 provides a vivid example of how one company has designed incentives linked directly to outcomes reflecting good execution.

# Nucor Corporation: Tying Incentives Directly to Strategy Execution

The strategy at Nucor Corporation, one of the three largest steel producers in the United States, is to be *the* low-cost producer of steel products. Because labor costs are a significant fraction of total cost in the steel business, successful implementation of Nucor's low-cost leadership strategy entails achieving lower labor costs per ton of steel than competitors' costs. Nucor management uses an incentive system to promote high worker productivity and drive labor costs per ton below those of rivals. Each plant's workforce is organized into production teams (each assigned to perform particular functions), and weekly production targets are established for each team. Base-pay scales are set at levels comparable to wages for similar manufacturing jobs in the local areas where Nucor has plants, but workers can earn a 1 percent bonus for each 1 percent that their output exceeds target levels. If a production team exceeds its weekly production target by 10 percent, team members receive a 10 percent bonus in their next paycheck; if a team exceeds its quota by 20 percent, team members earn a 20 percent bonus. Bonuses, paid every two weeks, are based on the prior two weeks' actual production levels measured against the targets.

Nucor's piece-rate incentive plan has produced impressive results. The production teams put forth exceptional effort; it is not uncommon for most teams to beat their weekly production targets by 20 to 50 percent. When added to employees' base pay, the bonuses earned by Nucor workers make Nucor's workforce among the highest-paid in the U.S. steel industry. From a management perspective, the incentive system has resulted in Nucor having labor productivity levels 10 to 20 percent above the average of the unionized workforces at several

of its largest rivals, which in turn has given Nucor a significant labor cost advantage over most rivals.

After years of record-setting profits, Nucor struggled in the economic downturn of 2008–2010, along with the manufacturers and builders who buy its steel. But while bonuses have dwindled, Nucor showed remarkable loyalty to its production workers, avoiding layoffs by having employees get ahead on maintenance, perform work formerly done by contractors, and search for cost savings. Morale at the company remained high, and Nucor's CEO at the time, Daniel DiMicco, was inducted into *IndustryWeek* magazine's Manufacturing Hall of Fame because of his no-layoff policies. As industry growth has resumed, Nucor has retained a well-trained workforce, more committed than ever to achieving the kind of productivity for which Nucor is justifiably famous. DiMicco had good reason to expect Nucor to be "first out of the box" following the crisis, and although he has since stepped aside, the company's culture of making its employees think like owners has not changed.

*Sources:* Company website (accessed March 2012); N. Byrnes, "Pain, but No Layoffs at Nucor," *Bloomberg Businessweek,* March 26, 2009; and J. McGregor, "Nucor's CEO Is Stepping Aside, but Its Culture Likely Won't," *The Washington Post* Online, November 20, 2012 (accessed April 3, 2014).

## Additional Guidelines for Designing Incentive Compensation Systems

The first principle in designing an effective incentive compensation system is to tie rewards to performance outcomes directly linked to good strategy execution and targeted strategic and financial objectives, as explained earlier. But for a company's reward system to truly motivate organization members, inspire their best efforts, and sustain high levels of productivity, it is equally important to observe the following additional guidelines in designing and administering the reward system:

- *Make the performance payoff a major, not minor, piece of the total compensation package.* Performance bonuses must be at least 10 to 12 percent of base salary

> The first principle in designing an effective incentive compensation system is to tie rewards to performance outcomes directly linked to good strategy execution and the achievement of financial and strategic objectives.

to have much impact. Incentives that amount to 20 percent or more of total compensation are big attention-getters, likely to really drive individual or team efforts. Incentives amounting to less than 5 percent of total compensation have a comparatively weak motivational impact. Moreover, the payoff for high-performing individuals and teams must be meaningfully greater than the payoff for average performers, and the payoff for average performers meaningfully bigger than that for below-average performers.

- *Have incentives that extend to all managers and all workers, not just top management.* It is a gross miscalculation to expect that lower-level managers and employees will work their hardest to hit performance targets just so a few senior executives can get lucrative rewards.

- *Administer the reward system with scrupulous objectivity and fairness.* If performance standards are set unrealistically high or if individual and group performance evaluations are not accurate and well documented, dissatisfaction with the system will overcome any positive benefits.

- *Ensure that the performance targets set for each individual or team involve outcomes that the individual or team can personally affect.* The role of incentives is to enhance individual commitment and channel behavior in beneficial directions. This role is not well served when the performance measures by which company personnel are judged are outside their arena of influence.

- *Keep the time between achieving the performance target and receiving the reward as short as possible.* To combat problems with late-arriving flights, Continental pays employees a cash bonus each month whenever actual on-time flight performance meets or beats the monthly on-time target. Annual bonus payouts work best for higher-level managers and for situations where the outcome target relates to overall company profitability.

- *Avoid rewarding effort rather than results.* While it is tempting to reward people who have tried hard, gone the extra mile, and yet fallen short of achieving performance targets because of circumstances beyond their control, it is ill advised to do so. The problem with making exceptions for unknowable, uncontrollable, or unforeseeable circumstances is that once "good excuses" start to creep into justifying rewards for subpar results, the door opens to all kinds of reasons why actual performance has failed to match targeted performance. A "no excuses" standard is more evenhanded, easier to administer, and more conducive to creating a results-oriented work climate.

The unwavering standard for judging whether individuals, teams, and organizational units have done a good job must be whether they meet or beat performance targets that reflect good strategy execution.

For an organization's incentive system to work well, the details of the reward structure must be communicated and explained. Everybody needs to understand how his or her incentive compensation is calculated and how individual and group performance targets contribute to organizational performance targets. The pressure to achieve the targeted financial and strategic performance objectives and continuously improve on strategy execution should be unrelenting. People at all levels must be held accountable for carrying out their assigned parts of the strategic plan, and they must understand that their rewards are based on the caliber of results achieved. But with the pressure to perform should come meaningful rewards. Without an attractive payoff, the system breaks down, and managers are left with the less workable options of issuing orders, trying to enforce compliance, and depending on the goodwill of employees.

# KEY POINTS

1. Implementing a new or different strategy calls for managers to identify the resource requirements of each new strategic initiative and then consider whether the current pattern of resource allocation and the budgets of the various subunits are suitable.

2. Company policies and procedures facilitate strategy execution when they are designed to fit the strategy and its objectives. Anytime a company alters its strategy, managers should review existing policies and operating procedures and replace those that are out of sync. Well-conceived policies and procedures aid the task of strategy execution by (1) providing top-down guidance to company personnel regarding how things need to be done and what the limits are on independent actions, (2) enforcing consistency in the performance of strategy-critical activities, thereby improving the quality of the strategy execution effort and coordinating the efforts of company personnel, however widely dispersed, and (3) promoting the creation of a work climate conducive to good strategy execution.

3. Competent strategy execution entails visible unyielding managerial commitment to best practices and continuous improvement. Benchmarking, best-practice adoption, business process reengineering, total quality management (TQM), and Six Sigma programs are important process management tools for promoting better strategy execution.

4. Company strategies can't be implemented or executed well without a number of support systems to carry on business operations. Real-time information systems and control systems further aid the cause of good strategy execution.

5. Strategy-supportive motivational practices and reward systems are powerful management tools for gaining employee commitment and focusing their attention on the strategy execution goals. The key to creating a reward system that promotes good strategy execution is to make measures of good business performance and good strategy execution the *dominating basis* for designing incentives, evaluating individual and group efforts, and handing out rewards. Positive motivational practices generally work better than negative ones, but there is a place for both. While financial rewards provide high-powered incentives, nonmonetary incentives are also important. For an incentive compensation system to work well, (1) the performance payoff should be a major percentage of the compensation package, (2) the use of incentives should extend to all managers and workers, (3) the system should be administered with objectivity and fairness, (4) each individual's performance targets should involve outcomes the person can personally affect, (5) rewards should promptly follow the achievement of performance targets, and (6) rewards should be given for results and not just effort.

# ASSURANCE OF LEARNING EXERCISES

**LO 1**  **1.** Implementing a new or different strategy calls for new resource allocations. Using your university's access to LexisNexis or EBSCO, search for recent articles that discuss how a company has revised its pattern of resource allocation and divisional budgets to support new strategic initiatives.

**LO 2**  **2.** Policies and procedures facilitate strategy execution when they are designed to fit the company's strategy and objectives. Using your university's access to LexisNexis or EBSCO, search for recent articles that discuss how a company has revised its policies and procedures to provide better top-down guidance to company personnel on how to conduct their daily activities and responsibilities.

**LO 3**  **3.** Illustration Capsule 11.1 discusses Whirlpool Corporation's Operational Excellence initiative and its use of Six Sigma practices. How did the implementation of the program change the culture and mindset of the company's personnel? List three tangible benefits provided by the program. Explain why a commitment to quality control is important in the appliance industry?

**LO 3**  **4.** Read some of the recent Six Sigma articles posted at **www.isixsigma.com**. Prepare a one-page report to your instructor detailing how Six Sigma is being used in two companies and what benefits the companies are reaping as a result. Further, discuss two to three criticisms of, or potential difficulties with, Six Sigma implementation.

**LO 4**  **5.** Company strategies can't be executed well without a number of support systems to carry on business operations. Using your university's access to LexisNexis or EBSCO, search for recent articles that discuss how a company has used real-time information systems and control systems to aid the cause of good strategy execution.

**LO 5**  **6.** Illustration Capsule 11.2 provides a sampling of motivational tactics employed by several prominent companies (many of which appear on *Fortune*'s list of the 100 best companies to work for in America). Discuss how rewards at SAS, Salesforce.com, DPR Construction, and Hilcorp aid in the strategy execution efforts of each company.

# EXERCISE FOR SIMULATION PARTICIPANTS

**LO 1**  **1.** Have you and your co-managers allocated ample resources to strategy-critical areas? If so, explain how these investments have contributed to good strategy execution and improved company performance.

**LO 2, LO 3, LO 4**  **2.** What actions, if any, is your company taking to pursue continuous improvement in how it performs certain value chain activities?

**LO 3**  **3.** Is benchmarking data available in the simulation exercise in which you are participating? If so, do you and your co-managers regularly study the benchmarking data to see how well your company is doing? Do you consider the benchmarking information provided to be valuable? Why or why not? Cite three recent instances in which your examination of the benchmarking statistics has caused you and your co-managers to take corrective actions to boost company performance.

4. What hard evidence can you cite that indicates your company's management team is doing a *better* or *worse* job of achieving operating excellence and executing strategy than are the management teams at rival companies?

**LO 3**

5. Are you and your co-managers consciously trying to achieve operating excellence? Explain how you are doing this and how you will track the progress you are making.

**LO 2, LO 3, LO 4**

6. Does your company have opportunities to use incentive compensation techniques? If so, explain your company's approach to incentive compensation. Is there any hard evidence you can cite that indicates your company's use of incentive compensation techniques has worked? For example, have your company's compensation incentives actually increased productivity? Can you cite evidence indicating that the productivity gains have resulted in lower labor costs? If the productivity gains have *not* translated into lower labor costs, is it fair to say that your company's use of incentive compensation is a failure?

**LO 5**

## ENDNOTES

[1] Christopher E. Bogan and Michael J. English, *Benchmarking for Best Practices: Winning through Innovative Adaptation* (New York: McGraw-Hill, 1994); Mustafa Ungan, "Factors Affecting the Adoption of Manufacturing Best Practices," *Benchmarking: An International Journal* 11, no. 5 (2004), pp. 504–520; Paul Hyland and Ron Beckett, "Learning to Compete: The Value of Internal Benchmarking," *Benchmarking: An International Journal* 9, no. 3 (2002), pp. 293–304; Yoshinobu Ohinata, "Benchmarking: The Japanese Experience," *Long-Range Planning* 27, no. 4 (August 1994), pp. 48–53.

[2] M. Hammer and J. Champy, *Reengineering the Corporation: A Manifesto for Business Revolution* (New York: HarperCollins, 1993).

[3] James Brian Quinn, *Intelligent Enterprise* (New York: Free Press, 1992); Ann Majchrzak and Qianwei Wang, "Breaking the Functional Mind-Set in Process Organizations," *Harvard Business Review* 74, no. 5 (September–October 1996), pp. 93–99; Stephen L. Walston, Lawton R. Burns, and John R. Kimberly, "Does Reengineering Really Work? An Examination of the Context and Outcomes of Hospital Reengineering Initiatives," *Health Services Research* 34, no. 6 (February 2000), pp. 1363–1388; Allessio Ascari, Melinda Rock, and Soumitra Dutta, "Reengineering and Organizational Change: Lessons from a Comparative Analysis of Company Experiences," *European Management Journal* 13, no. 1 (March 1995), pp. 1–13; Ronald J. Burke,

"Process Reengineering: Who Embraces It and Why?" *The TQM Magazine* 16, no. 2 (2004), pp. 114–119.

[4] www.answers.com (accessed July 8, 2009); "Reengineering: Beyond the Buzzword," *Businessweek,* May 24, 1993, www.businessweek.com (accessed July 8, 2009).

[5] Gene Hall, Jim Rosenthal, and Judy Wade, "How to Make Reengineering Really Work," *Harvard Business Review* 71, no. 6 (November–December 1993), pp. 119–131.

[6] M. Walton, *The Deming Management Method* (New York: Pedigree, 1986); J. Juran, *Juran on Quality by Design* (New York: Free Press, 1992); Philip Crosby, *Quality Is Free: The Act of Making Quality Certain* (New York: McGraw-Hill, 1979); S. George, *The Baldrige Quality System* (New York: Wiley, 1992); Mark J. Zbaracki, "The Rhetoric and Reality of Total Quality Management," *Administrative Science Quarterly* 43, no. 3 (September 1998), pp. 602–636.

[7] Robert T. Amsden, Thomas W. Ferratt, and Davida M. Amsden, "TQM: Core Paradigm Changes," *Business Horizons* 39, no. 6 (November–December 1996), pp. 6–14.

[8] Peter S. Pande and Larry Holpp, *What Is Six Sigma?* (New York: McGraw-Hill, 2002); Jiju Antony, "Some Pros and Cons of Six Sigma: An Academic Perspective," *TQM Magazine* 16, no. 4 (2004), pp. 303–306; Peter S. Pande, Robert P. Neuman, and Roland R. Cavanagh, *The Six Sigma Way: How GE, Motorola and Other Top Companies Are Honing Their*

*Performance* (New York: McGraw-Hill, 2000); Joseph Gordon and M. Joseph Gordon, Jr., *Six Sigma Quality for Business and Manufacture* (New York: Elsevier, 2002); Godecke Wessel and Peter Burcher, "Six Sigma for Small and Medium-Sized Enterprises," *TQM Magazine* 16, no. 4 (2004), pp. 264–272.

[9] www.isixsigma.com (accessed November 4, 2002); www.villanovau.com/certificate-programs/six-sigma-training.aspx (accessed February 16, 2012).

[10] Kennedy Smith, "Six Sigma for the Service Sector," *Quality Digest Magazine,* May 2003; www.qualitydigest.com (accessed September 28, 2003).

[11] www.isixsigma.com/implementation/financial-analysis/six-sigma-costs-and-savings/ (accessed February 23, 2012).

[12] "A Dark Art No More," *The Economist* 385, no. 8550 (October 13, 2007), p. 10; Brian Hindo, "At 3M, a Struggle between Efficiency and Creativity," *Businessweek,* June 11, 2007, pp. 8–16.

[13] Charles A. O'Reilly and Michael L. Tushman, "The Ambidextrous Organization," *Harvard Business Review* 82, no. 4 (April 2004), pp. 74–81.

[14] Terry Nels Lee, Stanley E. Fawcett, and Jason Briscoe, "Benchmarking the Challenge to Quality Program Implementation," *Benchmarking: An International Journal* 9, no. 4 (2002), pp. 374–387.

[15] Milan Ambrož, "Total Quality System as a Product of the Empowered Corporate Culture,"

*TQM Magazine* 16, no. 2 (2004), pp. 93–104; Nick A. Dayton, "The Demise of Total Quality Management," *TQM Magazine* 15, no. 6 (2003), pp. 391–396.

[16] Judy D. Olian and Sara L. Rynes, "Making Total Quality Work: Aligning Organizational Processes, Performance Measures, and Stakeholders," *Human Resource Management* 30, no. 3 (Fall 1991), pp. 310–311; Paul S. Goodman and Eric D. Darr, "Exchanging Best Practices Information through Computer-Aided Systems," *Academy of Management Executive* 10, no. 2 (May 1996), p. 7.

[17] Thomas C. Powell, "Total Quality Management as Competitive Advantage," *Strategic Management Journal* 16 (1995), pp. 15–37; Richard M. Hodgetts, "Quality Lessons from America's Baldrige Winners," *Business Horizons* 37, no. 4 (July–August 1994), pp. 74–79; Richard Reed, David J. Lemak, and Joseph C. Montgomery, "Beyond Process: TQM Content and Firm Performance," *Academy*

*of Management Review* 21, no. 1 (January 1996), pp. 173–202.

[18] www.otiselevator.com (accessed February 16, 2012).

[19] Fred Vogelstein, "Winning the Amazon Way," *Fortune* 147, no. 10 (May 26, 2003), pp. 60–69.

[20] Robert Simons, "Control in an Age of Empowerment," *Harvard Business Review* 73 (March–April 1995), pp. 80–88.

[21] David C. Band and Gerald Scanlan, "Strategic Control through Core Competencies," *Long Range Planning* 28, no. 2 (April 1995), pp. 102–114.

[22] Stanley E. Fawcett, Gary K. Rhoads, and Phillip Burnah, "People as the Bridge to Competitiveness: Benchmarking the 'ABCs' of an Empowered Workforce," *Benchmarking: An International Journal* 11, no. 4 (2004), pp. 346–360.

[23] Jeffrey Pfeffer and John F. Veiga, "Putting People First for Organizational Success," *Academy of Management Executive* 13,

no. 2 (May 1999), pp. 37–45; Linda K. Stroh and Paula M. Caliguiri, "Increasing Global Competitiveness through Effective People Management," *Journal of World Business* 33, no. 1 (Spring 1998), pp. 1–16; articles in *Fortune* on the 100 best companies to work for (various issues).

[24] As quoted in John P. Kotter and James L. Heskett, *Corporate Culture and Performance* (New York: Free Press, 1992), p. 91.

[25] Clayton M. Christensen, Matt Marx, and Howard Stevenson, "The Tools of Cooperation and Change," *Harvard Business Review* 84, no. 10 (October 2006), pp. 73–80.

[26] Steven Kerr, "On the Folly of Rewarding A While Hoping for B," *Academy of Management Executive* 9, no. 1 (February 1995), pp. 7–14; Doran Twer, "Linking Pay to Business Objectives," *Journal of Business Strategy* 15, no. 4 (July–August 1994), pp. 15–18.

### CHAPTER 12

# Corporate Culture and Leadership

## Keys to Good Strategy Execution

## Learning Objectives

**LO 1**  The key features of a company's corporate culture and the role of a company's core values and ethical standards in building corporate culture.

**LO 2**  How and why a company's culture can aid the drive for proficient strategy execution.

**LO 3**  The kinds of actions management can take to change a problem corporate culture.

**LO 4**  What constitutes effective managerial leadership in achieving superior strategy execution.

> The key to successful leadership today is influence, not authority.
>
> Kenneth Blanchard – *Author and Management Expert*

> As we look ahead into the next century, leaders will be those who empower others.
>
> Bill Gates – *Cofounder and Former CEO and Chairman of Microsoft*

> If you want to change the culture, you will have to start by changing the organization.
>
> Mary Douglas – *Social Anthropologist and Expert on Culture*

In the previous two chapters, we examined eight of the managerial tasks that drive good strategy execution: staffing the organization, acquiring the needed resources and capabilities, designing the organizational structure, allocating resources, establishing policies and procedures, employing process management tools, installing operating systems, and providing the right incentives. In this chapter, we explore the two remaining managerial tasks that contribute to good strategy execution: creating a strategy-supportive corporate culture and exerting the internal leadership needed to drive the implementation of strategic initiatives forward.

# INSTILLING A CORPORATE CULTURE CONDUCIVE TO GOOD STRATEGY EXECUTION

Every company has its own unique **corporate culture**—the shared values, ingrained attitudes, and company traditions that determine norms of behavior, accepted work practices, and styles of operating.[1] The character of a company's culture is a product of the core values and beliefs that executives espouse, the standards of what is ethically acceptable and what is not, the "chemistry" and the "personality" that permeate the work environment, the company's traditions, and the stories that get told over and over to illustrate and reinforce the company's shared values, business practices, and traditions. In a very real sense, the culture is the company's automatic, self-replicating "operating system" that defines "how we do things around here."[2] It can be thought of as the company's psyche or *organizational DNA*.[3] A company's culture is important because it influences the organization's actions and approaches to conducting business. As such, it plays an important role in strategy execution and may have an appreciable effect on business performance as well.

Corporate cultures vary widely. For instance, the bedrock of Walmart's culture is zealous pursuit of low costs and frugal operating practices, a strong work ethic, ritualistic headquarters meetings to exchange ideas and review problems, and company executives' commitment to visiting stores, listening to customers, and soliciting suggestions from employees. The culture of General Electric (GE) under CEO Jeff Immelt entails a commitment to creativity and bold innovation that wires the company for growth. It drives a willingness to accept the risk of embracing new ventures with the potential to grow GE revenues by at least $100 million, real prowess in improving customer service, pressure to produce good business results, and cross-business sharing of ideas, best practices, and learning.[4] At Publix, the most profitable grocery store chain in the United States, corporate culture is centered on delivering exceptional service to customers; the company's reputation for never disappointing its customers is "legendary in the industry."[5] Its "people first" culture is focused not only on its customers but on its employees as well, who are also the company's largest collective shareholders.[6] Publix makes a point of promoting employees from within so that they are motivated not only by an ownership stake in the company but by opportunities for advancement in the company as well. Illustration Capsule 12.1 describes the corporate culture of another exemplar company—W. L. Gore & Associates, the inventor of GORE-TEX.

## Identifying the Key Features of a Company's Corporate Culture

A company's corporate culture is mirrored in the character or "personality" of its work environment—the features that describe how the company goes about its business and the workplace behaviors that are held in high esteem. Some of these features are readily apparent, and others operate quite subtly. The chief things to look for include:

- The values, business principles, and ethical standards that management preaches and *practices*—these are the key to a company's culture, but actions speak much louder than words here.
- The company's approach to people management and the official policies, procedures, and operating practices that provide guidelines for the behavior of company personnel.
- The atmosphere and spirit that pervades the work climate—whether the workplace is competitive or cooperative, innovative or resistant to change, political or collegial, all business or fun-loving, and the like.
- The way managers and employees interact and relate to one another—whether and to what extent good camaraderie exists, whether people tend to work independently or collaboratively, whether communications among employees are free-flowing or infrequent, whether people are called by their first names, whether co-workers spend little or lots of time together outside the workplace, and so on.
- The strength of peer pressure to do things in particular ways and conform to expected norms.
- The actions and behaviors that management explicitly encourages and rewards and those that are frowned upon.
- The company's revered traditions and oft-repeated stories about "heroic acts" and "how we do things around here."
- The manner in which the company deals with external stakeholders—whether it treats suppliers as business partners or prefers hard-nosed, arm's-length business arrangements and whether its commitment to corporate citizenship and environmental sustainability is strong and genuine.

# The Culture That Drives Innovation at W. L. Gore & Associates

W. L. Gore & Associates is best known for GORE-TEX, the waterproof, breathable fabric highly prized by outdoor enthusiasts. But the company has developed a wide variety of other revolutionary products, including Elixir guitar strings, Ride-On bike cables, and a host of medical devices such as cardiovascular patches and synthetic blood vessels. As a result, it is now one of the largest privately held companies in the United States, with more than $3 billion in revenue and 10,000 employees in 30 countries worldwide.

When Gore developed the core technology on which most of its more than 2,000 worldwide patents is based, the company's unique culture played a crucial role in allowing Gore to pursue multiple end-market applications simultaneously, enabling rapid growth from a niche business into a diversified multinational company. The company's culture is team-based and designed to foster personal initiative. It is described on the company's website as follows:

> There are no traditional organizational charts, no chains of command, nor predetermined channels of communication. Instead, we communicate directly with each other and are accountable to fellow members of our multidiscipline teams. We encourage hands-on innovation, involving those closest to a project in decision making. Teams organize around opportunities and leaders emerge.

Personal stories posted on the website describe the discovery process behind a number of breakthrough products developed by particular teams at W. L. Gore & Associates. Employees are encouraged to use 10 percent of their time to tinker with new ideas and to take

the long view regarding the idea's development. Promising ideas attract more people who are willing to work on them without orders from higher-ups. Instead, self-managing associates operating in self-developed teams are simply encouraged to pursue novel applications of Gore technology until these applications are fully commercialized or have had their potential exhausted. The encouragement comes both from the culture (norms and practices) of the organization and from a profit-sharing arrangement that allows employees to benefit directly from their successes.

This approach makes Gore a great place to work and has helped it attract, retain, and motivate top talent globally. Gore has been on *Fortune* magazine's list of the 100 best companies to work for in the United States for the last 17 years. Gore places similarly on the lists of other countries in which it operates, such as the United Kingdom, Germany, France, Italy, and Sweden.

*Note:* Developed with Kenneth P. Fraser.

*Sources:* Company websites; www.gore.com/en_xx/news/FORTUNE-2011.html; www.director.co.uk/magazine/2010/2_Feb/WLGore_63_06.html; and www.fastcompany.com/magazine/89/open_gore.html (accessed March 10, 2012).

---

The values, beliefs, and practices that undergird a company's culture can come from anywhere in the organizational hierarchy. Typically, key elements of the culture originate with a founder or certain strong leaders who articulated them as a set of business principles, company policies, operating approaches, and ways of dealing with employees, customers, vendors, shareholders, and local communities where the company has operations. They also stem from exemplary actions on the part of company personnel and evolving consensus about "how we ought to do things around here."[7] Over time, these cultural underpinnings take root, come to be accepted by company managers and employees alike, and become ingrained in the way the company conducts its business.

### The Role of Core Values and Ethics

The foundation of a company's corporate culture nearly always resides in its dedication to certain core values and the bar it sets for ethical behavior. The culture-shaping significance of core values and ethical behaviors accounts for why so many companies have developed a formal value statement and a code of ethics. Of course, sometimes a company's stated core values and code of ethics are cosmetic, existing mainly to impress outsiders and help create a positive company image. But usually they have been developed to purposely mold the culture and communicate the kinds of actions and behavior that are expected of all company personnel. Many executives want the work climate at their companies to mirror certain values and ethical standards, partly because of personal convictions but mainly because they are convinced that adherence to such principles will promote better strategy execution, make the company a better performer, and positively impact its reputation.[8] Not incidentally, strongly ingrained values and ethical standards reduce the likelihood of lapses in ethical and socially approved behavior that mar a company's public image and put its financial performance and market standing at risk.

> A company's culture is grounded in and shaped by its core values and ethical standards.

As depicted in Figure 12.1, a company's stated core values and ethical principles have two roles in the culture-building process. First, a company that works hard at putting its stated core values and ethical principles into practice fosters a work climate in which company personnel share strongly held convictions about how the company's business is to be conducted. Second, the stated values and ethical principles provide company personnel with guidance about the manner in which they are to do their jobs—which behaviors and ways of doing things are approved (and expected) and which are out-of-bounds. These value-based and ethics-based cultural norms serve as yardsticks for gauging the appropriateness of particular actions, decisions, and behaviors, thus helping steer company personnel toward both doing things right and doing the right thing.

> A company's value statement and code of ethics communicate expectations of how employees should conduct themselves in the workplace.

**FIGURE 12.1**    The Two Culture-Building Roles of a Company's Core Values and Ethical Standards

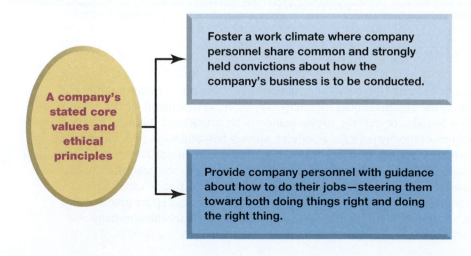

**Embedding Cultural Norms in the Organization and Perpetuating the Culture**    Once values and ethical standards have been formally adopted, they must be institutionalized in the company's policies and practices and embedded in the conduct of company personnel. This can be done in a number of different ways.[9] Tradition-steeped companies with a rich folklore rely heavily on word-of-mouth indoctrination and the power of tradition to instill values and enforce ethical conduct. But most companies employ a variety of techniques, drawing on some or all of the following:

1.  Screening applicants and hiring those who will mesh well with the culture.
2.  Incorporating discussions of the company's culture and behavioral norms into orientation programs for new employees and training courses for managers and employees.
3.  Having senior executives frequently reiterate the importance and role of company values and ethical principles at company events and in internal communications to employees.
4.  Expecting managers at all levels to be cultural role models and exhibit the advocated cultural norms in their own behavior.
5.  Making the display of cultural norms a factor in evaluating each person's job performance, granting compensation increases, and deciding who to promote.
6.  Stressing that line managers all the way down to first-level supervisors give ongoing attention to explaining the desired cultural traits and behaviors in their areas and clarifying why they are important.
7.  Encouraging company personnel to exert strong peer pressure on co-workers to conform to expected cultural norms.
8.  Holding periodic ceremonies to honor people who excel in displaying the company values and ethical principles.

To deeply ingrain the stated core values and high ethical standards, companies must turn them into *strictly enforced cultural norms.* They must make it unequivocally clear that living up to the company's values and ethical standards has to be "a way of life" at the company and that there will be little toleration for errant behavior.

**The Role of Stories**    Frequently, a significant part of a company's culture is captured in the stories that get told over and over again to illustrate to newcomers the importance of certain values and the depth of commitment that various company personnel have displayed. One of the folktales at Zappos, known for its outstanding customer service, is about a customer who ordered shoes for her ill mother from Zappos, hoping they would remedy her mother's foot pain and numbness. When the shoes didn't work, the mother called the company to ask how to return them and explain why she was returning them. Two days later, she received a large bouquet of flowers from the company, along with well wishes and a customer upgrade giving her free expedited service on all future orders. Specialty food market Trader Joe's is similarly known for its culture of going beyond the call of duty for its customers. When a World War II veteran was snowed in without any food for meals, his daughter called several supermarkets to see if they offered grocery delivery. Although Trader Joe's technically doesn't offer delivery, it graciously helped the veteran, even recommending items for his low-sodium diet. When the store delivered the groceries, the veteran wasn't charged for either the groceries or the delivery. When Apple's iPad 2 was launched, one was returned to the company almost immediately, with a note attached that said

"Wife said No!"[10] Apple sent the customer a refund, but it also sent back the device with a note reading "Apple says Yes!" Such stories serve the valuable purpose of illustrating the kinds of behavior the company reveres and inspiring company personnel to perform similarly. Moreover, each retelling of a legendary story puts a bit more peer pressure on company personnel to display core values and do their part in keeping the company's traditions alive.

**Forces That Cause a Company's Culture to Evolve**  Despite the role of time-honored stories and long-standing traditions in perpetuating a company's culture, cultures are far from static—just like strategy and organizational structure, they evolve. New challenges in the marketplace, revolutionary technologies, and shifting internal conditions—especially an internal crisis, a change in company direction, or top-executive turnover—tend to breed new ways of doing things and, in turn, drive cultural evolution. An incoming CEO who decides to shake up the existing business and take it in new directions often triggers a cultural shift, perhaps one of major proportions. Likewise, diversification into new businesses, expansion into foreign countries, rapid growth that brings an influx of new employees, and the merger with or acquisition of another company can all precipitate significant cultural change.

## Strong versus Weak Cultures

Company cultures vary widely in strength and influence. Some are strongly embedded and have a big influence on a company's operating practices and the behavior of company personnel. Others are weakly ingrained and have little effect on behaviors and how company activities are conducted.

<table>
<tr><td>

**CORE CONCEPT**

In a **strong-culture company,** deeply rooted values and norms of behavior are widely shared and regulate the conduct of the company's business.

</td></tr>
</table>

**Strong-Culture Companies**  The hallmark of a **strong-culture company** is the dominating presence of certain deeply rooted values and behavioral norms that "regulate" the conduct of company personnel as they go about the company's business.[11] Strong cultures enable a company to operate like a well-oiled machine, smoothly operating without a lot of intervention from management. Senior managers in strong-culture companies embody the cultural norms in their own actions and expect the same of others within the company. An unequivocal expectation that company personnel will act and behave in accordance with the adopted values and ways of doing business leads to two important outcomes: (1) Over time, the values come to be widely shared by rank-and-file employees—people who dislike the culture tend to leave—and (2) individuals encounter strong peer pressure from co-workers to observe the culturally approved norms and behaviors. Hence, a strongly implanted corporate culture ends up having a powerful influence on behavior because so many company personnel are accepting of cultural traditions and because this acceptance is reinforced by both management expectations and co-worker peer pressure to conform to cultural norms.

Strong cultures emerge only after a period of deliberate and rather intensive culture building that generally takes years (sometimes decades). Two factors contribute to the development of strong cultures: (1) a founder or strong leader who established core values, principles, and practices that are viewed as having contributed to the success of the company, and (2) a sincere, long-standing company commitment to operating the business according to these established traditions and values. Continuity of leadership, low workforce turnover, geographic concentration, and considerable organizational success all contribute to the emergence and sustainability of a strong culture.[12]

In strong-culture companies, values and behavioral norms are so ingrained that they can endure leadership changes at the top—although their strength can erode over time if new CEOs cease to nurture them or move aggressively to institute cultural adjustments. The cultural norms in a strong-culture company typically do not change much as strategy evolves, either because the culture constrains the choice of new strategies or because the dominant traits of the culture are somewhat strategy-neutral and compatible with evolving versions of the company's strategy. As a consequence, *strongly implanted cultures provide a huge assist in executing strategy* because company managers can use the traditions, beliefs, values, common bonds, or behavioral norms as levers to mobilize commitment to executing the chosen strategy.

**Weak-Culture Companies**   In direct contrast to strong-culture companies, weak-culture companies lack widely shared and strongly held values and principles. As a result, they also lack cultural mechanisms for aligning, constraining, and regulating the actions, decisions, and behaviors of company personnel. In the absence of any long-standing top management commitment to particular values, beliefs, operating practices, and behavioral norms, individuals encounter little pressure to do things in particular ways. Such a dearth of companywide cultural influences and revered traditions produces a work climate where there is no strong employee allegiance to what the company stands for or to operating the business in well-defined ways. While individual employees may well have some bonds of identification with and loyalty toward their department, their colleagues, their union, or their immediate boss, there's neither passion about the company nor emotional commitment to what it is trying to accomplish—a condition that often results in many employees' viewing their company as just a place to work and their job as just a way to make a living.

As a consequence, *weak cultures provide little or no assistance in executing strategy* because there are no traditions, beliefs, values, common bonds, or behavioral norms that management can use as levers to mobilize commitment to executing the chosen strategy. Without a work climate that channels organizational energy in the direction of good strategy execution, managers are left with the options of either using compensation incentives and other motivational devices to mobilize employee commitment, supervising and monitoring employee actions more closely, or trying to establish cultural roots that will in time start to nurture the strategy execution process.

# Why Corporate Cultures Matter to the Strategy Execution Process

Even if a company has a strong culture, the culture and work climate may or may not be compatible with what is needed for effective implementation of the chosen strategy. When a company's present culture promotes attitudes, behaviors, and ways of doing things that are *in sync with the chosen strategy* and conducive to first-rate strategy execution, the culture functions as a valuable ally in the strategy execution process. For example, a corporate culture characterized by frugality and thrift prompts employee actions to identify cost-saving opportunities—the very behavior needed for successful execution of a low-cost leadership strategy. A culture that celebrates taking initiative, exhibiting creativity, taking risks, and embracing change is conducive to successful execution of product innovation and technological leadership strategies.[13]

**LO 2**

How and why a company's culture can aid the drive for proficient strategy execution.

A culture that is grounded in actions, behaviors, and work practices that are conducive to good strategy implementation supports the strategy execution effort in three ways:

1. *A culture that is well matched to the chosen strategy and the requirements of the strategy execution effort focuses the attention of employees on what is most important to this effort.* Moreover, it directs their behavior and serves as a guide to their decision making. In this manner, it can align the efforts and decisions of employees throughout the firm and minimize the need for direct supervision.

2. *Culture-induced peer pressure further induces company personnel to do things in a manner that aids the cause of good strategy execution.* The stronger the culture (the more widely shared and deeply held the values), the more effective peer pressure is in shaping and supporting the strategy execution effort. Research has shown that strong group norms can shape employee behavior even more powerfully than can financial incentives.

3. *A company culture that is consistent with the requirements for good strategy execution can energize employees, deepen their commitment to execute the strategy flawlessly, and enhance worker productivity in the process.* When a company's culture is grounded in many of the needed strategy-executing behaviors, employees feel genuinely better about their jobs, the company they work for, and the merits of what the company is trying to accomplish. Greater employee buy-in for what the company is trying to accomplish boosts motivation and marshals organizational energy behind the drive for good strategy execution. An energized workforce enhances the chances of achieving execution-critical performance targets and good strategy execution.

> A strong culture that encourages actions, behaviors, and work practices that are in sync with the chosen strategy and conducive to good strategy execution is a valuable ally in the strategy execution process.

In sharp contrast, when a culture is in conflict with the chosen strategy or what is required to execute the company's strategy well, the culture becomes a stumbling block.[14] Some of the very behaviors needed to execute the strategy successfully run contrary to the attitudes, behaviors, and operating practices embedded in the prevailing culture. Such a clash poses a real dilemma for company personnel. Should they be loyal to the culture and company traditions (to which they are likely to be emotionally attached) and thus resist or be indifferent to actions that will promote better strategy execution—a choice that will certainly weaken the drive for good strategy execution? Alternatively, should they go along with management's strategy execution effort and engage in actions that run counter to the culture—a choice that will likely impair morale and lead to a less-than-wholehearted commitment to good strategy execution? Neither choice leads to desirable outcomes. Culture-bred resistance to the actions and behaviors needed for good strategy execution, particularly if strong and widespread, poses a formidable hurdle that must be cleared for a strategy's execution to be successful.

> It is in management's best interest to dedicate considerable effort to establishing a corporate culture that encourages behaviors and work practices conducive to good strategy execution.

The consequences of having—or not having—an execution-supportive corporate culture says something important about the task of managing the strategy execution process: *Closely aligning corporate culture with the requirements for proficient strategy execution merits the full attention of senior executives.* The culture-building objective is to create a work climate and style of operating that mobilize the energy of company personnel squarely behind efforts to execute strategy competently. The more deeply management can embed execution-supportive ways of doing things, the more management can rely on the culture to automatically steer company personnel toward behaviors and work practices that aid good strategy execution and veer from doing things that impede it. Moreover, culturally astute managers understand that nourishing the right cultural environment not only adds power to their push for proficient strategy execution but also promotes strong employee identification with, and commitment to, the company's vision, performance targets, and strategy.

# Healthy Cultures That Aid Good Strategy Execution

A strong culture, provided it fits the chosen strategy and embraces execution-supportive attitudes, behaviors, and work practices, is definitely a healthy culture. Two other types of cultures exist that tend to be healthy and largely supportive of good strategy execution: high-performance cultures and adaptive cultures.

**High-Performance Cultures**    Some companies have so-called "high-performance" cultures where the standout traits are a "can-do" spirit, pride in doing things right, no-excuses accountability, and a pervasive results-oriented work climate in which people go all out to meet or beat stretch objectives.[15] In high-performance cultures, there's a strong sense of involvement on the part of company personnel and emphasis on individual initiative and effort. Performance expectations are clearly delineated for the company as a whole, for each organizational unit, and for each individual. Issues and problems are promptly addressed; there's a razor-sharp focus on what needs to be done. The clear and unyielding expectation is that all company personnel, from senior executives to frontline employees, will display high-performance behaviors and a passion for making the company successful. Such a culture—permeated by a spirit of achievement and constructive pressure to achieve good results—is a valuable contributor to good strategy execution and operating excellence.[16]

The challenge in creating a high-performance culture is to inspire high loyalty and dedication on the part of employees, such that they are energized to put forth their very best efforts. Managers have to take pains to reinforce constructive behavior, reward top performers, and purge habits and behaviors that stand in the way of high productivity and good results. They must work at knowing the strengths and weaknesses of their subordinates, so as to better match talent with task and enable people to make meaningful contributions by doing what they do best. They have to stress learning from mistakes and must put an unrelenting emphasis on moving forward and making good progress—in effect, there has to be a disciplined, performance-focused approach to managing the organization.

**Adaptive Cultures**    The hallmark of adaptive corporate cultures is willingness on the part of organization members to accept change and take on the challenge of introducing and executing new strategies. Company personnel share a feeling of confidence that the organization can deal with whatever threats and opportunities arise; they are receptive to risk taking, experimentation, innovation, and changing strategies and practices. The work climate is supportive of managers and employees who propose or initiate useful change. Internal entrepreneurship (often called *intrapreneurship*) on the part of individuals and groups is encouraged and rewarded. Senior executives seek out, support, and promote individuals who exercise initiative, spot opportunities for improvement, and display the skills to implement them. Managers openly evaluate ideas and suggestions, fund initiatives to develop new or better products, and take prudent risks to pursue emerging market opportunities. As in high-performance cultures, the company exhibits a proactive approach to identifying issues, evaluating the implications and options, and moving ahead quickly with workable solutions. Strategies and traditional operating practices are modified as needed to adjust to, or take advantage of, changes in the business environment.

But why is change so willingly embraced in an adaptive culture? Why are organization members not fearful of how change will affect them? Why does an

> As a company's strategy evolves, an adaptive culture is a definite ally in the strategy-implementing, strategy-executing process as compared to cultures that are resistant to change.

adaptive culture not break down from the force of ongoing changes in strategy, operating practices, and behavioral norms? The answers lie in two distinctive and dominant traits of an adaptive culture: (1) Changes in operating practices and behaviors must *not* compromise core values and long-standing business principles (since they are at the root of the culture), and (2) changes that are instituted must satisfy the legitimate interests of key constituencies—customers, employees, shareholders, suppliers, and the communities where the company operates. In other words, what sustains an adaptive culture is that organization members perceive the changes that management is trying to institute as *legitimate,* in keeping with the core values, and in the overall best interests of stakeholders.[17] Not surprisingly, company personnel are usually more receptive to change when their employment security is not threatened and when they view new duties or job assignments as part of the process of adapting to new conditions. Should workforce downsizing be necessary, it is important that layoffs be handled humanely and employee departures be made as painless as possible.

Technology companies, software companies, and Internet-based companies are good illustrations of organizations with adaptive cultures. Such companies thrive on change—driving it, leading it, and capitalizing on it. Companies like Facebook, Twitter, Adobe, Groupon, Cisco Systems, Google, Yahoo, and Yelp cultivate the capability to act and react rapidly. They are avid practitioners of entrepreneurship and innovation, with a demonstrated willingness to take bold risks to create altogether new products, new businesses, and new industries. To create and nurture a culture that can adapt rapidly to shifting business conditions, they make a point of staffing their organizations with people who are flexible, who rise to the challenge of change, and who have an aptitude for adapting well to new circumstances.

In fast-changing business environments, a corporate culture that is receptive to altering organizational practices and behaviors is a virtual necessity. However, adaptive cultures work to the advantage of all companies, not just those in rapid-change environments. Every company operates in a market and business climate that is changing to one degree or another and that, in turn, requires internal operating responses and new behaviors on the part of organization members.

## Unhealthy Cultures That Impede Good Strategy Execution

The distinctive characteristic of an unhealthy corporate culture is the presence of counterproductive cultural traits that adversely impact the work climate and company performance. Five particularly unhealthy cultural traits are hostility to change, heavily politicized decision making, insular thinking, unethical and greed-driven behaviors, and the presence of incompatible, clashing subcultures.

### Change-Resistant Cultures    Change-resistant cultures—where skepticism about the importance of new developments and a fear of change are the norm—place a premium on not making mistakes, prompting managers to lean toward safe, conservative options intended to maintain the status quo, protect their power base, and guard their immediate interests. When such companies encounter business environments with accelerating change, going slow on altering traditional ways of doing things can be a serious liability. Under these conditions, change-resistant cultures encourage a number of unhealthy behaviors—avoiding risks, not capitalizing on emerging opportunities, taking a lax approach to both product innovation and continuous improvement

in performing value chain activities, and responding more slowly than is warranted to market change. In change-resistant cultures, word quickly gets around that proposals to do things differently face an uphill battle and that people who champion them may be seen as something of a nuisance or a troublemaker. Executives who don't value managers or employees with initiative and new ideas put a damper on product innovation, experimentation, and efforts to improve.

Hostility to change is most often found in companies with stodgy bureaucracies that have enjoyed considerable market success in years past and that are wedded to the "We have done it this way for years" syndrome. Blockbuster, Yahoo, Toys 'R Us, Sears, and Eastman Kodak are classic examples of companies whose change-resistant bureaucracies have damaged their market standings and financial performance; clinging to what made them successful, they were reluctant to alter operating practices and modify their business approaches when signals of market change first sounded. As strategies of gradual change won out over bold innovation, all four lost market share to rivals that quickly moved to institute changes more in tune with evolving market conditions and buyer preferences. While IBM and GM have made strides in building a culture needed for market success, Sears and Kodak are still struggling to recoup lost ground.

## Politicized Cultures
What makes a politicized internal environment so unhealthy is that political infighting consumes a great deal of organizational energy, often with the result that what's best for the company takes a backseat to political maneuvering. In companies where internal politics pervades the work climate, empire-building managers pursue their own agendas and operate the work units under their supervision as autonomous "fiefdoms." The positions they take on issues are usually aimed at protecting or expanding their own turf. Collaboration with other organizational units is viewed with suspicion, and cross-unit cooperation occurs grudgingly. The support or opposition of politically influential executives and/or coalitions among departments with vested interests in a particular outcome tends to shape what actions the company takes. All this political maneuvering takes away from efforts to execute strategy with real proficiency and frustrates company personnel who are less political and more inclined to do what is in the company's best interests.

## Insular, Inwardly Focused Cultures
Sometimes a company reigns as an industry leader or enjoys great market success for so long that its personnel start to believe they have all the answers or can develop them on their own. There is a strong tendency to neglect what customers are saying and how their needs and expectations are changing. Such confidence in the correctness of how the company does things and an unflinching belief in its competitive superiority breed arrogance, prompting company personnel to discount the merits of what outsiders are doing and to see little payoff from studying best-in-class performers. Insular thinking, internally driven solutions, and a must-be-invented-here mindset come to permeate the corporate culture. An inwardly focused corporate culture gives rise to managerial inbreeding and a failure to recruit people who can offer fresh thinking and outside perspectives. The big risk of insular cultural thinking is that the company can underestimate the capabilities and accomplishments of rival companies while overestimating its own—all of which diminishes a company's competitiveness over time.

## Unethical and Greed-Driven Cultures
Companies that have little regard for ethical standards or are run by executives driven by greed and ego gratification are

scandals waiting to happen. Executives exude the negatives of arrogance, ego, greed, and an "ends-justify-the-means" mentality in pursuing overambitious revenue and profitability targets.[18] Senior managers wink at unethical behavior and may cross over the line to unethical (and sometimes criminal) behavior themselves. They are prone to adopt accounting principles that make financial performance look better than it really is. Legions of companies have fallen prey to unethical behavior and greed, most notably Enron, Rite Aid, Xerox, Olympus, Peregrine Financial Group, Pilot Flying J, Marsh & McLennan, Siemens, Countrywide Financial, and JPMorgan Chase, with executives being indicted and/or convicted of criminal behavior.

**Incompatible Subcultures**    Although it is common to speak about corporate culture in the singular, it is not unusual for companies to have multiple cultures (or subcultures). Values, beliefs, and practices within a company sometimes vary significantly by department, geographic location, division, or business unit. As long as the subcultures are compatible with the overarching corporate culture and are supportive of the strategy execution efforts, this is not problematic. Multiple cultures pose an unhealthy situation when they are composed of incompatible subcultures that embrace conflicting business philosophies, support inconsistent approaches to strategy execution, and encourage incompatible methods of people management. Clashing subcultures can prevent a company from coordinating its efforts to craft and execute strategy and can distract company personnel from the business of business. Internal jockeying among the subcultures for cultural dominance impedes teamwork among the company's various organizational units and blocks the emergence of a collaborative approach to strategy execution. Such a lack of consensus about how to proceed is likely to result in fragmented or inconsistent approaches to implementing new strategic initiatives and in limited success in executing the company's overall strategy.

# Changing a Problem Culture

*When a strong culture is unhealthy or otherwise out of sync with the actions and behaviors needed to execute the strategy successfully, the culture must be changed as rapidly as can be managed.* This means eliminating any unhealthy or dysfunctional cultural traits as fast as possible and aggressively striving to ingrain new behaviors and work practices that will enable first-rate strategy execution. The more entrenched the unhealthy or mismatched aspects of a company culture, the more likely the culture will impede strategy execution and the greater the need for change.

Changing a problem culture is among the toughest management tasks because of the heavy anchor of ingrained behaviors and attitudes. It is natural for company personnel to cling to familiar practices and to be wary of change, if not hostile to new approaches concerning how things are to be done. Consequently, it takes concerted management action over a period of time to root out unwanted behaviors and replace an unsupportive culture with more effective ways of doing things. *The single most visible factor that distinguishes successful culture-change efforts from failed attempts is competent leadership at the top.* Great power is needed to force major cultural change and overcome the stubborn resistance of entrenched cultures—and great power is possessed only by the most senior executives, especially the CEO. However, while top management must lead the change effort, the tasks of marshaling support for a new culture and instilling the desired cultural behaviors must involve a company's whole management team. Middle managers and frontline supervisors play a key role in implementing the new work practices and operating approaches, helping win rank-and-file acceptance of and support for changes, and instilling the desired behavioral norms.

As shown in Figure 12.2, the first step in fixing a problem culture is for top management to identify those facets of the present culture that are dysfunctional and pose obstacles to executing strategic initiatives. Second, managers must clearly define the desired new behaviors and features of the culture they want to create. Third, they must convince company personnel of why the present culture poses problems and why and how new behaviors and operating approaches will improve company performance— the case for cultural reform has to be persuasive. Finally, and most important, all the talk about remodeling the present culture must be followed swiftly by visible, forceful actions to promote the desired new behaviors and work practices—actions that company personnel will interpret as a determined top-management commitment to bringing about a different work climate and new ways of operating. The actions to implant the new culture must be both substantive and symbolic.

**Making a Compelling Case for Culture Change**    The way for management to begin a major remodeling of the corporate culture is by selling company personnel on the need for new-style behaviors and work practices. This means making a compelling case for why the culture-remodeling efforts are in the organization's best interests and why company personnel should wholeheartedly join the effort to do things somewhat differently. This can be done by:

- Explaining why and how certain behaviors and work practices in the current culture pose obstacles to good strategy execution.
- Explaining how new behaviors and work practices will be more advantageous and produce better results. Effective culture-change leaders are good at telling stories

## FIGURE 12.2    Changing a Problem Culture

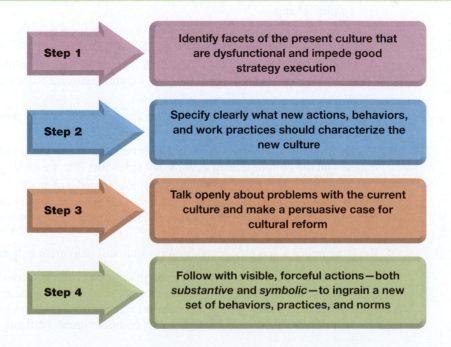

**Step 1** → Identify facets of the present culture that are dysfunctional and impede good strategy execution

**Step 2** → Specify clearly what new actions, behaviors, and work practices should characterize the new culture

**Step 3** → Talk openly about problems with the current culture and make a persuasive case for cultural reform

**Step 4** → Follow with visible, forceful actions—both *substantive* and *symbolic*—to ingrain a new set of behaviors, practices, and norms

to describe the new values and desired behaviors and connect them to everyday practices.

- Citing reasons why the current strategy has to be modified, if the need for cultural change is due to a change in strategy. This includes explaining why the new strategic initiatives will bolster the company's competitiveness and performance and how a change in culture can help in executing the new strategy.

It is essential for the CEO and other top executives to talk personally to personnel all across the company about the reasons for modifying work practices and culture-related behaviors. For the culture-change effort to be successful, frontline supervisors and employee opinion leaders must be won over to the cause, which means convincing them of the merits of *practicing* and *enforcing* cultural norms at every level of the organization, from the highest to the lowest. Arguments for new ways of doing things and new work practices tend to be embraced more readily if employees understand how they will benefit company stakeholders (particularly customers, employees, and shareholders). Until a large majority of employees accept the need for a new culture and agree that different work practices and behaviors are called for, there's more work to be done in selling company personnel on the whys and wherefores of culture change. Building widespread organizational support requires taking every opportunity to repeat the message of why the new work practices, operating approaches, and behaviors are good for company stakeholders and essential for the company's future success.

### Substantive Culture-Changing Actions
No culture-change effort can get very far when leaders merely talk about the need for different actions, behaviors, and work practices. Company executives must give the culture-change effort some teeth by initiating *a series of actions* that company personnel will see as unmistakably indicative of the seriousness of management's commitment to cultural change. The strongest signs that management is truly committed to instilling a new culture include:

- Replacing key executives who are resisting or obstructing needed organizational and cultural changes.
- Promoting individuals who have stepped forward to spearhead the shift to a different culture and who can serve as role models for the desired cultural behavior.
- Appointing outsiders with the desired cultural attributes to high-profile positions—bringing in new-breed managers sends an unambiguous message that a new era is dawning.
- Screening all candidates for new positions carefully, hiring only those who appear to fit in with the new culture.
- Mandating that all company personnel attend culture-training programs to better understand the culture-related actions and behaviors that are expected.
- Designing compensation incentives that boost the pay of teams and individuals who display the desired cultural behaviors. Company personnel are much more inclined to exhibit the desired kinds of actions and behaviors when it is in their financial best interest to do so.
- Revising policies and procedures in ways that will help drive cultural change.

Executives must take care to launch enough companywide culture-change actions at the outset so as to leave no room for doubt that management is dead serious about changing the present culture and that a cultural transformation is inevitable. Management's commitment to cultural change in the company must be made credible. The series of actions initiated by top management must command attention, get the change process off to a fast start, and be followed by unrelenting efforts to firmly establish the new work practices, desired behaviors, and style of operating as "standard."

**Symbolic Culture-Changing Actions** There's also an important place for symbolic managerial actions to alter a problem culture and tighten the strategy–culture fit. The most important symbolic actions are those that top executives take to *lead by example.* For instance, if the organization's strategy involves a drive to become the industry's low-cost producer, senior managers must display frugality in their own actions and decisions. Examples include inexpensive decorations in the executive suite, conservative expense accounts and entertainment allowances, a lean staff in the corporate office, scrutiny of budget requests, few executive perks, and so on. At Walmart, all the executive offices are simply decorated; executives are habitually frugal in their own actions, and they are zealous in their efforts to control costs and promote greater efficiency. At Nucor, one of the world's low-cost producers of steel products, executives fly coach class and use taxis at airports rather than limousines. Top executives must be alert to the fact that company personnel will be watching their behavior to see if their actions match their rhetoric. Hence, they need to make sure their current decisions and actions will be construed as consistent with the new-culture values and norms.[19]

Another category of symbolic actions includes holding ceremonial events to single out and honor people whose actions and performance exemplify what is called for in the new culture. Such events also provide an opportunity to celebrate each culture-change success. Executives sensitive to their role in promoting strategy–culture fit make a habit of appearing at ceremonial functions to praise individuals and groups that exemplify the desired behaviors. They show up at employee training programs to stress strategic priorities, values, ethical principles, and cultural norms. Every group gathering is seen as an opportunity to repeat and ingrain values, praise good deeds, expound on the merits of the new culture, and cite instances of how the new work practices and operating approaches have produced the desired results.

The use of symbols in culture building is widespread. Numerous businesses have employee-of-the-month awards. The military has a long-standing custom of awarding ribbons and medals for exemplary actions. Mary Kay Cosmetics awards an array of prizes ceremoniously to its beauty consultants for reaching various sales plateaus, including the iconic pink Cadillac.

**How Long Does It Take to Change a Problem Culture?** Planting the seeds of a new culture and helping the culture grow strong roots require a determined, sustained effort by the chief executive and other senior managers. Changing a problem culture is never a short-term exercise; it takes time for a new culture to emerge and take root. And it takes even longer for a new culture to become deeply embedded. The bigger the organization and the greater the cultural shift needed to produce an execution-supportive fit, the longer it takes. In large companies, fixing a problem culture and instilling a new set of attitudes and behaviors can take two to five years. In fact, it is usually tougher to reform an entrenched problematic culture than it is to instill a strategy-supportive culture from scratch in a brand new organization.

Illustration Capsule 12.2 discusses the approaches used at America Latina Logistica (ALL) to change a culture that was grounded in antiquated practices and bureaucratic management.

# Culture Transformation at America Latina Logistica

For many, a steam-engine locomotive's stocky profile, billowing exhaust, and hiss evoke nostalgia for a bygone era. For the managers at America Latina Logistica (ALL), which had just acquired the southern freight lines of the Brazilian Rail Network (RFFSA), such antiquated locomotives represented the difficulties they faced in fixing their ailing railroad.

When ALL assumed control of the RFFSA's Southern Line in 1997, it was losing money, struggling from decades of underinvestment, and encumbered by bureaucratic management. Half the network's bridges required repairs, over three-quarters of its rails were undersized for supporting standard-sized loads, and the system still relied on 20 steam-engine locomotives to move industrial customers' cargo.

CEO Alexandre Behring's priority was to transform ALL into a performance-oriented organization with the strong cost discipline necessary to support an overdue modernization program. He decided that this would require a complete cultural transformation for the company. His first step was to recruit a new management team and fire the dozens of political appointees previously administering the railroad. In his first 10 days, he and his COO interviewed the top-150 managers to evaluate their suitability. They selected 30 for additional responsibility and removed those who did not embrace the new direction. The company established a trainee program, and in four years hired 500 recent college graduates. In Behring's first year, he introduced a performance-based bonus program; in his second year, the company began comparing performance on operational indicators like car utilization and on-time delivery between divisions.

The top managers also took symbolic steps to demonstrate their commitment to the new culture and to reinforce the personnel and process changes they implemented. They sold cars previously reserved for officers' use and fired the chauffeurs retained to drive them. Behring became certified as a train conductor and spent a week each month working in the field, wearing the conductor uniform. For the first time, managers visited injured workers at home. The company created the "Diesel Cup" to recognize conductors who most effectively reduced fuel consumption.

Behring's new direction energized the company's middle managers and line employees, who had been demoralized after years of political interference and ineffectual leadership. In three years Behring transformed a company that hadn't made a hire in over a decade into one of the most desirable employers in Brazil, attracting 9,000 applications for 18 trainee positions. In 2000 ALL achieved profitability, enabled by the company's cultural transformation.

*Note:* Developed with Peter Jacobson.

*Sources:* Company website, **pt.all-logistica.com**; **www.strategy-business.com/article/ac00012?pg=1**; **blogs.hbr.org/2012/09/shape-strategy-with-simple-rul/**; and Donald N. Sull, Fernando Martins, and Andre Delbin Silva, "America Latina Logistica," Harvard Business School case 9-804-139, January 14, 2004.

# LEADING THE STRATEGY EXECUTION PROCESS

For an enterprise to execute its strategy in truly proficient fashion, top executives must take the lead in the strategy implementation process and personally drive the pace of progress. They have to be out in the field, seeing for themselves how well operations are going, gathering information firsthand, and gauging the progress being made. Proficient strategy execution requires company managers to be diligent and adept in spotting problems, learning what obstacles lay in the path of good execution, and then clearing the way for progress—the goal must be to produce better results speedily and productively. There must be constructive, but unrelenting, pressure on organizational units to (1) demonstrate excellence in all dimensions of strategy execution and (2) do so on a consistent basis—ultimately, that's what will enable a well-crafted strategy to achieve the desired performance results.

The specifics of how to implement a strategy and deliver the intended results must start with understanding the requirements for good strategy execution. Afterward comes a diagnosis of the organization's preparedness to execute the strategic initiatives and decisions on how to move forward and achieve the targeted results.[20] In general, leading the drive for good strategy execution and operating excellence calls for three actions on the part of the managers in charge:

- Staying on top of what is happening and closely monitoring progress.
- Putting constructive pressure on the organization to execute the strategy well and achieve operating excellence.
- Initiating corrective actions to improve strategy execution and achieve the targeted performance results.

## Staying on Top of How Well Things Are Going

To stay on top of how well the strategy execution process is going, senior executives have to tap into information from a wide range of sources. In addition to communicating regularly with key subordinates and reviewing the latest operating results, watching the competitive reactions of rival firms, and visiting with key customers and suppliers to get their perspectives, they usually visit various company facilities and talk with many different company personnel at many different organizational levels—a technique often labeled **managing by walking around (MBWA).** Most managers attach great importance to spending time with people at company facilities, asking questions, listening to their opinions and concerns, and gathering firsthand information about how well aspects of the strategy execution process are going. Facilities tours and face-to-face contacts with operating-level employees give executives a good grasp of what progress is being made, what problems are being encountered, and whether additional resources or different approaches may be needed. Just as important, MBWA provides opportunities to give encouragement, lift spirits, shift attention from the old to the new priorities, and create some excitement—all of which generate positive energy and help boost strategy execution efforts.

Jeff Bezos, Amazon.com's CEO, is noted for his practice of MBWA, firing off a battery of questions when he tours facilities and insisting that Amazon managers spend time in the trenches with their people to prevent getting disconnected from the reality of what's happening.[21] Walmart executives have had a long-standing practice of spending two to three days every week visiting Walmart's stores and talking with store managers and employees. Sam Walton, Walmart's founder, insisted, "The key is to get out into the store and listen to what the associates have to say." Jack Welch, the highly effective former CEO of General Electric, not only spent several days each month personally visiting GE operations and talking with major customers but also arranged his schedule so that he could spend time exchanging information and ideas with GE managers from all over the world who were attending classes at the company's leadership development center near GE's headquarters.

Many manufacturing executives make a point of strolling the factory floor to talk with workers and meeting regularly with union officials. Some managers operate out

---

**LO 4**

What constitutes effective managerial leadership in achieving superior strategy execution.

---

**CORE CONCEPT**

**Management by walking around (MBWA)** is one of the techniques that effective leaders use to stay informed about how well the strategy execution process is progressing.

of open cubicles in big spaces filled with open cubicles for other personnel so that they can interact easily and frequently with co-workers. Managers at some companies host weekly get-togethers (often on Friday afternoons) to create a regular opportunity for information to flow freely between down-the-line employees and executives.

# Mobilizing the Effort for Excellence in Strategy Execution

Part of the leadership task in mobilizing organizational energy behind the drive for good strategy execution entails nurturing a results-oriented work climate, where performance standards are high and a spirit of achievement is pervasive. Successfully leading the effort is typically characterized by such leadership actions and managerial practices as:

- *Treating employees as valued partners.* Some companies symbolize the value of individual employees and the importance of their contributions by referring to them as cast members (Disney), crew members (McDonald's), job owners (Graniterock), partners (Starbucks), or associates (Walmart, LensCrafters, W. L. Gore, Edward Jones, Publix Supermarkets, and Marriott International). Very often, there is a strong company commitment to training each employee thoroughly, offering attractive compensation and benefits, emphasizing promotion from within and promising career opportunities, providing a high degree of job security, and otherwise making employees feel well treated and valued.

- *Fostering an esprit de corps that energizes organization members.* The task here is to skillfully use people-management practices calculated to build morale, foster pride in working for the company, promote teamwork and collaborative group effort, win the emotional commitment of individuals and organizational units to what the company is trying to accomplish, and inspire company personnel to do their best in achieving good results.[22]

- *Using empowerment to help create a fully engaged workforce.* Top executives—and, to some degree, the enterprise's entire management team—must seek to engage the full organization in the strategy execution effort. A fully engaged workforce, where individuals bring their best to work every day, is necessary to produce great results.[23] So is having a group of dedicated managers committed to making a difference in their organization. The two best things top-level executives can do to create a fully engaged organization are (1) delegate authority to middle and lower-level managers to get the strategy execution process moving and (2) empower rank-and-file employees to act on their own initiative. Operating excellence requires that everybody contribute ideas, exercise initiative and creativity in performing his or her work, and have a desire to do things in the best possible manner.

- *Setting stretch objectives and clearly communicating an expectation that company personnel are to give their best in achieving performance targets.* Stretch objectives—those beyond an organization's current capacities—can sometimes spur organization members to increase their resolve and redouble their efforts to execute the strategy flawlessly and ultimately reach the stretch objectives. When stretch objectives are met, the satisfaction of achievement and boost to employee morale can result in an even higher level of organizational drive.

- *Using the tools of benchmarking, best practices, business process reengineering, TQM, and Six Sigma to focus attention on continuous improvement.* These are proven approaches to getting better operating results and facilitating better strategy execution.

- *Using the full range of motivational techniques and compensation incentives to inspire company personnel, nurture a results-oriented work climate, and reward high performance.* Managers cannot mandate innovative improvements by simply exhorting people to "be creative," nor can they make continuous progress toward operating excellence with directives to "try harder." Rather, they must foster a culture where innovative ideas and experimentation with new ways of doing things can blossom and thrive. Individuals and groups should be strongly encouraged to brainstorm, let their imaginations fly in all directions, and come up with proposals for improving the way that things are done. This means giving company personnel enough autonomy to stand out, excel, and contribute. And it means that the rewards for successful champions of new ideas and operating improvements should be large and visible. It is particularly important that people who champion an unsuccessful idea are not punished or sidelined but, rather, encouraged to try again. Finding great ideas requires taking risks and recognizing that many ideas won't pan out.

- *Celebrating individual, group, and company successes.* Top management should miss no opportunity to express respect for individual employees and appreciation of extraordinary individual and group effort.[24] Companies like Google, Tupperware, and McDonald's actively seek out reasons and opportunities to give pins, ribbons, buttons, badges, and medals for good showings by average performers—the idea being to express appreciation and give a motivational boost to people who stand out in doing ordinary jobs. Whole Foods, Cisco Systems, and 3M Corporation make a point of ceremoniously honoring individuals who believe so strongly in their ideas that they take it on themselves to hurdle the bureaucracy, maneuver their projects through the system, and turn them into improved services, new products, or even new businesses. Taj Hotels Resorts and Palaces credits its ability to deliver unprecedented levels of service to its guests to its Special Thanks and Recognition System (STARS) program, which rewards employees for exceptional effort, tracked on a yearly basis using a variety of metrics.[25]

While leadership efforts to instill a results-oriented, high-performance culture usually accentuate the positive, negative consequences for poor performance must be in play as well. Managers whose units consistently perform poorly must be replaced. Low-performing workers and people who reject the results-oriented cultural emphasis must be weeded out or at least employed differently. Average performers should be candidly counseled that they have limited career potential unless they show more progress in the form of additional effort, better skills, and improved ability to execute the strategy well and deliver good results.

## Leading the Process of Making Corrective Adjustments

There comes a time at every company when managers have to fine-tune or overhaul the approaches to strategy execution since no action plan for executing strategy can foresee all the problems that will arise. Clearly, when a company's strategy execution effort is not delivering good results, it is the leader's responsibility to step forward and initiate corrective actions, although sometimes it must be recognized that unsatisfactory performance may be due as much or more to flawed strategy as to weak strategy execution.[26]

Success in making corrective actions hinges on (1) a thorough analysis of the situation, (2) the exercise of good business judgment in deciding what actions to take, and (3) good implementation of the corrective actions that are initiated. Successful managers are skilled in getting an organization back on track rather quickly. They (and their staffs) are good at discerning what actions to take and in bringing them to a successful conclusion. Managers who struggle to show measurable progress in implementing corrective actions in a timely fashion are candidates for being replaced.

The *process* of making corrective adjustments in strategy execution varies according to the situation. In a crisis, taking remedial action quickly is of the essence. But it still takes time to review the situation, examine the available data, identify and evaluate options (crunching whatever numbers may be appropriate to determine which options are likely to generate the best outcomes), and decide what to do. When the situation allows managers to proceed more deliberately in deciding when to make changes and what changes to make, most managers seem to prefer a process of incrementally solidifying commitment to a particular course of action.[27] The process that managers go through in deciding on corrective adjustments is essentially the same for both proactive and reactive changes: They sense needs, gather information, broaden and deepen their understanding of the situation, develop options and explore their pros and cons, put forth action proposals, strive for a consensus, and finally formally adopt an agreed-on course of action. The time frame for deciding what corrective changes to initiate can be a few hours, a few days, a few weeks, or even a few months if the situation is particularly complicated.

The challenges of making the right corrective adjustments and leading a successful strategy execution effort are, without question, substantial.[28] There's no generic, by-the-books procedure to follow. Because each instance of executing strategy occurs under different organizational circumstances, the managerial agenda for executing strategy always needs to be situation-specific. But the job is definitely doable. Although there is no prescriptive answer to the question of exactly what to do, any of several courses of action may produce good results. As we said at the beginning of Chapter 10, executing strategy is an action-oriented, make-the-right-things-happen task that challenges a manager's ability to lead and direct organizational change, create or reinvent business processes, manage and motivate people, and achieve performance targets. If you now better understand what the challenges are, what tasks are involved, what tools can be used to aid the managerial process of executing strategy, and why the action agenda for implementing and executing strategy sweeps across so many aspects of managerial work, then the discussions in Chapters 10, 11, and 12 have been a success.

# A FINAL WORD ON LEADING THE PROCESS OF CRAFTING AND EXECUTING STRATEGY

In practice, it is hard to separate leading the process of executing strategy from leading the other pieces of the strategy process. As we emphasized in Chapter 2, the job of crafting and executing strategy consists of five interrelated and linked stages, with much looping and recycling to fine-tune and adjust the strategic vision, objectives, strategy, and implementation approaches to fit one another and to fit changing circumstances. The process is continuous, and the conceptually separate acts of crafting and executing strategy blur together in real-world situations. *The best tests of good strategic leadership are whether the company has a good strategy and business model, whether the strategy is being competently executed, and whether the enterprise is meeting or beating its performance targets.* If these three conditions exist, then there is every reason to conclude that the company has good strategic leadership and is a well-managed enterprise.

# KEY POINTS

1. Corporate culture is the character of a company's internal work climate—the shared values, ingrained attitudes, core beliefs and company traditions that determine norms of behavior, accepted work practices, and styles of operating. A company's culture is important because it influences the organization's actions, its approaches to conducting business, and ultimately its performance in the marketplace. It can be thought of as the company's organizational DNA.

2. The key features of a company's culture include the company's values and ethical standards, its approach to people management, its work atmosphere and company spirit, how its personnel interact, the strength of peer pressure to conform to norms, the behaviors awarded through incentives (both financial and symbolic), the traditions and oft-repeated "myths," and its manner of dealing with stakeholders.

3. A company's culture is grounded in and shaped by its core values and ethical standards. Core values and ethical principles serve two roles in the culture-building process: (1) They foster a work climate in which employees share common and strongly held convictions about how company business is to be conducted, and (2) they provide company personnel with guidance about the manner in which they are to do their jobs—which behaviors and ways of doing things are approved (and expected) and which are out-of-bounds. They serve as yardsticks for gauging the appropriateness of particular actions, decisions, and behaviors.

4. Company cultures vary widely in strength and influence. Some cultures are *strong* and have a big impact on a company's practices and behavioral norms. Others are *weak* and have comparatively little influence on company operations.

5. Strong company cultures can have either positive or negative effects on strategy execution. When they are in sync with the chosen strategy and well matched to the behavioral requirements of the company's strategy implementation plan, they can be a powerful aid to strategy execution. A culture that is grounded in the types of actions and behaviors that are conducive to good strategy execution assists the effort in three ways:

    • By focusing employee attention on the actions that are most important in the strategy execution effort.

    • By inducing peer pressure for employees to contribute to the success of the strategy execution effort.

    • By energizing employees, deepening their commitment to the strategy execution effort, and increasing the productivity of their efforts

    It is thus in management's best interest to dedicate considerable effort to establishing a strongly implanted corporate culture that encourages behaviors and work practices conducive to good strategy execution.

6. Strong corporate cultures that are conducive to good strategy execution are healthy cultures. So are high-performance cultures and adaptive cultures. The latter are particularly important in dynamic environments. Strong cultures can also be unhealthy. The five types of unhealthy cultures are those that are (1) change-resistant, (2) heavily politicized, (3) insular and inwardly focused, (4) ethically unprincipled and infused with greed, and (5) composed of incompatible subcultures. All five impede good strategy execution.

7. Changing a company's culture, especially a strong one with traits that don't fit a new strategy's requirements, is a tough and often time-consuming challenge. Changing a culture requires competent leadership at the top. It requires making a compelling case for cultural change and employing both symbolic actions and substantive actions that unmistakably indicate serious and credible commitment on the part of top management. The more that culture-driven actions and behaviors fit what's needed for good strategy execution, the less managers must depend on policies, rules, procedures, and supervision to enforce what people should and should not do.

8. Leading the drive for good strategy execution and operating excellence calls for three actions on the part of the manager in charge:
   - Staying on top of what is happening and closely monitoring progress. This is often accomplished through managing by walking around (MBWA).
   - Mobilizing the effort for excellence in strategy execution by putting constructive pressure on the organization to execute the strategy well.
   - Initiating corrective actions to improve strategy execution and achieve the targeted performance results.

## ASSURANCE OF LEARNING EXERCISES

**connect**
LO 1

1. Go to the company website for REI (www.rei.com). Click on the Stewardship tab, and then click on some of the tabs below to learn more about the company's culture and values. What are the key features of its culture? Do features of REI's culture influence the company's ethical practices? If so, how?

LO 2

2. Based on what you learned about REI from answering the previous question, how do you think the company's culture affects its ability to execute strategy and operate with excellence?

**connect**
LO 1, LO 2

3. Illustration Capsule 12.1 discusses W. L. Gore's strategy-supportive corporate culture. What are the standout features of Gore's corporate culture? How does Gore's culture contribute to innovation and creativity at the company? How does the company's culture make Gore a good place to work?

LO 3

4. If you were an executive at a company that had a pervasive yet problematic culture, what steps would you take to change it? Using Google Scholar or your university library's access to EBSCO, LexisNexis, or other databases, search for recent articles in business publications on "culture change." What role did the executives play in the culture change? How does this differ from what you would have done to change the culture?

LO 4

5. Leading the strategy execution process involves staying on top of the situation and monitoring progress, putting constructive pressure on the organization to achieve operating excellence, and initiating corrective actions to improve the execution effort. Using your university's access to business periodicals, discuss a recent example of how a company's managers have demonstrated the kind of effective internal leadership needed for superior strategy execution.

## EXERCISE FOR SIMULATION PARTICIPANTS

1.  If you were making a speech to company personnel, what would you tell employees about the kind of corporate culture you would like to have at your company? What specific cultural traits would you like your company to exhibit? Explain.   **LO 1, LO 2**

2.  What core values would you want to ingrain in your company's culture? Why?   **LO 1**

3.  Following each decision round, do you and your co-managers make corrective adjustments in either your company's strategy or the way the strategy is being executed? List at least three such adjustments you made in the most recent decision round. What hard evidence (in the form of results relating to your company's performance in the most recent year) can you cite that indicates that the various corrective adjustments you made either succeeded at improving or failed to improve your company's performance?   **LO 3, LO 4**

4.  What would happen to your company's performance if you and your co-managers stick with the status quo and fail to make any corrective adjustments after each decision round?   **LO 4**

## ENDNOTES

[1] Jennifer A. Chatham and Sandra E. Cha, "Leading by Leveraging Culture," *California Management Review* 45, no. 4 (Summer 2003), pp. 20–34; Edgar Shein, *Organizational Culture and Leadership: A Dynamic View* (San Francisco, CA: Jossey-Bass, 1992).

[2] T. E. Deal and A. A. Kennedy, *Corporate Cultures: The Rites and Rituals of Corporate Life* (Harmondsworth, UK: Penguin, 1982).

[3] Joanne Reid and Victoria Hubbell, "Creating a Performance Culture," *Ivey Business Journal* 69, no. 4 (March–April 2005), p. 1.

[4] Diane Brady, "The Immelt Revolution," *Businessweek,* March 27, 2005, www.businessweek.com (accessed April 4, 2013).

[5] www.publix.com/about/PublixHistory.do (accessed February 22, 2014).

[6] www.forbes.com/sites/briansolomon/2013/07/24/the-wal-mart-slayer-how-publixs-people-first-culture-is-winning-the-grocer-war/ (accessed February 22, 2014).

[7] John P. Kotter and James L. Heskett, *Corporate Culture and Performance* (New York: Free Press, 1992), p. 7. See also Robert Goffee and Gareth Jones, *The Character of a Corporation* (New York: HarperCollins, 1998).

[8] Joseph L. Badaracco, *Defining Moments: When Managers Must Choose between Right and Wrong* (Boston: Harvard Business School Press, 1997); Joe Badaracco and Allen P. Webb, "Business Ethics: A View from the Trenches," *California Management Review* 37, no. 2 (Winter 1995), pp. 8–28; Patrick E. Murphy, "Corporate Ethics Statements: Current Status and Future Prospects," *Journal of*

*Business Ethics* 14 (1995), pp. 727–740; Lynn Sharp Paine, "Managing for Organizational Integrity," *Harvard Business Review* 72, no. 2 (March–April 1994), pp. 106–117.

[9] Emily F. Carasco and Jang B. Singh, "The Content and Focus of the Codes of Ethics of the World's Largest Transnational Corporations," *Business and Society Review* 108, no. 1 (January 2003), pp. 71–94; Patrick E. Murphy, "Corporate Ethics Statements: Current Status and Future Prospects," *Journal of Business Ethics* 14 (1995), pp. 727–740; John Humble, David Jackson, and Alan Thomson, "The Strategic Power of Corporate Values," *Long Range Planning* 27, no. 6 (December 1994), pp. 28–42; Mark S. Schwartz, "A Code of Ethics for Corporate Codes of Ethics," *Journal of Business Ethics* 41, no. 1–2 (November–December 2002), pp. 27–43.

[10] mentalfloss.com/article/30198/11-best-customer-service-stories-ever (accessed February 22, 2014).

[11] Terrence E. Deal and Allen A. Kennedy, *Corporate Cultures* (Reading, MA: Addison-Wesley, 1982); Terrence E. Deal and Allen A. Kennedy, *The New Corporate Cultures: Revitalizing the Workplace after Downsizing, Mergers, and Reengineering* (Cambridge, MA: Perseus, 1999).

[12] Vijay Sathe, *Culture and Related Corporate Realities* (Homewood, IL: Irwin, 1985).

[13] Avan R. Jassawalla and Hemant C. Sashittal, "Cultures That Support Product-Innovation Processes," *Academy of Management Executive* 16, no. 3 (August 2002), pp. 42–54.

[14] Kotter and Heskett, *Corporate Culture and Performance,* p. 5.

[15] Reid and Hubbell, "Creating a Performance Culture," pp. 1–5.

[16] Jay B. Barney and Delwyn N. Clark, *Resource-Based Theory: Creating and Sustaining Competitive Advantage* (New York: Oxford University Press, 2007), chap. 4.

[17] Rosabeth Moss Kanter, "Transforming Giants," *Harvard Business Review* 86, no. 1 (January 2008), pp. 43–52.

[18] Kurt Eichenwald, *Conspiracy of Fools: A True Story* (New York: Broadway Books, 2005).

[19] Judy D. Olian and Sara L. Rynes, "Making Total Quality Work: Aligning Organizational Processes, Performance Measures, and Stakeholders," *Human Resource Management* 30, no. 3 (Fall 1991), p. 324.

[20] Larry Bossidy and Ram Charan, *Confronting Reality: Doing What Matters to Get Things Right* (New York: Crown Business, 2004); Larry Bossidy and Ram Charan, *Execution: The Discipline of Getting Things Done* (New York: Crown Business, 2002); John P. Kotter, "Leading Change: Why Transformation Efforts Fail," *Harvard Business Review* 73, no. 2 (March–April 1995), pp. 59–67; Thomas M. Hout and John C. Carter, "Getting It Done: New Roles for Senior Executives," *Harvard Business Review* 73, no. 6 (November–December 1995), pp. 133–145; Sumantra Ghoshal and Christopher A. Bartlett, "Changing the Role of Top Management: Beyond Structure to Processes," *Harvard Business Review* 73, no. 1 (January–February 1995), pp. 86–96.

[21] Fred Vogelstein, "Winning the Amazon Way," *Fortune,* May 26, 2003, p. 64.

[22] For a more in-depth discussion of the leader's role in creating a results-oriented culture that nurtures success, see Benjamin Schneider, Sarah K. Gunnarson, and Kathryn Niles-Jolly, "Creating the Climate and Culture of Success," *Organizational Dynamics,* Summer 1994, pp. 17–29.

[23] Michael T. Kanazawa and Robert H. Miles, *Big Ideas to Big Results* (Upper Saddle River, NJ: FT Press, 2008).

[24] Jeffrey Pfeffer, "Producing Sustainable Competitive Advantage through the Effective Management of People," *Academy of Management Executive* 9, no.1 (February 1995), pp. 55–69.

[25] www.forbes.com/sites/kevinkruse/2012/10/08/employee-recognition/.

[26] Cynthia A. Montgomery, "Putting Leadership Back into Strategy," *Harvard Business Review* 86, no. 1 (January 2008), pp. 54–60.

[27] James Brian Quinn, *Strategies for Change: Logical Incrementalism* (Homewood, IL: Irwin, 1980).

[28] Daniel Goleman, "What Makes a Leader," *Harvard Business Review* 76, no. 6 (November–December 1998), pp. 92–102; Ronald A. Heifetz and Donald L. Laurie, "The Work of Leadership," *Harvard Business Review* 75, no. 1 (January–February 1997), pp. 124–134; Charles M. Farkas and Suzy Wetlaufer, "The Ways Chief Executive Officers Lead," *Harvard Business Review* 74, no. 3 (May–June 1996), pp. 110–122; Michael E. Porter, Jay W. Lorsch, and Nitin Nohria, "Seven Surprises for New CEOs," *Harvard Business Review* 82, no. 10 (October 2004), pp. 62–72.

# PART 2

## Cases in Crafting and Executing Strategy

# Mystic Monk Coffee

connect

## David L. Turnipseed
University of South Alabama

As Father Daniel Mary, the prior of the Carmelite Order of monks in Clark, Wyoming, walked to chapel to preside over Mass, he noticed the sun glistening across the four-inch snowfall from the previous evening. Snow in June was not unheard of in Wyoming, but the late snowfall and the bright glow of the rising sun made him consider the opposing forces accompanying change and how he might best prepare his monastery to achieve his vision of creating a new Mount Carmel in the Rocky Mountains. His vision of transforming the small brotherhood of 13 monks living in a small home used as makeshift rectory into a 500-acre monastery that would include accommodations for 30 monks, a Gothic church, a convent for Carmelite nuns, a retreat center for lay visitors, and a hermitage presented a formidable challenge. However, as a former high school football player, boxer, bull rider, and man of great faith, Father Prior Daniel Mary was unaccustomed to shrinking from a challenge.

Father Prior had identified a nearby ranch for sale that met the requirements of his vision perfectly, but its current listing price of $8.9 million presented a financial obstacle to creating a place of prayer, worship, and solitude in the Rockies. The Carmelites had received a $250,000 donation that could be used toward the purchase, and the monastery had earned nearly $75,000 during the first year of its Mystic Monk coffee-roasting operations, but more money would be needed. The coffee roaster used to produce packaged coffee sold to Catholic consumers at the Mystic Monk Coffee website was reaching its capacity, but a larger roaster could be purchased for $35,000. Also, local Cody, Wyoming, business owners had begun a foundation for those

wishing to donate to the monks' cause. Father Prior Daniel Mary did not have a great deal of experience in business matters but considered to what extent the monastery could rely on its Mystic Monk Coffee operations to fund the purchase of the ranch. If Mystic Monk Coffee was capable of making the vision a reality, what were the next steps in turning the coffee into land?

## THE CARMELITE MONKS OF WYOMING

Carmelites are a religious order of the Catholic Church that was formed by men who traveled to the Holy Land as pilgrims and crusaders and had chosen to remain near Jerusalem to seek God. The men established their hermitage at Mount Carmel because of its beauty, seclusion, and biblical importance as the site where Elijah stood against King Ahab and the false prophets of Jezebel to prove Jehovah to be the one true God. The Carmelites led a life of solitude, silence, and prayer at Mount Carmel before eventually returning to Europe and becoming a recognized order of the Catholic Church. The size of the Carmelite Order varied widely throughout the centuries with its peak in the 1600s and stood at approximately 2,200 friars living on all inhabited continents at the beginning of the 21st century.

The Wyoming Carmelite monastery was founded by Father Daniel Mary, who lived as a Carmelite hermit in Minnesota before moving to Clark, Wyoming, to establish the new monastery. The Wyoming Carmelites were a cloistered order and were allowed to leave the monastery only by permission of the bishop for medical needs or the death of a family member. The Wyoming monastery's abbey bore little resemblance to the great stone cathedrals and monasteries of Europe and was confined to a rectory that had once been a four-bedroom ranch-style home and an adjoining 42 acres of land that had been donated to the monastery.

There were 13 monks dedicated to a life of prayer and worship in the Wyoming Carmelite monastery. Since the founding of the monastery six years ago, there had been more than 500 inquiries from young men considering becoming a Wyoming Carmelite. Father Prior Daniel Mary wished to eventually have 30 monks who would join the brotherhood at age 19 to 30 and live out their lives in the monastery. However, the selection criteria for acceptance into the monastery were rigorous, with the monks making certain that applicants understood the reality of the vows of obedience, chastity, and poverty and the sacrifices associated with living a cloistered religious life.

## The Daily Activities of a Carmelite Monk

The Carmelite monks' day began at 4:10 a.m., when they arose and went to chapel for worship wearing traditional brown habits and handmade sandals. At about 6:00 a.m., the monks rested and contemplated in silence for one hour before Father Prior began morning Mass. After Mass, the monks went about their manual labors. In performing their labors, each brother had a special set of skills that enabled the monastery to independently maintain its operations. Brother Joseph Marie was an excellent mechanic, Brother Paul was a carpenter, Brother Peter Joseph (Brother Cook) worked in the kitchen, and five-foot, four-inch Brother Simon Mary (Little Monk) was the secretary to Father Daniel Mary. Brother Elias, affectionately known as Brother Java, was Mystic Monk Coffee's master roaster, although he was not a coffee drinker.

Each monk worked up to six hours per day; however, the monks' primary focus was spiritual, with eight hours of each day spent in prayer. At 11:40 a.m., the monks stopped work and went to Chapel. Afterward they had lunch, cleaned the dishes, and went back to work. At 3:00 p.m., the hour that Jesus was believed to have died on the cross, work stopped again for prayer and worship. The monks then returned to work until the bell was rung for Vespers (evening prayer). After Vespers, the monks had an hour of silent contemplation, an evening meal, and more prayers before bedtime.

## The New Mount Carmel

Soon after arriving in Wyoming, Father Daniel Mary had formed the vision of acquiring a large parcel of land—a new Mount Carmel—and building a monastery with accommodations for 30 monks, a retreat center for lay visitors, a Gothic church, a convent for Carmelite nuns, and a hermitage. In a letter to supporters posted on the monastery's website, Father Daniel Mary succinctly stated his vision: "We beg your prayers, your friendship and your support that this vision, our vision may come to be that Mount Carmel may be refounded in Wyoming's Rockies for the glory of God."

The brothers located a 496-acre ranch for sale that would satisfy all of the requirements to create a new Mount Carmel. The Irma Lake Ranch was located about 21 miles outside Cody, Wyoming, and included a remodeled 17,800-square-foot residence, a 1,700-square-foot caretaker house, a 2,950-square-foot guesthouse, a hunting cabin, a dairy and horse barn, and forested land. The ranch was at the end of a seven-mile-long private gravel road and was bordered on one side by the private Hoodoo Ranch (100,000 acres) and on the other by the Shoshone National Park (2.4 million acres). Although the asking price was $8.9 million, the monks believed they would be able to acquire the property through donations and the profits generated by the monastery's Mystic Monk Coffee operations. The $250,000 donation they had received from an individual wishing to support the Carmelites could be applied toward whatever purpose the monks chose. Additionally, a group of Cody business owners had formed the New Mount Carmel Foundation to help the monks raise funds.

## OVERVIEW OF THE COFFEE INDUSTRY

About 150 million consumers in the United States drank coffee, with 89 percent of U.S. coffee drinkers brewing their own coffee at home rather than purchasing ready-to-drink coffee at coffee shops and restaurants such as Starbucks, Dunkin' Donuts, or McDonald's. Packaged coffee for home brewing was easy to find in any grocery store and typically carried a retail price of $4 to $6 for a 12-ounce package. About 30 million coffee drinkers in the United States preferred premium-quality specialty coffees that sold for $7 to $10 per 12-ounce package. Specialty coffees are made from high-quality Arabica beans instead of the mix of low-quality Arabica beans and bitter, less flavorful Robusta beans that makers of value brands use. The wholesale price of Robusta coffee beans averaged $1.15 per pound, while mild Columbian Arabica wholesale prices averaged $1.43 per pound.

Prior to the 1990s, the market for premium-quality specialty coffees barely existed in the United States, but Howard Schultz's vision for Starbucks of bringing the Italian espresso bar experience to America helped specialty coffees become a large and thriving segment of the industry. The company's pursuit of its mission, "To inspire and nurture the human spirit—one person, one cup, and one neighborhood at a time," had allowed Starbucks to become an iconic brand in most parts of the world. The company's success had given rise to a number of competing specialty coffee shops and premium brands of packaged specialty coffee, including Seattle's Best, Millstone, Green Mountain Coffee Roasters, and First Colony Coffee and Tea. Some producers such as First Colony had difficulty gaining shelf space in supermarkets and concentrated on private-label roasting and packaging for fine department stores and other retailers wishing to have a proprietary brand of coffee.

Specialty coffees sold under premium brands might have been made from shade-grown or organically grown coffee beans, or have been purchased from a grower belonging to a World Fair Trade Organization (WFTO) cooperative. WFTO cooperative growers were paid above-market prices to better support the cost of operating their farms—for example, WFTO-certified organic wholesale prices averaged $1.55 per pound. Many consumers who purchased specialty coffees were willing to pay a higher price for organic, shade-grown, or fair trade coffee because of their personal health or social concerns—organic coffees are grown without the use of synthetic fertilizers or pesticides, shade-grown coffee plants are allowed to grow beneath the canopies of larger indigenous trees, and fair trade pricing makes it easier for farmers in developing countries to pay workers a living wage. The specialty coffee segment of the retail coffee industry had grown dramatically in the United States, with retail sales increasing from $8.3 billion to $13.5 billion during the last seven years. The retail sales of organic coffee accounted for about $1 billion of industry sales and had grown at an annual rate of 32 percent for each of the last seven years.

# MYSTIC MONK COFFEE

Mystic Monk Coffee was produced using high-quality fair trade Arabica and fair trade/organic Arabica beans. The monks produced whole-bean and ground caffeinated and decaffeinated varieties in dark, medium, and light roasts and in different flavors. The most popular Mystic Monk flavors were Mystical Chants of Carmel, Cowboy Blend, Royal Rum Pecan, and Mystic Monk Blend. With the exception of sample bags, which carried a retail price of $2.99, all varieties of Mystic Monk Coffee were sold via the monastery's website (**www.mysticmonkcoffee.com**) in 12-ounce bags at a price of $9.95. All purchases from the website were delivered by United Parcel Service (UPS) or the U.S. Postal Service. Frequent customers were given the option of joining a "coffee club," which offered monthly delivery of one to six bags of preselected coffee. Purchases of three or more bags qualified for free shipping. The Mystic Monk Coffee website also featured T-shirts, gift cards, CDs featuring the monastery's Gregorian chants, and coffee mugs.

Mystic Monk Coffee's target market was the segment of the U.S. Catholic population who drank coffee and wished to support the monastery's mission. More than 69 million Americans were members of the Catholic Church—making it four times larger than the second-largest Christian denomination in the United States. An appeal to Catholics to "use their Catholic coffee dollar for Christ and his Catholic church" was published on the Mystic Monk Coffee website.

## Mystic Monk Coffee-Roasting Operations

After the morning religious services and breakfast, Brother Java roasted the green coffee beans delivered each week from a coffee broker in Seattle,

Washington. The monks paid the Seattle broker the prevailing wholesale price per pound, which fluctuated daily with global supply and demand. The capacity of Mystic Monk Coffee's roaster limited production to 540 pounds per day; production was also limited by time devoted to prayer, silent meditation, and worship. Demand for Mystic Monk Coffee had not yet exceeded the roaster's capacity, but the monastery planned to purchase a larger, 130-pound-per-hour-roaster when demand further approached the current roaster's capacity. The monks had received a quote of $35,000 for the new larger roaster.

## Marketing and Website Operations

Mystic Monk Coffee was promoted primarily by word of mouth among loyal customers in Catholic parishes across the United States. The majority of Mystic Monk's sales were made through its website, but on occasion telephone orders were placed with the monks' secretary, who worked outside the cloistered part of the monastery. Mystic Monk also offered secular website operators commissions on its sales through its Mystic Monk Coffee Affiliate Program, which placed banner ads and text ads on participating websites. Affiliate sites earned an 18 percent commission on sales made to customers who were directed to the Mystic Monk site from their site. The affiliate program's ShareASale participation level allowed affiliates to refer new affiliates to Mystic Monk and earn 56 percent of the new affiliate's commission. The monks had also just recently expanded Mystic Monk's business model to include wholesale sales to churches and local coffee shops.

## Mystic Monk's Financial Performance

At the conclusion of Mystic Monk Coffee's first year in operation, its sales of coffee and coffee accessories averaged about $56,500 per month. Its cost of sales averaged about 30 percent of revenues, inbound shipping costs accounted for 19 percent of revenues, and broker fees were 3 percent of revenues—for a total cost of goods sold of 52 percent. Operating expenses such as utilities, supplies, telephone, and website maintenance averaged 37 percent of revenues. Thus, Mystic Monk's net profit margin averaged 11 percent of revenues.

# REALIZING THE VISION

During a welcome period of solitude before his evening meal, Father Prior Daniel Mary again contemplated the purchase of the Irma Lake Ranch. He realized that his vision of purchasing the ranch would require careful planning and execution. For the Wyoming Carmelites, coffee sales were a means of support from the outside world that might provide the financial resources to purchase the land. Father Prior understood that the cloistered monastic environment offered unique challenges to operating a business enterprise, but it also provided opportunities that were not available to secular businesses. He resolved to develop an execution plan that would enable Mystic Monk Coffee to minimize the effect of its cloistered monastic constraints, maximize the potential of monastic opportunities, and realize his vision of buying the Irma Lake Ranch.

# BillCutterz.com: Business Model, Strategy, and the Challenges of Exponential Growth

connect

### John E. Gamble
Texas A&M University–Corpus Christi

### Randall D. Harris
Texas A&M University–Corpus Christi

Barry Gross, founder and president of BillCutterz .com, celebrated his birthday on January 21, 2014, by inviting friends and family to his Corpus Christi, Texas, home to watch the airing of his previously taped interview with Diane Sawyer on *ABC World News Tonight.* His four-year-old bill negotiation company, BillCutterz.com, was being featured on that evening's "Real Money" segment, which explained how his company was saving its customers hundreds or thousands of dollars each year on their monthly bills. The segment described how BillCutterz.com negotiated on behalf of its enrolled customers to reduce the amounts of their cable, Internet, mobile phone, and other service provider bills by as much as 50 percent. BillCutterz .com's negotiation tactic centered on convincing the provider that it was less costly to lower the customer's monthly bill than to go through the expense of acquiring a new customer to replace a dissatisfied customer. The segment also featured interviews with BillCutterz.com customers who discussed how the company's bill negotiation service had saved them $1,500 or more per year on their monthly expenses.

Those gathered to celebrate Gross's birthday marveled at how much his customers benefited from the service provided by his company and many asked about how they could enroll to have their bills lowered as well. Gross explained that customers could enroll at BillCutterz.com and upload copies of their most recent bills to begin the process. After telling his guests more about his business and enjoying the evening, he received a call from an employee telling him that 6,500 new customers had enrolled and 19,500 bills had been uploaded in the first 1½ hours since the segment aired. Gross expected the segment to boost enrollees, but he was not prepared for such a spike in new business.

Within days of the *ABC World News Tonight* segment, Gross also appeared live on *Fox Business News* to discuss his company's approach to saving money for its customers on their monthly bills. The exposure from the two news segments brought in more than 30,000 new enrollees by February 2014. The vast increase in enrollees immediately focused Gross's activities on recruiting, selecting, and training new employees and ensuring that the bills of its new customers were properly negotiated to receive the greatest possible savings. At the end of its first quarter in 2014, BillCutterz.com was adding 20 to 30 new enrollments every day and had seen its revenues increase by more than 400 percent over the same period in 2013. However, it was far too early to tell if the company's business model, strategy, and operating approaches could withstand the challenges of exponential growth.

## COMPANY HISTORY

BillCutterz.com was launched in May 2009 when Barry Gross decided to pursue a business opportunity presented to him by a close friend. During a visit with long-time friend and mortgage banker Mindy

Niles, Gross asked if she could give him advice for lowering his mortgage payment. Niles told Gross he should request that his lender eliminate his PMI insurance requirement since the equity in his home had grown since the time of purchase. Gross called his lender and was able to save $180 per month. He thanked his friend and told her he had successfully negotiated reductions in his monthly cable and mobile phone bills and he could try to lower hers as well if she wished. Niles agreed and was later thrilled when she learned that Gross had reduced the amounts she was charged for the services by 50 percent. It was then that Niles pushed Gross to turn his negotiating skills into a business.

Before becoming a stockbroker in 1980, Gross had spent four years in telephone sales, most notably with the Houston, Texas, originator of crime scene tape. As marketing manager for Reef Industries, he was assigned responsibility for marketing the company's products, including Banner Guard. The company's caution tape had annual sales of only about $60,000 in 1976 when Gross began calling police chiefs and sheriffs across the United States to explain how the product could be used to keep curious citizens from disturbing and contaminating crime scenes. He shipped free samples after each call and later set up accounts with third-party distributors after demand from police departments began to grow. Within two years, Gross's strategy and near-constant television broadcasts of taped-off crime scenes produced a 5,000 percent increase in sales to $3 million. Reef Industries' caution tape soon became ubiquitous in law enforcement and extended its application to construction and industrial sites. When Gross left the company in 1980, Reef Industries' annual sales had grown to $18 million from $4 million in 1976.

Gross's career later focused on telephone sales at E. F. Hutton before he launched an investor relations firm in 1993. Gross's representation of publicly traded companies for investor communications matters continued in 2014. However, Gross ensured that his schedule included time for fishing off the Texas Gulf Coast since fishing was something that had been important to him most of his life. In fact, his career included a stint as a professional bass fisherman between 1990 and 1993.

Gross actually had quite a bit more time for fishing and serving his four investor relations clients until the January 2014 Diane Sawyer interview. The interviews on ABC and Fox resulted from e-mails sent to eight consumer blogger sites by BillCutterz.com's marketing director in April 2013. Sydney Alcala offered to work the personal bills of the bloggers to demonstrate BillCutterz.com's effectiveness. A blogger at lifehacker.com accepted the offer and within 24 hours of enrolling with BillCutterz.com, the blogger saved $400. The blogger wrote about the experience the very next day, which led to 3,000 enrollees at BillCutterz.com within the next three weeks. Among those impressed with the lifehacker.com review of BillCutterz.com was a contributor at *Men's Health,* who featured the company in the magazine's "How to Do Everything Better" section. Employees at both ABC News and Fox News saw the lifehacker.com piece and decided that BillCutterz.com would make a great story for television as well.

## BILLCUTTERZ.COM'S BUSINESS MODEL AND STRATEGY

BillCutterz.com's customer value proposition was easy for potential customers to understand. The company would negotiate lower rates on their monthly bills for such services as electricity and utilities, Internet, phone, waste management, and cable or satellite television. No fee was charged for BillCutterz.com's services unless savings were negotiated on behalf of its customer. Once savings were obtained and the customer had received revised bills from providers, BillCutterz.com would receive one-half of the savings for the first year. Customers could elect to pay the fee to BillCutterz.com in a single payment or in 12 equal payments over one year. Customers paying in a single payment received a 10 percent discount on the bill negotiation fee. Service providers usually provided the discount for 12 months, at which time the discount could be renegotiated.

The company's profit formula was largely dependent on the efficiency of the company's Savings Experts in coming to terms with customers' service providers since its fixed expenses were very small. BillCutterz.com was a business incubator client of the Coastal Bend Business Innovation Center, which provided Corpus Christi, Texas, entrepreneurs with low-cost, all-inclusive office space and mentoring on issues typically confronted by startup businesses. With low fixed costs limited mostly to computer hardware and software and office furniture purchases, labor expense became the determining factor on the profitability of the company. Gross explained the variability of this cost by commenting, "Our largest expense is payroll. Our profitability boils down to time and money. We train our Savings Experts to be as proficient and efficient as possible. They all know that the more calls they make, the more money we make."

Gross believed that nearly every U.S. citizen over the age of 18 was a potential customer since all adults had some type of monthly bill. Any bill other than a regulated utility bill could be negotiated. "People would be shocked at how many bills they really have that can be negotiated. It's not just power and cable. Things like landscaping, pet boarding, health club memberships can be negotiated as well," said Gross. In addition, the company sought to negotiate bills for businesses and nonprofit organizations. Just like individuals, businesses and other organizations had Internet provider bills, utilities, and maintenance contracts. For example, BillCutterz.com successfully obtained an $800-per-year discount on an elevator maintenance contract for a local church. The savings for organizations and businesses tended to be much larger than those obtained for households because of the larger expense amounts and greater number of services.

The company's strategy was also keyed to gaining referrals from existing clients, asking clients to provide more bills to negotiate, and building name recognition through social media marketing. The exposure from *Men's Health, ABC World News Tonight,* and *Fox Business News* had resulted in tens of thousands of new enrollees in just a matter of weeks. Gross was excited about the rapid growth in clients but was also investigating the possibility of developing a referral system to produce a steady stream of new enrollees. The only drawback to free media exposure was that it had produced large spikes in enrollments that stressed the company's ability to serve new customers in a timely manner. Barry Gross believed that a referral system would provide predictable growth that would allow personnel to be added and trained on a planned schedule. The appeal of BillCutterz.com's business model and strategy had allowed its revenues to grow to $92,000 during the first five months of 2014. The company's income statements for 2013 through May 31, 2014, are presented in Exhibit 1. The company's balance sheets for 2013 and the first five months of 2014 are presented in Exhibit 2.

# OVERVIEW OF THE BILL NEGOTIATION INDUSTRY

While no formal bill negotiation industry existed, BillCutterz.com did have indirect competition. Mint.com and Billshrink.com provided tools to help consumers monitor their budgets and compare the prices of competing service providers. Barriers to entry in the bill negotiation industry were limited primarily to experience in negotiating with service providers and capital necessary for office space and equipment. However, as of mid-2014, Gross knew of no direct competitor providing bill negotiation services.

Any leverage that BillCutterz.com had with creditors or service providers was related to a service provider's churn rate. *Churn rate,* sometimes called the *attrition rate,* was a measure of the number of customers leaving a service provider or other business over a specific period of time. For subscription-based businesses, even a small reduction in the churn rate of customers could have a large impact on the company's revenues and profitability.[1] Customer churn tended to occur when either (1) the quality of the customer's experience fell below a specific threshold relative to the competition (comparison churn) or (2) the quality of the customer's

**EXHIBIT 1**   Income Statements for BillCutterz.com, 2013 and Five Months Ending May 31, 2014

|  | Jan–May 2014 | 2013 |
|---|---|---|
| Revenues | $92,170 | $89,612 |
| Wages | 76,496 | 16,429 |
| Computer and Internet | 656 | 685 |
| Merchant processing fees | 2,686 | 1,117 |
| Office supplies | 5,037 | 4,209 |
| Rent | 4,066 | 7,188 |
| Telephone | 1,164 | 1,830 |
| Other expenses | 2,028 | 568 |
| Total expenses | 92,133 | 32,027 |
| Net Income | $    37 | $57,585 |

*Note:* Financials have been disguised for confidentiality purposes but reflect actual growth rates and percentage composition.

**EXHIBIT 2**  Balance Sheets for BillCutterz.com, 2013 and Five Months Ending May 31, 2014

| | Jan–May 2014 | 2013 |
|---|---|---|
| **Assets** | | |
| Current assets | | |
| Cash | $32,810 | $24,054 |
| Accounts receivable | 4,337 | 24,621 |
| Total current assets | 37,147 | 48,675 |
| Furniture and equipment | 8,223 | 8,222 |
| Total assets | $45,370 | $56,896 |
| **Liabilities and shareholders' equity** | | |
| Current liabilities | | |
| Revolving line of credit | $ 1,724 | $    387 |
| Total current liabilities | 1,724 | 387 |
| Long-term liabilities | | |
| Bank loan | 20,400 | 17,017 |
| Total long-term liabilities | 20,400 | 17,017 |
| Total liabilities | 22,124 | 17,403 |
| Shareholders' equity | 13,676 | 13,676 |
| Retained earnings | 9,569 | 25,817 |
| Total equity | 23,245 | 39,493 |
| Total liabilities and shareholders' equity | $45,370 | $56,896 |

*Note:* Financials have been disguised for confidentiality purposes but reflect actual growth rates and percentage composition.

experience fell below a threshold relative to his or her own expectations (frustration churn).[2]

Unfortunately for service providers and subscription-based businesses, customer satisfaction surveys rarely predicted the possibility that a customer might leave. Customer satisfaction surveys could not measure the desire to leave after a customer had already left.[3] Exit surveys were also of little utility; information provided by these surveys was often too generic to provide company management with insights regarding where to focus company retention efforts. Also, retention efforts with dissatisfied customers were difficult since most customers canceled after they had established a relationship with a competing service provider.[4] However, many service providers were willing to negotiate with dissatisfied customers if they had the opportunity. Such a

willingness to negotiate new terms with a customer made BillCutterz.com's business model possible. The degree to which service providers would negotiate with customers or their representatives over terms varied based on the importance of customer retention to the provider. One of the company's customers in Corpus Christi explained how much success BillCutterz.com had in negotiating with service providers:

> When I registered with BillCutterz.com, I really didn't expect much. I thought that I might get free HBO for six months or a better data plan on my cell phone bill. I was amazed when BillCutterz.com saved me $100 per month on my power bill alone. After paying BillCutterz.com their fee, I still saved $1,200 per year.

## BILLCUTTERZ.COM'S COMPETITIVE RESOURCES AND CAPABILITIES

Barry Gross's 30-plus years' experience in telephone marketing was among the company's greatest competitive assets. Gross was skilled at politely keeping customers on topic if they began to wander into a conversation unrelated to their bills and was effective in convincing customer retention personnel to accept his proposed terms. He honed his negotiating techniques over time to ensure that BillCutterz.com used the best possible leverage points with service providers to achieve large savings.

Much of Gross's daily activity involved training and coaching existing employees to become more skilled Savings Experts and recruiting new employees. The company's spike in enrollments in early 2013 created pressure on its existing three Savings Experts, with contact wait times increasing to seven days in some cases. By March 2014, Gross had been able to add new employees to handle the volume of calls to service providers, but he was still heavily involved in employee training. The bill negotiation process and the company's training focused on minimizing negotiation time and maximizing savings. A bill negotiation phone call could be completed in as little as 3 minutes or as much as 30 minutes—depending on the experience and expertise of the Savings Expert.

The training program for Savings Experts began with instructions on how to conduct consultations with customers to determine whether their current services matched their specific needs. Gross explained that the consultation was not the biggest factor in reducing the amounts of monthly bills. "We never try to convince the customer to eliminate features that they wish to keep. The point is to not convince the customer to accept less value, but to help the customer obtain more value," said Gross. After features were confirmed, Savings Experts contacted the customer's service providers to go through the bill line-by-line to negotiate the lowest possible rate for the service. New Savings Experts needed to learn negotiation tactics such as not only how to overcome objections but also how to find all the potential leverage points and how to avoid long hold times. Gross commented, "We know what to say and how best to say it to ensure the highest possible savings for the customer. The key to negotiating is to have all of your ducks in a row and be prepared to overcome all possible objections." The company utilized a proprietary software system that tracked all communications with customers and service providers.

Once all of a customer's bills had been negotiated, BillCutterz.com notified the customer by e-mail of the amount of the negotiated savings for each bill. Typically, service providers would agree to the discount for one year and require a new negotiation at the end of the agreement period. The savings would appear on the customers' regular bills from their service providers. Then BillCutterz.com invoiced the customer for one-half of the savings approximately 7 to 10 days after service provider bills were made available. Customers could pay BillCutterz.com the fee in monthly installments or in a one-time, pay-in-full, lump-sum payment that included a 10 percent discount. BillCutterz.com contacted customers during the end of their discount period to determine whether they wished to have their bills renegotiated for another year.

## THE FUTURE

Going into the close of the company's 2014 second quarter, Barry Gross was thrilled with the

company's ability to obtain discounts for thousands of its new customers. However, the company's Savings Experts had yet to successfully work through the backlog of new enrollees, and Gross believed too much of his time was spent on training rather than business development. The strain of large enrollment spikes following favorable media exposure did not seem sustainable to Gross. A referral-based customer acquisition approach would allow the company to grow at a more predicable rate that would require perhaps one or two new employees per month to be added and trained rather than several. Gross was attempting to determine what type of company would be interested in creating an alliance that would yield 1,000 new customers per month on an annual basis. Of course, certain types of companies would be unable to enter into such an alliance because of customer privacy matters. Gross also believed that with the company's growing volume, BillCutterz.com could enter into prenegotiated savings agreements with high-volume service providers like Verizon, T-Mobile, Time Warner Cable, and AT&T. Such agreements would eliminate the need for individual negotiations unless an account involved a large amount needing nonroutine negotiation.

Until Gross was able to modify the company's business model and strategy to better accommodate scale, much of his daily effort would be put into selecting and training new employees. In addition, the company had grown to such a size that it would soon become a graduate of the Coastal Bend Business Innovation Center. Ample office space was available in the community for the growing company, but relocating to a new space would be another task that would take away from Barry's time and would alter the company's cost structure. The company's meteoric growth had made it a standout among entrepreneurial startups, but its rise had also created a need for new strategies and operating practices to flourish as an established business.

## ENDNOTES

[1] M. Kon, "Customer Churn: Stop It before It Starts," *Mercer Management Journal* 17 (2005), pp. 53–60.
[2] Ibid.
[3] Ibid.
[4] Ibid.

# Whole Foods Market in 2014:
# Vision, Core Values, and Strategy

connect

## Arthur A. Thompson
### The University of Alabama

Founded in 1980, Whole Foods Market had evolved from a local supermarket for natural and health foods in Austin, Texas, into the most visible and best-known leader of the natural and organic food movement across the United States, helping the industry gain acceptance among growing numbers of consumers concerned about the food they ate. The company had 2013 sales revenues of $12.9 billion and in spring 2014 had 379 stores in the United States, Canada, and Great Britain. Over the past 22 years, sales had grown at a compound annual rate of 25.2 percent, and profits had grown at a compound average rate of 30.4 percent. In 2013, Whole Foods was the 8th-largest food and drug retailer in the United States (up from 21st in 2009) and ranked 232nd on *Fortune* magazine's 2013 list of the 500 largest companies in the United States. Over 7 million customers visited Whole Foods stores in 41 U.S. states, Canada, and the United Kingdom each week, and Whole Foods was the number-two retail brand on Twitter, with 4 million followers.

Whole Foods' mission was "to promote the vitality and well-being of all individuals by supplying the highest quality, most wholesome foods available." The core of the mission involved promoting organically grown foods, healthy eating, and the sustainability of the world's entire ecosystem. For many years, the company used the slogan "Whole Foods, Whole People, Whole Planet" to capture the essence of its mission. John Mackey, the company's cofounder and co-CEO, was convinced that Whole Foods' rapid growth and market success had much to do with its having "remained a uniquely mission-driven company—highly selective about what we sell, dedicated to our core values and stringent quality standards, and committed to sustainable agriculture."

Mackey's vision was for Whole Foods to become an international brand synonymous with carrying the highest-quality natural and organic foods available and being the best food retailer in every community in which a Whole Foods store was located. The company sought to offer the highest-quality, least processed, most flavorful and naturally preserved foods available, and it marketed them in appealing store environments that made shopping at Whole Foods interesting and enjoyable. Mackey believed that marketing high-quality natural and organic foods to more and more customers in more and more communities would, over time, gradually transform the diets of individuals in a manner that would help them live longer, healthier, more pleasurable lives.

## THE NATURAL AND ORGANIC FOODS INDUSTRY

The retail grocery industry in the United States—which included conventional supermarkets, supercenters, and limited-assortment and natural/gourmet-positioned supermarkets—had sales of approximately $603 billion in 2012, up 3 percent over 2011.[1] Within this broader category, retail sales of food products labeled "natural" were approximately $81 billion, a 10 percent increase over the prior year.[2]

Foods labeled "organic" generated estimated retail sales across North America approaching $35 billion in 2013, up from $9 billion in 2002. *Natural foods* were (1) minimally processed, (2) largely or completely free of artificial ingredients, preservatives, and other non–naturally occurring chemicals, and (3) as near to their whole, natural state as possible. The U.S. Department of Agriculture's Food and Safety Inspection Service defined *natural food* as "a product containing no artificial ingredient or added color and that is minimally processed." *Organic foods* were a special subset of the natural food category and had to be grown and processed without the use of pesticides, antibiotics, hormones, synthetic chemicals, artificial fertilizers, preservatives, dyes or additives, or genetic engineering. Organic foods included fresh fruits and vegetables, meats, and processed foods that had been produced using:

1. Agricultural management practices that promoted a healthy and renewable ecosystem and that used no genetically engineered seeds or crops, petroleum-based fertilizers, fertilizers made from sewage sludge, or long-lasting pesticides, herbicides, and fungicides.

2. Livestock management practices that involved organically grown feed, fresh air and outdoor access for the animals, and no use of antibiotics or growth hormones.

3. Food processing practices that protected the integrity of the organic product and disallowed the use of radiation, genetically modified ingredients, or synthetic preservatives.

Organic food sales accounted for 5 to 6 percent of total U.S. retail sales of food and beverages in 2013.

In 1990, passage of the Organic Food Production Act started the process of establishing national standards for organically grown products in the United States, a movement that included farmers, food activists, conventional food producers, and consumer groups. In October 2002, the U.S. Department of Agriculture (USDA) officially established labeling standards for organic products, overriding both the patchwork of inconsistent state regulations for what could be labeled as organic and the different rules of some 43 agencies for certifying organic products. The new USDA regulations established four categories of food with organic ingredients, with varying levels of organic purity:

1. *100 percent organic products.* Such products were usually whole foods, such as fresh fruits and vegetables, grown by organic methods—which

meant that the product had been grown without the use of synthetic pesticides or sewage-based fertilizers, had not been subjected to irradiation, and had not been genetically modified or injected with bioengineered organisms, growth hormones, or antibiotics. Products that were 100 percent organic could carry the green USDA organic certification seal provided the merchant could document that the food product had been organically grown (usually by a certified-organic producer).

2. *Organic products.* Such products, often processed, had to have at least 95 percent organically certified ingredients. These could also carry the green USDA organic certification seal.

3. *Made with organic ingredients.* Such products had to have at least 70 percent organic ingredients; they could be labeled "made with organic ingredients" but could not display the USDA seal.

4. *All other products with organic ingredients.* Products with less than 70 percent organic ingredients could not use the word *organic* on the front of a package, but organic ingredients could be listed among other ingredients in a less prominent part of the package.

The USDA's labeling standards were intended to enable shoppers who were ingredient-conscious or wanted to buy pesticide-free or support sustainable agricultural practices to evaluate product labels on which the word *organic* appeared. The standards were not meant to imply anything about the health or safety of organic products (because there was no credible scientific evidence that organic products were more nutritious or safer to eat than conventionally grown products). The USDA also issued regulations requiring documentation on the part of growers, processors, exporters, importers, shippers, and merchants to verify that they were certified to grow, process, or handle organic products carrying the USDA's organic seal. In 2003, Whole Foods was designated as the first national "Certified Organic" grocer by Quality Assurance International, a federally recognized independent third-party certification organization.

Major food processing companies like Kraft, General Mills, Danone (the parent of Dannon Yogurt), Dean Foods, and Kellogg had all purchased organic food producers in an effort to capitalize on growing consumer interest in purchasing organic products. Heinz had introduced an organic ketchup and bought a 19 percent stake in Hain Celestial

**3NCB68oo6WAK**

**Crafting & Executing Strategy: The Quest for Competitive Advantage:  Concepts and Cases ((**

**Shelf 24 Bay A      Item 771**

Thank you for buying from **GOODWILL OF SOUTH FLORIDA** on Amazon Marketplace.

**Ship To**
Myra Mings
2494 WOODRUM RIDGE RD
LIBERTY, KY 42539-7769

**Order Details**

| | |
|---|---|
| Order ID | 114-2022806-7733854 |
| Order Date | 12/19/2019 1:47:11 PM |
| Shipping Service | Standard |
| Buyers Name | Myra |

| SKU / Listing ID | Title / Condition | Location / Comments |
|---|---|---|
| 3NCB68oo6WAK | Crafting & Executing Strategy: The Quest for Competitive Advantage: Concepts and Cases (Crafting & | Shelf 24 - Bay A - Item 771 |

Executing Strategy: Text and Readings)

107134760822242  Good

Most of our items we sell are used and are in good condition. Since our items are mostly used, digital codes are not always valid. We cannot and do not guarantee codes will be unused, redeemable, or included. Our books may contain highlighting or writing. We ship Monday – Friday. Thank you for supporting Goodwill Industries of South Florida.

**GOODWILL OF SOUTH FLORIDA strives to have each and every customer 100% satisfied with their purchase. If for any reason you are not 100% satisfied please contact us through the Amazon marketplace.**

**If we need to make something right, we will, <u>Guaranteed!</u>**

**Thanks for buying on Amazon Marketplace.**

Group, one of the largest organic and natural food producers. Campbell Soup had introduced organic tomato juice. Starbucks, Green Mountain Coffee, and several other premium coffee marketers were marketing organically grown coffees; Coca-Cola's Odwalla juices were organic; Del Monte and Hunt's were marketing organic canned tomatoes; and Tyson Foods and several other chicken producers had introduced organic chicken products. Producers of organically grown beef were selling all they could produce in 2011–2013, with demand growing an estimated 20 to 25 percent annually; headed into 2014, the market share of natural, organic, and grass-fed beef was estimated to be 5 percent based on dollars and 3 percent based on volume.

According to the most recent data from the U.S. Department of Agriculture, U.S. producers dedicated approximately 5.4 million acres of farmland—3.1 million acres of cropland and 2.3 million acres of rangeland and pasture—to certified-organic production systems in 2011, up from a total of 2.1 million acres in 2001.[3] Only About 0.8 percent of all U.S. cropland and 0.5 percent of all U.S. pasture were certified-organic in 2011. There were approximately 13,000 certified-organic producers in the United States in 2011, and perhaps another 9,000 small farmers growing organic products. All 50 states had some certified-organic farmland, with California, Oregon, New York, North Dakota, Montana, Minnesota, Wisconsin, and Texas having the most acres of certified-organic cropland.

Farmers were becoming increasingly interested in and attracted to organic farming, chiefly because of the substantially higher prices they could get for organically grown fruits, vegetables, and meats. Since 2005, health-conscious chefs at many fine-dining restaurants had begun sourcing ingredients for their dishes from local organic farmers and touting the use of organically grown products on their menus. Growing restaurant use of organically grown herbs, lettuces, vegetables, and fruits, as well as organic cheeses and organic meats, was spurring the growth of organic farming (since supplying local restaurants gave organic producers a ready market for their crops). Likewise, there was growing demand for locally grown organic fruits and vegetables on the part of many supermarkets—growing numbers had begun promoting fresh, locally grown organic produce in their stores. Organic farmers were also experiencing strong demand for their products among consumers who shopped at local farmers' markets.

## Retailing of Organic Foods

Organic foods and beverages were available in nearly every food category in 2014 and were available in over 90 percent of U.S. retail food stores. Increasingly, the vast majority of retail sales of organic products in 2013–2014 were made through mainstream supermarkets and grocery stores and through leading organic and natural food supermarket chains such as Whole Foods, Trader Joe's, and Fresh Market. Only a small portion of organic sales occurred through independent, small-chain natural grocery stores.

Over the past decade, mainstream supermarkets had gradually expanded their offerings of natural and organic products for two reasons. One was because mounting consumer enthusiasm for organic products allowed retailers to earn attractively high profit margins on organics (compared to other grocery items, for which intense price competition among rival supermarket chains on general food products limited profit margins). The other was because consumer demand for organics was growing two to three times faster than the demand for traditional grocery products. Several factors had combined to transform organic food retailing, once a niche market, into the fastest-growing segment of U.S. food sales:

- A "wellness," or health-consciousness, trend among people of many ages and ethnic groups.
- Heightened awareness of the role that food, nutrition, and good eating patterns played in long-term health. Among those most interested in organic products were aging, affluent people concerned about maintaining their health and eating better-for-you foods.
- Increasing consumer concerns over the purity and safety of food due to the presence of pesticide residues, growth hormones, artificial ingredients and other chemicals, and genetically engineered ingredients.
- The growing belief that organic farming had positive environmental effects, particularly in contributing to healthier soil and water conditions and to sustainable agricultural practices.

Organic food products were between 10 and 40 percent more expensive than nonorganic foods, chiefly because of the higher production, distribution, and marketing costs for organic products. Such higher prices were the primary barrier for most consumers in trying or using organic products.

As of 2014, most supermarket chains stocked a selection of natural and organic food items—including fresh produce, canned and frozen fruits and vegetables, milk, cheeses, yogurt, vinegars, salad dressings, cereals, pastas, and meats—and the number and variety of organic items on supermarket shelves were growing. Fresh fruits and vegetables accounted for close to 40 percent of total organic food sales, with organic lettuces, spinach, broccoli, cauliflower, celery, carrots, and apples among the biggest sellers. Meat, dairy, grains, and snack foods were among the fastest-growing organic product categories.

Leading supermarket chains like Walmart, Kroger, Safeway, Supervalu/Save-a-Lot, and Publix had created special "organic and health food" sections for nonperishable natural foods and organics in most of their stores. Kroger, Publix, and several other chains also had special sections for fresh organic fruits and vegetables in their produce cases in almost all of their stores. Walmart, Target, Safeway, Publix, and Kroger were stocking organic chicken and organic, pasture-raised beef at most of their stores.

# WHOLE FOODS MARKET

Whole Foods Market was founded in Austin, Texas, when John Mackey, the current co-CEO, and three other local natural food grocers in Austin decided the natural food industry was ready for a supermarket format. The original Whole Foods Market opened in 1980 with a staff of only 19. It was an immediate success. At the time, there were less than half a dozen natural food supermarkets in the United States. By 1991, the company had 10 stores, revenues of $92.5 million, and net income of $1.6 million. Whole Foods became a public company in 1992, with its stock trading on the NASDAQ. In February 2014, Whole Foods operated 358 stores in 41 U.S. states and the District of Columbia, 8 stores in Canada, and 7 in Great Britain. Its stores averaged 38,000 square feet in size and $37.4 million in sales annually. More than 50 Whole Foods stores had average sales volumes of more than $1 million per week in fiscal 2013, up from just 6 stores in 2005; several Whole Foods stores averaged sales of over $2 million per week. Exhibit 1 presents highlights of

the company's financial performance for fiscal years 2009–2013 (Whole Foods' fiscal year ended the last Sunday in September).

## Core Values

In 1997, when Whole Foods developed the "Whole Foods, Whole People, Whole Planet" slogan to characterize its mission, John Mackey, known as a go-getter with a "cowboy way of doing things," said:

> This slogan taps into perhaps the deepest purpose of Whole Foods Market. It's a purpose we seldom talk about because it seems pretentious, but a purpose nevertheless felt by many of our Team Members and by many of our customers (and hopefully many of our shareholders too). Our deepest purpose as an organization is helping support the health, well-being, and healing of both people (customers and Team Members) and of the planet (sustainable agriculture, organic production and environmental sensitivity). When I peel away the onion of my personal consciousness down to its core in trying to understand what has driven me to create and grow this company, I come to my desire to promote the general well-being of everyone on earth as well as the earth itself. This is my personal greater purpose with the company and the slogan perfectly reflects it.

Complementing the "Whole Foods, Whole People, Whole Planet" mission was a statement of eight core values that governed how the company endeavored to conduct its business (see Exhibit 2). Whole Foods' managers and employees (referred to as *team members*) took pride in "walking the talk" when it came to the company's core values. The prevailing philosophy at Whole Foods was that the company's success and long-term profitability depended on its ability to simultaneously satisfy the needs and desires of its customers, team members, investors, and suppliers while also demonstrating a genuine concern for the communities in which it operated and for the environment.

## Growth Strategy

Since going public in 1991, Whole Foods' growth strategy had been to expand via a combination of opening its own new stores and acquiring small, owner-managed chains that had capable personnel and were located in desirable markets. During 1992–2001, Whole Foods' most significant acquisitions

**EXHIBIT 1**  Select Financial Information, Whole Foods Market, Fiscal Years 2009–2013 (in millions, except per share amounts)

| | Fiscal Year Ending: | | | | |
|---|---|---|---|---|---|
| | Sept. 29, 2013 | Sept. 30, 2012 | Sept. 25, 2011 | Sept. 26, 2010 | Sept. 27, 2009 |
| **Income statement data** | | | | | |
| Sales | $12,917 | $11,699 | $10,108 | $9,006 | $8,032 |
| Cost of goods sold and occupancy costs | 8,288 | 7,543 | 6,571 | 5,870 | 5,277 |
| Gross profit | 4,629 | 4,156 | 3,537 | 3,136 | 2,754 |
| Direct store expenses | 3,285 | 2,983 | 2,629 | 2,377 | 2,146 |
| Store contribution[1] | 1,344 | 1,173 | 908 | 759 | 608 |
| General and administrative expenses | 397 | 372 | 311 | 272 | 244 |
| Preopening and relocation costs | 52 | 47 | 41 | 38 | 49 |
| Relocation, store closure, and lease termination costs | 12 | 10 | 8 | 11 | 31 |
| Operating income | 883 | 743 | 548 | 438 | 284 |
| Interest expense, net | — | — | (4) | (33) | (37) |
| Investment and other income | 11 | 8 | 8 | 7 | 4 |
| Income before income taxes | 894 | 752 | 552 | 412 | 251 |
| Provision for income taxes | 343 | 286 | 209 | 166 | 104 |
| Net income | 551 | 466 | 343 | 246 | 147 |
| Preferred stock dividends | — | — | — | 6 | 28 |
| Net income available to common shareholders | $ 551 | $ 466 | $ 343 | $ 240 | $ 119 |
| Basic earnings per share | $1.48 | $1.28 | $0.98 | $0.72 | $0.42 |
| Weighted average shares outstanding | 371.2 | 364.8 | 350.5 | 332.5 | 280.8 |
| Diluted earnings per share | $1.47 | $1.26 | $0.97 | $0.72 | $0.42 |
| Weighted-average shares outstanding, diluted basis | 374.5 | 368.9 | 354.6 | 343.4 | 280.8 |
| Dividends declared per share | $1.40 | $0.28 | $0.20 | — | — |
| **Balance sheet data** | | | | | |
| Net working capital[2] | $ 892 | $ 1,126 | $ 574 | $ 414 | $ 371 |
| Total assets | 5,538 | 5,294 | 4,292 | 3,987 | 3,783 |
| Long-term debt (including current maturities) | 27 | 24 | 18 | 509 | 739 |
| Shareholders' equity | 3,878 | 3,802 | 2,991 | 2,373 | 1,628 |
| **Cash flow data** | | | | | |
| Net cash provided by operating activities | $ 1,009 | $ 920 | $ 759 | $ 585 | $ 588 |
| Development costs of new locations | (339) | (262) | (203) | (171) | (288) |
| Other property and equipment expenditures | (67) | (85) | (162) | (194) | (198) |
| Free cash flow | $ 273 | $ 328 | $ 390 | $ 464 | $ 472 |

*Note:* Whole Foods' fiscal year ends the last Sunday in September.
[1]Store contribution is defined as gross profit less direct store expenses.
[2]Net working capital is defined as total current assets minus total current liabilities.

*Sources:* 2013 10-K report, pp. 20 and 40; and 2011 10-K report, p. 36.

consisted of seven small chains with a total of 45 stores ranging in size from 5,000 to 20,000 square feet. The company entered the Atlanta market in 2001 by acquiring Harry's Market, which operated three 55,000-square-foot supermarkets. Starting in 2002, Whole Foods' management decided to drive growth by opening 10 to 15 decidedly bigger stores in metropolitan areas each year—stores that ranged

# EXHIBIT 2    Whole Foods Market's Eight Core Values

**Our Core Values**

The following list of core values reflects what is truly important to us as an organization. These are not values that change from time to time, situation to situation or person to person, but rather they are the underpinning of our company culture.

1. **We Sell the Highest Quality Natural and Organic Products Available**
   - **Passion for Food**—We appreciate and celebrate the difference natural and organic products can make in the quality of one's life.
   - **Quality Standards**—We have high standards and our goal is to sell the highest quality products we possibly can. We define quality by evaluating the ingredients, freshness, safety, taste, nutritive value and appearance of all of the products we carry. We are buying agents for our customers and not the selling agents for the manufacturers.

2. **We Satisfy, Delight and Nourish Our Customers**
   - **Our Customers**—They are our most important stakeholders in our business and the lifeblood of our business. Only by satisfying our customers first do we have the opportunity to satisfy the needs of our other stakeholders.
   - **Extraordinary Customer Service**—We go to extraordinary lengths to satisfy and delight our customers. We want to meet or exceed their expectations on every shopping trip. We know that by doing so we turn customers into advocates for our business. Advocates do more than shop with us, they talk about Whole Foods to their friends and others. We want to serve our customers competently, efficiently, knowledgeably and with flair.
   - **Education**—We can generate greater appreciation and loyalty from all of our stakeholders by educating them about natural and organic foods, health, nutrition and the environment.
   - **Meaningful Value**—We offer value to our customers by providing them with high quality products, extraordinary service and a competitive price. We are constantly challenged to improve the value proposition to our customers.
   - **Retail Innovation**—We value retail experiments. Friendly competition within the company helps us to continually improve our stores. We constantly innovate and raise our retail standards and are not afraid to try new ideas and concepts.
   - **Inviting Store Environments**—We create store environments that are inviting and fun, and reflect the communities they serve. We want our stores to become community meeting places where our customers meet their friends and make new ones.

3. **We Support Team Member Happiness and Excellence**
   - **Empowering Work Environments**—Our success is dependent upon the collective energy and intelligence of all of our Team Members. We strive to create a work environment where motivated Team Members can flourish and succeed to their highest potential. We appreciate effort and reward results.
   - **Self-Responsibility**—We take responsibility for our own success and failures. We celebrate success and see failures as opportunities for growth. We recognize that we are responsible for our own happiness and success.
   - **Self-Directed Teams**—The fundamental work unit of the company is the self-directed team. Teams meet regularly to discuss issues, solve problems and appreciate each others' contributions. Every Team Member belongs to a team.
   - **Open & Timely Information**—We believe knowledge is power and we support our Team Members' right to access information that impacts their jobs. Our books are open to our Team Members, including our annual individual compensation report. We also recognize everyone's right to be listened to and heard regardless of their point of view.
   - **Incremental Progress**—Our company continually improves through unleashing the collective creativity and intelligence of all of our Team Members. We recognize that everyone has a contribution to make. We keep getting better at what we do.
   - **Shared Fate**—We recognize there is a community of interest among all of our stakeholders. There are no entitlements; we share together in our collective fate. To that end we have a salary cap that limits the compensation (wages plus profit incentive bonuses) of any Team Member to nineteen times the average total compensation of all full-time Team Members in the company.

4. **We Create Wealth through Profits & Growth**
   - **Stewardship**—We are stewards of our shareholders' investments and we take that responsibility very seriously. We are committed to increasing long term shareholder value.
   - **Profits**—We earn our profits everyday through voluntary exchange with our customers. We recognize that profits Satisfaction and job security are essential to creating capital for growth, prosperity, opportunity, job.

5. **We Serve and Support Our Local and Global Communities**
   Our business is intimately tied to the neighborhood and larger community that we serve and in which we live. Caring for the communities in which we reside is hugely important to our organization.
   - **Local**—First off, it's a given that each store donates food to area food banks and shelters. We have food; they know how to get it to people who need it. Done. Then, several times a year, our stores hold community-giving days (otherwise known as "5% Days") where five percent of that day's net sales are donated to a local nonprofit or educational organization. The groups that benefit from these "5% Days" are as varied as the communities themselves. Last but not least, Team Members are constantly volunteering their time and expertise to an assortment of local non-profits.
   - **Global**—While our store donations provide the backbone of our community giving, we also give back to the larger national and global community.
     Whole Planet Foundation works toward poverty alleviation in developing-world communities where Whole Foods Market sources product. Through microcredit, Whole Planet Foundation seeks to unleash the energy and creativity of every human being they work with in order to create wealth and prosperity in emerging economies.
     Whole Kids Foundation supports schools and inspires families to improve children's nutrition and wellness. Through partnerships with innovative organizations, schools and educators they work to provide children access to fresh, nutritious meals.
     Our Local Producer Loan Program provides up to $10 million in low-interest loans to small, local producers. Why? Because we believe in supporting local farmers and producers.
6. **We Practice and Advance Environmental Stewardship**
   - **Sustainable Agriculture**—We support organic farmers, growers and the environment through our commitment to sustainable agriculture and by expanding the market for organic products.
   - **Wise Environmental Practices**—We respect our environment and recycle, reuse, and reduce our waste wherever and whenever we can.
7. **We Create Ongoing Win-Win Partnerships with Our Suppliers**
   - **Integrity in All Business Dealings**—Our supplier partners are our allies in serving the interests of our other stakeholders in bringing to market the safest highest quality products available. We treat them with respect, fairness and integrity at all times and expect the same in return. We seek supplier partnerships that share our concern for social responsibility and the environment.
   - **Honesty and Communication**—We are committed to honesty, timeliness and clarity in communicating with our suppliers and we expect the same in return.
   - **Transparency**—We seek to create transparency from "farm to fork" with respect to production, planning, sourcing, ingredients, product safety and efficacy in order to bring to market the safest highest quality products available. We work with our supplier partners in eliminating all unnecessary production and distribution costs to help ensure the best possible price.
   - **Education**—We partner with our suppliers to educate, inspire and communicate the outstanding quality and benefits of our products to promote a lifestyle of health, balance and well-being.
   - **Innovation/Differentiation**—We foster supplier partnerships that enable us to remain at the forefront of the retail food industry, by creating new, unique and innovative products.
8. **We Promote the Health of Our Stakeholders through Healthy Eating Education**
   - **Education**—Healthy eating is a basic foundation for optimum health and well-being. By providing healthy eating education we inspire and empower our stakeholders to make the best health-supportive, delicious food choices to maximize personal health and vitality.

*Source:* www.wholefoodsmarket.com (accessed February 14, 2014).

from 40,000 square feet to as much as 80,000 square feet and were on the same scale as or larger than the conventional supermarkets operated by Kroger, Safeway, Publix, and other chains. However, the company did opt to enter Great Britain in 2004 by purchasing Fresh and Wild, an operator of seven small stores in the London area.

Then, in 2007, Whole Foods began what proved to be a largely successful, but contentious, 2½-year battle to purchase struggling Wild Oats Markets—Whole Foods' biggest competitor in natural and organic foods—for an acquisition price of $700 million. Wild Oats operated 109 older and smaller stores (averaging 24,000 square feet in size) in 23 states under the Wild Oats Market, Henry's Farmer's Market, and Sun Harvest brands and had total annual sales of about $1.2 billion. The Federal Trade Commission opposed the acquisition on grounds that competition in the organic food retailing segment would be weakened; however, a U.S. district court ruled that the FTC's position lacked merit. Whole Foods went forward and completed its acquisition of Wild Oats in late August 2007. Acquiring Wild Oats gave Whole Foods entry into five new states and 14 new metropolitan markets. Whole Foods then quickly sold 35 Henry's and Sun Harvest stores in California and Texas that had been previously acquired by Wild Oats, along with a California distribution center, to Los Angeles food retailer Smart & Final, realizing approximately $165 million from the sale and reducing its net purchase price for Wild Oats Market to about $535 million (which included the assumption of $148 million in Wild Oats' debt).[4] In addition, Whole Foods immediately closed nine Wild Oats stores that did not fit with its brand strategy or real estate strategy and began planning to relocate seven smaller Wild Oats stores to existing or soon-to-be-opened Whole Foods locations. In fiscal 2008, Whole Foods launched a program to spend nearly $45 million renovating Wild Oats stores and rebranding them as Whole Foods stores.

In a surprising move in July 2008, the U.S. Court of Appeals for the District of Columbia reversed the lower-court order allowing Whole Foods to acquire Wild Oats and directed the U.S. district court to reopen proceedings for further evidentiary hearings. Separately, the FTC reopened its administrative actions challenging the acquisition on antitrust grounds. To resolve the dispute, the FTC and Whole Foods entered into a consent agreement in March 2009 whereby Whole Foods would sell:

- Twelve of the former Wild Oats stores it was currently operating and one Whole Foods store.
- The leases and related fixed assets for 19 former Wild Oats stores (10 of which were closed by Wild Oats prior to the acquisition and 9 of which were closed by Whole Foods Market).
- Wild Oats' trademarks and other intellectual property associated with the Wild Oats stores.

The divestiture period was later extended until 2010 to allow for the finalization of good-faith offers for 6 of the 13 operating stores and 2 of the closed stores, as well as Wild Oats' trademark and intellectual property; Whole Foods was allowed to keep the seven remaining operating stores without further obligation to attempt to divest them. This resulted in 51 former Wild Oats stores operating under the Whole Foods name. In his Letter to Stakeholders in the company's 2009 annual report, John Mackey expressed confidence that sales and profits at these stores would continue to improve in coming years, enabling the company to realize a solid return for shareholders on the Wild Oats acquisition. However, senior management indicated that, going forward, acquisitions would be a minor element of the company's growth strategy, used only as a means of entering desirable geographic areas and gaining experienced team members.[5] The company acquired only eight stores during fiscal years 2010–2013, opting to drive growth by opening additional stores and striving to increase sales at existing stores. However, in February 2014, Whole Foods seized the opportunity to acquire leases from Safeway for seven Dominick's supermarket stores in Chicago; plans were under way to remodel these stores and reopen them as Whole Foods stores in 2015. The addition of these seven stores, along with three other new Chicago-area stores that Whole Foods already had under development, represented a major strategic initiative to significantly expand the company's presence in the greater Chicago area. Then, in March 2014, Whole Foods purchased four stores from New Frontiers Natural Marketplace; the stores averaged 22,000 square feet and were in Flagstaff, Prescott, and Sedona, Arizona, and San Luis Obispo, California.

Exhibit 3 shows the growth in the number of Whole Foods stores and the extent to which sales at existing stores have grown.

## Store Location Strategy

Whole Foods had its own internally developed model to analyze potential markets according to education levels, population density, and income within certain drive times. After picking a target metropolitan area, the company's store development group considered several possible sites, developing sales and profit projections for each location and working with regional teams to estimate the costs of opening a store at each site under consideration. Before Whole Foods entered into a lease for the best apparent site, the project had to meet an internal economic value added (EVA) hurdle return, based on Whole Foods' internal weighted-average cost of capital (which was 8 percent in fiscal year 2013). EVA is equivalent to net operating profits after taxes minus a charge for the cost of invested capital necessary to generate

**EXHIBIT 3**  Number of Stores in the Whole Foods Markets Chain, 1991–2014, and Select Store Operating Statistics, Fiscal Years 2000–2014

**A. Growth in the Number of Whole Foods Stores**

| Year | Number of Stores, End of Fiscal Year | Year | Number of Stores, End of Fiscal Year |
|---|---|---|---|
| 1991 | 10 | 2003 | 145 |
| 1992 | 25 | 2004 | 163 |
| 1993 | 42 | 2005 | 175 |
| 1994 | 49 | 2006 | 186 |
| 1995 | 61 | 2007 | 276 |
| 1996 | 68 | 2008 | 275 |
| 1997 | 75 | 2009 | 284 |
| 1998 | 87 | 2010 | 299 |
| 1999 | 100 | 2011 | 311 |
| 2000 | 117 | 2012 | 335 |
| 2001 | 126 | 2013 | 362 |
| 2002 | 135 | May 2014 | 379 |

**B. Store-Related Performance and Operating Statistics**

| | Fiscal Year | | | | |
|---|---|---|---|---|---|
| | 2000 | 2005 | 2006 | 2007 | 2008 |
| Sales, all stores (000s) | $1,839,000 | $4,701,000 | $5,607,000 | $6,592,000 | $7,954,000 |
| Average weekly sales | $325,000 | $537,000 | $593,000 | $617,000 | $570,000 |
| Comparable-store sales growth* | 8.6% | 12.8% | 11.0% | 7.1% | 4.9% |
| Identical-store sales increase* | 7.0% | 11.3% | 10.3% | 5.8% | 3.6% |
| Sales increases contributed by stores opened or acquired during the fiscal year | Not available | Not available | Not available | $421 million | $236 million |
| Total square footage of all stores, end of year | 3,180,000 | 5,819,000 | 6,377,000 | 9,312,000 | 9,895,000 |
| Average store size | 27,000 | 33,000 | 34,000 | 34,000 | 36,000 |
| | 2009 | 2010 | 2011 | 2012 | 2013 |
| Sales, all stores (000s) | $8,032,000 | $9,006,000 | $10,108,000 | $11,699,000 | $12,917,000 |
| Average weekly sales | $549,000 | $588,000 | $636,000 | $682,000 | $711,000 |
| Comparable-store sales growth* | −3.1% | 7.1% | 8.5% | 8.7% | 6.9% |
| Identical-store sales increase* | −4.3% | 6.5% | 8.4% | 8.4% | 6.6% |
| Sales increases contributed by stores opened or acquired during the fiscal year | $235 million | $252 million | $222 million | $294 million | $345 million |
| Total square footage of all stores, end of year | 10,566,000 | 11,231,000 | 11,832,000 | 12,735,000 | 13,779,000 |
| Average store size | 37,000 | 38,000 | 38,000 | 38,000 | 38,000 |

*Sales of a store start to be included in the comparable-store sales calculation in the 53rd full week after the store was opened. Stores acquired in purchase acquisitions enter the comparable-store sales growth calculation store base in the 53rd full week following the date of acquisition.

Identical-store sales exclude sales from relocated and remodeled stores with square-footage changes greater than 20% from the comparable calculation to reduce the impact of square-footage changes on the comparison.

Stores closed for eight or more days are excluded from the comparable- and identical-store bases from the first fiscal week of closure until reopened for a full fiscal week. Comparable and identical sales growth is calculated on a same-calendar-week to same-calendar-week basis.

*Source:* Whole Foods Market's 10-K reports, 2005, 2009, and 2013.

those profits. For a new store project to go forward, the projections had to show a cumulative positive EVA in five years or less. New stores opened 12 to 24 months after a lease was signed.

The cash investment needed to get a new Whole Foods Market site ready for opening varied with the metropolitan area, store size, amount of work performed by the landlord, and the complexity of site development issues—the average capital cost for new stores was about $8 million in 2010–2012 (versus capital costs averaging $15.1 million per new store in 2007).[6] In addition to the capital cost of a new store, it took about $850,000 to stock a store with inventory, a portion of which was financed by vendors. Preopening expenses (including rent) for most stores were in the $2 million to $3 million range.

Most Whole Foods stores were in high-traffic shopping locations on premier real estate sites; some were freestanding, some were in strip centers, and some were in high-density mixed-use projects. For a number of years, Whole Foods favored store locations on high-traffic thoroughfares in the upscale areas of large metropolitan areas. The company's "sweet spot" for the mostly metropolitan markets it entered during 2001–2009 was a store footprint between 45,000 and 60,000 square feet (the new stores of supermarket chains like Safeway and Kroger averaged around 55,000 square feet). As of year-end 2010, Whole Foods had over 90 stores that were 40,000 square feet or larger. But it had also opened a number of showcase or "flagship" stores, including a 99,800-square-foot store in London; a 71,000-square-foot store in the Bowery area of New York City; a 74,500-square-foot store in Columbus, Ohio; a 78,000-square-foot store in Austin, Texas; a 77,000-square-foot store in Pasadena, California; a 75,000-square-foot store in Chicago; and two 75,000-square-foot stores in the suburbs of Atlanta, Georgia. All told, Whole Foods had 17 stores in excess of 65,000 square feet as of 2014.

But the economic slowdown that began in 2007 and then quickly accelerated into a deep recession in 2008–2009 forced a major overhaul of Whole Foods' store expansion strategy. In November 2007, when Whole Foods had 87 new stores in varying stages of development, the company announced it was scaling back its store expansion program. The leases for 14 of the new stores were downsized by an average of 12,000 square feet each, and planned openings of some stores were delayed. Then, in 2008–2009, when the recession in the United States hit full force, management terminated 18 leases for stores in development and downsized others, determining that planned store openings during 2010–2012 would be reduced and that the majority of new Whole Foods stores would be in the 35,000- to 50,000-square-foot range. In addition to the company's cutbacks in developing new stores, Whole Foods' construction and store development teams adopted a leaner and more disciplined approach to design and building, including plans for smaller stores with simpler decor and smaller, less labor-intensive perishable departments. These moves were expected to result in lower costs on both a per-store and per-square-foot basis. Average preopening costs dropped to $2 million per store in 2012–2013.

However, as the effects of the recession gradually wore off and modest economic growth resumed in 2011–2013, Whole Foods became more confident about its growth prospects and began to accelerate its new store openings. By May 2014, the company had a record 114 new stores averaging 40,000 square feet in varying stages of development. Management expected to have a base of more than 400 Whole Foods stores open and operating by year-end 2014 and to cross the 500-store mark in fiscal year 2017. Longer term, management expressed confidence that there was opportunity for Whole Foods to grow its geographic coverage and market penetration to 1,200 stores in the United States alone. While management acknowledged that, going forward, some new Whole Foods stores would likely range in size from as small as 15,000 square feet to as large as 75,000 square feet, the majority were expected to fall in the range of 35,000 to 45,000 square feet. Exhibit 4 provides store development statistics for 2005–2014.

## Product Line Strategy

Because Whole Foods stores were different sizes and had different shopper clienteles, the product and brand selections varied from about 10,000 items in small stores to as many as 50,000 items in the largest stores—the all-store average was about 21,000 items. Whole Foods' product line included natural, organic, and gourmet food and nonfood items in the following principal categories:

- *Fresh produce*—fruits; vegetables; displays of fresh-cut fruits; and a selection of seasonal, exotic, and specialty products like cactus pears, cipollini onions, and Japanese eggplant.

**EXHIBIT 4**  New Store Development Statistics, Whole Foods Market, 2005–2014

|  | Nov. 9, 2005 | Nov. 2, 2006 | Nov. 20, 2007 | Nov. 5, 2008 | Nov. 4, 2009 |
|---|---|---|---|---|---|
| New stores in development | 65 | 88 | 87 | 66 | 52 |
| Average size (gross square feet) | 55,000 | 56,000 | 51,000 | 49,000 | 45,000 |
| Total gross square footage in development | 3,626,000 | 5,003,000 | 4,485,000 | 3,294,000 | 2,410,000 |
| Development footage as a percentage of existing square footage | 60% | 77% | 48% | 33% | 23% |
| Development costs of new locations | $208 million | $209 million | $389 million | $358 million | $248 million |

|  | Nov. 3, 2010 | Nov. 2, 2011 | Nov. 7, 2012 | Nov. 6, 2013 | May 6, 2014 |
|---|---|---|---|---|---|
| New stores in development | 53 | 62 | 79 | 94 | 114 |
| Average size (gross square feet) | 39,000 | 35,000 | 37,000 | 38,000 | 40,000 |
| Total gross square footage in development | 2,052,000 | 2,192,000 | 2,896,000 | 3,605,000 | 4,607,000 |
| Development footage as a percentage of existing square footage | 18% | 18% | 22% | 26% | 32% |
| Development costs of new locations | $171 million | $203 million | $262 million | $339 million | Not available |

*Sources:* Company 10-K reports, 2006, 2007, 2009, 2011, and 2013; and company press release, May 6, 2014.

- *Meat and poultry*—natural and organic meats, house-made sausages, turkey, and chicken products from animals raised on wholesome grains, pastureland, and well water (and not raised with the use of by-products, hormones, or steroids).
- *Fresh seafood*—some wild-caught and some farmed using safe and environmentally responsible practices. A portion of the fresh-fish selections came from the company's four seafood processing and distribution facilities (Pigeon Cove, Select Fish, South Seafood, and Mid-Atlantic Seafood). Seafood items coming from distant supply sources were flown in to stores to ensure maximum freshness.
- *Bakery goods*—a selection of daily baked breads, cakes, pies, cookies, bagels, muffins, and scones.
- *Prepared foods*—soups, packaged salads and sandwiches, oven-ready meals, rotisserie meats, hearth-fired pizza, pastas, a salad bar, a sandwich station, and a selection of entrees and side foods prepared daily.
- *Specialty foods*—fine-quality cheeses, olives (up to 40 varieties in the largest stores), chocolates and confections.
- *Frozen goods*—foods, juices, yogurt and dairy products, smoothies, and bottled waters.

- *Dried foods*—a selection of dried fruits, nuts, grains, and spices (some prepackaged and some dispensed from bins).
- *Beer and wines.*
- *Coffees and teas*—specialty and organic coffees that spanned the roasting spectrum from light to extra-dark roast, supplied to all stores by the company's Allegro coffee subsidiary; tea selections that included fine and exotic teas from all the major tea-growing regions of the world.
- *Grocery and household products*—canned and packaged goods, pastas, soaps, cleaning products, and other conventional household items that helped make the larger Whole Foods stores a one-stop grocery shopping destination where people could get everything on their shopping list.
- *Body care and nutrition products*—natural and organic body care and cosmetics products, vitamin supplements, homeopathic remedies, and aromatherapy products. All items entailed the use of non-animal-testing methods and contained no artificial ingredients.
- *Private-label and exclusive brand offerings*—a family of goods that were a key component of the company's differentiations strategy. The private-label offerings were led by Whole Foods' "365"

and "365 Organic Everyday Value" brands that spanned many product categories and were less expensive than comparable name brands. Whole Foods had also created a "Whole" family of brands (including Whole Foods Market, Whole Catch, Whole Fields, Whole Pantry, Whole Living, and Whole Paws) with consistent logos and packaging for specific departments and product categories. In addition, Whole Foods had a grouping of "exclusive" and "control brand" products that outside suppliers produced and packaged exclusively for sale in Whole Foods stores, including Allegro Coffee, Engine 2, Wellshire Farms, and Nature's Rancher.

- *Pet supplies*—natural and organic pet foods, treats, toys, and pest control remedies.
- *Floral items*—sophisticated flower bouquets and a selection of plants for inside and outside the home.
- *Educational items*—materials and books relating to healthy eating, cooking, healing and alternative health care, and lifestyle.

Whole Foods was the world's biggest seller of organic produce. Organic products, excluding bakery goods and prepared foods, accounted for an estimated 30 percent of Whole Foods' total sales in fiscal 2013. In fiscal year 2013, Whole Foods' private-label and exclusive brands accounted for approximately 16 percent of the company's nonperishable sales and approximately 12 percent of total retail sales, up slightly from 15 and 11 percent, respectively, in fiscal year 2012. The 365 and 365 Organic Everyday Value brands accounted for approximately half of the sales of private-label and exclusive brand items.

Prepared foods, fresh fruits and vegetables, fresh meats and seafood, bakery goods, and other perishable items accounted for about 66 percent of Whole Foods' sales in 2011–2013, considerably higher than the 40 to 50 percent that such perishables represented at conventional supermarkets. The 2001 acquisition of the Harry's Market superstores in Atlanta, at which 75 percent of sales were perishables, had provided Whole Foods with personnel having valuable intellectual capital in creatively merchandising all major perishables categories. Management believed that the company's emphasis on fresh fruits and vegetables, bakery goods, meats, seafood, and other perishables differentiated Whole

Foods stores from other supermarkets and attracted a broader customer base. According to John Mackey:[7]

> First-time visitors to Whole Foods Market are often awed by our perishables. We devote more space to fresh fruits and vegetables, including an extensive selection of organics, than most of our competitors. Our meat and poultry products are natural—no artificial ingredients, minimal processing, and raised without the use of artificial growth hormones, antibiotics or animal by-products in their feed. Our seafood is either wild-caught or sourced from aquaculture farms where environmental concerns are a priority. Also, our seafood is never treated with chlorine or other chemicals, as is common practice in the food retailing industry. . . . We bake daily, using whole grains and unbleached, unbromated flour and feature European-style loaves, pastries, cookies and cakes as well as gluten-free baked goods for those allergic to wheat. We also offer many vegetarian and vegan products for our customers seeking to avoid all animal products. Our cheeses are free of artificial flavors, colors, and synthetic preservatives, and we offer an outstanding variety of both organic cheeses and cheeses made using traditional methods.

**Quality Standards**    One of Whole Foods Market's foremost commitments to its customers was to sell products that met strict standards and were of high quality in terms of nutrition, freshness, appearance, and taste—Exhibit 5 shows the company's quality standards. Whole Foods guaranteed 100 percent satisfaction on all items purchased and went to great lengths to live up to its core value of satisfying and delighting customers. Buyers personally visited the facilities of many of the company's suppliers and were very picky about the items they chose and the ingredients they contained.

## Pricing Strategy

Whole Foods' strategy was to sell the highest-quality products that it could find at the most competitive prices possible. While the majority of the company's private-label products and some of its other offerings were "value-priced," prices at Whole Foods were normally higher than those at conventional supermarkets. This was in part because the costs of growing, distributing, and marketing organic products were 10 to 40 percent higher than the costs for nonorganic items and in part because Whole Foods' strategy was to carry the highest-quality natural and organic foods available. Likewise, the earth-friendly detergents, toilet papers, and other household items that

**EXHIBIT 5**  Whole Foods' Quality Standards

| Whole Foods' Statement |
| --- |
| Our business is to sell the highest quality foods we can find at the most competitive prices possible. We evaluate quality in terms of nutrition, freshness, appearance, and taste. Our search for quality is a never-ending process involving the careful judgment of buyers throughout the company. <br><br> • We carefully evaluate each and every product we sell. <br> • We feature foods that are free of artificial preservatives, colors, flavors, sweeteners, and hydrogenated fats. <br> • We are passionate about great tasting food and the pleasure of sharing it with others. <br> • We are committed to foods that are fresh, wholesome and safe to eat. <br> • We seek out and promote organically grown foods. <br> • We provide food and nutritional products that support health and well-being. <br><br> Whole Foods Market's Quality Standards team maintains an extensive list of unacceptable ingredients [see below]. However, creating a product with no unacceptable ingredients does not guarantee that Whole Foods Market will sell it. Our buyers are passionate about seeking out the freshest, most healthful, minimally processed products available. |
| **Additional Information on Whole Foods' Standards** |
| In addition to the above standards, the company had more explicit and detailed quality standards regarding seafood, meat and animal welfare, supplements and body care products, and food safety. <br> In 2014, there were 78 chemicals on Whole Foods' list of unacceptable ingredients, including artificial colors, artificial flavors, aspartame, bleached flour, cyclamates, hydrogenated fats, irradiated foods, nitrates and nitrites, saccharin, sorbic acid, sucralose, and sulfites (sulfur dioxide). |

*Source:* Quality Standards section of **www.wholefoodsmarket.com** (accessed February 21, 2014).

Whole Foods merchandised frequently had higher price tags than did the name brands of comparable products found in traditional supermarkets. The higher prices that Whole Foods charged for many of its products had prompted some media critics to dub Whole Foods as "Whole Paycheck," a term that resonated with price-sensitive grocery shoppers who had visited a Whole Foods store. Nonetheless, Whole Foods' customers were sufficiently enchanted with the company's product offerings and shopping experience that they overlooked the pricing and patronized Whole Foods stores in increasing numbers. Sales revenues at Whole Foods had grown at a robust compound average rate of 25 percent over the past 22 years. Observers attributed this to several factors. One grocery industry analyst said, "If people believe that the food is healthier and they are doing something good for themselves, they are willing to invest a bit more, particularly as they get older. It's not a fad."[8] Another analyst noted that while Whole Foods served a growing niche, it had managed to attract a new kind of customer, one who was willing to pay a premium to dabble in health food without being totally committed to vegetarianism or an organic lifestyle.[9] Shopping at

Whole Foods was also attractive to food lovers and fine-food connoisseurs who saw food as being about pleasurable taste and indulgence and were willing to pay a premium for what they saw as a high-quality gourmet experience.

However, despite all the attractions of shopping at a Whole Foods store, the company was hit hard when the U.S. economy collapsed in fall 2008, a deep recession ensued, and concerned consumers cut back on spending. According to John Mackey, "We knew that 2009 was going to be a tough year but did not predict just how challenging the economic environment would be. For the first time in 30 years, we experienced a decline in our comparable store sales."[10] As was the case with the company's store expansion strategy, the Great Recession of 2008–2009 caused Mackey and other Whole Foods' executives to act swiftly and decisively to change the company's strategy to better match the economic climate and allay customer concerns about the higher costs of doing their grocery shopping at Whole Foods. An aggressive campaign was launched to increase the number of value-priced items at Whole Foods stores, to better communicate to customers how Whole Foods' prices stacked up against those of rivals, and to improve the perception of customers about the value of shopping at Whole Foods. The strategy shift had several elements:

- Drawing on new pricing research capabilities to monitor the prices of its supermarket rivals, Whole Foods trimmed the prices of items it considered as "key" to boosting the value perceptions of shoppers. Signs were placed on store shelves calling attention to items with price reductions and to hundreds of value-priced items, many of which were at such popular price points as 99 cents, $1.09, $1.49, $1.99, and $2.99. In a number of areas (like cheeses and packaged nuts), Whole Foods instituted programs to get deals from suppliers that enabled it to provide better values for customers without sacrificing its gross margins. The goal was to strike the right balance between spurring higher sales and maintaining profit margins.

- To help put good value front and center, the company began using aisle displays with accompanying signage to feature "this week's hot deals," everyday low-priced products, budget-priced cheeses and wines, and out-of-the-ordinary products with budget prices; formerly, the practice was to use most aisle displays to promote gourmet cheeses, upscale wines, exotic fresh produce, and novel but premium-priced items. In addition, grocery bags at checkout counters had such printed messages as "365 Everyday Value Products. Cut Costs. Not Quality" and "365 Everyday Value Products. Comparison Shopping Strongly Encouraged."

- Stores began featuring new family-sized prepared food selections for $17.99, prepared food items in "sizes for every budget," and family-sized value packs of fruits, vegetables, meats, and chicken.

- An in-store value guide, *The Whole Deal,* was created that featured supplier-sponsored and Whole Foods Market store-brand coupons, products throughout the store with everyday low prices, budget-conscious recipes, and meal-planning advice to help shoppers stretch their food dollars. Customer use of *The Whole Deal* proved quite popular, prompting the company to begin a *Whole Deal* e-newsletter (which enabled shoppers to see the specials and print out the coupons before they left home).

- The company took advantage of opportunity buys offered by suppliers and lower costs in several product categories, including fresh produce and meat, using them to push strong promotions and pass the savings on to customers in the form of lower prices. In-store signs announced "Great Buys" and "More of the good stuff for less than you think!"

The strategic initiatives were effective. Sales growth per store for the first quarter of fiscal 2010 was 3.5 percent (versus −4 percent in the first quarter of fiscal 2009), and total revenues were up 7 percent over the first quarter of fiscal 2009. Whole Foods' management was pleased with these results, indicating that the strategy modifications had changed the dialogue about the company's prices and improved customer perceptions about the value of doing their grocery shopping at Whole Foods.

Because comparable-store and identical-store sales growth continued to be strong in succeeding quarters and years (see Section B of Exhibit 3), top executives opted to make the new pricing strategy and emphasis on value a permanent part of Whole Foods' strategy. Going into 2014, Whole Foods had competitively matched prices on thousands of items, extended the range of value-priced choices to its perishables departments, regularly featured "Sure Deals" in *The Whole Deal* and used in-store signage to highlight everyday value pricing on various products, and started promoting regional and national one-day sales, all in an ongoing effort to broaden and strengthen customer awareness about the value being offered in Whole Foods stores.

**New Strategic Moves to Control Expenses in 2008–2009**   When the sharp economic downturn began in September 2008, Whole Foods' management moved swiftly to institute a series of cost-containment measures relating to cost of goods sold, direct store expenses, and general and administrative expenses. Purchases from suppliers were scrutinized for possible cost savings. A hiring and salary freeze was imposed, which remained in effect until July 2009. To trim back on labor costs at its stores, the company used a set of tools on a daily basis to monitor and adjust the work hours of some store employees on the basis of hourly shopper traffic and sales volumes. The size of the company's overall workforce was reduced by normal attrition (as team members retired or left the company), but there were no involuntary layoffs. Team members joined forces with managers throughout the company to find ways to operate the business in a more frugal manner.

## Merchandising Strategy

The layout of each Whole Foods store was customized to fit the particular site and building configuration and to best show off the particular product mix chosen for that store's target clientele. The driving concept of Whole Foods' merchandising strategy was to create an inviting and interactive store atmosphere that turned shopping for food from a chore into a fun, pleasurable experience. Stores had a colorful decor, and products were displayed in an attractive manner that both welcomed close inspection and stimulated purchases (see Exhibit 6). The effect projected Whole Foods as an authentic retailer of natural and organic products, a lifestyle brand, and a supermarket playground with both a unique environment and unusually appealing food selections (some wholesome and safe to eat, some "must try," and some definitely calorific with mouthwatering eye appeal). According to one industry analyst, Whole Foods had "put together the ideal model for the foodie who's a premium gourmet and the natural foods buyer. When you walk into a Whole Foods store, you're overwhelmed by a desire to look at everything you see."[11]

Most stores featured hand-stacked produce, appealing displays of fresh seafood and meats, open kitchens and teams of in-store chefs, scratch bakeries, prepared food stations, salad bars, gourmet food sections with items from around the world, multiple opportunities to sample products, and ever-changing merchandise displays. To further a sense of community and interaction with customers, Whole Foods stores typically included sit-down eating areas, customer comment boards, customer service booths, and multiple displays containing brochures on such topics as sustainable agriculture, organics, the sustainability of seafood supplies and overfishing problems, food safety, product quality, the environment, and healthy eating. Whole Foods' 78,000-square-foot flagship Austin store was a top central Texas tourist destination and downtown Austin landmark; it had an intimate village-style layout, six mini-restaurants within the store, a raw food and juice bar, more than 600 varieties of cheese and 40 varieties of olives, a selection of 1,800 wines, a "Candy Island" with handmade lollipops and popcorn balls, a hot-nut bar with an in-house nut roaster, a world food section, a walk-in beer cooler with hundreds of selections, pastry chefs making a variety of items, a natural home section with organic cotton apparel and household linens, an extensive meat department with an in-house smoker and 50 oven-ready items prepared by in-house chefs, and a theaterlike seafood department with more than 150 fresh seafood items and on-the-spot shucking, cooking, smoking, slicing, and frying to order. When the three-floor, 99,800-square-foot store in London opened, it had 55 in-store chefs, 13 dining venues (including a tapas bar, a champagne and oyster bar, a pub, and a sushi and dim sum eatery) that accommodated 350 diners, a self-service bulk food center with 100 selections, and a 12-meter display of fresh seafood (many of the seafood selections were hook-and-line caught off the shores of the United Kingdom). Management believed that the extensive and attractive displays of fresh produce, seafood, meats and house-made sausages, baked goods, and prepared foods in its larger stores appealed to a broader customer base and were responsible for stores bigger than 35,000 square feet performing better than smaller stores. Management's intent was for Whole Foods stores to play a unique role as a third place, besides the home and office, where its customers could gather, interact, and learn while discovering the many joys of eating and sharing food.

Whole Foods got very high marks from merchandising experts and customers for its presentation—from the bright colors of the produce displays, to the quality of the foods and customer service, to the wide aisles and cleanliness. Management was continually experimenting with new merchandising concepts to keep stores fresh and exciting for customers. According to a Whole Foods regional manager, "We take the best ideas from each of our stores and try to incorporate them in all our other stores. We're constantly making our stores better."[12] Whole Foods' merchandising skills were said to be a prime factor in its success in luring shoppers back time and again—sales at Whole Foods stores in the first quarter of 2014 averaged $983 per square foot, about double the sales per square foot of leading supermarket chains.

## Marketing and Customer Service

Whole Foods spent much less than other supermarkets on advertising and marketing, preferring

## EXHIBIT 6   Scenes from Whole Foods Stores

instead to rely primarily on word-of-mouth recommendations and testimonials from customers. Expenditures for advertising and marketing, treated as direct store expenses, totaled $56 million in fiscal 2013, $51 million in fiscal 2012, and $43 million in fiscal 2011. The corporate marketing budget was divided among national and regional programs, *The*

*Whole Deal* in-store value guide and e-newsletter, and activities for individual stores.

There were marketers in every store dedicated to giving shoppers the best possible in-store experience and managing store participation in local events and community programs. Stores spent most of their marketing budgets on in-store promotional signage, product samplings, and related merchandising efforts that engaged shoppers and induced them to put more items in their shopping baskets.

Since one of Whole Foods' core values was to satisfy and delight customers, store personnel were empowered to exert their best efforts to meet or exceed customer expectations on every shopping trip. They were personable and chatty with shoppers. Customers could get personal attention in every department of the store. When customers asked where an item was located, team members often took them to the spot, making conversation along the way and offering to answer any questions. Team members were quite knowledgeable and enthusiastic about the products in their particular department and tried to take advantage of opportunities to inform and educate customers about natural foods, organics, healthy eating, and food-related environmental issues. They took pride in helping customers choose among the various product options. Seafood and meat department personnel provided customers with custom cuts, cooking instructions, and personal recommendations. Management wanted competent, knowledgeable, and friendly service to be a hallmark of shopping at a Whole Foods Market. The aim was to turn highly satisfied customers into advocates for Whole Foods who talked to close friends and acquaintances about their positive experiences shopping at Whole Foods. Top management believed word-of-mouth advocacy was more effective than traditional advertising.

**Social Media**   Whole Foods also connected and engaged with customers through social media and the company's website and blog at **www.wholefoods market.com**. Management believed social media provided the company with a powerful way to communicate and interact with Internet-savvy customers and thereby gain useful insight into how Whole Foods was viewed and what customers wanted and expected when shopping at a Whole Foods store. On a companywide basis, Whole Foods published roughly 1,000 messages per day across 900 social media channels. Its footprint on Facebook and Twitter was approximately 7 million, with 3 million Facebook "likes" and 4 million Twitter followers, including both global brand accounts and individual store accounts. The individual store accounts were particularly useful to local marketing personnel

in building deeper community ties and connecting more directly to the tastes and needs of local customers.

## Store Operations and Work Environment

Whole Foods employed a decentralized, team-based approach to store operations. Each store was headed by a store team leader and one or more associate team leaders. Depending on store size and traffic volume, Whole Foods stores employed between 50 and 650 team members, who were organized into 10 self-managed teams per store, each responsible for a different product category or aspect of store operations and each led by a team leader. These teams were empowered to make many decisions regarding the operations of their respective department, including merchandising and the means they would use to please customers shopping in their department. Team leaders screened candidates for job openings on their team, but a two-thirds majority of the whole team had to approve a new hire—approval came only after a 30-day trial for the candidate. The store team leader worked with one or more associate store team leaders, as well as with all the department team leaders, to operate the store as efficiently and profitably as possible. Store team leaders reported directly to a regional president. Top executives at Whole Foods were acutely aware that the company's decentralized team approach to store operations— whereby many personnel, merchandising, and operating decisions were made by teams at the individual store level—made it critical to have an effective store team leader.

All the teams at each store were continuously evaluated on measures relating to sales, operations, and morale; the results were made available to team members and to headquarters personnel.[13] Teams competed not only against the goals they had set for themselves but also against other teams at their stores or in their region—competition among teams was encouraged. In addition, stores went through two review processes—a store tour and a "customer snapshot." Each store was toured periodically and subjected to a rigorous evaluation by personnel from another region; the group included region heads, store team leaders, associate team leaders, and department team leaders. Customer snapshots involved a surprise inspection by a headquarters official or regional president who rated the store on 300 items; each store had 10 surprise inspections annually, with the results distributed to every store and included in the reward system. Rewards were team-based and tied to performance metrics.

Whole Foods promoted from within as much as possible, with team members often moving up to assume positions at stores soon to be opened or at stores in other regions. There were online, self-paced training programs to inform and educate team members on such topics as organic products, dietary supplements and the law, the company's numerous quality standards, and how the company's compensation and incentive reward system worked. These programs were intended to better connect team members to the company's core values, aspects of the company's operations, and the organic food and supermarket industries. All stores had budgets for enhancing team member job skills and performance.

Whole Foods' commitment to team-based management of store operations stemmed from the conviction that the company's long-term success was dependent on the collective efforts of energetic and intelligent team members who were motivated to (1) go to great lengths to satisfy and delight customers and (2) operate the store as efficiently and profitably as possible. The team approach, complemented by a strong emphasis on empowering employees and tying a part of their compensation to store profitability and stock option awards, was seen as promoting a strong corporate culture and contributing to a work environment in which motivated team members could flourish, build a career, and reach their highest potential. Management also believed that team members were further motivated and inspired by the company's strategic vision—many team members felt good about their jobs and had a greater sense of purpose because the work they did contributed to better diets and eating habits on the part of Whole Foods' shoppers and to the overall well-being of society at large. Indeed, many job candidates were drawn to interview at Whole Foods because their personal philosophy and lifestyle matched well with the company's "Whole Foods, Whole People, Whole Planet" mission of selling natural and organic foods, advancing the cause of long-term sustainable agricultural practices, and promoting a cleaner environment. Management believed that voluntary turnover of full-time team members at Whole Foods, which fell from 23 percent in fiscal year 2008 to 12 percent

in fiscal year 2009 and to 10 percent in fiscal 2013, was very low for the food retailing industry and helped the company do a better job of satisfying its customers and operating its stores efficiently.

Whole Foods Market had about 80,000 team members in early 2014, including approximately 57,800 full-time, 19,000 part-time, and 3,200 seasonal team members; 44 percent were minorities and 43 percent were women.[14] None were represented by unions, although there had been a couple of unionization attempts. John Mackey was viewed as fiercely antiunion and had once said: "The union is like having herpes. It doesn't kill you, but it's unpleasant and inconvenient and it stops a lot of people from becoming your lover."[15]

Whole Foods had made *Fortune*'s "100 Best Companies to Work For" list for 17 consecutive years (1998–2014), one of only 13 companies to make the list every year since its inception. In scoring companies, *Fortune* placed two-thirds weight on responses to a 57-question survey of approximately 400 randomly selected employees and one-third on *Fortune*'s own evaluation of a company's demographic makeup, pay and benefits, and culture.

## Compensation, Incentives, Benefits, and the Use of Economic Value Added Measures of Performance

Management wanted the company's compensation policy, incentive and reward programs, and benefits package to be perceived as fair to all stakeholders. Compensation levels were attractive. Wages and salary differentials between store employees and executives reflected a philosophy of egalitarianism. Whole Foods had a salary cap that limited the compensation (wages plus profit incentive bonuses) of any team member or officer to 19 times the average total compensation of all full-time team members in the company—a policy mandated in the company's core values (see Exhibit 2). The salary cap was raised from 14 to 19 times the average total compensation in 2007—it had been 8 times in 2003; the increases stemmed from the need to attract and retain key executives. Thus, if the average total compensation of a Whole Foods team member was $35,000, then a cap of 19 times the average meant that an executive could not be paid more than $665,000. All team members had access to the company's financial books, including an annual compensation report listing the gross pay of each team member and company executive. Cofounder and CEO John Mackey had voluntarily set his annual salary at $1 and received no cash bonuses or stock option awards.

In addition, Whole Foods strived to create a "shared-fate consciousness" on the part of team members by uniting the self-interests of team members with those of shareholders. One way management reinforced this concept was through a gain-sharing program (which was equivalent to profit-sharing plans that some companies employed) based on an economic value added (EVA) management and incentive system adopted by Whole Foods in 1999. As indicated earlier, EVA equaled company net operating profits after taxes minus a charge for the cost of capital necessary to generate that profit. Senior executives managed the company with the goal of *improving* EVA at the store level and companywide; they believed that an EVA-based bonus system was the best financial framework for team members to use in helping make decisions that created sustainable shareholder value. At Whole Foods, EVA at the store level was based on store contribution (store revenues minus cost of goods sold minus store operating expenses) relative to store investment over and above the prevailing weighted-average cost of capital. The teams in all stores were challenged to find ways to boost store contribution and store EVA, and all gain-sharing bonuses for store-level team members (except store leaders and assistant store leaders) were tied to these two measures of store performance. Typically, gain-sharing distributions added 5 to 7 percent to team member wages.

In 2009, approximately 1,000 senior executives, regional managers, store team leaders, and assistant store team leaders throughout the company were also on an EVA-based incentive compensation plan. The primary measure determining the payout for these officers and team leaders was EVA *improvement*. The company's overall EVA climbed from a negative $30.4 million in fiscal 2001 to $2.6 million in fiscal 2003, $15.6 million in fiscal 2004, $25.8 million in 2005, and $64.4 million in 2006, but then it dropped sharply to $35.4 million in 2007. The company did not publicly report overall EVA data for fiscal years 2008 and 2009. [*Note:* In addition to using EVA measures for its incentive system, Whole Foods utilized EVA calculations to (1) determine whether the sales and profit projections for new stores would yield a positive and large-enough EVA to justify the investment, (2) to guide decisions on store closings, and (3) to evaluate new acquisitions.] Whole Foods executives believed the emphasis on empowered teams and EVA-based incentives helped harness the collective energy and intelligence of team members to operate their departments effectively and efficiently—thereby enabling Whole Foods to manage its stores better than rival supermarket chains managed their stores.

A second way that Whole Foods endeavored to link the interests of team members with those of shareholders was through three kinds of stock ownership programs:

1. *A team member stock option plan.* All full-time and part-time team members—once they had accumulated 6,000 service hours (about three years of full-time employment)—were eligible to receive stock option grants each year based on their leadership performance and their length of service; the number of shares available for these grants was determined annually by the company's board of directors. Stock option grants based on outstanding leadership performance were awarded on the basis of the recommendation of a team member's regional president. Stock option grants based on length of service were made to full- or part-time nonseasonal team members with more than 6,000 service hours. Options were granted at a price equal to the market value of the stock at the grant date and were exercisable over a four-year period beginning one year from the date of the grant. Since the inception of the plan in 1992, approximately 95 percent of the stock options granted were to team members who were not executive officers. In fiscal year 2013, more than 14,000 team members exercised over 4 million stock options worth approximately $120 million in gains before taxes, or an average of about $8,400 per team member.

2. *A team member stock purchase plan.* Through payroll deductions, all full-time team members with a minimum of 400 hours of service could purchase shares of Whole Foods common stock at 95 percent of the market price on the purchase date. Team members purchased 120,000 shares in fiscal 2011, 120,000 shares in fiscal 2012, and 80,000 shares in fiscal 2013

3. *A team member 401(k) retirement savings plan.* Team members with a minimum of 1,000 service

hours in any one year were eligible to participate in a "Growing Your Future" 401(k) plan. Team members were automatically enrolled unless they opted out of the plan. Whole Foods made matching contributions to the 401(k) plan totaling $6 million in fiscal 2013 and $5 million in fiscal years 2011 and 2012. Whole Foods Market stock was one of the investment options in the 401(k) plan.

**The Benefits Package for Team Members**
Since 2002, team members across the company have been encouraged to actively contribute ideas about the benefits they would like the company to offer. By participating in Whole Foods' companywide benefits vote every three years, team members could take an active role in choosing the benefits made available by the company and how they shared in the cost. In the most recent vote, held in September 2012, 82 percent of eligible team members cast a ballot to determine the company's benefits package for fiscal years 2013–2015. Under medical care coverage, part of the package approved by team members, Whole Foods provided health care coverage at no cost to full-time team members working 30 or more hours per week and having a minimum of 20,000 service hours (approximately 10 years of full-time employment). Full-time team members with 800 to 19,999 service hours paid a premium of $10 per paycheck. In addition, Whole Foods provided personal wellness dollars in the form of either a health reimbursement arrangement (HRA) or a health savings account (HSA). Team members could receive from $300 to $1,800 per year (based on years of service) to help cover the cost of deductibles and other allowable out-of-pocket health care expenses not covered by health insurance.

In addition, Whole Foods promoted the health of team members through two initiatives, the Total Health Immersion Program and the Healthy Discount Incentive Program. The Total Health Immersion Program provided educational opportunities for team members that were fully paid by the company. Since launching the program in 2009, more than 2,400 team members had participated. The Healthy Discount Incentive Program offered additional store discounts of up to 35 percent, going beyond the standard 20 percent store discount that all team members received, based on meeting designated biometric criteria (cholesterol/low-density lipoprotein, body mass index or waist-height ratio, blood

pressure) and being nicotine-free. In fiscal year 2013, more than 14,000 team members participated in biometric screenings, with approximately 9,200 receiving higher-level discount cards.

Other key benefits included:

- *Paid time off based on hours worked.* The paid time off could be used for vacations, holidays, illness, and personal days, as a team member saw fit.
- *A 20 percent discount on all purchases at Whole Foods.* This benefit became available on a team member's first day of employment.
- *Dental and eye care plans.* Coverage was available for both team members and their dependents.
- *Life insurance and disability insurance plans.*
- *A dependent care reimbursement plan.* This plan allowed team members to contribute pretax funds to pay for anticipated day care expenses incurred while at work.
- *Assistance for unforeseeable emergencies.* This benefit was funded by voluntary team member paycheck deductions (usually $1), by paid-time-off donations (from team member to team member), and by the company (in situations where there was a major disaster).

## Purchasing and Distribution

Whole Foods had a centralized buying group that purchased most of the items retailed in the company's stores from regional and national wholesale suppliers and vendors in order to negotiate better volume discounts with major vendors and distributors. United Natural Foods was the company's single largest third-party supplier, accounting for approximately 32 percent of the company's total purchases in fiscal year 2013. Whole Foods' long-term relationship with United as the primary supplier of dry grocery and frozen food products extended through 2020. Whole Foods had a produce procurement center that facilitated the procurement and distribution of the majority of the produce Whole Foods sold. The company also operated four seafood processing and distribution facilities, a specialty coffee and tea procurement and roasting operation, and 11 regional distribution centers that focused primarily on perishables distribution to Whole Foods stores across the United States, Canada, and the United Kingdom. In addition, Whole Foods had three regional commissary kitchens and five regional bake house facilities that supplied certain fresh-baked goods and prepared foods to area stores. Other products were typically procured through a combination of specialty wholesalers and direct distributors.

Local store buyers sourced some fruits and vegetables from local organic farmers as part of the company's commitment to promote and support organic farming methods. In fiscal 2013, about 25 percent of the produce sold in Whole Foods stores came from local farms. Store buyers also sourced select other products (such as cheeses, soups, and other condiments) that were produced locally to help give their store a local flavor and to support community enterprises making quality food products with appeal to Whole Foods shoppers. In 2007, Whole Foods established a Local Producer Loan Program with a budget of up to $10 million to promote local production; in 2013, the budget was increased to $25 million. At the end of fiscal 2013, Whole Foods had disbursed $10 million in loans to 147 local food producers companywide.

## Whole Foods' Social Responsibility Strategy and Community Citizenship Initiatives

Whole Foods was pursuing a comprehensive social responsibility strategy. Key elements of this strategy included standards relating to animal welfare, support for organic farming and sustainable agriculture, healthy-eating education, actions to promote responsible and sustainable seafood practices, comprehensive actions to implement wise environmental practices and display good environmental stewardship, a policy of donating at least 5 percent of after-tax profits (in cash or products) to nonprofit or educational organizations, the Local Producer Loan Program, a Whole Trade Guarantee program, the activities of the company's Whole Planet Foundation, the activities of the company's Whole Kids Foundation, and a variety of community citizenship activities. Select elements of Whole Foods social responsibility strategy are summarized below:

- Whole Foods had implemented a Five-Step Animal Welfare Rating system that laid out a set of "animal compassionate" standards expected of Whole Foods' meat and poultry suppliers. These standards entailed a requirement of humane living conditions for animals, prohibited the use of antibiotics and growth hormones, prohibited the use of feeds containing animal by-products, and specified other permissible and prohibited production and handling techniques (e.g., there were prohibitions against raising animals in crates, cages, or crowded facilities). Whole Foods ceased selling live lobsters in 2006 because the process of handling live lobsters throughout the supply chain (from capture to in-store tank conditions) was not in line with the company's commitment to humane treatment. In early 2008, Whole Foods created a Global Animal Partnership foundation for the purpose of working with farms, ranches, and others to foster continuous improvement of the environment and conditions for each species that supported the animal's natural physical, emotional, and behavioral well-being. Whole Foods refused to sell commercial veal from tethered calves, foie gras from force-fed ducks, and eggs from caged hens.

- Whole Foods was committed to supporting wise environmental practices and being a leader in environmental stewardship. Internally, the company employed environmentally sound practices for every aspect of store and facility operations, including paperless ordering systems, use of biodegradable supplies for food and wine sampling, composting, use of recycled paper, conducting company and community recycling drives for electronics, providing receptacles for glass and plastic recycling in dining areas, the use of Green Seal products for cleaning and maintenance, and installation of flushless urinals (each of which saved an average of 40,000 gallons of water annually). Since 2004, Whole Foods had purchased over 4.3 billion kilowatt hours of wind-based renewable energy, earning seven Green Power awards from the Environmental Protection Agency. It had 14 stores and one distribution center using or hosting rooftop solar systems, four stores with fuel cells, one store with a rooftop farm, and a commissary kitchen that used biofuel from internally generated waste cooking oil. Electric vehicle charging stations had been installed at over 35 stores. The company had committed to reducing energy consumption at all of its stores by 25 percent per square foot by 2015. New stores were built with the environment in mind, using green building innovations whenever possible. In 2008, Whole Foods began using all-natural fiber packaging at its salad and food bars, and it ended the use of disposable plastic bags at the checkout lanes of all its stores, chiefly because such bags did not break down in landfills. Whole Foods distribution vehicles had been converted to the use of biodiesel fuel. Unless located in a community that did not support recycling and composting, all stores were involved in a recycling program, and most participated in a composting program in which food waste and compostable paper items were regenerated into compost. Whole Foods was working to eliminate the use of Styrofoam in packing materials shipped to the company and in product packaging in its stores. It had a goal of achieving zero waste (defined by the EPA as a 90 percent diversion rate of waste from landfills) in at least 90 percent of its stores by 2017.

In April 2011, Whole Foods introduced its exclusive Eco-Scale rating system and became the first national retailer to launch its own comprehensive set of green cleaning standards to help shoppers make environmentally friendly choices. Under the Eco-Scale rating system, producers of all household cleaning products in Whole Foods stores were required to list all ingredients on their packaging. Using the Eco-Scale rating system's red-orange-yellow-green color scale, shoppers easily identified a product's environmental impact and safety. Whole Foods was committed to working with its suppliers to evaluate and independently audit every product in its cleaning products category, with a goal of having all brands in its stores meet a minimum baseline standard of orange.

- In October 2005, Whole Foods established its not-for-profit Whole Planet Foundation, which was charged with combating poverty and promoting self-sufficiency in third-world countries that supplied Whole Foods with some of the products it sold. Most of the foundation's efforts involved providing loans, training, and other financial services to aspiring entrepreneurs and the self-employed poor. As of the end of fiscal 2013, the Whole Planet Foundation had partnered with various microfinance institutions to facilitate approximately $42 million in various donor-funded grants for 91 projects in 58 countries where the company sourced products. Over 330,000 borrower families (88 percent women) had received loans used to support such home-based businesses as poultry and pig farming, agriculture, furniture making, tailoring, and selling handicrafts, homemade foods, clothing, and footwear.

- In March 2007, Whole Foods launched its Whole Trade Guarantee program, which committed the company to paying small-scale producers (chiefly in impoverished, low-wage countries where living standards were low) a price for their products that more than covered the producer's costs. The goal was to make sure that the producers of products meeting Whole Foods' quality standards could always afford to create, harvest, or grow their product so that they did not have to abandon their work or jeopardize the well-being of their family to make ends meet. The commitment to paying such producers a premium price was viewed as an investment in the producers and their communities, a way for producers to be able to put money back into their operations, invest in training and education for their workers, and have sufficient take-home pay to help support a better life. In 2014, the Whole Trade Guarantee label was featured on 400 items at Whole Foods' stores. Whole Foods donated 1 percent of the retail sales of all Whole Trade Guarantee products sold to the Whole Planet Foundation.

- In 2011, Whole Foods established the Whole Kids Foundation, a nonprofit organization dedicated to improving children's nutrition by supporting schools and inspiring families. The foundation provided grants for school gardens and salad bars and offered cooking and nutrition education for teachers and staff. As of 2014, through the generosity of Whole Foods customers, suppliers, and community donors, approximately 1,600 schools in the United States and Canada had received school garden grants since 2011. Whole Foods Market and the Whole Kids Foundation, in partnership with Let's Move Salad Bars to Schools, had provided more than 2,600 salad bars for schools in the United States. Team members and customers donated approximately $3 million during the foundation's fall 2013 fund-raising campaign. Whole Foods Market covered all operating costs for the foundation, allowing 100 percent of public donations to be dedicated to program support.

- A renewed drive to make customers more aware of healthy-eating choices began in 2009 and was in full force by 2010. Whole Foods had partnered with Eat Right America and the creator of The Engine 2 Diet to create Getting Started programs. In addition, Whole Foods had initiated its Health Starts Here campaign that included a growing selection of new, healthy prepared foods, an educational booth where team members dispensed information and provided healthy-eating materials, and Health Starts Here logos and signage adjacent to items considered to be good healthy-eating choices. Whole Foods viewed Health Starts Here as "a mindful approach to healthy eating rooted in four simple principles to build better meals—Whole Food, Plant-Strong™, Healthy Fats, and Nutrient Dense. Products such as frozen items, breads and prepared foods that meet these guidelines carry our 'Health Starts Here' logo. In addition, our stores feature signage on the Aggregate Nutrient Density Index ('ANDI®'), a proprietary scoring system that ranks foods based on nutrient density (vitamins, minerals, antioxidants and phytochemicals) per calorie."[16]

In 2010, John Mackey launched a program to better engage the company's team members in the healthy-eating campaign (because they were the ones that interfaced with customers) by giving them a monetary incentive to get healthier. Team members who scored well on three of four biomarkers of good health (having a good body mass index, being a nonsmoker, having a good cholesterol count, and having good blood pressure) received 25 percent discounts on store purchases; team members with acceptable scores on all four markers received a 30 percent discount (later increased to 35 percent). Mackey also envisioned instituting competitions for the healthiest team in a store, the healthiest store in each region, and the healthiest region in the company. At the time, Mackey said, "I fully expect that I am going to get a [30 percent discount]. I see in my mind's eye how this is going to play out. I'm into it."[17]

- In September 2013, Whole Foods announced plans to launch a three-tier, science-based rating system for the produce and flowers sold in its stores whereby items would be labeled "good," "better," and "best." The rating system, developed by Whole Foods Market with help from sustainable agriculture experts and input from suppliers, measured performance on such sustainable farming practices

and concerns as pest management, pollinator protection, water conservation, soil health, ecosystems, biodiversity, energy, waste, climate, and the welfare of farm workers. Whole Foods management believed the new ratings would enable shoppers to make more informed decisions, as well as recognize growers for responsible practices that went beyond compliance with organic standards.

- Team members at every Whole Foods store were heavily involved in such community citizenship activities as sponsoring blood donation drives, preparing meals for seniors and the homeless, holding fund-raisers to help the disadvantaged, growing vegetables for a domestic violence shelter, participating in housing renovation projects, and working as delivery people for Meals on Wheels. Each store donated food to area food banks and shelters. Several times a year, individual Whole Foods stores held "5% Days" (or community giving days) on which 5 percent of that day's sales were donated to a local nonprofit or educational organization. Each store had latitude in deciding what activities it would undertake to support the local community.

## Mackey's Ethics Are Called into Question

*Business Ethics* named Whole Foods Market to its "100 Best Corporate Citizens" list in 2004, 2006, and 2007. However, during 2007, CEO John Mackey was the center of attention in two ethics-related incidents. The first involved the discovery that, over a seven-year period, Mackey had typed out more than 1,100 entries on Yahoo Finance's message board touting his company's stock and occasionally making uncomplimentary remarks about rival Wild Oats Markets. Mackey's postings stopped several months prior to Whole Foods' offer to buy Wild Oats Market. In making his postings, Mackey used the alias Rahodeb—a variation of Deborah, his wife's name. The *Wall Street Journal* reported that in January 2005 Rahodeb posted that no one would buy Wild Oats at its current price of $8 per share and that Whole Foods had nothing to gain by buying Wild Oats because its stores were too small.[18] A *New York Times* article reported that on March 28, 2006, Rahodeb wrote, "OATS has lost their way and no longer has a sense of mission or even a well-thought-out theory of the business. They lack a viable business model that they can replicate. They are floundering around hoping to find a viable strategy that may stop their erosion. Problem is they lack the time and the capital now."[19] The *New York Times* article quoted Mackey as saying, "I posted on Yahoo! under a pseudonym because I had fun doing it. I never intended any of those postings to be identified with me." Mackey's postings, which came to light in June and July 2007 and spurred calls for his resignation on grounds that he breached his fiduciary responsibility, were first discovered by the Federal Trade Commission in Whole Foods' documents that the FTC obtained in the course of challenging the Wild Oats acquisition. According to Mackey, the views he expressed in his Rahodeb postings sometimes represented his personal beliefs and sometimes were different because he would occasionally play the role of devil's advocate. He said no proprietary information about Whole Foods was disclosed.[20]

In the days following the media reports of the postings, Mackey expressed remorse for his postings, apologized for his behavior, and asked stakeholders to forgive him for exercising bad judgment. Nonetheless, the content of certain Mackey postings was cited in court documents filed by the FTC as reasons why the Whole Foods' acquisition of Wild Oats should be blocked. On July 17, 2007, the Securities and Exchange Commission announced that it had begun an investigation of the postings. That same day, Whole Foods announced that the company's board of directors had formed a special committee to investigate the postings and retained legal counsel to advise it during the investigation. Whole Foods said it would cooperate fully with the SEC inquiry.

In October 2007, Whole Foods announced that the special committee had completed its investigation of Mackey's message board postings and that the board of directors affirmed its support of CEO John Mackey; the company indicated the special committee's findings would be turned over to the SEC and that the company would have no further comment pending the SEC investigation.[21] In April 2008, the SEC closed its investigation into Mackey's online chat activities and took no actions against Mackey or Whole Foods.

A second controversy-stirring incident involved a Mackey-authored blog entitled "Whole Foods, Wild Oats and the FTC" that was posted on the company's website on June 19, 2007. Mackey, who objected strenuously to the grounds on which the Federal Trade Commission was trying to block Whole Foods' acquisition of Wild Oats, authored a blog that was dedicated to providing updates and information regarding the FTC proceeding and to making the case for why the company's acquisition of Wild Oats Market should be allowed to go forward. Mackey explained the basis for the blog posting:

> My blog posting provides a detailed look into Whole Foods Market's decision-making process regarding the merger, as well as our company's experience interacting with the FTC staff assigned to this merger. I provide explanations of how I think the FTC, to date, has neglected to do its homework appropriately, especially given the statements made regarding prices, quality, and service levels in its complaint. I also provide a glimpse into the bullying tactics used against Whole Foods Market by this taxpayer-funded agency. Finally, I provide answers in my FAQ section to many of the questions that various Team Members have fielded from both the media and company stakeholders. As previously announced, we set an intention as a company to be as transparent as possible throughout this legal process, and this blog entry is my first detailed effort at transparency.

The blog posting by Mackey addressed:

- Why Whole Foods Market wants to buy Wild Oats.
- Whole Foods Market's objections to the FTC's investigation.
- What the FTC is claiming in its objections to the merger.
- FAQs.

Critics of the Mackey blog posting said it was inappropriate for a CEO to publicly air the company's position, to take issue with the FTC, and to make the company's case for why the acquisition should be allowed to proceed. At the least, some critics opined, the blog should be toned down.[22] When the SEC announced on July 17, 2007, that it would investigate John Mackey's financial message board postings, Mackey put a hold on further blog postings regarding the FTC's actions to try to block the Wild Oats acquisition.

In 2010, Ethisphere Institute named Whole Foods as one of the world's most ethical companies; Ethisphere is a leading research-based international think tank dedicated to the creation, advancement, and sharing of best practices in business ethics, corporate social responsibility, anticorruption, and environmental sustainability.

## Whole Foods Market's Outlook for Fiscal Year 2014

In February 2014, Whole Foods provided the following guidance for fiscal year 2014, ending September 28:[23]

- Sales growth of 11 to 12 percent
- Comparable-store sales growth in the range of 5.5 to 6.2 percent
- Diluted earnings per share in the range of $1.58 to $1.65
- New openings of 33 to 38 stores (followed by the opening of 38 to 45 new stores in fiscal 2015)
- Percentage of total sales contributed by new stores of about 6 percent
- Capital expenditures in the range of $600 million to $650 million

# COMPETITORS

The food retailing business was intensely competitive. The degree of competition Whole Foods faced varied from locality to locality, and to some extent from store location to store location within a given locale, depending on the proximity of stores of its two closest competitors in the natural food and organic segment of the food retailing industry, Fresh Market and Trader Joe's. Other competitors included local supermarkets, small chains, local independent retailers of natural and health foods, regional and national supermarkets (most of which had begun stocking a growing and more diverse selection of natural and organic products), and national superstores (Walmart and Target). Whole Foods also faced competition in parts of its product line from specialty grocery stores (with upscale delicatessen offerings and prepared foods), small-scale health food stores, retailers of vitamins and nutritional supplements, local farmers' markets, and warehouse clubs (Costco and Sam's Club). Whole Foods' executives had said it was to the company's benefit for conventional supermarkets to offer natural and organic foods for two reasons: First, it helped fulfill the company's mission of improving the health and well-being of people and the planet, and, second, it helped create new customers for Whole Foods by providing a gateway experience. They contended that as more people were exposed to natural and organic products, they were more likely to become a Whole Foods customer because Whole Foods was the category leader for natural and organic products, offered the largest selection at competitive prices, and provided the most informed customer service.

## The Fresh Market

The Fresh Market, headquartered in Greensboro, North Carolina, operated over 150 stores in 26 states in the Southeast, Midwest, Mid-Atlantic, Northeast, and West; the company opened 22 new stores in fiscal 2013 and had signed leases for 25 future store locations to be opened in 2014. Founded by Ray Berry, a former vice president with Southland Corporation who had responsibility over some 3,600 7-Eleven stores, the first Fresh Market store opened in 1982 in Greensboro. Berry's concept was to deliver a differentiated food shopping experience—a small, rustically decorated, neighborhood store with a warm, inviting atmosphere that featured friendly, knowledgeable service and a focus on premium perishable goods. The Greensboro store, which had low-level lighting and classical music playing in the background, was a hit with customers and Berry began to open similar stores in other locales. Between 1982 and 2010, The Fresh Market steadily expanded its geographic presence into additional states, and, as sales approached $1 billion in late 2010, the company opted to become a public company via an initial public offering of its common stock. The company had sales of $1.51 billion (up 13.7 percent over the prior year) and net income of $50.8 million (down 20.8 percent) for fiscal year 2013, ending January 26, 2014.

Fresh Market stores were typically in the 17,000- to 22,000-square-foot range (the average was 21,190 square feet) and were located mostly in high-traffic and/or upscale neighborhood shopping areas. Fresh Market stores were organized around distinct departments with engaging merchandise displays. Accent lighting, classical background music, terra-cotta-colored tiles, and colorful product presentations made Fresh Market stores a cozier, more inviting place to shop than a typical supermarket. The atmosphere was meant to encourage customers to slow down, interact with employees, and have an enjoyable shopping experience.

Fresh Market's product line consisted of 9,000 to 10,000 items that included meats, seafood, fresh fruits and vegetables, fresh baked goods, prepared foods, premium coffees and teas, a small selection of grocery and dairy items, bulk products, more than

200 varieties of domestic and imported cheeses, deli items (including rotisserie meats, sandwiches, wraps, soups, and sandwiches), wine and beer, and a small assortment of cookbooks, candles, kitchen items, and seasonal gift baskets. The emphasis was on variety, freshness, and quality. Management characterized the company as a specialty food retailer, with a store atmosphere and product selection that were distinct from those of competitors. Based on operating experience and market research, management believed that the market in the United States could support at least 500 Fresh Market stores operating under the current format.

The typical Fresh Market store was staffed with approximately 70 to 80 full- and part-time employees including a store manager, two to three assistant store managers, and five department heads. The store management team was responsible for all aspects of store execution including managing inventory and cash, maintaining a clean and engaging store environment, and hiring, training, and supervising store employees. Store employees, especially store managers, were encouraged to engage regularly with customers. To facilitate interaction between staff and customers, store managers were stationed on the selling floor, near the service counters. Special efforts were devoted to hiring, training, retaining, developing, and promoting qualified and enthusiastic employees who displayed a passion for delivering an extraordinary food shopping experience. Because Fresh Market was opening new stores at a rapid pace, management believed it was important to maintain a sufficient pipeline of people qualified to be store managers and assistant store managers. Nearly all store managers and district managers were promoted from within.

After 60 days, all full-time employees who worked at least 30 hours per week were eligible to enroll in plans providing medical, prescription medication, dental, life, and disability coverage; coverage could be extended to spouses or domestic partners and children. In addition, there were employee discounts on most products, a paid annual-leave program, a 401(k) plan with 50 percent company matching of employee contributions, an employee assistance program, and a discounted stock purchase plan.

## Trader Joe's

Founded in 1967 and headquartered in Monrovia, California, Trader Joe's was a specialty supermarket chain with 408 stores in 31 states and Washington, D.C.; about half of the stores were in California. Owned by Germany's Albrecht family, Trader Joe's sales in 2013 were an estimated $10.5 billion. Trader Joe's was ranked number 21 on the *Supermarket News* 2013 list of the top-75 retailers. The company had an ongoing strategy to open additional stores.

The company's mission and business were described on its website as follows:[24]

> At Trader Joe's, our mission is to bring our customers the best food and beverage values and the information to make informed buying decisions. There are more than 2000 unique grocery items in our label, all at honest everyday low prices. We work hard at buying things right: Our buyers travel the world searching for new items and we work with a variety of suppliers who make interesting products for us, many of them exclusive to Trader Joe's. All our private label products have their own "angle," i.e., vegetarian, Kosher, organic or just plain decadent, and all have minimally processed ingredients.
>
> Customers tell us, "I never knew food shopping could be so much fun!" Some even call us "The home of cheap thrills!" We like to be part of our neighborhoods and get to know our customers. And where else do you shop that even the CEO, Dan Bane, wears a loud Hawaiian shirt.
>
> Our tasting panel tastes every product before we buy it. If we don't like it, we don't buy it. If customers don't like it, they can bring it back for a no-hassle refund.
>
> We stick to the business we know: good food at the best prices! Whenever possible we buy direct from our suppliers, in large volume. We bargain hard and manage our costs carefully. We pay in cash, and on time, so our suppliers like to do business with us.
>
> Trader Joe's Crew Members are friendly, knowledgeable and happy to see their customers. They taste our items too, so they can discuss them with their customers. All our stores regularly cook up new and interesting products for our customers to sample.

Trader Joe's stores had open layouts, with wide aisles, appealing displays, cedar plank walls, a nautical decor, and crew members wearing colorful Hawaiian shirts; store sizes ranged from 8,000 to 12,000 square feet. Prices and product offerings varied somewhat by region and state. There were no weekly specials or cents-off coupons or glitzy promotional discounts. Customers could choose from an eclectic and somewhat upscale variety of baked goods, organic foods, fresh fruits and vegetables, imported and domestic cheeses, gourmet chocolates and candies, coffees, fresh salads, meatless entrees and other vegan products, low-fat and low-carbohydrate foods, frozen fish and seafood, heat-and-serve entrees, packaged meats, juices, wine and beer, snack foods, energy bars, vitamins, nuts and trail mixes, and whatever other exotic items the company's buyers had come upon. About 20 to 25 percent of Trader Joe's products were imported. There were very few brand-name items; more than 2,000 items carried the Trader Joe's label and the company's other quirky labels for particular foods: Trader Jose's (Mexican food), Trader Ming's (Chinese food), Trader Giotto's (Italian food), Pilgrim Joe's (seafood), Trader Jacques' (imported French soaps), Joe's Diner (certain frozen entrees), and Joe's Kids (children's food); these items accounted for about 70 percent of total sales. Items with a Trader Joe's logo contained no artificial flavors, colors, or preservatives and no trans fats, monosodium glutamate (MSG), or genetically modified ingredients. About 10 to 15 new, seasonal, or one-time-buy items were introduced each week. Products that weren't selling well were dropped. Trader Joe's was the exclusive retailer of Charles Shaw wine, popularly known as "Two Buck Chuck" because of its $1.99 price tag in California—raised to $2.49 in 2013; outside California, the price ranged as high as $3.79 because of higher liquor taxes and transportation costs.

The appealingly low prices at Trader Joe's enabled the company to draw large numbers of bargain-hunting shoppers, as well as upscale shoppers intrigued by the quirky product offerings. Because of its combination of low everyday prices, emporiumlike atmosphere, intriguing selections, friendly service, and fast checkout lanes, customers viewed shopping at Trader Joe's as an enjoyable experience. The company was able to keep the prices of its unique products low because of (1) discount buying (its buyers were always on the lookout for exotic items they could buy at a discount—all products had to pass a taste test and a cost test), (2) less expensive store locations and decor, (3) lower labor costs (it had fewer employees per store compared with competitors), (4) the very high percentage of products sold under labels exclusive to Trader Joe's, and (5) high sales volumes per square foot of store space (reputed to be in excess of $1,000 per square foot).

Most cities and towns that did not have a Trader Joe's were anxious to get one, particularly those with residents who had shopped at Trader Joe's regularly when they lived in places with a Trader Joe's store. Trader Joe's owed much of its reputation to the glowing word-of-mouth experiences of highly satisfied customers. However, Trader Joe's revealed scant information about its operations and plans—the locations and opening dates of soon-to-be-opened stores were closely guarded secrets. Many sizable markets, like Tampa–St. Petersburg, Houston, Denver, Kansas City, and Milwaukee typically had only one or two stores, making shopping at Trader Joe's more of a destination trip for loyal customers.

## Sprouts Farmers Market

Founded in 2002, Sprouts Farmers Market had grown into a regional chain with 170 stores in Arizona, California, Colorado, Kansas, Nevada, New Mexico, Oklahoma, Texas, and Utah. A total of 19 new stores were opened in 2013. Sprouts had 2013 sales of $2.4 billion and net income of $51.3 million. The company completed an initial public offering of common stock in August 2013. It used $340 million of the net proceeds of $344 million to repay a portion of its outstanding debt.

Management viewed Sprouts Farmers Market as a fast-growing differentiated specialty retailer of natural and organic food, offering a complete shopping experience that included fresh produce, bulk foods, vitamins and supplements, grocery items, meat and seafood, bakery goods, dairy items, frozen foods, body care products, and natural household items catering to consumers' growing interest in eating and living healthier. Sprouts mission was "Healthy Living for Less." The foundation of the company's value proposition was fresh, high-quality produce offered at prices significantly below those of conventional food retailers and even further below high-end natural and organic food retailers.

In 2014, Sprouts management was pursuing a number of strategies designed to continue the company's growth, including expanding the store base, driving comparable-store sales growth, enhancing operating margins, and building the Sprouts brand. The strategy to expand the store base included opening new stores in existing markets, expanding into adjacent markets, and penetrating new markets. The plan was to expand the store base primarily through new store openings, but management expected the company to grow through strategic acquisitions if it identified suitable targets and was able to negotiate acceptable terms and conditions for acquisition.

The strategic objective was to achieve 12 percent or more annual new store growth for at least the next five years.

## Independent and Small-Chain Retailers of Natural and Organic Products

In 2014 there were approximately 12,000 to 13,000 independent and small-chain retailers of natural and organic foods, vitamins and supplements, and natural personal care products. While there were a few regional chains like Natural Grocers by Vitamin Cottage (70 stores in 13 states) and several hundred multistore retailers, the majority were single-store, owner-managed enterprises serving small to medium-sized communities and particular neighborhoods in metropolitan areas. Product lines and range of selection at the stores of independent natural and health food retailers varied from narrow to moderately broad, depending on a store's size and market focus and the shopper traffic it was able to generate.

Over half of the independent stores had less than 2,500 square feet of retail sales space and generated revenues of less than $1 million annually; the core product offerings of these retailers were vitamins and mineral and herbal supplements, complemented by a limited selection of organic and natural foods and some prepared foods, as many as 5,000 items in total. But there were roughly 1,000 natural and health food retailers with store sizes exceeding 6,000 square feet and sales per store of about $10 million annually. Sales of vitamins and supplements at many small independent stores were beginning to flatten, chiefly because conventional supermarket chains and most large drugstore chains had begun to carry a sizable selection of vitamins and supplements. Sales at small retailers of natural and organic foods were also under pressure because conventional supermarkets had a growing selection of organic and natural foods, while chains like Whole Foods and Trader Joe's had a far wider selection of organic and natural products of all types. As one industry expert noted, "Shoppers can pick up a bag of mixed organic salad greens, a half-gallon of organic milk, some hormone-free chicken, trans-fat-free cookies and crackers, non-dairy beverages and—brace yourself—even gluten-free foods, right in the aisles of their regular supermarkets."[25]

## Walmart

Over the past decade or so, Walmart had opened hundreds of new Walmart Supercenters that included a full-line supermarket; food items were also sold at Walmart Discount Stores and Walmart Neighborhood Markets. As of 2014, Walmart was far and away the biggest seller of food, grocery, and household products in the United States, with sales of such products exceeding $150 billion. In April 2014, Walmart announced that it had struck a deal with Yuciapa Companies, a private investment firm that owned the Wild Oats trademarks, to begin selling 100 mostly organic Wild Oats–branded products in the food sections of its 3,290 Supercenters and 346 Neighborhood Markets and also in the pantry sections of its 508 Discount Stores. Because of concerns about adequate supplies, the Wild Oats products would initially be introduced in about 2,000 stores and then gradually rolled out to the more than 2,100 remaining stores.[26] Walmart said it would enter into long-term agreements with suppliers to lock in the large-volume requirements of Wild Oats products it expected it would need to supply its network of stores in the United States.

The lines of Wild Oats products to be offered at Walmart's stores included:

- *Wild Oats Marketplace Organic*—a selection of items that adhered to USDA guidelines for organic certification and included everything from canned vegetables (15 ounces) at $0.88 to spices such as paprika and curry powder (2 ounces) starting at $2.48. This Wild Oats line of organic items represented nearly 90 percent of the 100 Wild Oats products that Walmart would initially offer its customers.

- *Wild Oats Marketplace*—a selection of items with simple and natural ingredients such as ready-to-prepare skillet meals (5.8 ounces) at $1.50.

- *Wild Oats Marketplace Originals*—a selection of new and uniquely formulated items that Walmart expected to introduce in late 2014.

Walmart indicated that it planned to sell the Wild Oats–branded items at prices that would undercut national brand-name organic competitors by 25 percent or more—see Exhibit 7. Walmart said that its internal research found that 91 percent of Walmart shoppers would consider purchasing products from an affordable organic brand at the company's stores.

**EXHIBIT 7**   Expected Price Savings for Walmart Consumers on Select Wild Oats Marketplace Organic Products

| Wild Oats' Product | Wild Oats' Price at Walmart | Price of Comparable National-Brand Organic Item | Price Difference |
|---|---|---|---|
| Organic Tomato Paste (6 oz.) | $0.58 | $0.98 | 41% |
| Organic Chicken Broth (32 oz.) | 1.98 | 3.47 | 43 |
| Organic Cinnamon Applesauce Cups (24 oz.) | 1.98 | 2.78 | 29 |
| Organic Tomato Sauce (15 oz.) | 0.88 | 1.38 | 36 |

*Source:* Walmart press release, April 10, 2014.

# ENDNOTES

[1] According to Nielsen's TDLinx and *Progressive Grocer,* as cited by Whole Foods Market in its 2013 10-K report, p. 1.

[2] According to *Natural Foods Merchandiser,* a leading trade publication for the natural foods industry, as cited by Whole Foods Market in its 2013 10-K report, p. 1.

[3] Economic Research Service, U.S. Department of Agriculture, www.ers.usda.gov, September 27, 2013 (accessed February 14, 2014).

[4] 2009 10-K report, p. 51.

[5] 2009 10-K report, p. 10.

[6] Company press releases, February 19, 2008, and February 16, 2010.

[7] Letter to Shareholders, 2003 annual report.

[8] Hollie Shaw, "Retail-Savvy Whole Foods Opens in Canada," *National Post,* May 1, 2002, p. FP9.

[9] See Karin Schill Rives, "Texas-Based Whole Foods Market Makes Changes to Cary, N.C. Grocery Store," *News and Observer,* March 7, 2002.

[10] Letter to Stakeholders, 2009 annual report.

[11] As quoted in Marilyn Much, "Whole Foods Markets: Austin, Texas Green Grocer Relishes Atypical Sales," *Investors Business Daily,* September 10, 2002.

[12] As quoted in "Whole Foods Market to Open in Albuquerque, N.M.," *Santa Fe New Mexican,* September 10, 2002.

[13] Information contained in John R. Wells and Travis Haglock, "Whole Foods Market, Inc.," Harvard Business School case 9-705-476.

[14] Company 2009 10-K report, p. 14; company press release, January 21, 2010.

[15] As quoted in John K. Wilson, "Going Whole Hog with Whole Foods," *Bankrate.com,* December 23, 1999 (accessed March 21, 2010). Mackey made the statement in 1991 when efforts were being made to unionize the company's store in Berkeley, California.

[16] Company 2013 annual report.

[17] "Frank Talk from Whole Foods' John Mackey," *Wall Street Journal,* August 4, 2009, online.wsj.com (accessed March 13, 2010).

[18] David Kesmodel and John. R. Wilke, "Whole Foods Is Hot, Wild Oats a Dud—So Said Rahodeb," *Wall Street Journal,* July 12, 2007, online.wsj.com/article/SB118418782959963745 .html (accessed April 7, 2007).

[19] Andrew Martin, "Whole Foods Executive Used Alias," *New York Times,* July 12, 2007, www.nytimes.com/2007/07/12/ business/12foods.html (accessed April 7, 2008).

[20] Ibid.

[21] Company press release, October 5, 2007.

[22] According to a July 13, 2007, posting on a *Business Week* message board, www.businessweek.com/careers/managementiq/ archives/2007/07/who_advises_joh.html (accessed March 26, 2010).

[23] Company press release, February 12, 2014.

[24] Information posted at www.traderjoes.com (accessed December 1, 2005).

[25] Jay Jacobwitz, "Independent Retailers Need New Customers: The New 'Integrated' Foods Shopper," *Merchandising Insights,* November 2009, wfcgreenbook.com (accessed March 30, 2010).

[26] Walmart press release, April 10, 2014.

# Papa John's International, Inc.: Its Strategy in the Pizza Restaurant Industry

**A. J. Strickland**
The University of Alabama

**Joyce Meyer**
The University of Alabama

**Christopher Harrington,**
MBA 2013

The University of Alabama

Papa John's International, Inc., had become the world's third-largest pizza chain by focusing on a high-quality product made from the best ingredients, responsive customer service and convenient ordering systems, extensive marketing campaigns, employee training and development, and franchising. In 2013, the company operated 723 company-owned and 3,705 franchised establishments throughout all 50 states and in 34 countries. Papa John's had opened 265 new restaurants in 2013, of which 82 were in North America and 183 were in international markets. The addition of 183 new international units pushed the total number of Papa John's restaurants in international locations to 1,159. The company planned to open more than 1,000 new units over the next five years, with about 95 percent of these units being franchised and 70 percent being located in international markets. Papa John's management believed that the company could support as many as 4,000 units in North America and thousands more internationally.

The company was performing at a high level in 2014, with average sales per restaurant slightly exceeding $1 million, operating income averaging $186,000 per unit, and cash flow averaging $127,000 per location. Corporate revenues had increased from $1,218 million in 2011 to $1,439 million in 2013. Papa John's net income had increased from $4.7 million to $69.5 million over the same time period. However, the company faced considerable challenges from its rival pizza chains and from external trends in the marketplace, including greater health awareness among consumers, the growing use of technology in the industry, and unstable economic conditions in many countries' markets where Papa John's did business. As 2015 approached, Papa John's top management needed to develop new strategies to strengthen the company's competitive position in the industry and continue its impressive rate of growth. A summary of Papa John's International's financial performance for 2009 through 2013 is presented in Exhibit 1.

**EXHIBIT 1**   Financial Summary for Papa John's International, Inc., 2009–2013 (in thousands, except per share data)

|  | Dec. 29, 2013 (52 weeks) | Dec. 30, 2012 (53 weeks) | Dec. 25, 2011 (52 weeks) | Dec. 26, 2010 (52 weeks) | Dec. 27, 2009 (52 weeks) |
|---|---|---|---|---|---|
| **Income statement data** | | | | | |
| North America revenues: | | | | | |
| Domestic company-owned restaurant sales | $  635,317 | $  592,203 | $  525,841 | $  503,272 | $  503,818 |
| Franchise royalties | 81,692 | 79,567 | 73,694 | 69,631 | 62,083 |
| Franchise and development fees | 1,181 | 806 | 722 | 610 | 912 |
| Domestic commissary sales | 578,870 | 545,924 | 508,155 | 454,506 | 417,689 |
| Other sales | 53,322 | 51,223 | 50,912 | 51,951 | 54,045 |
| International revenues: | | | | | |
| Royalties and franchise and development fees | 21,979 | 19,881 | 16,327 | 13,265 | 11,780 |
| Restaurant and commissary sales | 66,661 | 53,049 | 42,231 | 33,162 | 28,223 |
| Total revenues | 1,439,022 | 1,342,653 | 1,217,882 | 1,126,397 | 1,078,550 |
| Operating income | 106,503 | 99,807 | 87,017 | 86,744 | 95,218 |
| Investment income | 589 | 750 | 755 | 875 | 629 |
| Interest expense | (983) | (2,162) | (2,981) | (4,309) | (11,660) |
| Income before income taxes | 106,109 | 98,395 | 84,791 | 83,310 | 84,187 |
| Income tax expense | 33,130 | 32,393 | 26,324 | 27,247 | 26,702 |
| Net income before attribution to noncontrolling interests | 72,979 | 66,002 | 58,467 | 56,063 | 57,485 |
| Income attributable to noncontrolling interests | (3,442) | (4,342) | (3,732) | (3,485) | (3,756) |
| Net income attributable to the company | $   69,537 | $   61,660 | $   54,735 | $   52,578 | $   53,729 |
| Net income attributable to common shareholders | $   68,497 | $   61,660 | $   54,735 | $   52,578 | $   53,729 |
| Basic earnings per common share | $1.58 | $1.31 | $1.09 | $1.00 | $0.97 |
| Earnings per common share— assuming dilution | $1.55 | $1.29 | $1.08 | $0.99 | $0.96 |
| Basic weighted-average common shares outstanding | 43,387 | 46,916 | 50,086 | 52,656 | 55,476 |
| Diluted weighted-average common shares outstanding | 44,243 | 47,810 | 50,620 | 52,936 | 55,818 |
| Dividends declared per common share | $0.25 | — | — | — | — |
| **Balance sheet data** | | | | | |
| Total assets | $  464,291 | $  438,408 | $  390,382 | $  417,492 | $  396,009 |
| Total debt | 157,900 | 88,258 | 51,489 | 99,017 | 99,050 |
| Mandatorily redeemable noncontrolling interests | 10,786 | 11,837 | 11,065 | 9,972 | 10,960 |
| Redeemable noncontrolling interests | 7,024 | 6,380 | 3,965 | 3,512 | 3,215 |
| Total stockholders' equity | 138,184 | 181,514 | 205,647 | 195,608 | 173,145 |

*Source:* Papa John's International, Inc., 10-K report, 2013.

# THE HISTORY OF PAPA JOHN'S PIZZA

John Schnatter's interest in the pizza business began in high school when he worked part-time as a dishwasher in a Jeffersonville, Indiana, pizza and sandwich shop. He enjoyed working in the restaurant and dreamed of one day owning his own pizza restaurant. While attending Ball State University, Schnatter continued to be involved in the pizza industry by working as a delivery driver for another pizzeria. Working there solidified his dream of opening his own pizza place one day.

After graduating with a bachelor's degree in business, Schnatter returned home to Jeffersonville to work in his father's tavern—Mick's Lounge. The tavern was struggling, and Schnatter ended up selling his most prized possession, his 1972 Camaro Z28, in order to pump more money into the business. It was then that he saw an opportunity to salvage his father's business for good while pursuing his lifelong dream.

In 1984, at the age of 22, Schnatter invested $1,600 in a used pizza oven and began selling pizzas out of the back of Mick's Lounge. Combining his years of experience in the pizza industry with the strong work ethic instilled in him by his father and grandfather, Schnatter's start in the pizza business was almost immediately successful. Later in the year, he was able to realize his dream when he opened the first Papa John's restaurant. Schnatter slowly began to expand but kept the business plan simple. His early success was founded on the ideas of superior customer service, a quality product, and a limited menu. Schnatter began franchising the Papa John's concept in 1986, and in 1993 he launched a successful initial public offering that raised $12 million. By 1996, the 1,000th Papa John's location was opened. The company expanded internationally, with restaurants in Mexico and Puerto Rico in 1998, and by 1999 it had expanded to 2,000 locations.

In addition to maintaining a focus on superior product quality, the company applied marketing innovations that contributed greatly to its success. Papa John's had consistently achieved the highest customer satisfaction ratings among pizza chains, and its frequent advertising during NFL games made it the most identified NFL sponsor in 2013. Also, the company had been a pioneer in online food ordering, with its first online order accepted in 1997.

The company rolled out its online ordering program nationwide in 2001, added text orders in 2007, launched apps for iPhone and Android in 2010 and 2011, respectively, and launched an online ordering app for Kindle Fire in 2012. By 2014, more than 50 percent of Papa John's orders were made digitally.

As of 2013, with a market share of approximately 6 percent, Papa John's was the world's third-largest pizza chain, trailing only Pizza Hut and Domino's, whose market shares were 11.5 and 10 percent, respectively. Headquartered in Louisville, Kentucky, Papa John's operated 723 company-owned and 3,705 franchised establishments in all 50 states and 34 countries. Schnatter owned roughly 20 percent of the company's shares and served as chairman, having stepped down as CEO in 2005. He remained actively involved in the company's marketing campaigns and often appeared in the company's commercials, always touting the slogan "Better Ingredients. Better Pizza. Papa John's." Also, in 2009, Schnatter was able to track down the Z28 that he had sold to fund the company's startup, and he purchased it back for $250,000.

# OVERVIEW OF THE PIZZA RESTAURANT INDUSTRY

Pizza was the number-one meal of choice for Americans, with 93 percent of them eating pizza at least once a month. Pizza was consumed so frequently that in the United States alone people ate, on average, 100 acres of pizza every day at a pace of 350 slices per second. In 2012, the pizza industry recorded worldwide sales of $42.8 billion, with a total of 74,400 pizzerias, and was projected to grow to $49.5 billion in worldwide industry sales by 2017. The number of pizza establishments worldwide was expected to increase to 86,493 by 2017.

The industry comprised two segments: pizza chains and independent pizzerias. Independently owned restaurants accounted for 57 percent of locations and 48 percent of industry sales. The four largest pizza chains were Pizza Hut, Domino's, Papa John's, and Little Caesars, which together accounted for 32 percent of industry sales and 28 percent of locations.

There were four channels of distribution for the industry, with some pizzerias falling into multiple categories. The first was the traditional sit-down option. A big portion of the sit-down establishments consisted of independent pizzerias along with many Pizza Hut locations. Delivery was another form that was associated with all of the major chains. Customers typically had the option of calling in their order or placing it online. Although this was the most convenient option for consumers, it involved a trade-off because most pizzerias charged a delivery fee. Carryout allowed consumers to place their order via phone or online and pick it up in person at the pizzeria. This correlated with the delivery option but had the opposite trade-off: It was more inconvenient for customers but was cheaper since they did not have to pay a delivery charge. Little Caesars was the most well-known pizzeria that allowed only carryout. The final option was a somewhat newer concept known as *take n' bake,* in which pizzerias provided premade, uncooked pizzas for consumers to bring home and bake at their own convenience. Many pizzerias fell into multiple categories, and of these four means of obtaining a pizza the most popular option was carryout. Establishments combining both carryout and delivery accounted for 66.2 percent of pizzerias.

Pizza restaurants also competed against the frozen-pizza selections found in outlets such as Kroger and Walmart stores. According to market research firm Mintel, more than 1,100 new frozen-pizza products were introduced between 2005 and 2009. Also, more food retailers were offering partially baked (par-baked) pizzas in the refrigerated section and touting them as having high-quality, restaurant-style flavor and ingredients. These products were particularly popular among price-conscious consumers who wanted quality pizza but at a lower price.

The biggest consumer demographic for the pizza industry was the 25-to-44 age group, which made up 46.3 percent of all consumers. Many consumers in this segment had young children, and pizza, whether delivered or picked up, provided busy parents with a meal option for the whole family that took very little time. At 22.8 percent, the second-largest group was patrons between the ages of 45 and 64, followed by consumers under 25 and those over 65, at 16.2 and 14.7 percent, respectively.

A big determinant of success for a pizza restaurant was location. A prime location not only allowed for easier pickup options for consumers and shorter driving distances for deliveries and suppliers but also improved restaurant visibility. The pizza restaurant industry was also strongly linked to the disposable income of patrons and to the economy as a whole. When the economy was down and people faced financial uncertainty, consumers were more likely to use takeout and delivery options for pizza. As the economy turned around and people began to make more money, consumers had an increasing tendency to dine out for pizza. However, regardless of the economy, those strapped for cash took advantage of the cheaper takeout and delivery services with coupons and discounts, while those with high incomes typically satisfied their pizza cravings by dining out at a gourmet pizza restaurant.

## Health Concerns Affecting Pizza Restaurants

In recent years, a trend within the entire restaurant industry was that consumers were seeking out healthier menu choices. In a 2010 survey conducted by the National Restaurant Association (NRA), 7 out of 10 consumers stated that compared to two years earlier, they were now trying to eat healthier when eating out. In the same survey, two-thirds of restaurant operators responded that their guests paid more attention to the nutritional content in their food and ordered healthier items compared to a few years earlier.

The pizza industry took notice of this growing trend toward healthier eating and responded in various ways. All of the major pizza chains posted their nutritional content on their websites. Some made it easier for the consumer and included a calorie counter so that consumers could see how their customizable pizzas and orders stacked up in nutritional content. Some pizzerias that offered sit-down dining, such as Pizza Hut and Cici's Pizza, started to offer salad bars for consumers. In addition, some pizzerias began to add gluten-free and low-carbohydrate items to their menus and cut down on trans fat in their menu items.

Pizza is not an awful food choice as long as one doesn't overindulge. The problem lies in the choice of toppings and crust; some pizzas can have as many as 750 calories per slice. However, pizza can actually be a good source of vegetables, calcium, and protein. The key for consumers is ordering the right kinds of pizza, those that avoid unhealthy toppings and crusts. As a result, many of the higher-end pizzerias began to offer organic, locally grown, and whole wheat products in an effort to attract more health-conscious consumers.

## Expanded Menu Options

Traditionally, pizzeria chains served the obvious: pizza. Over the years they began to add some items that would go hand in hand with pizzas, such as breadsticks. But a trend that emerged in recent years was expanding the menu even further to include all sorts of items. All of the main players in the pizza industry added chicken to the menu. Wings became a staple on any menu, with multiple flavors available. In addition, each chain had its own unique offerings of chicken, from chicken tenders to chicken bites. Some chains also began to add pasta and sandwiches to their menus, as well as a multitude of desserts. Most establishments added bottled soft drinks or water. Long gone were the days when ordering from a pizzeria meant you had to actually order a pizza.

These increases in menu items served not only to differentiate pizza chains from one another but also to expand their customer base. Pizzerias were considered a part of the quick-serve industry and competed with fast-food giants like McDonald's and Burger King. By expanding their menus, pizzerias were able to attract new customers who wanted to choose from a broader selection of menu items than just pizza.

Along with offering new items, pizzerias tried to differentiate from one another by expanding their actual pizza options. Every chain allowed customers to customize their pizzas with different crusts, sauces, and toppings. In addition, many pizzerias featured specialty pizzas ranging from Hawaiian Barbeque Chicken to Bacon Cheeseburger. Some of these pizzas remained staples on the menu, while others were offered for limited periods and then dropped to make room for new ones.

Originally, to place an order, a customer went to a pizzeria in person or telephoned the establishment. Over the years, to provide more options for ordering, the pizza industry took advantage of the ever-increasing advances in technology. Most of the major pizza chains instituted order placement via their websites, with a few pizzerias allowing customers to track their order online. Pizza chains also designed apps for smartphones to provide yet another way for customers to order.

Social media was also a growing trend in society, and the pizza industry began to utilize this medium as well. According to Hudson Riehle, the senior vice president of the Research and Knowledge Group for the National Restaurant Association, "Social media has become very important to the [entire restaurant] industry and social media users are much more active and likely to dine-out, to connect with restaurants online and post reviews." Utilizing social media sites such as Facebook and Twitter also allowed pizza franchises to broaden their marketing campaigns and reach more potential customers. These sites provided customers with an opportunity to interact with the franchises in a multitude of ways, including through promotions and games. Also, besides using traditional mailing lists, some pizzerias began to dabble in using text messaging and e-mails to inform consumers about the latest specials and promotions.

## Delivery Driver Safety

Pizza delivery drivers were put in harm's way every time they delivered a pizza. These drivers were appearing at total strangers' homes, often after dark. According to the U.S. Bureau of Labor Statistics, pizza delivery drivers fell into the category of "drivers-sales workers," which was ranked as the fifth most dangerous job category. The top four were military personnel, police officers, stunt performers, and firefighters. There were many instances in which a pizza delivery driver was robbed or killed while making a delivery. Pizza chains had to take steps to protect their drivers by creating some "do not deliver" zones. These were areas where it was deemed too dangerous to send pizza delivery drivers due to high crime rates or previous instances of a delivery driver being assaulted or killed.

A controversial issue was whether pizza delivery drivers should be allowed the right to bring a concealed weapon with them when making a delivery. Some pizza chains allowed this, while others were completely against it. In one instance, a Pizza Hut driver shot and killed a man who was trying to rob him at gunpoint. The driver was acquitted of any wrongdoing, as the courts found that he acted in self-defense, but it was against Pizza Hut's policy to carry a firearm and he was fired. Afterward, the driver delivered pizzas for a competitor that allowed its drivers to carry a weapon.

## Ingredient Costs

During the early 2000s, pizza restaurants faced increasing operating expenses, particularly in the cost of ingredients. Between 2007 and 2012, the world price of wheat increased an average of 3.4 percent per year. Also, the price of milk, the main ingredient used in making cheese, increased 27.3 percent in 2010 and 9.2 percent in 2011. These commodities influenced the price of making pizza; therefore, as their costs increased, profit margins for the industry declined. Operators tried to offset the costs by increasing product prices, but price sensitivity by consumers did not allow all costs to be recovered through price increases. In 2012, it was estimated that the average profit margin for U.S. pizza establishments was 6.4 percent of revenue.

## PAPA JOHN'S STRATEGY

Papa John's International's strategic intent was to build the strongest brand loyalty in the pizza industry. The company expected to achieve that objective through a strategy with five major components: high-quality menu offerings, efficient operating systems, employee training and development, effective marketing programs, and a strong franchise system. Papa John's believed that high-quality pizzas and side items such as breadsticks, chicken poppers and wings, and dessert items were essential to its success. The company used only fresh dough, 100 percent real mozzarella cheese, vine-ripened tomatoes rather than tomato paste, and 100 percent beef and pork in its pizza products. Franchisees were required to purchase all ingredients from Papa John's Quality Control Centers to ensure consistency across locations. The Quality Control Centers also specified operating practices and restaurant layouts for franchisees to facilitate efficient restaurant operations in all locations. Papa John's Quality Control Centers were operated in the United States; Mexico City, Mexico; the United Kingdom; and Beijing, China.

The company recognized that employee performance affected the profitability of company-owned and franchised units and provided regular training and development programs to its team members. In addition, the company created opportunities for advancement for restaurant personnel and offered performance-based financial incentives for employees at all levels.

Papa John's marketing approach varied by geography, with its marketing program in the United States consisting of national television, print, and social media marketing and advertising as well as locally targeted promotions. In international markets, the company focused its marketing effort within a small radius of areas where Papa John's restaurants were located. The company used television, radio, and print advertising internationally only when the local market was of sufficient size to justify such expenditures.

The company's franchising system was a major component of its strategy. Papa John's actively recruited operators with experience in the restaurant industry or retailing to open one or more new establishments. After meeting the financing qualifications, franchisees were charged $25,000 for each unit, plus a royalty fee of 5 percent of net sales each month. In addition, franchisees were required to pay a marketing fee of 7 percent of monthly sales to support corporate marketing. In 2014, the typical initial investment required to franchise a Papa John's restaurant was $280,000. Also in 2014, the company initiated a development incentive plan that waived the $25,000 franchise fee, reduced the royalty fee, provided two pizza ovens at no charge, and allowed a credit that was applied to the franchisee's first food order. The incentive package lowered the initial startup cost for a Papa John's unit by $60,000. The company was recognized by *Quick Service Restaurant* as one of the best franchise opportunities in the restaurant industry in 2013.

Papa John's opened 265 new locations in 2013—82 in North America and 183 in international markets. The company closed 121 units in 2013. Papa John's management believed that an opportunity for 4,000 units in North America existed and planned to add 220 to 250 new units per year. Seventy percent of the new units would be located in international markets. Exhibit 2 presents financial information for Papa John's International's domestic company-owned and franchised restaurants, its international restaurants, and its commissaries in North America.

### Community Service

Papa John's was very active within the community across a wide range of causes. It chose to sponsor organizations that aligned with the company's core values. Junior Achievement (JA) Worldwide and Papa John's formed a nationwide partnership. Junior Achievement was an organization that focused on providing kids with the tools and skills necessary to succeed once they started on their career paths. In addition to providing financial donations, certain Papa John's locations offered "job shadow" events at which students could witness what it would be like

**EXHIBIT 2**  Revenue and Income before Tax Contribution for Papa John's Operating Divisions, 2011–2013

|  | 2013 | 2012 | 2011 |
|---|---|---|---|
| **Revenues from external customers** | | | |
| Domestic company-owned restaurants | $  635,317 | $  592,203 | $  525,841 |
| Domestic commissaries | 578,870 | 545,924 | 508,155 |
| North America franchising | 82,873 | 80,373 | 74,416 |
| International | 88,640 | 72,930 | 58,558 |
| All others | 53,322 | 51,223 | 50,912 |
| Total revenues from external customers | $1,439,022 | $1,342,653 | $ 1,217,882 |
| **Intersegment revenues** | | | |
| Domestic commissaries | $  191,756 | $  171,212 | $  151,423 |
| North America franchising | 2,222 | 2,267 | 2,163 |
| International | 280 | 229 | 215 |
| Variable interest entities | — | — | 25,117 |
| All others | 14,197 | 11,606 | 10,468 |
| Total intersegment revenues | $  208,455 | $  185,314 | $  189,386 |
| **Income (loss) before income taxes** | | | |
| Domestic company-owned restaurants | $  34,590 | $  38,114 | $  28,980 |
| Domestic commissaries | 37,804 | 34,317 | 30,532 |
| North America franchising | 70,201 | 69,332 | 66,222 |
| International | 2,803 | 3,063 | (165) |
| All others | 3,490 | 2,889 | (441) |
| Unallocated corporate expenses | (41,025) | (48,958) | (39,727) |
| Elimination of intersegment profits | (1,754) | (362) | (610) |
| Total income before income taxes | $  106,109 | $  98,395 | $  84,791 |

*Source:* Papa John's International, Inc., 10-K report, 2013.

to own and run a Papa John's franchise. Employees were encouraged to volunteer to teach JA classes within their communities.

Papa John's was also an avid supporter of The Boy Scouts of America. This organization worked to foster character development, worldwide citizenship, and moral, mental, and physical fitness among young people. Papa John's chose this organization to inspire kids and help provide them with a more well-rounded education. In 2010, Papa John's donated a significant portion of profits to the Make-A-Wish Foundation, an organization that helped make dreams come true for ailing children across the nation.

Papa John's, along with John Schnatter personally, has donated over $20 million to the University of Louisville, primarily to the athletic facilities. This led to the University of Louisville constructing and

naming its football stadium the Papa John's Cardinal Stadium in 1996. In addition, every year Papa John's sponsored the Papa John's 10 Miler. The proceeds from this running event benefited the WHAS Crusade for Children, an organization that aided in improving the lives of children with special needs in the states of Indiana and Kentucky. Papa John's also encouraged its employees to suggest events or programs the company could sponsor within their local communities.

# PAPA JOHN'S RIVAL PIZZA CHAINS

## Pizza Hut

Yum! Brands, based in Louisville, Kentucky, was the parent company of the Pizza Hut, KFC, and Taco

Bell quick-service restaurant chains. Yum! Brands recorded 2013 system revenues and net earnings of approximately $11.2 billion and $1.1 billion, respectively. In 2014, its Pizza Hut division operated and franchised restaurants in 88 countries, with 7,846 units in the United States, 1,264 units in China, and 5,490 units in other international markets.

Pizza Hut was known for its dine-in restaurant locations but had begun to open more units dedicated to delivery and carryout only. Between 2011 and 2013, 600 of its new locations did not offer dine-in seating. The company had also expanded the number of its Express (carryout-only) units in shopping malls, large retail chains, travel centers, and military bases. However, the majority of its new locations, especially those in international markets, were dine-in pizza restaurants. Pizza Hut had also developed its WingStreet subbrand in the United States that delivered chicken and complete chicken dinners.

Among the "Big Four" pizza chains, Pizza Hut was unique in that, in addition to its takeout and delivery options, it had many locations that offered a dine-in option for consumers. The dine-in menu included a lunch buffet that offered healthy options and featured a salad bar. Pizza Hut's signature dish was its Pan Pizza. In addition, it had a variety of other types of crusts including Thin n' Crispy, Stuffed Crust, Hand Tossed, and Sicilian. Pizza Hut also offered one of the widest menu selections and constantly innovated by serving pastas, wings, calzones, stuffed pizza rollers, breadsticks, desserts, and drinks. Catering was also available. Nutritional information for every product was provided on the company's website.

Like most major pizza chains, Pizza Hut franchised its restaurants, with only 15 percent being company-owned. It offered online ordering for consumers, and it was the first to take advantage of smartphones by creating the first pizza ordering app in 2009. The company was heavily involved with social media, providing links from its website to its Facebook and Twitter pages, along with other interactive social media outlets like Tumblr, Flickr, and YouTube.

Pizza Hut gave back to the community with various programs. One of these was the Share a Slice of Hope campaign, in which the company raised almost $2 million and supplied 8 million meals during the World Hunger Relief campaign in 2011. Pizza Hut was also an avid sponsor of the Book It! National Incentive Reading program that offered kids free personal pan pizzas and pizza parties if they met their reading goals.

Yum! Brands' net earnings declined by 9 percent during 2013, but the company expected earnings to increase by 20 percent in 2014. The decline in sales in 2013 was primarily related to declining KFC sales and profits in China that resulted from an avian flu outbreak and declining Pizza Hut and KFC revenues in the United States.

## Domino's

Domino's Pizza operated and franchised more than 10,800 carryout and delivery pizza units in all 50 states and in more than 70 countries in 2014. The company added 631 units in 2013, 573 of which were outside the United States. The company's revenues had increased from $1,652 million in 2011 to $1,802 million in 2013. Same-store sales for its U.S. units increased by 5.4 percent from 2012 to 2013, while its same-store sales in international markets increased by 6.2 percent over the same two-year period. The company's global retail sales exceeded $8 billion in 2013. Net income for the company had increased from $105.4 million in 2011 to $143 million in 2013.

Domino's sales were primarily generated through its pizza delivery business. As such, the company focused on securing its number-two ranking among pizza chains by acquiring convenient store locations and operating an efficient supply chain. The focus on operations and convenient locations also benefited carryout sales. Domino's strategy includes expanding its global presence to take advantage of emerging markets outside the United States. The company operated and franchised 5,900 international units in 2013.

Until the late 1980s, Domino's was known for keeping its menu very simple in an attempt to ensure the utmost consistency. At the time, the company offered only one type of pizza in two sizes with 11 toppings to choose from and Coke as the only drink option. Since then, the menu expanded greatly to many types of pizzas, including four types of crust, artisan pizzas, specialty pizzas, four types of sauce, and 26 toppings. In addition to its wide pizza selection, Domino's also offered pasta, bread bowls, sandwiches, wings, breadsticks, stuffed bread, bread bites, chips, desserts, and six drink selections. Nutritional information was provided online for every product, and Domino's website pointed out "healthy" selections on its menu by recommending certain items for health-conscious consumers.

The year 2010 marked the 50th anniversary of Domino's. Shortly after, the company changed its entire pizza recipe "from the crust up" by making changes to the sauce, dough, and cheese used in each pizza. It marketed the changes by admitting that its pizza quality and taste had not been up to par. The company listened to its customers and came up with the current recipe. The changes to the recipe were received well by the majority of consumers.

Domino's marketing campaign relied heavily on TV commercials in which its CEO, J. Patrick Doyle, informed consumers that the pizza chain had heard their complaints and responded with big changes. The campaign started in 2009 by filming customers complaining about the poor taste and quality of Domino's pizzas and showing chefs working to fix the recipe. Simultaneously, chefs really were working to fix the recipe, and the chain completely revamped its pizza. Commercials then touted the new recipe and focused on how customers spoke out and the company listened. The campaign was immensely successful.

Domino's partnered with St. Jude Children's Research Hospital in 2004, and through 2012 it raised more than $12 million for the hospital. St. Jude was an organization dedicated to exhaustive research and treatment for children affected by cancer and other catastrophic diseases. Domino's also allowed people to go online and submit a request for the company to supply pizzas for a charity function or event. In 2011, this resulted in Domino's donating more than $400,000 in monetary and in-kind gifts to local and national organizations. Domino's also took care of its team members via the Partners Foundation, established in 1986. This program provided financial aid to team members who were affected by extreme tragedies such as fires, natural disasters, medical emergencies, immediate family member deaths, and on-the-job accidents. After 25 years, Domino's had provided team members in need with over $6 million.

Domino's utilized the ever-increasing advances of technology to its advantage. Domino's offered consumers the ability to order online and even track their pizza, seeing where their order was in the process and when it was ready for delivery or pickup. Consumers also had the option of ordering via smartphones or the traditional over-the-phone method. Domino's website included a link to company-created pizza games consumers could play and a section where consumers could voice their opinions or suggestions. Domino's also had a large presence on Facebook and Twitter, where consumers could interact with the company.

## Little Caesars

Little Caesars was the fourth-largest pizza chain, with a 4.7 percent share of the market and operations in more than 20 countries with over 2,500 units. The company was founded in 1959 in Garden City, Michigan, by Michael and Marian Ilitch when they put their life savings of $10,000 into opening the first restaurant. It was immensely successful, and they expanded the business through franchising. Over the years, franchises grew to account for about 80 percent of the company's locations. As of 2014, Little Caesars remained privately held by the original founders.

The majority of Little Caesars restaurants offered only a takeout service. They were well known for offering Hot-N-Ready pizzas, which were large pizzas with standard toppings for only $5 and were constantly being made so that they were ready as soon as the customer ordered. Customers could order a custom pizza as well by calling ahead or ordering in the restaurant. A few other specialty pizzas were also available. Apart from pizza, the menu was relatively simple for the industry, with product offerings of breadsticks, cheese bread, and wings. The website provided nutritional information for every product. The company tended to focus on cutting down costs rather than expanding its product line.

Little Caesars was synonymous with the catchphrase "Pizza! Pizza!" This phrase originally came about because the company offered two pizzas for the price of one. The company also had its own mascot, "Little Caesar." Most of its advertising focused on touting its Hot-N-Ready pizzas and emphasizing the ease for the consumer of being able to walk in and have a pizza already waiting. The chain utilized modern technology by providing consumers with a smartphone app and having its own Facebook and Twitter pages.

## Other Competition

Besides the Big Four chains, there were many other pizza chains that together had a 19.6 percent share of the market. These chains all varied on their pizza offerings and were located all over the country. Independent pizzerias made up 48 percent of the market share and operated 57 percent of pizza stores. A good portion of these independent pizzerias were sit-down restaurants that offered higher-end pizzas and a wide variety of menu options. Additionally, there were many small pizza stores that relied solely on delivery and takeout. It was expected that there would be an increase in independent sit-down pizzerias that offered healthier products and more diverse products that could satisfy complex tastes.

## What Course of Action Should Papa John's Take?

John Schnatter grew his company from a broom closet to the third-largest pizza chain in the United States. But how was he going to overtake the other two big players—Pizza Hut and Domino's? Did Schnatter have to expand his company's product line as the other two chains had? How would he adapt to the new health-conscious trend? Keeping these and other issues in mind, "Papa" needed to make a decision fast because, on average, Americans were eating 350 slices of pizza every second.

# Under Armour's Strategy in 2014: Potent Enough to Win Market Share from Nike and Adidas?

Mc Graw Hill **connect**

## Arthur A. Thompson
The University of Alabama

Founded in 1996 by former University of Maryland football player Kevin Plank, Under Armour (UA) was the originator of performance sports apparel—gear engineered to keep athletes cool, dry, and light throughout the course of a game, practice, or workout. It started with a simple plan to make a T-shirt that provided compression and wicked perspiration off the wearer's skin, thereby regulating body temperature and avoiding the discomfort of sweat-absorbed apparel. Under Armour's innovative synthetic performance-fabric T-shirts were an instant hit.

Seventeen years later, with 2013 revenues of $2.3 billion, Under Armour had a growing brand presence in the roughly $63 billion multisegment retail market for sports apparel, active wear, and athletic footwear in the United States. Its interlocking "U" and "A" logo had become almost as familiar and well-known as industry-leader Nike's swoosh. In 2013, Under Armour had a 14.7 percent share of the U.S. market for sports apparel (up from 12.7 percent in 2012 and 11.1 percent in 2011), which compared quite favorably with Nike's 27 percent market share and adidas's 7.4 percent market share.[1] In the synthetic performance-apparel segment—a market niche with estimated sales of $3 to $4 billion in 2013—Under Armour had an approximate 60 percent market share.

Across all segments (sports apparel, active wear, and athletic footwear), however, Under Armour still had a long way to go to overtake the two long-time industry leaders—Nike and The adidas Group. In fiscal 2013, Nike had U.S. sales of $11.3 billion and global sales of $25.3 billion, and it dominated both the U.S. and global markets for athletic footwear. In the United States, Nike's share of athletic footwear sales approached 60 percent (counting its Nike-branded footwear and sales of its Jordan and Converse brands) versus Under Armour's 2.25 percent share. Nike's 2013 global sales of athletic footwear totaled almost $16 billion (over 1 million pairs per day), dwarfing Under Armour's 2013 footwear sales of $299 million. The adidas Group—the industry's second-ranking company—had 2013 global sales of €14.5 billion (including €6.9 billion in athletic footwear and €5.8 billion in sports apparel) and 2013 North American sales of €3.4 billion. But Under Armour was gaining ground. From 2008 through 2013, Under Armour's sales revenues grew at a compound annual rate of 26.3 percent. Nike's revenues during its most recent five fiscal years (July 1, 2008, to June 30, 2013) grew at only a 6.3 percent compound rate; the revenues of The adidas Group—the second-largest company in the global sporting goods industry—grew at a compound rate of 6.3 percent during 2008–2013.

Founder and CEO Kevin Plank believed Under Armour's potential for long-term growth was exceptional for three reasons: (1) The company had built an incredibly powerful and authentic brand in a relatively short time, (2) there were significant opportunities to expand the company's narrow product lineup and brand-name appeal into product categories where it currently had little or no market presence, and (3) the company was only in the early stages of establishing its brand and penetrating markets outside North America.

# COMPANY BACKGROUND

Kevin Plank honed his competitive instinct growing up with four older brothers and playing football. As a young teenager, he squirmed under the authority of his mother, who was the town mayor of Kensington, Maryland. When he was a high school sophomore, he was tossed out of Georgetown Prep for poor academic performance and ended up at Fork Union Military Academy, where he learned to accept discipline and resumed playing high school football. After graduation, Plank became a walk-on special-teams football player for the University of Maryland in the early 1990s, ending his college career as the special teams' captain in 1995. Throughout his football career, he regularly experienced the discomfort of practicing on hot days and the unpleasantness of peeling off sweat-soaked cotton T-shirts after practice. At the University of Maryland, Plank sometimes changed the cotton T-shirt under his jersey as it became wet and heavy during the course of a game.

During his later college years and in classic entrepreneurial fashion, Plank hit upon the idea of using newly available moisture-wicking, polyester-blend fabrics to make next-generation, tighter-fitting shirts and undergarments that would make it cooler and more comfortable to engage in strenuous activities during high-temperature conditions.[2] While Plank had a job offer from Prudential Life Insurance at the end of his college days in 1995, he couldn't see himself being happy working in a corporate environment—he told the author of a 2011 *Fortune* article on Under Armour, "I would have killed myself."[3] Despite a lack of business training, Plank opted to try to make a living selling high-tech microfiber shirts. Plank's vision was to sell innovative, technically advanced apparel products engineered with a special fabric construction that provided supreme moisture management. A year of fabric and product testing produced a synthetic compression T-shirt that was suitable for wear beneath an athlete's uniform or equipment, provided a snug fit (like a second skin), and remained drier and lighter than a traditional cotton shirt. Plank formed KP Sports as a subchapter S corporation in Maryland in 1996 and commenced selling the shirt to athletes and sports teams.

## The Company's Early Years

Plank's former teammates at high school, military school, and the University of Maryland included about 40 National Football League (NFL) players whom he knew well enough to call and offer the shirt he had come up with. He worked the phone and, with a trunk full of shirts in the back of his car, visited schools and training camps in person to show his products. Within a short time, Plank's sales successes were good enough that he convinced Kip Fulks, who played lacrosse at Maryland, to become a partner in his enterprise. Fulks's initial role was to leverage his connections to promote use of the company's shirts by lacrosse players. Their sales strategy was predicated on networking and referrals. But Fulks had another critical role—he had good credit and was able to obtain 17 credit cards that were used to make purchases from suppliers and charge expenses.[4] Operations were conducted on a shoestring budget out of the basement of Plank's grandmother's house in Georgetown, a Washington, D.C., suburb. Planks and Fulks generated sufficient cash from their sales efforts that Fulks never missed a minimum payment on any of his credit cards. When cash flows became particularly tight, Plank's older brother Scott made loans to the company to help keep KP Sports afloat (in 2011 Scott owned 4 percent of the company's stock). It didn't take long for Plank and Fulks to learn that it was more productive to direct their sales efforts more toward equipment managers than to individual players. Getting a whole team to adopt use of the T-shirts that KP Sports was marketing meant convincing equipment managers that it was more economical to provide players with a pricey $25 high-performance T-shirt that would hold up better in the long-run than a cheap cotton T-shirt.

In 1998, the company's sales revenues and growth prospects were sufficient to secure a $250,000 small-business loan from a tiny bank in Washington, D.C.; the loan enabled the company to move its basement operation to a facility on Sharp Street in nearby Baltimore.[5] As sales continued to gain momentum, the D.C. bank later granted KP Sports additional small loans from time to time to help fund its needs for more working capital. Then Ryan Wood, one of Plank's acquaintances from high school, joined the company in 1999 and became a partner. The company consisted of three jocks trying to gain a foothold in a growing, highly competitive industry against more than 25 brands, including those of Nike, adidas, Columbia, and Patagonia. Plank functioned as president and CEO; Kip Fulks was vice president of sourcing and quality assurance; and Ryan Wood was vice president of sales.

Nonetheless, KP Sports' sales grew briskly as it expanded its product line to include high-tech undergarments tailored for athletes in different sports and for cold temperatures as well as hot temperatures, plus jerseys, team uniforms, socks, and other accessories. Increasingly, the company was able to secure deals not just to provide gear for a particular team but for most or all of a school's sports teams. However, the company's partners came to recognize the merits of tapping the retail market for high-performance apparel and began making sales calls on sports apparel retailers. In 2000, Galyan's, a large retail chain later acquired by Dick's Sporting Goods, signed on to carry KP Sports' expanding line of performance apparel for men, women, and youth. Sales to other sports apparel retailers began to explode, quickly making the retail segment of the sports apparel market the biggest component of the company's revenue stream. Revenues totaled $5.3 million in 2000, with operating income of $0.7 million. The company's products were available in 500 retail stores. Beginning in 2000, Scott Plank, Kevin's older brother, joined the company as vice president of finance, with operational and strategic responsibilities as well.

## Rapid Growth Ensues

Over the next 13 years, the company's product line evolved to include a widening variety of shirts, shorts, underwear, outerwear, gloves, and other offerings. The strategic intent was to grow the business by replacing products made with cotton and other traditional fabrics with innovatively designed performance products that incorporated a variety of technologically advanced fabrics and specialized manufacturing techniques, all in an attempt to make the wearer feel "drier, lighter, and more comfortable." In 1999 the company began selling its products in Japan through a licensee. On January 1, 2002, prompted by growing operational complexity, increased financial requirements, and plans for further geographic expansion, KP Sports revoked its "S" corporation status and became a "C" corporation. The company opened a Canadian sales

office in 2003 and began efforts to grow its market presence in Canada. In 2004, KP Sports became the outfitter of the University of Maryland football team and was a supplier to about 400 women's sports teams at NCAA Division 1-A colleges and universities. The company used independent sales agents to begin selling its products in the United Kingdom in 2005. SportsScanINFO estimated that as of 2004, KP Sports had a 73 percent share of the U.S. market for compression tops and bottoms, more than seven times that of its nearest competitor.[6]

Broadening demand for the company's product offerings among professional, collegiate and Olympic teams and athletes, active outdoor enthusiasts, elite tactical professionals, and consumers with active lifestyles propelled revenue growth from $5.3 million in 2000 to $263.4 million for the 12 months ending September 30, 2005, equal to a compound annual growth rate of 127 percent. Operating income increased from $0.7 million in 2000 to $32.7 million during the same period, a compound annual growth rate of 124 percent. About 90 percent of the company revenues came from sales to 6,000 retail stores in the United States and 2,000 stores in Canada, Japan, and the United Kingdom. In addition, sales were being made to high-profile athletes and teams, most notably in the National Football League, Major League Baseball, the National Hockey League, and major collegiate and Olympic sports. KP Sports had 574 employees at the end of September 2005.

Throughout 2005, KP Sports increased its offerings to include additional men's and women's performance products and, in particular, began entry into such off-field outdoor sports segments as hunting, fishing, running, mountain sports, skiing, and golf. Management expected that its new product offerings in 2006 would include football cleats.

## KP Sports Is Renamed Under Armour

In late 2005, the company changed its name to Under Armour and became a public company with an initial public offering of 9.5 million shares of Class A common stock that generated net proceeds of approximately $114.9 million. Simultaneously, existing stockholders sold 2.6 million shares of Class A stock from their personal holdings. The shares were all sold at just above the offer price of $13 per share; on the first day of trading after the IPO, the shares closed at $25.30, after opening at $31 per share. Following these initial sales of Under Armour stock to the general public, Under Armour's outstanding shares of common stock consisted of two classes: Class A common stock and Class B common stock; both classes were identical in all respects except for voting and conversion rights. Holders of Class A common stock were entitled to one vote per share, and holders of Class B common stock were entitled to 10 votes per share, on all matters to be voted on by common stockholders. Shares of Class A and Class B common stock voted together as a single class on all matters submitted to a vote of stockholders. All of the Class B common stock was beneficially owned by Kevin Plank, which represented 83 percent of the combined voting power of all of the outstanding common stock. As a result, Plank was able to control the outcome of substantially all matters submitted to a stockholder vote, including the election of directors, amendments to Under Armour's charter, and mergers or other business combinations.

At the time of Under Armour's IPO, Kevin Plank, Kip Fulks, and Ryan Wood were all 33 years old; Scott Plank was 39 years old. After the IPO, Kevin Plank owned 15.2 million shares of Under Armour's Class A shares (and all of the Class B shares); Kip Fulks owned 2.125 million Class A shares, Ryan Wood owned 2.142 million Class A shares, and Scott Plank owned 3.95 million Class A shares. All four had opted to sell a small fraction of their common shares at the time of the IPO—these accounted for a combined 1.83 million of the 2.6 million shares sold from the holdings of various directors, officers, and other entities. Ryan Wood decided to leave his position as senior vice president of sales at Under Armour in 2007 to run a cattle farm. Kip Fulks assumed the position of chief operating officer at Under Armour in September 2011, after moving up the executive ranks in several capacities, chiefly those related to sourcing, quality assurance, product development, and product innovation; beginning October 2013, Kip Fulks's title was expanded to chief operating officer and president of product. In September 2012, Scott Plank, who was serving as the company's executive vice president of business development after holding several other positions in the company's executive ranks, retired from the company to start a real estate development company and pursue his passion for building sustainable urban environments.

Exhibit 1 summarizes Under Armour's financial performance during 2008–2013. Exhibit 2 shows the growth of Under Armour's quarterly revenues in 2010 through 2013. The company's strong financial performance had propelled its stock price from $46 in early January 2013 to a high of $124 in March 2014; the stock split 2 for 1 in April 2014—over the past five years, the stock price had risen more than 1,300 percent. Top executives at Under Armour expected sales revenues to reach $4 billion by 2016.[7]

# UNDER ARMOUR'S STRATEGY

Under Armour's mission was "to make all athletes better through passion, design, and the relentless pursuit of innovation." The company's principal business activities in 2014 were the development, marketing, and distribution of branded performance apparel, footwear, and accessories for men, women, and youth. The brand's moisture-wicking fabrications were engineered in many designs and styles for wear in nearly every climate to provide a performance alternative to traditional products. Its products were worn by athletes at all levels, from youth to professional, and by consumers with active lifestyles. In 2012–2013, about 75.5 percent of Under Armour's sales were apparel items, with athletic footwear products and accessories accounting for the remainder—see Exhibit 3, panel A. Just over 94 percent of Under Armour's sales were in North America; although sales to distributors and retailers outside North America were growing, UA's international presence was still in the infant stage (Exhibit 3, panel B).

## Growth Strategy

Under Armour's announced sales objective was to achieve sales revenues of $4 billion by 2016, some 71 percent above 2013 sales. The company's growth strategy in 2014 consisted of several strategic initiatives:

- Continuing to broaden the company's product offerings to men, women, and youth for wear in a widening variety of sports and recreational activities.
- Targeting additional consumer segments for the company's ever-expanding lineup of performance products.
- Increasing its sales and market share in the athletic footwear segment.
- Securing additional distribution of Under Armour products in the retail marketplace in North

**EXHIBIT 1**    Select Financial Data for Under Armour, Inc., 2008–2013
(in thousands, except per share amounts)

| Select income statement data | 2013 | 2012 | 2011 | 2010 | 2008 |
|---|---|---|---|---|---|
| Net revenues | $2,332,051 | $1,834,921 | $1,472,684 | $1,063,927 | $725,244 |
| Cost of goods sold | 1,195,381 | 955,624 | 759,848 | 533,420 | 372,203 |
| Gross profit | 1,136,670 | 879,297 | 712,836 | 530,507 | 353,041 |
| Selling, general and administrative expenses | 871,572 | 670,602 | 550,069 | 418,152 | 276,116 |
| Income from operations | 265,098 | 208,695 | 162,767 | 112,355 | 76,925 |
| Interest expense, net | (2,933) | (5,183) | (3,841) | (2,258) | (850) |
| Other expense, net | (1,172) | (73) | (2,064) | (1,178) | (6,175) |
| Income before income taxes | 260,993 | 203,439 | 156,862 | 108,919 | 69,900 |
| Provision for income taxes | 98,663 | 74,661 | 59,943 | 40,442 | 31,671 |
| Net income | $ 162,330 | $ 128,778 | $ 96,919 | $ 68,477 | $ 38,229 |
| | | | | | |
| Net income per common share | | | | | |
| Basic | $1.54 | $1.23 | $0.94 | $0.67 | $0.39 |
| Diluted | 1.50 | 1.21 | 0.92 | 0.67 | 0.38 |
| | | | | | |
| Weighted-average common shares outstanding | | | | | |
| Basic | 105,348 | 104,343 | 103,140 | 101,595 | 98,171 |
| Diluted | 107,979 | 106,380 | 105,052 | 102,563 | 100,685 |
| **Select balance sheet data** | | | | | |
| Cash and cash equivalents | $ 347,489 | $ 341,841 | $175,384 | $203,870 | $102,042 |
| Working capital* | 702,181 | 651,370 | 506,056 | 406,703 | 263,313 |
| Inventories at year-end | 469,006 | 319,286 | 324,409 | 215,355 | 182,232 |
| Total assets | 1,577,741 | 1,157,083 | 919,210 | 675,378 | 487,555 |
| Total debt and capital lease obligations, including current maturities | 52,923 | 61,889 | 77,724 | 15,942 | 45,591 |
| Total stockholders' equity | 1,053,354 | 816,922 | 636,432 | 496,966 | 331,097 |
| **Select cash flow data** | | | | | |
| Net cash provided by operating activities | $ 120,070 | $ 199,761 | $ 15,218 | $ 50,114 | $ 69,516 |

*Working capital is defined as current assets minus current liabilities.
*Source:* Company 10-K reports for 2013, 2012, 2010, and 2008.

America not only via store retailers and catalog retailers but also through Under Armour factory outlet and specialty stores and sales at the company's website.
- Expanding the sale of Under Armour products in foreign countries and becoming a global competitor in the world market for sports apparel, athletic footwear, and performance products.

- Growing global awareness of the Under Armour brand name and strengthening the appeal of Under Armour products worldwide.

## Product Line Strategy

For a number of years, expanding the company's product offerings and marketing them at

**EXHIBIT 2    Growth in Under Armour's Quarterly Revenues, 2010–2013 (dollar amounts in thousands)**

|  | Quarter 1 (Jan.–Mar.) | | Quarter 2 (Apr.–June) | | Quarter 3 (July–Sept.) | | Quarter 4 (Oct.–Dec.) | |
|---|---|---|---|---|---|---|---|---|
|  | Revenues | Change from Prior Year's Quarter 1 | Revenues | Change from Prior Year's Quarter 2 | Revenues | Change from Prior Year's Quarter 3 | Revenues | Change from Prior Year's Quarter 4 |
| **2010** | $229,407 | 14.7% | $204,786 | 24.4% | $328,568 | 21.9% | $301,166 | 35.5% |
| **2011** | 312,699 | 36.3 | 291,336 | 42.3 | 465,523 | 41.7 | 403,126 | 33.9 |
| **2012** | 384,389 | 23.0 | 369,473 | 26.8 | 575,196 | 23.6 | 505,863 | 25.5 |
| **2013** | 471,608 | 22.7 | 454,541 | 23.0 | 723,146 | 25.7 | 682,756 | 35.0 |

*Source:* Company 10-K reports, 2013, 2012, and 2010.

multiple price points had been a key element of Under Armour's strategy. The goal for each new item added to the lineup of offerings was to provide consumers with a product that was a *superior* alternative to the traditional products of rivals—striving to always introduce a superior product would, management believed, help foster and nourish a culture of innovation among all company personnel.

**Apparel** The company designed and merchandised three lines of apparel gear intended to regulate body temperature and enhance comfort, mobility, and performance regardless of weather conditions: HeatGear for hot weather conditions; ColdGear for cold weather conditions; and AllSeasonGear for temperature conditions between the extremes.

**EXHIBIT 3    Composition of Under Armour's Revenues, 2010–2013 (dollar amounts in thousands)**

**A. Net Revenues by Product Category**

|  | 2013 | | 2012 | | 2011 | | 2010 | |
|---|---|---|---|---|---|---|---|---|
|  | Dollars | Percent | Dollars | Percent | Dollars | Percent | Dollars | Percent |
| Apparel | $1,762,150 | 75.6% | $1,385,350 | 75.5% | $1,122,031 | 76.2% | $ 853,493 | 80.2% |
| Footwear | 298,825 | 12.8 | 238,955 | 13.0 | 181,684 | 12.3 | 127,175 | 12.0 |
| Accessories | 216,098 | 9.3 | 165,835 | 9.0 | 132,400 | 9.0 | 43,882 | 4.1 |
| Total net sales | $2,277,073 | 97.6% | $1,790,140 | 97.6% | $1,436,115 | 97.5% | $1,024,550 | 96.3% |
| License revenues | 54,978 | 2.4 | 44,781 | 2.4 | 36,569 | 2.5 | 39,377 | 3.7 |
| Total net revenues | $2,332,051 | 100.0% | $1,385,350 | 100.0% | $1,122,031 | 100.0% | $ 853,493 | 100.0% |

**B. Net Revenues by Geographic Region**

|  | 2013 | | 2012 | | 2011 | | 2010 | |
|---|---|---|---|---|---|---|---|---|
|  | Dollars | Percent | Dollars | Percent | Dollars | Percent | Dollars | Percent |
| North America | $2,193,739 | 94.1% | $1,726,733 | 94.1% | $1,383,346 | 93.9% | $ 997,816 | 93.8% |
| Other foreign countries | 138,312 | 5.9 | 108,188 | 5.9 | 89,338 | 6.1 | 66,111 | 6.2 |
| Total net revenues | $2,332,051 | 100.0% | $1,834,921 | 100.0% | $1,472,684 | 100.0% | $1,063,927 | 100.0% |

*Source:* Company 10-K reports, 2013, 2012, and 2010.

*HeatGear*   HeatGear was designed to be worn in warm to hot temperatures under equipment or as a single layer. The company's first compression T-shirt was the original HeatGear product and was still one of the company's signature styles in 2013. In sharp contrast to a sweat-soaked cotton T-shirt that could weigh 2 to 3 pounds, HeatGear was engineered with a microfiber blend featuring what Under Armour termed a "Moisture Transport System" that ensured the body would stay cool, dry, and light. HeatGear was offered in a variety of tops and bottoms in a broad array of colors and styles for wear in the gym or outside in warm weather.

*ColdGear*   Under Armour high-performance fabrics were appealing to people participating in cold-weather sports and vigorous recreational activities like snow skiing who needed both warmth and moisture-wicking protection from a sometimes overheated body. ColdGear was designed to wick moisture from the body while circulating body heat from hotspots to maintain core body temperature. All ColdGear apparel provided dryness and warmth in a single light layer that could be worn beneath a jersey, uniform, protective gear or ski vest, or other cold weather outerwear. ColdGear products generally were sold at higher price levels than other Under Armour gear lines. A new ColdGear Infrared line, with a new fabric technology, was introduced in fall 2013.

*AllSeasonGear*   AllSeasonGear was designed to be worn in changing temperatures and used technical fabrics to keep the wearer cool and dry in warmer temperatures while preventing a chill in cooler temperatures.

Each of the three apparel lines contained three fit types: compression (tight fit), fitted (athletic fit), and loose (relaxed). Most recently, Under Armour had partnered with DC Comics and Marvel Entertainment to introduce Under Armour Alter Ego superhero apparel for boys, featuring the images of Superman, Spiderman, Ironman, and Captain America.

In 2014, Under Armour was actively pursuing efforts to grow its apparel sales in the men's, women's, and youth segments. The specific sales targets for each segment were:[8]

- Men's apparel—sales revenues of $1.5 billion in 2016 (up from approximately $960 million in 2013).

- Women's apparel—sales revenues of $960 million in 2016 (up from $500 million in 2013).

- Youth apparel—sales revenues of $470 million in 2016 (up from approximately $220 million in 2013).

**Footwear**   Under Armour began marketing footwear products for men, women, and youth in 2006 and had expanded its footwear line every year since. Its current offerings included football, baseball, lacrosse, softball and soccer cleats, slides, performance training footwear, running footwear, basketball footwear, and hunting boots. Under Armour's athletic footwear was light, breathable, and built with performance attributes for athletes. Innovative technologies were used to provide stabilization, directional cushioning, and moisture management, and all models and styles were engineered to maximize the athlete's comfort and control.

Under Armour ended 2013 with athletic footwear sales of $298.8 million and a U.S. market share of about 2.4 percent, far below Nike's industry-leading 59 percent share.[9] Under Armour was targeting $600 million in athletic footwear sales in 2016. In early 2014, UA introduced a new premium running shoe, the SpeedForm Apollo, with a retail price of $100. Kevin Plank believed this new shoe model, which was a follow-on to the $120 SpeedForm RC introduced in 2013, had the potential to be one of the company's defining products and help take UA to the next level in the market for athletic footwear, particularly in the running-shoe category, where the company was striving to make major inroads. The company's marketing tagline for the SpeedForm Apollo was "This is what fast feels like."

**Accessories**   Under Armour's accessory line in 2013 included gloves, socks, headwear, bags, kneepads, custom-molded mouth guards, inflatable basketballs and footballs, and eyewear designed to be used and worn before, during, and after competition. All of these items featured performance advantages and functionality similar to other Under Armour products. For instance, the company's baseball batting, football, golf, and running gloves included HeatGear and ColdGear technologies and were designed with advanced fabrications to provide various high-performance attributes that differentiated Under Armour gloves from those of rival brands.

**Licensing**   Under Armour had licensing agreements with a number of firms to produce and market its various accessories except for headgear and bags. Under Armour product, marketing, and sales teams were actively involved in all steps of the design process for licensed products in order to maintain brand standards and consistency.

In December 2013, Under Armour acquired MapMyFitness, which served one of the largest fitness communities in the world at its website, **www .mapmyfitness.com**, and offered a diverse suite of websites and mobile applications under its flagship brands, MapMyRun and MapMyRide. Utilizing GPS and other advanced technologies, MapMyFitness provided users with the ability to map, record, and share their workouts. MapMyFitness had 22 million registered users as of March 2014, 30 percent of whom were located outside the United States. Under Armour executives believed the MapMyFitness acquisition would enable the company to be a leader in the Connected Fitness market space and deliver game-changing solutions to athletes and fitness-minded consumers—outcomes that would complement the company's strategic efforts to grow global sales over the long term. Revenues generated from the sale of licensed accessories, including MapMyFitness digital platform licenses and subscriptions, are included in the licensing revenue amounts shown in Exhibit 2, panel A.

## Marketing, Promotion, and Brand Management Strategies

Under Armour had an in-house marketing and promotion department that designed and produced most of its advertising campaigns to drive consumer demand for its products and build awareness of Under Armour as a leading performance athletic brand. The company's total marketing expenses were $246.5 million in 2013, $205.4 million in 2012, $167.9 million in 2011, $128.2 million in 2010, and $108.9 million in 2009. These totals included the costs of sponsorships (of events and sports teams), athlete endorsements, and ads placed in a variety of television, print, radio, and social media outlets. All are included as part of selling, general, and administrative expenses in Exhibit 1.

**Sports Marketing**   A key element of Under Armour's marketing and promotion strategy was to promote the sales and use of its products to high-performing athletes and teams on the high school, collegiate, and professional levels. This strategy included entering into outfitting agreements with a variety of collegiate and professional sports teams, sponsoring an assortment of collegiate and professional sports events, and selling Under Armour products directly to team equipment managers and to individual athletes.

Management believed that having audiences see Under Armour products (with the interlocking UA logo prominently displayed) being worn by athletes on the playing field helped the company establish on-field authenticity of the Under Armour brand with consumers. Considerable effort went into giving Under Armour products broad exposure at live sporting events, as well as on television, in magazines, and at a wide variety of Internet sites.

In 2013–2014, Under Armour was the official outfitter of *all* the men's and women's athletic teams at Notre Dame, Boston College, Texas Tech University, the University of Maryland, the University of South Carolina, the U.S. Naval Academy, Auburn University, and the University of South Florida and *select* sports teams at the University of Illinois, Northwestern University, the University of Minnesota, the University of Utah, the University of Indiana, the University of Missouri, Georgetown University, the University of Delaware, the University of Hawaii, Southern Illinois University, Temple University, Wichita State University, South Dakota State University, Wagner College, Whittier College, and La Salle University. All told, it was the official outfitter of over 100 Division I men's and women's collegiate athletic teams, growing numbers of high school athletic teams, and several Olympic sports teams; and it supplied sideline apparel and fan gear for many collegiate teams as well. In addition, Under Armour sold products to high-profile professional athletes and teams, most notably in the National Football League, Major League Baseball, the National Hockey League, and the National Basketball Association (NBA). Since 2006, Under Armour had been an official supplier of football cleats to the National Football League. Under Armour became the official supplier of gloves to the NFL beginning in 2011, and in 2012 it began supplying the NFL with training apparel for athletes attending NFL tryout camps. In 2011 Under Armour became the official performance footwear supplier of Major League Baseball. Starting with the 2011–2012 season, UA was granted rights by the NBA to show ads and promotional displays of players who were official endorsers of Under Armour products in their NBA game uniforms wearing UA-branded basketball footwear.

In 2014, Under Armour was the official supplier of competition suits, uniforms, and training resources for a number of U.S. teams in the Winter Olympics in Sochi, Russia. During the 2014 Winter Games, when the U.S. speedskating team performed poorly and failed to win any medals, there was much speculation about whether UA's specially designed, high-tech competition suits for the team had a flawed design in the rear ventilation panels that slowed the U.S. skaters down and contributed to their poor performance. Despite the disparagement, Under Armour steadfastly stood behind the technology and design of its skin suits, as did the executive director of the U.S. speedskating team. Fears that Under Armour's brand had suffered considerable damage from the incident quickly dissipated, however, and prior to the conclusion of the games in Sochi, Under Armour and the directors of the U.S. speedskating team formally extended their partnership through the 2022 Olympic Games.

Internationally, Under Armour was using sponsorships to broaden consumer awareness of its brand in Canada, Europe, and South America. In Canada, it was an official supplier of performance apparel to Hockey Canada, had advertising rights at many locations in the Air Canada Center during the Toronto Maple Leafs' home games, and was the official performance product sponsor of the Toronto Maple Leafs. In Europe, Under Armour was the official supplier of performance apparel to the Hannover 96 and Tottenham Hotspur soccer teams and the Welsh Rugby Union, among others. In 2014, Under Armour became the official kit supplier for the Colo-Colo soccer club in Chile and the Cruz Azul soccer team in Mexico.

In addition to sponsoring teams and events, another part of Under Armour's brand-building strategy was securing the endorsement of individual athletes. One facet of this strategy was to sign endorsement contracts with newly emerging sports stars—examples included Milwaukee Bucks point guard Brandon Jennings, Golden State Warriors point guard Stephen Curry, Charlotte Bobcats point guard Kemba Walker, U.S. professional skier and Olympic gold-medal winner Lindsey Vonn, professional lacrosse player Paul Rabil, Baltimore Orioles catcher Matthew Wieters, 2012 National League (baseball) Most Valuable Player and World Series Champion Buster Posey, UFC welterweight champion Georges St-Pierre, 2012 National League Rookie of the Year Bryce Harper of the Washington Nationals, Derrick Williams (the number-two pick in the 2011 NBA draft), tennis phenomenon Sloane Stephens, WBC super-welterweight boxing champion Canelo Alvarez, and former world number-one amateur golfer Jordan Spieth. But the company's growing roster of athletes also included established stars: NFL football players Tom Brady, Ray Lewis, Brandon Jacobs, Arian Foster, Miles Austin, Julio Jones, Devon Hester, Vernon Davis, Patrick Willis, Santana Moss, and Anquan Boldin; triathlon champion Chris "Macca" McCormack; professional baseball players Ryan Zimmerman, José Reyes, and eight others; U.S. Women's National Soccer Team players Heather Mitts and Lauren Cheney; U.S. Olympic and professional volleyball player Nicole Branagh; Olympic snowboarder Lindsey Jacobellis; U.S. Olympic swimmer Michael Phelps; and professional golfer Hunter Mahan. In January 2014, Under Armour signed ballerina soloist Misty Copeland to a multiyear contract; later in 2014, Copeland was featured in Under Armour's largest advertising campaign to date for its women's brand of apparel offerings. In 2014 Under Armour was actively pursuing efforts to boost its market profile in foreign countries by signing high-profile foreign sports celebrities to endorsement contracts.

During 2010–2013, Under Armour hosted over 125 combines, camps, and clinics for male and female athletes in many sports at various regional sites in the United States. It sponsored American Youth Football (an organization that promoted the development of youth and a variety of camps and clinics), the Under Armour Senior Bowl (a televised annual competition between the top seniors in college football), the Under Armour (Baltimore) Marathon, the Under Armour All-America Lacrosse Classic, and a collection of high school All-America games in a variety of sports. Under Armour had partnered with Ripken Baseball to outfit some 35,000 Ripken Baseball participants at camps and clinics and to be the title sponsor for all Ripken youth baseball tournaments. It had partnered with the Baseball Factory to outfit top high school baseball athletes from head to toe and serve as the title sponsor for nationally recognized baseball tryouts, training camps, and tournament teams.

Under Armour spent approximately $57.8 million in 2013 for athlete endorsements, various team and league sponsorships, athletic events, and other marketing commitments, compared to about $53.0 million in 2012, $43.5 million in 2011, and $29.4 million in 2010.[10] The company was contractually obligated to spend a minimum of $222 million for endorsements, sponsorships, events, and other marketing commitments in 2014–2018.[11] Under Armour did not know precisely what its future endorsement and sponsorship costs would be because its contractual agreements with most athletes were subject to certain performance-based variables and because it was actively engaged in efforts to sign additional endorsement contracts and sponsor additional sports teams and athletic events.

**Retail Marketing and Product Presentation**
The primary thrust of Under Armour's retail marketing strategy was to increase the floor space *exclusively* dedicated to Under Armour products in the stores of its major retail accounts. The key initiative here was to design and fund Under Armour "concept shops"—including flooring, in-store fixtures, product displays, life-size athlete mannequins, and lighting—within the stores of its major retail customers. This shop-in-shop approach was seen as an effective way to gain the placement of Under Armour products in prime floor space, educate consumers about UA products, and create a more engaging and sales-producing way for consumers to shop for UA products.

In stores that did not have Under Armour concept shops, the company worked with retailers to establish optimal placement of its products. In big-box sporting goods stores, it was important to be sure that Under Armour's growing variety of products gained visibility in all of the various departments (hunting apparel in the hunting goods department, footwear and socks in the footwear department, and so on). Except for the retail stores with Under Armour concept shops, company personnel worked with retailers to employ in-store fixtures and displays that highlighted the UA logo and conveyed a performance-oriented, athletic look (chiefly through

the use of life-size athlete mannequins). The merchandising strategy was not only to enhance the visibility of Under Armour products but also to reinforce the message that the company's brand was distinct from those of competitors.

**Media and Promotion**   Under Armour advertised in a variety of national digital, broadcast, and print media outlets, and its advertising campaigns included a variety of lengths and formats. The company's "Protect This House" and "Click-Clack" campaigns featured several NFL players, and the Protect This House campaign had been used in several NFL and collegiate stadiums during games as a crowd prompt. Beginning in 2003–2004 and continuing through 2012, Under Armour utilized an ongoing series of TV commercials in which the UA brand asked athletes engaged in sporting events at their home field to "Protect This House" and athletes responded to the request with a resounding "I Will" to familiarize consumers with the UA brand. Top executives believed the long-standing Protect This House—I Will campaign had been instrumental in making the Under Armour brand a widely recognized household name.

In February 2013, Under Armour launched a global marketing campaign featuring its now iconic I Will trademark. The campaign's principal 60-second spot ads on TV and online depicted four of Under Armour's up-and-coming celebrity endorsers—Canelo Alvarez, Sloane Stephens (the only teenager ranked in the top 20 in the World Tennis Association), Bryce Harper, and Kemba Walker—in their authentic training environments outfitted in the company's most technologically advanced products. The campaign showcased UA's new Spine Venom and Micro G Toxic 6 performance footwear collections, the new ColdGear Infrared insulated apparel collection, and the Armour39 system. The first-of-its-kind Armour39 system was a digital performance-measuring device that enabled users to track their heart rate, calories burned, and intensity during a workout; the headline attribute of the Armour 39 system was a single numerical "WILL-power score" that reflected an individual's overall effort during a workout session and that served as a gauge of the person's training and athletic potential.

On several occasions, the company had secured the use of Under Armour products in movies, television shows, and video games; management believed the appearance of Under Armour products in these media reinforced authenticity of the brand and provided brand exposure to audiences that may not have seen Under Armour's other advertising campaigns. Starting in 2011, Under Armour began efforts to significantly grow the company's "fan base" via social marketing at sites like Facebook and Twitter; the company's goal in using social media was to engage consumers and promote conversation about its products and brand.

## Distribution Strategy

Under Armour products were available in over 25,000 retail stores worldwide at the end of 2011, of which about 18,000 retail stores were in North America. Under Armour also sold its products directly to consumers through its own factory outlet and specialty stores, website, and catalogs.

**Wholesale Distribution**   In 2011–2013, close to 70 percent of Under Armour's net revenues were generated from sales to retailers. The company's two biggest retail accounts were Dick's Sporting Goods and The Sports Authority, which in 2013 accounted for a combined 22 percent of the company's net revenues. Other important retail accounts in the United States included Academy Sports and Outdoors, Hibbett Sporting Goods, Modell's Sporting Goods, Bass Pro Shops, Cabela's, Footlocker, Finish Line, The Army and Air Force Exchange Service, and such well-known department store chains as Macy's, Dillards, Belk, and Lord & Taylor. In Canada, the company's biggest customers were Sportchek International and Sportman International. Roughly 75 percent of all sales made to retailers were to large-format national and regional retail chains. The remaining 25 percent of wholesale sales were to smaller-sized outdoor and other specialty retailers, institutional athletic departments, leagues, teams, and fitness specialists. Sales to independent and specialty retailers were made by a combination of in-house sales personnel and third-party commissioned manufacturer's representatives.

**Direct-to-Consumer Sales**   In 2013, 30.4 percent of Under Armour's net revenues were generated through direct-to-consumer sales, versus 23 percent in 2010 and 6 percent in 2005; the direct-to-consumer channel included sales of discounted merchandise at Under Armour's Factory House stores and full-price

sales at company-owned retail stores, at the company's global website (www.underarmour.com), and through periodically distributed Under Armour catalogs. Over the past seven years, Under Armour had opened increasing numbers of Factory House stores. Not only did these stores give the company added brand exposure and help familiarize consumers with UA's growing lineup of products, but they also functioned as an important channel for selling discontinued, out-of-season, and/or overstocked products at discount prices without undermining the prices of Under Armour merchandise being sold at the stores of retailers, the company's Brand Houses, and the company's website. Going into April 2014, Under Armour had 121 factory outlet stores in 39 states and Canada. The company was on track to at least meet and possibly exceed its previously stated goal of having 141 Factory House locations averaging 7,700 square feet by late 2016.[12]

In late 2007, Under Armour opened its first company-owned retail store to showcase its branded apparel at a mall in Annapolis, Maryland. Over the next several years, a few more retail stores (which the company called Brand Houses) were opened in a select number of high-traffic locations in the United States. In spring 2014, the company was operating six Under Armour full-price Brand House stores in the United States (three in Maryland and one each in New York, Virginia, and Colorado)—two previously opened Brand House stores, one in a Chicago suburb and one outside Boston, had been closed. The first Under Armour retail store outside North America was opened in Edinburgh, Scotland—it was owned and operated by First XV, a rugby store that was situated next door.

Under Armour management's website strategy called for e-commerce sales at www.underarmour.com to be one of the company's principal vehicles for sales growth in upcoming years. To help spur website sales, the company was endeavoring to establish a clearer connection between its website offerings and the brand initiatives being undertaken in retail stores. It was also enhancing the merchandising techniques and storytelling regarding the UA products being marketed at its website. Management estimated that in 2016 some 90 million customers would shop at the company's website and that website sales would likely exceed $1.25 billion.[13]

**Product Licensing**   In 2013, 2.4 percent of the company's net revenues came from licensing arrangements to manufacture and distribute Under Armour–branded products. Under Armour preapproved all products manufactured and sold by its licensees, and the company's quality assurance team strived to ensure that licensed products met the same quality and compliance standards as company-sold products. Under Armour had relationships with several licensees for team uniforms, eyewear, and custom-molded mouth guards, as well as the distribution of Under Armour products to college bookstores and golf pro shops.

**Distribution outside North America**   Sales of Under Armour products outside North America accounted for only 5.9 percent of the company's net revenues in both 2012 and 2013, down fractionally from 6.1 percent in 2011 and 6.2 percent in 2010 (see Exhibit 3, panel B). But despite the small percentage declines, dollar sales had risen briskly from $66.1 million in 2010 to $89.3 million in 2011 to $108.2 million in 2012 and to $138.3 million in 2013. Under Armour saw growth in foreign sales as a huge market opportunity for the company in upcoming years, partly because management was convinced that the trend toward using performance products was global and partly because there were vast numbers of people outside the United States who could be attracted to patronize the Under Armour brand. As a consequence, the company had begun entering foreign country markets as rapidly as was prudent. In his Letter to Shareholders in the company's 2013 annual report, Kevin Plank said, "We are committed to being a global brand with global stories to tell, and we are on our way."

Under Armour's first strategic move to gain international distribution occurred in 2002 when it established a relationship with a Japanese licensee, Dome Corporation, that gave Dome exclusive rights to distribute Under Armour products in Japan. The relationship evolved, and Under Armour made a minority equity investment in Dome Corporation in January 2011. As of 2014, Dome was producing, marketing, and selling Under Armour–branded apparel, footwear, and accessories in Japan and South Korea. Dome sold Under Armour products to professional sports teams, large sporting goods retailers (including Alpen, Himaraya, The Sports Authority, and Xebio), and several thousand independent retailers of sports apparel. Under Armour worked closely with Dome to develop variations of Under Armour products for the different sizes, sports interests, and preferences of Japanese and Korean consumers.

A UA European headquarters was opened in 2006 in Amsterdam, Netherlands, to conduct and oversee sales, marketing, and logistics activities across Europe. The strategy was to first sell Under Armour products directly to teams and athletes and then leverage visibility in the sports segment to access broader audiences of potential consumers. By 2011, Under Armour had succeeded in selling products to Premier League Football clubs and multiple running, golf, and cricket clubs in the United Kingdom and to soccer teams in France, Germany, Greece, Ireland, Italy, Spain, and Sweden, as well as First Division Rugby clubs in France, Ireland, Italy, and the United Kingdom. Sales to European retailers quickly followed on the heels of the gains being made in the sports team segment. By year-end 2012, Under Armour had 4,000 retail customers in Austria, France, Germany, Ireland, and the United Kingdom and was generating revenues from sales to independent distributors that resold Under Armour products to retailers in Italy, Greece, Scandinavia, and Spain. In 2013–2014, gradual expansion into other countries in Europe, the Middle East, and Africa was under way.

In 2010–2011, Under Armour began selling its products in parts of Latin America and Asia. In Latin America, Under Armour sold directly to retailers in some countries and in other countries sold its products to independent distributors that then were responsible for securing sales to retailers. In 2014, Under Armour launched sales in Brazil via arrangements to make its products available in over 70 of the country's premium points of sale and e-commerce hubs, such as Centauro, Netshoes and Paquetá; expanded sales efforts were also under way in Chile and Mexico. Under Armour was utilizing its four retail locations in China to learn about Chinese consumers and what it would take to succeed in selling its products in China on a much wider scale. In 2013, distribution to the retail stores in China was handled through a third-party logistics provider based in Hong Kong.

In 2011, Under Armour opened a retail store in Shanghai, China, the first of a series of steps to begin the long-term process of introducing Chinese athletes and consumers to the Under Armour brand, showcase Under Armour products, and learn about

Chinese consumers. Additional retail locations in Shanghai and Beijing soon followed (some of them were operated by UA's franchise partners in China). In October 2013, Under Armour CEO Kevin Plank and Olympic gold medalist Michael Phelps, an Under Armour endorser, hosted a grand opening event for the new Under Armour Retail Theatre Experience at the Jing An Kerry Centre, a new mall development in Shanghai, China. The first-of-its-kind retail environment placed storytelling at the forefront through a multidimensional short film shot with 360-degree camera technology and displayed on a 270-degree screen. The film, hosted by Phelps, used a series of vignettes to depict different moments defining the will of an athlete, including a training session with NBA star Brandon Jennings, rooftop yoga in Shanghai, and the exhilaration of running out onto the field before a soccer match at White Hart Lane, home of the Tottenham Hotspurs. When the film ended, performance trainers guided guests to a separate section of the store featuring a limited selection of the brand's footwear and apparel including the new UA Speedform RC running shoe. As of April 2014, there were five company-owned and franchised retail locations in mainland China that merchandised Under Armour products; additionally, the Under Armour brand had been recently introduced in Hong Kong through a partnership with leading retail chain GigaSports.

Also in 2014, Under Armour was selling its branded apparel, footwear, and accessories to independent distributors in Australia, New Zealand, and Taiwan; these distributors were responsible for securing retail accounts to merchandise Under Armour products to consumers. The distribution of Under Armour products to retail accounts in Asia was handled by a third-party logistics provider based in Hong Kong.

In June 2013, Under Armour organized its international activities into four geographic regions—North America (the United States and Canada), Latin America, Asia, and Europe/Middle East/Africa (EMEA), and it established a target of boosting sales outside North America to 12 percent of total revenues in 2016. By comparison, in 2013 Nike generated about 55 percent of its revenues outside the United States, and adidas, based in Germany, got about 60 percent of its sales outside its home market of Europe—these big international sales percentages for Nike and adidas were a big reason why Under Armour executives were confident that growing UA's international sales represented an enormous market opportunity for the company, despite the stiff competition it could expect from these two rivals.

## Product Design and Development

Top executives believed that product innovation—in terms of both technical design and aesthetic design—was the key to driving Under Armour's sales growth and building a stronger brand name.

Under Armour products were manufactured with technically advanced specialty fabrics produced by third parties. The company's product development team collaborated closely with fabric suppliers to ensure that the fabrics and materials used in UA's products had the desired performance and fit attributes. Under Armour regularly upgraded its products as next-generation fabrics with better performance characteristics became available and as the needs of athletes changed. Product development efforts also aimed at broadening the company's product offerings in both new and existing product categories and market segments. An effort was made to design products with "visible technology," utilizing color, texture, and fabrication that would enhance customers' perception and understanding of the use and benefits of Under Armour products.

Under Armour's product development team had significant prior industry experience at leading fabric and other raw-material suppliers and branded athletic apparel and footwear companies throughout the world. The team worked closely with Under Armour's sports marketing and sales teams as well as professional and collegiate athletes to identify product trends and determine market needs. Collaboration among the company's product development, sales, and sports marketing team had proved important in identifying the opportunity and market for four recently launched product lines and fabric technologies:

- *Charged Cotton products*, which were made from natural cotton but performed like the products made from technically advanced synthetic fabrics, drying faster and wicking moisture away from the body.
- *Storm Armour Fleece products*, which had a unique, water-resistant finish that repelled water without stifling airflow.
- *ColdBlack,* a technology fabric that repelled heat from the sun and kept the wearer cooler outside.

- *ColdGear Infrared*, a ceramic print technology that was applied to the inside of garments and provided wearers with lightweight warmth.

Under Armour executives projected that the innovative Charged Cotton and Storm Armour Fleece product lines would generate combined revenues of $500 million in 2016.[14] Under Armour had partnered with the Swiss company Schoeller in 2012 to introduce the ColdBlack technology product line.

## Sourcing, Manufacturing, and Quality Assurance

Many of the high-tech specialty fabrics and other raw materials used in UA products were developed by third parties and sourced from a limited number of preapproved specialty fabric manufacturers; no fabrics were manufactured in-house. Under Armour executives believed outsourcing fabric production enabled the company to seek out and utilize whichever fabric suppliers were able to produce the latest and best performance-oriented fabrics to Under Armour's specifications, while also freeing more time for UA's product development staff to concentrate on upgrading the performance, styling, and overall appeal of existing products and expanding the company's overall lineup of product offerings.

In 2013, approximately 50 to 55 percent of the fabric used in UA products came from six suppliers, with primary locations in China, Malaysia, Mexico, Taiwan, and Vietnam. Because a big fraction of the materials used in UA products were petroleum-based synthetics, fabric costs were subject to crude oil price fluctuations. The cotton fabrics used in the Charged Cotton products were also subject to price fluctuations and varying availability based on cotton harvests.

In 2013, substantially all UA products were made by 26 primary manufacturers, operating in 19 countries; 14 manufacturers produced approximately 65 percent of UA's products. Approximately 66 percent of UA's products were manufactured in Asia, 14 percent in Central and South America, 15 percent in the Middle East, and 5 percent in Mexico. All manufacturers purchased the fabrics they needed from the six fabric suppliers preapproved by Under Armour. All of the makers of UA products were evaluated for quality systems, social compliance, and financial strength by Under Armour's quality assurance team prior to being selected and also on an ongoing basis. The company strived to qualify multiple manufacturers for particular product types and fabrications and to seek out contractors that could perform multiple manufacturing stages, such as procuring raw materials and providing finished products, which helped UA control its cost of goods sold. All contract manufacturers were required to adhere to a code of conduct regarding quality of manufacturing, working conditions, and other social concerns. However, the company had no long-term agreements requiring it to continue to use the services of any manufacturer, and no manufacturer was obligated to make products for UA on a long-term basis. Under Armour had an office in Hong Kong to support its manufacturing, quality assurance, and sourcing efforts for apparel and had offices in Guangzhou, China, to support its manufacturing, quality assurance, and sourcing efforts for footwear and accessories.

Under Armour had a 17,000-square-foot Special Make-Up Shop located at one of its distribution facilities in Maryland, where it had the capability to make and ship customized apparel products on tight deadlines for high-profile athletes and teams. While these apparel products represented a tiny fraction of Under Armour's revenues, management believed the facility helped provide superior service to select customers.

## Distribution Facilities and Inventory Management

Under Armour packaged and shipped the majority of its products for the North American market at two distribution facilities located approximately 15 miles from its Baltimore, Maryland, headquarters and at a third distribution facility in Rialto, California; all three facilities were leased. The two facilities in Maryland had a total space of 830,000 square feet, and the California facility had 1.2 million square feet of space.

Distribution to European retail accounts and to European customers making purchases at www.underarmour.com was handled by a third-party logistics provider based in Venlo, Netherlands; the current agreement with this distributor extended until 2015. Under Armour had contracted with a third-party logistics provider based in Hong Kong to handle packing and shipment to customers in

Asia. Until recently, shipments of apparel, footwear, and accessories to independent distributors in Latin America were generally handled by the company's distribution facilities in the United States, although in a few instances Under Armour arranged to have products shipped from the independent factories that made its products directly to customer-designated facilities. In June 2013, Under Armour signed an agreement to acquire certain facilities of its distributor in Mexico. In early 2014, Under Armour began using these facilities to ship its products to retailers in Mexico, Brazil, and Chile. Under Armour planned to add additional company-owned distribution facilities in the future, as might be needed to keep shipping costs to distant locations economically low.

Under Armour based the amount of inventory it needed to have on hand for each item in its product line on existing orders, anticipated sales, and the need to rapidly deliver orders to customers. Its inventory strategy was focused on (1) having sufficient inventory to fill incoming orders promptly and (2) putting strong systems and procedures in place to improve the efficiency with which it managed its inventories of individual products and total inventory. The amounts of seasonal products it ordered from manufacturers were based on current bookings, the need to ship seasonal items at the start of the shipping window in order to maximize the floor space productivity of retail customers, the need to adequately stock its Factory House and Brand House stores, and the need to fill customers' orders placed at the company's website. Excess inventories of particular products were either shipped to its Factory House stores or earmarked for sale to third-party liquidators.

However, the growing number of individual items in UA's product line and uncertainties surrounding upcoming consumer demand for individual items made it difficult to accurately forecast how many units to order from manufacturers and what the appropriate stocking requirements were for many items. Under Armour's year-end inventories rose from $148.4 million in 2009 to $215.4 million in 2010 to $324.4 million in 2011—percentage increases that exceeded the gains in companywide revenues and that caused days of inventories to climb from 121.4 days in 2009 to 148.4 days in 2010 and to 155.8 days in 2011. The increases were due, in part, to long lead times for the design and production of some products and to the need to begin manufacturing seasonal

products and soon-to-be introduced products before receiving any orders for them. In January 2012, management announced that because inventory growth of 118 percent over the past two years had outstripped revenue growth of 72 percent, it was instituting a review of UA's entire product line with the objectives of reducing production lead times, curtailing the number of distinct individual items included in the company's lineup of product offerings (frequently referred to as SKUs, or stock-keeping units), and doing a better job of planning and executing shipments of excess inventory to the company's factory outlet stores. Year-end inventories of $319.3 million in 2012 equated to 120 days of inventory and an inventory turnover of 2.99 turns per year. Year-end inventories of $469 million in 2013 equated to 143.2 days of inventory and an inventory turnover of 2.56 turns per year. The company's stated target for inventory turns in 2013 was 3; the 2016 target was for turns in the 3-to-3.3 range.[15]

## COMPETITION

The multisegment global market for sports apparel, athletic footwear, and related accessories was fragmented among some 25 brand-name competitors with diverse product lines and varying geographic coverage and numerous small competitors with specialized-use apparel lines that usually operated within a single country or geographic region. Industry participants included athletic and leisure shoe companies, athletic and leisure apparel companies, sports equipment companies, and large companies having diversified lines of athletic and leisure shoes, apparel, and equipment. In 2012, the global market for athletic footwear was about $75 billion and was forecast to reach about $85 billion in 2018; growth was expected to be driven by rising population, increasing disposable incomes, rising health awareness, and the launch of innovative footwear designs and technology.[16] The global market for athletic and fitness apparel, estimated to be $135 billion in 2012, was forecast to grow about 4 percent annually and reach about $178 billion by 2019.[17] Exhibit 4 shows a representative sample of the best-known companies and brands in select segments of the sports apparel, athletic footwear, and sports equipment industry.

As Exhibit 4 indicates, the sporting goods industry consisted of many distinct product categories

**EXHIBIT 4**   Major Competitors and Brands in Select Segments of the Sports Apparel, Athletic Footwear, and Accessory Industry, 2013

| Performance apparel for sports (baseball, football, basketball, softball, volleyball, hockey, lacrosse, soccer, track and field, and other action sports) | Performance-driven athletic footwear | Training/fitness clothing |
|---|---|---|
| • Nike | • Nike | • Nike |
| • Under Armour | • Reebok | • Under Armour |
| • Eastbay | • adidas | • Eastbay |
| • adidas | • New Balance | • adidas |
| • Russell | • Saucony | • Puma |
| | • Puma | • Fila |
| | • Rockport | • lululemon athletica |
| | • Converse | • Champion |
| | • Ryka | • Asics |
| | • Asics | • SUGOI |
| | • Li Ning | • Li Ning |

| Performance activewear and sports-inspired lifestyle apparel | Performance skiwear | Performance golf apparel |
|---|---|---|
| • Polo Ralph Lauren | • Salomon | • Footjoy |
| • Lacoste | • North Face | • Polo Golf |
| • Izod | • Descente | • Nike |
| • Cutter & Buck | • Columbia | • adidas |
| • Timberland | • Patagonia | • Puma |
| • Columbia | • Marmot | • Under Armour |
| • Puma | • Helly Hansen | • Ashworth |
| • Li Ning | • Bogner | • Cutter & Buck |
| • Many others | • Spyder | • Greg Norman |
| | • Many others | • Many others |

and market segments. Because the product mixes of different companies varied considerably, it was common for the product offerings of industry participants to be extensive in some segments, moderate in others, and limited to nonexistent in still others. Consequently, the leading competitors and the intensity of competition varied significantly from market segment to market segment. Nonetheless, competition tended to be intense in almost every segment with substantial sales volume and typically revolved around performance and reliability, the breadth of product selection, new product development, price, brand-name strength and identity through marketing and promotion, the ability of companies to convince retailers to stock and effectively merchandise

their brands, and capabilities of the various industry participants to sell directly to consumers through their own retail and factory outlet stores and/or at their company websites. It was common for the leading companies selling athletic footwear, sports uniforms, and sports equipment to actively sponsor sporting events and clinics and to contract with prominent and influential athletes, coaches, professional sports teams, colleges, and sports leagues to endorse their brands and use their products.

Nike was the clear global market leader in the sporting goods industry, with a global market share in athletic footwear of about 21 percent and a sports apparel share of about 4.8 percent. The adidas Group, with businesses that produced athletic footwear, sports uniforms, fitness apparel, sportswear, and a variety of sports equipment and marketed them across the world, was the second-largest global competitor. Both were major competitors of Under Armour and are profiled below.

## Nike, Inc.

Incorporated in 1968, Nike was engaged in the design, development, and worldwide marketing and selling of footwear, sports apparel, sports equipment, and accessory products. Its principal businesses in fiscal years 2012 and 2013 are shown in the table just above Exhibit 5.

Total companywide sales were $23.3 billion in fiscal 2012 and $25.3 billion in fiscal 2013. Nike was the world's largest seller of athletic footwear, athletic apparel, and athletic equipment and accessories, with over 40,000 retail accounts, 753 company-owned stores, 23 distribution centers, and selling arrangements with independent distributors and licensees in over 190 countries—see Exhibit 5. About 55 percent of Nike's sales came from outside the United States in 2013. Nike's retail account base in the United States included a mix of footwear stores; sporting goods stores; athletic specialty stores; department stores; skate, tennis and golf shops; and other retail accounts. During fiscal 2013, Nike's three largest customers accounted for approximately 25 percent of U.S. sales; its three largest customers outside the United States accounted for about 6 percent of total non-U.S. sales. In fiscal 2013, Nike had sales of $4.3 billion at its company-owned stores and website, up from $3.5 billion in fiscal 2012.

In 2011, Nike established a fiscal 2015 revenue target of $28 billion to $30 billion and reaffirmed its ongoing target of annual earnings per share growth in the 14 to 16 percent range.

**Principal Products**  Nike's athletic footwear models and styles were designed primarily for specific athletic use, although many were worn for casual or leisure purposes. Running, training, basketball, soccer, sport-inspired casual shoes, and kids'

| Business | Fiscal 2012 Revenues (millions) | Fiscal 2013 Revenues (millions) |
|---|---|---|
| Nike Brand footwear (over 800 models and styles) | $13,428 | $14,539 |
| Nike Brand apparel | 6,336 | 6,820 |
| Nike Brand equipment for a wide variety of sports | 1,204 | 1,405 |
| Converse (a designer and marketer of athletic footwear, apparel, and accessories) | 1,324 | 1,449 |
| Nike Golf (footwear, apparel, golf equipment, accessories) | 726 | 791 |
| Hurley (a designer and marketer of action sports and youth lifestyle footwear and apparel, including shorts, tees, tanks, hoodies, and swimwear) | 248 | 260 |

## EXHIBIT 5    Nike's Worldwide Retail and Distribution Network, 2013

| United States | Foreign Countries |
|---|---|
| • ~ 20,000 retail accounts | • More than 20,000 retail accounts |
| • 171 Nike factory outlet stores | • 388 Nike factory outlet stores |
| • 33 Nike and Niketown stores | • 59 Nike and Niketown stores |
| • 72 Converse retail and factory outlet stores | • 3 Converse retail and factory outlet stores |
| • 27 Hurley stores | • — |
| • 7 distribution centers | • 16 distribution centers |
| • Company website (www.nike.com) | • Independent distributors and licensees in over 190 countries |
| | • Company website (www.nike.com) |

shoes were the company's top-selling footwear categories. It also marketed footwear designed for baseball, football, golf, lacrosse, cricket, outdoor activities, tennis, volleyball, walking, and wrestling. The company designed and marketed Nike-branded sports apparel and accessories for almost all of these sports categories, as well as sports-inspired lifestyle apparel, athletic bags, and accessory items. Footwear, apparel, and accessories were often marketed in "collections" of similar design or for specific purposes. It also marketed apparel with licensed college and professional team and league logos. Nike-brand offerings in sports equipment included bags, socks, sport balls, eyewear, timepieces, electronic devices, bats, gloves, protective equipment, and golf clubs.

Exhibit 6 shows a breakdown of Nike's sales of footwear, apparel, and equipment by geographic region for fiscal years 2010 through 2013.

**Marketing, Promotions, and Endorsements**
Nike responded to trends and shifts in consumer preferences by (1) adjusting the mix of existing product offerings, (2) developing new products, styles, and categories, and (3) striving to influence sports and fitness preferences through aggressive marketing, promotional activities, sponsorships, and athlete endorsements. Nike spent $2.75 billion in fiscal 2013, $2.61 billion in fiscal 2012, and $2.45 billion in fiscal 2011 for what it termed "demand creation expenses" that included advertising and

**EXHIBIT 6**   Nike's Sales of Nike Brand Footwear, Apparel, and Equipment, by Geographic Region, Fiscal Years 2010–2013 (dollar amounts in millions)

| | Fiscal Year Ending May 31 | | | |
|---|---|---|---|---|
| **Sales Revenues and Earnings** | **2013** | **2012** | **2011** | **2010** |
| **North America** | | | | |
| Revenues—Nike Brand footwear | $ 6,687 | $5,887 | $5,111 | $4,610 |
| Nike Brand apparel | 3,028 | 2,482 | 2,103 | 1,740 |
| Nike Brand equipment | 672 | 470 | 365 | 346 |
| Total Nike Brand revenues | $10,387 | $8,839 | $7,579 | $6,696 |
| Earnings before interest and taxes | $ 2,534 | $2,007 | $1,736 | $1,538 |
| Profit margin | 24.4% | 22.7% | 22.9% | 23.0% |
| **Western Europe** | | | | |
| Revenues—Nike Brand footwear | $2,646 | $2,526 | $2,345 | $2,320 |
| Nike Brand apparel | 1,261 | 1,377 | 1,303 | 1,325 |
| Nike Brand equipment | 221 | 241 | 220 | 247 |
| Total Nike Brand revenues | $4,128 | $4,144 | $3,868 | $3,892 |
| Earnings before interest and taxes | $  640 | $  597 | $  730 | $  856 |
| Profit margin | 15.5% | 14.4% | 18.9% | 22.0% |
| **Central and Eastern Europe** | | | | |
| Revenues—Nike Brand footwear | $  714 | $  671 | $  605 | $558 |
| Nike Brand apparel | 483 | 441 | 359 | 354 |
| Nike Brand equipment | 90 | 88 | 76 | 81 |
| Total Nike Brand revenues | $1,287 | $1,200 | $1,040 | $993 |
| Earnings before interest and taxes | $  259 | $  234 | $  244 | $253 |
| Profit margin | 20.1% | 19.5% | 23.5% | 25.5% |

*(Continued)*

**EXHIBIT 6**    (*Continued*)

| Sales Revenues and Earnings | Fiscal Year Ending May 31 | | | |
|---|---|---|---|---|
| | 2013 | 2012 | 2011 | 2010 |
| **Greater China** | | | | |
| Revenues—Nike Brand footwear | $1,493 | $1,518 | $1,164 | $  53 |
| Nike Brand apparel | 829 | 896 | 789 | 684 |
| Nike Brand equipment | 131 | 125 | 107 | 105 |
| Total Nike Brand revenues | $2,453 | $2,539 | $2,060 | $1,742 |
| Earnings before interest and taxes | $ 809 | $ 911 | $ 777 | $ 637 |
| Profit margin | 33.0% | 35.9% | 37.7% | 36.6% |
| **Japan** | | | | |
| Revenues—Nike Brand footwear | $429 | $439 | $396 | $433 |
| Nike Brand apparel | 301 | 325 | 302 | 357 |
| Nike Brand equipment | 61 | 71 | 68 | 92 |
| Total Nike Brand revenues | $791 | $835 | $766 | $882 |
| Earnings before interest and taxes | $133 | $136 | $114 | $180 |
| Profit margin | 16.8% | 16.3% | 14.9% | 20.4% |
| **Emerging markets** | | | | |
| Revenues—Nike Brand footwear | $2,570 | $2,386 | $1,897 | $1,458 |
| Nike Brand apparel | 918 | 815 | 657 | 577 |
| Nike Brand equipment | 230 | 209 | 182 | 164 |
| Total Nike Brand revenues | $3,718 | $3,410 | $2,736 | $2,199 |
| Earnings before interest and taxes | $1,011 | $ 853 | $ 688 | $ 521 |
| Profit margin | 27.2% | 25.0% | 25.1% | 23.7% |
| **All regions** | | | | |
| Revenues—Nike Brand footwear | $14,539 | $13,426 | $11,518 | $10,332 |
| Nike Brand apparel | 6,820 | 6,333 | 5,513 | 5,037 |
| Nike Brand equipment | 1,405 | 1,202 | 1,018 | 1,035 |
| Total Nike Brand revenues | $22,764 | $20,961 | $18,145 | $16,404 |
| Earnings before interest and taxes | $ 5,386 | $ 4,738 | $ 4,289 | $ 3,932 |
| Profit margin | 23.7% | 22.6% | 23.6% | 24.0% |
| **Other businesses** | | | | |
| Revenues—Converse | $1,449 | $1,324 | $1,131 | $ 983 |
| Nike Golf | 791 | 726 | 658 | 670 |
| Hurley | 260 | 248 | 252 | 222 |
| Total revenues | $2,500 | $2,298 | $2,041 | $1,875 |
| Earnings before interest and taxes | $  456 | $  385 | $  353 | Not available |
| Profit margin | 18.2% | 16.8% | 17.3% | — |

*Note:*  The revenue and earnings figures for all geographic regions include the effects of currency exchange fluctuations.

*Sources:* Nike's 10-K report for fiscal year 2012, pp. 21–25; and Nike's 10-K report for fiscal year 2013, pp. 24–29.

promotion expenses and the costs of endorsement contracts. Well over 500 professional, collegiate, club, and Olympic sports teams in football, basketball, baseball, ice hockey, soccer, rugby, speed skating, tennis, swimming, and other sports wore Nike uniforms with the Nike swoosh prominently visible. There were over 1,000 prominent professional athletes with Nike endorsement contracts in 2011–2013, including former basketball great Michael Jordan; NFL players Drew Brees, Tim Tebow, Tony Romo, Aaron Rodgers, and Clay Matthews; Major League Baseball players Albert Pujols and Alex Rodriguez; NBA players LeBron James and Dwayne Wade; professional golfers Tiger Woods and Michelle Wie; and professional tennis players Victoria Azarenka, Maria Sharapova, Venus and Serena Williams, Roger Federer, and Rafael Nadal. When Tiger Woods turned pro, Nike signed him to a five-year $100 million endorsement contract and made him the centerpiece of its campaign to make Nike a factor in the golf equipment and golf apparel marketplace. Nike's long-standing endorsement relationship with Michael Jordan led to the introduction of the highly popular line of Air Jordan footwear and, more recently, to the launch of the Jordan brand of athletic shoes, clothing, and gear. In 2003 LeBron James signed an endorsement deal with Nike worth $90 million over seven years. Golfer Rory McIlroy's 2013 deal with Nike was reportedly in the range of $150 million over 10 years. Because soccer was such a popular sport globally, Nike had more endorsement contracts with soccer athletes than with athletes in any other sport; track and field athletes had the second-largest number of endorsement contracts.

**Research and Development**   Nike management believed R&D efforts had been and would continue to be a key factor in the company's success. Technical innovation in the design of footwear, apparel, and athletic equipment received ongoing emphasis in an effort to provide products that helped reduce injury, enhance athletic performance, and maximize comfort.

In addition to Nike's own staff of specialists in the areas of biomechanics, chemistry, exercise physiology, engineering, industrial design, and related fields, the company utilized research committees and advisory boards made up of athletes, coaches, trainers, equipment managers, orthopedists, podiatrists, and other experts who reviewed designs, materials, concepts for product improvements, and compliance with product safety regulations around the world. Employee athletes, athletes engaged under sports marketing contracts, and other athletes wear-tested and evaluated products during the design and development process.

**Manufacturing**   In fiscal 2013, about 98 percent of Nike's footwear was produced by contract manufacturers in Vietnam, China, and Indonesia, but the company had manufacturing agreements with independent factories in Argentina, Brazil, India, and Mexico to manufacture footwear for sale primarily within those countries. Nike-branded apparel was manufactured outside the United States by independent contract manufacturers located in 28 countries; most of the apparel production occurred in China, Vietnam, Thailand, Indonesia, Sri Lanka, Pakistan, Malaysia, Turkey, Mexico, and Cambodia.

## The adidas Group

The mission of The adidas Group was to be the global leader in the sporting goods industry with brands built on a passion for sports and a sporting lifestyle. Headquartered in Germany, its businesses and brands consisted of:

- *adidas*—a designer and marketer of active sportswear, uniforms, footwear, and sports products in football, basketball, soccer, running, training, outdoor, and six other categories (76.3 percent of The adidas Group's sales in 2013).
- *Reebok*—a well-known global provider of athletic footwear for multiple uses, sports and fitness apparel, and accessories (11.0 percent of Group sales in 2013).
- *TaylorMade-adidas Golf*—a designer and marketer of TaylorMade golf equipment, Adams Golf equipment, adidas golf shoes and golf apparel, and Ashworth golf apparel (8.9 percent of Group sales in 2013).
- *Rockport*—a designer and marketer of dress, casual, and outdoor footwear that largely targeted metropolitan professional consumers (2.0 percent of Group sales in 2013).
- *Reebok-CCM Hockey*—one of the world's largest designers, makers, and marketers of ice hockey equipment and apparel under the brand names Reebok Hockey and CCM Hockey (1.8 percent of Group sales in 2013).

Exhibit 7 shows the company's financial highlights for 2010–2013.

The company sold products in virtually every country of the world. In 2013, its extensive product offerings were marketed through thousands of third-party retailers (sporting goods chains, department stores, independent sporting goods retailer buying groups, lifestyle retailing chains, and Internet retailers), 1,661 company-owned and franchised adidas- and Reebok-branded "concept" stores, 779 company-owned adidas and Reebok factory outlet stores, 300 other adidas and Reebok stores with varying formats, and various company websites (such as **www.adidas.com, www.reebok.com,** and **www .taylormadegolf.com**). Wholesale sales to third-party retailers in 2013 were €9.1 billion (62.8 percent of

## EXHIBIT 7    Financial Highlights for The adidas Group, 2010–2013 (euro amounts in millions)

|  | 2013 | 2012 | 2011 | 2010 |
|---|---|---|---|---|
| **Income statement data** | | | | |
| Net sales | €14,492 | €14,883 | €13,322 | €11,990 |
| Gross profit | 7,140 | 7,103 | 6,329 | 5,730 |
| Gross profit margin | 49.3% | 47.7% | 47.5% | 47.8% |
| Operating profit | 1,254 | 1,185 | 953 | 894 |
| Operating profit margin | 8.7% | 6.2% | 7.2% | 7.5% |
| Net income | 839 | 791 | 613 | 567 |
| Net profit margin | 5.8% | 5.3% | 4.6% | 4.7% |
| **Balance sheet data** | | | | |
| Inventories | €2,634 | €2,486 | €2,502 | €2,119 |
| Working capital | 2,125 | 2,503 | 1,990 | 1,972 |
| **Net sales by brand** | | | | |
| adidas | €11,059 | €11,344 | €9,867 | €8,714 |
| Reebok | 1,599 | 1,667 | 1,940 | 1,913 |
| TaylorMade-adidas Golf | 1,285 | 1,344 | 1,044 | 909 |
| Rockport | 289 | 285 | 261 | 252 |
| Reebok-CCM Hockey | 260 | 243 | 210 | 200 |
| **Net sales by product** | | | | |
| Footwear | €6,873 | €6,992 | €6,275 | €5,389 |
| Apparel | 5,813 | 6,290 | 5,734 | 5,380 |
| Equipment | 1,806 | 1,691 | 1,335 | 1,221 |
| **Net sales by region** | | | | |
| Western Europe | €3,800 | €4,076 | €3,922 | €3,543 |
| European emerging markets | 1,894 | 1,947 | 1,596 | 1,385 |
| North America | 3,362 | 3,410 | 3,102 | 2,805 |
| Greater China | 1,655 | 1,562 | 1,229 | 1,000 |
| Other Asian markets | 2,206 | 2,407 | 2,125 | 1,972 |
| Latin America | 1,575 | 1,481 | 1,368 | 1,285 |

*Source:* Company annual reports, 2013, 2012, 2011, and 2010.

the company's 2013 total net sales of €14.5 billion), while retail sales at the company's various stores and websites were €3.45 billion (23.8 percent of 2013 net sales).

Like Under Armour and Nike, both adidas and Reebok were actively engaged in sponsoring major sporting events, teams, and leagues and in using athlete endorsements to promote their products. Recent high-profile sponsorships and promotional partnerships included official sportswear partner of the 2012 Olympic Games (adidas), outfitting all volunteers, technical staff, and officials as well as all the athletes in Team Great Britain; official sponsors and ball supplier of the 2010 FIFA World Cup, the 2011 FIFA Women's World Cup in Germany, the 2014 FIFA World Cup in Brazil (adidas), and numerous other important soccer tournaments held by FIFA and the Union of European Football Associations, or UEFA (adidas); official outfitters of NHL (Reebok), NFL (Reebok), NBA (adidas), WNBA (adidas), and NBA-Development League (adidas); official apparel and footwear outfitter for the Boston Marathon and the London Marathon (adidas); and official licensee of Major League Baseball fan and lifestyle apparel (Reebok). Athletes who were under contract to endorse various adidas Group brands included NBA players Derrick Rose, Tim Duncan, and John Wall; professional golfers Paula Creamer (LPGA), Jim Furyk, Sergio Garcia, Retief Goosen, Dustin Johnson, Kenny Perry, Justin Rose, and Mike Weir; soccer player David Beckham; tennis stars Andy Murray and Caroline Wozniacki; and various participants in the 2012 Summer Olympics in London and 2014 Winter Olympics in Sochi, Russia. In 2003, David Beckham, who had been wearing adidas products since the age of 12, signed a $160 million lifetime endorsement deal with adidas that called for an immediate payment of $80 million and subsequent payments said to be worth an average of $2 million annually for the next 40 years.[18] Adidas had been anxious to sign Beckham to a lifetime deal not only because doing so would prevent Nike from trying to sign him but also because soccer was considered the world's most lucrative sport and adidas management believed that Beckham's endorsement of adidas products would result in more sales than all of the company's other athlete endorsements combined. Companywide expenditures for advertising, event sponsorships, athlete endorsements, public relations, and other marketing activities were €1.46 billion in 2013, €1.50 billion in 2012, €1.36 billion in 2011, and €1.29 billion in 2010.

Research and development activities commanded considerable emphasis at The adidas Group. Management had long stressed the critical importance of innovation in improving the performance characteristics of the company's products. New apparel and footwear collections featuring new fabrics, colors, and the latest fashion were introduced on an ongoing basis to heighten consumer interest, as well as to provide performance enhancements— there were 39 "major product launches" in 2010, 48 in 2011, 36 in 2012, and 43 in 2013. About 1,000 people were employed in R&D activities at 10 locations, of which 4 were devoted to adidas products, 3 to Reebok products, and 1 each for TaylorMade-adidas Golf, Rockport, and Reebok-CCM Hockey. In addition to its own internal activities, the company drew upon the services of well-regarded researchers at universities in Canada, the United States, England, and Germany. Expenditures on R&D in 2013 were €128 million, versus €123 million in 2012, €115 million in 2011, and €102 million in 2010.

Over 95 percent of production was outsourced to 322 independent contract manufacturers located in China and other Asian countries (78 percent), the Americas (14 percent), Europe (7 percent), and Africa (less than 1 percent). The adidas Group operated 10 relatively small production and assembly sites of its own in Germany (1), Sweden (1), Finland (1), the United States (4), and Canada (3). Close to 96 percent of the Group's production of footwear was performed in Asia; annual volume sourced from footwear suppliers had ranged from a low of 171 million pairs to a high of 257 million pairs during 2009–2013. During the same time frame, apparel production ranged from 239 million to 321 million units, and the production of hardware products ranged from 34 million to 54 million units.

Executives at The adidas Group expected that the Group's global sales would reach €17 billion in 2015; management also wanted to achieve an 11 percent operating margin and grow annual earnings at a compound annual rate of 15 percent.

# ENDNOTES

1 "What's Driving Big Growth for Under Armour," www.trefis.com (accessed April 24, 2013); "Factors Underlying Our $74 Valuation of Under Armour, Part 1," www.trefis.com, February 28, 2014 (accessed March 18, 2014); Andria Cheng, "Underdog Under Armour Still Has a Long Way to Go to Catch Up with Nike," Marketwatch, www.marketwatch.com, October, 24, 2013 (accessed March 18, 2014).

2 Daniel Roberts, "Under Armour Gets Serious," Fortune, October 26, 2011, p. 156.

3 Ibid.

4 Ibid.

5 Ibid.

6 As stated on p. 53 of Under Armour's Prospectus for its initial public offering of common stock, November 17, 2005.

7 As stated in the company's slide presentation for Investors Day 2013, June 5, 2013.

8 Information contained in management's slide presentation for Investors Day 2013, June 5, 2013.

9 Sarah Meehan, "This $100 Premium Running Shoe Could Be Under Armour's Breakout Footwear Product," Baltimore Business Journal, January 31, 2014, www.bizjournals.com (accessed February 13, 2014).

10 Company 10-K reports, 2009, 2010, 2011, 2012, and 2013.

11 Company 10-K report, 2013, p. 55.

12 Presentation by Brad Dickerson (UA's CFO) to Raymond James Institutional Investors Conference, March 3, 2014, www.underarmour.com (accessed March 24, 2014).

13 According to information in the company's slide presentation for Investors Day 2013, June 5, 2013.

14 Ibid.

15 As stated in ibid.

16 According to a report by Transparency Market Research, "Athletic Footwear Market—Global Industry Size, Market Share, Trends, Analysis and Forecast, 2012–2018," as summarized in a September 26, 2012, press release by PR Newswire, www.prnewsire.com (accessed May 1, 2013).

17 Ibid. and "Factors Underlying Our $74 Valuation of Under Armour (Part 1)," www.trefis.com, February 28, 2014 (accessed March 18, 2014).

18 Steve Seepersaud, "5 of the Biggest Athlete Endorsement Deals," www.askmen.com (accessed February 5, 2012).

# Lululemon Athletica, Inc. in 2014: Can the Company Get Back on Track?

connect

## Arthur A. Thompson
### The University of Alabama

In April 2014, shareholders of lululemon athletica—a designer and retailer of high-tech athletic apparel under the lululemon athletica and ivivva athletica brand names that offered performance, fit, and comfort—were concerned whether customers were losing enthusiasm for the company's stylish, premium-priced products. Revenue growth of 16.1 percent in fiscal 2013 was well below the 36.9 percent increase in fiscal 2012. Sales at lululemon's retail stores open more than 12 months grew an average of only 2 percent (4 percent excluding the effect of adverse changes in foreign currency exchange rates) in fiscal 2013, compared to average sales growth of 16 percent in fiscal 2012 (both with and without the effects of changes in currency exchange rates). Of equal or greater concern, however, was the extent to which the company's brand image had been damaged by product quality problems encountered in March 2013 when shipments of women's black Luon pants proved to be sheer and revealing of the garments being worn underneath. Customer complaints about the see-through and unflattering nature of the fabric—which were quickly reported by the media because of the company's rapid growth and high public profile—prompted the company to quickly pull all of the affected items from the shelves of its retail stores (amounting to 17 percent of the company's inventory of yoga pants) and initiate expedited actions to work with the fabric supplier to correct the problem and with its garment manufacturers to get replacement products into its stores as quickly as possible. The lost sales, the additional costs incurred, and the write-downs on the affected inventory all had a significant negative bottom-line impact and were a big reason why lululemon's net income rose a meager 3.3 percent in fiscal 2013 after increasing a resounding 47 percent in fiscal 2012.

But the more pressing concern was the extent to which the incident with the overly sheer Luon pants and apparent lingering damage to lululemon's brand image in the last three quarters of 2013 would continue to haunt lululemon in upcoming years. Would strong sales growth at lululemon retail stores resume in 2014, or would sales stagnation continue, especially in light of the fact that several important competitors (Under Armour, Nike, adidas, and The Gap's new Athleta-brand retail stores) were broadening their product lines to include a bigger selection of fashionable, high-performance athletic and fitness apparel for women? Might the heretofore "must have" appeal of lululemon's functional and stylish apparel among fitness-conscious women be fading? Were a significant fraction of the company's customers switching to lower-priced brands and/or brands they considered to be more cutting edge, more trendsetting, or more appealingly designed? Was the market signaling that the "fad for lululemon apparel" was ending? What strategic actions could lululemon's management initiate to get strong revenue growth back on track? And, given whatever actions top management decided to take to rejuvenate sales growth, how long would it be before the company's stock price climbed from around $50 per share (where it traded for most of the first three months of 2014) back to around $80 per share (where it was trading in March 2013 when the problems with the black Luon pants first surfaced)?

# COMPANY BACKGROUND

A year after selling his eight-store surf-, skate- and snowboard-apparel chain called Westbeach Sports, Chip Wilson took the first commercial yoga class offered in Vancouver, British Columbia, and found the result exhilarating. But he found the cotton clothing used for sweaty, stretchy power yoga completely inappropriate. Wilson's passion was technical athletic fabrics, and in 1998 he opened a design studio for yoga clothing that also served as a yoga studio at night to help pay the rent. He began offering upscale yoga clothing made of performance fabrics and asked local yoga instructors to wear the products and give him feedback. Gratified by the positive response to yoga apparel, Wilson opened lululemon's first real store, in the beach area of Vancouver called Kitsilano, in November 2000.

While the store featured Wilson-designed yoga clothing, Chip Wilson's vision was for the store to be a community hub where people could learn and discuss the physical aspects of healthy living—from yoga and diet to running and cycling, plus the yoga-related mental aspects of living a powerful life of possibilities. But the store's clothing proved so popular that dealing with customers crowded out the community-based discussions and training about the merits of living healthy lifestyles. Nonetheless, Chip Wilson and store personnel were firmly committed to healthy, active lifestyles, and Wilson soon came to the conclusion that for the store to provide staff members with the salaries and opportunities required to experience fulfilling lives, the one-store company needed to expand into a multistore enterprise. Wilson believed that the increasing number of women participating in sports, and specifically yoga, provided ample room for expansion, and he saw lululemon athletica's yoga-inspired performance apparel as a way to address a void in the women's athletic apparel market. Wilson also saw the company's mission as one of providing people with the components for living a longer, healthier, and more fun life.

Several new stores were opened in the Vancouver area, with operations conducted through a Canadian operating company, initially named Lululemon Athletica, Inc., and later renamed lululemon canada inc. In 2002, the company expanded into the United States and formed a sibling operating company, Lululemon Athletica USA Inc. (later renamed as lululemon usa, inc.), to conduct its U.S. operations.

Both operating companies were wholly owned by affiliates of Chip Wilson. In 2004, the company contracted with a franchisee to open a store in Australia as a means of more quickly disseminating the lululemon athletica brand name, conserving on capital expenditures for store expansion (since the franchisee was responsible for the costs of operating the store), and boosting revenues and profits. The company wound up its fiscal year ending January 31, 2005, with 14 company-owned stores, 1 franchised store, and net revenues of $40.7 million. A second franchised store was opened in Japan later in 2005. Franchisees paid lululemon a one-time franchise fee and an ongoing royalty based on a specified percentage of net revenues; lululemon supplied franchised stores with garments at a discount to the suggested retail price.

Five years after the first retail store opened, it was apparent that lululemon apparel was fast becoming something of a cult phenomenon and a status symbol among yoga fans in areas where lululemon stores had opened. Avid yoga exercisers were not hesitating to purchase $120 color-coordinated lululemon yoga outfits that felt comfortable and made them look good. Mall developers and mall operators quickly learned about lululemon's success and began actively recruiting lululemon to lease space for stores in their malls.

In December 2005, with 27 company-owned stores, 2 franchised stores, and record sales approaching $85 million annually, Chip Wilson sold 48 percent of his interest in the company's capital stock to two private equity investors: Advent International Corporation, which purchased 38.1 percent of the stock, and Highland Capital Partners, which purchased a 9.6 percent ownership interest. In connection with the transaction, the owners formed lululemon athletica inc. to serve as a holding company for all of the company's related entities, including the two operating subsidiaries, lululemon canada inc. and lululemon usa inc. Robert Meers, who had 15 years' experience at Reebok and was Reebok's CEO from 1996 to 1999, joined lululemon as CEO in December 2005. Chip Wilson headed the company's design team and played a central role in developing the company's strategy and nurturing the company's distinctive corporate culture; he was also chairman of the company's board of directors, a position he had held since founding the company in 1998. Wilson and Meers assembled a management team with a mix of retail, design, operations, product sourcing, and marketing experience from such leading apparel and retail companies as Abercrombie & Fitch, Limited Brands, Nike, and Reebok.

Brisk expansion ensued. The company ended fiscal 2006 with 41 company-owned stores, 10 franchised stores, net revenues of $149 million, and net income of $7.7 million. In 2007, the company's owners elected to take the company public. The initial public offering took place on August 2, 2007, with the company selling 2,290,909 shares to the public and various stockholders selling 15,909,091 shares of their personal holdings. Shares began trading on the NASDAQ under the symbol "LULU" and on the Toronto Exchange under the symbol "LLL."

In 2007, the company's announced growth strategy had five key elements:

1. *Grow the company's store base in North America.* The strategic objective was to add new stores to strengthen the company's presence in locations where it had existing stores and then selectively enter new geographic markets in the United States and Canada. Management believed that the company's strong sales in its U.S. stores demonstrated the portability of the lululemon brand and retail concept.

2. *Increase brand awareness.* This initiative entailed leveraging the publicity surrounding the opening of new stores with grassroots marketing programs that included organizing events and partnering with local fitness practitioners.

3. *Introduce new product technologies.* Management intended to continue to focus on developing and offering products that incorporated technology-enhanced fabrics and performance features that differentiated lululemon apparel and helped broaden the company's customer base.

4. *Broaden the appeal of lululemon products.* This initiative entailed (1) adding a number of apparel items for men, (2) expanding product offerings for women and young females in such categories as athletic bags, undergarments, outerwear, and sandals, and (3) adding products suitable for additional sports and athletic activities.

5. *Expand beyond North America.* In the near term, the company planned to expand its presence in Australia and Japan and then, over time, pursue opportunities in other Asian and European markets that offered similar, attractive demographics.

The company grew rapidly. Fitness-conscious women began flocking to the company's stores not only because of the fashionable products but also because of the store ambience and attentive, knowledgeable store personnel. Dozens of new lululemon athletic retail stores were opened annually, and the company pursued a strategy of embellishing its product offerings to create a comprehensive line of apparel and accessories designed for athletic pursuits such as yoga, running, and general fitness; technical clothing for active female youths; and a selection of fitness and recreational items for men. Revenues topped $1 billion in fiscal 2011 and reached almost $1.6 billion in fiscal 2013. Headed into fiscal year 2014, the company's products could be bought at its 254 retail stores in the United States, Canada, Australia, and New Zealand; at the company's website, www.lululemon.com; and at assorted other locations. In the company's most recent fiscal year, ending February 2, 2014, retail store sales accounted for 81.7 percent of company revenues, website sales accounted for 16.5 percent, and sales in all other channels (showroom sales, sales at outlet centers, and wholesale sales to premium yoga studios, health clubs, and fitness centers) accounted for 7.7 percent.

Exhibit 1 presents highlights of the company's performance for fiscal years 2009–2013. Exhibit 2 shows lululemon's revenues by business segment and geographic region for the same period.

## Lululemon's Evolving Senior Leadership Team

In January 2008, Christine M. Day joined the company as executive vice president, Retail Operations. Previously, she had worked at Starbucks, functioning in a variety of capacities and positions, including president, Asia Pacific Group (July 2004 to February 2007); co-president, Starbucks Coffee International (July 2003 to October 2003); senior vice president, North American Finance & Administration; and vice president of sales and operations, Business Alliances. In April 2008, Day was appointed as lululemon's president and chief operating officer, and she was named chief executive officer and member of the board of directors in July 2008. During her tenure as CEO, Day expanded and strengthened the company's management team to support its expanding operating activities and geographic scope, favoring the addition of people with relevant backgrounds and

**EXHIBIT 1    Financial and Operating Highlights, Lululemon Athletica, Fiscal Years 2009–2013**

| | Fiscal Year 2013 (ending Feb. 2, 2014) | Fiscal Year 2012 (ending Feb. 3, 2013) | Fiscal Year 2011 (ending Jan. 29, 2012) | Fiscal Year 2010 (ending Jan. 30, 2011) | Fiscal Year 2009 (ending Jan. 31, 2010) |
|---|---|---|---|---|---|
| **Select income statement data (in millions, except per share data)** | | | | | |
| Net revenues | $1,591.2 | $1,370.4 | $1,000.8 | $711.7 | $452.9 |
| Cost of goods sold | 751.1 | 607.5 | 431.6 | 316.8 | 229.8 |
| Gross profit | 840.1 | 762.8 | 569.3 | 394.9 | 223.1 |
| Selling, general, and administrative expenses | 448.7 | 386.4 | 282.3 | 212.8 | 136.2 |
| Operating profit | 391.4 | 376.4 | 287.0 | 180.4 | 86.5 |
| Net profit (loss) | 279.5 | 271.4 | 185.0 | 121.8 | 58.3 |
| | | | | | |
| Earnings per share | | | | | |
| Basic | $1.93 | $1.88 | $1.29 | $0.86 | $0.41 |
| Diluted | 1.91 | 1.85 | 1.27 | 0.85 | 0.41 |
| **Balance sheet data (in millions)** | | | | | |
| Cash and cash equivalents | $ 698.6 | $ 590.2 | $409.4 | $316.3 | $159.6 |
| Inventories | 186.1 | 155.2 | 104.1 | 57.5 | 44.1 |
| Total assets | 1,250.0 | 1,051.1 | 734.6 | 499.3 | 307.3 |
| Stockholders' equity | 1,096.7 | 887.3 | 606.2 | 394.3 | 233.1 |
| **Cash flow and other data (in millions)** | | | | | |
| Net cash provided by operating activities | $278.3 | $280.1 | $203.6 | $180.0 | $118.0 |
| Capital expenditures | 106.4 | 93.2 | 116.7 | 30.4 | 15.5 |
| **Store data** | | | | | |
| Number of corporate-owned stores open at end of period | 254 | 211 | 174 | 133 | 110 |
| Number of franchised stores open at end of period | 0 | 0 | 0 | 4 | 14 |
| Sales per gross square foot at corporate-owned stores open at least 1 full year | $1,894 | $2,058 | $2,004 | $1,726 | $1,318 |
| Average sales at corporate-owned stores open at least 1 year | $5,440,000 | $5,830,000 | $5,330,000 | $4,960,000 | $3,760,000 |

*Source:* Company 10-K reports, fiscal years 2010, 2011, 2012, and 2013.

experiences at such companies as Nike, Abercrombie & Fitch, The Gap, and Speedo International. She also spent a number of hours each week in the company's stores observing how customers shopped, listening to their comments and complaints, and using the information to tweak product offerings, merchandising, and store operations.

Company founder Chip Wilson stepped down from his executive role as lululemon's chief innovation and branding officer on January 29, 2012, and moved

**EXHIBIT 2**   Lululemon Athletica's Revenues and Income from Operations, by Business Segment and Geographic Region, Fiscal Years 2009–2013 (dollar amounts in millions)

| | Fiscal Year 2013 (ending Feb. 2, 2014) | Fiscal Year 2012 (ending Feb. 3, 2013) | Fiscal Year2011 (ending Jan. 29, 2012) | Fiscal Year 2010 (ending Jan. 30, 2011) | Fiscal Year 2009 (ending Jan. 31, 2010) |
|---|---|---|---|---|---|
| **Revenues by business segment** | | | | | |
| Corporate-owned stores | $1,229.0 | $1,090.2 | $816.9 | $590.4 | $393.4 |
| Direct-to-consumer (e-commerce) sales | 263.1 | 197.3 | 106.3 | 57.3 | 18.3 |
| All other channels* | 99.1 | 82.9 | 77.6 | 64.0 | 41.2 |
| Total | $1,591.2 | $1,370.4 | $1,000.8 | $ 711.7 | $452.9 |
| **Percentage distribution of revenues by business segment** | | | | | |
| Corporate-owned stores | 77.3% | 79.6% | 81.6% | 83.0% | 86.9% |
| Direct-to-consumer (e-commerce) sales | 16.5% | 14.4% | 10.6% | 8.1% | 4.0% |
| All other channels* | 6.2% | 6.0% | 7.8% | 8.9% | 9.1% |
| Total | 100.0% | 100.0% | 100.0% | 100.0% | 100.0% |
| **Income from operations (before general corporate expenses), by business segment** | | | | | |
| Corporate-owned stores | $372.6 | $375.5 | $297.8 | $215.1 | $121.6 |
| Direct-to-consumer (e-commerce) sales | 109.6 | 84.7 | 44.2 | 16.4 | 6.3 |
| All other channels* | 16.1 | 19.9 | 21.1 | 18.0 | 10.8 |
| Total income from operations (before general corporate expenses) | $498.3 | $480.1 | $363.1 | $249.5 | $138.7 |
| **Revenues by geographic region** | | | | | |
| United States | $1,052.2 | $ 839.9 | $ 536.2 | $323.5 | $181.1 |
| Canada | 454.2 | 461.6 | 425.7 | 371.6 | 271.2 |
| Outside North America | 84.8 | 68.9 | 38.9 | 16.6 | 0.6 |
| Total | $1,591.2 | $1,370.4 | $1,000.8 | $ 711.7 | $452.9 |
| **Percentage distribution of revenues by geographic region** | | | | | |
| United States | 66.1% | 61.3% | 53.6% | 45.5% | 40.0% |
| Canada | 28.5% | 33.7% | 42.5% | 52.2% | 59.9% |
| Outside North America | 5.3% | 5.0% | 3.9% | 2.3% | 0.1% |
| Total | 99.9% | 100.0% | 100.0% | 100.0% | 100.0% |

*Includes showroom sales, sales at outlet centers, wholesale sales to premium yoga studios, health clubs, and fitness centers, and—in fiscal years 2009 and 2010—sales to franchised stores.

*Source:* Company 10-K reports, fiscal years 2011, 2012, and 2013.

his family to Australia; however, he continued in his role of chairman of the company's board of directors and focused on becoming a better board chairman, even going so far as to take a four-day course on board governance at Northwestern University.[1] Christine Day promoted Sheree Waterson, who had joined the company in 2008 and had over 25 years of consumer and retail industry experience, as chief product officer to assume responsibility for product design, product development, and other executive tasks that Wilson had been performing. Shortly after the quality problems with the black Luon pants occurred, Sheree Waterson resigned her position and left the company. In October 2013, lululemon announced that Tara Poseley had been appointed to its Senior Leadership Team as chief product officer and would have responsibility for overseeing lululemon's design team, product design activities, merchandising, inventory activities, and strategic planning. Previously, Poseley held the positions of interim president at Bebe Stores, Inc., president of Disney Stores North America (The Children's Place), and CEO of Design Within Reach (DWR), as well as a range of senior merchandising and design management positions during her 15-year tenure at The Gap Inc.

In the aftermath of the pants recall in March 2013, the working relationship between Christine Day and Chip Wilson deteriorated. Wilson made it clear that he would have handled the product recall incident differently and that he did not think there were problems with the design of the product or the quality of the fabric. But the differences between Day and Wilson went beyond the events of March 2013, especially when some consumers began to complain about the quality of the replacement pants. Wilson returned from Australia in May 2013, and weeks later Christine Day announced she would step down as CEO when her successor was named. A lengthy search for Day's replacement ensued.

In the meantime, Chip Wilson triggered a firestorm when, in an interview with Bloomberg TV in November 2013, he defended the company's design of the black Luon pants, saying, "Quite frankly, some women's bodies just actually don't work" with the pants. Although a few days later he publicly apologized for his remarks, which suggested that the company's product quality issues back in March 2013 were actually the fault of overweight women, his apology was not well received. In December 2013, Wilson resigned from his position as chairman of lululemon's board of directors and took on the lesser role of nonexecutive chairman. A few months later, Wilson announced that he intended to give up his position as nonexecutive chairman prior to the company's annual stockholders meeting in June 2014 but would continue as a member of the company's board of directors (in 2013–2014, Wilson was the company's largest stockholder and controlled 29.2 percent of the company's common stock).

In early December 2013, lululemon announced that its board of directors had appointed Laurent Potdevin as the company's chief executive officer and a member of its board of directors; Potdevin stepped into his role in January 2014, and, to help ensure a smooth transition, Christine Day remained with lululemon through the end of the company's fiscal year (February 2, 2014). Before joining lululemon, Potdevin served as president of TOMS Shoes, a company founded on the mission that it would match every pair of shoes purchased with a pair of new shoes given to a child in need. Prior to TOMS, Potdevin held numerous positions at Burton Snowboards for more than 15 years, including president and CEO from 2005 to 2010. Burton Snowboards, headquartered in Burlington, Vermont, was considered to be the world's premier snowboard company, with a product line that included snowboards and accessories (bindings, boots, socks, gloves, mitts, and beanies); men's, women's, and youths' snowboarding apparel; and bags and luggage. Burton grew significantly under Potdevin's leadership, expanding across product categories and opening additional retail stores.

## THE YOGA MARKETPLACE

According to a "Yoga in America" study funded by the *Yoga Journal,* as of 2012 there were 20.4 million people in the United States who practiced yoga, up from 15.8 million in a previous 2008 study. About 82 percent of the people who engaged in yoga exercises were women, and close to 63 percent of all yoga practitioners were in the 18–44 age range.[2] Just over 60 percent of the people who practiced yoga had done so for more than one year. The level of yoga expertise varied considerably: 44.8 percent of yoga practitioners considered themselves to be beginners, 39.6 percent considered themselves to be "intermediate," and 15.6 percent considered themselves to be in the expert or advanced category. Spending on yoga classes, yoga apparel, and related items was an estimated $10.3 billion in 2012, up from $5.7 billion in 2008.[3]

The market for sports and fitness apparel was considerably larger, of course, than just the market for yoga apparel, which was in the $2 billion to $2.5 billion range in 2013. In the United States, sales of activewear and all types of gym and fitness apparel in 2014 were expected to be approximately $8 billion to $10 billion by some estimates and as high as $13 billion by other estimates, which included both items made with high-tech performance fabrics that wicked away moisture and items made mostly of cotton, polyester, stretch fabrics, and certain other man-made fibers that lacked moisture-wicking and other high-performance features. In the United States (as well as in many other countries), the market for all types of activewear was the fastest-growing segment of the apparel industry.[4] The global market for all types of sportswear, activewear, and athletic apparel, estimated to be $135 billion in 2012, was forecast to grow about 4 percent annually and reach about $178 billion by 2019.[5]

## LULULEMON'S STRATEGY AND BUSINESS IN 2014

Lululemon athletica viewed its core mission as "creating components for people to live longer, healthier, fun lives."[6] The company's primary target customer was:

> a sophisticated and educated woman who understands the importance of an active, healthy lifestyle. She is increasingly tasked with the dual responsibilities of career and family and is constantly challenged to balance her work, life and health. We believe she pursues exercise to achieve physical fitness and inner peace.[7]

In the company's early years, lululemon's strategy was predicated on management's belief that other athletic apparel companies were not effectively addressing the unique style, fit, and performance needs of women who were embracing yoga and a variety of other fitness and athletic activities. Lululemon sought to address this void in the marketplace by incorporating style, feel-good comfort, and functionality into its yoga-inspired apparel products and by building a network of lululemon retail stores, along with an online store at the company's website, to market its apparel directly to these women. However, while the company was founded to address the unique needs and preferences of women, management recognized the merits of broadening the company's market target to include fitness apparel for activities other than yoga and apparel for population segments other than adult women. Recently, it had begun designing and marketing products for

men and athletic female youths who appreciated the technical rigor and premium quality of athletic and fitness apparel. Management also believed that participation in athletic and fitness activities was destined to climb as people over 60 years of age became increasingly focused on living longer, healthier, active lives in their retirement years and engaged in regular exercise and recreational activities. Another demand-enhancing factor was that consumers' decisions to purchase athletic, fitness, and recreational apparel were being driven not only by an actual need for functional products but also by a desire to create a particular lifestyle perception through the apparel they wore. Consequently, over the past three to four years, senior executives had been transitioning lululemon's strategy from one of focusing exclusively on the market for yoga apparel for women to one aimed at designing and marketing a wider range of fitness apparel to a wider segment of the population.

As lululemon began fiscal year 2014, the company's business strategy had seven core components, five of which were essentially carryovers from the strategy that top management had launched when lululemon athletica became a public company in mid-2007:

- Broaden the lululemon product line beyond yoga, running, and general fitness (specifically swimming, golf, and tennis) and include offerings for both males and females of many ages.
- Grow the store base in North America, primarily the United States.
- Open additional stores outside North America.
- Broaden awareness of the lululemon and ivivva brands and the nature and quality of the company's apparel offerings.
- Provide a distinctive in-store shopping experience, complemented with strong ties to fitness instructors and fitness establishments, local athletes and fitness-conscious people, and various community-based athletic and fitness events.
- Grow traffic and sales at the company's websites to provide a distinctive and satisfying online shopping experience and to extend the company's products into geographic markets where it did not have retail stores.
- Incorporate next-generation fabrics and technologies in the company's products to strengthen consumers' association of the lululemon and ivivva

brands with technically advanced fabrics and innovative features, thereby enabling lululemon to command higher prices for its products compared to the prices of traditional fitness and recreational apparel products made of cotton, rayon, polyester, and/or other man-made fibers lacking the performance features of high-tech fabrics.

## Product Line Strategy

In 2014, lululemon offered a diverse and growing selection of premium-priced performance apparel and accessories for women, men, and female youths that were designed for healthy lifestyle activities such as yoga, running, and general fitness. While many of its products were specifically intended for the growing number of people who participated in yoga, the company had, for some years, been broadening its product range to address the needs of other activities. Swimwear selections for women had been introduced in fiscal 2013, and several men's swimwear items were introduced in spring 2014. Management had indicated that apparel suitable for golf and tennis would soon be forthcoming. In 2014, the company's range of offerings included a growing number of categories (see the table below).

Exhibit 3 shows a sampling of lululemon's products for men and women.

Most of the company's products for female youths were sold at ivivva stores and at the ivivva website, www.ivivva.com. The ivivva product line, while featuring dancing apparel, also included apparel for yoga and running; specific apparel items available under the ivivva label included leotards, shorts, dance pants, crop pants, tights, sports bras, tank tops, tees, jackets, hoodies, pullovers, caps, headbands, socks, bags, and other accessories.

**Lululemon's Strategy of Offering Only a Limited Range of Apparel Sizes**    In the months following the product recall of the too-sheer pants in March 2013, lululemon officially revealed in a posting on its Facebook page that it did not offer clothing in plus sizes because focusing on sizes 12 and below was an integral part of its business strategy; according to the company's posting and to the postings of lululemon personnel who responded to comments made by Facebook members who read the lululemon posting:[8]

> Our product and design strategy is built around creating products for our target guest in our size range of 2–12. While we know that doesn't work for everyone and recognize fitness and health come in all shapes and sizes, we've built our business, brand and relationship with our guests on this formula.
>
> We agree that a beautiful healthy life is not measured by the size you wear. We want to be excellent at what we do, so this means that we can't be everything to everybody and need to focus on specific areas. Our current focuses are in innovating our women's design, men's brand, and building our international market.
>
> At this time, we don't have plans to change our current sizing structure which is 2–12 for women.

## Retail Distribution and Store Expansion Strategy

After several years of experience in establishing and working with franchised stores in the United States, Australia, Japan, and Canada, top management in 2010 determined that having franchised stores was not in lululemon's best long-term strategic interests.

| Women | | Men |
|---|---|---|
| • Sports bras | • Swimwear | • Tops |
| • Tanks | • Socks and underwear | • Jackets and hoodies |
| • Tops | • Gear bags | • Shorts |
| • Jackets | • Caps and headbands | • Pants |
| • Hoodies | • Sweat cuffs and gloves | • Gear bags |
| • Pants | • Water bottles | • Swimwear |
| • Crops | • Yoga mats and props | • Socks and underwear |
| • Shorts | • Instructional yoga DVDs | • Caps and gloves |
| • Skirts and dresses | | • Yoga mats, props, and instructional DVDs |

# EXHIBIT 3    Examples of Lululemon Apparel Items

*Source:* All photos provided by lululemon; used with permission.

A strategic initiative was begun to either acquire the current stores of franchisees and operate them as company stores or convert the franchised stores to a joint venture arrangement in which lululemon owned the controlling interest in the store and the former franchisee owned a minority interest. In some cases, contracts with franchisees contained a clause allowing lululemon to acquire a franchised store at a specified percentage of trailing 12-month sales. The three franchised stores in Canada became company-owned in 2009 and 2010. The franchise rights of nine store locations in Australia, in which lululemon already had an ownership interest, were acquired during 2010; five of nine franchised stores in the United States were converted to company-owned in 2010. The franchised store established in Japan in 2005 was converted to a company-owned

store months after it opened. The last four franchised stores—three in Colorado and one in California—were reacquired in 2011.

As of February 2014, lululemon's retail footprint included:

- 54 stores in Canada scattered across seven provinces, but mainly located in British Columbia, Alberta, and Ontario.
- 171 company-owned stores in the United States (38 states and the District of Columbia).
- 25 stores in Australia.
- 4 stores in New Zealand.

Virtually all these stores were branded lululemon athletica, but 12 company-owned stores were branded ivivva athletica and specialized in dance-inspired apparel for female youths. Lululemon's management evaluated the company's portfolio of company-owned store locations on an ongoing basis. Since 2009, five underperforming stores had been closed.

Management had announced that near-term store expansion efforts would be concentrated mainly in the United States and that lululemon would gradually expand into additional countries, primarily in Asia and Europe, either by opening company-owned stores or by entering into joint ventures with experienced and capable retail partners. In fiscal 2014, the company planned to open 39 new stores (including 10 ivivva athletica stores) in North America, 2 new lululemon stores in Australia, and 2 new international lululemon stores.

Management believed its sales-per-square-foot performance (see the bottom portion of Exhibit 1) had consistently been among the best in the retail apparel sector—for example, the stores of specialty fashion retailers like Old Navy, Banana Republic, The Gap, and Abercrombie & Fitch typically had annual sales averaging less than $500 per square foot of store space.

**Lululemon's Retail Stores: Locations, Layout, and Merchandising**    The company's retail stores were located primarily on street locations, in upscale strip shopping centers, in lifestyle centers, and in malls. Typically, stores were leased and were 2,500 to 3,000 square feet in size. Almost all stores included space for product display and merchandising, checkout, fitting rooms, a restroom, and an office and storage area. While the leased nature of the store spaces meant that each store had its own customized layout and arrangement of fixtures and displays, each store was carefully decorated and laid out in a manner that projected the ambience and feel of a homespun local apparel boutique rather than the more impersonal, cookie-cutter atmosphere of many apparel chain stores.

The company's merchandising strategy was to sell all of the items in its retail stores at full price.[9] Special colors and seasonal items were in stores for only a limited time—such products were on 3-, 6-, or 12-week life cycles so that frequent shoppers could always find something new. Store inventories of short-cycle products were deliberately limited to help foster a sense of scarcity, condition customers to buy when they saw an item rather than wait,

and avoid any need to discount unsold items. In one instance, a hot-pink color that launched in December was supposed to have a two-month shelf life, but supplies sold out in the first week. However, supplies of core products that did not change much from season to season were more ample to minimize the risk of lost sales due to items being out of stock. Approximately 95 percent of the merchandise in lululemon stores was sold at full price.[10]

One unique feature of lululemon's retail stores was that the floor space allocated to merchandising displays and customer shopping could be sufficiently cleared to enable the store to hold an in-store yoga class before or after regular shopping hours. Every store hosted a complimentary yoga class each week that was conducted by a professional yoga instructor from the local community who had been recruited to be a "store ambassador"; when the class concluded, the attendees were given a 15 percent–off coupon to use in shopping for products in the store. From time to time, each store's yoga ambassadors demonstrated their moves in the store windows and on the sales floor. Exhibit 4 shows the exteriors and interiors of representative lululemon athletica stores.

**Lululemon's    Showroom    Strategy**    Over the years, lululemon had opened "showrooms" in numerous locations both inside and outside North America as a means of introducing the lululemon brand and culture to a community, developing relationships with local fitness instructors and fitness enthusiasts, and hosting community-related fitness events, all in preparation for the grand opening of a new lululemon athletica retail store in the weeks ahead. Showroom personnel:

• Hosted get-acquainted parties for fitness instructors and fitness enthusiasts.

• Recruited a few well-regarded fitness instructors in the local area to be store ambassadors for lululemon products and periodically conduct in-store yoga classes when the local lululemon retail store opened.

• Advised people visiting the showroom on where to find great yoga or Pilates classes, fitness centers, and health and wellness information and events.

• Solicited a select number of local yoga studios, health clubs, and fitness centers to stock and retail a small assortment of lululemon's products.

**EXHIBIT 4**   Representative Exterior and Interior Scenes at Lululemon Stores

*Source:* Photos provided by lululemon, used with permission.

Showrooms were open only part of the week so that personnel could be out in the community meeting people, participating in local yoga and fitness classes, promoting attendance at various fitness activities and wellness events, and stimulating interest in the soon-to-open retail store.

As of February 2014, lululemon had 17 showrooms in operation outside North America, up from 5 such showrooms a year earlier. In fiscal 2008, lululemon opened its first company-operated showroom in Hong Kong, and in fiscal 2012 it opened the first company-operated showroom in the United Kingdom. In fiscal 2013, additional showrooms in Hong Kong and the United Kingdom were opened, and the first showrooms were opened in Germany, Singapore, the Netherlands, and mainland China. In fiscal 2014 and 2015, management expected to open additional showrooms in Asia and Europe as a means of "preseeding" the opening of retail stores in the Asian and European markets. In North America, lululemon's management in 2010 began cutting back on opening showrooms as a prelude to opening its first retail store in a new geographic area because of the growing number of retail store locations, increased consumer awareness of the lululemon brand, and accelerating traffic and sales at the company's website, **www.lululemon.com**.

## Wholesale Sales Strategy

Lululemon marketed its products to select premium yoga studios, health clubs, and fitness centers as a way to gain the implicit endorsement of local fitness personnel for lululemon-branded apparel, familiarize its customers with the lululemon brand, and give them an opportunity to conveniently purchase lululemon apparel. Also, when certain styles, colors, and sizes of apparel items at lululemon retail stores were selling too slowly for the company to rid itself of the volumes ordered from contract manufacturers, lululemon typically shipped the excess inventories to one or more of the nine lululemon factory outlet stores in North America to be sold at discounted prices.

Lululemon's management did not want to grow wholesale sales to these types of establishments into a significant revenue contributor. Rather, the strategic objective of selling lululemon apparel to yoga studios, health clubs, and fitness centers was to build brand awareness, especially in new geographic markets in both North America and other international locations where the company intended to open new stores. Wholesale sales to outlet stores were made only to dispose of excess inventories and thereby avoid in-store markdowns on slow-selling items. The company's wholesale sales to all these channels accounted for just 1.4 percent of net revenues in fiscal 2013, versus 1.5 percent in fiscal 2012 and 2.2 percent in fiscal 2011.

## Direct-to-Consumer Sales Strategy

In 2009, lululemon launched its e-commerce website, **www.lululemon.com**, to enable customers to make online purchases, supplement its already-functioning phone sales activities, and greatly extend the company's geographic market reach. Management saw online sales as having three strategic benefits: (1) providing added convenience for core customers, (2) securing sales in geographic markets where there were no lululemon stores, and (3) helping build brand awareness, especially in new markets, including those outside North America. As of early 2014, the company operated country- and region-specific websites in Australia, Europe, and Asia and brand-specific websites for both lululemon and ivivva (www.ivivva.com) products in North America. Lululemon provided free shipping on all lululemon and ivivva orders to customers in North America; a shipping fee was charged to a number of international destinations.

The merchandise selection that lululemon offered to online buyers differed somewhat from what was available in the company's retail stores. A number of the items available in stores were not sold online; a few online selections were not available in the stores. Styles and colors available for sale online were updated weekly. On occasion, the company marked down the prices of some styles and colors sold online to clear out the inventories of items soon to be out of season and make way for newly arriving merchandise—online customers could view the discounted merchandise by clicking on the We Made Too Much link.

Since 2009, direct-to-consumer sales at the company's websites had become an increasingly important part of the company's business, with net revenues climbing from $18.3 million in fiscal 2009 when e-commerce sales first began to $263.1 million in fiscal 2013—equal to a hefty compound annual growth rate of 94.7 percent.

In addition to making purchases, website visitors could browse information about what yoga was, what the various types of yoga were, and what their benefits were; learn about fabrics and technologies used in lululemon's products; read recent posts on lululemon's yoga blog; and stay abreast of lululemon activities in their communities. The company planned to continue to develop and enhance its e-commerce websites in ways that would provide a distinctive online shopping experience and strengthen its brand reputation.

## Product Design and Development Strategy

Lululemon's product design efforts were led by a team of designers based in Vancouver, British Columbia, who partnered with various international designers. The design team included athletes and users of the company's products who embraced lululemon's design philosophy and dedication to premium quality. Design team members regularly visited retail stores in a proactive effort to solicit feedback on existing products from store customers and fitness ambassadors and to gather their ideas for product improvements and new products. In addition, the design team used various market intelligence sources to identify and track market trends. On occasion, the team hosted meetings in several geographic markets to discuss the company's products with local athletes, trainers, yogis, and members of the fitness industry. The design team incorporated all of this input to make fabric selections, develop new products, and make adjustments in the fit, style, and function of existing products.

The design team worked closely with its apparel manufacturers to incorporate innovative fabrics that gave lululemon garments such characteristics as stretch ability, moisture-wicking capability, colorfastness, feel-good comfort, and durability. Fabric quality was evaluated via actual wear tests and by a leading testing facility. Before bringing out new products with new fabrics, lululemon used the services of leading independent inspection, verification, testing, and certification companies to conduct a battery of tests on fabrics for such performance characteristics as pilling, shrinkage, abrasion resistance, and colorfastness. Lastly, lululemon design personnel worked with leading fabric suppliers to identify opportunities to develop fabrics that lululemon could trademark and thereby gain added brand recognition and brand differentiation. Trademarked fabrics currently incorporated in lululemon products included Luon, Silverescent, VitaSea, Boolux, Luxtreme, Luxchange, Groove Pant, Light as Air, and Power Y. In addition to trademarks, the company owned 29 industrial-design registrations in Canada that protected its distinctive apparel and accessory designs, as well as a number of corresponding design patents in the United States and registered community designs in Europe.

Where appropriate, product designs incorporated convenience features, such as pockets to hold credit cards, keys, digital audio players, and clips for heart-rate monitors and long sleeves that covered the hands for cold-weather exercising. Product specifications called for the use of advanced sewing techniques, such as flat seaming, that increased comfort and functionality, reduced chafing and skin irritation, and strengthened important seams. All of these design elements and fabric technologies were factors that management believed enabled lululemon to price its high-quality technical athletic apparel at prices above those of traditional athletic apparel.

Typically, it took 8 to 10 months for lululemon products to move from the design stage to availability in its retail stores; however, the company had the capability to bring select new products to market in as little as two months. Management believed its lead times were shorter than those of most apparel brands due to the company's streamlined design and development process, the real-time input received from customers and ambassadors at its store locations, and the short times it took to receive and approve samples from manufacturing suppliers. Short lead times facilitated quick responses to emerging trends or shifting market conditions.

Lululemon's management believed that its design process enhanced the company's capabilities to develop top-quality products and was a competitive strength.

## Sourcing and Manufacturing

Production was the only value chain activity that lululemon did not perform internally. Lululemon did not own or operate any manufacturing facilities to produce fabrics or make garments. Fabrics were sourced from a group of approximately 65 fabric manufacturers. Luon, which constituted about 30 percent of the fabric in lululemon's garments, was supplied by a single fabric maker. Garments were sourced from approximately 30 contract manufacturers, 5 of which produced approximately 67 percent of the company's products in fiscal 2013. However, the company deliberately refrained from entering into long-term contracts with any of its fabric suppliers or manufacturing sources, preferring instead to transact business on an order-by-order basis and rely on the close working relationships it had developed with its various suppliers over the years. During fiscal 2013, approximately 67 percent of the company's products were produced in South and Southeast Asia, approximately 23 percent in China, approximately 3 percent in North America, and the remainder in other countries.

Lululemon took great care to ensure that its manufacturing suppliers shared its commitment to quality and ethical business conduct. All manufacturers were required to adhere to a vendor code of ethics regarding quality of manufacturing, working conditions, environmental responsibility, fair wage practices, and child labor laws, among other factors. Lululemon utilized the services of a leading inspection and verification firm to closely monitor each supplier's compliance with applicable law, lululemon's vendor code of ethics, and other business practices in which noncompliance could reflect badly on lululemon's choice of suppliers.

The company's North American manufacturers were the reason lululemon had the capability to speed select products to market and respond quickly to changing trends and unexpectedly high buyer demand for certain products. While management expected to utilize manufacturers outside North America to supply the bulk of its apparel requirement in the years to come, it intended to maintain production in Canada and the United States whenever possible.

## Distribution Facilities

Lululemon shipped products to its stores in North America from a leased 102,000-square-foot facility in Vancouver, British Columbia, and a leased 82,000-square-foot facility in Sumner, Washington. Both were modern and cost-efficient. In 2011, the company began operations at a leased 54,000-square-foot distribution center in Melbourne, Australia, to supply its stores in Australia and New Zealand. During fiscal 2013, lululemon purchased a distribution facility in Columbus, Ohio, that it expected to open in 2014. Management believed these four facilities would be sufficient to accommodate its expected store growth and expanded product offerings over the next several years. Merchandise was typically shipped to retail stores through third-party delivery services multiple times per week, providing them with a steady flow of new inventory.

## Lululemon's Community-Based Marketing Approach and Brand-Building Strategy

One of lululemon's differentiating characteristics was its community-based approach to building brand awareness and customer loyalty. Local fitness practitioners chosen to be ambassadors introduced their fitness class attendees to the lululemon brand, thereby leading to interest in the brand, store visits, and word-of-mouth marketing. Each yoga-instructor ambassador was also called upon to conduct a complimentary yoga class every four to six weeks at the local lululemon store the ambassador was affiliated with. In return for helping drive business to lululemon stores and conducting classes, ambassadors were periodically given bags of free products, and billboard-sized portraits of each ambassador wearing lululemon products and engaging in physical activity at a local landmark were posted in his or her local lululemon store, which helped the ambassadors expand their clientele.

Every lululemon store had a dedicated community coordinator who developed a customized plan for organizing, sponsoring, and participating in local athletic, fitness, and philanthropic events. In addition, each store had a community events bulletin board for posting announcements of upcoming activities, providing fitness education information and brochures, and promoting the local yoga studios and fitness centers of ambassadors. There was also a chalkboard in each store's fitting-room area on which customers could scribble comments about lululemon products, their yoga class experiences, or store personnel; these comments were relayed to lululemon headquarters every two weeks. Customers could use a lululemon micro-website to track their progress regarding fitness or life goals.

Lululemon made little use of traditional print or television advertisements, preferring instead to rely on its various grassroots, community-based marketing efforts and the use of social media (like Facebook and Twitter) to increase brand awareness, reinforce its premium-brand image, and broaden the appeal of its products.

## Store Personnel

As part of the company's commitment to providing customers with an inviting and educational store environment, lululemon's store sales associates, who the company referred to as *educators,* were coached to personally engage and connect with each guest who entered the store. Educators, many of whom had prior experience as a fitness practitioner or were avid runners or yoga enthusiasts, received approximately 30 hours of in-house training within the first three months of their employment.

Training was focused on (1) teaching educators about leading a healthy and balanced life, exercising self-responsibility, and setting lifestyle goals, (2) preparing them to explain the technical and innovative design aspects of all lululemon products, and (3) providing the information needed for educators to serve as knowledgeable references for customers seeking information on fitness classes, instructors, and events in the community. New hires who lacked knowledge about the intricacies of yoga were given subsidies to attend yoga classes so that they could understand the activity and better explain the benefits of lululemon's yoga apparel.

People who shopped at lululemon stores were called *guests,* and store personnel were expected to educate guests about lululemon's apparel, not sell to them. To provide a personalized, welcoming, and relaxed experience, store educators referred to their guests on a first-name basis in the fitting and changing area, allowed them to use store restrooms, and offered them complimentary fresh-filtered water. Management believed that such a soft-sell, customer-centric environment encouraged product trial, purchases, and repeat visits.

## Core Values and Culture

Consistent with the company's mission of "providing people with the components to live a longer, healthier and more fun life," lululemon's executives sought to promote and ingrain a set of core values centered on developing the highest-quality products, operating with integrity, leading a healthy, balanced life, and instilling in employees a sense of self-responsibility and the value of goal setting. The company sought to provide employees with a supportive and goal-oriented work environment; all employees were encouraged to set goals aimed at reaching their full professional, health, and personal potential. The company offered personal development workshops and goal coaching to assist employees in achieving their goals. Many lululemon employees had a written set of professional, health, and personal goals. All employees had access to a "learning library" of personal development books that included Stephen Covey's *The 7 Habits of Highly Effective People,* Rhonda Byrne's *The Secret,* and Brian Tracy's *The Psychology of Achievement.*

Chip Wilson had been the principal architect of the company's culture and core values, and the company's work climate through 2013 reflected his business and lifestyle philosophy. Wilson had digested much of his philosophy about life in general and personal development into a set of statements and prescriptions that he called "the lululemon manifesto" (see Exhibit 5). The manifesto was considered to be a core element of lululemon's culture. Senior executives believed the company's work climate and core values helped it attract passionate and motivated employees who were driven to succeed and who would support the company's vision of "elevating the world from mediocrity to greatness"—a phrase coined by Chip Wilson in the company's early years.

Top management believed that its relationship with company employees was exceptional and a key contributor to the company's success.

## COMPETITION

Competition in the market for athletic and fitness apparel was principally centered on product quality, performance features, innovation, fit and style, distribution capabilities, brand image and recognition, and price. Rivalry among competing brands was vigorous, involving both established companies that were expanding their production and marketing of performance products and recent entrants that were attracted by the growth opportunities.

Lululemon competed with wholesalers and direct sellers of premium performance athletic apparel made of high-tech fabrics, especially Nike, The adidas Group AG (which marketed athletic and sports apparel under its adidas, Reebok, and Ashworth brands), and Under Armour. Nike had a powerful and well-known global brand name, an extensive and diverse line of athletic and sports apparel, 2013 apparel sales of $6.8 billion ($3 billion in North America), and 2013 total revenues (footwear, apparel, and equipment) of $25.3 billion. Nike was the world's largest seller of athletic footwear and athletic apparel, with over 40,000 retail accounts, 753 company-owned stores, 23 distribution centers, and selling arrangements with independent distributors and licensees in over 190 countries; its retail account base for sports apparel in the United States included a mix of sporting goods stores, athletic specialty stores, department stores, and skate, tennis, and golf shops.

Reebok and adidas were both global brands that generated worldwide sports apparel revenues of approximately $7.8 billion in 2013; their product lines consisted of high-tech performance garments for a wide variety of sports and fitness activities, as well as recreational sportswear. The adidas Group sold products in virtually every country of the world. In 2013, its extensive product offerings were marketed through third-party retailers (sporting goods chains, department stores, independent sporting goods retailer buying groups, lifestyle retailing chains, and Internet retailers), 1,661 company-owned and franchised adidas and Reebok "concept" stores, 779 company-owned adidas and Reebok factory outlet stores, 300 other adidas and Reebok stores with varying formats, and various company websites (including **www.adidas.com** and **www.reebok.com**).

Under Armour, an up-and-coming designer and marketer of performance sports apparel, had total sales of $2.33 billion in 2013, of which $1.76 billion was in apparel. Like lululemon, Under Armour's apparel products were made entirely of technically advanced, high-performance fabrics and were designed to be aesthetically appealing as well as highly functional and comfortable. Under Armour regularly upgraded its products as next-generation fabrics with better performance characteristics became available. Under Armour's product line included men's apparel (2013 sales of approximately $960 million), women's apparel (2013 sales of approximately $500 million), and youths' apparel (2013 sales of about $220 million). Management was actively pursuing efforts to grow its apparel sales in the men's, women's, and youths' segments, with an apparel sales target of $2.9 billion in 2016. Under Armour's business was currently concentrated in North America (94 percent of 2013 sales revenues), but it was upping its efforts to expand globally. Under Armour's products were available in 25,000 retail stores worldwide, 18,000 of which were in Canada and the United States. Under Armour also sold its products directly to consumers through its own factory outlet and specialty stores and its website.

Nike, The adidas Group, and Under Armour all aggressively marketed and promoted their high-performance apparel products and spent heavily to grow consumer awareness of their brands and build brand loyalty. All three sponsored numerous athletic events, provided uniforms and equipment with their logos to collegiate and professional sports teams,

# EXHIBIT 5   The Lululemon Manifesto

- Drink FRESH water and as much water as you can. Water flushes unwanted toxins from your body and keeps your brain sharp.
- A daily hit of athletic-induced endorphins gives you the power to make better decisions, helps you be at peace with yourself, and offsets stress.
- Do one thing a day that scares you.
- Listen, listen, listen, and then ask strategic questions.
- Write down your short and long-term GOALS four times a year. Two personal, two business and two health goals for the next 1, 5, and 10 years. Goal setting triggers your subconscious computer.
- Life is full of setbacks. Success is determined by how you handle setbacks.
- Your outlook on life is a direct reflection of how much you like yourself.
- That which matters the most should never give way to that which matters the least.
- Stress is related to 99 percent of all illness.
- Jealousy works the opposite way you want it to.
- The world is changing at such a rapid rate that waiting to implement changes will leave you 2 steps behind. Do it now, do it now, do it now!
- Friends are more important than money.
- Breathe deeply and appreciate the moment. Living in the moment could be the meaning of life.
- Take various vitamins. You never know what small mineral can eliminate the bottleneck to everlasting health.
- Don't trust that an old age pension will be sufficient.
- Visualize your eventual demise. It can have an amazing effect on how you live for the moment.
- The conscious brain can only hold one thought at a time. Choose a positive thought.
- Live near the ocean and inhale the pure salt air that flows over the water (Vancouver will do nicely).
- Observe a plant before and after watering and relate these benefits to your body and brain.
- Practice yoga so you can remain active in physical sports as you age.
- Dance, sing, floss and travel.
- Children are the orgasm of life. Just like you did not know what an orgasm was before you had one, nature does not let you know how great children are until you have them.
- Successful people replace the words "wish," "should" and "try," with "I will."
- Creativity is maximized when you're living in the moment.
- Nature wants us to be mediocre because we have a greater chance to survive and reproduce. Mediocre is as close to the bottom as it is to the top, and will give you a lousy life.
- Lululemon athletica creates components for people to live longer, healthier and more fun lives. If we can produce products to keep people active and stress-free, we believe the world will become a much better place.
- Do not use cleaning chemicals on your kitchen counters. Someone will inevitably make a sandwich on your counter.
- SWEAT once a day to regenerate your skin.
- The perfect tombstone would read "all used up."
- 10–15 friends allows for real relationships.
- Communication is COMPLICATED. We are all raised in a different family with slightly different definitions of every word. An agreement is an agreement only if each party knows the conditions for satisfaction and a time is set for satisfaction to occur.
- What we do to the earth we do to ourselves.
- The pursuit of happiness is the source of all unhappiness.

*Source:* www.lululemon.com (accessed February 12, 2012).

and paid millions of dollars annually to numerous high-profile male and female athletes to endorse their products. Like lululemon, they designed their own products but outsourced the production of their garments to contract manufacturers.

## Three New Formidable Competitors Emerge

Headed into 2014, lululemon was confronted with increasingly stiff competition from three specialty retailers that had taken note of lululemon's success and opted to significantly expand their offerings of women's activewear and fitness apparel:

- *Athleta.* Athleta was a relatively new chain and online retailer (**athleta.gap.com**) that specialized in comfortable, fashionable, high-performance women's apparel for workouts, sports, physically active recreational activities, and leisure wear. The chain had grown from 1 retail store in 2011 to 65 retail stores coast to coast as of early 2014; more Athleta stores were expected to open in 2014 and beyond. Athleta's expanding product line included swimwear, tops, bras, jackets, sweaters, pants, tights, shorts, T-shirt dresses, performance footwear, sneakers, sandals, bags, headwear, and gear. Items were colorful, stylish, and functional. In April 2014, the array of apparel items and color selections at Athleta's website exceeded those at lululemon's website; Athleta's online sales grew 21 percent in 2013. A number of items in Athleta's retail stores and at its website were available in tall and petite sizes, as well as large and extra-large sizes. According to Nancy Green, Athleta's general manager, "Many of our competitors offer performance or lifestyle apparel, but we have extraordinary expertise and strength in both categories. It's about owning the fusion of premium performance, fashion, and lifestyle." Athleta utilized well-known women athletes and local fitness instructors to serve as brand ambassadors by blogging for Athleta's website, teaching classes at local stores, and testing Athleta garments. In 2012, Athleta initiated its first national advertising campaign, "Power to the She," to promote the Athleta brand. In addition, Athleta had a special social media website, **www.athleta.net/chi**, that connected women with interests in sports and fitness, nutrition and health, tutorials and training plans, and travel and adventure. Athleta was a subsidiary of The Gap, Inc.; in 2013, Gap had 3,095 company-operated retail stores worldwide and 312 franchised stores that operated under such brand names as Gap, Old Navy, Banana Republic, Athleta, and Intermix. The product offerings at the 1,236 Gap-branded stores included a GapFit collection of fitness and lifestyle products for women.

- *Lucy.* Lucy was a women's activewear brand designed for style, performance, and fit that was intended for yoga, running, training, and other fitness and active recreational activities; the product offerings included tops, bottoms, skirts, dresses, jackets, hoodies, sports bras, socks, caps, headbands, and bags and totes. Apparel was made from five lucy signature fabrics, each with different combinations of performance features that included moisture-wicking, odor-inhibiting, seamless, stretch, thermal warmth, wind resistant, and water resistant. Many garments were offered in three distinct fits: relaxed, body skimming, and body hugging. Pants came in three lengths (short, regular, and tall). Garments were typically offered in six sizes: XXS, XS, S, M, L, and XL. Lucy-branded performance apparel was sold at 63 company-owned lucy stores in 15 states and the District of Columbia and at **www.lucy.com**; plans called for opening additional stores. Lucy had recently initiated new advertising campaigns and remodeled all its existing stores, using a design that featured more social space, communal tables and benches, soft canopy lighting, and nice dressing rooms. Lucy was a wholly owned subsidiary of VF Corp., a designer, marketer, wholesaler, and retailer of over 30 brands of apparel and footwear, with 2013 sales of $11.4 billion. Sales at lucy stores in 2013 were in the range of $110 million.

- *Bebe stores.* Bebe touted its stores as upscale, visually stimulating boutiques that were a go-to destination for chic, contemporary fashion. The company's bebe Sport collection consisted of apparel for a variety of fitness and recreational activities and included sports bras, tops, pants, shorts, jackets, hoodies, and tennis outfits. Garments were offered in two size ranges: regular (XS, S, M, and L) and petite (S and M/L). Bebe marketed its bebe Sport collection through more than 250 retail stores, more than 100 international-licensee operated stores, and bebe.com.

A number of other national and regional retailers of women's apparel, seeking to capitalize on growing sales of activewear made of high-tech fabrics, had created their own labels for fitness apparel suitable for yoga, running, gym exercise, and outdoor activities, For example, Nordstrom, a nationally respected department store retailer, had recently introduced its own Zella line of attire for yoga, cross-training, workouts, swimming, and "beyond the workout"; many of the initial products in the Zella collection were designed by a former member of lululemon's design team. Zella-branded products were offered in regular sizes (XXS, XS, S, M, L, XL, and XXL)

and plus sizes (1X, 2X, and 3X). Nordstrom was also marketing several other brands of activewear for women, men, and juniors, including Nike, Under Armour, Patagonia, Reebok, and adidas. In 2014, Nordstrom's activewear offerings could be purchased at 117 Nordstrom full-line department stores (typically 140,000 to 250,000 square feet in size) and 148 Nordstrom Rack stores (typically 30,000 to 50,000 square feet in size) in 36 states, as well as online at Nordstrom's website, www.nordstrom.com.

Typically, the items in the Gapfit, Athleta, lucy, bebe Sport, and Zella collections were priced 10 to 25 percent below similar kinds of lululemon products. Likewise, Nike, Under Armour, adidas, and Reebok apparel items were usually less expensive than comparable lululemon-branded items.

## ENDNOTES

[1] Beth Kowitt and Colleen Leahey, "Lululemon: In an Uncomfortable Position," *Fortune,* September 16, 2013, p. 118.

[2] "Yoga in America" (press release), *Yoga Journal,* December 5, 2012, www.yogajournal.com (accessed April 7, 2014).

[3] Ibid.

[4] Renee Frojo, "Yoga Clothing Retailers Go to the Mat for Market Share," *San Francisco Business Times,* December 28, 2012,

www.bizjournals.com/sanfrancisco (accessed April 10, 2014).

[5] Ibid.; and "Factors Underlying Our $74 Valuation of Under Armour (Part 1)," www.trefis.com, February 28, 2014 (accessed March 18, 2014).

[6] As posted on www.lululemon.com (accessed April 3, 2014).

[7] Company 10-K report for the fiscal year ending February 2, 2014, p. 2.

[8] Kim Basin, "Lululemon Admits Plus-Size Clothing Is Not Part of Its 'Formula,'" *Huffington Post,* August 2, 2013, www.huffingtonpost.com (accessed April 7, 2014).

[9] Dana Mattioli, "Lululemon's Secret Sauce," *Wall Street Journal,* March 22, 2012, pp. B1–B2.

[10] Ibid.

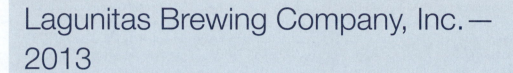

# Lagunitas Brewing Company, Inc. — 2013

**Armand Gilinsky, Jr.**
Sonoma State University

**Steve Bowden**
University of Waikato

**Jack Eldredge, Shawn Purcell, and Clark Rupp III**
MBA Students at Sonoma State University

I'd been digging getting drunk at the famous Marin Brewing Co. pub and thought the "gear" of brewing was pretty sexy looking. For me, cool and functional "stuff" has always been sexy. Like a nice reverb unit, or a great speaker, or a vintage guitar—and brewing "stuff" fit right in. I went down to the local homebrew supply shop and got the standard 5-gallon plastic pail, a strainer, the hop packets, and the malt syrup, everything you needed.
—Tony Magee, Founder and CEO, Lagunitas Brewing Company

On August 1, 2013, Tony Magee, the founder and CEO of Lagunitas Brewing Company (LBC), stood in Chicago, Illinois, 2,100 miles away from the current brewery in Petaluma, California. He had chosen to build his second brewery, providing him the capacity to meet current and expected future demand of his LBC brand. The new brewery, which would immediately allow LBC to increase its production of beer and quadruple capacity, was scheduled to open in early 2014. However, as Magee visualized his future in Chicago, he couldn't help but wonder what the future held and if expansion was the right move. How was LBC to manage and maintain control of its expansion? If demand projections were off, did LBC have enough capacity or too much? Did LBC have the financial resources to withstand more competition or another recession?

Nevertheless, LBC's chief marketing officer, Ron Lindenbusch, showed high levels of confidence and held lofty expectations for the Chicago operation:

> We are building an identical brewery to the one that we have built in Petaluma; the equipment is exactly the same. One way we are controlling costs is by not having the typical frills and thrills of other breweries:

> We don't install fancy copper pipes or stone on the platforms around the tanks, it's not necessary. The Chicago brewery will be all enclosed with a tasting room suspended above the brewery floor, so that visitors can take in all the wonder that is beer making. We want our customers to feel connected to our products and felt that by putting them in the front row, to really see the production process, we could start to build deep-rooted connections for the Lagunitas brand.

## U.S. BREWING INDUSTRY

The United States and brewing have been inexorably linked since the founding of the American colonies. In 1607, the first shipment of English ales arrived and by 1612 the first New World brewery was established in New Amsterdam. By the mid-1800s, German immigrants founded many of the breweries that built the foundation of the U.S. brewing industry, including Anheuser-Busch, Coors, Miller, and Schlitz. In 1865, American breweries produced 3.66 million barrels (bbl; 1 barrel = 31 U.S. gallons) of alcoholic beverages. The Prohibition movements started within the states during 1880–1919 and sought to ban the sale of alcohol. Local Prohibition laws prompted consolidation within the industry. With the passage of the Webb-Kenyon Act in 1914, the U.S. Congress put 1,568 businesses out of brewing operations. After Prohibition was repealed in 1933 by the ratification of the Twenty-First Amendment, the number of domestic breweries climbed to approximately 700 in just five years (Exhibit 1).

The latter half of the 20th century saw large-scale breweries exiting the market, as they could not produce sufficient volumes at low-enough costs amid growing competition. There was a need to produce and market beers on a national scale, which increased capital requirements, forcing the more inefficient producers out of the market. The brewers that survived did so mainly by remaining small and regional, like Anchor Brewing located in San Francisco. Federal legislation changed again in 1976, allowing smaller, independent brewers to sell their creations onsite. Responding to changes in consumer tastes, these new brewers began producing darker and fuller-flavored beverages like ales, porters, stouts, and dark lagers.

Conditions in the U.S. beer market were challenging from 1981 to 1994, with a growth rate of only 1 percent. In contrast, the 1980s were a decade of pioneering in the craft-brewing segment (Exhibit 2) and were followed by high growth during the 1990s. Annual volume growth was 35 percent in 1991 and continued to grow every year until reaching a high of 58 percent in 1995. From 1997 to 2003, the craft-brewing-segment growth declined to under 5 percent annually. Independent breweries and local brewers saw the beer-drinking clientele gravitate toward their styles of production, and, as a result, from 2004 to 2008 annual volume growth rates held steady, ranging from 6 to 12 percent. Craft brewers represented 6.5 percent of U.S. beer sales in 2012 and grew 15 percent in volume in that year. In 1980, there were 8 craft breweries, and the number grew to 2,360 breweries by 2013, according to the Brewers Association (Exhibit 3).

# COMPANY HISTORY

## Founding (1992–1997)

In the early 1990s, Magee began home brewing in his Lagunitas, California, kitchen as a hobby. During the first five years of brewing, Magee worked as a printing salesman to earn his living. He confessed, "[I] wanted out of printing very badly."

By early 1993, Magee's wife "evicted him from the kitchen." He then rented a small space in the back of Richard's Grocery Store, in the small town of Forest Knolls, California. He expanded the operation by installing a three-tier brewing system and purchasing an all-electric plug-n-play cargo container. Despite no longer brewing in the town of Lagunitas, all the permits and legal documents were under the "Lagunitas" name and Magee thought the name was cool and catchy, so he kept it.

## EXHIBIT 1    Growth in the Number of U.S. Breweries, 1887–2012

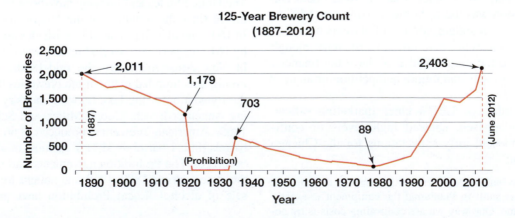

*Source:* Brewers Association, www.brewersassociation.org.

## EXHIBIT 2   Market Segments

The **craft beer industry** is defined by six distinct markets: brewpubs, microbreweries, regional craft breweries, and contract brewing companies.

*Microbrewery:* A brewery that produces less than 15,000 barrels of beer per year with 75% or more of its beer sold off-site. Microbreweries sell to the public by one or more of the following methods: the traditional three-tier system (brewer to wholesaler to retailer to consumer); the two-tier system (brewer acting as wholesaler to retailer to consumer); and, directly to the consumer through carry-outs and/or on-site tap-room or restaurant sales.

*Brewpub:* A restaurant-brewery that sells 25% or more of its beer on site. The beer is brewed primarily for sale in the restaurant and bar. The beer is often dispensed directly from the brewery's storage tanks. Where allowed by law, brewpubs often sell beer "to go" and/or distribute to off-site accounts. Note: BA re-categorizes a company as a microbrewery if its off-site (distributed) beer sales exceed 75%.

*Contract Brewing Company:* A business that hires another brewery to produce its beer. It can also be a brewery that hires another brewery to produce additional beer. The contract brewing company handles marketing, sales, and distribution of its beer, while generally leaving the brewing and packaging to its producer-brewery (which, confusingly, is also sometimes referred to as a contract brewery).

*Regional Brewery:* A brewery with an annual beer production of between 15,000 and 6,000,000 barrels.

*Regional Craft Brewery:* An independent regional brewery who has either an all malt flagship or has at least 50% of its volume in either all malt beers or in beers which use adjuncts to enhance rather than lighten flavor.

*Large Brewery:* A brewery with an annual beer production over 6,000,000 barrels.

*Source:* Brewers Association, **www.brewersassociation.org**.

## EXHIBIT 3   Number of U.S. Breweries and Volume Produced, 2012

| U.S. Breweries in Operation | Quantity | Volume (bbl) |
|---|---|---|
| Brewpubs | 1,124 | 870,371 |
| Microbreweries | 1,139 | 1,905,212 |
| Regional craft breweries | 97 | 10,237,632 |
| Total U.S. craft breweries | 2,360 | |
| Large noncraft breweries | 23 | |
| Other noncraft breweries | 33 | 227,702 |
| Total U.S. breweries | 2,416 | |

*Source:* Brewers Association, **www.brewersassociation.org**.

From the beginning, Magee had a clear idea of how he would make money in the beer business:

I would do it the way another great San Francisco brewery did it: wholesale. The margins would be thin, but I would do all the work myself and whatever crumbs were left over, I'd feast on them. I was only planning on producing unfiltered draught beer and to market it as a "private label" product to the 20 or so bars and restaurants in San Francisco and in the tourism heavy West Marin coastal area where I lived. I would brew, filter, keg, sell, deliver, and service it all solo.

By 1994, the brewing operation of Lagunitas overwhelmed the capacity of the small grocery store's septic system. Magee was forced to quickly relocate to Petaluma, California. Once LBC moved into an 8,500-square-foot location in Petaluma, Magee purchased a 14-barrel brew system and the company's first bottling line. With production of six-packs of beer starting in 1995, the bottling line was easy to justify to Magee: "The current 20 ounce bottles were easy to hand-fill. But a $2,500 bottling line for 12 ounce bottles would allow $1 million in product."

Over the next three years, LBC grew production from 600 barrels to nearly 10,000 barrels annually by adding tanks and fermenters, one at a time. As Magee recalled:

> At some point—in June of 1994—it all got to be too much, and while the little brewery was just beginning to carry its own weight financially, selling only the private-label draft beer, I needed to hire some help. This single decision to increase the brewery's daily "burn-rate," and the resultant need for increased sales volume to support the first payroll position, was the beginning of what I can only describe as 12 crazy years of being chased down the street by a rabid pack of wild dogs.

Even with incredible growth, financing remained an issue, as no bank believed in the craft beer movement or in Magee:

> There is too much work and too many good customers for you to do a good job by yourself, so you hire one guy, and your daily cost of operation goes up. Now you need to sell more beer to pay for this change, which you can, so you do. To make this extra tasty brew you need to buy more ingredients, which you can, so you do. Unless you sell the beer COD, you will probably need to pay for these ingredients before you get to collect for the beer the ingredients will become, which means you need a little more cash. It's all about the "time of arrival" of the money to your checking account. Your little brewery is a little profitable, but you are growing quickly and the "time of arrival" of money thing is getting harder to manage because you seem to need more than the little bit of money that you are generating in profits if you are going to pay your bills on time—so you need a little more money to put into the bank account to cover the checks that are clearing the account faster and faster. But you have a day job and you just put your paychecks in the brewery because things seem to be going so well.
>
> So you grow a little bit more, you pay for materials—and now salary—before you collect for the brew you're delivering, and you are a little profitable, but actual cash somehow remains scarce. Suddenly, you realize that you need another fermenter and a few more kegs because you are growing and you are starting to short customers' orders, so you buy another fermenter, which also takes more money than you are making. Maybe you have a bank that will lend you money, but in 1996, I didn't.

## Bootstrapping (1997–2007)

In 1997, the craft beer industry hit hard times. Financing dried up and many breweries folded. Magee remembered those difficult years:

> I counted 23 serious brands that had recently been important brewers and were now gone from the market. There was beer running in the streets. Distributors started getting tired of all the brands, retailers were just numb, beer fans were more than a little bowled over. But, it was also a good time to be buying used equipment for the same reasons.

As many breweries were closing or stagnating, LBC was thriving and growing fast (Exhibit 4). In 1998, Magee leased a 17,000-square-foot facility across the street from the original 14-barrel brew house in Petaluma. The new facility was built with growth in mind. The 30-barrel brew house was composed of cheaply procured used equipment from casualties of the industry downturn, specifically Wisconsin Brewing Co. and Napa Ale Works. While the old plant was slowly phased out, the new one was similarly phased in. Magee fondly remembered moving day:

> When we had the new place mostly ready, we had a big moving party of 1,200 or so of our best friends, and after a 10 beer tasting and some live music while getting loaded at the old plant, a loud horn blew and everybody grabbed anything they could carry that was not nailed down and we all literally marched over to the new McDowell plant in a massive parade led by a mime, a guy on stilts, a purple bear, and a tragic little civil war style marching band.

The new facility required large amounts of new capital, and Magee sought private equity to provide the financing:

> Eventually, when I had to move the brewery into a larger space, buy bigger brewing stuff, and do a bunch of building renovations, I needed to raise money. I got it from some old friends, and from some new friends, and in 1998, I traded about half ownership of the brewery for $650,000. At that time, I couldn't borrow it from anywhere, so I had to raise it by selling stock.

In 2000, increased debt and overhead expenses pushed LBC to pursue faster growth. The next several years were used to "clean up" production with efficiency purchases, such as a new bottling line that did not waste as much beer and a new high-speed centrifuge separator. Both strategies paid for themselves by getting more beer to the consumer without additional inputs. By the end of 2007, production was reaching maximum capacity again.

**EXHIBIT 4** Lagunitas Brewing Company: Capacity, Revenues, and Profits, 1992–2013

| Period | Year | Petaluma Maximum Annual Capacity (bbl) | Sales Revenue (000s of US$) | Net Profit (000s of US$) |
|---|---|---|---|---|
| Founding | 1992 | n/a | n/a | n/a |
| | 1993 | n/a | n/a | n/a |
| | 1994 | n/a | n/a | n/a |
| | 1995 | 3,420 | 513 | n/a |
| | 1996 | 5,420 | 813 | n/a |
| | 1997 | 8,420 | 1,263 | n/a |
| | 1998 | 10,420 | 1,615 | n/a |
| | 1999 | 14,420 | 2,278 | n/a |
| | 2000 | 17,420 | 2,787 | n/a |
| | 2001 | 19,420 | 3,165 | n/a |
| Bootstrapping | 2002 | 23,420 | 3,888 | n/a |
| | 2003 | 24,420 | 4,151 | n/a |
| | 2004 | 26,420 | 4,544 | 270 |
| | 2005 | 32,420 | 5,674 | 400 |
| | 2006 | 37,420 | 6,600 | 503 |
| | 2007 | 43,420 | 9,500 | 804 |
| | 2008 | 57,420 | 12,900 | 595 |
| Evolution | 2009 | 72,420 | 17,100 | 563 |
| | 2010 | 101,420 | 24,600 | 1,500 |
| | 2011 | 165,420 | 39,700 | 1,737 |
| Expansion | 2012 | 235,420 | 59,000 | 3,107 |
| | 2013 | 400,420 | 105,000 | 8,500 |

Source: Lagunitas Brewing Company, private communication.

## Exceeding Capacity (2008–2010)

In 2008, Magee purchased an automated 80-barrel brew house manufactured in Germany by Rolec, a company renowned for quality brewing products. The new equipment allowed for significant growth. With the installation complete, Magee told local newspapers that it would take 10 years to reach maximum production and that after reaching that level he would be "happy to stop growing for a while."

At that time, LBC's beer was distributed in 35 states. Four trucks a week shipped beer to Manhattan and five trucks a week to Chicago. According to Magee, "If you look at Highway 80 going across the country, it's literally a pipeline of Lagunitas [beer] being transported all the time."

Two years later, LBC was quickly approaching the brew house's maximum production level, running the plant "flat out to keep up with orders." The expansion that was supposed to last 10 years lasted only two. In March 2010, amid an annual growth rate of 46 percent, Magee announced an additional new 250-barrel automated brew house, which would allow for annual capacity of over 150,000 barrels, at a cost of $9.2 million. Magee recalled:

> It was like making decisions on the back of a galloping horse, without quite enough information to know exactly what your next step has to be. . . . [There was] tremendous growth, from day to day, there was no such thing as standard operating procedure, it was scary, you look around, there was something new every day.

## National Expansion (2011–2013)

After unprecedented 60 percent growth in the first two quarters of 2011, Magee revised his initial demand estimates and increased annual capacity to just under 200,000 barrels in Petaluma. With a total cost just over $14 million, Magee revised his expansion predictions and said, "I can see us growing three to four times in size in the next five to ten years." In 2012 and 2013, LBC expanded again to nearly 230,000 and 400,000 barrels annual capacity, respectively.

While the Petaluma brewery continued its expansion with a new building and bottling line (now at 130,000 square feet), LBC began planning a second brewery. The planning included brewery designs, capacity requirements, brewing processes, and ways to finance the expansion.

The location choice of Chicago was a natural one: Chicago, home to some 8 million people, represented the largest LBC market outside Northern California. A Chicago brewery gave LBC easier access to its Midwest and East Coast customers and suppliers by taking advantage of Chicago's distribution lines. For example, Magee claimed that $1.5 million per year was spent to truck beer bottles from a glassmaker in Oklahoma to Petaluma and, after filling them up, back across the country to the Midwest and East Coast.

Additionally, Lindenbusch was optimistic that LBC would be considered a hometown beer by Chicagoans: "Lagunitas has deep connections to Chicago. Tony is originally from Chicago and still has family living there. Tony loves Chicago and Chicago loves Tony."

Securing financing for the new 300,000-square-foot brewery and its initial operating costs was a top priority for Magee. He knew he couldn't finance this expansion phase in the same way he had in Petaluma, that is, borrowing from friends and family and taking second mortgages. In the early days, LBC was paying 1.5 percent on receivables and 10 to 14 percent on equipment. This made it difficult for LBC to acquire bank loans or further investors. Before 1995, LBC had been bleeding cash and showed little profits. Once the debts were all paid, LBC was flush with cash. This made its Chicago endeavor an attractive opportunity for banks and investors, as the investors saw the brewery was growing.

The company secured $17.5 million in funding in 2011 and purchased a plot of land inside the city limits of Chicago. While the cost to do business was much higher inside the city limits, LBC felt it was more valuable to be officially located within the historic city. While other well-known breweries had sought tax advantages for placing their new breweries inside certain states, Magee had been adamant about profitable beer companies not taking advantage of these types of tax deals.

Setting up the Chicago brewery identically to the one in Petaluma was crucial to Magee. Everything from the water and physical brewery to the culture inside—all of it had to be the same. LBC set and reset the Chicago annual capacity from 150,000 barrels to 250,000 as the planning continued. Eventually the 300,000-square-foot Chicago facility would support a 500,000-barrel annual operation. A brewery's capacity (i.e., "bottleneck") was determined by the number of fermenters on site. In Chicago, each fermenter produced 750 barrels per batch, with a turnover rate of about 20 times per year.

Jeremy Marshall, the head brewer, was to be stationed in Chicago during the early days of operation, because, according to Lindenbusch, "the beer recipes are so solid, the first batch is usually good, and just needs a bit of tweaking from Jeremy." The plan was for Marshall to travel back and forth between Petaluma and Chicago, being responsible for both. The beers in production would be the same at both locations, and according to Magee, "A customer should not be able to distinguish between batches brewed in Chicago versus Petaluma."

Lindenbusch commented in July 2013:

> One of the reasons we chose Chicago was the water supply. Chicago has very similar water to that in Petaluma. Water is the lifeblood of beer making and really affects the flavor profile. So choosing the right water was important in our decision to select Chicago. We don't want the customer to have a different tasting beer depending on where it was brewed. Both Petaluma and Chicago have no minerals in their water so all we have to do in order to get the correct pH balance, is to add in some gypsum. This really helps in guaranteeing continuity in our beers.

During that growth period, LBC added key people from major corporations and placed them in upper-management roles to help guide the expansion. Much like a traditional corporation, LBC employed a CEO, CFO, COO, VP of marketing, VP of sales, and VP of packaging. Most of the executive team had been with LBC for over 10 years and expressed little interest in early retirement. Most of these executives were in their 50s and empathized with Magee when he said, "I'll die while still on payroll."

By 2012, LBC had grown from 13 salespeople to 56 and had added six regional sales managers. As LBC began to increase its national exposure, the need to support its sales team on the ground became paramount. Leon Sharyon, LBC's chief financial officer, explained:

> We realized that we needed a CRM (customer relationship management software) to specifically deal with our needs, so we went out and hired an IT director. Then I called up the Dean of the Computer Science program at Sonoma State (University) and asked him to send me his best three students to work on a project for me. They did so well we offered the students jobs and they have built us a great tool that our sales team uses every day. The impact of arming our sales team with the proper tools as they go into bars, restaurants and events has really helped.

## MISSION AND VALUES

In July 2013, Lindenbusch explained how LBC wanted to be viewed:

> We want to be known as an American brewery with American owners and American employees. Our vision is to be known more as an American beer like Bud. We don't want the label of craft or microbrew placed upon us. The craft definition is becoming blurred by various tax and trade association guideline changes. We don't feel we fit the craft mold. Lagunitas is more about getting our beer to as many people as possible.

LBC believed that with profitability came responsibility to not only maintain high brewing standards but also support the communities that supported them. This "pay it forward" attitude typically involved helping charities raise money through LBC donations. But rather than extol its virtuous side, LBC preferred to focus its PR efforts on highlighting the fund-raising group's mission. As Lindenbusch saw it, Lagunitas and music went hand in hand:

> Our marketing efforts primarily revolve around music, in some way or another, whether it's a festival or concert. Sponsoring bands that are hitting the road is one of our next ventures. It will be called "Fueled by Lagunitas," and we basically donate beer and gas. Often we deal with LiveNation for concerts and intend to participate more in various capacities with college radio, PBS and music festivals. Recently we added our mini amp (amphitheater) at our Petaluma brewery and host concerts and benefits of all types. And we have live music that goes on in our tasting room four nights a week. Our motivation is to help music and the arts.

However, as LBC became a larger player in the craft beer segment, it encountered considerable competition from other craft brewers. Lindenbusch insisted that LBC was now blocked from participating in certain music festivals. Other brewers had already secured exclusive distribution rights to certain events, which stifled the organic expansion and word-of-mouth strategy that LBC had been following since its inception.

## COMPETITION

As LBC left its small startup roots, it set its eyes on the big domestic competitors, like MillerCoors and Anheuser-Busch. As the craft-brewing segment matured, major American brewers had started to offer similar craft brew–like products such as Blue-Moon (MillerCoors) and Shock Top (Anheuser-Busch). Additionally, some craft brewers, such as Sam Adams (Boston Brewing Co.), chose to be contract-brewed by the big American brewers.

In 2013 LBC occupied the 6th spot in the rankings of domestic craft brewers (Exhibit 5), and the 13th spot for overall U.S. brewers (Exhibit 6). There were over 100 distributors that sold LBC nationwide and in a few foreign countries. LBC expected further expansion internationally in the next few years.

Besides competing with the big American brewers, LBC continued to compete with existing and new craft brewers that entered the market. In addition to the more than 2,400 breweries that existed in the United States, an estimated 1,500 new breweries were under construction in 2013, according to the Brewers Association. California had the greatest number of craft breweries with 312 but was only midrange in breweries per capita (Exhibit 7). According to Lindenbusch, LBC considered itself "the low-end of the high-end beers (in terms of popularity), such as Corona, Heineken, Sierra Nevada, and a tier above Anchor and Stone."

While flavorful beer was one aspect of a successful company, capacity and distribution were other keys. Similar to LBC, many of the craft brewers were expanding operations to fulfill the growing craft beer demand. Sierra Nevada and New Belgium Brewing Co., both major craft brewers, planned to open second breweries in North Carolina.

## MARKETING AND DISTRIBUTION

Lagunitas had built a successful and identifiable brand with little traditional articulation or consistent messaging. The brand was developed, predominantly

**EXHIBIT 5    Top U.S. Craft-Brewing Companies (based on 2012 beer sales volume)**

| Rank | U.S. Craft Brewing Company | City | State | Barrels Sold |
|------|---------------------------|------|-------|--------------|
| 1 | Boston Beer Co. | Boston | MA | 2,100,000 |
| 2 | Sierra Nevada Brewing Co. | Chico | CA | 966,000 |
| 3 | New Belgium Brewing Co. | Fort Collins | CO | 765,000 |
| 4 | The Gambrinus Co.* | San Antonio | TX | n/a |
| 5 | Deschutes Brewery | Bend | OR | 255,000 |
| **6** | **Lagunitas Brewing Co.** | **Petaluma** | **CA** | **244,000** |

*Includes BridgePort, Shiner, Trumer, Tappeto Volant, and Pete's Wicked brands.

*Source:* Brewers Association, **www.brewersassociation.org**.

**EXHIBIT 6    Top Overall U.S. Brewing Companies (based on 2012 beer sales volume)**

| Rank | U.S. Overall Brewing Company | City | State |
|------|------------------------------|------|-------|
| 1 | Anheuser-Busch Inc. (a) | St. Louis | MO |
| 2 | MillerCoors (b) | Chicago | IL |
| 3 | Pabst Brewing Co. (c) | Los Angeles | CA |
| 4 | D. G. Yuengling and Son Inc. | Pottsville | PA |
| 5 | Boston Beer Co. (d) | Boston | MA |
| 6 | North American Breweries (e) | Rochester | NY |
| 7 | Sierra Nevada Brewing Co. | Chico | CA |
| 8 | New Belgium Brewing Co. | Fort Collins | CO |
| 9 | Craft Brew Alliance, Inc. (f) | Portland | OR |
| 10 | The Gambrinus Co. (g) | San Antonio | TX |
| 11 | Minhas Craft Brewery (h) | Monroe | WI |
| 12 | Deschutes Brewery | Bend | OR |
| **13** | **Lagunitas Brewing Co.** | **Petaluma** | **CA** |

(a) Includes Bass, Beck's, Bud Light, Budweiser, Busch, Goose Island, Landshark, Michelob, Rolling Rock, Shock Top, and Wild Blue brands—does not include partially owned Coastal, Craft Brew Alliance, Fordham, Kona, Old Dominion, Omission, Red Hook, and Coastal, Fordham, and Craft Brew Alliance brands;

(b) includes A.C. Golden, Batch 19, Blue Moon, Colorado Native, Coors, Keystone, Killian's, Leinenkugel's, Miller, and Tenth & Blake brands;

(c) includes Pabst, Schlitz and 28 other brand families;

(d) includes Alchemy & Science and Sam Adams brands;

(e) includes Dundee, Genesee, Labatt Lime, Magic Hat, and Pyramid brands;

(f) includes Kona, Omission, Red Hook, and Coastal, Fordham, and Craft Brew Alliance brands;

(g) includes BridgePort, Shiner, Trumer, Tappeto Volant, and Pete's Wicked brands;

(h) includes Mountain Crest and 10 other brand families.

*Source:* Brewers Association, **www.brewersassociation.org**.

from Magee's personality, through catchy and quirky labels with simple typeface and interesting copy. LBC found an industry niche and continued to lead the craft industry by producing strong-flavored and high-alcohol-content beers that failed to be categorized in traditional categories.

Lagunitas' marketing methodology lacked traditional media promotions, minimal-pricing incentives,

**EXHIBIT 7**   Capita per Craft Brewery by State (select states), 2012

| Capita per Craft Brewery Rank | State | Total Craft Breweries | Capita per Craft Brewery |
|---|---|---|---|
| 1 | Vermont | 25 | 25,030 |
| 2 | Oregon | 140 | 27,365 |
| 3 | Montana | 36 | 27,484 |
| 4 | Alaska | 22 | 32,283 |
| 5 | Colorado | 151 | 33,306 |
| 6 | Maine | 37 | 35,902 |
| 7 | Wyoming | 15 | 37,575 |
| 8 | Washington | 158 | 42,560 |
| 9 | Idaho | 29 | 54,055 |
| 10 | Wisconsin | 83 | 68,518 |
| **20** | **California** | **316** | **117,892** |
| 35 | Illinois | 67 | 191,502 |
| 39 | New York | 88 | 220,206 |
| 42 | Texas | 84 | 299,352 |
| 44 | Florida | 57 | 329,848 |
| 51 | Mississippi | 3 | 989,099 |

*Source:* Brewers Association, **www.brewersassociation.org**.

and push marketing techniques. Magee described his hesitation to categorize his brand:

> This is a delicate thing to talk about because I don't want to limit the possible interpretations of what Lagunitas is in your minds or in our own. Having started this ball rolling down the alley, I have never been certain where it would land and there have been more than enough interesting and unforeseeable inputs over the years. If I said we are irreverent does that preclude our being traditional? Is saying that we are funny ruling out our displaying gravitas? If you say we're extreme should people infer that we're challenging to have in the fridge? If I said that our labels are literate, could you infer that we're pretentious . . . ? Like Joseph Campbell's *Hero with a Thousand Faces,* I've always liked the idea of a brand that is equal parts legend, material, and myth, and always a mirror—a chimerical presence, where everyone that apprehends it sees something in it that is unique to their own point of view.

The company had found a promotional niche for itself by "giving away beer and making friends," according to Lindenbusch. For example, in 2012 LBC donated 11,212 cases of beer to festivals and events, and in 2013 it had already donated 10,045 cases by July. Magee was telling a story, through the label artwork and the taste and quality of the beer.

The artwork on the bottle matched the art that went into brewing any batch of Lagunitas. LBC realized its "secret" was still in the quality of its beers, as Lindenbusch noted:

> Our labels have personality, humor, intelligence, and art. They are similar to a J. Peterman catalogue, describing a lifestyle rather than a product. However, a consumer may buy our beer for the artwork or story on the bottle, but it is what is inside that keeps them coming back.

Word of mouth and quality products had been the backbone of LBC's marketing. As the craft brew market expanded, LBC had witnessed revenue growth of 46 percent in 2010 and 60 percent in the first two quarters of 2011. Its major markets at that time were California, Colorado, Texas, Florida, New York, and Illinois. LBC's marketing strategy was quite simple: Continue to be Lagunitas. Magee talked about what he called "the personality of Lagunitas":

> We kept the name "Lagunitas" after moving away from that town for a few reasons: it's a beautiful little word, it's hard to say, once you said it you're in, and it looks lovely in type. I work very hard to get personality into the recipes. Not to emulate styles that have gone before us, but I like to think that none of our beers are

today's version of yesterday's anything. We are always trying to find new material within those four ingredients: malt, hops, yeast and water that make up beer. I think that independence of thought and independence of spirit show up in the brand.

Pricing strategy played an important role in the formation of the brand. From the beginning, LBC realized that how it priced its product would make huge differences in sales and brand image. When the company first started to produce six-packs in 1998, Magee needed to select a price segment:

I had a lot of decisions to make about the new bottled brand, but the heaviest one was what we would charge for it. I looked at some market-info (IRI) reports and saw that the average selling price of most every six-pack brand in the top twenty was $5.99 and some even less. This seemed really, really cheap, but it was the world around us. They all had frontline six-pack prices of $6.99, but they all did every other month promotional prices of $4.99, and so the average fell in the middle.

I wanted to make sure that at every opportunity I would aim Lagunitas at participating in the market with only the best brands. That didn't just mean other craft brewers (although we all fished in the same pond) but also it meant imports. I needed to price similarly and participate in the market similarly. These were huge breweries, but I wanted them to be my peers. We weren't sophisticated enough to do effective promotional pricing yet but I felt that if we wanted to play with the big boys, I'd have to ante-up. So, we set our everyday price at $5.99 for a six-pack.

## ECONOMIC DEVELOPMENT ISSUES

LBC had always had problems in regard to wastewater. Excessive wastewater was a major reason for moving brewery operations often during the early days. The city of Petaluma explored whether additional industrial wastewater treatment capacity was needed. This wastewater issue directly affected Lagunitas. If LBC continued to grow, its wastewater requirements would proportionately increase.

High levels of organic matter in the brewing process caused problems for municipal treatment systems. Breweries commonly pretreated their wastewater to meet municipal standards of biological

oxygen demand (BOD) and total suspended solids (TSS). Even though LBC pretreated its wastewater, it still incurred thousands of dollars in fines from the city of Petaluma. The company also had costs associated with the excess wastewater that it couldn't release into the sewers. By 2013, LBC was paying $250,000 every month to truck its wastewater 60 miles away into a neighboring municipal district. LBC purchased a nearby plot of land, two lots south of the brewery in Petaluma, to build its own wastewater treatment plant. Petaluma had, to date, shown a willingness to work with Lagunitas when it came to permits and fees.

## FUTURE CHALLENGES

With 2,400 craft breweries and another 1,500 in various stages of development and completion in mid-2013, the U.S. craft beer market appeared to be in the midst of explosive growth in production. The galloping horse that was LBC had been at the forefront of the growth in capacity. But LBC had also evolved beyond the craft origins, with a clear focus on national distribution and an increasing orientation toward taking on the "big boys." The Petaluma brewery was in a good location from a West Coast distribution standpoint, and the Chicago brewery would be in an excellent location for East Coast distribution. Chicago, one of the major distribution centers in the United States, would allow LBC to harness the city's distribution network to get products out to consumers more efficiently.

Lagunitas expected continued growth for the immediate future, but Magee was all too conscious of the cyclical nature in the craft industry. He admitted that he feared the next "unknowable step." The fast-paced nature and increased competition in the craft industry segment of the beer industry seemed to all but guarantee difficult times ahead. But looking at LBC's history, the company was in a good position to weather anything. The Chicago expansion was a key step to being able to break out of the craft beer label and compete on the larger national—and perhaps eventually global—stage. Magee and Lindenbusch expressed hope that the personality of LBC would not get lost in the process.

# Cooper Tire & Rubber Company in 2014: Competing in a Highly Competitive Market for Replacement Tires

**Javad Kargar**
North Carolina Central University

**Houtan Kargar**
North Carolina Central University

**Robert Moffie**
North Carolina Central University

I n 2014, Cooper Tire & Rubber Company, a U.S.-based independent tire manufacturer, was ranked as the 11th-largest tire producer worldwide and as North America's 4th-largest tire producer. However, its capacity of 97,000 consumer tires a day was still 20 percent below what it had been four years earlier, before the closing of its Albany, Georgia, plant. With a mix equally divided between proprietary house brand and private label, Cooper Tire & Rubber marketed its tires in more than 100 countries around the world.

Cooper Tire & Rubber was one of only a few companies to achieve both consistent high growth and strong returns for more than a decade. With the exception of 2005, 2006, and 2008, Cooper Tire had earned a profit in every year since its inception—a remarkable accomplishment in a mature business where it was common for industry members to post losses when demand for tires sagged. Cooper Tire had paid dividends every year since 1980, when the company first began paying dividends. However, in 2014 the company found itself competing in an industry characterized by increasingly fierce competition. In addition, the company was still attempting to recover from a failed merger in late-2013 and reverse its recent sharp decline in revenues and earnings. It was imperative that the company's management evaluate the appropriateness of its strategic direction and operating approaches in 2014.

## COMPANY HISTORY

Cooper Tire & Rubber Company began its journey from obscurity to a tire industry leader nearly a century ago, in 1914, when brothers-in-law John F. Schaefer and Claude E. Hart purchased M and M Manufacturing Company, an Akron, Ohio, producer of tire patches, tire cement, and tire repair kits. The following year, they purchased the Giant Tire & Rubber Company of Akron, a tire rebuilding business, and two years later they moved the business to Findlay, Ohio. By 1920, they had broadened the scope of the firm, repositioning it as a tire manufacturer. At that time, the firm had more than 130 domestic competitors, 40 in the state of Ohio alone. In 1930, Giant Tire & Rubber merged with the Falls Rubber Company and Cooper Corporation to form the Master Tire & Rubber Company. Within a year, the combined production of the plants totaled 2,850 tires per day.

The firm changed its name to Cooper Tire & Rubber Company in 1946 and, in 1960, became a publicly held corporation and was listed on the New York Stock Exchange. Throughout the next five decades, the company expanded its products, manufacturing plants, distribution system, and marketplace.

The 1980s were years of significant change for Cooper Tire & Rubber and the tire industry overall.

Many American tire manufacturers scrambled to lower production capacity as the domestic market became saturated. From 1979 to 1987, a total of 23 U.S. tire plants were closed in the rush to downsize. Cooper Tire & Rubber executives calmly delineated strategies for continued growth and even expansion of production. As its competitors deserted plants, Cooper Tire bought them and upgraded them. By overhauling older facilities, Cooper Tire added capacity for one-third the cost of building new ones. Research and development (R&D) at Cooper Tire was enhanced by several capital investments during the 1980s. Distribution was also improved during the 1980s, with centers opening or expanding in Moraine, Ohio; Atlanta, Georgia; and Tacoma, Washington. Cooper Tire's warehousing capacity totaled 3.2 million tires by 1985. By the end of the 1980s, distribution centers at Findlay and Moraine were granted foreign trade subzone status from the U.S. Department of Commerce. The designation diminished and suspended Cooper Tire's payment of duty on imported raw materials. Cooper Tire & Rubber joined the ranks of Fortune 500 companies in 1983 as one of the largest industrial companies in the United States. In the following year, its net sales exceeded $500 million, and its net income was more than $24 million. In 1985, Cooper Tire made its first foreign acquisition in Mexico. In the same year, Cooper Tire & Rubber was named one of the 100 best-performing companies in America.

Capital investments continued to grow in the 1990s: The company purchased a 1.8-million-square-foot tire manufacturing plant in Albany, Georgia, in 1990, and expanded its Findlay and Bowling Green locations in 1993. Despite a lingering U.S. recession, Cooper Tire's net sales topped the $1 billion mark in 1991, and the company added almost a quarter of a billion dollars more the following year. Construction of a new plant at Mt. Sterling, Kentucky, got under way in 1995, and a $10.5 million upgrade of the Clarksdale, Mississippi, facility began in 1994. Cooper Tire acquired British-based Avon Tyres in early 1997, which manufactured products for the replacement-tire industry in the United Kingdom and western Europe. The company also had a strategic alliance with Pirelli Tyres of Milan, Italy, which involved contractual arrangements. This alliance provided revenue to Cooper Tire primarily through commissions on sales of Pirelli tires by Cooper Tire dealers. By 1999,

Cooper Tire had 50 manufacturing facilities in nine countries. Much of the company's growth came through the acquisition of the Standard Products Company, a move that added 10,000 employees to its payroll.

Cooper Tire's capital investments, ongoing cost-cutting efforts, and focus on the replacement market almost doubled its operating margin from the late 1980s to the early 1990s. In fact, the company's efficient means of production propelled it to the highest gross profit margins in the industry, at 33 percent. When larger competitors turned to the replacement market and tried to undercut Cooper Tire's prices, those high margins gave the company leeway to join in the price wars.

Cooper Tire acquired Avon Tyres in 1997 and Mickey Thompson Performance Tires & Wheels in 2003. The company also entered into a joint venture with Kenda Rubber Industrial Company Ltd. for construction of a plant outside Shanghai, China, to produce radial passenger and light-truck tires in 2003. Cooper Tire sold its automotive business, Cooper Tire & Rubber–Standard Automotive in 2004 for approximately $1.165 billion. Cooper Tire & Rubber–Standard Automotive, which was a global manufacturer of fluid-handling systems, body-sealing systems, and active and passive vibration control systems, primarily for automotive original-equipment manufacturers.

In 2005, Cooper formed a new commercial division encompassing both the Oliver Rubber Company and commercial tires. Also in 2005, the company announced an agreement to obtain 51 percent ownership in China's third-largest tire manufacturer. The company also entered into a joint venture with Resilient Technologies. In 2008, Cooper Tire acquired an approximate 38 percent ownership share of a Mexican tire manufacturing plant that was the second-largest plant in Mexico. In 2011, Cooper Tire acquired an additional 21 percent ownership in its Mexican plant, leading to a 58 percent ownership. In January 2012, Cooper Tire acquired the assets of an existing tire plant in Krusevac, Serbia, to supply tires to the European and Russian markets. By 2014, Cooper Tire & Rubber had over 65 manufacturing, sales, and design facilities located in 11 countries.

The company's current CEO, Roy Armes, had spearheaded the positive transformation since 2005, creating a stronger, more resilient, and more sustainable Cooper Tire & Rubber and better positioned the company to drive long-term value. Nearly all of the financial and performance goals in Armes's ambitious strategic agenda had been achieved by 2012. In fact, 2012 was a record-setting year for Cooper Tire, as the company generated record full-year net sales of $4.2 billion and a record operating profit of $379 million. Cooper Tire's business stalled in 2013 and was still in the recovery stage in 2014. Exhibit 1 presents a financial and operating summary for Cooper Tire & Rubber for 2009–2013.

# COOPER TIRE & RUBBER COMPANY'S STRATEGIC PLAN

Starting in 2008, Cooper Tire embarked on a strategic growth plan to drive the company in creating shareholder value. The vision of Cooper Tire was "together, around the world. One company . . . one team . . . one goal: creating superior value, for our customers, employees, partners and shareholders."[1]

**EXHIBIT 1**   Summary of Cooper Tire & Rubber Company's Financial and Operating Performance, 2009—2013 (dollar amounts in millions, except per share data)

| | 2013 | 2012 | 2011 | 2010 | 2009 |
|---|---|---|---|---|---|
| Net sales | $3,439.2 | $4,200.8 | $3,907.8 | $3,342.7 | $2,778.9 |
| Cost of products sold | 2,923.0 | 3,546.6 | 3,562.8 | 2,940.3 | 2,359.9 |
| Gross profit | 516.2 | 654.2 | 345.0 | 402.4 | 419.0 |
| Selling, general & administrative | 275.5 | 257.3 | 181.7 | 193.4 | 207.0 |
| Impairment of goodwill | — | — | — | — | — |
| Restructuring | — | — | — | 20.6 | 48.7 |
| Operating profit before taxes | 240.7 | 396.9 | 163.3 | 188.4 | 156.3 |
| Interest expense | (27.9) | (29.5) | (36.2) | (36.6) | (47.2) |
| Interest income | 0.8 | 2.6 | 3.2 | 5.2 | 5.2 |
| Other income–expense | (0.6) | (1.5) | 3.8 | 2.8 | 1.3 |
| Income (loss) before income taxes | 213.0 | 368.4 | 134.1 | 159.8 | 115.5 |
| Provision (benefit) for income taxes | 79.4 | (116.0) | 135.5 | (20.1) | (0.2) |
| Income (loss) from continued operations | 133.6 | 252.5 | 269.6 | 139.7 | 115.3 |
| Noncontrolling shareholders' interests | (22.6) | (32.1) | (16.1) | (23.4) | (31.9) |
| Income (loss) from operations attributable to Cooper Tire & Rubber stockholders | $  111.0 | $  220.4 | $ 253.5 | $  116.3 | $   83.4 |
| Net earnings (loss) per share: | | | | | |
|   Basic | $   1.75 | $   3.52 | $   4.08 | $   1.90 | $   1.57 |
|   Diluted | $   1.73 | $   3.49 | $   4.02 | $   1.86 | $   1.54 |
| Dividends declared per share | $   0.42 | $   0.42 | $   0.42 | $   0.42 | $   0.42 |
| Percentage of net earnings to net sales | 3.2% | 5.3% | 6.5% | 4.2% | 1.9% |
| Return on average stockholders' equity | 9.6% | 24.3% | 36.3% | 26.8% | 11.2% |
| Capital expenditures | $  180.4 | $  187.3 | $ 155.4 | $  119.7 | $   79.3 |
| Depreciation & amortization | 134.8 | 128.9 | 122.9 | 123.7 | 123.5 |
| Cash, cash equivalents | 397.7 | 351.8 | 233.7 | 413.4 | 427.0 |
| Current assets | 1,454.8 | 1,449.7 | 1,264.0 | 1,340.2 | 1,131.8 |

*(Continued)*

## EXHIBIT 1   (Continued)

| | 2013 | 2012 | 2011 | 2010 | 2009 |
|---|---|---|---|---|---|
| Current liabilities | 564.6 | 655.1 | 651.0 | 694.2 | 636.3 |
| Working capital | 890.2 | 794.6 | 613.0 | 646.0 | 495.5 |
| Current ratio | 2.58 | 2.21 | 1.94 | 1.93 | 1.78 |
| Net property, plant, and equipment | 974.3 | 929.3 | 899.0 | 824.7 | 839.4 |
| Total assets | 2,738.1 | 2,801.2 | 2,510.0 | 2,305.5 | 2,100.3 |
| Long-term liabilities | 320.9 | 336.1 | 329.5 | 320.7 | 331.0 |
| Total liabilities | 1,581.3 | 1,892.7 | 1,812.0 | 1,782.4 | 1,636.2 |
| Stockholders' equity | 1,156.8 | 908.4 | 697.9 | 523.1 | 464.1 |
| Average common shares (000s) | 63,327 | 62,561 | 62,150 | 61,299 | 59,439 |
| Employees | 13,280 | 13,550 | 12,890 | 12,898 | 12,568 |

*Source:* Cooper Tire & Rubber Company 10-K report, 2013.

The key imperatives of the strategic plan involved developing a competitive cost structure and improving profitability, driving top-line profitable growth, and building organizational capabilities.

After development of the plan, Cooper Tire encountered floods, earthquakes, hurricanes, and the meltdown of the credit markets and oil prices, which started in 2008 around $75 per barrel, spiked mid-year at nearly $150 per barrel, and ended the year at around $45 per barrel. Cooper Tire also entered into what some had termed a global recession. Demand for replacement tires declined for the second of three years, an extremely unusual pattern for the industry. All of these factors impacted Cooper Tire & Rubber's 2008 results.

While implementing elements of the strategic plan in 2008, the company's existing operations were able to lower production costs, excluding the impacts of shutdowns due to soft demand. In the past, to address the top line, Cooper Tire had launched new premium products that positioned the company very well for growth in that segment of the market. In fact, over 30 percent of the company's sales in 2008 were from products launched in the previous two years. The Cooper Tire & Rubber brand continued with a strong performance. This effort delivered results over the year with the successful implementation of channel strategies at the national, regional, wholesale, and independent retail levels. Cooper Tire also continued investing in facilities in lower-cost countries. This positioned the company for improved operating costs, greater geographic flexibility, and the ability to penetrate markets outside

the United States. To enhance its capabilities, the company continued to shift the culture at Cooper Tire to a continuous-improvement mindset. To that end, the company trained black and green belts as part of its Lean Six Sigma efforts, as well as made internal changes in the organization's structure to support quick and sustainable improvements to its operations. The company also aggressively pursued business that would position its products in market channels where it was underrepresented. Cooper Tire had cash and untapped credit lines available for capital spending. The company continued to tightly monitor spending and capital expenditures during 2008 and suspended the repurchase of shares and debt. Raw-material costs were extremely volatile in 2008.

In 2009, Cooper Tire & Rubber had a strong focus on the first of its strategic imperatives. In North America, the company closed its Albany, Georgia, plant and successfully moved products from the plant to its remaining two plants, making the transition virtually invisible to its customers and, at the same time, improving efficiency and reducing waste. Its international operations were aggressively attacking costs while continuously improving quality. From a supply standpoint, Cooper Tire was faced with continually adjusting its production to weakening levels of demand across the industry. Raw-material costs declined in the first half of 2009 from their peak in 2008 but rapidly escalated again in the second half of the year. Across the organization, Cooper Tire did an excellent job of managing its costs against difficult headwinds. These challenges did not detract from its unwavering focus on safety and quality. Cooper Tire also had substantial resources and energy directed at top-line growth initiatives in 2009. The company developed and introduced successful new products, including an entry-level tire and a more fuel-efficient tire to meet market demands, driven by the economic downturn, in both product segments. In Asia and Europe, Cooper Tire launched products that were extremely popular in those markets. In the second half of 2009, Cooper Tire & Rubber began to see the results of these efforts, and its performance compared to the market improved noticeably. From an organizational capability perspective, Cooper Tire & Rubber concentrated on talent development and continued implementation of Lean Six Sigma and automation projects.

Among the company's highlights of 2010, Cooper Tire & Rubber completed the move to a 24/7 operation in Texarkana, Arkansas, and increased production at six of the seven tire manufacturing locations. The company also boosted its ownership stake in Cooper Tire & Rubber Chengshan Tire (CCT) to 65 percent from 51 percent and increased ownership in Corporación de Occidente SA de CV to 58 percent from 38 percent and of Cooper Tire & Rubber Company de Mexico SA de CV to approximately 100 percent from 50 percent. The company's Cooper Tire Lean Six Sigma (CTLSS) program, in its second year, continued to bring forward successful results as employees around the world embraced and used Six Sigma methodology to improve the company's overall business. The company's new product launches during the year were extremely well received by its customers.

In 2011, Cooper Tire & Rubber made long-term investments in money and resources, including ownership levels at Cooper Tire & Rubber Kunshan Tire Corporation de Occidente and Cooper Tire & Rubber Company de Mexico, as well as agreeing to purchase assets in Serbia. These investments complemented ongoing investments at the company's legacy facilities, targeted to enhance competitiveness. Meanwhile, the company successfully rolled out a rebranding initiative of the Cooper Tire & Rubber brand that better connected consumers to the great qualities and values the company offered.

Cooper Tire continued to reinvest in its business throughout 2013, with capital investments that were higher than historical norms but necessary to maintain growth momentum. These investments included initiatives such as its ERP deployment, which would ultimately provide a seamless flow of information on a global basis in real time, greatly enhancing the efficiency of its operations. Cooper Tire also invested in the continued ramp-up of its tire manufacturing facility in Serbia, which the company purchased in January 2012. This facility ended the year with production of 1 million tires and was a factor, along with operations in China, in the 12 percent year-over-year sales growth that the company's international segment achieved in 2012. In North America, the company maintained vigilance in driving cost reductions and invested in automation, equipment, and other enhancements while achieving a 4 percent sales increase. The increase was led by strong performance in premium passenger, light-truck and truck-bus radial tires.

## COOPER TIRE & RUBBER IN 2014

In 2014, Cooper Tire & Rubber, with its subsidiaries, was the 4th-largest tire manufacturer in North America and the 11th-largest tire company in the world based on sales. Cooper Tire focused on the manufacture and sale of passenger and light- and medium-truck replacement tires. As of December 2013, Cooper Tire operated 9 manufacturing facilities and 38 distribution centers in 11 countries and employed 13,280 persons worldwide. The company was organized into two separate business divisions: North American Tire Operations and International Tire Operations. Each division was managed separately.

**North American Tire Operations Division**
The North American Tire Operations division manufactured and marketed passenger-car and light-truck tires, primarily for sale in the U.S. replacement-tire market. As of 2014, Cooper Tire operated three manufacturing facilities in the United States and one in Mexico—see Exhibit 2. This Cooper Tire division operated in a highly competitive market, which included Bridgestone, Goodyear, and Michelin. These competitors were substantially larger than Cooper Tire and served the original-equipment manufacturer (OEM) market as well as the replacement-tire market. Cooper Tire's North American division also faced competition from low-cost producers in Asia, Mexico, South America, and central Europe.

**EXHIBIT 2**   Plant Capacity of North American Tire Manufacturers, 2014 (in thousands of units per day)

| Company and Plant Location | Number of Plants | Capacity per Day | | | | |
|---|---|---|---|---|---|---|
| | | Passenger Car | Light Truck | Truck | Other | Total |
| Bridgestone Americas Inc. | 10 | 79.3 | 24.3 | 15.2 | 4.91 | 123.71 |
| Carlisle Tire & Wheels Co., USA | 2 | 0.0 | 0.0 | 0.0 | 41.0 | 41.0 |
| Continental Tire, the Americas | 2 | 31.9 | 3.6 | 6.0 | 0.0 | 41.5 |
| Cooper Tire & Rubber Co., USA | 3 | 73.0 | 24.0 | 0.0 | 0.0 | 97.0 |
| Goodyear Tire & Rubber Co. | 8 | 131.0 | 26.0 | 18.8 | 19.3 | 195.1 |
| GTY (General/Yokohama), USA | 1 | 0.0 | 0.0 | 3.9 | 0.0 | 3.9 |
| Michelin North America Inc. | 14 | 163.5 | 33.0 | 7.0 | 5.11 | 208.61 |
| Mitas Tires North America Inc. | 1 | 0.0 | 0.0 | 0.0 | 0.5 | 0.5 |
| Pirelli Tire North America Inc. | 2 | 4.0 | 1.7 | 0.0 | 0.0 | 5.7 |
| Specialty Tires of America Inc. | 2 | 0.0 | 0.4 | 0.0 | 6.2 | 6.6 |
| Titan Tire Corp., USA | 3 | 0.0 | 0.0 | 0.0 | 19.68 | 19.68 |
| Toyo Tire North America, USA | 1 | 7.8 | 7.8 | 0.0 | 0.0 | 15.6 |
| Yokohama Tire Corp., USA | 1 | 25.7 | 1.1 | 0.0 | 0.0 | 26.8 |
| Grupo Carson/Euzkadi (Continental AG), Mexico | 1 | 15.0 | 5.0 | 0.0 | 0.0 | 20.0 |
| JK Tyre & Industries, Mexico | 3 | 10.0 | 5.0 | 2.0 | 1.04 | 18.04 |
| Corporación de Occidente SA de CV (Cooper Tire & Rubber), Mexico | 1 | 10.0 | 7.2 | 2.8 | 0.0 | 20.0 |
| U.S. Totals | 40 | 442.1 | 105.1 | 50.9 | 79.7 | 677.8 |
| Canadian Totals | 6 | 46.3 | 11.2 | 0.0 | 17.0 | 74.5 |
| Mexican Totals | 9 | 62.8 | 22.8 | 4.8 | 1.04 | 91.44 |
| **Total** | **55** | **551.2** | **139.1** | **55.7** | **97.74** | **843.74** |
| 2014 vs. 2013 | +5 | +0.4% | +0.9% | +1.1% | −0.1% | +0.5% |

Source: *Modern Tire Dealer,* 48th Annual Facts issue.

Some of these producers were foreign affiliates of the division's competitors in North America. The division also participated in the U.S. medium-truck replacement market. In addition to manufacturing tires in the United States, the division had a joint venture manufacturing operation in Mexico. Only a small portion of the products manufactured by the division were exported throughout the world. Exhibit 3 presents market shares for the leading sellers of replacement tires in the United States in 2013.

Success in competing for the sale of replacement tires was dependent upon many factors, the most important of which were price, quality, performance, line coverage, availability through appropriate distribution channels, and relationship with dealers. Other factors included warranty, credit terms, and other value-added programs. The North American division had built close working relationships with independent dealers. Cooper Tire management believed those relationships had enabled the company to obtain a competitive advantage in that channel of the market. As a steadily increasing percentage of replacement tires were sold by large regional and national tire retailers, the division has increased its penetration of those distribution channels while maintaining a focus on its traditionally strong network of independent dealers.

**International Tire Operations Division**

The International Tire Operations division had two manufacturing operations in the United Kingdom,

**EXHIBIT 3**    Market Shares of the Leading Brands of U.S. Replacement Tires, 2013

| Passenger-Car Tires (based on 201.6 million units) | | Light-Truck Tires (based on 28.3 million units) | |
|---|---|---|---|
| Goodyear | 13.0% | Goodyear | 12.0% |
| Michelin | 8.5 | BF Goodrich | 9.0 |
| Bridgestone | 8.0 | Bridgestone | 8.0 |
| Firestone | 7.5 | Michelin | 7.0 |
| Cooper Tire & Rubber | 5.5 | Firestone | 6.5 |
| BF Goodrich | 4.5 | Cooper Tire & Rubber | 6.0 |

Source: *Modern Tire Dealer*, 48th Annual Facts issue.

one in the Republic of Serbia, and two in China. The U.K. entity manufactured and marketed passenger-car, light-truck, motorcycle, and racing tires and tire retread material for the global market. The Republic of Serbia entity manufactured light-vehicle tires for the European markets. The division's entity in China manufactured only light-vehicle tires. Under an agreement with the government of China, all of the tires produced at the facility were exported. The division also had a joint venture in China, Cooper Tire & Rubber Chengshan Tire, which manufactured and marketed radial bias medium-truck tires as well as passenger-car and light-truck tires for the global market.

As with the North American division, the International division operated in a highly competitive industry, which included Bridgestone, Goodyear, and Michelin. The division also faced competition from low-cost producers in certain markets.

## Quality Control

Cooper Tire & Rubber's quality control policies and procedures were managed by specific staff, but a great deal of the responsibility for quality rested with the individual workers, who were trained to do their own quality-assurance checks. Cooper Tire's employee-centered organization resulted in high product quality. Employees received as many as 900 hours of training, and signs bearing such slogans as "Quantity is Important, but Quality is MORE Important" hung from factory walls. To symbolize a personal commitment to quality, each tire carried not only a brand name but also a sticker identifying the worker who made it. It was believed that this helped foster pride in workmanship among Cooper

Tire's workers and created a bond with the consumers buying the tires.

## Market Positioning

One factor in Cooper Tire & Rubber's success was that it confined itself to the replacement-tire market. Although Cooper Tire was a midget among the world's tire makers, it was the only major U.S. tire producer that refused to compete for low-profit-margin OEM sales to automakers. Instead, it concentrated on the replacement-tire market, which was about four times larger than the OEM market and was growing faster because the owners of highly durable cars were keeping them longer. Although the major competitors controlled more than 50 percent of the replacement market, Cooper Tire & Rubber made about 5.6 percent of the 230 million replacement tires sold in North America in 2013 (see Exhibit 3).

## Distribution and Marketing

Cooper Tire had a broad customer base in North America, including purchasers of private-label tires (which were manufactured by Cooper Tire but marketed and distributed by its customers) and purchasers of house-brand tires (which were marketed and distributed by Cooper Tire).

The company attracted private-label customers and earned retailer loyalty by pledging not to open its own sales outlets—a strategy that also allowed Cooper Tire to avoid the headaches of the retail market. Rather than selling through its own retail chains, as Goodyear and Bridgestone/Firestone did, Cooper Tire continued to sell about half of its production as private labels to store chains, mass merchants, and discounters. Private brands included Sears, TBC, Hercules, Pep Boys, American Car Care Centers, ProComp Tires, and Tires Les Schwab. Over recent years, price pressure on private-label tires had increased as the price differential between major brands and private labels had been squeezed. But Cooper Tire management believed that private-label tires still played a very important role in the replacement-tire market. Private-label tires were an excellent value and provided the distributors and dealers with the ability to call their marketing shots and maintain product control in their local markets. It was believed that the strong private brands with distributors and dealers that provided good service would continue to prosper. In 1997 and 1998, Cooper Tire & Rubber was honored by private-brand customer Sears and received the Sears Partners in Progress award out of more than 10,000 vendors vying for this recognition.

The other half of the company's output was primarily sold under its Mastercraft, Starfire, Dick Cepek, Chengshan, Dean, Avon, and Roadmaster brands through independent tire dealers and wholesale distributors. Independent dealers and distributors remained crucial to the company's success. They accounted for an estimated 67 percent of replacement-tire sales since they were the main suppliers to car dealer franchises, muffler shops, and service stations. According to the Retail Tire Customer Survey, "The independent dealers helped customers choose a brand of tires to buy 79 percent of the time. The customers were more likely to stay with the recommended replacement tire brand suggested by the dealer for the first set of tires than for subsequent sets."[2] In 2007 and 2008, Cooper Tire received high marks from independent dealers. Cooper Tire & Rubber and Mastercraft house brands were ranked at the top of a national survey of tire dealers conducted by *Tire Review*, with dealers ranking Mastercraft first and Cooper Tire & Rubber second.

Cooper Tire focused its relatively modest marketing budget on supporting its independent dealers, mainly by providing superior service and delivery and by offering a value-priced product. Cooper Tire advertising programs assisted dealers and distributors with promotional materials in their local markets. Co-op advertising allowances were based on annual dealer purchases and were applicable to all types of media. The Cooper Tire's house brands were growing a little faster than its private-label business.

To broaden brand awareness among customers, at the beginning of 1997, Cooper Tire signed Arnold Palmer as company spokesman and stepped up its advertising media expenditures. It was believed that these moves were beginning to pay off, with all the house brands showing healthy sales increases. Dealers loved Cooper Tire & Rubber because unlike Goodyear, it did not have company retail stores to compete against the dealers and it provided them with the highest gross profit margins in the industry—33 percent versus an average of 28 percent for competing brands.

Product shipments to customers were directed through a strategic, nationwide network of distribution centers, which ensured timely deliveries to customers. A new management information system was introduced to further streamline inventory and order-processing operations and to provide even better service to customers.

Over the years, Cooper Tire & Rubber had expanded exports of its products. The company's new acquisition of British-based Avon Tyres had added $169 million to annual sales, increasing Cooper Tire's international sales exposure from its 8 percent preacquisition level and providing a strong base for future global expansion.

## Research and Development

The company also saved on R&D. Cooper Tire generally directed its research activities toward product development, improvements in quality, and operating efficiency. While other tire makers incurred high R&D expenses to capture a share of the original-equipment tire market segment, Cooper Tire was able to produce tires with a proven track record and sell them to value-oriented customers. Instead of pioneering its own designs, the company waited to see what sold well as original equipment, and then it produced its own versions. Original tires on new cars normally lasted up to four years; therefore, the company was able to reduce speculative R&D expenditures and had ample time to produce its own versions.

Cooper Tire & Rubber did not just copy others' designs, however; it had very active R&D departments in both tires and its engineered rubber products divisions. There was very good communication between the R&D departments and other organizational units. Engineers in R&D were cross-trained in manufacturing procedures and spent a lot of time on the floor so that they would not be working in isolation.

Computer technology was used in product design and development, machine design, and mold design. The major tire companies were spending freely, 2.5 to 3 percent of revenues, on R&D. They were using computers to test tire durability, traction, fuel efficiency, compatibility with new car designs, and even noise. Analysts considered Goodyear the research leader. A decade earlier, designing a tire for a new automobile model required testing 200 to 300 tires. In 2011, doing so took about 65 tires. In the last few years, tire designing moved from an empirical art to a science, mainly because of advancements in computer technology. Goodyear spent $369 million on R&D in 2011, or 3.5 percent of revenues, up from 2.5 percent five years earlier.

Research and development expenditures at Cooper Tire & Rubber amounted to approximately $35.7 million in 2009, $39.7 million in 2010, and $44.6 million in 2011. The amount spent in 2011 on R&D represented 1.1 percent of its revenues. Cooper Tire's innovative application of advanced computer technology provided the company with a competitive advantage in bringing new, high-quality products to market quickly. Data collection devices on a wide range of equipment throughout the production process provided accurate information on the components being made. Comparing the component data with product orders from customers ensured that the proper tires were scheduled for production.

Other main tire companies were also using research to cut costs for original equipment, the tires that automakers buy for new cars. Although original-equipment sales accounted for just a quarter of production, nearly 70 percent of consumers replaced their tires with the brand that came with the car. Since auto companies wanted a distinctive tire design for each new model, tire makers were striving to develop lines more quickly. At Goodyear, computer-aided design helped cut development time from 117 weeks in 1980 to 65 weeks in 1995, and the goal was to reduce the time to less than 20 weeks by 2011.

## Choosing Plant Locations

Moving into low-cost regions was one of Cooper Tire & Rubber's winning strategies, and the company intended to continue utilizing this strategy in the future for further growth. Having its plants in small-town locations was another factor in Cooper Tire's superior performance. The company wasted no money on frills, not even on utilization of its headquarters in the small town of Findlay, Ohio. Getting attention wasn't Cooper Tire's style. When the company wanted to add capacity, it did so cheaply by buying old plants and retrofitting them. This was made possible by the fact that more than 35 tire plants had been shut down since the 1970s. Cooper Tire & Rubber had a good engineering department, which not only designed and built the company's own production equipment but also adapted and modified other equipment to meet its own needs and specifications. The engineering team also continually monitored advances in new technology for possible incorporation into Cooper Tire's manufacturing processes. At its plant in Texarkana, Arkansas, changes in materials flow and production scheduling meant that inventory got turned 10 times a year instead of 3 to 5 times.

Cooper Tire & Rubber's tire plants were in places like Tupelo, Mississippi, and Texarkana, Arkansas, where the company was a master employer. In these small towns, Cooper Tire employees at all levels and their families constantly interacted in community churches and organizations. This developed the feeling that everyone had a stake in the future of the company. Some analysts believed that Cooper Tire's small-town locations permitted it to pay lower salaries and to reap other savings over companies in urban locations. Most Cooper Tire employees grew up in and around the rural areas where the company's tire plants were located. Employees drawn from these smaller communities tended to make a longer-term commitment to the firm and to exhibit a stronger work ethic than did employees from larger and more mobile communities.

Cooper Tire & Rubber ran its plants at 100 percent capacity, while other companies operated at about 80 percent. In a capital-intensive industry, running at full capacity created lots of leverage for Cooper Tire. Its Tupelo, Mississippi, factory ran 24 hours a day, seven days a week.

## Raw-Material Strategy

Over 200 raw materials were used in manufacturing tires. The primary raw materials used for tire production were synthetic rubber, carbon black, natural rubber, rubber chemicals, steel wire, steel cord, polyester, and adhesives. Petroleum and natural gas were important for production of some of these materials, such as rubber and carbon black. Crude oil accounted for the largest raw-material cost; about 10 gallons of crude oil was consumed when manufacturing an average-sized passenger-car radial tire. Large economies of scale were very helpful in the industry, as the tire buyers were price-sensitive. A historical cost-of-goods-sold (COGS) percentage composition breakdown for Cooper Tire & Rubber can be found in Exhibit 4.

In 1993, Cooper Tire opened a purchasing office in Singapore to acquire natural rubber and various materials directly from producers in the Far East. This purchasing operation enabled the company to work directly with producers to improve the consistency of quality and to reduce the costs of materials, delivery, and transactions. Cooper Tire's inventory control policies and procedures were believed to be highly efficient—buying ahead on occasion to get the best deals but not hedging on raw materials.

The industry did not experience any significant raw-material shortages over the past years. In fact, all of the raw materials were commodities, available in bulk from a variety of sources on world markets.

**EXHIBIT 4    Historical Percentage Composition Breakdown of Cooper Tire & Rubber Company's Cost of Goods Sold**

| Input | Percent of COGS |
|---|---|
| Labor | 20–30 |
| Other | 15–30 |
| Raw materials | 50–55 |

| Raw Material | Percent of Raw Materials |
|---|---|
| Natural rubber | 20–25 |
| Synthetic rubbers | 25–30 |
| Carbon black | 10–15 |
| Reinforcing fabrics | 10–15 |
| Steel | 10–15 |
| Other raw materials | 10–15 |

*Source:* www.docstoc.com/docs/79573233/Cooper Tire & Rubber-Tire-_amp-Rubber-Company-Strategic-Plan-and-Vision.

Raw-material prices in 2012 demonstrated volatility: Prices started the year at an elevated level and declined steadily through the end of the year, with the full-year average index down 7 percent compared to 2011. Like all companies within the tire industry, Cooper Tire & Rubber benefited from lower raw-material prices in 2012. However, on a longer-term basis, it expected prices to generally increase as the global economy gained momentum.

In 2012, there was a worldwide crunch for natural rubber (NR), and the rapidly rising NR prices were a major concern for all tire manufacturers. The worldwide shortage of NR was arising mainly because of production cuts in Malaysia (where plantations were shifting more toward palm oil), the growing usage of NR in radial tires, and an increasing demand in China. In the future, the usage of more synthetic rubber and the partial replacement of NR by synthetic polyisoprene were expected to increase. Even though natural rubber was traded above $2 per kilogram, it was still the first choice for radial truck tire manufacturers because of its excellent physical and mechanical properties, and its better adhesion to steel cord. The increasing price of crude oil had built up the pressure on the tire and automobile industries to develop low-rolling-resistance tires with better traction.

Several tire manufacturers had integrated backward into rubber manufacturing and tire fabric supply. However, there was no evidence that these manufacturers had gained a meaningful cost advantage or had a better ability to differentiate their products on the basis of quality.

Volatility in raw-material pricing was a factor in Cooper Tire & Rubber's pursuit of alternative material sources that required innovative technology. In 2012, Cooper Tire, along with partner organizations, received a $6.9 million grant from the U.S. Department of Agriculture to evaluate the U.S.-grown guayule plant as an alternative source of natural rubber.

## COOPER TIRE & RUBBER'S EFFORTS TO EXECUTE ITS STRATEGY

Much of the credit for Cooper Tire & Rubber's success, said Alec Reinhardt, the company's chief financial officer, should go to its workforce for being motivated in a way that fitted nicely with management's unending search for new ways to hold down costs. The company made great strides in developing a participative, cooperative, less hierarchical work climate. Cooper Tire management had long recognized that the performance of dedicated employees could make a difference in an industry where competitors sell products that differ very little from one another. Employees became involved at all levels of the organization, especially in the areas of productivity, quality assurance, and customer service. Monthly meetings were held in each department to update workers on new developments and to solicit their suggestions and information about problems.

Cooper Tire's employee recruiting process was operated by examining applicants through a series of screening procedures. The applicants who passed the initial screening were motivated people—team players and good communicators—with the right attitude and personality to fit the job for which they had applied. Then they took two pencil-and-paper tests, one of which was keyed to a video tape, followed by a one-on-one behavioral-type interview with a supervisor. Those who made it through the preliminary screening were placed in groups, working on problem solving in situations involving some stress.

All new Cooper Tire employees received a basic, two-week training and orientation course. Each new employee's spouse was also asked to come in to learn what it meant to work for Cooper Tire & Rubber and why the company considered an employee's spouse to be part of the team. Training courses were designed to meet the specific needs of each employee. After the basic course, an employee's training could continue for a period of three days to over a year. Management scheduled working hours and shifts in ways that allowed employees ample days off for participating in community activities, thereby developing a family atmosphere at the plants.

Cooper Tire's innovative incentive system was a driving force for employees. The compensation system—in which the earnings of everyone, from the CEO to line workers, rose and fell with the individual's performance and contribution to productivity—instilled loyalty. Executive compensation was tied to performance benchmarks and provided for

cuts, as well as raises, of up to 30 percent. Profit-sharing opportunities and paid incentives also augmented the paychecks of the company's blue-collar and clerical workers. Hourly workers were paid extra for producing more, and salaried employees could earn bonuses of up to 7.5 percent based on the return on assets they worked with. In fact, although incentive programs were offered to every employee, none of them were based on market share.

Employee turnover was discouraged by Cooper Tire's stock option plan. The company had a very low (3.1 percent) turnover rate, and absenteeism was at one-tenth of 1 percent. For staff and management alike, a long tenure with the company was the norm. Some analysts pointed to Cooper Tire's tight fiscal controls, its high productivity, and its low-cost manufacturing efficiencies as the key ingredients of its strategy. But Gorr insisted that the heart of Cooper Tire's success wasn't anything more complicated than a lot of hard work, an obsession with quality, and a devotion to the dealers.

All of the company's managers were substantial stockholders, as were many workers. Reinhardt estimated that employees held 20 percent of Cooper Tire's stock. The company's stock purchase program had been profitable for many employees. The stock rose an astonishing 6,800 percent during the 1980s, richly rewarding long-time employees who had invested in the company.

## COMPETITION IN THE GLOBAL AUTOMOTIVE TIRE INDUSTRY

Tire manufacturing became an important industry in the first half of the 20th century as motor vehicles became the dominant mode of transportation. While the tire industry was certainly mature in developed countries, having been around for more than 160 years, it was a vastly different business in 2013 than it had been even five years earlier. The challenges were many, but so were the opportunities. In the United States, production of passenger-vehicle and light-truck tires had undergone significant change over the last two decades. What was once considered a major U.S. manufacturing sector was now part of a global industry that was largely controlled by foreign-headquartered corporations.

Rubber chemistry had become much more complex since the day, 152 years ago, when Charles Goodyear invented strong, vulcanized rubber by accidentally dropping sulfur and crude rubber onto his stove. Tire company chemists were now stirring up exotic synthetic rubbers to improve traction on wet streets without sacrificing fuel efficiency. Steel belts—actually steel and polyester woven into a tough fabric—were being improved as well, beginning 20 years ago. The average radial tire lasted 50,000 miles; the average bias tire lasted 18,000 to 20,000 miles. James A. Thiese, director of passenger and light-truck tire development for Firestone, credited the work of the chemists: "That's what now allows a tire to perform with the same efficiency in 20 degree-below-zero weather as it does in 95-degree heat."[3]

A decade ago, a dozen major tire manufacturers, half of them American, competed for world leadership. In 2013, just four giant global tire companies were dominant, accounting for about 50 percent of worldwide tire sales, and they included only one U.S.-headquartered company: Goodyear Tire and Rubber Company. Consolidation had come about because of slackening demand and global competition. Goodyear, the leader for decades, was contending for fourth place. In the previous six years, foreign companies had bought out most of the best-known American labels, including Firestone and Armstrong. The recent agreement by Groupe Michelin of France to buy Uniroyal Goodrich Tire Company would create the world's largest tire maker—if, as expected, American antitrust regulators approve. In the United States, aside from Goodyear, only the smaller Cooper Tire & Rubber Company has remained independent. Exhibit 5 shows the world's largest sellers of new tires in 2012 and 2013.

Confronted with sharp declines in output, employment, and the number of plants in the consumer tire sector, numerous members of Congress expressed concerns about the future of tire manufacturing in the United States. Congress appeared to have few policy levers with which to support tire manufacturing in the United States. To the extent that government policy encouraged domestic production of small vehicles, most of which were imported, there might have been additional demand for U.S.-made OEM tires. More stringent

federal standards for tires also might have encouraged domestic production, albeit at the cost of higher prices for consumers. In response to a petition filed by the United Steel Workers with the U.S. International Trade Commission, the Obama administration imposed punitive tariffs on Chinese tires for three years, starting in September 2009. A World Trade Organization (WTO) panel determined in December 2010 that the U.S. tariff measures were in compliance with the nation's WTO obligations. The higher tariffs caused an increase in imports of low-cost tires from countries other than China, notably Thailand and Mexico, but did not lead manufacturers to shift production back to the United States.

Companies within the tire manufacturing industry often chose certain distribution channels. For example, Bridgestone and Goodyear sold tires to their own retail stores, which sold them directly to end users, but Cooper Tire & Rubber did not

### EXHIBIT 5    Leading Sellers of New Tires, by Worldwide Revenue, 2012–2013 (in billions of U.S. dollars)

| Company | Country | 2013 | 2012 |
|---|---|---|---|
| Bridgestone Corp. | Japan | $31.2 | $32.0 |
| Groupe Michelin | France | 26.8 | 27.4 |
| Goodyear Tire & Rubber Co. | United States | 18.9 | 20.2 |
| Continental AG | Germany | 13.0 | 12.4 |
| Pirelli & Cie SpA | Italy | 8.0 | 7.7 |
| Sumitomo Rubber Industries Ltd. | Japan | 6.9 | 7.7 |
| Hankook Tire Co. | South Korea | 6.6 | 6.3 |
| Yokohama Rubber Corp. | Japan | 4.9 | 5.6 |
| Cheng Shin Rubber Ind. Co. Ltd. | Taiwan | 4.5 | 4.4 |
| Kumho Tire Co. Ltd. | South Korea | 3.4 | 3.6 |
| Cooper Tire & Rubber Co. | United States | 3.2 | 4.2 |
| Toyo Tire & Rubber Co. Ltd. | Japan | 3.0 | 3.6 |

*Source: Modern Tire Dealer, 48th Annual Facts issue.*

have its own company-owned retail stores. Cooper Tire also did not sell tires to OEMs. The account managers had to make wise decisions and choose their distribution channel carefully. Service stations typically stocked one or two manufacturers' brand tires and sometimes a private-label brand. Retail tire outlets owned and franchised by the tire manufacturers carried only the manufacturer's name brands and perhaps a private-label made by the manufacturer. Department stores and the major retail chains usually marketed their own private-label brands, but occasionally also carried manufacturers' label tires.

The global automotive tire market was highly consolidated and consisted of passenger-car tires, heavy-truck tires, and other segments. North America dominated this market with about 30 percent of the global total in 2012. Europe emerged as the highest potential market, followed by the Asia-Pacific (APAC) region and North America. Competition in the global automotive tire industry was high. A combination of factors such as vehicle sales, government regulations, and environmental factors impacted market dynamics significantly.

Year 2012 was a record year for the global production and shipment of light-vehicle tires, with worldwide production reaching 1,460 million tires in 2012 (see Exhibit 6). Over the years, tire supply and demand was tight globally and particularly in North America. Tire manufacturers had increasingly moved production of replacement tires from the United States to Asia, especially China, as imports undercut sales of domestically produced tires. Chinese production capacity far exceeded Chinese domestic demand for tires, and China had pursued an aggressive export agenda. The Asia-Pacific region was by far the largest production region for light-vehicle tires, accounting for more than half of the global light-vehicle tire production in 2012. Sales of motor vehicle tires in China were the second highest in the world, behind only sales in the United States. The massive Chinese light-vehicle tire market, which accounted for more than 12 percent of global light-vehicle tire demand in 2012, was on course to record the strongest gains, compared to that market in any country, through 2015. Global light-vehicle tire demand was forecast to rise 3.3 percent per year through 2015. The tire markets in North America and western Europe were expected to continue to see advances below the global average.

Although tire manufacturing was relatively capital-intensive, there was significant labor content—labor costs ran from about 15 to 40 percent of total costs, depending on wage rates and labor productivity. Industry observers were predicting increased worldwide sourcing of tires from countries having the lowest labor costs, with Korea, Mexico, and Brazil becoming increasingly attractive production locations. Several major tire manufacturers were considering plant locations in low-wage countries.

According to Lucintel, a leading market research firm, the global automotive tire industry held opportunities for industry players due to the strong expected demand for replacement tires and increasing sales of passenger and commercial vehicles in developing countries. The Asia-Pacific region was expected to attain the highest growth in rubber demand during the 2012–2017 forecast period, reflecting strength in China, India, Thailand, and Vietnam. The global

**EXHIBIT 6**    Global Light-Vehicle Tire Production, 2007–2012 (in millions of tires)

| Year | North America | South America | Europe | Asia | Other | Global |
|------|---------------|---------------|--------|------|-------|--------|
| 2007 | 215 | 63 | 380 | 580 | 57 | 1,295 |
| 2008 | 200 | 66 | 335 | 624 | 65 | 1,290 |
| 2009 | 180 | 58 | 320 | 580 | 47 | 1,185 |
| 2010 | 200 | 64 | 340 | 735 | 48 | 1,387 |
| 2011 | 200 | 65 | 345 | 770 | 49 | 1,429 |
| 2012 | 200 | 65 | 345 | 800 | 50 | 1,460 |

*Source:* Moderntiredealer.com.

automobile tire industry market was forecast to reach an estimated $187 billion in 2017, with a compound annual growth rate (CAGR) of 4 percent over the forecast five years. The passenger-car segment was forecast to see the strongest growth during the forecast period. Lucintel's research also indicated that although volatile raw-material prices and higher dependency of suppliers on the OEMs were market challenges, the increasing per capita income in developing nations, population growth, new infrastructure projects, urbanization, increase in middle-class population, and green movement were all expected to drive growth in the industry.

The tire industry consisted of two distinct markets: (1) the original-equipment (OE) market, and (2) the replacement market. Both markets included passenger-car tires; light-, medium-, and heavy-truck tires; and farm-vehicle tires.

**Original-Equipment Market**   Auto manufacturers bought all of their tires directly from tire manufacturers. No auto producers had integrated backward into tire manufacturing as they had done into other component vehicle parts. Competition among the tire manufacturers to supply tires to the auto manufacturers was fierce. Since tires were such a small-cost item in the overall price of new vehicles, changes in OE tire prices had virtually no effect on total OE tire demand. The demand for OE tires was directly related to the number of vehicles produced, and it was highly elastic in regard to the ease with which motor vehicle manufacturers could switch to other tire manufacturers' brands. However, the vast majority of OE tires used on American-made vehicles were made in the United States in order to reduce car makers' supply chain risks and to protect the tire manufacturers' proprietary production processes. All the major tire manufacturers were eager to have new vehicles equipped with their own brands in order to enhance replacement-tire sales. In fact, increasing automation was allowing tire manufacturers to meet OE demand with fewer plants and fewer workers. The sale of OE tires was thus seen as strategically important, not only as a way to strengthen sales in the more profitable replacement segment but also to achieve economies of scale in manufacturing.

Vehicle manufacturers set detailed tire specifications for each of their vehicle models, and tire producers had to meet those specifications if their tires were to be considered original equipment. It was more typical for automobile and truck manufacturers to establish quality standards for the OE tires they purchased than for replacement tires. The automobile companies bought tires in large quantities, and since the number of buyers was low, they could usually negotiate low prices. Using this leverage over the years, the automakers had managed to negotiate an average price for an OE tire that was several dollars below what wholesale distributors paid tire manufacturers for a replacement tire of similar quality. In effect, the auto companies bought OE tires for roughly half the retail price commanded by replacement tires. As a result, the original-equipment market had become a low-margin one relative to the replacement-tire market.

**Replacement-Tire Market**   The larger portion of the consumer tire market involved replacement tires that were sold to consumers through various retail channels. The postwar era was one of expansion for the tire industry as a result of several converging growth factors. More disposable income enabled more Americans to own cars. Americans experienced the expansion of the interstate highway system and the postwar trend toward suburbanization. This meant more wear and tear on tires and increasing demand for replacement tires. Furthermore, the rail system was being replaced rapidly by buses, taxis, and trucks for local and long-distance transportation.

The demand for replacement tires depended on factors such as per capita disposable income, the average age of a car, the durability of the tire tread, the number of cars in circulation, the average number of miles driven, and gasoline prices. Any reduction in new-car sales was considered good news in the replacement market because it meant that drivers were hanging on to their cars longer. Even in a strong economy, used-car sales rose along with those of new cars, and motorists also spent more time on the road, further increasing the demand for replacement tires. The per capita income was low during the recession, thus tire sales suffered especially in 2008 and 2009. Consumers were cutting back on spending by holding back on tire replacement, and the OEs halted production lines. Since 2010, unit shipments of replacement tires have been flat every year. Exhibit 7 presents shipment volume trends in the United States by segment for 2009 through 2013.

**EXHIBIT 7**   U.S. Tire Shipments, 2009–2013 (in millions of tires)

| Tire Type | 2009 | 2010 | 2011 | 2012 | 2013 |
|---|---|---|---|---|---|
| Passenger: | | | | | |
| Replacement | 184.0 | 198.7 | 195.5 | 192.0 | 201.6 |
| OE | 25.0 | 34.6 | 36.0 | 40.5 | 44.0 |
| Light truck: | | | | | |
| Replacement | 26.0 | 28.5 | 28.6 | 28.3 | 28.3 |
| OE | 2.6 | 3.5 | 4.1 | 4.2 | 4.4 |
| Medium truck/bus: | | | | | |
| Replacement | 12.7 | 15.3 | 17.0 | 16.0 | 15.7 |
| OE | 2.1 | 3.3 | 4.9 | 5.3 | 5.0 |

Source: *Modern Tire Dealer*, 48th Annual Facts issue.

**EXHIBIT 8**   U.S. Consumer Tire Retail Market Share, by Distribution Channel, 2011–2013

| Distribution Channel | 2011 | 2012 | 2013 |
|---|---|---|---|
| Independent tire dealers | 61.0% | 60.5% | 60.5% |
| Mass merchandisers | 14.0 | 14.0 | 14.0 |
| Warehouse clubs | 8.5 | 8.5 | 8.5 |
| Tire company–owned stores | 7.5 | 7.5 | 7.5 |
| Auto dealerships | 2.5 | 7.0 | 7.5 |
| Miscellaneous outlets | 2.5 | 2.5 | 2.0 |

Source: *Modern Tire Dealer*, 48th Annual Facts issue.

The total vehicle miles were also a useful indicator in determining replacement-tire demand, because high usage of tires would have resulted in the increase of replacement-tire sales. Due to the recession in 2008–2009, budget-conscious consumers had increased, and these consumers wanted tires that could increase the gasoline efficiency of their vehicles. This demand caused tire manufacturers to invest in technologies to produce tires such as those with low-roll resistance.

Consumers were also holding on to their vehicles longer. According to R.I. Polk & Co., the average age of light-duty vehicles on the road stood at a record 10.8 years, compared to 11.1 years for passenger cars and 10.4 years for light trucks. "The increasing age of the vehicle fleet, together with the increasing length of ownership, offers significant business growth opportunity for the automotive aftermarket," says Mark Seng, Polk's global aftermarket-practice leader.[4]

Replacement tires were marketed to vehicle owners through a variety of retail channels, including independent tire dealers, service stations, manufacturer-owned retail stores, major department stores with auto centers, retail chains, automobile dealerships, and warehouse clubs. Independent tire dealers usually carried the brands of several different major manufacturers as well as a discount-priced private-label brand, providing replacement buyers with a full assortment of brands with varying tread designs,

widths, durability, quality, and price attributes. Over the years, independent tire dealers handled about 61 percent of the replacement-tire market—see Exhibit 8.

Surveys showed that dealers were able to influence a car owner's choice of replacement tires. Studies also showed that most replacement-tire buyers did not have strong tire-brand preferences, making it easy for tire salespeople to switch customers to the tire brands and grades with the highest dealer margins. Dealers normally pushed their private-label tires because their profit margins on them were higher than the margins on the name-brand tires of major manufacturers. Independent tire dealers frequently ran price promotion ads in the local newspapers, making it easy for price-sensitive buyers to watch for sales and buy at off-list prices.

**Technology—Recent Advances and Future Trends**   Advances in tire materials, tire constructions, and tire technologies had led to new products and the development of new market segments. Tire manufacturing technology had progressed in parallel with tire construction technology so that tires were designed not only to meet specific performance targets but also to enable improved manufacturability (i.e., more efficient, lower-cost, and more uniform production).

With all-around development, the expectations of tire customers had also grown. Increasing automobile manufacturers' requirements and ever-growing customer expectations resulted in the evolution of new product technology. Such technology continued to develop to accommodate new applications, safety, health, and environmental issues. Customers were more demanding and were looking for better mileage (tread wear), lower heat buildup, better ride and handling (dry and wet traction), and environmentally friendly features (e.g., low-rolling resistance, reduced noise, more durability, and less pollution). Keeping customers' expectations in mind, major tire manufacturers introduced several innovative products. Super single tires, run-flat technology, active wheel systems, the tweel tire, solid tires, and multi-air-chamber tires were among the major recent pathbreaking achievements of the tire industry.

Over a few decades, tire manufacturing technology had undergone a series of changes, and the tire had become a high-technology product. New expressways and highways increased demands for low-cost tires with more speed capability, high mileage, and energy-efficiency. New tire technology faced demands arising out of changes in modern vehicles with faster speeds, safety regulations, mechanization in agriculture and construction work, continuous crude oil price increases, and aggressive competition.

Reduction in tire development time and improvement in quality continued to be advanced by the use of computers. The possibility existed that, in the future, different vehicles would require different tires, fine-tuned to the specific features of each vehicle and its suspensions. The development of a tire able to run some distance after air loss continued to be pursued to eliminate the requirement for a spare tire.

**Recapped or Retreaded Tire**   The retread tire was made by retaining the tire's casing and removing its old (worn) tread professionally, by machine buffering, and replacing it with a new tread. The new tread was put on the casing through a process of pressure and heat and was mold-cured. This added better grip, improved reliability, and top-grade tire performance at a reasonable price. New tires were built in layers. The tread layer was the portion of the tire that had the most contact with the road. Retread tires were not used tires but, rather, refurbished tires with newly added grip and improved performance in all road conditions. In the past, retread tires had been widely used by some vehicle users. Retread-tire buyers were very price-conscious. In 2014, the retread-tire segment was very small and declining partly because buyers could purchase a new, more reliable set of tires for about $100 more than the cost of retreads.

## COOPER TIRE & RUBBER'S COMPETITIVE STANDING IN THE TIRE INDUSTRY

Cooper Tire & Rubber had always operated under a "price umbrella" created by the original-equipment tire manufacturers, so as that umbrella rose higher, so did Cooper Tire's profitability. However, the industry was becoming extremely competitive as major tire makers realized the attractiveness of the replacement-tire market. Cooper Tire would not have the luxury of watching how that market performed for two or three years before deciding whether to copy it. Furthermore, competitors had recently narrowed the gap between themselves and low-cost-producer Cooper Tire, with the closer rivalry apt to cause the company's margins to rise more slowly than in past years. Recently, more tire manufacturers provided longer-mileage warranties to the buyers of replacement tires. The longer warranty of 60,000 to 80,000 miles was likely to create intermediate-term demand problems. This would likely signal the beginning of heightened price competition.

The future of Cooper Tire & Rubber was expected to include periods of continuing and new challenges, with increased threats of competition in the replacement-tire market and major changes in the new products of the big-three tire companies. Cooper Tire believed that significant numbers of Chinese tires would be imported immediately following the expiration of the special U.S. tariff on such tires. However, it was expected that the company would continue doing business as it had over the past few years or, in the worst-case scenario, would manage to grow earnings and margins at a slightly lower rate. For 2014, Cooper Tire anticipated growth equal to or higher than the industry norm in key markets, allowing it to recover unit volumes lost in 2013.

Cooper Tire & Rubber operated in a highly competitive industry, which included a number of competitors larger than Cooper Tire. At the lower end of the replacement-tire market, there was additional competition from low-cost tire producers located in Asia and South America. Tire imports into the United States, especially from China, were growing each year but had slowed with the introduction of a 35 percent tariff. After the tariff implementation, the imports started to decrease significantly—see Exhibit 9. The tariff also had an effect on U.S.-based companies that operated in China. However, Cooper Tire benefited from the tariff even though it had operations in China. The company had gains in revenue despite the tariff because it was able to fight the price war by maintaining its prices. Overall, China still ranked number one as the country with the most tire imports in the United States in 2014.

Cooper Tire & Rubber competed in the markets for a wide variety of passenger-car, light- and medium-truck, motorsport, and motorcycle tires. Cooper Tire executives considered all these markets to be highly competitive and populated with both domestic and many foreign firms. Competition in the replacement-tire market centered mainly on price and price terms, quality, reputation, availability, warranty terms, credit terms, consumer convenience, and overall customer service. A combination of factors, such as vehicle sales, government regulations, and environmental concerns, also impacted market dynamics significantly.

Over the years, the recession and the uncertainty about job security had forced many consumers to become more price-conscious and less brand-loyal. Furthermore, with the demand for cars having declined over the years, the market for OE tires had shrunk, making competition fiercer in the replacement-tire market. Thus, many tire producers dumped entire inventories into the replacement-tire market, lowering prices and making profit margins even leaner. Many of the vehicles on the road were old—the average age of the U.S. vehicle fleet was over eight years. While such cars and trucks were maintained, the owners often did not want to spend a lot of money on them because there was a new car in the future. This mentality, fostered by the prevailing economic climate, played right into the hands of the low-cost tire producers. Overall, tire quality and performance were on the upswing. The longer tread life of OE and replacement tires threatened to radically reduce the number of sets of replacement tires needed per vehicle in service.

Yet it looked as though 2012 was a year of distinction for Cooper Tire & Rubber, which demonstrated that it could meet or beat the competition across a wide range of industry and global conditions. For Cooper Tire, driving growth within an industry and a global economy in which customers were looking for new ways to get an edge, new competitors from around the world continued to enter the market, the speed of technology demanded constant innovation, and upcoming government regulations and requirements could be game changers, 2012 was a proving ground. That proving ground not only tested Cooper Tire but also allowed the company to demonstrate that it was capable of mastering the toughest challenges and delivering strong value to its stakeholders. Delivering innovative, high-quality products was key to Cooper Tire's success and central to its value proposition. During 2012, the company continued to see strong consumer demand for tires such as its Zeon RS3-A and Discoverer A/T3, both of which continued to take hold in the marketplace and earned significant third-party endorsements. In fact, the RS3-A was the tire selected by Ford Motor Company as original equipment on its 2013 Ford Focus Titanium and SE models. This was Cooper Tire & Rubber's first U.S. passenger-car OE tire.

## A SUDDEN ANNOUNCEMENT OF MERGER

On June 12, 2013, it was announced that Apollo Tyres Ltd., an Indian tire company, had signed an agreement to acquire Cooper Tire & Rubber under

**EXHIBIT 9   U.S. Consumer Tire Imports from China, 2009–2013**

| Year | Units (millions) | Year-to-Year Change |
|------|------------------|---------------------|
| 2009 | 43.0 | −7.5% |
| 2010 | 31.0 | −27.9 |
| 2011 | 26.0 | −16.1 |
| 2012 | 32.5 | +25.0 |
| 2013 | 51.2 | +57.5 |

*Source:* U.S. Government data in *Modern Tire Dealer,* 48th Annual Facts issue.

a wholly owned subsidiary of Apollo via an all-cash transaction, valued at approximately US$2.5 billion, for $35 a share. Before the news was out, Cooper Tire's stock price was $24.56 a share; at the end of the day, it was $34.66. John Healy, an industry analyst for Northcoast Research in Cleveland, Ohio, and coauthor of *Modern Tire Dealer*'s monthly "Your Marketplace" column, said that Apollo wanted a stronger presence in the U.S. tire industry and knew this would be difficult to achieve on its own. Healy believed that a merger with Cooper Tire & Rubber would give Apollo a jump start for growth in this market with a valuable partner. He further stated that even with the merger, the company would be the world's seventh-largest tire company and the merger would not change the dynamics of the industry very much.

The price of $35 a share that Apollo agreed to pay seemed doomed from the start, and it immediately struck some analysts and investors as too high. Cooper Tire's margins were viewed as already being near their peaks, and competition in the United States was likely to pick up because of increased competition from Chinese manufacturers. "It was a relatively full price being paid for Apollo to gain some North American exposure," said Bret D. Jordan, an analyst with BB&T Capital Markets. "They were paying at peak margin prices."[5] Apollo shares declined 39 percent on news of the deal, even as Indian executives pledged to press on. Analysts had concluded that Apollo was borrowing too much to finance the deal and that Cooper Tire & Rubber was too big. Apollo was the minnow swallowing the whale.

Yet despite the full price being paid to Cooper Tire, problems at the company immediately arose. The United Steelworkers union filed grievances with Cooper Tire & Rubber, contending that the union was contractually allowed to approve any change in ownership and using that as an opportunity to try to renegotiate its contract. Apollo said that it would negotiate a new collective bargaining agreement but argued that this meant it should be able to pay a lower price for Cooper Tire & Rubber. Cooper Tire said that Apollo knew about the steelworkers' contract and that no price adjustment was warranted.

The issues with the steelworkers, however, were small compared with the problems Cooper Tire suddenly faced with its joint venture in China. Cooper Tire & Rubber Chengshan Tire, the joint venture, was originally 51 percent owned by Cooper Tire & Rubber, which teamed up with a local businessman. In 2010, Chengshan's Chinese partner sold Cooper Tire a significant portion of his stake for just $18 million, a figure that might have been much higher based on the size of Apollo's offer. But after the deal with Apollo was originally announced in June 2013, the Chinese factory, which had accounted for about a quarter of Cooper Tire's 2012 sales, stopped producing Cooper Tire–branded tires, and management revoked Cooper Tire's access to the factory's financial records. This cut into Cooper Tire's revenue and made it impossible for the company to provide Apollo with the updated financial information it needed to secure financing for the deal. Cooper Tire's joint venture partner suggested that the opposition was the result of concerns about Indian management of Chinese workers. In an advertisement it placed in *The Wall Street Journal,* the partner said, "Who can guarantee the success of integration between Chinese culture and Indian culture?" But Chengshan's opposition ultimately appeared to be less about Indian ownership than about compensation. Locking Cooper Tire out of the factory was seen by many as a ploy to extract a higher price, and when Cooper Tire failed to force arbitration of the dispute into courts in Hong Kong, the partner was able to keep the case mired in local courts. The partner demanded as much as $400 million to be bought out of his minority stake, Cooper Tire executives later said in court.

The problems with the union and in China led Apollo to delay the closing of the deal, saying Cooper Tire had agreed to lower its asking price. In October 2013, Cooper Tire dragged Apollo to a Delaware court, trying to force it to complete the deal under the agreed conditions, while the Indian company sought a discount on the purchase price of up to $9 a share, citing labor problems and other issues at Cooper Tire's U.S. and China units. In December 2013, the Delaware court ruled in favor of Apollo, saying the Indian company had not breached its obligations.

Cooper Tire & Rubber terminated the agreement on December 30, 2013, and said that it made the decision after Apollo's lenders refused to extend their financing commitments beyond December 31, 2013. Apollo blamed Cooper Tire for not submitting a complete picture of the working of its joint venture in China, which Apollo claimed was a key obstacle in its efforts to raise the $1.87 billion in debt that was needed for the deal. Apollo had planned to borrow the money from Morgan Stanley, Deutsche Bank AG, Goldman Sachs Group, and Standard Chartered Bank Ltd. Then, on December 30, 2013, Cooper Tire management announced that it would pursue a breakup fee, plus possible damages, from the same Delaware judge who in December 2013 declined to force Apollo to close on the original transaction. According to the contract, if the deal did not stretch beyond December 31, 2013, Apollo would be liable to pay $112.5 million to Cooper Tire for breach of contract, while Cooper Tire would have to pay a $50 million breakup penalty if it chose to withdraw from the deal.

The turmoil left Cooper Tire unable to file financial reports for the calendar third and fourth quarters of 2013 until the middle of March 2014. Cooper Tire was one of only a few companies to achieve both consistent high growth and strong returns for more than a decade. The company posted net income of $92 million on net sales of $1,746 million for the six months ended June 30, 2013. That compared to net income of $74 million on net sales of $2,043 million for the same period in 2012. Its operating profit rose 16 percent, from $143 million to a six months' record of $166 million. But Cooper Tire reported measurably lower operating and net income for the second six months and year 2013, largely due to the costs associated with the failed merger with Apollo and the negative effects of markedly lower sales.

For fiscal 2013, Cooper Tire's operating income fell 39.4 percent to $240.7 million, while net income was cut nearly in half, to $111 million. Sales were off 18.1 percent, down to $3.44 billion. According to management, fourth-quarter profits were impacted by $27 million in unusual items related to the negative effects of labor actions taken at the Cooper Tire & Rubber Chengshan Tire Company joint venture. This figure included $25 million from lower volumes and $2 million of manufacturing inefficiencies in the international business segment. The results also included $9 million of costs stemming from the terminated merger agreement with Apollo. In addition, management indicated that an unfavorable price and product mix reduced profits by $68 million, offset in part by $31 million of lower raw-material costs.

While Apollo was back where it started when the merger was announced in June 2013, Cooper Tire & Rubber still had to work to undo the damage caused by the aborted deal. "Cooper Tire & Rubber had made the point that the world is a tough place for a small tire manufacturer," Mr. Jordan said. "Now they're going it alone. I don't see any obvious second strategic buyer out there." [6]

## ENDNOTES

[1] Cooper Tire & Rubber, Cooper Tire & Rubbertire.com/About-Us/Our-Company.aspx.
[2] Holzinger, "A Successful Competition?" Nation's Business, April 1993.

[3] news.google.com/newspapers?nid=1876&dat=19900211&id=obItAAAAIBAJ&sjid=Z84EAAAAIBAJ&pg=3250,3483320.
[4] www.moderntiredealer.com/files/stats/stats/s013-facts-section-pdf.

[5] dealbook.nytimes.com/2013/12/30/Cooper Tire & Rubber-tire-abandons-merger/?_php-=true&_type=blogs&_r=0.
[6] Ibid.

# Panera Bread Company in 2014: Can a Slowdown in the Company's Growth Be Avoided?

connect

## Arthur A. Thompson
The University of Alabama

In spring 2014, Panera Bread was widely regarded as the clear leader of the "fast-casual" segment of the restaurant industry—fast-casual restaurants were viewed as being a cut above traditional quick-service restaurants like McDonald's because of better food quality, limited table service, and, in many instances, often wider and more upscale menu selections. On average, close to 8 million customers patronized Panera Bread restaurants each week, and Panera baked more specialty breads daily than any other bakery-café enterprise in North America. There were 1,777 company-owned and franchised bakery-cafés in operation in 45 states, the District of Columbia, and Ontario, Canada, under the Panera Bread, Saint Louis Bread Co., and Paradise Bakery & Café names. In 2013, the company had corporate revenues of $2.4 billion, systemwide store revenues of $4.3 billion, and average sales of almost $2.5 million per store location.

The number of Panera Bread locations was up from 1,027 units in 36 states at the end of 2006, but well short of the ambitious target the company set in 2006 to have 2,000 outlets in operation by the end of 2010. While the Great Recession of 2008–2009 had forced management to scale back Panera's expansion plans, the company decided to reinstitute its rapid-growth strategy by opening a net of 76 new company-operated and franchised units in 2010, 88 new units in 2011, 111 new units in 2012, and 125 units in 2013. Plans called for opening 115 to 125 new company-operated and franchised units in 2014.

But despite the recent acceleration of store openings, there were signs in 2014 that the company's revenue growth in 2014 would not match the robust 19.9 percent compound average growth achieved from 2009 through year-end 2013. Top management in February 2014 indicated that it was expecting 2014 sales gains of just 2 to 4 percent at Panera bakery-cafés open at least one year, below the percentage gains in each of the past three years. Moreover, diluted earnings per share in 2014 were projected to increase only 5 to 8 percent, well below the company's targeted long-term EPS growth rate of 15 to 20 percent annually.

## COMPANY BACKGROUND

In 1981, Louis Kane and Ron Shaich founded a bakery-café enterprise named Au Bon Pain Co., Inc. Units were opened in malls, shopping centers, and airports along the east coast of the United States and internationally throughout the 1980s and 1990s; the company prospered and became the dominant operator within the bakery-café category. In 1993, Au Bon Pain Co. purchased Saint Louis Bread Company, a chain of 20 bakery-cafés located in the St. Louis area. Ron Shaich and a team of Au Bon Pain managers then spent considerable time in 1994 and 1995 traveling the country and studying the market for fast-food and quick-service meals. They concluded that many patrons of fast-food chains like

McDonald's, Wendy's, Burger King, Subway, Taco Bell, Pizza Hut, and KFC could be attracted to a higher-quality quick dining experience. Top management at Au Bon Pain then instituted a comprehensive overhaul of the newly acquired Saint Louis Bread locations, altering the menu and the dining atmosphere. The vision was to create a specialty café anchored by an authentic, fresh-dough, artisan bakery and upscale, quick-service menu selections. Between 1993 and 1997, average unit volumes at the revamped Saint Louis Bread units increased by 75 percent, and over 100 additional Saint Louis Bread units were opened. In 1997, the Saint Louis Bread bakery-cafés were renamed Panera Bread in all markets outside St. Louis.

By 1998, it was clear the reconcepted Panera Bread units had connected with consumers. Au Bon Pain's management concluded that the Panera Bread format had broad market appeal and could be rolled out nationwide. Ron Shaich believed Panera Bread had the potential to become one of the leading "fast-casual" restaurant chains in the nation. Shaich also believed that growing Panera Bread into a national chain required significantly more management attention and financial resources than the company could marshal if it continued to pursue expansion of both the Au Bon Pain and Panera Bread chains. He convinced the Au Bon Pain board of directors that the best course of action was for the company to go exclusively with the Panera Bread concept and divest the Au Bon Pain cafés. In August 1998, the company announced the sale of its Au Bon Pain bakery-café division for $73 million in cash to ABP Corp.; the transaction was completed in May 1999. With the sale of the Au Bon Pain division, the company changed its name to Panera Bread Company. The restructured company had 180 Saint Louis and Panera Bread bakery-cafés and a debt-free balance sheet.

Between January 1999 and December 2006, close to 850 additional Panera Bread bakery-cafés were opened, some company-owned and some franchised. In February 2007, Panera purchased a 51 percent interest in Arizona-based Paradise Bakery & Café, which operated 70 company-owned and franchised units in 10 states (primarily in the West and Southwest) and had sales close to $100 million. At the time, Paradise Bakery units had average weekly sales of about $40,000 and an average check size of $8 to $9. Panera purchased the remaining 49 percent ownership of Paradise Bakery in June 2009. In 2008, Panera expanded into Canada, opening two locations in Ontario; since then, 10 additional units in Canada had been opened.

In May 2010, William W. Moreton, Panera's executive vice president and co-chief operating officer, was appointed president and chief executive officer and a member of the company's board. Ron Shaich, who had served as Panera's president and CEO since 1994 and as chairman or co-chairman of the board of directors since 1988, transitioned to the role of executive chairman of the board. In addition to handling the normal duties of board chairman, Shaich maintained an active strategic role, with a particular focus on how Panera Bread could continue to be the best competitive alternative in the market segments the company served. However, on March 15, 2012, the company announced that Ron Shaich and Bill Moreton would become co-CEOs, effective immediately; Shaich's formal title was changed to chairman of the board and co-CEO, and Moreton's title became president and co-CEO. In August 2013, Shaich and Moreton took on new titles because of family-related issues that required more of Bill Moreton's time— Shaich became chairman of the board and CEO, and Moreton was named executive vice chairman, with a role of helping oversee Panera's business operations.

Over the years, Panera Bread had received a number of honors and awards. In 2011, 2012, and 2013, Harris Poll EquiTrend Rankings named Panera Bread as Casual Dining Restaurant Brand of the Year.[1] Zagat's 2012 Fast Food Survey of 10,500 diners ranked Panera as fourth for Top Food, second for Top Decor, and fifth for Top Service among national chains with fewer than 5,000 locations.[2] For 9 of the past 12 years (2002–2013), customers had rated Panera Bread as tops on overall satisfaction among large chain restaurants in Sandelman & Associates' Quick-Track study "Awards of Excellence" surveys; in Sandelman's 2012 Quick-Track study of more than 110,000 customers of quick-service restaurants, Panera ranked number one in the Attractive/Inviting restaurant category.[3] Panera scored the highest level of customer loyalty among quick-casual restaurants, according to a 2011 research study conducted by TNS Intersearch.[4]

A summary of Panera Bread's recent financial performance is shown in Exhibit 1. Exhibit 2 provides select operating statistics for Panera's company-owned and franchised bakery-cafés.

**EXHIBIT 1**   Select Consolidated Financial Data for Panera Bread, 2002–2013 (in thousands, except per share amounts)

| | 2013 | 2012 | 2011 | 2009 | 2002 |
|---|---|---|---|---|---|
| **Income statement data** | | | | | |
| Revenues: | | | | | |
| Bakery-café sales | $2,108,908 | $1,879,280 | $1,592,951 | $1,153,255 | $212,645 |
| Franchise royalties and fees | 112,641 | 102,076 | 92,793 | 78,367 | 27,892 |
| Fresh-dough and other product sales to franchisees | 163,453 | 148,701 | 136,288 | 121,872 | 41,688 |
| Total revenues | 2,385,002 | 2,130,057 | 1,822,032 | 1,353,494 | 282,225 |
| Bakery-café expenses: | | | | | |
| Food and paper products | 625,622 | 552,580 | 470,398 | 337,599 | 63,370 |
| Labor | 625,457 | 559,446 | 484,014 | 370,595 | 63,172 |
| Occupancy | 148,816 | 130,793 | 115,290 | 95,996 | 15,408 |
| Other operating expenses | 295,539 | 256,029 | 216,237 | 155,396 | 27,971 |
| Total bakery-café expenses | 1,695,434 | 1,498,848 | 1,285,939 | 959,586 | 169,921 |
| Fresh-dough and other product costs of sales to franchisees | 142,160 | 131,006 | 116,267 | 100,229 | 38,432 |
| Depreciation and amortization | 106,523 | 90,939 | 79,899 | 67,162 | 13,794 |
| General and administrative expenses | 123,335 | 117,932 | 113,083 | 83,169 | 24,986 |
| Preopening expenses | 7,794 | 8,462 | 6,585 | 2,451 | 1,051 |
| Total costs and expenses | 2,075,246 | 1,847,187 | 1,601,773 | 1,212,597 | 248,184 |
| Operating profit | 309,756 | 282,870 | 220,259 | 140,897 | 34,041 |
| Interest expense | 1,053 | 1,082 | 822 | 700 | 32 |
| Other (income) expense, net | (4,017) | (1,208) | (466) | 273 | 467 |
| Income taxes | 116,551 | 109,548 | 83,951 | 53,073 | 12,242 |
| Less net income (loss) attributable to noncontrolling interest | — | — | — | 801 | — |
| Net income to shareholders | $ 196,169 | $ 173,448 | $ 135,952 | $ 86,050 | $ 21,300 |
| Earnings per share | | | | | |
| Basic | $6.85 | $5.94 | $4.59 | $2.81 | $0.74 |
| Diluted | 6.81 | 5.89 | 4.55 | 2.78 | 0.71 |
| Weighted-average shares outstanding | | | | | |
| Basic | 28,629 | 29,217 | 29,601 | 30,667 | 28,923 |
| Diluted | 28,794 | 29,455 | 29,903 | 30,979 | 29,891 |
| **Balance sheet data** | | | | | |
| Cash and cash equivalents | $ 125,245 | $ 297,141 | $ 222,640 | $ 246,400 | $ 29,924 |
| Short-term investments | — | — | 186 | — | 9,149 |
| Current assets | 302,716 | 478,842 | 353,119 | 322,084 | 59,262 |
| Total assets | 1,180,862 | 1,268,163 | 1,027,322 | 837,165 | 195,431 |
| Current liabilities | 303,325 | 277,540 | 238,334 | 142,259 | 32,325 |
| Total liabilities | 480,970 | 446,244 | 372,246 | 240,129 | 32,587 |
| Stockholders' equity | 699,892 | 821,919 | 655,076 | 597,036 | 151,503 |
| **Cash flow data** | | | | | |
| Net cash provided by operating activities | $ 348,417 | $ 289,456 | $ 236,889 | $ 214,904 | $ 46,323 |
| Net cash used in investing activities | (188,307) | (195,741) | (152,194) | (49,219) | (40,115) |
| Net cash (used in) provided by financing activities | (332,006) | (19,214) | (91,354) | 6,005 | 5,664 |
| Net (decrease) increase in cash and cash equivalents | (171,896) | 74,501 | (6,659) | 171,690 | 11,872 |

*Sources:* 2013 10-K report, pp. 41–43; 2011 10-K report, pp. 41–43; 2010 10-K report, pp. 29–30, 46–48; and 2003 10-K report, pp. 29–31.

## EXHIBIT 2  Select Operating Statistics, Panera Bread Company, 2002–2013

|  | 2013 | 2012 | 2011 | 2009 | 2002 |
|---|---|---|---|---|---|
| Revenues at company-operated stores (in millions) | $2,108.9 | $1,879.3 | $1,593.0 | $1,153.3 | $ 212.6 |
| Revenues at franchised stores (in millions) | $2,175.2 | $1,981.7 | $1,828.2 | $1,640.3 | $ 542.6 |
| Systemwide store revenues (in millions) | $4,284.1 | $3,861.0 | $3,421.2 | $2,793.6 | $ 755.2 |
| Average annualized revenues per company-operated bakery-café (in millions) | $ 2.483 | $ 2.435 | $ 2.292 | $ 2.031 | $ 1.764 |
| Average annualized revenues per franchised bakery-café (in millions) | $ 2.448 | $ 2.419 | $ 2.315 | $ 2.109 | $ 1.872 |
| Average weekly sales, company-owned cafés | $ 47,741 | $ 46,836 | $ 44,071 | $ 39,050 | $33,924 |
| Average weekly sales, franchised cafés | $ 47,079 | $ 46,526 | $ 44,527 | $ 40,566 | $35,997 |
| Comparable-bakery-café sales percentage increases* |  |  |  |  |  |
|   Company-owned outlets | 4.5% | 6.5% | 4.9% | 2.4% | 4.1% |
|   Franchised outlets | 3.9% | 5.0% | 3.4% | 2.0% | 6.1% |
| Company-owned bakery-cafés open at year-end | 867 | 809 | 740 | 585 | 132 |
| Franchised bakery-cafés open at year-end | 910 | 843 | 801 | 795 | 346 |
|   Total bakery-cafés open | 1,777 | 1,652 | 1,541 | 1,380 | 478 |

*The percentages for comparable-bakery-café sales are based on annual changes at bakery-cafés that opened before the first day of the prior fiscal year (meaning that a bakery-café had to be open for all 12 months of the year to be included in this statistic).

*Source:* Company 10-K reports for 2013, 2011, 2010, and 2003.

# Panera Bread's Concept and Strategy

Panera Bread's identity was rooted in its fresh-baked, artisan breads made with a craftsperson's attention to quality and detail, and its breads and baked products were the platform for the dining experience at its bakery-cafés and a major basis for differentiating Panera from its competitors. The featured menu offerings at Panera locations included breads and pastries baked in-house, breakfast items and smoothies, made-to-order sandwiches, signature soups and salads, and café beverages. Recognizing that diners chose a dining establishment based on individual food preferences and mood, Panera strived to be the first choice for diners craving fresh-baked goods, a sandwich, soup, a salad, or a beverage served in a warm, friendly, comfortable dining environment. Its target market was urban workers and suburban dwellers looking for a quick-service meal or light snack and an aesthetically pleasing dining experience. Management's long-term objective and strategic intent was to make Panera Bread a nationally recognized brand name and to be the dominant restaurant operator in upscale, quick-service dining. Top management believed that success depended on "being better than the guys across the street" and making the experience of dining at Panera so attractive that customers would be willing to pass by the outlets of other fast-casual restaurant competitors to dine at a nearby Panera Bread bakery-café.[5]

Panera management's blueprint for attracting and retaining customers was called Concept Essence. Concept Essence underpinned Panera's strategy and embraced several themes that, taken together, acted to differentiate Panera from its competitors:

- Offering an appealing selection of artisan breads, bagels, and pastry products that were handcrafted and baked daily at each café location.
- Serving high-quality food at prices that represented a good value.
- Developing a menu with sufficiently diverse offerings to enable Panera to draw customers from breakfast through the dinner hours each day.
- Providing courteous, capable, and efficient customer service.
- Designing bakery-cafés that were aesthetically pleasing and inviting.
- Offering patrons such a sufficiently satisfying dining experience that they were induced to return again and again.

Panera Bread's menu, store design and ambience, and unit location strategies enabled it to compete successfully in multiple segments of the restaurant business—breakfast, AM "chill" (when customers visited to take a break from morning-hour activities), lunch, PM "chill" (when customers visited to take a break from afternoon activities), dinner, and take-home—through both on-premise sales and off-premise catering. It competed with a wide assortment of specialty food, casual-dining, and quick-service establishments operating nationally, regionally, and locally. Its close competitors varied according to the menu item, meal, and time of day. For example, breakfast and AM-chill competitors included Starbucks and McDonald's; close lunch and dinner competitors included such chains as Chili's, Applebee's, California Pizza Kitchen, Jason's Deli, Cracker Barrel, Ruby Tuesday, T.G.I. Friday's, Chipotle Mexican Grill, and Five Guys Burgers and Fries. In the bread and pastry segment, Panera competed with Corner Bakery Café, Atlanta Bread Company, Au Bon Pain, local bakeries, and supermarket bakeries.

Except for bread and pastry products, Panera's strongest competitors were dining establishments in the so-called fast-casual restaurant category. Fast-casual restaurants filled the gap between fast-food outlets and casual, full-table-service restaurants. A fast-casual restaurant provided quick-service dining (much like that in fast-food enterprises) but was distinguished by enticing menus, higher food quality, and more inviting dining environments; typical meal costs per guest were in the $7-to-$12 range. Some fast-casual restaurants had full table service, some had partial table service (with orders being delivered to the tables after customers order and pay at the counter), and some were self-service (like fast-food establishments, with orders being taken and delivered at the counter). Exhibit 3 provides information on prominent national and regional dining chains that competed against Panera Bread in some or many geographic locations.

Panera Bread's growth strategy was to capitalize on Panera's market potential by opening both company-owned and franchised Panera Bread locations as fast as was prudent. So far, working closely with franchisees to open new locations had been a key component of the company's efforts to broaden its market penetration. Panera Bread had organized its business around company-owned bakery-café operations, franchise operations, and fresh-dough operations; the fresh-bread unit supplied dough and other products to all Panera Bread stores, both company-owned and franchised.

## Panera Bread's Product Offerings and Menu

Panera Bread's artisan signature breads were made from four ingredients—water, natural yeast, flour, and salt; no preservatives or chemicals were used. Carefully trained bakers shaped every step of the process, from mixing the ingredients, to kneading the dough, to placing the loaves on hot stone slabs to bake in a traditional European-style stone deck bakery oven. Breads, as well as bagels, muffins, cookies, and other pastries, were baked fresh throughout the day at each café location. Exhibit 4 shows Panera's lineup of breads.

The Panera Bread menu was designed to provide target customers with products built on the company's bakery expertise, particularly its varieties of breads and bagels. The key menu groups were fresh baked goods, hot breakfast selections, bagels and cream cheese spreads, hot panini, made-to-order sandwiches and salads, soups, fruit smoothies, frozen drinks, beverages, and espresso bar selections. Exhibit 5 summarizes the menu offerings at Panera Bread locations as of March 2014.

Menu offerings were regularly reviewed and revised to sustain the interest of regular customers, satisfy changing consumer preferences, and be responsive to various seasons of the year. Special soup offerings, for example, appeared seasonally. Product development was focused on providing food that customers would crave and trust to be tasty. New menu items were developed in test kitchens and then introduced in a limited number of bakery-cafés to determine customer response and verify that preparation and operating procedures resulted in product consistency and high-quality standards. If successful, they were then rolled out systemwide. New product introductions were integrated into periodic or seasonal menu rotations, referred to as "celebrations." Panera introduced 10 new menu items in 2010, added 14 new or improved items in 2011, featured 8 different selections (5 new ones and 3 that had been put back on the menu after being removed in prior periods) in 2012, and introduced 20 new menu items during the course of five celebrations held throughout 2013.

**EXHIBIT 3**    Representative Fast-Casual Restaurant Chains and Select Full-Service Restaurant Chains in the United States, 2013–2014

| Company | Number of Locations, 2013 | Select Financial Data, 2013–2014 | Key Menu Categories |
|---|---|---|---|
| Applebee's Neighborhood Grill and Bar* (a subsidiary of DineEquity) | 2,010 locations in 49 states, 1 U.S. territory, and 15 countries outside the U.S. | 2013 average annual sales of about $2.4 million per U.S. location | Beef, chicken, pork, seafood, and pasta entrees, plus appetizers, salads, sandwiches, a selection of under-500-calorie Weight Watchers–branded menu alternatives, desserts, and alcoholic beverages (about 12 percent of total sales) |
| Atlanta Bread Company | Approximately 100 bakery-cafés in 21 states | Not available (privately held company) | Fresh-baked breads, salads, sandwiches, soups, wood-fired pizza and pasta (select locations only), baked goods, and desserts |
| Au Bon Pain | 300+ company-owned and franchised bakery-cafés in 23 states and 5+ foreign countries | Not available (privately held company) | Baked goods (with a focus on croissants and bagels), soups, salads, sandwiches and wraps, and coffee drinks |
| Bruegger's Bagels | 315+ bakery-cafés in 26 states, the District of Columbia, and Canada | Not available (privately held company) | Fresh-baked bagels and breads, sandwiches, salads, soups, and desserts |
| California Pizza Kitchen* (a subsidiary of Golden Gate Capital) | 270+ locations in 32 states and 10 foreign countries | Average annual sales of about $3.2 million per location | Signature California-style hearth-baked pizzas, plus salads, pastas, soups, sandwiches, appetizers, desserts, beer, wine, coffees, teas, and assorted beverages |
| Chili's Grill and Bar* (a subsidiary of Brinker International) | 1,265 locations in 50 states and 282 locations in 32 foreign countries and 2 U.S. territories | 2013 average revenues of about $2.9 million per location; average check size per customer of $13.99 | Chicken, beef, and seafood entrees, plus steaks, appetizers, salads, sandwiches, desserts, and alcoholic beverages (13.6 percent of sales) |
| Chipotle Mexican Grill | 1,580+ units | 2013 revenues of $3.2 billion; average unit sales of $2.2 million | Gourmet burritos and tacos, salads, beverages (including margaritas and beers) |
| Corner Bakery Café (a subsidiary of Roark Capital Group) | 130 locations in 10 states and the District of Columbia (planning to double number of locations by 2015 | Menu price range: $0.99 to $7.99 | Specialty breads, hot breakfasts, signature sandwiches, grilled panini, pastas, soups and chili, salads, sweets, coffees, and teas |
| Cracker Barrel* | 626 combination retail stores and restaurants in 42 states | Restaurant-only sales of $2.1 billion in 2013; average sales per restaurant of $3.4 million; average guest check of $9.68; approximately 6,800 customers served per week per location | Two menus (breakfast and lunch/dinner; rated in Zagat's 2010 Consumer Survey as "Best Breakfast" among family-dining chains and by Technomics as "Top of the Full-Service Restaurants in family and casual dining" |

| Company | Number of Locations, 2013 | Select Financial Data, 2013–2014 | Key Menu Categories |
|---|---|---|---|
| Culver's | 450 locations in 19 states | Not available (a privately held company) | Signature hamburgers served on buttered buns, fried battered cheese curds, value dinners (chicken, shrimp, cod with potato and slaw), salads, frozen custard, milkshakes, sundaes, and fountain drinks |
| Einstein Noah Restaurant Group (Einstein Bros. Bagels, Noah's New York Bagels, Manhattan Bagel) | Approximately 850 company-owned, franchised, and licensed locations in 40 states | Annual sales revenues of $434 million; annual sales per company-owned unit of about $850,000 | Fresh-baked bagels, hot breakfast sandwiches, made-to-order lunch sandwiches, creamed cheeses and other spreads, salads, soups, and gourmet coffees and teas |
| Fazoli's (a subsidiary of Sun Capital Partners) | 220+ locations in 26 states | Revenues of $226 million (2012) | Spaghetti and meatballs, fettuccine alfredo, lasagna, ravioli, submarinos and panini sandwiches, pizza, entrée salads, garlic breadsticks, and desserts |
| Firehouse Subs | 730+ locations in 38 + states | Average unit sales of about $750,000 | Hot and cold subs, salads, sides, and drinks, plus catering |
| Five Guys Burgers and Fries | 1,200+ locations in 46 states and 6 Canadian provinces | Not available (a privately held company) | Hamburgers (with choice of 15 toppings), hot dogs, fries, Coca-Cola, and beverages |
| Fuddruckers | Approximately 200 locations in 32 states, the District of Columbia, Puerto Rico, and Canada | Not available (a privately held company) | Exotic hamburgers (the feature menu item), chicken and fish sandwiches, french fries and other sides, soups, salads, and desserts |
| Jason's Deli | 240+ locations in 28 states | Not available (a privately held company) | Sandwiches, extensive salad bar, soups, loaded potatoes, and desserts, plus catering services, party trays, and box lunches |
| Moe's Southwest Grill (a subsidiary of Roark Capital Group) | 500+ locations in 37 states and the District of Columbia | 2013 sales of $526 million; average annual sales per restaurant of about $1.05 million | Burritos, quesadillas, fajitas, tacos, nachos, rice bowls (chicken, pork, or tofu), salads with a choice of two homemade dressings, a kid's menu, five side items (including queso and guacamole), two desserts (cookie or brownie), soft drinks, iced tea, and bottled water, plus catering |
| McAlister's Deli (a subsidiary of Roark Capital Group) | 310+ locations in 23 states | Not available (a privately held company) | Deli sandwiches, loaded baked potatoes, soups, salads, and desserts, plus sandwich trays, lunch boxes, and catering |
| Noodles & Company | 380+ urban and suburban locations in 29 states and the District of Columbia | 2013 sales of $351 million; comparable-store sales growth of 3% in 2013 | Customizable Asian, Mediterranean, and American noodle/pasta entrées, soups, salads, sandwiches, and alcoholic beverages |

*(Continued)*

## EXHIBIT 3    (Concluded)

| Company | Number of Locations, 2013 | Select Financial Data, 2013–2014 | Key Menu Categories |
|---|---|---|---|
| Qdoba Mexican Grill (a subsidiary of Jack in the Box, Inc.) | 615 company-owned and franchised locations in 46 states, the District of Columbia, and Canada | Average unit sales per location of $1,017,000 in 2013 | Signature burritos, tacos, taco salads, quesadillas, three-cheese nachos, Mexican gumbo, tortilla soup, and five signature salsas, plus breakfast selections at some locations |
| Ruby Tuesday* | 783 company-owned and franchised locations in 45 states, 11 foreign countries, and Guam | Fiscal 2013 sales of $1.39 billion; average restaurant sales of $1.73 million; typical entrée price ranges of $7.49 to $19.99 | Appetizers, handcrafted burgers, 35-item salad bar, steaks, fresh chicken, crab cakes, lobster, salmon, tilapia, ribs, desserts, and nonalcoholic and alcoholic beverages, plus catering |
| Starbucks | Approximately 11,500 company-operated and licensed locations in the U.S. and 8,300+ international locations | 2013 global revenues of $14.9 billion; sales of $1.36 million per company-operated location in the Americas | Italian-style espresso beverages, teas, sodas, juices, and assorted pastries and confections, plus sandwiches and salads at some locations |
| T.G.I. Friday's* (a subsidiary of Carlson's Restaurants) | 930 locations in 60 foreign countries and territories | Not available (a privately held company) | Appetizers, salads, soups, burgers and other sandwiches, chicken, seafood, steaks, pasta, desserts, and nonalcoholic and alcoholic beverages, plus party platters |

*A full-service restaurant.

*Sources:* Company websites; and FastCasual.com's "2013 Top 100 Movers and Shakers," **www.fastcasual.com** (accessed March 3, 2014).

Over the past 10 years, Panera had responded to growing consumer interest in healthier, more nutritious menu offerings. In 2004, whole grain breads were introduced, and in 2005 Panera switched to the use of natural, antibiotic-free chicken in all of its chicken-related sandwiches and salads. Other recent health-related changes included using organic and all-natural ingredients in select items, using unbleached flours in breads, adding a yogurt-granola-fruit parfait and reduced-fat spreads for bagels to the menu, introducing fruit smoothies, increasing the use of fresh ingredients (like fresh-from-the-farm lettuces and tomatoes), and revising ingredients and preparation methods to yield 0 grams of artificial trans fat per serving. All of the menu boards and printed menus at company-owned Panera bakery-cafés included the calories for each food item. Also, Panera's website had a nutritional calculator showing detailed nutritional information for each individual menu item or combination of menu selections.

**Off-Premises Catering**  In 2004–2005, Panera Bread introduced a catering program to extend its market reach to the workplace, schools, and parties and gatherings held in homes and to grow its breakfast-, lunch-, and dinner-hour sales without making capital investments in additional physical facilities. The first menu consisted of items appearing on the regular menu and was posted for viewing at the company's website. A catering coordinator was available to help customers make menu selections, choose between assortments or boxed meals, determine appropriate order quantities, and arrange pickup or delivery times. Orders came complete with plates, napkins, and utensils, all packaged and presented in convenient, ready-to-serve-from packaging.

In 2010, Panera boosted the size of its catering sales staff and introduced sales training programs and other tools—factors that helped drive a 26 percent increase in catering sales in 2010. In 2011, Panera introduced an online catering system that catering customers

## EXHIBIT 4    Panera's Line of Fresh-Baked Breads, March 2014

| Artisan Breads | Specialty Breads |
| --- | --- |
| **Country**<br>A crisp crust and nutty flavor. *Available in Loaf, Miche.* | **Sourdough**<br>Panera's signature sourdough bread with no fat, oil, sugar, or cholesterol. *Available in Loaf, XL Loaf, Roll, Bread Bowl.* |
| **French**<br>Slightly blistered crust, wine-like aroma. *Available in Baguette, Miche.* | **Asiago Cheese**<br>Standard sourdough recipe with Asiago cheese baked in and sprinkled on top. *Available in Demi, Loaf.* |
| **Ciabatta**<br>A moist, chewy crumb with a thin crust and light olive oil flavor. *Available in Loaf.* | **Honey Wheat**<br>Sweet and hearty with honey and molasses. *Available in Loaf.* |
| **Focaccia**<br>Italian flatbread baked with olive oil and topped with either Asiago Cheese or Sea Salt. *Available in Loaf.* | **All-Natural White Bread**<br>Soft and tender white sandwich bread. *Available in Loaf.* |
| **Rye**<br>With chopped rye kernels and caraway seeds. *Available in Loaf, Miche.* | **Tomato Basil**<br>Sourdough bread made with tomatoes and basil, and sweet streusel topping. *Available in Loaf.* |
| **Three Cheese**<br>Made with Parmesan, Romano, and Asiago cheeses. *Available in Demi, Loaf, Miche.* | **Cinnamon Raisin Swirl**<br>Fresh dough made with flour, whole butter, and eggs, swirled with Vietnamese and Indonesian cinnamons, raisins, and brown sugar, topped with Panera's cinnamon crunch topping. *Available in Loaf.* |
| **Three Seed**<br>Sesame, poppy, and fennel seeds. *Available in Demi.* | |
| **Whole Grain**<br>Moist and hearty, sweetened with honey. *Available in Loaf, Miche, Baguette.* | |
| **Sesame Semolina**<br>Delicate and moist, topped with sesame seeds. *Available in Loaf, Miche.* | |

*Source:* www.panerabread.com (accessed March 5, 2014).

could use to view the catering menu, place orders, specify whether the order was to be picked up or delivered to a particular location, and pay for purchases. The catering menu in 2014 included breakfast assortments, sandwiches, salads, soups, pasta dishes, drinks, and bakery items. Going forward, top executives at Panera believed that off-premise catering was an important revenue growth opportunity for both company-operated and franchised locations.

**The MyPanera Loyalty Program**  In 2010, Panera initiated a loyalty program to reward customers who dined frequently at Panera Bread locations. The introduction of the MyPanera program was completed systemwide in November, and by the end of December about 4.5 million customers had signed up and become registered card members. Members presented their MyPanera card when ordering.

When the card was swiped, the specific items being purchased were automatically recorded to learn what items a member liked. As Panera got an idea of a member's preferences over the course of several visits, a member's card was "loaded" with such "surprises" as complimentary bakery-café items, exclusive previews and tastings, cooking and baking tips, invitations to special events, ideas for entertaining, or recipe books. On a member's next visit, when an order was placed and the card swiped, order-taking personnel informed the member of the surprise award. Members could also go online at **www.MyPanera.com** and see if a reward was waiting for their next visit. Going into 2014, the company's MyPanera program had over 16 million members, and during 2013 approximately 50 percent of the transactions at Panera Bread bakery-cafés were attached to a MyPanera loyalty card.

**EXHIBIT 5**    Panera Bread's Menu Selections, March 2014

**Bakery**
Artisan and Specialty Breads (15 varieties) – Bagels
(10 varieties) – Scones (4 varieties) – Sweet Rolls
(3 varieties) – Muffins and Muffies (6 varieties) – Artisan
Pastries (7 varieties) – Brownies – Cookies (6 varieties)

**Bagels & Cream Cheese Spreads**
(10 varieties of bagels, 5 varieties of spreads)

**Hot Breakfast**
Breakfast Sandwiches (9 varieties)
Baked Egg Soufflés (4 varieties)

**Strawberry Granola Parfait**

**Steel Cut Oatmeal**

**Fruit Smoothies** (5 varieties)

**Fruit Cup**

**Signature Hot Paninis**
Frontega Chicken – Chipotle Chicken –
Smokehouse Turkey – Tomato and
Mozzarella

**Signature Sandwiches**
Napa Almond Chicken Salad – Asiago Roast Beef –
Italian Combo – Bacon Turkey Bravo – Fontina Grilled
Cheese

**Café Sandwiches**
Smoked Ham and Swiss – Roasted Turkey and
Avocado BLT – Tuna Salad – Mediterranean Veggie –
Sierra Turkey – Classic Grilled Cheese

**Signature Pastas**
Chicken Sorrentina – Chicken Tortellini Alfredo – Mac &
Cheese – Basil Pesto Sacchettini – Tortellini Alfredo

**Soups (5 selections varying daily, plus seasonal specialties)**
Options include: Broccoli Cheddar – Bistro French Onion –
Baked Potato – Low Fat All-Natural Chicken Noodle –
Cream of Chicken and Wild Rice – New England Clam
Chowder – Low Fat Vegetarian Garden Vegetable with
Pesto – Low Fat Vegetarian Black Bean – Low Fat Chicken
Tortilla – Vegetarian Creamy Tomato – Turkey Chili

**Café Salads**
Caesar – Classic – Greek

**Signature Salads**
Chicken Cobb – Chicken Cobb with Avocado –Chicken
Caesar – Asian Sesame Chicken – Fuji Apple Chicken –
Thai Chicken – Spinach Power Salad – Mediterranean
Shrimp Couscous – Greek with Shrimp – Classic with
Chicken – Greek with Chicken

**Panera Kids**
Grilled Cheese Sandwich – Peanut Butter and Jelly
Sandwich – Smoked Ham Sandwich – Smoked Turkey
Sandwich – Mac & Cheese – Buttered Ribbon Noodles –
10 varieties of regular and seasonal soups – 3 salads

**Beverages**
Coffee (4 varieties) – Hot Teas – Iced Tea – Iced Green
Tea – Pepsi beverages – Bottled Water – Organic Milk
or Chocolate Milk – Orange Juice – Organic Apple
Juice – Lemonade

**Frozen Drinks**
Frozen Caramel – Frozen Mocha

**Espresso Bar**
Espresso – Cappuccino – Caffe Latte – Caffe Mocha
– Vanilla Latte – Caramel Latte – Skinny Caffe Mocha –
Chai Tea Latte (hot or iced) – Hot Chocolate

*Source:* www.panerabread.com (accessed March 5, 2014).

Management believed that the loyalty program had two primary benefits. One was to entice members to dine at Panera more frequently and thereby deepen the bond between Panera Bread and its most loyal customers. The second was to provide Panera's management with better marketing research data on the purchasing behavior of customers and enable Panera to "get as close to one on one marketing with our customers as possible."[6]

**Panera's Nonprofit Pay-What-You-Want Bakery-Café Locations**    In May 2010, Panera Bread converted one of its restaurants in a wealthy St. Louis suburb into a nonprofit pay-what-you-want Saint Louis Bread Cares bakery-café with the idea of helping to feed the needy and raising

money for charitable work. A sign in the bakery-café said, "We encourage those with the means to leave the requested amount or more if you're able. And we encourage those with a real need to take a discount." The menu board listed "suggested funding levels," not prices. Payments went into a donation box, with the cashiers providing change and handling credit card payments. The hope was that enough generous customers would donate money above and beyond the menu's suggested funding levels to subsidize discounted meals for those who were experiencing economic hardship and needed help. The restaurant was operated by Panera's charitable Panera Bread Foundation; all profits from the store were donated to community programs.

After several months of operation, the Saint Louis Bread Cares store was judged to be successful enough that Ron Shaich, who headed the Panera Bread Foundation, opted to open two similar Panera Cares cafés—one in the Detroit suburb of Dearborn, Michigan, and one in Portland, Oregon. At one juncture, Panera statistics indicated that roughly 60 percent of store patrons left the suggested amount; 20 percent left more, and 20 percent less.[7] Of course, there were occasional instances in which a patron tried to game the system. Ron Shaich cited the case of a college student who ordered more than $40 worth of food and charged only $3 to his father's credit card; Shaich, who happened to be working in the store behind the counter, had to restrain himself and later said, "I wanted to jump over the counter."[8] One person paid $500 for a meal, the largest single payment. Although in May 2011 Panera had intentions to open a new pay-what-you-want store every three months or so, the company still had only three pay-what-you-want café locations as of April 2012, but two locations were added in the next nine months—one in Chicago and one in Boston. Panera expected to serve over 1 million people at the five pay-what-you-can locations in 2013.[9] The latest statistics continued to indicate that 60 percent of store patrons left the suggested amount, 20 percent left more, and 20 percent less, often significantly less.[10]

In March 2013, Panera introduced its special "Meal of Shared Responsibility"—turkey chili in a bread bowl—at a suggested retail price of $5.89 (tax included) at 48 locations in the St. Louis area. The idea was that the needy could get a nutritious 850-calorie meal for whatever they could afford to pay, while those who paid above the company's cost made up the difference.[11] The program was supported by heavy media coverage at launch, extensive in-store signage, and employees explaining how the meal worked. For the first three weeks, customers on average paid above the retail value, but then payments dropped off to an average of around 75 percent of retail value. After six weeks, in-store signage was taken down to promote other meal options, and conversation about the Meal of Shared Responsibility faded into the background. Then, in July 2013, after serving about 15,000 of the turkey chili meals, Panera canceled the program, chiefly because few needy people were participating—an outcome attributed largely to the fact that most Panera cafés in the St. Louis area were located in middle-class and affluent neighborhoods. Management indicated it would rethink its approach to social responsibility and possibly retool the program and bring it back as a seasonal offering in winter 2014 (but that had not occurred as of March 2014). Nonetheless, the five Panera Cares locations remained open in 2014 and were continuing to generate enough revenues to cover operating costs on average.

## Marketing

In the company's early years, marketing had played only a small role in Panera's success. Brand awareness had been built on customers' satisfaction with their dining experience at Panera and their tendency to share their positive experiences with friends and neighbors. From time to time, Panera had utilized focus groups to determine customer food and drink preferences and price points. In 2006, Panera's marketing research indicated that about 85 percent of consumers who were aware that there was a Panera Bread bakery-café in their community or neighborhood had dined at Panera on at least one occasion; 57 percent of consumers who had "ever tried" dining at Panera Bread had been customers in the past 30 days.[12] Panera's research also showed that people who dined at Panera Bread very frequently or moderately frequently typically did so for only one part of the day, although 81 percent indicated "considerable willingness" to try dining at Panera Bread at other parts of the day.

This data prompted management to pursue three marketing initiatives during 2006–2007. One aimed at raising the quality of awareness about Panera by continuing to feature the caliber and appeal of its breads and baked goods, by hammering home the theme "food you crave, food you can trust," and by enhancing the appeal of its bakery-cafés as neighborhood gathering places. The second initiative sought to raise awareness and boost customer trials of dining at Panera Bread at multiple meal times (breakfast, lunch, "chill out" times, and dinner). The third initiative aimed to increase perception of Panera Bread as a viable evening-meal option by introducing a number of new entrée menu selections. Panera avoided hard-sell or "in-your-face" marketing approaches, preferring instead to employ a range of ways to softly drop the Panera Bread name into the midst of consumers as they moved through their lives and let them "gently collide" with the brand. The idea was to let consumers "discover" Panera Bread and then convert them into loyal repeat customers by providing a very satisfying dining experience when they tried Panera bakery-cafés for the first time or opted to try dining at Panera at a different part of the day, particularly during breakfast or dinner as opposed to the busier lunchtime hours. These initiatives were only partially successful, partly because of the difficult economic environment that emerged in 2008–2009 and partly because the new dinner entrées that were introduced did not prove popular enough to significantly boost dinner-hour traffic and were dropped from the menu—in 2011–2012, the only hot entrée on the menu was Mac & Cheese. But a variety of new pasta entrées began appearing on the menu in 2012–2013 (see Exhibit 5).

Panera management was committed to growing sales at existing and new unit locations, continuously improving the customer experience at its restaurants, and encouraging frequent customer visits via the new menu items featured during the periodic celebrations, increased enrollment of patrons in the MyPanera loyalty programs, and efforts to strengthen relationships with customers who, management believed, would then recommend dining at Panera to their friends and acquaintances. Panera hired a new chief marketing officer and a new vice president of marketing in 2010; both had considerable consumer marketing experience and were playing an important role in crafting the company's long-term marketing strategy to increase awareness of the Panera brand, develop and promote appealing new menu selections, expand customer participation in the MyPanera loyalty program, and otherwise make dining at Panera bakery-cafés a pleasant and satisfying experience.

To promote the Panera brand and menu offerings to target customer groups, Panera employed a mix of radio, billboard, social networking, Internet, and periodic cable television advertising campaigns. In recent years, Panera had put considerable effort into (1) improving its advertising messages to better capture the points of difference and the soul of the Panera concept and (2) doing a better job of optimizing the media mix in each geographic market.

Whereas it was the practice at many national restaurant chains to spend 3 to 5 percent of revenues on media advertising, Panera's advertising expenses had typically been substantially lower, running as low as 0.6 percent of systemwide sales at company-owned and franchised bakery-cafés in 2008. But in the past five years, Panera had started upping its advertising effort to help spur sales growth. Advertising expenses totaled $33.2 million in 2011

(1 percent of systemwide bakery-café sales), $44.5 million in 2012 (1.15 percent of systemwide bakery-café sales), and $55.6 million in 2013 (1.3 percent of systemwide bakery-café sales). In 2014, advertising expenses were scheduled to climb further to support Panera's first-ever national television advertising campaign. This new initiative was being financed by both Panera and its franchisees.

Panera's franchise agreements required franchisees to contribute a specified percentage of their net sales to advertising. In 2013, Panera's franchise-operated bakery-cafés were required to contribute 1.8 percent of their sales to a national advertising fund and to pay Panera a marketing administration fee equal to 0.4 percent of their sales—Panera contributed the same net sales percentages from company-owned bakery-cafés toward the national advertising fund and the marketing administration fee. Franchisees were also required in 2013 to spend amounts equal to 1.6 percent of their net sales on advertising in their local markets. Over the past eight years, Panera had raised the contribution of both company-owned and franchised bakery cafés to the national advertising fund—from 0.4 percent of net sales prior to 2006 to 0.7 percent beginning January 2006 to 1.2 percent beginning July 2010 to 1.6 percent starting April 2012. However, to help offset these increases, the amounts franchisees were expected to spend for local advertising had been reduced from 2 percent of net sales beginning July 2010 to 1.6 percent of net sales beginning April 2012. Under the terms of its franchise agreements, Panera had the right to increase national advertising fund contributions to a maximum of 2.6 percent of net sales.

To support its new national advertising campaign beginning in 2014, Panera exercised its right to require franchisees to pay the maximum 2.6 percent of net sales to the company's national advertising fund. However, the marketing administration fee of 0.4 percent of net sales remained unchanged, and the required percentage franchisees had to spend on advertising in their respective local market areas was reduced from 1.6 percent to 0.8 percent beginning January 2014.

## Franchise Operations

Opening additional franchised bakery-cafés was a core element of Panera Bread's strategy and management's initiatives to achieve the company's revenue growth and earnings targets. Panera Bread did not grant single-unit franchises, so a prospective franchisee could not open just one bakery-café. Rather, Panera Bread's franchising strategy was to enter into franchise agreements that required the franchise developer to open a number of units, typically 15 bakery-cafés in a period of six years. Franchisee candidates had to be well-capitalized, have a proven track record as excellent multiunit restaurant operators, and agree to meet an aggressive development schedule. Applicants had to meet eight stringent criteria to gain consideration for a Panera Bread franchise:

- Experience as a multiunit restaurant operator.
- Recognition as a top restaurant operator.
- Net worth of $7.5 million.
- Liquid assets of $3 million.

- Infrastructure and resources to meet Panera's development schedule for the market area the franchisee was applying to develop.
- Real estate experience in the market to be developed.
- Total commitment to the development of the Panera Bread brand.
- Cultural fit and a passion for fresh bread.

Exhibit 6 shows the estimated costs of opening a new franchised Panera Bread bakery-café. The franchise agreement typically required the payment of a $5,000 development fee for each bakery-café contracted for in a franchisee's "area development agreement," a franchise fee of $30,000 per bakery-café (payable in a lump sum at least 30 days prior to the scheduled opening of a new bakery-café), and continuing royalties of 5 percent on gross sales at each franchised bakery-café. Franchise-operated

### EXHIBIT 6    Estimated Initial Investment for a Franchised Panera Bread Bakery-Café, 2012

| Investment Category | Actual or Estimated Amount | To Whom Paid |
|---|---|---|
| Development fee | $5,000 per bakery-café contracted for in the franchisee's area development agreement | Panera |
| Franchise fee | $35,000 ($5,000 of the development fee was applied to the $35,000 franchise fee when a new bakery-café was opened) | Panera |
| Real property | Varies according to site and local real estate market conditions | — |
| Leasehold improvements | $334,000 to $938,500 | Contractors |
| Equipment | $198,000 to $310,000 | Equipment vendors, Panera |
| Fixtures | $32,000 to $54,000 | Vendors |
| Furniture | $28,500 to $62,000 | Vendors |
| Consultant fees and municipal impact fees (if any) | $51,500 to $200,250 | Architect, engineer, expeditor, others |
| Supplies and inventory | $19,150 to $24,350 | Panera, other suppliers |
| Smallwares | $24,000 to $29,000 | Suppliers |
| Signage | $15,000 to $84,000 | Suppliers |
| Additional funds (for working capital and general operating expenses for 3 months) | $175,000 to $245,000 | Vendors, suppliers, employees, utilities, landlord, others |
| **Total** | **$917,150 to $1,984,100, plus real estate and related costs** | |

*Source:* **www.panerabread.com** (accessed April 5, 2012).

bakery-cafés followed the same standards for in-store operations, product quality, menu, site selection, and building construction as did company-owned bakery-cafés. Franchisees were required to purchase all of their dough products from sources approved by Panera Bread. Panera's fresh-dough facility system supplied fresh-dough products to substantially all franchise-operated bakery-cafés. Panera did not finance franchisee construction or area development agreement payments or hold an equity interest in any of the franchise-operated bakery-cafés. All area development agreements executed after March 2003 included a clause allowing Panera Bread the right to purchase all bakery-cafés opened by the franchisee at a defined purchase price, at any time five years after the execution of the franchise agreement. In 2010, Panera purchased 37 bakery-cafés from the franchisee in the New Jersey market and sold 3 bakery-cafés in the Mobile, Alabama, market to an existing franchisee. In 2011, Panera completed the purchase of 25 bakery-cafés owned by its Milwaukee franchisee and 5 bakery-cafés owned by an Indiana franchisee; also in 2011, Panera sold 2 Paradise Bakery & Café units to a Texas franchisee and terminated the franchise agreements for 13 Paradise bakery-cafés that were subsequently rebranded by the former franchisee. In 2012, Panera acquired 16 bakery-cafés from a North Carolina franchisee, and in 2013 it acquired 1 bakery-café from a Florida franchisee.

As of January 2014, Panera Bread had agreements with 37 franchise groups that operated 910 bakery-cafés. Panera's largest franchisee operated nearly 200 bakery-cafés in Ohio, Pennsylvania, West Virginia, Kentucky, and Florida. The company's franchise groups had committed to open an additional 117 bakery-cafés. If a franchisee failed to develop bakery-cafés on schedule, Panera had the right to terminate the franchise agreement and develop its own company-operated locations or develop locations through new franchisees in that market. However, Panera from time to time agreed to modify the commitments of franchisees to open new locations when unfavorable market conditions or other circumstances warranted the postponement or cancellation of new unit openings.

Panera provided its franchisees with support in a number of areas: market analysis and site selection assistance, lease review, design services and new bakery-café opening assistance, a comprehensive 10-week initial training program, a training program for hourly employees, manager and baker certification, bakery-café certification, continuing education classes, benchmarking data regarding costs and profit margins, access to company-developed marketing and advertising programs, neighborhood marketing assistance, and calendar planning assistance.

## Site Selection and Café Environment

Bakery-cafés were typically located in suburban, strip mall, and regional mall locations. In evaluating a potential location, Panera studied the surrounding trade area, demographic information within that area, and information on nearby competitors. Based on analysis of this information, including utilization of predictive modeling using proprietary software, Panera developed projections of sales and return on investment for candidate sites. Cafés had proved successful as free-standing units and as both in-line and end-cap locations in strip malls and large regional malls.

The average Panera bakery-café size was approximately 4,500 square feet. Almost all company-operated locations were leased. Lease terms were typically for 10 years, with one, two, or three 5-year-renewal option periods. Leases typically entailed charges for minimum base occupancy, a proportionate share of building and common-area operating expenses and real estate taxes, and a contingent percentage rent based on sales above a stipulated amount. Some lease agreements provided for scheduled rent increases during the lease term. The average construction, equipment, furniture and fixture, and signage cost for the 63 company-owned bakery-cafés opened in 2013 was $1,050,000 (excluding capitalized development overhead expenses), compared to average costs of $750,000 for 42 company-owned bakery-cafés opened in 2010 and $920,000 for 66 company-owned bakery-cafés opened in 2005.

Each bakery-café sought to provide a distinctive and engaging environment (what management referred to as "Panera Warmth"), in many cases using fixtures and materials complementary to the neighborhood location of the bakery-café. All Panera cafés used real china and stainless silverware, instead of paper plates and plastic utensils. In 2005–2006, the company had introduced a new café design aimed at further refining and enhancing the appeal of Panera bakery-cafés as a warm and appealing neighborhood gathering place. The design incorporated higher-quality furniture, cozier seating, comfortable gathering areas, and relaxing decor. A number of locations had fireplaces to further create an alluring and hospitable atmosphere that patrons would flock to on a regular basis, sometimes for a meal with or without friends and acquaintances and sometimes to take a break for a light snack or beverage. Many locations had outdoor seating, and all company-operated and most franchised locations had free wireless Internet to help make the bakery-cafés community gathering places where people could catch up on some work, hang out with friends, read the paper, or just relax (a strategy that Starbucks had used with great success).

In 2006, Panera began working on store designs and operating systems that would enable free-standing and end-cap locations to incorporate a drive-thru window. In 2010–2011, increasing numbers of newly opened locations, both company-owned and franchised, featured drive-thru windows. Some existing units had undergone renovation to add a drive-thru window. Going into 2012, about 50 Panera Bread locations had drive-thru windows. Sales at these locations were running about 20 percent higher on average than units without drive-thru capability.

## Bakery-Café Operations

Panera's top executives believed that operating excellence was the most important element of Panera Warmth and that without strong execution and operational skills and energized café personnel who were motivated to provide pleasing service, it would be difficult to build and maintain a strong relationship with the customers patronizing its bakery-cafés. Additionally, top management believed that high-quality restaurant management was critical to the company's long-term success. Bakery-café managers were provided with detailed operations manuals, and all café personnel received hands-on training, both in small-group and individual settings. The company had created systems to educate and prepare café personnel to respond to a customer's questions and do their part to create a better dining experience. Management strived to maintain adequate staffing at each café and had instituted competitive compensation for café managers and both full-time and part-time café personnel (who were called *associates*).

Panera executives had established the Joint Venture Program, whereby selected general managers and multiunit managers of company-operated bakery-cafés could participate in a bonus program based on a percentage of the store profit of the bakery-cafés they operated. The bonuses were based on store profit percentages generally covering a period of five years, and the percentages were subject to annual minimums and maximums. Panera's management believed that the program's multiyear approach (1) improved operator quality and management retention, (2) created team stability that generally resulted in a higher level of operating consistency and customer service for a particular bakery-café, (3) fostered a low rate of management turnover, and (4) helped drive operating improvements at the company's bakery-cafés. In 2013, approximately 45 percent of the bakery-café operators at Panera's company-owned locations participated in the Joint Venture Program.

Going into 2014, Panera Bread had approximately 40,100 employees. Approximately 37,700 were employed in Panera's bakery-café operations as bakers, managers, and associates; approximately 1,300 were employed in the fresh-dough facility operations; and approximately 1,100 were employed in general or administrative functions, principally in the company's support centers. Roughly 22,700 worked, on average, at least 25 hours per week. Panera had no collective bargaining agreements with its associates and considered its employee relations to be good.

## Panera's Bakery-Café Supply Chain

Panera operated a network of 24 facilities (22 company-owned and 2 franchise-operated) to supply fresh dough for breads and bagels on a daily basis to almost all of its company-owned and franchised bakery-cafés—one of the company's 22 facilities was a limited-production operation colocated at a company-owned bakery-café in Ontario, Canada, that supplied dough to 12 Panera bakery-cafés in that market. All of the company's facilities were leased. Most of the 1,300 employees at these facilities were engaged in preparing dough for breads and bagels, a process that took about 48 hours. The dough-making process began with the preparation and mixing of starter dough, which then was given time to rise; other all-natural ingredients were then

*Competitive advantage*

added to create the dough for each of the different bread and bagel varieties (no chemicals or preservatives were used). Another period of rising then took place. Next, the dough was cut into pieces, shaped into loaves or bagels, and readied for shipment in fresh-dough form. There was no freezing of the dough, and no partial baking was done at the fresh-dough facilities. Trained bakers at each bakery-café performed all of the baking activities, using the fresh doughs delivered daily.

Distribution of the fresh bread and bagel doughs (along with tuna, cream cheese spreads, and certain fresh fruits and vegetables) was accomplished through a leased fleet of about 220 temperature-controlled trucks operated by Panera personnel. The optimal maximum distribution route was approximately 300 miles; however, routes as long as 500 miles were sometimes necessary to supply cafés in outlying locations. In 2013, the various distribution routes for regional facilities entailed making daily deliveries to an average of eight bakery-cafés.

Panera obtained ingredients for its doughs and other products manufactured at its regional facilities from suppliers. While a few ingredients used at these facilities were sourced from a single supplier, there were numerous suppliers of each ingredient needed for fresh dough and cheese spreads. Panera contracted externally for the manufacture and distribution of sweet goods to its bakery-cafés. After delivery, sweet-goods products were finished with fresh toppings and other ingredients (based on Panera's own recipes) and baked to Panera's artisan standards by professionally trained bakers at each café location.

Panera had arrangements with several independent distributors to handle the delivery of sweet-goods products and other items to its bakery-cafés, but the company had contracted with a single supplier to deliver the majority of ingredients and other products to its bakery-cafés two or three times weekly. Virtually all other food products and supplies for the bakery-cafés, including paper goods, coffee, and smallwares, were contracted for by Panera and delivered by the vendors to designated independent distributors for delivery to the bakery-cafés. Individual bakery-cafés placed orders for the needed supplies directly with a distributor; distributors made deliveries to bakery-cafés two or three times per week. Panera maintained a list of approved suppliers and distributors that all company-owned and franchised cafés could select from in obtaining food products and other supplies not sourced from the company's regional facilities or delivered directly by contract suppliers.

Although many of the ingredients and menu items sourced from outside vendors were prepared to Panera's specifications, the ingredients for a big majority of menu selections were generally available and could be obtained from alternative sources when necessary. In a number of instances, Panera had entered into annual and multiyear contracts for certain ingredients in order to decrease the risks of supply interruptions and cost fluctuation. However, Panera had only a limited number of suppliers of antibiotic-free chicken; because there were relatively few producers of meat products from animals raised without antibiotics—as well as certain other organically grown items—it was difficult or more costly for Panera to find alternative suppliers.

Management believed the company's fresh-dough-making capability provided a competitive advantage by ensuring consistent quality and dough-making efficiency (it was more economical to concentrate the dough-making operations in a few facilities dedicated to that function than it was to have each bakery-café equipped and staffed to do all of its baking from scratch). Management also believed that the company's growing size and scale of operations gave it increased bargaining power and leverage with suppliers to improve ingredient quality and cost and that its various supply chain arrangements entailed little risk that its bakery-cafés would experience significant delivery interruptions from weather conditions or other factors that would adversely affect café operations.

The fresh dough made at the regional facilities was sold to both company-owned and franchised bakery-cafés at a delivered cost not to exceed 27 percent of the retail value of the product. Exhibit 7 provides financial data relating to each of Panera's three business segments: company-operated bakery-cafés, franchise operations, and the operations of the regional facilities that supplied fresh dough and other products. The sales and operating profits of the fresh-dough and other-products segment shown in Exhibit 7 represent only those transactions with franchised bakery-cafés. The company classified any operating profits of the regional facilities stemming from supplying fresh dough and other products to

**EXHIBIT 7**   Business Segment Information, Panera Bread Company, 2009–2013 (in thousands)

| | 2013 | 2012 | 2011 | 2010 | 2009 |
|---|---|---|---|---|---|
| **Segment revenues** | | | | | |
| Company bakery-café operations | $2,108,908 | $1,879,280 | $1,592,951 | $1,321,162 | $1,153,255 |
| Franchise operations | 112,641 | 102,076 | 92,793 | 86,195 | 78,367 |
| Fresh-dough and other-product operations at regional facilities | 347,922 | 312,308 | 275,096 | 252,045 | 216,116 |
| Intercompany sales eliminations | (184,469) | (163,607) | (138,808) | (116,913) | (94,244) |
| Total revenues | $2,385,002 | $2,130,057 | $1,822,032 | $1,542,489 | $1,353,494 |
| **Segment operating profit** | | | | | |
| Company bakery-café operations | $ 413,474 | $ 380,432 | $ 307,012 | $ 249,177 | $ 193,669 |
| Franchise operations | 106,395 | 95,420 | 86,148 | 80,397 | 72,381 |
| Fresh-dough and other-product operations at regional facilities | 21,293 | 17,695 | 20,021 | 24,146 | 21,643 |
| Total segment operating profit | $ 541,162 | $ 493,547 | $ 413,181 | $ 353,720 | $ 287,693 |
| **Depreciation and amortization** | | | | | |
| Company bakery-café operations | $ 90,872 | $ 78,198 | $ 68,651 | $ 57,031 | $ 55,726 |
| Fresh-dough and other-product operations at regional facilities | 8,239 | 6,793 | 6,777 | 7,495 | 7,620 |
| Corporate administration | 7,412 | 5,948 | 4,471 | 4,147 | 3,816 |
| Total | $ 106,523 | $ 90,939 | $ 79,899 | $ 68,673 | $ 67,162 |
| **Capital expenditures** | | | | | |
| Company bakery-café operations | $ 153,584 | $ 122,868 | $ 94,873 | $ 66,961 | $ 46,408 |
| Fresh-dough and other-product operations at regional facilities | 11,461 | 13,434 | 6,483 | 6,452 | 3,681 |
| Corporate administration | 26,965 | 16,026 | 6,576 | 8,813 | 4,595 |
| Total capital expenditures | $ 192,010 | $ 152,328 | $ 107,932 | $ 82,226 | $ 54,684 |
| **Segment assets** | | | | | |
| Company bakery-café operations | $ 867,093 | $ 807,681 | $ 682,246 | $ 581,193 | $ 498,806 |
| Franchise operations | 10,156 | 10,285 | 7,502 | 6,679 | 3,850 |
| Fresh-dough and other-product operations at regional facilities | 62,854 | 60,069 | 47,710 | 48,393 | 48,616 |
| Total segment assets | $ 940,103 | $ 878,035 | $ 737,458 | $ 636,265 | $ 551,272 |

*Sources:* Panera Bread's 2013 10-K report, p. 67, and 2011 10-K report, p. 69.

company-owned bakery-cafés as a reduction in the cost of food and paper products. The costs of food and paper products for company-operated bakery-cafés are shown in Exhibit 1.

## Panera Bread's Management Information Systems

Each company-owned bakery-café had programmed point-of-sale registers that collected transaction data used to generate transaction counts, product mix, average check size, and other pertinent statistics. The prices of menu selections at all company-owned bakery-cafés were programmed into the point-of-sale registers from the company's data support centers. Franchisees were allowed access to certain parts of Panera's proprietary bakery-café systems and systems support. Franchisees were responsible for providing the appropriate menu prices, discount rates, and tax rates for system programming.

The company used in-store enterprise application tools to (1) assist café managers in scheduling work hours for café personnel and controlling food costs, in order to provide corporate and retail operations management with quick access to retail data, (2) enable café managers to place online orders with distributors, and (3) reduce the time café managers spent on administrative activities. The information collected electronically at café registers was used to generate daily and weekly consolidated reports regarding sales, transaction counts, average check size, product mix, sales trends, and other operating metrics, as well as detailed profit-and-loss statements for company-owned bakery-cafés. These data were incorporated into the company's "exception-based reporting" tools.

Panera's regional facilities had software that accepted electronic orders from bakery-cafés and monitored delivery of the ordered products to the bakery-cafés. Panera also had developed proprietary digital software to provide online training to employees at bakery-cafés and online baking instructions for the baking personnel at each café.

Most of Panera's bakery-cafés provided customers with free Internet access through a managed WiFi network that was among the largest free public WiFi networks in the United States.

## The Restaurant Industry in the United States

According to the National Restaurant Association, total food-and-drink sales at some 990,000 food service locations of all types in the United States were projected to reach a record $683 billion in 2014, up 3.6 percent over 2013 and up from $379 billion in 2000 and $239 billion in 1990.[13] Of the projected $683 billion in food-and-drink sales industrywide in 2014, about $456 billion was expected to occur in commercial restaurants, with the remainder divided among bars and taverns, lodging-place restaurants, managed food service locations, military restaurants, and other types of retail, vending, recreational, and mobile operations with food service capability. In 2011, unit sales averaged $874,000 at full-service restaurants and $777,000 at quick-service restaurants; however, very popular restaurant locations achieved annual sales volumes in the $2.5 million to $5 million range.

Restaurants were the nation's second-largest private employer in 2013, with about 13.5 million employees. Nearly half of all adults in the United States had worked in the restaurant industry at some point in their lives, and close to one out of three adults got their first job experience in a restaurant. More than 90 percent of all eating-and-drinking-place businesses had fewer than 50 employees, and more than 70 percent of these places were single-unit operations.

Even though the average U.S. consumer ate 76 percent of their meals at home, on a typical day about 130 million U.S. consumers were food service patrons at an eating establishment—sales at commercial eating places were projected to average about $1.87 billion daily in 2014. Average household expenditures for food away from home in 2011 were $2,505, equal to about 48 percent of total household expenditures for food and drink.

The restaurant business was labor-intensive, extremely competitive, and risky. Industry members pursued differentiation strategies of one variety or another, seeking to set themselves apart from rivals via pricing, food quality, menu theme, signature menu selections, dining ambience and atmosphere, service, convenience, and location. To further enhance their appeal, some restaurants tried to promote greater customer traffic via happy hours, lunch and dinner specials, children's menus, innovative or trendy dishes, diet-conscious menu selections, and beverage and appetizer specials during televised sporting events (important at restaurants and bars with big-screen TVs). Most restaurants were quick to adapt their menu offerings to changing consumer tastes and eating preferences, frequently featuring heart-healthy, vegetarian, organic, low-calorie, and/or low-carb items on their menus. Research conducted by the Natural Restaurant Industry in 2013 indicated that:[14]

- 81 percent of consumers believed there were more healthy options at restaurants than there were two years ago.
- 72 percent of consumers were more likely to visit a restaurant that offered healthy menu options.
- 72 percent of consumers would consider dining out more often if menu prices were lower during off-peak times.

It was the norm at many restaurants to rotate some menu selections seasonally and to periodically introduce creative dishes in an effort to keep regular patrons coming back, attract more patrons, and remain competitive.

The profitability of a restaurant location ranged from exceptional to good to average to marginal to money-losing. Consumers (especially those who ate out often) were prone to give newly opened eating establishments a trial, and if they were pleased with their experience, they might return, sometimes frequently—loyalty to existing restaurants was low when consumers perceived there were better dining alternatives. It was also common for a once-hot restaurant to lose favor and confront the stark realities of a dwindling clientele, forcing it to either reconcept its menu and dining environment or go out of business. Many restaurants had fairly short lives. There were multiple causes for a restaurant's failure—a lack of enthusiasm for the menu or dining experience, inconsistent food quality, poor service, a poor location, meal prices that patrons deemed too high, and being outcompeted by rivals with comparable menu offerings.

## ENDNOTES

[1] Harris Interactive press releases, March 16, 2011 and May 10, 2012, and information at www.harrisinteractive.com (accessed March 7, 2014).

[2] "Zagat Announces 2012 Fast-Food Survey Results," www.prnewswire.com, September 27, 2012 (accessed March 7, 2014).

[3] Sandelman and Associates Quick-Track surveys and Fast-Food Awards of Excellence Winners, and information in "Press Kit," www.panerabread.com (accessed March 7, 2014).

[4] According to information at Panera Bread's website, www.panerabread.com (accessed March 30, 2012).

[5] As stated in a presentation to securities analysts, May 5, 2006.

[6] CEO William Moreton's letter to the stockholders, in Panera's 2010 annual report, April 18, 2011.

[7] Ron Ruggless, "Panera Cares: One Year Later," Nation's Restaurant News, May 16, 2011, www.nrn.com (accessed July 19, 2011).

[8] Sean Gregory-Clayton, "Sandwich Philanthropy," Time Magazine, August 2, 2010, www.time.com (accessed July 19, 2011).

[9] Annie Gasparro, "A New Test for Panera's Pay-What-You-Can," Wall Street Journal, June 4, 2013, www.wsj.com (accessed March 7, 2014).

[10] Ibid.

[11] Jim Salter, "Panera Suspends Latest Pay-What-You-Can Experiment in Stores," Huffington Post, July 10, 2013, www.huffingtonpost.com (accessed March 7, 2014).

[12] As cited in Panera Bread's presentation to securities analysts on May 5, 2006.

[13] The statistical data in this section is based on information posted at www.restaurant.org (accessed July 26, 2011, April 8, 2012, and March 17, 2014).

[14] National Restaurant Industry, "2014 Restaurant Industry Pocket Factbook," www.restaurant.org (accessed March 17, 2014).

# Chipotle Mexican Grill in 2014: Will Its Strategy Become the Model for Reinventing the Fast-Food Industry? connect

**Arthur A. Thompson**

The University of Alabama

In early 2014, it was obvious that founder, co-CEO, and Chairman Steve Ells's vision and strategy for Chipotle Mexican Grill had resulted in a home run. Ells's vision for Chipotle (pronounced "chi-POAT-lay") was "to change the way people think about and eat fast food." Taking his inspiration from features commonly found in many fine-dining restaurants, Ells's strategy for Chipotle Mexican Grill was predicated on six elements:

- Serving a focused menu of burritos, tacos, burrito bowls (a burrito without the tortilla), and salads.

- Using high-quality, fresh ingredients and classic cooking methods to create great-tasting, reasonably-priced dishes prepared to order and ready to be served one to two minutes after they were ordered.

- Enabling customers to select the ingredients they wanted in each dish by speaking directly to the employees assembling the dish on the serving line.

- Creating an operationally efficient restaurant with an aesthetically pleasing interior.

- Building a special people culture that consisted of friendly, high-performing people motivated to take good care of each customer and empowered to achieve high standards.

- Doing all of this with increasing awareness and respect for the environment and with the use of organically grown fresh produce and meats from animals raised in a humane manner without hormones and antibiotics.

Since 1993, the company had grown from a 1-unit operation in Denver into a 1,595-unit operation serving nearly 1 million customers a day in 43 states, the District of Columbia, Canada, London, Paris, and Frankfurt as of February 2014. In 2013, Chipotle reported revenues of $3.2 billion, net income of $327.4 million, and diluted earnings per share of $10.47. When the company went public in January 2006, the stock doubled on its first day of trading, jumping from the initial offering price of $22 per share to a closing price of $44 per share. In April 2012, Chipotle Mexican Grill's stock price reached a record high of $440, but then it took a sharp dive to $243 six months later on fears of slowing growth and increased competition from Taco Bell's recently introduced upscale menu offerings. But the fears were short-lived. Over the next 28 months, Chipotle's stock price trended steadily upward, reaching an all-time high of $611 in March 2014.

But Steve Ells was not content to capitalize on the growing demand for healthier, more wholesome fast foods and continue on a path of opening several hundred new domestic and international Chipotle Mexican Grill locations annually, perhaps eventually mounting a challenge to McDonald's, the solidly entrenched global leader of the fast-food industry and the company that had invented the fast-food concept in the 1950s—McDonald's currently had 35,000 company-owned and franchised restaurant locations serving about 70 million customers in 119 countries daily. Beginning in 2011, Ells launched a strategic initiative to begin testing and refining a second restaurant concept, ShopHouse Southeast Asian Kitchen, predicated on the same strategic principles as Chipotle Mexican Grill but with a different menu. Ells believed that the Chipotle model—a limited menu, fresh ingredients, classic cooking methods, and customer customization of the dishes ordered—could work well with a variety of different cuisines. The first ShopHouse restaurant opened in Washington, D.C., in the summer of 2011, and, by year-end 2013, there were six ShopHouse locations.

Then, in December 2013, Chipotle announced it was partnering with two Colorado restaurateurs to launch a fast-casual pizza restaurant concept called Pizzeria Locale that incorporated the Chipotle model. Seven months earlier, Chipotle and the two restaurateurs had partnered to open the first Pizzeria Locale in Denver; it featured a focused menu with a selection of classic pizzas and customer-created pizzas using high-quality ingredients. The pizzas were then fired in a special Chipotle-designed, high-temperature pizza oven that baked the pizzas in less than two minutes and delivered results like those from an Italian wood-burning oven. The menu also included salads, meatballs, sliced-to-order prosciutto, a caramel chocolate pudding, and red and white Italian wines. Plans called for opening the second and third Pizzeria Locale locations in Denver in 2014. Co-CEO Steve Ells said the following about the speed with which the company could open larger numbers of ShopHouse and Pizzeria Locale restaurants, once he was satisfied that the ShopHouse and Pizzeria Locale concepts had been "perfected":[1]

> When we are ready to expand at a faster rate, we certainly have the infrastructure in place. . . . [W]e have so much information on 1,600 specific sites now in the U.S. with Chipotles, and so we know exactly what regions, what markets, what intersections we would want to go to with these new concepts.

Part of Chipotle's lofty stock price in 2014 was predicated on investors' belief that the potential was there not only to open hundreds more Chipotle restaurants but also to open 1,500 or more domestic locations of both ShopHouse and Pizzeria Locale restaurants—as well as hundreds of international restaurants for all three concepts, in which case Chipotle was likely to hit a second home run with ShopHouse and a third home run with Pizzeria Locale,

a rare and unusual feat for a relatively young company still rounding the bases on its first home run. However, over the previous two years, at least six other food enterprises—all very small compared to Chipotle—had opened locations featuring the build-your-own-pizza concept; the menus consisted of artisan and gourmet pizzas, with a variety of crust options and premium toppings, that were baked in high-temperature ovens and ready to serve in around three minutes. Some restaurant industry analysts speculated that "better pizza" might become the next fast-casual restaurant category.[2]

## CHIPOTLE MEXICAN GRILL'S EARLY YEARS

Steve Ells graduated from the Culinary Institute of America and then worked for two years at Stars Restaurant in San Francisco. Soon after moving to Denver, he began working on plans to open his own restaurant. Guided by a conviction that food served fast did not have to be low quality and that delicious food did not have to be expensive, he came up with the concept of Chipotle Mexican Grill. When the first Chipotle restaurant opened in Denver in 1993, it became an instant hit. Patrons were attracted by the experience of getting better-quality food served fast and dining in a restaurant setting that was more upscale and appealing than those of traditional fast-food enterprises. Over the next several years, Ells opened more Chipotle restaurants in Denver and other Colorado locations.

Intrigued by what it saw happening at Chipotle, McDonald's acquired an initial ownership stake in the fledgling company in 1998 and then acquired a controlling interest in early 2000. But McDonald's recognized the value of Ells's visionary leadership and kept him in the role of Chipotle's chief executive after it gained majority ownership. Drawing on the investment capital provided by McDonald's and its decades of expertise in managing supply chain logistics, expanding a restaurant chain, and operating restaurants efficiently, Chipotle—under Ells's watchful and passionate guidance—embarked on a long-term strategy to open new restaurants and expand its market coverage. By year-end 2005, Chipotle had 489 locations in 24 states. As 2005 drew to a close, in somewhat of a surprise move, McDonald's top management determined that instead of continuing to parent Chipotle's growth, it would take the company public and give Chipotle's management a free rein in charting the company's future growth and strategy. An initial public offering of shares was held in January 2006, and Steve Ells was designated as Chipotle's CEO and chairman of the board. During 2006—through the January IPO, a secondary offering in May 2006, and a tax-free exchange offer in October 2006—McDonald's disposed of its entire ownership interest in Chipotle Mexican Grill.

When Chipotle became an independent enterprise, Steve Ells and the company's other top executives kept the company squarely on a path of rapid expansion and continued to employ the same basic strategy elements that were the foundation of the company's success. Steve Ells functioned as the company's principal driving force for ongoing innovation and constant improvement. He pushed especially hard for new ways to boost "throughput"—the number of customers whose orders could be taken, prepared, and served per hour.[3] By 2012, Ells's mantra of "slow food, fast" had resulted in throughputs of 300 customers per hour at Chipotle's best restaurants.

Between 2007 and 2013, Chipotle's revenues grew at a robust compound average rate of 19.8 percent. Net income grew at a compound rate of 29.1 percent, due to gains in operating efficiency that boosted profit margins. Average annual sales for restaurants open at least 12 full calendar months climbed from $1,085,000 in 2007 to $2,169,000 in 2013, owing to increased customer visits and higher expenditures per customer visit. The average tab per customer ran $8 to $9 in 2011–2013.[4] Exhibit 1 presents recent financial and operating data for Chipotle Mexican Grill.

## MENU AND FOOD PREPARATION

The menu at Chipotle Mexican Grill restaurants was quite limited—burritos, burrito bowls, tacos, and salads, plus soft drinks, fruit drinks, and milk. Except in restaurants where there were restrictions on serving alcoholic beverages, the drink options also included a selection of beers and margaritas. However, customers could customize their burritos, burrito bowls, tacos, and salads to their liking. Options included four different meats—marinated and grilled chicken and steak, carnitas (seasoned and braised pork), and barbacoa (spicy shredded beef)—pinto beans, vegetarian black beans, brown or white rice tossed with lime juice and fresh-chopped cilantro, and such extras as sautéed peppers and onions, salsas, guacamole, sour cream, shredded cheese, lettuce, and tortilla chips seasoned with fresh lime and salt. In addition, it was restaurant policy to make special dishes for customers if the requested dish could be made from the ingredients on hand. Exhibit 2 shows some of the dishes served at Chipotle Mexican Grill restaurants.

From the outset, Chipotle's menu strategy had been to keep it simple, do a few things exceptionally well, and not include menu selections (like coffee and desserts) that complicated restaurant operations and impaired efficiency. While it was management practice to consider menu additions, the menu offerings had remained fundamentally the same since the addition of burrito bowls in 2005. However, in early 2013, Chipotle began testing a new vegetarian menu item called Sofritas in seven restaurants in the San Francisco Bay Area. The feature ingredient of Sofritas was shredded organic tofu braised with chipotle chilis, roasted poblanos, and a blend of aromatic spices. The item proved popular with vegan, vegetarian, and meat-eating customers and was rolled out to about 40 percent of Chipotle's restaurants by year-end 2013. Sofritas accounted for about 3 percent of the sales in the restaurants where they were on the menu; company analysis revealed that about 40 percent of the Sofritas being sold were ordered by people who normally ate meat. Chipotle planned to make Sofritas available in more restaurants as soon as it was able to secure bigger supplies of the special organic tofu. So far, Steve Ells had rejected the idea of adding a breakfast menu and opening earlier in the day—although serving breakfast was rumored to be under serious consideration in early 2014.

The food preparation area of each restaurant was equipped with stoves and grills, pots and pans, and an assortment of cutting knives, wire whisks, and other kitchen utensils. A walk-in refrigerator was stocked with ingredients, and there were supplies of herbs, spices, and dry goods such as rice. The workspace more closely resembled the layout of the kitchen in a fine-dining restaurant than the cooking area of a typical fast-food restaurant that made extensive use of automated cooking equipment and microwaves. All of the menu selections and optional

**EXHIBIT 1** Financial and Operating Highlights for Chipotle Mexican Grill, 2007–2013 (financial data in 000s of dollars, except for per share items)

| | 2013 | 2012 | 2011 | 2009 | 2007 |
|---|---|---|---|---|---|
| **Income statement data** | | | | | |
| Total revenue | $3,214,591 | $2,731,224 | $2,269,548 | $1,518,417 | $ 1,085,782 |
| Food, beverage, and packaging costs | 1,073,514 | 891,003 | 738,720 | 466,027 | 346,393 |
| As % of total revenue | 33.4% | 32.6% | 32.5% | 30.7% | 31.9% |
| Labor costs | 739,800 | 641,836 | 543,119 | 385,072 | 289,417 |
| As % of total revenue | 23.0% | 23.5% | 23.9% | 25.4% | 26.7% |
| Occupancy costs | 199,107 | 171,435 | 147,274 | 114,218 | 75,891 |
| As % of total revenue | 6.2% | 6.3% | 6.5% | 7.5% | 7.0% |
| Other operating costs | 347,401 | 286,610 | 251,208 | 174,581 | 131,512 |
| As % of total revenue | 10.8% | 10.5% | 11.1% | 11.5% | 12.1% |
| General and administrative expenses | 203,733 | 183,409 | 149,426 | 99,149 | 75,038 |
| As % of total revenue | 6.3% | 6.7% | 6.6% | 6.5% | 6.9% |
| Depreciation and amortization | 96,054 | 84,130 | 74,938 | 61,308 | 43,595 |
| Preopening costs | 15,511 | 11,909 | 8,495 | 8,401 | 9,585 |
| Loss on disposal of assets | 6,751 | 5,027 | 5,806 | 5,956 | 6,168 |
| Total operating expenses | 2,681,871 | 2,275,359 | 1,918,986 | 1,314,712 | 977,599 |
| Operating income | 532,720 | 455,865 | 350,562 | 203,705 | 108,183 |
| Interest and other income (expense) net | 1,751 | 1,820 | (857) | 520 | 5,819 |
| Income before income taxes | 534,471 | 457,685 | 349,705 | 204,225 | 114,002 |
| Provision for income taxes | (207,033) | (179,685) | (134,760) | (77,380) | (43,439) |
| Net income | $ 327,438 | $ 278,000 | $ 214,945 | $ 126,845 | $ 70,563 |
| Earnings per share | | | | | |
| Basic | $10.58 | $8.82 | $6.89 | $3.99 | $2.16 |
| Diluted | 10.47 | 8.75 | 6.76 | 3.95 | 2.13 |
| Weighted-average common shares outstanding | | | | | |
| Basic | 30,957 | 31,513 | 31,217 | 31,766 | 32,672 |
| Diluted | 31,281 | 31,783 | 31,775 | 32,102 | 33,146 |
| **Selected balance sheet data** | | | | | |
| Total current assets | $ 666,307 | $ 546,607 | $ 501,192 | $ 297,454 | $ 201,844 |
| Total assets | 2,009,280 | 1,668,667 | 1,425,308 | 961,505 | 722,115 |
| Total current liabilities | 199,228 | 186,852 | 157,453 | 102,153 | 73,301 |
| Total liabilities | 470,992 | 422,741 | 381,082 | 258,044 | 160,005 |
| Total shareholders' equity | 1,538,288 | 1,245,926 | 1,044,226 | 703,461 | 562,110 |
| **Other financial data** | | | | | |
| Net cash provided by operating activities | $ 528,780 | $ 419,963 | $ 411,096 | $ 260,673 | $ 146,923 |
| Capital expenditures | 199,926 | 197,037 | 151,147 | 117,200 | 141,000 |
| **Restaurant data (in actual amounts)** | | | | | |
| Restaurants open at year-end | 1,595 | 1,410 | 1,230 | 956 | 704 |
| Average annual sales for restaurants open at least 12 full calendar months | $2,169,000 | $2,113,000 | $2,013,000 | $1,728,000 | $1,085,000 |
| Comparable-restaurant sales increases* | 5.6% | 7.1% | 11.2% | 2.2% | 10.8% |
| Development and construction costs per newly-opened restaurant | $ 800,000 | $ 800,000 | $ 800,000 | $ 850,000 | $ 880,000 |

*The change in period-over-period sales for restaurants beginning in their 13th full calendar month of operation.

*Source:* Company 10-K reports, 2013, 2012, 2011, and 2008.

## EXHIBIT 2    Representative Dishes Served at Chipotle Mexican Grill Restaurants

extras were prepared from scratch—hours went into preparing food onsite, but some items were prepared from fresh ingredients in nearby commissaries. Kitchen crews used classic cooking methods: They marinated and grilled the chicken and steak, hand-cut produce and herbs, made fresh salsa and guacamole, and cooked rice in small batches throughout the day. While the food preparation methods were labor-intensive, the limited menu created efficiencies that helped keep costs down.

### Serving Orders Quickly

One of Chipotle's biggest innovations had been creating the ability to have a customer's order ready quickly. As customers moved along the serving line, they selected which ingredients they wanted in their burritos, burrito bowls, tacos, and salads by speaking directly to the employees who prepared the food and were assembling the order behind the counter. Much experimentation and fine-tuning had gone into creating a restaurant layout and serving-line design that made the food-ordering and dish-creation process intuitive and time-efficient, thereby enabling a high rate of customer throughput. The throughput target was at least 200 and up to 300 customers per hour, in order to keep the number of customers waiting in line at peak hours to a tolerable minimum. Management was focused on further improving the speed at which customers moved through the service line in all restaurants so that orders placed by fax, online, or via an iPhone ordering app could be accommodated without slowing service to in-restaurant customers and compromising the interactions between customers and crew members on the service line. The attention to serving orders quickly was motivated by management's belief that while customers returned because of the great-tasting food, they also liked their orders served fast without having a "fast-food" experience (even when they were not in a hurry).

## Chipotle's New Catering Program

In January 2013, Chipotle introduced an expanded catering program to help spur sales at its restaurants. The rollout began in the company's Colorado restaurants and was available at every Chipotle Mexican Grill in 2014. The program involved setting up a portable version of its service line for groups of 20 or more people; guests could create tacos and bowls with the same ingredients offered in Chipotle's restaurant. For customers wanting to accommodate a smaller group of six or more people, Chipotle offered its Burritos by the Box option (this was the only meal option prior to the expanded catering offering). By early 2014, catering sales had jumped to almost 1 percent of average restaurant sales from a prior volume of less than 0.1 percent of sales. In larger metropolitan markets like Denver, Seattle, St. Louis, and San Francisco, catering sales were averaging about 1.5 percent of sales. To support catering going into the 2013 holiday season, Chipotle had run digital, print, and outdoor advertising in all of its geographic markets throughout December, a move that more than doubled page views regarding catering at Chipotle's website.

## The Commitment to "Food With Integrity"

In 2003–2004, Chipotle began a move to increase its use of organically grown local produce, organic beans, organic dairy products, and meats from animals that were raised in accordance with animal welfare standards and were never given feeds containing antibiotics and growth hormones to speed weight gain. This shift in ingredient usage was part of a long-term management campaign to use top-quality, nutritious ingredients and improve "the Chipotle experience"—an effort that Chipotle designated as "Food With Integrity" and that top executives deemed critical to the company's vision of changing the way people think about and eat fast food. The thesis was that purchasing fresh ingredients and preparing them by hand were not enough.

To implement the Food With Integrity initiative, the company began working with experts in the areas of animal ethics to try to support more humane farming environments, and it started visiting the farms and ranches from which it obtained ingredients. It also began investigating the use of more produce supplied by farmers who respected the environment, avoided use of chemical fertilizers and pesticides, followed U.S. Department of Agriculture standards for growing organic products, and used agriculturally sustainable methods like conservation tillage methods that improved soil conditions and reduced erosion. Simultaneously, efforts were made to source a greater portion of products locally (within 350 miles of the restaurants where they were used) while they were in season. Chipotle's limited menu enabled it to concentrate on the sources of each ingredient—this was the cornerstone of the company's effort to improve its food.

The transition to using organically grown local produce and meats from naturally raised animals occurred gradually, rather than being an all-at-once 100 percent switch, because it took time for Chipotle to develop sufficient sources of supply to accommodate the requirements of all of its restaurants. The process of switching to 100 percent organic ingredients and natural meats was still under way in 2014. But substantial progress had been made. By year-end 2011, all of the sour cream and cheese Chipotle purchased was made from milk that came from cows that were not given recombinant bovine growth hormone (rBGH). The milk used to make much of the purchased cheese and a portion of the purchased sour cream was sourced from dairies that provided pasture access for their cows rather than housing them in confined spaces. There had been progress in other areas as well. A portion of the beans the company used was organically grown and a portion was being grown by farmers who used sustainable agricultural practices. As of 2014, all Chipotle restaurants normally served only meats from animals that were raised without the use of subtherapeutic antibiotics or added hormones and met other Chipotle standards; these meats were branded and promoted under the "Responsibly Raised" label. Chipotle served more than 15 million pounds of locally grown produce in 2013, up from about 10 million pounds in 2012. Also, in 2013, Chipotle began an initiative to stop using ingredients grown with genetically modified seeds in all of its dishes;

the process of shifting to ingredients not grown from genetically modified seeds was expected to be complete by year-end 2014.

However, there were ongoing challenges. Supplies of organic products, locally grown produce, and natural meats were sometimes constrained because consumers were purchasing growing volumes of these items at their local farmers' markets and supermarkets and because the chefs at many fine-dining establishments were making concerted efforts to incorporate organic, locally grown produce and natural meats into their dishes. Moreover, the costs incurred by organic farmers and by those raising animals naturally were typically higher. Organic crops often took longer to grow, and crop yields could be lower than nonorganic yields. Among chickens, cattle, and pigs, growth rate and weight gain was typically lower for those that were fed only vegetarian diets containing no subtherapeutic antibiotics and for cattle that were not given growth hormones. Hence the prices of organically grown produce and natural meat were higher. As a consequence, periodic supply–demand imbalances produced market conditions under which certain organic products and natural meats were sometimes either unavailable or prohibitively high-priced. For example, some Chipotle restaurants were forced to serve chicken or steak from conventionally raised animals for much of 2011. Chipotle restaurants in a few markets reverted to the use of conventional beef in early 2012. Some restaurants served conventional beef and chicken for periods during 2013, and some were continuing to serve conventional beef in early 2014, due to supply constraints for Responsibly Raised meats. When certain Chipotle restaurants were forced to serve conventional meat, it was company practice to disclose this temporary change on signage in each affected restaurant so that customers could avoid those meats if they chose to do so.

The ongoing challenges in sourcing adequate supplies of organic produce and Responsibly Raised meats had resulted in an upward creep in the prices that Chipotle had to pay for food ingredients. Rising market prices for organically grown ingredients and natural meats largely accounted for why Chipotle's costs for food, beverages, and packing rose from 30.7 percent of revenues in 2009 to 32.6 percent of revenues in 2012 and to 33.4 percent in 2013 (see Exhibit 1).

Going forward, Chipotle executives were firmly committed to continuing the Food With Integrity initiative, despite the attendant price-cost challenges and supply chain complications. They wanted Chipotle to be at the forefront in responding to mounting consumer concerns about food nutrition, where their food came from, how fruits and vegetables were grown, and how animals used for meat were raised. And they wanted customers to view Chipotle Mexican Grill as a place that used high-quality, "better-for-you" ingredients in its menu selections. Nonetheless, top management expected that there would be times when prohibitively high prices for certain organic products and natural meats would temporarily revert to using conventional produce and meats in its dishes in the interest of preserving the company's reputation for providing great food at reasonable prices and protecting profit margins. Over the longer term, top executives anticipated that the price volatility and shortages of organically grown ingredients and natural meats would gradually dissipate as growing demand for such products attracted more small farmers and larger agricultural enterprises to boost supplies. But it was also anticipated that most of these organic and natural ingredients would remain more expensive than conventionally raised, commodity-priced equivalents.

## SUPPLY CHAIN MANAGEMENT PRACTICES

Top executives were acutely aware that maintaining high levels of food quality in Chipotle restaurants depended in part on acquiring high-quality, fresh ingredients and other necessary supplies that met company specifications. Over the years, the company had developed long-term relationships with a number of reputable food industry suppliers that could meet Chipotle's quality standards and understood the importance of helping Chipotle live up to its Food With Integrity mission. It then worked with these suppliers on an ongoing basis to establish and implement a set of forward, fixed, and formula pricing protocols for determining the prices that suppliers charged Chipotle for various items. Reliable suppliers that could meet Chipotle's quality specifications and were willing to comply with Chipotle's set of pricing protocols and guidelines for certain products were put on Chipotle's list of approved suppliers. The number of approved suppliers was small for such key ingredients as beef, pork, chicken, beans, rice, sour cream, and tortillas, but Chipotle was constantly working to increase the number of approved suppliers for ingredients subject to volatile prices and short supplies. In addition, Chipotle personnel diligently monitored industry news, trade issues, weather, exchange rates, foreign demand, crises, and other world events to better anticipate potential impacts on ingredient prices.

Instead of making purchases directly from approved suppliers, Chipotle utilized the services of 23 independently owned and operated regional distribution centers to purchase and deliver ingredients and other supplies to Chipotle restaurants. These distribution centers were required to make all purchases from Chipotle's list of approved suppliers in accordance with the agreed-on pricing guidelines and protocols.

## QUALITY ASSURANCE AND FOOD SAFETY

Chipotle had a quality assurance department that established and monitored quality and food safety throughout the company's supply chain and all the way through the serving lines at restaurants. There were quality and food safety standards for certain farms that grew ingredients used by company restaurants, approved suppliers, and the regional distribution centers that purchased and delivered products to the restaurants. Chipotle's training and risk management departments developed and implemented operating standards for food quality, preparation, cleanliness, and safety in company restaurants. The food safety programs for suppliers and restaurants were designed to ensure compliance with applicable federal, state, and local food safety regulations.

## RESTAURANT MANAGEMENT AND OPERATIONS

Chipotle's strategy for operating its restaurants was based on the principle that "the front line is key." The restaurant and kitchen designs intentionally placed most personnel up front where they could speak to customers in a personal and hospitable manner, whether preparing food items or customizing the meal ordered by a customer moving along the service line. The open kitchen design allowed customers to see employees preparing and cooking ingredients, reinforcing that Chipotle's food was freshly made each day. Restaurant personnel, especially those who prepared dishes on the serving line, were expected to deliver a customer-pleasing experience "one burrito at a time," give each customer individual attention, and make every effort to respond positively to customer requests and suggestions. Special effort was made to hire and retain people who were personable and could help deliver a positive customer experience. Management believed that creating a positive and interactive experience helped build loyalty and enthusiasm for the Chipotle brand not only among customers but among the restaurant's entire staff.

## Restaurant Staffing and Management

Each Chipotle Mexican Grill typically had a general manager (a position top management characterized as the most important in the company), an apprentice manager (in about 75 percent of the restaurants), one to three hourly service managers, one or two hourly kitchen managers, and an average of 23 full- and part-time crew members. Busier restaurants had more crew members. Chipotle generally had two shifts at its restaurants, which simplified scheduling and facilitated assigning hourly employees with a regular number of work hours each week. Most employees were cross-trained to work at a variety of stations, both to provide people with a variety of skills and to boost labor efficiency during busy periods. Personnel were empowered to make decisions within their assigned areas of responsibility.

One of Chipotle's top priorities was to build and nurture a people-oriented, performance-based culture in each Chipotle restaurant; executive management believed that such a culture led to the best possible experience for both customers and employees. The foundation of that culture started with hiring good people to manage and staff the company's restaurants. One of the prime functions of a restaurant's general manager was to hire and retain crew members who had a strong work ethic, took pride in preparing food items correctly, enjoyed interacting with other people, exhibited enthusiasm in serving customers, and were team players in striving to operate the restaurant in accordance with the high standards expected by top management. A sizable number of Chipotle's crew members had been attracted to apply for a job at the company because of either encouragement from an acquaintance who worked at Chipotle or their own favorable impressions of the work atmosphere while going through the serving line and dining at a Chipotle Mexican Grill. New crew members received hands-on, shoulder-to-shoulder training. In 2012–2013, full-time crew members had average earnings of nearly $18,250 (regular compensation and bonuses), plus benefits of about $2,830 [clothes, meals, insurance, and 401(k) contributions].[5] Total earnings and benefits averaged $27,000 for hourly managers, $50,000 for apprentice managers, and $63,000 for general managers.

Top-performing store personnel could expect to be promoted because of the company's unusually heavy reliance on promotion from within—about 85 percent of salaried managers and about 96 percent of hourly managers had been promoted from positions as crew members. In several instances, a newly hired crew member had risen rapidly through the ranks and become the general manager of a restaurant in 9 to 12 months; many more high-performing crew members had been promoted to general managers within 2 to 4 years. The long-term career opportunities for Chipotle employees were quite attractive because of the company's rapid growth and the speed with which it was opening new stores in both new and existing markets.

## The Position and Role of Restaurateur

The general managers who ran high-performing restaurants and succeeded in developing a strong, empowered team of hourly managers and crew members were promoted to *restaurateur,* a position that entailed greater leadership and culture-building responsibility. In addition to continuing to run their assigned restaurant, restaurateurs were typically given responsibility for mentoring one or more nearby restaurants and using their leadership skills to help develop the managers and build high-performing teams at the restaurants they mentored. At year-end 2013, Chipotle had over 400 restaurateurs overseeing nearly 40 percent of the company's Chipotle restaurants, including their home restaurant and others that they mentored. The average salary of Chipotle restaurateurs was $106,000 in 2013.

Restaurateurs could earn bonuses up to $23,000 for their people development and team-building successes and for creating a culture of high standards, constant improvement, and empowerment in each of their restaurants. Restaurateurs whose mentoring efforts resulted in high-performing teams at four restaurants and the promotion of at least one of the four restaurant managers to restaurateur could be promoted to the position of apprentice team leader and become a full-time member of the company's field support staff.

Chipotle's field support system included apprentice team leaders, team leaders or area managers, team directors, executive team directors or regional directors, and restaurant support officers—over 100 of the people in these positions in 2014 were former restaurateurs. In 2014, over two-thirds of Chipotle's restaurants were under the leadership and supervision of the company's 500 existing and former restaurateurs. The principal task of field support personnel was to foster a culture of employee empowerment, high standards, and constant improvement in each of Chipotle's restaurants. One of Chipotle's field support staff members had been hired as a crew member in 2003, was promoted to general manager in 12 months, and—8 years after starting with Chipotle—was appointed as a team director (with responsibilities for 57 restaurants and more than 1,400 employees in 2013).[6]

## A New Diagnostic and Planning Tool for Field Support Personnel

In 2013, Chipotle brought its entire field support team together for the purposes of (1) establishing clear expectations of what they were supposed to accomplish and (2) introducing a new restaurant diagnostic and planning tool developed by the company's co-CEO, Monty Moran. The tool was designed to help field leaders more effectively recognize what was keeping a restaurant general manager from achieving restaurateur status and to develop a clear plan of action to help general managers become a restaurateur more quickly. Use of the tool required field leaders to visit their restaurants, interview all crew members, determine the degree to which the restaurant had a team of empowered top performers, identify the root causes of weaker-than-desired financial and operating performance, create a corrective action plan, go over the plan with the restaurant's general manager, and indicate how they planned to help the general manager on an ongoing basis. Field leaders followed up each quarter to conduct more interviews, gauge progress, and create an updated plan, watching closely to see how the restaurant team was evolving and developing toward becoming a restaurateur-caliber team.

Monty Moran believed the new tool was producing tangible benefits:[7]

> In using the tool, our field leaders become aware of a great deal of information, including the strength of the team, the depth of the people pipeline to be sure the restaurant has the right people in place for continued development, the training systems that are in place, the scheduling, the financial metrics, and how well the restaurant is implementing the four pillars of great [customer] throughput [on the serving line]. We're hearing over and over how excited managers are to have this tool in place. For nearly all of our restaurants, this tool is providing a new level of understanding as to our expectations and giving clear direction to our GMs about how to become Restaurateurs by taking some of the mystery out of what it takes to build this special culture. As of now, all of our non-Restaurateur restaurants have plans in place to put them on the road to Restaurateur, and our field teams will create new plans for each restaurant every quarter.

During the fourth quarter of 2013, there was solid evidence that the new diagnostic and planning tool was delivering dividends: Customer throughput on the service line at Chipotle restaurants increased by an average of six transactions during the peak lunch hour and by an average of five transactions during the peak dinner hour.

## MARKETING

Chipotle executives believed that word-of-mouth publicity from customers telling others about their favorable experiences at Chipotle restaurants was the most powerful marketing of all. But they also recognized the need to introduce the Chipotle brand to consumers and emphasize what made Chipotle different from other restaurants. Over the past 10 years, Chipotle had generated considerable media coverage from scores of publications that had largely favorable articles describing its food, restaurant concept, and business; the company had also been featured in a number of television programs. There was an ongoing effort to monitor public awareness of Chipotle and customer sentiment.

Marketing personnel paid close attention to presenting the Chipotle brand consistently and keeping advertising and promotional programs and in-restaurant communications closely aligned with what Chipotle was, what the Chipotle experience was all about, and what differentiated Chipotle from other fast-food competitors. When the company opened restaurants in new markets, it initiated a range of promotional activities to introduce Chipotle to the local community and to create interest in the restaurant. In markets where there were existing Chipotle restaurants, newly opened restaurants typically attracted customers in volumes at or near market averages without having to initiate special promotions or advertising to support a new opening.

Chipotle's advertising mix typically included print, outdoor, transit, theater, radio, and online ads. In February 2012, Chipotle Mexican Grill ran its first-ever national TV commercial during the broadcast of the Grammy Awards. The commercial was actually a short film, *Back to the Start,* that Chipotle had shown in 2011 in theaters and online and was an unusually long commercial for a national broadcast. The company had increased its use of digital, mobile, and social media in its overall marketing mix because these media gave customers greater opportunity to access Chipotle in ways that were convenient for them and broadened Chipotle's ability to engage with its customers individually. Most recently, the company had run an ad campaign featuring its newly expanded catering program.

In 2012–2013, Chipotle started utilizing more "owned media" in its overall marketing effort, such as new video and music programs, and a more visible event strategy that included increasing its participation in local community events and conducting what the company called "cultivate festivals" featuring food, music, and information about healthy foods, organic agriculture, and the overuse of antibiotics in livestock farming. Cultivate festivals had been held in Chicago, San Francisco, Dallas, and Minneapolis, drawing total audiences exceeding 120,000 and reaching a much bigger audience with the attendant advertising and public relations activities. Postevent research revealed that more than 90 percent of attendees in each market would attend such events again.

Some food-related issues were complex and sometimes hard for consumers to understand—for example, the pros and cons of ingredients grown with genetically modified seeds, the pros and cons of organically grown fruits and vegetables, the reasons people ought to consider eating meats that come from animals raised humanely and without the use of antibiotics, the benefits of eating nutritious foods, and the reasons Chipotle was deeply committed to its Food With Integrity mission. To increase customer awareness, Chipotle recently created marketing programs designed to make people more curious about these food-related issues in the belief that the more curious people became and the more they learned, the more likely they would be to eat at Chipotle. In 2013, Chipotle introduced its Scarecrow marketing program, which included a three-minute animated film and a game (for iPads and iPhones) that were intended to spark conversation about issues in industrial food production. The *Scarecrow* film had been viewed online nearly 12 million times as of early 2014, and the companion game had been downloaded nearly 600,000 times. Resulting discussions about these food issues had generated 500 million media impressions through news coverage of the program—a volume of coverage that Chipotle management believed would cost $5 million to purchase as advertising.[8]

Continuing in the tradition of *Scarecrow,* Chipotle then launched *Farmed and Dangerous,* an original scripted comedy series that hysterically explored the world of industrial agriculture in America. *Farmed and Dangerous* consisted of four 30-minute episodes that ran on Hulu in early 2014. The series focused on the introduction of a new petroleum-based animal feed created by the fictional agribusiness company Animoil. By using satire and doing so in an entertaining way, Chipotle hoped to make people more curious about their food and how it was produced. Executive management believed these newer programs allowed the company to forge stronger emotional connections with customers and communicate its story better and with more nuance than it could do through traditional advertising.

Top executives believed that Chipotle's collective marketing efforts, together with the considerable word-of-mouth publicity from customers telling others about their favorable experiences at Chipotle restaurants, had enabled the company to build good brand awareness among consumers with relatively low advertising expenditures—even in the highly competitive fast-food and fast-casual segments of the restaurant industry—and to differentiate Chipotle as a company that was committed to doing the right things in every facet of its business. Chipotle's advertising and marketing costs totaled $44.4 million in 2013 versus $35 million in 2012, $31.9 million in 2011, and $21 million in 2009 (these costs are included in "Other operating costs" in Exhibit 1).

## RESTAURANT SITE SELECTION

Chipotle had an internal team of real estate managers that devoted substantial time and effort to evaluating potential locations for new restaurants. The site selection process entailed studying the surrounding trade area, demographic and business information within that area, and available information on competitors. In addition, advice and recommendations were solicited from external real estate brokers with expertise in specific markets. Locations proposed by the internal real estate team were visited by a team of operations and development management as part of a formal site ride; the team toured the surrounding trade area, reviewed demographic and business information on the area, and evaluated the food-establishment operations of competitors. On the basis of this analysis, along with the results of predictive modeling based on proprietary formulas, the company came up with projected sales and targeted returns on investment for a new location. Chipotle Mexican Grills had proved successful in a number of different types of locations, including in-line or end-cap locations in strip or power centers, regional malls, and downtown business districts, as well as freestanding buildings and even a location at Dulles International Airport outside Washington, D.C. The company had also explored locating new restaurants in areas where it had little or no prior experience, including smaller or more economically mixed communities, highway sites, outlet centers, and locations in airports, in food courts, and on military bases.

Recently, Chipotle began locating a bigger fraction of its new restaurants in freestanding locations because restaurants in such locations were drawing greater customer traffic. In 2014, the company planned to open about 40 percent of its new restaurants in freestanding locations.

# DEVELOPMENT AND CONSTRUCTION COSTS FOR NEW RESTAURANTS

Chipotle opened a net of 146 restaurants in 2011, 180 restaurants in 2012, and 185 restaurants in 2013. Plans called for opening between 180 and 195 restaurants in 2014—new restaurants typically had opening-year sales of $1.6 to $1.7 million. About 75 percent of the restaurants opened in 2014 were expected to be in proven and established geographic markets, with the remainder in new or developing markets.

Approximately 30 percent of the 2012 openings were slightly scaled-back "A Model" restaurants located primarily in secondary trade areas with attractive demographics. A Model restaurants typically had lower investment and occupancy costs than did the restaurants that Chipotle had traditionally opened. To lower the average development costs for new restaurants, Chipotle had recently begun using a new, simpler design for its restaurants that incorporated some A Model design elements. Exhibit 3 shows the interiors and exteriors of several Chipotle Mexican Grills.

The company's average development and construction costs per restaurant decreased from about $850,000 in 2009 to around $800,000 in 2011, 2012, and 2013 (see Exhibit 1), chiefly because of cost savings realized from building more lower-cost A Model restaurants and the growing use of its new, simpler restaurant design. Chipotle anticipated that average development costs for new restaurants to be opened in 2014 would rise about 5 percent, due to opening more freestanding restaurants (which were more expensive than end-caps and in-line sites in strip centers) and opening proportionately more sites in the northeastern United States, where construction costs (and also sales volumes) were typically higher. Also, the company's normal capital reinvestment in existing restaurants was expected to rise from an average of $15,000 per restaurant to $20,000 per restaurant in 2014 because of performing a full remodel on many of the company's oldest restaurants. Chipotle also planned to invest about $10 million to perform a significant network redesign in all of its restaurants that would (1) enhance the way the company communicated with and trained restaurant employees and (2) provide better security, improved reliability, and greater capabilities, including accepting mobile payments at checkout.

Total capital expenditures in 2014 were expected to be about $225 million. Capital expenditures in prior years are shown in Exhibit 1. Chipotle's chief financial officer expected that the company's annual cash flows from operations, together with current cash on hand, would be adequate to meet ongoing capital expenditures, working-capital requirements, planned repurchases of common stock, and other cash needs for the foreseeable future.

# THE SHOPHOUSE SOUTHEAST ASIA KITCHEN TEST CONCEPT

The ShopHouse format grew out of Steve Ells's belief that the fundamental principles on which Chipotle Mexican Grill restaurants were based—finding the very best sustainably raised ingredients, preparing and cooking them using classical methods in front of the customer, and having the food served in an interactive format by special people dedicated to providing a great dining experience—could be adapted to other cuisines. To test the Chipotle model with different ingredients and a different style of food, the company opened its first ShopHouse Southeast Asian Kitchen on DuPont Circle in Washington, D.C., in September 2011. ShopHouse served a focused menu consisting of rice bowls, noodle bowls, and banh mi sandwiches, made with a choice of grilled steak, grilled chicken satay, pork and chicken meatballs, or organic tofu. In addition to a choice of meats or tofu, the rice and noodle bowls included choices of four fresh vegetables, a sauce (red or green curry or tamarind vinaigrette), and a garnish and topping (including chili-jam marmalade, roast corn with scallions, Chinese broccoli, pickled vegetables, and assorted aromatic herbs). Customers could have their meals flavored from mega-spicy to mild. The flavors were a blend of Thai, Vietnamese, and Malaysian flavors.

As was the case at Chipotle, customers moved along a cafeteria-style line, with servers behind the counter customizing each order; there was room for seating or customers could have orders readied for takeout. The interior of the Dulles Circle Shop-House had a resemblance to Chipotle interiors—sparse and a bit industrial, with an attention to such

**EXHIBIT 3**    Representative Interiors and Exteriors of Chipotle Mexican Grills

environmentally green detail as high-efficiency lighting. Much of the dining area was constructed with recycled materials, including dark maple treated to look like teak.

In 2012–2013, Chipotle continued to refine the ShopHouse menu and restaurant designs and gauge customer response at two locations in Washington, D.C., one location in Bethesda, Maryland, and three locations in the Los Angeles area (Hollywood, Santa Monica, and Westwood).

## COMPETITION

Chipotle competed with national and regional fast-casual, quick-service, and casual-dining restaurant chains, as well as locally owned restaurants and food-service establishments. The number, size, and strength of competitors varied by region, local market area, and a particular restaurant's location within a given community. Competition among the various types of restaurants and food-service establishments was based on such factors as type of food served, menu selection (including the availability of low-calorie and nutritional items), food quality and taste, speed of service, price and value, dining ambience, name recognition and reputation, convenience of location, and customer service.

There were a myriad of dining establishments that specialized in Mexican food. The leading fast-food chain in the Mexican-style food category was Taco Bell. Chipotle's two biggest competitors in the fast-casual segment were Moe's Southwest Grill and Qdoba Mexican Grill. Two smaller chains, Baja Fresh and California Tortilla, were also competitors in a small number of geographic locations.

### Taco Bell

Since 2005, Taco Bell locations had been struggling to attract customers. Throughout 2005–2011, the total number of Taco Bell restaurants, both domestically and internationally, declined as more underperforming locations were closed than new Taco Bell units were opened.

In 2010, Taco Bell had U.S. sales of $6.9 billion at combined company-owned and franchised Taco Bell locations, compared with $6.8 billion in 2009 and $6.7 billion in 2008. Average sales at Taco Bell restaurants were $1.28 million in 2011, versus averages of $1.29 million in 2010 and $1.26 million in 2009. Sales at company-owned Taco Bell restaurants in the United States that were open at least 12 or more months declined by 2 percent in 2011.[9] The sluggish sales performance at Taco Bell restaurants, most especially those in the United States, was viewed as mainly attributable to a loss of customers to Chipotle Mexican Grill, Moe's Southwest Grill, and Qdoba Mexican Grill, all of which had more upscale menu selections and used better-quality ingredients. Several fast-food hamburger chains, including McDonald's, had recently introduced upscaled hamburgers to better compete with the quality of the made-to-order burgers available at Five Guys and Smashburger locations, two up-and-coming fast-casual chains. A September 2011 survey by *Nation's Restaurant News* and consultant WD Partners found that Taco Bell scored the lowest in food quality and atmosphere among limited-service Mexican eateries, a group that included Chipotle Mexican Grill and Qdoba Mexican Grill.[10]

In late 2011, Taco Bell's parent company, Yum! Brands, began a multiyear campaign to reduce company ownership of Taco Bell locations from 23 percent of total locations to about 16 percent; a total of 1,276 company-owned Taco Bell locations were sold to franchisees in 2010–2012. Yum! Brands also owned Pizza Hut and KFC (Kentucky Fried Chicken); the company sold its A&W All American and Long John Silver's brands in December 2011.

To counter stagnant sales and begin a strategy to rejuvenate Taco Bell, during 2010–2011 Taco Bell restaurants began rolling out a new taco with a Doritos-based shell called Doritos Locos Taco, which management termed a "breakthrough product designed to reinvent the taco." The launch was supported with an aggressive advertising campaign to inform the public about the new Doritos Locos Taco. The effort was considered a solid success, driving record sales of 375 million tacos in one year. In March 2012, Taco Bell began introducing its new Cantina Bell menu, a group of upgraded products conceptualized by celebrity Miami chef Lorena Garcia that included such ingredients and garnishes as black beans, cilantro rice, and corn salsa.[11] The new Cantina Bell menu items had undergone extensive testing in select geographic areas. In addition to adding the upscaled Cantina Bell selections, Taco Bell also introduced several new breakfast selections. According to Taco Bell's president, Greg Creed, it was Taco Bell's biggest new product launch ever. The upscaled menu at Taco Bell was a competitive response to growing consumer preferences for the higher-caliber, made-to-order dishes they could get at fast-casual Mexican-food chains like Chipotle, Moe's, and Qdoba. Taco Bell's new Cantina Bell items were priced below similar types of Chipotle products—the average ticket price for the new Cantina Bell selections was about $4.50 (compared to averages of $7 to $9 for meals at Chipotle, Moe's, and Qdoba). The rollout of the Cantina Bell menu was supported with a new slogan and brand campaign. Within a few months, it was clear that the new tacos and Cantina Bell menu selections were boosting customer traffic and sales at Taco Bell locations. As of year-end 2012, Taco Bell was the leader in the U.S. Mexican quick-service restaurant segment, with a 49 percent market share, and the outlook for Taco Bell seemed much more promising.[12] Sales growth at Taco Bell restaurants in 2012 was an estimated 6.8 percent.[13]

In 2012–2013, expansion of Taco Bell locations resumed, with the vast majority of the new additions being franchised. In early 2013, Yum! Brands announced the long-term goal of growing the number of Taco Bell locations worldwide from 5,000 units to 8,000 units. Going into 2013, Taco Bell had 5,695 company-owned and franchised restaurant locations in the United States, plus another 285 international locations. About 20 percent of the locations in the United States were company-owned and just three of the foreign locations (all in India) were company-owned.

## Moe's Southwest Grill

Moe's Southwest Grill was founded in Atlanta, Georgia, in 2000 and acquired in 2007 by Atlanta-based Focus Brands, an affiliate of Roark Capital, a private equity firm. Focus Brands was a global franchisor and operator of over 4,300 ice cream shops, bakeries, restaurants, and cafes under the brand names Carvel, Cinnabon, Schlotzsky's, Moe's Southwest Grill, Auntie Anne's, and McAlister's Deli. In 2013, there were more than 500 fast-casual Moe's Southwest Grill locations in 37 states and the District of Columbia. Most Moe's locations were franchised.

Moe's had systemwide sales of $526 million in 2013, a 12 percent increase from 2012. Sales at Moe's locations that were open at least 12 months rose 4.5 percent in 2013, pushing average annual sales per restaurant to about $1,050,000. In 2013, Moe's opened 54 new restaurants and signed 155 new franchise deals in a move to accelerate new restaurant openings and achieve significantly greater geographic coverage. The company planned to open nearly 100 new restaurants in 2014.

The menu at Moe's featured burritos, quesadillas, tacos, nachos, burrito bowls (with selections of chicken, pork, or tofu), and salads with a choice of two homemade dressings. Main dishes could be customized with a choice of 20 items that included protein (sirloin steak, chicken breast, pulled pork,

ground beef, or organic tofu); grilled peppers, onions, and mushrooms; black olives; cucumbers; fresh chopped or pickled jalapenos; pico de gallo (handmade fresh daily); lettuce; and six salsas. Moe's also offered a kids' menu and vegetarian, gluten-free, and low-calorie options, as well as a selection of five side items (including queso and guacamole), two desserts (cookie or brownie), soft drinks, iced tea, and bottled water. All meals were served with chips and salsa. Moe's used high-quality ingredients, including all-natural, cage-free, white-breast-meat chicken; steroid-free, grain-fed pulled pork; 100% grass-fed sirloin steak; and organic tofu. No dishes included trans fats or monosodium glutamate (MSG)—a flavor enhancer—and no use was made of microwaves.

Moe's provided catering services; the catering menu included a fajitas bar, a taco bar, a salad bar, mini-burrito appetizers, a burrito box, a selection of dips, cookies, and drinks. At some locations, customer orders could be taken online.

The company and its franchisees emphasized friendly hospitable service. When customers entered a Moe's location, it was the practice for employees to do a "Welcome to Moe's!" shout-out.

## Qdoba Mexican Grill

The first Qdoba Mexican Grill opened in Denver in 1995. Rapid growth ensued and the company was acquired by Jack in the Box, Inc., a large operator and franchisor of Jack in the Box quick-service restaurants best known for its hamburgers. Jack in the Box had fiscal year 2013 revenues of $1.5 billion (the company's fiscal year was October 1 through September 30), and its Jack in the Box system included 2,251 company-owned and franchised locations in 21 states. Corporate management at Jack in the Box was executing a long-term campaign to sell company-owned Jack in the Box restaurants to franchisees and to boost the number and percentage of company-owned Qdoba restaurants by acquiring locations from franchisees.

In October 2013, there were 615 Qdoba restaurants in 46 states, the District of Columbia, and Canada, of which 296 were company-operated and 319 were franchise-operated; 62 underperforming company-owned Qdoba restaurants were closed during fiscal year 2013. However, management believed Qdoba had significant long-term growth potential—perhaps as many as 2,000 locations. A total of 34 new company-owned and 34 franchised Qdoba restaurants opened in fiscal 2013. A net of 44 new Qdoba locations had opened in fiscal year 2012, versus 58 units in fiscal 2011, 15 units in fiscal 2010, and 56 in fiscal 2009. Plans for fiscal 2014 were to open 60 to 70 new company-owned and franchised restaurants.

Qdoba was the second-largest fast-casual Mexican brand in the United States as of early 2014, based on number of restaurants. In 2013, sales revenues at all company-operated and franchise-operated Qdoba restaurant locations averaged $1,017,000, compared to $969,000 in fiscal 2012 and $961,000 in fiscal 2011. Sales at Qdoba restaurants that were open more than 12 months rose 0.8 percent in fiscal 2013, 2.4 percent in fiscal 2012, 5.3 percent in fiscal 2011, and 2.8 percent in fiscal 2010.

## Menu Offerings and Food Preparation

Qdoba Mexican Grill billed itself as an "artisanal Mexican kitchen" where dishes were handcrafted with fresh ingredients and innovative flavors by skilled cooks. The menu included burritos, tacos, taco salads, three-cheese nachos, grilled quesadillas, tortilla soup, Mexican gumbo, chips and dips, five meals for kids, and, at select locations, a variety of breakfast burritos and breakfast quesadillas. Burritos and tacos could be customized with choices of five meats or just vegetarian ingredients. Salads were served in a crunchy flour tortilla bowl with a choice of two meats, or vegetarian, and included black bean corn salsa and fat-free picante ranch dressing.

Throughout each day at Qdoba restaurants, guacamole was prepared onsite using fresh avocados, black and pinto beans were slow-simmered, shredded beef and pork were slow-roasted, and adobo-marinated chicken and steak were flame-grilled. Orders were prepared in full view, with customers having multiple options to customize meals to their individual taste and nutritional preferences. Qdoba restaurants offered a variety of catering options that could be tailored to feed groups of five to several hundred. Most Qdoba restaurants operated from 10:30 a.m. to 10 p.m. and had seating capacity for 60 to 80 persons, including outdoor patio seating at many locations. The average check at company-operated restaurants in fiscal 2012 was $10.43.

## Site Selection and New Restaurant Development

Site selections for all new company-operated Qdoba restaurants were made after an economic analysis and a review of demographic data and other information relating to population density, traffic, competition, restaurant visibility and access, available parking, surrounding businesses, and opportunities for market penetration. Restaurants developed by franchisees were built to the parent company's specifications on sites it had reviewed. Most Qdoba restaurants were located in leased spaces in conventional large-scale retail projects and food courts in malls, in smaller neighborhood retail strip centers, on or near college campuses, and in airports. Development costs for new Qdoba restaurants typically ranged from $0.6 million to $1 million, depending on the geographic region and specific location.

## Restaurant Management and Operations

At Qdoba's company-owned restaurants, emphasis was placed on attracting, selecting, engaging, and retaining people who were committed to creating long-lasting, positive impacts on operating results. The company's core development tool was a "Career Map" that provided employees with detailed education requirements, skill sets, and performance expectations by position, from entry level to area manager. High-performing general managers and hourly team members were certified to train and develop employees through a series of on-the-job and classroom training programs that focused on knowledge, skills, and behaviors. The Team Member Progression program within the Career Map tool recognized and rewarded three levels of achievement for cooks and line servers who displayed excellence in their positions. Team members had to possess, or acquire, specific technical and behavioral skill sets to reach an achievement level. All restaurant personnel were expected to contribute to delivering a great guest experience in the company's restaurants.

There was a four-tier management structure for company-owned Qdoba restaurants. Division vice presidents supervised regional operations managers, who supervised district managers, who in turn supervised restaurant managers. All four levels were eligible for periodic performance bonuses based on goals related to restaurant sales, profit optimization, guest satisfaction, and other operating performance standards

## Purchasing and Distribution

Beginning in March 2012, Qdoba and 90 percent of its franchisees entered into a five-year contract with an independent distributor to provide purchasing and distribution services for food ingredients and other supplies to Qdoba restaurants.

**Advertising and Promotion**  The goals of Qdoba's advertising and marketing activities were to build brand awareness and generate customer traffic. Both company-owned and franchised restaurants contributed to a fund primarily used for producing media ads and running regional or local advertising campaigns—so far, Qdoba had not undertaken any national advertising or promotions, although it did have a national presence on several social media networks. The majority of Qdoba's marketing was done at the local level and entailed engaging and partnering with local schools, sports teams, community organizations, and businesses. There was growing use of digital marketing.

## RESTAURANT INDUSTRY STATISTICS

Restaurant industry sales were forecast to be a record-high $683 billion in 2014 at some 990,000 food establishments in the United States; the forecast represented a compound average growth rate of 3.9 percent since 2010.[14] According to survey data reported in the National Restaurant Association's *2014 Restaurant Industry Forecast*, 64 percent of consumers said they were more likely to visit a restaurant that offered locally produced food items; 72 percent said they were more likely to visit a restaurant that offered healthier options; and 54 percent said they were more likely to visit restaurants pursuing environmental sustainability initiatives.

The fast-casual segment represented less than 2 percent of food establishments in the United States and accounted for about 5 percent of total industry sales. Fast-casual chains—which included Chipotle Mexican Grill, Moe's Southwest Grill,

and Qdoba—were perceived to have enhanced service and higher-quality food than traditional quick-service restaurants like McDonald's and Taco Bell. Fast-casual restaurants were the fastest-growing restaurant category, having boosted their share of all quick-service restaurant sales from 5 to 15 percent over the past 10 years.[15] According to NDP Group, the unit counts of restaurant locations classified as fast-casual had risen over the past five years:[16]

|      | Unit Count | Increase over Prior Year |
|------|------------|--------------------------|
| 2007 | 11,013     | 11%                      |
| 2008 | 12,108     | 10                       |
| 2009 | 12,801     | 6                        |
| 2010 | 13,161     | 4                        |
| 2011 | 13,643     | 7                        |
| 2012 | 15,312     | 12                       |
| 2013 | 16,215     | 6                        |

Overall, restaurant customers had been trading down during the past five years, foregoing some of their visits to full-service places while increasing the number of visits made to fast-casual restaurants. Traffic at fast-casual restaurants was up 6 percent in 2010, 6 percent in 2011, 8 percent in 2012, and 9 percent in 2013; over the same period, traffic at quick-service restaurants was flat.[17] According to a 2013 Technomic study, 85 percent of consumers surveyed said they ate at fast-casual restaurants at least once a month.[18] Guest check sizes at fast-casual restaurants on average were $7.40 in 2013, higher than the average quick-service restaurant visit check of $5.30, but still much lower than the average full-service restaurant visit check of $13.66.[19]

## ENDNOTES

[1] "Chipotle Mexican Grill's CEO Discusses 2013 Results—Earnings Call Transcript," www.seekingalpha.com, January 30, 2014 (accessed February 8, 2014).
[2] See Alice Kelso, "Is 'Better Pizza' the Next Fast Casual Category?" www.fastcasual.com, February 19, 2013 (accessed February 12, 2014).
[3] David A. Kaplan, "Chipotle's Growth Machine," *Fortune,* September 26, 2011, p.138.

[4] Ibid.; Aimee Picchi, "Chipotle Hints at a Price Increase," *MSN Money,* January 18, 2013, www.money.msn.com (accessed May 13, 2013); "Chipotle Prices May Rise on Higher Food Costs," *Huffington Post,* January 17, 2013, www.huffingtonpost.com (accessed May 13, 2013).
[5] According to information posted in the Careers section at www.chipotle.com (accessed February 18, 2012, and May 13, 2013).

[6] Ibid.
[7] "Chipotle Mexican Grill's CEO Discusses 2013 Results."
[8] Ibid.
[9] Company press release, February 6, 2012.
[10] Ibid.
[11] Leslie Patton, "Taco Bell Sees Market Share Recouped with Chipotle Menu," *Bloomberg News,* January 11, 2012, www.bloomberg.com (accessed February 20, 2012).

[12] According to The NPD Group, Inc./Crest, year ending December 2012, based on consumer spending; this market share statistic was cited in Yum! Brands 2012 10-K report, p. 4.

[13] According to information in "Fast Casuals Leading Restaurant Growth," www.fastcasual.com, March 21, 2013 (accessed May 14, 2013).

[14] National Restaurant Association, *2014 Restaurant Industry Forecast* and "Fact at a Glance," www.restaurant.org (accessed February 12, 2014).

[15] "Top 100 Movers and Shakers: Fast Casual Trends," www.fastcasual.com, January 24, 2013 (accessed May 14, 2013).

[16] NPD Group, "Fast Casual Is Only Restaurant Segment to Grow Traffic in 2013,"

www.fastcasual.com, February 5, 2014 (accessed February 11, 2014).

[17] Ibid.

[18] Joe Satran, " 'Fast-Casual' Restaurants Are Visited by 85% of Americans at Least Once a Month," *Huffington Post,* February 13, 2013, www.huffingtonpost.com (accessed May 14, 2013).

[19] Ibid.

# Sirius XM Satellite Radio Inc. in 2014: On Track to Succeed after a Near-Death Experience?

McGraw Hill Education **connect**

## Arthur A. Thompson

The University of Alabama

In February 2009, the outlook for Sirius XM Satellite Radio was grim. Despite having 2008 revenues of nearly $1.7 billion and some 19 million subscribers, the company's stock price had dropped to a low of $0.05 per share, and the company was mired in a deep financial crisis, with debts totaling more than $3 billion. Years of big spending and annual losses in the hundreds of billions had depleted the company's ability to secure additional credit to pay its bills, and the company lacked the cash to make a scheduled debt payment of $171.6 million due on February 17. But hours before filing for Chapter 11 bankruptcy (in order to avoid defaulting on the scheduled debt payment), Sirius XM got a lifeline from Liberty Media, a $2 billion company with business interests in the media, communications, and entertainment industries; Liberty was headed by cable TV pioneer and financial tycoon John Malone, who not only owned a controlling interest in Liberty Media but also was known for making big investments in troubled or undervalued companies having what he believed were good prospects for long-term profitability. Liberty agreed to provide an aggregate of $530 million in loans to Sirius in return for (1) 12.5 million shares of Sirius XM preferred stock convertible into 40 percent of common stock of Sirius XM and (2) seats on the Sirius XM board of directors proportional to its equity ownership. Two of these seats were to be occupied by John Malone, Liberty's chairman, and Greg Maffei, Liberty's CEO. Many outsiders viewed the terms to be a sweetheart deal for Liberty Media.

Headed into 2014, Sirius XM had 25.6 million subscribers, 2013 revenues of $3.8 billion, operating income of $1 billion, net income of $377 million, and cash flows from operations of $1.1 billion. The company's stock price had rebounded nicely and traded mostly in the $3.50 to $4 range during the last three months of 2013, equal to a market capitalization of $21 billion to $24 billion.

## COMPANY BACKGROUND

Sirius XM Satellite Radio was the product of a 2008 merger of Sirius Satellite Radio and XM Satellite Radio. The two predecessor companies had begun operations in 2001–2002, spending hundreds of millions to launch satellites for broadcasting signals, arrange for the manufacture of satellite radio receivers and other equipment, install terrestrial signal repeaters and other necessary networking equipment, develop programming, conduct market research, and attract subscribers. The primary target market for satellite radio service included the owners of the more than 230 million registered vehicles in North America and, secondarily, the over 120 million households in the United States and Canada.

Market research done in 2000–2001 indicated that as many as 49 million people might subscribe to satellite radio service by 2012, assuming a monthly fee of $9.95 and radio receiver prices of $150 to $399, depending on the car or home model chosen. A 2002 market research study conducted for XM concluded there would be a total of about 15 million satellite radio subscribers by the end of 2006. Considering that in spring 2005 both XM and Sirius raised their subscription rates to $12.95 monthly, the forecast turned out to be fairly close to the actual 13.6 million satellite radio subscribers in the United States reported at year-end 2006.

Both Sirius and XM employed a subscription-based business model to generate revenues. Subscribers received discounts if they had multiple XM or Sirius satellite radios (for different vehicles or for home and office use) or if they signed up for prepaid plans of two to three years. Both companies did not expect to cover the high startup costs and become profitable until acquiring at least 8 million to 10 million subscribers.

## Competition between XM and Sirius Quickly Becomes Spirited and Expensive

Early on, the two companies became embroiled in a fierce market battle waged on multiple fronts:

- Creating a programming lineup that was more attractive than its rival's programming lineup.
- Convincing automakers to factory-install its brand of satellite radio (the radios of the two rivals were incompatible—XM radios could not receive signals broadcast by Sirius, and vice versa).
- Gaining broad retail distribution of its various satellite radio models and equipment for use at home or in used vehicles.
- Building brand awareness and stimulating consumer demand for satellite radio service.

**The Race to Differentiate Programming Content**  While each company's programming strategy was to offer a diverse, appealing selection of digital-quality radio programs that would attract listeners willing to subscribe to mostly commercial-free programming, each company recognized that the key to gaining a competitive edge was having differentiated programming content capable of attracting and retaining the greatest number of subscribers. Each company quickly moved to create one or more channels for almost every music genre and a big assortment of channels devoted to news and commentary, sports, comedy and entertainment, family and health, religion, politics, traffic, and weather. By

2007, XM had a programming lineup of over 170 channels that included 69 commercial-free music channels; 5 commercial music channels; 37 news, talk, and commentary channels; 38 sports channels; and 21 instant traffic and weather channels. Sirius was broadcasting on 133 channels that included 69 channels of 100 percent commercial-free music and 64 channels providing sports programming, news, talk, information, entertainment, traffic, and weather. To achieve differentiation, both companies spent large, sometimes lavish, sums for contracts to:

- Obtain broadcast rights for the audio portions of programs on National Public Radio and such cable TV channels as Fox News, CNN, CNBC, MSNBC, ESPN News, and ESPN Radio.
- Gain *exclusive* rights to air live play-by-play broadcasts of various sporting events (Major League Baseball games, National Football League games, National Basketball Association games, National Hockey League games, college football and basketball games for all major conferences, professional golf and tennis tournaments, NASCAR races, horse races, FIFA World Cup soccer games, etc.). As an example of the large amounts spent to acquire exclusive rights for high-profile programming, XM paid $60 million annually for a six-year agreement to broadcast Major League Baseball games live nationwide for the years 2007 through 2012.
- Secure the services of well-known personalities and brands (like Howard Stern, Oprah Winfrey, and Martha Stewart Living) and create special channels featuring their shows and content. In 2004, Sirius signed a five-year contractual agreement with Howard Stern said to be worth $400 million to $500 million in salaries for Stern and his staff plus stock bonuses for Stern and his agent that were based on exceeding specified subscriber targets; Howard Stern broadcasts began on two Sirius channels in January 2006.

At XM, expenditures for programming and content were $101 million in 2005, $165.2 million in 2006, and $183.9 million in 2007. Sirius Satellite Radio's expenditures for programming were $100.8 million in 2005, $520.4 million in 2006, and $236.1 million in 2007. Apart from battling to achieve differentiated programming content, the two competitors also strived to attain overall product differentiation by offering greater geographic coverage, more commercial-free programming choices, and digital sound quality.

**Partnering with Automakers and Gaining Broad Distribution in the Retail Marketplace** Simultaneously, both XM and Sirius aggressively launched well-funded strategic initiatives to gain broad distribution of their satellite radios via partnerships with motor vehicle manufacturers, making satellite radios available at national and regional consumer electronics retailers and mass merchandisers (Best Buy, Walmart, and Target), and selling radios at their websites—all were sources of new subscribers. The battle was particularly fierce in the automobile segment for three reasons:

1. A big majority of the new subscribers for satellite radio service were the owners of newly purchased vehicles equipped with a satellite radio.
2. A majority of the satellite radios for new vehicles were factory-installed, although automobile dealers could install satellite radios in some models.
3. The incompatibility of XM and Sirius radios forced vehicle manufacturers to choose which brand to install in factory-assembled vehicles.

Each of the competitors lobbied hard for vehicle manufacturers to sign contractual agreements to exclusively install only its brand of satellite radio in vehicles scheduled to be equipped with a satellite radio. Both XM and Sirius used liberal subsidies and commissions to induce manufacturers to sign exclusivity agreements: Each rival paid automakers a subsidy if its brand of satellite radio and a prepaid trial subscription (usually for three months but sometimes for six months) was included in the sale or lease price of a new vehicle. As a further incentive, each paid automakers either a commission or a share of the subscription revenues to purchase, install, and activate its brand of satellite radio. There were also revenue-sharing payments on subsequent subscriptions by new vehicle owners after the trial period expired. For instance, XM had a long-term distribution agreement with General Motors whereby GM agreed to exclusively install only XM's brand of satellite radios in return for GM being paid a portion of the revenues derived from all subscribers using GM vehicles equipped to receive XM's service—this was in addition to the incentives XM paid to GM to subsidize a portion of the costs of installing XM radios in GM vehicles. Indeed, it was common practice for XM and Sirius to reimburse automakers for certain hardware-related costs, tooling expenses, and promotional and advertising expenses directly related to including a satellite radio as a vehicle option.

For the 2007 model year, Sirius radios were available as a factory-installed option in 89 vehicle models and as a dealer-installed option in 19 vehicle models; Sirius service was also offered to renters of Hertz vehicles at 55 airport locations nationwide. For the same model year, XM's satellite radios were available as original equipment in over 140 vehicle models.

In addition to offering subsidies and incentives to automakers, XM and Sirius also offered subsidies and incentives to (1) the manufacturers of their satellite radios, (2) the makers of chip sets and other components used in manufacturing satellite radios, (3) the various distributors and retailers of satellite radio devices and equipment, and (4) automotive dealers that installed satellite radios on vehicles not having a factory-installed satellite radio. Moreover, there were device royalties for certain types of satellite radios, subsidies for handling product warranty obligations, price protection for distributor inventories, and provisions for inventory allowances.

All of these expenses (except for revenue-sharing payments) were incurred in advance of acquiring a subscriber and were classified as subscriber acquisition costs. For XM, subscriber acquisition costs were $245.6 million in 2005, $224.9 million in 2006, and $259.1 million in 2007; Sirius incurred subscriber acquisition costs of $399.4 million in 2005, $451.6 million in 2006, and $407.6 million in 2007.

In 2006, the Federal Communications Commission, which had jurisdiction for satellite radio communications and had regulatory authority for issuing operating licenses for satellite radio enterprises, responded to growing numbers of consumer complaints about being locked into subscribing to the service of one company or the other, depending on the brand of satellite radio they had purchased. The FCC brought pressure on XM and Sirius to resolve the signal reception incompatibility and issued rules requiring the interoperability of both licensed satellite radio systems. Late in 2006, XM and Sirius signed an agreement to develop a unified standard for satellite radios to enable consumers to purchase one radio capable of receiving either company's broadcast signal and thus subscribe to whichever company's service they wished. The agreement called for the technology relating to this unified standard to be developed, jointly funded, and jointly owned by the two companies. Satellite radio manufacturers began including both XM and Sirius chip sets in their satellite radios to enable dual-signal reception in 2008; within months, all satellite radios were being manufactured with dual-reception capability.

**Building Brand Awareness and Stimulating Demand for Satellite Radio Service**  Both XM and Sirius pursued aggressive marketing strategies, spending heavily on a variety of sizable sales, marketing, and promotional activities calculated to build brand awareness, communicate the appealing features of satellite radio service compared to traditional radio, and attract, first, hundreds of thousands and, then, millions of new subscribers annually. Advertising and promotional activities were conducted via television, radio, print, and the Internet; brochures illustrating the array of available channels and programs, along with other satellite radio features, were distributed at retail outlets, concert venues, and motor sports events and on the Internet to generate consumer interest; some major retailers participated in jointly funded local advertising campaigns. In-store promotions typically included displays at electronics and music stores, car audio retailers and other retailers that stocked and promoted sales of satellite radios, automobile dealerships, and rental car agencies with vehicles equipped with a satellite radio.

At XM, expenses for marketing and advertising were $182.4 million in 2005, $164.4 million in 2006, and $178.7 million in 2007. Sirius had sales and marketing expenses of $197.7 million in 2005, $203.7 million in 2006, and $173.6 million in 2007.

## The Competitive Battle between XM and Sirius Inflicted Major Financial Damage

The heavy expenses incurred by the efforts of the two rivals as each tried to gain an edge over the other produced gigantic losses every year of their existence, despite having attracted millions of subscribers. Comparative performance statistics for 2005–2007 are shown in Exhibit 1.

With both companies burdened by sizable negative cash flows from operations, balance sheets that were becoming precariously weaker as long-term borrowings and stockholders' deficits mounted, waning ability to raise additional equity capital from increasingly anxious investors, and growing concerns about the viability of their business models, there was much speculation in 2006–2007 about whether either XM or Sirius could obtain the financing needed to survive for much longer. Executives at both companies concluded that after six years of battling for subscribers and bidding up programming costs, the only long-term solution was to merge and bring a halt to the destructive competitive battle that was unlikely to end short of bankruptcy. The executives and boards of directors of the two companies hammered out a planned merger agreement that was announced on February 19, 2007.

But there were significant hurdles to overcome because the merger, if approved by the FCC and the Antitrust Division of the U.S. Department of Justice, would create a satellite radio monopoly, although the merged company would still face competition for listeners from multiple sources, including terrestrial AM/FM radio, both free and paid Internet streaming services (from Clear Channel, CBS Radio, Pandora, and others), the music channels offered by cable TV providers, digital music devices such as iPods and MP3 players, and the music and other programming that could be stored on or streamed to smartphones. Traditional AM/FM radio enterprises offered free broadcast reception paid for by commercial advertising rather than by a subscription fee. Sirius and XM argued that the free broadcast programs of AM/FM enterprises (as well as all the other free and paid music programming that was widely available) not only reduced the likelihood that customers would be willing to pay for satellite radio subscription service but also imposed limits on what a merged XM-Sirius could charge for its service. Thus, it was alleged by XM and Sirius that competitive forces would be adequate to protect consumers from any "monopoly pricing" or other monopolistically abusive practices stemming from an XM-Sirius merger. However, many AM/FM enterprises, along with consumer interest groups and other interested parties, expressed opposition to the merger, largely on grounds that it would be anticompetitive and injurious to satellite radio subscribers.

After 17 months of regulatory scrutiny and despite the objections of various concerned parties, the proposed merger won approval from the FCC and the Antitrust Division of the U.S. Department of

**EXHIBIT 1**   Comparative Performance, XM Satellite Radio and Sirius Satellite Radio, 2005–2007 (dollar amounts in thousands, except per-subscriber data)

| | 2005 | 2006 | 2007 |
|---|---|---|---|
| **XM Radio** | | | |
| Number of subscribers, year-end | 5,933,000 | 7,629,000 | 9,027,000 |
| Gross subscriber additions | 4,130,000 | 3,866,000 | 3,891,000 |
| Deactivated subscribers | 1,427,000 | 2,170,000 | 2,493,000 |
| Net subscriber additions | 2,703,000 | 1,696,000 | 1,398,000 |
| Subscriber revenues | $   502,612 | $   825,626 | $ 1,005,479 |
| Total revenues | 558,266 | 933,417 | 1,136,542 |
| Operating expenses | 1,113,801 | 1,336,515 | 1,647,979 |
| Loss from operations | (555,535) | (403,098) | (511,437) |
| Net loss | (666,715) | (718,872) | (682,381) |
| Long-term debt | 1,035,584 | 1,286,179 | 1,480,639 |
| Total stockholders' (deficit) equity | 80,948 | (397,880 | (984,303) |
| Cash flows from operations | $(166,717) | $(462,091) | $(154,730) |
| Average monthly revenue per subscriber | $10.57 | $11.41 | $11.48 |
| Subscriber acquisition costs per gross subscriber addition* | $109 | $108 | $121 |
| **Sirius Satellite Radio** | | | |
| Number of subscribers, year-end | 3,316,560 | 6,024,555 | 8,321,785 |
| Gross subscriber additions | 2,519,301 | 3,758,163 | 4,183,901 |
| Deactivated subscribers | 345,999 | 1,050,168 | 1,886,671 |
| Net subscriber additions | 2,173,302 | 2,707,995 | 2,297,230 |
| Subscriber revenues | $   223,615 | $   575,404 | $   854,933 |
| Total revenues | 242,245 | 637,235 | 922,066 |
| Operating expenses | 1,071,385 | 1,704,959 | 1,435,156 |
| Loss from operations | (829,140) | (1,067,724) | (513,090) |
| Net loss | (862,997) | (1,104,867) | (562,252) |
| Long-term debt | 1,084,437 | 1,068,249 | 1,278,617 |
| Total stockholders' (deficit) equity | 324,968 | (389,071) | (792,737) |
| Cash flows from operations | $(269,994) | $(421,702) | $(148,766) |
| Average monthly revenue per subscriber | $10.34 | $11.01 | $10.46 |
| Subscriber acquisition costs per gross subscriber addition* | $139 | $114 | $101 |

*Subscriber acquisition costs include hardware subsidies paid to radio manufacturers, distributors, and automakers, including subsidies paid to automakers that included a satellite radio and subscription to Sirius or XM service in the sale or lease price of a new vehicle; subsidies paid for chip sets and certain other components used in manufacturing satellite radios; device royalties for certain radios and chip sets; commissions paid to automakers as incentives to purchase, install, and activate satellite radios; payments for handling product warranty obligations; freight; and provisions for inventory allowances associated with factory-installations of satellite radios by automakers and the orders and sales of satellite radio equipment by distributors and retailers.

*Source:* Company 10-K report for 2007.

Justice in July 2008 after XM and Sirius voluntarily agreed to:

1. Pay a $20 million fine for failure to previously comply with certain FCC regulations.

2. Sign a consent decree to cease such practices and bring their operating activities into full compliance with FCC regulations.

3. Not raise the retail price for, or reduce the number of channels in, the basic $12.95-per-month subscription package, or any new programming packages, before July 28, 2011.

4. Offer a variety of subscription plans (as opposed to a single all-channel option priced at $12.95 per month) that allowed subscribers to choose any of

several combinations of channels, including an à la carte subscription option.

The two companies quickly began preparations to finalize the merger. On August 5, 2008, Sirius Satellite Radio Inc. changed its name to Sirius XM Radio Inc. In April 2010, XM Satellite Radio Holdings Inc. merged with and into XM Satellite Radio Inc.; and in January 2011, XM Satellite Radio Inc., a wholly owned subsidiary of Sirius XM Radio, was merged into Sirius XM Radio Inc.

## SIRIUS XM'S STRATEGY

In the period since the merger, Sirius XM's strategy had been aimed at:

- Recruiting new subscribers and rapidly growing the size of the company's customer base.
- Eliminating largely duplicative programming and thereby significantly reducing the combined programming costs of the two former companies.
- Cutting the "bloated" operating costs stemming from the mutually destructive and unprofitable "arms race" between XM and Sirius to outcompete one another.
- Streamlining operations in ways that would enable the merged company to become profitable within a few years.
- Reducing long-term debt, taking advantage of low interest rates to refinance existing debt, increasing the company's operating margins, boosting cash flows from operations, and getting the company on a strong financial footing.

Top executives believed it was essential to generate near-term results that would convince investors and creditors that the merged company's subscription-based business model was capable of producing attractive long-term profitability. This required progressively reducing the company's net losses per year and turning the corner to positive net profits in the 2011–2012 time frame.

Financial performance data for 2010–2013 is shown in Exhibit 2. Income from operations had climbed from $465.4 million in 2010 to $1.04 billion in 2013. From August 2012 to the end of 2013, Sirius refinanced $2.5 billion of debt, pushed the average maturities out from 4.7 years to 6.7 years, and reduced its weighted-average interest rates from 9.2 to 5.1 percent.

Assorted subscriber metrics are shown in Exhibit 3. Sirius XM Radio had a 38 percent equity interest in Sirius XM Canada, which offered satellite radio services in Canada and had 2 million subscribers in early 2014. However, subscribers to the Sirius XM Canada service were not included in Sirius XM's subscriber count.

## Programming Strategy

Since the 2008 merger, the programming strategy had centered on three key elements:

1. *Bargaining hard for lower prices on programming content so as to reduce the company's overall programming costs.* Sirius XM executives were acutely aware that the fierce rivalry between XM and Sirius during 2002–2007 had led to significant "overbidding" for content. The overbidding resulted from trying to match or beat the content recently acquired by one's rival and/or sometimes agreeing to pay a big price premium to keep the other firm from winning exclusive rights to high-profile content with considerable listener appeal (like Howard Stern or play-by-play sporting events). Hence, as the contracts expired for programming content negotiated prior to the merger, the central objective during contract renegotiation was to reduce the premium prices the company was paying for high-profile broadcast rights, most particularly for sporting events and talk-show personalities (like Howard Stern).

2. *Curbing the costs of duplicate programming,* particularly in the case of music channels where both XM and Sirius were incurring the costs of programming "look-alike" channels, each operated as an individual station, in every music genre. For example, XM had four country-music channels, each with its own format, style, mix of recordings, and branding, that were programmed and hosted by a team of country-music experts, while Sirius also had four country-music channels, each with its own slightly different format, style, recordings mix, and branding, that were programmed and hosted by a different set of country-music experts. The same sort of duplication and overlap existed for the rock, pop, hip-hop, gospel, dance, jazz, Latin, and classical channels the two companies were broadcasting. Sirius XM executives promptly began a multiyear initiative

**EXHIBIT 2**    Select Financial Statement Data for Sirius XM Satellite Radio, 2010–2013 (in thousands, except per share data)

| | 2010 | 2011 | 2012 | 2013 |
|---|---|---|---|---|
| **Income statement data** | | | | |
| Revenue: | | | | |
| Subscriber revenue[1] | $2,414,174 | $ 2,55,414 | $2,962,665 | $3,824,660 |
| Advertising revenue,[2] net of agency fees | 64,517 | 73,672 | 82,320 | 89,288 |
| Equipment revenue[3] | 71,355 | 71,051 | 73,456 | 80,573 |
| Other revenue[4] | 266,946 | 274,387 | 283,599 | 344,574 |
| Total revenue | 2,816,992 | 3,014,524 | 3,402,040 | 3,799,095 |
| Operating expenses: | | | | |
| Royalty and revenue-sharing payments | 435,410 | 471,149 | 551,012 | 677,642 |
| Programming and content | 305,914 | 281,234 | 278,997 | 290,323 |
| Customer service and billing | 241,680 | 259,719 | 294,980 | 320,755 |
| Satellite and transmission | 80,947 | 75,902 | 72,615 | 79,292 |
| Cost of equipment | 35,281 | 33,095 | 31,766 | 26,478 |
| Subscriber acquisition costs | 413,041 | 434,482 | 474,697 | 495,610 |
| Sales and marketing | 215,454 | 222,773 | 248,905 | 291,024 |
| Engineering, design and development | 45,390 | 53,435 | 48,843 | 57,969 |
| General and administrative | 240,970 | 238,738 | 261,905 | 262,135 |
| Depreciation and amortization | 273,691 | 267,880 | 266,295 | 253,314 |
| Restructuring, impairments, and related costs | 63,800 | — | — | — |
| Total operating expenses | 2,351,578 | 2,338,407 | 2,530,015 | 2,754,542 |
| Income from operations | 465,414 | 676,117 | 872,025 | 1,044,553 |
| Other income (expense): | | | | |
| Interest expense, net of amounts capitalized | (295,643) | (304,938) | (265,321) | (204,671) |
| Loss on extinguishment of debt and credit facilities, net | (120,120) | (7,206) | (132,726) | (190,577) |
| Interest and investment income (loss) | (5,375) | 73,970 | 716 | 6,976 |
| Loss on change in value of derivatives | — | — | — | (20,393) |
| Other (loss) income | 3,399 | 3,252 | (226) | 1,204 |
| Total other expense | (417,739) | (234,922) | (397,557) | (407,461) |
| Income before income taxes | 47,675 | 441,195 | 474,468 | 636,092 |
| Income tax benefit (expense) | (4,620) | (14,234) | 2,998,234 | (259,877) |
| Net income | $    43,055 | $   426,961 | $3,472,702 | $    377,215 |
| Net income per common share: | | | | |
| Basic | $0.01 | $0.07 | $0.55 | $0.06 |
| Diluted | $0.01 | $0.07 | $0.51 | $0.06 |
| Dividends paid on common stock | — | — | $0.05 | — |
| Weighted-average common shares outstanding: | | | | |
| Basic | 3,693,259 | 3,744,606 | 4,209,073 | 6,277,646 |
| Diluted | 6,391,071 | 6,500,822 | 6,873,786 | 6,384,791 |
| **Balance sheet data** | | | | |
| Cash and cash equivalents: | $ 586,691 | $ 773,990 | $ 520,945 | $ 134,805 |
| Total current assets | 991,775 | 1,276,954 | 1,828,182 | 1,419,013 |
| Total assets | 7,383,086 | 7,495,996 | 9,054,843 | 8,844,760 |
| Total current liabilities | 2,349,709 | 2,247,596 | 2,314,588 | 2,948,904 |
| Long-term debt, including related-party debt | 3,021,763 | 3,012,351 | 2,430,986 | 3,093,821 |
| Total stockholders' equity | $    207,636 | $ 704,145 | $ 4,039,565 | $ 2,745,742 |

| | 2010 | 2011 | 2012 | 2013 |
|---|---|---|---|---|
| **Cash flow data** | | | | |
| Net cash provided by operating activities | $   512,895 | $   543,630 | $   806,765 | $ 1,102,832 |
| Repayment of long-term borrowings | 1,262,396 | 234,976 | 1,041,824 | 1,982,160 |
| Proceeds from long-term borrowings and revolving credit facility, net of costs | 1,274,707 | — | 383,641 | 3,156,063 |

[1] Includes revenues from all the various subscription plans, activation fees (including those for radios activated on vehicles rented at participating car rental agencies), and other fees.
[2] Includes the sale of advertising on certain nonmusic channels, net of agency fees. Agency fees are based on a contractual percentage of the gross advertising revenue.
[3] Includes revenue and royalties associated with the sale of satellite radios, components, and accessories.
[4] Includes amounts charged to subscribers for the U.S. music royalty fee (this fee was a surcharge on all subscription plans involving music channels), royalties earned from the operations of the company's Canadian affiliate, and ancillary fees earned on weather, traffic, data and Backseat TV services.

*Source:* Company 10-K reports, 2011, 2012, and 2013.

to consolidate the roughly 70 music channels broadcast by XM and the 70 or so music channels broadcast by Sirius into a new set of about 70 music channels that were jointly broadcast to XM subscribers and to Sirius subscribers.

3. *Refreshing and expanding the company's programming lineup.* Sirius executives viewed programming as the foundation of the company's business. To complement and strengthen Sirius XM's broad channel lineup and offering of exclusive programs,

## EXHIBIT 3    Select Subscriber Statistics, Sirius XM Satellite Radio, 2010–2013

| | 2010 | 2011 | 2012 | 2013 |
|---|---|---|---|---|
| **Subscriber data** | | | | |
| Beginning subscribers | 18,772,758 | 20,190,964 | 21,892,824 | 23,900,336 |
| Gross subscriber additions | 7,768,827 | 8,696,020 | 9,617,771 | 10,136,391 |
| Deactivated subscribers | (6,350,621) | (6,994,160) | (7,610,259) | (8,477,407) |
| Net additions | 1,418,206 | 1,701,860 | 2,007,512 | 1,658,974 |
|     Self-pay | 982,867 | 1,221,943 | 1,661,532 | 1,511,543 |
|     Paid promotional (trial) | 435,339 | 479,917 | 345,980 | 147,431 |
| Ending subscribers | 20,190,964 | 21,892,824 | 23,900,336 | 25,559,310 |
|     Self-pay | 16,686,799 | 17,908,742 | 19,570,274 | 21,081,817 |
|     Paid promotional (trial) | 3,504,165 | 3,984,082 | 4,330,062 | 4,477,493 |
| **Subscriber metrics** | | | | |
| Daily weighted-average number of subscribers | 19,385,055 | 20,903,908 | 22,794,170 | 24,886,300 |
| Average self-pay monthly churn* | 1.9% | 1.9% | 1.9% | 1.8% |
| New-vehicle conversion rate from trial to self-pay | 46% | 45% | 45% | 44% |
| Average revenue per subscriber | $11.53 | $11.73 | $12.00 | $12.27 |
| Subscriber acquisition cost, per gross subscriber addition | $59 | $55 | $54 | $50 |
| Customer service and billing expense per average subscriber | $1.03 | $1.03 | $1.07 | $1.07 |

*Derived from the average of the quarterly average self-pay monthly churn during the year. The average self-pay monthly churn for a quarter is calculated by dividing the monthly average of self-pay deactivations for a quarter by the average self-pay subscriber balance for a quarter.

*Sources:* Company 10-K report, 2012, pp. 30 and 32; and company 10-K report, 2013, pp. 31 and 33.

management continuously looked for new and unique brands and personalities to collaborate with and develop content that was unavailable to terrestrial radio and online competitors. The strategic objective was to continue to build record numbers of subscribers by producing innovative and appealing content.

Company efforts to cut programming costs had been successful. When interviewed by a *Barron's* reporter in fall 2013, Sirius XM CEO Jim Meyer was quoted as saying:[1]

> Before we merged, our programming cost was $450 million for everything besides music. Now, it's under $300 million. And that's not going to change a lot.

One industry analyst estimated that Sirius XM's monthly programming costs were $0.96 per subscriber in 2013 and would likely fall to $0.76 per subscriber by 2016 because of flat programming costs and growing numbers of subscribers.[2]

**Music Programming**   Sirius XM's music offerings were regularly adjusted and fine-tuned to remain in step with the ongoing changes in the tastes and preferences of music listeners and the shifting popularity of music artists. The channels created by the company were broadcast commercial-free, but certain music channels were programmed by third parties and aired commercials. The 2013 channel lineup also featured interviews and performances of some of the biggest names in music, a *Town Hall* series that featured concerts and interviews before a live audience, and several "pop-up" channels featuring the music of particular artists.

In 2013, music programming accounted for about 60 percent of the company's total programming costs.[3] Sirius XM had to pay royalties to the music publishers, recording studios and record companies, songwriters, and performing artists whose musical works were broadcast on its channels. In some cases, the royalty rate was negotiated directly with the copyright owners or their representatives; but if no agreements were reached, the laws in the United States governing copyrights called for the royalty rates to be determined by the Copyright Royalty Board (CRB) of the Library of Congress. In December 2012, the CRB determined that the royalties paid on sound recordings broadcast over satellite radio for the five-year period starting January 1, 2013, and ending December 31, 2017,

would be based on subscription revenue from U.S. satellite digital audio radio subscribers and advertising revenue from channels other than those channels that make only incidental performances of sound recordings and that the royalty rates would be 9 percent for 2013, 9.5 percent for 2014, 10 percent for 2015, 10.5 percent for 2016, and 11 percent for 2017. The rate for 2012 was 8 percent. However, revenues derived from the following were not subject to CRB-mandated royalty payments: (1) channels, programming, and products or other services offered for a separate charge when such channels make only incidental performances of sound recordings, (2) equipment sales, (3) current and future data services, and (4) certain other services and activities. In addition, the regulations allowed Sirius XM to reduce its monthly royalty fee in proportion to the percentage of its music performances that featured pre-1972 recordings (which were not subject to federal copyright protection) as well as those that were licensed directly from the copyright holder, rather than through a statutory license. Sirius XM charged all U.S. subscribers a U.S. music royalty fee, as an add-on to the regular subscription price, to cover the music royalty payments required by the CRB.

**Sports Programming**   Live play-by-play sports were an important part of Sirius XM's programming strategy. In 2013–2014, Sirius XM was the Official Satellite Radio Partner of the National Football League (NFL), the National Hockey League (NHL), and the PGA TOUR, and it broadcast most major college sports, including NCAA Division I regular-season football and basketball games, over 30 college football bowl games, and all tournament games of the NCAA Division 1 Men's Basketball Championship. There were broadcasts of soccer matches from the Barclays Premier League, FIS Alpine Skiing events, FIFA World Cup events, and horse racing. In addition, the sports lineup included a number of exclusive talk channels and programs such as MLB Network Radio, SiriusXM NASCAR Radio, Sirius XM NFL Radio, College Sports Nation, and Chris "Mad Dog" Russo's *Mad Dog Unleashed* on Mad Dog Radio, as well as two ESPN channels (ESPN Radio and ESPN Xtra). Simulcasts of select ESPN television shows, including *SportsCenter,* were broadcast on the company's ESPN Xtra channel.

Sirius XM's contract to broadcast every Major League Baseball game ran through 2021. Its agreement with the National Football League was up for renewal at the end of 2015.

**Talk and Entertainment Programming** Sirius XM's channel lineup included about 30 talk and entertainment channels that were designed for a broad variety of audiences and thus differentiated the company's programming from terrestrial radio and other audio entertainment providers. The talk-radio listening options featured a multitude of popular talk personalities, some with their own radio shows that aired exclusively on Sirius XM, including Howard Stern, Oprah Winfrey, Dr. Laura Schlessinger, Opie and Anthony, Bob Edwards, former senator Bill Bradley, and doctors from the NYU Langone Medical Center. Subscribers could listen to a range of humor on Sirius XM's comedy channels, including Jamie Foxx's The Foxxhole, Laugh USA, Blue Collar Comedy, and Raw Dog Comedy. Other talk and entertainment channels included a full-time channel devoted to business and management, SiriusXM Book Radio, Kids Place Live, Radio Disney, Rural Radio, Cosmo Radio, OutQ, Road Dog Trucking, and Playboy Radio. Religious programming included The Catholic Channel (programmed with the archdiocese of New York), EWTN (Catholic programming and news programming from around the world), and Family Talk.

The company's contract with Howard Stern was up for renewal at the end of 2015. According to media reports, the five-year contract Sirius XM and Howard Stern signed in December 2010 called for Sirius XM to pay an estimated $80 million annually for Howard Stern programming, down 20 percent from the approximately $100 million annual payments (including bonuses) for the initial five-year contract signed in 2004. Some observers had speculated that Stern's declining popularity and listener base might give Sirius XM greater leverage in negotiating to renew its contract with Stern in 2015. Sirius had already made some progress in reducing the prices of its highest-paid radio personalities—both Martha Stewart and Bubba the Love Sponge Clem had already agreed to reduced compensation.

**News and Information Programming** There was a wide range of national, international, and financial news, including news from CNBC, CNN, Fox News, HLN, Bloomberg Radio, MSNBC, NPR, BBC World Service News, and World Radio Network, plus several political call-in talk shows on a variety of channels and Sirius XM's exclusive channel, POTUS. Subscribers could get local traffic reports for 22 metropolitan markets throughout the United States.

**Internet Radio** Sirius XM streamed music channels and select nonmusic channels over the Internet, including several channels and features that were not available to satellite radio subscribers. Access to the company's Internet services was offered to satellite radio subscribers for an additional fee. Sirius XM marketed devices that enabled access to its Internet services without the need for a personal computer. It had also developed apps that allowed consumers to access the company's Internet services on certain smartphones and tablet computers.

In 2012, the company launched SiriusXM On Demand that gave Internet subscribers listening on the company's online media player and on smartphones the ability to choose their favorite episodes from a library of more than 300 shows and over 3,000 hours of content that included regularly updated feature content, commercial-free music from many genres, *Town Hall* specials, music specials, interviews with a wide range of celebrities, *The Howard Stern Show,* Dr. Laura, Jimmy Buffett concerts, Coach K, *Bob Dylan's Theme Time Radio Hour,* and selected shows from the company's lineup of sports, comedy, and exclusive talk and entertainment channels.

More recently, Sirius had introduced MySXM that permitted listeners to personalize the company's existing commercial-free music and comedy channels to create a more tailored listening experience. Channel-specific sliders allowed users to create over 100 variations of each of more than 50 channels by adjusting characteristics like library depth, familiarity, music style, tempo, region, and multiple other channel-specific attributes. SiriusXM On Demand and MySXM were offered to Internet subscribers at no extra charge.

In 2013 Sirius expanded its online offering to further enhance the appeal of subscribing to Sirius XM Internet Radio. Top management believed that coordinating the content and programming attractions across its satellite and streaming platforms would allow the company to provide subscribers with an "unparalleled experience."[4]

**Dynamic Programming Content and Channel Content** Sirius XM monitored the popularity of the content on each channel and the size of the audience listening to each channel. Channels with uneconomically low listener appeal either were dropped or had their content revised. Programming of existing channels was periodically refreshed. From time to time, new channels with altogether new content were added to the lineup of channel offerings. In 2012, the company launched a Comedy Central Radio channel and added Michael Smerconish, a nationally syndicated terrestrial talk-radio star, to its lineup in its ongoing campaign to bring the best audio entertainment to subscribers. In 2013, prominent programming additions included numerous *Town Hall* special events with high-profile personalities, dozens of new weekly programs and special events on existing channels, and the launch of a David Bowie channel, an expanded Pink Floyd channel, a Just for Laughs comedy channel, a Tom Petty Radio channel, an Entertainment Weekly channel (in partnership with *Entertainment Weekly,* which was the content provider), a The Girls' Room channel, and a Bon Jovi channel.

Several times each month, the company sent e-mails to subscribers calling attention to upcoming programs, shows, and events of interest scheduled for broadcast across its entire channel lineup. The e-mails also announced the launch of new shows on particular channels, temporary switches to seasonal music on particular channels, and any other noteworthy items (contests to win tickets to live performances and major sporting events, the appearance of special guests and/or the discussion of particular topics on regularly scheduled talk and entertainment shows, and the availability of certain videos that could be watched on the company's website or streamed to subscribers' tablets or smartphones). The e-mails served to heighten subscriber interest in satellite radio and build awareness of the dynamic and unique nature of Sirius XM's programming and how its diverse channel lineup and content offered "something for everyone and every mood."

**Programming Studios**   Sirius XM's programming activities were conducted principally in studio facilities occupying a full floor at the company's corporate headquarters building in midtown Manhattan and at studios in Washington, D.C. The company also operated smaller studio facilities in Cleveland, Los Angeles, Memphis, Nashville, and Austin. Both the New York City and Washington, D.C., offices housed facilities for programming origination, programming personnel, and programming transmission to the company's 140-plus channels.

## Radio Distribution Strategy

Following the merger in 2008, Sirius XM continued to employ the strategy of gaining access to new subscribers by distributing its satellite radios through three channels: automakers, assorted retail locations nationwide (including rental car companies), and the company's website. As had been the case during 2002–2008, when XM and Sirius battled each other for new subscribers, the merged Sirius XM continued to use subsidies and incentives to induce automakers to install a satellite radio and to partner with Sirius XM in promoting satellite radio service to customers who bought or leased a new vehicle equipped with a satellite radio.

**Automakers**   Just as had been the case prior to the merger, Sirius XM's primary means of distributing satellite radios (and gaining new subscribers) was through the sale and lease of new vehicles equipped with satellite radios. The purchasers of new or leased motor vehicles had, from the onset of satellite radio service, been the chief source of new subscribers. Listening to satellite radio broadcasts while driving had gained in popularity in the years since broadcasts began in 2002, spurring vehicle manufacturers to equip an increasing fraction of new vehicles, particularly models selling for $30,000 or more, with factory-installed satellite radios. About 70 percent of the 15.6 million new vehicles sold in the United States in 2013 had satellite radios (up from 33 percent in 2007), and the percentage was to grow in coming years. New vehicle sales were forecast to be around 16.3 million in 2014. Sirius XM's subscriber growth since 2009 had been driven largely by the recovery in automotive sales that had been under way since the Great Recession of 2008–2009, when annual sales in the United States in 2009 fell to 10.4 million vehicles.

To help boost the percentage of vehicles equipped with satellite radios, Sirius XM had continued the practice of using subsidies and incentives to induce automakers to offer satellite radios as a factory- or dealer-installed option in substantially all vehicle makes sold in the United States. Since the merger, Sirius XM had been successful in signing agreements with almost all vehicle makers whereby Sirius XM paid certain specified subsidies and incentives for each satellite radio installed in a new or leased vehicle. Sirius executives believed that these subsidies and incentives, coupled with growing driver enthusiasm for satellite radio service, would continue to broaden the distribution of satellite radios and boost the company's ability to attract growing numbers of new subscribers.

**The Retail Channel**    Sirius distributed and marketed its satellite and Internet radios through major national and regional retailers; to secure broader distribution, the company relied heavily on subsidies and incentives to induce retailers to stock satellite radios and promote Sirius XM's satellite radio service. Sirius also provided these retailers with an assortment of in-store merchandising materials to support their efforts to sell satellite radios to consumers, and it provided sales force training for several retailers.

In addition, the company's distribution strategy in the retail channel included:

- Using subsidies and incentives to induce distributors to stock satellite radio equipment and fill the orders of retailers who sold satellite radios.
- Selling satellite and Internet radios directly to consumers at the company's website.
- Working with certain rental car companies to equip a portion of the vehicles in their rental car fleets with satellite radios and to offer satellite radio service to their car rental customers.

## Sales and Marketing Strategy

Because Sirius XM's primary source of revenue was subscription fees, the company's sales and marketing strategy was concentrated on programs and initiatives to attract and retain new subscribers and rapidly grow its subscriber base. Going into 2014, Sirius XM radios were installed in close to 60 million vehicles in the United States, a number that represented 30 percent of the 200 million nonfleet registered vehicles on the road. With new vehicle sales in the United States running at 15 million to 16 million vehicles annually, roughly 11 million new vehicles per year were being equipped with a satellite radio. Approximately 110 million satellite-equipped vehicles were expected to be on the road in 2019.

Sirius CEO Jim Meyer expected the company to easily get to 30 million subscribers and believed that reaching 40 million subscribers was feasible in the not too distant future.[5] To achieve those numbers, Sirius was concentrating its sales and marketing efforts to gain new subscribers in both the new vehicle and used-vehicle segments, using subsidies and incentives to automakers, the retailers of used vehicles, and the retailers of satellite radios, complemented with telemarketing efforts to nonsubscribing owners of vehicles equipped with satellite radios.

However, the company had over $500 million in annual revenues from other sources, including the sale of advertising on select nonmusic channels, equipment revenues and royalties associated with the sale of satellite radios and accessories, amounts earned from subscribers through the U.S. music royalty fee, royalties from the company's Canadian affiliate, and ancillary fees from weather, traffic, data, and Backseat TV services—see Exhibit 2. Consequently, a portion of the company's sales and marketing strategy was aimed at growing these revenue streams.

**Subsidies and Incentives for Automakers**    Far and away the biggest marketing effort to secure new subscribers continued to be directed at people who purchased or leased new vehicles. This effort began with the long-standing practice of rewarding automakers for installing a satellite radio in new vehicles and including a three-month or six-month trial subscription to Sirius satellite service in the sale or lease price of these vehicles. The incentive package Sirius offered had induced every major automaker to offer satellite radios as a factory or dealer-installed option in substantially all makes of vehicles sold in the United States.

As a general rule, Sirius received trial subscription payments from automakers in advance of activating the trial subscription on the day the vehicle was purchased or leased from franchised dealers. Furthermore, Sirius reimbursed various automakers for certain costs associated with the satellite radios installed in their vehicles, including hardware costs, tooling expenses associated with installing satellite radios, and promotional and advertising expenses. And it shared with certain automakers a portion of the revenues it got from subscribers driving their satellite radio–equipped models. All of these subsidies, incentives, and expenses for cooperative marketing programs were classified as subscriber acquisition costs. To complement this effort, Sirius had been using outbound telemarketing campaigns to contact the nonsubscribing owners of new vehicles and try to convert them into becoming subscribers.

**Trial Subscriptions with Purchase or Lease of Used Vehicles Equipped with a Satellite Radio** In recent years, Sirius XM had accelerated its sales and marketing efforts to help induce people who bought or leased previously owned vehicles with factory-installed or dealer-installed satellite radios to subscribe to Sirius XM service. The company had recently developed systems and methods to identify these people and had established marketing programs to promote its programming to these potential subscribers. The company worked directly with franchised and independent vehicle dealers to promote and sell Sirius XM subscriptions for both certified and noncertified used vehicles equipped with satellite radios. It had launched subscriber programs at large used-car retailers, such as CarMax, AutoNation, and Penske, and over 11,000 other dealer locations to enhance its capabilities to gain new subscribers when satellite radio–enabled vehicles changed ownership. The centerpiece of Sirius XM's program with these participating used-vehicle retailers was giving a three-month Sirius XM trial subscription to customers buying any preowned vehicle with a factory-equipped satellite radio; in addition, the dealers reported the sale of such vehicles to Sirius. About 34 percent of used-car owners converted their three-month trial subscriptions to self-paying subscriptions.

In 2013, Sirius XM began enrolling dealers in its Service Lane Program to provide a complimentary two-month Sirius XM subscription to qualifying customers who brought their vehicles with a factory-equipped satellite radio in for service; there were over 2,500 dealers participating in the Service Lane Program as of February 2014. Both the used-car dealer and Service Lane programs also involved providing subsidies and/or revenue-sharing incentives of one kind or another, as well as providing promotional materials and participating in various cooperative marketing activities. The company was also using telemarketing to promote Sirius XM to nonsubscribing owners of satellite radio–equipped used vehicles.

The strategic target was to convert some of the 30 million vehicles on the road with inactive satellite radios into vehicles with active subscriptions to Sirius XM's service. At the end of the 2013 third quarter, Sirius was on track to gain 1.5 million in gross subscriber additions in the used-vehicle segment in 2013 (up from 1 million in 2012); the used-vehicle conversion rate from trial subscriptions to paid subscriptions was running above 30 percent.

**Subsidies and Incentives for the Retailers of Satellite Radios** Subsidies and incentives were also used to induce retailers to stock satellite radios and promote Sirius XM's satellite radio service. They included hardware subsidies paid to retail distributors, inventory allowances, in-store merchandising materials, sales force training for large-volume retailers, the handling of product warranty obligations on radios sold, loyalty payments, commissions (or some other sort of revenue-sharing arrangement) on subsequent subscriptions, and payments to reimburse retailers for the cost of advertising and other product awareness activities performed on Sirius XM's behalf.

Share-based payments of subscription revenues to automakers, franchised dealers, independent used-car dealers, and the retailers of satellite radios totaled $68.9 million in 2013, $63.8 million in 2012, $53.4 million in 2011, and $63.3 million in 2010. These payments appeared on the company's income statement in the operating expense category labeled "Royalty and revenue-sharing payments"—see Exhibit 2.

**A Variety of Subscription Plans and Subscription Packages** Sirius marketers had created a variety of subscription plans for customers to choose from—Exhibit 4 shows the three most popular plans. Most customers, especially newer subscribers, opted for annual, semiannual, quarterly, or sometimes monthly subscription plans. To entice customers whose subscriptions were expiring to sign up for a longer term, Sirius offered discounts for prepaid subscriptions and for automatic-renewal plans that ran for terms of two or three years. There were also discounts for customers who subscribed for service for two or more vehicles or had multiple radios for home and/or office use—roughly 80 percent of car-owning households in the United States owned two or more vehicles. The percentages of subscribers taking advantage of the discounts for longer-term plans and multiple-vehicle service were rising. From time to time, Sirius ran special promotions offering slightly deeper discounts on these plans.

Subscribers having an à la carte–capable radio (Sirius Starmate 8) could customize the programming they received; there were two à la carte

**EXHIBIT 4**   Sirius XM's Most Popular Subscription Plans, February 2014

|  | Sirius or XM Select | Sirius or XM All Access | Sirius or XM Mostly Music |
|---|---|---|---|
| Monthly subscription | $14.99 | $18.99 | $9.99 |
| Quarterly subscription | $44.97 ($14.99 per month) | $56.97 ($18.99 per month) | $27.97 ($9.99 per month) |
| Annual subscription | $164.89 ($13.74 per month) 1 free month | $199.00 ($16.58 per month) 1 free month | $119.88 ($9.99 per month) |
| 2-year subscription | $314.79 ($13.12 per month) 3 free months | $398.00 ($16.58 per month) 3 free months | $239.76 ($9.99 per month) |
| 3-year subscription | $464.69 ($12.91 per month) 5 free months | $588.69 ($16.35 per month) 5 free months | $359.64 ($9.99 per month) |
| Addition of a second radio | $9.99 per month | $13.99 per month | $9.99 per month |
| Number of channels | Over 140 channels | Over 150 channels plus online listening | Over 80 channels |
| Internet Radio | Add $4 per month | Included | Add $4 per month |
| Howard Stern | √ | √ | x |
| Oprah Radio, Opie and Anthony, Bob Edwards | x | √ | x |
| Every NFL game | √ | √ | x |
| Every NASCAR race | √ | √ | x |
| Every MLB game | x | √ | x |
| NBA and NHL games and PGA Tour coverage | x | √ | x |
| Up-to-the-minute traffic and weather coverage for 22 locations | √ | √ | x |

*Source:* Company website (accessed February 4, 2014).

subscription plans—one allowed subscribers to pick their 50 favorite channels within the Select package for a monthly price of $7.99, and the other allowed subscribers to choose 100 channels (not including live sports broadcast channels) for a monthly price of $15.99. There were also two family-friendly packages that did not contain adult-themed channels and had $1-per-month cheaper subscription prices, a 50+ channel news-sports-talk package priced at $9.99 per month, and a 155-channel Internet-only plan (for people who preferred to listen on a computer, tablet, smartphone, or other Internet-enabled device) priced at $14.99 per month—people who signed up for the Internet-only plan got a 30-day free trial. Because a substantial number of subscribers were driving older motor vehicles equipped with XM or Sirius radios that did not permit dual-signal reception, the company still had to broadcast both

XM signals and Sirius signals rather than just a single signal. But the subscription plan packages and prices for customers with either XM or Sirius radios were identical.

**Sales and Marketing Expenses**   Sirius XM's costs for sales and marketing activities are shown in Exhibit 2. These expenses included (1) expenditures for advertising, promotional events, and sponsorships, (2) reimbursement payments to automakers and retailers for advertising costs, certain cooperative marketing activities, and other product awareness activities performed on Sirius XM's behalf, (3) expenses related to direct mail, outbound telemarketing, and e-mail, and (4) personnel costs. Management anticipated that future sales and marketing expenses would increase as the company launched seasonal advertising, expanded promotional initiatives to attract new subscribers, and boosted efforts to retain existing subscribers and win back former subscribers.

## Customer Service and Customer Care Strategy

One of Sirius XM's top strategic priorities was to help boost subscriber retention rates through improvements in customer service and overall customer satisfaction. To improve customer retention and customer satisfaction metrics by making it easier and more satisfying to be a Sirius XM subscriber, the company had:

- Made significant investments in customer care and assembled a team of experienced customer service personnel to perform an assortment of customer support activities.
- Increased its capabilities to "chat" with online customers—a function that online customers liked and used when trying to manage their accounts, purchase equipment, and resolve other questions or issues they had.
- Expanded the customer self-service options that enabled subscribers to perform more transactions online.
- Integrated its subscriber management systems to enable Sirius radios and XM radios to exist on a single consolidated account.
- Launched a mobile service app to allow transactions and account management from a subscriber's smartphone.

## Satellite Systems and Operations Strategies

In 2014 Sirius had a fleet of 10 orbiting satellites, costing an average of $300 million each; four were manufactured by Boeing Satellite Systems and six were manufactured by Space Systems/Loral. The company used launch and in-orbit insurance to mitigate the potential financial impact of satellite launch and in-orbit failures unless the premium costs were considered to be uneconomical relative to the risk of satellite failure. The satellite fleet provided clear reception in most areas despite terrain variations, buildings, and other obstructions. Subscribers could receive transmissions at all outdoor locations in the continental United States where the satellite radio

had an unobstructed line of sight with one of the satellites or was within range of one of the company's 700 terrestrial repeaters to supplement satellite coverage.

Sirius controlled and communicated with the satellites from facilities in North America and also maintained earth stations in Panama and Ecuador to control and communicate with several satellites. The satellites were monitored, tracked, and controlled by a third-party satellite operator.

**Satellite Radios**    Sirius did not manufacture satellite radios. Rather, it designed the radios, established their specifications, either sourced or specified the needed parts and components, and managed various aspects of the logistics and production of its satellite and Internet radios. It had authorized manufacturers and distributors to produce and distribute radios, and it had licensed the company's technology to various electronics manufacturers to develop, manufacture, and distribute radios under brands other than Sirius XM. It also was responsible for obtaining FCC certification of its radios. Sirius purchased radios from these manufacturers for distribution through the company's website. To facilitate the sale of its radios, Sirius typically subsidized a portion of the radio manufacturing costs to reduce the hardware price to consumers—the majority of these subsidies were paid to the makers of the chip sets (microprocessors) used in its radios and to the suppliers of certain other parts and components.

Radios were manufactured in four principal configurations—in-dash radios for new and used motor vehicles, Dock & Play radios, home or commercial units, and portable radios. In 2011, Sirius introduced the Sirius XM Edge, a Dock & Play radio featuring a technology that expanded the company's available channel lineup and data bandwidth. At the time, the Edge was the only Sirius XM radio able to access Sirius XM's new 2.0 technology; it was sold at retail locations and on the Sirius XM website for $139.99. Later, Sirius XM introduced the Lynx model, a portable radio with Sirius XM 2.0 satellite and Internet radio capability. In addition, there was an interoperable radio, MiRGE, which had a unified control interface allowing for easy switching between the XM and Sirius satellite radio networks. Sirius's other important radio model was the XM SkyDock, which connected to an Apple iPhone and iPod touch and provided live XM satellite radio using the control capability of the iPhone or iPod touch. A new model, the Sirius XM Onyx Plus Dock & Play radio, priced at $99.99, was introduced in November 2013. The Onyx Plus had the capability to receive all of the channels of the company's previous satellite radios plus Sirius XM's expanded channel lineup and SiriusXM Latino, a suite of Spanish-language channels, and was packed with advanced features. With Onyx Plus, the listener was able to:

- Store up to 20 channels for one-touch access, including 18 Smart Favorite channels.
- Automatically start songs from the beginning when tuned to a Smart Favorite music channel with TuneStart.
- Create a customized music channel that was a blend of the Smart Favorite music channels with TuneMix.
- Scan and select songs that had already played on the Smart Favorite music channels with TuneScan.
- Pause, rewind, and replay live satellite radio plus go back and replay music, news, talk, or sports segments on all Smart Favorite channels.
- Browse what was playing on other channels while listening to the current one.
- Get alerts so that the listener wouldn't miss any favorite artists, songs, and games.
- Get score alerts when scores occurred in games that involved the user's favorite teams.
- Catch up on the latest sports scores with Sports Ticker.
- Jump back to the previous channel with One-Touch Jump.
- Lock and unlock channels with mature content.

Onyx Plus also boasted a large color graphic display for viewing album art and channel logos, program and channel information, and song and show titles.

**New Technology and Expanded Online and Two-Way Wireless Capabilities**  In 2013, Sirius introduced the SiriusXM Internet Radio app for smartphones and other connected devices to make Sirius XM programming more widely available. In 2013–2014, Sirius accelerated efforts to develop and deliver in-vehicle technology and systems with greater capabilities and connectivity. It was participating in an initiative with Nissan to provide a comprehensive suite of services that would allow for crash notification, stolen or parked vehicle locator service, remote vehicle diagnostics, roadside assistance, monitoring of vehicle emissions, and other safety and convenience measures. In November 2013, Sirius completed the acquisition of the connected-vehicle services business of Agero, Inc., giving it significantly greater capability to develop a connected-vehicle platform and begin delivering connected-vehicle services to a host of major automotive manufacturers. Agreements had already been negotiated with Acura, BMW, Honda, Hyundai, Infiniti, Lexus, Nissan, and Toyota, with several others in the pipeline, making Sirius the current leader in providing connected-vehicle services to automakers. Sirius XM's offerings included safety, security, and convenience services for drivers and end-to-end, turnkey solutions for automakers. The company expected to earn revenues of $100 million from providing these services in 2014 and expected these revenues to reach $200 million in the next three years.

## COMPETITION

Despite being the monopoly provider of satellite radio service in the United States, Sirius XM nonetheless faced significant competition for both listeners and advertisers from a number of diverse sources—in addition to prerecorded, disc-based music entertainment that consumers could purchase and play in cars and homes and on various portable devices.

### Broadcasters of Analog and Digital AM/FM Radio Programs

The broadcasters of AM/FM programs had a loyal listener base numbering in the tens of millions and long-standing demand for their product offerings They utilized an advertising-based business model that provided free broadcast reception paid for by commercial advertising. Stations chose one of several basic programming formats (music, talk, sports, religious, news, educational, ethnic), put their own differentiating spin on the selected programming format, and then tried to make money by selling a sufficient number of advertising spots at rates commensurate with their audience ratings to produce a profitable revenue stream. Radio stations competed for listeners and advertising revenues with other radio stations in their geographic listening area based on such factors as program content, on-air talent, transmitter power, and audience demographics; these factors, along with audience size and the number and characteristics of other radio stations in the area, affected the rates they were able to charge for advertising. Some AM/FM radio stations had reduced the number of commercials per hour, expanded the range of music played on the air, and experimented with new formats in order to lure customers away from satellite radio.

In recent years, most AM/FM radio stations had begun broadcasting digital signals as well as the older analog signals. Digital signals had clarity similar to Sirius XM signals but made a difference only to listeners with a digital or HD radio. Many AM/FM broadcasters were also complementing their HD radio efforts by aggressively pursuing Internet radio, wireless Internet-based distribution arrangements, and data services. Several automakers had installed HD radio equipment as factory standard equipment in select models, and more were planning to shift from installing analog radios as standard equipment to installing digital radios.

## Internet Radio Broadcasters and Internet-Enabled Smartphones

Internet radio broadcasts typically had no geographic limitations and provided listeners with radio programming from across the country and around the world. Major media companies and online-only providers, including Clear Channel, CBS and Pandora, made high-fidelity digital streams available through the Internet for free or, in some cases, for a fraction of the cost of a satellite radio subscription. Pandora, for example, had 70 million listeners and 3 million paying subscribers. Online broadcasters competed directly with Sirius XM's services in automobiles, at home, on mobile devices, and wherever audio entertainment was consumed. Internet-enabled smartphones, most of which had the capability of interfacing with vehicles, could play recorded or cached content and access Internet radio via dedicated applications or browsers. These applications were often free to the user and offered music and talk content as long as the user had subscribed to a sufficiently large mobile data plan. Leading audio smartphone radio applications included Pandora, last.fm, Slacker, iheartradio, and Stitcher. Certain of these applications also included

advanced functionality, such as personalization, and allowed the user to access large libraries of content and podcasts on demand.

Spotify had launched a music-streaming service in the United States that allowed its users unlimited, on-demand access to a large library of song tracks, enabling the sharing of playlists with other listeners through the Facebook platform. Other similar services had launched Facebook integration, including MOG and Rdio. These services, which usually required a monthly subscription fee, were currently available on smartphones but were likely to become integrated into connected vehicles in the future.

Third-generation (G3) and fourth-generation (G4) mobile networks had enabled a steady increase in the audio quality and reliability of mobile Internet radio streaming, and this was expected to further increase as G4 networks became standard. Sirius executives expected that improvements from higher bandwidths, wider programming selection, and advancements in functionality would continue making Internet radio and smartphone applications an increasingly significant competitor, particularly in vehicles.

Because the audio entertainment marketplace was evolving rapidly and new media platforms and portable devices emerged periodically, it was likely that new companies would enter the marketplace and begin to compete with Sirius XM's programming and services.

## Advanced In-Dash Infotainment Systems

In 2014, nearly all automakers had deployed or were in the process of installing integrated multimedia systems in the dashboards of their models. These systems could combine control of audio entertainment from a variety of sources, including AM/FM/HD radio broadcasts, satellite radio, Internet radio, smartphone applications, and stored audio, with navigation and other advanced applications such as restaurant bookings, movie show times, and stock-trading information. Internet radio and other data were typically connected to the system via a Bluetooth link to an Internet-enabled smartphone, and the entire system could be controlled via dashboard touchscreens or voice recognition. These systems significantly enhanced the attractiveness of the services of Sirius XM's Internet-based competitors by making such applications more prominent, easier to access, and safer to use in the car. Similar systems were also available in the aftermarket for automobile accessories and were being sold by retailers.

## Direct Broadcast Satellite and Cable Audio

Such providers of TV programming as DirecTV, Dish, Comcast, Time Warner, Charter, and others typically included a package of audio programs (mostly music) as part of their packages of video programming services. Customers generally did not pay an additional monthly charge for the audio channels, and such programming was accessible only at the fixed locations where customers' TVs were connected.

## Providers of Traffic News Services

A number of providers competed with Sirius XM's traffic news services. Clear Channel and Tele Atlas had partnered to deliver nationwide traffic information for the top-50 markets to in-vehicle navigation systems with RDS-TMC traffic reception capability; RDS-TMC was the radio broadcast standard technology for delivering traffic and travel information to drivers. Moreover, the market for in-dash navigation systems was being invaded by increasingly capable smartphones that provided advanced navigation functionality, including live traffic information. Android, BlackBerry, and Apple iOS-based smartphones all included GPS mapping and navigation functionality, often with turn-by-turn navigation.

## GOVERNMENT REGULATION

As operators of a privately owned satellite system, Sirius XM was regulated by the Federal Communications Commission under the Communications Act of 1934. Any assignment or transfer of control of the company's FCC licenses had to be approved by the FCC. Sirius XM's licenses for its five Sirius satellites expired in 2017; its FCC licenses for several XM satellites expired in 2014 and 2018. Management anticipated that, absent significant misconduct, the FCC would renew the licenses to permit operation of these satellites for their useful lives and would also grant a license for any replacement satellites. The FCC had established rules governing terrestrial repeaters and had granted Sirius XM a license to operate its repeater network. Sirius had to obtain FCC certification for all of its satellite radios.

Sirius XM was required to obtain export licenses from the U.S. government to export certain ground control equipment, satellite communications and control services, and technical data related to its satellites and their operations. The delivery of such equipment, services, and technical data to destinations outside the United States and to foreign persons was subject to strict export control and prior approval requirements.

## IMPORTANT NEW DEVELOPMENTS

In October 2013, Sirius XM announced that its board of directors had approved an additional $2 billion common stock repurchase program to be funded by cash on hand, future cash flow from operations, and future borrowings. The company also announced that it had agreed to repurchase $500 million of common stock from Liberty Media and its affiliates in three installments, in November 2013, January 2014, and April 2014. These purchases were in addition to Sirius XM's recent repurchases of 476.5 million shares of common stock at an aggregate cost of approximately $1.6 billion.

Meanwhile, Liberty Media brought its ownership of Sirius XM common stock to about 53 percent of the shares outstanding, and three new directors chosen by Liberty Media were added to Sirius XM's board. This resulted in a "change of control" at the corporate level since Liberty Media became the controlling owner. On January 3, 2014, Sirius XM's board of directors received a nonbinding letter from Liberty Media Corporation proposing a tax-free transaction whereby all outstanding shares of Sirius XM's common stock not owned by Liberty Media would be converted into the right to receive 0.0760 share of Liberty Series C common stock, which would have no voting rights. Liberty Media indicated that immediately prior to the conversion, it intended to distribute, on a 2-to-1 basis, shares of its Series C common stock to all holders of record of Liberty Media's Series A and B common stock. Liberty Media also indicated that it expected that upon the completion of the proposed transaction, Sirius XM's public stockholders would own approximately 39 percent of Liberty Media's then-outstanding common stock. Sirius XM's board of directors formed a special committee of independent directors to consider Liberty Media's proposal.

In addition to its 53 percent ownership of Sirius XM, Liberty Media owned interests in a broad range of media, communications, and entertainment businesses, including:

- 100 percent ownership of the Atlanta National League Baseball Club and TruePosition, Inc., a global leader in location determination and intelligence solutions that help protect citizens, combat crime, and save lives.

- 67 percent ownership of MacNeil/Lehrer Productions, producer of *The PBS NewsHour,* documentaries, interactive DVDs, civic engagement projects, and educational programs.

- Minority interests in Charter Communications (27 percent); Live Nation Entertainment (26 percent)—the largest live entertainment company in the world; Barnes & Noble (17 percent); Mobile Streams (16 percent)—a global mobile content retailer of full-track downloads, ringtones, videos, graphics, and games; Kroenke Arena Co. (7 percent)—the owner of the Pepsi Center, a sports and entertainment facility in Denver, Colorado; and Crown Media Holdings (3 percent)—the owner-operator of the Hallmark Channel and the Hallmark Movie Channel.

- Small common stock investments (generally 1 percent or less) in CenturyLink, Time Warner Cable, and media companies Time Warner, Inc., and Viacom.

Analysts speculated that Liberty Media's offer to Sirius XM shareholders—which they valued at $3.67 per share based on then-prevailing conditions—was predicated on strengthening its balance sheet and gaining access to Sirius XM's $1.1 billion in annual cash flows from operations, cash that it could use to join forces with Charter Communications in a bid to acquire Time Warner Cable (TWC). Charter had offered to buy Time Warner Cable for $127 in October 2013 and had upped its offer to $132.50 in January 2014; TWC had rejected both offers as grossly inadequate. Then in mid-February 2014, TWC agreed to be acquired by Comcast in an all-stock deal worth about $155 per share to Time Warner shareholders. Shortly thereafter, Liberty Media turned its attention to making some acquisitions in Europe and, on March 13, 2014, officially announced it was abandoning its offer to acquire all of the outstanding shares of Sirius XM. A day later, Sirius XM issued a press release saying that it was resuming the common stock repurchase program previously announced in October 2013.

## Decline in the Number of Subscribers, Fourth Quarter 2013

On February 4, 2014, Sirius XM announced its financial and operating performance for both full-year 2013 and the fourth quarter of 2013. While the company's performance was on the whole positive, Sirius XM's reported decline in the number of subscribers from the third quarter to the fourth quarter was a red flag that quickly caught the attention of stockholders and industry analysts. Gross subscriber additions of 2,409,804 in Q4 of 2013 were about 155,000 below the gross subscriber additions of 2,561,175 in Q3 of 2013, but a big jump in subscriber deactivations to an all-time record high (up 384,493 over the prior quarter) led to a net decline of 22,756 subscribers in the 2013 fourth quarter—recent quarterly subscriber data for Sirius XM are presented in Exhibit 5.

Several factors contributed to the negative subscriber growth in 2013's last quarter:

- Sirius XM began paying automakers lower subsidy rates per satellite radio–equipped vehicle. Indeed, the lower subsidy payments resulted in subscriber acquisition costs of $124 million in the fourth quarter, or just 12 percent of revenue, the lowest percentage in the company's history. And subscriber acquisition cost per gross subscriber addition was a record low $44, which was 18.5 percent below the $54 average for the fourth quarter of 2012.

- A major automaker shifted to unpaid trial subscriptions in Q4 of 2013, accounting for most of the 434,240 decline in paid promotional (trial) subscriptions from Q3 to Q4.

- The new vehicle conversion rate from trial to self-pay was only 42 percent in Q4, as compared to the normal 45 to 46 percent rates that prevailed during 2010–2012 (see Exhibit 3).

It was unclear whether the jump in deactivations reflected resistance to the costs of subscribing to one of the company's numerous subscription plans. Subscription prices, which ranged from $6.99 to $16.99 per month until mid-2011, were increased shortly after the agreement with the FCC to not raise prices expired in July 2011—the base rate was increased

**EXHIBIT 5   Quarterly Gross Subscriber Additions, Deactivated Subscribers, and Net Subscriber Additions, Sirius XM Satellite Radio, 2011–2013**

|  | Gross Subscriber Additions | Deactivated Subscribers | Net Subscriber Additions |
|---|---|---|---|
| **2011** | | | |
| Quarter 1 | 2,052,367 | 1,679,303 | 373,064 |
| Quarter 2 | 2,179,348 | 1,727,201 | 452,147 |
| Quarter 3 | 2,138,131 | 1,804,448 | 333,683 |
| Quarter 4 | 2,326,174 | 1,783,208 | 542,966 |
| **2012** | | | |
| Quarter 1 | 2,161,693 | 1,757,097 | 404,596 |
| Quarter 2 | 2,481,004 | 1,858,962 | 622,042 |
| Quarter 3 | 2,421,586 | 1,975,665 | 445,921 |
| Quarter 4 | 2,553,489 | 2,018,536 | 534,953 |
| **2013** | | | |
| Quarter 1 | 2,509,914 | 2,057,024 | 452,890 |
| Quarter 2 | 2,655,488 | 1,939,726 | 715,762 |
| Quarter 3 | 2,561,175 | 2,048,067 | 513,078 |
| Quarter 4 | 2,409,804 | 2,432,560 | (22,756) |

*Sources:* Company 10-Q reports; and company press releases of fourth-quarter and full-year results, February 5, 2013, and February 4, 2014.

by an average of $1.54. Another $0.50 increase went into effect in January 2014, resulting in subscription plan prices ranging from $9.99 to $18.99 per month. But many new vehicles had in-dash connections that enabled drivers to plug in smartphones and other mobile devices and listen to downloaded or streamed music from sources other than Sirius. However, the data plans that drivers had for their connected devices could often result in paying more to listen to streamed programs than the cost of a Sirius subscription, especially if they listened to a lot of hours of streamed programming in their vehicles each month.

The performance of Sirius XM's stock price in the first three months of 2014 was disappointing. After jumping to $3.86 per share in the days following Liberty Media's offer on January 3, 2014, to acquire all of the remaining shares of Sirius XM's common stock that it did not already own, Sirius XM's stock price drifted down to $3.43 the day after the company announced its fourth-quarter and full-year results for 2013. On March 31, 2014, the company's stock price closed at $3.20 per share.

## Sirius XM's Guidance for 2014

In announcing the company's full-year 2013 financial and operating results on February 4, 2014, Sirius's management reiterated its guidance for the company's performance for 2014:

- Revenue of over $4 billion.
- Net subscriber additions of approximately 1.25 million.
- Income from operations of approximately $1.30 billion
- Free cash flow approaching $1.1 billion.

This guidance was reaffirmed in an April 24, 2014, press release.

## ENDNOTES

[1] Alexander Eule, "Sound of Success," *Barron's*, November 25, 2013, p. 26.

[2] Ibid.
[3] Ibid.

[4] Letter to Shareholders, 2012 annual report.
[5] Eule, "Sound of Success."

# Sony Music Entertainment and the Evolution of the Music Industry

A. J. Strickland
The University of Alabama

Andrew Pharaoh
2015 Undergraduate,
The University of Alabama

Seth Kennedy
2014 Undergraduate,
The University of Alabama

"At such a pivotal time for music, it's more important than ever to develop a fertile, creative environment that generates the highest quality of artists and music, while seeking to fully exploit the many opportunities that new digital services and products provide in reaching audiences around the world."[1]

The remarks of Sony Music Entertainment CEO Doug Morris in 2011 illustrated an accurate understanding of the environment of music sales. Morris, a globally influential executive and music innovator, agreed to join Sony Music Entertainment as chief executive officer effective July 1, 2011. In a time of great change in the music marketplace, it was absolutely necessary that Sony take active steps to remain competitive. Morris took the job graciously, but he placed himself into a business whose margins were becoming thinner and thinner. With a declining industry that had been made less lucrative by the wide availability of substitutes, Morris was forced to develop a strategy to contend with industry change and unfavorable competitive forces in 2014.

## HISTORY OF SONY MUSIC ENTERTAINMENT

American Record Company, the company that would later become Sony Music Entertainment, was founded in 1929 and then acquired by Columbia Broadcasting Company in 1938. In March 1968, Sony, at that time a Japanese company, began a joint venture with the American company CBS to form CBS/Sony Records Inc. In September 1976, Sony introduced the optical digital audio disc, now known as the compact disc (CD). In 1983, CBS Inc., as an American company, allowed introduction of the CD to American markets. In January 1988, CBS Records Inc. was absorbed, and in January 1991, the new company was renamed Sony Music Entertainment Inc.

In August 2004, Sony BMG Music Entertainment was established as a new joint venture with Bertelsmann AG. Later, in August 2008, Sony acquired BMG's 50 percent stake in Sony Music Entertainment and began operation once again as Sony Music Entertainment, a wholly owned subsidiary of Sony Corporation. In July 2012, Sony/ATV Music Publishing, a joint venture between Sony and the Michael Jackson Family Trust, along with a consortium of other investment firms, bought the publishing arm of the EMI Group, which solidified Sony's position as the world's largest music publisher.

## OVERVIEW OF THE MUSIC INDUSTRY

Before the 1900s, music and entertainment media had a strong emphasis on performance. If theater, magic, or music was wanted in a certain venue, individuals who could perform the art personally were found and paid to do so. At the beginning of the 20th century, music began to become ownership-driven. Listening to music was still done live, but, as the quality of technology improved, artists began to produce recordings of their music. Recordings initially made the music industry more efficient, because artists were able to receive royalties on physical recordings and were able to reach a wider audience with their songs. This allowed more time to be spent on creating new music, and the field became more lucrative and more attractive. However, after a short-lived heyday came a long decline, beginning in the early 2000s, as a result of piracy (discussed later) and digital distribution.

The 1993 release of the MP3 algorithm enabled the reduction of song files to a size that made Internet broadcasting and uploading and downloading feasible. Shortly afterward, in 1994, WXYC (89.3 FM, Chapel Hill, North Carolina) became the first traditional radio station to announce broadcasting on the Internet. In 1998, the newfound portability of music was coupled with a naming service and comprehensive databases of music information developed by Gracenote (later purchased by Sony in 2008 for $260 million), making it possible to retain the information associated with the song files. Technologies like these opened the floodgates of digital distribution. Napster, the popular (illegal) file-sharing service, was started shortly afterward, in 1999, and iTunes, a legal online music store, was launched by Apple in 2001.

In February 2003, Warehouse Music, a retail music store selling physical albums, declared bankruptcy. The following year, in February 2004, Tower Records filed for the first of three bankruptcies, which ended with the closing of its 93 stores across the United States. Virgin and Circuit City lasted somewhat longer, until 2009, but were also eventual fodder to digital music. Sellers of other types of physical media, such as Borders (books) and Blockbuster (DVDs), also chose to shut their doors in the 2000s as a result of the digital music and video age. These companies, however, tended to blame piracy for their financial downturn, not digital media, and certainly not an outdated business model.

Album sales continued the decline that put brick-and-mortar record stores out of business, with sales falling from about 575 million in 2006 to about 290 million in 2013. Internet and digital track sales, on the other hand, continued to rise, topping out at an estimated 1.34 billion tracks in 2012. Digital sales declined slightly in 2013 to 1.26 billion. This roughly 6 percent decline was the first decline in digital sales since the iTunes store debuted more than a decade earlier. However, industry revenues steadily declined from a peak of $17 billion in 2000 to $7.9 billion in 2013.

## Copyright Infringement and Piracy

The early 2000s saw a huge increase in copyright infringement in the music world. For products such as Rolex watches and Gucci bags, imitations had always existed. Third-party manufacturers, especially abroad, re-created the look of the original product with cheaper raw materials and sold the counterfeits at a discount. With music, however (and most digital media, for that matter), the duplicates were identical in quality, simple and costless to the duplicator, and able to be redistributed digitally. To make matters worse for the profitability of the industry, the likelihood of being held responsible for the crime was quite low. Sharing music was so easy, so ubiquitous, and so socially acceptable that it was not long before it gave birth to popular file sharing on a much larger scale, like that through Napster (1999), LimeWire (2000), and Kazaa (2006)—not to mention sharing by individuals who burned physical CDs to give to friends.

As of May 2014, two bills were under consideration by the U.S. Congress that addressed digital piracy. The Stop Online Piracy Act (SOPA) and the Protect IP Act (PIPA) aimed to stop copyright infringement and to stop the trafficking of copyright material by requiring that search engines abstain from linking to websites violating copyright laws and that Internet service providers block access to these websites. Both bills were met with public opposition, and votes on the bills were postponed until the issues regarding the bills could be resolved.

The Institute for Policy Innovation estimated that "global music piracy causes $12.5 billion of economic losses every year, 71,060 U.S. jobs lost, a loss of $2.7 billion in workers' earnings, and a loss of $422 million in tax revenues, $291 million in personal income tax and $131 million in lost corporate income and production taxes."

## Music Publishing

Record labels scout for promising musicians and bands, sign them to publishing contracts, and help them through the process of creating and marketing their music. Record labels (or the artists themselves) will typically own all rights to the master recordings that their artists produce and then compensate the artists according to the amount of sales that the specific sound recording produces. Labels record the music of artists in studios, manufacture recordings, and promote and distribute that music by various means to the consumer. Through copyrights, labels are responsible for the protection of the music and artists they sponsor.

There was an increasing simplicity to digital music distribution, and it was becoming easier and easier for artists to record, publish, and promote their music themselves without the help of corporations. The trend of using the Internet and technology that was more accessible than ever had initiated a bypass of the middlemen and was a difficult obstacle for music companies to overcome.

In January 2014, Sony Music Entertainment was the second-largest record label, with 20 percent of total industry market share. In terms of total album sales, Sony Music Entertainment was positioned with 30.4 percent of market share, behind the leader Universal by 7.3 percent; however, Sony's artist Justin Timberlake was the top-selling artist in 2013. In digital sales, Sony still lagged behind Universal by 6.2 and 9.5 percent in album sales and individual-track sales, respectively. Sony/ATV Music Publishing was the largest music publisher, with 16.9 percent of the total market share.

Whereas record companies owned the physical sound recording, publishers (or the artists themselves) typically owned the rights to license and collect royalties on the specific melody, lyrics, rhythm, and so on, every time they were used. A "use" of a song was typically classified as falling under one of three "rights" controlled by a publisher: Mechanical rights represented the ability of an owner to collect royalties when the song was digitally downloaded; performing arts royalties were collected when a song was played on the radio; and synchronization royalties would be collected when a song was used in a movie or commercial. Publishers typically worked closely with record labels in the same way that a hardware store might have worked with a carpenter or plumber. In the case of Sony Music Entertainment and the other two leading music industry giants, both the publisher and the label were vertically integrated as subsidiaries

of the same parent company. Publishers also helped to market recordings and performed services for a musician much as a bank did for a businessperson—providing advances and loans with future income as collateral.

# DIGITAL MUSIC DISTRIBUTION IN 2014

In 2014, there were three main methods of digital music distribution: digital download, Internet radio, and interactive streaming. For the digital purchases of music, iTunes was the clear leader, accounting for 63 percent of digital music sales in 2013, and it had facilitated over $25 billion in digital music sales since its inception. According to Apple's 2013 10-K report, filed October 30, 2013, the iTunes Store generated a total of $9.3 billion in net sales during 2013, representing a 24 percent increase over 2012 sales. The iTunes sales figure included digital music downloads through iTunes, purchases through the App Store, and purchases on iBooks. In September 2013, iTunes had launched its own free Internet radio service, iTunes Radio. The service tailored radio stations on the basis of users' iTunes libraries and user input. The service was available in Australia and the United States and boasted over 20 million users.

## Self-Publishing in the Music Industry

The same technologies and social environment that facilitated the rise in digital distribution through services like iTunes and Amazon were also facilitating self-publishing, and in 2014 the allure to an artist was strong. The creator had control over the creation; the profit margin was much higher and paid monthly, in contrast to the annual royalty remuneration typical of labels; and the whole process was completed much faster. Avoiding the 30 percent cut that distributors like iTunes and Amazon took was an incentive in and of itself, if avoiding the typical 10 percent cut to record labels wasn't enough.

For example, the band Radiohead digitally self-published two albums, *In Rainbows* (October 2007) and *King of Limbs* (February 2011), by means of the band's website, **radiohead.com**. Additionally, *In Rainbows* was released on a donation-based system, which effectively allowed fans to download the album free. In the first month after its release,

40 percent of the approximately 1 million fans who had downloaded the album paid an average of $6, earning almost $3 million for the band.

Artists without a substantial preexisting constituency also had options to bypass the record labels through a growing number of services such as Amazon's Create Space and CD Baby. Exhibit 1 presents a breakdown of the split in royalties with CD Baby.

## Interactive Streaming and Internet Radio

There were many Internet radio and subscription streaming services in 2014, but Spotify, Slacker Radio, Rdio, Pandora, Last.fm, Beats Music, Napster, Zune Marketplace, Grooveshark, Myspace, iTunes Radio, and Rhapsody were among the largest. From 2008 to 2013, Internet radio grew at an annual rate of 42 percent, to a $767 million industry. It was projected that Internet and streaming radio would continue to grow at an annual rate of 12.7 percent a year until 2018 and that in 2016 almost 161 million consumers would be subscribing to a streaming music or Internet radio service. Increasingly, many music companies saw revenue from music streaming and Internet radio as a substitute for sales. This meant that, instead of purchasing a physical CD or even downloading a CD on iTunes, the consumer would instead turn to a cheaper (in many cases, free), more convenient Internet streaming source. A business model that relied on scarcity to force consumers to buy, download, or have ownership of the product in any way waned in efficacy.

Despite manifold flaws in licensing models and remuneration of artists (Grooveshark, another popular interactive streaming service, had been sued by all of the Big Three record labels over licensing problems since its inception), the period from 2010 to 2012 saw rapid growth of Internet distribution. Possibly stimulated by the threat of file sharing and reductions in physical CD sales, record labels and music publishers were willing to look to new monetization methods, such as streaming services, that might save their profitability. A common goal of salespeople was to make their product as attractive and accessible as possible to the consumer. In the early to mid-2000s, the constraints of technology were still a problem, but advancements quickly progressed to reduce these constraints. Music streaming services weren't a new idea by any means, but in 2010–2011 new streaming services were accompanied by the ubiquity of the smartphone. In 2014, any smartphone, computer, and Internet-enabled automobile (as of January 2014, Pandora had partnered with 140 different car models to offer its in-car radio service) was able to stream music directly and quickly. It was estimated that, in 2014, 58 percent of Americans had a smartphone and 63 percent of cell phone owners used their phones to access the Internet. Content owners had been reluctant to embrace the services because of very low profit margins, but

## EXHIBIT 1  Split of CD Baby Royalties

| How Much CD Baby Pays You | | |
|---|---|---|
| **Type of Sale** | **You Get** | **Our Cut** |
| **CDs and vinyl** (includes sales through our distribution partners) | Your chosen purchase price minus $4 | We keep $4 per unit sold. If your album sells for $13, you get paid $9. |
| **CDBaby.com downloads** (single tracks and full-album) | 75% of your chosen purchase price | We keep only 25% and pay you a whopping 75% per download sold on our store—more than iTunes, Amazon, and other retailers. So if you set your single-song download price at 99¢ you'll get paid 74¢ per song! |
| **Digital distribution sales** (from iTunes, Amazon MP3, Rhapsody, and many more) | 91% of net income | We keep 9% of the net income paid to us by our partners and you keep the rest. |
| **Credit card swiper sales** | 87.2% | We keep 9% plus 3.8% for credit card fees (12.8% total). |

*Source:* CDBaby.com.

it had become clear that consumers were enjoying the services' flexibility, freedom, and access.

Interactive streaming services like Rhapsody and Spotify licensed music from artists and record labels and then provided it to users through a client available on their respective websites. Spotify and Rhapsody were very similar in terms of business model, as both companies relied most heavily on payments from subscribers in order to fund their high cost of sales, or licensing fees. The main difference was the content available to unsubscribed users. Whereas Rhapsody allowed a short, 30-day trial of its premium service, nonpaying Spotify users were able to listen to much of its paid content for free, as long as they were willing to listen to ads played between every few songs.

Spotify seemed to be off to an inauspicious start in October 2008, with heavy losses totaling $42 million. Exhibit 2 shows the change in the number of paying customers for Spotify. Since its inception, Spotify had not turned a profit but had seen explosive revenue growth. The company increased its revenues from $99 million in 2009 to $578 million in 2012.

## YouTube

YouTube was an unlikely but very significant player in the music industry. An integral part of YouTube's success in the music scene was the introduction of Content ID, a service that identified the music in videos posted by users. With this information, instead of removing videos that contained a song whose use was a copyright infringement, YouTube simply identified the owner of the copyright and paid a royalty to the record label or artist after a short verification process.

Like Spotify and Rhapsody, YouTube paid licensing fees to record labels and artists, and it was better able to absorb the costs paid to content owners because

of the higher price advertisers paid for video ads. Below the video would be a link to a digital distributor, such as iTunes or Amazon, from which the song could be purchased, as well as a link to the YouTube account run by the artist. In this way, YouTube was somewhat able to harness what was once copyright infringement in order to gain legal entry into the market of interactive streaming. Of course, the technology was still flawed, but it had come far. YouTube is also rumored to be planning to unveil a subscription music and video service to directly rival Spotify, Rdio, and other competitors. YouTube would offer a free version along with a premium service for a monthly fee of $9.99.

To put the rivalry between YouTube and streaming services in perspective, Spotify announced in February 2014 that its most popular song was Avicii's "Wake Me Up," with more than 200 million plays since it was released in June 2013. On YouTube, "Wake Me Up" had over 450 million plays and that number did not include other uploads featuring the song, such as uploads from fans, live performances, or remixes.

## SONY MUSIC ENTERTAINMENT'S BUSINESS MODEL AND STRATEGY

In 2007, Sony Music Entertainment, in collaboration with BMG, focused on two things: finding promising new talent and collecting more fans for its stars such as Daughtry, Alicia Keys, Avril Lavigne, Celine Dion, Bruce Springsteen, and Foo Fighters. The year 2007 was an excellent one for innovation. Sony began Myspace Music as a joint venture "as an interactive online platform for music sales, subscription services and ad supported entertainment"; access to many of the company's artists' greatest hits

### EXHIBIT 2    Change in Spotify's Number of Paying Subscribers, 2010–2013

|                                | 2010 | 2011 | 2012 | 2013 | 2012–2013 Change |
|--------------------------------|------|------|------|------|------------------|
| Number of paying subscribers   | 8m   | 13m  | 20m  | 28m  | +40%             |

*Source:* online.wsj.com/news/articles/SB10001424052702304791704579212152163448852.

was included on stock mobile phones, and an agreement was made with Amazon to sell MP3s, which were compatible with iPods and other MP3 players. All this was accompanied by the promise in Sony's 2008 annual report that the company would maximize the potential of the digital distribution age.

A change in strategy came on October 1, 2009, when Sony Music Entertainment became a wholly owned subsidiary of Sony Corporation. Previously, the company had been a 50-50 joint venture with Bertelsmann AG, but the remaining 50 percent stake was acquired by Sony for $1.2 billion. This was done to lower costs through increased efficiency, and, according to Sony's 2009 annual report, it was envisioned that the acquisition would allow the company to work more effectively with the electronics, game, and pictures businesses.

## VEVO

In December 2009, Sony Music entered into a joint venture with Abu Dhabi Media and Universal Music Group to form VEVO, a music video licensor and aggregator. The videos were uploaded by VEVO, and users viewed and listened for free as advertisements scrolled simultaneously. The company operated at a loss in 2010 and 2011, but it was projected to be profitable sometime in the middle of 2012, with revenue jumping from $150 million in 2011 to $280 million in 2012. In 2013, VEVO had 227 million viewers from 13 countries and 5.5 billion monthly video views. The company had seen a transition from videos being viewed on smart TVs and computers to 65 percent of videos being viewed on mobile phones. The company was valued at $500 million in 2013.

## Music Unlimited

In December 2010, Sony Music announced Music Unlimited, a cloud-based music streaming service powered by Qriocity, the company's video distribution platform. Music Unlimited had a library of approximately 15 million songs and allowed both radio and interactive streaming capabilities. In January 2012, Music Unlimited had more than 1 million active users. Sony was not the first to develop a cloud-based music listening service, so the company made use of its market share in consumer electronics to bundle the software with Sony-made devices, like gaming systems, Blu-ray players, and TVs, in order to gain an initial audience. Holding true to the strategy of October 2009, Sony aimed to blend the business of Sony Music Entertainment and Sony Corporation for the sake of efficiency. This strategy paid dividends, with nearly 38 percent of all song streams occurring on Sony's PlayStation 4 gaming device as of January 2014.

On June 15, 2011, Sony introduced the Music Unlimited app for Android-enabled devices; the app was, therefore, compatible with all Sony Corporation tablets and smartphones. Sony Corporation also partnered with various other music services, most notably Pandora and Slacker Radio, whose applications were compatible with Sony TVs, MP3 players, smartphones, and tablets. The Sony Entertainment Network allowed linking of devices, so the same preferences, library, and account could be used on multiple machines.

Upon creation of an account, Music Unlimited provided certain benefits free, with progressive benefits based upon the subscription type. New users were given a free 30-day preview of premium service. There were two subscription levels:

- For $4.99 per month, the basic subscription included Spotify-like full interactive streaming from a consumer's home PC and game console.
- For $9.99 per month, the premium subscription included Spotify-like full interactive streaming from the devices covered in the basic subscription as well as Androids, iPhones, and tablets.

Interestingly, Music Unlimited was not Sony's first attempt at a digital music medium. In December 2001, Sony Music (then Sony Music Entertainment Inc.) and the Universal Music Group began Pressplay, an online, subscription-based music service that allowed tracks to be streamed, downloaded, and burned onto a CD while protecting artists' rights. Pressplay had many of the features that characterized subsequent popular services such as Spotify—for example, playlist sharing and access to music charts and new release information. However, the initiative was discontinued in mid-2003 because of intense criticism of the heavy-handed implementation, shallow variety of music, and inefficient licensing.

Beginning in 2012, under new CEO Kazuo Hirai, Sony launched a four-part plan to save the company, which was hemorrhaging cash. Hirai wanted to focus the company on its core business, which he identified as gaming, mobile products, and digital imaging, while curtailing the company's diverse business portfolio and exiting the LCD TV market. In 2012, Sony Publishing completed the purchase of EMI

Music Publishing for $2.2 billion. The purchase gave Sony Publishing access to 1.3 million songs, raising its total to over 2 million songs. In 2012 and 2013, Sony sold Gracenote, an ownership stake in M3, and Sony Chemical.

Sony Corporation's revenues from the sale of music increased from ¥441.7 billion in 2012 to ¥503.3 billion in 2013, and its operating income for the division increased from ¥37.2 billion to ¥50.2 billion over the same period. This increase in operating income was mainly the result of lower restructuring costs than in previous years and growth in digital revenue. A summary of Sony Corporation's financial performance between 2009 and 2013 is presented in Exhibit 3. Exhibit 4 presents the revenue and operating profit contributions for Sony Corporation's various divisions for 2011 through 2013.

## COMPETITION IN THE DIGITAL MUSIC INDUSTRY

In the record label business in 2014, Sony Records was second in terms of market share, with 20 percent.

Universal Music Group boasted a slight edge at 25.5 percent, and Warner Music Group lagged somewhat behind, with 11.6 percent. The Big Three music companies collectively held 57.1 percent of the industry market share. In music publishing, the same players held 35.9 percent of the industry market share: Sony/ATV had 16.9 percent; Universal Music Group, 13.9 percent; and Warner Music Group, 5.1 percent. In 2013, Universal Music Group (a 100% Vivendi subsidiary) had revenues of $6.7 billion and employed 6,500 employees. On November 11, 2011, Vivendi announced that it had signed a definitive agreement to purchase EMI's recorded music division for $1.9 billion, which was seven times EBITDA prior to synergies.

## Mobile Applications

In the age of data streaming and smartphones, mobile application downloads were an apt way to track the success of services. For comparison with the ratings below, Clash of Clans, the most popular free app in the Apple Store in 2014, received 752,024 ratings with an average of 4.5 stars.

**EXHIBIT 3**   Financial Summary for Sony Corporation, 2009–2013 (in millions of yen, except per share amounts)

| | 2013 | 2012 | 2011 | 2010 | 2009 |
|---|---|---|---|---|---|
| Sales and operating revenue | ¥6,800,851 | ¥6,493,212 | ¥7,181,273 | ¥7,213,998 | ¥7,729,993 |
| Operating income | 230,100 | −67,275 | 199,821 | 31,772 | −227,783 |
| Income (loss) before income taxes | 245,681 | −83,186 | 205,013 | 26,912 | −174,955 |
| Income taxes | 141,505 | 315,239 | 425,339 | 13,958 | −72,741 |
| Net income (loss) attributable to Sony Corporation's stockholders | ¥43,034 | −¥456,660 | −¥259,585 | −¥40,802 | −¥98,938 |
| Data per share of common stock: | | | | | |
| Basic | ¥42.80 | −¥455.03 | −¥258.66 | −¥40.66 | −¥98.59 |
| Diluted | ¥40.19 | −¥455.03 | −¥258.66 | −¥40.66 | −¥98.59 |
| Cash dividends | ¥25.00 | ¥25.00 | ¥25.00 | ¥25.00 | ¥42.50 |
| **At year-end** | | | | | |
| Net working capital (deficit) | −¥668,556 | −¥775,019 | −¥291,253 | ¥64,627 | −¥190,265 |
| Long-term debt | 938,428 | 762,226 | 812,235 | 924,207 | 660,147 |
| Sony Corporation's stockholders' equity | 2,197,766 | 2,028,891 | 2,547,987 | 2,965,905 | 2,964,653 |
| Common stock | 630,923 | 630,923 | 630,921 | 630,822 | 630,765 |
| Total assets | 14,206,383 | 13,295,667 | 12,911,122 | 12,862,624 | 11,983,480 |

*Source:* Sony Corporation 2013 annual report.

- *Pandora.* Pandora received 811,124 ratings with an average of 4 stars at the Apple Store and 1,428,724 ratings with an average of 4.5 stars at Google Play in 2013. As of the first quarter of 2014, Pandora had over 250 million registered users, who listened to 4.8 billion hours of music, and had total revenue of $194.3 million. Pandora had been downloaded more than 1 billion times and claimed 73.6 percent of the market share of streaming Internet radio listening in 2013.

- *Music Unlimited.* At $9.99 per month, Music Unlimited was far less popular than Pandora. It received 688 ratings with an average of 3 stars at the Apple Store and 24,029 ratings with an average of 3.7 stars at Google Play. Music Unlimited had approximately 10 million downloads by 2014.

- *Spotify.* Spotify had 303,200 ratings with an average of 4.5 stars at the Apple Store and 568,870 ratings with an average of 4 stars at Google Play in 2013. It was estimated that Spotify had been downloaded more than 100 million times by 2014. In May 2014, Spotify had over 24 million active users, 5 million of whom were paying for the interactive streaming service. The company was based in Sweden and operated globally in 56 countries.

The bulk of an average band's or artist's income in 2013 came from live performances—this was true even for a band like Radiohead, which was able to self-publish a CD that earned almost $3 million. Under such circumstances, the publishing industry still continued to struggle with monetizing streaming music and saw an average annual growth of

## EXHIBIT 4   Sony Corporation's Revenues and Operating Income, by Division, 2012–2013 (in millions of yen)

|  | 2013 | 2012 |
|---|---|---|
| **Sales and operating revenue** | | |
| Mobile Products & Communications | ¥1,257,618 | ¥622,677 |
| Game | 707,078 | 804,966 |
| Imaging Products & Solutions | 756,201 | 785,116 |
| Home Entertainment & Sound | 994,827 | 1,286,261 |
| Devices | 848,575 | 1,026,568 |
| Pictures | 732,739 | 657,721 |
| Music | 441,708 | 442,789 |
| Financial Services | 1,002,389 | 868,661 |
| All other, corporate and eliminations | 59,716 | −1,547 |
| Consolidated | ¥6,800,851 | ¥6,493,212 |
| **Operating income** | | |
| Mobile Products & Communications | −¥97,170 | ¥7,246 |
| Game | 1,735 | 29,302 |
| Imaging Products & Solutions | 1,442 | 19,641 |
| Home Entertainment & Sound | −84,315 | −199,461 |
| Devices | 43,895 | −22,126 |
| Pictures | 47,800 | 34,130 |
| Music | 37,218 | 36,887 |
| Financial Services | 142,209 | 129,283 |
| All other, corporate and eliminations | 137,286 | −102,177 |
| Consolidated | ¥230,100 | −¥67,275 |

*Source:* Sony Corporation 2013 annual report.

negative 3.8 percent from 2008 to 2013. This was only slightly better than the performance of its big-brother industry, record labels, which recorded a negative 4.3 percent growth rate from 2009 to 2014. Prior to CD duplication and digital distribution, consumers either paid the price to hear the entire album (even if they liked only five songs on it) or didn't hear the music at all. In the same scenario in 2014, consumers were likely to simply download the music illegally from a file-sharing site. The small number of people who purchased music legitimately would buy only the five songs they liked.

Whatever the model of access to music, something that seemingly was dropped by the wayside was remuneration of artists. In an industry where the consumer was becoming increasingly important, it was equally important for record labels like Sony Music Entertainment to keep in mind that without the promise of profitability, sustainability, and means of financial support, artists might return to their roots, heavily focused on live performances, whereby the product was much harder to steal. The stimulation and motivation for an artist to record a song decreased significantly if there was no way to support oneself financially, and, although the world would never stop making music, profitability incentives and disincentives were just as real in the music industry as they were in any other industry that produced a product for sale.

Although the way of the future seemed to be interactive streaming and Internet radio funded by subscription or advertisements, there was much debate in the music community about the effects that such a shift would have on the industry. Streaming services were growing very rapidly, as evidenced by the success of a wide variety of new services and the continued decreases in physical and digital CD sales. While these services were growing rapidly, in 2014 they still represented only 6.6 percent of the total revenue to labels and even less to the average artist. A subscriber had no idea where his or her $9.99 subscription went, but it certainly didn't go straight to the artist. Label agreements with artists were traditionally confidential, so it was difficult to discern exactly how much money was being transferred to the original creators of the product, that is, the music. This was why many popular artists, such as Coldplay, Adele, and the Black Keys, resisted or even denied access to their music through subscription-based services.

However, despite the downside risk of the shift in the way that music was monetized, subscription services still represented significant opportunity. They were much more accessible and convenient to the consumer than was purchasing an MP3, and such convenience represented an addition in value. Additions in value were typically commensurate with an increase in demand and therefore an increase in revenue, and most agreed that an increase in the "revenue pie" of the industry would help solve problems. Subscription services also proved to be helpful to new bands whose focus was more on promotion and development of a fan base than on immediate profit. Exploring new music on a Pandora radio station or through the Related Artists feature on Spotify was much more accessible, as it was not necessary to purchase each individual song. Streaming had also proved to be an excellent medium for advertising and publicity for concerts, downloads, and merchandise.

Rhapsody, a subscription service available only in the United States, had been around for nearly 10 years and had experienced slow, steady growth. Rhapsody had been stagnant at 800,000 subscribers for several years, but in December 2011, the company experienced tremendous growth, hitting 1 million paying customers for the first time. Since the large increase, Rhapsody made only incremental gains, reaching an estimated 1.2 million subscribers in 2013. With Spotify and other streaming services posting wild growth increases, the only question was the sustainability of such increases.

According to David Hyman, CEO of Beats Music and former CEO of MOG (a popular interactive streaming service that shut down in 2014), an average iTunes user spent $40 a year on music, the average American spent $17 a year on music, and premium subscribers to MOG paid $120. Hyman attested, "When it comes to individual deals between artists and labels, I do know that the content owners, the labels and the publishers are getting a lot more money out of these subscription services than they're getting from iTunes." Like iTunes, MOG had forwarded an average of 65 percent of income to labels.

In another interesting use of technology to monetize music, Denison Witmer, a solo artist who got his start playing with Sufjan Stevens, began what he called an "Everywhere at Once" tour in 2012. By paying $25 at his website, fans were able to order a personal show of one to two songs played by Witmer himself live from his kitchen over Skype or Apple's FaceTime.

In terms of forecasting the future of the music industry, the movie industry offered some clues, especially with services like VEVO and YouTube blurring the line between video and music. Quite recently, Netflix superseded physical DVD stores, driving companies like Blockbuster and Movie Gallery to Chapter 11 bankruptcy in September 2010 and February 2010, respectively.

In the words of Sony founder Masaru Ibuka, "Creativity comes from looking for the unexpected and stepping outside your own experience."[2] Sony as a company showed great innovation and clever execution in the past, earning a significant market share in many diffuse markets, both in terms of geography and in terms of products. The question of the future was always: How would the current position be used to press forward?

## ENDNOTES

[1] As quoted in a Sony Corporation press release, March 2, 2011.

[2] Quote from Masaru Ibuka at quotes.lifehack .org.

# Vera Bradley in 2014: Will the Company's Strategy Reverse Its Downward Trend? McGraw Hill Education connect

## David L. Turnipseed
University of South Alabama

## John E. Gamble
Texas A&M University–Corpus Christi

Vera Bradley had grown rapidly since the mid-2000s with a strategy keyed to offering a distinctive line of colorful, patterned women's luggage, handbags, and accessories sold in department stores, in company-owned full-price retail stores and factory outlet stores, and over the Internet. As the mid-2010s approached, the company's standing seemed less certain as competition intensified in the market for ladies' handbags and accessories. Its meteoric growth had stalled in fiscal 2014, with revenues slipping by only 1 percent but net income declining by nearly 15 percent. This decline in revenues and profits came on the heels of the company's rollout of its new strategic plan in early 2014 that would focus the company on a product line of a limited assortment of the highest-quality ladies' handbags and accessories, expanded distribution channels with an emphasis on outlets and e-commerce, and an enhanced marketing approach.

The strategic plan appeared to match the company's external market conditions and internal situation, but it provided little uniqueness since Vera Bradley's rivals were all competing with similar strategies. Vera Bradley's management believed that the quality of the plan, coupled with the company's management expertise, would yield a competitive advantage. Robert Wallstrom, Vera Bradley's chief executive officer, commented shortly after the new strategic plan was announced that the company's strategies and talented and seasoned team of retail executives would reverse the company's recent decline in revenue and profits and return it to an impressive growth trajectory.

## COMPANY HISTORY

The inspiration for Vera Bradley occurred in 1982 when two traveling friends, Barbara Bradley Baekgaard and Patricia Miller, observed that passersby in the Hartsfield Atlanta International Airport all had similar, bland luggage and that a market for colorful, stylish luggage might exist. Almost immediately upon their return to Fort Wayne, Indiana, the two women began creating colorful, quilted fabric duffel bags from their homes. They named the company after Barbara Baekgaard's mother, Vera Bradley, and initially focused only on duffel bags, handbags, and sports bags.

As consumer interest in the brand grew, the company developed additional assortments of patterns and products to reach a broader range of customers. The focus of the company's merchandising was changed to highlight Vera Bradley as a lifestyle brand. The company enhanced its marketing function to work collaboratively with the design group in 2012 to improve the product development to market process. In 2014, the company designed, manufactured, marketed, and retailed accessories for women, including luggage, purses, wallets, cell phone and computer covers, jewelry, a wide variety of bags, lunch sacks, scarves, beach accessories, and baby clothing.

As the company grew, Vera Bradley's management realized the importance of a strong infrastructure and began strengthening its supply chain capabilities and IT systems early on. These improvements resulted in significant cost savings and a more flexible and scalable operating structure. In 2005, the company shifted its production from primarily domestic manufacturing to global sourcing, which was substantially more cost-effective. A new state-of-the-art distribution facility was built in Roanoke, Indiana, in 2007 and was expanded in 2013 to approximately 400,000 square feet, which was double its original size.

Vera Bradley's products were initially sold wholesale to department stores and other retailers specializing in women's accessories. The company also maintained specialty retailer accounts that marketed Vera Bradley bags and other distinctive items as corporate gifts. By 2014, the company's products were sold through indirect department store and specialty retailer channels and through direct channels that included the Internet, full-price retail stores, and factory outlet stores. As of February 2014, the company had about 3,100 indirect retail partners, with about 30 percent of the indirect retailers accounting for over 70 percent of the indirect revenue in 2013. The company entered into direct sales in 2006 with the launch of an e-commerce site in the United States, and in 2007 it opened its first retail store. The company operated 84 full-price retail stores in the United States in 2014. Vera Bradley retail stores were about 1,800 square feet in size and were designed to reflect the casual comfort of a home. The company also operated 15 factory outlet stores in the United States and 7 full-price retail stores in Japan. Vera Bradley also launched an e-commerce site in Japan in 2012.

Vera Bradley executed its initial public offering in October 2010 and was listed on the NASDAQ with the symbol "VRA." According to Vera Bradley's management, the company's direct competitors were manufacturers and marketers of handbags and accessories, such as Coach, Michael Kors, and Kate Spade. Miller and Baekgaard had been honored by the U.S. Small Business Administration as "Outstanding Women Entrepreneurs" and by the Indiana Historical Society as "Indiana Living Legends." The Vera Bradley Foundation for Breast Cancer had pledged over $35 million to the Indiana University Melvin and Bren Simon Cancer Center to support cancer research. Exhibit 1 presents a financial summary for Vera Bradley for fiscal 2010 through fiscal 2014. The company's balance sheets for fiscal 2013 and fiscal 2014 are presented in Exhibit 2.

## OVERVIEW OF THE HANDBAG AND LEATHER ACCESSORIES MARKET IN 2014

The handbag and leather accessories market was estimated about $96 billion in 2013, with the largest markets being the United States with 36 percent of industry sales, Europe with 21 percent of industry sales, Japan with 16 percent of industry sales, and China with 11 percent of industry sales. The retail market for global luxury goods was affected significantly by general economic

**EXHIBIT 1**    Financial Summary for Vera Bradley, Inc., Fiscal 2010–Fiscal 2014 (dollar amounts in thousands, except per share and store data)

| | Fiscal Year Ended | | | | |
|---|---|---|---|---|---|
| | February 1, 2014 | February 2, 2013 | January 28, 2012 | January 29, 2011 | January 29, 2010 |
| **Consolidated statement of income data** | | | | | |
| Net revenues | $536,021 | $541,148 | $460,843 | $366,057 | $288,940 |
| Cost of sales | 240,589 | 232,867 | 203,220 | 156,910 | 137,803 |
| Gross profit | 295,432 | 308,281 | 257,623 | 209,147 | 151,137 |
| Selling, general, and administrative expenses | 205,957 | 204,412 | 169,427 | 163,053 | 116,168 |
| Other income | 4,776 | 6,277 | 7,975 | 7,225 | 10,743 |
| Operating income | 94,251 | 110,146 | 96,171 | 53,319 | 45,712 |
| Interest expense, net | 382 | 679 | 1,147 | 1,625 | 1,604 |

*(Continued)*

## EXHIBIT 1 (Continued)

| | Fiscal Year Ended | | | | |
|---|---|---|---|---|---|
| | February 1, 2014 | February 2, 2013 | January 28, 2012 | January 29, 2011 | January 29, 2010 |
| Income before income taxes | 93,869 | 109,467 | 95,024 | 51,694 | 44,108 |
| Income tax expense | 35,057 | 40,597 | 37,103 | 5,496 | 889 |
| Net income | $ 58,812 | $ 68,870 | $ 57,921 | $ 46,198 | $ 43,219 |
| Basic weighted-average shares outstanding | 40,599 | 40,536 | 40,507 | 36,813 | 35,441 |
| Diluted weighted-average shares outstanding | 40,648 | 40,571 | 40,542 | 36,851 | 35,441 |
| Basic net income per share | $1.45 | $1.70 | $1.43 | $1.25 | $1.22 |
| Diluted net income per share | 1.45 | 1.70 | 1.43 | 1.25 | 1.22 |
| **Net revenues by segment** | | | | | |
| Direct | $326,217 | $ 292,564 | $225,287 | $ 151,118 | $ 96,111 |
| Indirect | 209,804 | 248,584 | 235,556 | 214,939 | 192,829 |
| Total | $536,021 | $ 541,148 | $460,843 | $366,057 | $288,940 |
| **Store data** | | | | | |
| Total stores open at end of year | 99 | 76 | 56 | 39 | 27 |
| Comparable-store sales (decrease) increase | (5.7)% | 3.4% | 10.9% | 25.8% | 36.4% |
| Total gross square footage at end of year | 207,096 | 156,310 | 113,504 | 74,426 | 50,506 |
| Average net revenues per gross square foot | $887 | $1,083 | $1,042 | $851 | $615 |
| **Consolidated balance sheet data** | | | | | |
| Cash and cash equivalents | $ 59,215 | $ 9,603 | $ 4,922 | $ 13,953 | $ 6,509 |
| Working capital | 186,543 | 145,641 | 106,234 | 91,919 | 61,238 |
| Total assets | 332,927 | 277,319 | 219,513 | 206,039 | 153,752 |
| Long-term debt, including current portion | — | 15,095 | 25,184 | 67,017 | 30,136 |
| Shareholders' equity | 255,147 | 194,255 | 124,007 | 64,322 | 77,893 |

*Source:* Vera Bradley, Inc., 10-K report, 2014.

conditions, with consumers curtailing expenditures for luxury goods in general during recessions and economic slowdowns. For example, the poor general economic conditions between 2006 and 2010 contributed to a 0.6 percent annual decline in industry sales during those years. Continued growth in China and other emerging markets was expected to allow luxury goods sales to increase by 7.8 percent annually through 2015 and reach a staggering $350 billion.

*Euromonitor* predicted that by 2018, the Asia-Pacific region would be the largest market in the world for luxury goods. This growth was due primarily to China but also to other emerging Asian markets such as Indonesia, Malaysia, and India. Emerging markets, especially China and India, were expected to provide a major boost to the luxury goods market because of rapidly increasing wealth levels and standard-of-living gains. China surpassed Japan in 2010 as the third-largest luxury market, with sales of luxury goods approaching $32 billion. The Chinese market for luxury goods was predicted to increase substantially over the next several years, which would make it possibly the world's largest market for luxury goods.

**EXHIBIT 2**  Vera Bradley, Inc.'s Balance Sheets, Fiscal 2013–Fiscal 2014 (in thousands)

| | Fiscal Year Ended | |
| --- | --- | --- |
| | February 1, 2014 | February 2, 2013 |
| **Assets** | | |
| Current assets: | | |
| Cash and cash equivalents | $ 59,215 | $ 9,603 |
| Accounts receivable, net | 27,718 | 34,811 |
| Inventories | 136,923 | 131,562 |
| Prepaid expenses and other current assets | 9,952 | 11,016 |
| Deferred income taxes | 13,094 | 11,348 |
| Total current assets | 246,902 | 198,340 |
| Property, plant, and equipment, net | 84,940 | 77,211 |
| Other assets | 1,085 | 1,768 |
| Total assets | $332,927 | $277,319 |
| **Liabilities and shareholders' equity** | | |
| Current liabilities: | $ 27,745 | $ 14,853 |
| Accrued employment costs | 10,586 | 14,162 |
| Other accrued liabilities | 20,403 | 16,532 |
| Income taxes payable | 1,625 | 7,094 |
| Current portion of long-term debt | — | 58 |
| Total current liabilities | 60,359 | 52,699 |
| Long-term debt | — | 15,037 |
| Deferred income taxes | 4,643 | 6,078 |
| Other long-term liabilities | 12,778 | 9,250 |
| Total liabilities | 77,780 | 83,064 |
| Commitments and contingencies | | |
| Shareholders' equity: | | |
| Preferred stock; 5,000 shares authorized, no shares issued or outstanding | — | — |
| Common stock; without par value; 200,000 shares authorized, 40,607 and 40,563 shares issued and outstanding, respectively | — | — |
| Additional paid-in capital | 78,153 | 75,675 |
| Retained earnings | 178,002 | 119,190 |
| Accumulated other comprehensive loss | (1,008) | (610) |
| Total shareholders' equity | 255,147 | 194,255 |
| Total liabilities and shareholders' equity | $332,927 | $277,319 |

*Source:* Vera Bradley, Inc., 10-K report, 2014.

The most valuable luxury leather-goods brands in terms of annual revenues were Louis Vuitton, Gucci, Hermès, and Cartier. Luxury brands, in general, relied on creative designs, high quality, and brand reputation to attract customers and build brand loyalty. Price sensitivity for luxury goods was driven by brand exclusivity, customer-centric marketing, and, to a large extent, some emotional sense of status

and value. The market for luxury goods was divided into three main categories: haute couture, traditional luxury, and the growing submarket "accessible luxury." The apex of the market was haute couture with its very high-end "custom" product offering that catered to the extremely wealthy. Leading brands in the traditional-luxury category included such fashion design houses as Prada, Burberry, Hermès,

Gucci, Polo Ralph Lauren, Calvin Klein, and Louis Vuitton. Some of these luxury goods makers also broadened their appeal with diffusion lines in the accessible-luxury market to compete with Coach, DKNY, and other lesser luxury brands. For example, while Dolce & Gabbana (D&G) dresses sold for $1,000 to $1,500, dresses of similar appearance under the D&G affordable luxury brand were priced at $400 to $600. Giorgio Armani's Emporio Armani line and Gianni Versace's Versus lines typically sold for about 50 percent less than similar-looking items carrying the marquee labels.

Profit margins on marquee brands approximated 40 to 50 percent, while most diffusion brands carried profit margins of about 20 percent. Luxury goods manufacturers believed that the diffusion brands' lower profit margins were offset by the opportunity for increased sales volume, the growing size of the accessible-luxury market, and the protected margins available on such products by sourcing production to low-wage countries. In 2013, Bain & Company reported that online sales were continuing to grow faster than the rest of the market, with 28 percent annual growth for the year, reaching almost $14 billion. Online sales were about 5 percent of total luxury sales and more than the luxury sales for Germany.

Industry sales in the United States had become more dependent on the success of diffusion lines in the accessible-luxury category. Although primary traditional-luxury consumers in the United States were among the top 1 percent of wage earners, with household incomes of $300,000 or more, consumers who earned substantially less also aspired to own products with higher levels of quality and styling. The growing desire for luxury goods among middle-income consumers was thought to be a result of a wide range of factors, including effective advertising and television programming that promoted conspicuous consumption. The demanding day-to-day rigor of a two-income household was another factor, suggested as urging middle-income consumers to reward themselves with luxuries. An additional factor contributing to rising sales of luxury goods in the United States was the "trade up, trade down"[1] shopping strategy, whereby consumers would balance their spending by offsetting gains made with lower-priced necessities purchased at major retailers (e.g., Walmart and Target) to enable more discretionary spending for luxury goods.

# VERA BRADLEY'S STRATEGIC PLAN FOR 2015–2019

In March 2014, Vera Bradley announced a comprehensive five-year strategic plan designed to improve the company's competitive standing, financial performance, and long-term shareholder value. The company's plan focused on three key areas: product, distribution channels, and marketing.

## Product Strategy

Vera Bradley's major product categories in 2014 were handbags; accessories such as wallets, wristlets, eyeglass cases, cosmetics cases, and paper and gifts; and travel and leisure items such as duffel bags, garment bags, rolling luggage, and travel cosmetics cases. The company's new strategic emphasis was on improving its product assortment by focusing on its core designs, with "halo" products used to expand price points without creating an overly broad product line. The strategy would put the greatest focus on the company's strongest product categories such as travel, backpacks, bags, and accessories. However, the company planned to invest in emerging growth and brand-enhancing opportunities that would strengthen the future product core, such as scarves and jewelry. Management also intended to add products targeted to career-focused women to expand the customer base.

Vera Bradley planned to limit the number of signature patterns launched each year and add more solids to the pattern assortment to better showcase the signature patterns. The company's product release strategy involved the introduction of two to four patterns per season that were used in each of its key product categories. Production of poor-selling patterns was to be quickly discontinued, with remaining inventory sold through the company's website, outlet stores, and annual outlet sale. Also, management decided to develop new products with a predetermined life cycle in mind and alter product launch campaigns based on the potential of the product. In prior years, all products utilized a similar launch strategy and were intended to be marketed as long as demand permitted. The percentage of Vera Bradley's net revenues accounted for by each major product category for fiscal 2012 through fiscal 2014 is presented in Exhibit 3.

**EXHIBIT 3**   Vera Bradley's Net Revenue Contributions, by Major Product Category, Fiscal 2012–Fiscal 2014

| | Fiscal Year Ended | | |
| --- | --- | --- | --- |
| | February 1, 2014 | February 2, 2013 | January 28, 2012 |
| Handbags | 40.0% | 40.4% | 43.1% |
| Accessories | 30.1 | 31.7 | 32.2 |
| Travel and leisure items | 14.8 | 14.7 | 15.2 |
| Other* | 15.1 | 13.2 | 9.5 |
| Total† | 100.0% | 100.0% | 100.0% |

*Includes primarily home, merchandising, freight, and licensing revenues.

†Excludes net revenues generated by the annual outlet sale.

*Source:* Vera Bradley, Inc., 10-K report, 2014.

## Distribution Channels

Vera Bradley's strategic plan intended to utilize a tightly integrated multichannel distribution strategy that included department stores and specialty retailers, full-line stores, factory outlet stores, and e-commerce. The company believed that its legacy gift channel would remain important, but it planned to reduce the product assortment in the channel. Vera Bradley's long-term strategic objective was to expand to 300 full-price retail stores and 100 factory outlet stores. Vera Bradley planned to add 13 new full-line stores in fiscal 2015 and accelerate that pace, beginning in fiscal 2016, to add approximately 20 to 25 new stores per year for at least the next four years. The company also planned to add at least seven new outlet stores in fiscal 2015. Management believed that the company could accelerate this growth rate going forward to approximately 10 to 15 new stores per year for at least the next four years. Within three years, the company expected that approximately 40 percent of the products sold in factory outlet stores would be designed specifically for the outlet channel. Management expected that 70 percent of the factory outlet items would be unique to the factory outlet channel by 2019. The company believed this made-for-outlet (MFO) strategy would boost gross margins in the factory outlet channel.

E-commerce was also intended to be a key distribution channel and provide support for the Vera Bradley brand and marketing strategies. The goal was for the e-commerce experience to mirror the in-store shopping experience by segregating the full-line and factory outlet products onto different sites. The company placed greater focus on department store relationships and continued to explore other expansion opportunities in department store space, especially since department stores were the largest handbag channel for career professionals.

## Marketing

The marketing objective for the company was to make Vera Bradley an aspirational brand for consumers and to generate excitement around new product launches. The company hoped that its marketing approach would expand its customer base while strengthening its connections with loyal customers. The majority of its advertising expenditures were to be allocated to fresh, new products and halo assortments building upon the brand equity of established lines. The company believed its iconic products and styles needed little reinforcement with consumers through additional advertising expenditures. Its brand-building efforts were focused primarily on advertising in ladies' fashion magazines, direct-mail and digital communications, and database analytics to better personalize communications with consumers.

# VERA BRADLEY'S COMPETITIVE RESOURCES AND CAPABILITIES

Vera Bradley's new strategy was based on competencies that were closely related to success in the markets for handbags, luggage, and women's accessories. The company believed it had a well-developed ability to understand the needs and wants of its customers, valuable product design skills, marketing and brand-building expertise, and strong distribution capabilities. Other capabilities that enabled the company's strategy included site-location expertise and manufacturing efficiencies.

## Product Development

Vera Bradley had implemented a fully integrated, cross-functional product development process that aligned its design, market research, merchandise management, sales, marketing, and sourcing functions. The company's product development teams in New York City and Roanoke, Indiana, combined an understanding of target customers' needs with knowledge of approaching color and fashion trends to design new collections as well as totally new product categories that would fit well in their markets. The development cycle for new products for the Vera Bradley portfolio began about 12 to 18 months in advance of their release. Each new pattern included the design of an overall print, a fabric backing that complemented the pattern, and three sizes of coordinating trim materials.

Vera Bradley also collaborated with independent designers to create unique patterns for each season, but the company retained final approval of all patterns and designs. All new patterns, including the print, fabric backing, and coordinating trim, were protected by a copyright. The company believed that great designs were fundamental to its product development and were a central part of its brand development and growth strategies. Vera Bradley routinely updated its classic styles and also actively pursued new lines and brand extensions to increase its product offerings.

Vera Bradley's product development group attended major trend shows in Europe and the United States, subscribed to trend-monitoring services, and engaged in comparison shopping to monitor fashion trends and customer needs. Product development personnel were also responsible for assortment planning, pricing, forecasting, promotional development, and product life-cycle management. Forecasting was based on seasonal market research and in-store testing. Seasonal market data were obtained through seasonal in-store testing by releasing test products in full-price stores and evaluating their success in the marketplace prior to introducing the product on a larger scale.

## Product Launch Process

Vera Bradley introduced two to four new patterns each season that were incorporated into the designs of a wide range of products, including handbags, accessories, and travel and leisure items. The seasonal product assortments could be classic styles, updates of older designs, or totally new product introductions. Patterns were discontinued at regular intervals to keep the assortment current and fresh and to focus the inventory investment on top-performing patterns. The remaining inventory of retired products was sold primarily through the company's website, factory outlet stores, and annual outlet sale.

## Site Location

Vera Bradley's management believed that ample opportunity for expansion existed since none of its geographic markets had been saturated. The company saw expansion of company-operated full-price and factory outlet stores as complementary to its indirect channels since the visibility of Vera Bradley retail stores increased brand awareness and bolstered its brand image. The site-location process involved analyzing area economic conditions, the specific location within a shopping center, the size and shape of the space, and the presence of desirable cotenants. Management attempted to achieve a balanced mix of moderate and high-end retailers and cotenants that shared Vera Bradley's target customers to encourage high levels of traffic. The ideal full-price store size was about 1,800 square feet, but the company could work with spaces as small as 1,000 square feet. Depending on the market strategy and relevant economic factors, spaces as large as 2,800 square feet could be used.

Opening expenses for new locations averaged about $400,000 to provide for space renovation costs, initial inventory, and preopening expenses. New full-price stores generated, on average, between

$1.2 million and $1.4 million in net revenues during the first 12 months. The typical payback period for recovering the company's initial investment in a new location was approximately 18 months.

## PROFILES OF VERA BRADLEY'S CHIEF RIVALS

### Coach, Inc.

In 2013, Coach operated 351 full-price stores and 193 factory outlet stores in North America and maintained over 1,000 wholesale department store accounts. The company operated 191 stores in Japan and 218 stores in other Asian nations. Coach products were also available in 183 locations in other international markets. Coach also operated e-commerce websites in the United States, Canada, Japan, and China and had informational websites in over 20 other countries. Coach viewed its websites as a key communication vehicle for promoting traffic in Coach's retail stores and department store locations and for building brand awareness. With approximately 74 million online visits to its e-commerce websites in fiscal 2013, Coach's online store provided a virtual showcase environment where customers could browse selected offerings of the latest styles and colors. Coach's e-commerce strategy also included invitation-only factory flash

sites and third-party flash sites. In addition to its direct retail businesses, Coach had built a strong presence globally through Coach boutiques located within select department stores and specialty retailer locations in North America and through distributor-operated shops in Asia, Latin America, the Middle East, Australia, and Europe.

Coach was one of the most recognized fine-accessories brands in the United States and in its targeted international markets. The company offered attractively priced, premium lifestyle accessories to a loyal and growing customer base, and it provided consumers with well-made, appealing, and innovative products. Coach's product offerings of fine accessories and gifts for women and men included handbags, men's bags, women's and men's small leather goods, footwear, outerwear, watches, weekend and travel accessories, scarves, sunwear, fragrances, jewelry, and related accessories. Continuing development of new categories had further established the signature style and distinctive identity of the Coach brand. With its licensing partners, the company offered watches, footwear, eyewear, and fragrances bearing the Coach brand name in select department stores and specialty retailer locations.

Coach's high-fashion ladies' handbags and accessories were manufactured using a wide range of high-quality leathers, fabrics, and materials. Responding to customer demands for both fashion and function,

**EXHIBIT 4**   Financial Summary for Coach, Inc., Fiscal 2009–Fiscal 2013 (dollar amounts in thousands, except per share data)

|  | Fiscal Year Ended | | | | |
|---|---|---|---|---|---|
|  | June 29, 2013 | June 30, 2012 | July 2, 2011 | July 3, 2010 | June 27, 2009 |
| Net sales | $5,075,390 | $4,763,180 | $4,158,507 | $3,607,636 | $3,230,468 |
| Gross profit | 3,698,148 | 3,466,078 | 3,023,541 | 2,633,691 | 2,322,610 |
| Selling, general, and expenses | 2,173,607 | 1,954,089 | 1,718,617 | 1,483,520 | 1,350,697 |
| Operating income | 1,524,541 | 1,511,989 | 1,304,924 | 1,150,171 | 971,913 |
| Net income | 1,034,420 | 1,038,910 | 880,800 | 734,940 | 623,369 |
| Net income: |  |  |  |  |  |
| Per basic share | $3.66 | $3.60 | $2.99 | $2.36 | $1.93 |
| Per diluted share | 3.61 | 3.53 | 2.92 | 2.33 | 1.91 |
| Weighted-average basic shares outstanding | 282,494 | 288,284 | 294,877 | 311,413 | 323,714 |
| Weighted-average diluted shares outstanding | 286,307 | 294,129 | 301,558 | 315,848 | 325,620 |
| Dividends declared per common share | $1.238 | $0.975 | $0.675 | $0.375 | $0.075 |

*Source:* Coach Inc., 10-K report, 2013.

Coach offered updated styles and several product categories that met an increasing share of its customers' accessory needs. The company created a sophisticated, modern, and appealing environment to showcase its product collection and reinforce its brand position. The company used a flexible, cost-effective global sourcing model, with independent manufacturers supplying its products, which allowed Coach to get its broad line of products to market rapidly and cost-efficiently.

**Coach's Strategic Initiatives in 2014** Coach's strategic plan was to sustain growth in the global business by focusing on four key strategic initiatives. The company planned to move from a leading international accessories company to a global lifestyle brand encompassing a wide range of accessories for men and women. Coach management believed that men's products, particularly in North America and Asia, created a unique growth opportunity. Coach capitalized on men's products by opening new stand-alone and dual-gender stores and broadening the men's assortment in existing stores. The company also intended to raise brand awareness and market share in markets where Coach was underpenetrated, most notably in Europe, Asia, and Central and South America. Finally, the company planned to accelerate the development of its digital programs and capabilities in North America and worldwide, reflecting the changing global consumer shopping behavior.

Coach believed that these growth strategies would allow the company to produce superior long-term returns on its investments and increased cash flows from operating activities. Coach's management realized that intensified competition, the promotional environment, and the current macroeconomic environment had created a challenging retail market. The company believed that sustained, long-term growth could be achieved by strict cost control, a focus on innovation to enhance productivity, and a brand transformation that would include expanded product offerings and additional distribution. A summary of the company's financial performance for fiscal 2009 through fiscal 2013 is presented in Exhibit 4.

## Michael Kors Holdings

In 2014, Michael Kors was among the leading American luxury lifestyle brands, with sales in 74 countries and a product line focused on handbags, accessories, footwear, and apparel. The company's design team was personally led by Michael Kors, who directed the team in conceptualizing and designing all of the company's products. Michael Kors had been recognized with numerous awards, including the Council of Fashion Designers (CFDA) Women's Fashion Designer of the Year (1999), the CFDA Men's Fashion Designer of the Year (2003), the Accessories Council Excellence (ACE) Accessory Designer of the Year (2006), and the CFDA Lifetime Achievement (2010) awards.

Michael Kors's strategy involved the design, manufacturing, and marketing of two primary collections: the Michael Kors luxury collection and the MICHAEL Michael Kors accessible-luxury collection. The Michael Kors luxury line was introduced in 1981 and was sold in the company's retail stores and in luxury department stores throughout the world, including Bergdorf Goodman, Saks Fifth Avenue, Neiman Marcus, Holt Renfrew, Harrods, Harvey Nichols, and Printemps. The Michael Kors collection included accessories, handbags, footwear, and apparel, including ready-to-wear and small leather goods. The MICHAEL Michael Kors accessible-luxury line was added in 2004 to capitalize on the brand strength of the Michael Kors collection in order to meet the significant demand for moderately priced luxury goods. Although the MICHAEL Michael Kors collection was focused on accessories, it also offered footwear and apparel and was designed to appeal to younger customers. The MICHAEL Michael Kors collection was carried in the company's lifestyle stores as well as in leading department stores throughout the world, including Bloomingdale's, Nordstrom, Macy's, Harrods, Harvey Nichols, Galeries Lafayette, Lotte, Hyundai, Isetan, and Lane Crawford.

As of 2014, Michael Kors operated in three market segments: retail, wholesale, and licensing. In fiscal 2013, the retail segment accounted for approximately 48.7 percent of total revenue. As of March 30, 2013, the retail segment included 231 retail stores in North America and 73 international retail stores in Europe and Japan. The wholesale segment comprised about 2,215 department and specialty stores in North America and approximately 1,034 international department and specialty stores. In fiscal 2013, licensing produced approximately 4 percent of total revenue and consisted primarily of royalties on licensed products and geographic licenses. A financial summary for Michael Kors Holdings for fiscal 2010–fiscal 2014 is presented in Exhibit 5. The exhibit also presents the number of stores at the end of each period and comparable-store sales growth per year for 2010 through 2014.

**Michael Kors's Strategic Initiatives in 2014**
Michael Kors's business strategy was focused on increasing brand awareness, expanding the retail store base in North America, increasing comparable-store sales, and expanding internationally. The company's management planned to increase the North American retail store base to about 400 locations in the long term. Newly added stores were to be located in

**EXHIBIT 5**   Financial Summary for Michael Kors Holdings, Fiscal 2010–Fiscal 2014 (dollar amounts in thousands, except per share and store data)

| | Fiscal Year Ended | | | | |
| --- | --- | --- | --- | --- | --- |
| | March 29, 2014 | March 30, 2013 | March 31, 2012 | April 2, 2011 | April 3, 2010 |
| **Statement of operations data** | | | | | |
| Net sales | $3,170,522 | $2,094,757 | $1,237,100 | $757,800 | $483,452 |
| Licensing revenue | 140,321 | 86,975 | 65,154 | 45,539 | 24,647 |
| Total revenue | 3,310,843 | 2,181,732 | 1,302,254 | 803,339 | 508,099 |
| Cost of goods sold | 1,294,773 | 875,166 | 549,158 | 357,274 | 241,365 |
| Gross profit | 2,016,070 | 1,306,566 | 753,096 | 446,065 | 266,734 |
| Selling, general, and administrative expenses | 926,913 | 621,536 | 464,568 | 279,822 | 191,717 |
| Depreciation and amortization | 79,654 | 54,291 | 37,554 | 25,543 | 18,843 |
| Impairment of long-lived assets | 1,332 | 725 | 3,292 | 3,834 | — |
| Total operating expenses | 1,007,899 | 676,552 | 505,414 | 309,199 | 210,560 |
| Income from operations | 1,008,171 | 630,014 | 247,682 | 136,866 | 56,174 |
| Interest expense, net | 393 | 1,524 | 1,495 | 1,861 | 2,057 |
| Foreign currency loss (gain) | 131 | 1,363 | (2,629) | 1,786 | (830) |
| Income before provision for income taxes | 1,007,647 | 627,127 | 248,816 | 133,219 | 54,947 |
| Provision for income taxes | 346,162 | 229,525 | 101,452 | 60,713 | 15,699 |
| Net income | 661,485 | 397,602 | 147,364 | 72,506 | 39,248 |
| Net income applicable to preference shareholders | — | — | 21,227 | 15,629 | 8,460 |
| Net income available for ordinary shareholders | $    661,485 | $    397,602 | $    126,137 | $    56,877 | $    30,788 |
| Weighted-average ordinary shares outstanding: | | | | | |
| Basic | 202,582,945 | 196,615,054 | 158,258,126 | 140,554,377 | 140,554,377 |
| Diluted | 205,638,107 | 201,540,144 | 189,299,197 | 179,177,268 | 179,177,268 |
| Net income per ordinary share: | | | | | |
| Basic | $3.27 | $2.02 | $0.80 | $0.40 | $0.22 |
| Diluted | $3.22 | $1.97 | $0.78 | $0.40 | $0.22 |
| **Operating data** | | | | | |
| Comparable-retail-store sales growth | 26.2% | 40.1% | 39.2% | 48.2% | 19.2% |
| Retail stores, including concessions, at end of period | 405 | 304 | 237 | 166 | 106 |

*Source:* Michael Kors Holdings, 10-K report, 2014.

high-traffic street and mall locations in high-income demographic areas. The new stores would be consistent with the company's successful retail store formats to reinforce the Michael Kors brand image and generate strong sales per square foot. The company also planned to increase wholesale sales in North America by increasing the number of shop-in-shops. Michael Kors believed that its proprietary shop-in-shop fixtures were effective in projecting its brand image within department stores and enhancing the presentation of Michael Kors merchandise.

The company intended to increase global comparable-store sales by increasing the size and frequency of purchases by existing customers and attracting new customers. Management initiatives to achieve those goals included increasing the size of existing stores, creating more stimulating store environments, and offering new products such as logo products, footwear, small leather goods, and fashion jewelry. Michael Kors planned to continue international expansion in targeted regions in Europe and other international markets and to continue to leverage existing European and Japanese operations to drive continued expansion. Plans included increasing international retail stores, including concessions, wholesale locations, and shop-in-shop conversions at select department stores.

## Kate Spade & Company

Kate Spade, a former accessories editor at *Mademoiselle,* decided in 1993 to launch a company focused on what she believed were the ideal handbag styles. Her initial designs were clustered around just six silhouettes, as she combined sleek, utilitarian shapes and colorful palettes in an entirely new way. In 2014, Kate Spade & Company was organized under three lifestyle brands that were marketed globally through multiple channels. The company's kate spade new york brand was its marquee global brand of ladies' handbags, apparel, and accessories and was sold in company-owned specialty retail stores in the United States and other countries and in U.S. and foreign factory outlet stores. The company's Kate Spade Saturday line was a stylish, casual line of handbags and accessories and was primarily sold in company-owned locations in the United States. The company's Jack Spade brand of men's leather bags and accessories was also primarily sold in the United States. All of the company's brands maintained e-commerce sites for Internet sales. Kate Spade & Company

also owned the Adelington Design Group, a private-brand jewelry design and development group that marketed brands through department stores. The company had owned the Juicy Couture and Lucky Brand apparel businesses, which were divested in late 2013 and early 2014, respectively. The company received $195 million from the sale of Juicy Couture and $225 million from the sale of Lucky Brand. Kate Spade also had a license for the Liz Claiborne New York brand, available at QVC, and Lizwear, which was distributed through the club store channel.

In 2013, total revenue for Kate Spade brands increased by 61 percent, to $743 million. In the fourth quarter of 2013, the company had its 14th consecutive quarter of annualized comparable-store productivity growth and achieved industry-leading growth across categories. The company added new product categories in its kate spade new york stores that included stationery, desk accessories, and fragrances. The company also expanded globally, with new stores in North America, China, Japan, Brazil, Mexico, Turkey, and the Middle East and international concessions in Japan and France.

**Kate Spade & Company's Strategic Initiatives in 2014**   In 2014, Kate Spade's management team was focused on aggressively expanding the business, identifying new opportunities, and continuing the company's positive growth trend. Management planned to increase the profit margin by adding additional product category licenses, which would enable the company to enter new product lines quickly and with minimal investment. As the company grew, management intended to evaluate appropriate business models for international expansion. Kate Spade's management believed that being able to concentrate solely on Kate Spade & Company would enhance the company's progress. Exhibit 6 presents a financial summary for Kate Spade & Company for 2009 through 2013. At year-end 2013, Kate Spade had 118 specialty retail stores and 42 factory outlet stores in the United States and 22 foreign specialty stores and 9 foreign factory outlet stores.

## VERA BRADLEY'S PERFORMANCE IN FISCAL 2015

In June 2014, Vera Bradley's strategic direction seemed adrift as its revenues and earnings slipped

## EXHIBIT 6   Financial Summary for Kate Spade & Company, 2009–2013 (dollar amounts in thousands, except per share data)

|  | 2013 | 2012 | 2011 | 2010 | 2009 |
|---|---|---|---|---|---|
| Net sales | $1,264,935 | $1,043,403 | $1,100,508 | $1,236,300 | $1,489,171 |
| Gross profit | 725,581 | 599,169 | 598,331 | 602,875 | 622,240 |
| Operating loss | (45,513) | (52,528) | (102,772) | (42,832) | (169,630) |
| Income (loss) from continuing operations | 73,924 | (70,221) | 138,206 | (81,048) | (125,372) |
| Net income (loss) | 72,995 | (74,505) | (171,687) | (251,467) | (305,767) |
| Working capital | 206,473 | 36,407 | 124,772 | 39,043 | 244,379 |
| Total assets | 977,511 | 902,523 | 950,004 | 1,257,659 | 1,605,903 |
| Total debt | 394,201 | 406,294 | 446,315 | 577,812 | 658,151 |
| Total stockholders' (deficit) equity | (32,482) | (126,930) | (108,986) | (24,170) | 216,548 |
| Per common share data: |  |  |  |  |  |
| Basic |  |  |  |  |  |
| Income (loss) from continuing operations | $0.61 | $(0.64) | $1.46 | $(0.86) | $(1.34) |
| Diluted |  |  |  |  |  |
| Income (loss) from continuing operations | $0.60 | $(0.64) | $1.22 | $(0.86) | $(1.34) |
| Weighted-average shares outstanding, basic | 121,057 | 109,292 | 94,664 | 94,243 | 93,880 |
| Weighted-average shares outstanding, diluted | 124,832 | 109,292 | 120,692 | 94,243 | 93,880 |

*Source:* Kate Spade & Company, 10-K report, 2013.

further. The company's fiscal first-quarter 2015 revenues declined by 12 percent and its net earnings had fallen by 25 percent compared to the same period in fiscal 2014. The declines resulted from an unanticipated decline in sales in company-owned retail stores. Robert Wallstrom stated that the company's "traditional patterns and products simply are not attracting enough new customers to our brand, and overall traffic is down substantially."[2] He continued, "This will be an important year of transition and transformation for Vera Bradley. We believe that the product, distribution and marketing initiatives we previously outlined as part of our long-term strategic plan are absolutely the right ones for the future."[3]

# ENDNOTES

[1] As quoted in "Stores Dancing Chic," *Houston Chronicle,* May 6, 2000.

[2] As quoted in "Vera Bradley Announces Fiscal Year 2015 First Quarter Results," *Global Newswire,* June 5, 2014.

[3] Ibid.

# J.Crew in 2014: Will Its Turnaround Strategy Improve Its Competitiveness?

## A. J. Strickland
The University of Alabama

## Ellen Lindsay
2015 MBA Student, The University of Alabama

In early 2014, Mickey Drexler, CEO of J.Crew Group, Inc., had some important decisions to make. In 2012, after J.Crew customers complained that the company's latest product offerings consisted of far too many funky patterns with a younger-looking style—as opposed to consisting of a wide and fashionable selection of preppy button downs and classic khakis— Drexler decided that J.Crew's 2013 fall line should, once again, feature conservative, but fashionably appealing, button-down shirts, classic blouses, sweaters, skirts, and trousers. However, fall sales were lackluster, producing an alarming 42 percent drop in profits from the fourth quarter of 2012. Drexler was perplexed, feeling that he and the company's designers had tried their best to listen to customers' feedback and respond to their complaints and dislikes.

As he prepared for a meeting with Jenna Lyons, creative director, he wanted to consider a range of economic, cultural, and financial factors in deciding on the company's approach to its fall 2014 lineup of offerings. It was important for the company to arrive at the best strategy to rejuvenate sales and rekindle consumer interest in shopping at J.Crew. If it did not, J.Crew risked losing the sales boost that came from news reports that such high-profile personalities as First Lady Michelle Obama and Britain's Prince William and Kate Middleton shopped at J.Crew. Most important, of course, was developing a strategy to reverse the company's recent decline and achieve the following objectives:

- Attract consumers to J.Crew's stores in much greater numbers.
- Boost the company's revenue, profitability, and overall brand strength.
- Position the company for profitable long-term growth.

## COMPANY HISTORY AND BACKGROUND

J.Crew was founded in 1947 under the name Popular Sales Club. It was a startup company that specialized in door-to-door sales of women's clothing. Over the years, the firm grew, and in the 1980s, its executives saw a new opportunity. Catalog sales for companies such as L.L.Bean and Lands' End were booming, and the executives wanted their company to share in the boom. In 1983, Popular Sales Club mailed out its first 100-page catalog, filled with models wearing the latest fashions. As sales began to grow, the company changed its name to J.Crew in hopes of catching the preppy, affluent consumer's attention. Over the following years, J.Crew developed a loyal following by having a distinct image that the younger generations found appealing. By 1992, J.Crew had reached $70 million in sales. In 1989, J.Crew opened its first retail store at South Street Seaport in Manhattan. However, during the early 90s annual sales from the catalog business started to stagnate, and J.Crew realized it was time to make a change in its strategy.

A new CEO was named in 2003, Mickey Drexler, and he was ready to watch J.Crew expand into the fashion-forward company he dreamed it could be. Drexler is better known as the man who grew The

Gap from a $400 million company to a $14 billion competitor. After he became CEO of J.Crew, the company rolled out an expansion plan. The store opened entirely new lines, such as Crewcuts, for children, and Weddings, for the entire bridal party. Crewcuts had almost 100 shopping locations throughout the United States in 2014, while the Weddings line had nine retail stores. In 2008, Drexler hired Jenna Lyons to be the new creative director. Lyons, known for her fashion-forward thinking, quickly decided that J.Crew needed to revamp its classic image. At the company website, instead of finding pages and pages of classic button downs and nautical sweaters, now the consumer found edgy vests, bold patterns, and even stiletto heels.

Not all of J.Crew's loyal followers were impressed with the new change, with many disappointed that the company had abandoned its loyal customers who had been attracted to its traditional styles. Drexler responded by admitting that the styling might have gone too far and that changes should be made in the upcoming collection. The company's strategic changes had produced hoped-for revenue gains, but its net income and liquidity had steadily declined since 2009. On March 7, 2011, J.Crew Group, Inc., was acquired by TPG Capital, LP, and Leonard Green & Partners for approximately $3.1 billion, including the incurrence of $1.6 billion of debt. A summary of the company's financial and operating performance for fiscal 2009 through fiscal 2013 is presented in Exhibit 1. The company's complete consolidated balance sheets for fiscal 2012 and fiscal 2013 are presented in Exhibit 2.

# OVERVIEW OF THE U.S. APPAREL INDUSTRY

The U.S. women's apparel industry was a $42 billion industry made up of over 29,000 different businesses, with a projected growth rate of 3.6 percent from 2013 to 2018. This would result in its becoming a $50 billion industry annually. Because of the recession, the industry took a large hit in 2008 and its profitability fell by 3.1 percent. The recession, coupled with the rising price of cotton, caused less demand for discretionary products, such as women's clothing. However, it was expected that as the economy picked up, women would begin to purchase all the clothing they postponed purchasing during the recession.

The projected compound growth of cotton prices between 2009 and 2014 was 7.3 percent due to an increased demand for cotton. China had been slowly building a stockpile of cotton, and this was causing a global shortage of cotton, which in turn was causing a spike in the price. The global price of cotton drastically jumped from 62.75 cents per pound to 103.55 cents per pound in the year 2010. The increase in the price of cotton caused the retailers' overhead costs to increase as well. Because of the increased price of cotton, it became essential for the retailers to manage their purchases and overhead costs. The U.S. apparel industry was highly driven by imports. It was projected that by 2018, 78.6 percent of the products in the market would be imported from countries such as China and Vietnam.

Despite the negative downturn, the industry continued to grow, and the number of stores was expected to continue to increase at a rate of 2.3 percent annually to roughly 61,200 by 2018. As consumer spending continued to increase, it would entice more companies to enter the industry. Although the industry was in the mature stage, the forecast growth potential and the increasing consumer attitude would keep the industry fully functional.

Demand inside this industry was highly dependent on women aged 20 to 64 but, more specifically, on those aged 20 to 39 due to their larger amount of disposable income. The number of women in this age demographic was predicted to increase slowly through 2018. Almost one-third of the revenues inside the industry came from purchases of tops and blouses. Pants, denims, and shorts made up 24 percent of the total sales, followed closely by dresses and outerwear, with 18 and 17 percent, respectively. The remaining 9 percent was from sportswear and other garments, including custom-made items. Demand in the apparel industry was also driven by factors such as brand name, disposable income, and fashion trends. Companies had to be on the forefront of the new fashion trends and had to anticipate what consumers' demands would be for the next fashion season.

## J.Crew's Strategy in 2014

J.Crew delivered its products to customers through two main channels: retail stores and direct, which included websites and catalogs. J.Crew's U.S. retail stores accounted for over 60 percent of the company's overall revenue. The percentage of sales

**EXHIBIT 1    Summary of J.Crew Group, Inc.'s Financial and Operating Performance, Fiscal 2009–Fiscal 2013 (in thousands, unless otherwise indicated)**

| | Year Ended | | For the Period | | Year Ended | |
| --- | --- | --- | --- | --- | --- | --- |
| | February 1, 2014 (Successor) | February 2, 2013 (Successor) | March 8, 2011–January 28, 2012 (Successor) | January 30, 2011–March 7, 2011 (Predecessor) | January 29, 2011 (Predecessor) | January 30, 2010 (Predecessor) |
| **Income statement data** | | | | | | |
| Total revenues | $2,428,257 | $2,227,717 | $1,721,750 | $133,238 | $1,722,227 | $1,578,042 |
| Cost of goods sold, including buying and occupancy costs | 1,422,143 | 1,240,989 | 1,042,197 | 70,284 | 975,230 | 882,385 |
| Gross profit | 1,006,114 | 986,728 | 679,553 | 62,954 | 746,997 | 695,657 |
| Selling, general and administrative expenses | 756,219 | 733,070 | 574,877 | 79,736 | 533,029 | 484,396 |
| Income (loss) from operations | 249,895 | 253,658 | 104,676 | (16,782) | 213,968 | 211,261 |
| Interest expense, net | 104,221 | 101,684 | 91,683 | 1,166 | 3,914 | 5,384 |
| Provision (benefit) for income taxes | 57,550 | 55,887 | 584 | (1,798) | 88,549 | 82,517 |
| Net income (loss) | $ 88,124 | $ 96,087 | $ 12,409 | $ (16,150) | $ 121,505 | $ 123,360 |
| **Operating data** | | | | | | |
| Revenues | | | | | | |
| Stores | $1,638,170 | $1,546,619 | $1,194,276 | $ 86,474 | $1,192,876 | $1,110,932 |
| Direct | 755,915 | 651,480 | 502,033 | 43,642 | 490,594 | 428,186 |
| Other | 34,172 | 29,618 | 25,441 | 3,122 | 38,757 | 38,924 |
| Total revenues | $2,428,257 | $2,227,717 | $1,721,750 | $133,238 | $1,722,227 | $1,578,042 |
| Increase in comparable company sales | 3.1% | 12.6% | N/A | N/A | 6.7% | 3.9% |
| Stores | | | | | | |
| Sales per gross square foot | $671 | $686 | N/A | N/A | $601 | $577 |
| Stores open at end of period | 451 | 401 | 362 | 334 | 333 | 321 |

| | Year Ended | Year Ended | For the Period | For the Period | Year Ended | Year Ended |
|---|---|---|---|---|---|---|
| | February 1, 2014 (Successor) | February 2, 2013 (Successor) | March 8, 2011–January 28, 2012 (Successor) | January 30, 2011–March 7, 2011 (Predecessor) | January 29, 2011 (Predecessor) | January 30, 2010 (Predecessor) |
| **Direct** | | | | | | |
| Millions of catalogs circulated | 30.6 | 39.6 | N/A | N/A | 41.1 | 36.4 |
| Billions of pages circulated | 3.7 | 4.2 | N/A | N/A | 3.9 | 4.0 |
| Capital expenditures: | | | | | | |
| New stores | $ 54,635 | $ 51,868 | $ 29,820 | $ 626 | $ 14,873 | $ 19,954 |
| Other | 76,590 | 80,142 | 63,088 | 2,018 | 37,478 | 24,751 |
| Total capital expenditures | $ 131,225 | $ 132,010 | $ 92,908 | $ 2,644 | $ 52,351 | $ 44,705 |
| Depreciation of property and equipment | $ 79,394 | $ 72,471 | $ 59,595 | $ 3,929 | $ 49,756 | $ 51,765 |
| Amortization of intangible assets | $ 9,342 | $ 9,805 | $8,988 | $ — | $ — | $ — |

| | As of | As of | As of | As of | As of |
|---|---|---|---|---|---|
| | February 1, 2014 (Successor) | February 2, 2013 (Successor) | January 28, 2012 (Successor) | January 29, 2011 (Predecessor) | January 30, 2010 (Predecessor) |
| **Balance sheet data** | | | | | |
| Cash and cash equivalents | $ 156,649 | $ 68,399 | $ 221,852 | $381,360 | $298,107 |
| Working capital | $ 159,792 | $ 85,764 | $ 210,431 | $364,220 | $283,972 |
| Total assets | $3,682,220 | $3,486,714 | $3,573,522 | $860,166 | $738,558 |
| Total debt | $1,567,000 | $1,579,000 | $1,594,000 | $ — | $ 49,229 |
| Stockholders' equity | $1,190,420 | $1,091,491 | $ 1,177,052 | $511,121 | $375,878 |

*Source:* J.Crew Group, Inc., 10-K report, 2013.

**EXHIBIT 2**   J.Crew Group, Inc.'s Consolidated Balance Sheets, Fiscal 2012–Fiscal 2013 (in thousands, except share data)

| | Fiscal Year Ended | |
|---|---|---|
| | February 1, 2014 | February 2, 2013 |
| **Assets** | | |
| Current assets | | |
| Cash and cash equivalents | $  156,649 | $   68,399 |
| Merchandise inventories | 353,976 | 265,628 |
| Prepaid expenses and other current assets | 56,434 | 51,105 |
| Deferred income taxes, net | 11,831 | 14,686 |
| Prepaid income taxes | 2,782 | 11,620 |
| Total current assets | 581,672 | 411,438 |
| Property and equipment, at cost | 495,659 | 399,270 |
| Less accumulated depreciation | (120,567) | (75,159) |
| Property and equipment, net | 375,092 | 324,111 |
| Favorable lease commitments, net | 26,560 | 35,104 |
| Deferred financing costs, net | 41,911 | 51,851 |
| Intangible assets, net | 966,175 | 975,517 |
| Goodwill | 1,686,915 | 1,686,915 |
| Other assets | 3,895 | 1,778 |
| Total assets | $3,682,220 | $3,486,714 |
| **Liabilities and stockholders' equity** | | |
| Current liabilities | | |
| Accounts payable | $   237,019 | $   141,119 |
| Other current liabilities | 154,796 | 153,743 |
| Interest payable | 18,065 | 18,812 |
| Current portion of long-term debt | 12,000 | 12,000 |
| Total current liabilities | 421,880 | 325,674 |
| Long-term debt | 1,555,000 | 1,567,000 |
| Unfavorable lease commitments and deferred credits, net | 93,788 | 71,146 |
| Deferred income taxes, net | 389,403 | 392,984 |
| Other liabilities | 31,729 | 38,419 |
| Total liabilities | 2,491,800 | 2,395,223 |
| Stockholders' equity | | |
| Common stock $0.01 par value; 1,000 shares authorized, issued and outstanding | — | — |
| Additional paid-in capital | 1,008,984 | 1,003,184 |
| Accumulated other comprehensive loss | (15,184) | (20,189) |
| Retained earnings | 196,620 | 108,496 |
| Total stockholders' equity | 1,190,420 | 1,091,491 |
| Total liabilities and stockholders' equity | $3,682,220 | $3,486,714 |

*Source:* J.Crew Group, Inc., 10-K report, 2013.

accounted for by women's clothing had declined from 58 percent in 2011 to 55 percent in 2013. Accessories approximated 13 percent each year between 2011 and 2013. Children's clothing accounted for 6 percent of sales for all three years. Sales of men's clothing had increased from 23 percent of sales in 2011 to 25 percent in 2013. In 2013, the company sourced its merchandise from buying agents, as well as by purchasing directly from trading companies and manufacturers. The buying agents received commissions for placing orders with vendors, ensuring on-time deliveries, inspecting finished merchandise, and obtaining samples of the products during production. The top-10 vendors supplied 46 percent of J.Crew's merchandise.

The company focused on projecting a consistent brand image by placing creative messages throughout its stores, websites, and catalogs that were designed to capture the attention of its shoppers. J.Crew perfected its consistency by keeping control over the pricing, production, and design of all its products. Senior management was highly involved in all phases of production, from early design to the display of the final products throughout the stores. To promote its brand, J.Crew relied heavily on its catalog for advertising. In fiscal 2013, total catalog costs were around $45 million, while the company's other advertising expenditures were about $39 million for the year.

As of early 2014, J.Crew operated 265 J.Crew retail stores, 121 J.Crew Factory stores, and 65 Madewell stores, as well as its e-commerce websites. In 2014, J.Crew opened a third store in London and its first two stores in Hong Kong. Introduced in 2006, Madewell offered products exclusively for women, including perfect-fitting, heritage-inspired jeans, vintage-influenced tees, cardigans and blazers, boots, and jewelry and other accessories. Madewell products were sold through Madewell retail stores and the Madewell website. Exhibit 3 presents J.Crew Group's revenues by retail brand for fiscal 2011 through fiscal 2013. The company's revenue by distribution channel for 2011 through 2013 is presented in Exhibit 4.

## EXPANSION

J.Crew worked hard to stay at the forefront of fashion and deliver exactly what consumers desired. In 1989, J.Crew opened its first retail store in downtown Manhattan. It was there that J.Crew developed its classic style and gained a loyal following. The store focused on upper-middle-class customers and aimed to provide them with leisurewear at a price point between Ralph Lauren and The Limited.

Originally, the store offered products such as blouses, pants, and jackets. Over the years, J.Crew increased its product offerings exponentially, and the store offered products such as swimwear, loungewear, sweaters, tees, suits, and accessories. A typical shirt cost between $65 and $350 and pants cost $75 to $750 depending on fabrics and collections.

J.Crew extended not only its product depth but also its product breadth. The company engaged in major expansion and added lines for children, men, and even the wedding party.

In 1988, J.Crew Factory was launched. While many people assumed this store was a typical outlet store that just offered last season's leftovers, it was actually a different line created with slightly different fabrics or designs that enabled a lower price point. All products were created on the basis of other popular designs. J.Crew Factory offered products such as tops, jackets, pants, swimwear, and dresses. A typical shirt cost between $25 and $100, depending on the fabric used. The Factory stores were often located in strip malls and focused on selling styles that had already been proved successful.

## EXHIBIT 3    Revenue Contribution by J.Crew Group Retail Brand, Fiscal 2011–Fiscal 2013 (dollar amounts in millions)

|  | Fiscal 2013 | | Fiscal 2012 | | Fiscal 2011 | |
|---|---|---|---|---|---|---|
|  | Amount | Percent of Total | Amount | Percent of Total | Amount | Percent of Total |
| J.Crew | $2,212.7 | 91.1% | $2,066.2 | 92.8% | $1,740.8 | 93.8% |
| Madewell | 181.4 | 7.5 | 131.9 | 5.9 | 85.6 | 4.6 |
| Shipping and handling fees | 34.2 | 1.4 | 29.6 | 1.3 | 28.6 | 1.6 |
| Total | $2,428.3 | 100.0% | $ 2,227.7 | 100.0% | $1,855.0 | 100.0% |

Source: J.Crew Group, Inc., 10-K report, 2013.

**EXHIBIT 4    J.Crew Group's Revenue by Distribution Channel, Fiscal 2011–Fiscal 2013 (dollar amounts in millions)**

|  | Fiscal 2013 | | Fiscal 2012 | | Fiscal 2011 | |
| --- | --- | --- | --- | --- | --- | --- |
|  | Amount | Percent of Total | Amount | Percent of Total | Amount | Percent of Total |
| Stores | $1,638.2 | 67.5% | $1,546.6 | 69.4% | $1,280.7 | 69.0% |
| Direct | 755.9 | 31.1 | 651.5 | 29.3 | 545.7 | 29.4 |
| Shipping and handling fees | 34.2 | 1.4 | 29.6 | 1.3 | 28.6 | 1.6 |
| Total | $2,428.3 | 100.0% | $2,227.7 | 100.0% | $1,855.0 | 100.0% |

*Source:* J.Crew Group, Inc., 10-K report, 2013.

In 2006, Madewell, a subsidiary of J.Crew, was opened to exclusively target the younger female generation by offering more trendy clothing at a lower price point. Madewell offered products such as denims, dresses, shoes, and tops. The cost of shirts ranged from $25 to $150, while jeans cost, on average, $130 a pair.

Crewcuts offered products for boys and girls between the ages of 2 and 12, thus serving parents who wanted to dress their kids in trendy clothes. Crewcuts featured products such as shirts, skirts, dresses, sweaters, pants, and swimwear. Shirt prices ranged from about $25 to $50, and pants cost around $50 to $80.

J.Crew Wedding provided styles for the entire wedding party. The bride could pick out her dream gown while also selecting a new suit for her groom. The store also offered over 50 different styles and colors for bridesmaid's dresses. In the suiting department, groomsmen could choose from a wide selection of suits and tuxedos, as well as ties, shoes, and belts. The Weddings line also offered choices for ring bearers and flower girls.

In the early 2000s, J.Crew began to think about global expansion, and it opened its first store in Canada in 2011. In 2013, it was reported that London's Regent Street would be J.Crew's first European location and that locations would soon be announced for cities such as Tokyo and Hong Kong. The company was already shipping to over 100 countries worldwide as a result of sales on its e-commerce website. As the company expanded, there were important factors to consider. Drexler had mentioned that with expansion comes unfamiliar territory. One major factor that had to be considered was sizing. J.Crew

was known for its consistent sizing; however, in some areas of the world, people had smaller body frames than Americans. Also, less tangible factors needed to be considered, such as culture. Did all cultures dress as conservatively as the American loyal followers of J.Crew?

## J.CREW'S RIVALS IN THE SPECIALTY RETAILING INDUSTRY

The women's apparel industry was a competitive market with many factors that could determine success. Companies had to compete with other women's clothing stores on factors such as marketing, product availability, designs, price, quality, service, shipping prices, and brand image. The retail industry also had to compete with one-stop shops such as Walmart and Costco. These stores often offered lower prices, and they were very successful during the recession. The continued growth of e-commerce companies was another factor that retail stores had to consider, because e-commerce competitors often offered lower prices, free shipping, and promotional offers.

The Mid-Atlantic region had the highest-level concentration of revenues, at 25 percent. The concentration was highly dependent on population as well as per capita income. The higher the income and the larger the population in an area, the more concentrated the retail stores were in that area. In a close second place was the Southeast region, which accounted for 23.2 percent of all revenues in the industry. While the national income level was

$62,900, the average income in the Mid-Atlantic region was higher, at $72,800. The average income in the Southeast was considerably lower, at $55,000 annually. These statistics showed that the Southeast population had less disposable income to spend on women's clothing.

Firms had to work hard to establish their brand name. While the barriers to entry in this market were low, there was a high level of competition among successful brands. Concentration inside the industry was low, and the top-four major players held about 20 percent of the revenues in 2013. The four largest players were Ascena Retail Group Inc., Ann Inc., Forever 21, and Hennes & Mauritz (H&M) AB. The major players had several retail stores scattered throughout the country, while the independent retailers had fewer stores, typically operated on a local scale. The apparel industry was highly fragmented, with no one chain holding above 8 percent total market share. This was because of the high number of independent retailers and the vast availability of clothing and accessories. Between 2008 and 2013, concentration increased, and it was predicted to continue increasing over the coming years.

## Ascena Retail Group, Inc.

Ascena was one of the largest specialty retailers in the United States in the women's apparel industry, with 7.1 percent of the total market share. Ascena operated approximately 3,900 stores throughout the United States, Puerto Rico, and Canada. Some of its more popular stores were Justice, Dress Barn, Lane Bryant, and Catherines. In 2012, Ascena purchased the Charming Shoppes, which helped diversify its portfolio. The company focused on offering women comfortable, trendy clothes at a moderate price. Its diversified portfolio allowed the company to target girls and women from age 7 to age 50 in both regular and plus-sized attire. Lane Bryant offered items such as casual clothing and lingerie in women's sizes 12 to 32. The Justice line was focused on young girls aged 7 to 14 and offered trendy skirts and tops.

Ascena's moderately priced clothing allowed the company to be very successful during the recession and enabled it to gain a loyal following. The appeal of Ascena's brands, product lines, and pricing allowed the company's annual revenues to increase from approximately $1.7 billion in 2009 to more than $3.3 billion in 2013—see Exhibit 5.

**EXHIBIT 5   Ascena Retail Group's Revenues and Operating Income, 2009—2013 (in millions)**

| Year | Revenues | Operating Income |
|------|----------|------------------|
| 2009 | $1,662.7 | $158.4 |
| 2010 | 1,764.0 | 160.5 |
| 2011 | 2,046.6 | 120.0 |
| 2012 | 3,001.8 | 101.2 |
| 2013 | 3,346.7 | 101.4 |

Source: www.ibisworld.com.

## Ann Inc.

Ann Inc. had the second-largest market share inside the U.S. women's apparel industry, with 5.6 percent of the market. In 2013, it operated approximately 1,000 stores in the United States, Puerto Rico, and Canada. Ann's approach was to target women aged 25 to 55 who were willing to spend a little more income in order to wear more fashionable clothes. A financial summary for Ann Inc. for 2009 through 2013 is provided in Exhibit 6. The company focused on offering a wide selection of merchandise, such as tops, dresses, loungewear, pants, suits, skirts, accessories, and shoes. Ann Inc. operated Ann Taylor, Ann Taylor Loft, and Ann Taylor Factory. In 2000, the company launched its website to compete on the e-commerce platform. Ann Inc. was projected to grow by 3 percent annually through

**EXHIBIT 6   Ann Inc.'s Revenues and Operating Income, 2009—2013 (in millions)**

| Year | Revenues | Operating Income |
|------|----------|------------------|
| 2009 | $1,828.5 | $(24.0) |
| 2010 | 1,980.2 | 119.8 |
| 2011 | 2,212.5 | 145.5 |
| 2012 | 2,375.5 | 166.8 |
| 2013 | 2,548.5 | 189.0 |

Source: www.ibisworld.com.

2014, making it a $2.5-billion-a-year company. The company claimed its success was based on its new product lines as well as its new locations, with over 60 additional stores opened recently. Because Ann Inc. competed at the "upper moderate" price point, sales numbers were affected due to the recession and profits dropped $371.1 million in 2009.

## Forever 21

Forever 21 was a women's apparel company that focused on attracting the 15-to-30 age demographic. In 2013, it had an estimated 4 percent of the U.S. market share and had 500 stores in the United States. The company had expanded globally and operated stores in Europe, Asia, and the Middle East. As a result of this expansion, Forever 21 almost doubled its revenues, to a record $3 billion, in 2013. Because Forever 21 focused on the budget-conscious consumer, it was able to continue growing during the recession. The company's main focus was offering low-priced, trendy clothing to its consumers, as well as maintaining a quick turnover by introducing new styles weekly.

## Hennes & Mauritz

Hennes & Mauritz was a clothing and cosmetics company that held a 4 percent share of the U.S. apparel industry in 2013. The company operated on a global scale and had 3,000 stores in almost 50 markets. H&M offered products at an affordable price for children, men, and women. The company's estimated revenues in the United States were $1.7 billion in 2013. H&M worked with high-end designers to develop styles that consumers desired. A key component of its strategy was to continuously expand its merchandise selection by offering new product lines.

# THE STATE OF THE TURNAROUND IN MID-2014

As the recession of the late 2000s hit, the industry experienced a decrease in demand for women's apparel. Consequently, many retailers had to offer large discounts on clothing between 2008 and 2009. Because many consumers did not have large amounts of disposable income, a trend emerged: Rather than being concerned about the brand of their clothing as they had been in the past, consumers instead focused on the price and quality of merchandise. Some consumers changed their shopping preferences altogether and became more loyal to stores that offered trendy clothes at a lower price point.

While J.Crew's top management was at a crossroads of many different dilemmas, there was no clear path ahead. As the economy recovered, would consumers return to their previous habits of spending? Or would they be more conservative with their purchases in fear of another recession hitting? In addition, the increasing price sensitivity among consumers had put considerable pressure on J.Crew's margins, and its recent acquisition by investment groups had added more than $1.5 billion in debt. As Mickey Drexler and the company's chief managers prepared to meet to discuss the future of the company, they had many factors to consider. The most important questions were, What was the best strategy moving forward, and what changes would be necessary to provide attractive returns to the company's shareholders?

# The United Methodist Church: Challenges to Its Ministerial Mission in 2014

**A. J. Strickland**
The University of Alabama

**Rebecca Livingston**
2015 MBA Student,
The University of Alabama

As Martha Tipton prepared her words for a presentation at the United Methodist Church (UMC) General Conference, a wave of apprehension swept over her. Martha was one of many who had volunteered for the Sustainability Advisory Group (SAG), which was tasked with examining the financial implications of sustaining UMC's mission over the previous year. After the 2007–2009 economic recession, critical research in 2010 indicated that current compensation packages, benefit structures, and infrastructures were no longer included in many UMC congregations' capabilities. As a member of SAG, Tipton had joined leaders and bishops from different conferences around the United States to share financial information and best practices in order to discover what was affordable for UMC. At the next General Conference, the SAG coalition aimed to present the Council of Bishops with possible strategies for overcoming the hardships that had plagued the church. The coalition members were aware that efforts to restructure and cut costs would be highly scrutinized by other leaders in the church, so they had to provide conclusive evidence for any changes they sought to implement.

While her own church in the South Central Conference was able to sustain its financial structure, Tipton was acutely aware that this was due to the much larger size of its congregation. Many congregations across the United States were struggling to remain vital and were facing severe declines in membership. According to the constituting law and doctrine of the United Methodist Church, *The Book of Discipline,* a vital congregation is considered to have grown over some time period, engaged with the community it seeks to serve, involved more people with ministry and mission, and invited people to give generously to the mission. By the end of 2010, only 15 percent of UMC congregations across the United States were considered "highly vital." This staggering statistic indicated a flaw in the current methods and sparked discussion on how to help UMC become fiscally accountable once more.

Many individual churches within the United Methodist Church were having a difficult time attracting new members and maintaining their current memberships. Members supplied the vast majority of UMC's financial resources, so their involvement and commitment were essential for sustainability in the long run. Tipton knew that without a shift in the current strategy, UMC would continue on its wayward path. However, determining what approach to take seemed overwhelming. There were so many conflicting views from the numerous congregations and individual leaders that change seemed impossible, but the future was unclear without it. Was UMC to continue with the structure it currently operated under, or could a radical change be implemented to restore dwindling congregations across the country?

## HISTORY OF THE UNITED METHODIST CHURCH

The United Methodist Church was founded in Dallas, Texas, on April 23, 1968, as a union of the Evangelical United Brethren Church and the Methodist

Church. On that day, Bishops Reuben H. Mueller and Lloyd C. Wicke joined hands, and with the words "Lord of the Church, we are united in Thee, in Thy Church and now in The United Methodist Church," a new denomination was born.[1] Its theological traditions stemmed from the Protestant Reformation and Wesleyanism ideals that had been established for over 200 years in Great Britain. Methodism was organized in America in the late 1700s on the basis of the lives and ministries of the English missionaries John and Charles Wesley. These men had begun a renewal within the Church of England that emphasized inclusion of the poor or average person, a systematic approach to building the person, Arminian doctrine, and, most prominently, a deep conviction for missionary work. While early Methodist followers spanned all levels of society, Methodist preachers took the message to laborers and criminals, who tended to be left outside organized religion at the time. Additionally, under the leadership of John Wesley, Methodists became leaders in many social issues of the day, such as prison reform and abolitionism.

At its inception in 1968, the United Methodist Church had approximately 11 million members, making it one of the largest Protestant churches in the world. As technology and time progressed, UMC enhanced its global presence with members and conferences in Africa, Asia, Europe, and the United States. However, while significant growth was recorded in Africa and Asia, membership in Europe and the United States visibly declined. To further the vision for inclusion, UMC extended ordained ministry appointments to an increasing number of women. For instance, in 1980 Marjorie Matthews was the first woman elected to the church's episcopacy. These changes were a direct result of UMC's effort to become a community in which all persons could participate in the ministry. However, like many religious organizations, the United Methodist Church struggled with numerous controversial social issues, such as nuclear power, human sexuality, the environment, abortion, AIDS, evangelism, and world mission.

By 2008, UMC's membership included nearly 8 million U.S. citizens, a decrease of over 3 million members from the church's 1968 inception date. Additionally, the average attendance at weekly worship barely exceeded 3 million. In the 2012 *State of the Church Report,* it was observed that central and southern European nations and the United States had declines in membership of 25.6 and 7.8 percent,

respectively. This drastic decrease in membership was examined for a 10-year period, beginning in 2000, through statistical data provided by the General Council on Finance and Administration.[2]

## THE UNITED METHODIST CHURCH'S FINANCIAL SITUATION

In 2011, the General Conference budgeted $149,472,006 to the general fund for use by annual conferences, but because of decreased giving, only 87.6 percent of this financial commitment was fulfilled. The distribution, or apportionment, of the general fund is how the World Service, Ministerial Education, Black College, Africa University, Episcopal, Interdenominational Cooperation, and General Administration funds were financed. Historical general-fund apportionments are presented in Exhibit 1.

Most local church income came from congregational giving, which varied by conference from a high of 96 percent of total church income to a low of 74 percent. Other sources of income were dividends, sales of assets, building-use fees, and fund-raisers. Stan Sutten, of the West Ohio Conference, reported that the total debt of local churches from 2000 to 2007 increased about 6 percent faster than the rate of inflation. Over the same period, total debt rose from about 45 percent of annual expenditures to approximately 62 percent.

According to a report from SAG in 2010, a church needed to have about 125 congregants to raise the funds needed for a full-time pastor. In 2007, fewer than 8,700 churches out of 33,000 could report that they had an average attendance rate of 100 congregants or more. This left an estimated surplus of 784 to 942 UMC clergy in the United States. Additionally, because of declining membership, operating costs per attendee had increased for many churches.

In 2007, it was reported that the annual operating expense for the 6,099 growing churches was $257 per attendee, while the annual operating expense for the 11,260 declining churches was $406 per attendee.[3] As the congregation size declined, operating expenses per member or attendee increased to an unsustainable level. A small UMC Church in Galesville, Alabama, that was shut down after the congregation could only declare 17 congregants is shown in Exhibit 2.

## EXHIBIT 1   Percentage Apportionments for General-Fund Budgets for the United Methodist Church, 1986–2011

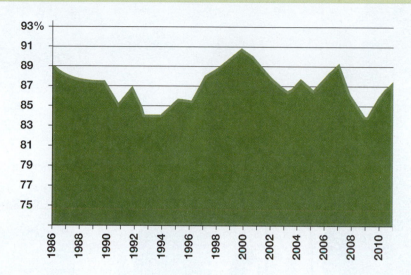

Source: s3.amazonaws.com/Website_Properties/state-of-the-church/documents/2012-state-of-the-church-report.PDF.

# MEMBERSHIP TRENDS IN THE UNITED METHODIST CHURCH

As shown in Exhibit 3, the decline in membership was drastic in European nations and areas that had strong economic stability, but the decline was slower in the United States. Conversely, mass growth was recorded in areas of the world that were less developed. The membership figures were attributed to research that suggested that as education and standards of living improve, individuals' faith in religion tends to waver. Hence, it was expected that as the richer nations continued to improve their economic structure, decreased levels of membership would be recorded.

It was clear that the current ministries, infrastructures, and systems of UMC would not be sustainable in the long run and that the organization could soon face a financial crisis. Many of the organization's experts began to question how practical the United Methodist Church's outdated approach was in a 21st-century global economy. However, many leaders were reluctant to change the procedures, and because the structure of UMC was based on *The Book of Discipline,* they were able to rule organizational change as unconstitutional. After a heated 2012 General Conference, Bishop Scott Jones said that he had witnessed "the death throes of a 1970s institution." The president of the Council of Bishops, Bishop Rosemarie Wenner, wrote, "Many people were not ready to do bold steps into a new model of structure and oversight and we fettered ourselves with a constitution that saves a dysfunctional system." Additionally, a defeated pastor, Andy Langford, wrote, "I believe that The United Methodist Church in 2012 has become the stagnant Church of England, which Mr. Wesley sought to reform."[4]

# GIVING TO RELIGIOUS ORGANIZATIONS

Religious organizations across the United States reported nearly $98.2 billion in giving in 2013. As of 2013, Protestantism was considered the most widely practiced religion in the United States. This led to Protestant worship services accounting for the largest share of giving, at 64 percent. However, the Protestant segment had experienced some decline in recent years as younger generations demonstrated less interest in organized religion; the characteristic conservative viewpoints of many Protestant organizations may have distanced younger individuals from the church. Catholicism was the second-largest religion in the United States by 2013 and accounted for about 21 percent of giving to

**EXHIBIT 2    Historic United Methodist Church in Galesville, Alabama**

*Source:* Photograph by A. J. Strickland.

religious organizations. While Catholic individuals typically contributed lower monetary obligations than did Protestants, the number of Catholics was expected to grow as immigration to the United States expanded.

Giving to organized religions experienced an average annual growth rate of negative 2.3 percent from 2008 to 2013. This negative growth rate occurred during a time of economic recession, and much of the decline in charitable donations at that time can be attributed to Americans having less disposable income. The peak recession year of 2009 was an especially tough year for organized religions as annual giving fell nearly 6.4 percent. As the effects of the recession weakened and the unemployment rate declined, giving was expected to grow at an annualized rate of 1.4 percent through 2018.

Research showed that increased disposable income, higher education levels, and improved standards of living resulted in diminishing devotion to religion in most developed countries. According to the U.S. Bureau of the Census, college attendance in the United States was expected to grow at a rate of 1.7 percent per year in the five years leading to 2013. Because higher education could involve educational studies that cause some to question religion, this would suggest that the participation in religious organizations could further decrease. However, when compared to other developed nations, the United States experienced a slower rate of decline in religious faith.

**EXHIBIT 3**   Membership Trends for the United Methodist Church, 2000 and 2010

| Central Conference/Region | Members | | Change in Membership | |
|---|---|---|---|---|
| | 2000 | 2010 | Number | Percent |
| Africa | 166,434 | 450,686 | 284,252 | 170.8% |
| Central Congo | 630,697 | 2,210,726 | 1,601,029 | 253.9 |
| West Africa | 379,425 | 1,508,696 | 1,129,271 | 297.6 |
| Central Europe and Eurasia | 21,725 | 16,162 | −5,563 | −25.6 |
| Germany | 38,536 | 32,305 | −6,231 | −16.2 |
| Northern Europe and Eurasia | 19,110 | 15,293 | −3,817 | −20.0 |
| Philippines | 56,780 | 145,642 | 88,862 | 156.5 |
| United States | 8,292,531 | 7,570,541 | −721,990 | −7.8 |
| Total | 9,605,238 | 11,971,051 | 2,365,813 | 25.0% |

*Source:* **s3.amazonaws.com/Website_Properties/state-of-the-church/documents/2012-state-of-the-church-report.PDF.**

# CHURCH MEMBERSHIP CHARACTERISTICS

Religious organizations across the United States raised resources through gaining and maintaining a strong and capable following. Without charitable followers, the organizations could not raise the funds required to fully pursue their ministerial missions. The majority of giving to organized religions was done by individuals over the age of 50. In 2013, the baby-boomer generation accounted for the largest portion of the U.S. population and, in turn, the largest portion of the membership in religious organizations, at 39.9 percent. Baby boomers were considered the second most religious generation in the United States, and much of their charitable giving could be attributed to this.

The "silent generation," people born before 1945, made up the second-largest membership portion of religious organizations, at 27.7 percent. This generation was most likely to contribute to charity, with 79 percent of individuals making at least one donation per year. The silent generation was regarded as the most religious generation and usually contributed more money per capita than any other generation.

The third-largest membership group, at 24.4 percent, was the Generation X demographic group. This generation comprised individuals born sometime after the baby boom, with birth years ranging from the early 1960s to the early 1980s. Gen-X individuals were considered less religious than older generations and were the hardest hit by the economic recession. Many individuals in this demographic group experienced a significant decrease in their income over the previous five years, and due to this decline in expendable income, the group was less likely to make charitable donations.

The smallest membership group in 2013, at 8 percent, was the generation known as the Millennials, which consisted of individuals born in the 1980s or early 1990s. This generation was thought to have the least desire to be religiously affiliated compared to older generations. The Pew Research Forum's U.S. Religious Landscape Survey discovered that one in four Americans between the ages of 18 and 29 did not affiliate with any specific religion. Conversely, among the entire population, only 16.1 percent of individuals were not affiliated with a religion. Many individuals in this generation felt a strain between themselves and religious organizations due to scandals and the conservative stances of many religious groups. Some reports indicated that confidence in organized religion could fall to 42 percent in 2018, which would be a decrease of over 10 percent compared to the 2004 confidence level of 53 percent. In addition, the members of this generation were the least likely to make donations because the unemployment rate for Millennials was much higher than that for the overall population.

# RELIGIOUS ORGANIZATIONS IN THE UNITED STATES

Four primary Christian church groups accounted for almost 90 percent of the entire religious population of the United States: Evangelical Protestants, Mainline

Protestants, Roman Catholic Church, and Historically Black churches. Each group was composed of a broad range of denominations that had similar religious traditions. Although religious organizations operated as nonprofit entities, their evangelism and outreach approaches resulted in a sort of competition for giving.

The largest group was the Evangelical Protestants, at 34.7 percent of the religious population in the United States. The largest denominations included in this group were Southern Baptist Convention, Church of Christ, Assemblies of God, Lutheran Church, and Missouri Synod. Modern Evangelical Protestant leaders were known to have strong media presence and typically held conservative social or political viewpoints. These leaders had strong convictions for their beliefs, which provided a strong leadership platform to attract and maintain membership. Compared to the other primary groups, the Evangelical Protestants were still increasing their membership. In addition to their strong leaders, Evangelical Protestants remained successful because they were able to secure donations, effectively control costs, attract new members, and maintain a positive reputation. The set of beliefs that defined this group and differed from those of Mainline Protestants included the following:

- The Bible was to be interpreted literally.
- Salvation was attainable only through Jesus Christ.
- Individuals had to accept salvation for themselves.
- Believers needed to proselytize.

Many of the so-called Megachurches were part of the Evangelical Protestant group. The Megachurches had unusually large congregations, some reaching 45,000 members, and they were able to create growth and draw in unprecedented revenues given the time period. However, many of their tactics were highly scrutinized. Some observers argued that these large churches stole members from the characteristically smaller churches in the United States and that they took advantage of their tax benefits as religious institutions. Megachurches were known to add membership programs that offered entertainment options such as basketball courts, pools, and, in some cases, movie theaters to attract new followers. Additionally, these churches made use of technology and online services to reach more people and further their brand image.

In 2013, the second-largest faith group was Mainline Protestants, with 23.6 percent of religious organization membership. The denominations included in this group were United Methodist Church, Evangelical Lutheran Church in America, American Baptist Churches USA, Presbyterian Church USA, Episcopal Church, and United Church of Christ. While Mainline Protestantism was once the largest market segment, it experienced decline since the 1950s. Most Mainline Protestant churches did not actively recruit new members, furthering the decline. Furthermore, the Evangelical Protestants were more proactive in recruiting younger members than were Mainline Protestants, so competition had played a major role in the market share decline. Mainline Protestants were typically characterized by their support of social gospel and application of Christian ethics to social problems. Due to these beliefs, Mainline Protestants were considered more economically and socially liberal than their counterparts.

The Roman Catholic Church accounted for 22.3 percent of religious membership in the United States. Globally, it was considered the world's largest Christian church, with more than 1 billion followers. The pope in the Vatican led the church, and the community was made up of ordained ministry and laity. The Catholic Church sought to spread the word of Christ and operated social programs, such as schools, hospitals, and missions, around the world. The church considered itself as the original church, founded by Jesus, and its bishops as successors of the apostles. The number of Catholics in the United States had risen in recent years, partly due to the fact that 50 percent of recent immigrants in the United States stemmed from Latin America and affiliated with Catholicism. However, many members of Catholic congregations were in a lower income level than the national median. It was reported that Catholics typically contributed 50 percent less to their respective churches than Protestants, and this resulted in a lower market share.

The smallest of the four large Christian groups was the Historically Black churches, which accounted for 9.1 percent of church membership. Major denominations in this group included the National Baptist Convention and the Church of God in Christ. Most Historically Black congregations consisted primarily of African-American members and were formed in the 19th century. These churches thrived and developed during segregation in the 20th century, when they played a major role in the civil rights movement. Additionally, a Gallup survey found that the attendance rates of these churches were over 50 percent, which was much higher than the attendance rate among the overall churchgoing population.

The other religions that made up the final 10.3 percent of faith membership were not as widely practiced as the four largest religious traditions in the United States. Some of the larger religious affiliations in this category included Islam, Buddhism, and Judaism. While these religions controlled only a small market share, they experienced some growth in the years leading up to 2013. According to the Pew Research Forum, more individuals were changing faith at that time than ever before, but such changes were unlikely to occur outside the major Protestant denominations.

## CHANGING SOCIETAL VIEWS

A major social issue that churches of every religion had struggled with was the issue of gay marriage and nontraditional families. While *The Book of Discipline* in the United Methodist Church called same-gender relationships "incompatible with Christian teaching," many clergy members were defying UMC laws and presiding over same-sex weddings. In March 2014, the Council of Bishops dropped the trial of Reverend Thomas Ogletree, a retired Yale Divinity School dean and retired elder in the church's New York district, for officiating at the same-sex marriage of his son; just months earlier, the UMC had defrocked another pastor, Frank Schaefer, for the same offense. Many theologically conservative Methodists had formed groups, such as the Wesleyan Covenant Network, to press church leaders to discipline clergy members for breaking church law, and this led to a strong division in the organization. These more conservative members believed that breaking the covenant that founded the church would lead to its ultimate demise. With an organizational split forming over this issue, some members of the clergy were electing to leave the denomination.[5]

The United Methodist Church was not alone in the battle on the social front. Other religious organizations around the world were dealing with similar problems, and the consequences had become dire. The Episcopal Church, once the largest denomination in the Colonies, was near collapse by 2013 because of the gay-marriage issue. It was forced to sell its headquarters in New York City because members were leaving the church at record rates.

Some churches considered altering their viewpoint on nontraditional families. Under new leadership, the Roman Catholic Church had become increasingly flexible to further its teachings that all persons should be treated with dignity and respect. In a 2013 interview, Pope Francis declared, "If someone is gay and seeks the Lord with good will, who am I to judge?" and the world gasped. Although Pope Francis was not publically acknowledging tolerance for same-sex marriage, his words revealed that acceptance within the Catholic Church could be possible.

## MARTHA TIPTON'S DECISION

As the economy recovered from the recession, the United Methodist Church expected an improvement in charitable giving compared to previous years. However, with an aging membership base, would the donations continue as membership rates steadily declined? The current financial situation and the decline in U.S. membership could jeopardize UMC's ministerial mission. Already, UMC's declining membership made it increasingly difficult for its small congregations to remain as organized churches.

Active recruitment of young members was critical to the success of any plan for the United Methodist Church. Martha Tipton knew that UMC had reached a turning point, but with so much division forming within the organization, she would have to settle on what measures needed to be taken. It was important to consider the doctrine and foundational principles of the church, but what if this foundation was no longer capable of supporting the mission?

## ENDNOTES

1 www.umc.org/who-we-are/history.
2 s3.amazonaws.com/Website_Properties/ state-of-thechurch/documents/2012-state-of-the-church-report.PDF.
3 www.gbophb.org/assets/1/7/SAGReport_ 052110.pdf.
4 pastorandylangford.com/2012/05/15/.
5 bigstory.ap.org/article/methodists-crisis-over-gay-marriage-church-law.

# Nucor Corporation in 2014: Combating Low-Cost Foreign Imports and Depressed Market Demand for Steel Products

McGraw Hill Education **connect**

## Arthur A. Thompson
### The University of Alabama

In 2014, Nucor Corporation, with a production capacity approaching 27 million tons, was the largest manufacturer of steel and steel products in North America and ranked as the 14th-largest steel company in the world based on tons shipped in 2013. It was regarded as a low-cost producer, and it had a sterling reputation for being a global leader in introducing innovative steelmaking technologies throughout its operations. Nucor began its journey from obscurity to a steel industry leader in the 1960s. Operating under the name of Nuclear Corporation of America in the 1950s and early 1960s, the company was a maker of nuclear instruments and electronics products. After suffering through several money-losing years and facing bankruptcy in 1964, Nuclear Corporation of America's board of directors opted for new leadership and appointed F. Kenneth Iverson as president and CEO. Shortly thereafter, Iverson concluded that the best way to put the company on sound footing was to exit the nuclear instrument and electronics business and rebuild the company around its profitable South Carolina–based Vulcraft subsidiary that was in the steel joist business—Iverson had been the head of Vulcraft prior to being named president. Iverson moved the company's headquarters from Phoenix, Arizona, to Charlotte, North Carolina, in 1966, and he proceeded to expand the joist business with new operations in Texas and Alabama. Then, in 1968, top management decided to integrate backward into steelmaking, partly because of the benefits of supplying the company's own steel requirements for producing steel joists and partly because Iverson saw opportunities to capitalize on newly emerging technologies to produce steel more cheaply. In 1972 the company adopted the name Nucor Corporation, and Iverson initiated a long-term strategy to grow Nucor into a major player in the U.S. steel industry.

By 1985 Nucor had become the seventh-largest steel company in North America, with revenues of $758 million, six joist plants, and four state-of-the-art steel mills that used electric arc furnaces to produce new steel products from recycled scrap steel. Nucor was regarded as an excellently managed company, an accomplished low-cost producer, and one of the most competitively successful manufacturing companies in the country.[1] A series of articles in *The New Yorker* related how Nucor, a relatively small American steel company, had built an enterprise that led the whole world into a new era of making steel with recycled scrap steel. NBC did a business documentary that used Nucor to make the point that American manufacturers could be successful in competing against low-cost foreign manufacturers.

During the 1985–2000 period, Nucor continued to construct additional steelmaking capacity, adopt trailblazing production methods, and expand its lineup of steel products. By 2000, Nucor was the second-largest steel producer in the United States and was charging to overtake long-time leader United States Steel. Nucor continued its long-term growth strategy between 2006 and 2013, constructing additional plants and acquiring other (mostly troubled) steel facilities at bargain-basement prices, enabling it to enter new product segments and offer customers a diverse variety of steel shapes and steel products. Heading into 2014, Nucor was solidly entrenched as the largest steel producer in North America (based on production capacity); it had 23 plants with the capacity to produce 27 million tons of assorted steel shapes (steel bars, sheet steel, steel plate, and structural steel) and had additional steel-manufacturing facilities with the capacity to make 4.6 million tons of steel joists, steel decking, cold-finish bars, steel buildings, steel mesh, steel grating, steel fasteners, and fabricated-steel reinforcing products. The company had 2013 revenues of $19.1 billion and net profits of $488.0 million, well below its prerecession peak in 2008 of $23.7 billion in revenues and $1.8 billion in net profits.

With the exception of three quarters in 2009 and one quarter in 2010 (when the steel industry in the United States was in the midst of a deep economic downturn and the demand for steel was unusually weak), Nucor had earned a profit in every quarter of every year since 1966—a truly remarkable accomplishment in a mature and cyclical business in which it was common for industry members to post losses when demand for steel sagged. As of April 2014, Nucor had paid a dividend for 164 consecutive quarters and had raised the base dividend it paid to stockholders every year since 1973, when the company first began paying cash dividends. (In years when earnings and cash flows permitted, it was Nucor's practice to pay a supplemental year-end dividend in addition to the base quarterly dividend.) Exhibit 1 provides highlights of Nucor's growth since 1970.

## NUCOR IN 2014

Former CEO Ken Iverson, the architect of Nucor's climb to prominence in the steel industry, was regarded by many as a "model company president." Under Iverson, who served as Nucor's CEO from

**EXHIBIT 1**   Nucor's Growing Presence in the Market for Steel, 1970–2013

| Year | Total Tons Sold to Outside Customers | Average Price per Ton | Net Sales (millions) | Earnings before Taxes (millions) | Pretax Earnings per Ton | Net Earnings (millions) |
|------|------|------|------|------|------|------|
| 1970 | 207,000 | $245 | $ 50.8 | $ 2.2 | $ 10 | $ 1.1 |
| 1975 | 387,000 | 314 | 121.5 | 11.7 | 30 | 7.6 |
| 1980 | 1,159,000 | 416 | 482.4 | 76.1 | 66 | 45.1 |
| 1985 | 1,902,000 | 399 | 758.5 | 106.2 | 56 | 58.5 |
| 1990 | 3,648,000 | 406 | 1,481.6 | 111.2 | 35 | 75.1 |
| 1995 | 7,943,000 | 436 | 3,462.0 | 432.3 | 62 | 274.5 |
| 2000 | 11,189,000 | 425 | 4,756.5 | 478.3 | 48 | 310.9 |
| 2001 | 12,237,000 | 354 | 4,333.7 | 179.4 | 16 | 113.0 |
| 2002 | 13,442,000 | 357 | 4,801.7 | 227.0 | 19 | 162.1 |
| 2003 | 17,473,000 | 359 | 6,265.8 | 70.0 | 4 | 62.8 |
| 2004 | 19,109,000 | 595 | 11,376.8 | 1,725.9 | 96 | 1,121.5 |
| 2005 | 20,465,000 | 621 | 12,701.0 | 2,027.1 | 104 | 1,310.3 |
| 2006 | 22,118,000 | 667 | 14,751.3 | 2,692.4 | 129 | 1,757.7 |
| 2007 | 22,940,000 | 723 | 16,593.0 | 2,253.3 | 104 | 1,471.9 |
| 2008 | 25,187,000 | 940 | 23,663.3 | 2,790.5 | 116 | 1,831.0 |
| 2009 | 17,576,000 | 637 | 11,190.3 | (470.4) | (28) | (293.6) |
| 2010 | 22,019,000 | 720 | 15,844.6 | 194.9 | 9 | 134.1 |
| 2011 | 23,044,000 | 869 | 20,023.6 | 1,169.9 | 53 | 778.2 |
| 2012 | 23,092,000 | 841 | 19,429.3 | 764.4 | 34 | 504.6 |
| 2013 | 23,730,000 | 803 | 19,052.0 | 693.6 | 30 | 488.0 |

*Source:* Company records, **www.nucor.com** (accessed April 15, 2014).

the time the company was formed until late 1998, Nucor was known for its aggressive pursuit of innovation and technical excellence, rigorous quality systems, strong emphasis on employee relations and workforce productivity, cost-conscious corporate culture, and ability to achieve low costs per ton produced. The company had a very streamlined organizational structure, incentive-based compensation systems, and steel mills that were among the most modern and efficient in the United States. Iverson proved himself as a master in crafting and executing a low-cost provider strategy, and he made a point of making sure that he practiced what he preached when it came to holding down costs. The offices of executives and division general managers were simply furnished. There were no company planes and no company cars, and executives were not provided with company-paid country club memberships, reserved parking spaces, executive dining facilities, or other perks. To save money on his own business expenses and set an example for other Nucor managers, Iverson flew coach class and took the subway when he was in New York City.

When Iverson left the company in 1998 following disagreements with the board of directors, he was succeeded briefly by John Correnti and then Dave Aycock, both of whom had worked in various roles under Iverson for a number of years. In 2000,

Daniel R. DiMicco, who had joined Nucor in 1982 and risen up through the ranks to executive vice president, was named president and CEO. DiMicco was Nucor's chairman and CEO through 2012. Like his predecessors, DiMicco continued to pursue a strategy to aggressively grow the company's production capacity and product offerings. DiMicco expanded the company's production capabilities via both acquisition and new plant construction; tons sold rose from 11.2 million in 2000 to 25.2 million in 2008. Then the unexpected financial crisis in the fourth quarter of 2008 and the subsequent economic fallout caused tons sold in 2009 to plunge to 17.6 million and revenues to nose-dive from $23.7 billion in 2008 to $11.2 billion in 2009. Nucor's business remained in the doldrums in 2010–2013 (see Exhibit 2) because of a lackluster economy in the United States and almost everywhere else, depressed global demand for steel and steel products, global overcapacity in the steel industry, and fierce competition from foreign imports.

In the 12 years of Dan DiMicco's leadership, Nucor was quite opportunistic in initiating actions to strengthen its competitive position during periods when the demand for steel was weak and then to capitalize on these added strengths in periods of strong market demand for steel products and significantly boost financial performance. According to Dan DiMicco:[2]

## EXHIBIT 2 Five-Year Financial and Operating Summary, Nucor Corporation, 2009–2013 (dollar amounts in millions, except per share data and sales per employee)

|  | 2013 | 2012 | 2011 | 2010 | 2009 |
|---|---|---|---|---|---|
| **For the year** | | | | | |
| Net sales | $19,052.0 | $19,429.3 | $20,023.6 | $15,844.6 | $11,190.3 |
| Costs, expenses and other: | | | | | |
| Cost of products sold | 17,641.4 | 17,915.7 | 18,142.1 | 15,060.9 | 11,090.2 |
| Marketing, administrative and other expenses | 481.9 | 454.9 | 439.5 | 331.5 | 296.9 |
| Equity in (earnings) losses of minority-owned enterprises | (9.3) | 13.3 | 10.0 | 32.1 | 82.3 |
| Impairment of noncurrent assets | — | 30.0 | 13.9 | — | — |
| Interest expense, net | 146.9 | 162.4 | 166.1 | 153.1 | 134.8 |
| Total | 18,260.9 | 18,576.3 | 18,771.8 | 15,577.5 | 11,604.3 |
| Earnings (loss) before income taxes and noncontrolling interests | 791.1 | 852.9 | 1,251.8 | 267.1 | (414.0) |
| Provision for (benefit from) income taxes | 205.6 | 259.8 | 390.8 | 60.8 | (176.8) |

(*Continued*)

## EXHIBIT 2    (Continued)

| | 2013 | 2012 | 2011 | 2010 | 2009 |
|---|---|---|---|---|---|
| Net earnings (loss) | 585.5 | 593.1 | 861.0 | 206.3 | (237.2) |
| Less earnings attributable to the minority-interest partners of Nucor's joint ventures* | 97.5 | 88.5 | 82.8 | 72.2 | 56.4 |
| Net earnings (loss) attributable to Nucor stockholders | $   488.0 | $   504.6 | $   778.2 | $   134.1 | $   (293.6) |
| Net earnings (loss) per share: | | | | | |
|   Basic | $1.52 | $1.58 | $2.45 | $0.42 | $(0.94) |
|   Diluted | 1.52 | 1.58 | 2.45 | 0.42 | (0.94) |
| Dividends declared per share | $1.4725 | $1.4625 | $1.4525 | $1.4425 | $1.41 |
| Percentage of net earnings to net sales | 2.6% | 2.6% | 3.9% | 0.8% | −2.6% |
| Return on average stockholders' equity | 6.4% | 6.7% | 10.7% | 1.8% | −3.8% |
| Capital expenditures | $1,230.4 | $1,019.3 | $450.6 | $345.3 | $390.5 |
| Acquisitions (net of cash acquired) | — | 760.8 | 4.0 | 64.8 | 32.7 |
| Depreciation | 535.9 | 534.0 | 522.6 | 512.1 | 494.0 |
| Sales per employee (000s) | 859 | 906 | 974 | 777 | 539 |
| **At year-end** | | | | | |
| Cash, cash equivalents, and short-term investments | $ 1,511.5 | $ 1,157.1 | $ 2,563.3 | $2,479.0 | $ 2,242.0 |
| Current assets | 6,410.0 | 5,661.4 | 6,708.1 | 5,861.2 | 5,182.2 |
| Current liabilities | 1,960.2 | 2,029.6 | 2,396.1 | 1,504.4 | 1,227.1 |
| Working capital | 4,449.8 | 3,631.8 | 4,312.0 | 4,356.8 | 3,995.1 |
| Cash provided by operating activities | 1,077.9 | 1,200.4 | 1,032.6 | 873.4 | 1,173.2 |
| Current ratio | 3.3 | 2.8 | 2.8 | 3.9 | 4.2 |
| Property, plant, and equipment | $ 4,917.0 | $ 4,283.1 | $ 3,755.6 | $ 3,852.1 | $ 4,013.8 |
| Total assets | 15,203.3 | 14,152.1 | 14,570.4 | 13,921.9 | 12,571.9 |
| Long-term debt (including current maturities) | 4,380.2 | 3,630.2 | 4,280.2 | 4,280.2 | 3,086.2 |
| Percentage of long-term debt to total capital[†] | 35.6% | 31.5% | 35.7% | 36.9% | 28.9% |
| Stockholders' equity | $7,645.8 | $7,641.6 | $7,474.9 | $7,120.1 | $7,390.5 |
| Shares outstanding (000s) | 318,328 | 317,663 | 316,749 | 315,791 | 314,856 |
| Employees | 22,300 | 22,200 | 20,800 | 20,500 | 20,400 |

*The principal joint venture responsible for these earnings is the Nucor-Yamato Steel Company, of which Nucor owns 51 percent. This joint venture operates a structural steel mill in Blytheville, Arkansas, and it is the largest producer of structural steel beams in the Western Hemisphere.

[†]Total capital is defined as stockholders' equity plus long-term debt.

*Source:* Nucor's 2013 annual report, p. 43.

Our objective is to deliver improved returns at every point in the economic cycle. We call it delivering higher highs and higher lows. In the last major economic slump, from 2001 through 2003, Nucor had total net earnings of $339.8 million. During the even deeper slump of 2009 through 2011, Nucor earned $618.7 million, an increase of 82 percent. The most recent peak to peak earnings grew from $310.9 million in 2000 to $1.83 billion in 2008, an increase of 489 percent.

Nucor uses each economic downturn as an opportunity to grow stronger. We use the good times to prepare for the bad, and we use the bad times to prepare for the good. Emerging from downturns stronger than we enter them is how we build long-term value for our stockholders. We get stronger because our team is focused on continual improvement and because our financial strength allows us to invest in attractive growth opportunities throughout the economic cycle.

During DiMicco's tenure, Nucor completed more than 50 acquisitions from 2000 to 2012, expanding from 18 facilities to more than 200 and boosting revenues from $4.8 billion in 2000 to $19.4 billion at the end of 2012. DiMicco retired as

Nucor's CEO at the end of 2012 and was succeeded by John J. Ferriola, who had served as Nucor's president and COO since 2011. DiMicco continued on as chairman of Nucor's board of directors during 2013 and then relinquished that role to John Ferriola at the beginning of 2014.

In his first year as Nucor's CEO, Ferriola continued to pursue Nucor's core strategy of investing in down markets to better position the company for success when the economy strengthened and market demand for steel products became more robust. In the company's 2013 annual report, Ferriola said:

> We are finding ways to grow our company and be successful despite the lackluster economy by continually looking for ways to improve our performance and lower our costs, investing in projects that will move us up the value chain and providing superior customer service.

## NUCOR'S EVER-GROWING PRODUCT LINE, 1967–2014

Over the years, Nucor had expanded progressively into the manufacture of a wider and wider range of steel shapes and steel products, enabling it in 2014 to offer steel users the broadest product lineup of any North American steel producer. Steel shapes and steel products were considered commodities. While some steelmakers had plants whose production quality was sometimes inconsistent or, on occasion, failed to meet customer-specified metallurgical characteristics, most steel plants turned out products of comparable metallurgical quality—one producer's reinforcing bar was essentially the same as another producer's reinforcing bar, and a particular type and grade of sheet steel made at one plant was essentially identical to the same type and grade of sheet steel made at another plant. The commodity nature of steel products forced steel producers to be very price-competitive, with the market price of each particular steel product being driven by demand–supply conditions for that product.

### Finished Steel Products

Nucor's first venture into steel in the late 1960s, via its Vulcraft division, was principally one of fabricating steel joists and joist girders from steel that was purchased from various steelmakers. Vulcraft expanded into the fabrication of steel decking in 1977. The division expanded its operations over the years, and, as of 2014, Nucor's Vulcraft division was the largest producer and leading innovator of open-web steel joists, joist girders, and steel deck in the United States. It had seven plants with annual capacity of 715,000 tons that made steel joists and joist girders and nine plants with 530,000 tons of capacity that made steel deck; in 2012–2013, about 85 percent of the steel needed to make these products was supplied by various Nucor steelmaking plants. Vulcraft's joist, girder, and decking products were used mainly for roof and floor support systems in retail stores, shopping centers, warehouses, manufacturing facilities, schools, churches, hospitals, and, to a lesser extent, multistory buildings and apartments. Customers for these products were principally nonresidential construction contractors.

In 1979, Nucor began fabricating cold-finished steel products. These consisted mainly of cold drawn and turned, ground, and polished steel bars or rods of various shapes—rounds, hexagons, flats, channels, and squares—made from carbon, alloy, and leaded steels based on customer specifications or end-use requirements. Cold-finished steel products were used in tens of thousands of other products, including anchor bolts, hydraulic cylinders, farm machinery, air conditioner compressors, electric motors, motor vehicles, appliances, and lawn mowers. Nucor sold cold-finish steel directly to large-quantity users in the automotive, farm machinery, hydraulic, appliance, and electric motor industries and to steel service centers that in turn supplied manufacturers needing only relatively small quantities. In 2013, Nucor Cold Finish was the largest producer of cold-finished bar products in North America and had facilities in Missouri, Nebraska, South Carolina, Utah, Wisconsin, and Ontario, Canada, with a capacity of about 860,000 tons per year. It obtained most of its steel from Nucor's mills that made steel bar. This factor, along with the fact that all of Nucor's cold-finished facilities employed the latest technology and were among the most modern in the world, resulted in Nucor Cold Finish having a highly competitive cost structure. It maintained sufficient inventories of cold-finish products to fulfill anticipated orders.

Nucor produced metal buildings and components throughout the United States under several brands: Nucor Building Systems, American Buildings Company, Kirby Building Systems, Gulf States Manufacturers, and CBC Steel Buildings. In 2014, the Nucor Buildings Group had 11 metal buildings plants, with an annual capacity of approximately 465,000 tons. Sales were 280,000 tons in 2013, an increase of 2 percent over 274,000 tons in 2010. Nucor's Buildings Group began operations in 1987 and currently had the capability to supply customers with buildings ranging from less than 1,000 square feet to more than 1,000,000 square feet. Complete metal buildings packages could be customized and combined with other materials such as glass, wood, and masonry to produce a cost-effective, aesthetically pleasing building built to a customer's particular requirements. The buildings were sold primarily through an independent builder distribution network. The primary markets served were commercial, industrial, and institutional buildings, including distribution centers, automobile dealerships, retail centers, schools, warehouses, and manufacturing facilities. Nucor's Buildings Group obtained a significant portion of its steel requirements from the Nucor bar and sheet mills.

Another Nucor division produced steel mesh, grates, and fasteners. Various steel mesh products were made at two facilities in the United States and one in Canada that had a combined annual production capacity of about 128,000 tons. Steel and aluminum bar grating, safety grating, and expanded metal products were produced at several North American locations that had a combined annual production capacity of 103,000 tons. Nucor Fastener, located in Indiana, began operations in 1986 with the construction of a $25 million plant. At the time, imported steel fasteners accounted for 90 percent of the U.S. market because U.S. manufacturers were not competitive on cost and price. Iverson said, "We're going to bring that business back; we can make bolts as cheaply as foreign producers." Nucor built a second fastener plant in 1995, giving it the capacity to supply about 20 percent of the U.S. market for steel fasteners. In 2013, these two facilities had annual capacity of over 75,000 tons and produced carbon and alloy steel hex-head cap screws, hex bolts, structural bolts, nuts and washers, finished hex nuts, and custom-engineered fasteners that were used for automotive, machine tool, farm implement, construction, military, and various other applications. Nucor Fastener obtained much of the steel it needed from Nucor's mills that made steel bar.

Beginning in 2007, Nucor—through its newly acquired Harris Steel subsidiary—began fabricating, installing, and distributing steel reinforcing bars (rebars) for highways, bridges, schools, hospitals, airports, stadiums, office buildings, high-rise residential complexes, and other structures where steel reinforcing was essential to concrete construction. Harris Steel had over 70 fabrication facilities in the United States and Canada, with each facility serving the surrounding local market. Since acquiring Harris Steel, Nucor had more than doubled its rebar fabrication capacity to over 1,700,000 tons annually. Total fabricated rebar sales in 2013 were 1,065,000 tons, down 10 percent from 1,180,000 tons in 2012. Much of the steel used in making fabricated rebar products was obtained from Nucor steel plants that made steel bar. Fabricated reinforcing products were sold only on a contract bid basis.

## Steelmaking

In 1968 Nucor got into basic steelmaking, building a mill in Darlington, South Carolina, to manufacture steel bars. The Darlington mill was one of the first plants of major size in the United States to use electric arc furnace technology to melt scrap steel and cast molten metal into various shapes. Electric arc furnace technology was particularly appealing because the labor and capital requirements for melting steel scrap and producing crude steel were far lower than those at conventional integrated steel mills, where raw steel was produced using coke ovens, basic oxygen blast furnaces, ingot casters, and multiple types of finishing facilities to make crude steel from iron ore, coke, limestone, oxygen, scrap steel, and other ingredients. By 1981, Nucor had four steel mills making carbon and alloy steels in bars, angles, and light structural shapes; since then, Nucor had undertaken extensive capital projects to keep these facilities modernized and globally competitive.

In 2000–2011, Nucor aggressively expanded its market presence in steel bars, and by 2012 it had 13 bar mills located across the United States that produced concrete-reinforcing bars, hot-rolled bars, rods, light shapes, structural angles, channels, and guard rails in carbon and alloy steels; in 2014, these 13 plants had total annual capacity of approximately 9.1 million tons. Four of the 13 mills made hot-rolled special quality bar manufactured to exacting specifications. The products of the 13 bar mills had wide usage and were sold primarily to customers in the agricultural, automotive, construction, energy, furniture, machinery, metal buildings, railroad, recreational equipment, shipbuilding, heavy truck, and trailer industries.

Nucor began work in 2012 on a $290 million project to expand its wire rod and special-quality steel bar production capabilities at three existing bar mills by 1 million tons annually; the purpose of the investment was to enable Nucor to produce engineered bars for the most demanding applications (and realize a significantly higher price) while maintaining its market share in commodity bar products by shifting production to its other bar mills that were operating below capacity. Completion of the added capacity to make special-quality bar products was expected sometime in 2014, with production startup following shortly thereafter. In addition, the company had recently renovated an existing wire rod and bar mill in Kingman, Arizona, to boost production capacity from 200,000 tons annually to 500,000 tons annually, thereby putting Nucor in a strong position to serve wire rod and rebar customers in the southwestern U.S. market. Nucor executives expected that the added capacity at the three special-quality bar mills and at the Kingman plant would be an important source of revenue and profit growth in upcoming years.

In the late 1980s, Nucor entered into the production of sheet steel at a newly constructed plant in Crawfordsville, Indiana. Flat-rolled sheet steel was used in the production of motor vehicles, appliances, steel pipes and tubes, and other durable goods. The Crawfordsville plant was the first in the world to employ a revolutionary thin-slab casting process that substantially reduced the capital investment and costs to produce flat-rolled sheet steel. Thin-slab casting machines had a funnel-shaped mold to squeeze molten steel down to a thickness of 1.5 to 2.0 inches, compared to the typically 8- to 10-inch-thick slabs produced by conventional casters. It was much cheaper to then build and operate facilities to roll thin-gauge sheet steel from 1.5- to 2-inch-thick slabs than from 8- to 10-inch-thick slabs. When the Crawfordsville plant first opened in 1989, it was said to have cost $50 to $75 per ton below the costs of traditional sheet steel plants, a highly significant cost advantage in a commodity market where the going price at the time was $400 per ton. *Forbes* magazine described Nucor's pioneering use of thin-slab casting as the most substantial, technological industrial innovation in the past 50 years.[3] By 1996 two additional sheet steel mills that employed

thin-slab casting technology were constructed and a fourth mill was acquired in 2002, giving Nucor the capacity to produce 11.3 million tons of sheet steel products annually. Nucor also operated two Castrip sheet production facilities, one built in 2002 at the Crawfordsville plant and a second built in Arkansas in 2009; these facilities used the breakthrough strip-casting technology that involved the direct casting of molten steel into the final shape and thickness without further hot or cold rolling. The process allowed for lower capital investment, reduced energy consumption, smaller-scale plants, and improved environmental impact (because of significantly lower emissions).

Also in the late 1980s, Nucor added wide-flange steel beams, pilings, and heavy structural steel products to its lineup of product offerings. Structural steel products were used in buildings, bridges, overpasses, and similar projects where strong weight-bearing support was needed. Customers included construction companies, steel fabricators, manufacturers, and steel service centers. To gain entry to the structural steel segment, in 1988 Nucor entered into a joint venture with Yamato-Kogyo, one of Japan's major producers of wide-flange beams, to build a new structural steel mill in Arkansas; a second mill was built on the same site in the 1990s that made the Nucor-Yamato venture in Arkansas the largest structural beam facility in the Western Hemisphere. In 1999, Nucor started operations at a third structural steel mill in South Carolina. The mills in Arkansas and South Carolina both used a special continuous-casting method that was quite cost-effective. In 2014, the Nucor-Yamato mill completed a $115 million project to add several new sheet-piling sections, increase production of single-sheet widths by 22 percent, and provide customers with a lighter, stronger sheet covering more area at a lower installed cost. Going into 2014, Nucor had the capacity to make 3.7 million tons of structural steel products annually.

Starting in 2000, Nucor began producing steel plate of various thicknesses and lengths that was sold to manufacturers of heavy equipment, ships, barges, bridges, railcars, refinery tanks, pressure vessels, pipes and tubes, wind towers, and similar products. Steel plate was made at two mills in Alabama and North Carolina having combined capacity of about 2.9 million tons. In early 2011, Nucor started operations at a newly constructed 125,000-ton heat-treating facility at the plate mill in North Carolina. Heat-treated steel plate was used in applications requiring higher strength, abrasion resistance, and toughness. During 2012, the North Carolina plate mill began using a newly constructed vacuum-tank degasser and started operations on a new 120,000-ton normalizing line in 2013. Collectively, these investments allowed Nucor to broaden its product offerings in the markets for pressure vessels, tank cars, tubular structures for offshore oil rigs, and naval and commercial shipbuilding.

All of Nucor's 23 steel mills used electric arc furnaces, whereby scrap steel and other metals were melted and the molten metal was then poured into continuous-casting systems. Sophisticated rolling mills converted the billets, blooms, and slabs produced by various casting equipment into rebars, angles, rounds, channels, flats, sheets, beams, plates, and other finished steel products. Nucor's steel mill operations were highly automated, typically requiring fewer operating employees per ton produced than the mills of rival companies. High worker productivity at all Nucor steel mills resulted in labor costs roughly 50 percent lower than the labor costs at the integrated mills of companies using union labor and conventional blast furnace technology. Nucor's value chain (anchored in using electric arc furnace technology to recycle scrap steel) involved far fewer production steps, far less capital investment, and considerably less labor than the value chains of companies with integrated steel mills that made crude steel from iron ore.

The breadth of Nucor's product line in steel mill products and finished steel products made it the most diversified steel producer in North America, and all of its steel mills were among the most modern and efficient mills in the United States. In 2013, the company was the North American market leader in nine product categories—steel bars, structural steel, steel reinforcing bars, steel joists, steel deck, cold-finished bar steel, metal buildings, steel piling distribution, and rebar fabrication, distribution, and installation.[4] It ranked number two in 2013 sales of plate steel, and number three in sales of sheet steel. Exhibit 3 shows Nucor's sales by product category for 1990 to 2013.

However, despite Nucor's long-standing reputation for being a cost-efficient producer, it had been stymied throughout the 2010–2013 period in its quest to operate its 23 steel mills as cost-efficiently as they were capable of being operated. Ever since the Great Recession of 2008–2009, the combination of an anemic economic recovery, depressed market demand for steel products, industrywide overcapacity, and fierce competition from foreign imports in certain product categories had forced Nucor to operate its steel mills well below full capacity. Whereas in the first three quarters of 2008, Nucor's steel mills operated at an average of 91 percent of full capacity, the average capacity utilization rates at Nucor's 23 steel mills were 54 percent in 2009, 70 percent in 2010, 74 percent in 2011, 75 percent in 2012, and just over 76 percent in 2013 (including tons shipped to outside customers and tons shipped to Nucor facilities making finished steel products). Likewise, subpar average capacity utilization rates at Nucor's facilities for producing finished steel products— 54 percent in 2010, 57 percent in 2011, 58 percent in 2012, and 61 percent in 2013—had impaired Nucor's ability to keep overall production costs for finished steel products as low as it would have been able to keep them at higher production levels. Market conditions in the steel industry still remained challenging in 2014, making the 2009–2014 period one of the longest and deepest economic slumps in several decades.

One of Nucor's biggest challenges in boosting its sales and profitability concerned the unusually weak demand for steel products used in nonresidential construction. As the company stated in its 2013 10-K report:[5]

> Sales of many of our products are dependent upon capital spending in the nonresidential construction markets in the United States, including in the industrial and commercial sectors, as well as capital spending on infrastructure that is publicly funded such as bridges, schools, prisons and hospitals. Unlike recoveries from past recessions, the recovery from the recession of 2008–2009 has not included a strong recovery in the severely depressed nonresidential construction market. In fact, while capital spending on nonresidential construction projects is slowly improving, it continues to lack sustained momentum, which is posing a significant challenge to our business. We do not expect to see strong growth in our net sales until we see a sustained increase in capital spending on these types of construction projects.

## Pricing and Sales

In both 2012 and 2013, approximately 86 percent of the steel shipped from Nucor's steel mills went to external customers. The balance of the company's

**EXHIBIT 3** Nucor's Sales of Steel and Steel Products to Outside Customers, by Product Category, 1990–2013

| | Tons Sold to Outside Customers (thousands) | | | | | | | | | |
|---|---|---|---|---|---|---|---|---|---|---|
| | Steel Mill Products | | | | | Finished Steel Products | | | | |
| Year | Sheet Steel (2013 capacity of ~11.3 million tons) | Steel Bars (2013 capacity of ~9.1 million tons) | Structural Steel (2013 capacity of ~3.7 million tons) | Steel Plate (2013 capacity of ~2.9 million tons) | Total (2013 capacity of ~27 million tons) | Steel Joists (2013 capacity of ~715,000 tons) | Steel Deck (2013 capacity of ~530,000 tons) | Cold Finished Steel (2013 capacity of ~860,000 tons) | Rebar Fabrication (2013 capacity of ~1.7 million tons) and Other Products* | Total Tons |
| 2013 | 7,491 | 5,184 | 2,695 | 2,363 | 17,733 | 342 | 334 | 474 | 4,847 | 23,730 |
| 2012 | 7,622 | 5,078 | 2,505 | 2,268 | 17,473 | 291 | 308 | 492 | 4,528 | 23,092 |
| 2011 | 7,500 | 4,680 | 2,338 | 2,278 | 16,796 | 288 | 312 | 494 | 5,154 | 23,044 |
| 2010 | 7,434 | 4,019 | 2,139 | 2,229 | 15,821 | 276 | 306 | 462 | 5,154 | 22,019 |
| 2009 | 5,212 | 3,629 | 1,626 | 1,608 | 12,075 | 264 | 310 | 330 | 4,596 | 17,576 |
| 2008 | 7,505 | 5,266 | 2,934 | 2,480 | 18,185 | 485 | 498 | 485 | 4,534 | 25,187 |
| 2007 | 8,266 | 6,287 | 3,154 | 2,528 | 20,235 | 542 | 478 | 449 | 1,236 | 22,940 |
| 2006 | 8,495 | 6,513 | 3,209 | 2,432 | 20,649 | 570 | 398 | 327 | 174 | 22,118 |
| 2005 | 8,026 | 5,983 | 2,866 | 2,145 | 19,020 | 554 | 380 | 342 | 169 | 20,465 |
| 2004 | 8,078 | 5,244 | 2,760 | 1,705 | 17,787 | 522 | 364 | 271 | 165 | 19,109 |
| 2003 | 6,954 | 5,530 | 2,780 | 999 | 16,263 | 503 | 353 | 237 | 117 | 17,473 |
| 2002 | 5,806 | 2,947 | 2,689 | 872 | 12,314 | 462 | 330 | 226 | 110 | 13,442 |
| 2001 | 5,074 | 2,687 | 2,749 | 522 | 11,032 | 532 | 344 | 203 | 126 | 12,237 |
| 2000 | 4,456 | 2,209 | 3,094 | 20 | 9,779 | 613 | 353 | 250 | 194 | 11,189 |
| 1995 | 2,994 | 1,799 | 1,952 | — | 6,745 | 552 | 234 | 234 | 178 | 7,943 |
| 1990 | 420 | 1,382 | 1,002 | — | 2,804 | 443 | 134 | 163 | 104 | 3,648 |

*Includes steel fasteners (steel screws, nuts, bolts, washers, and bolt assemblies), steel mesh, steel grates, metal buildings systems, light-gauge steel framing, and scrap metal.

*Source:* Company records, www.nucor.com (accessed April 15, 2014).

steel mill shipments went to supply the steel needs of the company's joist, deck, rebar fabrication, fastener, metal buildings, and cold-finish operations.

The commodity nature of steel products meant that the prices a company could command were governed by market demand–supply conditions that shifted more or less constantly and caused the spot market price for commodity steel to bounce around on a weekly and sometimes daily basis. The big majority of Nucor's steel sales were to customers that placed orders monthly based on their immediate upcoming needs; Nucor's pricing strategy was to charge customers the going spot price on the day an order was placed. Ongoing shifts in market demand–supply conditions and the resulting spot market price

caused Nucor's average sales prices per ton to fluctuate from quarter to quarter, sometimes by considerable amounts—see Exhibit 4. It was Nucor's practice to quote the same payment terms to all customers and for customers to pay all shipping charges.

Nucor marketed the output of its steel mills and steel product facilities mainly through an in-house sales force; there were salespeople located at almost every Nucor production facility. In 2012 and 2013, approximately 65 percent of Nucor's sheet steel sales were to contract customers (versus 40 percent in 2010 and 30 percent in 2009); the contracts for sheet steel were usually for periods of 6 to 12 months and permitted price adjustments to reflect changes in the market pricing for steel and/or raw-material costs.

## EXHIBIT 4 Nucor's Average Quarterly Sales Prices for Steel Products, by Product Category, 2011–2013

| Period | Sheet Steel | Steel Bars | Structural Steel | Steel Plate | Average of All Steel Mill Products | Average of All Finished Steel Products* |
|---|---|---|---|---|---|---|
| **2011** | | | | | | |
| Qtr 1 | $755 | $779 | $831 | $ 880 | $789 | $1,274 |
| Qtr 2 | 894 | 803 | 923 | 1,029 | 891 | 1,361 |
| Qtr 3 | 800 | 811 | 901 | 1,021 | 847 | 1,381 |
| Qtr 4 | 744 | 796 | 891 | 946 | 806 | 1,395 |
| **2012** | | | | | | |
| Qtr 1 | 780 | 823 | 866 | 929 | 824 | 1,387 |
| Qtr 2 | 759 | 795 | 905 | 922 | 812 | 1,395 |
| Qtr 3 | 707 | 745 | 973 | 837 | 775 | 1,371 |
| Qtr 4 | 690 | 723 | 956 | 778 | 751 | 1,420 |
| **2013** | | | | | | |
| Qtr 1 | 699 | 732 | 949 | 769 | 756 | 1,380 |
| Qtr 2 | 676 | 731 | 959 | 765 | 746 | 1,374 |
| Qtr 3 | 693 | 708 | 923 | 753 | 741 | 1,369 |
| Qtr 4 | 724 | 709 | 969 | 767 | 763 | 1,378 |

*An average of the steel prices for steel deck, steel joists and girders, steel buildings, cold-finished steel products, steel mesh, fasteners, fabricated rebar, and other finished steel products.

*Source:* Company records, www.nucor.com (accessed April 15, 2014).

The other 35 percent of Nucor's sheet steel shipments and virtually all of the company's shipments of plate, structural, and bar steel were sold at the prevailing spot market price—customers not purchasing sheet steel rarely ever wanted to enter into a contract sales agreement. Nucor's steel mills maintained inventory levels deemed adequate to fill the expected incoming orders from customers.

Nucor sold steel joists, joist girders, and deck on the basis of firm, fixed-price contracts that, in most cases, were won in competitive bidding against rival suppliers. Longer-term supply contracts for these items that were sometimes negotiated with customers contained clauses permitting price adjustments to reflect changes in prevailing raw-material costs. Steel joists, girders, and deck were manufactured to customers' specifications and shipped immediately; Nucor's plants did not maintain inventories of steel joists, girders, and deck. Nucor also sold fabricated reinforcing products only on a construction contract bid basis. However,

cold-finished steel, steel fasteners, steel grating, wire, and wire mesh were all manufactured in standard sizes, with each facility maintaining sufficient inventories of its products to fill anticipated orders; almost all sales of these items were made at the prevailing spot price. The average prices Nucor received for its various finished steel products are shown in the last column of Exhibit 4.

## NUCOR'S STRATEGY TO GROW AND STRENGTHEN ITS BUSINESS AND COMPETITIVE CAPABILITIES

Starting in 2000, Nucor embarked on a five-part growth strategy that involved new acquisitions, new plant construction, continued plant upgrades and cost reduction efforts, international growth through joint ventures, and greater control over raw-material costs.

## Strategic Acquisitions

Beginning in the late 1990s, Nucor management concluded that growth-minded companies like Nucor might well be better off purchasing existing plant capacity rather than building new capacity, provided the acquired plants could be bought at bargain prices, economically retrofitted with new equipment if need be, and then operated at costs comparable to (or even below) those of newly constructed state-of-the-art plants. At the time, the steel industry worldwide had far more production capacity than was needed to meet market demand, forcing many companies to operate in the red. Nucor had not made any acquisitions since about 1990, and a team of five people was assembled in 1998 to explore acquisition possibilities that would strengthen Nucor's customer base, geographic coverage, and lineup of product offerings.

For almost three years, no acquisitions were made. But then the economic recession that hit Asia and Europe in the late 1990s reached the United States in full force in 2000–2001. The September 11, 2001, terrorist attacks further weakened steel purchases by such major steel-consuming industries as construction, automobiles, and farm equipment. Many steel companies in the United States and other parts of the world were operating in the red. Market conditions in the United States were particularly grim. Between October 2000 and October 2001, 29 steel companies in the United States, including Bethlehem Steel Corp. and LTV Corp., the nation's third- and fourth-largest steel producers respectively, filed for bankruptcy protection. Bankrupt steel companies accounted for about 25 percent of U.S. capacity. The *Economist* noted that of the 14 steel companies tracked by Standard & Poor's, only Nucor was indisputably healthy. Some experts believed that close to half of the U.S. steel industry's production capacity might be forced to close before conditions improved; about 47,000 jobs in the U.S. steel industry had vanished since 1997.

One of the principal reasons for the distressed market conditions in the United States was a surge in imports of low-priced steel from foreign countries. Outside the United States, weak demand and a glut of capacity had driven commodity steel prices to 20-year lows in 1998. Globally, the industry had about 1 billion tons of annual capacity, but puny demand had kept production levels in the range of 750 to 800 million tons per year during 1998–2000. A number of foreign steel producers, anxious to keep their mills running and finding few good market opportunities elsewhere, began selling steel in the U.S. market at cut-rate prices in 1997–1999. Nucor and other U.S. companies reduced prices to better compete, and several filed unfair trade complaints against foreign steelmakers. The U.S. Department of Commerce concluded in March 1999 that steel companies in six countries (Canada, South Korea, Taiwan, Italy, Belgium, and South Africa) had illegally dumped stainless steel in the United States and that the governments of Belgium, Italy, and South Africa further facilitated the dumping by giving their steel producers unfair subsidies that at least partially made up for the revenue losses of selling at below-market prices. Congress and the Clinton administration opted to not impose tariffs or quotas on imported steel, which helped precipitate the number of bankruptcy filings. However, the Bush administration was more receptive to protecting the U.S. steel industry from the dumping practices of foreign steel companies. In October 2001, the U.S. International Trade Commission (ITC) ruled that increased steel imports of semi-finished steel, plate, hot-rolled sheet, strip and coils, cold-rolled sheet and strip, and corrosion-resistant and coated sheet and strip were a substantial cause of serious injury, or threat of serious injury, to the U.S. industry. In March 2002, the Bush administration imposed tariffs of up to 30 percent on imports of select steel products to help provide relief from Asian and European companies dumping steel in the United States at ultra-low prices.

Even though market conditions were tough for Nucor, management concluded that oversupplied steel industry conditions and the number of beleaguered U.S. companies made it attractive to expand Nucor's production capacity via acquisition. Starting in 2001 and continuing through 2013, the company proceeded to make a series of strategic acquisitions to strengthen Nucor's competitiveness, selectively expand its product offerings, improve its ability to serve customers in particular geographic locations, and boost the company's overall prospects for excellent profitability in times when market demand for steel was strong:

- In 2001, Nucor paid $115 million to acquire substantially all of the assets of Auburn Steel Company's 400,000-ton steel bar facility in Auburn, New York. This acquisition gave Nucor expanded market presence in the Northeast and was seen as a good source of supply for a new Vulcraft joist plant being constructed in Chemung, New York.

- In November 2001, Nucor announced the acquisition of ITEC Steel Inc. for a purchase price of $9 million. ITEC Steel had annual revenues of $10 million and produced load-bearing light-gauge steel framing for the residential and commercial markets at facilities in Texas and Georgia. Nucor was impressed with ITEC's dedication to continuous improvement and intended to grow ITEC's business via geographic and product line expansion. ITEC Steel's name was changed to Nucor Steel Commercial Corporation in 2002.

- In July 2002, Nucor paid $120 million to purchase Trico Steel Company, which had a 2.2-million-ton sheet steel mill in Decatur, Alabama. Trico Steel was a joint venture of LTV (which owned a 50 percent interest) and two leading international steel companies—Sumitomo Metal Industries and British Steel. The joint venture partners had built the mill in 1997 at a cost of $465 million, but Trico was in Chapter 11 bankruptcy proceedings at the time of the acquisition and the mill was shut down. The Trico mill's capability to make thin sheet steel with a superior surface quality added competitive strength to Nucor's strategy to gain sales and market share in the flat-rolled sheet segment. By October 2002, two months ahead of schedule, Nucor had restarted operations at the Decatur mill and was shipping products to customers.

- In December 2002, Nucor paid $615 million to purchase substantially all of the assets of Birmingham Steel Corporation, which included four bar mills in Alabama, Illinois, Washington, and Mississippi. The four plants had a capacity of approximately 2 million tons annually. The purchase price also included approximately $120 million in inventory and receivables, the assets of Port Everglade Steel Corp., the assets of Klean Steel, Birmingham Steel's ownership interest in Richmond Steel Recycling, and a mill in Memphis, Tennessee, that was not currently in operation. Top executives believed the Birmingham Steel acquisition would broaden Nucor's customer base and build profitable market share in bar steel products.

- In August 2004, Nucor acquired a cold-rolling mill in Decatur, Alabama, from Worthington Industries for $80 million. This 1-million-ton mill, which opened in 1998, was located adjacent to the previously acquired Trico mill and gave Nucor added ability to serve the needs of sheet steel buyers located in the southeastern United States.

- In June 2004, Nucor paid a cash price of $80 million to acquire a plate mill owned by Britain-based Corus Steel that was located in Tuscaloosa, Alabama. The Tuscaloosa mill, which currently had a capacity of 700,000 tons that Nucor management believed was expandable to 1 million tons, was the first U.S. mill to employ a special technology that enabled high-quality wide steel plate to be produced from coiled steel plate. The mill produced coiled steel plate and plate products that were cut to customer-specified lengths. Nucor intended to offer these niche products to its commodity-plate and coiled-plate customers.

- In February 2005, Nucor completed the purchase of Fort Howard Steel's operations in Oak Creek, Wisconsin; the Oak Creek facility produced cold-finished bars in sizes up to 6-inch rounds and had approximately 140,000 tons of annual capacity.

- In June 2005, Nucor purchased Marion Steel Company located in Marion, Ohio, for a cash price of $110 million. Marion operated a bar mill with annual capacity of about 400,000 tons; the Marion location was within close proximity to 60 percent of the steel consumption in the United States.

- In May 2006, Nucor acquired Connecticut Steel Corporation for $43 million in cash. Connecticut Steel's bar-products mill in Wallingford had annual capacity to make 300,000 tons of wire rod and rebar and approximately 85,000 tons of wire mesh fabrication and structural mesh fabrication, products that complemented Nucor's present lineup of steel bar products provided to construction customers.

- In late 2006, Nucor purchased Verco Manufacturing Co. for approximately $180 million; Verco produced steel floor and roof decking at one location in Arizona and two locations in California. The Verco acquisition further solidified Vulcraft's market-leading position in steel decking, giving it total annual capacity of over 500,000 tons.

- In January 2007, Nucor acquired Canada-based Harris Steel for about $1.07 billion. Harris Steel had 2005 sales of Cdn$1.0 billion and earnings of Cdn$64 million. The company's operations consisted of (1) Harris Rebar, which was involved in the fabrication and placement of concrete-reinforcing steel and the design and installation of concrete post-tensioning systems;

(2) Laurel Steel, which manufactured and distributed wire and wire products, welded wire mesh, and cold-finished bar; and (3) Fisher & Ludlow, which manufactured and distributed heavy industrial steel grating, aluminum grating, and expanded metal. In Canada, Harris Steel had 24 reinforcing-steel fabricating plants, two steel-grating distribution centers, and one cold-finished bar and wire processing plant; in the United States, it had 10 reinforcing-steel fabricating plants, two steel-grating manufacturing plants, and three cold-finished bar and wire processing plants. Harris had customers throughout Canada and the United States and employed about 3,000 people. For the past three years, Harris had purchased a big percentage of its steel requirements from Nucor. Nucor management opted to operate Harris Steel as an independent subsidiary.

- Over several months in 2007 following the Harris Steel acquisition, Nucor, through its new Harris Steel subsidiary, acquired rebar fabricator South Pacific Steel Corporation, Consolidated Rebar, Inc., and a 90 percent equity interest in rebar fabricator Barker Steel Company, as well as completing several smaller transactions—all aimed at growing its presence in the rebar fabrication marketplace.

- In August 2007, Nucor acquired LMP Steel & Wire Company for a cash purchase price of approximately $27.2 million, adding 100,000 tons of cold-drawn steel capacity.

- In October 2007, Nucor completed the acquisition of Nelson Steel, Inc., for a cash purchase price of approximately $53.2 million, adding 120,000 tons of steel mesh capacity.

- In the third quarter of 2007, Nucor completed the acquisition of Magnatrax Corporation, a leading provider of custom-engineered metal buildings, for a cash purchase price of approximately $275.2 million. The Magnatrax acquisition enabled Nucor's Buildings Group to become the second-largest metal buildings producer in the United States.

- In August 2008, Nucor's Harris Steel subsidiary acquired Ambassador Steel Corporation for a cash purchase price of about $185.1 million. Ambassador Steel was one of the largest independent fabricators and distributors of concrete-reinforcing steel—in 2007, Ambassador shipped 422,000 tons of fabricated rebar and distributed another 228,000 tons of reinforcing steel. Its business complemented that of Harris Steel, and the acquisition represented another in a series of moves to greatly strengthen Nucor's competitive position in the rebar fabrication marketplace.

- Another small rebar fabrication company, Free State Steel, was acquired in late 2009, adding to Nucor's footprint in rebar fabrication.

- In June 2012, Nucor acquired Skyline Steel, LLC, and its subsidiaries for a cash price of approximately $675.4 million. Skyline was primarily a distributor of steel pilings, and it also processed and fabricated spiral-weld pipe piling, rolled and welded pipe piling, cold-formed sheet piling, and threaded bar. The Skyline acquisition paired Skyline's leadership position in the steel piling distribution market with Nucor's own Nucor-Yamato plant in Arkansas, which was the market leader in steel piling manufacturing. To capitalize upon the strategic fits between Skyline's business and Nucor's business, Nucor immediately announced that its Nucor-Yamato mill in Arkansas would begin a capital project to (1) add several new sheet-piling sections, (2) increase the production of single-sheet widths by 22 percent, and (3) produce a lighter, stronger sheet covering more area at a lower installed cost—outcomes that would broaden the range of hot-rolled steel piling products that could be marketed through Skyline's distribution network in the United States, Canada, Mexico, and the Caribbean that supplied customers needing steel pilings for marine construction, bridge and highway construction, heavy civil construction, storm protection, underground commercial parking, and environmental containment projects.

## Commercialization of New Technologies and New Plant Construction

The second element of Nucor's growth strategy was to continue to be a technology leader and to be opportunistic in constructing new plant capacity that would enable the company to expand its presence in attractive new or existing market segments. From its earliest days, Nucor had been an early and aggressive investor in two types of steelmaking breakthroughs:

- *Disruptive technological innovations*—production processes and equipment that would give Nucor a commanding market advantage and thus be disruptive to the efforts of competitors in matching Nucor's cost competitiveness and/or product quality.

- *Leapfrog technological innovations*—production processes and equipment that would enable Nucor to overtake competitors in terms of product quality, cost per ton, or market share.

One of Nucor's biggest and most recent successes in pioneering new technology had been at its Crawfordsville facilities, where Nucor had the world's first installation of direct strip casting of carbon sheet steel—a process called Castrip. After several years of testing and process refinement at Crawfordsville, Nucor announced in 2005 that the Castrip process was ready for commercialization; Nucor had exclusive rights to Castrip technology in the United States and Brazil. The process, which had proved to be quite difficult to bring to commercial reality, was a major technological breakthrough for producing flat-rolled, carbon, and stainless steels in very thin gauges; it involved far fewer process steps to cast metal at or very near customer-desired thicknesses and shapes. The Castrip process drastically reduced capital outlays for equipment and produced savings on operating expenses as well—major expense savings resulted from the ability to use lower-quality scrap metal and to expend 90 percent less energy to process liquid metal into hot-rolled steel sheets. A big environmental benefit of the Castrip process was that it cut greenhouse gas emissions by up to 80 percent. Nucor's Castrip facility at Crawfordsville had the capacity to produce 500,000 tons annually. In 2006, Nucor built a second Castrip facility on the site of its structural steel mill in Arkansas.

Nucor's growth strategy also included investing in the construction of new plant capacity or enhanced production capabilities whenever management spotted opportunities to strengthen its competitive position vis-à-vis rivals:

- In 2006, Nucor announced that it would construct a new $27 million facility to produce metal buildings systems in Brigham City, Utah. The new plant, Nucor's fourth buildings systems plant, had a capacity of 45,000 tons and gave Nucor national market reach in buildings systems products.

- In 2006, Nucor initiated construction of a $230 million state-of-the-art steel mill in Memphis,

Tennessee, with the annual capacity to produce 850,000 tons of special-quality steel bars. Management believed this mill, together with the company's other special-quality bar mills in Nebraska and South Carolina, would give Nucor the broadest, highest-quality, and lowest-cost special-quality steel bar offering in North America.

- In 2009, Nucor opened an idle and newly renovated $50 million wire rod and bar mill in Kingman, Arizona, that had been acquired in 2003. Production of straight-length rebar, coiled rebar, and wire rod began in mid-2010; the plant had an initial capacity of 100,000 tons and the ability to increase annual production to 500,000 tons.

- Also in 2009, Nucor began production at a new facility in Blytheville, Arkansas, which used the breakthrough Castrip technology to cast molten steel into near-final shape and thickness with minimal hot or cold rolling. This innovative production process entailed both lower capital investment and lower operating costs, plus it reduced the environmental impact of producing steel.

- A new $150 million galvanizing facility located at the company's sheet steel mill in Decatur, Alabama, began operations in mid-2009. This facility gave Nucor the ability to make 500,000 tons of 72-inch-wide galvanized sheet steel, a product used by motor vehicle and appliance producers and in various steel frame and steel stud buildings. The galvanizing process entailed dipping steel in melted zinc at extremely high temperatures; the zinc coating protected the steel surface from corrosion.

## The Drive for Plant Efficiency and Low-Cost Production

A key part of Nucor's production strategy was to make ongoing capital investments to improve efficiency and lower production costs at each and every facility it operated. From its earliest days in the steel business, Nucor had built state-of-the-art facilities in the most economical fashion possible and then made it standard company practice to invest in plant modernization and efficiency improvements as technology advanced and new cost-saving opportunities emerged. Nucor management made a point of staying on top of the latest advances in steelmaking around the world, diligently searching for emerging cost-effective technologies it could adopt or adapt in its facilities. Executives at Nucor had a long-standing commitment to provide the company's workforce with the best technology available to get the job done safely and to do it in an environmentally responsible manner. When Nucor acquired plants, it immediately began bringing them up to Nucor standards—a process it called "Nucorizing." This included increasing operational efficiency by reducing the amount of time, space, energy, and manpower it took to produce steel or steel products and paying close attention to worker safety and environmental protection practices.

Nucor management also stressed continual improvement in product quality and cost at each one of its production facilities. Almost all of Nucor's production locations were ISO 9000– and ISO 14000–certified. The company had a "BESTmarking" program aimed at being the industrywide best performer on a variety of production and efficiency measures. Managers at all Nucor plants were accountable for demonstrating that their operations were competitive on both product quality and cost vis-à-vis the plants of rival companies. One trait of Nucor's corporate culture was the expectation that plant-level managers would be persistent in implementing methods to improve product quality and keep costs per ton low relative to rival plants. Nucor's capital expenditures for new technology, plant improvements, and equipment upgrades in 2000–2013 are shown in Exhibit 5.

Nucor management viewed the task of optimizing its manufacturing operations as a continuous process. According to former CEO Dan DiMicco:[6]

> We talk about "climbing a mountain without a peak" to describe our constant improvements. We can take pride in what we have accomplished, but we are never satisfied.

## Shift of Production from Lower-End Steel Products to Value-Added Products

During 2010–2013, Nucor undertook a number of actions to shift more of the production tonnage at its steel mills and steel product facilities to "value-added products" that could command higher prices and yield better profit margins than could be had by producing lower-end or commodity steel products. Examples included:

- Adding new galvanizing capability at the Decatur, Alabama, mill that enabled Nucor to sell 500,000 tons of corrosion-resistant, galvanized sheet steel for high-end applications.

- Expanding the cut-to-length capabilities at the Tuscaloosa, Alabama, mill that put the mill in position to sell as many as 200,000 additional tons per year of cut-to-length and tempered steel plate.

- Shipping 250,000 tons of new steel plate and structural steel products in 2010 that were not offered in 2009, and further increasing shipments of these new products to 500,000 tons in 2011.

- Completing installation of a heat-treating facility at the Hertford County plate mill in 2011 that gave Nucor the capability to produce as much as 125,000 tons annually of heat-treated steel plate ranging from 3/16 of an inch through 2 inches thick.

- Installing new vacuum degassers at the Hickman, Arkansas, sheet mill and Hertford County, North Carolina, mill to enable these two facilities to produce increased volumes of higher-grade sheet steel and steel plate. The degasser at the Hickman plant facilitated production of higher-value steel piping and tubular products used in the oil and gas industry.

**EXHIBIT 5**    Nucor's Capital Expenditures for New Plants, Plant Expansions, New Technology, Equipment Upgrades, and Other Operating Improvements, 2000–2013

| Year | Capital Expenditures (millions) | Year | Capital Expenditures (millions) |
|------|------|------|------|
| 2000 | $415.0 | 2007 | $ 520.4 |
| 2001 | 261.0 | 2008 | 1,019.0 |
| 2002 | 244.0 | 2009 | 390.5 |
| 2003 | 215.4 | 2010 | 345.2 |
| 2004 | 285.9 | 2011 | 450.6 |
| 2005 | 331.5 | 2012 | 1,019.3 |
| 2006 | 338.4 | 2013 | 1,230.4 |

*Sources:* Company records, www.nucor.com; data for 2009–2013 are from the 2013 10-K report, p. 43.

- Investing $290 million at its three steel bar mills to enable the production of steel bars and wire rods for the most demanding engineered bar applications and also put in place state-of-the-art quality inspection capabilities. The project enabled Nucor to offer higher-value steel bars and wire rods to customers in the energy, automotive, and heavy truck and equipment markets (where the demand for steel products had been particularly strong in recent years).

- Completing installation of a new 120,000-ton "normalizing" process for making steel plate at the Hertford County mill in June 2013; the new normalizing process allowed the mill to produce a higher grade of steel plate that was less brittle and had a more uniform fine-grained structure (which permitted the plate to be machined to more precise dimensions). Steel plate with these qualities was more suitable for armor plate applications and for certain uses in the energy, transportation, and shipbuilding industries. Going into 2014, the normalizing process, coupled with the company's recent investments in a vacuum tank degasser and a heat-treating facility at the same plant, doubled the Hertford mill's capacity to produce higher-quality steel plate products that commanded a higher market price.

- Modernizing the casting, hot-rolling, and downstream operations at the Berkeley, South Carolina, mill to enable, starting in the first quarter of 2014, the production of 72-inch-wide sheet steel and lighter-gauge hot-rolled and cold-rolled steel products with a finished width of 72 inches that were used in an assortment of high-strength and ultra-high-strength applications. This product line expansion opened opportunities for Nucor to sell higher-value sheet steel products to customers in the agricultural, pipe and tube, industrial equipment, automotive, and heavy equipment industries.

Several product upgrades had also been undertaken at several Nucor facilities making cold-finished and fastener products. Senior management believed that all of these upgraded product offerings would contribute to higher revenues and earnings when market demand for steel products turned upward.

## Global Growth via Joint Ventures

In 2007, Nucor management decided it was time to begin building an international growth platform. The company's strategy to grow its international revenues had two elements:

- *Establishing foreign sales offices and exporting U.S.-made steel products to foreign markets.* Because about 60 percent of Nucor's steelmaking capacity was located on rivers with deep-water transportation access, management believed that the company could be competitive in shipping U.S.-made steel products to customers in a number of foreign locations.

- *Entering into joint ventures with foreign partners to invest in steelmaking projects outside North America.* Nucor executives believed that the success of this strategy element was finding the right partners to grow with internationally.

Nucor opened a trading office in Switzerland and proceeded to establish international sales offices in Mexico, Brazil, Colombia, the Middle East, and Asia. The company's trading office bought and sold steel and steel products that Nucor and other steel producers had manufactured. In 2010, approximately 11 percent of the shipments from Nucor's steel mills were exported. Customers in South and Central America presented the most consistent opportunities for export sales, but there was growing interest from customers in Europe and other locations.

In January 2008, Nucor entered in a 50-50 joint venture with the European-based Duferco Group to establish the production of beams and other long products in Italy, with distribution in Europe and North Africa. A few months later, Nucor acquired 50 percent of the stock of Duferdofin-Nucor S.r.l. for approximately $667 million (Duferdofin was Duferco's Italy-based steelmaking subsidiary). In 2013, Duferdofin-Nucor operated, at various locations, a steel melt shop and bloom/billet caster with an annual capacity of 1.1 million tons, two beam-rolling mills with a combined capacity of 1.1 million tons, a 495,000-ton merchant bar mill, and a 60,000-ton trackshoes/cutting edges mill. The customers for the products produced by Duferdofin-Nucor were primarily steel service centers and distributors located both in Italy and throughout Europe. So far, the joint venture project had not lived up to the partners' financial expectations because all of the plants made construction-related products. The European construction industry had been hard hit by the economic events of 2008–2009, and the construction-related demand for steel products in Europe was very slowly creeping back toward precrisis levels. During the second quarter of 2012, Nucor recorded an impairment charge of $30 million against its investment in Duferdofin-Nucor. In 2013, the Duferdofin-Nucor venture was unprofitable, but the loss was smaller than that in 2012. Nucor's investment in Duferdofin-Nucor at December 31, 2013, was $465.4 million.

In early 2010, Nucor invested $221.3 million to become a 50-50 joint venture partner with Mitsui USA to form NuMit LLC—Mitsui USA was the largest wholly owned subsidiary of Mitsui & Co., Ltd., a diversified global trading, investment, and service enterprise headquartered in Tokyo, Japan. NuMit LLC owned 100 percent of the equity interest in Steel Technologies LLC, an operator of 25 sheet steel processing facilities throughout the United States, Canada, and Mexico. The NuMit partners agreed that Nucor's previously announced plans to construct a new flat-rolled processing center in Monterrey, Mexico, would be implemented by Steel Technologies. The NuMit joint venture was profitable in both 2012 and 2013. At the end of 2013, Nucor's investment in NuMit was $318.4 million, which consisted of the initial investment plus additional capital contributions and equity method earnings less distributions to Nucor; Nucor had loaned Steel Technologies $40 million that

was due in October 2014 and had also extended a $100 million line of credit to Steel Technologies (of which $17 million was outstanding as of December 31, 2013).

## Nucor's Raw-Materials Strategy

Scrap metal and scrap substitutes were Nucor's single biggest cost—all of Nucor's steel mills used electric arc furnaces to make steel products from recycled scrap steel, scrap iron, pig iron, hot briquetted iron (HBI), and direct reduced iron (DRI). On average, it took approximately 1.1 tons of scrap and scrap substitutes to produce a ton of steel—the proportions averaged about 70 percent scrap steel and 30 percent scrap substitutes. Nucor was the biggest user of scrap metal in North America, and it also purchased millions of tons of pig iron, HBI, DRI, and other iron products annually—top-quality scrap substitutes were especially critical in making premium grades of sheet steel, steel plate, and special-quality bar steel at various Nucor mills. Scrap prices were driven by market demand–supply conditions and could fluctuate significantly—see Exhibit 6. Rising scrap prices adversely impacted the company's costs and ability to compete against steelmakers that made steel from scratch using iron ore, coke, and traditional blast furnace technology.

## EXHIBIT 6     Nucor's Costs for Scrap Steel and Scrap Substitute, 2000–2013

| Period | Average Cost of Scrap and Scrap Substitute per Ton Used | Period | Average Cost of Scrap and Scrap Substitute per Ton Used |
|---|---|---|---|
| 2000 | $120 | 2012 | |
| 2001 | 101 | Quarter 1 | $445 |
| 2002 | 110 | Quarter 2 | 427 |
| 2003 | 137 | Quarter 3 | 380 |
| 2004 | 238 | Quarter 4 | 372 |
| 2005 | 244 | Full-year average | 407 |
| 2006 | 246 | 2013 | |
| 2007 | 278 | Quarter 1 | $379 |
| 2008 | 438 | Quarter 2 | 377 |
| 2009 | 303 | Quarter 3 | 372 |
| 2010 | 351 | Quarter 4 | 377 |
| 2011 | 439 | Full-year average | 376 |

*Sources:* Nucor's annual reports, 2011, 2009, 2007; and information in the Investor Relations section at www.nucor.com (accessed October 25, 2006, April 12, 2012, and April 15, 2014).

Nucor's raw-materials strategy was aimed at achieving greater control over the costs of all types of metallic inputs (both scrap metal and iron-related substitutes) used at its steel plants. A key element of this strategy was to backward-integrate into the production of 6 million to 7 million tons per year of high-quality scrap substitutes (chiefly pig iron and direct reduced iron) either at its own wholly owned and operated plants or at plants jointly owned by Nucor and other partners—integrating backward into supplying a big fraction of its own iron requirements held the promise of raw-material savings and less reliance on outside iron suppliers. The costs of producing pig iron and DRI were not as subject to steep swings as was the price of scrap steel.

Nucor's first move to execute its long-term raw-material strategy came in 2002 when it partnered with The Rio Tinto Group, Mitsubishi Corporation, and Chinese steelmaker Shougang Corporation to pioneer Rio Tinto's HIsmelt technology at a new plant to be constructed in Kwinana, Western Australia. The HIsmelt technology entailed converting iron ore to liquid metal or pig iron and was both a replacement for traditional blast furnace technology and a hot-metal source for electric arc furnaces. Rio Tinto had been developing the HIsmelt technology for 10 years and believed the technology had the potential to revolutionize iron making and provide low-cost, high-quality iron for making steel. Nucor had a 25 percent ownership in the venture and had a joint global marketing agreement with Rio Tinto to license the technology to other interested steel companies. The Australian plant represented the world's first commercial application of the HIsmelt technology; it had a capacity of over 880,000 tons and was expandable to 1.65 million tons at an attractive capital cost per incremental ton. Production started in January 2006. However, the joint venture partners opted to permanently close the HIsmelt plant in December 2010 because the project, while technologically acclaimed, proved to be financially unviable. Nucor's loss in the joint venture partnership amounted to $94.8 million.

In April 2003, Nucor entered a joint venture with Companhia Vale do Rio Doce (CVRD) to construct and operate an environmentally friendly $80 million pig iron project in northern Brazil. The project, named Ferro Gusa Carajás, utilized two conventional mini-blast furnaces to produce about 418,000 tons of pig iron per year, using iron ore from CVRD's Carajás mine in northern Brazil. The charcoal fuel for the plant came exclusively from fast-growing eucalyptus trees in a cultivated forest in northern Brazil owned by a CVRD subsidiary. The cultivated forest removed more carbon dioxide from the atmosphere than the blast furnace emitted, thus counteracting global warming—an outcome that appealed to Nucor management. Nucor invested $10 million in the project and was a 22 percent owner. Production of pig iron began in the fourth quarter of 2005; the joint venture agreement called for Nucor to purchase all of the plant's production. However, Nucor sold its interest in the project to CVRD in April 2007.

Nucor's third raw-material sourcing initiative came in 2004 when it acquired an idled direct reduced iron plant in Louisiana, relocated all of the plant assets to Trinidad (an island off the coast of South America, near Venezuela), and expanded the project (named Nu-Iron Unlimited) to a capacity of 2 million tons. The plant used a proven technology that converted iron ore pellets into direct reduced iron. The Trinidad site was chosen because it had a long-term and very cost-attractive supply of natural gas (large volumes of natural gas were consumed in the plant's production process), along with favorable logistics for receiving iron ore and shipping direct reduced iron to Nucor's steel mills in the United States. Nucor entered into contracts with natural gas suppliers to purchase natural gas in amounts needed to operate the Trinidad plant through 2028. Production began in January 2007. Nu-Iron personnel at the Trinidad plant had recently achieved world-class product quality levels in making DRI; this achievement allowed Nucor to use an even larger percentage of DRI in producing the most demanding steel products.

In September 2010, Nucor announced plans to build a $750 million DRI facility with an annual capacity of 2.5 million tons on a 4,000-acre site in St. James Parish, Louisiana. This investment moved Nucor two-thirds of the way to its long-term objective of being able to supply 6 million to 7 million tons of its requirements for high-quality scrap substitutes. However, the new DRI facility was the first phase of a multiphase plan that included a second 2.5-million-ton DRI facility, a coke plant, a blast furnace, an iron ore pellet plant, and a steel mill. Permits for both DRI plants were received from the Louisiana Department of Environmental Quality in January 2011. Construction of the first DRI unit at the St. James site began in 2011, and production began in late 2013 and was rapidly ramped up toward capacity in 2014. Because producing DRI was a natural gas–intensive process, Nucor had entered into a long-term, onshore natural gas working-interest drilling program with Encana Oil & Gas, one of North America's largest producers of natural gas, to help offset the company's exposure to future increases in the price of natural gas consumed by the DRI facility in St. James Parish. Nucor entered into a second and more significant drilling program with Encana in 2012. All natural gas from Nucor's working-interest drilling program was being sold to outside parties. In December 2013, Nucor and Encana agreed to temporarily suspend drilling new gas wells because of expectations that the natural gas pricing environment would be weak in 2014. By the middle of 2014, when all of the in-process wells were completed, Nucor management believed that the over 300 producing wells would provide a full hedge against the Louisiana DRI plant's expected consumption of natural gas into 2015. Nucor had the option to resume drilling operations in the event that a higher natural gas pricing environment made it prudent to do so.

In 2014, a Nucor official indicated that Nucor's use of DRI in its steel mills gave the company an approximate $75-per-ton cost advantage in producing a ton of steel over traditional integrated steel mills using conventional blast furnace technology.[7]

**Acquisition of the David J. Joseph Company**   In February 2008, Nucor acquired the David J. Joseph Company (DJJ) and related affiliates for a cash purchase price of approximately $1.44 billion, the largest acquisition in Nucor's history. DJJ was one of the leading scrap metal companies in the United States, with 2007 revenues of $6.4 billion. It processed about 3.5 million tons of scrap iron and steel annually at 35 scrap yards and brokered over 20 million tons of iron and steel scrap and over 500 million pounds of nonferrous materials in 2007. It obtained scrap from industrial plants, the manufacturers of products that contained steel, independent scrap dealers, peddlers, auto junkyards, demolition firms, and other sources. The DJJ Mill and Industrial Services business provided logistics and metallurgical blending operations and offered onsite handling and trading of industrial scrap. The DJJ Rail Services business owned over 2,000 railcars dedicated to the movement of scrap metals and offered complete railcar fleet management and leasing services. Nucor was familiar with DJJ and its various operations because it

had obtained scrap from DJJ since 1969. Most importantly, though, all of DJJ's businesses had strategic value to Nucor in helping gain control over its scrap metal costs. Within months of completing the DJJ acquisition (which was operated as a separate subsidiary), the DJJ management team acquired four other scrap-processing companies. Additional scrap processors were acquired during 2010–2012, and several new scrap yards were opened. As of early 2014, DJJ had expanded to 76 operating facilities in 16 states (along with multiple brokerage offices in the United States and certain foreign countries) and added over 1.7 million tons of scrap-processing capacity, giving Nucor a total annual scrap-processing capacity of 5.2 million tons. And, because of DJJ's railcar fleet, Nucor had the ability to improve the cost and speed with which scrap could be delivered to its steel mills.

## Nucor's Commitment to Being a Global Leader in Environmental Performance

Every Nucor facility was evaluated for actions that could be taken to promote greater environmental sustainability. Measurable objectives and targets relating to such outcomes as reduced use of oil and grease, more efficient use of electricity, and sitewide recycling were in place at each plant. Computerized controls on large electric motors and pumps and energy-recovery equipment to capture and reuse energy that otherwise would be wasted had been installed throughout Nucor's facilities to lower energy usage—Nucor considered itself to be among the most energy-efficient steel companies in the world. All of Nucor's facilities had water-recycling systems. Nucor even recycled the dust from its electric arc furnaces because scrap metal contained enough zinc, lead, chrome, and other valuable metals to recycle into usable products; the dust was captured in each plant's state-of-the-art baghouse air pollution control devices and then sent to a recycler that converted the dust into zinc oxide, steel slag, and pig iron. The first Nucor mill received ISO 14001 Environmental Management System (EMS) certification in 2001; as of year-end 2013, 49 Nucor facilities has ISO 14001 EMS certifications in place and efforts were under way for dozens more to receive certification in the future.

Nucor's sheet mill in Decatur, Alabama, used a measuring device called an *opacity monitor,* which gave precise, minute-by-minute readings of the air quality that passed through the bag house and out of the mill's exhaust system. While rival steel producers had resisted using opacity monitors (because they documented any time a mill's exhaust was out of compliance with its environmental permits, even momentarily), Nucor's personnel at the Decatur mill viewed the opacity monitor as a tool for improving environmental performance. They developed the expertise to read the monitor so well that they could pinpoint in just a few minutes the first signs of a problem in any of the nearly 7,000 bags in the bag house—before those problems resulted in increased emissions. Their early-warning system worked so well that the division applied for a patent on the process, with an eye toward licensing it to other companies.

## Organization and Management Philosophy

Nucor had a simple, streamlined organizational structure to allow employees to innovate and make quick decisions. The company was highly decentralized, with most day-to-day operating decisions made by group or plant-level general managers and their staff. Each group or plant operated independently as a profit center and was headed by a general manager, who in most cases also had the title of vice president.

The organizational structure at a typical plant had four layers:

- General manager
- Department manager
- Supervisor or professional
- Hourly employee

Group managers and general managers of plants reported to one of five executive vice presidents at corporate headquarters. Nucor's corporate staff was exceptionally small, consisting of about 100 people in 2013, the philosophy being that corporate headquarters should consist of a small cadre of executives who would guide a decentralized operation where liberal authority was delegated to managers in the field. Each plant had a sales manager who was responsible for selling the products made at that particular plant; such staff functions as engineering, accounting, and personnel management were performed at the group and/or plant level. There was a minimum of paperwork and bureaucratic systems. Each group or plant was expected to earn about a 25 percent return on total assets before

corporate expenses, taxes, interest, or profit sharing. As long as plant managers met their profit targets, they were allowed to operate with minimal restrictions and interference from corporate headquarters. A very friendly spirit of competition existed among the plants to see which facility could be the best performer, but since all of the vice presidents and general managers shared the same bonus systems, they functioned pretty much as a team despite operating their facilities individually. Top executives did not hesitate to replace group or plant managers who consistently struggled to achieve profitability and operating targets.

## Workforce Compensation Practices

Nucor was a largely nonunion, "pay-for-performance" company with an incentive compensation system that rewarded goal-oriented individuals and did not put a maximum on what they could earn. All employees, except those in the recently acquired Harris Steel and DJJ subsidiaries that operated independently from the rest of Nucor, worked under one of four basic compensation plans, each featuring incentives related to meeting specific goals and targets:

1. *Production Incentive Plan.* Production line jobs were rated on degree of responsibility required and were assigned a base wage comparable to the wages paid by other manufacturing plants in the area where a Nucor plant was located. But in addition to their base wage, operating and maintenance employees were paid weekly bonuses based on the number of tons by which the output of their production team or work group exceeded the "standard" number of tons. All operating and maintenance employees were members of a production team that included the team's production supervisor, and the tonnage produced by each work team was measured for each work shift and then totaled for all shifts during a given week. If a production team's weekly output beat the weekly standard, team members (including the team's production supervisor) earned a specified percentage bonus for each ton produced above the standard— production bonuses were paid weekly (rather than quarterly or annually) so that workers and supervisors would be rewarded immediately for their efforts. The standard rate was calculated based on the capabilities of the equipment employed (typically at the time plant operations began), and no bonus was paid if the equipment was not operating

(which gave maintenance workers a big incentive to keep a plant's equipment in good working condition)—Nucor's philosophy was that when equipment was not operating, everybody suffered and the bonus for downtime ought to be zero. Production standards at Nucor plants were seldom raised unless a plant underwent significant modernization or important new pieces of equipment were installed that greatly boosted labor productivity. It was common for production incentive bonuses to run from 50 to 150 percent of an employee's base pay, thereby pushing compensation levels up well above those at other nearby manufacturing plants. Worker efforts to exceed the standard and get a bonus were less involved with working harder than with engaging in good teamwork and close collaboration to resolve problems and figure out how best to exceed the production standards.

2. *Department Manager Incentive Plan.* Department managers earned annual incentive bonuses based primarily on the percentage of net income generated to dollars of assets employed for their division. These bonuses could be as much as 80 percent of a department manager's base pay.

3. *Professional and Clerical Bonus Plan.* A bonus based on a division's net income return on assets was paid to employees who were not on the production worker or department manager plan.

4. *Senior Officers Annual Incentive Plan.* Nucor's senior officers did not have employment contracts and did not participate in any pension or retirement plans. Their base salaries were set at approximately 90 percent of the median base salary for comparable positions in other manufacturing companies with comparable assets, sales, and capital. The remainder of their compensation was based on Nucor's annual overall percentage of net income to stockholders' equity (ROE) and was paid out in cash and stock. Once Nucor's ROE reached a threshold of not less than 3 percent or more than 7 percent (as determined annually by the compensation committee of the board of directors), senior officers earned a bonus equal to 20 percent of their base salary. If Nucor's annual ROE was 20 percent or higher, senior officers earned a bonus equal to 225 percent of their base salary. Officers could earn an additional bonus up to 75 percent of their base salary based on a comparison of Nucor's net sales growth with the net sales growth of members of a steel industry peer group. There was also a long-term incentive plan that provided for stock awards and stock options. The structure of these officer incentives was such that bonus compensation for Nucor officers fluctuated widely—from close to zero (in years like 2003 when industry conditions were bad and Nucor's performance was subpar) to 400 percent (or more) of base salary (when Nucor's performance was excellent, as had been the case in 2004–2008). Based on Nucor's 2013 ROE of 6.4 percent and its second-place ranking in net sales performance within the steel industry peer group, Nucor's executive officers earned an annual incentive award of (1) 60.97 percent of base salary for the ROE performance measure and (2) an additional 60 percent of base salary for favorable net sales performance relative to the peer group.

*Senior Officers Long-Term Incentive Plan.* The long-term incentive was intended to balance the short-term focus of the annual incentive plan by rewarding performance over multiyear periods. Long-term incentives were received in the form of cash (50 percent) and restricted stock (50 percent) and covered a performance period of three years; 50 percent of the long-term award was based on how Nucor's three-year return on average invested capital (ROAIC) compared against the three-year ROAIC of the steel industry peer group, and 50 percent was based on how Nucor's three-year ROAIC compared against a multi-industry group of well-respected companies in capital-intensive businesses similar to that of steel. Nucor's ROAIC of 15.23 percent for the long-term incentive plan performance period that began January 1, 2011, and ended December 31, 2013, ranked 2nd relative to the 6 members of the steel industry peer group and ranked 10th relative to the 11 members of the multi-industry peer group. This produced stock issue and cash awards of 80 percent of the maximum payout based on the peer-group comparison and zero stock and cash awards based on the multi-industry peer-group comparison.

Nucor management had designed the company's incentive plans for employees so that bonus calculations involved no discretion on the part of a plant or division manager or top executives. This was done to eliminate any concerns on the part of workers that managers or executives might show favoritism or otherwise be unfair in calculating or awarding incentive awards.

There were two other types of extra compensation:

- *Profit sharing.* Each year, Nucor allocated 10 percent of its operating profits to profit-sharing bonuses for all employees (except senior officers). Depending on company performance, the bonuses could run anywhere from 1 percent to over 20 percent of pay. Of the bonus amount, 20 percent was paid to employees in the following March as a cash bonus, and the remaining 80 percent was put into a trust for each employee, with each employee's share being proportional to his or her earnings as a percentage of total earnings by all workers covered by the plan. An employee's share of profit sharing became vested after one full year of employment. Employees received a quarterly statement of their balance in profit sharing.
- *401(k) plan.* Both officers and employees participated in a 401(k) plan whereby the company matched from 5 to 25 percent of each employee's first 7 percent of contributions; the amount of the match was based on how well the company was doing.

In 2013, an entry-level worker at a Nucor plant could expect to earn about $47,000 to $50,000 annually (including bonuses). Total compensation for Nucor's plant employees in 2013 was in the range of $70,000 to $100,000 annually. It was common for worker compensation at Nucor plants to be double or more the average earned by workers at other manufacturing companies in the states where Nucor's plants were located. At Nucor's plant in Hertford County, North Carolina, where jobs were scarce and poverty was common, Nucor employees earned three times the local average manufacturing wage. Nucor management philosophy was that workers ought to be excellently compensated because the production jobs were strenuous and the work environment in a steel mill was relatively dangerous.

Employee turnover in Nucor mills was extremely low (6 percent in 2013); absenteeism and tardiness were minimal. Each employee was allowed four days of absences and could also miss work for jury duty, military leave, or the death of close relatives. After this, a day's absence cost a worker the entire performance bonus pay for that week, and being more than a half-hour late to work on a given day resulted in no bonus payment for the day. When job vacancies did occur, Nucor was flooded with applications from people wanting to get a job at Nucor; plant personnel screened job candidates very carefully, seeking people with initiative and a strong work ethic.

## Employee Relations and Human Resources

Employee relations at Nucor were based on four clear-cut principles:

1. Management is obligated to manage Nucor in such a way that employees will have the opportunity to earn according to their productivity.
2. Employees should feel confident that if they do their jobs properly, they will have a job tomorrow.
3. Employees have the right to be treated fairly and must believe that they will be.
4. Employees must have an avenue of appeal when they believe they are being treated unfairly.

The hallmarks of Nucor's human resource strategy were its incentive pay plan for production exceeding the standard and the job security provided to production workers—despite being in an industry with strong down cycles, Nucor had made it a practice not to lay off workers. Instead, when market conditions were tough and production had to be cut back, workers were assigned to plant maintenance projects, cross-training programs, and other activities calculated to boost the plant's performance when market conditions improved.

Nucor took an egalitarian approach to providing fringe benefits to its employees; employees had the same insurance programs, vacation schedules, and holidays as upper-level managers. However, certain benefits were not available to Nucor's officers. The fringe-benefit package at Nucor included:

- *Medical and dental plans.* The company had a flexible and comprehensive health benefit program for officers and employees that included wellness and health care spending accounts.
- *Tuition reimbursement.* Nucor reimbursed up to $3,000 of an employee's approved educational expenses each year and up to $1,500 of a spouse's educational expenses for two years.
- *Service awards.* After each five years of service with the company, Nucor employees received a service award consisting of five shares of Nucor stock.
- *Scholarships and educational disbursements.* Nucor provided the children of every employee

(except senior officers) with college funding of $3,000 per year for four years to be used at accredited academic institutions. As of 2011, Nucor had paid out over $61 million.

- *Other benefits.* Long-term disability, life insurance, vacation time.

Most of the changes Nucor made in work procedures came from employees. The prevailing view at Nucor was that the employees knew the problems of their jobs better than anyone else and were thus in the best position to identify ways to improve how things were done. Most plant-level managers spent considerable time in the plant, talking and meeting with frontline employees and listening carefully to suggestions. Promising ideas and suggestions were typically acted upon quickly and implemented—management was willing to take risks to try worker suggestions for doing things better and to accept the occasional failure when the results were disappointing. Teamwork, a vibrant team spirit, and a close worker–management partnership were much in evidence at Nucor plants.

Nucor plants did not utilize job descriptions. Management believed job descriptions caused more problems than they solved, given the teamwork atmosphere and the close collaboration among work-group members. The company saw formal performance appraisal systems as a waste of time and added paperwork. If a Nucor employee was not performing well, the problem was dealt with directly by supervisory personnel and the peer pressure of work-group members (whose bonuses were adversely affected).

Employees were kept informed about company and division performance. Charts showing the division's results in return-on-assets and bonus payoff were posted in prominent places in the plant. Most all employees were quite aware of the level of profits in their plant or division. Nucor had a formal grievance procedure, but grievances were few and far between. The corporate office sent all news releases to each division, where they were posted on bulletin boards. Each employee received a copy of Nucor's annual report; it was company practice for the cover of the annual report to consist of the names of all Nucor employees.

All of these practices had created an egalitarian culture and a highly motivated workforce that grew out of former CEO Ken Iverson's radical insight: Employees, even hourly clock punchers, would put forth extraordinary effort and be exceptionally productive if they were richly rewarded, treated with respect, and given real power to do their jobs as best they saw fit.[8] There were countless stories of occasions when managers and workers had gone beyond the call of duty to expedite equipment repairs (in many instances even using their weekends to go help personnel at other Nucor plants solve a crisis); the company's workforce was known for displaying unusual passion and company loyalty even when no personal financial stake was involved. As one Nucor worker put it, "At Nucor, we're not 'you guys' and 'us guys.' It's all of us guys. Wherever the bottleneck is, we go there, and everyone works on it."[9]

It was standard procedure for a team of Nucor veterans, including people who worked on the plant floor, to visit their counterparts as part of the process of screening candidates for acquisition.[10] One of the purposes of such visits was to explain the Nucor compensation system and culture face-to-face, gauge reactions, and judge whether the plant would fit into "the Nucor way of doing things" if it was acquired. Shortly after making an acquisition, Nucor management moved swiftly to institute its pay-for-performance incentive system and to begin instilling the egalitarian Nucor culture and idea sharing. Top priority was given to looking for ways to boost plant production by using fewer people and without making substantial capital investments; the take-home pay of workers at newly acquired plants typically went up rather dramatically. At the Auburn Steel plant, acquired in 2001, it took Nucor about six months to convince workers that they would be better off under Nucor's pay system; during that time Nucor paid people under the old Auburn Steel system but posted what they would have earned under Nucor's system. Pretty soon, workers were convinced to make the changeover—one worker saw his pay climb from $53,000 in the year prior to the acquisition to $67,000 in 2001 and to $92,000 in 2005.[11]

**New Employees**    Each plant and division had a "consul" who provided new employees with general advice about becoming a Nucor teammate and who served as a resource for inquiries about how things were done at Nucor, how to navigate the division and company, and how to resolve issues that might come up. Nucor provided new employees with a personalized plan that set forth who would give them feedback about how well they were doing and when and how this feedback would be given;

from time to time, new employees met with the plant manager for feedback and coaching. In addition, there was a new employee orientation session that provided a hands-on look at the plant or division operations; new employees also participated in product-group meetings to provide exposure to broader business and technical issues. Each year, Nucor brought all recent college hires to the Charlotte headquarters for a forum intended to give the new hires a networking opportunity and to provide senior management with guidance on how best to leverage their talent.

# THE WORLD STEEL INDUSTRY

Both 2012 and 2013 were record years for the global production of crude steel, with worldwide production reaching 1,703 million tons in 2012 and 1,744 million tons in 2013—see Exhibit 7. Steelmaking capacity worldwide was approximately 2,300 million tons in 2013, resulting in a 2013 capacity utilization rate of 75.8 percent (up from a historically unprecedented low of 52 percent in 2009, but largely unchanged from 2012). Worldwide demand for steel mill products grew an average of about 5.5 percent annually from 2000 to 2013, but the annual growth rate was quite volatile, ranging from a low of 0.01 percent (2007–2008) to a high of 14.5 percent (2010–2011). Worldwide steel demand grew 3.6 percent in 2013 and was forecast to increase about 3.1 percent in 2014 and 3.3 percent in 2015.[12] In North America, after a 2.4 percent decline in steel demand in 2013, the forecast was for increases of 3.8 percent in 2014 and 3.4 percent in 2015.[13]

The six biggest steel-producing countries in 2013 were:

| Country | Total Production of Crude Steel | Percent of Worldwide Production |
|---|---|---|
| China | 859 million tons | 49.2 |
| Japan | 121 million tons | 7.0 |
| United States | 96 million tons | 5.5 |
| India | 89 million tons | 5.1 |
| Russia | 76 million tons | 4.4 |
| South Korea | 73 million tons | 4.2 |

Exhibit 8 shows the world's 15 largest producers of steel in 2013.

## Steelmaking Technologies

Steel was produced either by integrated steel facilities or by "mini-mills" that employed electric arc furnaces. Integrated mills used blast furnaces to produce hot metal typically from iron ore pellets, limestone, scrap steel, oxygen, assorted other metals, and coke (coke was produced by firing coal in large coke ovens and was the major fuel used in blast furnaces to produce molten iron). Melted iron from the blast furnace process was then run through the basic oxygen process to produce liquid steel. To make flat rolled steel products, liquid steel was either fed into a continuous-caster machine and cast into slabs or else cooled in slab form for later processing. Slabs were further shaped or rolled at a plate mill or hot-strip mill. In making certain sheet steel products, the hot-strip mill process was followed by various finishing processes, including pickling, cold rolling, annealing, tempering, galvanizing, or other coating procedures. These various processes for converting raw steel into finished steel products were often distinct steps undertaken at different times and in different onsite or offsite facilities rather than being done in a continuous process in a single plant facility—an integrated mill was thus one that had multiple facilities at a single plant site and could therefore not only produce crude (or raw) steel but also run the crude steel through various facilities and finishing processes to make hot-rolled and cold-rolled sheet steel products, steel bars and beams, stainless steel, steel wire and nails, steel pipes and tubes, and other finished steel products. The steel produced by integrated mills tended to be purer than steel produced by electric arc furnaces since less scrap was used in the production process (scrap steel often contained nonferrous elements that could adversely affect metallurgical properties). Some steel customers required purer steel products for their applications.

Mini-mills used an electric arc furnace to melt steel scrap or scrap substitutes into molten metal that was then cast into crude steel slabs, billets, or blooms in a continuous-casting process. As was the case at integrated mills, the crude steel was then run through various facilities and finishing processes to make hot-rolled and cold-rolled sheet steel products, steel bars and beams, stainless steel, steel wire and nails, steel pipes and tubes, and other finished steel products. Mini-mills could accommodate short production runs and had a relatively fast product-changeover time. The electric

**EXHIBIT 7**    Worldwide Production of Crude Steel, with Compound Average Growth Rates, 1975–2013

| Year | World Crude Steel Production (millions of tons) | Compound Average Growth Rate in World Crude Steel Production | |
|------|------------------------------------------------|-------------------------------------------------------------|--|
| | | Period | Percentage Rate |
| 1975 | 709   | 1975–1980 | 2.2% |
| 1980 | 789   | 1980–1985 | 0.1% |
| 1985 | 793   | 1985–1990 | 1.4% |
| 1990 | 849   | 1990–1995 | −0.5% |
| 1995 | 827   | 1995–2000 | 4.5% |
| 2000 | 1,029 | 2000–2005 | 4.2% |
| 2001 | 1,032 | 2005–2010 | 4.6% |
| 2002 | 996   | 2010–2013 | 3.3% |
| 2003 | 1,069 | | |
| 2004 | 1,170 | | |
| 2005 | 1,264 | | |
| 2006 | 1,377 | | |
| 2007 | 1,486 | | |
| 2008 | 1,480 | | |
| 2009 | 1,364 | | |
| 2010 | 1,580 | | |
| 2011 | 1,694 | | |
| 2012 | 1,703 | | |
| 2013 | 1,744 | | |

*Sources:* Worldsteel Association, *Steel Statistical Yearbook,* various years, and "Crude Steel Production 2013," **www.worldsteel.org** (accessed April 23, 2014).

arc technology employed by mini-mills offered two primary competitive advantages: capital investment requirements that were 75 percent lower than those of integrated mills and a smaller workforce (which translated into lower labor costs per ton shipped).

Initially, companies that used electric arc furnace technology were able to make only low-end steel products (such as reinforcing rods and steel bars). But when thin-slab casting technology came on the scene in the 1980s, mini-mills were able to compete in the market for flat-rolled carbon sheet and strip products; these products sold at substantially higher prices per ton and thus were attractive market segments for mini-mill companies. Carbon sheet and strip steel products accounted for about 50-60 percent of total steel production and represented the last big market category controlled by the producers employing basic oxygen furnace and blast furnace technologies. Thin-slab casting technology, which had been developed by SMS

Schloemann-Siemag AG of Germany, was pioneered in the United States by Nucor at its plants in Indiana and elsewhere. Other mini-mill companies in the United States and across the world were quick to adopt thin-slab casting technology because the low capital costs of thin-slab casting facilities, often coupled with lower labor costs per ton, gave mini-mill companies a cost and pricing advantage over integrated steel producers, enabling them to grab a growing share of the global market for flat-rolled sheet steel and other carbon steel products. Many integrated producers also switched to thin-slab casting as a defensive measure to protect their profit margins and market shares.

In 2011–2013, about 70 percent of the world's steel mill production was made at large integrated mills and about 29 percent was made at mills that used electric arc furnaces. In the United States, however, roughly 60 percent of the steel was produced at mills employing electric arc furnaces and 40 percent at mills using

**EXHIBIT 8**  Top 15 Producers of Crude Steel Worldwide, 2013

| 2013 Rank | Company (Headquarters) | Crude Steel Production (millions of tons) | | |
|---|---|---|---|---|
| | | 2005 | 2010 | 2013 |
| 1 | ArcelorMittal (Luxembourg) | 120.9 | 98.2 | 96.1 |
| 2 | Nippon Steel (Japan) | 35.3 | 35.0 | 50.1 |
| 3 | Hebei Group (China) | — | — | 45.8 |
| 4 | Baosteel (China) | 25.0 | 37.0 | 43.9 |
| 5 | Wuhan Group (China) | 14.3 | 16.6 | 39.3 |
| 6 | POSCO (South Korea) | 33.6 | 35.4 | 38.4 |
| 7 | Shagang Group (China) | — | 23.2 | 35.1 |
| 8 | Ansteel Group (China) | 13.1 | 22.1 | 33.7 |
| 9 | Shougang Group (China) | — | — | 31.5 |
| 10 | JFE (Japan) | 32.9 | 31.1 | 31.2 |
| 11 | Tata Steel Group (India) | — | 23.2 | 25.3 |
| 12 | Shandong Steel Group (China) | — | — | 22.8 |
| 13 | United States Steel (USA) | 21.3 | 22.3 | 20.4 |
| 14 | Nucor (USA) | 20.3 | 18.3 | 20.2 |
| 15 | Tianjin Bohai Iron and Steel Group (China) | — | — | 19.3 |

*Source:* Worldsteel Association, "Top Steel Producers 2013," www.worldsteel.org (accessed July 13, 2014).

blast furnaces and basic oxygen processes. Large integrated steel mills using blast furnaces, basic oxygen furnaces, and assorted casting and rolling equipment typically had the ability to manufacture a wide variety of steel mill products but faced significantly higher energy costs and were often burdened with higher capital and fixed operating costs. Electric arc furnace mill producers were challenged by increases in scrap prices but tended to have lower capital and fixed operating costs compared than the integrated steel producers. However, the quality of the steel produced using blast furnace technologies tended to be superior to that of electric arc furnaces unless, as at many of Nucor's facilities, the user of electric arc furnaces invested in additional facilities and processing equipment to enable the production of upgraded steel products.

The global marketplace for steel was considered to be relatively mature and highly cyclical as a result of ongoing ups and downs in the world economy or the economies of particular countries. However, in 2010–2013, the world steel market was divided into "two separate worlds." In places like Europe, the United States, and Japan, where recovery from the 2008–2009 financial crisis and economic recession was slow, the demand for steel was weak and there was abundant excess steelmaking capacity. In fast-developing areas of the world—like Asia (especially China and India) and a number of countries in Latin America and the Middle East—the demand for steel was much stronger and sometimes exceeded the capacity of local steelmakers, many of which were adding new capacity.

In general, competition within the global steel industry was intense and expected to remain so. Companies with excess production capacity were active in seeking to increase their exports of steel to foreign markets. During 2005–2013, the biggest steel-exporting countries were China, Japan, South Korea, Russia, the Ukraine, and Germany; the biggest steel-importing countries during the same period were the United States, Germany, South Korea, Thailand, China, Italy, France, and Turkey. China, Germany, and South Korea were both big exporters and big importers because they had more capacity to make certain types and grades of steel than was needed inside their borders (and thus local steelmakers sought to export supplies to other countries) but lacked sufficient internal capacity to supply local steel users with other types and grades of steel.

**Industry Consolidation** Both in the United States and across the world, industry downturns and the overhang of excess production capacity had over the years precipitated numerous mergers and acquisitions. Some of the mergers and acquisitions were the result of a financially and managerially strong company seeking to acquire a high-cost or struggling steel company at a bargain price and then pursue cost reduction initiatives to make the newly acquired steel mill operations more cost-competitive. Other mergers and acquisitions, particularly in China, where very significant mergers and acquisitions occurred in the 2005–2012 period, reflected the strategies of growth-minded steel companies that wanted to expand their production capacity and/or geographic market presence.

## NUCOR AND COMPETITION IN THE U.S. MARKET FOR STEEL

Nucor's broad product lineup meant that it was an active participant in the markets for a wide variety of finished steel products and unfinished steel products, plus the markets for scrap steel and scrap substitutes. Nucor executives considered all the market segments and product categories in which the company competed to be intensely competitive, with many segments and categories populated with both domestic and foreign rivals. For the most part, competition for steel mill products and finished steel products was centered on price and the ability to meet customer delivery requirements. And, due to global overcapacity, almost all steelmakers were actively seeking new business in any geographic markets where they could find willing buyers.

Since the beginning of 2010, Nucor had encountered escalating competitive pressures in the market for sheet steel in the United States due to:

- The opening of a newly constructed 5-million-ton sheet steel mill in Alabama owned by Thyssen Krupp, a Germany-based steelmaker.
- Capacity additions at several existing domestic sheet mills.
- The reopening of a previously shuttered sheet mill in Maryland.

In addition, Nucor was continually locked in a competitive battle with rivals to win orders from buyers engaged in nonresidential construction. Headed into 2014, Nucor management did not foresee any signs of a meaningful and sustained upswing in nonresidential construction activity, meaning that the company's sales and profits that were based on the many different construction-related steel products included in its product offering would remain under competitive pressure.

Furthermore, over the past four years, Nucor had to contend with mounting competition in a number of product categories from foreign steelmakers seeking to export some of their production to the United States and win customers by undercutting the prices of domestic producers. Imports of foreign steel into the United States more than doubled from 2009 through 2012 (see Exhibit 9). In Nucor's 2013 10-K report, management said:[14]

> Imported steel and steel products continue to present unique challenges for us because foreign producers often benefit from government subsidies, either directly through government-owned enterprises or indirectly through government-owned or controlled financial institutions. Foreign imports of finished and semi-finished steel accounted for approximately 30% of the U.S. steel market in 2013 despite significant unused domestic capacity. Rebar and hot-rolled bar were impacted especially hard by imports in 2013 as imports of these products increased by 23% and 15%, respectively, over 2012 levels. Increased imports of bar have translated into even lower domestic utilization rates for that product—utilization in the mid-60% range—and significant decreases in domestic bar pricing in 2013. Competition from China, the world's largest producer and exporter of steel, which produces more than 45% of the steel produced globally, is a major challenge in particular. We believe that Chinese producers, many of which are government-owned in whole or in part, benefit from their government's manipulation of foreign currency exchange rates and from the receipt of government subsidies, which allow them to sell steel into our markets at artificially low prices.

> China is not only selling steel at artificially low prices into our domestic market but also across the globe. When they do so, steel products which would otherwise have been consumed by the local steel customers in other countries are displaced into global markets, which compounds the issue. In a more indirect manner, but still significant, is the import of fabricated steel products, such as oil country tubular goods, wind towers and other construction components that were produced in China.

Many foreign steel producers had costs on a par with or even below those of Nucor, although their competitiveness in the U.S. market varied significantly according to the prevailing strength of their local currencies versus the U.S. dollar and the extent to which they received government subsidies.

## Nucor's Two Largest Domestic Competitors

Consolidation of the industry into a smaller number of larger and more efficient steel producers had heightened competitive pressures for Nucor and most other steelmakers. Nucor had two major rivals in the United States—the USA division of Arcelor-Mittal and United States Steel.

**ArcelorMittal USA**   In 2013, ArcelorMittal USA operated 17 major production facilities, including four large integrated steel mills, six electric arc furnace plants, and four rolling and finishing plants. Its facilities were considered to be modern and efficient. Its product lineup included hot-rolled and cold-rolled sheet steel, steel plate, steel bars, railroad rails, high-quality wire rods, rebars, grinding balls, structural steel, tubular steel, and tin mill products. Much of its production was sold to customers in the automotive, trucking, off-highway, agricultural equipment, and railway industries, with the balance being sold to steel service centers and companies in the appliance, office furniture, electric motor, packaging, and industrial machinery sectors.

Globally, ArcelorMittal was the world's largest steel producer, with 2013 annual production capacity of 119 million tons of crude steel and 2013 steel shipments of 84.3 million tons. It had worldwide sales revenues of $79.4 billion and a net loss of $2.5 billion in 2013 and worldwide sales revenues of $84.2 billion and a net loss of $3.4 billion in 2012.[15] ArcelorMittal's financial reports suggested that its steel operations in the United States were probably profitable in 2013. A portion of ArcelorMittal USA's steel operations were included in the overall company's Flat Carbon Americas business group, which reported 2013 sales of $19.3 billion (down 3 percent from 2012) and operating income of $852 million

**EXHIBIT 9**   Apparent Consumption of Steel Mill Products in the United States, 2000–2012 (in millions of tons)

| Year | U.S. Shipments of Steel Mill Products | U.S. Exports of Steel Mill Products | U.S. Imports of Steel Mill Products | Apparent U.S. Consumption of Steel Mill Products* |
|---|---|---|---|---|
| 2000 | 109.1 | 6.5 | 38.0 | 140.6 |
| 2001 | 99.1 | 6.4 | 30.8 | 123.5 |
| 2002 | 100.7 | 6.2 | 33.3 | 127.8 |
| 2003 | 103.0 | 8.5 | 23.8 | 118.3 |
| 2004 | 109.6 | 8.6 | 36.0 | 137.0 |
| 2005 | 104.4 | 10.4 | 33.2 | 127.2 |
| 2006 | 108.4 | 10.5 | 46.4 | 144.3 |
| 2007 | 107.9 | 10.8 | 30.5 | 127.6 |
| 2008 | 100.5 | 13.2 | 27.1 | 114.4 |
| 2009 | 64.0 | 10.2 | 16.9 | 70.7 |
| 2010 | 88.5 | 13.0 | 24.8 | 100.3 |
| 2011 | 95.2 | 14.6 | 29.4 | 110.0 |
| 2012 | 97.8 | 14.9 | 34.0 | 116.9 |

*Apparent U.S. consumption equals total shipments minus exports plus imports.

*Source:* Worldsteel Association, *Steel Statistical Yearbook,* 2011 and 2013, www.worldsteel.org (accessed April 24, 2014).

(down from $1.0 billion in 2012). The remaining portion of ArcelorMittal USA's steel business was part of the overall company's Long Carbon Americas and Europe business group, which had 2013 sales of $21.0 billion (down 4 percent from 2012) and operating income of $1.1 billion (up from a loss of $512 million in 2012).

**U.S. Steel**    United States Steel was an integrated steel producer of flat-rolled and tubular steel products with major production operations in the United States and Europe. In 2013, it had a crude steel production capacity of 27 million tons, of which 22 million tons was in North America. At the end of 2013, U.S. Steel permanently closed its Hamilton facilities in Ontario, Canada, reducing its North American capacity by 2.3 million tons. In 2012, the company sold all of its steel operations in Serbia to the Republic of Serbia for one dollar, resulting in a loss on the sale of approximately $400 million. In North America, U.S. Steel's production of crude steel was 17.9 million tons in 2013, 19.1 million tons in 2012, and 18.6 million tons in 2011, equal to capacity utilization rates of 74 percent in 2013, 79 percent in 2012, and 77 percent in 2011.

U.S. Steel's operations were organized into three business segments: flat-rolled products (which included all of its integrated steel mills that produced steel slabs, rounds, steel plate, sheet steel, and tin mill products), U.S. Steel Europe, and the tubular product operations. The flat-rolled segment primarily served North American customers in the transportation (including automotive), construction, container, appliance, and electrical industries, plus steel service centers and manufacturers that bought steel mill products for conversion into a variety of finished steel products. In addition, this segment supplied steel rounds and hot-rolled bands needed to produce steel casing and tubular products to the company's tubular business segment; shipments from the flat-rolled segment to the tubular segment totaled 1.7 million tons in 2013, 1.9 million tons in 2012, and 2.2 million tons in 2011. U.S. Steel's flat-rolled business segment had 2013 sales of $11.5 billion and operating income of $105 million, 2012 sales of $12.9 billion and operating income of $400 million, and 2011 sales of $12.4 billion and operating income of $469 million.

U.S. Steel's tubular product operations, located primarily in the United States, produced steel casing and tubing marketed chiefly to customers in the oil, gas, and petrochemicals industries. With annual production capability of 2.8 million tons, U.S. Steel was the largest supplier of steel casing and tubing products in North America. Sales of steel casing and tubular products were $2.8 billion in 2013, $3.3 billion in 2012, and $3 billion in 2011; the tubular segment had operating income of $190 million in 2013, $366 million in 2012, and $316 million in 2011.

U.S. Steel's exports of steel products from the United States totaled 365,000 tons in 2013, 409,000 tons in 2012, and 572,000 tons in 2011. U.S. Steel had a labor cost disadvantage versus Nucor and ArcelorMittal USA, partly due to the lower productivity of its unionized workforce and partly due to its retiree pension costs. In 2013, U.S. Steel launched a series of internal initiatives to "get leaner faster, right-size, and improve our performance."[16]

# ENDNOTES

[1] Tom Peters and Nancy Austin, *A Passion for Excellence: The Leadership Difference,* (New York: Random House, 1985), and "Other Low-Cost Champions," *Fortune,* June 24, 1985.

[2] Nucor's 2011 annual report, p. 4.

[3] According to information at **www.nucor.com** (accessed October 11, 2006).

[4] March 2014 Investor Presentation, **www.nucor.com** (accessed April 22, 2014).

[5] 2013 10-K report, p. 22.

[6] Nucor's 2008 annual report, p. 5.

[7] March 2014 Investor Presentation.

[8] Nanette Byrnes, "The Art of Motivation," *Businessweek,* May 1, 2006, p. 57.

[9] Ibid., p. 60.

[10] Ibid.

[11] Ibid.

[12] Worldsteel Association press release, April 9, 2014.

[13] Ibid.

[14] Company 10-K report, 2011, p. 6.

[15] Company annual report, 2013.

[16] Company 10-K report, 2013, p. 12.

# Tesla Motors' Strategy to Revolutionize the Global Automotive Industry

**Arthur A. Thompson**

The University of Alabama

In his February 2014 Letter to Shareholders, Elon Musk—an early investor in Tesla Motors and its current chairman and CEO—was pleased with the company's future prospects. Tesla's strategy was producing rapidly improving results, and by all indications the company's execution of the strategy was very much on track. Musk's report left little doubt that Tesla Motors was making good progress in its journey to manufacture premium-quality, high-performance electric vehicles capable of winning widespread customer acceptance and accelerating the world's transition from carbon-producing, gasoline-powered vehicles to energy-efficient, environmentally responsible electric vehicles.

After suffering five years of losses totaling $943.5 million on combined revenues of just $861 million between 2008 and 2012, Tesla delivered 22,477 of its recently introduced Model S vehicles to customers in 2013. Production rates had recently increased to 600 vehicles per week and were expected to reach 1,000 vehicles per week by year-end 2014. Tesla reported global revenues of $2.0 billion in 2013 and over $100 million in net income on a non-GAAP basis. Deliveries to customers in Europe began in August 2013, and deliveries to China were set to begin in spring 2014—the company's sales showroom in Beijing was already generating the heaviest traffic of any of Tesla's showrooms worldwide. Musk was confident that sales of Tesla vehicles in Europe and China would exceed sales in the United States in two, or no more than three, years. Tesla was well along on its plan to begin producing two new models in 2014–2016—an SUV and a mid-priced sedan. The company's stock price had climbed from $34 in January 2013 to over $250 in March 2014.

The Tesla Model S had received widespread praise and acclaim not only as the world's best electric vehicle but also as a product far superior to any other brand or model of electric vehicle currently on the market. In 2013, the Model S was the most awarded car in the United States. In picking the 2014 Tesla Model S as the "best overall" model out of 260 cars tested, *Consumer Reports* awarded the Model S a score of 99 out of 100 (the highest score any vehicle had ever received from the magazine) and described it as "a technological tour de force" with "blistering acceleration, razor-sharp handling, compliant ride, and versatile cabin."[1] The sleek styling and politically correct power source of the Tesla Model S was thought to explain why thousands of wealthy individuals in North America and Europe—anxious to be a part of the migration from gasoline-powered vehicles to electric-powered vehicles and to publicly display support for a cleaner environment—had become early purchasers and advocates for the vehicle. Indeed, word-of-mouth praise for the Model S among current owners and glowing articles in the media were so pervasive that Tesla had not yet spent any money on advertising to boost customer traffic in its showrooms. In a presentation to investors, a Tesla officer said, "Tesla owners are our best salespeople."[2]

In fall 2013, the Model S ranked as the best-selling car in 8 of the 25-wealthiest zip codes in the United States, as ranked by Forbes.[3] At the top of that list was Atherton, California, a Silicon Valley town near Tesla's Palo Alto headquarters where the median home price in 2013 was $6.65 million. Other posh Silicon Valley zip codes where the Model S had a leading market share included Los Altos Hills, Portola Valley, Montecito, and Woodside. Almost 5,000 new Model S Teslas were registered in California in the first six months of 2013, equal to 1 Tesla for each 108 registrations of new passenger cars. However, Washington state had the distinction of having the highest ratio of Model S registrations relative to all other new car registrations in the first half of 2013—1 Model S per 100 new passenger car registrations. The high densities of Model S sales in California and Washington were attributed partly to the relatively large percentages of residents in these states who were "green-minded." But the popularity of the Model S relative to other premium-priced luxury cars in the United States was widespread. In the first nine months of 2013 in the United States, unit sales of Tesla's Model S sedan (14,200 vehicles) were higher than sales of Mercedes' top-of-the line S-Class sedan (9,600 vehicles), BMW's 700 series luxury sedan (9,600 vehicles), the Lexus LS 460 luxury sedan (9,200 vehicles), BMW's 600 series (8,000 vehicles), Audi's premium-priced A7 series (6,700 vehicles), and the Porsche Panamera sedan (4,300 vehicles).[4]

According to Jessica Caldwell, senior analyst at Edmunds.com (a respected website for automotive industry data):[5]

> Influential people set trends while the mainstream aspires to follow. We've seen this countless times in many different retail sectors. Cars are no different, albeit more expensive than most other purchases. Additionally, with the proclivity of tech geek being chic, the Silicon Valley area will set trends faster than traditional high-income markets like New York that have roots in (highly vilified) banking.
>
> So, as Tesla increases the number of models on offer and price points, it could find itself in demand by more than just those in these wealthy enclaves. After all, most luxury car companies find the most volume in their entry-level vehicles.

Headed into 2014, Tesla Model S owners in 20 countries were driving their vehicles almost 1 million miles every day—and had driven their vehicles a total of 200 million cumulative miles. Management believed that more than 80 percent of Model S owners were using their Model S as their primary vehicle. All the available evidence pointed to Tesla's Model S as being the best electric vehicle the world had ever seen.

## COMPANY BACKGROUND

Tesla Motors was incorporated in July 2003 by Martin Eberhard and Marc Tarpenning, two Silicon Valley engineers who believed it was feasible to produce an "awesome" electric vehicle. The namesake of Tesla Motors was the genius Nikola Tesla (1856–1943), an electrical engineer and scientist who once worked with Thomas Edison and later became known for his impressive inventions (of which more than 700 were patented) and his contributions to the design of modern alternating-current (AC) power transmission systems and electric motors. Tesla Motors' first vehicle, the Tesla Roadster (an all-electric sports car) introduced in early 2008, was powered by an AC motor that descended directly from Nikola Tesla's original 1882 design.

### Financing Early Operations

Eberhard and Tarpenning financed the company until Tesla Motors' first round of investor funding in February 2004. Elon Musk contributed $6.35 million of the $6.5 million in initial funding and, as the company's majority investor, assumed the position of chairman of the company's board of directors. Martin Eberhard put up $75,000 of the initial $6.5 million, with two private equity investment groups and a number of private investors contributing the remainder to Tesla's initial funding as well.[6] Shortly thereafter, the company had a second round of investor funding amounting to $13 million, with Musk and a third private equity investment group being the principal capital contributors.

In May 2006, a third round of investor funding raised $40 million in additional capital for the young company, the majority of which was contributed by Elon Musk and an investment group called Technology Partners. This third round included capital contributions from Google cofounders Sergey Brin and Larry Page, former eBay president Jeff Skoll, Hyatt heir Nick Pritzker, and three other venture capital firms. A fourth round of private financing in May 2007 brought in an additional $45 million in new investment capital. But the company continued to burn through the investment capital that had been raised—largely because of heavy product R&D expenditures and several product design changes. These costs forced a fifth financing round that raised $40 million in investment capital in February 2008.

Of the $145 million in investment capital raised in these first five financing rounds, Elon Musk contributed about $74 million, making him the company's largest shareholder.[7]

In May 2009, when the company was struggling to cope with still another cash crunch and also overcome a series of glitches in getting the Model S into production, Germany's Daimler AG, the maker of Mercedes vehicles, announced that it was acquiring an equity stake of almost 10 percent in Tesla for a reported $50 million and that a Daimler executive would become a member of Tesla's board of directors.[8] Daimler's investment signaled a strategic partnership with Tesla to accelerate the development of Tesla's lithium-ion battery technology and electric drive train technology and to collaborate on electric cars being developed at Mercedes. In July 2009, Daimler announced that Abu Dhabi's Aabar Investments had purchased 40 percent of Daimler's ownership interest in Tesla.[9]

In June 2009, following two years of lobbying effort by Tesla on behalf of its loan applications, the company received approval for about $465 million in low-interest loans from the U.S. Department of Energy (DOE) to accelerate the production of affordable, fuel-efficient electric vehicles; the loans were part of the DOE's $25 billion Advanced Technology Vehicle Manufacturing Program, created in 2007 during the George Bush administration and funded in September 2008, which provided incentives to new and established automakers to build more fuel-efficient vehicles and reduce the country's dependence on foreign oil. Tesla intended to use $365 million for production engineering and assembly of its forthcoming Model S and $100 million for a powertrain manufacturing plant employing about 650 people that would supply all-electric powertrain solutions to other automakers and help accelerate the availability of relatively low-cost, mass-market electric vehicles.

In September 2009, Tesla Motors raised $82.5 million from Daimler, Fjord Capital Partners, Aabar Investments, and other undisclosed investors; Elon Musk did not contribute to this funding round. Tesla indicated that the funds raised would be used primarily to open additional sales and service centers for its vehicles.

In June 2010, Tesla Motors became a public company, raising $226 million with an initial public offering of 13,300,000 shares of common stock sold at a price of $17 per share; of the shares sold to the public, 11,880,600 shares were offered by the company and 1,419,400 shares were offered by selling stockholders. In addition, the selling stockholders granted the underwriters a 30-day option to purchase up to an additional aggregate of 1,995,000 shares of common stock to cover overallotments, if any. Tesla's shares began trading on Tuesday, June 29, 2010, on the NASDAQ under the ticker symbol "TSLA." Tesla Motors was the first American car company to go public since Ford Motor Company's IPO in 1956. In October 2012, Tesla completed a follow-on offering of 7.97 million shares from which it received net proceeds of $222.1 million.

## Management Changes

In August 2007, with the company plagued by production delays, cofounder Martin Eberhard was ousted as Tesla's CEO and replaced with an interim CEO who headed the company until Ze'ev Drori, an Israeli-born American technology entrepreneur and avid car enthusiast, was named the company's president and CEO in November 2007. Drori was specifically tasked by the company's board of directors to get the delayed Tesla Roadster into production and start deliveries to customers as fast as possible. To combat continuing production delays (the latest of which involved problems in designing and developing a reliable, tested transmission that would last many miles) and "out-of-control" costs that were burning through the company's investment capital at a rate that disturbed investors, Drori conducted a performance review of the company's more than 250 employees and contractors and proceeded to fire or lay off roughly 10 percent of the workforce, including several executives, high-ranking members of the company's automotive engineering team, and other heretofore key employees.[10] Although Drori succeeded in getting the Tesla Roadster into production in March and initiating deliveries to customers, in October 2008 Musk decided it made more sense for him to take on the role as Tesla's chief executive—while continuing to serve as chairman of the board—because he was making all the major decisions anyway. Drori was named vice chairman but then opted to leave the company in December 2008. By January 2009, Tesla had raised $187 million and delivered 147 cars. Musk declared that the company would be cash flow–positive by mid-2009.

# Elon Musk

Elon Musk was born in South Africa, taught himself computer programming, and, at age 12, made $500 by selling the computer code for a video game he invented.[11] In 1992, after spending two years at Queen's University in Ontario, Canada, Musk transferred to the University of Pennsylvania, where he earned an undergraduate degree in business and a second degree in physics. During his college days, Musk spent some time thinking about two important matters that he thought would merit his time and attention later in his career: One was that the world needed an environmentally clean method of transportation; the other was that it would be good if humans could colonize another planet.[12] After graduating from the University of Pennsylvania, he decided to move to California and pursue a PhD in applied physics at Stanford but with the specific intent of working on energy storage capacitors that could be used in electric cars. However, he promptly decided to leave the program after two days to pursue his entrepreneurial aspirations instead.

Musk's first entrepreneurial venture was to join up with his brother, Kimbal, and establish Zip2, an Internet software company that developed, hosted, and maintained some 200 websites involving "city guides" for media companies, including the *New York Times,* the *Chicago Tribune,* and other newspapers in the Hearst, Times Mirror, and Pulitzer Publishing chains. In 1999 Zip2 was sold to a wholly owned subsidiary of Compaq Computer for $307 million in cash and $34 million in stock options—Musk received a reported $22 million from the sale.[13]

In March 1999, Musk cofounded X.com, a Silicon Valley online financial services and e-mail payment company. One year later, X.com acquired Confinity, which operated a subsidiary called PayPal. Musk was instrumental in the development of the person-to-person payment platform and, seeing a big market opportunity for such an online payment platform, decided to rename X.com as PayPal. Musk pocketed about $150 million in eBay shares when PayPal was acquired by eBay for $1.5 billion in eBay stock in October 2002.

In June 2002, Elon Musk, with an investment of $100 million of his own money, founded his third company, Space Exploration Technologies (SpaceX), to develop and manufacture space launch vehicles, with a goal of revolutionizing the state of rocket technology and ultimately enabling people to live on other planets. He vowed to revolutionize the space industry with a low-cost, reliable satellite launcher that charged $6 million a flight—less than half the going rate for small payloads. Upon hearing of Musk's new venture into the space flight business, David Sacks, one of Musk's former colleagues at PayPal, said, "Elon thinks bigger than just about anyone else I've ever met. He sets lofty goals and sets out to achieve them with great speed."[14] In 2011, Musk vowed to put a man on Mars in 10 years.[15] In May 2012, a SpaceX Dragon cargo capsule powered by a SpaceX Falcon Rocket completed a near flawless test flight to and from the International Space Station; the successful test flight prompted Musk to say that the mission, in his view, marked a turning point toward rapid advancement in space transportation technology, one that would pave the way for routine cargo deliveries and commercial space flights.[16] Since May 2012, under a $1.6 billion contract with NASA, the SpaceX Dragon had delivered cargo to and from the Space Station three times, in the first of at least 12 cargo resupply missions. As of 2013, SpaceX was both profitable and cash flow–positive; it had completed nearly 50 launches, representing some $5 billion in contracts, and had 3,000 employees. Headquartered in Hawthorne, California, SpaceX was owned by management, employees, and private equity firms; Elon Musk was the company's CEO and chief designer.

Elon Musk's other active business venture was SolarCity Inc., a full-service provider of solar system design, financing, solar panel installation, and ongoing system monitoring for homeowners, municipalities, businesses (including Toyota, Walmart, Walgreens, and eBay), over 100 schools (including Stanford University), nonprofit organizations, and military bases. Going into 2014, SolarCity managed more solar systems for homes than any other solar company in the United States. SolarCity had revenues of $163.8 million in 2013, but the company had lost money every year it had been in business, with the losses growing in size every year since 2009. Nonetheless, investors were bullish on SolarCity's future prospects; the company's stock price ranged from a low of $48 to a high of $86 in the first five months of 2014. Elon Musk was the chairman of SolarCity's board of directors and owned 22.9 percent of the outstanding shares of the company as of April 4, 2014.

On August 12, 2013, Musk published a blog post detailing his design for a solar-powered, city-to-city elevated transit system called the Hyperloop that could take passengers and cars from Los Angeles to San Francisco (a distance of 380 miles) in 30 minutes. He then held a press call to go over the details. In Musk's vision, the Hyperloop would transport people via aluminum pods enclosed inside steel tubes. He described the design as looking like a shotgun, with the tubes running side by side for most of the route and closing the loop at either end.[17] The tubes would be mounted on columns 50 to 100 yards apart, and the pods inside would travel up to 800 miles per hour. The pods could be enlarged to ferry cars, as well as people—with enlarged pods, Musk said, "You just drive on, and the pod departs." Musk estimated that a Los Angeles–to–San Francisco Hyperloop could be built for $6 billion with people-only pods, or $10 billion for the larger pods capable of holding people and cars. Musk claimed his Hyperloop alternative would be four times as fast as California's proposed $70 billion high-speed train, with ticket costs being "much cheaper" than a plane ride. While pods would be equipped with an emergency brake for safety reasons, Musk said the safe distance between the pods would be about 5 miles, so you could have about 70 pods between Los Angeles and San Francisco that departed every 30 seconds. Musk stated that riding on the Hyperloop would be quite pleasant. "It would have less lateral acceleration—which is what tends to make people feel motion sick—than a subway ride, as the pod banks against the tube like an airplane," he says. "Unlike an airplane, it is not subject to turbulence, so there are no sudden movements. It would feel supersmooth." Musk envisioned the Hyperloop as an ideal way to link cities less than 1,000 miles apart that had high amounts of traffic between them (like Los Angeles and San Francisco, New York and Washington, and New York and Boston). Travel between cities less than 1,000 miles apart via a Hyperloop system would be quicker than flying because of the time it took to board and unboard airline passengers and the time it took for planes to take off and land at busy airports. Musk believed the costs of Hyperloop transportation for routes over 1,000 miles would prove prohibitive, not to mention the visual and logistical problems that would accrue from having Hyperloop tubes crisscrossing the country. Musk announced that he would not form a company to build Hyperloop systems;

rather, he was releasing his design in hopes that others would take on such projects.

Since 2008, many business articles had been written about Musk's brilliant entrepreneurship in creating companies with revolutionary products that either spawned new industries or disruptively transformed existing industries. In a 2012 *Success* magazine article, Musk indicated that his commitments to his spacecraft, electric car, and solar panel businesses were long-term and deeply felt.[18] The author quoted Musk as saying, "I never expect to sort of sell them off and do something else. I expect to be with those companies as far into the future as I can imagine." Musk indicated he was involved in SolarCity and Tesla Motors "because I'm concerned about the environment," while "SpaceX is about trying to help us work toward extending life beyond Earth on a permanent basis and becoming a multiplanetary species." The same writer described Musk's approach to a business as one of rallying employees and investors without creating false hope.[19] The article quoted Musk as saying:

> You've got to communicate, particularly within the company, the true state of the company. When people really understand it's do or die but if we work hard and pull through, there's going to be a great outcome, people will give it everything they've got.

Asked if he relied more on information or instinct in making key decisions, Musk said he makes no bright-line distinction between the two:[20]

> Data informs the instinct. Generally, I wait until the data and my instincts are in alignment. And if either the data or my instincts are out of alignment, then I sort of keep working the issue until they are in alignment, either positive or negative.

Musk was widely regarded as being an inspiring and visionary entrepreneur with astronomical ambition and willingness to invest his own money in risky and highly problematic business ventures—on several occasions, Musk's ventures had approached the brink of failure in 2008–2009 and then unexpectedly emerged with seemingly bright prospects. He set stretch performance targets and high product-quality standards, and he pushed hard for their achievement. He exhibited perseverance, dedication, and an exceptionally strong work ethic—he typically worked 85 to 90 hours a week. Most weeks, Musk split his time between SpaceX and Tesla. He was at SpaceX's Los Angeles–based headquarters on Monday and Thursday and at various Tesla facilities in the San Francisco Bay area on Tuesday and Wednesday.[21] On Friday he split his time between both companies—Tesla Design had offices in the same office park in a southern Los Angeles suburb as SpaceX; Musk's personal residence was about 18 miles away in a northern Los Angeles suburb.

However, Musk got mixed marks on his management style. He was praised for his grand vision of what his companies could become and his ability to shape the culture of his startup companies but was criticized for being hard to work with, partly because of his impatience for action and results, his intensity and sometimes hands-on micromanagement of certain operational and product design issues, and the frequency with which he overruled others and imposed his wishes when big decisions had to be made. In 2000, while on vacation, he was forced out as CEO at PayPal after seven months.[22] Several lawsuits had been filed against him by disgruntled former colleagues and employees. A number of articles had made mention of assorted minor annoyances and criticisms of the ways he did things and his frequently prickly manner when responding to probing or unpleasant questions from reporters. But virtually no one had disparaged his brilliant intellect, inventive aptitude, and exceptional entrepreneurial abilities. In 2014, it was hard to dispute that Musk—at the age of 43—had already made a name for himself in two ways:[23]

- He had envisioned the transformative possibilities of the Internet, a migration from fossil fuels to sustainable energy, and the expansion of life beyond Earth.
- His companies (Tesla, SpaceX, and SolarCity) had put him in position to personally affect the path the world would take in migrating from fossil fuels to sustainable energy and in expanding life beyond Earth. Musk won the 2010 Automotive Executive of the Year Innovator Award for expediting the development of electric vehicles throughout the global automotive industry. *Fortune* magazine named Elon Musk its 2013 Businessperson of the Year.

In 2014 Elon Musk's base salary as Tesla's CEO was $33,280, an amount required by California's minimum wage law; however, he was accepting only $1 in salary. Musk controlled over 33 million shares of common stock in Tesla Motors (worth some $8.3 billion in March 2014) and had been granted options for an additional 89 million shares, 78 million shares of which were subject to Tesla Motors' achieving specified increases in market capitalization and 10 designated performance milestones by 2023.[24]

## Recent Financial Performance and Financing Activities

Exhibits 1 and 2 present recent financial statement data for Tesla Motors.

In May 2013, Tesla raised over $1 billion by issuing 4.5 million shares of common stock at a price of $92.24 per share and $660 million of 1.5 percent convertible senior notes. Elon Musk personally purchased 1.08 million of these shares at the public offering price, boosting his investment in Tesla by another $100 million. Tesla used about $450 million of the offering proceeds to fully pay off its 2009 loan from the U.S. Department of Energy, including an $11 million fee for early payment.

Tesla ended 2013 with $848.9 million in cash and cash equivalents and current restricted cash, an increase of $52.5 million from the end of the third quarter. Executive management expected that the current level of liquidity, coupled with projected future cash flows from operating activities, was likely to provide adequate liquidity based on current plans. However, if market conditions proved favorable, management said it would evaluate the merits of opportunistically pursuing actions to further boost the company's cash balances and overall liquidity.

Tesla had capital expenditures of $264 million in 2013, aimed chiefly at expanding its factory production capabilities and opening additional sales galleries, service centers, and Supercharger stations. Capital expenditures of $650 million to $850 million were planned for 2014.

## TESLA'S STRATEGY TO BECOME THE WORLD'S BIGGEST AND MOST HIGHLY REGARDED PRODUCER OF ELECTRIC VEHICLES

Elon Musk's vision for Tesla Motors was to utilize the company's proprietary batteries and powertrain technology to put millions more electric cars on the

## EXHIBIT 1    Consolidated Statement of Operations, Tesla Motors, 2010–2013 (in thousands, except share and per share data)

| | Fiscal Year Ending December 31 | | | |
| --- | --- | --- | --- | --- |
| | 2013 | 2012 | 2011 | 2010 |
| **Income statement data** | | | | |
| Revenues: | | | | |
| Sales of vehicles, options and accessories, vehicle service, and regulatory credits | $ 1,952,684 | $   354,344 | $ 101,748 | $   75,459 |
| Sales of powertrain components, battery packs, and drive units to other vehicle manufacturers | 45,102 | 31,355 | 46,860 | 21,619 |
| Development of powertrain components and systems for other vehicle manufacturers | 15,710 | 27,557 | 55,674 | 19,666 |
| Total revenues | 2,013,496 | 413,256 | 204,242 | 116,744 |
| Cost of revenues: | | | | |
| Vehicle sales and sales of powertrain components and related systems to other manufacturers | 1,543,878 | 371,658 | 115,482 | 79,982 |
| Development of powertrain systems and components for other vehicle manufacturers | 13,356 | 11,531 | 27,165 | 6,031 |
| Total cost of revenues | 1,557,234 | 383,189 | 142,647 | 86,013 |
| Gross profit (loss) | 456,262 | 30,067 | 61,595 | 30,731 |
| Operating expenses: | | | | |
| Research and development | 231,976 | 273,978 | 208,981 | 92,996 |
| Selling, general, and administrative | 285,569 | 150,372 | 104,102 | 84,573 |
| Total operating expenses | 517,545 | 424,350 | 313,083 | 177,569 |
| Loss from operations | (961,283) | (394,283) | (251,488) | (146,838) |
| Interest income | 189 | 288 | 255 | 258 |
| Interest expense | (32,934) | (254) | (43) | (992) |
| Other income (expense), net | 22,602 | (1,828) | (2,646) | (6,583) |
| Loss before income taxes | (71,426) | (396,077) | (253,922) | (154,155) |
| Provision for income taxes | 2,588 | 136 | 489 | 173 |
| Net loss | $    (74,014) | $ (396,213) | $(254,411) | $ (154,328) |
| Net loss per share of common stock, basic and diluted | $(0.62) | $(3.69) | $(2.53) | $(3.04) |
| Weighted-average shares used in computing net loss per share of common stock, basic and diluted | 119,421,414 | 107,349,188 | 100,388,815 | 50,718,302 |
| **Balance sheet data** | | | | |
| Cash and cash equivalents | $    845,889 | $   201,890 | $255,266 | $    99,558 |
| Inventory | 340,355 | 268,504 | 50,082 | 45,182 |
| Total current assets | 1,265,939 | 524,768 | 372,838 | 235,886 |
| Property, plant, and equipment, net | 738,494 | 552,229 | 298,414 | 114,636 |
| Total assets | 2,416,930 | 1,114,190 | 713,448 | 386,082 |
| Total current liabilities | 675,160 | 539,108 | 191,339 | 85,565 |
| Long-term debt, less current portion | — | 401,495 | 268,335 | 71,828 |
| Total stockholders' equity | 667,121 | 124,700 | 224,045 | 207,048 |

*(Continued)*

## EXHIBIT 1   (Continued)

| | Fiscal Year Ending December 31 | | | |
|---|---|---|---|---|
| | 2013 | 2012 | 2011 | 2010 |
| **Cash flow data** | | | | |
| Cash flows from operating activities | $257,994 | $(266,081) | $(128,034) | ($127,817) |
| Proceeds from issuance of common stock in public offerings | 360,000 | 221,496 | 172,410 | 188,842 |
| Purchases of property and equipment excluding capital leases | (264,224) | (239,228) | (184,226) | (40,203) |
| Net cash used in investing activities | (249,417) | (206,930) | (162,258) | (180,297) |
| Net cash provided by financing activities | 635,422 | 419,635 | 446,000 | 338,045 |

*Source:* Company 10-K reports for years 2011–2013.

road and dramatically curtail global dependence on petroleum-based transportation. The company's overriding strategic objective was "to drive the world's transition to electric mobility by bringing a full range of increasingly affordable electric cars to market."[25] At its core, the company's strategy was aimed squarely at disrupting the world automotive industry in ways that were sweeping and revolutionary. If Tesla's strategy proved to be as successful as Elon Musk believed it would be, industry observers expected that the competitive positions and market standing of Tesla and its automotive rivals would likely be vastly different in 2025 than they were in 2014.

## Product Line Strategy

So far, Tesla had introduced two models—the Tesla Roadster and the Model S, but two new models were rapidly advancing through the pipeline. It was the company's strategic intent to broaden its customer base by offering not only a bigger model variety but also by introducing substantially cheaper models. Because the lithium-ion battery pack in Tesla vehicles reputedly cost upward of $25,000 and was far and away the biggest cost component, the speed with which the company could profitably introduce new vehicles with prices of $35,000 to $50,000 depended largely on how fast and how far it was able to drive down the costs of its battery pack via greater scale economies in battery production and cost-saving advances in battery technology.

**The Tesla Roadster**   Following Tesla's initial funding in 2004, Musk took an active role within the company. Although he was not involved in day-to-day business operations, he did exert strong influence in the design of the company's first model, the Tesla Roadster, a two-seat convertible that could accelerate from zero to 60 miles per hour in as little as 3.7 seconds, had a maximum speed of about 120 miles per hour, could travel about 245 miles on a single charge, and had a base price of $109,000 (€84,000). Musk insisted from the beginning that the Roadster have a lightweight, high-strength carbon fiber body, and he influenced the design of components of the Roadster ranging from the power electronics module to the headlamps and other styling features.[26] Prototypes of the Roadster were introduced to the public in July 2006, and the first "Signature One Hundred" set of fully equipped Roadsters sold out in less than three weeks; the second hundred sold out by October 2007. General production began on March 17, 2008. New models of the Roadster were introduced in July 2009 (including the Roadster Sport, with a base price of $128,500, equivalent to €112,000) and in July 2010. Sales of Roadster models to countries in Europe and Asia began in 2010. From 2008 through 2012, Tesla sold more than 2,450 Roadsters in 31 countries.[27] Tesla Roadsters sold in 2006–2007 had a warranty of three years or 36,000 miles; beginning with sales of the 2008 Roadster, the warranty period was

**EXHIBIT 2    Tesla's Financial Performance by Quarter, GAAP vs. Non-GAAP, Quarter 1, 2013, through Quarter 1, 2014**

| | Q1, 2013 | Q2, 2013 | Q3, 2013 | Q4, 2013 | Q1, 2014 |
|---|---|---|---|---|---|
| Revenues (GAAP) | $561,792 | $405,139 | $431,346 | $615,219 | $620,542 |
| Model S revenues deferred due to lease accounting | — | 146,812 | 171,229 | 146,125 | 92,506 |
| Revenues (non-GAAP) | 561,792 | 551,951 | 602,575 | 761,344 | 713,048 |
| Gross profit (loss) (GAAP) | 96,320 | 100,483 | 102,868 | 156,590 | 155,128 |
| Model S gross profit deferred due to lease accounting | — | 19,349 | 28,732 | 29,796 | 21,384 |
| Stock-based compensation expense | 1,563 | 1,063 | 3,017 | 3,455 | 3,106 |
| Gross profit (loss) (non-GAAP) | 97,856 | 120,895 | 134,617 | 189,641 | 179,618 |
| Research and development expenses (GAAP) | 54,859 | 52,312 | 56,351 | 68,454 | 81,544 |
| Stock-based compensation expense | (7,644) | (8,565) | (8,707) | (10,578) | (13,545) |
| Research and development expenses (non-GAAP) | 47,215 | 43,747 | 47,644 | 57,876 | 67,999 |
| Selling, general, and administrative expenses (GAAP) | 47,045 | 59,963 | 77,071 | 101,489 | 117,551 |
| Stock-based compensation expense | (5,688) | (9,631) | (9,715) | (14,056) | (20,387) |
| Selling, general and administrative expenses (non-GAAP) | 41,357 | 50,332 | 67,356 | 87,443 | 97,164 |
| Net loss (GAAP) | (11,248) | (30,502) | (38,496) | (16,264) | (49,800) |
| Stock-based compensation expense | 14,868 | 19,259 | 21,439 | 28,089 | 37,038 |
| Change in fair value of warrant liability | (10,692) | — | — | — | — |
| Non-cash interest expense related to convertible notes | — | 1,791 | 4,260 | 4,299 | 8,393 |
| Early extinguishment of DOE loans | — | 16,386 | — | — | — |
| Model S gross profit deferred due to lease accounting | — | 19,349 | 28,732 | 29,796 | 21,384 |
| Net income (loss) (non-GAAP) | $ 15,424 | $ 26,283 | $ 15,935 | $ 45,920 | $ 17,015 |
| Net income (loss) per common share, basic (GAAP) | $0.10 | $(0.26) | $(0.32) | $(0.32) | $(0.40) |
| Net income (loss) per common share, basic (non-GAAP) | 0.13 | 0.22 | 0.13 | 0.37 | 0.14 |
| Shares (in 000s) used in per share calculation, basic (GAAP and non-GAAP) | 114,712 | 118,194 | 121,862 | 122,802 | 123,473 |
| Net loss per share, diluted (GAAP) | $0.00 | $(0.23) | $(0.28) | $(0.12) | $(0.36) |
| Net income (loss) per share, diluted (non-GAAP) | 0.12 | 0.20 | 0.12 | 0.33 | 0.12 |
| Shares (in 000s) used in per share calculation, diluted (non-GAAP) | 124,265 | 130,503 | 137,131 | 137,784 | 140,221 |

*Special note on GAAP vs. non-GAAP treatments:* Under generally accepted accounting principles (GAAP), revenues and costs of leased vehicles must be recorded and apportioned across the life of the lease; with non-GAAP lease accounting, all revenues and costs of a leased vehicle are recorded at the time the lease is finalized. Under GAAP, stock compensation must be expensed and allocated to the associated cost category; non-GAAP excludes stock compensation as a cost because it is a non-cash item. Many companies, including Tesla Motors, believe non-GAAP treatments are useful in understanding company operations and actual cash flows. In Tesla's case, the non-GAAP treatments exclude such non-cash items as stock-based compensation, the change in fair value related to Tesla's warrant liability, and non-cash interest expense related to Tesla's 1.5 percent convertible senior notes, as well as one-time expenses associated with the early repayment of the 2010 loan Tesla received from the Department of Energy.

*Source:* Tesla Motors' Letters to Shareholders, first through fourth quarters 2013 and first quarter 2014.

extended to four years or 50,000 miles. Tesla Roadster customers could purchase an extended warranty to cover an additional three years or 36,000 miles. Sales of Roadster models ended in December 2012 so that the company could concentrate exclusively on producing and marketing the Model S.

**The Model S**    Tesla Motors began shipments of its second vehicle, the Model S sedan, in June. The Model S was a fully electric, four-door, five-passenger luxury sedan with an all-glass panoramic roof, no tailpipe and zero emissions, a high-definition backup camera, keyless entry, xenon headlights, dual USB

ports, and numerous other features that were standard in most luxury vehicles. Tesla had designed the Model S to give buyers the option of having a third row with two rear-facing child seats, thus providing seating for five adults and two children. Buyers had a choice of two battery-pack options and a "Performance Plus" model with a high-performance powertrain. Exhibit 3 provides comparative data on the three Model S battery packs. Tesla executives believed the Model S offered a compelling combination of functionality, convenience, and styling without compromising performance and energy efficiency. With the battery pack in the floor of the vehicle and the motor and gearbox

## EXHIBIT 3    Features, Performance, and Pricing of Tesla's Three Model S Offerings

| | 60-kWh Lithium-Ion Battery Pack | 85-kWH Lithium-Ion Battery Pack | 85-kWH Lithium-Ion Performance Battery Pack |
|---|---|---|---|
| Estimated range at 55 mph | 230 miles | 300 miles | 300 miles |
| EPA-certified range | 208 miles | 265 miles | 265 miles |
| 0 to 60 mph | 5.9 seconds | 5.4 seconds | 4.2 seconds |
| Top speed | 120 mph | 125 mph | 130 mph |
| Peak motor power | 302 horsepower | 362 horsepower | 416 horsepower |
| Powertrain | Rear-wheel drive, with a liquid-cooled powertrain that includes the battery, electric motor, drive inverter, and gearbox | | |
| Electronic stability control and traction control | Standard | Standard | Standard |
| Base price | $69,900 | $81,200 | $94,900 |
| Vehicle warranty | 4 years or 50,000 miles, whichever comes first; owners could buy an extended warranty covering an additional 4 years or 50,000 miles | 4 years or 50,000 miles, whichever comes first; owners could buy an extended warranty covering an additional 4 years or 50,000 miles | 4 years or 50,000 miles, whichever comes first; owners could buy an extended warranty covering an additional 4 years or 50,000 miles |
| Battery warranty | 8 years, 125,000 miles | 8 years, unlimited miles | 8 years, unlimited miles |
| Tesla Supercharger | Optional ($2,000) | Standard | Standard |
| Supercharging capability: | | | |
| Standard 110-volt wall outlet | Complete recharge overnight | Complete recharge overnight | Complete recharge overnight |
| 240-volt outlet with a single onboard charger | 29 miles of range per hour | 29 miles of range per hour | 29 miles of range per hour |
| 240-volt outlet with twin onboard chargers | 58 miles of range per hour | 58 miles of range per hour | 58 miles of range per hour |
| Tesla Supercharger-enabled | 50% in 20 minutes 80% in 40 minutes 100% in 75 minutes | 50% in 20 minutes 80% in 40 minutes 100% in 75 minutes | 50% in 20 minutes 80% in 40 minutes 100% in 75 minutes |

| | 60-kWh Lithium-Ion Battery Pack | 85-kWH Lithium-Ion Battery Pack | 85-kWH Lithium-Ion Performance Battery Pack |
|---|---|---|---|
| Instrument cluster | 17-inch high-resolution touchscreen display with integrated controls for media (radio, Bluetooth, and USB audio devices), navigation, Internet communications, cabin comfort, energy consumption, and other vehicle data | 17-inch high-resolution touchscreen display with integrated controls for media (radio, Bluetooth, and USB audio devices), navigation, Internet communications, cabin comfort, energy consumption, and other vehicle data | 17-inch high-resolution touchscreen display with integrated controls for media (radio, Bluetooth, and USB audio devices), navigation, Internet communications, cabin comfort, energy consumption, and other vehicle data |
| Rear-facing, fold-down seating for 2 children under age 10 | Optional ($2,500) | Optional ($2,500) | Optional ($2,500) |
| Airbags | 8 | 8 | 8 |
| Body structure | State-of-the-art aluminum-intensive design that was strong, rigid, and light; high-strength boron steel was used in key areas to enhance occupant safety | State-of-the art aluminum-intensive design that was strong, rigid, and light; high-strength boron steel was used in key areas to enhance occupant safety | State-of-the art aluminum-intensive design that was strong, rigid, and light; high-strength boron steel was used in key areas to enhance occupant safety |
| Overall length | 196.0" | 196.0" | 196.0" |
| Overall width (mirrors extended) | 86.2" | 86.2" | 86.2" |
| Height | 56.5" | 56.5" | 56.5" |
| Ground clearance | 6" | 6" | 6" |

*Sources:* Information at www.teslamotors.com, February 27, 2014; pricing data is based on information at www.edmunds.com, November 20, 2013.

in line with the rear axle, the Tesla Model S provided best-in-class storage space of 63.4 cubic feet, including storage inside the cabin (58.1 cubic feet) and under the hood (5.3 cubic feet). This compared quite favorably with the 14.0-cubic-foot trunk capacity of BMW's large 7-series sedan, the 16.3-cubic-foot capacity of a Mercedes S-class sedan, and the 18.0 cubic-foot trunk capacity of the large Lexus 460 sedan. The battery-charging port in the Model S, located in the driver's side taillight, opened with the press of a button; the charging port accepted charges from both 110-volt and 240-volt outlets, as well as Supercharging devices. The Model S was designed to allow a fast battery swap when driving long distances; at any of Tesla's hundreds of Supercharging stations, drivers could exchange their car's battery pack for a fully charged one in less than half the time it took to refill a gas tank.

In the second quarter of 2013, Tesla announced several new options for the Model S, including a subzero weather package, parking sensors, upgraded leather interior, several new wheel options, and a yacht-style floor center console. Xenon headlights and a high-definition backup camera were made standard equipment on all Model S cars.

Customers who purchased any of the three Model S versions were eligible for a federal tax credit of $7,500; a number of states also offered rebates on electric vehicle purchases, with states like California and New York offering rebates as high as $7,500. Customers who leased a Model S were not entitled to rebates.

The Model S was the most-awarded car of 2013, including *Motor Trend*'s 2013 Car of the Year award and *Automobile* magazine's 2013 Car of the Year award. The National Highway Traffic Safety Administration (NHTSA) in 2013 awarded the Tesla Model S a 5-star safety rating, both overall and in every subcategory (a score achieved by approximately 1 percent of all cars tested by the NHTSA); however, the Model S achieved an overall Vehicle Safety

Score of 5.4 stars, the highest of any vehicle ever tested. Of all vehicles tested, including every major make and model approved for sale in the United States, the Model S set a new record for the lowest likelihood of injury to occupants in front, side, rear, and rollover accidents.[28] *Consumer Reports* gave the Model S a score of 99 out of 100 points, saying it was "better than anything we've ever tested."

### The Forthcoming Model X Crossover SUV

Tesla was adapting the platform architecture of the Model S to develop its Model X crossover—about 60 percent of the Model S platform was to be shared with the Model X, greatly reducing the development costs for the Model X. The Model X was designed to seat 7 adults and fill the niche between the roominess of a minivan and the style of an SUV, while having high-performance features such as a dual-motor all-wheel-drive system and a driving range of 214- to 267 miles per charge. A prototype of the Model X was released in February 2012; it had "falcon-wing doors" that provided easy access to the third-row seats and resembled a sedan more than an SUV. Initial production of the Model X was expected to begin in late 2014, with production volume increasing to approximately 300 vehicles per week by mid-2015. The Tesla Model X crossover was expected to cost slightly more than the Model S.

### The Forthcoming Mass Market Tesla Model 3 Vehicle

Tesla had also announced its intent to introduce a third-generation electric vehicle (named the Model 3) in 2017 that would be sold at a lower price point—perhaps as low as $35,000 if sufficient cost-reductions could be achieved. Plans called for it to be produced at Tesla's assembly plant in Fremont, California, and, in the case of units delivered to customers in Europe, to undergo final assembly at Tesla's plant in Tilburg, Netherlands. During 2014, Tesla intended to continue to make progress on the design work and styling of the Model 3 vehicle.

## Technology and Product Development Strategy

Since its founding, Tesla had spent over $900 million on research and development (R&D) activities to design, develop, test, and refine the components and systems needed to produce top-quality electric vehicles and, further, to design and develop prototypes of the Tesla Roadster, the Model S, and the forthcoming Model X and Gen III vehicles (see Exhibit 1 for R&D spending during 2010–2013). In the fourth quarter of 2013, the company increased its R&D spending by about 25 percent in order to accelerate product development efforts on Model S and Model X enhancements.

By 2014, top executives believed that the company had developed core competencies in powertrain and vehicle engineering and that the company's core intellectual property was contained in its electric powertrain technology—the battery pack, power electronics, induction motor, gearbox, and control software that enabled these key components to operate as a system. As of year-end 2013, Tesla had been issued 203 patents and had more than 280 pending patent applications domestically and internationally in a broad range of areas.

Tesla personnel had designed a compact, modular powertrain system with far fewer moving parts than the powertrains of traditional gasoline-powered vehicles, a feature that enabled Tesla to implement powertrain enhancements and improvements as fast as they could be identified, designed, and tested. Tesla had incorporated its latest powertrain technology into the Model S and also into the powertrain components that it built and sold to other makers of electric vehicles; plus, it was planning to use much of this technology in its forthcoming electric vehicles.

**Battery Pack**   Over the years, Tesla had tested hundreds of battery cells of different chemistries and performance features. It had an internal battery-cell testing lab and had assembled an extensive performance database of the many available lithium-ion cell vendors and chemistry types. Based on this evaluation, it had elected to use "18650 form-factor" lithium-ion battery cells, chiefly because a battery pack containing 18650 cells offered two to three times the driving range of the lithium-ion cells used by other makers of electric vehicles—see Exhibit 4. Moreover, Tesla had been able to obtain large quantities of the 18650 lithium-ion cells for its battery pack (each pack had about 7,000 of the 18650 cells) at attractive prices because global lithium-ion battery manufacturers were suffering from a huge capacity glut, having overbuilt production capacity in anticipation of fast-growing buyer demand for electric vehicles that so far had failed to materialize.

**EXHIBIT 4    Comparative Miles per Charge of Select Electric Vehicles, 2013**

| Vehicle | Miles per Charge (based on EPA 5-cycle test) |
|---|---|
| Tesla Model S (85-kWh battery pack) | 265 miles |
| Tesla Model S (60-kWh battery pack) | 208 |
| Nissan LEAF | 84 |
| Honda Fit EV | 82 |
| Chevrolet Spark | 82 |
| Ford Focus EV | 76 |
| Mitsubishi 1-MiEV | 62 |

*Source:* Tesla Motors Investor Presentation, September 14, 2013, www.teslamotors.com (accessed December 1, 2013).

Management believed that the company's accumulated experience and expertise had produced a core competence in battery-pack design and safety, putting Tesla in position to capitalize on the substantial battery-cell investments and advancements being made globally by battery-cell manufacturers and to benefit from ongoing improvements in the energy storage capacity, longevity, power delivery, and costs per kilowatt-hour (kWh) of the battery packs used in its current and forthcoming models. Tesla's battery-pack design gave it the ability to change battery-cell chemistries and vendors while retaining the company's existing investments in software, electronics, testing, and other powertrain components. The long-term plan was to incorporate whichever battery-cell chemistries delivered the best combination of performance and value to the buyers of Tesla vehicles.

The driving range of Tesla's vehicles on a single charge declined over the life of the battery on the basis of a customer's use of the vehicle and the frequency with which the customer charged the battery. Tesla estimated that the Tesla Roadster battery pack would retain approximately 60 to 65 percent of its ability to hold its initial charge after approximately 100,000 miles or seven years, which would result in a decrease to the vehicle's initial range. In addition, based on internal testing, the company estimated that the Tesla Roadster would have a 5 to 10 percent reduction in range when operated in temperatures at or below −20°C. The battery charge deterioration for Model S battery packs was expected to be less than that for the Roadster.

**Power Electronics**   The power electronics in Tesla's powertrain system had two primary functions: the control of torque generation in the motor while driving and the control of energy delivery back into the battery pack while charging. The first function was accomplished through the drive inverter, which was directly responsible for the performance, energy-use efficiency, and overall driving experience of the vehicle. The second function, charging the battery pack, was accomplished by the vehicle's charger, which converted alternating current (usually from a wall outlet or other electricity source) into direct current that could be accepted by the battery. Most Model S owners ordered vehicles equipped with twin chargers in order to cut the charging time in half. Owners could use any available source of power to charge their vehicle. A standard 12-amp/110-volt wall outlet could charge the battery pack to full capacity in about 42 hours for vehicles equipped with a single charger, or 21 hours with a twin charger. Tesla recommended that owners install *at least* a 24-amp/240-volt outlet in their garage or carport (the same voltage used by many electric ovens and clothes dryers), which permitted charging at the rate of 34 miles of range per hour of charging time on vehicles equipped with a twin charger. But Tesla strongly recommended the installation of a more powerful 40-amp/240-volt outlet that charged at the rate of 58 miles of range per hour of charge if the Model S was equipped with twin chargers. Model S vehicles came standard with three adapters: a 12-amp/110-volt adapter, a 40-amp/240-volt adapter, and a J1772 public charging station adapter; other adapters could be purchased online.

**Induction Motors**   Tesla had developed custom-designed three-phase alternating-current induction motors for its powertrain system. Company personnel had incorporated several important innovations, including a proprietary fabricated copper rotor and more optimized winding patterns that allowed for both the use of more copper wire and easy manufacture. The outcomes were higher power and greater efficiency (because of reduced resistance and lower energy losses).

**Gearbox**    Tesla R&D personnel had also designed custom, single-speed gearboxes for the Tesla Roadster and Model S. These gearboxes combined low mass with high efficiency and could match both the speed and torque capabilities of the alternating-current induction motors. Compared to gasoline-powered vehicles, the elimination of gear changes enhanced the rapid acceleration characteristics of Tesla's vehicles. The gearbox for the Model S was being manufactured in-house.

**Control Software**    The battery pack and the performance and safety systems of Tesla vehicles required the use of numerous microprocessors and sophisticated software. For example, computer-driven software monitored the charge state of each of the cells of the battery pack and managed all of the safety systems. The flow of electricity between the battery pack and the motor had to be tightly controlled in order to deliver the performance and behavior expected in the vehicle. There were software algorithms that enabled the vehicle to mimic the "creep" feeling that drivers expected from an internal combustion engine vehicle without having to apply pressure on the accelerator. Other algorithms controlled traction, vehicle stability, and the sustained acceleration and regenerative braking of the vehicle. Drivers used the vehicle's information systems to optimize performance and charging modes and times. In addition to developing the vehicle control software, Tesla had developed software for the infotainment system of the Model S. Many of the software programs had been developed and written by Tesla personnel.

Tesla routinely enhanced the performance of its Model S vehicles by sending wireless software updates to the microprocessors on board each Model S it had sold.

## Vehicle Design and Engineering

Tesla had devoted considerable effort to creating significant in-house capabilities related to designing and engineering portions of its vehicles, and it had become knowledgeable about the design and engineering of the parts, components, and systems that it purchased from suppliers. Tesla personnel had designed and engineered the body, chassis, and interior of the Model S and were working on the designs and engineering of the same components for the Model X and Gen III. As a matter of necessity, Tesla was forced to redesign the heating, cooling, and ventilation system for its vehicles to operate without the energy generated from an internal combustion engine and to integrate with its own battery-powered thermal management system. In addition, the low-voltage electric system, which powered such features as the radio, power windows, and heated seats, had to be designed specifically for use in an electric vehicle. Tesla had developed expertise in integrating these components with the high-voltage power source in the Model S and in designing components that significantly reduced their load on the vehicle's battery pack, thus maximizing the available driving range.

Tesla personnel had accumulated considerable expertise in lightweight materials, since an electric vehicle's driving range was heavily impacted by the vehicle's weight and mass. The Tesla Roadster had been built with an in-house-designed carbon fiber body to provide a good balance of strength and mass. The Model S was being built with a lightweight aluminum body and a chassis that incorporated a variety of materials and production methods to help optimize vehicle weight, strength, safety, and performance. In addition, top management believed that the company's design and engineering team had core competencies in computer-aided design and crash test simulations; this expertise was expected to reduce the product development time of new models.

In December 2013, Tesla hired a former Apple executive as senior director of manufacturing technology to be in charge of the company's efforts to make design advances in battery, powertrain, and vehicle technologies.

## Manufacturing Strategy

Tesla contracted with Lotus Cars, Ltd., to produce Tesla Roadster "gliders" (a complete vehicle minus the electric powertrain) at a Lotus factory in Hethel, England. The Tesla gliders were then shipped to a Tesla facility in Menlo Park, California, where the battery pack, induction motors, and other powertrain components were installed as part of the final assembly process. The production of Roadster gliders ceased in January 2012.

In May 2010, Tesla purchased the major portion of a recently closed automobile plant in Fremont, California, for $42 million; months later, Tesla purchased some of the plant's equipment for $17 million. The facility—formerly a General Motors (GM) manufacturing plant (1960–1982) and then operated as a joint venture between GM and Toyota (1984–2010) to showcase Toyota's famed production system and produce Toyota Corolla and Tacoma vehicles—was closed in 2010 when GM pulled out of the joint venture and Toyota elected to cease its production of several thousand vehicles per week and permanently lay off about 4,700 workers. Tesla executives viewed the facility as one of the largest, most advanced, and cleanest automotive production plants in the world, and the space inside the 5.5-million-square-foot main building was deemed sufficient for Tesla to produce about 500,000 vehicles annually (approximately 1 percent of the total worldwide car production), thus giving Tesla plenty of room to grow its output of electric vehicles. Elon Musk felt the Fremont plant was superior to two other Southern California sites being considered because Fremont's location in the northern section of Silicon Valley facilitated hiring talented engineers already residing nearby and because the short distance between Fremont and Tesla's Palo Alto headquarters ensured "a tight feedback loop between vehicle engineering, manufacturing, and other divisions within the company."[29] Tesla officially took possession of the 350-acre site in October 2010, renamed it the Tesla Factory, and launched efforts to get a portion of the massive facility ready to begin manufacturing components and assembling the Model S in 2012. The first retail delivery of the Model S took place during a special event held at the Tesla Factory on June 22, 2012.

In December 2012, Tesla opened a new 60,000-square-foot facility in Tilburg, Netherlands, about 50 miles from the port of Rotterdam, to serve as the final assembly and distribution point for all Model S vehicles sold in Europe and Scandinavia. The facility, called the Tilburg Assembly Plant, received nearly complete Model S units shipped from the Tesla Factory, performed certain final-assembly activities, conducted final vehicle testing, and handled the delivery to customers throughout the European market. It also functioned as Tesla's European service and parts headquarters. Tilburg's central location and its excellent rail and highway network to all major markets on the European continent allowed Tesla to distribute to anywhere across the continent in about 12 hours. By fall 2013, the Tilburg operation had been expanded to over 200,000 square feet—including facilities for technical training, parts remanufacturing, and collision repair activities for Tesla's European operations—and was receiving about 200 Model S vehicles weekly for final assembly, testing, and customer delivery.

Tesla's manufacturing strategy was to source a number of parts and components from outside suppliers but to design, develop, and manufacture in-house the key components for which it had considerable intellectual property and core competencies (namely, lithium-ion battery packs, electric motors, gearboxes, and other powertrain components) and to perform all assembly-related activities itself. In early 2014, the Tesla Factory contained several production-related activities, including the manufacturing of battery packs and other powertrain components, a hydraulic press line that stamped aluminum into paint-ready body panels, robotic body assembly, paint operations, final vehicle assembly, and end-of-line quality testing. Activities were under way to ramp annual production volume of the Model S up from about 21,500 vehicles in 2013 to over 40,000 vehicles in 2014.

Initially, production costs for the Model S were high due to an assortment of startup costs at the Tesla Factory, manufacturing inefficiencies associated with inexperience and low-volume production, higher prices for component parts during the first several months of production runs, and higher logistics costs associated with the immaturity of Tesla's supply chain. However, as Tesla engineers redesigned various elements of the Model S for greater ease of manufacturing, supply chain improvements were instituted, and production volumes approached 600 vehicles per week in 2013, manufacturing efficiency rose, the costs of some parts decreased, and overall production costs per vehicle trended downward. Management expected that further cost-saving initiatives being undertaken by both Tesla and its suppliers, together with further boosts in production volume, would result in still lower production costs per vehicle at least until mid-2014. Elon Musk expected that continued execution of the company's road map for reducing production costs would enable Tesla to achieve a gross margin of 28 percent in the fourth quarter of 2014.

**Supply Chain Strategy**   The Model S contained over 2,000 parts and components that Tesla was sourcing globally from over 300 direct suppliers, the majority of which were currently single-source suppliers. It was the company's practice to obtain the needed parts and components from multiple sources whenever feasible, and Tesla management expected to secure alternate sources of supply for most single-sourced components within a year or two. However, qualifying alternate suppliers for certain highly customized components—or producing them internally—was thought to be both time-consuming and costly, perhaps even requiring modifications to a vehicle's design. Tesla had developed close relationships with the suppliers of lithium-ion battery cells and certain other key system parts, but it did not maintain long-term agreements with many of its suppliers.

## Distribution Strategy: A Company-Owned and Operated Network of Retail Stores and Service Centers

Tesla sold its vehicles directly to buyers and also provided them with after-sale service through a network of company-owned sales galleries and service centers. This contrasted sharply with the strategy of rival motor vehicle manufacturers, all of which sold vehicles and replacement parts at wholesale prices to their networks of franchised dealerships that in turn handled retail sales, maintenance and service, and warranty repairs. Management believed that integrating forward into the business of traditional automobile dealers and operating the company's own retail sales and service network had three important advantages:

1. *The ability to create and control Tesla's own version of a compelling customer buying experience,* one that was differentiated from the buying experience consumers had with sales and service locations of franchised automobile dealers. Having customers deal directly with Tesla-employed sales and service personnel enabled Tesla to (a) engage and inform potential customers about electric vehicles in general and the advantages of owning a Tesla in particular and (b) build a more personal relationship with customers and, hopefully, instill a lasting and favorable impression of Tesla Motors, its mission, and the caliber and performance of its vehicles.

2. *The ability to achieve greater operating economies in performing sales and service activities.* Management believed that a company-operated sales and service network offered substantial opportunities to better control inventory costs of both vehicles and replacement parts, manage warranty service and pricing, maintain and strengthen the Tesla brand, and obtain rapid customer feedback.

3. *The opportunity to capture the sales and service revenues of traditional automobile dealerships.* When Tesla buyers purchased a vehicle at a Tesla-owned sales gallery, Tesla captured the full retail sales price, roughly 10 percent greater than the wholesale price realized by vehicle manufacturers selling through franchised dealers. And, by operating its own service centers, it captured service revenues not available to vehicle manufacturers that relied upon their franchised dealers to provide needed maintenance and repairs. Furthermore, Tesla management believed that company-owned service centers avoided the conflict of interest between vehicle manufacturers and their franchised dealers in which the sale of warranty parts and repairs by a dealer were a key source of revenue and profit for the dealer but warranty-related costs were typically a substantial expense for the vehicle manufacturer.

**Tesla Sales Galleries and Showrooms**   Currently, all of Tesla's sales galleries and showrooms were in or near major metropolitan areas; some were in prominent regional shopping malls, and others were on highly visible sites along busy thoroughfares. Most sales locations had only several vehicles in stock. While some customers purchased their vehicles from the available inventory, most preferred to order a custom-equipped car in their preferred color.

Tesla was aggressively expanding its network of sales galleries and service centers to broaden its geographic presence and to provide better maintenance and repair service in areas with a high concentration of Model S customers. In 2013, Tesla began combining its sales and service activities at a single location (rather than having separate locations, as had been the case earlier); experience indicated that combination sales and service locations were more cost-efficient and facilitated faster expansion of the company's retail footprint. At the end of 2013, Tesla had 116 sales and service locations around the world, and it planned to open approximately 85 to 90 more stores, galleries, and service centers in 2014, including 30 combination sales–service center facilities in Europe. Tesla's strategy was to have sufficient service locations to ensure that after-sale services were available to owners when and where needed.

However, there was a lurking problem with Tesla's strategy of bypassing distribution through franchised Tesla dealers and selling directly to consumers.

Going back many years, franchised automobile dealers in the United States had feared that automotive manufacturers might one day decide to integrate forward into selling and servicing the vehicles they produced. To foreclose any attempts by manufacturers to compete directly against their franchised dealers, automobile dealers in every state had formed statewide franchised-dealer associations to lobby for legislation blocking motor vehicle manufacturers from becoming retailers of new and used cars and from providing maintenance and repair services to vehicle owners. Legislation either forbidding or severely restricting the ability of automakers to sell vehicles directly to the public had been passed in 48 states; these laws had been in effect for many years, and franchised-dealer associations were diligent in pushing for strict enforcement of the laws. As sales of the Model S rose briskly in 2013 and Tesla continued opening more sales galleries and service centers, both franchised dealers and statewide dealer associations became increasingly anxious about "the Tesla problem" and what actions might need to be taken. Dealers and dealer trade associations in a number of states were openly vocal about their concerns and actively began lobbying state legislatures to consider either enforcement actions against Tesla or amendments to existing legislation that would bring a halt to Tesla's efforts to sell vehicles at company-owned showrooms.

In mid-December 2013, a group of Ohio car dealers filed a lawsuit against Tesla, the Ohio Bureau of Motor Vehicles, and the Ohio Department of Public Safety in a Franklin County court, alleging violations of Ohio law in granting Tesla a license to sell new cars and asking for an injunction to immediately rescind Tesla's license and prevent the Bureau of Motor Vehicles from issuing additional licenses to Tesla for other new locations. However, a settlement was reached in March 2014 that allowed Tesla to own and operate a maximum of three sales galleries in Ohio as long as it produced only all-electric cars and was not acquired by another company.

In March 2014, the New Jersey Motor Vehicle Commission announced that it would enforce New Jersey's state law forbidding automotive manufacturers from selling cars directly to consumers—at the time, Tesla had two showrooms in New Jersey. A controversy ensued, with some New Jersey lawmakers introducing legislation that would exempt Tesla and other electric car makers from the rule.

In New York state, legislation was pending in April 2014 that would require all automakers to sell their vehicles only through registered third-party dealers.

So far, automobile dealers and statewide dealer associations in Texas, Arizona, and Colorado (in addition to New Jersey) had succeeded in gaining enforcement of existing legislation banning direct sales to consumers and effectively blocking Tesla from taking orders for the Model S at Tesla showrooms in their states. Battles were pending in several other states—Massachusetts, Virginia, North Carolina, Minnesota, Maryland, and Georgia.

As of early 2014, it seemed very unlikely that Tesla would back away from its strategy and business model without first trying to sway public opinion in its favor and test whether the courts would uphold the monopoly that franchised dealers had been able to create for themselves. A Tesla spokesperson told an *Automotive News* reporter in September 2013 that dealerships around the country "object to the fact that we're trying to educate our consumers directly, sell them cars directly and service their vehicles directly because this runs entirely counter to the virtual monopoly they have in most states."[30] Tesla had also asserted it was not violating state franchising laws because it did not have any franchises. In the opinion of a senior editor at Edmunds.com, the real fear of automobile dealers was not Tesla but rather that other automakers would follow in Tesla's footsteps.[31]

**Tesla Service Centers**  Tesla's strategy was to have sufficient service locations to ensure that after-sale services were available to owners when and where needed. The company had over 70 service locations as of February 2014, and was rapidly adding new locations to serve Tesla owners in a widening number of geographic locations.

Tesla Roadster owners could upload data from their vehicle and send them to a service center on a memory card; Model S owners had an on-board system that could communicate directly with a service center, allowing service technicians to diagnose and remedy many problems before ever looking at the vehicle. When maintenance or service was required, a customer could schedule service by contacting a Tesla service center. Some service locations offered valet service, whereby the owner's car was picked up, replaced with a very well-equipped Model S loaner car, and then returned when the service was completed—there was no additional charge for valet service. Owners could also opt to have service performed at their home, office, or other remote location by a Tesla Ranger mobile technician who had the capability to perform a variety of services that did not require a vehicle lift. Tesla Rangers could perform most warranty repairs, but the cost of their visit was not covered under the new vehicle limited warranty. Ranger service pricing was based on a per-visit, per-vehicle basis. Ranger service was not immediately available in all areas in early 2014.

**Prepaid Maintenance Program**    Tesla offered a prepaid maintenance program to Model S buyers that included plans covering maintenance for four years or up to 50,000 miles and an additional four years or up to an additional 50,000 miles. The new vehicle limited warranty covered the Model S battery for a period of eight years or 125,000 miles (or in some instances unlimited miles). These plans covered annual inspections and the replacement of wear and tear on parts, excluding tires and the battery, with either a fixed fee per visit for Tesla Ranger service or unlimited Tesla Ranger visits for a higher initial purchase price. For owners with vehicles not covered by new vehicle limited warranties or extended-service plans, the fees for Tesla Ranger service were higher.

**Tesla's Supercharger Network: Providing Recharging Services to Owners on Long-Distance Trips**    A major component of Tesla's strategy to build rapidly growing long-term demand for its vehicles was to make battery recharging while driving long distances convenient and worry-free for all Tesla vehicle owners. Tesla's solution to providing owners with ample and convenient recharging opportunities was to establish an extensive geographic network of recharging stations. Superchargers were strategically placed along major highways connecting city centers, usually at locations with such nearby amenities as roadside diners, cafés, and shopping centers that enabled owners to have a brief rest stop or get a quick meal during the recharging process—about 90 percent of Model S buyers opted to have their vehicle equipped with Supercharging capability when they ordered their vehicle. Access to the Supercharger network was free of charge to owners of Model S vehicles with the 85-kWh battery-pack options or could be purchased as an up-front option

for vehicles equipped with a 60-kWh battery pack. As of fall 2013, nearly one-third of all Model S cars had been Supercharged at least once.

Initially, Tesla had installed 90-kWh fast-charging equipment at its charging stations that could replenish 50 percent of the battery pack in as little as 30 minutes. But in May 2013 the company began rolling out 120-kWh Superchargers, which were 33 percent faster and could replenish half a charge in just 20 minutes (3 hours' driving time), 80 percent in 40 minutes, and 100 percent in 75 minutes, for free. And it had begun a program of expanding the size of some locations to enable charging of 10 to 12 Model S vehicles simultaneously. The company had plans to upgrade to even faster 135-kWh Superchargers in Germany in 2014. As of February 19, 2014, Tesla had 90 Supercharger stations open in North America and Europe; close to 270 stations were expected to be operational in North America, Europe, and China by year-end 2014. By the end of 2014, Tesla expected that its Supercharging station network in Europe would enable Model S owners to travel almost everywhere in Europe using only Supercharging stations. Exhibit 5 shows Tesla's planned network of Supercharger stations in the United States by year-end 2015.

Tesla executives expected that the company's planned Supercharger network would relieve much of the "range anxiety" associated with driving on a long-distance trip. However, even with many Supercharger locations strategically positioned along major travel routes, it was likely that Tesla owners traveling to more remote locations would still be inconvenienced by having to deviate from the shortest direct route and detour to the closest Supercharger station for needed recharging. The degree to which range anxiety and "detour frustration" might prompt future vehicle shoppers to steer away from buying a Tesla was a risk that Tesla had to prove it could hurdle.

**Battery-Swap Service—An Even Faster Battery Replenishment Option**    The design of the Model S permitted the entire battery pack to be lowered from the bottom of the vehicle chassis and swapped out within a span of five minutes or less. In 2013 Tesla began offering Model S owners the option of pulling into a Supercharging station and paying a fee to exchange their vehicle's partially discharged battery pack for a fully charged battery

**EXHIBIT 5**   Tesla's Planned Network of Supercharger Locations in the United States, Year-End 2015

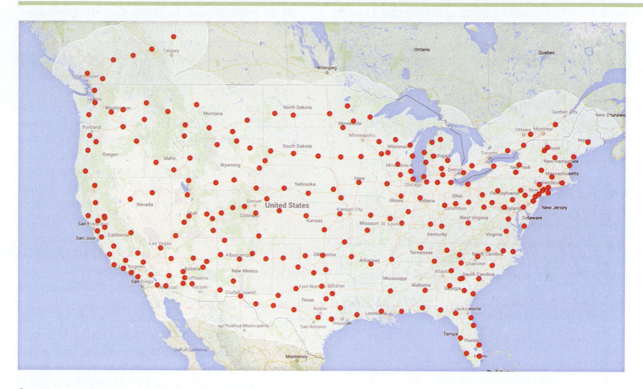

Source: www.teslamotors.com (accessed February 27, 2014).

pack. This meant that when Model S owners pulled into a Tesla Supercharger station, they only had to answer one question: Do you prefer faster (battery-pack swap) or free (charging)?

## Marketing Strategy

In 2014, Tesla's principal marketing goals and functions were to:

- Generate demand for the company's vehicles and drive sales leads to personnel in Tesla's showrooms and sales galleries.
- Build long-term brand awareness and manage the company's image and reputation.
- Manage the existing customer base to create brand loyalty and generate customer referrals.
- Obtain feedback from the owners of Tesla vehicles and make sure their experiences and suggestions for improvement were communicated to Tesla personnel engaged in designing, developing,

and/or improving the company's current and future vehicles.

As the first company to commercially produce a federally-compliant, fully electric vehicle that achieved market-leading range on a single charge, Tesla had been able to generate significant media coverage of the company and its vehicles. Management expected this would continue to be the case for some time to come. So far, the extensive media coverage, glowing praise from both new Model S owners and admiring car enthusiasts (which effectively enlarged Tesla's sales force at zero cost), and the decisions of many green-minded affluent individuals to help lead the movement away from gasoline-powered vehicles had combined to drive good traffic flows at Tesla's sales galleries and create a backlog of orders for the Model S. As a consequence, going into 2014, the company had achieved a growing volume of sales without traditional advertising and at relatively low marketing costs. Nonetheless, Tesla did make use of pay-per-click advertisements on websites and mobile applications relevant to its target clientele. It also displayed and demonstrated its vehicles at such widely attended public events as the Detroit, Los Angeles, and Frankfurt auto shows and at a few small private events attended by people who were likely to be intrigued by its vehicles.

## Tesla's Innovative Resale Guarantee Program for New Vehicle Purchases

During the second quarter of 2013, Tesla instituted its first big internal marketing and sales promotion campaign to spur demand for its Model S vehicles and give owners complete peace of mind about the long-term value of the product. In partnership with Wells Fargo Bank and U.S. Bank, Model S customers were offered unique financing terms that combined the best elements of ownership and leasing. The financing program had three important features:

1. U.S. Bank and Wells Fargo provided 10 percent–down financing and loan terms of up to 72 months to Model S buyers with approved credit. The interest rate on the loans varied according to current credit market conditions, but in the second half of 2013 the rates were in the 3.3 to 3.5 percent range.

2. Depending on the total cost of the Model S vehicle being purchased, Model S buyers could recoup most or all of the 10 percent down payment via federal and state tax credits. All Model S buyers were eligible for a federal tax credit of $7,500, and six states (California, Colorado, Georgia, Illinois, Utah, and West Virginia) offered their residents tax credits ranging from $600 to $7,500 on electric vehicle purchases. New Jersey, Washington, and the District of Columbia also had no sales tax on electric vehicle purchases. Tax credits were not available to persons who leased an electric vehicle. Further, under the financing arrangements with U.S. Bank and Wells Fargo, Model S buyers could opt not to pay some or all of the 10 percent down payment in cash and, instead, give the two banks the right to collect the owner's $7,500 federal electric car tax-credit incentive (plus any state credits) and apply the tax-credit money toward the down payment.

3. Model S customers were given the option of selling their vehicle back to Tesla within a window of 36 to 39 months after delivery for a guaranteed 50 percent of the base vehicle selling price and 43 percent of the price of any vehicle options. Tesla management believed that its guaranteed repurchase price would be as high as or higher than the top resale value of any comparably-equipped three-year-old premium luxury sedan (Mercedes, BMW, Audi, Jaguar, or Lexus), but in the event the guaranteed buyback value turned out to be less than the top resale value of any of the comparable vehicles, Elon Musk personally guaranteed to pay the difference to owners choosing to sell a three-year-old vehicle back to Tesla. Tesla's analysis indicated that the benchmarked premium luxury sedans (Mercedes, BMW, Audi, Jaguar, and Lexus) tended to retain *on average* about 43 percent of their original value after three years.

During the fourth quarter of 2013, approximately 48 percent of Model S buyers in North America financed their purchase using the innovative buyback guarantee program, an increase from 44 percent in the third quarter and 31 percent in the second quarter.[32]

Tesla's offer to buy back Model S cars from customers using its lease-buyback financing option had the potential to provide Tesla with another profitable revenue stream—selling used Tesla vehicles at prices above the buyback price. According to one analyst, "Buying back three-year-old cars at a set price means Tesla to a great extent can control the secondary market for Model S and other cars it brings out. The company's going to be the main buyer and get a chance to earn a second gross profit on the same car."[33] The analyst estimated that sales of used Model S vehicles in 2016 could mean an added $350 million to $370 million in revenues for Tesla in 2016 and perhaps an added $40 million in annual gross profit.

Even though Tesla received full up-front payment for the vehicles sold under the resale guarantee financing program, generally accepted accounting principles (GAAP) required Tesla to treat transactions under the resale guarantee program as leased vehicles and to spread the recognition of revenue and cost over the contractual term of the resale-value guarantee (36 to 39 months). If a Model S owner decided not to sell his or her vehicle back to Tesla by the end of the resale-value guarantee term, any deferred revenue and the vehicle's undepreciated book value were then recognized as revenues from automotive sales and as a cost of automotive sales, respectively.

The resale guarantee program exposed Tesla to the risk that the vehicles' resale value could be lower than its estimates and also to the risk that the volume of vehicles sold back to Tesla at the guaranteed resale price might be higher than the company's estimates. GAAP required such risks to be accounted for on Tesla's financial statements by establishing a reserves account (a contingent liability in the current liabilities section of the balance sheet) deemed sufficient to cover these risks.

Tesla's website contained a section where prospective buyers could calculate the out-of-pocket cost to own a Model S when considering the savings from using electricity instead of gasoline, depreciation benefits, and other factors. In many instances, these calculations resulted in a net monthly cost under $800 per month.

## Sales of Regulatory Credits to Other Automotive Manufacturers

Because Tesla's electric vehicles had no tailpipe emissions of greenhouse gases or other pollutants, Tesla earned zero emission vehicle (ZEV) and greenhouse gas (GHG) credits on each vehicle sold in the United States. Moreover, it also earned corporate average fuel economy (CAFE) credits on its sales of vehicles because of their high equivalent-miles-per-gallon ratings. All three of these types of regulatory credits had significant market value because the manufacturers of traditional gasoline-powered vehicles were subject to assorted emission and mileage requirements set by the U.S. Environmental Protection Agency (EPA) and by certain state agencies charged with protecting the environment within their borders; automotive manufacturers whose vehicle sales did not meet prevailing emission and mileage requirements were allowed to achieve compliance by purchasing credits earned by other automotive manufacturers. Tesla had entered into contracts for the sale of ZEV and GHG credits with several automotive manufacturers, and it also routinely sold its CAFE credits. Tesla's sales of ZEV, GHG, and CAFE credits produced revenues of $2.8 million in 2010, $2.7 million in 2011, $40.5 million in 2012, and $194.5 million in 2013—the proceeds were included on Tesla's income statement as part of the item labeled "Sales of vehicles, options and accessories, vehicle service, and regulatory credits" (see Exhibit 1).

Wall Street analysts, many of whom were openly skeptical of whether Tesla's profit prospects justified such a lofty stock price, attributed the company's improving financial performance to the revenues earned from the sales of regulatory credits. Without these revenues, their argument went, Tesla's bottom line would look significantly worse in 2012 and especially in 2013. While Tesla planned to pursue opportunities to sell regulatory credits earned from future sales of its vehicles, the company repeatedly asserted in its 10-K and 10-Q reports to the Securities and Exchange Commission that it was not relying on these sales to be a significant contributor to the company's gross margin and that the long-term viability and profitability of Tesla's business model was not predicated on revenues from the sale of regulatory credits.

## Strategic Partnerships

Going into 2014, Tesla had entered into long-term strategic partnerships with Panasonic Corp., Daimler AG (the parent of Mercedes-Benz), and Toyota Motor Corp.

**The Panasonic Partnership**  In 2010, Tesla began collaborating with Panasonic on the development of next-generation battery cells for electric vehicles that were based on the 18650 form-factor and nickel-based lithium-ion chemistry. In November 2010, Tesla sold 1,418,573 shares of its common stock to an entity affiliated with Panasonic at a price of $21.15, producing $30 million in new investor capital. In October 2011, Tesla and Panasonic finalized an agreement whereby Panasonic would supply Tesla with sufficient battery cells to build more than 80,000 vehicles over the next four years. In October 2013, Tesla and Panasonic agreed to extend the supply agreement though the end of 2017, with Tesla agreeing to purchase a minimum of 1.8 billion lithium-ion battery cells and Panasonic agreeing to provide Tesla with preferential prices.

In the last quarter of 2013, Tesla's sales volume was not constrained in any way by slack buyer demand for the Model S but rather was constrained by difficulties in ramping up production due to Panasonic's inability to deliver sufficient battery cells. Panasonic and Tesla were working in close collaboration to alleviate the tight supply conditions for battery cells.

**The Daimler Partnership**  Shortly after Daimler purchased an ownership stake in Tesla for $50 million in 2009, the two companies began working out an arrangement whereby Tesla would provide certain research and development services for a battery pack and charger to Daimler for its Smart Fortwo electric vehicle. When this development work was completed at the end of 2009, Tesla began supplying battery packs and chargers for the Smart Fortwo vehicle—some 2,100 battery packs and chargers were sold to Daimler through December 2011. In early 2010, Daimler engaged Tesla to assist with the development and production of a battery pack and charger for a pilot fleet of Mercedes A-Class electric vehicles to be introduced in Europe during 2011. When the development work was completed in October 2010, Tesla began shipping production parts in February 2010; through December 2011, Tesla sold Daimler over 500 battery packs and chargers for Mercedes A-Class electric vehicles. In early 2010, Tesla also completed the development and sale of modular battery packs for electric delivery vans for Freightliner, an affiliate of Daimler; Freightliner tested the use of these electric vans with a limited number of customers.

During the fourth quarter of 2011, Daimler engaged Tesla to assist with the development of a full electric powertrain for a Mercedes B-Class electric vehicle; in 2012, formal arrangements were established for Daimler to pay Tesla for the successful completion of certain at-risk development milestones and the delivery of prototype samples. During 2013, Tesla completed various milestones, delivered prototype samples, and recognized $15.7 million in development services revenues.

**The Toyota Partnership**    In May 2010, Tesla and Toyota announced their intention to cooperate on the development of electric vehicles and to have Tesla receive Toyota's support with sourcing parts and production and engineering expertise for the Model S. In July 2010, Tesla and Toyota entered into an early-phase agreement to develop an electric powertrain system for Toyota's popular compact RAV4 sports utility vehicle and to provide prototype samples. Also in July 2010, Tesla sold 2,941,176 shares of its common stock to Toyota at its IPO price of $17 per share, which provided Tesla with new investor capital of $50 million.

Tesla began developing and delivering electric powertrains for the RAV4 for Toyota's evaluation in September 2010, and the following month Tesla entered into a $60.1 million contract services agreement with Toyota for the development of a validated RAV4 powertrain system (including a battery pack, charging system, inverter, motor, gearbox, and associated software). In July 2011, Tesla contracted with Toyota to supply an electric powertrain system for the RAV4 model. All of the development services for the RAV4 electric vehicle were completed in the first quarter of 2012, and Tesla began producing and delivering RAV4 powertrain systems to Toyota in the first half of 2012. Tesla was also providing Toyota with certain services related to the supply of the RAV4 electric powertrain system. Powertrain production for the RAV4 and the provision of associated services were expected to continue through 2014. During 2013, Tesla recorded revenues of $45.1 million from powertrain system sales to Toyota.

Tesla performed its electric powertrain component and systems activities principally at a company facility in Palo Alto. This facility, which also served as Tesla's corporate headquarters, housed the company's research and development services, including cell and component testing and prototyping, as well as the manufacturing of powertrain components for sales to Daimler and Toyota.

**Tesla's Strategic Partnership to Build a New Gigafactory to Produce Battery Packs**    On February 26, 2014, Tesla announced that it and unnamed partners (one of which was expected to be Panasonic) would invest $4 billion to $5 billion through 2020 in a "gigafactory" capable of producing enough lithium-ion batteries to make battery packs for 500,000 vehicles (plus stationary storage applications for solar-powered generating facilities)—the planned output of the battery factory by 2020 exceeded the *total global production of lithium batteries in 2013*. Tesla said its direct investment in the project would be $2 billion. Tesla indicated that the new gigafactory would reduce the company's battery-pack cost by more than 30 percent—to around $200 per kilowatt-hour by some estimates (from the current estimated level of about $300 per kilowatt-hour). The schedule called for facility construction in 2014–2015, equipment installation in 2016, and initial production in 2017. The plant was expected to be built on a 500- to 1,000-acre site, employ about 6,500 workers, have about 10 million square feet of space on two levels, and be powered by wind and solar generating facilities located nearby. Evaluation of finalist plant sites in five states (Nevada, Arizona, New Mexico, California, and Texas) began immediately and was still under way in mid-2014.

Shortly after its gigafactory announcement, Tesla announced that it had sold $920 million of convertible senior notes due 2019 carrying an interest rate of 0.25 percent and $1.38 billion in convertible senior notes due 2021 carrying an interest rate of 1.25 percent. The senior notes due 2019 were convertible into cash, shares of Tesla's common stock, or a combination thereof, at Tesla's election. The senior notes due 2021 were convertible into cash and, if applicable, shares of Tesla's common stock (subject to Tesla's right to deliver cash in lieu of shares of common stock). Both bonds had an equity conversion premium of 42.5 percent above the last reported sale price of Tesla's common stock price ($252.54) at the time of the debt issue (which equated to almost $360 per share)—in other words, Tesla's stock had to be trading above $360 per share for the holders of the convertible bonds to be eligible to receive 2.8 shares of Tesla common stock for every $1,000 of bonds they chose to convert (but again that was subject to Tesla's right to deliver cash in lieu of shares of common stock). Moreover, to further protect existing shareholders against ownership dilution that might result from the senior notes being converted into additional shares of Tesla stock, Tesla immediately entered into convertible-note hedge transactions and warrant transactions at an approximate cost of $186 million that management expected would reduce potential dilution of existing shareholder interests and/or offset cash payments that Tesla was required to make in excess of the principal amounts upon any conversion of the 2019 notes and 2021 notes.

Tesla originally intended to issue only $1.6 billion in convertible debt, but increased the amount to $2.0 billion due to the strong demand and the attractively low interest rates. An overallotment provision in the offering granted underwriters a 30-day option to purchase an additional $240 million in convertible senior notes.

## QUESTIONS ARISE ABOUT THE SAFETY OF THE MODEL S BATTERY PACK

Within the space of five weeks in October–November 2013, three Model S vehicles (two in the United States and one in Mexico) were involved in traffic accidents that resulted in fires in the battery pack. All three fires occurred after high-speed collisions, and none resulted in serious injuries or deaths. In all three cases, wreck debris penetrated the quarter-inch-thick aluminum case housing the battery pack and punctured a number of the lithium-ion battery cells—one characteristic of all lithium-ion battery cells is that a puncture of the cell wall causes the materials inside the cell to ignite. A battery fire results as spiking internal temperatures from the ignited cells cause other cells to ignite; such fires, while not violent, are difficult to extinguish, allowing the fire to spread to other combustible parts of the vehicle.

Because the sharp rise in Model S sales during 2013 had greatly raised Tesla's public profile, all three battery fire incidents received national and international media coverage—a video of the first vehicle fire was posted on YouTube and quickly went viral. According to eyewitness reports, a modest fire began from the initially punctured cells; then when these flames caused the thermal temperatures of adjacent cells to spike, they exploded into flames and sparked temperature increases that caused another series of cells to explode, producing a rather spectacular fire. Firemen at the scene had trouble completely extinguishing the fire because it kept reigniting as additional battery cells exploded. The media headlines and accompanying stories (some of which contained pictures from the YouTube video) immediately brought the safety of Tesla's high-energy-density lithium-ion battery pack into question. In the ensuing days and weeks, there was considerable debate and uncertainty surrounding the answers to two questions:

1. Did the use of 18650 lithium-ion cells make Tesla vehicles more prone to battery fires and thus less safe than originally thought?

2. How life threatening was Tesla's decision to use 18650 lithium-ion batteries in the Model S battery back?

As both journalists and concerned investors researched the characteristics and safety profiles of various types of lithium-ion batteries, it quickly became apparent that there were two risks associated with the 18650 form-factor battery cells in the Model S battery pack that combined to produce a less desirable safety profile in comparison to the safety profiles of the low-energy-density lithium-ion cells used in the battery packs of the electric vehicles made by all other automotive manufacturers.[34] One risk concerned the fact that the fires arising from punctured cells were significantly more intense in high-energy-density cells than in low-energy-density cells—due to the different amounts of energy stored in the two types of cells. The second risk had to do with the fact that between 1 in 10 million and 1 in 40 million of the lithium-ion cells that were produced had an internal short circuit created during manufacturing that was not detectable at the point of manufacture; cells with such short circuits would fail at some point during "normal" operation in the field. These so-called field failures produced instant and very high temperature spikes, possibly resulting in thermal runaway, and caused fires and explosions with varying intensities that depended on the chemistries of the materials used and the cell design. Although the risk of a field failure was tiny, each cell in a battery pack represented an independent field-failure risk. Thus the Model S battery pack, which contained about 7,000 cells, was alleged to have a much bigger field-failure risk than the battery pack of the Nissan Leaf, which reportedly had only 192 cells.

Tesla had opted to use the 18650 form-factor lithium-ion cells in the Model S battery pack because the higher energy density of these cells was precisely what enabled the driving range of the Model S to be so much greater than the driving ranges of other electric vehicles whose battery packs contained only low-energy-density cells.

Because the flurry of publicity about the Model S fires precipitated a 20 percent drop in Tesla's stock price and heightened the concerns of both Tesla investors and Model S owners, Elon Musk decided to address the issue of the safety of the Model S battery pack head-on in a November 18, 2013, blog post at www.teslamotors.com; in his blog posting, Elon Musk said in part:

Since the Model S went into production last year, there have been more than a quarter million gasoline car fires in the United States alone, resulting in over 400 deaths and approximately 1,200 serious injuries. . . . However, the three Model S fires, which only occurred after very high-speed collisions and caused no serious injuries or deaths, received more national headlines than all 250,000+ gasoline fires combined. The media coverage of Model S fires vs. gasoline car fires is disproportionate by several orders of magnitude, despite the latter actually being far more deadly.

. . . A gasoline tank has 10 times more combustion energy than our battery pack. Moreover, the Model S battery pack also has internal firewalls between the 16 modules and a firewall between the battery pack and passenger compartment. This effectively limits the fire energy to a few percent that of a gasoline car. . . .

While we believe the evidence is clear that there is no safer car on the road than the Model S, we are taking three specific actions.

First, we have rolled out an over-the-air update to the air suspension that will result in greater ground clearance at highway speeds. To be clear, this is about reducing the chances of underbody impact damage, not improving safety. The theoretical probability of a fire injury is already vanishingly small and the actual number to date is zero. Another software update expected in January [2014] will give the driver direct control of the air suspension ride height transitions.

Second, we have requested that the National Highway Traffic Safety Administration conduct a full investigation as soon as possible into the fire incidents. While we think it is highly unlikely, if something is discovered that would result in a material improvement in occupant fire safety, we will immediately apply that change to new cars and offer it as a free retrofit to all existing cars. . . .

Third, to reinforce how strongly we feel about the low risk of fire in our cars, we will be amending our warranty policy to cover damage due to a fire, even if due to driver error. Unless a Model S owner actively tries to destroy the car, they are covered. Our goal here is to eliminate any concern about the cost of such an event and ensure that over time the Model S has the lowest insurance cost of any car at our price point. Either our belief in the safety of our car is correct and this is a minor cost or we are wrong, in which case the right thing is for Tesla to bear the cost rather than the car buyer.

All of these actions are taken in order to make clear the confidence we have in our product and to eliminate any misperceptions regarding the integrity of our technology and the safety of our cars.

A fourth Model S–related fire incident occurred in a residential garage on the campus of the University of California–Irvine on November 15, 2013. A blaze broke out in the garage at a wall socket where a Model S was plugged in for charging; the fire was noticed by the car's owner and was extinguished by fire crews. The report of the Orange County Fire Authority stated that the most likely cause was either a faulty high-resistance connection at the wall socket or problems with the car's charging cable; the report further said that the fire had nothing to do with the battery.[35] The Fire Authority report noted that cardboard boxes stacked near the 240-volt wall outlet aided the spread of the fire, thus contributing to the estimated damages of up to $25,000. A review of the car's logs by Tesla officials who went to the scene indicated that the car was charging normally, with no fluctuations in temperature and no malfunctions within the battery or the charge electronics capable of causing a fire. They said, "The cable was fine on the vehicle side; the damage was on the wall side. Our inspection of the car and the battery made clear that neither were the source" of the fire.[36]

Nonetheless, Tesla responded to the garage fire incident by immediately redesigning the Model S charging cable to automatically cut off the charging process when a faulty wall-socket problem was detected. Furthermore, it provided all Model S owners with the newly redesigned charging cable free of cost.

In December 2013, the National Highway Traffic Safety Administration reaffirmed the 5-star safety rating of the Tesla Model S overall and in all subcategories for Model Year 2014, despite the fact that its investigation of the recent Model S fire incidents was still ongoing. On March 6 2014, Tesla began adding titanium shielding and an aluminum deflector bar and plate to the underbody of its Model S luxury electric car to prevent possible battery fires that could be caused by running over objects; the company said it would retroactively install the shielding on existing cars upon the owner's request or during scheduled service. On March 28, 2014, the NHTSA announced it had closed the investigation of Tesla Model S fires and the safety of the Model S battery pack as a result of the company's decision to add increased underbody protection to reduce the risk of fires if the car ran over an object; the agency further noted, "A defect trend has not been identified."

# THE ELECTRIC VEHICLE SEGMENT OF THE GLOBAL AUTOMOTIVE INDUSTRY

Global production of passenger cars totaled about 65 million in 2013, accounting for about 74 percent of the world's total annual production of motor vehicles. The remaining 26 percent, close to 23 million vehicles, consisted of light trucks (commonly termed *pickup trucks*), heavy or cargo-carrying trucks, recreational vehicles, buses, and minibuses. In 2013, global sales of plug-in electric vehicles were less than 1 percent of the global vehicle sales—plug-in vehicles included both battery-only vehicles and so-called plug-in hybrid electric vehicles equipped with a gasoline or diesel engine for use when the vehicle's battery pack (rechargeable only from an external plug-in source) was depleted, usually after a distance of 10 to 40 miles for current models. However, global sales of hybrid electric vehicles were roughly 3 percent of global vehicle sales. Hybrid vehicles were jointly powered by an internal combustion engine and an electric motor that ran on batteries charged by "regenerative braking"[37] and the internal combustion engine; the batteries in a hybrid vehicle could not be restored to a full charge by connecting a plug to an external power source.

Total motor vehicle sales in the United States in 2013 were 15.6 million units (up 7.6 percent from 2012); the forecast for 2014 was for sales of 16 million vehicles. Going into 2014, the all-time best month for sales of plug-in electric vehicles in the United States was August 2013, with a volume of 11,073 units—see Exhibit 6.[38] Plug-in sales for October 2013 ranked as the second-best all-time sales month, with a volume of 9,695 units. Sales of plug-in electric vehicles in the United States in 2013 totaled just over 95,000 units, equal to a market share of just 0.8 percent. The three best-selling electric vehicles in the United States in 2013—the Chevrolet Volt, Nissan LEAF, and Tesla Model S—accounted for almost twice as many units as the other 12 models combined (Exhibit 6). In 2013, U.S. sales of hybrid electric vehicles were just under 500,000 units, roughly a 2.8 percent market share. But with gasoline prices drifting lower in the United States during most of 2013, the vehicle models posting the biggest sales gains were pricey pickup trucks, SUVs, and luxury passenger cars rather than the smaller, more fuel-efficient and plug-in vehicles that the Obama administration had been pushing automakers to focus on since 2008.

A forecast by IHS Automotive, a supplier of information and research to the automotive industry, predicted that global electric vehicle production (including hybrids) would increase 67 percent in 2014, as a number of major automakers introduced new models and expanded their efforts to sell them in more geographic markets.[39] According to IHS, Europe would account for 40 percent of all electric vehicle production, followed by Asia at 30 percent, and the United States with 27 percent.

## EXHIBIT 6   Sales of Plug-In Electric Vehicles in the United States, 2013

| | Jan | Feb | Mar | Apr | May | Jun | Jul | Aug | Sep | Oct | Nov | Dec | Total |
|---|---|---|---|---|---|---|---|---|---|---|---|---|---|
| Chevrolet Volt | 1,140 | 1,626 | 1,478 | 1,306 | 1,607 | 2,698 | 1,788 | 3,351 | 1,766 | 2,022 | 1,920 | 2,392 | 23,094 |
| Nissan LEAF | 650 | 653 | 2,236 | 1,937 | 2,138 | 2,225 | 1,864 | 2,420 | 1,953 | 2,002 | 2,003 | 2,529 | 22,610 |
| Tesla Model S | 1,200 | 1,400 | 2,300 | 2,100 | 1,700 | 1,350 | 1,800 | 1,300 | 1,000 | 800 | 1,200 | 1,500 | 17,650 |
| Toyota Prius PHV | 874 | 693 | 786 | 599 | 678 | 584 | 817 | 1,791 | 1,152 | 2,095 | 1,100 | 919 | 12,088 |
| Ford C-Max Energi | 338 | 334 | 494 | 411 | 450 | 455 | 433 | 621 | 758 | 1,092 | 941 | 827 | 7,154 |
| Ford Fusion Energi | 0 | 119 | 295 | 364 | 416 | 390 | 407 | 600 | 750 | 1,087 | 870 | 791 | 6,089 |
| Ford Focus Electric | 81 | 158 | 180 | 147 | 157 | 177 | 150 | 175 | 110 | 115 | 130 | 158 | 1,738 |
| Toyota RAV4 EV | 25 | 52 | 133 | 70 | 84 | 44 | 109 | 231 | 167 | 91 | 62 | 28 | 1,096 |
| Mitsubishi i-MiEV | 257 | 337 | 31 | 127 | 91 | 39 | 46 | 30 | 20 | 28 | 12 | 11 | 1,029 |
| smart ED | 2 | 0 | 0 | 0 | 60 | 53 | 58 | 182 | 137 | 111 | 153 | 167 | 923 |
| Fiat 500e | 0 | 0 | 0 | 0 | 0 | 0 | 150 | 160 | 50 | 40 | 125 | 120 | 645 |
| Honda Fit EV | 8 | 15 | 23 | 22 | 15 | 208 | 63 | 66 | 35 | 40 | 23 | 51 | 569 |
| Chevrolet Spark EV | 0 | 0 | 0 | 0 | 0 | 27 | 103 | 102 | 78 | 66 | 87 | 76 | 539 |
| Honda Accord PHV | 2 | 17 | 26 | 55 | 58 | 42 | 54 | 44 | 51 | 71 | 68 | 38 | 526 |
| Porsche Panamera S-E | 0 | 0 | 0 | 0 | 0 | 0 | 0 | 0 | 0 | 0 | 35 | 4 | 47 | 86 |
| Cadillac ELR | 0 | 0 | 0 | 0 | 0 | 0 | 0 | 0 | 0 | 0 | 0 | 6 | 6 |
| | 4,577 | 5,404 | 7,982 | 7,138 | 7,454 | 8,292 | 7,842 | 11,073 | 8,027 | 9,695 | 8,698 | 9,660 | 95,842 |

*Note:* The falloff in monthly Tesla sales in the United States beginning in August 2013 was the result of Tesla's shipping a big fraction of the Model S units assembled each month at the Tesla Factory in Fremont, California, to fill customer orders throughout Europe.

*Source:* "Monthly Plug-In Sales Scorecard," *Inside EVs,* www.insideevs.com (accessed February 27, 2014).

Toyota Motor Corp. was the global leader in sales of hybrids and plug-ins, with cumulative sales approaching 6 million units at the end of 2013 and expected annual sales in excess of 1 million units in 2014–2015.[40] In 2013, Toyota sold 19 hybrid models and 1 plug-in model in approximately 80 countries around the world and planned to introduce 18 new hybrid models between May 2013 and the end of 2015.

Despite the low sales and market shares for plug-in electric vehicles and hybrids in the United States and other countries, executives at automotive companies across the world were closely watching the strategic moves that Elon Musk was making and the waves that Tesla's Model S was making in the marketplace. Headed into 2014, there were 15 automobile manufacturers feverishly working on next-generation electric vehicles. Developmental efforts were aimed chiefly at extending the distance electric car battery packs would go on a single charge

and keeping production costs low enough to make a profit selling large quantities of compact electric vehicles for prices of about $30,000. In mid-2013, Volkswagen said it intended to become the world's largest seller of electric vehicles by 2018. Volkswagen planned to introduce its fully electric e-Golf in 2014.

The publicity that Tesla's Model S received and the rapid climb of the company stock price in 2013 prompted the CEO of General Motors not only to closely monitor what Tesla was doing but also to set up a special team to study how Tesla products might disrupt the automotive industry in upcoming years. Executives at GM were acutely aware that cures were needed for the disappointingly small sales volume of the much ballyhooed Chevrolet Volt and that the Volt had failed to spark consumer interest in electric vehicles—sales totaled only 23,100 units in 2013. To boost sales of the Volt, GM reduced the Volt's 2013 base price of $39,995 to a base price of $34,995 for the 2014 Volt. General Motors was rumored to be working on a next-generation compact electric car that could go 200 miles on a charge and that would be equipped with a generator for battery charging; supposedly the car would be introduced in 2016 and have a base price close to $30,000.

In late 2013, BMW began selling its all-new i3 series electric car models that had a lightweight, carbon fiber–reinforced plastic body, lithium-ion batteries with a driving range of 80 to 100 miles on a single charge, a 170-horsepower electric motor, and a base price of $41,350; customers could also get the BMW i3 with a range-extender package (base price of $45,200) that included a 34-horsepower motor used only to maintain the charge of the lithium-ion battery at an approximate 5 percent charge and extend the driving range to 160 to 180 miles per charge. BMW had nearly 10,000 i3s on order and expected global sales for the i3 to be approximately 21,400 units in 2014 and 22,500 units in 2015. In mid-2014, BMW began selling a super-premium sporty, high-tech electric vehicle called the i8 (base price of $136,000) that had a three-cylinder electric motor, a supplemental gasoline engine for higher speeds, scissor doors, flamboyant aerodynamic flourishes, and an electric-only driving range of about 22 miles. Preliminary forecasts called for i8 sales of close to 2,000 units in 2014 and 5,100 units in 2015.

In January 2014 General Motors began selling its first Cadillac electric car—the ELR Coupe (base price of $75,995), which had a stylish exterior and a luxurious interior but was mechanically similar to the Chevrolet Volt. The hybrid plug-in ELR had lithium-ion batteries with an electric-only range of 37 miles, a four-cylinder, 84-horsepower gasoline engine that powered a generator to keep the battery pack charged up, and regenerative braking to also help recharge the batteries. Test-drive reviewers at *Car and Driver* and **Edmunds.com** praised the ELR's looks, comfort, and interior quality but were highly critical of its driving performance and technological sophistication—especially when compared to Tesla's Model S. The ELR's electric powertrain system was a slightly upgraded version of the powertrain system in the Chevrolet Volt and, in the opinion of the test-drive reviewers, did not have the performance capabilities one would expect in a vehicle with the ELR's price tag.

Mercedes-Benz was set to launch sales of its premium compact B-Class electric vehicle in the United States in summer 2014; the four-door, five-passenger vehicle (base price of $41,450) was built on an entirely new platform compared to other B-Class models with traditional gasoline engines, had an estimated driving range of 115 miles on a single charge, accelerated from 0 to 60 miles per hour in less than 10 seconds, delivered 174 horsepower, had a top speed of 100 miles per hour, utilized an electric powertrain system custom-designed and produced by Tesla, and was loaded with safety features. Mercedes B-Class electric vehicles with a range-extender package were also available. The new electric B-Class models were expected to compete directly with BMW's i3 series electric car.

At the January 2014 Consumer Electronics Show, Ford debuted a solar-powered concept car, a version of the C-Max Energi plug-in car that it was already selling (Ford delivered 35,200 units of its C-Max plug-in hybrid models to dealers in 2013).[41] The roof of the C-Max concept car was covered with solar cells supplied by SunPower Corp. Because it took the solar cells a while to charge the battery pack, Ford had teamed with Georgia Tech engineers to offer a special carport (called an *off-vehicle solar concentrator*) that was essentially a magnifying glass designed to track the sun as it moved across the sky. According to Ford, this carport boosted the power that could be collected from sunlight by a factor of eight, allowing a full 8-kilowatt charge over the course of a day. In 2013, Ford sold about 85,000 hybrids, plug-in hybrids, and all-electric vehicles; it sold more plug-in vehicles in October and November 2013 than both Toyota and Tesla. Going into 2014, Ford was the world's second-leading seller of traditional hybrid cars that did not have a plug-in option (behind only Toyota). Still, Ford's sales of hybrids trailed far behind the company's best-selling model line—Ford delivered 763,400 F-series pickup trucks to dealers in 2013.

Exhibit 7 shows how the expected price and electric-only driving range of Tesla's forthcoming Model 3 mid-priced sedan (2016–2017) compared against the price and electric-only driving range of other electric vehicles on the market in 2014.

**EXHIBIT 7**   Comparative Prices and Driving Ranges of Tesla's Forthcoming Model 3 Sedan and Other 2014 Model Electric Vehicles

| Electric Vehicle | Manufacturer's Suggested Retail Price (base model, no options) | EPA-Estimated Driving Range (all electric, full charge) |
|---|---|---|
| 2014 Nissan LEAF Hatchback | $28,980 | 84 miles |
| 2014 Chevrolet Spark EV | $26,695 | 82 miles |
| 2014 Chevrolet Volt | $34,185 | 38 miles |
| 2014 Ford Focus electric | $35,170 | 76 miles |
| 2014 Fiat 500e | $32,600 | 87 miles |
| 2014 Honda Fit EV | $37,415 | 82 miles |
| 2014 BMW i3 Hatchback | $41,350 | 80–100 miles |
| 2014 Mercedes B-Class | $41,450 | 115 miles |
| 2016–2017 Tesla Model 3 | ~$35,000–$40,000 | 200 miles |

*Sources*: www.edmunds.com; company websites; and "The Tesla Model E Will Have a 48 kWh Battery, and Will Be 20% Smaller," www.cleantechnica.com, March 5, 2014 (accessed March 20, 2014). Note: In July 2014, Tesla announced it was changing the name of the Model E to Model 3 because of a lawsuit from Ford Motor claiming it had rights to the name Model E.

# ENDNOTES

[1] *Consumer Reports,* April 2014, p. 10.

[2] Ibid.

[3] Jessica Caldwell, "Drive by Numbers—Tesla Model S Is the Vehicle of Choice in Many of America's Wealthiest Zip Codes," www.edmunds.com, October 31, 2013 (accessed November 18, 2013).

[4] Jeff Evanson, Tesla Motors Investor Presentation, September 14, 2013, www.teslamotors.com (accessed November 29, 2013).

[5] Ibid.

[6] John Reed, "Elon Musk's Groundbreaking Electric Car," *FT Magazine,* July 24, 2009, www.ft.com (accessed September 26, 2013).

[7] Ibid.

[8] Tesla press release, May 19, 2009; Michael Arrington, "Tesla Worth More than Half a Billion after Daimler Investment," www.techcrunch.com, May 19, 2009 (accessed September 30, 2013).

[9] According to an article titled "Abu Dhabi Takes Part of Daimler's Investment Stake," www.marketwatch.com, July 13, 2009.

[10] Chris Morrison, "Tesla's Layoffs: Bad Blood, a Bloodbath, or Business as Usual?" www.venturebeat.com, January 11, 2008 (accessed September 24, 2013).

[11] Josh Friedman, "Entrepreneur Tries His Midas Touch in Space," *Los Angeles Times,* April 23, 2003, www.latimes.com (accessed September 16, 2013).

[12] David Kestenbaum, "Making a Mark with Rockets and Roadsters," *National Public Radio,* August 9, 2007, www.npr.org (accessed September 17, 2013).

[13] Ibid.

[14] Ibid.

[15] Video interview with Alan Murray, "Elon Musk: I'll Put a Man on Mars in 10 Years," *Market Watch,* December 1, 2011, marketwatch.com (accessed September 16, 2013).

[16] William Harwood, "SpaceX Dragon Returns to Earth, Ends Historic Trip," *CNET,* May 31, 2012, www.cbsnews.com (accessed September 16, 2013).

[17] Ashlee Vance, "Revealed: Elon Musk Explains the Hyperloop, the Solar-Powered High-Speed Future of Inter-City Transportation," *Bloomberg Businessweek,* August 12, 2013, www.businessweek.com (accessed September 25, 2013).

[18] Mike Seemuth, "From the Corner Office—Elon Musk," *Success,* April 10, 2011, www.success.com (accessed September 25, 2013).

[19] Ibid.

[20] Ibid.

[21] Jay Yarow, "A Day in the Life of Elon Musk, the Most Inspiring Entrepreneur in the World," *Business Insider,* July 24, 2012, www.businessinsider.com (accessed September 25, 2013).

[22] April Dembosky, "The Entrepreneur with Astronomical Ambition," *Financial Times,* May 25, 2012, www.ft.com (accessed September 25, 2013).

[23] Terry Dawes, "Why Critics Love to Hate Elon Musk," www.cantechletter.com, June 10, 2013 (accessed September 25, 2013).

[24] According to information in the company's Proxy Statement issued April 17, 2013, pp. 28–30.

[25] Jeff Evanson, Tesla Motors Investor Presentation, January 15, 2014, www.teslamotors.com (accessed February 24, 2014).

[26] According to information in Martin Eberhard's blog titled "Lotus Position," July 25, 2006, www.teslamotors.com/blog/lotus-position (accessed September 17, 2013).

[27] 2013 10-K report, p. 4.

[28] Company press release, August 19, 2013.

[29] Company press release, May 20, 2010.

[30] See Vince Bond, Jr., "Tesla's Plan to Sell in Ohio Dodges Bullet," *Automotive News,* December 4, 2013, www.autonews.com (accessed December 27, 2013).

[31] Dan Gearino, "Ohio Car Dealers Sue to Block Tesla Dealership," *Columbus Dispatch,* December 19, 2013, www.dispatch.com (accessed December 27, 2013).

[32] Calculated by the case author from information on total fourth-quarter Model S sales in the United States and the number of Model S vehicles delivered in the United States in Q4 2013 with a resale-value guarantee, as cited in Tesla's press release of February 19, 2014.

[33] As quoted in Alan Ohnsman, "Tesla Model S Buyback Offer May Generate More Revenue," www.bloomberg.com, September 10, 2013 (accessed December 10, 2013).

[34] John Peterson, "Understanding Tesla's Life Threatening Battery Decisions," www.seekingalpha.com, November 22, 2013 (accessed December 19, 2013).

[35] Anthony Ingram, "Tesla, Irvine Fire Dept Disagree over Cause of Garage Fire," *Green Car Reports,* December 19, 2013, www.greencar-reports.com (accessed December 21, 2013); Alan Ohnsman, "Tesla Says Model S, Charger Didn't Cause Garage Fire," *Bloomberg Technology,* December 19, 2013, www.bloomberg.com (accessed December 21, 2013).

[36] Ibid.

[37] Regenerative braking involved capturing the energy lost during braking by using the electric motor as a generator and storing the captured energy in the battery. Hybrids could not use off-board sources of electricity to charge the batteries—hybrids could use only regenerative braking and the internal combustion engine to charge. The extra power provided by the electric motor in a hybrid vehicle enabled faster acceleration and also allowed for use of a smaller internal combustion engine.

[38] "Monthly Plug-In Sales Scorecard," *Inside EVs,* www.insideevs.com (accessed February 27, 2014).

[39] "Global Production of Electric Vehicles to Surge by 67 Percent This Year," press.ihs.com, February 4, 2014 (accessed February 28, 2014).

[40] Green Car Congress, "Toyota Cumulative Global Hybrid Sales Pass 5M, nearly 2M in US," www.greencarcongress.com, April 17, 2013 (accessed December 16, 2013).

[41] Chris Isidore, "Ford to Debut Solar Car," *CNN Money,* January 2, 2014, www.money.cnn.com (accessed January 6, 2014).

# Tata Motors in 2014: Its Multibrand Approach to Competing in the Global Automobile Industry

**David L. Turnipseed**
University of South Alabama

**John E. Gamble**
Texas A&M University–Corpus Christi

Tata Motors, Ltd., was India's leading automobile manufacturer by revenue and the number-three passenger-vehicle brand in India in 2012. However, in 2013 and 2014, the company's namesake brand slid into a decline, both domestically and internationally, with the company eventually losing its number-three rank in automobile sales in India to Honda. Also, the company's sales of commercial vehicles declined in 2013 and 2014, causing the company to drop from fourth-largest seller of commercial vehicles to fifth.

Some of the company's poor performance could be attributed to poor macro-economic conditions in India, increasing competition, and a variety of other external factors such as the possible elimination of diesel subsidies by the Indian government. However, much of the company's poor performance was a result of a flawed strategy and poor execution. For example, it was imperative that the company's managers consider how to expand the market for its low-priced Nano, which had required substantial investment during its development and had fallen far short of sales expectations. Plus, the company's entire strategy for its Tata-branded vehicles seemed to be in disarray.

However, the company's Jaguar Land Rover division was achieving great success, with a 23 percent year-over-year increase in revenues and a 55 percent year-over-year increase in profit after tax in fiscal 2014. In fact, Jaguar Land Rover accounted for 88 percent of the company's total automotive revenues in fiscal 2014 and 89 percent of its income before other income, finance cost, tax, and exceptional items in fiscal 2014. Tata Motors' management would be forced to evaluate its strategy for its Tata passenger cars, Tata commercial vehicles, and Jaguar Land Rover division if it was to compete successfully with the world's leading automobile producers.

## THE HISTORY OF TATA MOTORS

Tata Motors was a division of the Tata Group, which was India's largest corporation, owning more than 90 companies spanning seven business sectors (chemicals, information technology and communications, consumer products, engineering, materials, services, and energy). In 2012, the corporation had operations in over 80 countries, and it had gross revenues of $83.5 billion in 2011. The company's gross revenues dipped to $96.8 million in fiscal 2013, after having reached $100 million in 2012. Nearly 60 percent of the Tata Group's revenues were generated outside India. The Tata Group was a powerful symbol of India's emergence as a world economic power and was India's largest private-sector employer, with over 425,000 employees. A financial summary for the Tata Group for fiscal 2010 through fiscal 2013 is presented in Exhibit 1.

**EXHIBIT 1**    Financial Summary for the Tata Group, Fiscal 2010–Fiscal 2013 (in billions of U.S. dollars)

|  | Fiscal 2013 | Fiscal 2012 | Fiscal 2011 | Fiscal 2010 |
|---|---|---|---|---|
| Total revenue | $96.79 | $100.09 | $83.30 | $67.40 |
| Sales | 95.59 | 99.10 | 82.20 | 65.63 |
| Total assets | 107.17 | 108.55 | 68.90 | 52.77 |
| International revenues | 60.70 | 59.09 | 48.30 | 38.36 |
| Net forex earnings | 3.05 | 1.59 | 5.80 | −0.16 |

*Note:* Financial year is April to March.

*Source:* www.tata.com.

Tata Motors' history began in 1945 when the Tata Engineering and Locomotive Company began manufacturing locomotives and engineering products. In 1948, Tata began production of steam road rollers, in collaboration with U.K. manufacturer Marshall Sons. In 1954, the company entered into a 15-year collaborative agreement with Daimler-Benz AG, of Germany, to manufacture medium-sized commercial vehicles. The company began producing hydraulic excavators in collaboration with Japan's Hitachi in 1985. The first independently designed light commercial vehicle, the Tata 407 "pickup," was produced in 1986, followed by the Tata 608 light truck. Tata Engineering began manufacturing passenger cars in 1991 and entered into a joint agreement with Cummins Engine Co. to manufacture high-horsepower and low-emission diesel engines for cars and trucks in 1993.

In 1994, the company began a joint venture with Daimler-Benz to manufacture Mercedes-Benz passenger cars in India. Also that year, Tata signed a joint venture agreement with Tata Holset, a U.K. firm, to manufacture turbochargers for the Cummins engines. India's first sports utility vehicle, the Tata Safari, was launched in 1998, and its independently designed Indica V2 became the number-one car in its segment in India in 2001. Also during 2001, Tata exited its joint venture with Daimler-Benz, and it entered into a product agreement with U.K.-based MG Rover in 2002.

Tata Engineering changed its name to Tata Motors Limited in 2003, and in that year the company produced its three-millionth vehicle. Tata's stock was listed in the New York Stock Exchange on September 27, 2004, under the symbol "TTM." Also in 2004, Tata Motors and South Korea's Daewoo Commercial Vehicle Co. Ltd. entered into a joint venture that produced and marketed heavy-duty commercial trucks in South Korea. Tata Motors acquired a 21 percent interest in the Spanish bus manufacturer Hipo Carrocera SA in 2005 and began production of several new vehicles, including small trucks and SUVs.

Tata Motors produced its four-millionth vehicle in 2006. In the same year, it began a joint venture with Brazil's Marcopolo to manufacture buses for India and foreign markets, expanded Tata Daewoo's product line to include tractor-trailer trucks powered by liquefied natural gas (LNG), and established three joint ventures with Fiat. The company formed a joint venture with Thonburi Automotive Assembly Plant Co. in Thailand to manufacture, assemble, and market pickup trucks. In 2007, Tata sold all its interest in Tata Holset to Cummins, Inc.

In 2008, Tata purchased the iconic British brands Land Rover and Jaguar, began selling passenger cars and pickup trucks in the Democratic Republic of the Congo, and announced its "People's Car," named the Nano. The Nano hit the market in 2009 at a base price of about $2,250 and won India's Car of the Year award. Tata began exporting the Nano to South Africa, Kenya, and developing countries in Asia and Africa. Also in 2009, Tata purchased the remaining 79 percent of Hipo Carrocera and a 50.3 percent interest in Miljø Grenland/Innovasjon, a Norwegian firm specializing in electric vehicle technology. Tata also entered into an agreement with Motor Development International (MDI), of Luxembourg, to develop an air-powered car. In 2010, the Tata Nano Europa was set up for sale in developed economies, especially country markets in Europe.

Tata celebrated its 50th year in international business in 2011. During that year, the company announced the opening of a commercial-vehicle assembly plant in South Africa and a Land Rover assembly plant in India. Two long-distance buses, the Tata Divo Luxury Coach and the Tata Starbus Ultra, were introduced, and two new SUVs—the Tata Sumo Gold and the Range Rover Evoque—went on the market. Also in 2011, the upscale Tata Manza and the Prima heavy truck were launched in South Africa.

During 2011, Tata won two prestigious awards, which helped bring the company to global prominence. The Jaguar C-X75 won the Louis Vuitton award in Paris, and the Range Rover Evoque won Car Design of the Year. The new Pixel, Tata's city-car concept for Europe, was displayed at the 81st Geneva Motor Show, and the Tata 407 light truck celebrated its silver anniversary in 2011, accounting for 7 out of every 10 vehicles sold in the light-commercial-vehicle (LCV) category. The company began exporting the Nano to Sri Lanka, and it launched the Tata Magic IRIS, a four- to five-seat vehicle (top speed of 34 miles per hour) for public transportation. Also in 2011, the company introduced the Tata Ace Zip, a small "micro truck" for deep-penetration goods transport on the poor roads of rural India, and the new Tata Indica eV2, the most fuel-efficient car in India.

Continuing its innovative operations, Tata signed an agreement of cooperation in 2012 with Malaysia's DRB-HICOM's Defense Technologies. Tata also introduced its Anti-Terrorist Indoor Combat Vehicle concept at DEFEXPO-India. The company brought out three new vehicles at the 2012 Auto Expo: Tata Safari Storme, a large SUV; Tata Ultra, a light commercial vehicle (truck); and Tata LPT 3723, a medium-duty truck and India's first five-axle rigid truck. The air-powered car developed with Luxembourg's MDI was showing promise and would possibly serve a large market niche that wanted ultra-economical transportation.

In fiscal 2014, the company launched two compact car models: The Zest was designed to compete with the Suzuki DZire, Hyundai Xcent, and Honda Amaze. The Bolt, a smaller version of the Zest, was positioned against the Suzuki Swift, Honda Brio, and Hyundai Grand i10. Tata also introduced 10 new products in its Prima truck series and launched its new Ultra line of intermediate light trucks.

Tata Motors' joint ventures, subsidiaries, and associated companies are presented in Exhibit 2. Consolidated income statements and balance sheets for Tata Motors are presented in Exhibits 3 and 4, respectively.

# MACROECONOMIC CONDITIONS IN INDIA

India was the seventh-largest nation in area, with about one-third the land size of the United States. As of 2013, it was the second-most-populous country on Earth, with 1.2 billion people (versus the United States with 319 million). The average age in India was 27 years (39 in the United States), and the population growth was 1.3 percent per year (0.77 percent in the United States); however, 29.9 percent were below the poverty line in 2013. The Indian gross domestic product (GDP), adjusted for purchasing power parity, in 2014 ranked fourth in the world, at about $4.99 trillion, and was growing at about 3.2 percent per year (the 108th-highest growth rate in the world). Indian per capita GDP was about $4,000 in 2013 (versus $48,000 in the United States).

India's economy recovered well from the global recession, primarily because of strong domestic demand, with economic growth over 8 percent. However, in 2011, this growth slowed due to the lack of progress on economic reforms, high interest rates, and continuing high inflation, and it averaged 5 percent in 2012 and 2013. Also, a slowdown in key sectors of the economy such as manufacturing and mining, as well as growth in developed markets, made India less attractive for foreign investors. The exchange rate for the Indian rupee was 53 per U.S. dollar in 2012. It then dropped almost 25 percent against the dollar, and although it recovered somewhat, the rate was still down about 12 percent at the beginning of 2014. By June 2014, the rupee was trading at approximately 60 rupees per U.S. dollar.

The Indian government subsidized several fuels (including diesel, which is a component in its inflation index), and as crude prices remained high, the fuel subsidy expenditures caused an increasing fiscal deficit and current account deficit. Between 2010 and 2012, India suffered from numerous serious corruption scandals that sidetracked legislative work, and as a result, little economic reform occurred.

## EXHIBIT 2   Tata Motors' Joint Ventures and Subsidiaries, 2014

Tata Motors has a 51 percent share in a joint venture with Marcopolo (49 percent), the Brazil-based maker of bus and coach bodies. Tata Motors (SA) (Proprietary) Ltd. is Tata Motors' joint venture with Tata Africa Holding (Pty) Ltd.; the joint venture's assembly plant at Rosslyn, Pretoria, assembles light, medium, and heavy commercial vehicles ranging from 4 to 50 tons from semi-knocked-down kits. Other associates include the following:

- *Tata Daewoo Commercial Vehicle Company* is a 100 percent subsidiary of Tata Motors in the business of heavy commercial vehicles (**www.tata-daewoo.com**).
- *Tata Motors European Technical Centre* is a U.K.-based, 100 percent subsidiary engaged in design engineering and development of products.
- *Telco Construction Equipment Company* makes construction equipment and provides allied services (**www.telcon.co.in/**). Tata Motors has a 60 percent holding; the rest is held by Hitachi Construction Machinery Company, of Japan.
- *Tata Technologies* provides specialized engineering and design services, product life-cycle management, and product-centric information technology services (**www.tatatechnologies.com/**).
- *Tata Motors (Thailand) Ltd.* is a joint venture between Tata Motors (70 percent) and Thonburi Automotive Assembly Plant Co. (30 percent) to manufacture and market the company's pickup vehicles in Thailand (**www.tatamotors .co.th/**).
- *Tata Cummins* manufactures high-horsepower engines used in the company's range of commercial vehicles.
- *HV Transmissions* and *HV Axles* are 100 percent subsidiaries that make gearboxes and axles for heavy and medium commercial vehicles.
- *TAL Manufacturing Solutions* is a 100 percent subsidiary that provides factory automation solutions and designs and manufactures a wide range of machine tools (**www.tal.co.in/**).
- *Hispano Carrocera* is a Spanish bus manufacturing company in which Tata Motors acquired a 100 percent stake in 2009 (**www.hispano-net.com/**).
- *Concorde Motors* is a 100 percent subsidiary retailing Tata Motors' range of passenger vehicles (**www.concordemotors.com/**).
- *Tata Motors Finance* is a 100 percent subsidiary in the business of financing customers and channel partners of Tata Motors (**www.tmf.co.in**).

Despite the scandals, poor infrastructure, a lack of nonagricultural employment, limited access to education, and the rapid migration of the population to unprepared urban centers, growth over the next three to five years was projected to approach 7 percent. The Reserve Bank of India suggested that inflation, which had ranged between 7 and 10 percent since 2009, dropped to 6.6 percent in early 2012. However, the inflationary situation worsened in 2013, with inflation reaching 11.2 percent, due in large part to energy prices. There was the very real probability that spikes in crude oil prices could bring additional inflation to India.

Education was highly valued in India, and the Indian workforce was well educated, which allowed India to become a major provider of engineering, design, and information technology services. However, continuing problems such as significant over-population, environmental degradation, extensive poverty, widespread corruption, and the slowing economic development were hampering India's rise on

the world stage and putting downward pressure on its domestic automobile industry.

# OVERVIEW OF THE AUTOMOTIVE INDUSTRY IN INDIA

The automobile industry in India had evolved during three relatively unique periods: protectionism (until the early 1990s), economic liberalism (early 1990s–2007), and then a period of globalization. The protectionist years were characterized by a closed economy with high duties and sales taxes. The automobile industry at that time was a seller's market with long waits for automobiles.

The period of economic liberalism that began in the early 1990s included the deregulation of industries, the privatization of state-owned businesses, and reduced controls on foreign trade and investment, which increased the entry of foreign businesses. This

**EXHIBIT 3** Tata Motors' Summarized Profit and Loss Statement, Fiscal 2011–Fiscal 2014 (in core rupees, or 10 million rupees*)

| | Year Ending | | | |
|---|---|---|---|---|
| | 3/31/2014 | 3/31/2013 | 3/31/2012 | 3/31/2011 |
| **Income** | | | | |
| Revenue from operations | 234,469.9 | 193,584.0 | 170,677.6 | 126,414.2 |
| Less: Excise duty | 3,729.8 | 4,766.3 | 5,023.1 | 4,286.3 |
| | 230,677.1 | 188,817.6 | 165,654.5 | 122,127.9 |
| Other income | 2,156.6 | 811.5 | 661.8 | 429.5 |
| | 232,833.7 | 189,629.2 | 166,316.3 | 122,557.4 |
| **Expenditures** | | | | |
| Cost of materials consumed | 135,550.0 | 111,600.4 | 100,797.4 | 70,453.7 |
| Purchase of products for sale | 10,876.9 | 11,752.1 | 11,205.9 | 10,390.8 |
| Changes in inventories of finished goods, work-in-progress, and product for sale | (2,840.6) | (3,031.4) | (2,535.7) | (1,836.2) |
| Employee cost/benefits expense | 21,556.4 | 16,584.1 | 12,298.5 | 9,342.7 |
| Finance cost | 4,733.8 | 3,553.3 | 2,982.2 | 2,385.3 |
| Depreciation and amortization expense | 11,078.2 | 7,569.3 | 5,625.4 | 4,655.5 |
| Product development expense/engineering expenses | 2,565.2 | 2,021.6 | 1,389.2 | 997.6 |
| Other expenses | 43,825.8 | 35,535.6 | 28,454.0 | 21,703.1 |
| Expenditure transferred to capital and other accounts | (13,537.9) | (10,192.0) | (8,266.0) | (5,741.3) |
| Total expenses | 209,074.1 | 175,393.0 | 151,950.9 | 112,351.22 |
| Profit before exceptional items, extraordinary items, and tax | 19,854.4 | 14,236.2 | 14,365.4 | 10,206.2 |
| Exchange loss (net) including on revaluation of foreign currency, borrowings, deposits, and loan | 707.7 | 515.1 | 654.1 | (231.0) |
| Impairment of intangibles and other costs | 224.1 | 87.6 | 177.4 | — |
| **Profit before tax from continuing operations** | 18,868.9 | 13,633.5 | 13,533.9 | 10,437.2 |
| Tax expense/(credit) | 4,764.8 | 3,771.0 | (40.0) | 1,261.4 |
| **Profit after tax from continuing operations** | 14,104.2 | 9,862.5 | 13,573.9 | 9,220.8 |
| Share of profit of associates (net) | (53.8) | 113.8 | 24.9 | 101.4 |
| Minority interest | (59.5) | (83.7) | (82.3) | (48.5) |
| **Profit for the year** | 13,991.0 | 9,892.6 | 13,516.5 | 9,273.6 |

*Exchange rate:* US$1 = Rs54.45 for 2012–2013, 47.53 for 2011–2012, and 47.41 for 2010–2011.

*Source:* Tata Motors annual reports, 2011, 2012, 2013, and 2014.

period triggered economic growth that averaged over 7 percent annually between 1997 and 2011. During the economic liberalization period, automobile financing greatly expanded, and the automobile market became more competitive.

Auto sales in India reached record levels in the first quarter of 2012, as consumers increased their purchasing—primarily of diesel vehicles—due to

concerns that the government would raise taxes on diesel vehicles in the next fiscal year. Increased loan rates and higher fuel prices in 2011 reduced the demand for cars; however, the boom in diesel sales lifted overall sales to a new high of 211,402 autos in April 2012. The demand for diesel vehicles grew to 45 percent of total demand, up from 30 percent in 2010. Diesel was more fuel-efficient than gas, and the Indian

**EXHIBIT 4**   Tata Motors' Consolidated Summarized Balance Sheets, Fiscal 2011–Fiscal 2014 (in core rupees, or 10 million rupees*)

| | Year Ending | | | |
| --- | --- | --- | --- | --- |
| | 3/31/2014 | 3/31/2013 | 3/31/2012 | 3/31/2011 |
| **Assets** | | | | |
| Fixed assets | 97,375.4 | 69,483.6 | 56,212.5 | 43,221.1 |
| Goodwill | 4,978.8 | 4,102.4 | 4,093.7 | 3,584.8 |
| Noncurrent investments | 1,114.4 | 1,222.4 | 1,391.5 | 1,336.8 |
| Deferred tax assets (net) | 2,347.1 | 4,428.9 | 4,539.3 | 632.3 |
| Long-term loans and advances | 13,268.8 | 15,465.5 | 13,658.0 | 9,818.3 |
| Other noncurrent assets | 5,068.5 | 1,024.0 | 574.7 | 332.3 |
| Foreign currency monetary item translation difference account (net) | — | — | 451.4 | — |
| Current assets | 95,845.3 | 74,006.7 | 64,461.5 | 42,088.8 |
| Total assets | 219,998.3 | 170,026.5 | 145,382.6 | 101,014.2 |
| **Liabilities** | | | | |
| Long-term borrowings | 45,258.6 | 32,110.1 | 27,962.5 | 17,256.0 |
| Other long-term liabilities | 2,596.9 | 3,284.1 | 2,458.6 | 2,292.7 |
| Long-term provisions | 12,190.3 | 8,319.2 | 6,071.4 | 4,825.6 |
| Net worth | | | | |
| Share capital | 643.8 | 638.1 | 634.8 | 637.7 |
| Reserves and surplus | 64,959.7 | 36,999.2 | 32.515.18 | 18,533.8 |
| Minority interest | 420.6 | 307.5 | 307.1 | 246.6 |
| Deferred tax liabilities (net) | 1,572.3 | 2,019.5 | 2,165.1 | 2,096.1 |
| Current liabilities | 92,356.1 | 86.285.90 | 73,268.1 | 55,125.6 |
| Total liabilities | 219,998.3 | 170,026.5 | 145,382.6 | 101,014.2 |

*Exchange rate:* US$1 = Rs54.45 for 2012–2013, 47.53 for 2011–2012, and 47.41 for 2010–2011.

*Source:* Tata Motors annual reports, 2011, 2012, 2013, and 2014.

government instituted controls on the price of diesel because of its impact on inflation. In the first quarter of 2012, diesel was 40 percent cheaper than gasoline.

In 2012, the trend for the industry turned down, with domestic sales of automobiles falling by 6.7 percent—the first decline in a decade. In 2013, sales were down an additional 4.6 percent. Sales of commercial vehicles were hit even harder, declining 20.2 percent from the prior year. In his investor presentation in 2013, Tata's managing director, Karl Slym, emphasized the impact of the Indian government's banning mining in the Karnataka region. This ban impacted 200 mines and resulted

in idling about 17,000 to 20,000 heavy trucks, which severely reduced the replacement demand for these trucks.

Ongoing national urban and rural highway projects through 2014 had been expected to increase national and state highways by 110,000 kilometers (68,350 miles) and rural roads by 411,000 kilometers (255,000 miles). This large increase in roads was also expected to increase the demand for cars, especially the more affordable models targeted at rural customers. However, many of the infrastructure projects were put on hold due to India's economic downturn. The almost certainty of increasing fuel prices would force successful automakers to focus on increasing fuel efficiency and to search for alternative fuels, which was one of Tata's competencies.

# TATA MOTORS' BUSINESS STRATEGY IN 2014

## Tata Motors' Strategy in Passenger Cars

Tata Motors' management believed that future growth for the company's subsidiaries would come from both investments in India and opportunities in international markets. Management also believed that the Indian passenger-car industry would recover and experience strong growth over the next 10 years and that it would become the third-largest passenger-car market (after the United States and China) by 2021. Tata Motors' strategy for its passenger-car division was keyed to leveraging its broad product line and concentrating on all-around value, including fuel efficiency. The company offered compact-sized Indica and midsized Indigo passenger cars for sales primarily in India, although the company also exported passenger cars to parts of Europe and Africa. Tata's passenger cars were powered by 1.2- to 1.4-liter gasoline and diesel engines, and its lineup also included the electric-powered Indica Vista. The division also produced the widely publicized Nano microsized car.

The passenger-vehicle strategy focused on aggressive growth of new vehicle sales, service locations, and growth in the used-car business through Tata Motors Assured operations. Tata management believed that a better sales and service network would enhance customer care and increase sales. The Jaguar and Land Rover brands were targeted for international growth in developed markets and such key emerging markets as China, Russia, and Brazil. China was expected to increase its share of auto sales volume among the four BRIC countries (Brazil, Russia, India, and China) from 53 to 61 percent, and Brazil, which was the most stable and mature of the four countries, was expected to remain in second position. Equally as important as the BRIC countries' economic resilience, their passenger-car penetration was extremely low: The number of cars per 1,000 persons in Brazil was 259; Russia, 200; China, 44; and India, 13. Managing

Director Karl Slym felt that these countries had great futures as markets for Tata's passenger cars. However, the company's sales of automobiles in India declined by 37 percent between 2013 and 2014, and its exports of automobiles failed to grow during 2014. According to Slym's analysis, the BRIC nations were expected to account for 30 percent of global auto sales in 2014.

## The "People's Car"—Tata Nano

In 2009, even though India's population was the second-largest on Earth and its economy was rapidly growing, there were only 12 cars per thousand people (compared to 56 per thousand in China, 178 per thousand in Brazil, and 439 per thousand in the United States). In contrast, there were over 7 million scooters and motorcycles sold in India that year. The two-wheel-vehicle sales were the result of India's large population, high urban density, and low income level. Tata Motors recognized the huge market for very low-cost motorized transportation that was being filled by scooters and motorcycles.

The middle-class household income in India started at about $4,500 in 2007. Tata believed that a car costing about $2,500 would be able to take advantage of the very large market that was being served only by two-wheel vehicles. In 2007, about 7.75 million Indians owned automobiles; however, more than 17 million others had the financial ability to purchase an automobile. Tata Motors' management believed that the potential market for automobiles priced under $3,000 could grow to about 30 million consumers in India. Tata Motors created the Tata Nano to capture such demand for low-cost automobiles and switch a large portion of the demand for two-wheel vehicles to the Nano.

Ratan Tata, the chairman of Tata Motors' board, viewed the Nano as the "People's Car." Mr. Tata once remarked about the many families riding on scooters: The father would drive with a child standing in front of him and the mother seated behind him, holding a baby. The Nano was intended to be the means to keep Indian middle-class families from transporting the entire family on one scooter. The Nano was widely anticipated in India, and it was projected that the Nano might have an effect on the used-car market because of its low price.

Tata Motors began the Nano design with a comprehensive study of the potential customers and their needs, wants, and purchasing ability. In a unique pricing approach, the company set the base price at $2,500, which was the price Tata thought its customers could pay, and worked backward into the design. The base price at introduction was about $2,000; however, it quickly went up to $2,300, and by 2012, the price was about $2,600. A typical 2014 Nano model is presented in Exhibit 5.

The base Nano model had a 625-cubic-centimeter, two-cylinder engine that produced a top speed of 65 miles per hour and offered gas mileage of nearly 50 miles per gallon. The small engine was well-matched to the driving conditions in urban markets in India, which were characterized by crowded streets with an average speed of less than 20 miles per hour. The base Nano model did not include air conditioning, a radio, or a CD player, and access to the trunk was through the interior—there was no trunk door on the outside of the vehicle. Every possible cost-saving measure was implemented: There were only three lug nuts on the wheels, no airbags, and one windshield wiper, and the speedometer was in the middle of the dash rather than behind the steering wheel, which saved on parts and reduced cost. A supplier of suspension parts used a hollow steel tube to replace the solid steel tube normally used so as to save on steel costs.

The Nano was manufactured using a module design, which allowed components to be built separately and shipped to a location where they could be assembled. Tata Motors created a geographically dispersed network of Nano dealers in developing countries such as Brazil, China, Malaysia, Nepal, Bangladesh, Nigeria, Myanmar, and Indonesia. Tata Motors' distribution network also included dealers in the Middle East, South Africa, and the African continent.

Despite very high expectations, Nano sales were less than expected after its introduction. Sales for calendar year 2010 were 59,576. Unit shipments

## EXHIBIT 5   The 2014 Tata Nano

increased to 70,432 in 2011 and 74,527 in 2012 before falling to 53,847 in 2013 and 21,130 in 2014. Analysts estimated that approximately 200,000 to 250,000 Nanos per year would need to be sold for Tata Motors to achieve an acceptable return on its $400 million investment in the Nano's development.

The potential of a low-priced car in the global automobile marketplace was widely recognized, and several potential competitors had plans to enter the market. There were rumors in the industry that General Motors (GM) was working with Wuling Automotive in China to design and produce a car that would directly compete with the Nano. Ford opened its second plant in India in 2011 and invested over $2 billion in its manufacturing facilities in India. Ford's new Figo offered features close to those of American cars at a price of slightly over $7,000 for the base model. Volkswagen also opened a manufacturing plant in India and was selling its base VW Polo for $8,495, which was well equipped compared to the Nano and Ford's Figo. France's Renault also offered an economical car, the Pulse, which was very well equipped, for about $7,850. In turn, Nissan sold its Micra for about $7,650, Maruti offered the Ritz for $7,500, and Chevrolet put out the Beat, priced at $8,030.

These competitors, plus a reported Nano defect that could cause the vehicle to catch fire, combined to depress sales. However, Tata was determined to make the Nano a success. Tata was rumored to be redesigning the Nano for export to the United States. The cost of adjusting the Nano to meet American standards and the costs of emissions control, power steering, a larger engine, and more options would drive the price of the Nano to about $8,000. However, the $8,000 price would make the Nano the least expensive new car in the United States—less than either the Nissan Versa ($11,800) or the Hyundai Accent ($13,205).

At the Auto Expo in Delhi in 2014, Tata presented its new Nano Twist Active. This Nano had a new front grill and a more stylish design. It featured a tailgate, which allowed access to the trunk from the outside, power steering, keyless entry, Bluetooth connectivity, and six new bright colors. The new Nano Plus had a larger engine, front disc brakes, improved air conditioning, a newly designed dashboard, fog lights, LED headlights, bucket seats, and an operational tailgate. Tata was expected to offer a diesel Nano in the near future. Although it was

originally launched as the world's least expensive car, the redesigned Nano was named India's "Most Trusted Automobile" by *The Brand Trust Report, India Study 2014,* published by the Comniscient Group Company.

Although the initial launch of the Nano in 2009 did not produce the desired level of sales, Tata was clearly not giving up on the world's least expensive car, now repositioned as the car of the stylish youth. Safety, however, is apparently a big concern of lower-income buyers as well as more affluent customers. The poor safety ratings of the Nano and the lack of airbags continued to hold down sales. Tata appeared determined to salvage the Nano, and the second launch of the redesigned and improved automobile may prove to be the key to the car's success.

## Commercial Vehicles

Tata's commercial-vehicle strategy focused on providing a wide range of products that offered the lowest cost of ownership for truck users in developing countries. Tata's strategy was to continuously evaluate its entire commercial product range with the intent of offering a very strong combination of existing products and new commercial platforms and products. Tata Motors offered small commercial vehicles that could be used for local deliveries, light pickup trucks, and light commercial vehicles capable of carrying larger payloads. The company also produced a full line of large buses and coaches, as well as medium and heavy commercial vehicles suitable for long-haul trucking.

Growth in international markets was a strategic priority, which Tata planned to address by combining and expanding its international manufacturing. The company opened an assembly plant in South Africa in 2011 and was considering additional capacity expansion. Tata's commercial-vehicle strategy included plans to refurbish commercial vehicles, sell annual maintenance contracts, and provide parts and services to the defense department in India. However, Tata Motors' exports of commercial vehicles declined by 2 percent from 44,109 in 2013 to 43,083 in 2014.

The commercial division planned to invest up to 1,500 core rupees (US$325 million) in fiscal 2015 to develop new products and technologies for its commercial segment. The company had sufficient manufacturing capability for the next five years: It focused its capital on technology and new products so that its portfolio would be ready when the market improved. Tata launched a new low-priced truck, the Prima LX, in March 2014, and in the first quarter of 2014–2015, the company launched the Magic Iris, a three-seat automotive vehicle designed as a rickshaw replacement. New buses and new models of the Tata light-commercial-vehicle Ultra were also planned for fiscal 2015. Tata was working with Cummins diesel to develop a new series of engines to power several of its commercial vehicles, including the Ultra LCV.

Tata's strategy included a commitment to quality and the lowest total cost of ownership. This was to be achieved by drawing on the company's in-depth knowledge of the Indian market and leveraging its development and design capabilities. The company planned an increased customer-centric operation, which was to be accomplished by a focus on customer services throughout the entire product life cycle, the use of customer relationship technology, and an increase in the availability of customer financing. However, these strategies and tactics were failing in 2014, with the division's unit shipments declining by 30 percent from 2013 volumes.

## Jaguar and Land Rover

The Jaguar and Land Rover (JLR) brands were in a separate division within Tata Motors and had a significantly different target market than Tata-branded passenger cars. Tata Motors' strategy for JLR was to capitalize on growth opportunities in the premium market segments with the two globally recognized brands. The strategy included achieving additional synergy and benefits with the support of Tata Motors. There were plans for substantial investment in new JLR technologies and products, more competitive powertrain combinations, and new body styles. Revenues for the JLR division had increased by 23 percent from 2013 to 2014. The division's EBITDA improved by 41.6 percent between 2013 and 2014, and its after-tax profit improved by 37.3 percent between those years. The Jaguar Land Rover division contributed 88 percent of Tata Motors' total automotive revenue in fiscal 2014 and 89 percent of its income before other income, finance costs, tax, and exceptional items in fiscal 2014.

The division's unit sales increased from 314,433 in 2012 to 372,062 in 2013 to 429,861 in 2014. The division's rise in sales and profitability was largely

a result of the growing popularity of its Land Rover brand, which included the Defender, LR2, LR4, Range Rover Evoque, Range Rover Sport, and Range Rover models. Land Rover sales accounted for 82.8 percent of the luxury division's unit sales in 2013 and 84.5 percent of the division's sales in 2014. While Jaguar's XF and XJ sedans struggled to compete against BMW, Mercedes, and other luxury performance sedans, its XK and F-Type coupes and convertibles had received strong interest among luxury sports car enthusiasts. Unit sales for the Jaguar brand increased by 37 percent between 2013 and 2014.

Land Rover's strong performance led to the announcement of a new $392 million factory to be located in Brazil. The new plant would have a capacity of 24,000 cars per year, and production was expected to begin in 2016. Much of Jaguar Land Rover's growth had come from China, which bought 25 percent of the division's production. China had become Jaguar Land Rover's largest market: Jaguar sales more than doubled in China in fiscal 2014, and Land Rover sales increased by 23 percent. The large demand for Jaguars and Land Rovers had required the company to operate the three factories in the United Kingdom 24 hours a day. The new Jaguar Land Rover factories that were being built in China and Brazil would increase capacity by about 50 percent. A plant was also scheduled for Saudi Arabia.

## TATA MOTORS' SITUATION IN 2014

Tata Motors' management enjoyed a record-setting year, with revenues for the fiscal year-end March 31, 2014, increasing by 21 percent compared to the prior year. The increase was driven by the growing success of its Jaguar and Land Rover acquisitions, with combined sales of the two luxury brands increasing by nearly 23 percent during the past 12 months. However, the sales of its Tata-branded automobile and commercial vehicles fell by 31 percent during the year, with both domestic sales and exports suffering.

Problems at Tata Motors continued into fiscal 2015, with commercial-vehicle sales declining 24.5 percent during the first two months compared to the same period in fiscal 2014. In addition, the Nano, hailed by *Businessweek* in 2008 as a tale of "innovation and ingenuity," had not lived up to expectations.

Even in the domestic market, consumers were not buying the tiny car with a poor track record for reliability. Strong demand for Honda's diesel sedans Amaze and City pushed Honda past Tata (and Ford India), making it the number-three passenger-car manufacturer. Tata's compact brand Indica had poor sales because it was perceived as a fleet car, and the Nano was perceived as a poor man's car.

Also, the death of Managing Director Karl Slym, head of Tata's domestic operations, had disrupted the company's stability. Slym, a former GM executive, had been with Tata only two years but had been instrumental in developing a business plan to address the declining sales of its Tata-branded vehicles and expand into new international markets, especially the BRIC countries.

Following the death of Slym, Tata's management stated that the company would continue to follow Slym's turnaround strategy by introducing two new cars: the Bolt hatchback and the small Zest. There was hope among management that Tata's new Bolt and Zest compact cars, plus another new compact model with the code name Kite, which were scheduled to be introduced in late 2015, would be better able to compete against the three market leaders in the compact market. As Tata's management looked further into the 2015 fiscal year, there was a promising domestic market for motor vehicles as well as attractive markets around the world. The company's management team would be forced to make further strides to truly become a contender in the global automobile industry.

# Deere & Company in 2014: Its International Strategy in the Agricultural, Construction, and Forestry Equipment Industry

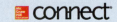

## Alen Badal
Author and Researcher

## John E. Gamble
Texas A&M University–Corpus Christi

Deere & Company had its best-ever year in fiscal 2013 with record net income for the third consecutive year. The company's sales and earnings of $37.8 billion and $3.54 billion, respectively, resulted from the success of its global strategy keyed to product innovation and quality, operating excellence, and best-in-industry customer service. Deere introduced dozens of technologically advanced agricultural and construction products during 2013 that helped boost productivity and lower the costs of its customers in farming and construction.

The company's prospects for even stronger financial performance were good as the global demand for agricultural products was expected to double by 2050. International markets such as China, Brazil, and Russia already accounted for more than 35 percent of the company's revenues in 2013, and they would likely make up a much larger percentage of sales in the long term as living standards in emerging markets improved. Deere & Company had recognized the importance of international expansion as early as 1956, when it first established operations outside the United States, but it was accelerating its efforts to prepare for rapid increases in the demand for food in international markets. The company built or acquired new plant capacity in Brazil, Germany, and China in 2013 and had plans for seven new factories in international markets in 2014.

Deere & Company achieved its record-setting year despite a slowdown in the construction industry,

where it also competed with a line of tractors, articulating dump trucks, backhoe loaders, motor graders, excavators, and bulldozers. The company also manufactured and marketed forestry equipment, turf equipment, and diesel engines for marine and construction equipment uses. The company's primary challenge in 2014 was how to best defend against the competitive pressures stemming from its chief rivals in the agricultural and construction equipment industries, who were also preparing for rapidly expanding industry growth.

## COMPANY HISTORY

Deere & Company began manufacturing and marketing farming equipment in 1837 when John Deere, a blacksmith and inventor, began forging steel plows for mule-drawn walking plows. The company added corn planters, wheeled sulky ploys, and cultivators during the late 1800s, but its walking plow accounted for the majority of its business until the company acquired motorized tractor producer Waterloo Boy in 1918. Deere's acquisition of Waterloo Boy dramatically changed the company's business model and scope of operations, but it was a necessity since Ford Motor Company was revolutionizing agriculture with the manufacture and sale of Fordson farm tractors. Ford sold more than 34,000 farm tractors in 1918 as farmers across the United States easily recognized how machinery could boost productivity in agriculture.

Deere's shift in strategy began with disastrous results, with the Waterloo Boy brand selling only 79 tractors in 1921. The first John Deere–branded tractor, the Model D, was launched in 1923 and was so popular that it remained in the company's product line for 30 years. Deere added more models to the product line throughout the 1920s. The appeal of the company's Model D, GP, Model 1, and Model 2 tractors allowed its revenues to soar until the depths of the Great Depression in 1922, when its revenues plunged to $8.7 million. However, even though Deere & Company was losing money, the company's management chose not to repossess farm equipment owned by farmers unable to make payments during the Depression—a decision that would solidify its bond with farmers for generations.

The company expanded internationally in 1956 when it opened an assembly plant in Mexico and acquired a German tractor manufacturer and a Spanish harvester manufacturer. Deere & Company expanded further internationally when it constructed a tractor and implement manufacturing plant in Argentina in 1958, built a plant in France in 1961, and acquired a cultivator manufacturer in South Africa in 1962. By 1963, John Deere was the world's largest producer of farm and industrial tractors and equipment. The company also began selling lawn and garden tractors that year. In 2014, with its world headquarters in Moline, Illinois, Deere & Company remained the largest agricultural equipment and machinery manufacturer in the world, with operations in more than 26 countries. The company's income statements for fiscal 2011 through fiscal 2013 are presented in Exhibit 1. Deere & Company's balance sheets for fiscal 2011 through fiscal 2013 are presented in Exhibit 2.

# OVERVIEW OF THE TRACTOR AND AGRICULTURAL EQUIPMENT INDUSTRY

The tractor and agricultural equipment industry was projected to grow at an attractive rate for decades because of increasing urbanization and rising standards of living in many countries around the world.

By 2050 the global population was expected to exceed 9 billion, up from approximately 7 billion in 2014, with Asia and Africa experiencing the greatest increases. It was also expected that a growing middle class would emerge in Latin America, China, and India, among other developing economies. Thus, agricultural output was projected to double by 2050 in order to maintain pace with the increase in global population, which would require the rate of production to grow. Also, an increase in urbanization would stir a need for infrastructure development, with the percentage of the world's population living in urban areas increasing from 50 percent in 2014 to 70 percent by 2050. The increase in urbanization was expected to result in increases in the demand for construction services and equipment.

The long-term macro-economic trends were favorable for the $41.6 billion tractor and agricultural industry, which had grown annually by 3.9 percent between 2009 and 2014. The industry consisted of dairy farm equipment and sprayers, dusters, blowers, and attachments, with harvesting machinery representing the largest segment—see Exhibit 3.

The steady growth in the industry since 2009 was brought about by favorable sociocultural forces and economic conditions that included farm interest rates supported by the U.S. federal government and subsidies of various sorts in countries outside the United States. Also, the weakening U.S. dollar and a rising demand for exporting helped rebuild the farming industry.

The farming industry was consolidating as large conglomerates took over smaller farms. As a result, total volume increases and economies of scale were taking place in the industry, along with more vertical integration across supply chains. A demand for better optimization of farming also resulted in reliance on technology to reduce operating costs and increase farming output. Precision agriculture was a growing trend in the industry that allowed farmers to spot-treat fields using aerial photography and geographic information systems (GIS) technology to precisely water, seed, and harvest in less time.

## Industry Competition

The tractor and agricultural equipment industry comprised more than 1,000 companies, with the top four generating half of all revenues. Industry production was concentrated primarily among Deere &

## EXHIBIT 1   Deere & Company Income Statements, Fiscal 2011–Fiscal 2013 (in thousands)

| Period Ending: | Oct 31, 2013 | Oct 31, 2012 | Oct 31, 2011 |
|---|---|---|---|
| Total revenue | $37,795,400 | $36,157,100 | $32,012,500 |
| Cost of revenue | 25,667,300 | 25,007,800 | 21,919,400 |
| Gross profit | 12,128,100 | 11,149,300 | 10,093,100 |
| Operating expenses | | | |
| Research and development | 1,477,300 | 1,433,600 | 1,226,200 |
| Selling, general, and administrative | 4,426,100 | 4,198,500 | 3,884,700 |
| Operating income | 6,224,700 | 5,517,200 | 4,982,200 |
| Interest expense | 741,300 | 782,800 | 759,400 |
| Income before tax | 5,483,400 | 4,734,400 | 4,222,800 |
| Income tax expense | 1,945,900 | 1,659,400 | 1,423,600 |
| Minority interest | (300) | (6,900) | (7,900) |
| Net income | $ 3,537,300 | $ 3,064,700 | $ 2,799,900 |

*Source:* **www.finance.yahoo.com**.

Company, CNH Industrial N.V., and AGCO Corporation. Mergers affected the industry, with CNH Industrial N.V. having gone through a merger with KamAZ in 2010 and Fiat Industrial in 2013. External factors, such as emission standards, continue to become more stringent in the United States. Quality control, research and development, and adoption of new technological advances were all strategic factors in the industry.

Agricultural equipment manufacturers were driving the use of technology with larger, more sophisticated equipment. Equipment manufacturers also recognized the importance of customer service and support and equipment financing as farming consolidated to a smaller group of farming corporations.

The average useful age for farming equipment was estimated to be 10 to 20 years. A preference of farmers was to prolong the life of equipment by purchasing replacement parts. The industry was expected to continue production of replacement parts for equipment and reap the profits of the segment. Interest rates on farm equipment loans had a direct impact on sales; lower rates and incentives helped boost sales of higher-end equipment.

Profits had increased over the five-year 2009–2014 period, with revenues increasing despite rising steel costs, which manufacturers had passed on to buyers. The weakened U.S. dollar had increased export sales for U.S. companies. An average industry

profit was projected as 6.2 percent of revenue. Wages in the industry had decreased as a result of the increased automation of the manufacturing process, which lessened dependence on labor. Because of technological advances in manufacturing, depreciation costs as a percentage of industry revenue had increased for manufacturers. Product quality, innovation, customer service, branding, and performance were essential areas rivals competed on. Generally, price competition between the three rivals was low; as a result, competition centered on overall value instead of price. Competitor barriers to entry into the industry ranged from low to medium; however, with such fierce competition among the top three, entrants were surely challenged.

Globalization had a significant effect on functions within the industry. Lower wages and overall production costs increased revenues. Between 2009 and 2014, both AGCO and Deere & Company increased their percentage of revenue generated internationally; CNH's tractor sales increased 25 percent in Latin America during 2011, with combined sales growth of 30 percent.

## International Markets for Agricultural Equipment

The declining U.S. dollar made it more affordable to export equipment from the United States. In 2013, total imports to the United States were estimated at

**EXHIBIT 2    Deere & Company Balance Sheets, Fiscal 2011–Fiscal 2013 (in thousands)**

| Period Ending: | Oct 31, 2013 | Oct 31, 2012 | Oct 31, 2011 |
|---|---|---|---|
| **Assets** | | | |
| Current assets | | | |
| Cash and cash equivalents | $ 3,504,000 | $ 4,652,200 | $ 3,647,200 |
| Short-term investments | 1,624,800 | 1,470,400 | 787,300 |
| Net receivables | 35,039,200 | 31,426,400 | 27,501,600 |
| Inventory | 4,934,700 | 5,170,000 | 4,370,600 |
| Total current assets | 45,102,700 | 42,719,000 | 36,306,700 |
| Long-term investments | 221,400 | 215,000 | 201,700 |
| Property, plant, and equipment | 9,124,100 | 7,539,700 | 6,502,300 |
| Goodwill | 844,800 | 921,200 | 999,800 |
| Intangible assets | 77,100 | 105,000 | 127,400 |
| Other assets | 1,825,800 | 1,485,500 | 1,210,900 |
| Deferred long-term asset charges | 2,325,400 | 3,280,400 | 2,858,600 |
| Total assets | $59,521,300 | $56,265,800 | $48,207,400 |
| **Liabilities** | | | |
| Current liabilities | | | |
| Accounts payable | $ 9,240,800 | $ 9,288,500 | $ 8,090,800 |
| Short/current long-term debt | 12,898,000 | 9,967,300 | 9,629,700 |
| Total current liabilities | 22,138,800 | 19,255,800 | 17,720,500 |
| Long-term debt | 21,577,700 | 22,453,100 | 16,959,900 |
| Other liabilities | 5,537,100 | 7,694,900 | 6,712,100 |
| Minority interest | 1,900 | 19,900 | 14,600 |
| Total liabilities | 49,255,500 | 49,423,700 | 41,407,100 |
| Stockholders' equity | | | |
| Common stock | 3,524,200 | 3,352,200 | 3,251,700 |
| Retained earnings | 19,645,600 | 16,875,200 | 14,519,400 |
| Treasury stock | (10,210,900) | (8,813,800) | (7,292,800) |
| **Other stockholders' equity** | (2,693,100) | (4,571,500) | (3,678,000) |
| Total stockholders' equity | 10,265,800 | 6,842,100 | 6,800,300 |
| Total liabilities and stockholders' equity | $59,521,300 | $56,265,800 | $48,207,400 |

*Source:* www.finance.yahoo.com.

$10.5 billion, while exports were estimated at $11.8 billion. Canada was the largest U.S export market, with a 34 percent share of exports, while Mexico, Australia, and Brazil were the next-largest export markets for U.S. agricultural equipment manufacturers. Germany was the largest exporter of farm equipment to the United States, accounting for 16 percent of U.S. imports. Canada, China, and Japan were also significant exporters of farm equipment to the United States—see Exhibit 4.

## Deere & Company's Strategy in 2014

Deere & Company's farming equipment product lines were aimed at supporting the farming of every owner of Deere equipment and compelling the thought of "should've got a John Deere" among those who farmed with rival equipment. Farming was arguably the most time-sensitive industry since harvesting windows could be limited to a matter of a few days. In addition, farming seasons were limited to specific months when weather

**EXHIBIT 3**   Product Segmentation of the Tractor and Agricultural Equipment Industry, 2013

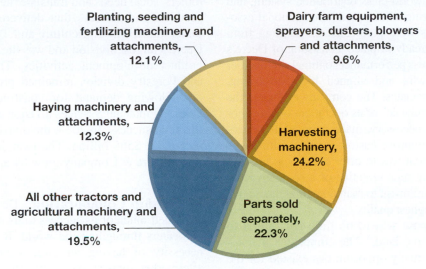

Total: $41.6 billion

*Source:* Adapted from *IBISWorld*, February 2014.

**EXHIBIT 4**   Leading U.S. International Trade Partners for Agricultural Products, 2013

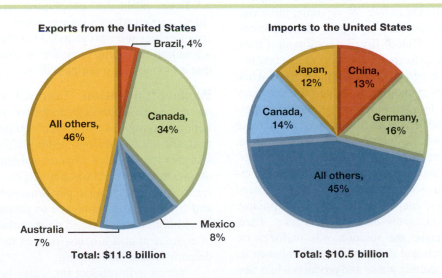

*Source:* Adapted from *IBISWorld*, February 2014.

was favorable to various types of crops. Deere's strategy of producing the highest-quality, most reliable farm equipment and offering farmers the highest level of customer service resulted in fiscal 2013 being the company's best financial year ever.

Deere & Company's strategic intent was to achieve $50 billion in sales by fiscal 2018 and 12 percent profit margins by fiscal 2014. Deere's strategy was keyed to expanding its business globally and enhancing its complementary businesses while supporting the overall business. In doing so, the company believed its critical business factors (CBFs) consisted of better understanding consumers at a root level, delivering value, offering a world-class distribution system, and grooming and hiring extraordinary international associates. The CBFs were predicated on building from the foundation already in place, consisting of Deere's exceptional business performance, optimal shareholder value-added growth, and aligned high-performing, team-oriented associates. The company evaluated the "health and performance" of its operations on an ongoing basis and, as necessary, made appropriate adjustments to further improve customer value. Ultimately, the overarching goal was to offer consumers farming products that were representative of a company with integrity and commitment to manufacturing innovative products of the highest quality.

Deere's purpose was to be fully committed to those "linked to the land." The company's managers believed that many opportunities existed for the company, such as an increase in the global population and income growth, which would require infrastructural needs on a global basis. Additional opportunities included new consumer segmentation and advances in technology.

The company identified challenges moving forward. Specifically, Deere foresaw capturing more customers across six identified key regions (United States/Canada, European Union, Brazil, CIS/Russia, China, and India), with a focus on meeting each country's local farming and agricultural equipment needs while leveraging global economies of scale. The company was strategizing forward progress without encountering any headwind. The company planned to increase its market share in developed markets. At the time, Deere was number two in market share in North America, a ranking it hoped to strengthen and increase. Perhaps a continuous focus on technology and increased customer services, coupled with competitive pricing, would help the company increase its market share. Alternatively, maybe the solution was to focus on additional research and development and enhance its domestic manufacturing plants and products while also focusing on optimally manufacturing equipment to meet the specific country demands of farming abroad.

**Deere & Company's Business Divisions**    In 2014, the company had three primary businesses: Agriculture and Turf Equipment, Construction and Forestry Equipment, and the Financial Services/ Power Systems/Global Parts/Intelligent Solutions Group. Deere's strategy in each of its two heavy-equipment divisions was to learn more about its customers' local needs and translate the knowledge into products and services that delivered superior customer value. The Agriculture and Turf division was Deere's largest division and was the focus of its new product development activities. The Construction and Forestry division remained profitable in spite of a slowing demand for construction machines. Deere's Financial Services division also experienced financial success. In 2013, the division achieved net income of $565 billion. The loan and lease portfolio of Deere & Company grew by approximately $5 billion.

**Dealership Collaboration**    Deere & Company attributed much of its success to its relationship with its dealers throughout the world. It emphasized the necessity of having an effective distribution and aftermarket support system. In the Commonwealth of Independent States, the number of dealerships increased by 50 percent between 2011 and 2013. The company also added new parts distribution centers in South Africa and Argentina and had additional expansion plans to begin operations in India and Brazil. Deere established cooperative banking relationships in seven African nations where additional sales opportunities were projected. Also, the company had a retailing-financing presence in over 40 countries that accounted for more than 90 percent of its sales.

**Product Innovation**    Deere & Company focused on the use of technology to better assist end users with managing and using their equipment. This was achieved via the MyJohnDeere platform. This wireless data transmission system enabled the collection of data that was used for analysis by John Deere, in regard to the mechanical performance of equipment, and by customers, in regard to production metrics. In addition, Deere focused on manufacturing dozens of equipment attachments, such as those utilized for demolition and landscaping.

Increases in product lines also helped the company with its goal of continued growth and profitability. In 2013, Deere introduced nine advanced agricultural equipment models, as well as flex-fuel premium lawn tractors, commercial mowers, and Deere's first hybrid-electric construction equipment. The company focused particularly on increasing efficiency and incorporating technology while reducing emissions and meeting consumers' requirements for power, reliability, and fluid and fuel efficiency. In a highly notable achievement, Deere's larger engines were certified as meeting the strict U.S. and European emission standards. Deere had reduced the emissions level of all its engines by over 99 percent since 1996 as a result of redesigning virtually all of its engines.

**Awards, Achievements, and Corporate Responsibility**  Deere & Company was named one of the top-100 innovators by a leading business media group on the basis of its patents and technology developments. The company received additional awards and recognition from organizations throughout the world, including special recognition for its new Chinese-made combine, which took top honors at China's largest machinery venue.

In 2013 Deere focused on identifying solutions to world hunger, improving educational opportunities, and helping to develop better communities in the locations where it operated. In most cases, Deere & Company employees volunteered to assist in the execution of its social initiatives. For example, to further the company's social mission, more than 3,000 U.S. employees prepared approximately 960,000 packaged meals for those in need in 2013, and 20 employees spent a week in northwest India training small farmers in new farming methods. In 2013, Deere & Company was named for the fifth time to *Fortune*'s "Most Admired Companies" list.

**Domestic Manufacturing Operations**  Deere's manufacturing plants in the United States were located in seven states (Iowa, Illinois, North Dakota, Georgia, Louisiana, Missouri, and Wisconsin). Deere manufactured tractor cabs and other assemblies in its Waterloo, Iowa, plant. Large combine harvesters and hydraulic cylinders and planting equipment were manufactured in East Moline, Illinois. The plant in Valley City, North Dakota, manufactured tilling and seeding equipment. The Davenport, Iowa, plant manufactured wheel loaders, motor graders, dump trucks, and forestry equipment. In neighboring Dubuque, Iowa, production consisted of backhoes, crawlers, tracked forestry equipment, and skid-steer loaders. The Springfield, Missouri, plant manufactured engines.

The Ankeny, Iowa, plant manufactured sprayers, while hay and pull-type mowers were made in Ottumwa, Iowa. Cane harvesting equipment and scrapers were made in Thibodaux, Louisiana. The plant in Horicon, Wisconsin, produced lawn and garden and turf care products, while the plant in Augusta, Georgia, manufactured the 5E, 5EN, and 5M Series tractors. The Fuquay Varina, North Carolina, plant made golf equipment and turf mowers.

**International Manufacturing Operations**  Expansion plans called for new manufacturing locations in key markets that were to be completed in 2013 and ready in 2014 to support increased production. Deere opened three locations in China to support construction equipment, engines, and large farm equipment; two locations in Brazil, one of which was in conjunction with Hitachi, for construction equipment; one location in India for manufacturing farm equipment; and one in Russia for manufacturing seeding and tillage machines. Additional plans included expansion into Germany to manufacture cab production and into Brazil to manufacture large tractors. In the United States, the company's expansion included new factories in Moline and Valley City, North Dakota, and extensive modernization at existing plants. Deere sold its landscape operation and purchased a manufacturer of ultra-wide planters.

Deere's international manufacturing operations spanned Mexico, India, Argentina, China, Canada, and Europe. Two plants in Mexico (Saltillo and Torreon) manufactured a variety of agricultural tractors. Power systems were manufactured in Fleury-les-Aubrais, France. Tractors, diesel engines, and header models for grain harvesting were built in Granadero Baigorria, Santa Fe, Argentina. The Pune, India, plant manufactured small agricultural tractors, while additional tractors were manufactured in the Mannheim, Germany, plant. The Zweibrücken, Germany, plant manufactured harvesting equipment, and the Horst, Netherlands, plant manufactured spraying equipment. Forwarders and wheeled harvesters were built in the Joensuu, Finland, plant. The Edmonton, Alberta, Canada, plant produced remanufactured equipment. Consumer and commercial lawn equipment was manufactured in Gummersbach, Germany.

# DEERE'S RIVALS IN THE TRACTOR AND AGRICULTURAL EQUIPMENT INDUSTRY

Deere & Company was the world's leading manufacturer of agricultural and forestry equipment, with a market share of 35.4 percent in 2013. Its

**EXHIBIT 5** Financial Summary for CNH Industrial N.V., 2009–2013 (in millions of euros)

| | 2013 | 2012 | 2011 | 2010 | 2009 |
|---|---|---|---|---|---|
| Net revenues | €25,778 | €25,785 | €24,289 | €21,342 | €17,968 |
| Trading profit | 1,985 | 2,063 | 1,690 | 1,096 | 322 |
| Operating profit (loss) | 1,868 | 1,846 | 1,633 | 1,021 | (19) |
| Profit (loss) before taxes | 1,507 | 1,460 | 1,162 | 567 | (470) |
| Profit (loss) | 917 | 900 | 694 | 369 | (503) |
| Total assets | 40,941 | 38,861 | 38,572 | 34,873 | 30,872 |
| Total equity | 5,556 | 5,376 | 5,252 | 4,556 | 5,718 |

*Source:* CNH Industrial 2013 annual report.

primary competitors in the tractors and agricultural equipment industry were CNH Industrial N.V., the maker of Case and New Holland tractors and construction equipment; AGCO Corporation, the maker of Massey Ferguson and other brands; and Caterpillar, Inc.

## CNH Industrial N.V.

CNH Industrial N.V., based in Basildon, United Kingdom, held an 11.7 percent market share and was Deere & Company's primary rival in agricultural equipment. CNH Industrial was formed in 2013 as a result of a merger between CNH Global and Fiat Industrial. The company marketed agricultural equipment under 12 global and regional brands, and it had 62 manufacturing plants, 48 research and development centers, and 6,000 dealers in 190 countries. The company's farming/agricultural and construction equipment was marketed under such brands as Case IH Agriculture, New Holland Agriculture, and Steyr. CNH Industrial also manufactured and marketed trucks, busses, and other commercial vehicles under the Iveco and Heuliez-Bus brands. The company's total revenues in 2013 were €25.8 billion. Approximately 62 percent of the company's revenues and 94 percent of its operating profits were generated from the sale of agricultural and construction equipment in 2013. Exhibit 5 provides a summary of the company's financial performance for 2009 through 2013.

## AGCO Corporation

AGCO Corporation, based in Duluth, Georgia, held an approximate 4 percent share of the global farm equipment market in 2013. The company's tractors, combines, planters, grain storage silos, and other agricultural equipment was sold in 140 countries. Sales from North America accounted for approximately 25 percent of the company's revenues in 2013. The company held a strong market presence in emerging markets, such as Brazil and other Latin American markets. Approximately 60 percent of its revenues were generated from tractor sales under brands such as Massey Ferguson, Fendt, and Challenger. The company had approximately 1,300 dealers in North America, 340 dealers in South America, 1,160 dealers in Europe and the Middle East, and 300 dealers in the Asia-Pacific region. A summary of AGCO's financial performance between 2009 and 2013 is presented in Exhibit 6.

## Caterpillar, Inc.

Caterpillar, Inc., manufactured construction and mining equipment, diesel and natural gas engines, gas turbines, and diesel-powered locomotives. The company also built and marketed small to medium-sized track-type tractors for use in the construction and mining industries. In 2013, the company's construction industry division recorded sales and operating profit of $18.5 billion and $1.8 billion, respectively. The company's construction equipment sales in North America for 2013 were approximately $7 billion, with sales in the Asia-Pacific region approximating $4.7 billion; sales in Europe, Africa, and the Middle East slightly exceeding $4 billion; and sales in Latin America approximating $2.7 billion. In 2013, the company's revenues for its energy and power systems were approximately $20.1 billion, its mining machinery

**EXHIBIT 6**    Financial Summary for AGCO Corporation, 2009–2013 (in millions)

|                        | 2013       | 2012      | 2011      | 2010      | 2009      |
|------------------------|-----------|-----------|-----------|-----------|-----------|
| Net revenues           | $10,786.9 | $9,962.2  | $8,773.2  | $6,896.6  | $6,516.4  |
| Gross profit           | 2,390.6   | 2,123.2   | 1,776.1   | 1,258.0   | 1,071.9   |
| Income from operations | 900.7     | 693.2     | 610.3     | 324.2     | 218.7     |
| Net income             | 592.3     | 516.4     | 585.3     | 220.2     | 135.4     |
| Total assets           | 8,438.8   | 7,721.8   | 7,257.2   | 5,436.9   | 4,998.9   |
| Total equity           | 4,044.8   | 3,481.5   | 3,031.2   | 2,259.2   | 2,394.4   |

Source: AGCO Corporation 2013 annual report.

**EXHIBIT 7**    Financial Summary for Caterpillar, Inc., 2009–2013 (in millions)

|                   | 2013     | 2012     | 2011     | 2010     | 2009     |
|-------------------|----------|----------|----------|----------|----------|
| Net revenues      | $55,656  | $65,875  | $60,138  | $42,588  | $32,396  |
| Operating profit  | 5,628    | 8,573    | 7,153    | 3,963    | 577      |
| Net profit        | 3,789    | 5,681    | 4,928    | 2,700    | 895      |
| Total assets      | 84,896   | 88,970   | 91,218   | 63,728   | 59,842   |

Source: Caterpillar, Inc., 2013 annual report.

revenues were approximately $13.3 billion, and its financial services revenues were nearly $3.2 billion. A summary of Caterpillar's financial performance for 2009 through 2013 is presented in Exhibit 7.

Caterpillar's strategy was focused on best-in-industry quality and after-the-sale service. The company maintained 178 global dealers, with an average dealer relationship of more than 88 years. The company's relationship with its dealers and its commitment to unmatched parts availability ensured that the 3 million Caterpillar products around the world were in top-notch operating condition and were able to keep construction projects on schedule. Caterpillar's strategy was also focused on developing new products and improving the company's cost structure to boost profitability. Even though Caterpillar was the industry leader in construction equipment sales, it experienced a dramatic decline in sales and profit in 2013 due to a slowdown in global construction.

## THE FUTURE FOR DEERE & COMPANY

Deere & Company's strategy seemed on track in 2014 as the company focused its efforts on entering emerging and new markets and utilizing technology to both help production and provide real data to customers that would support increased productivity. Deere management believed that in order to continue to achieve global business success, the company needed to understand its customers at a deeper level and deliver greater customer value. Management also understood that Deere's employee-associates and dealer allies were critical elements in its plan for long-term success. The overall aim was to deliver quality, stemming from a company with stellar integrity that was committed to providing innovative products and services for consumers.

Specifically, the company planned to advance operations and increase market share across six key markets: the United States and Canada, Brazil, China, Russia, India, and the European Union. However, the company's chief rivals all recognized the same trends in the macro-environment and the same opportunities for growth in revenues in profits. Deere & Company management would be compelled to develop an international strategy that yielded competitive advantage in domestic and rapidly growing emerging markets to capitalize on the industry's opportunities.

# Wal-Mart in Africa

### Adapa Srinivasa Rao
IBS Hyderabad

### Debapratim Purkayastha
IBS Hyderabad

"Africa is awakening. It's a huge market of almost a billion people with huge resources and a young population. People spend when they're young."[1]
—Christo Wiese, Chairman, Pepkor Ltd.[a] (Pepkor), in August, 2012.

"Whenever Walmart enters a new market, it introduces its global operating belief that being a responsible global citizen begins with being a responsible local citizen."[2]
—Doug McMillon, Wal-Mart International CEO, in June, 2011.

"Walmart, with sales of more than $405bn [£258bn—more than South Africa's GDP] in 2010, has massive power to dominate the world's global supply chains, and national retail sectors, and to dictate the conditions of trade to thousands of supply firms in other sectors."[3]
—A union spokesman, Cosatu, a South African Trades Union, in 2011.

On March 9, 2012, the Competition Appeal Court of South Africa ruled that US-based Wal-Mart Stores, Inc. (Wal-Mart), the world's biggest retailer, could go ahead with its US$ 2.4 billion purchase of stake in the South African retailer Massmart Holdings Limited (Massmart).[4] By ruling in favor of the deal, the Competition Appeal Court upheld the 2011 ruling of South Africa's Competition Tribunal[b]. Wal-Mart had started expanding into international markets in 1991. It experienced successes in international markets such as Mexico and bitter failure in markets such as Germany and South Korea. The financial crisis of 2008 resulted in Wal-Mart putting even more emphasis on the international markets to fuel its growth as there were limited growth opportunities in the domestic sector. Wal-Mart started to focus on Africa as other markets with good potential like India were still closed to foreign players.[c] Africa remained the last major market yet to be explored by big MNCs like Wal-Mart. Despite political instability and poor economic conditions plaguing the continent, some countries in Africa offered good potential for growth due to their stable political environment and rising disposable incomes.

---

[a]Pepkor Ltd., headquartered in Cape Town, South Africa, is the biggest clothing company in South Africa.

[b]The Competition Tribunal is the government agency of South Africa charged with promoting competition and protection of consumers.

[c]Wal-Mart entered into a joint venture with Indian major Bharti Enterprises to operate in India. As of early 2012, the JV operated 17 stores across the country. Multi-brand retailers like Wal-Mart were not allowed to sell directly to consumers in India. They were also required to invest at least US$100 million, half of which had to be spent on developing back-end infrastructure (Source: "Wal-Mart's Africa And India Plans Boost its International Outlook," www.forbes.com, March 25, 2012).

This case was written by **Adapa Srinivasa Rao**, under the direction of **Debapratim Purkayastha**, IBS Hyderabad. It was compiled from published sources, and is intended to be used as a basis for class discussion rather than to illustrate either effective or ineffective handling of a management situation.

Wal-Mart decided to expand its presence in Africa in the inorganic way and made a preliminary offer to buy South African Retailer, Massmart. Massmart was the second biggest retailer in South Africa and its operations were spread across many African countries. Wal-Mart's offer was accepted by Massmart's shareholders and South Africa's Competition Tribunal in June 2011. The deal was cleared with some conditions. But Wal-Mart quickly ran into trouble as the deal was opposed by some trade unions and government departments of South Africa. The coalition which was opposing the deal alleged that WM's entry would lead to huge job losses and adversely affect the domestic manufacturing sector of South Africa. Wal-Mart refuted the allegations and said that it was willing to create 15,000 new jobs within three years of the takeover. Wal-Mart's past record of being a low-wage, low-benefit employer which discouraged its employees from forming labor unions compounded the fears of the opposition coalition. While some analysts expressed optimism that Wal-Mart's low price model could prove successful in Africa due to its poverty and low income levels, others were skeptical. They said that much of the population in Africa lived below the poverty line and might not have good buying potential. Analysts also warned Wal-Mart of repeating the mistakes it had committed in Germany and South Korea like trying to use the same business model as it followed in the US market without understanding the needs of the local market.

## BACKGROUND NOTE

Wal-Mart was founded in 1962 by Samuel Moore Walton (Walton) in Rogers, Arkansas, USA. Walton worked at JC Penney Corporation, Inc.[d] before starting Wal-Mart. He also ran a franchise of Ben Franklin stores[e]. When working with other retailers and later running a franchise, the conviction grew on Walton that the changing buyer behavior in the US made discount stores the future of retailing, especially in the smaller towns. He traveled across the US before starting his own discount store and was convinced that Americans wanted a new type of discount store which would offer more discounts than the traditional

discount stores. Wal-Mart was founded on the principle of passing on the discounts that retailers could manage from the wholesalers to the consumers and making money through the higher volumes achieved.[5] Walton's business clicked and Wal-Mart made better profits than many of its competing stores. By 1967, Wal-Mart had 24 stores with sales of US$12.6 million. By 1968, it had expanded to Oklahoma and Missouri. Wal-Mart was incorporated as a company under the name Wal-Mart Stores, Inc. in 1969.

Wal-Mart achieved significant growth during the 1970s. It opened its first distribution center and Wal-Mart Home Office in Bentonville in the first year of the decade. In 1977, Wal-Mart acquired 16 Mohr-Value stores based in Michigan and Illinois—its first acquisition. Wal-Mart expanded its business into other retail formats in 1978 and set up pharmacy, auto service center, and jewelry divisions. In 1979, Wal-Mart's annual sales reached US$ 1 billion and it became the first company to reach that goal within the quickest time. It had expanded its stores to 276 by 1980. In the years 1981 and 1982, Wal-Mart entered new states in the US like Georgia, South Carolina, Florida, and Nebraska and expanded its reach. It opened its first Sam's Club in Midwest City, Oklahoma, in the year 1983. Sam's Club, a chain of membership-only warehouse clubs, proved highly successful. It was later expanded across 47 states in the US. Strong customer demand in small towns drove the rapid growth of Wal-Mart in the 1980s. In the 1980s, the number of Wal-Mart stores expanded to 640 with annual sales of US$ 4.5 billion.

Walton appointed David Glass (Glass) as the new CEO of Wal-Mart in 1988. Soon after taking over, Glass started a joint venture with Cullum Companies (a Dallas-based supermarket chain) called Hypermart USA. Wal-Mart bought out Cullum Companies' stake in the joint venture in 1989. Hypermart USA was a discount store/supermarket chain with an average space of over 200,000 sq. ft. It featured branch banks, fast food outlets, photo developers, and playrooms for shoppers' children. Hypermart USA stores were later renamed as Wal-Mart's Supercenters. In 1990, Wal-Mart became the largest retailer in the US after it entered California, Nevada, North Dakota, Pennsylvania, South Dakota, and Utah.[6] In the same year, it acquired McLane Company (a grocer and retail distributor) and launched a new retail format—Bud's Discount City. Walton died in 1992 after a prolonged illness. But Wal-Mart continued

---

[d]JC Penney Company, Inc., headquartered in Plano, Texas, US, was a chain of American mid-range department stores.

[e]Ben Franklin Stores was a chain of discount stores mostly spread across small towns in the US.

its impressive growth under the leadership of Glass. After Walton's death, Sam Robson Walton (Robson), Walton's eldest son, was named the chairman of the company. In 1997, Wal-Mart's annual sales crossed the US$100 billion mark. Even as Wal-Mart was enjoying successes, controversies regarding its business practices and labor issues began to surface. Wal-Mart faced several criticisms relating to its business practices (Refer to Exhibit 1 for criticisms faced by Wal-Mart).

Apart from following the strategy of selling products at a lower cost, Wal-Mart followed several unique practices in the US to emerge as the leader. It developed a strategy where it did not allow retailers any control over its merchandise. It limited the percentage of merchandise that it sourced from a single supplier to have good bargaining power over them. Wal-Mart was one of the first retailers to use information technology to its advantage. In the early 1980s, it adopted the barcode technology to track sales of items in its stores on specific days and to manage its inventory better than any other business in the world. The adoption of barcode technology helped the company in the communication process with its suppliers. It saved a lot of money through inventory management practices. Wal-Mart also started using a new technology called RFID[f] to track its merchandise better. Over the years, it used technology to gain good control over its supply chain. It hired some of the best people in the area of logistics and supply chain management. Wal-Mart developed the largest commercial satellite system in the world to collect and give information to its vendors. The vast amounts of data that Wal-Mart was able to gather gave it good control over its vendors. Through these practices, Wal-Mart could stock the latest merchandise in its stores and replenish it faster. The use of the latest technology also facilitated recruitment of employees who did not need to be trained heavily to handle store operations. This kept its employee recruitment and training costs under control. The savings which resulted from the use of technology, good logistics, supply chain management practices, and lower employee costs were passed on to the consumers in the form of lower prices. This helped Wal-Mart and cemented its leadership position in the US market.

## EXHIBIT I    Criticisms against Wal-Mart

| Issues | Description of Issues |
|---|---|
| Anti-unionist | Since the 1970s, Wal-Mart had been anti-unionist, taking the stand that it was adhering to an open-door employee policy. |
| Employee discrimination | The company was charged with discrimination against women employees in 2003. |
| Employee surveillance | A former employee of Wal-Mart contended that the retailer carried out a large surveillance operation involving employees, shareholders, critics, etc. |
| Poor working conditions | Wal-Mart was accused of forcing its workers to work off-the-clock, denying over-time payments, child-labor laws infringements, and of employing illegal immigrant workers. |
| Low wages | The retail giant was charged with discouraging labor costs and of paying lower wages to its workforce. |
| Health insurance | Critics alleged that employees were paid so little that they could not afford health insurance, and if they could afford it, they preferred the state's health insurance program to Wal-Mart's. |
| Overseas labor concerns | Critics accused Wal-Mart for its supervision of overseas operations, where issues like poor working conditions, employing prison labor, low wages, etc., were allegedly prevalent. |
| Predatory pricing and supplier issues | The company was also accused of intentionally selling the merchandize at low costs, driving competitors away from the market. It was also alleged that it used its scale to squeeze the margins of its suppliers. |

*Adapted from various sources.*

---

[f]Radio-frequency identification (RFID) is a wireless technology which facilitates automatic identification and tracking.

The 1990s also saw Wal-Mart expanding into international markets. In 1991, the company opened its first overseas store in Mexico City, Mexico. It entered Mexico through a joint venture with Mexican company Cifra and opened its first Sam's Club in the country. Wal-Mart's global expansion got a boost when an international division was created in 1993. Wal-Mart entered Canada in 1993 after acquiring 122 former Woolco stores from Woolworth in Canada. During the first five years of its global expansion (1991–1995), Wal-Mart concentrated on markets like Mexico, Canada, Argentina, and Brazil, which were close to its home market. For the fiscal year 2002, Wal-Mart's revenue stood at US$ 218 billion and it overtook ExxonMobil[g] as the biggest company in the world on the Fortune 500[h] list of 2002. By 2005, Wal-Mart had expanded to 10 countries across the world. It had 1,991 stores, which included 1,175 discount stores, 285 Super Centers, 91 Sam's Clubs, and 36 Neighbourhood Markets. But global expansion showed mixed results. While it had good results in some countries, it faced many problems in some countries and even had to exit some. Wal-Mart exited South Korea and Germany in 2006. Cultural discrepancies and intense competition from local retailers were cited as the reasons for its failure in these markets. At the same time, Wal-Mart experienced tremendous success in some global markets. It emerged as the largest retailer in Mexico, Argentina, Canada, and Puerto Rico. By 2005, it had emerged as one of the top three retailers in the UK. By 2012, Wal-Mart had a presence in 27 countries across the world with 10,130 retail stores (Refer to Exhibit 2 for the list of countries in which Wal-Mart operated in 2012). Its revenues for the fiscal year 2012 were US$ 443.85 billion (Refer to Exhibit 3 for Consolidated Income Statement of Wal-Mart from Fiscal Years 2010–2012).[7]

## WAL-MART'S PAST EXPERIENCE IN INTERNATIONAL MARKETS

Wal-Mart had mixed results in its operations in foreign countries. It operated very successfully in rich markets like Mexico, Canada, and the UK (Refer to Exhibit 4 for the Socio-Economic data of key countries where Wal-Mart operated). It operated in Mexico through its subsidiary called Wal-Mart de Mexico.

### EXHIBIT 2    Countries in which Wal-Mart Operated in 2012

| Country | Year of Entry |
| --- | --- |
| Argentina | 1995 |
| Botswana | 2011 |
| Brazil | 1995 |
| Canada | 1994 |
| Chile | 2009 |
| China | 1996 |
| Costa Rica | 2005 |
| El Salvador | 2005 |
| Ghana | 2011 |
| Guatemala | 2005 |
| Honduras | 2005 |
| India | 2007 |
| Japan | 2002 |
| Lesotho | 2011 |
| Malawi | 2011 |
| Mexico | 1991 |
| Mozambique | 2011 |
| Namibia | 2011 |
| Nicaragua | 2005 |
| Nigeria | 2011 |
| South Africa | 2011 |
| Swaziland | 2011 |
| Tanzania | 2011 |
| Uganda | 2011 |
| United Kingdom | 2000 |
| Zambia | 2011 |

*Source:* "Saving People Money so they can Live Better—Worldwide," http://www.walmartstores.com.

Right from the time it first started its overseas operations in Mexico in 1991 through a joint venture with a local retailer called Cifra, it had grown in size to become the biggest retailing company in the whole of Latin America. In 1997, Wal-Mart increased its stake in the joint venture with Cifra and acquired 51 percent in Cifra. After the acquisition of majority stake in Cifra, Wal-Mart expanded its operations across Mexico under different brands like Walmart,

---

[g]Exxon Mobil, headquartered in Irving, Texas, USA is an American multinational oil and gas corporation. It was formed after the merger of two major corporate entities, Exxon and Mobil, in 1999.

[h]Fortune 500 is the annual list of top 500 companies based on their gross revenue published by the Fortune Magazine.

**EXHIBIT 3**   Consolidated Income Statement of Wal-Mart for Fiscal Years 2010–2012 (in US$ Millions)

|  | 2012 | 2011 | 2010 |
|---|---|---|---|
| Net sales | $443,854 | $418,952 | $405,132 |
| Membership and other income | 3,096 | 2,897 | 2,953 |
| Cost of sales | 335,127 | 314,946 | 304,106 |
| Operating, selling, general and administrative expenses | 85,265 | 81,361 | 79,977 |
| Operating Income | 26,558 | 25,542 | 24,002 |
| Interest | 2,160 | 2,004 | 1,884 |
| Income from continuing operations before income taxes | 24,398 | 23,538 | 22,118 |
| Provision for income taxes | 7,944 | 7,579 | 7,156 |
| Consolidated net income | 16,387 | 16,993 | 14,883 |

*Source:* Wal-Mart 2012 Annual Report.

Superama, Suburbia, VIPS, Sam's Club, and Bodega Aurrerá. By the end of 2011, it had a total of 2,037 outlets and restaurants in Mexico. It was also the biggest employer in Mexico by the end of 2011. Though highly successful in Mexico, Wal-Mart faced fierce competition from local competitors. Some of Mexico's local retailers formed a purchasing association in 2004 called Sinergia to face up to the tremendous purchasing ability of Wal-Mart.[8]

Wal-Mart had also been operating successfully in Canada since it entered the Canadian market in 1993. By the end of January 2012, it operated 333 discount stores and supercenters across Canada through its subsidiary, Walmart Canada Corp.[9] Wal-Mart employed 82,000 people in Canada and was one of its largest employers. It was expected to face severe competition

in Canada with Target[i] announcing its intentions to enter the Canadian market by the spring of 2013.[10]

Wal-Mart experienced similar success in the UK market after it entered there through the acquisition of the third largest supermarket chain in the UK, Asda Stores Ltd., in 1999. Even after the takeover, Wal-Mart continued its operations in the UK under the Asda brand. Very soon, it opened the American-style supercenters in the UK which got a good response from customers. Wal-Mart expanded its operations in the UK quickly and very soon emerged as the second largest supermarket chain in the country. However, it experienced some problems in the UK related to labor issues as it was accused of following illegal practices. It was fined in 2006 for offering its staff a pay rise in return for their giving

**EXHIBIT 4**   Socio-Economic Data of Key Countries Where Wal-Mart Operated

| Country | GDP (US$ trillion) | GDP-Per Capita (US$) | GDP-Real Growth Rate | GNI-Per Capita (US$) | Population | Literacy Rate | Unemployment Rate |
|---|---|---|---|---|---|---|---|
| US | $15.040 | $48,100 | 1.5% | $47,310 | 313,847,465 | 99% | 9.0% |
| Mexico | 1.657 | 15,100 | 3.8% | 14,400 | 114,975,406 | 86% | 5.2% |
| Canada | 1.389 | 40,300 | 2.2% | 38,370 | 34,300,083 | 99% | 7.5% |
| UK | 2.250 | 35,900 | 1.1% | 35,840 | 63,047,162 | 99% | 8.1% |
| Japan | 4.389 | 34,300 | −0.5% | 34,610 | 127,368,088 | 99% | 4.6% |

*Sources:* https://www.cia.gov/library/publications/the-world-factbook, http://data.worldbank.org/indicator/NY.GNP.PCAP.PP.CD/countries.

---

[i]Target Corporation, headquartered in Minneapolis, Minnesota, US, is one of the leading retail companies in the world.

up a collective union agreement. But it quickly sorted out these issues before they escalated out of its control. Wal-Mart had 544 retail units including 32 supercenters in the UK as of May 31, 2012.[11]

On the other hand, Wal-Mart experienced its biggest fiasco in Germany. It entered Germany by acquiring the 21-hypermarket stores of Wertkauf in 1997.[12] It later acquired 74 hypermarket stores of another local retailer to increase its presence in Germany. But analysts pointed out that Wal-Mart had failed to understand the German market right from the beginning and had tried to implement the business model it followed in the US unchanged. Though it offered lower prices to German customers like it did in the US, its local competitors could easily match its prices. Germany was the most price sensitive market in Europe and Germans were accustomed to lower prices from domestic retailers. Wal-Mart also failed to build a good image for its stores in the German market. The stores which Wal-Mart acquired when entering Germany had a poor reputation, which compounded its problems. While not being able to differentiate itself on the price front, Wal-Mart also failed in offering any compelling value proposition to the German customers to visit its stores. Wal-Mart's vendors in Germany opposed the centralized distribution system followed by Wal-Mart globally. Another operational problem Wal-Mart faced in Germany was labor unrest. Wal-Mart paid lower wages and didn't encourage its employees to form unions. Wal-Mart's employees organized a two-day strike in protest against employee lay-offs and store closures in 2002 which further tarnished its reputation in Germany. Wal-Mart also faced problems on the legal front and was accused of violating various German competition laws. In May 2000, Wal-Mart reportedly sold some goods in its stores at a price which was lower than the cost price at which it bought them. Apart from regulatory issues, Wal-Mart also faced problems in integrating its culture with the culture of the retail businesses it acquired in Germany. Wal-Mart strongly discouraged office romance between employees in its stores, which many employees found to be intrusive. Commenting on Wal-Mart's attitude when it entered the German retail market, Bryan Roberts, an analyst at Planet Retail[j], said, "Wal-Mart was not very humble when they went in. They wanted to impose their own culture."[13] Analysts said that even by 2003, five years after it entered the German market, Wal-Mart was losing nearly US$ 200–300 million per annum. It remained a secondary player in the German retail market and was never able to recover.[14] Unable to understand the German market, Wal-Mart exited the country in 2006.

Wal-Mart similarly exited from the South Korean market retail in 2006 and struggled to establish itself in the Japanese retail market. It entered the South Korean market in 1998 and implemented its US business model of low prices just as it did in Germany. But the South Korean customers did not like Wal-Mart's offerings. The South Korean retail market was highly sophisticated with lavish stores and the South Korean customers did not like the 'warehouse style' environment of Wal-Mart's stores. Housewives were not satisfied with the food and beverage offerings in Wal-Mart's stores.[15] As a result, sales did not pick up in Wal-Mart's South Korean stores and the retailer could not open new stores in the country. Limited operations prevented Wal-Mart from extracting better discounts from its suppliers.[16] Analysts said that Wal-Mart had failed to localize its operations to suit the needs of the South Korean market unlike the other global retailing giant Tesco[k]. Homeplus, the South Korean subsidiary of Tesco, emerged as the second biggest retailer in South Korea by 2006 by localizing its operations to suit the needs of South Korean customers. Wal-Mart Korea reported sales of just US$ 800 million and a loss of US$ 10 million in 2005.[17] Unable to sustain its operations in South Korea, Wal-Mart sold its 16 stores in the country for US$ 882 million and exited the market in 2006.[18] Wal-Mart struggled to establish itself in Japan since it entered the Japanese retail market in 2002. But it later started adjusting its business model to suit the needs of the Japanese retail market. Japanese customers initially equated Wal-Mart's lower prices and unsophisticated stores to inferior products.[19] Wal-Mart rectified its problems in Japan through some measures like renovating its stores to look better and creating better consumer awareness about the quality of its products. Later, Wal-Mart expanded its operations in Japan and acquired 100 percent stake in its Japanese subsidiary in 2008.

[j]Planet Research, based in the UK, is a leading retail analyst firm in the world.

[k]Tesco, headquartered in Cheshunt, England, UK, is a multinational grocery and general merchandise retailer.

# WAL-MART EMBARKS ON AN AFRICAN SAFARI

Wal-Mart started putting more emphasis on the international markets to drive its expansion since the financial crisis of 2008[l]. The main reason for its enhanced international focus was the limited growth opportunities in its domestic (US) market since the financial crisis. Strong sales growth and a record number of new stores opened made its international segment grow faster. Wal-Mart's international segment grew by 15.2 percent year on year for the fiscal year 2012.[20] Its operating income from international operations for the fiscal year ending January 31, 2012, was US$ 6,241 million (Refer to Exhibit 5 for Wal-Mart's operating income from international operations for the fiscal years 2010–2012). According to an estimate by Forbes Magazine[m], Wal-Mart's international segment was approximately contributing 40 percent to its stock price in March 2012. This estimate highlighted the importance of international operations for Wal-Mart. It had been trying for a long time to enter the Indian retail market due to the tremendous growth opportunities for the retail sector there. The Indian retail sector was projected to grow from US$ 396 billion in 2012 to US$ 785 billion by 2015.[21] But the Indian retail market was still closed to foreign multi-brand retailers and Wal-Mart's operations were limited to some wholesale outlets there. That had left Wal-Mart to focus on Africa as another most important growth opportunity.

With most of the developed western markets reaching saturation levels and the Asian markets becoming highly competitive, many big multinational companies (MNCs) were turning their attention toward Africa. Africa was being considered the last major emerging market left to be captured by the MNCs. The unstable political environment in most of African countries made it unviable for businesses to set up shop there. But some African countries like South Africa and Nigeria with elected governments and rule of law were seen as viable options for big MNCs to enter the African continent. Wal-Mart decided to gain a foothold in the African market

## EXHIBIT 5   Operating Income from International Operations for Fiscal Years 2010–2012 (in US$ Millions)

| Fiscal year | Operating Income from International Operations | Percentage of Total Operating Income |
|---|---|---|
| 2012 | $6,214 | 23.4% |
| 2011 | 5,606 | 22.0% |
| 2010 | 4,901 | 20.4% |

Source: Wal-Mart 2012 Annual Report.

in the inorganic way by acquiring an established retailing company. Since 2008, Wal-Mart had been on the lookout for an acquisition target in Africa. South Africa had some sophisticated retailers such as Shoprite Holdings[n] (Shoprite), Massmart, Pick 'n Pay Stores Ltd.[o] (Pick 'n Pay), Spar[p], and Woolworths[q]. In September 2010, Wal-Mart announced that it had made a preliminary offer to buy the South African retailer, Massmart.[22] Analysts felt that Wal-Mart had gone in for Massmart rather than Africa's biggest grocer Shoprite, as Massmart had rapidly increased its presence into the food-retailing business and, by then, operated 40 grocery stores in South Africa.[23]

South Africa had a relatively mature organized retail market and some of South Africa's leading retailers like Pepkor were planning to expand their operations into other African markets like Nigeria.[24] Commenting on the preference given by Wal-Mart to South Africa, Andy Bond (Bond), Executive Vice President of Wal-Mart, said, "South Africa presents a compelling growth opportunity for Wal-Mart and offers a platform for growth and expansion in other

[l]The 2008 financial crisis was a major financial crisis that resulted in the meltdown of the global financial markets.

[m]Forbes Magazine is a biweekly business magazine published by the American publishing and media company Forbes.

[n]Shoprite Holdings, headquartered in Cape Town, South Africa, is a leading retail and fast food company. It has operations across 16 countries in Africa and the Indian Ocean Islands.

[o]Pick 'n Pay, headquartered in Cape Town, is the second largest supermarket chain in South Africa.

[p]Spar, headquartered in Amsterdam, Netherlands, is a leading retailer with operations across the globe. In Africa, its operations are spread across Nigeria, South Africa, Botswana, Namibia, Zimbabwe, Zambia, Swaziland, and Mauritius.

[q]Woolworths Group plc, headquartered in London, England, is a leading retail and distribution company.

African countries."[25] The preliminary offer was non-binding to Wal-Mart and it could withdraw the offer anytime after conducting due diligence.

Massmart was the second biggest retailer in Africa and owned several established local retail brands like Game, Makro, Builders' Warehouse, and CBW.[26] Massmart was founded in 1990 and the group comprised nine wholesale and retail chains (Refer to Exhibit 6 for the list of major retailers in South Africa). The group functioned through four operating divisions—Massdiscounters, Masswarehouse, Massbuild, and Masscash. Even though most of Massmart's operations were concentrated in South Africa, Massmart had operations across many sub-Saharan countries (Refer to Exhibit 7 for the list of countries in which Massmart operated in 2012). Wal-Mart hoped to gain an instant footprint across Africa through the acquisition of Massmart. Saying that "Walmart likes emerging markets and South Africa in particular,"[27] Bond said that Massmart hoped to open 40 new outlets a year in countries including South Africa, Nigeria, Malawi, and Zambia. It was also looking at opportunities in countries like Senegal, Cameroon, and Angola. The retailer said that its aim was not to change Massmart's strategy, but simply "to put the foot on the accelerator".[28]

However, the news of Wal-Mart's entry into South Africa led to huge protests from powerful trade unions and some government departments in South Africa who contended that Wal-Mart's entry would drive down wages and lead to unemployment. They threatened to respond with strike action, demonstrations, and boycotts. Faced with such opposition, Wal-Mart defended itself and also warned that it would walk away from the deal.[29]

After the negotiations were completed in June 2010, Wal-Mart's offer was accepted by the shareholders of Massmart and South Africa's Competition Tribunal in May 2011.[30] According to the tribunal, "The merging parties contend that the merger will indeed be good for competition by bringing lower prices and additional choice to South African consumers. We accept that this is a likely outcome of the merger based on Walmart's history in bringing about lower prices. However, the extent of this consumer benefit is by no means clear—Walmart itself has not been able to put a number to this claim, only that it is likely."[31]

According to the figures of United Nations Conference on Trade and Development, Wal-Mart's

### EXHIBIT 6    Major Retailers in South Africa

| Rank | Company |
|------|---------|
| 1 | Shoprite |
| 2 | Massmart |
| 3 | Pick 'n Pay |
| 4 | SPAR |
| 5 | Steinhoff International |
| 6 | Woolworths |

Source: http://www.prnewswire.com/news-releases/south-africa-retail-direct-selling-b2c-e-commerce-report-2012-150747085.html.

### EXHIBIT 7    List of Countries in Which Massmart Operated in 2012

| Country | No. of Stores |
|---------|---------------|
| Botswana | 9 |
| Lesotho | 2 |
| Ghana | 1 |
| Malawi | 2 |
| Mauritius | 1 |
| Mozambique | 1 |
| Namibia | 3 |
| Nigeria | 1 |
| South Africa | 188 |
| Tanzania | 1 |
| Uganda | 1 |
| Zambia | 1 |

Source: http://www.massmart.co.za/pdf/massmarts_operations_in_Africa_2011.pdf.

entry helped boost South Africa's foreign direct investment in 2011 to US$4.5 billion.[32]

## INITIAL HICCUPS

Wal-Mart's offer was to buy a controlling stake of 51 percent stake in the South African retailer. Its offer was accepted with some conditions. First of all, Wal-Mart would be restrained from cutting any jobs in Massmart for two years after the merger. Wal-Mart was also to give preference to the

503 Massmart employees who had been retrenched in June 2010 in its future recruitments.[r] Wal-Mart agreed to honor labor bargaining rights for at least three years after the merger. In a move to develop the local manufacturing sector, Wal-Mart agreed to implement a program to improve the competitiveness of local suppliers within three years of the merger approval date. It earmarked 100 million rand (US$13.37 million) for a supply-chain training program.[33]

Wal-Mart hoped to create at least 15,000 new jobs within three years of the merger.[34] But it started to run into trouble from various quarters in Africa who were opposed to the deal. The opposition to the deal was similar to the ones faced in markets like India against foreign participation in the retail sector. The main opposition was from some trade unions and government departments who feared job losses in the retail sector. People who were opposed to the deal included the organized labor unions of South Africa like The Congress of South African Trade Unions, The South African Commercial, and Catering and Allied Workers Union. Opposition to the deal also came from three government departments: Economic Development, Trade and Industry, and Agriculture, Forestry and Fisheries. In addition to the fear of job losses, the opposition was also opposed to some of the terms of the merger.

The opposition coalition to the deal claimed that there would be huge job losses due to the entry of Wal-Mart as it might import a large part of its merchandise from cheaper markets like China. They claimed that 4,000 jobs would be lost immediately even if Wal-Mart imported just one percent of its merchandise. They also claimed that importing the merchandise from cheaper markets like China would hit the manufacturing sector in South Africa. The main reason for opposition to Wal-Mart's entry into South Africa stemmed from the high levels of unemployment prevailing in that country. The South African government was wary of Wal-Mart's entry leading to huge job losses. The manufacturing and agriculture sectors in South Africa had been declining just before Wal-Mart decided upon entering South Africa. According to a report on the South African labor market published by the Development Policy Research Unit[s] (DPRU), the employment rate in the South African agriculture, forestry, and fishing sector contracted by 13 percent and the employment rate in the manufacturing sector contracted by 11 percent between second quarter of 2009 and the second quarter of 2010.[35] But Wal-Mart refuted the allegations made by the opposition coalition. Many analysts too supported the deal arguing that the fears expressed by the opposition coalition were ill founded. Some said that the fears raised by the opposition were misguided as the retrenchment ban forming part of the terms of the deal made it difficult for Wal-Mart to cut any jobs for at least two years after the merger. Some industry observers said that the supplier development program agreed upon by Wal-Mart at the time of the merger would help in improving the efficiency of South Africa's manufacturing sector.

Wal-Mart was also known for being a low-wage and low-benefit employer in the US. Its founder Walton feared and hated worker unions and Wal-Mart's workers were often discouraged from forming themselves into any labor unions. The opposition coalition feared that Wal-Mart might bring the same work culture to South Africa and other African countries. African countries like South Africa, Kenya, and Nigeria traditionally had a culture of very strong labor unions.

The three government departments opposed to the deal criticized the South Africa's Competition Tribunal approval to the deal saying that the commission had failed to consider some vital issues relating to public interest. Many labor unions in South Africa too voiced their opposition to the deal. Patrick Craven, spokesperson for the South African workers' union, Cosatu, said, "Walmart however is more likely to destroy jobs, by using its competitive advantage to force its competitors out of business, and destroying South African manufacturing businesses, which will not be able to compete with a flood of cheap imports. . . ."[36] The group opposed to the deal approached the Competition Appeal Court of South Africa for a review of the ruling by South Africa's Competition Tribunal. However, the Competition Appeal Court of South Africa ruled in favor of the deal on March 9, 2012, saying that the fears expressed over the deal were unfounded. The ruling by the appeals court finally paved the way for Wal-Mart to enter the South African retail market.

[r]Massmart CEO Grant Pattison had claimed that the retailer's decision to lay off workers had long preceded the merger talks with Wal-Mart.
[s]Development Policy Research Institute is a research unit at the University of Cape Town, Cape Town, South Africa.

Ruling in favor of the deal, the appeals court said, "There was insufficient evidence to conclude that the detrimental effects of the merger would outweigh the clear benefits."[37] As part of the ruling, the appeal court also ordered Wal-Mart to conduct a study to determine the best possible way to safeguard the interests of small producers who would not be able to compete against low cost foreign producers from whom Wal-Mart would be importing goods at cheaper rates.[38] Based on this study, the court would decide how Wal-Mart should use the 100 million rand fund that it had earmarked for improving the competitiveness of local industry. The court also ordered the retailer to reinstate the 503 workers who had been fired just before the merger.[39]

## SMOOTH RIDE?

As the court was deliberating on the appeal against the merger, Wal-Mart and Massmart were busy moving ahead with their integration, which included aligning product sourcing.[40] McMillon said, "Massmart is currently located in 12 markets so that's our focus. Building our business in the markets that we are currently in is our primary focus . . . We are excited about the region. We have a long-term view."[41]

Analysts were divided in their opinion about Wal-Mart's prospects in Africa. Just before the Competition Appeal Court of South Africa ruled in favor of Wal-Mart's deal with Massmart, Massmart announced that it was going to expand and open 20 more stores in Nigeria. Nigeria was another major market for retailing business in Africa with a population of 160 million. Announcing the expansion plans in Nigeria, Grant Pattison, CEO of Massmart, said that Nigeria had the potential to be a bigger market than South Africa. He said, "By all simple metrics, Nigeria has the potential to be larger than South Africa, but it has some way to go in terms of infrastructure and political stability."[42] This showed Massmart's desire to expand in all the major markets across Africa which could ultimately benefit Wal-Mart in its quest to gain a foothold across the African continent. Some analysts said that Wal-Mart's financial muscle could help Massmart to expand across the continent faster.

But some analysts expressed the view that Wal-Mart could face more problems in Africa than it had faced in countries like Germany. As the market potential of many individual African countries was limited, Wal-Mart would have to expand its operations to many countries across Africa to achieve good economies of scale and make its operations viable. Rampant poverty and low income levels would make operations in some African countries simply unviable to Wal-Mart, they said (Refer to Exhibit 8 for the socio-economic data of countries where Massmart operated). Nearly 61 percent of Nigeria's population lived on less than one US$1 per day which could limit

## EXHIBIT 8   Socio-Economic Data of Countries Where Massmart Operated

| Country | GDP (US$ billion) | GDP-Per Capita (US$) | GDP-Real Growth Rate | GNI-Per Capita (US$) | Population | Literacy Rate | Unemployment Rate |
|---|---|---|---|---|---|---|---|
| Botswana | $30.09 | $16,300 | 6.2% | $13,700 | 2,098,018 | 81.2% | 7.5% |
| Lesotho | 3.672 | 1,400 | 5.2% | 1,970 | 1,930,493 | 84.8% | 45.0% |
| Ghana | 74.77 | 3,100 | 13.5% | 1,620 | 25,241,998 | 57.9% | 11.0% |
| Malawi | 13.77 | 900 | 4.6% | 860 | 16,323,044 | 62.7% | NA |
| Mauritius | 19.28 | 15,000 | 4.2% | 13,980 | 1,313,095 | 84.4% | 7.8% |
| Mozambique | 23.87 | 1,100 | 7.2% | 930 | 23,515,934 | 47.8% | 21.0% |
| Namibia | 15.5 | 7,300 | 3.6% | 6,420 | 2,165,828 | 85.0% | 51.2% |
| Nigeria | 414.5 | 2,600 | 6.9% | 2,240 | 170,123,710 | 68.0% | 21.0% |
| South Africa | 554.6 | 11,000 | 3.4% | 10,360 | 48,810,427 | 86.4% | 24.9% |
| Tanzania | 63.44 | 1,500 | 6.1% | 1,440 | 43,601,796 | 69.4% | NA |
| Uganda | 45.9 | 1,300 | 6.4% | 1,250 | 35,873,253 | 66.8% | NA |
| Zambia | 21.93 | 1,600 | 6.7% | 1,380 | 14,309,466 | 80.6% | 14.0% |

*NA  Not available*

*Source:* https://www.cia.gov/library/publications/the-world-factbook, http://data.worldbank.org/indicator/NY.GNP.PCAP.PP.CD/countries.

the country's potential.[43] Some other problems cited by critics to the deal were unstable political environment and poor infrastructure in many parts of Africa that might hit Wal-Mart's ambitions there. David Strasser, an analyst at Janney Montgomery Scott[44], said, "For this deal to drive returns, we believe it is essential to succeed by using this acquisition as a springboard. For every relatively stable country like Botswana, there is a Zimbabwe."[45]

Some analysts were optimistic about the viability of Wal-Mart's US business model in Africa. They said that its business model of offering everyday low pricing for its customers would be very successful in a market like Africa where high poverty and very low income levels prevailed. Wal-Mart might not face the problem of being seen as a low quality retailer as it was seen in countries like Germany and South Korea. However, others warned Wal-Mart against repeating the mistakes it had made in countries like Germany and South Korea like failing to understand the needs of the local markets and trying to follow the same business model it followed in the US.

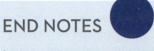

## END NOTES

[1] Sikonathi Mantshantsha, "Billionaire Wiese Targets Nigeria as Wal-Mart Enters Africa," http://www.businessweek.com, August 12, 2011.
[2] Max Clarke, "Walmart Enters Africa Despite Union Opposition," http://www.freshbusiness-thinking.com, June 1, 2011.
[3] Richard Wachman, "South Africa Resists March of Walmart," http://guardian.co.uk, October 10, 2011.
[4] Donna Bryson, "Wal-Mart Gets Go-ahead in South Africa," http://news.yahoo.com, March 9, 2012.
[5] TA Frank, "A Brief History of Wal-Mart," http://www.reclaimdemocracy.org.
[6] "History Timeline," http://www.walmart-stores.com.
[7] "About Us," http://www.walmartstores.com/AboutUs/.
[8] "Mexican Retailers Unite against Wal-Mart," http://www.expresstextile.com, July 29, 2004.
[9] Allison Martell and Jessica Wohl, "Target to Test Wal-Mart's Mettle in Canada," http://www.reuters.com, April 11, 2011.
[10] Ibid.
[11] www.walmartstores.com/AboutUs/275.aspx.
[12] Christine Lepisto, "Walmart Leaves Germany: Blame Smiles, Love or Plastic Bags," http://www.treehugger.com, June 30, 2006.
[13] Kate Norton, "Wal-Mart's German Retreat," http://www.businessweek.com, July 28, 2006.
[14] "Wal-Mart: Struggling in Germany," http://www.businessweek.com, April 11, 2005.
[15] Daniel Workman, "Wal-Mart Finally Gets It: Lessons from South Korea & Germany," http://daniel-workman.suite101.com, July 31, 2006.

[16] Choe Sang-Hun, "Wal-Mart Selling Stores and Leaving South Korea," http://www.nytimes.com, May 23, 2006.
[17] Daniel Workman, "Wal-Mart Finally Gets It: Lessons from South Korea & Germany," http://daniel-workman.suite101.com, July 31, 2006.
[18] Kelly Olsen, "Wal-Mart Pulls Out of South Korea, Sells 16 Stores," http://www.usatoday.com, May 22, 2006.
[19] Matthew Boyle, "Wal-Mart's Painful Lessons," http://www.businessweek.com, October 13, 2009.
[20] "Wal-Mart's Africa and India Plans Boost its International Outlook," http://www.forbes.com, March 25, 2012.
[21] Ibid.
[22] Stephanie Clifford, "Wal-Mart Bids for Massmart to Expand into Africa," http://www.nytimes.com, September 27, 2010.
[23] "Walmart in South Africa: The Beast in the Bush," www.economist.com, February 17, 2011.
[24] Sikonathi Mantshantsha, "Billionaire Wiese Targets Nigeria as Wal-Mart Enters Africa," www.businessweek.com, August 12, 2011.
[25] Stephanie Clifford, "Wal-Mart Bids for Massmart to Expand into Africa," www.nytimes.com, September 27, 2010.
[26] Tiisetso Motsoeneng, "Massmart Could Open Up To 20 Stores in Nigeria," http://af.reuters.com, February 22, 2012.
[27] Richard Wachman, "South Africa Resists March of Walmart," http://guardian.co.uk, October 10, 2011.
[28] "Walmart in South Africa: The Beast in the Bush," www.economist.com, February 17, 2011.
[29] David Smith, "Walmart Gets First Foothold in Africa," http://guardian.co.uk, May 31, 2011.

[30] Jennifer Booton, "Wal-Mart Enters South Africa with Massmart Deal," http://www.foxbusiness.com, June 20, 2011.
[31] David Smith, "Walmart Gets First Foothold in Africa," http://guardian.co.uk, May 31, 2011.
[32] Devon Maylie, "Wal-Mart, Massmart Merger Approved in South Africa," http://online.wsj.com, March 9, 2012.
[33] Ibid.
[34] Olumide Taiwo and Jessica Smith, "Big Box vs. Spring Boks: Wal-Mart's Troubles Entering the South African Retail Market," www.brookings.edu, November 1, 2011.
[35] Ibid.
[36] Max Clarke, "Walmart Enters Africa Despite Union Opposition," http://www.freshbusiness-thinking.com, June 1, 2011.
[37] Donna Bryson, "Wal-Mart Gets Go-ahead in South Africa," http://news.yahoo.com, March 9, 2012.
[38] Ibid.
[39] Devon Maylie, "Wal-Mart, Massmart Merger Approved in South Africa," http://online.wsj.com, March 9, 2012.
[40] Ibid.
[41] "Wal-Mart Focused on Existing Africa Markets," www.reuters.com, May 10, 2012.
[42] "Massmart Could Open up to 20 Stores in Nigeria," http://af.reuters.com, February 22, 2012.
[43] Ibid.
[44] Janney Montgomery Scott, headquartered in Philadelphia, Pennsylvania, US was a full-service financial services firm.
[45] Stephanie Clifford, "Wal-Mart Bids for Massmart to Expand into Africa," http://www.nytimes.com, September 27, 2010.

# PepsiCo's Diversification Strategy in 2014

connect

## John E. Gamble
Texas A&M University–Corpus Christi

PepsiCo was the world's largest snack and beverage company, with 2013 net revenues of approximately $66.4 billion. The company's portfolio of businesses in 2014 included Frito-Lay salty snacks, Quaker Chewy granola bars, Pepsi soft-drink products, Tropicana orange juice, Lipton Brisk tea, Gatorade, Propel, SoBe, Quaker Oatmeal, Cap'n Crunch, Aquafina, Rice-A-Roni, Aunt Jemima pancake mix, and many other regularly consumed products. The company viewed the lineup as highly complementary since most of its products could be consumed together. For example, Tropicana orange juice might be consumed during breakfast with Quaker Oatmeal, and Doritos and a Mountain Dew might be part of someone's lunch. In 2014, PepsiCo's business lineup included 22 $1 billion global brands.

The company's top managers were focused on sustaining the impressive performance through strategies keyed to product innovation, close relationships with distribution allies, international expansion, and strategic acquisitions. Newly introduced products such as Mountain Dew KickStart, Tostitos Cantina tortilla chips, Quaker Real Medleys, Starbucks Refreshers, and Gatorade Energy Chews accounted for 15 to 20 percent of all new growth in recent years. New product innovations that addressed consumer health and wellness concerns were important contributors to the company's growth, with PepsiCo's better-for-you and good-for-you products becoming focal points in the company's new product development initiatives.

In addition to focusing on strategies designed to deliver revenue and earnings growth, the company maintained an aggressive dividend policy, with more than $53 billion returned to shareholders between 2003 and 2012. The company bolstered its cash returns through carefully considered capital expenditures and acquisitions and a focus on operational excellence. Its Performance with Purpose plan utilized investments in manufacturing automation, a rationalized global manufacturing plan, reengineered distribution systems, and simplified organization structures to drive efficiency. In addition, the company's Performance with Purpose plan was focused on minimizing the company's impact on the environment by lowering energy and water consumption and reducing its use of packaging material, providing a safe and inclusive workplace for employees, and supporting and investing in the local communities in which it operated. PepsiCo had been listed on the Dow Jones Sustainability World Index for seven consecutive years and listed on the North America Index for eight consecutive years as of 2013.

Even though the company had recorded a number of impressive achievements over the past decade, its growth had slowed since 2011. In fact, the spikes in the company's revenue growth since 2000 had resulted from major acquisitions such as the $13.6 billion acquisition of Quaker Oats in 2001, the 2010 acquisition of the previously independent Pepsi Bottling Group and PepsiCo Americas for $8.26 billion, and the acquisition of Russia's leading food-and-beverage company, Wimm-Bill-Dann (WBD) Foods, for $3.8 billion in 2011. A summary of PepsiCo's financial performance for 2004 through 2013 is shown in Exhibit 1. Exhibit 2 tracks PepsiCo's market performance between 2004 and July 2014.

**EXHIBIT 1**  Financial Summary for PepsiCo, Inc., 2004–2013 (in millions, except per share amounts)

| | 2013 | 2012 | 2011 | 2010 | 2009 | 2008 | 2007 | 2006 | 2005 | 2004 |
|---|---|---|---|---|---|---|---|---|---|---|
| Net revenue | $66,415 | $65,492 | $66,504 | $57,838 | $43,232 | $43,251 | $39,474 | $35,137 | $32,562 | $29,261 |
| Net income | 6,740 | 6,178 | 6,443 | 6,320 | 5,946 | 5,142 | 5,599 | 5,065 | 4,078 | 4,212 |
| Income per common share— basic, continuing operations | $4.37 | $3.96 | $4.08 | $3.97 | $3.81 | $3.26 | $3.38 | $3.00 | $2.43 | $2.45 |
| Cash dividends declared per common share | $2.24 | $2.13 | $2.03 | $1.89 | $1.78 | $1.65 | $1.42 | $1.16 | $1.01 | $0.85 |
| Total assets | $77,478 | 74,638 | 72,882 | 68,153 | 39,848 | 35,994 | 34,628 | 29,930 | 31,727 | 27,987 |
| Long-term debt | 24,333 | 23,544 | 20,568 | 19,999 | 7,400 | 7,858 | 4,203 | 2,550 | 2,313 | 2,397 |

*Source:* PepsiCo 10-K reports, various years.

## COMPANY HISTORY

PepsiCo, Inc., was established in 1965 when Pepsi-Cola and Frito-Lay shareholders agreed to a merger between the salty-snack icon and soft-drink giant. The new company was founded with annual revenues of $510 million and such well-known brands as Pepsi-Cola, Mountain Dew, Fritos, Lay's, Cheetos, Ruffles, and Rold Gold. PepsiCo's roots can be traced to 1898 when New Bern, North Carolina, pharmacist Caleb Bradham created the formula for a carbonated beverage he named Pepsi-Cola. The company's salty-snack business began in 1932 when Elmer Doolin, of San Antonio, Texas, began manufacturing and marketing Fritos corn chips and Herman Lay started a potato chip distribution business in Nashville, Tennessee. In 1961, Doolin and Lay agreed to a merger between their businesses to establish the Frito-Lay Company.

During PepsiCo's first five years as a snack and beverage company, it introduced new products such as Doritos and Funyuns, entered markets in Japan and eastern Europe, and opened, on average, one new snack-food plant per year. By 1971, PepsiCo had more than doubled its revenues to reach $1 billion. The company began to pursue growth through acquisitions outside snacks and beverages as early as 1968, but its 1977 acquisition of Pizza Hut significantly shaped the strategic direction of PepsiCo for the next 20 years. The acquisitions of Taco Bell in 1978 and

Kentucky Fried Chicken in 1986 created a business portfolio described by Wayne Calloway (PepsiCo's CEO between 1986 and 1996) as a balanced three-legged stool. Calloway believed the combination of snack foods, soft drinks, and fast food offered considerable cost sharing and skill transfer opportunities, and he routinely shifted managers among the company's three divisions as part of the company's management development efforts.

PepsiCo strengthened its portfolio of snack foods and beverages during the 1980s and 1990s with the acquisitions of Mug Root Beer, 7-Up International, Smartfood ready-to-eat popcorn, Walker's Crisps (United Kingdom), Smith's Crisps (United Kingdom), Mexican cookie company Gamesa, and Sunchips. Calloway added quick-service restaurants Hot-n-Now in 1990; California Pizza Kitchens in 1992; and East Side Mario's, D'Angelo Sandwich Shops, and Chevy's Mexican Restaurants in 1993. The company expanded beyond carbonated beverages through a 1992 agreement with Ocean Spray to distribute single-serving juices, the introduction of Lipton ready-to-drink (RTD) teas in 1993, and the introduction of Aquafina bottled water and Frappuccino ready-to-drink coffees in 1994.

By 1996 it had become clear to PepsiCo management that the potential strategic-fit benefits existing between restaurants and PepsiCo's core beverage and snack businesses were difficult to capture. In addition, any synergistic benefits achieved

**EXHIBIT 2**   Monthly Performance of PepsiCo, Inc.'s Stock Price, 2004–July 2014

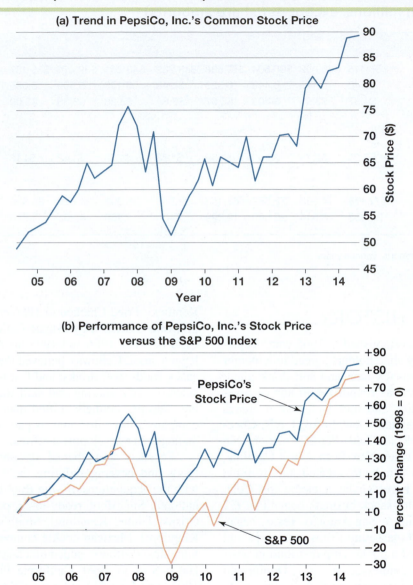

were more than offset by the fast-food industry's fierce price competition and low profit margins. In 1997, CEO Roger Enrico spun off the company's restaurants as an independent, publicly traded company to focus PepsiCo on food and beverages. Soon after the spin-off of PepsiCo's fast-food restaurants was completed, Enrico acquired Cracker Jack, Tropicana, Smith's Snackfood Company in Australia, SoBe teas and alternative beverages, Tasali Snack Foods (the leader in the

Saudi Arabian salty-snack market), and the Quaker Oats Company.

## The 2001 Acquisition of Quaker Oats

At $13.9 billion, Quaker Oats was PepsiCo's largest acquisition and gave it the number-one brand of oatmeal in the United States, with more than a 60 percent category share; the leading brand of rice cakes and granola snack bars; and other well-known grocery brands such as Cap'n Crunch, Rice-A-Roni, and Aunt Jemima. However, Quaker's most valuable asset in its arsenal of brands was Gatorade.

Gatorade was developed by University of Florida researchers in 1965, but it was not marketed commercially until the formula was sold to Stokely-Van Camp in 1967. When Quaker Oats acquired the brand from Stokely-Van Camp in 1983, Gatorade gradually made a transformation from a regionally distributed product with annual sales of $90 million to a $2 billion powerhouse. Gatorade was able to increase sales by more than 10 percent annually during the 1990s, with no new entrant to the sports beverage category posing a serious threat to the brand's dominance. PepsiCo, Coca-Cola, France's Danone Group, and Swiss food giant Nestlé all were attracted to Gatorade because of its commanding market share and because of the expected growth in the isotonic sports beverage category. PepsiCo became the successful bidder for Quaker Oats and Gatorade with an agreement struck in December 2000, but the merger would not receive U.S. Federal Trade Commission (FTC) approval until August 2001. The FTC's primary concern over the merger was that Gatorade's inclusion in PepsiCo's portfolio of snacks and beverages might give the company too much leverage in negotiations with convenience stores and ultimately force smaller snack-food and beverage companies out of convenience store channels. In its approval of the merger, the FTC stipulated that Gatorade and PepsiCo's soft drinks could not be jointly distributed for 10 years.

### Acquisitions after 2001

After the completion of the Quaker Oats acquisition in 2001, the company focused on integration of Quaker Oats' food, snack, and beverage brands into the PepsiCo portfolio. The company made a number of "tuck-in" acquisitions of small, fast-growing food and beverage companies in the United States and internationally to broaden its portfolio of brands. Tuck-in acquisitions in 2006 included Stacy's bagel and pita chips, Izze carbonated beverages, Netherlands-based Duyvis nuts, and Star Foods (Poland). Acquisitions made during 2007 included Naked Juice fruit beverages, Sandora juices in the Ukraine, New Zealand's Bluebird snacks, Penelopa nuts and seeds in Bulgaria, and Brazilian snack producer Lucky. The company also entered into a joint venture with the Strauss Group in 2007 to market Sabra—the top-selling and fastest-growing brand of hummus in the United States and Canada. The company acquired the Russian beverage producer Lebedyansky in 2008 for $1.8 billion, and in 2010 it acquired Marbo, a potato chip production operation in Serbia.

In 2010 and 2011, the company executed its largest acquisitions since the 2001 acquisition of Quaker Oats. In 2010, PepsiCo acquired the previously independent Pepsi Bottling Group and PepsiCo Americas for $8.26 billion in cash and PepsiCo common shares. The acquisition was designed to better integrate its global distribution system for its beverage business. In 2011, it acquired Russia's leading food and beverage company, Wimm-Bill-Dann Foods, for $3.8 billion. The combination of acquisitions and the strength of PepsiCo's core snacks and beverages business allowed the company's revenues to increase from approximately $29 billion in 2004 to more than $66 billion in 2013. Exhibit 3 presents PepsiCo's consolidated statements of income for 2011–2013, while the company's consolidated balance sheets for 2012–2013 are presented in Exhibit 4. The company's calculation of free cash flow for 2011–2013 is shown in Exhibit 5.

## BUILDING SHAREHOLDER VALUE IN 2014

Three people had held the position of CEO since the company began its portfolio restructuring in 1997. Even though Roger Enrico was the chief architect of the business lineup as it stood in 2007, his successor, Steve Reinemund, and Indra Nooyi, the company's CEO in 2007, were both critically involved in the restructuring. Nooyi joined PepsiCo in 1994 and developed a reputation as a tough negotiator who engineered the 1997 spin-off of Pepsi's restaurants, spearheaded the 1998 acquisition of Tropicana, and played a critical role in the 1999 IPO of Pepsi's bottling operations. After being promoted to chief financial officer, Nooyi was also highly involved in the 2001 acquisition of Quaker Oats. Nooyi was selected as the company's CEO upon Reinemund's retirement in October 2006. Nooyi had emigrated to the United States in 1978 to attend Yale's Graduate School of Business, and she worked with the

**EXHIBIT 3**    PepsiCo, Inc.'s Consolidated Statements of Income, 2011–2013
(in millions, except per share data)

| | 2013 | 2012 | 2011 |
|---|---|---|---|
| Net revenue | $66,415 | $65,492 | $66,504 |
| Cost of sales | 31,243 | 31,291 | 31,593 |
| Selling, general, and administrative expenses | 25,357 | 24,970 | 25,145 |
| Amortization of intangible assets | 110 | 119 | 133 |
| Operating profit | 9,705 | 9,112 | 9,633 |
| Interest expense | (911) | (899) | (856) |
| Interest income and other | 97 | 91 | 57 |
| Income before income taxes | 8,891 | 8,304 | 8,834 |
| Provision for income taxes | 2,104 | 2,090 | 2,372 |
| Net income | 6,787 | 6,214 | 6,462 |
| Less: Net income attributable to noncontrolling interests | 47 | 36 | 19 |
| Net income attributable to PepsiCo | $ 6,740 | $ 6,178 | $ 6,443 |
| Net income attributable to PepsiCo per common share: | | | |
| Basic | $4.37 | $3.96 | $4.08 |
| Diluted | $4.32 | $3.92 | $4.03 |
| Weighted-average common shares outstanding: | | | |
| Basic | 1,541 | 1,557 | 1,576 |
| Diluted | 1,560 | 1,575 | 1,597 |
| Cash dividends declared per common share | $2.24 | $2.1275 | $2.025 |

*Source:* PepsiCo, Inc., 10-K report, 2013.

Boston Consulting Group, Motorola, and Asea Brown Boveri before arriving at PepsiCo in 1994. In the eight years under Nooyi's leadership, PepsiCo's revenues had increased by nearly 90 percent, and its share price had grown by 50 percent.

In 2014, PepsiCo's corporate strategy had diversified the company into salty and sweet snacks, soft drinks, orange juice, bottled water, ready-to-drink teas and coffees, purified and functional waters, isotonic beverages, hot and ready-to-eat breakfast cereals, grain-based products, and breakfast condiments. Most PepsiCo brands had achieved number-one or number-two positions in their respective food and beverage categories through strategies keyed to product innovation, close relationships with distribution allies, international expansion, and strategic acquisitions. The company was committed to producing the highest-quality products in each category and was working diligently on product reformulations to make snack foods and beverages less unhealthy. The company believed that its efforts to develop good-for-you and better-for-you products would create growth opportunities from the intersection of business and public interests.

PepsiCo was organized into six business divisions, which all followed the corporation's general strategic approach. Frito-Lay North America manufactured, marketed, and distributed such snack foods as Lay's potato chips, Doritos tortilla chips, Cheetos cheese snacks, Fritos corn chips, Grandma's cookies, and Smartfood popcorn. Quaker Foods North America manufactured and marketed cereals, rice and pasta dishes, granola bars, and other food items that were sold in supermarkets. Latin American Foods manufactured, marketed, and distributed snack foods and many Quaker-branded cereals and snacks in Latin America. PepsiCo Americas Beverages manufactured, marketed, and sold beverage concentrates, fountain syrups, and finished goods under such brands as Pepsi, Gatorade, Aquafina, Tropicana, Lipton, Dole, and SoBe throughout North and South America. PepsiCo Europe manufactured,

**EXHIBIT 4**  PepsiCo, Inc.'s Consolidated Balance Sheets, 2012–2013 (in millions, except per share data)

| | 2013 | 2012 |
|---|---|---|
| **Assets** | | |
| Current assets | | |
| Cash and cash equivalents | $ 9,375 | $ 6,297 |
| Short-term investments | 303 | 322 |
| Accounts and notes receivable, net | 6,954 | 7,041 |
| Inventories | 3,409 | 3,581 |
| Prepaid expenses and other current assets | 2,162 | 1,479 |
| Total current assets | 22,203 | 18,720 |
| Property, plant, and equipment, net | 18,575 | 19,136 |
| Amortizable intangible assets, net | 1,638 | 1,781 |
| Goodwill | 16,613 | 16,971 |
| Other nonamortizable intangible assets | 14,401 | 14,744 |
| Nonamortizable intangible assets | 31,014 | 31,715 |
| Investments in noncontrolled affiliates | 1,841 | 1,633 |
| Other assets | 2,207 | 1,653 |
| Total assets | $ 77,478 | $74,638 |
| **Liabilities and Equity** | | |
| Current liabilities | | |
| Short-term obligations | $ 5,306 | $ 4,815 |
| Accounts payable and other current liabilities | 12,533 | 11,903 |
| Income taxes payable | — | 371 |
| Total current liabilities | 17,839 | 17,089 |
| Long-term debt obligations | 24,333 | 23,544 |
| Other liabilities | 4,931 | 6,543 |
| Deferred income taxes | 5,986 | 5,063 |
| Total liabilities | 53,089 | 52,239 |
| Commitments and contingencies | | |
| Preferred stock, no par value | 41 | 41 |
| Repurchased preferred stock | (171) | (164) |
| PepsiCo common shareholders' equity | | |
| Common stock, par value 1²/₃¢ per share (authorized 3,600 shares, issued, net of repurchased common stock at par value: 1,529 and 1,544 shares, respectively) | 25 | 26 |
| Capital in excess of par value | 4,095 | 4,178 |
| Retained earnings | 46,420 | 43,158 |
| Accumulated other comprehensive loss | (5,127) | (5,487) |
| Repurchased common stock, in excess of par value (337 and 322 shares, respectively) | (21,004) | (19,458) |
| Total PepsiCo common shareholders' equity | 24,409 | 22,417 |
| Noncontrolling interests | 110 | 105 |
| Total equity | 24,389 | 22,399 |
| Total liabilities and equity | $ 77,478 | $74,638 |

*Source:* PepsiCo, Inc., 10-K report, 2013.

## EXHIBIT 5   Net Cash Provided By PepsiCo's Operating Activities, 2011–2013

|  | 2013 | 2012 | 2011 |
|---|---|---|---|
| Net cash provided by operating activities | $9,688 | $8,479 | $8,944 |
| Capital spending | (2,795) | (2,714) | (3,339) |
| Sales of property, plant, and equipment | 109 | 95 | 84 |
| Free cash flow | $ 7,002 | $5,860 | $5,689 |

*Source:* PepsiCo, Inc., 10-K report, 2013.

marketed, and sold snacks and beverages through-out Europe, while the company's Asia, Middle East, and Africa division produced, marketed, and distrib-uted snack brands and beverages in more than 150 countries in those regions. A full listing of Frito-Lay snacks, PepsiCo beverages, and Quaker Oats prod-ucts is presented in Exhibit 6. Select financial infor-mation for PepsiCo's six reporting units is presented in Exhibit 7.

## Frito-Lay North America

As of 2014, three key trends that were shaping the industry were convenience, a growing awareness of the nutritional content of snack foods, and indul-gent snacking. A product manager for a regional snack producer explained, "Many consumers want to reward themselves with great-tasting, gourmet flavors and styles. . . . The indulgent theme carries into seasonings as well. Overall, upscale, restaurant-influenced flavor trends are emerging to fill con-sumers' desires to escape from the norm and taste snacks from a wider, often global, palate."[1] Most manufacturers had developed new flavors of salty snacks such as jalapeno and cheddar tortilla chips and pepper jack potato chips to attract the interest of indulgent snackers. Manufacturers had also begun using healthier oils when processing chips and had expanded lines of baked and natural salty snacks to satisfy the demands of health-conscious consumers. Snacks packaged in smaller bags not only addressed overeating concerns but also were convenient to take along on an outing. In 2013 Frito-Lay owned the top-selling chip brand in each U.S. salty-snack category and held more than a 2-to-1 lead over the next-largest snack-food maker in the United States. Frito-Lay's 36.6 percent market share of conve-nience foods sold in the United States was more than

five times greater than runner-up Kellogg's market share of 6.9 percent. Convenience foods included both salty and sweet snacks, such as chips, pretzels, ready-to-eat popcorn, crackers, dips, snack nuts and seeds, candy bars, and cookies.

PepsiCo's Performance with Purpose goals applied to all of its business units. Frito-Lay North Ameri-ca's (FLNA's) revenues increased by 3 percent dur-ing 2013, but its net revenue increased by 4 percent and its operating profit increased by 6 percent. The division's management believed that growth in snack foods remained possible since typical indi-viduals, on average, consumed snacks 67 times per month. On average, consumers chose Frito-Lay snacks only eight times per month. To increase its share of snack consumption, FLNA was focused on developing additional better-for-you (BFY) snacks like Baked Cheetos and Doritos packaged in smaller portion sizes. Between 2008 and 2013, improving the performance of the division's core salty brands and further developing health and wellness prod-ucts were key strategic initiatives. The company had eliminated trans fats from all Lay's, Fritos, Ruffles, Cheetos, Tostitos, and Doritos varieties, marketed a wide variety of gluten-free products, and was look-ing for further innovations to make its salty snacks more healthy. The company had introduced Lay's Classic Potato Chips cooked in sunflower oil that retained Lay's traditional flavor but contained 50% less saturated fat.

Good-for-you (GFY) snacks, such as Flat Earth fruit and vegetable snacks, offered an opportunity for the company to exploit consumers' desires for healthier snacks and address a deficiency in most diets. Americans, on average, consumed only about 50 percent of the U.S. Department of Agriculture's recommended daily diet of fruits and vegetables. Other GFY snacks included Stacy's Pita Chips,

# EXHIBIT 6  PepsiCo, Inc.'s Snack, Beverage, and Quaker Oats Brands, 2014

| Snack Brands | Beverage Brands | Quaker Oats Brands |
|---|---|---|
| • Lay's potato chips | • Pepsi-Cola | • Quaker Oatmeal |
| • Maui Style potato chips | • Mountain Dew | • Cap'n Crunch cereal |
| • Ruffles potato chips | • Mountain Dew AMP energy drink | • Life cereal |
| • Doritos tortilla chips | • Mug | • Quaker 100% Natural cereal |
| • Tostitos tortilla chips | • Sierra Mist | • Quaker Squares cereal |
| • Santitas tortilla chips | • Slice | • Quisp cereal |
| • Fritos corn chips | • Lipton Brisk (partnership) | • King Vitaman cereal |
| • Cheetos cheese-flavored snacks | • Lipton Iced Tea (partnership) | • Quaker Oh's! cereal |
| • Rold Gold pretzels and snack mix | • Dole juices and juice drinks (license) | • Mother's cereal |
| • Funyuns onion-flavored rings | • FruitWorks juice drinks | • Quaker grits |
| • Go Snacks | • Aquafina purified drinking water | • Quaker Oatmeal-to-Go |
| • Sunchips multigrain snacks | • Frappuccino ready-to-drink coffee (partnership) | • Aunt Jemima mixes & syrups |
| • Sabritones puffed-wheat snacks | • Starbucks DoubleShot (partnership) | • Quaker rice cakes |
| • Cracker Jack candy-coated popcorn | • SoBe juice drinks, dairy, and teas | • Quaker rice snacks (Quakes) |
| • Chester's popcorn | • SoBe energy drinks (No Fear and Adrenaline Rush) | • Quaker Chewy granola bars |
| • Grandma's cookies | • H2OH! | • Quaker Dipps granola bars |
| • Munchos potato crisps | • Gatorade | • Rice-A-Roni side dishes |
| • Smartfood popcorn | • Propel | • Pasta Roni side dishes |
| • Baken-ets fried pork skins | • Tropicana | • Near East side dishes |
| • Oberto meat snacks | • Tropicana Twister | • Puffed Wheat |
| • Rustler's meat snacks | • Tropicana Smoothie | • Harvest Crunch cereal |
| • Churrumais fried corn strips | • Izze | • Quaker baking mixes |
| • Frito-Lay nuts | • Naked Juice | • Spudz snacks |
| • Frito-Lay, Ruffles, Fritos, and Tostitos dips and salsas | **Outside North America** | • Crisp'ums baked crisps |
| • Frito-Lay, Doritos, and Cheetos snack crackers | • Mirinda | • Quaker Fruit & Oatmeal bars |
| • Fritos, Tostitos, Ruffles, and Doritos snack kits | • 7UP | • Quaker Fruit & Oatmeal Bites |
| • Grain Waves | • Pepsi | • Quaker Fruit and Oatmeal Toastables |
| • Lay's Stax potato crisps | • Kas | • Quaker Soy Crisps |
| • Miss Vickie's potato chips | • Teem | • Quaker Bakeries |
| • Munchies snack mix | • Manzanita Sol | **Outside North America** |
| • Stacy's Pita Chips | • Paso de los Toros | • FrescAvena beverage powder |
| • Flat Earth fruit and vegetable chips | • Fruko | • Toddy chocolate powder |
| • Red Rock Deli Chips | • Evervess | • Toddynho chocolate drink |
| • Sabra hummus | • Yedigun | • Coqueiro canned fish |
| **Outside North America** | • Shani | • Sugar Puffs cereal |
| • Bocabits wheat snacks | • Fiesta | • Puffed Wheat |
| • Crujitos corn snacks | • D&G (license) | • Cruesli cereal |
| | • Mandarin (license) | • Hot Oat Crunch cereal |
| | | • Quaker Oatso Simple hot cereal |
| | | • Scott's Porage Oats |

(Continued)

## EXHIBIT 6   (Continued)

| Snack Brands | Beverage Brands | Quaker Oats Brands |
|---|---|---|
| • Fandangos corn snacks | • Radical Fruit | • Scott's So Easy Oats |
| • Hamka's snacks | • Tropicana Touche de Lait | • Quaker bagged cereals |
| • Niknaks cheese snacks | • Alvalle gazpacho fruit juices and vegetable juices | • Quaker Mais Sabor |
| • Quavers potato snacks | | • Quaker Oats |
| • Sabritas potato chips | • Tropicana Season's Best juices and juice drinks | • Quaker oat flour |
| • Smiths potato chips | | • Quaker Meu Mingau |
| • Walkers potato crisps | • Loóza juices and nectars | • Quaker cereal bars |
| • Gamesa cookies | • Copella juices | • Quaker Oatbran |
| • Doritos Dippas | • Frui'Vita juices | • Corn goods |
| • Sonric's sweet snacks | • Sandora juices | • Magico chocolate powder |
| • Wotsits corn snacks | | • Quaker Vitaly Cookies |
| • Red Rock Deli | | • 3 Minutos Mixed Cereal |
| • Kurkure | | • Quaker Mágica |
| • Smiths Sensations | | • Quaker Mágica con Soja |
| • Cheetos Shots | | • Quaker pastas |
| • Quavers Snacks | | • Quaker Frut |
| • Bluebird Snacks | | |
| • Duyvis Nuts | | |
| • Müller yogurts | | |
| • Lucky snacks | | |
| • Penelopa nuts and seeds | | |
| • Marbo | | |
| • Wimm-Bill-Dann | | |

Source: Pepsico.com.

Sabra hummus, salsas and dips, and Quaker Chewy granola bars. In 2013, FLNA manufactured and marketed baked versions of its most popular products, such as Cheetos, Lay's potato chips, Ruffles potato chips, and Tostitos Scoops! tortilla chips.

## Quaker Foods North America

Quaker Foods produced, marketed, and distributed hot and ready-to-eat cereals, pancake mixes and syrups, and rice and pasta side dishes in the United States and Canada. The division recorded sales of approximately $2.6 billion in 2013. The sales volume of Quaker Foods products decreased by nearly 1 percent annually between 2011 and 2013 with Quaker Oatmeal, Life cereal, and Cap'n Crunch cereal volumes competing in mature industries with weak competitive positions relative to Kellogg's and General Mills. Sales of Aunt Jemima syrup and pancake mix and Rice-A-Roni rice and pasta kits also

declined between 2011 and 2013. Quaker Oats was the star product of the division, with a commanding share of the North American market for oatmeal in 2013. Rice-A-Roni also held a number-one market share in the rice and pasta side-dish segment of the consumer food industry. More than one-half of Quaker Foods' 2013 revenues was generated by BFY and GFY products.

## Latin American Foods

PepsiCo management believed international markets offered the company's greatest opportunity for growth since per capita consumption of snacks in the United States averaged 6.6 servings per month while per capita consumption in other developed countries averaged 4 servings per month and in developing countries averaged 0.4 serving per month. PepsiCo executives expected China and Brazil to become the two largest international markets for snacks. The United Kingdom

**EXHIBIT 7**    Select Financial Data for PepsiCo, Inc.'s Business Segments, 2011–2013 (in millions)

| | 2013 | 2012 | 2011 |
|---|---|---|---|
| **Net revenues** | | | |
| Frito-Lay North America | $14,126 | $13,574 | $13,322 |
| Quaker Foods North America | 2,612 | 2,636 | 2,656 |
| Latin American Foods | 8,350 | 7,780 | 7,156 |
| PepsiCo Americas Beverages | 21,068 | 21,408 | 22,418 |
| Europe | 13,752 | 13,441 | 13,560 |
| Asia, Middle East, Africa | 6,507 | 6,653 | 7,392 |
| Total division | 66,415 | 65,492 | 66,504 |
| **Operating profit** | | | |
| Frito-Lay North America | $ 3,877 | $ 3,646 | $ 3,621 |
| Quaker Foods North America | 617 | 695 | 797 |
| Latin American Foods | 1,242 | 1,059 | 1,078 |
| PepsiCo Americas Beverages | 2,955 | 2,937 | 3,273 |
| Europe | 1,293 | 1,330 | 1,210 |
| Asia, Middle East, Africa | 1,174 | 1,330 | 1,210 |
| Total division | 11,158 | 10,414 | 10,866 |
| **Capital expenditures** | | | |
| Frito-Lay North America | $ 423 | $ 365 | $ 439 |
| Quaker Foods North America | 38 | 37 | 43 |
| Latin American Foods | 384 | 436 | 413 |
| PepsiCo Americas Beverages | 716 | 702 | 1,006 |
| Europe | 550 | 575 | 588 |
| Asia, Middle East, Africa | 531 | 510 | 693 |
| Total division | 2,642 | 2,625 | 3,182 |
| **Total assets** | | | |
| Frito-Lay North America | $ 5,308 | $ 5,332 | $ 5,384 |
| Quaker Foods North America | 983 | 966 | 1,024 |
| Latin American Foods | 4,829 | 4,993 | 4,721 |
| PepsiCo Americas Beverages | 30,350 | 30,889 | 31,142 |
| Europe | 18,702 | 19,218 | 18,461 |
| Asia, Middle East, Africa | 5,754 | 5,738 | 6,038 |
| Total division | 65,926 | 67,146 | 66,770 |
| **Depreciation and other amortization** | | | |
| Frito-Lay North America | $ 430 | $ 445 | $ 458 |
| Quaker Foods North America | 51 | 53 | 54 |
| Latin American Foods | 253 | 248 | 238 |
| PepsiCo Americas Beverages | 863 | 855 | 865 |
| Europe | 525 | 522 | 522 |
| Asia, Middle East, Africa | 283 | 305 | 350 |
| Total division | 2,553 | 2,570 | 2,604 |

(Continued)

**EXHIBIT 7   (Continued)**

| | 2013 | 2012 | 2011 |
|---|---|---|---|
| **Amortization of other intangible assets** | | | |
| Frito-Lay North America | $    7 | $    7 | $    7 |
| Quaker Foods North America | — | — | — |
| Latin American Foods | 8 | 10 | 10 |
| PepsiCo Americas Beverages | 58 | 59 | 65 |
| Europe | 32 | 36 | 39 |
| Asia, Middle East, Africa | 5 | 7 | 12 |
| Total division | 110 | 119 | 133 |

Source: PepsiCo, Inc., 10-K report, 2013.

was estimated to be the third-largest international market for snacks, while developing markets Mexico and Russia were expected to be the fourth- and fifth-largest international markets, respectively.

Developing an understanding of consumer taste preferences was a key to expanding into international markets. Taste preferences for salty snacks were more similar from country to country than were preferences for many other food items, and this allowed PepsiCo to make only modest modifications to its snacks in most countries. For example, classic varieties of Lay's, Doritos, and Cheetos snacks were sold in Latin America. In addition, consumer characteristics in the United States that had forced snack-food makers to adopt better-for-you or good-for-you snacks applied in most other developed countries as well.

PepsiCo operated 50 snack-food manufacturing and processing plants and 640 warehouses in Latin America, with its largest facilities located in Guarulhos, Brazil; Monterrey, Mexico; Mexico City, Mexico; and Celaya, Mexico. PepsiCo was the second-largest seller of snacks and beverages in Mexico, and its Doritos, Marias Gamesa, Cheetos, Ruffles, Emperador, Saladitas, Sabritas, and Tostitos brands were popular throughout most of Latin America. The division's revenues had grown from $7.2 billion in 2011 to $8.3 billion in 2013 and accounted for 12 percent of 2013 total net revenues.

## PepsiCo Americas Beverages

PepsiCo was the largest seller of liquid refreshments in the United States, with a 24 percent share of the market in 2013. Coca-Cola was the second-largest nonalcoholic beverage producer, with a 21 percent

market share. Dr. Pepper Snapple Group was the third-largest beverage seller in 2013, with a market share of 8.9 percent. Private-label sellers of beverages collectively held an 8 percent market share in 2013. As with Frito-Lay, PepsiCo's beverage business contributed greatly to the corporation's overall profitability and free cash flows.

In 2013, PepsiCo Americas Beverages (PAB) accounted for 32 percent of the corporation's total revenues and 26 percent of its operating profits. The PAB division's $1 billion brands included Gatorade, Tropicana fruit juices, Lipton ready-to-drink tea, Pepsi, Diet Pepsi, Mountain Dew, Diet Mountain Dew, Aquafina, Miranda, Sierra Mist, Dole fruit drinks, Starbucks cold-coffee drinks, and SoBe. Gatorade was the number-one brand of sports drink sold worldwide; Tropicana was the number-two seller of juice and juice drinks globally; and PAB was the second-largest seller of carbonated soft drinks worldwide, with a 29 percent market share in 2014. Market leader Coca-Cola held a 40.5 percent share of the carbonated soft-drink (CSD) industry in 2014. Carbonated soft drinks were the most consumed type of beverage in the United States, with industry sales of $20.4 billion, but the industry had declined by 1 to 2 percent annually for nearly a decade. The overall decline in CSD consumption was a result of consumers' interest in healthier food and beverage choices. In contrast, flavored and enhanced water, energy drinks, ready-to-drink teas, and bottled water were growing beverage categories that were capturing a larger share of the stomachs in the United States and internationally.

### PepsiCo's Carbonated Soft-Drink Business
Among Pepsi's most successful strategies to sustain

volume and share in soft drinks was its Power of One strategy, which attempted to achieve the synergistic benefits of a combined Pepsi-Cola and Frito-Lay envisioned by shareholders of the two companies in 1965. The Power of One strategy called for supermarkets to place Pepsi and Frito-Lay products side by side on shelves. The company was also focused on soft-drink innovation to sustain sales and market share, including new formulations to lower the calorie content of nondiet drinks.

### PepsiCo's Noncarbonated Beverage Brands

Although carbonated beverages made up the largest percentage of PAB's total beverage volume, much of the division's growth was attributable to the success of its noncarbonated beverages. Aquafina was the number-one brand of bottled water in the United States. Gatorade, Tropicana, Aquafina, SoBe, Starbucks Frappuccino, Lipton RTD teas, and Propel were all leading BFY and GFY beverages in the markets where they were sold.

## PepsiCo Europe

All of PepsiCo's global brands were sold in Europe, as well as its country- or region-specific brands such as Domik v Derevne, Chjudo, and Agusha. PespiCo Europe operated 125 plants and approximately 525 warehouses, distribution centers, and offices in eastern and western Europe. The company's acquisition of Wimm-Bill-Dann Foods, along with sales of its long-time brands, made it the number-one food and beverage company in Russia, with a 2-to-1 advantage over its nearest competitor. It was also the leading seller of snacks and beverages in the United Kingdom. PepsiCo Europe management believed further opportunities in other international markets existed, with opportunities to distribute many of its newest brands and product formulations throughout Europe.

## Asia, Middle East, and Africa

PepsiCo's business unit operating in Asia, the Middle East, and Africa manufactured and marketed all of the company's global brands and many regional brands such as Kurkure and Chipsy. PepsiCo operated 45 plants, 490 distribution centers, warehouses, and offices located in Egypt, Jordan, and China and was the number-one brand of beverages and snacks in India, Egypt, Saudi Arabia, United Arab Emirates, and China. The division's revenues had declined from $7.4 billion in 2011 to $6.5 billion in 2013,

while its operating profit declined from $1,210 to $1,174 over the same period of time.

## Value Chain Alignment between PepsiCo Brands and Products

PepsiCo's management team was dedicated to capturing strategic-fit benefits within the business lineup throughout the value chain. The company's procurement activities were coordinated globally to achieve the greatest possible economies of scale, and best practices were routinely transferred among its more than 200 plants, over 3,500 distribution systems, and 120,000 service routes around the world. PepsiCo also shared market research information with its divisions to better enable each division to develop new products likely to be hits with consumers, and the company coordinated its Power of One activities across product lines.

PepsiCo management had a proven ability to capture strategic fits between the operations of new acquisitions and its other businesses. The Quaker Oats integration produced a number of noteworthy successes, including $160 million in cost savings resulting from corporatewide procurement of product ingredients and packaging materials and an estimated $40 million in cost savings attributed to the joint distribution of Quaker snacks and Frito-Lay products. In total, the company estimated that the synergies among its business units generated approximately $1 billion annually in productivity savings.

# PEPSICO'S STRATEGIC SITUATION IN 2014

For the most part, PepsiCo's strategies seemed to be firing on all cylinders in 2014. PepsiCo's chief managers expected the company's lineup of snack, beverage, and grocery items to generate operating cash flows sufficient to reinvest in its core businesses, provide cash dividends to shareholders, fund a $15 billion share-buyback plan, and pursue acquisitions that would provide attractive returns. Nevertheless, the low relative profit margins of PepsiCo's international businesses created the need for a continued examination of its strategy and operations to better exploit strategic fits between the company's international business units.

The company had developed a new divisional structure in 2008 to combine its food and beverage businesses in Latin America into a common division. Also, the company's international businesses were reorganized to boost profit margins in Europe and Asia, the Middle East, and Africa. However, more than five years after the reorganization, the performance of the company's international businesses continued to lag that of its North American businesses by a meaningful margin. Some food and beverage industry analysts had speculated that additional corporate strategy changes might also be required to improve the profitability of PepsiCo's international operations and to help restore previous revenue and earnings growth rates. Possible actions might include a reprioritization of internal uses of cash, new acquisitions, further efforts to capture strategic fits existing between the company's various businesses, or the divestiture of businesses with poor prospects of future growth and minimal strategic fit with PepsiCo's other businesses.

## ENDNOTES

[1] As quoted in "Snack attack," *Private Label Buyer,* August 2006, p. 26.

# The Walt Disney Company: Its Diversification Strategy in 2014

## John E. Gamble
### Texas A&M University–Corpus Christi

## David L. Turnipseed
### University of South Alabama

The Walt Disney Company was a broadly diversified media and entertainment company with a business lineup that included theme parks and resorts, motion picture production and distribution, cable television networks, the ABC broadcast television network, eight local television stations, and a variety of other businesses that exploited the company's intellectual property. The company's revenues had increased from $35.5 billion in fiscal 2007 to $45 billion in fiscal 2013 and its share price had consistently outperformed the S&P 500 since 2003. While struggling somewhat in the mid-1980s, the company's performance had been commendable in almost every year since Walt Disney created Mickey Mouse in 1928. During an investor's conference in May 2012, current Disney CEO Robert Iger commented on the company's performance since he had become its chief manager in 2005 and on its situation in 2012:[1]

> I inherited a great company seven years ago, obviously a strong brand in Disney and a strong business in ESPN. As I look back on the seven years, what I think I'm most proud of is that I made a strong company stronger with the acquisition of some very, very valuable and important brands for the company; notably, Pixar and Marvel. And the company today is extremely brand-focused. It's where we invest most of our capital. And those brands are not only stronger in the United States than they were before, but they are stronger globally.
>
> With that in mind, the company is also more diversified in terms of the territories that it does business in. So, while we are still predominantly a US-based company, meaning well more than 50% of our bottom line profits are generated from the US, we're far more global than we ever have been. And we've planted some pretty important seeds to make the international side of our business even bigger in the years ahead; notably, in some of the big, emerging markets but also in some of the more developed markets outside the US.
>
> We also adopted, I think, just at the right time, seven years ago, a technology-friendly approach, believing that nothing the company was going to do was going to stand in the way of technology and its developments. And, rather than watch technology throw threat after threat at us and disrupt our very valuable business models, we decided to embrace it and use it to not only enhance the quality of our product and the connection we have to our customers and make the company more efficient but, ultimately, to reach more people in more ways. And I'm pleased to say that that has definitely worked.
>
> The other thing that I think is very notable about the company is that, as many businesses as we are in, and as many territories as we operate in, the company is managed in a very cohesive fashion. The credit really belongs to a senior management team that knows where the value is created at the company, is invested in The Walt Disney Company and not in [their] individual business, and [strives for] coordination between the businesses. . . . [This mindset] is a real distinguishing factor or attribute of our company. And it sets us apart from many companies in the world, and it certainly sets us apart from all media companies.

As the company entered its second quarter of 2014, it was coming off a record-setting first quarter but faced several strategic issues. The company had invested nearly $15 billion in capital in its businesses during the past five years, including a 43 percent investment in a $4.5 billion theme park in China, the construction of two new 340-meter ships for its Disney Cruise Line, the acquisitions of Pixar and Marvel, and the acquisition of Maker Studios for $500 million with an additional $450 million performance-based payment. The company had also funded an aggressive share-buyback plan that had placed demands on its cash reserves. In addition, not all of the company's business units were providing sufficient returns on invested capital, and some business units competed in challenging industry environments. Going into 2015, Iger and Disney's management team would have to evaluate the corporation's diversification strategy under the growing cloud of layoffs at Maker Studios.

## COMPANY HISTORY

Walt Disney's venture into animation began in 1919 when he returned to the United States from France, where he had volunteered to be an ambulance driver for the American Red Cross during World War I. Disney volunteered for the American Red Cross only after being told that he was too young to enlist in the United States Army. Upon returning after the war, Disney settled in Kansas City, Missouri, and found work as an animator for Pesman Art Studio. Disney, and fellow Pesman animator Ub Iwerks, soon left the company to found Iwerks-Disney Commercial Artists in 1920. The company lasted only briefly, but Iwerks and Disney were both able to find employment with a Kansas City company that produced short animated advertisements for local movie theaters. Disney left his job again in 1922 to found Laugh-O-Grams, where he employed Iwerks and three other animators to produce short animated cartoons. Laugh-O-Grams was able to sell its short cartoons to local Kansas City movie theaters, but its costs far exceeded its revenues—forcing Disney to declare bankruptcy in 1923. Having exhausted his savings, Disney had only enough cash to purchase a one-way train ticket to Hollywood, California, where his brother, Roy, had offered a temporary room. Once in California, Walt Disney began to look for buyers for a finished animated live-action film he retained from Laugh-O-Grams. The film was never distributed, but New York distributors Margaret Winkler and Charles Mintz were impressed enough with the short film that they granted Disney a contract in October 1923 to produce a series of short films that blended cartoon animation with live-action motion picture photography. Disney brought Ub Iwerks

from Kansas City to Hollywood to work with Disney Brothers Studio (later to be named Walt Disney Productions) to produce the *Alice Comedies* series that would number 50-plus films by the series end in 1927. Disney followed the *Alice Comedies* series with a new animated cartoon for Universal Studios. After Disney's *Oswald the Lucky Rabbit* cartoons quickly became a hit, Universal terminated Disney Brothers Studio and hired most of Disney's animators to continue producing the cartoons.

In 1928, Disney and Iwerks created Mickey Mouse to replace Oswald as the feature character in Walt Disney Studios cartoons. Unlike the case with Oswald, Disney retained all rights over Mickey Mouse and all subsequent Disney characters. Mickey Mouse and his girlfriend, Minnie Mouse, made their cartoon debuts later in 1928 in the cartoons *Plane Crazy, The Gallopin' Gaucho,* and *Steamboat Willie. Steamboat Willie* was the first cartoon with synchronized sound and became one of the most famous short films of all time. The animated film's historical importance was recognized in 1998 when it was added to the National Film Registry by the U.S. Library of Congress. Mickey Mouse's popularity exploded over the next few decades with a Mickey Mouse Club being created in 1929, new accompanying characters such as Pluto, Goofy, Donald Duck, and Daisy Duck being added to Mickey Mouse cartoon storylines, and Mickey Mouse appearing in Walt Disney's 1940 feature-length film, *Fantasia.* Mickey Mouse's universal appeal reversed Walt Disney's series of failures in the animated film industry, and the character became known as the mascot of Disney Studios, Walt Disney Productions, and The Walt Disney Company.

The success of The Walt Disney Company was sparked by the Mickey Mouse cartoons, but Disney Studios also produced several highly successful animated feature films, including *Snow White and the Seven Dwarfs* in 1937, *Pinocchio* in 1940, *Dumbo* in 1941, *Bambi* in 1942, *Song of the South* in 1946, *Cinderella* in 1950, *Treasure Island* in 1950, *Peter Pan* in 1953, *Sleeping Beauty* in 1959, and *One Hundred and One Dalmatians* in 1961. What would prove to be Disney's greatest achievement began to emerge in 1954 when construction began on his Disneyland Park in Anaheim, California. Walt Disney's Disneyland resulted from an idea that Disney had many years earlier while sitting on an amusement park bench watching his young daughters play.

Walt Disney thought that there should be a clean and safe park that had attractions that both parents and children alike would find entertaining. Walt Disney spent years planning the park and announced the construction of the new park to America on his *Disneyland* television show, which had been launched to promote the new $17 million park. The park was an instant success when it opened in 1955, and it recorded revenues of more than $10 million during its first year of operation. After the success of Disneyland, Walt Disney began looking for a site in the eastern United States for a second Disney park. He settled on an area near Orlando, Florida, in 1963 and acquired more than 27,000 acres for the new park by 1965.

Walt Disney died of lung cancer in 1966, but upon his death, Roy O. Disney postponed retirement to become president and CEO of Walt Disney Productions and oversee the development of the Walt Disney World Resort. The resort opened in October 1971—only two months before Roy Disney's death in December 1971. The company was led by Donn Tatum from 1971 to 1976. Tatum had been with Walt Disney Productions since 1956, and he led the further development of the Walt Disney World Resort and began the planning of Epcot in Orlando and Tokyo Disneyland. Those two parks were opened during the tenure of Esmond Cardon Walker, who had been an executive at the company since 1956 and chief operating officer since Walt Disney's death in 1966. Walker also launched The Disney Channel before his retirement in 1983. Walt Disney Productions was briefly led by Ronald Miller, who was the son-in-law of Walt Disney. Miller was ineffective as Disney's CEO and was replaced by Michael Eisner in 1984.

Eisner formulated and oversaw the implementation of a bold strategy for Walt Disney Studios, including the acquisitions of ABC, ESPN, Miramax Films, the Anaheim Angels, and the Fox Family Channel; the development of Disneyland Paris, Disney-MGM Studios in Orlando, Disney California Adventure Park, Walt Disney Studios theme park in France, and Hong Kong Disneyland; and the launch of the Disney Cruise Line, the Disney Interactive game division, and the Disney Store retail chain. Eisner also restored the company's reputation for blockbuster animated feature films with the creation of *The Little Mermaid* in 1989 and *Beauty and the Beast* and *The Lion King* in 1994. Despite Eisner's

successes, his tendencies toward micromanaging and skirting board approval for many of his initiatives and his involvement in a long-running derivatives suit led to his removal as chairman in 2004 and his resignation in 2005.

The Walt Disney Company's CEO in 2012, Robert (Bob) Iger, became a Disney employee in 1996 when the company acquired ABC. Iger was president and CEO of ABC at the time of the acquisition and remained in that position until he was made president of Walt Disney International by Eisner in 1999. Iger was promoted to president and chief operating officer of The Walt Disney Company in 2000 and was named as Eisner's replacement as CEO in 2005. Iger's first strategic moves in 2006 included the $7.4 billion acquisition of Pixar animation studios and the purchase of the rights to Disney's first cartoon character, Oswald the Lucky Rabbit, from NBCUniversal. In 2007, Iger commissioned two new 340-meter ships for the Disney Cruise Line that would double its fleet size from two ships to four. The new ships were 40 percent larger than Disney's two older vessels and entered service in 2011 and 2012. Iger also engineered the acquisition of Marvel Entertainment in 2009, which would enable the Disney production of motion pictures featuring Marvel comic book characters such as Iron Man, Incredible Hulk, Thor, Spider-Man, and Captain America. All of the movies produced by Disney's Marvel unit performed exceptionally well at the box office, with *The Avengers,* which was released in May 2012, recording worldwide box office receipts of more than $1 billion. Disney's Miramax film production company and Dimension film assets were divested by Iger in 2010 for $663 million. A financial summary for The Walt Disney Company for 2007 through 2013 is provided in Exhibit 1. Exhibit 2 tracks the performance of The Walt Disney Company's common shares between June 2004 and June 2014.

## THE WALT DISNEY COMPANY'S CORPORATE STRATEGY AND BUSINESS OPERATIONS IN 2014

In 2014, The Walt Disney Company was broadly diversified into theme parks, hotels and resorts, cruise ships, cable networks, broadcast television

**EXHIBIT 1**    Financial Summary for The Walt Disney Company, Fiscal 2007–Fiscal 2013 (in millions, except per share data)

| | 2013 | 2012 | 2011[1] | 2010[2] | 2009[3] | 2008[4] | 2007[5] |
|---|---|---|---|---|---|---|---|
| **Revenues** | $45,041 | $42,278 | $40,893 | $38,063 | $36,149 | $37,843 | $35,510 |
| Income from continuing operations | 6,636 | 6,173 | 5,258 | 4,313 | 3,609 | 4,729 | 4,851 |
| Income from continuing operations attributable to Disney | 6,136 | 5,682 | 4,807 | 3,963 | 3,307 | 4,427 | 4,674 |
| Per common share | | | | | | | |
| Earnings from continuing operations attributable to Disney: | | | | | | | |
| Diluted | $3.38 | $3.13 | $2.52 | $2.03 | $1.76 | $2.28 | $2.24 |
| Basic | 3.42 | 3.17 | 2.56 | 2.07 | 1.78 | 2.34 | 2.33 |
| Dividends | 0.75 | 0.60 | 0.40 | 0.35 | 0.35 | 0.35 | 0.31 |
| **Balance sheets** | | | | | | | |
| Total assets | $81,241 | $74,898 | $72,124 | $69,206 | $63,117 | $62,497 | $60,928 |
| Long-term obligations | 17,337 | 17,876 | 17,717 | 16,234 | 16,939 | 14,889 | 14,916 |
| Disney shareholders' equity | 45,429 | 39,759 | 37,385 | 37,519 | 33,734 | 32,323 | 30,753 |
| **Statements of cash flows** | | | | | | | |
| Cash provided by operations | $9,452 | $7,966 | $6,994 | $6,578 | $5,319 | $5,685 | $5,519 |
| Investing activities: | | | | | | | |
| Investments in parks, resorts, and other property | (2,796) | (3,784) | (3,559) | (2,110) | (1,753) | (1,578) | (1,566) |
| Proceeds from dispositions | 397 | 15 | 564 | 170 | 185 | 14 | 1,530 |
| Acquisitions | (2,443) | (1,088) | (184) | (2,493) | (176) | (660) | (608) |
| Financing activities: | | | | | | | |
| Dividends | (1,324) | (1,076) | (756) | (653) | (648) | (664) | (637) |
| Repurchases of common stock | (4,087) | (3,015) | (4,993) | (2,669) | (138) | (4,453) | (6,923) |
| Supplemental cash flow information: | | | | | | | |
| Interest paid | 235 | 369 | 377 | 393 | 485 | 555 | 551 |
| Income taxes paid | (2,531) | (2,630) | 2,341 | 2,170 | 1,609 | 2,768 | 2,796 |

[1] The fiscal 2011 results include restructuring and impairment charges that rounded to $0.00 per diluted share and gains on the sales of Miramax and BASS ($0.02 per diluted share), which collectively resulted in a net adverse impact of $0.02 per diluted share.

[2] During fiscal 2010, the company completed a cash and stock acquisition for the outstanding capital stock of Marvel for $4.2 billion. In addition, results include restructuring and impairment charges ($0.09 per diluted share), gains on the sales of investments in two television services in Europe ($0.02 per diluted share), a gain on the sale of the Power Rangers property ($0.01 per diluted share), and an accounting gain related to the acquisition of The Disney Store Japan ($0.01 per diluted share). Including the impact of rounding, these items collectively resulted in a net adverse impact of $0.04 per diluted share.

[3] The fiscal 2009 results include restructuring and impairment charges ($0.17 per diluted share), a noncash gain in connection with the AETN-Lifetime merger ($0.08 per diluted share), and a gain on the sale of the company's investment in two pay-television services in Latin America ($0.04 per diluted share). Including the impact of rounding, these items collectively resulted in a net adverse impact of $0.06 per diluted share.

[4] The fiscal 2008 results include an accounting gain related to the acquisition of Disney Stores North America and a gain on the sale of movies.com (together, $0.01 per diluted share), the favorable resolution of certain income tax matters ($0.03 per diluted share), a bad-debt charge for a receivable from Lehman Brothers ($0.03 per diluted share), and an impairment charge ($0.01 per diluted share). These items collectively had no net impact on earnings per share.

[5] During fiscal 2007, the company concluded the spin-off of the ABC Radio business and thus reported ABC Radio as discontinued operations for all periods presented.

   The fiscal 2007 results include gains from the sales of E! Entertainment and Us Weekly (together $0.31 per diluted share), the favorable resolution of certain income tax matters ($0.03 per diluted share), an equity-based compensation plan modification charge ($0.01 per diluted share), and an impairment charge ($0.01 per diluted share). These items collectively resulted in a net benefit of $0.32 per diluted share.

*Source:* The Walt Disney Company 10-K reports, 2008 and 2013.

**EXHIBIT 2**   Performance of The Walt Disney Company's Stock Price, June 2004–June 2014

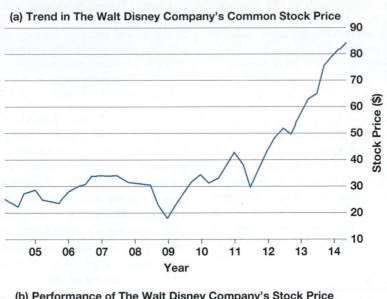

(a) Trend in The Walt Disney Company's Common Stock Price

(b) Performance of The Walt Disney Company's Stock Price versus the S&P 500 Index

networks, television production, television station operations, live-action and animated motion picture production and distribution, music publishing, live theatrical productions, children's book publishing, interactive media, and consumer products retailing. The company's corporate strategy was centered on (1) creating high-quality family content, (2) exploiting technological innovations to make entertainment experiences more memorable, and (3) expanding internationally. The company's 2006 acquisition of Pixar and 2009 acquisition of Marvel were executed to enhance the resources and capabilities of its core animation business with the addition of new animation skills and characters. The company's 2010 acquisition of Playdom gave it new online gaming capabilities, and its 2011 acquisition of UTV was engineered to facilitate its international expansion efforts. When asked about the company's recent acquisitions during a media, cable, and telecommunications conference in May 2012, Disney chief financial officer Jay Rasulo made the following comments:[2]

Our acquisition strategy is pretty clear. Either we are buying IP that is under-exploited, underused by the owners . . . or we're buying capabilities to reach consumers in new places or in new ways.

Marvel, like Pixar, was primarily an IP acquisition. We knew there was buried treasure there. The company was doing well to exploit it, but it was doing it largely through third parties.

We decided to make our big play on Avengers. . . . It's done $1.3 billion as of today in the worldwide box office. Hasn't even opened in Japan yet. So it's definitely still got some running room. And in addition to the box office, it's hitting in consumer products. There's a social game. It's just exactly what we envisioned when we purchased [Marvel].

If you look at the other end of the spectrum . . . Playdom did not own a lot of IP but had a capability in social gaming that we simply did not have. Certainly we could have built it, but it would have taken a long time. Social gaming, as you all know, was taking off and continues to rise like a rocket. And we wanted to jumpstart ourselves into that space, so we bought that company with the idea of using both IP we had and the creation of new IP to get into the social space.

UTV . . . is sort of a geographic. We want to grow in India. We want to grow in China. We want to grow in Russia and in Turkey, the big four and the ten after. But you need an entry strategy. And with UTV, we became the largest studio, an owner of nine television networks, and a bigger and more grounded distribution network for the Disney IP than we have in that market. Our ambition in India is clear. We want to be the family brand of India.

Disney's corporate strategy called for sufficient capital to be allocated to its core theme parks and resorts business to sustain its advantage in the industry. The company expanded the range of attractions at its Disney California Adventure park with the addition of the $75 million World of Color water and light show in 2010 and the $200 million Radiator Springs outdoor race track in Cars Land in 2012. During an investors' conference in May 2012, Iger, Disney's chairman and CEO, discussed the company's approach to allocating financial resources:[3]

Well, first of all, it begins with an overall evaluation of how we deploy capital across the company. So, if the theme park group comes to us with a proposal to renovate Fantasyland in Florida, we obviously look at it in a very discrete fashion, meaning what are the likely returns on that specific capital investment. But we look at it against the whole capital expenditure needs of the company over a given year, or over a given period of time.

So, if you look back in the seven years since I've been CEO, we've actually deployed capital in multiple ways. We've just increased our dividend. We've purchased a fair amount of our stock. We have now 103 Disney Channels worldwide, which took capital to do that. And, of course, we've invested more in our parks and resorts, which includes our theme parks.

Once we decide what kind of capital we believe we might be willing to invest over a period of time as a company, we take a very, very hard look at the specific opportunity or the specific request.

The Walt Disney Company's corporate strategy attempted to capture synergies existing among its business units. Two of the company's highest-grossing films, *Pirates of the Caribbean: On Stranger Tides* and *Cars 2,* were featured at the company's Florida and California theme parks. Disney had also made much of its content available digitally, including its WatchESPN services for Internet, smartphone, and tablet computer users; its growing list of Disney Publishing e-book offerings; and family content available through its Disney.com/YouTube partnership.

Disney's international expansion efforts were largely directed at exploiting opportunities in emerging markets. In 2012, the Disney Channel reached 75 percent of viewers in China and Russia and was available in more than 100 countries, compared to 19 countries in 2002. Disney opened a Toy Story Land attraction at Hong Kong Disneyland in 2011 and had two more lands planned for the Hong Kong resort. The company was also developing the Shanghai Disney Resort, which would include two themed hotels, attractions, and the largest interactive Magic Kingdom–style castle built at any Disney park. During the May 2012 investors' conference, Iger made the following comments about the company's international strategy:[4]

When we talk about growing internationally for instance, we know that we've had opportunities to invest in that business to, essentially, increase our footprint internationally. So the opening of Hong Kong Disneyland in 2005 and the expansion of Hong Kong Disneyland that's already underway—in fact, we're opening three new lands. One's already open, one is opening this summer, and then there's a third to come later in the year.

And then, of course, Shanghai Disneyland—and that's one where I think is probably the best opportunity the company's had since Walt Disney bought land in central Florida in the 1960s. This is a

7.5-square-kilometer piece of land sitting in Pudong, right in the heart of Shanghai. 330 million live within three hours commuting distance to this park. We stood on a tower overlooking a cleared piece of property recently. I couldn't believe its size. But I'm certain that it will fulfill its potential in what is the world's most populous country in the world.

In 2014, the company's business units were organized into five divisions: media networks, parks and resorts, studio entertainment, consumer products, and interactive media.

## Media Networks

The Walt Disney Company's media networks business unit included its domestic and international cable networks, the ABC television network, television production, and U.S. domestic television stations. The company's television production was limited to television programming for ABC, and its eight local television stations were all ABC affiliates. Six of Disney's eight domestic television stations were located in the 10 largest U.S. television markets. In all, ABC had 238 affiliates in the United States. When asked about Disney's ABC-related businesses, Iger suggested that the businesses made positive contributions to the company's overall performance:[5]

> The television studio, ABC, the network, and the eight stations that we own are a nicely profitable business for us and should continue to be nicely profitable. One of the reasons they're profitable is that, by using the studio and the network to support the creation of pretty high-quality, intellectual property or filmed entertainment, we've taken advantage of what has been a real growth market globally in the consumption of American-based filmed entertainment. We think we have distinctive, local news brands. Our stations tend to be—most of them are number one in the market. If they're not number one, they're number two. And they tend to rely on a very strong local news brand.

Exhibit 3 provides the market ranking for Disney's local stations and its number of subscribers and ownership percentage of its cable networks. The exhibit also provides a brief description of its ABC broadcasting and television production operations. The media networks division also included Radio Disney, which aired family-oriented radio programming on 34 terrestrial radio stations (31 of which were owned by Disney) in the United States. Radio Disney was also available on SiriusXM satellite radio, iTunes Radio Tuner and Music Store, XM/DirecTV, and mobile phones. In addition, Radio Disney was broadcast throughout most of South America on Spanish-language terrestrial radio stations. The company's 2011 acquisition of UTV would expand the division's television broadcasting and production capabilities to India.

Among the most significant challenges to Disney's media networks division was the competition for viewers, which impacted advertising rates and revenues. Not only did the company compete against other broadcasters and cable networks for viewers, but it also competed against other types of entertainment that consumers might enjoy. For example, consumers might prefer to watch DVD, play video games, or browse the Internet rather than watch television. The effect of the Internet on broadcast news had been significant, and the growth of streaming services had the potential to affect the advertising revenue potential of all of Disney's media businesses. However, Iger believed that technology provided great opportunities for Disney:[6]

> It's no longer just a television market . . . it's a media world. And it's rich. And it's no longer just in the home; it's everywhere. It's in school, in your car, walking down the street. You name it, you can consume media. And it's not just filmed entertainment, it's casual games and surfing websites and social networking.
>
> We're launching a TV everywhere app for the Disney Channel. This is like the WatchESPN app that we launched a while back, an app that will enable kids or anyone, for that matter, to watch the Disney Channel and its programs on a mobile device using our app, provided they are subscribers of a multi-channel service. . . . And I know that the adoption rate for the ESPN app has been great. It's a fantastic product. And, we're going to launch . . . ABC, ABC Family, and so on.

In summarizing his thoughts about the opportunities for Disney's media programming, Iger concluded:[7]

> We believe that high-quality, branded entertainment is going to continue to deliver real value to our shareholders, not just the value that we've delivered in the past but growth in a world that enables more and more distribution of that product and more consumption of it. Every one of our brands is in high demand by any new platform. You can't launch a platform today without some good content on it, and we're very well-positioned, probably better than anybody in the business, in that regard.

**EXHIBIT 3**    The Walt Disney Company's Media Networks, 2013

| Cable Networks | | |
|---|---|---|
| | Estimated Subscribers (millions)[1] | Ownership (%) |
| **ESPN**[2] | | |
| ESPN | 99 | 80.0 |
| ESPN2 | 99 | 80.0 |
| ESPNEWS | 73 | 80.0 |
| ESPN Classic | 33 | 80.0 |
| ESPNU | 72 | 80.0 |
| **Disney Channels Worldwide** | | |
| Disney Channel, domestic | 99 | 100.0 |
| Disney Channels, international[3] | 141 | 100.0 |
| Disney Junior[3] | 58 | 100.0 |
| Disney XD, domestic | 78 | 100.0 |
| Disney XD, international[3] | 91 | 100.0 |
| **ABC Family** | 98 | 100.0 |
| **SOAPnet** | 74 | 100.0 |
| **A&E/Lifetime** | | |
| A&E[2] | 99 | 42.1 |
| Lifetime Television | 99 | 42.1 |
| HISTORY | 99 | 42.1 |
| Lifetime Movie Network | 82 | 42.1 |
| The Biography Channel | 65 | 42.1 |
| History International | 64 | 42.1 |
| Lifetime Real Women[3] | 18 | 42.1 |
| **Broadcasting** | | |
| ABC Television Network (238 local affiliates reaching 99% of U.S. television households) | | |
| **Television Production** | | |
| ABC Studios and ABC Media Productions (daytime, prime-time, late-night, and news television programming) | | |

| Domestic Television Stations | | |
|---|---|---|
| Market | TV Station | Television Market Ranking[4] |
| New York, NY | WABC-TV | 1 |
| Los Angeles, CA | KABC-TV | 2 |
| Chicago, IL | WLS-TV | 3 |
| Philadelphia, PA | WPVI-TV | 4 |
| San Francisco, CA | KGO-TV | 6 |
| Houston, TX | KTRK-TV | 10 |
| Raleigh-Durham, NC | WTVD-TV | 24 |
| Fresno, CA | KFSN-TV | 55 |

[1] Estimated U.S. subscriber counts according to Nielsen Media Research as of September 2011.
[2] ESPN and A&E programming is distributed internationally through other networks.
[3] Subscriber counts are not rated by Nielsen and are based on an internal management report.
[4] Based on Nielsen Media Research, "U.S. Television Household Estimates," January 1, 2011.

*Source:* The Walt Disney Company 10-K report, 2013.

Operating results for Disney's media networks division for fiscal 2009 through fiscal 2013 are presented in Exhibit 4.

## Parks and Resorts

The Walt Disney Company's parks and resorts division included the Walt Disney World Resort in Orlando, the Disneyland Resort in California, the Aulani Disney Resort and Spa in Hawaii, the Disney Vacation Club, and the Disney Cruise Line. The company also owned a 51 percent interest in Disneyland Paris, a 47 percent interest in the Hong Kong Disneyland Resort, and a 43 percent interest in the Shanghai Disney Resort. Disney also licensed the operation of the Tokyo Disney Resort in Japan. Revenue for the division was primarily generated through park admission fees, hotel room charges, merchandise sales, food and beverage sales, sales and rentals of vacation club properties, and fees charged for cruise vacations.

Revenues from hotel lodgings and food and beverage sales were a sizable portion of the division's revenues. For example, at the 25,000-acre Walt Disney World Resort alone, the company operated 17 resort hotels with approximately 22,000 rooms. An 18th hotel with 2,000 rooms was added in 2012. The resort also included the 120-acre Downtown Disney retail, dining, and entertainment complex, where visitors could dine and shop during or after park hours. In addition, the Walt Disney World Resort in Orlando included four championship golf courses, full-service spas, tennis, sailing, water skiing, two water parks, and a 220-acre sports complex that was host to over 200 amateur and professional events each year.

Walt Disney's 461-acre resort in California included two theme parks—Disneyland and Disney California Adventure—along with three hotels and its Downtown Disney retail, dining, and entertainment complex. Disney California Adventure was opened in 2001 adjacent to the Disneyland property and included four lands—Golden State, Hollywood Pictures Backlot, Paradise Pier, and Bug's Land. The park was initially built to alleviate overcrowding at Disneyland and was expanded with the addition of World of Color in 2010 and Cars Land in 2012 to strengthen its appeal with guests. Rasulo discussed the history and shortcomings of Disney California Adventure in 2012:[8]

> We were starting to see rejection from Disneyland because it was simply too crowded every day. And we built [Disney California Adventure] both to expand the resort in terms of its offering, but also to pull people away from Disneyland.
>
> Well, the concept wasn't strong enough. It didn't have a great nighttime appeal, so the stays over there were very short, and the people would come back to Disneyland in the evening and accentuate the problem. Now you will see a totally renewed park with a real strong concept called Cars Land, built around the movie *Cars*. It's 12 acres. It's compelling. It's one of the biggest attractions we've ever done with a land around it. And we've already seen World of Color increase attendance at the resort.

## EXHIBIT 4 Operating Results for Walt Disney's Media Networks Business Unit, Fiscal 2009–Fiscal 2013 (in millions)

| | 2013 | 2012 | 2011 | 2010 | 2009 |
|---|---|---|---|---|---|
| Revenues: | | | | | |
| Affiliate fees | $10,018 | $ 9,360 | $ 8,790 | $ 8,082 | $ 7,407 |
| Advertising | 7,923 | 7,699 | 7,598 | 7,028 | 6,566 |
| Other | 2,415 | 2,377 | 2,326 | 2,052 | 2,236 |
| Total revenues | 20,356 | 19,436 | 18,714 | 17,162 | 16,209 |
| Operating expenses | 11,261 | 10,535 | 10,376 | 9,888 | 9,464 |
| Selling, general, administrative, and other | 2,768 | 2,651 | 2,539 | 2,358 | 2,341 |
| Depreciation and amortization | 251 | 258 | 237 | 222 | 206 |
| Equity in the income of investees | (742) | (627) | (584) | (438) | (567) |
| Operating Income | $ 6,818 | $ 6,619 | $ 6,146 | $ 5,132 | $ 4,765 |

*Source:* The Walt Disney Company 10-K report, 2013 and 2011.

Disney held a 51 percent ownership stake in Disneyland Paris and its seven hotels; convention center; shopping, dining, and entertainment complex; and 27-hole golf facility. The company had a 47 percent ownership interest in the Hong Kong Disneyland Resort, which included two hotels. A staged expansion of Hong Kong Disneyland that included three new lands—Toy Story Land, Grizzly Gulch, and Mystic Point—was expected to be completed by 2013. Disney received royalties from the operation of the Tokyo Disney Resort, which was owned and operated by the Oriental Land Company, a Japanese corporation in which Disney had no ownership interest. Disney would later have a 43 percent ownership interest in the Shanghai Disney Resort, a $4.5 billion project that would include Shanghai Disneyland; two theme hotels; a retail, dining, and entertainment complex; and an outdoor recreation area. The resort in China was expected to open in 2016.

The company also offered timeshare sales and rentals in 11 resort facilities through its Disney Vacation Club. The Disney Cruise Line operated ships out of Port Canaveral, Florida, and Los Angeles. Disney's cruise activities were developed to appeal to the interests of children and families. Its Port Canaveral cruises included a visit to Disney's Castaway Cay, a 1,000-acre private island in the Bahamas. The popularity of Disney's cruise vacations allowed its original two-ship fleet to be booked to full capacity year-round. While addressing investors in May 2012, Iger commented on the business's strong performance:[9]

The cruise ships [were] a solid business in that we had mid-teen returns on invested capital in two legacy ships that had been built in the 1990s. We believe that we had a quality product, that there was definitely room for us to add capacity, and that the market was there for us to expand in it. And we built two ships, the Dream, which launched in early 2011, and the Fantasy, which launched a couple of months ago. Again, a very specific look at return on invested capital for the two new ships. Interestingly enough, our four ships are about 90% booked for the year. The Dream, which we sailed, as I mentioned, in early 2011, was accretive, bottom line, the first full quarter of operation. The same thing will be true for the Fantasy. And it's just an incredible, high-quality product.

The division's operating results for fiscal 2009 through fiscal 2013 are presented in Exhibit 5.

## Studio Entertainment

The Walt Disney Company's studio entertainment division produced live-action and animated motion pictures, pay-per-view and DVD home entertainment, musical recordings, and *Disney on Ice* and *Disney Live!* live performances. The division's motion pictures were produced and distributed under the Walt Disney Pictures, Pixar, and Marvel banners. The division also distributed motion pictures under the Touchstone Pictures banner. Iger summarized the division's strategy in the following comments:[10]

The strategy for our motion picture group, or our studio, is very clear. We are likely to make two animated films a year, a Pixar and a Disney. There will be some times over the next five years that you could see two Pixar

---

**EXHIBIT 5**   Operating Results for Walt Disney's Parks and Resorts Business Unit, Fiscal 2009–Fiscal 2013 (in millions)

| | 2013 | 2012 | 2011 | 2010 | 2009 |
|---|---|---|---|---|---|
| Revenues | | | | | |
| Domestic | $11,394 | $10,339 | $9,302 | $8,404 | $8,442 |
| International | 2,693 | 2,581 | 2,495 | 2,357 | 2,225 |
| Total revenues | 14,087 | 12,920 | 11,797 | 10,761 | 10,667 |
| Operating expenses | 8,537 | 7,928 | 7,383 | 6,787 | 6,634 |
| Selling, general, administrative, and other | 1,960 | 1,849 | 1,696 | 1,517 | 1,467 |
| Depreciation and amortization | 1,370 | 1,241 | 1,165 | 1,139 | 1,148 |
| Operating Income | $2,220 | $ 1,902 | $1,553 | $1,318 | $1,418 |

*Source:* The Walt Disney Company 10-K report, 2013 and 2011.

films in one year and a Disney. But, basically, you're looking at two a year. We intend to make, probably, two Marvel films a year going forward, and that slate is pretty defined over the next three to four years. And then, somewhere in the neighborhood of six to eight, probably closer to six, Disney-branded live action films. . . . We're not in the business of making 20 films a year or more than that. We are only in the business of making those branded films—Disney, Pixar, and Marvel. We believe that our returns on investment in those branded movies are likely to be better than the overall industry. And, when we have success with a Disney, Pixar, or a Marvel film, we can leverage it much more broadly and deeply and for a longer period of time than we can in any other film that we might make.

Most motion pictures typically incurred losses during the theatrical distribution of a film because of production costs and the cost of extensive advertising campaigns accompanying the launch of the film. Profits for many films did not occur until the movie became available on DVD or Blu-ray discs for home entertainment, which usually began three to six months after the film's theatrical release. Revenue was also generated when a movie moved to pay-per-view (PPV) or video-on-demand (VOD) two months after the release of the DVD and when the motion picture became available on subscription premium cable channels, such as HBO, about 16 months after PPV or VOD availability. Broadcast networks such as ABC could purchase telecast rights to movies later, as could basic cable channels such as Lifetime, Hallmark Channel, and ABC Family.

Premium cable channels such as Showtime and Starz might also purchase telecast rights to movies long after their theatrical release. Telecast-right fees decreased as the length of time from initial release increased. Also, the decline in DVD sales and rentals had affected industry revenues as motion pictures moved to lower-revenue-generating telecasts more quickly. Operating results for The Walt Disney Company's studio entertainment division for fiscal 2009 through fiscal 2013 are shown in Exhibit 6.

## Consumer Products

The company's consumer products division included the company's Disney Store retail chain and businesses specializing in merchandise licensing and children's book and magazine publishing. In 2011, the company owned and operated 208 Disney Stores in North America, 103 stores in Europe, and 46 stores in Japan. Its publishing business included comic books, various children's book and magazine titles available in print and e-book format, and smartphone and tablet computer apps designed for children. The company's best-selling apps in 2011 were Disney Princess Dress-Up and Cars 2. Licensing revenues were generated from the use of Disney's portfolio of characters by manufacturers of toys, apparel, home decor, stationery, footwear, and consumer electronics. In 2011, Disney was the largest licensor of character-based merchandise in the world. The division's sales were primarily affected by seasonal shopping trends and changes

**EXHIBIT 6**    Operating Results for Walt Disney's Studio Entertainment Business Unit, Fiscal 2009–Fiscal 2013 (in millions)

|  | 2013 | 2012 | 2011 | 2010 | 2009 |
|---|---|---|---|---|---|
| Revenues: |  |  |  |  |  |
| Theatrical distribution | $1,870 | $1,470 | $1,733 | $2,050 | $1,325 |
| Home entertainment | 1,750 | 2,221 | 2,435 | 2,666 | 2,762 |
| Television distribution and other | 2,359 | 2,134 | 2,183 | 1,985 | 2,049 |
| Total revenues | 5,979 | 5,825 | 6,351 | 6,701 | 6,136 |
| Operating expenses | 3,012 | 2,908 | 3,136 | 3,469 | 3,210 |
| Selling, general, administrative, and other | 2,145 | 2,053 | 2,465 | 2,450 | 2,687 |
| Depreciation and amortization | 161 | 142 | 132 | 89 | 60 |
| Equity in the income of investees | — | — | — | — | (4) |
| Operating Income | $  661 | $  722 | $  618 | $  693 | $  175 |

*Source:* The Walt Disney Company 10-K report, 2013 and 2011.

in consumer disposable income. An overview of the division's operating results for fiscal 2009 through fiscal 2013 is presented in Exhibit 7.

## Interactive Media

Disney's interactive media business unit produced video games for handheld game devices, game consoles, and smartphone platforms. The division also developed games and other content for Disney.com and Disney's websites for its parks and resorts and studio entertainment divisions. The interactive media division had found it difficult to compete in the highly seasonal video game industry and had suffered losses each year between fiscal 2009 and fiscal 2013. In addition, the division's sales were affected dramatically by the timing of new console releases and the popularity of its game titles. In 2010, the company acquired Playdom, Inc., a company that developed online games for social networking sites, to help speed the company's product development capabilities in that area. In summing up the division's performance and future prospects, CEO Iger stated:[11]

> We have an interactive division that includes games and a number of our Disney-branded websites. We've lost money in that space. The division overall is small when you compare it with the other big divisions of the company and it will continue to be relatively small. We've said that we're targeting 2013 as a year of profitability. It's about time, because we've invested a fair amount. . . . Our goal now and our strategy is to diversify our gaming efforts. Some modest investment on the console front, very Disney-branded and

Marvel-branded, some investment on the mobile front, and investment on the social games front.

In March 2014, Disney laid off about 700 employees from its media units, the majority coming from Playdom. Operating results for Disney's interactive media division for fiscal 2009 through fiscal 2013 are presented in Exhibit 8.

The company's consolidated statements of income for fiscal 2009 through fiscal 2013 are presented in Exhibit 9. The Walt Disney Company's consolidated balance sheets for fiscal 2010 through fiscal 2013 are presented in Exhibit 10.

# THE WALT DISNEY COMPANY'S SECOND QUARTER 2014 PERFORMANCE AND ITS FUTURE PROSPECTS

The Walt Disney Company recorded record earnings per share during its first six months of fiscal 2014, with its media networks division achieving a 17 percent period-over-period increase in operating profit, its parks and resorts division seeing an 18 percent increase in operating profits, its studio entertainment division operating profit increasing by 250 percent, and its consumer electronics operating profit increasing by 29 percent between the first

**EXHIBIT 7**   Operating Results for Walt Disney's Consumer Products Business Unit, Fiscal 2009–Fiscal 2013 (in millions)

|  | 2013 | 2012 | 2011 | 2010 | 2009 |
|---|---|---|---|---|---|
| Revenues: | | | | | |
| Licensing and publishing | $2,254 | $2,056 | $1,933 | $1,725 | $1,584 |
| Retail and other | 1,301 | 1,196 | 1,116 | 953 | 841 |
| Total revenues | 3,555 | 3,252 | 3,049 | 2,678 | 2,425 |
| Operating expenses | 1,566 | 1,514 | 1,334 | 1,236 | 1,182 |
| Selling, general, administrative, and other | 731 | 686 | 794 | 687 | 597 |
| Depreciation and amortization | 146 | 115 | 105 | 78 | 39 |
| Equity in the income of investees | — | — | — | — | 2 |
| Operating Income | $1,112 | $ 937 | $ 816 | $ 677 | $ 609 |

*Source:* The Walt Disney Company 10-K report, 2012 and 2011.

**EXHIBIT 8   Operating Results for Walt Disney's Interactive Media Business Unit, Fiscal 2009–Fiscal 2013 (in millions)**

|  | 2013 | 2012 | 2011 | 2010 | 2009 |
|---|---|---|---|---|---|
| Revenues: | | | | | |
| Game sales and subscriptions | $ 798 | $ 613 | $ 768 | $ 563 | $ 565 |
| Advertising and other | 266 | 232 | 214 | 198 | 147 |
| Total revenues | 1,064 | 845 | 982 | 761 | 712 |
| Operating expenses | 658 | 583 | 732 | 581 | 623 |
| Selling, general, administrative, and other | 449 | 429 | 504 | 371 | 336 |
| Depreciation and amortization | 44 | 49 | 54 | 43 | 50 |
| Equity in the income of investees | — | — | — | — | 2 |
| Operating loss | $ (87) | $(216) | $(308) | $(234) | $(295) |

*Source:* The Walt Disney Company 10-K report, 2011, and company report, 2014.

six months of 2013 and the same period in 2014. Disney's interactive division earned a $69 million profit for the six months ending March 29, 2014, compared to a $45 million loss during the same period in 2013.

Chairman Iger summarized Disney's strong second-quarter performance and the company's position at mid-2014:

We're extremely pleased with our performance in Q2, with revenues up 10%, net income up 27%, and adjusted

**EXHIBIT 9   Consolidated Statements of Income for The Walt Disney Company, Fiscal 2009–Fiscal 2013 (in millions, except per share data)**

|  | 2013 | 2012 | 2011 | 2010 | 2009 |
|---|---|---|---|---|---|
| Revenues | $45,041 | $42,278 | $40,893 | $ 38,063 | $36,149 |
| Costs and expenses | 35,591 | 33,415 | 33,112 | 31,337 | 30,452 |
| Restructuring and impairment charges | 214 | 100 | 55 | 270 | 492 |
| Add: Other income | 69 | 239 | 75 | 140 | 342 |
| Net interest expense | 235 | 369 | 343 | 409 | 466 |
| Add: Equity in the income of investees | 688 | 627 | 585 | 440 | 577 |
| Income before income taxes | 9,620 | 9,260 | 8,043 | 6,627 | 5,658 |
| Income taxes | 2,984 | 3,087 | 2,785 | 2,314 | 2,049 |
| Net income | 6,636 | 6,173 | 5,258 | 4,313 | 3,609 |
| Less: Net income attributable to noncontrolling interests | 500 | 491 | 451 | 350 | 302 |
| Net income attributable to The Walt Disney Company (Disney) | $ 6,136 | $ 5,682 | $ 4,807 | $ 3,963 | $ 3,307 |
| Earnings per share attributable to Disney: | | | | | |
| Diluted | $3.38 | $3.13 | $2.52 | $2.03 | $1.76 |
| Basic | $3.42 | $3.17 | $2.56 | $2.07 | $1.78 |
| Weighted-average number of common and common equivalent shares outstanding: | | | | | |
| Diluted | 1,813 | 1,818 | 1,909 | 1,948 | 1,875 |
| Basic | 1,792 | 1,794 | 1,878 | 1,915 | 1,856 |

*Source:* The Walt Disney Company 10-K report, 2011, and company report, 2014.

**EXHIBIT 10**   Consolidated Balance Sheets for The Walt Disney Company, Fiscal 2010–Fiscal 2013 (in millions, except per share data)

| | Fiscal Year Ended | | | |
|---|---|---|---|---|
| | September 28, 2013 | September 29, 2012 | October 1, 2011 | October 2, 2010 |
| **Assets** | | | | |
| Current assets | | | | |
| Cash and cash equivalents | $ 3,931 | $ 3,387 | $ 3,185 | $ 2,722 |
| Receivables | 6,967 | 6,540 | 6,182 | 5,784 |
| Inventories | 1,487 | 1,537 | 1,595 | 1,442 |
| Television costs | 634 | 676 | 674 | 678 |
| Deferred income taxes | 485 | 765 | 1,487 | 1,018 |
| Other current assets | 605 | 804 | 634 | 581 |
| Total current assets | 14,109 | 13,709 | 13,757 | 12,225 |
| Film and television costs | 4,783 | 4,541 | 4,357 | 4,773 |
| Investments | 2,849 | 2,723 | 2,435 | 2,513 |
| Parks, resorts and other property, at cost: | | | | |
| Attractions, buildings and equipment | 41,192 | 38,582 | 35,515 | 32,875 |
| Accumulated depreciation | (22,459) | (20,687) | (19,572) | (18,373) |
| | 18,733 | 17,895 | 15,943 | 14,502 |
| Projects in progress | 2,476 | 2,453 | 2,625 | 2,180 |
| Land | 1,171 | 1,164 | 1,127 | 1,124 |
| | 22,380 | 21,512 | 19,695 | 17,806 |
| Intangible assets, net | 7,370 | 5,015 | 5,121 | 5,081 |
| Goodwill | 27,324 | 25,110 | 24,145 | 24,100 |
| Other assets | 2,426 | 2,288 | 2,614 | 2,708 |
| Total assets | $81,241 | $ 74,898 | $ 72,124 | $69,206 |
| **Liabilities and equity** | | | | |
| Current liabilities | | | | |
| Accounts payable and other accrued liabilities | $ 6,803 | $ 6,393 | $ 6,362 | $ 6,109 |
| Current portion of borrowings | 1,512 | 3,614 | 3,055 | 2,350 |
| Unearned royalties and other advances | 3,389 | 2,806 | 2,671 | 2,541 |
| Total current liabilities | 11,704 | 12,813 | 12,088 | 11,000 |
| Borrowings | 12,776 | 10,697 | 10,922 | 10,130 |
| Deferred income taxes | 4,050 | 2,251 | 2,866 | 2,630 |
| Other long-term liabilities | 4,561 | 7,179 | 6,795 | 6,104 |
| Authorized—100 million shares; Issued—none | — | — | — | — |
| Authorized—4.6 billion shares; Issued—2.7 billion shares | 33,440 | 31,731 | 30,296 | 28,736 |
| Retained earnings | 47,758 | 42,965 | 38,375 | 34,327 |
| Accumulated other comprehensive loss | (1,187) | (3,266) | (2,630) | (1,881) |
| | 80,011 | 71,430 | 66,041 | 61,182 |
| Treasury stock, at cost, 937.8 million shares at October 1, 2011, and 803.1 million shares at October 2, 2010 | (34,582) | (31,671) | (28,656) | (23,663) |
| Total Disney shareholders' equity | 45,429 | 39,759 | 37,385 | 37,519 |
| Noncontrolling interests | 2,721 | 2,199 | 2,068 | 1,823 |
| Total equity | 48,150 | 41,958 | 39,453 | 39,342 |
| Total liabilities and equity | $81,241 | $74,898 | $72,214 | $69,206 |

*Source:* The Walt Disney Company 10-K report, 2013 and 2011.

EPS up 41% to $1.11—the highest in the history of our company. And, once again, all of our business segments achieved double-digit increases, or more, in operating income. Our continued strong performance reflects the strength of our brands and the quality of our content, the extraordinary creative success we're having, and our unique ability to leverage it across the entire company. The unprecedented global success of Disney Animation's phenomenal *Frozen* continues—and it's now the world's highest-grossing animated film of all time and the best-selling title ever released on Blu-Ray and digital. The demand for Frozen merchandise remains extremely high, and the soundtrack was the #1 album in the U.S. again last week. And, as previously announced, Frozen is headed to Broadway.

The *Winter Soldier* has far surpassed the first Captain America in total global box office, which obviously bodes well for our Avengers franchise. We've had enormous success releasing Marvel movies on the first weekend of May—including the two biggest domestic openings of all time—and we'll continue this tradition with *The Avengers*: Age of Ultron next year and *Captain America* 3 in 2016. *Avengers*: Age of Ultron is currently shooting, and early footage looks great. This August 1st, we're looking forward to introducing the world to more fantastic Marvel storytelling with a great cast of new characters in *Guardians of the Galaxy*, which we screened last week—and we believe it has strong franchise potential.

Also on the Marvel front, we just announced that Disney Interactive's Infinity 2 will feature The Avengers, as well as their Marvel and Disney characters, when it's released in the fall. Since the first version of the game launched last August, more than three million Disney Infinity starter packs have been sold, and it was the best-selling interactive gaming toy of 2013 in the U.S. And we made some other news last week, when we announced the cast for *Star Wars*: Episode VII, which includes some very familiar faces as well as some exciting new talent, and the reaction has been tremendous. I was at Pinewood Studios with J.J. Abrams a couple of weeks ago and left more confident than ever that Episode VII will be the extraordinary movie Star Wars fans have been waiting for.

Our Parks and Resorts had another record quarter and we've completed the roll out of MyMagic+ to all guests, which Jay will get into in a few minutes. Guest reaction has been very positive and we believe the new program is delivering nicely on its promise of improving guest experience. Internationally, Hong Kong Disneyland set new attendance and occupancy records in Q2, and construction on Shanghai Disney Resort continues to go well. There are an estimated 330 million potential guests within a three-hour travel radius of our Shanghai resort, and by the time we open the gates in late 2015, China's travel market is expected to be 34% bigger than it was in 2012. And the number of upper middle-class and affluent households is expected to grow by 18% a year for most of the next decade. These trends factored into our recent decision with our partners in Shanghai to accelerate expansion with an additional $800 million investment.

Turning to Media Networks, both our Cable and Broadcast businesses had a solid quarter. We showcased the strength and long-term potential of ESPN at our investor day last month. It's an incredible brand that continues to drive tremendous value for us, and we've got a lot of reasons to be excited about what's coming up, including: a great NBA post-season, culminating with the finals on ABC; the World Cup from Brazil; a very promising Monday Night Football schedule; and ESPN's first foray into the NFL post-season. Finally, I'd like to share a few thoughts about our acquisition of the top online video network, Maker Studios. We're excited about entering the short-form video space in a much more assertive manner, to boost the presence of our brands and franchises in this increasingly valuable and fast-growing arena. Maker's production talent and leadership will create exciting new opportunities to drive value from our content and create new content as well.

By any measure, we had great success in Q2—creatively, financially, and strategically. In addition to our unique ability to leverage content across the entire company to create maximum value, our unparalleled portfolio of incredibly strong brands is a clear strategic advantage that we expect will be evident in our results for years to come.

**A new acquisition.** In April 2014, Disney purchased Maker Studios, a producer of online videos, for nearly $1 billion. The purchase price was paid by $500 million in cash and stock and a performance bonus of $450 million. Maker had a staff that was dedicated to creating and producing videos that were distributed via the Internet or mobile platforms. Disney was attracted by Maker Studios' distribution segment, which helped create and promote thousands of videos from users around the world. In announcing the deal, Disney chairman and CEO Iger said:[12]

Short-form online video is growing at an astonishing pace and with Maker Studios, Disney will now be at the center of this dynamic industry with an unmatched combination of advanced technology and programming expertise and capabilities.

Some of Maker's channels, such as *Epic Rap Battles of History,* received tens of millions of hits each, as well as tens of thousands of dollars in advertising money. Maker received a percentage of the advertising dollars.

Maker had 50,000 channels and about 5.5 million page views per month, and it was one of YouTube's largest multichannel networks. Disney's ownership of Maker provided access to thousands of popular YouTube videos and helped the company strike deals with hot creators. Google owned YouTube and received 45 percent of the ad revenue; the remainder was distributed to the content creators and Maker, which received 30 percent. Maker's videos had been earning between $1 and $3 in advertising revenue for every thousand views, and views often numbered in eight figures.

## ENDNOTES

[1] Bob Iger, chairman and chief executive officer of The Walt Disney Company, during the Sanford C. Bernstein Strategic Decisions Conference, May 30, 2012.

[2] Jay Rasulo, senior executive vice president and chief financial officer of The Walt Disney Company, during the Nomura U.S. Media, Cable, and Telecom Summit, May 30, 2012.

[3] Iger, Sanford C. Bernstein Strategic Decisions Conference.

[4] Ibid.

[5] Ibid.

[6] Ibid.

[7] Ibid.

[8] Rasulo, Nomura. U.S. Media, Cable, and Telecom Summit.

[9] Iger, Sanford C. Bernstein Strategic Decisions Conference.

[10] Ibid.

[11] Ibid.

[12] As quoted in Eddie Makuch, "Disney Pays $500M for YouTube Network That Distributes Gaming Content Like PewDiePie, TotalBiscuit," Gamespot.com, March 25, 2014, http://www.gamespot.com/articles/disney-pays-500m-for-youtube-network-that-distributes-gaming-content-like-pewdiepie-totalbiscuit/1100-6418525/.

# Robin Hood

## Joseph Lampel
City University London

It was in the spring of the second year of his insurrection against the High Sheriff of Nottingham that Robin Hood took a walk in Sherwood Forest. As he walked, he pondered the progress of the campaign, the disposition of his forces, the Sheriff's recent moves, and the options that confronted him.

The revolt against the Sheriff had begun as a personal crusade. It erupted out of Robin's conflict with the Sheriff and his administration. However, alone Robin Hood could do little. He therefore sought allies, men with grievances and a deep sense of justice. Later he welcomed all who came, asking few questions and demanding only a willingness to serve. Strength, he believed, lay in numbers.

He spent the first year forging the group into a disciplined band, united in enmity against the Sheriff and willing to live outside the law. The band's organization was simple. Robin ruled supreme, making all important decisions. He delegated specific tasks to his lieutenants. Will Scarlett was in charge of intelligence and scouting. His main job was to shadow the Sheriff and his men, always alert to their next move. He also collected information on the travel plans of rich merchants and tax collectors. Little John kept discipline among the men and saw to it that their archery was at the high peak that their profession demanded. Scarlock took care of the finances, converting loot to cash, paying shares of the take, and finding suitable hiding places for the surplus. Finally, Much the Miller's son had the difficult task of provisioning the ever-increasing band of Merry Men.

The increasing size of the band was a source of satisfaction for Robin, but also a source of concern. The fame of his Merry Men was spreading, and new recruits were pouring in from every corner of England. As the band grew larger, their small bivouac became a major encampment. Between raids the men milled about, talking and playing games. Vigilance was in decline, and discipline was becoming harder to enforce. "Why," Robin reflected, "I don't know half the men I run into these days."

The growing band was also beginning to exceed the food capacity of the forest. Game was becoming scarce, and supplies had to be obtained from outlying villages. The cost of buying food was beginning to drain the band's financial reserves at the very moment when revenues were in decline. Travelers, especially those with the most to lose, were now giving the forest a wide berth. This was costly and inconvenient to them, but it was preferable to having all their goods confiscated.

Robin believed that the time had come for the Merry Men to change their policy of outright confiscation of goods to one of a fixed transit tax. His lieutenants strongly resisted this idea. They were proud of the Merry Men's famous motto: "Rob the rich and give to the poor." "The farmers and the townspeople," they argued, "are our most important allies. How can we tax them, and still hope for their help in our fight against the Sheriff?"

Robin wondered how long the Merry Men could keep to the ways and methods of their early days. The Sheriff was growing stronger and becoming better organized. He now had the money and the men and was beginning to harass the band, probing for its weaknesses. The tide of events was beginning to turn against the Merry Men. Robin felt that the campaign must be decisively concluded before the Sheriff had a chance to deliver a mortal blow. "But how," he wondered, "could this be done?"

Robin had often entertained the possibility of killing the Sheriff, but the chances for this seemed increasingly remote. Besides, killing the Sheriff might satisfy his personal thirst for revenge, but it would not improve the situation. Robin had hoped that the perpetual state of unrest and the Sheriff's failure to collect taxes would lead to his removal from office. Instead, the Sheriff used his political connections to obtain reinforcement. He had powerful friends at court and was well regarded by the regent, Prince John.

Prince John was vicious and volatile. He was consumed by his unpopularity among the people, who wanted the imprisoned King Richard back. He also lived in constant fear of the barons, who had first given him the regency but were now beginning to dispute his claim to the throne. Several of these barons had set out to collect the ransom that would release King Richard the Lionheart from his jail in Austria. Robin was invited to join the conspiracy in return for future amnesty. It was a dangerous proposition. Provincial banditry was one thing, court intrigue another. Prince John had spies everywhere, and he was known for his vindictiveness. If the conspirators' plan failed, the pursuit would be relentless and retributions swift.

The sound of the supper horn startled Robin from his thoughts. There was the smell of roasting venison in the air. Nothing was resolved or settled. Robin headed for camp promising himself that he would give these problems his utmost attention after tomorrow's raid.

# Dilemma at Devil's Den

## Allan R. Cohen
Babson College

## Kim Johnson
Babson College

My name is Susan, and I'm a business student at Mt. Eagle College. Let me tell you about one of my worst experiences. I had a part-time job in the campus snack bar, The Devil's Den. At the time, I was 21 years old and a junior with a concentration in finance. I originally started working at the Den in order to earn some extra spending money. I had been working there for one semester and became upset with some of the happenings. The Den was managed by contract with an external company, College Food Services (CFS). What bothered me was that many employees were allowing their friends to take free food, and the employees themselves were also taking food in large quantities when leaving their shifts. The policy was that employees could eat whatever they liked free of charge while they were working, but it had become common for employees to leave with food and not to be charged for their snacks while off duty as well.

I felt these problems were occurring for several reasons. For example, employee wages were low, there was easy access to the unlocked storage room door, and inventory was poorly controlled. Also, there was weak supervision by the student managers and no written rules or strict guidelines. It seemed that most of the employees were enjoying freebies, and it had been going on for so long that it was taken for granted. The problem got so far out of hand that customers who had seen others do it felt free to do it whether they knew the workers or not. The employees who witnessed this never challenged anyone because, in my opinion, they did not care and they feared the loss of friendship or being frowned upon by others. Apparently, speaking up was more costly to the employees than the loss of money to CFS for the unpaid food items. It seemed obvious to me that

the employees felt too secure in their jobs and did not feel that their jobs were in jeopardy.

The employees involved were those who worked the night shifts and on the weekends. They were students at the college and were under the supervision of another student, who held the position of manager. There were approximately 30 student employees and 6 student managers on the staff. During the day there were no student managers; instead, a full-time manager was employed by CFS to supervise the Den. The employees and student managers were mostly freshmen and sophomores, probably because of the low wages, inconvenient hours (late weeknights and weekends), and the duties of the job itself. Employees were hard to come by; the high rate of employee turnover indicated that the job qualifications and the selection process were minimal.

The student managers were previous employees chosen by other student managers and the full-time CFS day manager on the basis of their ability to work and on their length of employment. They received no further formal training or written rules beyond what they had already learned by working there. The student managers were briefed on how to close the snack bar at night but still did not get the job done properly. They received authority and responsibility

This case was prepared by Kim Johnson under the supervision of Professor Allan R. Cohen, Babson College.
Copyright © 2004 by Babson College and licensed for publication to Harvard Business School Publishing.

over events occurring during their shifts as manager, although they were never actually taught how and when to enforce it! Their increase in pay was small, from a starting pay of just over minimum wage to an additional 15 percent for student managers. Regular employees received an additional nickel for each semester of employment.

Although I only worked seven hours per week, I was in the Den often as a customer and saw the problem frequently. I felt the problem was on a large enough scale that action should have been taken, not only to correct any financial loss that the Den might have experienced but also to help give the student employees a true sense of their responsibilities, the limits of their freedom, respect for rules, and pride in their jobs. The issues at hand bothered my conscience, although I was not directly involved. I felt that the employees and customers were taking advantage of the situation whereby they could "steal" food almost whenever they wanted. I believed that I had been brought up correctly and knew right from wrong, and I felt that the happenings in the Den were wrong. It wasn't fair that CFS paid for others' greediness or urges to show what they could get away with in front of their friends.

I was also bothered by the lack of responsibility of the managers to get the employees to do their work. I had seen the morning employees work very hard trying to do their jobs, in addition to the jobs the closing shift should have done. I assumed the night managers did not care or think about who worked the next day. It bothered me to think that the morning employees were suffering because of careless employees and student managers from the night before.

I had never heard of CFS mentioning any problems or taking any corrective action; therefore, I wasn't sure whether they knew what was going on, or if they were ignoring it. I was speaking to a close friend, Mack, a student manager at the Den, and I mentioned the fact that the frequently unlocked door to the storage room was an easy exit through which I had seen different quantities of unpaid goods taken out. I told him about some specific instances and said that I believed that it happened rather frequently. Nothing was ever said to other employees about this, and the only corrective action was that the door was locked more often, yet the key to the lock was still available upon request to all employees during their shifts.

Another lack of strong corrective action I remembered was when an employee was caught pocketing cash from the register. The student was neither suspended nor threatened with losing his job (nor was the event even mentioned). Instead, he was just told to stay away from the register. I felt that this weak punishment happened not because he was a good worker but because he worked so many hours and it would be difficult to find someone who would work all those hours and remain working for more than a few months. Although a customer reported the incident, I still felt that management should have taken more corrective action.

The attitudes of the student managers seemed to vary. I had noticed that one in particular, Bill, always got the job done. He made a list of each small duty that needed to be done, such as restocking, and he made sure the jobs were divided among the employees and finished before his shift was over. Bill also stared down employees who allowed thefts by their friends or who took freebies themselves; yet I had never heard of an employee being challenged verbally, nor had anyone ever been fired for these actions. My friend Mack was concerned about theft, or so I assumed, because he had taken some action about locking the doors, but he didn't really get after employees to work if they were slacking off.

I didn't think the rest of the student managers were good motivators. I noticed that they did little work themselves and did not show much control over the employees. The student managers allowed their friends to take food for free, thereby setting bad examples for the other workers, and allowed the employees to take what they wanted even when they were not working. I thought their attitudes were shared by most of the other employees: not caring about their jobs or working hard, as long as they got paid and their jobs were not threatened.

I had let the "thefts" continue without mention because I felt that no one else really cared and may even have frowned on me for trying to take action. Management thus far had not reported significant losses to the employees so as to encourage them to watch for theft and prevent it. Management did not threaten employees with job loss, nor did they provide employees with supervision. I felt it was not my place to report the theft to management, because I was just an employee and I would be overstepping the student managers. Also, I was unsure whether management would do anything about it anyway—maybe they did not care. I felt that talking to the student managers or other employees would be useless, because they were either abusing the rules themselves or clearly aware of what was going on and just ignored it. I felt that others may have frowned on me and made it uncomfortable for me to continue working there. This would be very difficult for me, because I wanted to become a student manager the next semester and did not want to create any waves that might have prevented me from doing so. I recognized the student manager position as a chance to gain some managerial and leadership skills, while at the same time adding a great plus to my résumé when I graduated. Besides, as a student manager, I would be in a better position to do something about all the problems at the Den that bothered me so much.

What could I do in the meantime to clear my conscience of the freebies, favors to friends, and employee snacks? What could I do without ruining my chances of becoming a student manager myself someday? I hated just keeping quiet, but I didn't want to make a fool of myself. I was really stuck.

# Southwest Airlines in 2014: Culture, Values, and Operating Practices

## Arthur A. Thompson
The University of Alabama

## John E. Gamble
Texas A&M University–Corpus Christi

In 2014, Southwest Airlines was the market share leader in domestic air travel in the United States; it transported more passengers from U.S. airports to U.S. destinations than any other airline, and it offered more regularly scheduled domestic flights than any other airline. Southwest also had the enviable distinction of being the only major air carrier in the United States that was consistently profitable, having reported a profit every year since 1973.

From humble beginnings as a scrappy underdog with quirky practices that flew mainly to "secondary" airports (rather than high-traffic airports like Chicago O'Hare, Dallas–Fort Worth, and New York's Kennedy airport), Southwest had climbed up through the industry ranks to become a major competitive force in the domestic segment of the U.S. airline industry. It had weathered industry downturns, dramatic increases in the price of jet fuel, cataclysmic falloffs in airline traffic due to terrorist attacks and economy-wide recessions, and fare wars and other attempts by rivals to undercut its business, all the while adding more and more flights to more and more airports. Since 2000, the number of passengers flying Southwest had increased from 72.6 million to 115.4 million, whereas domestic passenger traffic had remained flat or declined at American Airlines, Delta Air Lines, United Airlines, and US Airways—see Exhibit 1.

## COMPANY BACKGROUND

In late 1966, Rollin King, a San Antonio entrepreneur who owned a small commuter air service, marched into Herb Kelleher's law office with a plan to start a low-cost, low-fare airline that would shuttle passengers between San Antonio, Dallas, and Houston.[1] Over the years, King had heard many Texas businessmen complain about the length of time that it took to drive between the three cities and the expense of flying the airlines currently serving these cities. His business concept for the airline was simple: Attract passengers by flying convenient schedules, get passengers to their destination on time, make sure they have a good experience, and charge fares competitive with travel by automobile. Kelleher, skeptical that King's business idea was viable, dug into the possibilities during the next few weeks and concluded a new airline was feasible; he agreed to handle the necessary legal work and also to invest $10,000 of his own funds in the venture.

In 1967, Kelleher filed papers to incorporate the new airline and submitted an application to the Texas Aeronautics Commission for the new company to begin serving Dallas, Houston, and San Antonio.[2] But rival airlines in Texas pulled every string they could to block the new airline from commencing operations, precipitating a contentious four-year parade of legal and regulatory proceedings. Herb Kelleher led the fight on the company's behalf, eventually prevailing in June 1971 after winning two appeals to the Texas Supreme Court and a favorable ruling from the U.S. Supreme Court. Kelleher recalled, "The constant proceedings had gradually come to enrage me. There was no merit to our competitors' legal assertions. They were simply trying to use their superior economic power to squeeze us dry so we would collapse before we ever got into business. I was bound and determined to show that Southwest Airlines was going to survive and was going into operation."[3]

**EXHIBIT 1**   Total Number of Domestic and International Passengers Traveling on Select U.S. Airlines, 2000, 2005, 2010–2013 (in thousands)

| Carrier | Total Number of Enplaned Passengers[1] | | | | | |
|---|---|---|---|---|---|---|
| | 2000 | 2005 | 2010 | 2011 | 2012 | 2013 |
| American Airlines | | | | | | |
| Domestic | 68,319 | 77,297 | 65,774 | 65,253 | 65,027 | 65,070 |
| International | 17,951 | 20,710 | 20,424 | 20,887 | 21,430 | 19,962 |
| Total | 86,270 | 98,007 | 86,198 | 86,140 | 86,457 | 85,032 |
| Delta Air Lines[2] | | | | | | |
| Domestic | 97,965 | 77,581 | 90,141 | 92,864 | 95,641 | 98,590 |
| International | 7,596 | 8,359 | 19,390 | 19,344 | 19,568 | 18,925 |
| Total | 105,561 | 85,940 | 109,531 | 112,208 | 115,209 | 117,515 |
| **Southwest Airlines (domestic only, has no international flights)[3]** | **72,568** | **88,436** | **106,270** | **110,624** | **112,277** | **115,377** |
| **AirTran (Domestic)[3]** | — | — | — | **23,781** | **20,453** | **16,146** |
| **AirTran (International)** | — | — | — | **937** | **1,301** | **1,534** |
| **Southwest Airlines total** | | | | **135,342** | **134,031** | **133,057** |
| United Airlines[4] | | | | | | |
| Domestic | 72,450 | 55,173 | 43,323 | 39,551 | 67,629 | 65,221 |
| International | 10,625 | 10,356 | 9,727 | 10,091 | 23,998 | 22,209 |
| Total | 83,075 | 65,529 | 53,050 | 49,642 | 91,627 | 87,430 |
| US Airways[5] | | | | | | |
| Domestic | 56,667 | 37,040 | 45,180 | 46,208 | 47,481 | 50,037 |
| International | 3,105 | 4,829 | 6,670 | 6,749 | 6,794 | 6,480 |
| Total | 59,772 | 41,869 | 51,850 | 52,957 | 54,275 | 56,517 |

[1]Includes both passengers who paid for tickets and passengers who were traveling on frequent-flyer awards.
[2]Delta Air Lines and Northwest Airlines merged in October 2008; however, combined reporting did not begin until 2010.
[3]Southwest Airlines acquired AirTran in late 2010; by year-end 2014, all AirTran flights were scheduled to be rebranded as Southwest Airlines flights.
[4]United Airlines acquired Continental Airlines in 2010, and the two companies began joint reporting of passenger traffic in 2012. Prior to 2012, traffic count data are for only United flights.
[5]US Airways and America West merged in September 2005, but joint reporting of traffic counts did not begin until 2007; hence, data for 2000 and 2005 do not include America West, whereas the data for 2010–2013 do include the traffic counts of the combined companies. US Airways and American Airlines merged in December 2013 but continued to operate under their separate names through 2014.

*Source:* U.S. Department of Transportation, Bureau of Transportation Statistics, "Air Carrier Statistics," Form T-100.

In January 1971, Lamar Muse was brought in as the CEO to get operations under way. Muse was an aggressive and self-confident airline veteran who knew the business well and who had the entrepreneurial skills to tackle the challenges of building the airline from scratch and then competing head-on with the major carriers. Through private investors and an initial public offering of stock in June 1971, Muse raised $7 million in new capital to purchase planes and equipment and provide cash for startup. Boeing agreed to supply three new 737s from its inventory,

discounting its price from $5 million to $4 million and financing 90 percent of the $12 million deal. Muse was able to recruit a talented senior staff that included a number of veteran executives from other carriers. He particularly sought out people who were innovative, wouldn't shirk from doing things differently or unconventionally, and were motivated by the challenge of building an airline from scratch. Muse wanted his executive team to be willing to think like mavericks and not be lulled into instituting practices at Southwest that imitated what was done at other airlines.

## Southwest's Struggle to Gain a Market Foothold

In June 1971, Southwest initiated its first flights with a schedule that soon included 6 round-trips between Dallas and San Antonio and 12 round-trips between Houston and Dallas. But the introductory $20 one-way fares to fly the Golden Triangle, well below the $27 and $28 fares charged by rivals, attracted disappointingly small numbers of passengers. To try to gain market visibility and drum up more passengers, Southwest undertook some creative actions to supplement its ad campaigns publicizing its low fares:

- Southwest decided to have its flight hostesses dress in colorful hot pants and white knee-high boots with high heels. Recruiting ads for Southwest's first group of hostesses headlined "Attention, Raquel Welch: You can have a job if you measure up." Two thousand applicants responded, and those selected for interviews were asked to come dressed in hot pants to show off their legs—the company wanted to hire long-legged beauties with sparkling personalities. Over 30 of Southwest's first graduating class of 40 flight attendants consisted of young ladies who were cheerleaders and majorettes in high school and thus had experience performing skimpily dressed in front of people.

- A second attention-getting action was to give passengers free alcoholic beverages during daytime flights. Most passengers on these flights were business travelers. Management's thinking was that many passengers did not drink during the daytime and that with most flights being less than an hour's duration it would be cheaper to simply give the drinks away than collect the money.

- Taking a cue from being based at Dallas Love Field, Southwest began using the tagline "Now There's Somebody Else Up There Who Loves You." The routes between Houston, Dallas, and San Antonio became known as the "Love Triangle." Southwest's planes were referred to as "Love Birds," drinks became "Love Potions," peanuts were called "Love Bites," drink coupons were "Love Stamps," and tickets were printed on "Love Machines." The "love" campaign set the tone for Southwest's approach to its customers and its efforts to make flying Southwest Airlines an enjoyable, fun, and differentiating experience.

(Later, when the company went public, it chose "LUV" as its stock-trading symbol.)

- To add more flights without buying more planes, the head of Southwest's ground operations came up with a plan for ground crews to off-load passengers and baggage, refuel the plane, clean the cabin and restock the galley, on-load passengers and baggage, do the necessary preflight checks and paperwork, and push away from the gate in 10 minutes. The 10-minute turnaround became one of Southwest's signatures during the 1970s and 1980s. (In later years, as passenger volume grew and many flights were filled to capacity, the turnaround time gradually expanded to 30 minutes—because it took more time to unload and load 135 passengers compared to a half-full plane with just 60 to 65 passengers. Even so, the average turnaround times at Southwest during the 2000–2013 period were shorter than the 35- to 50-minute turnarounds typical at other major airlines.)

- In late November 1971, Lamar Muse came up with the idea of offering a $10 fare to passengers on the Friday night Houston-Dallas flight. With no advertising, the 112-seat flight sold out. This led Muse to realize that Southwest was serving two quite distinct types of travelers in the Golden Triangle market: (1) business travelers who were more time-sensitive than price-sensitive and wanted weekday flights at times suitable for conducting business, and (2) price-sensitive leisure travelers who wanted lower fares and had more flexibility about when to fly.[4] He came up with a two-tier on-peak and off-peak pricing structure in which all seats on weekday flights departing before 7 p.m. were priced at $26 and all seats on other flights were priced at $13. Passenger traffic increased significantly—and systemwide on-peak and off-peak pricing soon became standard across the whole airline industry.

- In 1972, the company decided to move its flights in Houston from the newly opened Houston Intercontinental Airport (where Southwest was losing money and where passengers faced a 45-minute trip to the city's downtown area) to the abandoned Houston Hobby Airport, located much closer to downtown Houston. Despite being the only carrier to fly into Houston Hobby, the results were spectacular— business travelers who flew to Houston frequently from Dallas and San Antonio found the Houston Hobby location far more convenient, and passenger traffic doubled almost immediately.

- In early 1973, in an attempt to fill empty seats on its San Antonio–Dallas flights, Southwest cut its regular $26 fare to $13 for all seats, all days, and all times. When Braniff International, at that time one of Southwest's major rivals, announced $13 fares of its own, Southwest retaliated with a two-page ad, run in the Dallas newspapers, headlining "Nobody is going to shoot Southwest Airlines out of the sky for a lousy $13" and containing copy stating that Braniff was trying to run Southwest out of business. The ad announced that Southwest would not only match Braniff's $13 fare but would also give passengers the choice of buying a regular-priced ticket for $26 and receiving a complimentary fifth of Chivas Regal scotch, Crown Royal Canadian whiskey, or Smirnoff vodka (or, for nondrinkers, a leather ice bucket). Over 75 percent of Southwest's Dallas-Houston passengers opted for the $26 fare, although the percentage dropped as the two-month promotion wore on and corporate controllers began insisting that company employees use the $13 fare. The local and national media picked up the story of Southwest's offer, proclaiming the battle as a David versus Goliath struggle in which the upstart Southwest did not stand much of a chance against the much larger and well-established Braniff; grassroots sentiment in Texas swung to Southwest's side.

All these moves paid off. The resulting gains in passenger traffic enabled Southwest to report its first-ever annual profit in 1973.

## More Legal and Regulatory Hurdles

During the rest of the 1970s, Southwest found itself embroiled in another round of legal and regulatory battles. One battle involved Southwest's refusal to move its flights from Dallas Love Field, located 10 minutes from downtown, out to the newly opened Dallas–Fort Worth (DFW) Regional Airport, which was 30 minutes from downtown Dallas. Local officials were furious because they were counting on fees from Southwest's flights in and out of DFW to help service the debt on the bonds issued to finance the construction of the airport. Southwest's position was that it was not required to move because it had not agreed to do so or been ordered to do so by the Texas Aeronautics Commission—moreover, the

company's headquarters were located at Love Field. The courts eventually ruled that Southwest's operations could remain at Love Field.

A second battle ensued when rival airlines protested Southwest's application to begin serving several smaller cities in Texas; their protest was based on arguments that these markets were already well served and that Southwest's entry would result in costly overcapacity. Southwest countered that its low fares would allow more people to fly and thus would grow the market. Again, Southwest prevailed, and its views about low fares expanding the market proved accurate. In the year before Southwest initiated service, 123,000 passengers flew from Harlingen Airport in the Rio Grande Valley to Houston, Dallas, or San Antonio; in the 11 months following Southwest's initial flights, 325,000 passengers flew to the same three cities.

Believing that Braniff and Texas International were deliberately engaging in tactics to harass Southwest's operations, Southwest convinced the U.S. government to investigate what it considered predatory tactics by its chief rivals. In February 1975, Braniff and Texas International were indicted by a federal grand jury for conspiring to put Southwest out of business—a violation of the Sherman Antitrust Act. The two airlines pleaded "no contest" to the charges, signed cease-and-desist agreements, and were fined a modest $100,000 each.

When Congress passed the Airline Deregulation Act in 1978, Southwest applied to the Civil Aeronautics Board (now the Federal Aviation Administration) to fly between Houston and New Orleans. The application was vehemently opposed by local government officials and airlines operating out of DFW because of the potential for passenger traffic to be siphoned away from DFW. The opponents solicited the aid of Fort Worth congressman Jim Wright, then the majority leader of the U.S. House of Representatives, who took the matter to the floor of the House; a rash of lobbying and maneuvering ensued. What emerged came to be known as the Wright Amendment of 1979: No airline may provide nonstop or through-plane service from Dallas Love Field to any city in any state except for locations in Texas, Louisiana, Arkansas, Oklahoma, and New Mexico. Southwest was prohibited from advertising, publishing schedules or fares, or checking baggage for travel from Dallas Love Field to any city it served outside the five-state "Wright Zone." The Wright amendment was expanded in 1997, when Alabama, Mississippi, and Kansas were added to the five-state zone; in 2005, Missouri was added to the Wright Zone. In 2006, after a heated battle in Congress, legislation was passed and signed into law that repealed the Wright amendment beginning in 2014.

## The Emergence of a Combative, Can-Do Culture at Southwest

The legal, regulatory, and competitive battles that Southwest fought in its early years produced a strong esprit de corps among Southwest personnel and a drive to survive and prosper despite the odds. With newspaper and TV stories reporting Southwest's difficulties regularly, employees were fully aware that the airline's existence was constantly on the line. Had the company been forced to move from Love Field, it would most likely have gone under, an outcome that employees, Southwest's rivals, and local government officials understood well. According to Southwest's former president, Colleen Barrett, the obstacles thrown in the company's path by competitors and local officials were instrumental in building Herb Kelleher's passion for Southwest Airlines and ingraining a combative, can-do spirit into the corporate culture:[5]

> They would put twelve to fifteen lawyers on a case and on our side there was Herb. They almost wore him to the ground. But the more arrogant they were, the more determined Herb got that this airline was going to go into the air—and stay there.
>
>    The warrior mentality, the very fight to survive, is truly what created our culture.

When Lamar Muse resigned in 1978, Southwest's board wanted Herb Kelleher to take over as chairman and CEO. But Kelleher enjoyed practicing law, so while he agreed to become chairman of the board, he insisted that someone else be CEO. Southwest's board appointed Howard Putnam, a group vice president of marketing services at United Airlines, as Southwest's president and CEO in July 1978. Putnam asked Kelleher to become more involved in Southwest's day-to-day operations, and over the next three years, Kelleher got to know many of the company's personnel and observe them in action. Putnam announced his resignation in fall 1981 to become president and COO at Braniff International. This time, Southwest's board succeeded in persuading Kelleher to take on the additional duties of CEO and president.

## Sustained Growth Transforms Southwest into the Domestic Market Share Leader, 1981–2013

When Herb Kelleher took over in 1981, Southwest was flying 27 planes to 14 destination cities and had $270 million in revenues and 2,100 employees. Over the next 20 years, Southwest Airlines prospered under Kelleher's leadership. When Kelleher stepped down as CEO in mid-2001, the company had 350 planes flying to 58 U.S. airports, annual revenues of $5.6 billion, over 30,000 employees, and 64 million fare-paying passengers annually.

Under the two CEOs who succeeded Kelleher, Southwest continued its march to becoming the market share leader in domestic air travel, growing to 2013 revenues of $17.7 billion and 44,800 employees, flying 680 planes to 96 airports in 41 states and 7 destinations outside the United States, and transporting more than 108 million fare-paying passengers and over 133 million total passengers (including those traveling on frequent-flyer awards) in 2013. In the process, the company won more industry Triple Crown awards—for best on-time record, best baggage handling, and fewest customer complaints—than any other U.S. airline. While Southwest fell short of its on-time performance and baggage-handling goals in 2013, it still led the domestic airline industry in customer satisfaction and received other awards and recognitions, including Best Domestic Airline for Customer Service, one of *Executive Travel Magazine*'s Leading Edge awards; Brand of the Year in the Value Airline Category, from the Harris Poll; and Best Customer Service and Best Loyalty Credit Card, from *InsideFlyer Magazine.*

Exhibit 2 provides a five-year summary of Southwest's financial and operating performance. Exhibit 3 on page C-347 provides select operating and financial data for major U.S. air carriers during the 1995–2013 period.

## HERB KELLEHER: THE CEO WHO TRANSFORMED SOUTHWEST INTO A MAJOR AIRLINE

Herb Kelleher majored in philosophy at Wesleyan University in Middletown, Connecticut, graduating

**EXHIBIT 2**   Summary of Southwest Airlines' Financial and Operating Performance, 2009–2013 (in millions, except per share and operating data)

| | Year Ended December 31 | | | | |
|---|---|---|---|---|---|
| | **2013** | **2012** | **2011** | **2010** | **2009** |
| **Financial data** | | | | | |
| Operating revenues | $ 17,699 | $17,088 | $ 15,658 | $ 12,104 | $10,350 |
| Operating expenses | 16,421 | 16,465 | 14,965 | 11,116 | 10,088 |
| Operating income | 1,278 | 623 | 693 | 988 | 262 |
| Other expenses (income), net | 69 | (62) | 370 | 243 | 98 |
| Income before taxes | 1,209 | 685 | 323 | 745 | 164 |
| Provision for income taxes | 455 | 264 | 145 | 286 | 65 |
| Net income | $   754 | $   421 | $   178 | $   459 | $   99 |
| Net income per share, basic | $1.06 | $0.56 | $0.23 | $0.62 | $0.13 |
| Net income per share, diluted | $1.05 | $0.56 | $0.23 | $0.61 | $0.13 |
| Cash dividends per common share | $0.1300 | $0.0345 | $ 0.0180 | $ 0.0180 | $0.0180 |
| Total assets at period-end | $19,345 | $18,596 | $18,068 | $15,463 | $14,269 |
| Long-term obligations at period-end | $ 2,191 | $ 2,883 | $ 3,107 | $ 2,875 | $ 3,325 |
| Stockholders' equity at period-end | $ 7,336 | $ 6,992 | $ 6,877 | $ 6,237 | $ 5,454 |
| **Operating data** | | | | | |
| Revenue passengers carried | 108,075,976 | 109,346,509 | 103,973,759 | 88,191,322 | 86,310,229 |
| Enplaned passengers | 133,155,030 | 133,978,100 | 127,551,012 | 106,227,521 | 101,338,228 |
| Revenue passenger-miles (RPMs) (000s)[1] | 104,348,216 | 102,874,979 | 97,582,530 | 78,046,967 | 74,456,710 |
| Available seat-miles (ASMs) (000s)[2] | 130,344,072 | 128,137,110 | 120,578,736 | 98,437,092 | 98,001,550 |
| Load factor[3] | 80.1% | 80.3% | 80.9% | 79.3% | 76.0% |
| Average length of passenger haul (miles) | 966 | 941 | 939 | 885 | 863 |
| Average length of each flight (miles) | 703 | 693 | 679 | 648 | 639 |
| Trips flown | 1,312,785 | 1,361,558 | 1,317,977 | 1,114,451 | 1,125,111 |
| Average passenger fare | $154.72 | $147.17 | $141.90 | $130.27 | $114.61 |
| Passenger revenue yield per RPM (cents)[4] | 16.02 | 15.64 | 15.12 | 14.72 | 13.29 |
| Operating revenue per ASM (cents)[5] | 13.58 | 13.34 | 12.99 | 12.30 | 10.56 |

*(Continued)*

## EXHIBIT 2 *(Continued)*

| | Year Ended December 31 | | | | |
|---|---|---|---|---|---|
| | **2013** | **2012** | **2011** | **2010** | **2009** |
| Passenger revenue per ASM (cents)[6] | ¢12.83 | ¢12.56 | ¢12.24 | ¢11.67 | ¢10.09 |
| Operating expenses per ASM (cents)[7] | ¢12.60 | ¢12.85 | ¢12.41 | ¢11.29 | ¢10.29 |
| Operating expenses per ASM, excluding fuel (cents) | ¢8.18 | ¢8.07 | ¢7.73 | ¢7.61 | ¢7.18 |
| Operating expenses per ASM, excluding fuel and profit sharing (cents) | ¢8.01 | ¢7.98 | ¢7.65 | ¢7.45 | ¢7.15 |
| Fuel costs per gallon, including fuel tax | $3.16 | $3.30 | $3.19 | $2.51 | $2.12 |
| Fuel costs per gallon, including fuel tax, economic | $3.12 | $3.28 | $3.19 | $2.39 | $1.97 |
| Fuel consumed, in gallons (millions) | 1,818 | 1,847 | 1,764 | 1,437 | 1,428 |
| Active full-time equivalent employees | 44,831 | 45,861 | 45,392 | 34,901 | 34,726 |
| Aircraft in service at period-end[8] | 680 | 694 | 698 | 548 | 537 |

[1]A revenue passenger-mile is one paying passenger flown 1 mile.
[2]An available seat-mile (ASM) is one seat (empty or full) flown 1 mile; also referred to as "capacity," which is a measure of the space available to carry passengers in a given period.
[3]Revenue passenger-miles divided by available seat-miles.
[4]Calculated as passenger revenue divided by revenue passenger-miles. It represents the average cost paid by a paying passenger to fly 1 mile.
[5]Calculated as operating revenue divided by available seat-miles. It is a measure of operating revenue production based on the total available seat-miles flown during a particular period.
[6]Calculated as passenger revenue divided by available seat-miles. It is a measure of passenger revenue production based on the total available seat-miles flown during a particular period.
[7]Calculated as operating expenses divided by available seat-miles. Also referred to as *unit costs* or *cost per available seat-mile*, this is the average cost of flying an aircraft seat (empty or full) 1 mile.
[8]Includes leased aircraft and excludes aircraft that were not available for service, in storage, held for sale, or held for return to the lessor.
*Source:* Company 10-K report, 2013.

with honors. He earned his law degree at New York University, again graduating with honors and also serving as a member of the law review. After graduation, he clerked for a New Jersey Supreme Court justice for two years and then joined a law firm in Newark. Upon marrying a woman from Texas and becoming enamored with Texas, he moved to San Antonio, where he became a successful lawyer and came to represent Rollin King's small aviation company.

When Herb Kelleher took on the role of Southwest's CEO in 1981, he made a point of visiting with maintenance personnel, to check on how well the planes were running, and talking with the flight attendants. Kelleher did not do much managing from his office, preferring instead to be out among the troops as much as he could. His style was to listen and observe and to offer encouragement. Kelleher attended most graduation ceremonies of flight attendant classes, and

**EXHIBIT 3    Select Operating and Financial Data for Major U.S. Airline Carriers, 1995, 2000, 2005, 2010–2013**

|  | 1995 | 2000 | 2005 | 2010 | 2011 | 2012 | 2013 |
|---|---|---|---|---|---|---|---|
| Passengers (millions) | 559.0 | 666.2 | 738.3 | 720.5 | 730.8 | 736.6 | 758.9 |
| Flights (thousands) | 8,062.0 | 9,035.0 | 11,564.0 | 9,521.0 | 9,478.0 | 9,284 | 9,161 |
| Revenue passenger-miles (billions) | 603.4 | 692.8 | 778.6 | 798.0 | 814.4 | 823.2 | 840.4 |
| Available seat-miles (billions) | 807.1 | 987.9 | 1,002.7 | 972.6 | 992.7 | 994.5 | 1,011.2 |
| Load factor (%) | 67.0 | 72.4 | 77.7 | 82.0 | 82.0 | 82.8 | 83.1 |
| Passenger revenues (millions) | $69,470 | $93,622 | $93,500 | $103,978 | $114,299 | $115,975 | $120,640 |
| Operating profit (loss) (millions) | $ 5,852 | $ 6,999 | $ 427 | $ 9,344 | $ 7,035 | $ 7,516 | $ 12,548 |
| Net profit (loss) excluding one-time charges and gains (millions) | $ 2,283 | $ 2,486 | ($5,782) | $ 3,665 | $ 1,392 | $ 360 | $ 12,771 |
| Total employees | 546,987 | 679,967 | 562,467 | 531,224 | 538,300 | 547,558 | n.a. |

*Source:* Air Transport Association, *2005 Economic Report,* p. 7; and U.S. Department of Transportation, Bureau of Transportation Statistics, "Airline Traffic Data" press releases, various years.

he often helped load bags on "Black Wednesday," the busy travel day before Thanksgiving. He knew the names of thousands of Southwest employees and was held in the highest regard by the employees. When he attended a Southwest employee function, he was swarmed like a celebrity.

Kelleher had an affinity for bold-print Hawaiian shirts, owned a tricked-out motorcycle, and made no secret of his love for smoking and Wild Turkey whiskey. He loved to make jokes and engage in pranks and corporate antics, prompting some people to refer to him as the "clown prince" of the airline industry. He once appeared at a company gathering dressed in an Elvis costume, and he had arm-wrestled a South Carolina company executive at a public event in Dallas for the right to use "Just Plane Smart" as an advertising slogan.[6] Kelleher was well known inside and outside the company for his combativeness, particularly when it came to beating back competitors. On one occasion, he reportedly told a group of veteran employees, "If someone says they're going to smack us in the face—knock them out, stomp them out, boot them in the ditch, cover them over, and move on to the next thing. That's the Southwest spirit at work."[7] On another occasion, he said, "I love battles. I think it's part of the Irish in me. It's like what Patton said, 'War is hell and I love it so.' That's how I feel. I've never gotten tired of fighting."[8]

While Southwest was deliberately combative and flamboyant in some aspects of its operations,

when it came to the financial side of the business, Kelleher insisted on fiscal conservatism, a strong balance sheet, comparatively low levels of debt, and zealous attention to bottom-line profitability. While believing strongly in being prepared for adversity, Kelleher had an aversion to Southwest personnel spending time drawing up all kinds of formal strategic plans, saying, "Reality is chaotic; planning is ordered and logical. The meticulous nit-picking that goes on in most strategic planning processes creates a mental straightjacket that becomes disabling in an industry where things change radically from one day to the next." Kelleher wanted Southwest managers to think ahead, have contingency plans, and be ready to act when it seemed that the future held significant risks or when new conditions suddenly appeared and demanded prompt responses.

Kelleher was a strong believer in the principle that employees—not customers—came first:[9]

> You have to treat your employees like your customers. When you treat them right, then they will treat your outside customers right. That has been a very powerful competitive weapon for us. You've got to take the time to listen to people's ideas. If you just tell somebody no, that's an act of power and, in my opinion, an abuse of power. You don't want to constrain people in their thinking.

Another indication of the importance that Kelleher placed on employees was the message he had penned in 1990 that was prominently displayed in the lobby of Southwest's headquarters in Dallas:

The people of Southwest Airlines are "the creators" of what we have become—and of what we will be.

Our people transformed an idea into a legend. That legend will continue to grow only so long as it is nourished— by our people's indomitable spirit, boundless energy, immense goodwill, and burning desire to excel.

Our thanks—and our love—to the people of Southwest Airlines for creating a marvelous family and a wondrous airline.

In June 2001, Herb Kelleher stepped down as CEO but continued on in his role as the chairman of Southwest's board of directors and the head of the board's executive committee; as chairman, he played a lead role in Southwest's strategy, expansion to new cities and aircraft scheduling, and government and industry affairs. In May 2008, after more than 40 years of leadership at Southwest, Kelleher retired as chairman (but he remained a full-time Southwest employee until July 2013 and carried the title of chairman emeritus in 2014).

# EXECUTIVE LEADERSHIP AT SOUTHWEST: 2001–2014

In June 2001 Southwest Airlines, responding to anxious investor concerns about the company's leadership succession plans, began an orderly transfer of power and responsibilities from Herb Kelleher, age 70, to two of his most trusted protégés: James F. Parker, 54, Southwest's general counsel, succeeded Kelleher as CEO; Colleen Barrett, 56, Southwest's executive vice president–customers and self-described keeper of Southwest's pep-rally corporate culture, became president and chief operating officer.

## James Parker, Southwest's CEO, 2001–2004

James Parker's association with Herb Kelleher went back 23 years to the time when they were colleagues at Kelleher's old law firm. Parker moved over to Southwest from the law firm in February 1986. Parker's profile inside the company as Southwest's vice president and general counsel had been relatively low, but he was Southwest's chief labor negotiator, and much of the credit for Southwest's good relations with employee unions belonged to Parker. Parker and Kelleher were said to think much alike, and Parker was regarded as having a good sense of humor, although he did not have as colorful and flamboyant a personality as Kelleher. Parker was seen as an honest, straight-arrow kind of person who had a strong grasp of Southwest's culture and market niche and who could be nice or tough, depending on the situation. When his appointment as CEO was announced, Parker said:[10]

There is going to be no change of course insofar as Southwest is concerned. We have a very experienced leadership team. We've all worked together for a long time. There will be evolutionary changes in Southwest, just as there have always been in our history. We're going to stay true to our business model of being a low-cost, low-fare airline.

Parker retired unexpectedly, for personal reasons, in July 2004, stepping down as CEO and vice chairman of the board and also resigning from the company's board of directors. He was succeeded by Gary C. Kelly.

## Colleen Barrett, Southwest's President, 2001–2008

Barrett began working with Kelleher as his legal secretary in 1967 and had been with Southwest since 1978. As executive vice president–customers, Barrett had a high profile among Southwest employees and spent most of her time on culture building, morale building, and customer service; her goal was to ensure that employees felt good about what they were doing and felt empowered to serve the cause of Southwest Airlines.[11] She and Kelleher were regarded as Southwest's guiding lights, and some analysts said she was essentially functioning as the company's chief operating officer prior to her formal appointment as president. Much of the credit for the company's strong record of customer service and its strong-culture work climate belonged to Barrett.

Barrett had been the driving force behind lining the hallways at Southwest's headquarters with photos of company events and trying to create a family atmosphere at the company. Believing it was important to make employees feel cared about and important, Barrett had put together a network of contacts across the company to help her stay in touch with what was happening with employees and their families. When network members learned about events that were worthy of acknowledgment, the word quickly got to Barrett—the information went into a database and an appropriate greeting card or gift was sent. Barrett had a remarkable ability to give gifts that were individualized and connected her to the recipient.[12]

Barrett was the first woman appointed as president and COO of a major U.S. airline. In October 2001, *Fortune* included Colleen Barrett on its list of the 50 most powerful women in American business (she was ranked number 20). Barrett retired as president in July 2008.

## Gary C. Kelly, Southwest's CEO, 2004–Present

Gary Kelly was appointed vice chairman of the board of directors and chief executive officer of Southwest effective July 15, 2004. Prior to that time, Kelly was executive vice president and chief financial officer from 2001 to 2004, and vice president–finance and chief financial officer from 1989 to 2001. He joined Southwest in 1986 as its controller. In 2008, effective with the retirement of Kelleher and Barrett, Kelly assumed the titles of chairman of the board and president, in addition to serving as CEO.

When Kelly was named CEO in 2004, Herb Kelleher said:[13]

> Gary Kelly is one of our brightest stars, well respected throughout the industry and well known, over more than a decade, to the media, analyst, and investor communities for his excellence. As part of our Board's succession planning, we had already focused on Gary as Jim Parker's successor, and that process has simply been accelerated by Jim's personal decision to retire. Under Gary's leadership, Southwest has achieved the strongest balance sheet in the American airline industry; the best fuel hedging position in our industry; and tremendous progress in technology.

In his first two years as CEO, Kelly and other top-level Southwest executives sharpened and fine-tuned Southwest's strategy in a number of areas, continued to expand operations (both adding more flights and initiating service to new airports), and worked to maintain the company's low-cost advantage over its domestic rivals.

Kelly saw four factors as keys to Southwest's recipe for success:[14]

- Hire great people, treat 'em like family.
- Care for our Customers warmly and personally, like they're guests in our home.
- Keep fares and operating costs lower than anybody else by being safe, efficient, and operationally excellent.

- Stay prepared for bad times with a strong balance sheet, lots of cash, and a stout fuel hedge.

To guide Southwest's efforts to be a standout performer on these four key success factors, Kelly had established five strategic objectives for the company:[15]

- Be the best place to work.
- Be the safest, most efficient, and most reliable airline in the world.
- Offer customers a convenient flight schedule with lots of flights to lots of places they want to go.
- Offer customers the best overall travel experience.
- Do all of these things in a way that maintains a low-cost structure and the ability to offer low fares.

In 2008–2009, Kelly initiated a slight revision of Southwest's mission statement and also spearheaded a vision statement that called for a steadfast focus on a triple bottom line of "Performance, People, and Planet"—see Exhibit 4.

In 2010, Kelly initiated one of the biggest strategic moves in the company's history: the acquisition of AirTran Airways, a low-fare, low-cost airline that served 70 airports in the United States, Mexico, and the Caribbean (19 of the airports AirTran served coincided with airports served by Southwest). In 2011, Kelly initiated a five-year strategic plan that featured five strategic initiatives:

- Integrating AirTran into Southwest.
- Modernizing Southwest Airlines' existing aircraft fleet.
- Adding over 100 new Boeing 737-800 aircraft to the Southwest fleet.
- Launching international service and a new reservation system.
- Growing membership in the company's Rapid Rewards frequent-flyer program.

In his Letter to the Shareholders in Southwest's 2013 annual report, Kelly said:

> We are now in the fourth year of a bold five-year strategic plan that began in 2011. We believe our five Strategic Initiatives are transformative with the potential to drive more revenue, reduce unit costs, and make Southwest more competitive. The world has changed dramatically since 2000. Our competitors took draconian measures, including massive layoffs and pay

**EXHIBIT 4**    Southwest Airlines' Mission, Vision, and Triple-Bottom-Line
Commitment to Performance, People, and Planet

**THE MISSION OF SOUTHWEST AIRLINES** The mission of Southwest Airlines is dedication to the highest quality of
Customer Service delivered with a sense of warmth, friendliness, individual pride, and Company Spirit.

**OUR VISION** Become the world's most loved, most flown, and most profitable airline.

**TO OUR EMPLOYEES** We are committed to provide our Employees a stable work environment with equal opportunity
for learning and personal growth. Creativity and innovation are encouraged for improving the effectiveness of
Southwest Airlines. Above all, Employees will be provided the same concern, respect, and caring attitude within the
organization that they are expected to share externally with every Southwest Customer.

**TO OUR COMMUNITIES** Our goal is to be the hometown airline of every community we serve, and because those
communities sustain and nurture us with their support and loyalty, it is vital that we, as individuals and in groups,
embrace each community with the SOUTHWEST SPIRIT of involvement, service, and caring to make those
communities better places to live and work.

**TO OUR PLANET** We strive to be a good environmental steward across our system in all of our hometowns, and one
component of our stewardship is efficiency, which, by its very nature, translates to eliminating waste and conserving
resources. Using cost-effective and environmentally beneficial operating procedures (including facilities and equipment)
allows us to reduce the amount of materials we use and, when combined with our ability to reuse and recycle material,
preserves these environmental resources.

**TO OUR STAKEHOLDERS** Southwest's vision for a sustainable future is one where there will be a balance in our
business model between Employees and Community, the Environment, and our Financial Viability. In order to protect
our world for future generations, while meeting our commitments to our Employees, Customers, and Stakeholders,
we will strive to lead our industry in innovative efficiency that conserves natural resources, maintains a creative and
innovative workforce, and gives back to the Communities in which we live and work.

*Source:* Southwest's "One Report, 2009," www.southwest.com (accessed August 20, 2010).

cuts, to adjust to today's economic realities and have
been given new life through the use of federal bankruptcy laws. Thanks to the hard work and extraordinary efforts of our Southwest Warriors, Southwest has
adjusted through incredible Teamwork and unwavering
resolve to execute our strategic plan. We have survived
the onslaught of challenges to remain profitable for 41
consecutive years, remain the nation's largest airline in
terms of domestic originating passengers boarded, and
operate the largest Boeing fleet in the world. The transformation hasn't been easy, but it was necessary, and
we made significant and successful progress in 2013.

## SOUTHWEST AIRLINES' STRATEGY IN 2014

From day one, Southwest had pursued a low-cost,
low-price, no-frills strategy to make air travel affordable to a wide segment of the population. While
specific aspects of the strategy had evolved over the
years, three strategic themes had characterized the
company's strategy throughout its existence and still
had high profiles in 2014:

- Charge fares that were very price-competitive
  and, in some cases, appealingly lower than what
  rival airlines were charging.
- Create and sustain a low-cost operating structure.
- Make it fun to fly on Southwest, and provide customers with a top-notch travel experience.

### Fare Structure Strategy

Southwest employed a relatively simple fare structure displayed in ways that made it easy for customers to choose the fare they preferred. In 2014,
Southwest's fares were bundled into four major categories: "Wanna Get Away," "Anytime," "Business
Select," and fares for seniors (people 65 and older):

1. *Wanna Get Away* fares were always the lowest fares and were subject to advance purchase
   requirements. No fee was charged for changing
   a previously purchased ticket to a different time
   or day of travel (rival airlines charged a change
   fee of $100 to $175), but applicable fare differences were applied. The purchase price was

nonrefundable, but the funds could be applied to future travel on Southwest, provided the tickets were not canceled or changed within 10 minutes of a flight's scheduled departure.

2. *Anytime* fares were refundable and changeable, and funds could be applied toward future travel on Southwest. Anytime fares included a higher frequent-flyer point multiplier under Southwest's Rapid Rewards frequent-flyer program than did Wanna Get Away fares.

3. *Business Select* fares were refundable and changeable, and funds could be applied toward future travel on Southwest. Business Select fares included additional perks such as priority boarding, a higher frequent-flyer point multiplier than other Southwest fares (including twice as many points per dollar spent as compared to Wanna Get Away fares), priority security and ticket counter access in select airports, and one complimentary adult-beverage coupon for the day of travel (for customers of legal drinking age). The Business Select fare had been introduced in 2007 to help attract economy-minded business travelers.

4. *Senior* fares were typically priced between the Wanna Get Away and Anytime fares. No fee was charged for changing a previously purchased ticket to a different time or day of travel, but applicable fare differences were applied. The purchase price was nonrefundable, but funds could be applied to future travel on Southwest, provided the tickets were not canceled or changed within 10 minutes of a flight's scheduled departure. Fares for seniors were not displayed on the list of fare options at the company's website unless customers checked a box indicating that one or more passengers were 65 years of age or older.

In 2008, rival airlines instituted a series of add-on fees—including a fuel surcharge for each flight, fees for checking bags, fees for processing frequent-flyer travel awards, fees for buying a ticket in person at the airport or calling a toll-free number to speak with a ticket agent to make a reservation, fees for changing a previously purchased ticket to a different flight, and fees for certain in-flight snacks and beverages—to help defray skyrocketing costs for jet fuel (which had climbed from about 15 percent of operating expenses in 2000 to 40 percent of operating expenses in mid-2008) and try to bolster their operating performance. In 2014, Frontier Airlines announced that it would begin charging passengers fees of $20 to $50 for using the overhead bins to store carry-on luggage and other items and fees of $3 to $15 to preselect a seat; Frontier also charged $1.99 for bottled water and soft drinks on its flights. Southwest, however, chose to forgo "à la carte" pricing and stuck with an all-inclusive fare price. During 2009 and periodically thereafter, Southwest ran "Bags Fly Free" ad campaigns to publicize the cost savings of flying Southwest rather than paying the $20 to $50 fees that rival airlines charged for a first or second checked bag. Southwest also ran ads promoting its policy of not charging a fee for changing a previously purchased ticket to a different flight.

When advance reservations were weak for particular weeks or times of the day or on certain routes, Southwest made a regular practice of initiating special fare promotions to stimulate ticket sales on flights that otherwise would have had numerous empty seats. The company's use of special fare sales and Bags Fly Free ads to combat slack air travel during much of the Great Recession in 2008–2009 resulted in company-record load factors (the percentage of all available seats on all flights that were occupied by fare-paying passengers) for every month from July through December 2009.

Southwest was a shrewd practitioner of the concept of price elasticity, proving in one market after another that the revenue gains from increased ticket sales and the volume of passenger traffic would more than compensate for the revenue erosion associated with low fares. When Southwest entered the Florida market with an introductory $17 fare from Tampa to Fort Lauderdale, the number of annual passengers flying the Tampa–Fort Lauderdale route jumped 50 percent, to more than 330,000. In Manchester, New Hampshire, passenger counts went from 1.1 million in 1997, the year prior to Southwest's entry, to 3.5 million in 2000, and average one-way fares dropped from just over $300 to $129. Southwest's success in stimulating higher passenger traffic at airports across the United States via low fares and frequent flights was coined the "Southwest Effect" by personnel at the U.S. Department of Transportation. (See Exhibit 6 for a list of the cities and airports Southwest Airlines served in July 2014.)

**AirTran's Fare Structure**  AirTran had a fare structure that included Business Class fares and competitively priced economy class fares. AirTran

Business Class fares were refundable and changeable and included such perks as priority boarding, oversized seats with additional leg room, bonus frequent-flyer credit, no first- or second-bag fees, and complimentary cocktails onboard. Business Class upgrades could be purchased within 24 hours of travel for a fee ranging from $69 to $139 (depending on the length of the flight). All other AirTran fares were nonrefundable but could be changed prior to departure for a service fee of $150 per person. AirTran also imposed fees for checked baggage ($25 for the first checked bag and $35 for the second checked bag), advance seat assignments, priority boarding, ticket booking through the customer call center, ticket cancellation ($150 per ticket), and assorted other services.

## Southwest's Strategy to Create and Sustain Low-Cost Operations

Southwest management fully understood that earning attractive profits by charging low fares necessitated the use of strategy elements that would enable the company to become a low-cost provider of commercial air service. There were three main components of Southwest's strategic actions to achieve a low-cost operating structure: using a single aircraft type for all flights, creating an operationally efficient point-to-point route structure, and striving to perform all value chain activities in a cost-efficient manner.

**Use of a Single Aircraft Type**    For many years, Southwest's aircraft fleets had consisted only of Boeing 737 aircraft. Operating only one type of aircraft produced many cost-saving benefits: minimizing the size of spare-parts inventories, simplifying the training of maintenance and repair personnel, improving the proficiency and speed with which maintenance routines could be done, and simplifying the task of scheduling planes for particular flights. In 2013, Southwest operated the biggest fleet of Boeing 737 aircraft in the world. Exhibit 5 provides information about Southwest's aircraft fleet.

**Southwest's Point-to-Point Route Structure Strategy**    Southwest's point-to-point scheduling of flights was more cost-efficient than the hub-and-spoke systems used by almost all rival airlines. Hub-and-spoke systems involved passengers on many different flights coming in from spoke locations (and sometimes another hub) to a central airport or

hub within a short span of time and then connecting to an outgoing flight to their destination—a spoke location or another hub. Most flights arrived at and departed from a hub during a two-hour window, creating big peak-valley swings in airport personnel workloads and gate utilization—airport personnel and gate areas were very busy when hub operations were in full swing and then were underutilized in the interval awaiting the next round of inbound and outbound flights. In contrast, Southwest's point-to-point routes permitted scheduling aircraft so as to minimize the time aircraft were at the gate, currently approximately 25 minutes, thereby reducing the number of aircraft and gate facilities that would otherwise be required. Furthermore, with a relatively even flow of incoming and outgoing flights and gate traffic, Southwest could staff its terminal operations to handle a fairly steady workload across a day, whereas hub-and-spoke operators had to staff their operations to serve 3 to 4 daily peak periods.

Exhibit 6 shows the cities and airports served by Southwest in mid-2014. Going into 2014, Southwest had nonstop service between 524 airports. In 2013, Southwest's average passenger airfare was $154.72 one way, and the average passenger trip length was approximately 966 miles.

**Striving to Perform All Value Chain Activities Cost-Effectively**    Southwest made a point of scrutinizing every aspect of its operations to find ways to trim costs. The company's strategic actions to reduce or at least contain costs were extensive and ongoing:

- Sharply rising prices for jet fuel over the past 12 years that caused fuel expenses to rise from 16.5 percent of total operating expenses in 2003 to between 28 and 38 percent of total operating expenses since 2006 had prompted a number of projects to increase fuel efficiency, including:
  - Installing "blended winglets" on all of Southwest's planes beginning in 2007 and then, in 2014, starting to upgrade its aircraft fleet with newly designed split-scimitar winglets—see Exhibit 7. These winglets reduced lift drag, allowed aircraft to climb more steeply and reach higher flight levels quicker, improved cruising performance, helped extend engine life and reduce maintenance costs, and reduced fuel burn.

## EXHIBIT 5   Southwest's Aircraft Fleet as of December 31, 2013

| Type of Aircraft | Number | Seats | Average Age (years) | Comments |
|---|---|---|---|---|
| Boeing 717-200 | 66 | 117 | 12 | All of these were AirTran aircraft that were in the process of being removed from the Southwest fleet and leased or subleased to Delta Air Lines. |
| Boeing 737-300 | 122 | 137/143 | 20 | Southwest was Boeing's launch customer for this model. |
| Boeing 737-500 | 15 | 122 | 22 | Southwest was Boeing's launch customer for this model. |
| Boeing 737-700 | 425 | 137/143 | 9 | Southwest was Boeing's launch customer for this model in 1997. As of April 2013, all were equipped with satellite-delivered broadband Internet-reception capability. |
| Boeing 737-800 | 52 | 175 | 1 | As of April 2013, all were equipped with satellite-delivered broadband Internet-reception capability. |
| Total | 541 | | | |

| Other Fleet-Related Facts | |
|---|---|
| Average age of aircraft fleet | Approximately 11 years |
| Average aircraft trip length | 708 miles, with an average duration of 1 hour and 59 minutes |
| Average aircraft utilization per day | Nearly 6 flights and 10 hours and 43 minutes of flight time |
| Fleet size: | 106 |
| 1990 | 224 |
| 1995 | 344 |
| 2000 | 537 |
| 2009 | |
| Firm orders for new aircraft: | 33 |
| 2014 | 19 |
| 2015 | 31 |
| 2016 | 225 |
| 2017–2024: | |

Source: Information at www.southwest.com (accessed May 7, 2014).

- Using auto-throttle and vertical navigation procedures to maintain optimum cruising speeds.
- Introducing new engine start procedures to support using a single engine for runway taxiing.
- Reducing engine aircraft idle speed while on the ground.

- Southwest was the first major airline to introduce ticketless travel (eliminating the need to print and process paper tickets); by 2007, ticketless travel accounted for more than 95 percent of all ticket sales.
- Southwest was also the first airline to allow customers to make reservations and purchase tickets at the company's website (thus bypassing the need to pay commissions to travel agents for handling the ticketing process and also reducing staffing requirements at Southwest's reservation centers). Selling a ticket on its website cost Southwest roughly $1, versus $3 to $4 for a ticket booked through its own internal reservation system and as much as $15 each for tickets purchased through travel agents and professional business travel partners. Online ticket sales at Southwest's website grew swiftly, accounting for 74 percent of Southwest's revenues in 2009 and 80 percent of all company bookings in 2013.
- For most of its history, Southwest stressed flights into and out of airports in medium-sized cities and less congested airports in major metropolitan

## EXHIBIT 6 Airports and Cities Served by Southwest Airlines, July 2014

| Southwest's Top-10 Airports, by Departures | | | |
|---|---|---|---|
| Airport/City | Daily Departures | Gates | Nonstop Cities Served |
| Chicago Midway | 233 | 32 | 64 |
| Las Vegas | 210 | 19 | 54 |
| Baltimore/Washington | 206 | 28 | 57 |
| Denver | 167 | 19 | 56 |
| Houston (Hobby) | 161 | 19 | 45 |
| Atlanta | 165 | 31 | 44 |
| Phoenix | 162 | 24 | 46 |
| Dallas (Love Field) | 124 | 15 | 18 |
| Orlando | 120 | 20 | 43 |
| Los Angeles | 104 | 12 | 23 |

| Other Airports Served by Southwest Airlines | | | |
|---|---|---|---|
| Akron, OH | Fort Myers/Naples | Norfolk | San Francisco |
| Albany | Greenville/Spartanburg, SC | Oakland | San Jose |
| Albuquerque | Harlingen/South Padre Island, TX | Oklahoma City | Seattle/Tacoma |
| Amarillo | Grand Rapids, MI | Omaha | Spokane |
| Austin | Hartford/Springfield | Ontario, CA | Tampa |
| Birmingham | Indianapolis | Orange County, CA | Tucson |
| Boise | Jacksonville | Panama City, FL | Tulsa |
| Boston Logan | Kansas City | Pensacola, FL | Washington, DC (Dulles) |
| Buffalo | Little Rock | Philadelphia | Washington, DC (Reagan National) |
| Burbank, CA | Long Island | Pittsburgh | |
| Charleston | Louisville | Portland, OR | West Palm Beach |
| Charlotte | Lubbock | Portland, ME | Wichita, KS |
| Cleveland | Manchester, NH | Providence | **International** |
| Columbus, OH | Memphis | Raleigh-Durham | Aruba |
| Corpus Christi, TX | Midland/Odessa, TX | Reno/Tahoe | Cabo San Lucas |
| Dayton, OH | Milwaukee | Richmond | Cancun |
| Detroit Metro | Minneapolis/St. Paul | Rochester | Mexico City |
| Des Moines | Nashville | Sacramento | Montego Bay |
| El Paso | Newark | St. Louis | Nassau |
| Flint, MI | New Orleans | Salt Lake City | Punta Cana, DOM |
| Fort Lauderdale | New York (LaGuardia) | San Antonio | San Juan |

*Source:* Company 10-K report, 2013; and information at www.southwest.com (accessed April 29, 2014).

areas (Chicago Midway, Detroit Metro, Houston Hobby, Dallas Love Field, Baltimore-Washington International, Burbank, Manchester, Oakland, San Jose, Providence, and Ft. Lauderdale–Hollywood). This strategy helped produce better-than-average on-time performance and reduce the fuel costs associated with planes sitting in line on crowded taxiways or circling airports waiting for clearance

to land. It further allowed the company to avoid paying the higher landing fees and terminal gate costs at such high-traffic airports as Atlanta's Hartsfield International, Chicago's O'Hare, and Dallas–Fort Worth, where landing slots were controlled and rationed to those airlines willing to pay the high fees. More recently, however, having already initiated service to almost all of the

## EXHIBIT 7  Southwest's Fuel-Saving Blended Winglets and Split-Scimitar Winglets

Blended Winglets: first installations began in 2007; fuel savings of about 3.5% per aircraft

Split-Scimitar Winglets: first installations began in 2014; fuel savings of about 5% to 5.5% per aircraft

*Source:* Southwest Airlines.

medium-sized cities and less congested airports where there were good opportunities for sustained growth in passenger traffic and revenues, Southwest had begun initiating service to airports in large metropolitan cities where air traffic congestion was a frequent problem—such as Los Angeles (LAX), Boston's Logan International, New York LaGuardia, Denver, San Francisco, Philadelphia, and Atlanta (when it acquired AirTran).

- To economize on the amount of time it took terminal personnel to check passengers in and to simplify the whole task of making reservations, Southwest dispensed with the practice of assigning each passenger a reserved seat. Initially, passengers were given color-coded plastic cards marked with the letter A, B, or C when they checked in at the boarding gate. Passengers then boarded in groups, according to their card color and letter, and sat in any seat that was vacant when they got on the plane. In 2002, Southwest abandoned the use of plastic cards and began printing a big, bold A, B, or C on the boarding pass when the passenger checked in at the ticket counter; passengers then boarded in groups according to the letter on their boarding pass. In 2007–2008, Southwest introduced an enhanced boarding method that automatically assigned each passenger a specific number within the passenger's boarding group at the time of check-in; passengers then boarded the aircraft in that numerical

order. All passengers could check in online up to 24 hours before departure time and print out a boarding pass, thus bypassing counter check-in (unless they wished to check baggage).

- Southwest flight attendants were responsible for cleaning up trash left by deplaning passengers and otherwise getting the plane presentable for passengers to board for the next flight. Rival carriers had cleaning crews come on board to perform this function until they incurred heavy losses in 2001–2005 and were forced to institute stringent cost-cutting measures that included abandoning use of cleaning crews and copying Southwest's practice.

- Southwest did not have a first-class section in any of its planes and had no fancy clubs for its frequent flyers to relax in at terminals.

- Southwest did not provide passengers with baggage transfer services to other carriers—passengers with checked baggage who were connecting to other carriers to reach their destination were responsible for picking up their luggage at Southwest's baggage claim and then getting it to the check-in facilities of the connecting carrier. (Southwest booked tickets involving only its own flights; customers connecting to flights on other carriers had to book such tickets through either travel agents or the connecting airline).

- Starting in 2001, Southwest began converting from cloth to leather seats; the team of Southwest employees that investigated the economics of the conversion concluded that an all-leather interior would be more durable and easier to maintain, more than justifying the higher initial costs.

- Southwest was a first mover among major U.S. airlines in employing fuel hedging and derivative contracts to counteract rising prices for crude oil and jet fuel. From 1998 through 2008, the company's fuel-hedging activities produced fuel cost savings of about $4 billion over what the company would have spent had it paid the industry's average price for jet fuel. But unexpectedly large declines in jet fuel prices in late 2008 and 2009 resulted in reported losses of $408 million on the fuel-hedging contracts that the company had in place during 2009. Since then, the company's fuel-hedging activities had continued to be ineffective in reducing fuel expenses; the company recognized losses on its fuel-hedging activities of $324 million in 2010, $259 million in 2011, $157 million in 2012, and $118 million in 2013. Southwest's fuel-hedging strategy involved modifying the amount of its future fuel requirements that were hedged based on management's judgments about the forward market prices of crude oil and jet fuel. As of January 2014, the company had fuel derivative contracts in place for about 20 percent of its expected fuel consumption in 2014, about 40 percent of its expected fuel consumption in 2015, and about 35 percent of its expected fuel consumption in 2016.

- Southwest regularly upgraded and enhanced its management information systems to speed data flows, improve operating efficiency, lower costs, and upgrade its customer service capabilities. In 2001, Southwest implemented the use of new software that significantly decreased the time required to generate optimal crew schedules and helped improve on-time performance. In 2007–2008, Southwest invested in next-generation technology and software to improve its ticketless system and its back-office accounting, payroll, and human resource information systems. During 2009, the company replaced or enhanced its point-of-sale, electronic ticketing and boarding, and revenue accounting systems. During 2010, it completed an initiative to convert to a new SAP enterprise resource planning application that would replace its general ledger, accounts payable, accounts receivable, payroll, benefits, cash

management, and fixed-asset systems; the conversion was designed to increase data accuracy and consistency and lower administrative support costs.

For many decades, Southwest's operating costs had been lower than those of rival U.S. airline carriers—see Exhibit 8 for comparative *costs per revenue passenger-mile* among the five major U.S. airlines during the 1995–2013 period. Exhibit 9 shows trends in Southwest's operating *costs per available seat-mile* rather than per passenger-occupied seat.

## Making It Fun to Fly Southwest: The Strategy to Provide a Top-Notch Travel Experience

Southwest's approach to delivering good customer service and building a loyal customer clientele was predicated on presenting a happy face to passengers, displaying a fun-loving attitude, and doing things in a manner calculated to provide passengers with a positive flying experience. The company made a special effort to employ gate personnel who enjoyed interacting with customers, had good interpersonal skills, and displayed cheery, outgoing personalities. A number of Southwest's gate personnel let their wit and sense of humor show by sometimes entertaining those in the gate area with trivia questions or contests such as "Who has the biggest hole in their sock?" Apart from greeting passengers coming onto planes and assisting them in finding vacant seats and stowing baggage, flight attendants were encouraged to be engaging, converse and joke with passengers, and go about their tasks in ways that made passengers smile. On some flights, attendants sang announcements to passengers on takeoff and landing. On one flight, while passengers were boarding, an attendant with bunny ears popped out of an overhead bin exclaiming "Surprise!" The repertoires to amuse passengers varied from flight crew to flight crew.

During their tenure, both Herb Kelleher and Colleen Barrett had made a point of sending congratulatory notes to employees when the company received letters from customers complimenting particular Southwest employees; complaint letters were seen as learning opportunities for employees and reasons to consider making adjustments. Employees were provided the following policy guidance regarding how far to go in trying to please customers:

**EXHIBIT 8**   Comparative Operating Cost Statistics per Revenue Passenger-Mile, Major U.S. Airlines, 1995, 2000, 2005, 2010–2013

| | Total Salaries and Fringe Benefits | | Costs Incurred per Revenue Passenger-Mile (in cents) | | | | | | | |
|---|---|---|---|---|---|---|---|---|---|---|
| | Pilots and Copilots | All Employees | Fuel and Oil | Maintenance | Rentals | Landing Fees | Advertising | General and Administrative | Other Operating Expenses | Total Operating Expenses |
| **American Airlines** | | | | | | | | | | |
| 1995 | 0.94¢ | 5.59¢ | 1.53¢ | 1.34¢ | 0.59¢ | 0.22¢ | 0.19¢ | 1.14¢ | 3.65¢ | 14.25¢ |
| 2000 | 1.16 | 5.77 | 2.04 | 1.90 | 0.48 | 0.23 | 0.18 | 0.58 | 3.30 | 14.48 |
| 2005 | 0.90 | 4.65 | 3.67 | 1.42 | 0.41 | 0.32 | 0.10 | 0.95 | 3.66 | 15.18 |
| 2010 | 0.88 | 5.18 | 4.57 | 1.92 | 0.47 | 0.35 | 0.13 | 1.23 | 3.68 | 17.53 |
| 2011 | 0.89 | 5.27 | 5.82 | 1.91 | 0.51 | 0.31 | 0.15 | 1.82 | 4.07 | 19.87 |
| 2012 | 0.86 | 5.17 | 6.10 | 1.87 | 0.43 | 0.30 | 0.12 | 1.91 | 3.70 | 19.61 |
| 2013 | 0.91 | 4.39 | 5.94 | 1.82 | 0.57 | 0.31 | 0.14 | 1.35 | 4.38 | 18.90 |
| **Delta Air Lines** | | | | | | | | | | |
| 1995 | 1.27¢ | 4.97¢ | 1.70¢ | 1.16¢ | 0.71¢ | 0.30¢ | 0.18¢ | 0.43¢ | 4.07¢ | 13.53¢ |
| 2000 | 1.27 | 5.08 | 1.73 | 1.41 | 0.54 | 0.22 | 0.12 | 0.74 | 3.03 | 12.85 |
| 2005 | 0.93 | 4.31 | 3.68 | 1.10 | 0.38 | 0.22 | 0.16 | 0.84 | 6.01 | 16.69 |
| 2010 | 0.91 | 4.15 | 4.51 | 1.33 | 0.14 | 0.28 | 0.10 | 0.64 | 6.26 | 17.41 |
| 2011 | 0.95 | 4.27 | 5.77 | 1.41 | 0.15 | 0.28 | 0.13 | 0.54 | 7.09 | 19.65 |
| 2012 | 0.99 | 4.57 | 5.97 | 1.53 | 0.15 | 0.28 | 0.14 | 0.71 | 6.85 | 20.21 |
| 2013 | 1.11 | 4.82 | 5.42 | 1.58 | 0.13 | 0.28 | 0.13 | 0.68 | 6.61 | 19.65 |
| **Southwest Airlines** | | | | | | | | | | |
| 1995 | 0.92¢ | 3.94¢ | 1.56¢ | 1.21¢ | 0.79¢ | 0.35¢ | 0.41¢ | 1.09¢ | 1.56¢ | 10.91¢ |
| 2000 | 0.86 | 4.22 | 1.95 | 1.22 | 0.48 | 0.31 | 0.35 | 1.42 | 0.96 | 10.91 |
| 2005 | 1.18 | 4.70 | 2.44 | 1.17 | 0.31 | 0.34 | 0.29 | 0.73 | 1.23 | 11.21 |
| 2010 | 1.37 | 4.97 | 4.63 | 1.47 | 0.28 | 0.46 | 0.26 | 0.83 | 1.32 | 14.23 |
| 2011 | 1.37 | 4.99 | 5.76 | 1.47 | 0.23 | 0.45 | 0.26 | 0.98 | 1.35 | 15.50 |
| 2012 | 1.57 | 5.66 | 6.70 | 1.86 | 0.42 | 0.51 | 0.26 | 1.29 | 1.72 | 18.43 |
| 2013 | 1.59 | 5.87 | 6.38 | 1.85 | 0.46 | 0.52 | 0.23 | 1.21 | 1.68 | 18.19 |

(Continued)

**EXHIBIT 8**  (*Continued*)

| | Total Salaries and Fringe Benefits | | Costs Incurred per Revenue Passenger-Mile (in cents) | | | | | | | |
|---|---|---|---|---|---|---|---|---|---|---|
| | Pilots and Copilots | All Employees | Fuel and Oil | Maintenance | Rentals | Landing Fees | Advertising | General and Administrative | Other Operating Expenses | Total Operating Expenses |
| **United Airlines** | | | | | | | | | | |
| 1995 | 0.86¢ | 4.73¢ | 1.51¢ | 1.51¢ | 0.90¢ | 0.29¢ | 0.17¢ | 0.53¢ | 2.92¢ | 12.58¢ |
| 2000 | 1.15 | 5.75 | 1.98 | 1.84 | 0.73 | 0.28 | 0.21 | 0.76 | 3.09 | 14.65 |
| 2005 | 0.62 | 3.72 | 3.53 | 1.60 | 0.35 | 0.30 | 0.16 | 0.60 | 5.09 | 15.35 |
| 2010 | 0.67 | 4.34 | 4.46 | 1.86 | 0.32 | 0.38 | 0.06 | 1.31 | 5.24 | 17.96 |
| 2011 | 0.69 | 4.38 | 5.60 | 2.14 | 0.32 | 0.36 | 0.08 | 1.38 | 6.07 | 20.34 |
| 2012 | 0.74 | 4.71 | 5.97 | 1.72 | 0.44 | 0.35 | 0.09 | 1.57 | 5.84 | 20.69 |
| 2013 | 0.95 | 5.01 | 5.59 | 1.70 | 0.41 | 0.35 | 0.10 | 1.38 | 6.19 | 20.74 |
| **US Airways** | | | | | | | | | | |
| 1995 | 1.55¢ | 7.53¢ | 1.59¢ | 2.09¢ | 1.05¢ | 0.29¢ | 0.13¢ | 0.73¢ | 4.32¢ | 17.73¢ |
| 2000 | 1.36 | 7.59 | 2.44 | 2.30 | 0.97 | 0.28 | 0.19 | 1.10 | 4.81 | 19.68 |
| 2005 | 0.78 | 3.74 | 3.89 | 1.50 | 1.06 | 0.31 | 0.06 | 0.66 | 7.26 | 18.49 |
| 2010 | 0.74 | 4.03 | 4.05 | 1.82 | 1.17 | 0.27 | 0.02 | 1.07 | 6.93 | 19.36 |
| 2011 | 0.72 | 3.96 | 5.57 | 1.82 | 1.09 | 0.27 | 0.03 | 1.02 | 7.47 | 21.24 |
| 2012 | 0.76 | 4.20 | 5.56 | 1.78 | 1.06 | 0.28 | 0.02 | 1.30 | 7.10 | 21.30 |
| 2013 | 0.75 | 4.29 | 5.24 | 1.69 | 0.93 | 0.29 | 0.02 | 1.93 | 6.68 | 21.06 |

*Note 1:* Cost per revenue passenger-mile for each of the cost categories in this table is calculated by dividing the total costs for each cost category by the total number of revenue passenger-miles flown, where a revenue passenger-mile is equal to one paying passenger flown 1 mile. Costs incurred per revenue passenger-mile thus represent the costs incurred per ticketed passenger per mile flown.

*Note 2:* US Airways and America West started merging operations in September 2005, and joint reporting of their operating costs began in late 2007. Effective January 2010, data for Delta Air Lines include the combined operating costs of Delta and Northwest Airlines; the merger of these two companies became official in October 2008. United Airlines acquired Continental Airlines in 2010, and the two companies began joint reporting of operating expenses in 2012.

*Source:* U.S. Department of Transportation, Bureau of Transportation Statistics, "Air Carrier Statistics," Form 298C, "Summary Data," and Form 41, Schedules P-6, P-12, P-51, and P-52, all for various years.

**EXHIBIT 9** Southwest Airline's Operating Costs per Available Seat-Mile, 1995–2013

| Expense Category | Costs per Available Seat-Mile (in cents) | | | | | | |
|---|---|---|---|---|---|---|---|
| | 2013 | 2012 | 2011 | 2010 | 2005 | 2000 | 1995 |
| Salaries, wages, bonuses, and benefits | 3.86¢ | 3.69¢ | 3.62¢ | 3.76 | 3.27¢ | 2.81¢ | 2.40¢ |
| Fuel and oil | 4.42 | 4.78 | 4.68 | 3.68 | 1.58 | 1.34 | 1.01 |
| Maintenance materials and repairs | .83 | .88 | .79 | .76 | .52 | .63 | .60 |
| Aircraft rentals | .28 | .28 | .26 | .18 | .19 | .33 | .47 |
| Landing fees and other rentals | .85 | .81 | .80 | .82 | .53 | .44 | .44 |
| Depreciation | .66 | .66 | .59 | .64 | .55 | .47 | .43 |
| Acquisition and integration | .07 | .14 | .11 | — | — | — | — |
| Other operating expenses | 1.63 | 1.61 | 1.56 | 1.45 | 1.41 | 1.71 | 1.72 |
| Total | 12.60¢ | 12.85¢ | 12.41¢ | 11.29¢ | 8.05¢ | 7.73¢ | 7.07¢ |

*Note:* The entries in this exhibit differ from those for Southwest in Exhibit 8 because the cost figures in Exhibit 8 are based on *cost per revenue passenger-mile,* whereas the cost figures in this exhibit are based on *cost per available seat-mile.* Costs per revenue passenger-mile represent the costs per ticketed passenger per mile flown, whereas costs per available seat-mile are the *costs per seat per mile flown (regardless of whether the seat was occupied or not).*

*Source:* Company 10-K reports and annual reports, various years.

No Employee will ever be punished for using good judgment and good old common sense when trying to accommodate a Customer—no matter what our rules are.[16]

When you empower People to make a positive difference everyday, you allow them to decide. Most guidelines are written to be broken as long as the Employee is leaning toward the Customer. We follow the Golden Rule and try to do the right thing and think about our Customer.[17]

Southwest executives believed that conveying a friendly, fun-loving spirit to customers was the key to competitive advantage. As one Southwest manager put it, "Our fares can be matched; our airplanes and routes can be copied. But we pride ourselves on our customer service."[18]

Southwest's emphasis on point-to-point flights enabled many passengers to fly nonstop to their destinations, thereby cutting total trip time and avoiding not only the added built-in travel time needed to make connections but also the oft-encountered delays associated with connecting flights (late incoming flights, potential equipment failures requiring repairs at the gate, and late departures). In recent years, about 72 percent of Southwest's passengers flew nonstop to their destination—nonstop travel was a major contributor to providing customers with a top-notch travel experience.

In 2007, Southwest invested in an "extreme gate makeover" to improve the airport experience of customers. The makeover included adding (1) a business-focused area with padded seats, tables with power outlets, power stations with stools, and a large-screen TV with news programming and (2) a family-focused area with smaller tables and chairs, power stations for charging electrical devices, and kid-friendly TV programming. Later, Southwest added free wireless Internet service for passengers waiting in its gate areas.

In 2013–2014, Southwest began offering in-flight satellite-based Internet service on all of its 737-700 and 737-800 aircraft, representing over 75 percent of Southwest's fleet. Southwest's arrangement with its Internet service provider enabled the company to control the pricing of in-flight Internet service (which in 2014 was $8 a day per device, including stops and connections). The addition of in-flight Internet service, coupled with the free wireless service available in all of Southwest's gate areas, meant that passengers traveling on a Southwest airplane equipped with satellite Internet service had gate-to-gate connectivity for small portable electronic devices—in early 2014, Southwest was the only carrier currently offering gate-to-gate connectivity on 75 percent of its total aircraft fleet.

In 2013, Southwest joined with DISH Network to give customers free access to 17 live channels and 75 on-demand recorded episodes from various TV series at no additional charge. This promotion was later extended through the end of 2014. Shortly thereafter, Southwest added a selection of movies on-demand (currently priced at $5 per movie) to its entertainment offerings and, in December 2013, became the first airline to offer a messaging-only option for $2 a day per device, including all stops and connections. Passengers did not have to purchase in-flight Internet service to access television offerings, movies on-demand, or the messaging-only service.

In 2013, Southwest introduced a completely redesigned Southwest mobile website and app for iPhone and Android that had more features and functionality. The app enabled passengers to begin using mobile boarding passes.

## Strategic Plan Initiatives, 2011–2015

**Integrating Southwest's and AirTran's Operations** The process of integrating AirTran into Southwest's operation began in 2013 and was expected to be completed by year-end 2014. Headed into 2014, Southwest had completed a number of integration milestones:

- Connecting capabilities between AirTran and Southwest flights had been fully deployed, thereby enabling customers of both Southwest and AirTran to book connecting itineraries between the two carriers and fly between any of the combined 96 Southwest and AirTran destinations on a single itinerary.

- Because AirTran utilized mainly a hub-and-spoke network system, with approximately half of its flights historically originating or terminating at its hub at Hartsfield-Jackson Atlanta International Airport, Southwest had begun gradually transitioning AirTran's Atlanta hub into a point-to-point operation to capture the efficiencies related to the scheduling of aircraft, flight crews, and ground staff. Converting AirTran's flight network into a point-to-point operation was in the final stages.

- In addition to converting AirTran's flight schedules into a point-to-point operation, Southwest had made excellent progress in merging and optimizing the combined Southwest-AirTran flight schedules. The optimization effort involved using a set of Southwest-developed tools for managing revenues and profitability to (1) discontinue service to unprofitable destinations (service to 15 AirTran destinations and 4 Southwest destinations was discontinued in 2011–2013) and redeploy the aircraft to other routes and markets, (2) adjust the frequencies and arrival-departure times of Southwest and AirTran flights to airports served by both Southwest and AirTran (to avoid having too many unsold seats and better optimize profitability), (3) establish point-to-point flights from airports currently served only by AirTran to select destinations currently served only by Southwest, and (4) establish point-to-point flights from airports currently served only by Southwest to destinations currently served only by AirTran. Southwest had established a Southwest presence in all AirTran cities not currently served by Southwest in preparation for rebranding all AirTran operations and activities as Southwest; already, AirTran operations in several airports had been rebranded as Southwest. Southwest management expected that optimization and alignment of the Southwest and AirTran flight schedules would produce significant cost savings, enable more efficient scheduling of airport employees, and free up aircraft for redeployment either to new destinations that looked appealing or to existing destinations where more flights were needed to serve the growing numbers of people choosing to fly Southwest Airlines.

- A total of 52 of AirTran's Boeing 737-700 aircraft had completed the process of being converted to the Southwest fleet. Conversion of AirTran's remaining 35 Boeing 737-700 aircraft was scheduled to occur when AirTran's flights to seven international destinations were redesignated as Southwest flights.

- Approximately 65 percent of AirTran employees had been converted to Southwest employees. The transfer of all remaining AirTran employees, including flight crews and dispatchers whose transitions were aligned with aircraft conversion, was scheduled for 2014.

- Southwest had made considerable headway in integrating Southwest's and AirTran's unionized workforces. AirTran's flight attendants, represented by the Association of Flight Attendants–CWA (AFA), had voted to ratify a new collective bargaining agreement with Southwest. The agreement with AFA applied to AirTran flight attendants until they transitioned to Southwest by the end of 2014 and automatically became members of the Transportation Workers of America union representing Southwest's flight attendants.

## Southwest's Fleet Modernization Initiative

Southwest had multiple efforts underway to modernize its aircraft fleet. One effort, referred to by Southwest as *Evolve—The New Southwest Experience,* entailed retrofitting and refreshing the cabin interior of its fleet of 425 Boeing 737-700 planes. The goal of the Evolve program was to enhance customer comfort, personal space, and the overall travel experience while improving fleet efficiency and being environmentally responsible. The cabin refresh featured recyclable carpet, a brighter color scheme, and more durable, ecofriendly, and comfortable seats that weighed less than the prior seats. By maximizing the space inside the plane, Evolve allowed for six additional seats on each retrofitted aircraft, along with more climate-friendly and cost-effective materials. Southwest retrofitted 78 of its 737-300 aircraft through Evolve in 2013. In addition, the new 737-800 aircraft entering the company's fleet had the Evolve interior. The 17 AirTran 737-700 aircraft that were transferred to Southwest's fleet at year-end 2013 were refreshed with the new Evolve interior, and the remaining 35 AirTran 737-700 aircraft were scheduled to be refreshed with the Evolve interior when they became a part of the Southwest fleet in the second half of 2014.

Furthermore, Southwest was divesting AirTran's fleet of Boeing 717-200 aircraft. It had negotiated an agreement with Delta Air Lines, Inc., and Boeing Capital Corp. to lease or sublease AirTran's 88 Boeing 717-200 aircraft to Delta. Deliveries to Delta began in September 2013 and were scheduled to continue at the rate of about three aircraft per month. The seating capacity of the AirTran Boeing 717-200 planes was being replaced by (1) extending the retirement dates for a portion of Southwest's 737-300 and 737-500 aircraft, (2) acquiring used Boeing 737 aircraft from other sources, and (3) the forthcoming deliveries of new Boeing 737 aircraft. The company did not want to keep Boeing 717-200 planes in its aircraft fleet because of the added maintenance and repair costs associated with having a second type of plane in the fleet. Moreover, replacing the Boeing 717 aircraft capacity with Boeing 737 capacity provided incremental revenue opportunities because the latter had more seats per aircraft yet cost approximately the same amount to fly on a per-trip basis as the smaller Boeing 717 aircraft.

**Incorporating Larger Boeing Aircraft into Southwest's Fleet**  Starting in 2012, Southwest began a long-term initiative to replace older Southwest aircraft with a new generation of Boeing aircraft that had greater seating capacity, a quieter interior, LED reading and ceiling lighting, improved security features, reduced maintenance requirements, increased fuel efficiency, and the capability to fly longer distances without refueling. Of the 680 active aircraft in Southwest's fleet at year-end 2013, the company had plans to remove 122 Boeing 737-300 aircraft (with 143 seats and an average age of 20 years), 15 Boeing 737-500 aircraft (with 122 seats and an average age of 22 years), and 12 Boeing 717-200 aircraft (with 117 seats and an average age of 12 years) from its fleet over the next five years and replace them with new Boeing 737-700s (143 seats), 737-800s (175 seats), and 737-MAX aircraft (up to 189 seats). While Southwest had added 54 new Boeing 737-700 and 737-800 planes to its fleet in 2012–2013, even bigger additions of new planes were scheduled for future delivery. As of early 2014, Southwest had placed firm orders for 52 Boeing 737-800 aircraft to be delivered in 2014–2015, 56 Boeing 737-700 aircraft to be delivered in 2016–2018 (with options to take delivery on an additional 36 planes), and 200 737-MAX aircraft to be delivered during 2017–2024 (with options to take delivery on an additional 83 planes—Southwest was Boeing's launch customer for the 737-MAX). Plans called for some of the new aircraft to be leased from third parties rather than be purchased—of the company's current fleet of 680 aircraft, 516 were owned and 164 were leased.

Southwest expected that the new Boeing 737-800 and 737-MAX aircraft would significantly enhance the company's capabilities to (1) more economically fly long-haul routes (the number of short-haul flights throughout the domestic airline industry had been declining since 2000), (2) improve scheduling flexibility and more economically serve high-demand, gate-restricted, slot-controlled airports by adding seats to such destinations without increasing the number of flights, and (3) boost overall fuel efficiency to reduce overall costs. Additionally, the aircraft would enable Southwest to profitably expand its operations to new, more distant destinations (including extended routes over water), such as Hawaii, Alaska, Canada, Mexico, and the Caribbean. Southwest management expected that the new Boeing 737-MAX planes would have the lowest operating costs of any single-aisle commercial airplane on the market.

**Launching International Service and a New Reservation System**    In January 2014, Southwest launched an international reservation system separate from its domestic reservation system (but linked to and accessible from **www.southwest. com**) and began selling tickets for its inaugural international daily nonstop service on Southwest aircraft beginning July 1, 2014, to Jamaica (Montego Bay), the Bahamas (Nassau), and Aruba (Oranjestad). During this first phase of Southwest's international conversion plan, AirTran continued service between Atlanta and Nassau and between Chicago Midway and Montego Bay, as well as flights to and from Cancun, Mexico City, and Cabo San Lucas, Mexico, and Punta Cana, Dominican Republic. AirTran service to all these destinations was scheduled to be converted to Southwest in the second half of 2014. Southwest worked with an outside vendor, Amadeus IT Group, to create and support its international reservation service. In 2014, Southwest was in the planning stages of replacing its existing domestic reservation system with a comprehensive domestic and international system; in May 2014, Southwest chose Amadeus IT Group to be the vendor for this multiyear project.

**Growing Southwest's Rapid Rewards Frequent-Flyer Program**    Southwest's current Rapid Rewards frequent-flyer program, launched in March 2011, linked free-travel awards to the number of points members earned purchasing tickets to fly Southwest (the previous version of the Rapid Rewards program had tied free-travel awards to the number of flight segments flown during a 24-month period). The amount of points earned was based on the fare and fare class purchased, with higher-fare products (like Business Select) earning more points than lower-fare products (like Wanna Get Away). Likewise, the amount of points required to be redeemed for a flight was based on the fare and fare

class purchased. Rapid Rewards members could also earn points through qualifying purchases with Southwest's Rapid Rewards Partners (which included car rental agencies, hotels, restaurants, and retail locations), and they could purchase points. Members who opted to obtain a Southwest cobranded Chase Visa credit card, which had an annual fee of $99, earned 2 points for every dollar spent on purchases of Southwest tickets and on purchases with Southwest's car rental and hotel partners, and they earned 1 point on every dollar spent everywhere else. Holders of Southwest's cobranded Chase Visa credit card could redeem credit card points for items other than travel on Southwest, including international flights on other airlines, cruises, hotel stays, rental cars, gift cards, event tickets, and other items. The most active members of Southwest's Rapid Rewards program qualified for priority check-in and security lane access (where available), standby priority, and free in-flight WiFi. In addition, members who flew 100 qualifying flights or earned 110,000 qualifying points in a calendar year automatically received a Companion Pass, which provided unlimited free round-trip travel for one year to any destination available via Southwest for a designated companion of the qualifying Rapid Rewards member.

Rapid Rewards members could redeem their points for any available seat, on any day, on any flight, with no blackout dates. Points did not expire as long as the Rapid Rewards member had points-earning activity during the most recent 24 months.

Headed into 2014, the current Rapid Rewards program had exceeded management's expectations with respect to the number of frequent-flyer members added, the amount spent per member on airfare, the number of flights taken by members, the number of Southwest's cobranded Chase Visa credit card holders added, the number of points sold to business partners, and the number of frequent-flyer points purchased by program members.

Southwest allowed both its Rapid Rewards members and the members of AirTran's A+ Rewards frequent-flyer program to transfer their loyalty rewards between the Southwest and AirTran frequent-flyer programs, thus giving them access to the benefits of the combined programs.

In 2013, members of the Southwest and AirTran frequent-flyer programs redeemed approximately 5.4 million flight awards, accounting for approximately 9.5 percent of the revenue passenger-miles flown. This was significantly higher than the 2012 redemptions of approximately 4.5 million flight awards (accounting for approximately 9.0 percent of the revenue passenger-miles flown) and the 2011 redemptions of approximately 3.7 million flight awards (accounting for approximately 8.6 percent of the revenue passenger-miles flown). Southwest's Rapid Rewards members redeemed 2.4 million free-ticket awards during 2009 and 2.8 million free-ticket awards in both 2007 and 2008.

## Southwest's Growth Strategy

Southwest's strategy to grow its business consisted of (1) adding more daily flights to the cities and airports it currently served and (2) adding new cities and airports to its route schedule.

It was normal for customer traffic to grow at the airports Southwest served. Hence, opportunities were always emerging for Southwest to capture additional revenues by adding more flights at the airports already being served. Sometimes these opportunities entailed adding more flights to one or more of the same destinations, and sometimes the opportunities entailed adding flights to a broader selection of Southwest destinations, depending on the mix of final destinations the customers departing from a particular airport were flying to.

To spur growth beyond that afforded by adding more daily flights to cities and airports currently being served, it had long been Southwest's practice to add one or more new cities and airports to its route schedule annually. In selecting new cities, Southwest looked for city pairs that could generate substantial amounts of both business and leisure traffic. Management believed that having numerous flights flying the same routes appealed to business travelers looking for convenient flight times and the ability to catch a later flight if they unexpectedly ran late.

As a general rule, Southwest did not initiate service to a city and/or airport unless it envisioned the potential for originating at least 8 flights a day there and saw opportunities to add more flights over time—in Denver, for example, Southwest had boosted the number of daily departures from 13 in January 2006 (the month in which service to and from Denver was initiated) to 79 daily departures in 2008, 129 daily departures in May 2010, and 167 daily departures in 2014.

On a number of occasions, when rival airlines had cut back flights to cities that Southwest served, Southwest had quickly moved in with more flights of its own, believing its lower fares would attract more passengers. When Midway Airlines ceased operations in November 1990, Southwest moved in overnight and quickly instituted flights to Chicago's Midway Airport. Southwest was a first mover in adding flights on routes where rivals cut their offerings following 9/11. When American Airlines closed its hubs in Nashville and San Jose, Southwest immediately increased the number of its flights into and out of both locations. When US Airways trimmed its flight schedule for Philadelphia and Pittsburgh, Southwest promptly boosted its flights into and out of those airports. Southwest initiated service to Denver when United, beset with financial difficulties, cut back operations at its big Denver hub. In 2014, it was clear that Southwest intended to pick up the pace in adding service to more locations, particularly larger metropolitan airports, places like Hawaii and Alaska, and international destinations.

## Marketing, Advertising, and Promotion Strategies

Southwest was continually on the lookout for novel ways to tell its story, make its distinctive persona come alive, and strike a chord in the minds of air travelers. Many of its print ads and billboards were deliberately unconventional and attention-getting to create and reinforce the company's maverick, fun-loving, and combative image. Previous campaigns had promoted the company's performance as "The Low-Fare Airline" and "The All-Time On-Time Airline" and its Triple Crown awards. One of the company's billboard campaigns touted the frequency of the company's flights with such phrases as "Austin Auften," "Phoenix Phrequently," and "L.A. A.S.A.P." Each holiday season since 1985 Southwest had run a "Christmas card" ad on TV featuring children and their families from the Ronald McDonald Houses and Southwest employees. Fresh advertising campaigns were launched periodically—Exhibit 10 shows four representative ads.

Southwest tended to advertise far more heavily than any other U.S. carrier. According to The Nielsen Company, during the first six months of 2009, Southwest boosted its ad spending by 20 percent to hammer home its "bags fly free" message. Passenger

that is to change a person's attitude. So we prefer an unskilled person with a good attitude . . . [to] a highly skilled person with a bad attitude.

Management believed that delivering superior service came from having employees who genuinely believed that customers were important and that treating them warmly and courteously was the right thing to do, not from training employees to *act* like customers are important. The belief at Southwest was that superior, hospitable service and a fun-loving spirit flowed from the heart and soul of employees who themselves were fun-loving and spirited, who liked their jobs and the company they worked for, and who were also confident and empowered to do their jobs as they saw fit (rather than being governed by strict rules and procedures).

Southwest recruited employees by means of newspaper ads, career fairs, and Internet job listings; a number of candidates applied because of Southwest's reputation as one of the best companies to work for in America and because they were impressed by their experiences as a customer on Southwest flights. Recruitment ads were designed to capture the attention of people thought to possess Southwest's "personality profile." For instance, one ad showed Herb Kelleher impersonating Elvis Presley and had the message:[21]

> Work In A Place Where Elvis Has Been Spotted. The qualifications? It helps to be outgoing. Maybe even a bit off center. And be prepared to stay for a while. After all, we have the lowest employee turnover rate in the industry. If this sounds good to you, just phone our jobline or send your resume. Attention Elvis.

Colleen Barrett elaborated on what the company looked for in screening candidates for job openings:[22]

> We hire People to live the Southwest Way [see Exhibit 11]. They must possess a Warrior Spirit, lead with a Servant's Heart, and have a Fun-LUVing attitude. We hire People who fight to win, work hard, are dedicated, and have a passion for Customer Service. We won't hire People if something about their behavior won't be a Cultural fit. We hire the best. When our new hires walk through the door, our message to them is you are starting the flight of your life.

All job applications were processed through the People and Leadership Development Department.

**Screening Candidates**   In hiring for jobs that involved personal contact with passengers, the company looked for people-oriented applicants who were extroverted and had a good sense of humor. It tried to identify candidates with a knack for reading peoples' emotions and responding in a genuinely caring, empathetic manner. Southwest wanted employees to deliver the kind of service that showed they truly enjoyed meeting people, being around passengers, and doing their jobs, as opposed to delivering the kind of service that came across as being forced or taught. Kelleher elaborated: "We are interested in people who externalize, who focus on other people, who are motivated to help other people. We are not interested in navel gazers."[23] In addition to seeking individuals with a "whistle while you work" attitude, Southwest was drawn to candidates whom it thought would be likely to exercise initiative, work harmoniously with co-employees, and be community-spirited.

## EXHIBIT 11   Personal Traits, Attitudes, and Behaviors That Southwest Wanted Employees to Possess and Display

| Living the Southwest Way | | |
| --- | --- | --- |
| **Warrior Spirit** | **Servant's Heart** | **Fun-LUVing Attitude** |
| • Work hard | • Follow the Golden Rule | • Have FUN |
| • Desire to be the best | • Adhere to the Basic Principles | • Don't take yourself too seriously |
| • Be courageous | • Treat others with respect | • Maintain perspective (balance) |
| • Display a sense of urgency | • Put others first | • Celebrate successes |
| • Persevere | • Be egalitarian | • Enjoy your work |
| • Innovate | • Demonstrate proactive Customer Service | • Be a passionate team player |
| | • Embrace the SWA Family | |

*Source:* www.southwest.com (accessed August 18, 2010).

Southwest did not use personality tests to screen job applicants, nor did it ask them what they would or should do in certain hypothetical situations. Rather, the hiring staff at Southwest analyzed each job category to determine the specific behaviors, knowledge, and motivations that jobholders needed and then tried to find candidates with the desired traits—a process called *targeted selection.* A trait common to all job categories was teamwork; a trait deemed critical for pilots and flight attendants was judgment. In exploring an applicant's aptitude for teamwork, interviewers often asked applicants to tell them about a time in a prior job when they went out of their way to help a co-worker or to explain how they had handled conflict with a co-worker. Another frequently asked question was, "What was your most embarrassing moment?" The thesis here was that having applicants talk about their past behaviors provided good clues about their future behaviors.

To test for unselfishness, Southwest interviewing teams typically gave a group of potential employees ample time to prepare five-minute presentations about themselves; during the presentations in an informal, conversational setting, interviewers watched the audience to see who was absorbed in polishing their presentations and who was listening attentively, enjoying the stories being told, and applauding the efforts of the presenters. Those who were emotionally engaged in hearing the presenters and giving encouragement were deemed more apt to be team players than those who were focused on looking good themselves. All applicants for flight attendant positions were put through such a presentation exercise before an interview panel consisting of customers, experienced flight attendants, and members of the People and Leadership Development Department. Flight attendant candidates who got through the group-presentation interviews then had to complete a three-on-one interview conducted by a recruiter, a supervisor from the hiring section of the People and Leadership Development Department, and a Southwest flight attendant; following this interview, the three-person panel tried to reach a consensus on whether to recommend or drop the candidate.

Southwest received 90,043 résumés and hired 831 new employees in 2009. In 2007, prior to the onset of the Great Recession, Southwest received 329,200 résumés and hired 4,200 new employees.

## Training

Apart from the FAA-mandated training for certain employees, training activities at Southwest were designed and conducted by Southwest Airlines University (formerly the University for people). The curriculum included courses for new recruits, employees, and managers. Learning was viewed as a never-ending process for all company personnel; the expectation was that each employee should be an "intentional learner," looking to grow and develop not just from occasional classes taken at Southwest Airlines University but also from his or her everyday on-the-job experiences.

Southwest Airlines University conducted a variety of courses offered to maintenance personnel and other employees to meet the safety and security training requirements of the Federal Aviation Administration (FAA), the U.S. Department of Transportation, the Occupational Safety and Health Administration, and other government agencies. And there were courses on written communications, public speaking, stress management, career development, performance appraisal, decision making, leadership, customer service, corporate culture, environmental stewardship and sustainability, and employee relations to help employees advance their careers.

Leadership development courses that focused on developing people, building teams, thinking strategically, and being a change leader were keystone offerings. New supervisors attended a four-week course "Leadership Southwest Style" that emphasized coaching, empowering, and encouraging, rather than supervising or enforcing rules and regulations. New managers attended a two-and-a-half-day course on "Next-Level Leadership." There were courses for employees wanting to explore whether a management career was for them and courses for high-potential employees wanting to pursue a long-term career at Southwest. From time to time supervisors and executives attended courses on corporate culture, intended to help instill, ingrain, and nurture such cultural themes as teamwork, trust, harmony, and diversity. All employees who came into contact with customers, including pilots, received customer care training. Altogether, Southwest employees spent over 1.4 million hours in training sessions of one kind or another in 2013 (see the table at the top of the next page).[24]

**The OnBoarding Program for Newly Hired Employees** Southwest had a program called

| Job Category | Amount of Training (hours) |
| --- | --- |
| Maintenance and support personnel | 145,100 |
| Customer support and services personnel | 57,800 |
| Flight attendants | 109,450 |
| Pilots | 193,600 |
| Ground operations personnel | 911,400 |

*OnBoarding* "to welcome New Hires into the Southwest Family" and provide information and assistance from the time they were selected until the end of their first year. All new hires attended a full-day orientation course that covered the company's history, an overview of the airline industry and the competitive challenges that Southwest faced, an introduction to Southwest's culture and management practices, the expectations of employees, and demonstrations on "Living the Southwest Way." The culture introduction included a video called *Southwest Shuffle* that featured hundreds of Southwest employees rapping about the fun they had on their jobs (at many Southwest gatherings, it was common for a group of employees to do the Southwest Shuffle, with the remaining attendees cheering and clapping). All new hires also received safety training. Anytime during their first 30 days, new employees were expected to access an interactive online tool—OnBoarding Online Orientation—to learn more about the company. During their first year of employment, new hires were invited to attend a "LUV@First Bite Luncheon" in the city where they worked; these luncheons were held on the same day as Leadership's Messages to the Field; at these luncheons, there were opportunities to network with other new hires and talk with senior leaders.

An additional element of the Onboarding program involved assigning each new employee to an existing Southwest employee who had volunteered to sponsor a new hire and be of assistance in acclimating the new employee to his or her job and to Living the Southwest Way; each volunteer sponsor received training from Southwest's Onboarding Team in what was expected of a sponsor. Much of the indoctrination of new employees into the company's culture was done by the volunteer sponsor, co-workers, and the new employee's supervisor. Southwest made active use of a one-year probationary employment period to help ensure that new employees fit in with its culture and adequately embraced the company's cultural values.

## Promotion

Approximately 80 to 90 percent of Southwest's supervisory positions were filled internally, reflecting management's belief that people who had "been there and done that" would be more likely to appreciate and understand the demands that people under them were experiencing and, also, more likely to enjoy the respect of their peers and higher-level managers. Employees could either apply for supervisory positions or be recommended by their present supervisor.

Employees being considered for managerial positions of large operations ("Up and Coming Leaders") received training in every department of the company over a six-month period in which they continued to perform their current jobs. At the end of the six-month period, candidates were provided with 360-degree feedback from department heads, peers, and subordinates; personnel in the People and Leadership Development Department analyzed the feedback in deciding on the specific assignment of each candidate.[25]

## Compensation and Benefits

Southwest's pay scales and fringe benefits were quite attractive compared to those of other major U.S. airlines (see Exhibit 12). Southwest's average pay for pilots in 2013 was between 31 and 92 percent higher than the average pay for pilots at American Airlines, Delta Air Lines, United Airlines, and US Airways; the average pay for Southwest's flight attendants ranged from as little as 12 percent higher to as much as 38 percent higher than the pay of their counterparts at those same rivals. Its benefit package was the best of any domestic airline in 2013.

In 2013, in addition to providing vacation time, paid holidays, and sick leave, Southwest offered full-time and part-time Southwest and AirTran employees a benefit package that included:

**EXHIBIT 12**  Employee Compensation and Benefits at Select U.S. Airlines, 2005, 2009, and 2013

| | Southwest Airlines | American Airlines | Delta Air Lines | United Airlines | US Airways |
|---|---|---|---|---|---|
| **Average pilot wage/salary:** | | | | | |
| 2005 | $157,420 | $137,734 | $155,532 | $114,789 | $128,056 |
| 2009 | 176,225 | 137,482 | 137,948 | 125,465 | 110,595 |
| 2013 | 229,290 | 144,266 | 174,196 | 153,786 | 119,268 |
| **Average flight attendant wage/salary:** | | | | | |
| 2005 | $42,045 | $46,191 | $40,037 | $35,450 | $35,902 |
| 2009 | 46,839 | 50,933 | 39,161 | 40,559 | 41,080 |
| 2013 | 61,277 | 52,000 | 45,945 | 47,588 | 38,896 |
| **All-employee average wage/salary:** | | | | | |
| 2005 | $62,122 | $57,889 | $57,460 | $49,863 | $48,873 |
| 2009 | 75,624 | 62,961 | 56,030 | 58,239 | 55,534 |
| 2013 | 81,675 | 68,269 | 72,960 | 68,056 | 59,118 |
| **Average benefits per employee:** | | | | | |
| 2005 | $26,075 | $24,460 | $39,379 | $20,980 | $14,607 |
| 2009 | 23,820 | 30,516 | 28,279 | 22,749 | 13,547 |
| 2013 | 34,573 | 27,028 | 32,638 | 32,222 | 26,552 |

*Source:* Information at **www.airlinefinancials.com** (accessed May 22, 2013).

- A 401(k) retirement savings plan
- A profit-sharing plan
- Medical and prescription coverage
- Mental health chemical dependency coverage
- Vision coverage
- Dental coverage
- Adoption assistance
- Mental health assistance
- Life insurance
- Accidental death and dismemberment insurance
- Long-term disability insurance
- Dependent life insurance
- Dependent care flexible spending account
- Health care flexible spending account
- Employee stock purchase plan
- Wellness program
- Flight privileges
- Health care for committed partners
- Early retiree health care

Company contributions to employee 410(k) and profit-sharing plans totaled $1.74 billion during the 2009–2013 period. In 2013, Southwest's contribution to the profit-sharing plan represented about 6 percent of each eligible employee's compensation. Employees participating in stock purchases via payroll deductions bought 1.7 million shares in 2011, 2.2 million shares in 2012, and 1.5 million shares in 2013 at prices equal to 90 percent of the market value at the end of each monthly purchase period.

## Employee Relations

About 83 percent of Southwest's 45,000 employees belonged to a union. An in-house union—the Southwest Airline Pilots Association—represented the company's pilots. The Teamsters Union represented Southwest's stock clerks and flight simulator technicians; a local of the Transportation Workers of America represented flight attendants; another local of the Transportation Workers of America represented baggage handlers, ground crews, and provisioning employees; the International Association of Machinists and Aerospace Workers represented customer service and reservation employees; and the Aircraft Mechanics Fraternal Association represented the company's mechanics.

Management encouraged union members and negotiators to research their pressing issues and to conduct employee surveys before each contract negotiation. Southwest's contracts with the unions representing its employees were relatively free of restrictive work rules and narrow job classifications that might impede worker productivity. All of the contracts allowed any qualified employee to perform any function—thus pilots, ticket agents, and gate personnel could help load and unload baggage when needed, and flight attendants could pick up trash and make plane cabins more presentable for passengers boarding the next flight.

Except for one brief strike by machinists in the early 1980s and some unusually difficult negotiations in 2000–2001, Southwest's relationships with the unions representing its employee groups were harmonious and nonadversarial for the most part—even though there were sometimes spirited disagreements over particular issues.

## The No-Layoff Policy

Southwest Airlines had never laid off or furloughed any of its employees since the company began operations in 1971. The company's no-layoff policy was seen as integral to how the company treated its employees and to management's efforts to sustain and nurture the culture. According to Kelleher:[26]

> Nothing kills your company's culture like layoffs. Nobody has ever been furloughed here, and that is unprecedented in the airline industry. It's been a huge strength of ours. It's certainly helped negotiate our union contracts. . . . We could have furloughed at various times and been more profitable, but I always thought that was shortsighted. You want to show your people you value them and you're not going to hurt them just to get a little more money in the short term. Not furloughing people breeds loyalty. It breeds a sense of security. It breeds a sense of trust.

Southwest had built up considerable goodwill with its employees and unions over the years by avoiding layoffs. Both senior management and Southwest employees regarded the three recent buyout offers as a better approach to workforce reduction than involuntary layoffs.

## Operation Kick Tail

In 2007, Southwest management launched an internal initiative called *Operation Kick Tail,* a multi-year call to action for employees to focus even more attention on providing high-quality customer service, maintaining low costs, and nurturing the Southwest culture. One component of this initiative involved giving a Kick Tail award to employees when they did something exemplary to make a positive difference in a customer's travel experience or in the life of a co-worker or otherwise stood out in exhibiting the values in Living the Southwest Way (Exhibit 11).

Gary Kelly saw this aspect of Operation Kick Tail as a way to foster the employee attitudes and commitment needed to provide "Positively Outrageous Customer Service"; he explained:

> One of Southwest's rituals is finding and developing People who are "built to serve." That allows us to provide a personal, warm level of service that is unmatched in the airline industry.

Southwest management viewed the Operation Kick Tail initiative as a means to better engage and incentivize employees to strengthen their display of the traits in Living the Southwest Way (and achieve a competitive edge keyed to superior customer service).

## Management Style

At Southwest, management strived to do things in a manner that would make Southwest employees proud of the company they worked for and its workforce practices. Managers were expected to spend at least one-third of their time out of the office, walking around the facilities under their supervision, observing firsthand what was going on, and listening to employees and being responsive to their concerns. A former director of people development at Southwest told of a conversation he had with one of Southwest's terminal managers:[27]

> While I was out in the field visiting one of our stations, one of our managers mentioned to me that he wanted to put up a suggestion box. I responded by saying that, "Sure—why don't you put up a suggestion box right here on this wall and then admit you are a failure as a manager?" Our theory is, if you have to put up a box so people can write down their ideas and toss them in, it means you are not doing what you are supposed to be doing. You are supposed to be setting your people up to be winners. To do that, you should be there listening to them and available to them in person, not via a suggestion box. For the most part, I think we have a very good sense of this at Southwest. I think that most people employed here know that they can call any one of our vice presidents on the telephone and get heard, almost immediately.

The suggestion box gives managers an out; it relinquishes their responsibility to be accessible to their people, and that's when we have gotten in trouble at Southwest—when we can no longer be responsive to our flight attendants or customer service agents, when they can't gain access to somebody who can give them resources and answers.

Company executives were very approachable, insisting on being called by their first names. At new employee orientations, people were told, "We do not call the company chairman and CEO Mr. Kelly, we call him Gary." Managers and executives had an open-door policy, actively listening to employee concerns, opinions, and suggestions for reducing costs and improving efficiency.

Employee-led initiatives were common. Southwest's pilots had been instrumental in developing new protocols for takeoffs and landings that conserved fuel. Another frontline employee had suggested not putting the company logos on trash bags, saving an estimated $250,000 annually. Rather than buy 800 computers for a new reservations center in Albuquerque, company employees determined that they could buy the parts and assemble the PCs themselves for half the price of a new PC, saving the company $1 million. It was Southwest clerks who came up with the idea of doing away with paper tickets and shifting to e-tickets.

There were only four layers of management between a frontline supervisor and the CEO. Southwest's employees enjoyed substantial authority and decision-making power. According to Kelleher:[28]

> We've tried to create an environment where people are able to, in effect, bypass even the fairly lean structures that we have so that they don't have to convene a meeting of the sages in order to get something done. In many cases, they can just go ahead and do it on their own. They can take individual responsibility for it and know they will not be crucified if it doesn't work out. Our leanness requires people to be comfortable in making their own decisions and undertaking their own efforts.

From time to time, there were candid meetings of frontline employees and managers at which operating problems and issues between or among workers and departments were acknowledged, openly discussed, and resolved.[29] Informal problem avoidance and rapid problem resolution were seen as managerial virtues.

## Southwest's Two Big Core Values—LUV and Fun

Two core values—LUV and fun—permeated the work environment at Southwest. LUV was much more than the company's ticker symbol and a recurring theme in Southwest's advertising campaigns. Over the years, *LUV* grew into Southwest's code word for treating individuals—co-employees and customers—with dignity and respect and demonstrating a caring, loving attitude. *LUV* and red hearts commonly appeared on banners and posters at company facilities, as reminders of the compassion that was expected toward customers and other employees. Practicing the Golden Rule, internally and externally, was expected of all employees. Employees who struggled to live up to these expectations were subjected to considerable peer pressure and usually were asked to seek employment elsewhere if they did not soon leave on their own volition.

*Fun* at Southwest was exactly what the word implies, and it occurred throughout the company in the form of the generally entertaining behavior of employees in performing their jobs, the ongoing pranks and jokes, and frequent company-sponsored parties and celebrations (which typically included the Southwest Shuffle). On holidays, employees were encouraged to dress in costumes. There were charity benefit games, chili cook-offs, Halloween parties, new Ronald McDonald House dedications, and other special events of various kinds at one location or another almost every week. According to one manager, "We're kind of a big family here, and family members have fun together."

## Culture-Building Efforts

Southwest executives believed that the company's growth was primarily a function of the rate at which it could hire and train people to fit into its culture and consistently display the traits and behaviors set forth in Living the Southwest Way. Kelly said, "Some things at Southwest won't change. We will continue to expect our people to live what we describe as the 'Southwest Way,' which is to have a Warrior Spirit, Servant's Heart, and Fun-Loving Attitude. Those three things have defined our culture for 36 years."[30]

**The Corporate Culture Committee**  Southwest formed its Corporate Culture Committee in 1990 to promote "Positively Outrageous Service" and devise tributes, contests, and celebrations intended to nurture and perpetuate the Southwest Spirit and Living the Southwest Way. The committee was composed of 100 employees who had demonstrated their commitment to Southwest's mission and values and their enthusiasm in exhibiting the Southwest Spirit and Living the Southwest Way. Members came from a cross-section of departments and locations and functioned as cultural ambassadors, missionaries, and storytellers during their two-year term.

The Corporate Culture Committee had four all-day meetings annually; ad hoc subcommittees that were formed throughout the year met more frequently. Over the years, the committee had sponsored and supported hundreds of ways to promote and ingrain the traits and behaviors embedded in Living the Southwest Way—examples included promoting the use of red hearts and LUV to embody the spirit of Southwest employees caring about each other and Southwest's customers and showing up at a facility to serve pizza or ice cream to employees or to remodel and decorate an employee break room. Kelleher indicated, "We're not big on Committees at Southwest, but of the committees we do have, the Culture Committee is the most important."[31]

In addition, there was a Culture Services Team in Southwest's executive office dedicated solely to ensuring that the culture of Southwest Airlines remained alive and well; the team's duties included coordinating the yearly Messages to the Field, planning Spirit Parties at various locations, writing commendations and congratulatory notes to employees exhibiting outstanding performance, organizing the company's Annual Awards Banquet, and supporting the Corporate Culture Committee. Each major department and geographic operating unit had a Local Culture Committee charged with organizing culture-building activities and nurturing the Southwest Spirit within its unit. More recently, the company created a new position in each of its major operating departments and largest geographic locations called *culture ambassador;* the primary function of culture ambassadors was to nurture the Southwest Spirit by helping ensure that the Local Culture Committee had the resources needed to foster the culture at its location, planning and coordinating departmental celebrations and employee appreciation events, and acting as a liaison between the local office and the corporate office on culture-related matters.

**Efforts to Nurture and Sustain the Southwest Culture**   Apart from the efforts of the Corporate Culture Committee, the Local Culture Committees, and the cultural ambassadors, Southwest management sought to reinforce the company's core values and culture via a series of employee recognition programs to single out and praise employees for their outstanding contributions to customer service, operational excellence, cost efficiency, and display of the Southwest Spirit. In addition to Kick Tail awards, there were "Heroes of the Heart" awards, *Spirit* magazine Star of the Month awards, President's awards, and LUV Reports whereby one or more employees could recognize other employees for an outstanding performance or contribution.

Other culture-supportive activities included the CoHearts mentoring program; the Day in the Field program, in which employees spent time working in another area of the company's operations; the Helping Hands program, in which volunteers from around the system traveled to work two weekend shifts at other Southwest facilities that were temporarily shorthanded or experiencing heavy workloads; and periodic Culture Exchange meetings to celebrate the Southwest Spirit and company milestones. Almost every event at Southwest was videotaped, which provided footage for creating multipurpose videos, such as *Keepin' the Spirit Alive,* that could be shown at company events all over the system and used in training courses. The concepts of LUV and fun were spotlighted in all of the company's training manuals and videos.

Southwest's monthly employee newsletter often spotlighted the experiences and deeds of particular employees, reprinted letters of praise from customers, and reported company celebrations of milestones. A quarterly news video, *As the Plane Turns,* was sent to all facilities to keep employees up to date on company happenings, provide clips of special events, and share messages from customers, employees, and executives. The company had published a book for employees that described "outrageous" acts of service.

In 2012, Southwest launched the Southwest Airlines Gratitude (SWAG) initiative, which included a software tool that enabled each employee to set up a profile that listed all the recognitions and awards she or he received. This tool also allowed the employee to send commendations to other employees, recognizing their hardworking efforts and/or exemplary performance. Employees who won Kick Tail, Heroes of the Heart, Star of the Month, or President's awards were credited with SWAG points that could be redeemed in the company's SWAG Shop, which contained thousands of items and enabled employees to reward themselves in ways they found most meaningful.

## Employee Productivity

Management was convinced the company's strategy, culture, esprit de corps, and people management practices fostered high labor productivity and contributed to Southwest having low labor costs in comparison to the labor costs at its principal domestic rivals (Exhibit 8). When a Southwest flight pulled up to the gate, ground crews, gate personnel, and flight attendants hustled to perform all the tasks required to turn the plane around quickly—employees took pride in doing their part to achieve good on-time performance. Southwest's turnaround times were in the 25-to-35-minute range, versus an industry average of around 45 minutes. In 2013, just as had been the case for many years, Southwest's labor productivity compared quite favorably with its chief domestic competitors:

|  | Productivity Measure | |
|---|---|---|
|  | Passengers Enplaned per Employee, 2013 | Employees per Plane, 2013 |
| **Southwest Airlines** | **2,412** | **66** |
| American Airlines | 1,461 | 96 |
| Delta Air Lines | 1,553 | 107 |
| United Airlines | 1,038 | 127 |
| US Airways | 1,775 | 98 |

*Source:* Information at www.airlinesfinancials.com (accessed May 22, 2014).

## System Operations

Under Herb Kelleher, instituting practices, procedures, and support systems that promoted operating excellence had become a tradition and a source of company pride. Much time and effort over the years had gone into finding the most effective ways to do aircraft maintenance, to operate safely, to make baggage handling more efficient and baggage transfers more accurate, and to improve the percentage of on-time arrivals and departures. Believing that air travelers were more likely to fly Southwest if its flights were reliable and on time, Southwest's managers constantly monitored arrivals and departures, making inquiries when many flights ran behind and searching for ways to improve on-time performance. One initiative to help minimize weather and operational delays involved the development of a state-of-the-art flight dispatch system.

Southwest's current CEO, Gary Kelly, had followed Kelleher's lead in pushing for operating excellence. One of Kelly's strategic objectives for Southwest was "to be the safest, most efficient, and most reliable airline in the world." Southwest managers and employees in all positions and ranks were proactive in offering suggestions for improving Southwest's practices and procedures; suggestions with merit were quickly implemented. Southwest was considered to have one of the most competent and thorough aircraft maintenance programs in the commercial airline industry and, going into 2008, was widely regarded as the best operator among U.S. airlines. Exhibit 13 presents data comparing Southwest against its four domestic rivals on four measures of operating performance.

**The First Significant Blemish on Southwest's Safety Record**  While no Southwest plane had ever crashed and there had never been a passenger fatality, there was an incident in 2005 in which a Southwest plane landing in a snowstorm with a strong tailwind at Chicago's Midway airport was unable to stop before overrunning a shorter-than-usual runway and rolled onto a highway, crashing into a car, killing one of the occupants, and injuring 22 of the passengers on the plane. A National Transportation Safety Board investigation concluded that "the pilot's failure to use available reverse thrust in a timely manner to safely slow or stop the airplane after landing" was the probable cause.

**Belated Aircraft Inspections Further Tarnish Southwest's Reputation**  In early 2008, various media reported that Southwest Airlines had, over a period of several months in 2006 and 2007, knowingly failed to conduct required inspections for early detection of fuselage-fatigue cracking on 46 of its older Boeing 737-300 jets. The company had voluntarily notified the Federal Aviation Administration about the lapse in checks for fuselage cracks, but it continued to fly the planes until the work was

**EXHIBIT 13**    Comparative Statistics on On-Time Flights, Mishandled Baggage, Boarding Denials due to Oversold Flights, and Passenger Complaints for Major U.S. Airlines, 2000, 2005, 2010–2013

| Percentage of Scheduled Flights Arriving within 15 Minutes of the Scheduled Time (during the previous 12 months ending in May of each year) | | | | | | |
|---|---|---|---|---|---|---|
| Airline | 2000 | 2005 | 2010 | 2011 | 2012 | 2013 |
| American Airlines | 75.8% | 78.0% | 79.6% | 77.8% | 76.9% | 77.6% |
| Delta Air Lines | 78.3 | 76.4 | 77.4 | 82.3 | 86.5 | 84.5 |
| **Southwest Airlines** | **78.7** | **79.9** | **79.5** | **81.3** | **83.1** | **76.7** |
| United Airlines | 71.6 | 79.8 | 85.2 | 80.2 | 77.4 | 79.3 |
| US Airways | 72.7 | 76.0 | 83.0 | 79.8 | 85.9 | 81.5 |

| Mishandled Baggage Reports per 1,000 Passengers (in May of each year) | | | | | | |
|---|---|---|---|---|---|---|
| Airline | 2000 | 2005 | 2010 | 2011 | 2012 | 2013 |
| American Airlines | 5.44 | 4.58 | 4.36 | 3.23 | 2.92 | 3.02 |
| Delta Air Lines | 3.64 | 6.21 | 4.90 | 2.28 | 2.22 | 2.15 |
| **Southwest Airlines** | **4.14** | **3.46** | **4.97** | **3.59** | **3.08** | **3.72** |
| United Airlines | 6.71 | 4.00 | 4.13 | 4.25 | 3.87 | 3.47 |
| US Airways | 4.57 | 9.73 | 3.49 | 2.42 | 2.14 | 2.52 |

| Involuntary Denied Boardings per 10,000 Passengers due to Oversold Flights (January–March of each year) | | | | | | |
|---|---|---|---|---|---|---|
| Airline | 2000 | 2005 | 2010 | 2011 | 2012 | 2013 |
| American Airlines | 0.59 | 0.72 | 0.75 | 0.78 | 0.75 | 0.36 |
| Delta Air Lines | 0.44 | 1.06 | 0.29 | 0.30 | 0.79 | 0.52 |
| **Southwest Airlines** | **1.70** | **0.74** | **0.76** | **0.49** | **0.75** | **0.66** |
| United Airlines | 1.61 | 0.42 | 1.00 | 0.94 | 1.52 | 1.37 |
| US Airways | 0.80 | 1.01 | 0.91 | 0.87 | 0.79 | 0.55 |

| Complaints per 100,000 Passengers Boarded (in May of each year) | | | | | | |
|---|---|---|---|---|---|---|
| Airline | 2000 | 2005 | 2010 | 2011 | 2012 | 2013 |
| American Airlines | 2.77 | 1.01 | 1.08 | 0.87 | 1.86 | 1.99 |
| Delta Air Lines | 1.60 | 0.91 | 1.21 | 0.90 | 0.43 | 0.53 |
| **Southwest Airlines** | **0.41** | **0.17** | **0.29** | **0.14** | **0.20** | **0.36** |
| United Airlines | 5.07 | 0.87 | 1.47 | 2.14 | 1.93 | 1.89 |
| US Airways | 1.63 | 0.99 | 1.15 | 1.56 | 0.91 | 1.27 |

*Source:* Office of Aviation Enforcement and Proceedings, "Air Travel Consumer Report," various years.

done—about eight days. The belated inspections revealed tiny cracks in the bodies of six planes, with the largest measuring 4 inches; none impaired flight safety. According to CEO Gary Kelly, "Southwest Airlines discovered the missed inspection area, disclosed it to the FAA, and promptly re-inspected all potentially affected aircraft in March 2007. The FAA approved our actions and considered the matter closed as of April 2007." Nonetheless, on March 12, 2008, shortly after the reports in the media surfaced about Southwest not meeting inspection deadlines, Southwest canceled 4 percent of its flights and grounded 44 of its Boeing 737-300s until it verified that the aircraft had undergone required inspections. Gary Kelly then initiated an internal review of the company's maintenance practices; the investigation raised "concerns" about the company's aircraft maintenance procedures, prompting Southwest to put three employees on leave. The FAA subsequently fined Southwest $10.2 million for its transgressions. In an effort to help restore customer confidence, Kelly publicly apologized for the company's wrongdoing, promised that it would not occur again, and reasserted the company's commitment to safety; he said:

> From our inception, Southwest Airlines has maintained a rigorous Culture of Safety—and has maintained that same dedication for more than 37 years. It is and always has been our number one priority to ensure safety.
>
> We've got a 37-year history of very safe operations, one of the safest operations in the world, and we're safer today than we've ever been.

In the days following the public revelation of Southwest's maintenance lapse and the tarnishing of its reputation, an industrywide audit by the FAA revealed similar failures to conduct timely inspections for early signs of fuselage fatigue at five other airlines. An air travel snafu ensued, with over a thousand flights subsequently being canceled due to FAA-mandated grounding of the affected aircraft while the overdue safety inspections were performed. Further public scrutiny, including a congressional investigation, turned up documents indicating that, in some cases, planes flew for 30 months after the inspection deadlines had passed. Moreover, high-level FAA officials were apparently aware of the failure of Southwest and other airlines to perform the inspections for fuselage skin cracking at the scheduled times and chose not to strictly enforce the inspection deadlines—according to some commentators, because of allegedly cozy relationships with personnel at Southwest and the other affected airlines. Disgruntled FAA safety supervisors in charge of monitoring the inspections conducted by airline carriers testified before Congress that senior FAA officials frequently ignored their reports that certain routine safety inspections were not being conducted in accordance with prescribed FAA procedures. Shortly thereafter, the FAA issued more stringent procedures to ensure that aircraft safety inspections were properly conducted.

## ENDNOTES

1 Kevin Freiberg and Jackie Freiberg, *NUTS! Southwest Airlines' Crazy Recipe for Business and Personal Success* (New York: Broadway Books, 1998), p.15.

2 Ibid., pp. 16–18.

3 Katrina Brooker, "The Chairman of the Board Looks Back," *Fortune,* May 28, 2001, p. 66.

4 Freiberg and Freiberg, *NUTS!* p. 31.

5 Ibid., pp. 26–27.

6 Ibid., pp. 246–247.

7 As quoted in *Dallas Morning News,* March 20, 2001.

8 Quoted in Brooker, "The Chairman of the Board Looks Back," p. 64.

9 Ibid., p. 72.

10 As quoted in *The Seattle Times,* March 20, 2001, p. C3.

11 Speech at Texas Christian University, September 13, 2007, www.southwest.com (accessed September 8, 2008).

12 Freiberg and Freiberg, *NUTS!* p. 163.

13 Company press release, July 15, 2004.

14 Speech to Greater Boston Chamber of Commerce, April 23, 2008, www.southwest.com (accessed September 5, 2008).

15 Speech to Business Today International Conference, November 20, 2007, www.southwest.com (accessed September 8, 2008).

16 As cited in Freiberg and Freiberg, *NUTS!* p. 288.

17 Speech by Colleen Barrett on January 22, 2007, www.southwest.com (accessed September 5, 2008).

18 Brenda Paik Sunoo, "How Fun Flies at Southwest Airlines," *Personnel Journal* 74, no. 6 (June 1995), p. 70.

19 Statement in the Careers section at www.southwest.com (accessed May 16, 2014). Kelly's statement has been continuously posted on www.southwest.com since 2009.

20 As quoted in James Campbell Quick, "Crafting an Organizational Structure: Herb's Hand at Southwest Airlines," *Organizational Dynamics* 21, no. 2 (Autumn 1992), p. 51.

21 Southwest's ad entitled "Work in a Place Where Elvis Has Been Spotted"; Sunoo, "How Fun Flies at Southwest Airlines," pp. 64–65.

22 Speech to the Paso Del Norte Group in El Paso, Texas, January 22, 2007, www.southwest.com (accessed September 5, 2008).

23 Quick, "Crafting an Organizational Structure," p. 52.

24 Southwest's "2013 One Report," p. 42, www.southwest.com (accessed May 16, 2014).

25 Sunoo, "How Fun Flies at Southwest Airlines," p. 72.

26 Brooker, "The Chairman of the Board Looks Back," p. 72.

27 Freiberg and Freiberg, *NUTS!* p. 273.

28 Ibid., p. 76.

29 Hallowell, "Southwest Airlines: A Case Study Linking Employee Needs Satisfaction and Organizational Capabilities to Competitive Advantage," *Human Resource Management* 35, no. 4 (Winter 1996), p. 524.

30 Speech to Business Today International Conference, November 20, 2007, www.southwest.com (accessed September 8, 2008).

31 Freiberg and Freiberg, *NUTS!* p. 165.

# Nordstrom: Focusing on a Culture of Service

## Indu Perepu
### IBS Hyderabad

"We keep it simple and follow a customer-focused strategy. It's not a brand, technology, price, merchandising, or any other kind of corporate strategy at Nordstrom—it's about staying focused on improving customer service and taking care of customers one at a time. While our focus doesn't change, the different tools and opportunities we have available to us continue to evolve, and so we're taking advantage of them to do a better job of serving the customer. Our hope is that we can find more ways to build on our culture of service going forward."[1]
—Colin Johnson, Public Relations Director, Nordstrom

"[At] Nordstrom they zero in like a laser pointer on the right customers . . . and shower them with love."[2]
—Lior Arussy, President of Strativity Group[3]

". . . and if you've never experienced the quality of service that is 'normal' there (at Nordstrom), you've really missed something special."[4]
—Mitch Schneider, Senior Editor, Motor Age[5]

## HAPPY EMPLOYEES— HAPPIER CUSTOMERS

In early 2013, US-based specialty fashion retailer Nordstrom Inc. (Nordstrom) was chosen as America's favorite fashion chain in a customer study conducted by research firm Market Force Information[6]. In the survey conducted among 4,000[7] customers, Nordstrom was ranked high on attributes like customer service, ambiance, return policy, merchandise selection, ease of finding items, designer lines, unique clothing, and dressing rooms. According to Janet Eden-Harris, chief marketing officer for Market Force, "Nordstrom has cultivated a distinctive brand over the past century, and while it's known for its selection of designer clothing, its real claim to fame is quality customer service."[8] The other retailers featured on the list included Kohl's and Macy's (Refer to Exhibit 1 for the companies that featured on the list of Market Force Information Study).

Nordstrom was also rated as one of the best organizations to work for. CareerBliss, an online

---

[1] "Nordstrom," Retail Merchandiser, May / June, 2011.

[2] Alexandra DeFelice, "A Century of Love," Customer Relationship Management, June 2005.

[3] Strativity Group is involved in customer experience strategy design and implementation. Lior Arussy authored a book titled "Passionate & Profitable: Why Customer Strategies Fail and 10 Steps to Do Them Right! "

[4] Mitch Schneider, ". . . Ya Gotta Wanna," www.motorage.com, September 2002.

[5] Motor Age is a monthly trade journal.

[6] Market Force Information is a US-based company providing customer intelligence solutions.

[7] The survey was conducted among male and female shoppers aged between 18 and 65.

[8] Dawn Kent, "America's Favorite Fashion Retailers: Nordstrom Tops List, New Study Shows," www.al.com, March 06, 2013

This case was written by **Indu Perepu,** IBS Hyderabad. It was compiled from published sources, and is intended to be used as a basis for class discussion rather than to illustrate either effective or ineffective handling of a management situation.

career community, came out with a list of Happiest Retailers in 2011. Nordstrom was ranked at the number one position[9]. In 2012, CareerBliss considered the reviews of 10,000 employees and once again ranked Nordstrom number one on the list. According to Heidi Golledge, CEO and co-founder of CareerBliss, "Nordstrom is one of the places on the planet that is consistently ranked on both customer service as well as employee happiness."[10]

Since its inception in 1901, Nordstrom had operated on the principles of exceptional service, selection, quality, and value. The company's customer service philosophy focused on doing everything to satisfy a customer. This was supported by the culture in the company that empowered its employees. The company's culture revolved around customer service excellence and all the employees were expected to focus on providing the best service to the customers. The ultimate goal was having satisfied customers. The employees were empowered to take any decision that would benefit the customers. According to Erik Nordstrom, president of stores at Nordstrom, "[Our] sales associates are empowered to make decisions. We have one rule: use good judgment. That covers 99.9 percent of all situations."[11]

Due to this philosophy, Nordstrom was able to provide exceptional service to its customers. Delighting the customers started right from the time they entered the stores. The huge, brightly lit stores with a lot of space to move around instantly attracted the customers. Nordstrom stocked a wide range of merchandise in various sizes—even uncommon sizes—with the idea of not sending any customer back empty handed from the store. The sales associates helped the customers in selecting the merchandise, designing a look, choosing the accessories, and even in billing for the items purchased.

Serving the customers did not stop when the customers left the store. The sales associates sent a thank you note to them and called them later to find out about their experience with Nordstrom and the products purchased there. Thus, the sales associates built up a long-term connection with the customers and kept in touch with them constantly. Nordstrom's liberal return policy allowed the customers to return the goods purchased without a receipt, even after they had been used. According to Shep Hyken, a customer service expert and business author, "Superior customer service is a cornerstone of what makes Nordstrom Inc. a top retailer. They're not as interested in

## EXHIBIT 1    America's Favorite Fashion Retailers—Market Force Information

| Nordstrom |
| --- |
| Kohl's |
| Macy's |
| Dillard's |
| J C Penney |
| T J Maxx |
| Banana Republic |
| Old Navy |
| Ross Dress for Less |
| Target |
| Walmart |
| Marshalls |
| American Eagle Outfitters |
| Express |

Source: www.marketforce.com

making money as they are in making their customers happy."[12]

## BACKGROUND NOTE

Nordstrom was started as a shoe store called Wallin & Nordstrom in Seattle in 1901 by John W Nordstrom[13] (John) and Carl Wallin. Nordstrom invested US$5,000 in the company while Wallin invested US$ 1,000. They bought shoes for US$ 3500. The first day sales were US$ 12.50. The annual sales reached US$ 47,000 in 1905. In 1915, John's sons started helping him in the store.

---

[9] CareerBliss evaluated factors that impact happiness at work. These included work-life balance, senior management, compensation, benefits, job security, work, culture, and work environment. Employees from different companies were asked to rate their company confidentially.

[10] "CareerBliss Announces the Top 10 Happiest Stores for Your Shopping Pleasure," www.marketwatch.com, November 19, 2012.

[11] Stores Seek An Edge With Better Service. WWD: Women's Wear Daily, August 06, 2012

[12] Christian Conte, "Nordstrom Built on Customer Service," www.bizjournals.com, September 07, 2012.

[13] John W Nordstrom emigrated to the US from Sweden. He and Carl Wallin made money in the Alaska Gold Rush.

The founders retired after opening the second store in Northeast Seattle in 1923. In 1929, Carl Wallin sold his stake to John's sons, Everett and Elmer. The brothers faced a major crisis during the 1930s due to the Great Depression. In 1932, John's youngest son, Lloyd, joined the business as a marketing specialist. When the brothers took over the business, they renovated the stores, increased the display and merchandising area, carpeted the floor, and improved lighting. The upholstery was changed and comfortable chairs were installed. In 1937, a new large store was started in the Fifth Avenue. At that time the three brothers decided that the posts of president, vice president and secretary / treasurer rotated among them every two years. The goal of the second generation of Nordstroms was to sell shoes to everyone in town. To achieve that, they stocked shoes in different sizes, styles, brands, and colors.

During World War II, merchandise was in short supply as the leather and footwear were supplied to the military. Retailers could sell shoes only as per a quota. Even in such a situation, Nordstrom sold all the shoes in its stock at their original price. The brothers travelled across the country to procure shoes and also persuaded salesmen to sell them extra stock.

During the 1950s, Nordstrom opened stores in Portland and Northgate mall, the first shopping mall in the US. In 1959, the store at Pike Street was remodeled and reopened. The store, spread over four floors, stocked 100,000 pairs of shoes and was the largest shoe store in the country. Nordstrom also convinced manufacturers to supply shoes in odd sizes.

By the early 1960s, Nordstrom became the largest independent shoe chain in the US, with eight stores in Washington and Seattle. In 1963, it acquired Best Apparel, a Seattle-based clothing store. Soon, Nordstrom added children's clothes and sportswear to its clothing line. In 1965, a store that housed both apparel and shoes was opened in Northgate Shopping Center in Seattle. In 1966, a complete line of men's suits was added to the collection. In the same year, it acquired a fashion retailer based in Oregon, Nicholas Ungar, and the company was renamed Nordstrom Best. By 1970, the third generation—Bruce (Everett's son), James, John (Elmer's sons) and Jack McMillan (Lloyd's son-in-law)—took over. In 1971, the company went public and was formally renamed Nordstrom Inc. In 1973, the company's sales crossed the US$ 100 million milestone.

During the year, the company opened Nordstrom Rack[14,15] as a clearance outlet for Nordstrom stores. In 1973, the company's name was formally changed to Nordstrom, Incorporated.

By 1977, sales had reached US$ 250 million and Nordstrom had become the third largest quality apparel retailer in the US. In 1978, Nordstrom entered California by opening a 124,000 square foot store in South Coast Plaza Shopping Center in Costa Mesa. It was the largest shoe store in California.

Between 1978 and 1995, Nordstrom opened 46 stores across the US. The size of the stores also saw an increase. While the average area of the stores was around 70,000 square feet during the 1970s, it was about 200,000 square feet by the mid 1990s. In 1993, a computer system was introduced all across Nordstrom stores. This helped in tracking inventory, buying trends, the merchandise available in other Nordstrom stores, among other things.

In 1995, Nordstrom operated 59 specialty stores, five smaller stores, and 13 Rack stores. In 1995, the third generation retired and the company appointed a Co-chairman who was not a family member. Six fourth generation Nordstroms became co-presidents of the company. In 2000, Bruce came back from retirement to become the Chairman.

The company's website **Nordstrom.com** was launched in October 1998. In 1999, **Nordstrom.com** became a partly-owned subsidiary of the company. The website focused on supporting the store sales. It provided data like availability of merchandise, inventory in stores, fashion suggestions, chat with sales representatives, store location and direction, etc.

In 2000, Nordstrom acquired France-based chain Façonnable boutiques, which carried high-end, fashionable merchandise, for US$ 169 million. The chain had 24 stores across Europe. In 2001, Nordstrom opened eight more Façonnable boutiques in Europe. In 2005, it acquired a majority interest in luxury fashion boutique Jeffrey, which operated from Atlanta and New York. In 2007, Nordstrom sold the Façonnable boutiques for US$ 210 million to M1 Group, based in Lebanon.

---

[14] Nordstrom Rack stores were smaller, occupying an area of around 26,000 to 60,000 square feet, as against the 600,000 square feet occupied by the Nordstrom stores.

[15] It also sold through Last Chance Apparel and footwear stores and through Nordstrom Factory Direct.

Nordstrom also acquired stakes in several companies that included Haute Look (2011), Kids wear brand Peek (2011), and Menswear brand Bonobos (2012). In 2011, the company recorded sales of US$10.5 billion.

As of March 2013, the company operated through 117 full line stores; 121 Nordstrom Rack stores, which sold off-price merchandise; Last Chance, a clearance store; online sales subsidiary HauteLook; two Jeffrey boutiques; one Treasure & Bond Store, which donated all its profits toward charity; and its online store **www.nordstrom.com**. The company also operated spas under the 'Spa Nordstrom' brand. As of 2012, the company had 61,000 employees, both full time and part time. (Refer to Exhibit 2 for the Financial Data of Nordstrom.)

# THE NORDSTROM EXPERIENCE

By the time the second store was opened, Nordstrom had realized that great service to customers was one aspect that would differentiate it from other retailers. Right from that time, the business philosophy of the company was based on exceptional service, selection, quality, and value. The Nordstrom family believed that customers would always talk about the service they received, be it good or bad. So it sought to create a positive impact on the customers.

Making shopping a pleasant experience for the customers began right from the time the customer stepped into the store. The store's interiors, layout, design, aisles, lighting, fitting rooms, rest rooms, café, lounge, etc., reflected Nordstrom's intention to delight the customers. The stores stocked a wide range of merchandise in different brands and sizes, so that no customer ever left the place without buying what he / she had come in for. The sales associates provided exceptional customer service, and helped the customers through their shopping. The customer service continued even after the customers' shopping trip. The employees sent 'Thank You' notes and greetings for birthdays and anniversaries. They also kept in touch with the customers to let them know about the arrival of new stock and discount sales. All this formed a part of the Nordstrom experience. According to Dave Lindsey, Vice President, store planning and architecture at Nordstrom, "It (Nordstrom Experience) is everything from walking into

**EXHIBIT 2**   Nordstrom, Inc.'s Consolidated Statements of Earnings, Fiscal 2011–Fiscal 2012 (in millions of US$)

|  | Year Ended | |
|---|---|---|
|  | Feb-2-2013 | Jan-28-2012 |
| Net sales | $11762 | $10497 |
| Credit card revenues | 386 | 380 |
| Total revenues | 12148 | 10877 |
| Cost of sales and related buying and occupancy costs | (7432) | (6592) |
| Selling, general and administrative expenses: |  |  |
| Retail | (3166) | (2807) |
| Credit | (205) | (229) |
| Earnings before interest and income taxes | 1345 | 1249 |
| Interest expense, net | (160) | (130) |
| Earnings before income taxes | 1185 | 1119 |
| Income tax expense | (450) | (436) |
| Net earnings | $  735 | $  683 |

Source: http://phx.corporate-ir.net

a comfortable space, being greeted by our salespeople, having pride in serving the customer and, in the end, having that customer leave happy. If our salespeople welcome the customer into their departments as if she is entering their living room, we've done our job."[16]

# APPEALING STORES & ATTRACTIVE DISPLAYS

Nordstrom believed in creating a memorable experience for the customers whenever they visited the store. The exteriors were fashioned in such a way that the façade matched the existing architecture of the area. Right from the time the customers entered the stores, they were made to feel special. All the stores had adequate parking facility within walking distance from the store. During the annual sale or holiday season, when the store attracted a lot of crowds, valet parking was provided. The external windows of the store had attractive displays, which were changed often.

The company believed that customers usually formed an opinion of their shopping experience within the first fifteen seconds. Keeping this in mind, the stores were made to look attractive and uncluttered and the décor was bright. Wide aisles allowed shoppers to stroll around the store and shop in a leisurely fashion. About half of the entire floor space was dedicated to selling, as against other retailers who used about 70% of the floor space for selling.

Seating arrangements were provided at the entrance to the store. The elevators / escalators were located in the middle of the store. All around them were aisles leading to different departments. At the end of the aisles were the gift department, restaurant, dressing rooms, lounge, etc.

The merchandise was displayed on either side of the aisles to make it convenient for customers to browse through. The stores were designed in such a way that customers could walk around the perimeter of the store. The aisles were wide enough to accommodate people on wheelchairs and mothers with strollers. The elevators were also large enough to accommodate these. The escalators were also wider than those in other stores.

The design of the stores was usually circular, without any walls between different departments.

This allowed customers to look across the entire store. Different departments were partitioned by curtains, aisles, lounge seating, showcases, display fixtures, etc. These were also placed low so that the shopper could get a complete view of the store. The stores were decorated with plush carpeting, warm furnishings, poster art, oak panels, etc.

Several comfortable chairs and sofas were placed around the store for the customers to sit down and relax. A concierge was always around to help the customer, not only with the shopping, but also with information about places or restaurants close by, or to call a cab if required.

Within the store, the layout was such that one department led to the other. Each department was organized in such a way as to attract the customers. New merchandise was displayed on the aisle ways leading to each department, on mannequins, tables, etc. The main department and the display area were not overstocked, and the salespeople quickly retrieved products from the storage area.

The display of apparel and footwear was changed frequently in order to retain the interest of customers who visited the store frequently.

The dressing rooms and fitting rooms were also well designed and maintained. They had plush carpets, and a customer lounge with comfortable seating. The lighting in the dressing room enabled the customers to perceive the original color of the item being tried. The dressing rooms were cooler than the rest of the store, to enable the customers to try on clothes in comfort. Nordstrom stores had a 'women's lounge' which was a sitting area where the shopper could relax. The lounge also had a mothers' room where mothers could relax with their babies. The area had comfortable chairs and changing tables. The lounge and dressing areas had televisions, video games, coloring books and crayons etc. to keep the kids engaged.

The sofas in the shoe department were plush, as customers spent a considerable time in the department. The chairs were higher, making it easy for the customers to get up after wearing the shoes to try them on.

To make the store ambiance appealing, Nordstrom employed live piano players at several of its stores.

Many times, based on feedback obtained from the customers, the display was changed. When customers found that shopping for cosmetics was not comfortable, Nordstrom replaced the glass counters with makeup stations, where customers could try

[16] Anne DiNardo, "Nordstrom," September 18, 2006.

out products. All the cosmetics were displayed on shelves with clear price tags.

Restaurants were a part of the Nordstrom stores. There were four kinds of restaurants—the Espresso bar was located at the entrance to the store. It sold coffee, soda, and pastries; Café served soup, salad, pastries, beverages, and sandwiches; The Garden Court was a full service dining restaurant; and the Pub served sandwiches, salads, and ale besides coffee and breakfast items. If the restaurants where the customer wished to dine were full, he/she could book a table and continue to shop in the store. The customer was informed once the table was available.

Nordstrom also had a spa and beauty clinic attached to several of its stores. So, a customer could not only shop at the store but could also eat food and go in for beauty treatments, thus spending several hours in the store.

## WIDE RANGE OF PRODUCTS

Nordstrom believed that one of the most important things to satisfy a customer was offering a wide range of merchandise in different sizes. It believed that if a lot of merchandise was available in the store the consumer would never walk out without buying anything.

All the stores of Nordstrom stocked merchandise like shoes, apparel, cosmetics, etc. in a wide range in different sizes. For example, shoes were available from sizes 2½ to 14 for women and from 5 to 18 for men. The store also carried many half sizes.

The merchandise was arranged style-wise, enabling people to assemble their wardrobe quickly. The merchandise was displayed in different departments, each functioning as an independent boutique. Some departments catered to young customers, while the others displayed designer wear from renowned designers. The merchandise was divided according to lifestyles. For example, the individualist section had contemporary goods in the mid price range; the narrative section featured classic styles from labels such as Lauren by Ralph Lauren and AK Anne Klein. Menswear ranged from moderately priced products to designer pieces. Footwear included inexpensive shoes to costly Italian leather shoes. Usually all the stores categorized the merchandise by brand.

Nordstrom carried designer merchandise from popular brands and designers like Lacoste, Gucci, Diesel, DKNY, Diane von Furstenberg, Elizabeth Arden, Hugo Boss, Issey Miyake, Lush, Nina Ricci, Oscar de la Renta, Max & Mia, Tommy Hilfiger, Versace, Chanel, Jimmy Choo, Givenchy, Burberry, etc. It also sold its own label products that included Nordstrom Collection, Nordstrom at Home, Nordstrom Baby, Classiques Entier, Halogen, Nordsport, and BP.

Different departments were located strategically in the store. The women's shoes department was located prominently at the entrance of the store. The department was larger than any other department in the store and stocked a wide range of shoes in different sizes. The inventory was stocked behind the department, which made it easy for employees to fetch different items. The inventory was also stored in stock rooms off the sales floor and several employees were present in the stock room to locate the merchandise needed.

The buying was decentralized and the merchandise was purchased at the regional level by buyers who were assigned separately for each store. This was done keeping in mind the different tastes of customers in different regions, and this enabled the buyers to procure items keeping in mind the local tastes and preferences. The buyers interacted with store managers to determine the merchandise that was selling well, and the items that needed to be procured. The salespeople provided feedback from the customers to the buyers about the products and also provided input on the demands of the buyers with regard to particular styles, colors, and sizes. Sometimes, the salespersons accompanied buyers to give them their perspective about the items being procured. The buyers also spent a considerable time in the store interacting with customers. The buyers also took the help of external agencies to predict fashion trends.

While opening new stores, buyers played an important role in stocking the store with merchandise and then adjusting it according to the demand. During sale events, the buyers were usually present on the floor.

Decentralized buying helped the company experiment with new merchandise in a few stores and understand the customers' reactions to those. Nordstrom also had lead buyers, who were responsible for procuring merchandise in a particular category. They negotiated with the vendors for purchasing a large quantity of merchandise. However, for merchandize that was imported, the buying was centralized.

# CUSTOMER SERVICE AT NORDSTROM

Nordstrom's management structure also supported its sales personnel and customer service initiatives. It followed a management structure that resembled an inverted pyramid. On the top layer were customers. They were followed by the sales and support people, as they were the ones who interacted with the customers. Department managers were on the next rung, with buyers, merchandise managers, store and regional managers forming the fourth layer. The bottom-most layer consisted of the executive team and the board of directors. According to Jamie Nordstrom, President of Nordstrom Direct and Executive Vice President, Nordstrom, "We don't like to make decisions about customer service in the board room. We leave it to the people closest to the customers. One rule is, use good judgment. By not having a lot of rules, you empower associates to innovate and come up with solutions for customers."[17]

Nordstrom made every customer feel special, and ensured that they were attended to when they visited the store. At the same time, the salespeople were not pushy. When customers entered Nordstrom, they were acknowledged, and were guided to the right department, and assisted if they enquired about a specific style or size. Otherwise, they were allowed to browse through the merchandise in a leisurely fashion without being disturbed. The sales associates were always around and helped whenever customers asked for assistance. The associates tried to make the customers feel comfortable. The ice breaking conversation usually started with the associates complimenting the customers on their attire or accessories and offering to show other pieces of clothing that would complement them.

When customers specified what they were looking for, the sales associates took them to wherever that item was stocked. Then the pieces they had were displayed and the customer was given some time to select. The associates also explained how the pieces were stitched, the cloth used, etc., when they were asked about these. Once the clothes were selected, the sales associates asked the customers if they were comfortable with the fit, if the dress was in keeping with what they had intended to buy, their other preferences, etc. They then asked the customers if they needed anything else, and showed them accessories to go with the clothes they had purchased. When it came to shoes, the customers were shown additional pieces apart from the ones they had asked for. The salespeople usually helped the customers put together the right look. This included a complete set of clothes and accessories.

There were several cases of customers walking in demanding a particular piece that they had seen in an advertisement. Even if the sales associates felt that that particular dress might not look as good on the customer as it had on the model, they showed what the customer demanded. However, they also showed other pieces, which they thought would suit the customer better.

Nordstrom was also known for its direct-to-customer sale. If a customer found a particular piece of interest, but it was not in the preferred size / color, he/she could request the salespeople to get a similar item in that size, color etc. The sales assistants then contacted other Nordstrom stores for that particular item, and got it shipped to the customer's house.

As the sales associates built an extensive association with the customers, customers often requested the sales associates to suggest dresses for a particular occasion, or clothes and accessories they would need on a holiday. Customers often called the sales associates asking for a dress or shoes that they needed urgently. The sales associates then selected the merchandise, packed it and kept it ready for them.

The sales associates were not restricted to the department in which they were based, but were encouraged to sell merchandize from any department of the store to fulfill the needs of the customers. They asked the customers what they wanted and offered them different options. They even went to other sections to bring shoes and accessories matching the dresses selected by the customers.

There were separate checkout counters for each department, unlike the central checkout at most of the other stores. Even then, the sales associates took the payment from the customers, and got them billed. It was not necessary for them to stand in checkout queues. All the sales associates had their

[17] Jordan K Speer, Nordstrom's Big Secret Revealed, Apparel Magazine, November 2012.

personal business cards, which were given to the customers along with the receipt. This helped the customers get in touch with that particular salesperson during the next visit and enabled Nordstrom to provide personalized service.

After finishing shopping in Nordstrom, if the customers planned to visit other shops in the mall, they could leave their bags with the sales associates and collect them later. The sales associates also helped the customers carry their bags to the parking area. Nordstrom accommodated customers who continued to shop even after closing time.

The sales associates kept in touch with the customers through email and phone. After the customers left the store, the sales associates sent them a handwritten 'Thank You' note. Then after a few weeks, the customers were called to ask how they felt about the new dress or the shoes they had bought.

If the customer had requested to be informed about the next discount sale, an email was sent to him/her before the beginning of the sale. If a customer looked for a particular item but it was not available, then the associates called him/her when the stock arrived. The sales associates were well aware of the preferences of their customers, and called them when items which they preferred arrived at the store.

Nordstrom also held pre-sales, where the sales associates informed the customers about the items that would be put up on sale to help them choose. Only some of the privileged customers were allowed for pre-sales. Before the beginning of discount sales, customers could choose the items they needed, and provide their credit / debit card number. The items were held for the customer. On the first day of the sale, the items were charged to the card.

Nordstrom provided the personal stylist service free to all the customers. The personal stylists helped the customers choose the merchandise that suited them, and built a wardrobe for different occasions. The customers could call or text the personal stylists about any item in the store or for finding what they needed. The stylists helped the customers manage outfits and put them together, and also helped them in selecting outfits and accessories.

When regular customers asked for a particular suit / dress before coming to the store, by the time they arrived, the sales associates usually picked up the pieces that the customer might like and placed them in a private room for him/her to check. They also displayed accessories to go with the dress.

When new customers asked for such a service, their measurements were taken, their preferences pertaining to material, price, etc, were noted down, and suitable items were displayed for them.

In the shoe section, the salespeople usually measured both the feet of the customers, to see if there was any size difference. The time taken to measure the feet was used to talk to the customer and know him / her better. There were several instances of the sales associates catering to the needs of the customers with two different foot sizes by breaking two pairs of shoes.

Nordstrom had a liberal return policy, which allowed customers to return goods they had purchased, even without a receipt. When Nordstrom was operating with two stores, Everett, Elmer, and Lloyd established the return policy of the company. Though there was the risk of facing unreasonable returns, they still decided to go with it. For the first year, they calculated the cost of the return policy and decided to continue with it. Nordstrom's return policy was initiated with the belief that 98% of the customers were honest, and they should be taken care of. The customers were told that if they had bought anything and did not like it, they could always return it. Even when the customers had used the product for some time, they could return it and it was replaced without hesitation. If a similar product was not available, the amount was refunded.

There were several instances of sales personnel exchanging clothes that looked worn and used, without a word. In one instance, a customer bought a pair of shoes and used them for more than a year. But she had always been feeling that one shoe was larger than the other. She mentioned this to the sales associate during one of her visits to the store. The associate asked the customer to get the shoes on her next trip, and they were replaced without any questions being asked. A customer purchased a velvet jacket at full price at Nordstrom and a week later, a similar piece was sold at a discount at Neiman Marcus[18]. The customer spoke to the sales associate at Nordstrom about it. The associate immediately said that the discount would be adjusted.

Every Nordstrom store had a register where customers could jot down their experiences about shopping at Nordstrom. Every morning, before the store was

---

[18] US-based Neiman Marcus is a luxury specialty department store.

opened, the store manager and the employees assembled at the central lobby of the store, and the store manager shared some of the best customer experiences of the previous day with the employees. Sales staff whose service had been appreciated were rewarded.

The fact that at Nordstrom salespeople went out of their way to accommodate customers and fulfill their shopping needs helped the company gain word of mouth publicity. Many customers who had received great customer service, recommended a particular sales associate to their friends, who asked for that associate when they visited the store. According to Deniz Anders, company spokeswoman, "We believe that word of mouth is extremely important. If [the customers] have a good experience, they will tell their friends."[19]

## THE RIGHT PEOPLE

For providing great customer service, it was necessary to have the right kind of staff. Hiring of sales personnel was decentralized, and each store could decide on the people to hire, the interview process, training interventions, etc. Nordstrom looked for people with entrepreneurial spirit to be a part of its sales team. It did not look for people with previous experience in sales. This was because it was felt that experienced people often found it difficult to adjust to Nordstrom's way of selling. The company essentially looked for self-starters with a desire to form a career and a sense of ambition. It hired people based on their behavior, rather than experience. It also looked for people who were self-motivated and were nice in their disposition. According to Bruce Nordstrom, former Chairman of Nordstrom, "We can hire nice people and teach them to sell, but we can't hire salespeople and teach them to be nice."[20]

During their interviews, potential employees were asked to narrate their worst customer service experience and how they had dealt with it. They were also asked about the best experience they had had, and why they thought it was the best.

Nordstrom believed that people were best trained by their parents and did not provide much of formal training. All the new employees were given a one-day orientation course, which had a daylong session on customer service. At that time the employees were introduced to the 'Nordstrom Rule Book'. The book consisted of just one page. (Refer to Exhibit 3 for Nordstrom Employee Handbook).

The main rule in the book was using good judgment in all situations. The company did not have many operating rules and procedures, as it considered these as an impediment to the work of the employees. Instead, the employees were required to focus entirely on creating a satisfied customer. James F Nordstrom, former co-Chairman, was of the view that rules were a hindrance to giving customers the best service and to empowering employees. He was of the view that if there were more rules, they become more important to the employees than the customers and the company would move farther away from the customers.

The employees were shown a video 'The Nordstrom Story', which had a history of the company, and interviews with some of the Nordstrom family members. Very little formal sales training was provided. The employees were told to do whatever was appropriate, based on their judgment.

Right at the beginning, the new recruits were told that it was impossible to know beforehand what a customer would like or how he / she would behave. So they were asked to use their best judgment all the time and in all situations. Sales associates who joined the company were asked to find a mentor in one of the senior personnel in the store and were asked to start working on the sales floor.

After completing three months, the new recruits discussed their job performance with their reporting head. Those who were involved in sales were rated on parameters like productivity, customer service, and team work. If they were found to be lagging in any of the three parameters, they were provided assistance (additional training, mentoring from a senior employee, etc). If the sales associates consistently missed their targets, they were given special coaching.

The salespeople could share their experiences and compare their sales techniques with their colleagues through frequent staff meetings and workshops. Video recording of interviews with top salespeople along with tips and advice on selling were circulated to all the sales associates.

Nordstrom introduced the commission system in the 1950s. In the footwear department for example, the commission was paid on net sales and ranged from 6.75% to 8.25% of the sales on men's shoes.

---

[19] Alexandra DeFelice, "A Century of Love," Customer Relationship Management, June 2005.

[20] Andris A. Zoltners, PK Sinha, Sally E. Lorimer, "In Sales, Hire for Personality, then Train for Skill," http://blogs.hbr.org, August 29, 2012

# EXHIBIT 3   Nordstrom Employee Handbook

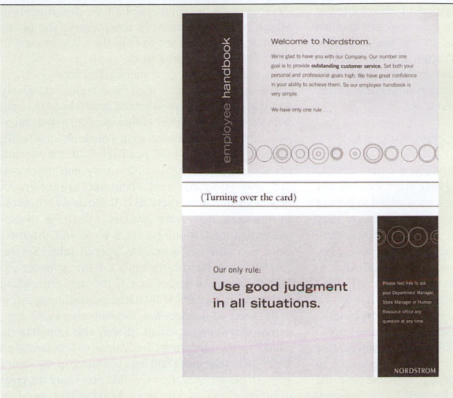

**Welcome to Nordstrom**

We're glad to have you with our Company. Our number one goal is to provide outstanding customer service. Set both your personal and professional goals high.

We have great faith in your ability to achieve them.

**Nordstrom Rules:**

Rule #1: Use your good judgment in all situations. There will be no additional rules.

Please feel free to ask your department manager, store manager, or division general manager any question at any time.

*Source:* Nordstrom Employee Handbook accessed from **http://blog.weekdone.com.**

9–10% on women's shoes, and 13% on children's shoes. The commission varied according to the area in which the store was located. The commission was paid on a draw system[21]. This meant that salespeople got either the base pay or the commission, whichever was higher. Employees also contributed 1–10% toward a tax-deferred investment retirement account, with matching contribution by the company.

At the same time, Nordstrom believed in encouraging employees to build business and in the process earn more money in the form of a commission. Thus, it encouraged competition among the employees. Right in the early days, the company used to conduct contests among the employees. Once it held a contest for selling a specific kind of shoes. The salesperson who sold the maximum number of shoes was given prizes like cash, dinner, trips, etc. Outstanding sales per hour and sales per month performances were rewarded with cash prizes, trips, awards, etc. In the monthly meetings, their contribution to the company was acknowledged.

---

[21] In the draw system, an employee is paid a base salary that is either supplemented or replaced by commission. In the case of Nordstrom, whichever was higher was paid to the employee.

The company's profit sharing and retirement plan was started in 1952. The Nordstroms wanted to make sure that the employees led a comfortable life after retirement. The profit to be shared was decided by the board of directors. The amount was deposited in a profit sharing trust. Nordstrom also had a 401(k) plan through which employees contributed 1 to 10% of their salary to an investment retirement account. The company also contributed to it.

# EMPOWERED EMPLOYEES

All the employees at Nordstrom were empowered to make their own decisions, and were given the authority to implement them. They were encouraged to behave like entrepreneurs running their own businesses. They were free to take decisions to provide the best service to the customers and create satisfied customers. They could take the initiative and act on it to add value to the customers. The employees were never criticized for providing service to the customers. It was not necessary for the sales associates to take the permission of their superiors to make a decision that was in favor of the customers. The sales associates were free to sell items at a lower price wherever necessary, to match the price of competitors. At the same time, the employees were asked not to hardsell, as the customer experience would take a back seat.

It was mandatory for all the sales associates to have thorough knowledge about the merchandise. They were required to be aware of different manufacturers, the reason for any difference in price, the unique aspects of different brands, price range, etc. The associates constantly updated themselves by reading about the trends in the industry. They were encouraged to attend seminars, watch videos, and also visit the vendors sometimes to know more about the products that they would sell. Before beginning their shift, the sales associates usually checked the department where they worked, to find out about the available stock, and made a note of any new stock that had arrived. They also checked if the merchandise demanded by their customers was available.

All the sales associates maintained a book that contained details about the customer's—name, telephone number, favorite brand, sizes, personal preferences, previous purchases, brand preferences, likes, other requirements, the time they usually shopped, etc. Customers' birthdays and anniversaries were also noted down in the book. The book also contained space where the associates could scribble daily and monthly goals, and to do lists, and a phone directory with the numbers of all the departments in all the Nordstrom stores in the country. The phone numbers were provided to help the salesperson call other Nordstrom stores to check the availability of particular items that customers asked for.

The sales associates used these books extensively to analyze customer preferences and to keep in touch with the customers. They called their customers regularly. In a day, the sales associates made about 40 calls. The sales associates took feedback from the customers about the merchandise that they had purchased and also informed them about the availability of new stock that they might like. If the items requested by the customers were available, then the associates called them to inform them about it. Customers were also informed about any special sales. Several employees in Nordstrom built a long customer list with thousands of names in it. Customers often asked for specific salespeople by name. According to a few of the successful associates, remembering customers' names was very important. It was also important to attend to the customers individually, accommodate them, and make them feel special. Some of the senior salespeople were of the view that providing the right experience was as important as providing the right merchandise.

Each Nordstrom store had a store manager and different departments in the store were headed by department managers. The store managers and the department managers were not hired from outside as Nordstrom believed that any person could appreciate the culture only when he/she had been a part of it and grown in it. People like department managers, store managers, and regional managers needed to know and understand the requirements of the salespeople, and only people who had been on the sales floor would understand this, according to the Nordstrom family. Most of the managers had worked with Nordstrom as sales personnel or in the stock department and were well aware about serving the customer.

The store managers were responsible for the store altogether. They too spent most of their time interacting with the customers and salespeople. They were asked not to micromanage things at the stores. The department managers were required to develop a sense of ownership. They were responsible for hiring people for their department and training, coaching, and nurturing the employees. They were also required to evaluate the employees and for scheduling daily activities. They had to take decisions about retaining and training employees. Every day, they spent some of their time on the sales floor interacting with the customers and staff. The managers were paid a commission and a bonus based on the increase in sales in a year.

Nordstrom was not much in favor of acquiring other companies. It preferred to open stores on its own, though this took more time. This it did in order to retain its culture. Several months before the new store was opened, experienced staff members from different stores were relocated to the new store. They helped in setting up the store and in recruiting and training new employees. According to some of the Nordstrom employees, it took a long time for the new employees to adjust to the culture of taking their own decisions. Time and again they had to be assured that they would not be criticized for doing their best for the customer. The company emphasized that they had to put customers above the company.

With the new stores being manned by old employees, the Nordstrom culture could be spread across these stores. The employees were also motivated as they knew that good work would be rewarded and they could get higher responsibility and positions in Nordstrom. With expansion, the people who were employed in the stores were given additional responsibility and a chance of advancement.

At the same time, doing customer service at Nordstrom was not everybody's cup of tea. The expectations from the salespeople were also very high. Only people who enjoyed selling were able to withstand the pressure that came with the job. If any employee was found to be earning only the hourly wage and the performance in sales was not up to the mark, that employee was either given extra training or moved to a non-sales position / support roles.

## MOTIVATING EMPLOYEES

All the employees including sales associates, buyers, and managers set daily, monthly, and yearly goals for themselves. All the employees worked toward meeting their own goals, along with the goals of the department, store, and region. They strove to surpass their previous year's achievements. If any department fell behind in achieving its daily target, the next day's target was increased. At the beginning of each work shift, the employees were reminded of their goals. The managers also constantly monitored the employees' goals and their achievements.

The best salespeople were designated as 'Pacesetters'. They were given a certificate and a 33% discount on purchases (13% more than what others got). When an employee became a 'Pacesetter' for the first time, he / she was given an engraved pen or a diamond lapel pin or other such trinkets. They were given business cards with 'Pacesetters' embossed against their name. The best performers were also assigned the best work-shifts. Each department had a different target to be considered a 'Pacesetter'. Depending on the number of associates who achieved 'Pacesetter' status, the target for becoming a 'Pacesetter' was changed. Salespeople who remained 'Pacesetters' for several years consistently were given generous rewards.

Employees who showed exemplary levels of customer service became a part of the weekly 'VIP Club'. The best performer of the month was chosen as 'Employee of the month'. The description of activities that made those employees 'Employee of the month' were circulated among the other employees. Their pictures were displayed in the customer service office in the store.

All the employees at Nordstrom had access to sales figures from different departments and different stores. The employees could compare their sales figures with those of other departments / stores. Sales per hour (SPH) was a measure that Nordstrom used to measure employee performance. Periodically, these figures were displayed in the backroom of the store, where all the employees could see their SPH figures. Employees with high SPH figures were rewarded at the end of the month. Similarly, the salesperson with the highest sales during the year was also given a cash prize and recognition.

When employees or departments reached their goals, the store manager made an announcement to that effect before the store opened the following morning. During the monthly store meetings, the managers shared with the other employees incidents of exemplary customer service and honored the salespersons who had provided such service. Letters received from customers were also read out during the meetings.

The Nordstrom family members were approachable and they kept the doors of their cabins open. Any employee could walk in and talk to them. All the family members answered their own phones. They visited the stores often, and interacted with the customers and salespeople. They made it a point to thank the salespeople for doing a great job and made them feel valued and appreciated. According to Jamie Nordstrom, "The cornerstone of the business has always been the people. We spend a lot of time talking about how we can improve our team. . . . It's the topic at most of our meetings."[22]

## CHALLENGES AND OPPORTUNITIES IN THE DIGITAL ERA

With the advent of new technologies like digital commerce, the concept of customer service had undergone a sea change. But Nordstrom used the technologies to serve the customers better.

However, the company experienced initial hitches when it started selling the merchandise online in 1999. At that time, the prices of merchandise available in the physical store and online were different, which confused the customers. Nordstrom then worked on the website and created a seamless shopping experience for the customers.

In 2002, Nordstrom introduced a perpetual inventory system through which sales associates could find sizes, colors, and styles of merchandise that was available at other outlets of Nordstrom. Later on, further improvements were made and the online inventory was combined with instore inventory. This enabled the customers to access any item that was available with Nordstrom at any of its stores.

In 2007, Nordstrom synchronized its store operations with the web catalogue. Through this, the sales personnel used the website to determine the kind of merchandise available for sale, and the merchandise available in all the Nordstrom stores and warehouses was viewed as the inventory that they had to sell.

In 2011, Nordstrom introduced mobile point of sale devices across its stores. It started using these units to help the customers find the items they were looking for in the store. The units helped in checking if the item was available in any other Nordstrom store. If it was available, the order was placed and the item was shipped to the customer. These devices also had a credit card reader, and the customer could sign for the purchase with his / her fingertip.

The registers that the sales personnel maintained, which contained details about the customers and their purchasing habits, were replaced by a tool 'Personal Book' which recorded all the details of the customers. The Personal Book generated reminders through which sales associates could contact customers about the availability of an item they had requested for, new stock in their favorite brand, sales, etc. The system was also used to gauge customers' response to the alerts. This made it easier for the sales associates to keep track of their customers. Personal Book automatically sent emails and alerts to the customers about upcoming sales and other events.

In a bid to give a boost to its online business, in September 2012, Nordstrom introduced free shipping and returns. It also worked to bring its famed customer experience online. According to Blake Nordstrom, "Our folks in the store do a good job with that, and we need to translate that online. For example, having a feature that suggests, 'If you like this, you might like these other items,' isn't new, but is something we need to improve upon."[23]

In the fourth quarter ended February 02, 2013, the company's online sales reached US$ 1 billion. The sales from mobile devices accounted for 20% of the total online sales. According to Blake Nordstrom, "We aspire to be the retailer of choice wherever and whenever customers choose to shop with us. And we understand that our customers' definition of services (is) changing."[24]

For companies like Nordstrom which relied on customer service to differentiate themselves from other retailers, e-commerce proved to be a huge challenge. According to Jamie Nordstrom, customers had higher expectations than they had before. "All the traditional definitions of customer service still exist, but e-commerce has changed those definitions, and added a lot of new ones,"[25] he said. He was of the view that customers looked for similar merchandise, sales, and prices whether they shopped at physical stores or online. But their expectations regarding customer services changed with the shopping channel. However Nordstrom maintained that customer service was important even in e-commerce.

---

[22] Jordan K Speer, Nordstrom's Big Secret Revealed, Apparel Magazine, November 2012.

[23] Catering to the Ever-Demanding Customer, WWD: Women's Wear Daily, October 24,2012.

[24] Anne D'innocenzio, Mae Anderson, High-End Spending, Improved Service Boosts Nordstrom's 4th Quarter Net Income 20 Per Cent, The Canadian Press, February 21, 2013

[25] Jordan K Speer, Nordstrom's Big Secret Revealed, Apparel Magazine, November 2012.

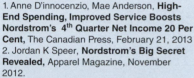

## SUGGESTED READINGS AND REFERENCES:

1. Anne D'innocenzio, Mae Anderson, **High-End Spending, Improved Service Boosts Nordstrom's 4th Quarter Net Income 20 Per Cent,** The Canadian Press, February 21, 2013

2. Jordan K Speer, **Nordstrom's Big Secret Revealed,** Apparel Magazine, November 2012.

3. **CareerBliss Announces the Top 10 Happiest Stores for Your Shopping Pleasure,** www.marketwatch.com, November 19, 2012.

4. **Catering to the Ever-Demanding Customer,** WWD: Women's Wear Daily, October 24,2012.

5. Christian Conte, **Nordstrom Built on Customer Service,** Jacksonville Business Journal, September 07, 2012.

6. **Stores Seek An Edge With Better Service,** WWD: Women's Wear Daily, August 06, 2012

7. Marina Strauss, **As Nordstrom's Arrival Looms, Rival Stores Sharpen up,** http://www.theglobeandmail.com, August 05, 2012.

8. Eric Savitz, **Help Your Organization Embrace the New Norm of Disruption,** Forbes.com, February 02, 2012.

9. Cotten Timberlake, **Nordstrom's Customer Service Catalyzes Growth,** Bloomberg Businessweek, August 14, 2011.

10. Cotten Timberlake, **How Nordstrom Bests Its Retail Rivals,** www.businessweek.com, August 11, 2011.

11. Summer Dennis, **Customer Service the Nordstrom Way!,** www.collectiveinktelligence.com, May 5, 2011.

12. **Deliver Customer Service,** WWD: Women's Wear Daily, July 28, 2008.

13. Suzanne Kapner, **Nordstrom,** Fortune, March 17, 2008.

14. **Nordstrom's Nexus,** Retailing Today, October 2007

15. **Nordstrom Synchronizing Channels for Sales Success,** SCT Week, August 20, 2007.

16. Jena McGregor, **Customer Service Champs,** BusinessWeek, March 05, 2007.

17. Jeffrey Gitomer, **Investment in People beats an Extreme Makeover,** The Central New York Business Journal, June 23, 2006.

18. Alexandra DeFelice, **A Century of Customer Love,** Customer Relationship Management, June 2005.

19. Jeffrey Gitomer, **Let's give them Something to Talk about,** The Enterprise, April 12–18, 2004.

20. Mitch Schneider, **. . .Ya Gotta Wanna,** www.motorage.com, September 2002.

21. Stanley Holmes, **Can the Nordstroms find the Right Style?** BusinessWeek, July 30, 2001.

## BOOKS

1. Robert Spector, Patrick D McCarthy, "*The Nordstrom Way, The Inside Story of America's #1 Customer Service Company,*" John Wiley & Sons, 2000.

2. Robert Spector, Patrick D McCarthy, "*The Nordstrom Way to Customer Service Excellence,*" John Wiley & Sons, 2012.

# Employee Training & Development at Ritz-Carlton: Fostering an Exceptional Customer Service Culture

## Debapratim Purkayastha

IBS Hyderabad

"As our Employee Promise states, the ladies and gentlemen of The Ritz-Carlton are the most important resource in our service commitment to our guests, members, and residents. That's why our commitment to learning and development is so important."[1]
—The Ritz-Carlton Company

"At a hotel you have a lineup three times a day for morning, afternoon, and night shifts. Four days a week we talk about our service values. We remind our ladies and gentlemen about the meaning of our service values.
"Once a week we share a best story of the week at every hotel. It's about reminding everyone about our commitment. They're not employees. They're ladies and gentlemen serving ladies and gentlemen."[2]
—Herve Humler, President and COO, The Ritz-Carlton Company, in 2013

A guest visited St. Thomas on a client incentive trip along with his girlfriend and checked in at the Ritz-Carlton. One day, during his stay at the hotel, he decided to rent standup paddle boards for a little fun on the beach. While paddling, he lost his balance and plunged into the water, losing his sunglasses in the process. Later that afternoon, a member of the hotel staff approached him and asked him if he had lost his sunglasses. When he said he had, the hotel staff handed over the missing sunglasses to him. Though the guest had not mentioned the sunglasses to anyone, one of the staff had overheard him talking about it. Some of the hotel staff indulged in a little snorkeling later in the day and recovered the glasses. Needless to say, the guest was delighted as it was way beyond his expectations. Such instances were a daily routine at the Ritz-Carlton hotels worldwide. The fulfillment of guests' unexpressed wishes and needs formed a part of the Ritz-Carlton mystique.

Ritz-Carlton was often cited as an example of a service company that had successfully leveraged the potential of its human resources to achieve excellence. It was also ranked first in the 'Training Top 125 Winners' list published by *Training* magazine in February 2007. The recognition was given based on the comprehensive training program that all its employees were asked to undergo to achieve service excellence. Ritz-Carlton was known for its sophisticated and elegant ambience and the exemplary quality of its service. The company cultivated its reputation by training its employees to provide high quality service that conformed to precise specifications and standards. The company invested sizeable resources (10% of its total payroll expenses[3]) in employee training and in developing the potential of its employees. It was one of the best employers in the US and had a voluntary attrition rate of 18%[4], which was significantly lower

This case was written by **Debapratim Purkayastha,** IBS Hyderabad. It was compiled from published sources, and is intended to be used as a basis for class discussion rather than to illustrate either effective or ineffective handling of a management situation.

To order copies, call +91 9640901313 or write to IBS Center for Management Research (ICMR), IFHE Campus, Donthanapally, Sankarapally Road, Hyderabad 501 203, Andhra Pradesh, India or email:
info@icmrindia.org, www.icmrindia.org

than the industry standard. According to Mandy Holloway (Holloway), senior director of global learning at Ritz-Carlton, "We take training and learning very seriously. We focus on the design of learning, measured competency, and whether the skills learned are truly being delivered to the customer."[5]

## ABOUT RITZ-CARLTON

The Ritz-Carlton Hotel Company, LLC, headquartered in Chevy Chase, Maryland, USA, was a wholly-owned subsidiary of Marriott International, Inc. As of September 2013, it operated 80 hotels and resorts in the Americas, Europe, Asia, the Middle East, Africa, and the Caribbean, with 30 more projects under development across the globe (*Refer to Exhibit 1 for Ritz's Lodging and Timesharing products*). The company had revenue of US$3billion for the year 2012 (Refer to Exhibit 2 for Marriott's Revenues). Ritz-Carlton was known for the luxury and world-class service its hotels offered to guests. Further, it was the only service company to have earned the prestigious Malcolm Baldrige National Quality Award twice—in 1992 and in 1999. In addition to this, the company had earned many other awards and certifications in recognition of its quality excellence and achievements.

The foundation for Ritz-Carlton's service quality excellence was laid in 1898 when Cesar Ritz, a Swiss hotelier (known as the 'king of hoteliers and hotelier to kings'[6]), opened the first Ritz hotel in Paris. Prior to this, Cesar Ritz had worked in several well-known hotels. He had definite ideas about what constituted a good hotel and he designed the Ritz Paris in keeping with these ideas. The hotel turned out to be one of the most elegant hotels of the time and became a great favorite with the wealthy and aristocratic members of society due to its design, furnishings, and meticulous service. During the early 1900s, Cesar Ritz focused on expanding the Ritz hotels across Europe. He opened the Carlton hotel in London during the same time. To franchise the Ritz-Carlton name and logo, he also set up the Ritz-Carlton Management Corporation (RCMC), which set the service and culinary standards that had to be adhered to by the franchisees.

In 1918, Cesar Ritz died and his wife continued to manage RCMC. In 1927, the first Ritz-Carlton in the US was established in Boston. Several others followed—in New York, Philadelphia, Pittsburgh, Atlantic City, and Boca Raton in the US and also across Europe. However, between the late 1920s and the 1940s, the business suffered a downturn due to the Great Depression and World War II (1939–1945). All the hotels, except the Boston Ritz-Carlton (set up in 1927), went bankrupt. After World War II, Charles Ritz, Cesar Ritz's son, took over the management of RCMC. He franchised the name to several new investors in Europe, as the European luxury hotel business had recovered quickly.

In 1983, Johnson Properties (Johnson), a company owned by William B. Johnson (a real estate businessman from Atlanta), purchased the Boston Ritz-Carlton and the US trademark for the Ritz-Carlton name for $75.5 million. Johnson then incorporated its hotel business as the Ritz-Carlton Hotel

## EXHIBIT 1  Total Lodging and Timeshare Products

| Luxury Lodging Segment | Properties | | | Rooms | | |
|---|---|---|---|---|---|---|
| | US | Non-US | Total | US | Non-US | Total |
| The Ritz-Carlton | 38 | 42 | 80 | 11,357 | 12,410 | 23,767 |
| Bulgari Hotels & Resorts | — | 3 | 3 | — | 202 | 202 |
| EDITION | — | 1 | 1 | — | 78 | 78 |
| The Ritz-Carlton Residential | 30 | 5 | 35 | 3,598 | 329 | 3,927 |
| The Ritz-Carlton Serviced Apartments | | 4 | 4 | — | 579 | 579 |
| Total | 68 | 55 | 123 | 14,955 | 13,598 | 28,553 |

*Source:* "Marriott International, Inc. 2012 Annual Report", http://files.shareholder.com/downloads/MAR/2734095087x0x651624/51819A94-F37F-4A6A-B735-E6F861259F1C/Marriott_2012AR.pdf, 2012.

**EXHIBIT 2**    Marriott International, Inc. Consolidated Statements of Income (2010–2012)

| | $ in millions, except per share amounts | | |
| --- | --- | --- | --- |
| | 2012 | 2011 | 2010 |
| Revenues | | | |
| Base Management Fees | $581 | $602 | $562 |
| Franchise Fees | 607 | 506 | 441 |
| Incentive Management fees | 232 | 195 | 182 |
| Owned, leased, corporate housing and other revenue | 989 | 1,083 | 1,046 |
| Timeshare sales and services | — | 1,088 | 1,221 |
| Cost reimbursements | 9,405 | 8,843 | 8,239 |
| **Total** | 11,814 | 12,317 | 11,691 |
| Operating Costs and Expenses | | | |
| Owned, leased and corporate housing-direct | 824 | 943 | 955 |
| Timeshare-direct | — | 929 | 1,022 |
| Timeshare strategy-impairment charges | — | 324 | — |
| Reimbursed costs | 9,405 | 8,843 | 8,239 |
| General, administrative and other | 645 | 752 | 780 |
| **Total** | 10,874 | 11,791 | 10,996 |
| Operating Income | 940 | 526 | 695 |
| Gains (losses) and other income | 42 | (7) | 35 |
| Interest expense | (137) | (164) | (180) |
| Interest income | 17 | 14 | 19 |
| Equity in losses | (13) | (13) | (18) |
| Income Before Income Taxes | 849 | 356 | 551 |
| Provision for income taxes | (278) | (158) | (93) |
| Net Income | $571 | $198 | $458 |
| Earnings Per Share-Basic | | | |
| Earnings per share | $1.77 | $0.56 | $1.26 |
| Earnings per share-Diluted | | | |
| Earnings per share | 1.72 | 0.55 | 1.21 |
| Cash Dividends Declared Per Share | 0.4900 | 0.3875 | 0.2075 |

Source: "Marriott International, Inc. 2012 Annual Report", http://files.shareholder.com/downloads/MAR/2734095087x0x651624/51819A94-F37F-4A6A-B735-E6F861259F1C/Marriott_2012AR.pdf, 2012.

Company LLC, with headquarters in Atlanta. In 1988, Johnson also bought the global rights to the Ritz-Carlton name (except for the Hotel-Ritz, Paris, and the Ritz-Carlton in Montreal). To turn around the Boston Ritz-Carlton and revive the hotel's reputation for service, he invested significant amounts in the company. In addition, he built several new hotels (wholly-owned) under the Ritz-Carlton name across the globe, of which only a few were built in partnership with other investors.

In the late 1980s, Horst Schulze (Schulze), a highly experienced hospitality industry executive, became the vice president of operations at Ritz-Carlton. Under his leadership, a conscious effort was made to ensure that the hotels projected an image of refined elegance and laid particular emphasis on providing an extraordinary level of service. As a result, in 1992, Ritz-Carlton received the Malcolm Baldrige National Quality Award for the first time.

But by the mid-1990s, Ritz-Carlton found itself floundering in debt. Analysts said the debt was the consequence of rapid expansion and the company's emphasis on high quality service which resulted in higher costs. In 1995, Marriott bought a 49% stake in Ritz-Carlton for $200 million in cash and assumed debt. In 1998, the stake was raised to 99%.[7] However, Marriott maintained an independent brand identity for the Ritz-Carlton chain. In 1999, Ritz-Carlton (with 35 hotels across the globe) received the Malcolm Baldrige Award for the second time.

In the early 2000s, Ritz-Carlton embarked on a diversification program. The company set up luxury residential condominiums called the 'Residences at the Ritz-Carlton', increased its focus on the Ritz-Carlton Club, a timeshare business that it had launched in 1999, and also opened spas and golf courses at some of its resort hotels. Schulze retired in 2001 and was succeeded by Simon Cooper (Cooper) as the president and COO of the company. In 2003, Ritz-Carlton shifted its headquarters from Atlanta to Chevy Chase in the State of Maryland to improve operational efficiencies. In the following years, it further expanded its properties and presence across the globe and by 2013, Ritz-Carlton operated 81 hotels in 26 nations (including Bahrain, Canada, Chile, China, Egypt, Germany, Grand Cayman, Indonesia, Italy, Jamaica, Japan, Korea, Malaysia, Mexico, Portugal, Qatar, Singapore, Spain, Turkey, the United Arab Emirates and the US) with 38,000 employees.

Ritz-Carlton had managed to maintain its reputation as an exceptional service organization over the years, and was branded as a "lifestyle company" that also managed golf resorts and spas and even sold bedding. According to the company, an average guest spent US$100,000 at the Ritz-Carlton over a lifetime.[8] So the company made every effort to keep each customer happy by providing exceptional customer service. It felt that service began with training.

## TRAINING AND DEVELOPMENT AT RITZ-CARLTON

Earlier in the 19th century, when the hotels and inns were small, the inn-keeper directed all the activities personally including managing the quality. But as they grew in size, managing them was beyond the capacity of the inn-keeper and delegation became necessary. Apprentices were trained and put in charge of managing various activities and quality, subject to inspection and audit by the inn-keeper. In the 20th century, the organization's size grew sharply and the hotels required functional departments. Here, planning was delegated to the division or department heads and execution was left to the first-line supervisors and workforce. Thereby, a factory concept emerged, in which people were assigned a single task rather than an entire sequence of tasks. Managers no longer managed quality directly and so quality suffered. However, the hotels remained profitable despite these quality concerns as competitors too faced similar problems.

In 1983, Horst Schulze (Schulze) joined Ritz-Carlton and faced the same challenge. Schulze realized that the management of quality could not be delegated. He and his team decided to personally take charge of managing quality. While the team's initiatives ranged across a broad spectrum, there were four most significant activities. First, the team defined the traits of all company products in The Credo. Second, it translated The Credo into basic standards to clarify the quality responsibilities of its products for its employees. Third, the team took up the responsibility of personally training the employees on the Gold Standards *(Refer to Exhibit 3 for the company's Gold Standards)*. Last, the passion for excellence was aggressively instilled in the employees.

Quality management and training were then undertaken by Ritz-Carlton with the President and other members of the top management as the senior quality management team which met every week to review product and service quality and guest satisfaction across the chain. The team prepared the overall strategic plan besides establishing and monitoring performance targets. Each hotel had a quality leader and monitored 720 work areas and recorded daily reports to provide early warning of quality and service problems. The company's aim was not just to satisfy guests, but to exceed their expectations and provide exceptional customized service. To track customer data, the staff was trained to note down both the stated and unstated preferences of customers during their stay, as it was felt that this information would be useful when the customer revisited the hotel chain.

Ritz-Carlton developed an organization culture that inspired its employees to go beyond conventional customer service and provide a 'WOW' experience to the guest. Employees here were referred to as 'The Ladies and Gentlemen of Ritz Carlton.' The

# EXHIBIT 3   The Ritz-Carlton Gold Standards

The Gold Standards are the foundation of The Ritz-Carlton Hotel Company, L.L.C. They encompass the values and philosophy by which we operate and include:

**The Credo**

- The Ritz-Carlton Hotel is a place where the genuine care and comfort of our guests is our highest mission.
- We pledge to provide the finest personal service and facilities for our guests who will always enjoy a warm, relaxed, yet refined ambience.
- The Ritz-Carlton experience enlivens the senses, instills well-being, and fulfills even the unexpressed wishes and needs of our guests.

**Motto**

- At The Ritz-Carlton Hotel Company, L.L.C., "We are Ladies and Gentlemen serving Ladies and Gentlemen." This motto exemplifies the anticipatory service provided by all staff members.

**Three Steps of Service**

1. A warm and sincere greeting. Use the guest's name.
2. Anticipation and fulfillment of each guest's needs.
3. Fond farewell. Give a warm good-bye and use the guest's name.

**Service Values: I Am Proud To Be Ritz-Carlton**

1. I build strong relationships and create Ritz-Carlton guests for life.
2. I am always responsive to the expressed and unexpressed wishes and needs of our guests.
3. I am empowered to create unique, memorable and personal experiences for our guests.
4. I understand my role in achieving the Key Success Factors, embracing Community Footprints and creating The Ritz-Carlton Mystique.
5. I continuously seek opportunities to innovate and improve The Ritz-Carlton experience.
6. I own and immediately resolve guest problems.
7. I create a work environment of teamwork and lateral service so that the needs of our guests and each other are met.
8. I have the opportunity to continuously learn and grow.
9. I am involved in the planning of the work that affects me.
10. I am proud of my professional appearance, language and behavior.
11. I protect the privacy and security of our guests, my fellow employees and the company's confidential information and assets.
12. I am responsible for uncompromising levels of cleanliness and creating a safe and accident-free environment.

**The 6th Diamond**

- Mystique
- Emotional Engagement
- Functional

**The Employee Promise**

- At The Ritz-Carlton, our Ladies and Gentlemen are the most important resource in our service commitment to our guests.
- By applying the principles of trust, honesty, respect, integrity and commitment, we nurture and maximize talent to the benefit of each individual and the company.
- The Ritz-Carlton fosters a work environment where diversity is valued, quality of life is enhanced, individual aspirations are fulfilled, and The Ritz-Carlton Mystique is strengthened.

*Source:* "Gold Standards", http://corporate.ritzcarlton.com/en/About/GoldStandards.htm.

company considered its employees as the cornerstone of its exceptional service culture and the most important resource in fulfilling its service commitment to its guests and therefore took great care of its employees. It also empowered them so that they had the freedom to contribute to creating guests for life. Training the selected talented individuals was the engine that drove Ritz-Carlton's growth strategy and helped it win in the competitive luxury hotel market. "The most important thing for us is the depth of our culture. We are ladies and gentlemen serving ladies and gentlemen. And the entire company culture is based around [this]: If we are treated with respect and dignity and there is pride and joy in the workplace, the automatic human reaction is that we will turn around and make magic for the customers,"[9] said Diana Oreck (Oreck), vice president and director of the Ritz-Carlton Leadership Center.

Considering the importance of training, each Ritz-Carlton hotel had a full time Director of Training and each department had one person with training responsibilities. Top performers from each department were provided with the responsibility of coaching in their own areas of expertise after attending a three-day "Train the Trainer" event.[10]

## RECRUITING THE SKILLED

As a service organization, Ritz-Carlton realized that the quality of its end product was only as good as the people providing it. Therefore, it took great care to recruit the right kind of employees and provide them with the necessary inputs to enable them to provide exceptional service.

Ritz-Carlton did not 'hire' employees; it 'selected' them. In fact, the company believed in 'casting' the right person for the right job, thereby ensuring the best customer service.[11] The selection process was rigorous and was based on 'benchmarking' and selecting ideal employees. The company prepared an ideal profile, job description, and qualification requirement based on the top performers from its hotel chain and other comparable organizations. This ensured that it brought the best people with the right qualifications and personality traits on board and was one of the reasons for Ritz-Carlton's low attrition rate. With five to ten applicants for each position, the selection process consisted of several stages. The initial screening was done through telephonic interviews. However, this screening was not done for skill-based jobs (like cooking) and the candidates were called for a demonstration. After the initial screening, the HR department issued a standard behavioral interview questionnaire to the candidates. This determined whether the candidate shared Ritz-Carlton's values and assessed his/her level of comfort when working with people. This was followed by several rounds of interviews with

different managers including the line manager, the division head, the HR Director, and finally the General Manager of the hotel. The General Manager's interview was intended to make the candidates feel important to the company. According to Bruce Seigel (Seigel), an area marketing director for several Ritz-Carlton properties, "The Ritz-Carlton doesn't hire; it selects its staff. A candidate must look you directly in the eye, be warm and friendly during the first interview. We are looking for ability to show empathy. If they can't do that in the first interview, how are they going to react with our guests?"[12]

In addition to the basic academic qualifications, Ritz-Carlton looked for a positive attitude, empathy, passion for service, and the ability to smile naturally in its recruits, and for people who sought a long-term career with the company, which made them ideal for the hospitality industry.[13] The company believed that these qualities would instill a commitment in the employee toward the company and its values and would thereby enable the candidate to serve guests better. The company felt that while technical skills could be taught to the candidates, bringing about a change in their attitude was a different matter. In addition, it also chose people with the special traits required for specific jobs. For example, a housekeeping position would need a person who was meticulous about his/her work whereas a front desk job would need a people-oriented person. As Sue Stephenson, Senior Vice President of HR, said, "If we don't select someone with a passion for service, everything we do around that is wasted. When it comes to the training we provide, particularly with employees who will interact with customers, the focus is on the talents of the individual, less so on the technical skills. We can teach those, but we can't really teach them to smile and to want to provide great service."[14]

## TRAINING AT RITZ-CARLTON

Training at Ritz-Carlton was a rigorous process. Once committed service individuals with varying levels of technical skills and backgrounds had been found, learning coaches were assigned to them. These coaches trained and certified them on the core competencies of their jobs. The company invested significant time and resources on its comprehensive training program to instill its values and educate its employees about its service standards. The

Ritz-Carlton training was conducted in five broad stages—initial orientation, 21-day certification, 365-day certification, ongoing training, and the daily lineup *(Refer to Exhibit 4 for Training & Development interventions at Ritz Carlton in the first year).*

# INITIAL ORIENTATION

Every new employee had to undergo a two-day orientation program before being assigned to their job at Ritz-Carlton. Ritz-Carlton ensured that no new recruit joined work without the two-day orientation.[15] The Director of Training and Organizational Effectiveness was responsible for the training activities at each hotel. As it was an important activity, the General Manager and people from the HR department conducted the initial orientation, where the new employee was familiarized with the company's history, culture, philosophy, values, standards, expectations, and benefits.

The new recruits were welcomed by a top manager who gave them handwritten welcome cards, and they were treated like hotel guests. They were also asked about their food preferences, and these were meticulously followed when refreshments were provided during orientation. The orientation program was conducted in the rooms used by the guests, and the recruits ate in the best restaurants of the hotel. According to Oreck, the company wanted to ensure that the new recruits felt that they had made the right decision in joining the company. A major part of the training was focused on team building, to bring about a sense of cohesion among the employees. The employees were also given a wallet-sized card with the company's Gold Standards printed on it. To reinforce the teachings of the orientation program, employees were required to carry this card with them at all times. "It's all about them and it's all about culture. We feel that orientation needs to be a significant emotional experience. Because think about it—you are making a very big decision in your life to either start a job or change a job. So our two days of orientation, they are solely revolving around our culture, which we call the gold standards. And the reason we

## EXHIBIT 4    Training & Development Interventions at Ritz Carlton in the First Year

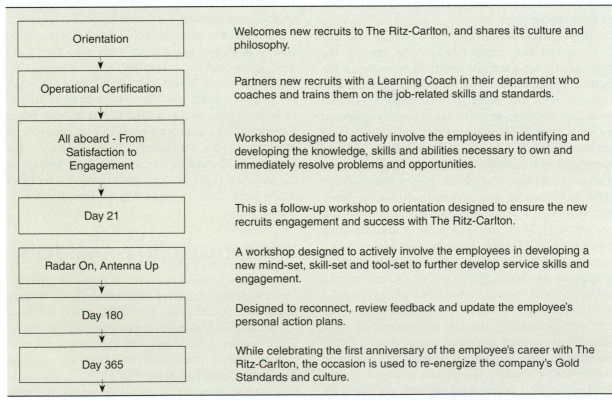

| | |
|---|---|
| Orientation | Welcomes new recruits to The Ritz-Carlton, and shares its culture and philosophy. |
| Operational Certification | Partners new recruits with a Learning Coach in their department who coaches and trains them on the job-related skills and standards. |
| All aboard - From Satisfaction to Engagement | Workshop designed to actively involve the employees in identifying and developing the knowledge, skills and abilities necessary to own and immediately resolve problems and opportunities. |
| Day 21 | This is a follow-up workshop to orientation designed to ensure the new recruits engagement and success with The Ritz-Carlton. |
| Radar On, Antenna Up | A workshop designed to actively involve the employees in developing a new mind-set, skill-set and tool-set to further develop service skills and engagement. |
| Day 180 | Designed to reconnect, review feedback and update the employee's personal action plans. |
| Day 365 | While celebrating the first anniversary of the employee's career with The Ritz-Carlton, the occasion is used to re-energize the company's Gold Standards and culture. |

Adapted from http://corporate.ritzcarlton.com/en/Careers/YourCareer/LearningAndDevelopment.htm.

do that is we know that the culture creates passion advocates of our employees,"[16] said Oreck.

## 'DAY 21' CERTIFICATION

After the initial orientation, each new recruit was assigned to an experienced employee (learning coach) from the department for three weeks of on-the-job training. This was done as the company realized that recruits might have varying levels of technical skill and backgrounds both inside and outside the hospitality industry.[17] The recruit accompanied the trainer to observe how the jobs/duties were carried out and the departmental trainer helped the recruit become familiar with the job and the company culture. This was the first time the new employees got to meet the guests and hence the trainers focused on developing their customer service skills and taught them the finer details related to these like addressing the guests properly, anticipating their needs, soothing them in case of complaints, and solving customer problems. The company believed that it could ensure the loyalty of customers only when customer problems were resolved efficiently by the employees as 51% of its guests were repeat customers.[18] The trainees also had access to online training modules and detailed operational manuals.[19]

In the third week of training, the new recruit was allowed to handle job responsibilities alone. The trainer later gave feedback on the recruit's performance. The company trained its recruits to use formal language like addressing the guests with a 'Good Morning' or 'Good Afternoon,' accompanied by the guest's name, instead of a 'Hello.' The trainees were also instructed on the kind of language to use, on dressing and appearance, and the behavior they should or should not use while interacting with the customers.

On the 21st day, the new recruits again met with the top management of the hotel to recall the company's values and standards along with their experiences about the training and to provide feedback on the training program. "The Day 21 meeting allows us to fill in any holes that were not covered in the initial orientation,"[20] said Tom Donavan, General Manager at the Ritz-Carlton Bachelor Gulch Hotel and Resort, Vail, Colorado. While the employee experience helped the management in assessing whether the behavior of the employees was in line with the company's standards, the feedback helped

it in identifying the shortcomings of the training program. The management then addressed the employee concerns, if any. The employees then took a test that gauged their technical skills and their understanding of the company philosophy. The trainees who cleared the test were certified while those who did not pass were given the option to leave or look for employment in a department more suited to their skills and abilities.[21]

## 365 DAY RECERTIFICATION

At Ritz-Carlton, training was an ongoing process. After the 21-day certification, employees were assigned their jobs, and formal on-the-job training continued till day 365. On the 365th day, the new employees were recertified after a written test, interview, and role-play session. The employees were recognized for their service and presented with 'service pins' indicating that they were now a formal part of the team. This one day meeting with lunch was used to remind them of the Gold Standards and reinforce these standards. Ritz-Carlton spent US$5000 on each new recruit. In one year, the recruits received about 310 hours of training on job skills, computer courses, and company culture.[22] The company also provided service recognition for five and ten years of employment at such events.[23]

## ONGOING TRAINING

Both the management and the non-management employees at Ritz-Carlton were provided with ongoing training and 70% of all learning was accomplished by on-the-job training.[24] They also had access to a number of instructor-led classes, workshops, and e-learning classes. "Those tools also are in alignment so that we can analyze operational skills acquisition against the results of mystery shopper and customer engagement surveys. In essence, secret shoppers are looking for the exact criteria that staff members are certified to meet. As such, we're not doing training for the sake of training,"[25] said Holloway.

After the first year, employees received 100 hours of training every year. All training programs were conducted by the Ritz-Carlton Leadership Center (started in the late 1990s). It consisted of three schools: The School of Performance Excellence (training and development programs for hourly employees); The School of Leadership and Business Excellence (provided leadership development and soft skills training); and The School of Service Excellence (dealt with benchmarking). The Leadership Center also conducted workshops for outsiders. Department specific workshops and general classes for the employees were conducted on a monthly or quarterly basis. CARE classes (Controlling Alcohol Risks Effectively) were meant for employees dealing with food and beverages. GLOW (Guest Loyalty Opportunity Workshop) and LEAP classes (Listen, Empathize, Act, Produce) were designed for customer-centric roles to enhance the employees' sales and problem-solving capabilities. Other workshops included the POSH training (Prevention of Sexual Harassment), leadership development, diversity training, and personality development.

New employees were also trained to anticipate the unexpressed needs of the guests through a workshop named "Radar on, Antenna Up, and Focus" where the trainees were provided with scenarios. "One of the scenarios might be a young couple comes into the restaurant with a two-year-old baby. What should you do? Then we discuss, you bring a high chair, you bring crayons, you bring our stuffed lion, Roarie. We have hundreds of scenarios like that. Because we know that it's going to be through the unique, memorable, and personable experiences that our customers are going to be fully delighted and engaged,"[26] explained Oreck.

Ritz-Carlton's managers had access to different types of instructor-led classes including Senior Leadership Development Certification and the Art of Facilitation. They could also enroll for Harvard Manager Mentor eLearning classes where they were provided inputs on financial essentials, managing their career, preparing business plans, and managing workplace stress. They were also encouraged to expand their learning by being part of the task force by taking up projects or volunteering for temporary assignments at other locations. Non-management employees too were encouraged to take advantage of such "lateral service".

## THE DAILY LINEUP

The Daily Lineup was a critical learning tool and a key component of Ritz-Carlton's learning strategy.[27] Every shift at Ritz-Carlton started with a 10–15 minute employee meeting within each department.

The main objective was to reinforce the Gold Standards and service values of the company. They also discussed the previous day's problems, menu items for that day, guests arriving for the day and their preferences, etc, which differed depending on location and department. The daily lineup was held thrice a day at every shift change. A speaker discussed one of the 20 Basics every day while others expressed their views about it or its implementation in the company (Refer to Exhibit 5 for the 20 basics). After all the basics were discussed, the cycle was repeated. Other topics like the events occurring at the corporate level were also a part of discussion sometimes. Monday had a special daily lineup known as the 'Monday Wow', as it included stories of employees who had gone the extra mile in delivering customer service. The stories were discussed at all locations and this motivated Ritz-Carlton employees to perform better. It was also a forum for discussing best practices and guidance from the industry. "This program energizes . . . You get to know everyone on your team, their desires, where they want to be,"[28] said Seigel.

The daily lineup was the most important tool for the company to keep its employees attuned to its corporate culture and it kept them focused on the company's expectations of them. Apart from that, it ensured good communication with employees and kept them informed about the events happening at the corporate level. It also acted as a platform for employees to express their concerns to their superiors and played a critical role in team building. According to Oreck, "We engage in our culture each and every day. Many companies have visions and missions and all of that, but they only refer to it when the numbers are going south, or they've had a shock or a customer complaint. We are engaging in the culture each and every day."[29] Oreck added, "Why bother with culture training? At Ritz-Carlton, we've quantified through research that happy customers spend more money."[30]

## EMPLOYEE EMPOWERMENT AND FEEDBACK

"It's all about empowerment. The thing our guests are most wowed about is that every single employee has $2,000 a day per guest to delight or make it

## EXHIBIT 5   The Twenty Basics

1. The Credo will be known, owned and energized by all employees.

2. Our motto is: "We are Ladies and Gentlemen serving Ladies and Gentlemen". Practice teamwork and "lateral service" to create a positive work environment.

3. The three steps of service shall be practiced by all employees.

4. All employees will successfully complete Training Certification to ensure they understand how to perform to the Ritz-Carlton standards in their position.

5. All employees will successfully understand their work area and Hotel goals as established in each strategic plan.

6. All employees will know the needs of their internal and external customers (guests and employees) so that we may deliver the products and services they expect. Use guest performance pads to record specific needs.

7. Each employee will continuously identify defects (Mr. BIV) throughout the Hotel.

8. Any employee who receives a customer complaint "owns" the complaint.

9. Instant guest pacification will be ensured by all. React quickly to correct the problem immediately. Follow-up with a telephone call within twenty minutes to verify the problem has been resolved to the customer's satisfaction. Do everything you possibly can to never lose a guest.

10. Guest incident action forms are used to record and communicate every incident of guest dissatisfaction. Every employee is empowered to resolve the problem and to prevent a repeat occurrence.

11. Uncompromising levels of cleanliness are the responsibility of every employee.

12. "Smile-We are on stage." Always maintain positive eye contact with our guests. (Use words like "Good Morning," "Certainly," "I will be happy to" and "My pleasure").

13. Be an ambassador of your hotel in and outside of the work place. Always talk positively. No negative comments.

14. Escort guests rather than pointing out directions to another area of the Hotel.

15. Be knowledgeable of Hotel information (hours of operation, etc.) to answer guest inquiries. Always recommend the Hotel's retail and food beverage outlet prior to outside facilities.

16. Use proper telephone etiquette. Answer within three rings and with a "smile." When necessary, ask the caller, "May I place you on hold." Do not screen calls. Eliminate call transfers when possible.

17. Uniforms are to be immaculate; Wear proper and safe footwear (clean and polished), and your correct name tag. Take pride and care in your personal appearance (adhere to all grooming standards).

18. Ensure all employees know their roles during emergency situations and are aware of fire and life safety processes.

19. Notify your supervisor immediately of hazards, injuries, equipment or assistance that you need. Practice energy conservation and proper maintenance and repair of Hotel property and equipment.

20. Protecting the assets of a Ritz-Carlton Hotel is the responsibility of every employee.

Source: "The Ritz-Carlton hotel," http://www.gwu.edu/~umpleby/mgt201/THE%20RITZ.doc.

right . . . we are saying to our employees—we trust you,"[31] said Oreck. Every employee, regardless of position or rank, was empowered to spend up to US$2,000 to correct a problem or handle a complaint, without having to ask a superior for permission. There was no limit on the number of times the employee could use this authority, as long as there was a valid reason. Employees were also expected to look out for 'Mr. Biv' (Mistakes, Rework, Breakdowns, Inefficiencies, and Variation) in their work process and contribute to continuous improvement. Once an employee spotted any of these, he/she was expected to report it to his/her superior for immediate corrective action (*Refer to Exhibit 6 for Employee Empowerment at Ritz-Carlton*). Employees could also give ideas for cutting costs or improving quality by giving in a formal report showing the implications of his/her idea. Any worthwhile suggestions were rewarded with cash bonuses and other prizes through an employee recognition program. Theo Gilbert-Jamison, Vice President of Leadership Development at the Ritz-Carlton, said, "We believe that to create pride and joy in the workplace, you must involve the employees. And you create that pride and joy by making employees feel like they are a part of the Ritz-Carlton."[32]

The company treated its employees with respect and dignity, making them feel important and

## EXHIBIT 6    Employee Empowerment at Ritz-Carlton

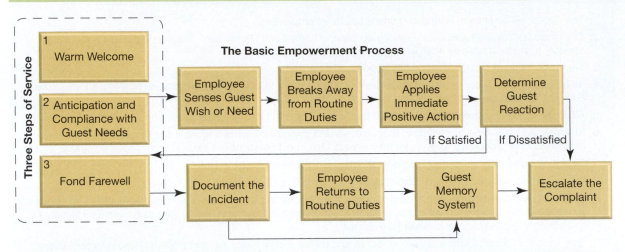

**The Basic Empowerment Process**

Three Steps of Service

1    Warm Welcome

2    Anticipation and Compliance with Guest Needs

3    Fond Farewell

Employee Senses Guest Wish or Need → Employee Breaks Away from Routine Duties → Employee Applies Immediate Positive Action → Determine Guest Reaction

If Satisfied    If Dissatisfied

Document the Incident → Employee Returns to Routine Duties → Guest Memory System → Escalate the Complaint

*Source:* "1999 Application Summary", http://corporate.ritzcarlton.com/NR/rdonlyres/22E2CEC9-62A4-4EA2-9C3C-51628265E10E/0/rcappsum.pdf.

increasing their job satisfaction. Though the salaries of the employees were not higher than those of other comparable organizations in the industry, Ritz-Carlton was a preferred employer because of its organizational culture and the way it treated its employees. "I've worked in a lot of places, but never anywhere where they treat me as nice as here,"[33] said a waiter at Ritz-Carlton. The company also had a policy of promoting from within to encourage employees to remain with the company for the long term.

The company believed that such empowerment motivated employees to take personal responsibility and deal with any guest complaint regardless of the position or department that they belonged to. Jeff Hargett, the corporate director of the Leadership Center, said, "If you're afraid of giving power to the staff because they're going to make a mistake, you're absolutely right. They're going to make a mistake. But employees also learned from their mistakes and gained confidence, which eventually benefited the company in the long run."[34]

## EVALUATING TRAINING

The company used mystery shoppers and guest surveys to evaluate the impact of its training interventions. Ritz-Carlton polled its customers once every month. The company enlisted the services of

Gallup, a leading agency providing research, analytics, and advisory services, for this. Gallup randomly sent out surveys to 38% of guests that had stayed at Ritz-Carlton the month before. The customers were asked 30 questions. According to Oreck, the questions included, "How likely is that guest to recommend Ritz-Carlton? Were they delighted and satisfied with their stay? If there was a problem, did we take care of their problem? We know that, if that guest engagement number goes up, our training programs have been successful."[35]

At times, this indicated the need for further training of some employees who had earlier been certified. "Even though the employees were at one time proficient and certified at that skill, the customer feedback affords the opportunity for what we call 'just-in-time learning' to take place to quickly refresh that service delivery standard,"[36] said Holloway.

## RESULTS

Ritz-Carlton's training and development initiatives were widely recognized. The company was ranked as the #1 Global Learning Company in the world by Training Magazine 2007 and in 2008 it was inducted into Training Magazine's Top 10 Training Hall of Fame.[37] Moreover, many professionals and companies wanted to emulate Ritz-Carlton and use its human resources, leadership, quality, and training practices as benchmarks. Many companies and individuals, cutting across industries, had benefited from the courses provided by the Ritz-Carlton Leadership Center, which was founded in 1999, to work with companies interested in benchmarking the business practices followed by Ritz-Carlton. The Ritz-Carlton Leadership Center headed by Oreck, offered courses on customer service, leadership development, executive training, changing corporate culture, etc. through Certified Leadership Center Ambassadors and expert consultants.[38] Over 3,000 clients from diverse industries such as Automotive, Finance, Healthcare, Transportation, Legal, Energy, Technology, Retail, Fitness, Insurance, Human Resources, and Hospitality, had benefited from these courses and advisory services at Ritz-Carlton properties and locations around the world.[39] Even very successful companies such as Apple, Inc. modeled its service after the Ritz-Carlton. Potential recruits were judged on whether they would be able to "offer a Ritz-Carlton level of service?"[40] In October 2011, The Leadership Center was ranked #2 out of 235 large organizations in Leadership Development by the Leadership Excellence Organization.[41] Earlier in September 2008, Oreck was also named as one of the top 100+ people in Learning & Development by Leadership Excellence Magazine.[42]

Analysts believed that it was Ritz-Carlton's training and development initiatives that helped it maintain its mystic, retain customers, and grow its sales. "We know that fully-engaged guests are spending more nights in a Ritz-Carlton every year than any other guest. There is a direct correlation to profitability. I can assure you we would not be spending the kind of money we do on training and reinforcement if we didn't think it was going to show us the money,"[43] said Oreck. Moreover, Ritz-Carlton's training and development interventions also helped it retain talent. According to Oreck. "It's about engagement . . . The lodging industry as a whole tends to run a 60–70 percent turnover in a year. Here at Ritz Carlton we run in the low 20's. It's a huge difference."[44]

However, some analysts opined that this kind of service put in detailed scripted format and its daily recitation by its employees was not a good way to motivate the employees. While they agreed that the selection and training at Ritz-Carlton was critical for its service excellence, they opined that the employees tended to follow the rules blindly as its

rituals had become repetitive and monotonous. Such an organization culture would make these employees reluctant to change. It would become a challenge for the company to prevent its rituals from becoming monotonous, they said. The analysts felt that effective customer service should be tailored according to guests' needs rather than having them scripted and standardized. Critics also opined that it put tremendous pressure on the employees and created inordinate amounts of stress for them. There were also some who opined that implementing and maintaining such an organization culture and training was very expensive for the company. However, Ritz-Carlton maintained that the company was evolving from a training organization into a learning environment. "We moved away from that heavily prescriptive, scripted approach and toward managing to outcomes. We're now saying, 'We won't tell you specifically how to get to the goal of a happy guest',"[45] quipped Oreck.

## LOOKING AHEAD

Over time, Ritz-Carlton developed a very refined process of making training a person-to-person continuous activity that led to the inculcation of its corporate values and mission. As the company was focusing on global expansion, the management felt that its commitment to training and skills certification provided it with a competitive advantage. Even in emerging markets such as China, where there was a lack of qualified hospitality staff, Ritz-Carlton was able to attract, train, and retain top talent. Recognizing that the issue of training new recruits for a new hotel was a far more daunting task than training new recruits in existing hotels, the company's senior management worked together to source the coaching needs of the new hotel by involving some of the most talented coaches and trainers from across the Ritz-Carlton system. The top management of Ritz-Carlton also saw to it that they were present during the opening of a new international hotel location. According to Bob Kharazmi, senior vice president of international operations, "No matter what we have going on at our corporate headquarters, we drop everything to make sure the hotel is launched from a solid cultural and operational foundation. We work with both the front line and leadership, helping them understand our Gold Standards and our approach to business."[46]

# ENDNOTES

[1] http://corporate.ritzcarlton.com/en/Careers/YourCareer/LearningAndDevelopment.htm

[2] Douglas Gollan, "In Conversation with Herve Humler, President, Ritz-Carlton Hotels," http://luxurysociety.com, February 12, 2013

[3] "Ritz-Carlton: Redefining Elegance (No. 1 of the Training Top 125)," www.trainingmag.com, March 1, 2007

[4] Ibid.

[5] "Training the Talented, the Ritz-Carlton Way," www.amanet.org, September 4, 2008

[6] "Our History," http://corporate.ritzcarlton.com/en/About/OurHistory.htm

[7] Ibid.

[8] "Putting on the Ritz: One Hotel Chain's Secret of Legendary Service," http://www.go2hr.ca, August 1, 2007

[9] Jacqueline Durett, "Ritz-Carlton-Plug in and Perform," www.cedma-europe.org, March 1, 2006

[10] "Ritz Carlton's Gold Standard Service," www.epmsonline.com, September 2011.

[11] Ibid.

[12] "Putting on the Ritz: One Hotel Chain's Secret of Legendary Service," http://www.go2hr.ca, August 1, 2007

[13] Ibid.

[14] Matt Damsker, "Fit for the Ritz," www.talentplus.com, March 2004

[15] "Ritz Carlton's Gold Standard Service," www.epmsonline.com, September 2011.

[16] Flavio Martins, "3 Keys to Customer Service Training and Retention from Ritz-Carlton VP Diana Oreck," www.customerthink.com, November 26, 2012

[17] "Training the Talented, the Ritz-Carlton Way," www.amanet.org, September 4, 2008.

[18] Bill Lampton, "Show and Tell - The Ritz Carlton Hotel PART III," www.expertmagazine.com, 2003

[19] "Training the Talented, the Ritz-Carlton Way," www.amanet.org, September 4, 2008

[20] "Ritz Carlton's Gold Standard Service," www.epmsonline.com, September 2011

[21] Jill Elswick, "Puttin' On The Ritz: Hotel Chain Touts Training to Benefit its Recruiting and Retention," Employee Benefit News, February 2000

[22] Duff McDonald, "Roll Out the Blue Carpet-How Ritz-Carlton Can Teach You to Serve Your Customers Better," http://money.cnn.com, May 1, 2004

[23] "Ritz Carlton's Gold Standard Service," www.epmsonline.com, September 2011.

[24] http://corporate.ritzcarlton.com/en/Careers/YourCareer/LearningAndDevelopment.htm

[25] "Training the Talented, the Ritz-Carlton Way," www.amanet.org, September 4, 2008.

[26] Ashley Furness, "An Interview with Diana Oreck of Ritz-Carlton," http://cxjourney.blogspot.in, November 2, 2012

[27] http://corporate.ritzcarlton.com/en/Careers/YourCareer/LearningAndDevelopment.htm

[28] "Putting on the Ritz: One Hotel Chain's Secret of Legendary Service," http://www.go2hr.ca, August 1, 2007

[29] Jacqueline Durett, "Ritz-Carlton-Plug in and Perform," http://www.cedma-europe.org, March 1, 2006

[30] Wanda Jankowski, "Ten Minutes With . . . Diana Oreck, vice president, Ritz-Carlton Leadership Center," www.remodeling.hw.net, August 26, 2008.

[31] Carmine Gallo, "How Wegmans, Apple Store and Ritz-Carlton Empower Employees to Offer Best-in-Class Service," www.retailcustomerexperience.com, December 27, 2012

[32] "The Ritz-Carlton Company: How It Became a 'Legend' in Service," Corporate University Review, January/February 2001.

[33] Martha H. Peak, "Puttin' on the Ritz," Management Review, January 1995

[34] Kirby Lee Davis, "Ritz-Carlton Executive Speaks on Building Quality Workforce," The Journal Record, April 10, 2007.

[35] Ashley Furness, "An Interview with Diana Oreck of Ritz-Carlton," http://cxjourney.blogspot.in, November 2, 2012

[36] "Training the Talented, the Ritz-Carlton Way," www.amanet.org, September 4, 2008

[37] http://corporate.ritzcarlton.com/en/Careers/YourCareer/LearningAndDevelopment.htm

[38] http://corporate.ritzcarlton.com/en/LeadershipCenter/Default.htm

[39] Ibid.

[40] Ashley Furness, "An Interview with Diana Oreck of Ritz-Carlton," http://cxjourney.blogspot.in, November 2, 2012

[41] Flavio Martins, "3 Keys to Customer Service Training and Retention from Ritz-Carlton VP Diana Oreck," www.customerthink.com, November 26, 2012

[42] http://corporate.ritzcarlton.com/en/LeadershipCenter/AboutUs/MeetTheTeam/Profiles/DianaOreck.htm

[43] Ashley Furness, "An Interview with Diana Oreck of Ritz-Carlton," http://cxjourney.blogspot.in, November 2, 2012

[44] Flavio Martins, "3 Keys to Customer Service Training and Retention from Ritz-Carlton VP Diana Oreck," www.customerthink.com, November 26, 2012

[45] "Ritz-Carlton: Redefining Elegance (No. 1 of the Training Top 125)," www.trainingmag.com, March 1, 2007

[46] "Training the Talented, the Ritz-Carlton Way," www.amanet.org, September 4, 2008

# Amazon's Big Data Strategy

## Adapa Srinivasa Rao
IBS Hyderabad

## Debapratim Purkayastha
IBS Hyderabad

"As Amazon's recommendation team, we asked ourselves, how do we take this data and make a little bit more money, how do we apply it in this channel differently and it was really neat. Now it is being called 'big data' in the marketing and media world, but at the time we were doing this stuff, it was just kind of putting one foot in front of the other."[1]

—David Sellinger, Former Software Manager (Customer Behavior Research), Amazon.com, Inc. (Amazon), in October 2013.

Leading e-commerce company Amazon.com, Inc. (Amazon) and its subsidiary Zappos were ranked among the top ten retailers in the National Retail Federation Foundation/American Express Customers' Choice Awards[a] for two years (2010 and 2011) in a row. Industry observers felt that the coveted recognition was the result of Amazon's use of its big data[b] resources to provide superior service quality. Right from the time it had emerged as a dominant provider of Internet services in the early 2000s, Amazon had started to focus on big data to improve its performance. Along with many other major Internet companies, it realized the importance of big data in the early 2000s, and had since then, focused on properly utilizing the huge databases of people who were shopping on its e-commerce portals.

Amazon leveraged its big data sources to give its customers good product recommendations and thereby improve the relationship with them. It utilized its big data resources to meticulously upgrade its famed customer recommendation system. Data on past purchases made by customers was used to give them highly customized product suggestions. Analysis of past customer data also helped Amazon in giving suggestions to new customers who were buying from its portal for the first time. Big data helped Amazon in developing 360 degree customer profiles and to create hyper-personalized marketing messages regarding the products based on the needs and preferences of individual customers. On the customer side, Amazon also utilized its big data resources to improve the quality of its customer care. Easy access to the profiles of customers and their past purchasing/browsing habits made it easy for the company's customer service executives to provide quick solutions to the complaints of customers. The

---

[a] The National Retail Federation Foundation/American Express Customers' Choice Awards were designed to know the consumer attitudes toward retailers' customer service. The survey collects data by polling consumers and is conducted by the marketing intelligence firm BIGinsight.

[b] Big data refers to the growth and availability of large volumes of data, both structured and unstructured. Such an exponential volume of data could not be analyzed by the traditional software used to handle databases. The latest trends in technology allowed decision making to be done largely based on data and analysis instead of past experience and intuition. According to a definition given by industry analyst, Doug Laney, big data spans three key dimensions, viz. Volume (amount of data generated), Velocity (speed at which data is streamed), and Variety (formats in which data comes in).

acquisition of Zappos[c] by Amazon in the year 2009 further facilitated the use of big data in improving customer service quality. Big data resources were also put to some innovative uses like checking fraud at the organizational level. Product catalogue data was analyzed thoroughly to identify which of the items were more likely to be stolen. The results of this analysis were fed back to the warehouses of the company to limit the theft of items.

Other than improving its own performance, Amazon also helped other smaller e-commerce companies by allowing them to use its big data resources and improve their performance. An innovative service called Amazon Webstore, launched in 2010, allowed smaller companies to build their portals around Amazon's e-commerce platform. Users of Amazon Webstore could advertise their products on Amazon's portals by paying a small part of the sales proceeds as a commission to Amazon. For a fixed monthly fee for utilizing the service, partnering businesses could use Amazon's big data resources. Amazon Webstore was quite successful and was adopted by both small as well as big retailers such as Timex and Samsonite who did not want to have their own e-commerce system. Amazon's suite of cloud based Internet services known as Amazon Web Services (AWS) had also come out with solutions for small companies so that they could implement big data easily. A new service known as Kinesis, announced in November 2013, could process high volumes of data flowing into AWS on a real time basis. According to some industry observers, this was Amazon's bid to close the loop on its integrated cloud stack and deliver an end-to-end solution for collecting and processing data. They felt that just by taking a relook at the various aspects of its big data capabilities and effectively leveraging on these, the company could emerge as a threat to the entire analytics eco-system.[2]

## BACKGROUND NOTE

Amazon was founded in the year 1994 by Jeffrey Preston Bezos (Bezos). It started its operations at a time when the reach of the Internet was increasing and the Internet was being considered as a potential business medium. Understanding the trend, Bezos came up with the idea of selling books through the Internet. He felt that books were the best products to sell online as millions of titles were in print and an e-commerce site could house and sell many more books than the conventional brick-and-mortar bookstores. Bezos calculated that the common brick-and-mortar stores could not house more than 200,000 books at a time[3] and aimed to build a large online bookstore which would be bigger than any physical bookstore in the world. Amazon was initially funded with the money that Bezos borrowed from friends and relatives. Bezos and his wife, along with some employees, built the website and tested it for over a year before launching it *(Refer to Exhibit 1 for Timeline of Amazon)*.

Amazon was finally opened to customers in the year 1995. Like many other technology giants, it was initially run from a garage—the one in Bezos' Washington home. At the time when Amazon started its operations, the book retailing market was highly fragmented and there was no major player except Barnes & Noble, Inc.[d] Barnes & Noble had one-tenth of the total market share but no online presence. Amazon thus got the first mover advantage and faced very little competition in its initial days of operation. Right from when it began its business operation, Bezos focused on customers and believed that customer loyalty was the key to penetrating the market and increasing sales. Amazon started to ship goods to all the 50 states in the US and 45 other countries within a month of its launch—and all this while still working from Bezos' garage. Amazon's popularity grew through word-of-mouth as customers recommended it to others. Within four months of its launch, Amazon was selling more than 100 books a day. The company's impressive performance attracted investors and Amazon got its first big investment of US$ 100,000 from Madrona Venture Group, Inc.[e] in 1995. The company reported net sales of US$ 511,000 during the first six months of its operations and Bezos' confidence that he could make a success of the company increased.

---

[c] Zappos, headquartered in Las Vegas, Nevada, USA was a leading online retailer of shoes and clothing products. This online shopping portal was founded by Nick Swinmurn in the year 1999.

[d] Barnes & Noble, Inc., headquartered in Manhattan, New York City, USA, is the largest book retailers in the United States.

[e] Madrona Venture Group, Inc., headquartered in Seattle, Washington, USA, is a venture capital which primarily focuses on investing in early-stage technology companies.

## EXHIBIT 1 Timeline of **Amazon.com**

| Year | Month | Event |
|------|-------|-------|
| 1994 | July | Amazon incorporated in Delaware |
| 1995 | July | Amazon.com launched. Sells its first book, "Fluid Concepts & Creative Analogies: Computer Models of the Fundamental Mechanisms of Thought" |
| 1996 | July | Amazon.com Associates Program launched |
| 1997 | May | Announces IPO and begins trading on NASDAQ |
| 1998 | June | Launches music store |
| 1999 | March | Launches Amazon.com Auctions, the company's Web auctions service |
|      | December | Jeff Bezos named Time Magazine "Person of the Year" |
| 2000 | August | Launches Amazon.fr (France) |
|      | November | Launches Amazon.co.jp (Japan) |
| 2001 | April | Amazon partners with Borders Group to run the company's online bookselling business |
| 2002 | July | Launches Amazon Web Services |
|      | November | Opens Apparel & Accessories Store |
| 2003 | June | Launches Amazon Services, Inc. subsidiary |
| 2004 | April | Opens Jewelery Store |
| 2005 | February | Introduces Amazon Prime |
| 2006 | September | Launches digital video download service, Amazon UnboxTM |
| 2007 | November | Launches Amazon Kindle |
| 2008 | November | Announces Frustration-Free Packaging initiative |
| 2009 | May | Introduces Kindle DX |
| 2010 | April | Amazon moves to new HQ in South Lake Union, Seattle |
| 2011 | July | Market capitalization of Amazon tops US$ 100 billion |
| 2012 | February | Amazon launches Sports Collectibles Store |
| 2013 | August | Jeff Bezos buys Washington Post |

*Source:* Compiled from various sources.

At the beginning of 1996, Amazon moved to new headquarters—a small warehouse in Seattle. The company employed 11 people and offered 2.5 million book titles. Following the Japanese model, Amazon had very limited inventory and thereby kept its costs under control. It started an innovative affiliate marketing program called Amazon Associates Program in July 1996. The program allowed third party websites to sell books through links to Amazon posted on their sites for a commission of 15 percent on the total sales made. The program was a huge success and helped in expanding Amazon's reach without the company having to spend much on advertising. Experts opined that the program not only generated traffic to Amazon but enhanced the brand's presence online as these third party sites carried Amazon's logo on their pages. The Amazon Associates Program was later extended to all the products sold on Amazon's portal. Amazon went public in the year 1997 and offered 3 million of its shares for sale. The shares opened at US$ 18 a share and the IPO raised US$ 54 million for the company. In the year 1998, Amazon started selling DVDs with the opening of its video store which was followed by the launch of Amazon.com auctions in March 1999.[4]

Amazon's success attracted many new competitors like Book Stacks and Book Zone to the market and this led to higher competition for the company. To counter the competition effectively, Amazon introduced new features like online product reviews where customers could write their own book review as well as read reviews written by others. By the year 2000, Amazon had made a big change in its business model and started selling other products. In 2000, it also expanded its presence and launched sites in France and Japan. In the year 2001, Amazon

## EXHIBIT 2    Financials of Amazon from 2008–2012 (in US$ Millions)

|  | 2012 | 2011 | 2010 | 2009 | 2008 |
|---|---|---|---|---|---|
| Total net sales | $61,093 | $48,077 | $34,204 | $24,509 | $19,166 |
| Total operating expenses | 60,417 | 47,215 | 32,798 | 23,380 | 18,324 |
| Income from operations | 676 | 862 | 1,406 | 1,129 | 842 |
| Interest income | 40 | 61 | 51 | 37 | 83 |
| Interest expense | (92) | (65) | (39) | (34) | (71) |
| Other income (expense), net | (80) | 76 | 79 | 29 | 47 |
| Total non-operating income (expense) | (132) | 72 | 91 | 32 | 59 |
| Income before income taxes | 544 | 934 | 1,497 | 1,161 | 901 |
| Provision for income taxes | (428) | (291) | (352) | (253) | (247) |
| Equity-method investment activity, net of tax | (155) | (12) | 7 | (6) | (9) |
| Net income (loss) | $ (39) | $ 631 | $ 1,152 | $ 902 | $ 645 |

*Source:* http://phx.corporate-ir.net/phoenix.zhtml?c=97664&p=irol-reportsannual.

allowed other retailers to sell their products through its site and took a part of the sales proceeds as its commission. In the last quarter of the year 2001, Amazon reported its first profit.[5]

Amazon's operations were further expanded in the year 2003 as it opened new websites in Asia-Pacific and European countries. In the year 2006, it launched a key subsidiary called Amazon Web Services.[6] Amazon Web Services provided an array of cloud based remote computing services to its customers. The advent of the digital era was changing the content consumption patterns of people. Many people started reading books and magazines on their desktops and laptops instead of buying physical copies. Responding to this change, Amazon introduced an e-book reader called Kindle in the year 2007. Kindle was a big hit in the market and heralded a new era of digital reading. Kindle was later released as an app for other devices working on operating systems like Android and iOS[f]. By the year 2011, the market capitalization of Amazon had reached the US$ 100 billion mark, making it one of the leading technology companies in the world. For the fiscal year 2012, Amazon had revenue of US$ 61.09 billion and a net loss of US$ 39 billion (*Refer to Exhibit 2 for the financials of Amazon*).

## BIG DATA AT AMAZON

Over the years, Amazon had evolved from being a pure e-commerce player into a giant Internet services firm which offered a large range of services for individuals and corporations. It started to focus heavily on big data and embarked on its transition from a pure online retailer into a giant big data company.[7] Amazon along with other major Internet giants like Yahoo! Inc.[g] (Yahoo) and Twitter, Inc.[h] (Twitter) realized in the early 2000s that they had huge amounts of data about their users which they could put to valuable use.[8] While the other companies did not concentrate on the importance of big data, Amazon was quick to cash in on the invaluable database of people who shopped on its e-commerce portals around the world. The product recommendation team at Amazon thought of innovative ways in which it could use the data accumulated by the company.[9] The result was the big data revolution which transformed the way Amazon did business.

As an e-commerce giant, Amazon's success had always depended on making the right products available to its customers. Making the right products available in turn depended on understanding the precise products that customers wanted. Understanding the

---

[f] Android and iOS are the two leading mobile OS promoted by Google and Apple respectively. They are used in mobile devices like smartphones and tablets.

[g] Yahoo, Inc., headquartered in Sunnyvale, California, USA, is a leading multinational Internet company.

[h] Twitter, Inc., headquartered in San Francisco, California, USA, is a leading social networking and microblogging service. It allows its users to send and receive text messages which are limited to 140 characters.

needs and tastes of customers involved doing proper market research as well as analyzing its own customer base. Since its inception, Amazon had been renowned for its product recommender system which provided product suggestions to customers depending upon their past purchasing behavior. Data collected from its customers was the primary driving force behind Amazon's recommender system. Being the leading e-commerce player, Amazon had a large bank of data regarding the likes and the past purchasing behavior of its customer base. It had used this data bank to build its recommender system. Its earlier recommender system had been based on showing more items similar to the ones which were being looked for by its customers. This item-by-item similarity method was built on the basis of collaborative filtering[i] and was hugely successful in deepening the relationship with its customers. Its recommender engine had since been improved and perfected to give better results.

Amazon later started utilizing the historical purchase data of consumers as well and the click-stream data of all its customers to show webpages with uniquely customized information.[10] Using such data helped Amazon in many ways other than showing the related and alternative products that the consumers had been looking for. Mining the vast amount of data helped in understanding the inner feelings and likings of customers which they could not express themselves. Commenting on the importance of data in understanding the behavior of customers, Michael Driscoll of Dataspora[j] said, "You can ask people what influences their desire to renew their cell phone contract, and what people say and what they do are often very different. Data is the key to differentiating between what people say in terms of sentiment and what they do in terms of actions."[11]

## UTILIZING BIG DATA

Amazon leveraged on big data to improve its relationship with its customers and provide superior customer service. The online retailer built a vast database of its customers and their buying preferences over a long period of time. It was one of the first e-commerce companies to start using the cross-selling/up-selling method. This customer recommendation system was later augmented by utilizing its big data resources. Using big data, Amazon started analyzing the past product purchases made from its online store by its customers and the other items that were purchased along with them. Data collected from its customers was used to give silent but highly customized suggestions to make them buy more. This analysis of data helped Amazon give product suggestions to existing as well as new customers who might not have otherwise bought a complementary product. This was the reason why Amazon's sites displayed 'Other customers who bought this item also purchased that item' kind of cross-selling recommendations.[12] Product related recommendations were also customized based on many factors such as the customer's location and demography. "It can even cross-correlate buying behavior between home and garden sales,"[13] said Jeff Kelly, lead big data analyst at Wikibon[k].

The bewildering range of products that were showcased on e-commerce portals made them seem unwieldy and incomprehensible to many customers. According to analysts, mining the treasure trove of information and providing relevant product recommendations could make e-commerce sites feel smaller and more intimate to the consumers.[14] Big data also helped Amazon in the development of its personalized marketing strategy—a tactic in which it excelled. Many e-commerce firms resorted to generic mass emailing of the products and offers that were available with them. This strategy led to the wastage of marketing efforts of many firms and the labeling of e-commerce mails as spam. Amazon created 360 degree customer profiles which tracked and stored everything related to customers like their browsing history, social data, tastes and preferences, past purchase history, etc. These 360 degree customer profiles facilitated the identification of discerning groups of customers who could be well targeted.[15] Amazon could create hyper-personalized marketing messages regarding the products based on the individual customer's needs and interests.[16]

Amazon also relied on big data to improve the quality of its after sales service to its customers.

[i] The Collaborative filtering system is a technique used in many recommender systems of e-commerce portals. Collaborative filtering involves filtering information or usage patterns through techniques involving multiple data bases, viewpoints, and agents.

[j] Dataspora, headquartered in Cambridge, Massachusetts, US is a leading big data and analytics consultancy.

[k] Wikibon, headquartered in Marlborough, Massachusetts, USA, is a community of practitioners and consultants on technology and business systems that use open source sharing of free advisory knowledge.

Most American customers were known to have a largely negative experience in their service interactions.[17] Amazon tried to solve this problem by leveraging on the large data it had regarding its customers. Having the right data helped it have a favorable exchange with its customers and to solve their problems quickly. Amazon's customer service executives had speedy access to data regarding the past purchases and browsing history of its customers. This enabled the company to provide quicker solutions to the problems and complaints of its customers. Complainants did not have to spell out their details like last names, contact numbers, and addresses repeatedly before their queries/problems were solved. This unique approach of utilizing big data to improve service quality gave spectacular results. After having a positive experience with Amazon's support team in one such encounter, Sean Madden, a top business blogger, said, "After nearly a decade of ordering stuff from Amazon, I never loved the company as much as I did at that moment."[18]

One of the factors which facilitated the use of big data for customer service was Amazon's acquisition of Zappos, the largest online retailer of shoes, in the year 2009. Amazon acquired Zappos for US$ 1.2 billion to expand its reach in product categories in which it was not strong.[19] Zappos was famed for using its customer database to provide a personal touch to its customers and turn them into its fans and cheerleaders.[20] Amazon adopted the customer service strategies of Zappos after it took over the company. The application of big data for improving customer service made Amazon and its subsidiary Zappos to rank among the top 10 retailers in National Retail Federation Foundation/American Express Customers' Choice Awards for the years 2010 and 2011 *(Refer to Exhibit 3 for top 10 retailers in National Retail Federation Foundation/American Express Customers' Choice Awards for 2010 and 2011).*[21]

Rather than using big data to just provide better product suggestions and improve the quality of service, Amazon used it to check fraud in the organization. An interesting area where Amazon benefited through using big data was in preventing warehouse theft. At any given point of time, Amazon had 1.5 billion items in its catalogues across its 200 fulfillment centers across the world. Theft of these items was a big threat to Amazon. The problem with identifying which of these items were more sought after by thieves was that both expensive and low-priced items were stolen. Inexpensive items too were often stolen due to reasons like their scarcity. To solve this problem, Amazon used big data and updated its product catalogue data nearly 50 million times a week.[22] Product catalogue data was collected, stored, and analyzed to identify which of the items were more likely to be stolen and the information was fed back to the warehouses *(Refer to Exhibit 4 for the five components of big data process).* This helped Amazon in preventing the theft of items in its catalogues. Werner Vogels (Vogels), Chief Technology Officer and Vice President of Amazon.com, felt that data and storage should be unconstrained. "In the old world of data analysis you knew exactly which questions you wanted to ask, which drove a

## EXHIBIT 3    Top 10 Retailers in National Retail Federation Foundation/American Express Customers' Choice Awards for 2010 and 2011

| Sl. No. | 2011 | 2010 |
|---|---|---|
| 1 | Amazon.com | Zappos |
| 2 | L.L. Bean | Amazon.com |
| 3 | Zappos | L.L. Bean |
| 4 | Overstock.com | Overstock.com |
| 5 | QVC | Lands' End |
| 6 | Kohl's Department Stores | JCPenney |
| 7 | Lands' End | Kohl's |
| 8 | JCPenney | QVC |
| 9 | Newegg | Nordstorm |
| 10 | Nordstorm | Newegg |

*Source:* "Customers' Choice Awards," http://www.nrffoundation.com.

## EXHIBIT 4 Five Components of the Big Data Process

| | |
|---|---|
| **Collect** | Collecting and getting the data to the place where the process can be started. |
| **Store** | Storing the collected data before it is put to proper use. |
| **Organize** | Controlling the quality of data by knowing which data to include in the stream. Organizing also involves validating data in order to make sure that correct data is used. |
| **Analytics** | Analysis of well-organized data to create usable information. |
| **Share** | Information that is created through analytics is shared with those who need it. |

*Source:* Eric Savitz, "CeBIT: Amazon CTO Werner Vogels Talks Big Data," www.forbes.com, August 3, 2012.

very predictable collection and storage model. In the new world of data analysis your questions are going to evolve and change over time and as such you need to be able to collect, store, and analyze data without being constrained by resources."[23]

## AIDING OTHER COMPANIES WITH BIG DATA

Other than utilizing big data for improving its own performance, Amazon also helped other e-commerce portals to leverage its big data resources. This it achieved through an innovative service for smaller e-commerce businesses called Amazon Webstore. Amazon Webstore, launched in 2010, allowed retailers to build their portals around Amazon's e-commerce platform.[24] Amazon Webstore was an independent store outside of Amazon's official e-commerce store built on the third party domain name and brand. Users of Amazon Webstore could place Amazon Product Ads[1] on Amazon's portals. People who clicked on these product ads would be redirected to the site of the partnering site where the sale would be completed. As part of this partnership, Amazon allowed its partnering sites to use its big data while maintaining their independent identity as a small online e-commerce store.[25] Amazon charged its merchant partners a fixed monthly fee as well as a fixed commission for using its resources and big data resources.[26]

An interesting case where Amazon Webstore improved the performance of a small retailer was Anaconda Sports. Anaconda Sports, a successful sports retailer from New York, USA, found itself stuck with an inefficient and expensive e-commerce system with issues like inability to store all the customer information, lack of unique experience based on customer preferences, and poor customer service quality.[27] Modifying its e-commerce portal through Amazon Webstore made it possible for it to develop an efficient store which solved all the problems it had been facing as well as increase its sales substantially.

Commenting on the benefits of Amazon's Webstore for small and medium businesses, Scott Pulsipher, director of Amazon Webstore, said, "By leveraging Amazon's technology and infrastructure, Amazon Webstore levels the playing field for small- and medium-sized businesses, helping them quickly and easily build their businesses and improve the customer experience."[28] Amazon Webstore was implemented even by big brands like Timex, MTV, Boeing, and Samsonite which allowed them to improve their engagement with their customers *(Refer to Exhibit 5 for the screenshot of Samsonite's website built using Amazon Webstore)*. Commenting on how Amazon Webstore helped to increase sales and cut costs at Timex[m], its e-commerce director Cal Crouch said, "When we launched our new Amazon Webstore, we saw an immediate lift of 40 percent in revenue and average order size. And on the support side, we have gained the flexibility to make most changes to content as well as brand ourselves—saving us thousands (of dollars) in development costs."[29]

Amazon's Amazon Web Services (AWS) helped a lot of companies to develop better applications, deploy new products and services, and cut their costs

---

[1] Amazon Product Ads was an advertising program that allowed sellers to promote their products on the official e-commerce portals of Amazon in different countries.

[m] Timex, headquartered in Hoofdorp, Netherlands, is a maker of timepieces and luxury goods.

**EXHIBIT 5**    Screenshot of Samsonite's Website Built Using Amazon Webstore

*Source:* http://webstore.amazon.com/client-showcase/b/6254207011.

*(Refer to Exhibit 6 for AWS architecture).* Amazon offered its solution using familiar tools such as Oracle Database and Microsoft SQL Server, while also pioneering and promoting new platforms such as DynamoDB[n], Hadoop[o], and Redshift[p].[30] "One of the core concepts of Big Data is being able to evolve analytics over time. For that, a company cannot be constrained by any resource. As such, Cloud Computing and Big Data are closely linked because for a company to be able to collect, store, organize,

analyze, and share data, they need access to infinite resources,"[31] said Vogels.

Small companies faced a lot of difficulties in adopting and deploying big data due to the limited resources at their disposal. Amazon came out with solutions for such companies so that they could implement big data easily. In November 2013, Amazon Web Service announced a new service for real time processing of big data. The service known as Kinesis, processed the high volumes of data flowing into Amazon's web-based storehouses on a real time basis. The tool had the capability to accept any number of data sources and could process terabytes of data per hour. It was intended to allow developers to create applications that worked on a real-time basis for tasks like website traffic analysis, business

---

[n] DynamoDB is a managed NoSQL database service which makes it simple and cheap to store and retrieve large amounts of data.

[o] Hadoop is an open-source software framework for storing and processing large data-sets.

[p] Redshift is a fast and powerful data warehouse service which is a part of AWS.

## EXHIBIT 6   AWS Infrastructure

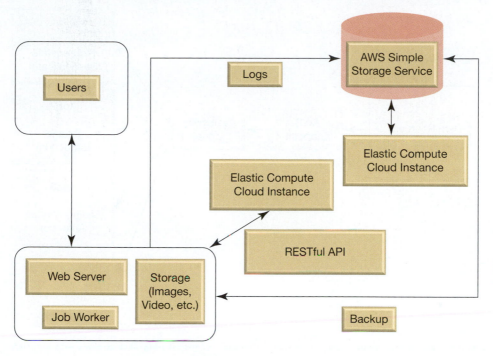

*Source:* http://d36cz9buwru1tt.cloudfront.net/pixnet_diagram_2.jpg.

transactions related to marketing and finance, social media data, and logs *(Refer to Exhibit 7 for Kinesis' architecture).* Commenting on the flexibility Kinesis would bring to businesses, an analyst at Neovise[q] Paul Burns said, "Sometimes people spend hours or days just collecting the data, then coming back and processing it, so it's out of date. . . . So Amazon said we'll take care of all that for you, just write your own program and connect to us."[32] The ability to create big data apps through Kinesis was expected to remove one of the biggest bottlenecks for smaller companies in adopting big data for their businesses. But one limitation of Kinesis was that all the data processing would be done at the data centers of Amazon itself instead of at the clients' location.

## LOOKING AHEAD

Analysts came up with suggestions on more ways in which Amazon could benefit from big data. Having

its roots in selling books, Amazon had built a review system for the books sold through its website. Amazon's review system was mainly based on text reviews written by customers and the number of stars (from one to five) given to a book or author. This review system allowed Amazon to build a community and a loyal customer base. Over the years, there were allegations that many authors had found a way to manipulate Amazon's review system and to get paid reviews for their books. Such paid reviews tended to be biased and in turn, they impacted the reliability of the review system.[33] To solve this problem, some industry experts suggested that Amazon create a big data solution which would allow readers to give a vast range of additional feedback and comments which could be used to check the veracity of the reviews. Analysts opined that apart from improving the reliability of its review system, a big data based review system would also make it possible for Amazon to show more relevant reviews to the customers just as it suggested relevant products.

Another suggestion regarding the use of big data to further Amazon's prospects was in giving

[q] Neovise, headquartered in Fort Collins, Colorado, USA, is an IT industry analyst firm.

## EXHIBIT 7    Kinesis' Architecture

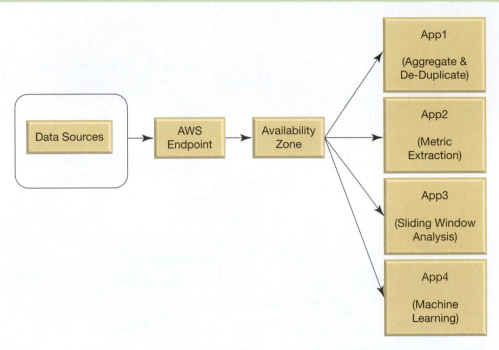

*Source:* http://arstechnica.com/information-technology/2013/11/amazon-wades-into-big-data-streams-with-kinesis/.

better competition to other big Internet companies like Google Inc.[r] and Facebook, Inc.[s] The business models of many of these Internet companies were based on online advertising. And according to an estimate by Google, 30 to 40 percent of its revenue from search advertising came from e-commerce sources.[34] The growth of Amazon as the Internet's one-stop shop and its increasing product base made it the primary destination for product searches, clearly bypassing Google. This unique position left Amazon in possession of more shopping data of people than any other Internet company. Some analysts

were of the view that using big data, Amazon could beat Google and Facebook in the long term. Bezos acquired The Washington Post[t] for US$ 250 million in August 2013.[35] This acquisition sparked speculation among industry observers that Bezos would use big data to revitalize the news business and find new revenue sources for the ageing business. The use of big data analytics could give better insights into the readers of The Washington Post. Amazon could thereby integrate the likings of readers in developing new products in the news business. According to analysts, Amazon's expertise in big data could transform the online news business in the same way as Bezos had transformed the 500-year-old book publishing business.[36] According to Wikibon's big data analyst Jeff Kelly, as of end 2013, Amazon had all the pieces of the big data puzzle but the firm would have put these together effectively to emerge as a dominant player in this space.[37]

---

[r] Google Inc., headquartered in Mountain View, California, USA, is a leading Internet-related products and services firm.

[s] Facebook, Inc., headquartered in Menlo Park, California, USA, is a leading social networking service.

[t] The Washington Post, headquartered in Washington, D.C., USA is a leading American newspaper.

# END NOTES

[1] Teresa Novellino, "At War with Amazon? Rich Relevance Offers Big Data Weaponry," http://upstart.bizjournals.com, October 9, 2013.

[2] Maria Deutscher, "Amazon Closes the Loop on Big Data," http://siliconangle.com, November 22, 2013.

[3] "History of AMAZON.COM," http://btmaushart.iweb.bsu.edu.

[4] "Timeline History Amazon.com," http://amazongenius.com.

[5] "History of AMAZON.COM," http://btmaushart.iweb.bsu.edu.

[6] "History and Timeline," http://phx.corporate-ir.net.

[7] "How Amazon is Leveraging Big Data," http://www.bigdata-startups.com.

[8] Bill Vorhies, "A Brief History of Big Data Technologies – From SQL to NoSQLtpHadoop and Beyond," http://data-magnum.com, October 31, 2013.

[9] Teresa Novellino, "At War with Amazon? Rich Relevance Offers Big Data Weaponry," http://upstart.bizjournals.com, October 9, 2013.

[10] "How Amazon is Leveraging Big Data," http://www.bigdata-startups.com.

[11] "Q&A: What Can Non-IT Companies Learn from Amazon and Facebook about How to Leverage Big Data?" www.hightable.com.

[12] Jodi Beuder, "How Can Big Data Improve the Customer Experience this Holiday Season?" http://www.icmi.com, November 5, 2013.

[13] Constance Gustke, "Retail Goes Shopping Through Big Data," www.cnbc.com, April 15, 2013.

[14] Adria Saracino, "Interesting Ways Businesses Use Big Data to Improve Personalization," http://www.clickz.com, April 23, 2013.

[15] Lisa Desjardins, "How Amazon Uses Marketing Personalization," http://www.nectarom.com, October 7, 2013.

[16] Lisa Desjardins, "How Amazon Uses Marketing Personalization," http://www.nectarom.com, October 7, 2013.

[17] Sean Madden, "How Companies like Amazon Use Big Data to Make You Love Them," http://www.fastcodesign.com, May 2, 2012.

[18] Sean Madden, "How Companies like Amazon Use Big Data to Make You Love Them," http://www.fastcodesign.com, May 2, 2012.

[19] "History and Timeline," http://phx.corporate-ir.net.

[20] Justin Amendola, "What Zappos.com can Teach you About Turning Customers into Mega Fans," http://www.business2community.com, May 19, 2012.

[21] Frank Reed, "Amazon Retains Top Spot in Customer Service Poll, Zappos Third," http://www.marketingpilgrim.com, January 19, 2012.

[22] Ryan Lawler, "How Amazon Uses Big Data to Prevent Warehouse Theft," www.gigaom.com, October 18, 2011.

[23] Roberto V. Zicari, "On Big Data: Interview with Dr. Werner Vogels, CTO and VP of Amazon.com," www.odbms.org, November 2, 2011.

[24] Chris Crum, "Amazon Launches New Webstore E-Commerce Product," http://www.webpronews.com, May 24, 2010.

[25] "Power of Amazon," http://webstore.amazon.com/power-of-amazon-your-brand/b/6254196011.

[26] "Amazon Webstore Pricing," http://webstore.amazon.com/amazon-webstore-pricing/b/6368778011.

[27] Adria Saracino, "Interesting Ways Businesses Use Big Data to Improve Personalization," http://www.clickz.com, April 23, 2013.

[28] Chris Crum, "Amazon Launches New Webstore E-Commerce Product," http://www.webpronews.com, May 24, 2010.

[29] Chris Crum, "Amazon Launches New Webstore E-Commerce Product," http://www.webpronews.com, May 24, 2010.

[30] Doug Henschen, "Amazon's Vogels: Big Data Belongs In The Cloud," www.informationweek.com, April 19, 2013

[31] Roberto V. Zicari, "On Big Data: Interview with Dr. Werner Vogels, CTO and VP of Amazon.com," www.odbms.org, November 2, 2011

[32] Andy Patrizio, "Why Amazon's Kinesis Tool is a Big Deal for Working with Big Data," www.citeworld.com, November 22, 2013.

[33] Amir Kurtovic, "A Better Review: Why Amazon Should Embrace Big Data to Fix Its Ratings System," http://www.amirkurtovic.com.

[34] David Hughes, "Big Data is the Only Way to Compete with Google," http://allthingsd.com, July 18, 2013.

[35] "Amazon Boss Jeff Bezos Buys Washington Post for $250m," http://www.bbc.co.uk, August 6, 2013.

[36] Karyl Scott, "How Bezos Could Apply Big Data and Other Amazon Tactics to the News Business," http://www.citeworld.com, August 14, 2013.

[37] Maria Deutscher, "Amazon Closes the Loop on Big Data," http://siliconangle.com, November 22, 2013.

# NCAA Athletics: Are Its Amateurism and Financial Assistance Policies Ethical?

A. J. Strickland

The University of Alabama

Garrett Moody

2015 MBA Student,
The University of Alabama

In 2014, more than 450,000 student athletes at approximately 1,100 universities participated in 23 National Collegiate Athletic Association (NCAA) sports. While at least 150,000 of these student athletes participated in college athletics without any financial assistance, scholarship athletes at NCAA Division I and Division II colleges and universities were awarded more than $1.5 billion in scholarships in 2013. Scholarships typically covered the cost of tuition, books, and room and board and had an average value of $13,821 for Division I schools in 2013. Student athletes in some sports could receive partial scholarships that provided less than the average $13,821 scholarship amount. The possibility of a future collegiate athletic scholarship was a motivating force to excel for many families and young athletes competing in Pee Wee, Little League, middle school, and high school sports.

College sports were regulated by the NCAA, which in 2013 recorded revenues of nearly $913 million and a budget surplus of $61 million. In 2013, the NCAA also had net assets of $627 million, which included an endowment balance of $326 million. The NCAA's revenues were generated primarily from NCAA Division I men's basketball tournament marketing and broadcast rights and from ticket sales for other championship events. The NCAA's 2013 expenses of $852 million included distributions to Division I member schools of $527.4 million. Some observers argued that the NCAA exploited the student athletes whose performances made revenue-generating sporting events possible, despite the financial support it provided to member universities.

In 2014, the NCAA was fighting a unionization movement at Northwestern University that was led by former quarterback Kain Colter, and it faced various lawsuits challenging its amateurism and financial assistance policies, which barred student athletes from receiving compensation for sports participation. The National Labor Relations Board (NLRB) ruled in March 2014 that college players had the right to organize as unions to bargain with schools as employers. Northwestern players voted on unionization in April 2014, but ballots were to remain sealed until an appeal of the NLRB ruling was resolved.

The Ed O'Bannon and Sam Keller lawsuits filed in 2009 charged that the NCAA illegally prevented players from receiving compensation from universities while their names and identities were used to generate billions in revenues for the universities, the NCAA, video game producers, and broadcasters. Keller was a former quarterback at Arizona State and the University of Nebraska, and O'Bannon played basketball at UCLA. The NCAA settled the Keller case in June 2014 and agreed to pay $20 million to current and former college athletes whose images and likenesses were used in EA Sports video games. In September 2013, EA Sports and Collegiate Licensing Company, the nation's largest collegiate trademark licensing firm, had agreed to a $40 million settlement in a similar case. In July 2013, the NCAA had ended its licensing agreement with EA Sports, which had produced NCAA football video games since 1998.

The O'Bannon lawsuit differed from the Keller suit in that it asked the judge to force the NCAA to alter its amateurism and financial assistance rules that prohibited college athletes from receiving compensation for use of their names and likenesses in broadcasts and video games. The NCAA's defense during the summer 2014 trial centered on the long-term economic value of a college education. The plaintiffs' case was summarized by an expert witness, Stanford economist Dr. Roger Noll, who testified that "the NCAA is a cartel that creates a price-fixing agreement among the member schools."[1] The NCAA's chief legal officer, Donald Remy, commented to reporters outside the courtroom that "by [Noll's] definition, every amateur organization would be a cartel."[2] After 15 days of testimony, on July 24, 2014, the NCAA and the O'Bannon plaintiffs were required to wait for Judge Claudia Wilken's decision. Regardless of the outcome of the trial, the NCAA was forced to evaluate the ethics of its amateurism and financial assistance policies.

# A BRIEF HISTORY OF AMATEURISM AND FINANCIAL ASSISTANCE FOR COLLEGE ATHLETES

The idea of giving some sort of compensation to college football players for playing a sport had been around almost since players began playing collegiate football. In the early 1900s, coaches and universities had "access to trust funds that they would allocate to male athletes who could not otherwise play football, attend college, and hold down a campus job because of the demands of the sport."[3] For years, members of the NCAA could never come to a consensus on the issue of scholarships and amateurism. Some universities gave no athletic scholarships, while others gave full benefits to student athletes.

The first movement toward a uniform system for all member institutions of the NCAA occurred in 1948, when the NCAA introduced the Sanity Code. The Sanity Code "abandoned the NCAA's forty-two-year-old commitment to amateur principles and allowed financial aid to be awarded on the basis of athletic ability."[4] Although this measure ultimately failed because a few NCAA members did not adopt the policy, it did signify the feeling the majority of NCAA members had toward compensation for its student athletes.

In 1951, Walter Byers became the first full-time director of the NCAA. He held the position for 36 years and brought a wealth of changes with him. Under Byers' direction, the NCAA passed a rule specifying that all member institutions had to provide athletic scholarships and grants to cover tuition, room, board, and other miscellaneous fees. The next, and final, major change occurred in 1973, when the NCAA decreed that athletic scholarships were no longer four-year contracts but were scholarships requiring yearly renewal. Student athletes were no longer guaranteed four years of compensation since their scholarships could be revoked for lack of performance on the field. There were minor tweaks throughout the years, but these changes laid the framework for what were considered legal and illegal payments for all student athletes.

In 2014, the NCAA Eligibility Center determined the amateurism eligibility of all student athletes for initial participation at an NCAA Division I or Division II college or university. Student athletes were prohibited from entering into contracts with professional teams, salaries for participation in athletics, prize money, benefits from agents, agreements with agents, or any financial assistance based on athletic talent or sports participation. Division I and Division II athletes were allowed to be reimbursed for travel and other expenses by professional sports teams or from prize money if the activity occurred prior to enrollment with a college or university.

# FINANCIAL VALUE OF A SCHOLARSHIP

NCAA Division I and Division II colleges and universities awarded more than $1.5 billion in scholarships to student athletes in 2013. Scholarships typically covered the cost of tuition, books, and room and board. Student athletes could receive full scholarships or partial scholarships. The number of financial awards to student athletes varied by the type of membership held by the institution. For example, Division I Football Bowl Subdivision (FBS) schools were allowed to provide 85 full scholarships in football, whereas Division I Football Championship Subdivision (FCS) schools were restricted to 65 equivalent full scholarships. Football, basketball, and ice hockey were the only men's head-count sports in 2014. That is, only full scholarships could be awarded in these sports. Partial scholarship awards were allowable in other men's sports. Women's basketball, gymnastics, tennis, and volleyball were NCAA head count sports requiring full scholarships, while partial scholarships were allowed in other women's sports.

The dollar amount of athletic scholarships offered in men's and women's sports was required to be proportional to the undergraduate enrollment under Title IX of the Education Amendments Act of 1972. For example, a university with a 50-50 proportion of men and women undergraduate students was required to provide equal scholarship dollars and other benefits to men and women student athletes. Title IX implementation at many universities with football programs resulted in the addition of several women's sports and, perhaps, the elimination of some men's sports, to ensure a proportional dollar value of scholarships and other benefits awarded to men and women student athletes. It was also not uncommon for a university with football programs to provide a greater number of scholarships for women's teams than men's teams participating in the same sport to offset the large dollar value of scholarships awarded to student athletes participating in football.

In 2014, there were 346 Division I, 291 Division II, and 439 Division III NCAA member schools. Division III schools did not provide student athletes with scholarships or other athletics-based financial aid. Approximately 150,000 student athletes participated in Division III athletics in 2013. Exhibit 1 presents the scholarship limits for select NCAA Division I and Division II men's and women's sports in 2013.

In 2013, the average number of athletic scholarships awarded by each Division I FBS school was approximately 600, and the average value of a full scholarship for NCAA Division I schools was $13,821. In the same year, the average full scholarship amount for NCAA Division II schools was $5,362, and approximately 400 student athletes, on average, participated in sports at each Division II football school. The average number of participants for nonfootball Division II schools was 250 per school in 2013.

According to a study done by Drexel University and the National College Players Association, college athletic scholarships fell short of covering the complete cost of attendance, and additional living expenses for transportation, various school supplies, and other miscellaneous expenses could exceed $3,000 per year.[5] Options for the students to pay for the costs not covered by their scholarships included student loans and Pell Grants. While student loans were available to any student athlete, Pell Grants were restricted to student athletes whose household income was below a certain threshold. Pell Grants up to $5,700 in 2014 were needs-based and did not require repayment since they were grants rather than loans. Pell Grants were not restricted to student athletes, but many student athletes did apply. Pell Grant spending on all postsecondary education was estimated at $31.7 billion in award year 2012–2013. The NCAA did not award athletics scholarships, but it did award scholarships to Division I and II athletes on the basis of financial need. The NCAA awarded $16.2 million in needs-based scholarships through its Special Assistance Fund in 2012.

## REVENUE GENERATION

The revenues needed to support athletic programs were generated through state appropriations to university budgets, ticket sales, and NCAA revenue distribution. NCAA revenues were generated from television and marketing rights fees, primarily from the Division I men's basketball championship, and from ticket sales for championship events. A small portion of NCAA revenues was generated from licensing fees for college sports video games. More than 90 percent of NCAA revenues were distributed to member institutions to support student athletes. The NCAA distributed $497.6 million to Division I schools in the 2013–2014 academic year.

Member institutions also collected revenues from ticket sales, concessions, royalties and licensing fees, broadcast fees, and direct institution support. Revenue generation from football averaged 44.3 percent of total athletic department revenues for FBS programs and 24 percent of total athletic department revenues for NCAA Division I FCS programs. Revenues to support university athletics programs varied widely: Division III schools relied almost exclusively on direct institutional support to fund programs, while the top-ranked Division I FBS programs generated between $50 million and $100 million each year to fund programs. In 2012, even with revenues from football, the expenses of average Division I schools exceeded revenues by $10 million to $12 million, and the average

**EXHIBIT 1**   Scholarship Limits for Select Division I and Division II Men's and Women's Sports, 2013

| Men's Varsity Sports | | |
| --- | --- | --- |
| | Scholarship Limit | |
| Sport | NCAA Division I | NCAA Division II |
| Baseball | 11.7 | 9.0 |
| Basketball | 13.0 | 10.0 |
| Football (FBS) | 85.0 | 36.0 |
| Golf | 4.5 | 3.6 |
| Soccer | 9.9 | 9.0 |
| Tennis | 4.5 | 4.5 |
| Track and field | 12.6 | 12.6 |
| Wrestling | 9.9 | 9.0 |

| Women's Varsity Sports | | |
| --- | --- | --- |
| | Scholarship Limit | |
| Sport | NCAA Division I | NCAA Division II |
| Basketball | 15.0 | 10.0 |
| Field hockey | 12.0 | 6.3 |
| Golf | 4.5 | 3.6 |
| Gymnastics | 12.0 | 6.0 |
| Lacrosse | 12.0 | 9.9 |
| Rowing | 20.0 | 20.0 |
| Soccer | 14.0 | 9.9 |
| Softball | 12.0 | 7.2 |
| Swimming & diving | 14.0 | 8.1 |
| Tennis | 8.0 | 6.0 |
| Track and field | 18.0 | 12.6 |
| Volleyball | 12.0 | 8.0 |

Source: ScholarshipStats.com.

budget shortfall for Division II schools was between $3.5 million and $4.5 million. Exhibit 2 presents the estimated total revenues and expenses for 25 of the top programs in the country for the 2011–2012 year. Median revenue and expenses for all Division I and Division II schools for 2004 and 2008–2012 are presented in Exhibits 3 and 4, respectively.

## A DAY IN THE LIFE OF A COLLEGE FOOTBALL PLAYER

A typical day in the life of a college football player was far different from that of the average college student. *The Wall Street Journal* examined the average day of a collegiate athlete in its October 14, 2011, profile of former Michigan quarterback Denard Robinson.

Robinson began the day with a 7 a.m. trip to the training room. Robinson had injured his knee in a game and received daily treatment from personal trainers and physical therapists to ensure that he would be able to participate in the upcoming practices and games. The various treatments lasted just over two and one-half hours, until 9:40. Robinson then rushed to make his first class, which began at 10:10 a.m. After class, he and a few teammates headed to the Michigan Student Union to grab lunch, which consisted of Wendy's spicy chicken nuggets. Following lunch, Robinson had a scheduled meeting with a professor to discuss a paper. At 2 p.m., Robinson headed back to the training room to take an ice bath and then went to a quarterbacks' meeting 30 minutes later. This meeting lasted an hour, and then came practice at 3:30. Once practice was completed, Robinson found himself back in the training room for more treatment on his knee. His final training-room session finished shortly after 7:30 p.m., and then came dinner. After a large meal (Robinson consumed, on average, 14,000 calories per day), he and some teammates headed to the film room to prepare for that week's upcoming game against rival Michigan State. The day finally concluded at 10:30 p.m., nearly 16 hours after it began.[6]

## PAYMENT SCANDALS

Under NCAA rules, it was strictly forbidden for players to be paid to play football at an amateur level. That did not mean that they weren't paid, but payment was highly illegal and had been the cause of many scandals at major institutions over the years. There were three main ways that the players were paid, involving three distinct sources. The first source was what was deemed "pay for play." Pay for play was essentially a system in which high-ranking boosters or school officials provided under-the-table money to a recruit or his family in order to secure

**EXHIBIT 2**   Financial Summary for the NCAA 2013 Preseason Top-25 Football Programs, 2011–2012

| Preseason Rank (2013) | University | Total Football Revenue (2011–2012) | Total Football Expenses (2011–2012) | Net Revenue (2011–2012) |
|---|---|---|---|---|
| 1 | Alabama | $ 81,993,762 | $36,918,963 | $45,074,799 |
| 2 | Ohio State | 58,112,270 | 34,026,871 | 24,085,399 |
| 3 | Oregon | 51,921,731 | 20,240,213 | 31,681,518 |
| 4 | Stanford | 25,564,646 | 18,738,731 | 6,825,915 |
| 5 | Georgia | 74,989,418 | 22,710,140 | 52,279,278 |
| 6 | Texas A&M | 44,420,762 | 17,929,882 | 26,490,880 |
| 7 | South Carolina | 48,065,096 | 22,063,216 | 26,001,880 |
| 8 | Clemson | 39,207,780 | 23,652,472 | 15,555,308 |
| 9 | Louisville | 23,756,955 | 18,769,539 | 4,987,416 |
| 10 | Florida | 74,117,435 | 23,045,846 | 51,071,589 |
| 11 | Notre Dame | 68,986,659 | 25,757,968 | 43,228,691 |
| 12 | Florida State | 34,484,786 | 22,052,228 | 12,432,558 |
| 13 | LSU | 68,804,309 | 24,049,282 | 44,755,027 |
| 14 | Oklahoma State | 41,138,312 | 26,238,172 | 14,900,140 |
| 15 | Texas | 103,813,684 | 25,896,203 | 77,917,481 |
| 16 | Oklahoma | 59,630,425 | 24,097,643 | 35,532,782 |
| 17 | Michigan | 85,209,247 | 23,640,337 | 61,568,910 |
| 18 | Nebraska | 55,063,437 | 18,649,947 | 36,413,490 |
| 19 | Boise State | 15,345,308 | 8,537,612 | 6,807,696 |
| 20 | TCU | 25,984,011 | 25,984,011 | — |
| 21 | UCLA | 25,168,004 | 19,193,346 | 5,974,658 |
| 22 | Northwestern | 27,547,684 | 20,148,403 | 7,399,281 |
| 23 | Wisconsin | 48,416,449 | 24,231,297 | 24,185,152 |
| 24 | USC | 34,410,822 | 23,123,733 | 11,287,089 |
| 25 | Oregon State | 20,666,946 | 11,903,213 | 8,763,733 |

*Source:* Alicia Jessop, "The Economics of College Football: A Look at the Top-25 Teams' Revenues and Expenses," *Forbes,* August 31, 2013, www.forbes.com/sites/aliciajessop/2013/08/31/the-economics-of-college-football-a-look-at-the-top-25-teams-revenues-and-expenses/.

the recruit's commitment to play football for the school in question. The second source of payment came in the form of what was called "impermissible benefits." Impermissible benefits could be anything from clothes to tattoos given to players for free or at a discounted price due to their status as a football player or in return for signed memorabilia. The third source of payment was professional sports agents who paid current collegiate players or their families in order to secure the player's commitment to sign with the agent's agency whenever the player decided

to become a professional football player. This problem had become more prevalent in recent years due to the absurdly high price of rookie contracts, but usually a few star players, guaranteed to command a large contract, were involved.

There had been hundreds of pay-for-play scandals throughout the past 50 years that resulted in penalties for university teams, ranging from probation to vacated victories and bowl bans, but one scandal of boosters and school officials' paying players stood above all others. In the early 1980s,

**EXHIBIT 3**  Median Revenue and Expenses for NCAA Division I Athletic Programs, 2004 and 2008–2012

|  | 2004 | 2008 | 2009 | 2010 | 2011 | 2012 |
|---|---|---|---|---|---|---|
| **Football Bowl Subdivision** | | | | | | |
| Total revenues | $22,864,000 | $30,494,000 | $ 32,264,000 | $35,336,000 | $ 38,781,000 | $ 40,581,000 |
| Total expenses | 28,991,000 | 41,363,000 | 45,887,000 | 46,688,000 | 50,774,000 | 56,267,000 |
| Median net revenue | $ (5,902,000) | $ (8,089,000) | $(10,164,000) | $ (9,446,000) | $(10,282,000) | $(12,272,000) |
| **Football Championship Subdivision** | | | | | | |
| Total revenues | $2,047,000 | $ 2,978,000 | $ 2,886,000 | $ 3,289,000 | $ 3,439,000 | $ 3,750,000 |
| Total expenses | 7,810,000 | 12,115,000 | 12,019,000 | 13,091,000 | 13,218,000 | 14,115,000 |
| Median net revenue | $(5,907,000) | $ (7,937,000) | $ (8,643,00) | $ (9,189,000) | $ (9,581,000) | $(10,219,000) |
| **Nonfootball programs** | | | | | | |
| Total revenues | $1,469,000 | $ 2,125,000 | $ 2,099,000 | $ 1,993,000 | $ 2,244,000 | $ 2,206,000 |
| Total expenses | 7,147,000 | 10,347,000 | 10,502,000 | 11,562,000 | 11,930,000 | 12,983,000 |
| Median net revenue | $(5,266,000) | $ (8,031,000) | $ (8,340,000) | $ (8,597,000) | $ (9,330,000) | $ (9,809,000) |

Source: *NCAA Division I Intercollegiate Athletics Programs Report,* 2013.

Southern Methodist University (SMU) was a football powerhouse in the Southwest conference. The university had a rich history of game victories, All-American players, and even a Heisman Trophy winner. In 1984, the SMU team was put on probation when an investigation discovered that SMU boosters and assistant coaches had paid an out-of-state recruit to commit to joining the university's football team in 1983. The team was placed on probation again for the 1985 and 1986 seasons, a probation that, among other penalties, banned the team from bowl games in those seasons.

In 1987, disaster struck the SMU program. Through a series of investigations ranging back to 1986, it was discovered that numerous SMU players were receiving illegal benefits from university boosters and coaches. These benefits ranged from a rent-free stay in a high-end Dallas apartment to a cash payment of $25,000 for a player to play at SMU. The money was coming from a so-called slush fund provided by high-ranking boosters. It was later discovered that high-ranking university officials and even the governor of Texas knew about the slush fund long before it was brought to public attention.

**EXHIBIT 4**  Median Revenue and Expenses for NCAA Division II Athletic Programs, 2004 and 2008–2012

|  | 2004 | 2008 | 2009 | 2010 | 2011 | 2012 |
|---|---|---|---|---|---|---|
| **Football programs** | | | | | | |
| Total revenues | $ 383,600 | $ 587,400 | $ 540,600 | $ 578,900 | $ 618,000 | $ 624,100 |
| Total expenses | 2,884,600 | 4,473,500 | 4,521,600 | 4,839,300 | 5,056,700 | 5,276,500 |
| Median net revenue | $(2,359,700) | $(3,637,500) | $(3,906,700) | $(4,004,200) | $(4,235,100) | $(4,521,600) |
| **Nonfootball programs** | | | | | | |
| Total revenues | $ 153,600 | $ 305,600 | $ 256,700 | $ 259,100 | $ 296,500 | $ 314,200 |
| Total expenses | 2,221,400 | 3,157,700 | 3,102,300 | 3,449,000 | 3,644,500 | 4,014,900 |
| Median net revenue | $ (2,000,200) | $(2,836,000) | $(2,926,200) | $(3,186,300) | $(3,351,600) | $(3,539,900) |

Source: *NCAA Division II Intercollegiate Athletics Programs Report,* 2013.

Given the nature of the violations at SMU, it was determined that the university would be punished with what was called the "death penalty." The death penalty essentially crippled the SMU football program for the next 20 years. Among the punishments doled out to the SMU team was a full cancellation of the 1987 season, a reduction of 55 scholarships over four years, and a ban from bowls or live television. Due to these penalties, SMU ended up canceling the 1988 season as well. While the situation at SMU was an extreme example of the effect that a pay-for-pay scandal can have on a university, there were multiple universities receiving lesser penalties every year for illegally paying players through boosters or university officials.

College football players at major universities were already high-profile young men, meaning items such as their memorabilia and autographs were in high demand. Many athletes and universities were punished because players had provided signed memorabilia or rings in order to receive various items. The fact that amateur athletes could not legally profit from their own signature, but the universities and athletic governing bodies could, was a major point among those in favor of providing some type of financial compensation for players.

A more recent major scandal involving impermissible benefits occurred at Ohio State University in 2010. It was discovered that eight Ohio State players had received roughly $14,000 worth of cash and tattoos in exchange for signed jerseys, memorabilia, and rings. It was later discovered that the Ohio State head coach had received information regarding the illegal activities of his players before it was made public and chose to remain silent about it. Following an investigation that discovered the illegal activities, the Ohio State team received a punishment that included a bowl ban, vacated wins, and a scholarship reduction. The Ohio State head coach lost his job because he had failed to inform a university official about the activities of his players despite his prior knowledge of those activities.

Another source of illegal payments to amateur athletes was professional agents. Agents would identify athletes who had the potential to be money-makers at a professional level and would offer them or their families illegal benefits in order to ensure that the athletes would sign with the agent's agency when they decided to go professional. The most famous case of this type occurred with Reggie Bush and the University of Southern California

(USC). Bush was a star player at USC. He was an All-American and Heisman Trophy winner who was drafted in the first round of the 2006 NFL draft. It was soon discovered that Bush and his family had received illegal benefits totaling over $290,000 from a professional sports agent. As a result, a full-scale investigation was launched into the USC athletic program, and it found that a high-profile basketball player had received similar benefits.

Although the investigation determined that the university itself had no knowledge of the illegal benefits being received by its players, it concluded that since the players had such high profiles, the university should have known. Normally, the punishment for playing an ineligible player (Bush was ineligible due to receiving illegal benefits) would be vacated wins in the games that player had played. In this case, because the university should have known what was going on, it was punished further, with probation, a scholarship reduction, and a two-year bowl ban. Bush was forced to give back his Heisman Trophy.

# EFFORTS TO PAY PLAYERS IN 2014

The debate over possible compensation for football players became more widespread in 2014 because of not only the various lawsuits against the NCAA over player compensation but also the National Labor Relations Board decision to allow college football players to unionize. In 2014, Northwestern football players had formed the College Athletes Players Association (CAPA) and filed a case with the NLRB in which they argued that they were, in fact, employees of the university and not student athletes and thus had the ability to form a union. Northwestern player Kain Colter argued, among other things, that playing college football was like a job due to the fact that players must spend over 50 hours a week preparing for games.[7] Colter did not argue for compensation specifically but just for the right to unionize. The Northwestern players hoped they would be able to engage in collective bargaining with their university similar to the type of negotiations that the NFL Players Association had with the NFL owners.

Once Colter and the CAPA brought their case to the NLRB, it took the board about a month to come to a decision. The local branch of the NLRB decided that players at Northwestern University did, in fact, have the right to unionize. This decision backed up the CAPA's belief that football players were employees of the university, rather than just student athletes. (Note: This ruling applied only to private schools. Players at public schools were subject to a different set of rules; if they wanted to unionize, they had to bring their case to their state's labor board.) The NLRB ruling was under appeal by Northwestern University in mid-2014.

The NCAA president, Mark Emmert, commented on unionization of college athletes during the 2014 State of the NCAA annual news conference:

> To be perfectly frank, the notion of using a union-employee model to address the challenges that exist in intercollegiate athletics is something that strikes most people as a grossly inappropriate solution to the problems.

While it was clear that Emmert and the NCAA leadership did not agree that players unions were appropriate, they didn't seem to be overly worried about them either. The general consensus among NCAA leaders was that, due to the complicated legal nature of unionization, there would not be any serious implications from players unions in the near future. Despite Emmert's opposition to players unions, he did seem open to some form of extra payment for players. In fact, he proposed a $2,000 stipend that would cover the extra costs that aren't covered by a scholarship. Emmert's proposal was eventually rejected by the NCAA board of directors.

Many observers recognized the NLRB ruling as a landmark event in college athletics. It marked the first legally recognized effort to consider independent unionization for a collective group of college athletes. However, not only did the ruling apply only to student athletes at private schools, but it did not address athletes' ability to unionize in any sports other than football.

There was one more issue that was being addressed by the NCAA in 2014 that would possibly have had an effect on the players: The NCAA was considering an overhaul of its governance system and introduced an initiative that would give conferences autonomy over how to use certain portions of their TV revenue. The initiative essentially said, "It's really this simple: If Ohio State wants to provide its athletes with a full cost of attendance scholarship—which it can easily afford—it doesn't feel it should need permission from Stony Brook."[8] The initiative

covered the following items, and thus the schools would decide whether to provide them to their student athletes:

- Financial aid, including full cost of attendance and scholarship guarantees
- Insurance, including policies that protect future earnings
- Academic support, particularly for at-risk student-athletes
- Other support, such as travel for families, free tickets to athletics events and expenses associated with practice and competition (such as parking)[9]

## WHY FOOTBALL PLAYERS?

No matter what the college sport was, a strong work ethic and an immense amount of talent were required for an athlete to be successful. Every student athlete in university-sponsored sports gave maximum effort for his or her team, both on and off the field. However, there were several reasons that the compensation issue focused on football players. First, football was, far and away, the most profitable sport in college athletics for some schools. While men's basketball could also generate positive revenue, there were some instances in which the revenue generated from a football program heavily contributed to the net revenues needed to support other athletic programs.

A second common argument for compensation for football players centered on NFL rules that did not allow players to enter the NFL draft unless they were three years out of high school. The NBA required that players spend only one year out of high school before entering the NBA draft. This essentially meant that college basketball players were required to spend only a semester or two in college before turning professional. Basketball players also had the option of playing professional basketball in another country for a year and then entering the NBA draft. In other sports, such as baseball and hockey, players had the option of playing professionally directly after high school, skipping college altogether.

Even though it was the dream of every college football player to one day play in the NFL, the odds of that happening were very slim. According to the NFL Players Association, out of the roughly 9,000 football players leaving college to possibly play in the NFL, only 315 were invited to the NFL Combine to show off their skills to potential draft suitors. The NFL draft consisted of only 254 picks, so only 2.8 percent of the eligible players were drafted, with a small group signing on as undrafted free agents. If a player was lucky enough to make an NFL roster, that did not mean that the player would instantly become a millionaire. In 2012, the NFL player minimum salary was $390,000 a year, and the average career for an NFL player was only three and one-half years.[10] Obviously, there were exceptions for the superstars in the league, but these were the numbers for most players.

An additional argument made by those who favored compensation for college football players was the fact that the risk of a long-term injury in football was much higher than that in any other sport. Of course, there was an injury risk for any player who played a sport at a competitive level, but the risk of injury, specifically head injury, was much higher in football. Concussion awareness had greatly increased in recent years at all levels of football as head injuries had greatly changed the way the sport was perceived. Measures had been taken, from penalties for targeting the head to improved helmet padding, to limit concussions, but they still occurred. College football players had to take a serious look at whether they wanted to put their bodies at risk day after day for the chance of, hopefully, playing professional football one day. Many individuals felt that amateur players who are putting their bodies at risk to such an extent deserved some type of compensation. Such thoughts mainly stemmed from the fact that universities and governing bodies were profiting from the players, who risked injury every day, yet the players themselves could not profit. However, student athletes in every sport had received career-ending injuries, with some suffering from limited mobility for the remainder of their lives.

Commenting on the various efforts to compensate student athletes for participation in NCAA football

and basketball, Big 12 Conference commissioner Bob Bowlsby stated, "It is hard to justify paying student athletes in football and men's basketball and not recognizing the significant effort that swimmers and wrestlers and lacrosse players and track athletes all put in. Football and basketball players don't work any harder than anybody else; they just happen to have the blessing of an adoring public who is willing to pay for the tickets and willing to buy the products on television that come with the high visibility. We have both a legal obligation and a moral obligation to do for female student athletes and male Olympic sports athletes just exactly what we do for football and basketball student athletes. I don't think it's even debatable."[11]

## CONCLUSION

While the settlement of the Keller lawsuit had resulted in an agreement to pay approximately 100,000 former Division I men's basketball and FBS football players $400 to $2,000 each for the possible inclusion of their likenesses in EA Sports video games, the issue of student athlete compensation was yet to be resolved. The ramifications of the O'Bannon lawsuit had the possibility of radically changing the nature of college athletics, and it was still uncertain how a final NLRB ruling concerning player unionization would affect universities and the NCAA. Also, the success of litigation against EA Sports and the NCAA had the potential to give rise to new lawsuits claiming that unethical or illegal student athlete policies were created and enforced by the NCAA. The developments of 2014 required that the NCAA closely evaluate its amateurism and financial assistance policies to ensure that the organization could meet the ethical expectations of the universities it represented and the consumers who enjoyed attending and viewing collegiate sporting events.

## ENDNOTES

[1] As quoted in Ben Strauss and Steve Edler, "NCAA Settles One Video Game Suit for $20 Million as a Second Begins," *New York Times,* June 9, 2014, www.nytimes.com/2014/06/10/sports/ncaafootball/ncaa-settles-sam-keller-video-game-suit-for-20-million.html?_r=0.
[2] Ibid.
[3] Ellen J. Staurowsky, "A Radical Proposal," *Marquette Sports Law Review,* May 8, 2012.
[4] Ibid.

[5] Ramogi Huma and Ellen J. Staurowsky, *The Price of Poverty in Big Time College Sport,* September 2011.
[6] online.wsj.com/news/articles/SB10001424052970204002304576629182093236092.
[7] www.huffingtonpost.com/2014/04/06/mark-emmert-union_n_5102239.html.
[8] college-football.si.com/2014/04/24/ncaa-board-of-directors-governance-restructuring/?eref=sircrc.

[9] Ibid.
[10] www.nflplayers.com/About-us/FAQs/NFL-Hopeful-FAQs/.
[11] As quoted in "Big 12 Commissioner Bob Bowlsby Says 'Cheating Pays' in Today's NCAA Landscape," *Bleacher Report,* July 21, 2014, http://bleacherreport.com/articles/2137073-big-12-commissioner-bob-bowlsby-says-cheating-pays-in-todays-ncaa-landscape.

# TOMS Shoes: A Dedication to Social Responsibility

**Margaret A. Peteraf**
Tuck School of Business, Dartmouth College

**Meghan L. Cooney**
Dartmouth College, Research Assistant

**Sean Zhang**
Dartmouth College, Research Assistant

While traveling in Argentina in 2006, Blake Mycoskie witnessed the hardships that children without shoes experienced and he became committed to making a difference. Rather than focusing on charity work, Mycoskie sought to build an organization capable of sustainable, repeated giving, where children would be guaranteed shoes throughout their childhood. He established Shoes for a Better Tomorrow, better known as TOMS, as a for-profit company based on the premise of the "One for One" pledge. For every pair of shoes TOMS sold, TOMS would donate a pair to a child in need. By year-end 2013, TOMS had given away over 10 million pairs of shoes in more than 40 different countries.[1]

As a relatively new and privately held company, TOMS experienced consistent and rapid growth despite the global recession that began in 2007. In 2013, TOMS had matured into an organization with nearly 400 employees and $210 million in revenues. TOMS shoes could be found in several major retail stores, such as Nordstrom, Bloomingdale's, and Urban Outfitters. In addition to providing shoes for underprivileged children, TOMS also expanded its mission to include restoring vision to those with curable sight-related illnesses by developing a new line of eyewear products. Exhibit 1 illustrates how quickly TOMS expanded in its first 8 years of business.

## COMPANY BACKGROUND

While attending Southern Methodist University, Blake Mycoskie founded the first of his six startups, a laundry service company that encompassed seven colleges and staffed over 40 employees.[2] Four startups and a short stint on *The Amazing Race* later, Mycoskie found himself vacationing in Argentina, where he not only learned about the Alpargata shoe originally used by local peasants in the 14th century but also witnessed the extreme poverty in rural Argentina.

Determined to make a difference, Mycoskie believed that providing shoes could more directly impact the children in these rural communities than delivering medicine or food. Aside from protecting children's feet from infections, parasites, and diseases, shoes were often required for a complete school uniform. In addition, research had shown that shoes were found to significantly increase children's self-confidence, help them develop into more active community members, and lead them to stay in school. Thus, by ensuring access to shoes, Mycoskie could effectively increase children's access to education and foster community activism, raising the overall standard of living for people living in poor Argentinian rural areas.

**EXHIBIT 1**   TOMS's Growth in Sales and Employees, 2006–2013

| Year | Total Employees | Pairs of Shoes Sold |
|------|-----------------|---------------------|
| 2006 | 4 | 10,000 |
| 2007 | 19 | 50,000 |
| 2008 | 33 | 110,000 |
| 2009 | 46 | 230,000 |
| 2010 | 72 | 700,000 |
| 2011 | 250 | 1,200,000 |
| 2012 | 320 | 2,500,000 |
| 2013 | 400 | 6,000,000 |

Source: PrivCo, "Private Company Financial Report: TOMS Shoes, Inc.," May 30, 2014.

Dedicated to his mission, Mycoskie purchased 250 pairs of Alpargatas and returned home to Los Angeles, where he subsequently founded TOMS Shoes. He built the company on the promise of "One for One," donating a pair of shoes for every pair sold. With an initial investment of $300,000, Mycoskie's business concept of social entrepreneurship was simple: Sell both the shoe and the story behind it. Building on a simple slogan that effectively communicated his goal, Mycoskie championed his personal experiences passionately and established deep and lasting relationships with customers.

Operating from his apartment with three interns he found through Craigslist, Mycoskie quickly sold out his initial inventory and expanded considerably, selling 10,000 pairs of shoes by the end of his first year. With family and friends, Mycoskie ventured back to Argentina, where they hand-delivered 10,000 pairs of shoes to children in need. Because he followed through on his mission statement, Mycoskie was able to subsequently attract investors to support his unique business model and expand his venture significantly.

When TOMS was initially founded, it operated as the for-profit financial arm while a separate entity entitled "Friends of TOMS" focused on charity work and giving. After 2011, operations at Friends of TOMS were absorbed into TOMS' own operations as TOMS itself matured. In Friends of TOMS's latest accessible 2011 501(c)(3) filing, assets were reported at less than $130,000.[3] Moreover, as of May 2013, the Friends of TOMS website was discontinued, while TOMS also ceased advertising its partnership with Friends of TOMS in marketing campaigns and on its corporate website. The developments suggested that Friends of TOMS became a defunct entity as TOMS incorporated all of its operations under the overarching TOMS brand.

## INDUSTRY BACKGROUND

Even though Mycoskie's vision for his company was a unique one, vying for a position in global footwear manufacturing was a risky and difficult venture. The industry was both stable and mature—one in which large and small companies competed on the basis of price, quality, and service. Competitive pressures came from foreign as well as domestic companies, and new entrants needed to fight for access to downstream retailers.

Further, the cost of supplies was forecast to increase between 2013 and 2020. Materials and wages constituted over 70 percent of industry costs—clearly a sizable concern for competitors. Supply purchases included leather, rubber, plastic compounds, foam, nylon, canvas, laces, and so on. While the price of leather rose steadily each year, the price of rubber also began to climb, at an average annual rate of 7.6 percent. Wages were expected to increase at a rate of 5.8 percent over a five-year period due to growing awareness of how manufacturers took advantage of cheap, outsourced labor.[4]

To thrive in the footwear manufacturing industry, firms needed to differentiate their products in a meaningful way. Selling good-quality products at a reasonable price was rarely enough; they needed to target a niche market that desired a certain image. Product innovation and advertising campaigns therefore became the most successful competitive weapons. For example, Clarks adopted a sophisticated design, appealing to a wealthier, more mature customer base. Nike, adidas, and Skechers developed athletic footwear and aggressively marketed their brands to reflect that image. Achieving economies of scale, increasing technical efficiency, and developing a cost-effective distribution system were also essential elements for success.

Despite the presence of established incumbents, global footwear manufacturing was an attractive industry to potential entrants based on the prediction of increased demand and therefore sales revenue. Moreover, the industry offered incumbents one of the highest profit margins in the fashion industry. But because competitors were likely to open new locations and expand their brands in order to discourage competition, new companies' only option was to attempt to undercut them on cost. Acquiring capital equipment and machinery to manufacture footwear on a large scale was expensive. Moreover, potential entrants also needed to launch costly large-scale marketing campaigns to promote brand awareness. Thus, successful incumbents were traditionally able to maintain an overwhelming portion of the market.

## Building the TOMS Brand

Due to its humble beginnings, TOMS struggled to gain a foothold in the footwear industry. While companies like Nike had utilized high-profile athletes like Michael Jordan and Tiger Woods to establish brand recognition, TOMS had relatively limited financial resources and tried to appeal to a more socially conscious consumer. Luckily, potential buyers enjoyed a rise in disposable income over time as the economy recovered from the recession. As a result, demand for high-quality footwear increased for affluent shoppers, accompanied by a desire to act (and be *seen* acting) charitably and responsibly.

While walking through the airport one day, Mycoskie encountered a girl wearing TOMS shoes. Mycoskie recounts:

> I asked her about her shoes, and she went on to tell me this amazing story about TOMS and the model that it uses and my personal story. I realized the importance

of having a story today is what really separates companies. People don't just wear our shoes, they tell our story. That's one of my favorite lessons that I learned early on.

Moving forward, TOMS focused more on selling the story behind the shoe rather than depending on product features or celebrity endorsements. Moreover, rather than relying on mainstream advertising, TOMS emphasized a grassroots approach using social media and word of mouth. With nearly 2 million Facebook "Likes" and over 2 million Twitter "Followers" in 2013, TOMS's social media presence eclipsed that of its much larger rivals, Skechers and Clarks. Based on 2013 data, TOMS had fewer Followers than Nike and fewer Likes than both Nike and adidas. However, TOMS had more Followers and Likes per dollar of revenue. Therefore, taking company size into account, TOMS also had a greater social media presence than the industry's leading competitors—see Exhibit 2.

TOMS's success with social media advertising can be attributed to the story crafted and championed by Mycoskie. Industry incumbents generally dedicated a substantial portion of revenue and effort to advertising since they were simply selling a product. TOMS, on the other hand, used its mission to ask customers to buy into a *cause,* limiting its need to devote resources to brand building. TOMS lets its charitable work and social media presence generate interest for the company organically. This strategy also increased the likelihood that consumers would make repeat purchases and share the story behind their purchases with family and friends. TOMS's

## EXHIBIT 2   TOMS's Use of Social Media Compared to Select Footwear Competitors, 2013

|  | 2013 Revenue (millions) | Facebook | | Twitter | |
|---|---|---|---|---|---|
|  |  | Number of Likes | Likes per Million $ in Revenue | Number of Followers | Followers per Million $ in Revenue |
| TOMS | $   210 (est.) | 2,215,283 | 7,384 | 2,173,377 | 7,245 |
| Clarks | 1,400 | 241,355 | 172 | 22,184 | 16 |
| Skechers | 1,854 | 1,200,911 | 648 | 18,005 | 10 |
| adidas | 19,640 | 16,340,675 | 832 | 961,065 | 49 |
| Nike | 25,280 | 18,020,656 | 713 | 3,138,584 | 124 |

*Source:* Author data.

customers took pride in supporting a grassroots cause instead of a luxury-footwear supplier and encouraged others to share in the rewarding act.

## A BUSINESS MODEL DEDICATED TO SOCIALLY RESPONSIBLE BEHAVIOR

Traditionally, the content of advertisements for many large apparel companies focused on the attractive aspects of the featured products. TOMS's advertising, on the other hand, showcased its charitable contributions and the story of its founder, Blake Mycoskie. While the CEOs of Nike, adidas, and Clarks rarely appeared in their companies' advertisements, TOMS ran as many ads with its founder as it did without

him, emphasizing the inseparability of the TOMS product from Mycoskie's story. In all of his appearances, Mycoskie was dressed in casual and friendly attire so that customers could easily relate to him and his mission. This advertising method conveyed a small-company feel and encouraged consumers to connect personally with the TOMS brand. It also worked to increase buyer patronage through differentiating the TOMS product from others. Consumers were convinced that every time they purchased a pair of TOMS, they became instruments of the company's charitable work. Exhibit 3 provides examples of TOMS's advertisements used in 2013.

The company's social message fueled buyer enthusiasm and led to repeat purchases by many customers. One reviewer commented, "This is my third pair of TOMS and I absolutely love them! . . . I can't

**EXHIBIT 3    Examples of TOMS's Advertisements**

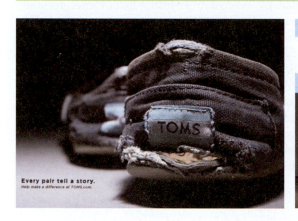

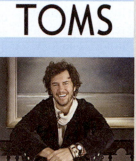

*Source:* **www.toms.com**.

wait to buy more!"[5] Another wrote, "Just got my 25th pair! Love the color! They . . . are my all-time favorite shoe for comfort, looks & durability. AND they are for a great cause!! Gotta go pick out my next pair."[6]

Virtually all consumer reports on TOMS shoes shared similar themes. Though not cheap, TOMS footwear was priced lower than rivals' products, and customers overwhelmingly agreed that the value was worth the cost. Reviewers described TOMS as comfortable, true to size, lightweight, and versatile ("go with everything"). The shoes had "cute shapes and patterns" and were made of canvas and rubber that molded to customers' feet with wear. Because TOMS products were appealing and trendy yet also basic and comfortable, they were immune to changing fashion trends and consistently attracted a variety of consumers.

In addition to offering a high-quality product that people valued, TOMS was able to establish a positive repertoire with its customers through efficient distribution. Maintaining an online shop helped TOMS save money on retail locations and also allowed it to serve a wide geographic range. Further, the company negotiated with well-known retailers like Nordstrom and Neiman Marcus to assist in distribution. Through thoughtful planning and structured coordination, TOMS limited its operation costs and provided prompt service for its customers.

## Giving Partners

As it continued to grow, TOMS sought to improve its operational efficiency by teaming up with "Giving Partners," nonprofit organizations that helped to distribute the shoes that TOMS donated. By teaming up with Giving Partners, TOMS streamlined its charity operations by shifting many of its distributional responsibilities to organizations that were often larger and more resourceful and were able to distribute TOMS shoes more efficiently. Moreover, these organizations possessed more familiarity and experience in dealing with the communities that TOMS was interested in helping and could therefore better allocate shoes that suited the needs of children in the area. Giving Partners also provided feedback to help TOMS improve upon its giving and distributional efforts.

Each Giving Partner also magnified the impact of TOMS shoes by bundling their distribution with other charity work that the organization specialized in. For example, Partners in Health, a nonprofit

organization that spent almost $100 million in 2012 on providing health care for the poor (more than TOMS's total revenue that year), dispersed thousands of shoes to schoolchildren in Rwanda and Malawi while also screening them for malnutrition. Cooperative giving further strengthened the TOMS brand by association with well-known and highly regarded Giving Partners. Complementary services expanded the scope of TOMS's mission, enhanced the impact that each pair of TOMS had on a child's life, and increased the number of goodwill and business opportunities available to TOMS.

To ensure quality of service and adherence to its fundamental mission, TOMS maintained five criteria for Giving Partners:[7]

- *Repeat giving.* Giving Partners must be able to work with the same communities in multiyear commitments, regularly providing shoes to the same children as they grow.
- *High impact.* Shoes must aid Giving Partners with their existing goals in the areas of health and education, providing children with opportunities they would not have otherwise.
- *Consideration of local economy.* Providing shoes cannot have negative socioeconomic effects on the communities where shoes are given.
- *Large-volume shipments.* Giving Partners must be able to accept large shipments of shoes.
- *Focus on health and education.* Giving Partners must give shoes only in conjunction with health and education efforts.

As of 2013, TOMS had built relationships with over 75 Giving Partners, including Save the Children, U.S. Fund for UNICEF, and IMA World Health. To remain accountable to its mission in these joint ventures, TOMS also performed unannounced audit reports that ensured shoes were distributed according to the One for One model.

## Building a Relationship with Giving Partners

Having Giving Partners offered TOMS the valuable opportunity to shift some of its philanthropic costs onto other parties. However, TOMS also proactively maintained strong relationships with its Giving Partners. Kelly Gibson, the program director of National Relief Charities (NRC), a Giving Partner and nonprofit organization dedicated to improving the lives of Native Americans, highlighted the respect with which TOMS treated its Giving Partners:

> TOMS treats their Giving Partners (like us) and the recipients of their giveaway shoes (the Native kids in this case) like customers. We had a terrific service experience with TOMS. They were meticulous about getting our shoe order just right. They also insist that the children who receive shoes have a customer-type experience at distributions.

From customizing Giving Partners' orders to helping pick up the tab for transportation and distribution, TOMS treated its Giving Partners as valuable customers and generated a sense of goodwill that extended beyond its immediate One for One mission. By ensuring that its Giving Partners and recipients of shoes were treated respectfully, TOMS developed a unique ability to sustain business relationships that other for-profit organizations more concerned with the financial bottom line did not.

# MAINTAINING A DEDICATION TO CORPORATE SOCIAL RESPONSIBILITY

Although TOMS manufactured its products in Argentina, China, and Ethiopia (countries that have all been cited as areas with a high degree of child and forced labor by the Bureau of International Labor Affairs), regular third-party factory audits and a Supplier Code of Conduct helped to ensure compliance with fair labor standards.[8] Audits were conducted on both an announced and unannounced basis, and the Supplier Code of Conduct was publicly posted in the local language of every work site. The Supplier Code of Conduct enforced standards such as minimum work age, requirement of voluntary employment, nondiscrimination, maximum workweek hours, and right to unionize. It also protected workers from physical, sexual, verbal, or psychological harassment in accordance with a country's legally mandated standards. Workers were encouraged to report violations directly to TOMS, and suppliers found in violation of TOMS's Supplier Code of Conduct faced termination.

In addition to ensuring that suppliers met TOMS's ethical standards, TOMS also emphasized its own dedication to ethical behavior in a number of ways. TOMS was a member of the American Apparel and Footwear Association (AAFA) and was registered with the Fair Labor Association (FLA). Internally, TOMS educated its own employees on human trafficking and slavery prevention and partnered with several organizations dedicated to raising awareness about such issues, including Hand of Hope.[9]

## Giving Trips

Aside from material shoe contributions, TOMS also held a series of "Giving Trips" that supported the broader notion of community service. Giving Trips were firsthand opportunities for employees of TOMS and selected TOMS's customers to participate in the delivery of TOMS shoes. These trips increased the transparency of TOMS's philanthropic efforts, further engaging customers and employees. They generated greater social awareness as well, since participants on these trips often became more engaged in local community service efforts at home.

From a business standpoint, the Giving Trips also represented a marketing success. First, a large number of participants were customers and journalists unassociated with TOMS who circulated their stories online through social media upon their return. Second, TOMS was able to motivate participants and candidates to become more involved in its mission by increasing public awareness. In 2013, instead of internally selecting customers to participate on the Giving Trips, TOMS opted to hold an open voting process that encouraged candidates to reach out to their known contacts and ask them to vote for their inclusion. This contest drew thousands of contestants and likely hundreds of thousands of voters, although the final vote tallies were not publicly released.

## Environmental Sustainability

Dedicated to minimizing its environmental impact, TOMS pursued a number of sustainable practices that included offering vegan shoes, incorporating recycled bottles into its products, and printing with soy ink. TOMS also used a blend of organic canvas and postconsumer recycled plastics to create shoes that were both comfortable and durable. By utilizing natural hemp and organic cotton, TOMS eliminated pesticide and insecticide use that adversely affected the environment.

In addition, TOMS supported several environmental organizations like Surfers Against Sewage, a movement that raised awareness about excess sewage discharge in the United Kingdom. TOMS was a member of the Textile Exchange, an organization dedicated to textile sustainability and protecting the environment. The company also participated actively in the AAFA's Environmental Responsibility Committee.

## Creating the TOMS Workforce

When asked what makes a great employee, Mycoskie blogged:

> As TOMS has grown, we've continued to look for these same traits in the interns and employees that we hire. Are you passionate? Can you creatively solve problems? Can you be resourceful without resources? Do you have the compassion to serve others? You can teach a new hire just about any skill . . . but you absolutely cannot inspire creativity and passion in someone that doesn't have it.[10]

The company's emphasis on creativity and passion was part of the reason that TOMS relied so heavily on interns and new hires rather than experienced workers. By hiring younger, more inexperienced employees, TOMS was able to be more cost-effective in terms of personnel. The company could also recruit young and energetic individuals who were more likely to think innovatively and out of the box. These employees were placed in specialized teams under the leadership of strong, experienced managerial talent. This human intellectual capital generated a competitive advantage for the TOMS brand.

Together with these passionate individuals, Mycoskie strove to create a familylike work atmosphere where openness and collaboration were celebrated. With his cubicle located in one of the most highly trafficked areas of the office (right next to customer service), Mycoskie made a point to interact with his employees on a daily basis, in all-staff meetings, and through weekly personal e-mails while traveling. Regarding his e-mails, Mycoskie reflected:

> I'm a very open person, so I really tell the staff what I'm struggling with and what I'm happy about. I tell them what I think the future of TOMS is. I want them to understand what I'm thinking. It's like I'm writing to a best friend.[11]

The notion of "family" was further solidified through company dinners, ski trips, and book clubs through which TOMS employees were encouraged to socialize in informal settings. These casual opportunities to interact with colleagues created a "balanced" work atmosphere where employees celebrated not only their own successes but the successes of their co-workers

Diversity and inclusion were also emphasized at TOMS. For example, cultural traditions like the Chinese Lunar New Year were celebrated publicly on the TOMS company blog. Moreover, as TOMS began expanding and distributing globally, the company increasingly sought to recruit a more diverse workforce by hiring multilingual individuals who were familiar with TOMS's diverse customer base and could communicate with its giving communities.[12]

The emphasis that Mycoskie placed on each individual employee was one of the key reasons why employees at TOMS often felt "lucky" to be part of the movement.[13] Coupled with the fact that TOMS employees knew their efforts fostered social justice, these "Agents of Change," as they referred to themselves, were generally quite satisfied with their work, making TOMS *Forbes*'s 18th "Most Inspiring Company" in 2011. Overall, the culture allowed TOMS to recruit and retain high-quality employees invested in achieving its social mission.

## FINANCIAL SUCCESS AT TOMS

While TOMS remained a privately held company with limited financial data, the estimated growth rate of TOMS's revenue was astounding. In the eight years after his company's inception, Mycoskie was able to turn his initial $300,000 investment into a company with estimated 2013 revenues of $210 million. Exhibit 4 presents the company's estimated revenues for 2006 through 2013. The exhibit also provides total footwear industry revenues for 2006 through 2013.

The fact that TOMS was able to experience consistent growth despite financial turmoil post-2008 illustrates the strength of the One for One movement to survive times of recession. Mycoskie attributed his success during the recession to two factors: (1) As consumers became more conscious of their spending during recessions, products like TOMS that gave to others actually became *more* appealing (according to Mycoskie); (2) the giving model that TOMS employed is not "priced in." Rather than commit a percentage of profits or revenues to charity, Mycoskie noted that TOMS simply gave away a pair for every pair it sold. This way, socially conscious consumers

## EXHIBIT 4 Estimated Annual Revenues for TOMS and the Footwear Industry, 2006–2013

| Year | TOMS | | Footwear Industry | |
| --- | --- | --- | --- | --- |
| | Revenue (millions) | Annual Growth Rate | Revenue (millions) | Annual Growth Rate |
| 2006 | $ 0.2 | — | $ 74 | 12.4% |
| 2007 | 1.2 | 457% | 87 | 16.8 |
| 2008 | 3.1 | 156 | 94 | 8.5 |
| 2009 | 8.4 | 168 | 98 | 4.0 |
| 2010 | 26.2 | 212 | 100 | 1.6 |
| 2011 | 43.5 | 66 | 106 | 6.2 |
| 2012 | 97.5 | 124 | 108 | 2.6 |
| 2013 | 210.0 | 115 | 117 | 7.5 |

*Source:* PrivCo; and "Global Footwear Manufacturing," *IBISWorld,* June 2, 2013, clients1.ibisworld.com/reports/gl/industry/currentperformance.aspx?entid=500.

knew exactly where their money was going without having to worry that TOMS would cut back on its charity efforts in order to turn a profit.[14]

## Production at TOMS

Although TOMS manufactured shoes in Argentina, Ethiopia, and China, only shoes made in China were brought to the retail market. Shoes made in Argentina and Ethiopia were strictly used for donation purposes. TOMS retailed its basic Alpargata shoes in the $50 price range, even though the cost of producing each pair was estimated at around $9.[15] Estimates for the costs of producing TOMS's more expensive lines of shoes were unknown, but they retailed for more than $150.

In comparison, manufacturing the average pair of Nike shoes in Indonesia cost around $20, and they were priced around $70.[16] Factoring in the giving aspect, TOMS seemed to have a slightly smaller markup than companies like Nike, yet it still maintained considerable profit margins. More detailed information on trends in TOMS's production costs and practices is limited due to the private nature of the company.

## The Future

Because demand and revenues were predicted to increase in the global footwear manufacturing industry, incumbents like TOMS needed to find ways to defend their position in the market. One method was to continue to differentiate products based on quality, image, or price. Another strategy was to focus

on R&D and craft new brands and product lines that appealed to different audiences. It was also recommended that companies investigate how to mitigate the threat posed by an increase in supply costs.

In an effort to broaden its mission and product offerings, TOMS began to expand both its consumer base and charitable-giving product lines. For its customers, TOMS started offering stylish wedges, ballet flats, and even wedding apparel in an effort to reach more customers and satisfy the special needs of current ones. For the children it sought to help, TOMS expanded past its basic, black canvas shoe offerings to winter boots in order to help keep children's feet dry and warm during the winter months in cold-climate countries.

On another front, TOMS entered the eyewear market in hopes of restoring vision to the 285 million blind or visually impaired individuals around the world. For every pair of TOMS glasses sold, TOMS restored vision to one individual either through donating prescription glasses or offering medical treatment for those suffering from cataracts and eye infections. TOMS recently focused its vision-related efforts in Nepal and planned to expand globally as the TOMS eyewear brand grew. As of 2013, TOMS had teamed up with 15 Giving Partners to help restore sight to 150,000 individuals in 13 countries. A challenge for Blake Mycoskie would be to remain focused on the company's social mission while meeting the managerial demands of a high-growth international company.

# ENDNOTES

[1] Groden, Claire. "TOMS Hits 10 Million Mark on Donated Shoes." *Time*. 26 June 2013. <http://style.time.com/2013/06/26/toms-hits-10-million-mark-on-donated-shoes/>.

[2] Mycoskie, Blake. Web log post. *The Huffington Post*. 26 May 2013. <http://www.huffingtonpost.com/blake-mycoskie/>.

[3] *501c3Lookup*. 2 June 2013. <http://501c3lookup.org/FRIENDS_OF_TOMS/>.

[4] "Global Footwear Manufacturing." *IBISWorld*. March 2014. <http://clients1.ibisworld.com/reports/gl/industry/keystatistics.aspx?entid=500>.

[5] Post by "Alexandria." *TOMS website*. 2 June 2013. <http://www.toms.com/red-canvas-classics-shoes-1>.

[6] Post by "Donna Brock." *TOMS website*. 13 January 2014. <http://www.toms.com/women/bright-blue-womens-canvas-classics>.

[7] *TOMS website*. 2 June 2013. <http://www.toms.com/our-movement-giving-partners>.

[8] "Trafficking Victims Protection Reauthorization Act." *U.S. Department of Labor.* 2 June 2013. <http://www.dol.gov/ilab/programs/ocft/tvpra.htm>. *TOMS website*. 2 June 2013. <http://www.toms.com/corporate-responsibility>.

[9] Hand of Hope. "Teaming Up with TOMS Shoes." *Joyce Meyer Ministries*. 2 June 2013. <http://www.studygs.net/citation/mla.htm>.

[10] Mycoskie, Blake. "Blake Mycoskie's Blog." *Blogspot*. 2 June 2013. <http://blakemycoskie.blogspot.com/>.

[11] Schweitzer, Tamara. "The Way I Work: Blake Mycoskie of TOMS Shoes." *Inc*. 2 June 2013.

<http://www.inc.com/magazine/20100601/the-way-i-work-blake-mycoskie-of-toms-shoes.html>.

[12] *TOMS Jobs website*. 2 June 2013. <http://www.toms.com/jobs/l>.

[13] Daniela. "Together We Travel." *TOMS Company Blog*. 3 June 2013. <http://blog.toms.com/post/36075725601/together-we-travel>.

[14] Zimmerman, Mike. "The Business of Giving: TOMS Shoes." *Success*. 2 June 2013. <http://www.success.com/articles/852-the-business-of-giving-toms-shoes>.

[15] Fortune, Brittney. "TOMS Shoes: Popular Model with Drawbacks." *The Falcon*. 2 June 2013. <http://www.thefalcononline.com/article.php?id=159>.

[16] *Behind the Swoosh*. Dir. Keady, Jim. 1995. Film.

# Samsung's Environmental Responsibility: Striking the Right Note for Corporate Survival

## Ms. Sushree Das
### Amity Research Centers

"When [Samsung's] technologies harmonize, amazing things happen. Advances in components are giving rise to a whole new era of possibility. At Samsung, we are passionate about Mobilizing Possibility. Not just for the privileged few, but possibility for all."[1]
—Dr. Stephen Woo, President of System LSI Business, Device Solutions Division, Samsung Electronics

Samsung Electronics (Samsung) was considered a pioneer in the field of electronics. It was one of the leaders in the global smartphone market because of its innovative products such as the Galaxy S. The Samsung Galaxy S2 was selected as the 'Best Smartphone of the year' in 2012, while the company was conferred with the 'Device Manufacturer of the Year' award at the Mobile World Congress in 2011. In addition, Samsung Electronics received 30 awards for innovation at the Consumer Electronics Show (CES) 2012 and 44 awards at the international iF Design Awards 2012.

In order to fulfill its environmental responsibility, Samsung Electronics introduced the 'Eco-Management 2013' initiative in 2009. As per the initiative, Samsung took up various environmental programs including reduction of greenhouse gas emissions and the development of best quality eco-friendly products. However, reports claimed that Samsung did not follow the guidelines related to environmental norms in many of its production plants. Though Samsung stepped up to compensate for the harm caused to the employees as well as repair the damages caused to the environment, apprehensions still lingered regarding its viability in the long run. The case study would be an attempt to highlight the environmental initiatives taken up by Samsung. It would also analyse the impacts of these initiatives and assess the sustainability of these initiatives.

This case was written by Sushree Das, Amity Research Centers Headquarters, Bangalore. It is intended to be used as the basis for class discussion rather than to illustrate either effective or ineffective handling of a management situation. The case was compiled from published sources. © 2013, Amity Research Centers Headquarters, Bangalore. No part of this publication may be copied, stored, transmitted, reproduced or distributed in any form or medium whatsoever without the permission of the copyright owner. Printed with permission from Amity Research Centres Headquarters and www.thecasecentre.org

# CORPORATE ENVIRONMENTAL SUSTAINABILITY: AN INSIGHT

In practice corporate environmental sustainability gained prominence in the business world since the concept of sustainable development grew in popularity during the late 1980s.[2] The mounting pressure for environmental protection forced organisations to implement a number of measures and technologies to minimise and control pollution and improve their ecological effectiveness. Of late researchers and practitioners developed several approaches for achieving corporate environmental sustainability. The approaches included eco-efficiency, triple bottom line, natural step, ecological footprint and carbon footprint, eco-effectiveness, and cradle-to-cradle design.[3] Analysts observed that these frameworks provided guidelines to reduce the ecological damage caused by organisations and offered assessment tools to support decision making by managers.[4] Through corporate sustainability, organisations were expected to generate long-term value for the consumer and the employees by adopting 'green' strategies for environmental protection and by considering the social, cultural, and economic aspects of the company's operations.

From a broader perspective, corporate sustainability described business practices revolving around social and environmental considerations. As per the Brundtland Commission's[5] Report—'Our Common Future', sustainable development was described as, "development that meets the needs of the present without compromising the ability of future generations to meet their own needs."[6] While experts analysed three strategic principles of corporate sustainable development such as transparency, employee development and resource efficiency, they highlighted the triple bottom-line approach as one of the commonly used approaches.[7] According to this approach, business goals were inseparable from the societies and environments in which they operated.[8] Analysts identified a number of organisations which accepted corporate sustainable development as a key strategy. Global companies such as Microsoft Corporation, Intel, Apple Inc, AT&T, and many other leading electronics companies focused on environmental issues in their corporate sustainability programs. (See Exhibit 1).

# SAMSUNG'S GREEN INITIATIVES: AN ASSESSMENT

Originating as a small export business in Taegu, Korea, during the 70s, Samsung Electronics (Samsung) went on to become one of the world's pioneering electronics companies.[9] Samsung was a specialist in manufacturing digital appliances and media, semiconductors, memory, and system integration. It had a wide range of businesses that connected speed and creativity and had the efficiency to invent, develop and market the products.[10] Samsung displayed all the qualities expected of a leader. It was a leader in digital technology, had ethical business practices, a wide range of companies and above all displayed global citizenship.[11] The company had a simple philosophy—to make proper utilisation of its talent and technology to create superior quality products and services for the benefit of the society across the globe. Samsung's core values consisted of its people, a passion for excellence, change and innovation, integrity in its operations, and co-prosperity.[12] Samsung's new vision for 2020 read as "Inspire the World, Create the Future", which reflected its commitment to inspire citizens by making efficient use of its strengths namely—new technology, innovative products, and creative solutions and promoting value for the industry, its partners and its employees.[13] To fulfill its vision, Samsung incorporated three strategic approaches in its management: such as creativity, partnership, and talent. Apart from this, Samsung had plans to explore new avenues in health, medicine and biotechnology.[14] As of 2011, while Samsung's total assets amounted to $343.7 billion, the net sales were recorded as $220.1 billion and net income was $21.2 billion.[15] As part of this vision, Samsung aimed to generate revenue of $400 billion and achieve the position among the world's top five brands by 2020.[16]

As a responsible global citizen, Samsung made efforts to generate economic profits and at the same time endeavoured to tackle global issues such as social, economic and environmental issues.[17] The key elements of its sustainability management agenda included the economic, social and environmental aspects of its operations. The organisation laid strong emphasis on shared growth in its business management. As part of its shared growth initiatives, Samsung introduced programmes such as 'Globally

# EXHIBIT 1    CER Activities of Selected Leading Companies

| Company | Activity/Performance |
|---|---|
| Intel | • At the end of 2011, Intel reduced their absolute emissions more than 60% below 2007 levels. In the same time frame, its annual revenue increased by 41%.<br>• In 2010 and 2011 new videoconferencing facilities resulted in cost savings of over $114 million and the avoidance of more than 87,500 metric tons of $CO_2$ emissions. |
| Apple Inc | • Apple's designers and engineers pioneered the development of smaller, thinner, and lighter products in 2011, thereby generating fewer carbon emissions.<br>• In addition to eliminating toxins and designing products with highly recyclable aluminum enclosures, Apple used recycled plastics, recycled paper, biopolymers, and vegetable-based inks in its products.<br>• Apple's global recycling exceeded its 70% goal in 2011.<br>• In 2011, there was a 61% increase in participation in the Commute Alternatives program which offered transit options that reduced traffic, smog, and $CO_2$ emissions associated with the use of single-occupancy vehicles. |
| Microsoft Corporation | • Saved resources by developing modular data centers that used up to 50% less energy and consumed only 1% of the water of traditional data centers.<br>• Helped reduce its reliance on electricity generated from coal and other traditional energy sources by purchasing more than 1.1 billion kilowatt-hours of green power in FY12.<br>• Eliminated unnecessary components from servers within its data centers, and used higher-efficiency supplies, converters, processors, and platforms. |
| AT&T | • Earned annualised savings of $86 million from 8,700 energy-saving projects implemented in 2010 and 2011.<br>• Deployed 5,114 alternative-fuel vehicles, including 3,469 CNG vehicles and 1,617 hybrid electric vehicles, as part of its $565 million commitment to deploy approximately 15,000 alternative-fuel vehicles (AFVs) over a 10-year period through 2018.<br>• Kept 50.1 million Pounds of network scrap materials out of landfills through reusing, selling and recycling materials.<br>• Collected approximately 3.0 million cell phones and 1.7 million pounds of batteries and accessories for reuse or recycling. |

*Source:* Compiled by the author from various sources.

Competitive SMEs', a 'Supplier Support Fund' and 'New Technology Development Contest' to facilitate financial assistance.[18] Samsung also took up measures for the benefit of second and third-tier suppliers from its shared growth initiatives. In 2011, Samsung launched a program titled 'Samsung Hope for Children' which dealt with various social contribution activities.[19] The programs included activities such as 'Hope Children's Learning Center' for students coming from low income households and the 'Stepping Stone Scholarship Program' for college students with disabilities. These programmes were organised in different regions of the world with the sole purpose of focusing on health and education of children and youth.[20]

Besides showing its concern towards social issues, Samsung was also aware of its responsibilities towards the environment. It not only practiced environmental leadership at the global level, but also demonstrated environmental leadership and citizenship in its own facilities, operations, and supply chain. The organisation worked to measure, report, and reduce its environmental impacts across all its operations. As per the 18th version of the 'Guide to Greener Electronics' published by Greenpeace International in November 2012, Samsung moved up to the 7th rank, with an overall score of 4.2 points in its performance scorecard[21] (See Exhibit 2). The guide ranked 16 global electronics companies considering their commitment and growth in three environment

**EXHIBIT 2    2012 Ranking of Electronics Companies**

| Rank | Companies | Points out of 10 |
|------|-----------|------------------|
| 1 | WIPRO | 7.1 (new) |
| 2 | HP | 5.7 (↓) |
| 3 | NOKIA | 5.4 (↑) |
| 4 | ACER | 5.1 (↑) |
| 5 | DELL | 4.6 (↓) |
| 6 | APPLE | 4.5 (↓) |
| 7 | **SAMSUNG** | 4.2 (↑) |
| 8 | SONY | 4.1 (↑) |
| 9 | LENOVO | 3.9 (↓) |
| 10 | PHILIPS | 3.8 (↓) |
| 11 | PANASONIC | 3.6 (↓) |
| 12 | LGE | 3.5 (↑) |
| 13 | HCL INFOSYSTEMS | 3.1 (new) |
| 13 | SHARP | 3.1 (↓) |
| 15 | TOSHIBA | 2.3 (↓) |
| 16 | RIM | 2.0 (↓) |

*Source:* Compiled from "Guide to Greener Electronics," http://www.greenpeace.org/international/en/campaigns/climate-change/cool-it/Campaign-analysis/Guide-to-Greener-Electronics/, November 2012.

criteria such as energy and climate, greener products and sustainable operations[22] (**Exhibit 3**). Samsung performed well on product life cycle criteria, as it provided detailed information on spare parts to extend product lifetime. Besides, Samsung almost scored maximum points on energy efficiency. The energy score increased as it continued to disclose information on its GHG emissions information, including its supply chain data. Samsung also scored major points for sustainable operations due to its relatively good e-waste take-back programme.[23]

Samsung strongly believed that it had the responsibility to run its operations in the most enriching ways. With this belief, Samsung carried out a range of environmental activities around the world (**Exhibit 4**). In 2009, Samsung established a mid-term environmental plan, Eco-Management 2013 (EM 2013), and accordingly framed strategies to achieve sustainable development.[24] The company manufactured eco-friendly products and was dedicated to products stewardship throughout the entire life cycle of its products.[25] Samsung's operations were guided by its focus on enhancement of a greener environment through greening of not only its products and technologies, but also the workplace and the communities. The company reiterated its concern for the environment through the 'PlanetFirst' approach.[26] It was a basic commitment that Samsung believed was essential for consumers to strike a balance between their aspiration for cutting edge technology and leading a greener way of life. Samsung made regular investments in green management. As of 2011, Samsung witnessed an increase of 86% in green investment compared to 2010.[27]

As part of its Vision 2020, Samsung identified climate change and energy management as one of its important management priorities.[28] The company implemented a number of measures to improve energy efficiency and developed technologies to reduce greenhouse gas (GHG) emissions (**Exhibit 5**). As per the mid-term environmental plan, Samsung set up a greenhouse gas emission management system to monitor direct as well as indirect sources of emissions related to all its business activities as well as its global partners'.[29] Samsung adopted a number of measures to accomplish its mid-term target of 50% reduction in GHG emissions by 2013 in comparison to 2008.[30] With respect to limiting electricity consumption during use of products, Samsung invested in developing energy efficient products. Moreover, the company participated in a carbon footprint labeling scheme set up by the Ministry of Environment in Korea as well as the one that was established by the Carbon Trust in the U.K.[31] The objective of the scheme was to convince manufacturers to reduce carbon emissions from their products by revealing information regarding GHG emissions through labeling and persuade consumers to purchase low carbon products. In 2011, Samsung Electronics selected around 2,630 models for eco-product labeling.[32] Samsung also took steps to monitor its carbon emissions emanating from transportation of its products, as well as supplier activities and business travel by employees.[33]

Achieving a 100% eco-product along with a 40% enhancement in energy efficiency rate were considered to be the key performance indicators for EM2013.[34] In 2011, the good eco-product and good eco-device rates crossed the specified targets and increased to 97% and 85% respectively.[35] Likewise product energy efficiency also went up by 25.6% in 2011.[36] Further, Samsung implemented the 'Eco-Design process' to address

## EXHIBIT 3   Samsung's Performance (as of November 2012)

| SAMSUNG | | ZERO | LOW | MEDIUM | HIGH |
|---|---|---|---|---|---|
| ENERGY | Disclose and set targets for operational GHG emissions and RE supply | | ■ | | |
| | Disclose and set targets for supply chain GHG emissions and RE supply | | ■ | | |
| | Clean Electricity Plan (CEP) | | ■ | | |
| | Clean Energy Policy Advocacy | | ■ | | |
| PRODUCTS | Product energy efficiency | | | ■ | |
| | Avoidance of hazardous substances in products | | ■ | | |
| | Use of recycled plastic in products | | ■ | | |
| | Product life cycle | | | ■ | |
| OPERATIONS | Chemicals management and advocacy | | | ■ | |
| | Policy and practice on sustainable sourcing of fibres for paper | | ■ | | |
| | Policy and practice on avoidance of conflict minerals | | ■ | | |
| | Provides effective voluntary take-back where there are no EPR laws | | | ■ | |

Source: "SAMSUNG'S PERFORMANCE IN DETAIL," http://www.greenpeace.org/international/en/Guide-to-Greener-Electronics/18th-Edition/SAMSUNG/, November 2012.

## EXHIBIT 4   Samsung's Green Management Policies

| | |
|---|---|
| **Global Green Management System** | Establish a top-class global green management system, ensure full compliance of all environment safety and health regulations in all our operation sites and enforce strict internal standards. |
| **Life Cycle Responsibility for Products and Services** | Take full responsibility for ensuring minimum environmental impact and the highest safety in all stages of the product life cycle including purchasing of parts/raw materials, development, manufacturing, transfer, product use and end-of-life. |
| **Green Manufacturing Process** | Establish manufacturing processes that minimize the release of greenhouse gas emissions and pollutants by employing best available clean manufacturing technologies that enable efficient resource and energy management. |
| **Zero-Accident Green Operation Sites** | Create recycling-centric production facilities and safe workplaces where wastes are recycled and accident prevention measures are implemented to ensure the health and safety of all employees. |
| **Preservation of the Global Environment** | Take actions to tackle climate change and protect local communities as well as the global environment. Disclose green management policies and achievements to both internal and external stakeholders. |

Source: "Global Harmony with people, society & environment," http://www.samsung.com/us/aboutsamsung/sustainability/sustainabilityreports/download/2012/2012_sustainability_rpt.pdf, 2012.

## EXHIBIT 5   Climate Change and Energy Management Activities in Samsung

- Installed F-gas treatment equipment to reduce SF6 and PFCs gases from the LCD and semiconductor manufacturing process which was equivalent to a reduction of one million and thirty thousand tons of CO2.

- Various energy efficiency improvement measures, including replacement with energy-efficient equipment system, installation of high efficiency transformers, and waste heat recovery facilities, were implemented which led to a reduction of 370 thousand tons of CO2. As a result, the company achieved its annual reduction targets since 2009 and achieved a 40% reduction in CO2 emissions intensity in 2011 compared to 2008.

- The estimated CO2 emission associated with use of Samsung products reduced by 17.63 million tons of CO2 in 2011 compared to 2008, with an estimated accumulated reduction of 32.92 million tons of CO2 during 2009–11.

- Optimised operation of manufacturing and utility facilities, introduced high energy efficient facilities, and waste heat recycling facilities to achieve the goal of a 2.5% reduction per year.

- Samsung Electronics first participated in the Korean scheme in 2009 and received the first carbon footprint reduction label for a LED TV, a Note PC and a memory chip product. Galaxy SII smartphone and Galaxy Note also became the first product in their category to receive a Carbon Footprint label issued by the Carbon Trust.

- Eliminated Polyvinyl Chloride (PVC) and brominated flame retardants (BFRs) in all mobile phones and MP3 players sold from April, 2010. For notebook PCs, it launched the first PVC-free and BFRs-free in October 2010, and eliminated PVC and BFRs in all 15 notebook PC models released in 2011.

- Reduced business travel-related emissions through measures including the encouragement of the use of mass transport and video-conferencing systems.

- Samsung received ISO 50001 certification in 2011 for Gumi, Giheung, Hwasung, Onyang and Tangjung plants in Korea. Also received 'Carbon Trust Standard' certification in April 2012 for significant GHG reductions achieved by all eight production plants in Korea.

*Source:* Compiled by the author from "Global Harmony with people, society & environment", http://www.samsung.com/us/aboutsamsung/sustainability/sustainabilityreports/download/2012/2012_sustainability_rpt.pdf, 2012.

energy efficiency and standby power of its products.[37] This was followed by its take back and global recycling programs. The company managed to increase the use of recycled plastic by 2.26%.[38] It continued to reduce its energy consumption from its operations and products to respond to the challenges thrown by climate change. In addition, to facilitate on-site energy management, Samsung adopted energy cost rate (%) to assess the financial benefits of reduction in energy consumption.[39] Furthermore, Samsung launched an Environmental Health & Safety (EHS) Certification management programme in its operation sites and earned ISO 14001 and OHSAS 18001 certifications.[40] Samsung planned to receive ISO 50001 certification in its units by 2015 with the objective of setting up a systematic energy management structure.[41]

Moreover, sustainable water management became an important global environmental issue for all electronic companies. Analysts observed that, the semiconductor industry consumed 7,500 to 15,000 tons of ultra pure water on a daily basis, which was sufficient to sustain a city with 50,000 residents per day.[42] Being a leading manufacturer of semiconductors, Samsung took up the responsibility to be an effective contributor to water resources management (**Exhibit 6**). For this the company incorporated water management policies in its agenda, and specified the reduction targets and strategies for preservation of sustainable water resources. With the goal of maximising water efficiency, Samsung Electronics established a 3% water usage reduction target per production unit by 2015.[43] After collecting the necessary data on water usage, Samsung identified plants where use of water was maximum, set up a monitoring structure, planned various reduction measures, and then implemented the most cost effective measures to curtail business risks related to water use and its environmental impacts. Samsung adopted new technologies to reduce discharge of water pollutants. In 2011 the company achieved a 30% reduction in water pollution by improving the efficiency of waste water processing facilities.[44]

In addition to water management, Samsung also had in place a waste management policy. It focused on enhancement of waste recycling and reduction of waste generation. In 2011, the company started recycling and utilising waste glass, waste plastics, and organic sludge which used to be either burnt

## EXHIBIT 6    Water Management Activities in Samsung

- Analysed water resource risk and developed alternative water supplies as well as an emergency response system to avoid any negative impact upon business.
- Established a comprehensive water management system which reduced the cost and pressure on water resources.
- Achieved reduction in water use by collecting ultra pure water used for the semiconductor and LCD production process and reusing it. The ultra pure water recycling rate at semiconductor and LCD production plants in 2011 decreased to 51% as compared to 2010 levels.
- Established on-site non-industrial waste water treatment and recycling facilities to reduce water use and sewage discharge.
- Samsung Electronics plant in India installed a rainwater collection system and used the collected rainwater for gardening and cleaning.
- Increasing waste water recycling rate by installing organic waste treatment and water recycling facilities to reduce discharge of water pollutants.

*Source:* Compiled by the author from "Global Harmony with people, society & environment", http://www.samsung.com/us/aboutsamsung/sustainability/sustainabilityreports/download/2012/2012_sustainability_rpt.pdf, 2012.

## EXHIBIT 7    Process of Strategy Development at Samsung

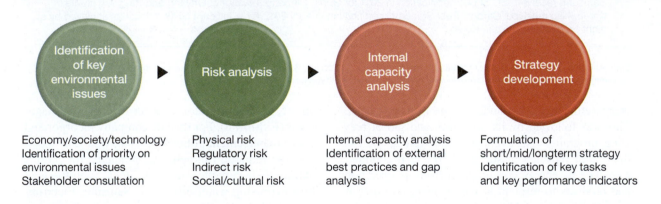

| Identification of key environmental issues | Risk analysis | Internal capacity analysis | Strategy development |
|---|---|---|---|
| Economy/society/technology Identification of priority on environmental issues Stakeholder consultation | Physical risk Regulatory risk Indirect risk Social/cultural risk | Internal capacity analysis Identification of external best practices and gap analysis | Formulation of short/mid/longterm strategy Identification of key tasks and key performance indicators |

*Source:* "Global Harmony with people, society & environment", http://www.samsung.com/us/aboutsamsung/sustainability/sustainabilityreports/download/2012/2012_sustainability_rpt.pdf, 2012.

or landfilled earlier. As per EM2013, Samsung aimed to achieve a waste recycling rate of 95% and a recycling-oriented waste management system to minimise waste generation. Its objective was to set a waste reduction target of 10% annually till 2015.[45] Besides, Samsung also strived to control handling of hazardous materials in its production units in compliance with Restriction of Hazardous Substances (RoHS)[46] regulation.[47] Regular inspection of storage facilities was carried out and adequate training was provided to workers handling the materials to prevent accidental leakage of hazardous materials. Samsung also continued to minimise the use of ozone depleting substances which were used as refrigerants and fire extinguishing agents in freezers and fire control systems respectively.[48]

Apart from these initiatives, Samsung also had a green communication system through which information and ideas on environmental affairs was exchanged. Employees were encouraged to live a greener life-style. Environmental education classes for children of employees were conducted and campaigns consisting of students, non-governmental organisations and green activists were flagged off. Samsung formulated green management strategies by assessing the impact on the environment and the management risks associated with the impacts **(Exhibit 7).**

**EXHIBIT 8**   **Climate Change Response—Risks and Opportunity Analysis**

| Category | Type of Risks | Opportunities | Risk Management Activities |
|---|---|---|---|
| Regulatory Risks | • Emission trading scheme<br>• Emission reporting obligations<br>• Product efficiency regulations and standards<br>• Product labeling regulations and standards<br>• Uncertainty on new regulations | • GHG Emissions trading scheme<br>• Product efficiency regulations and standards<br>• Voluntary agreements | • Developing CDM project within semiconductor manufacturing process<br>• Improving transparency on GHG emissions data through third party verification<br>• Increasing R&D on energy efficiency improvement on products and receiving energy marks<br>• Increasing number of eco-label certified products<br>• Monitoring on global environmental regulations |
| Physical Risks | • Change in precipitation and drought | • Extreme weather events<br>• Air and water pollution | • Identification of risks and response manuals on site facilities through regular/special review and 3rd party audit |
| Other Risks | • Reputation<br>• Change in consumer behavior | • Increased consumer demand on low carbon products<br>• Increase of brand value as a low carbon and energy efficient product provider<br>• Reduction in operation cost by improving energy efficiency of equipments | • Strategic response to Eco-Product exhibition and evaluations<br>• Developing products using insight from consumer research |

*Source:* "Global Harmony with people, society & environment", http://www.samsung.com/us/aboutsamsung/sustainability/sustainabilityreports/download/2012/2012_sustainability_rpt.pdf, 2012.

Samsung took up measures to reduce the negative impacts of its operations on the environment by analysing the opportunities and the risks associated with it. The risks included physical risks, regulatory risks, indirect and socio-cultural risks and were analysed with respect to all the green management activities.[49] Identification of risks associated with green management strategies led to the creation of the Green Management Committee whose objective was to approve the green management policies, review performance and take decisions on the establishment of new measures.[50] Samsung set up a Climate Change Response Committee to look into issues related to GHG emissions and energy management, as well as an Eco Council to look

into issues concerning eco-product development and green operations at the production units.[51] With respect to climate change response strategies, Samsung identified the opportunities associated with climate change and the risks associated with its impacts[52] (**Exhibit 8**).

Samsung adopted cost effective measures to minimise business risks associated with water use and environmental impact. While identifying the risk, the company turned the surplus water supply into an emergency response system to avoid any negative impact on its business. They expanded monitoring efforts to collect data from the production units and other facilities to verify the reliability of efficient water consumption. Additionally, Samsung monitored waste processing companies by visiting the site and checking their waste processing methods to stop illegal processing and illegal shipping of waste. Likewise, recognising the risks of waste water discharge and its impact on the environment, Samsung promoted ecosystem restoration projects and water conservation activities in its domestic as well as overseas operation sites. Further, Samsung implemented the 'Eco-Design Assessment process' through which environmental impact assessment at the product development stage became a mandatory requirement. Likewise the 'Eco-Design System (EDS)' enabled the execution of an 'Eco-Product Rating Program' for assessing the green attributes of each development project.

## THE ROAD AHEAD

In recognition of Samsung's green management practices, four of Samsung's products received Eco Design awards at the Consumer Electronics Show (CES) 2012.[53] Samsung received the Energy Star Partner of the Year award by the U.S. Environmental Protection Agency (EPA).[54] Moreover, the China Europe International Business School (CEBIS) identified Samsung as one of the 100 green foreign companies operating in China.[55] In spite of all its achievements, Samsung's practices were criticised by some organisations. Reports revealed that Samsung had violated labour rights and health rights of employees and was involved in environmental violations. In some of its production units, Samsung was said to have neglected unsafe working conditions, employed children as labourers, and illegally dumped hazardous waste.[56]

Moreover, in its sustainability report of 2011, Samsung mentioned that it had removed all brominated flame retardants (BFRs) and polyvinyl chloride (PVCs) from its mobile phones and several other products. However, Public Eye, which was a Switzerland based whistle-blower organisation and was organised by Greenpeace, emphasised that they had found certain cancer-causing solvents in some random samples and that Samsung had not disclosed information regarding 10 of 83 chemicals.[57] Further, Public Eye, whose objective was to criticise global businesses that operated with a profit motive and neglected their social responsibilities, claimed that Samsung "uses banned and highly-toxic substances in its factories, without informing and/or protecting its workers . . . Samsung has a history of over 50 years of environmental pollution, trade union repression, corruption and tax flight."[58] Furthermore, while Public Eye accused Samsung of around 140 cases of cancer as well as 50 deaths due to unsafe working conditions, it argued that its no-union policy covered the truth and obstructed investigation of the cases.[59]

Meanwhile, there were accusations that toxics were found in the cleaning rooms in Samsung facilities.[60] Worker groups in South Korea reported many cases of brain cancer and other serious diseases such as leukemia and lymphoma. Employees working at Samsung's semiconductor units and other chemically-intensive manufacturing units became victims of such diseases.[61] The occurrence of cancer among Samsung's employees was tracked by Dr. Jeong-ok Kong (Kong), an occupational health physician who worked for the Korea Institute of Labor Safety and Health (KILSH) and other non-profit organisations. Kong reported that most of the employees who were afflicted with serious diseases worked in Samsung's semiconductor plants.[62] These findings were reiterated by Supporters of Health and Rights of People in the Semiconductor Industry[63] (SHARPS).[64] However the accusations and the findings of the reports were rejected by Samsung officials. Reuben Staines (Staines), member of Samsung's corporate communications team in Seoul, was quoted as saying, "Samsung maintains a world-class environment, health, and safety infrastructure, and we continually make improvements and enhancements to ensure that it is state-of-the-art. We make these ongoing investments in the normal course of business, which includes careful review and implementation of recommendations that are presented to us through credible research."[65]

In addition, analysts raised concerns regarding the disclosure of used chemicals in products. Democratic Party Lawmaker Lee Mi-kyung (Lee) clarified this by saying that disclosure regarding used chemicals in the US was mandatory.[66] While the American branch of Samsung in USA followed this, its South Korean branch did not. Lee stressed that the company was expected to be more transparent in its operations.[67] While a news daily reported in 2011 that, Samsung was willing to bear the treatment costs of the cancer patients employed at its semiconductor and LCD plants, it also said that the eligibility conditions to avail this compensation package were so severe that many employees could not receive the treatment.[68] Reacting to this statement, Staines clarified that Samsung "has strengthened its support programs for employees who have developed serious illnesses" and that "the company is committed to providing support for hospital expenses and living expenses."[69] Likewise, members belonging to the Samsung Accountability Campaign alleged that the company operated "with impunity" and called it "one of the most corrupt operations on the planet."[70]

While many global electronics companies were successful in eliminating toxic chemicals from the products manufactured by them, their manufacturing and supply chains still relied on energy sources which contributed to climate change.[71] At the same time many of these companies lagged behind in effectively managing their e-waste. With the rapid growth of such companies, analysts were of the opinion that only corporate environmental leadership could prevent a rise in e-waste and ensure that the industry shifted its focus on using clean energy to manufacture

necessary products.[72] They also observed that since electronics companies gained political power in several countries, their support for clean energy had the potential to impact government policy.[73] Analysts were apprehensive that even if Samsung initiated measures to reduce its environmental footprint, they were uncertain about the viability of these initiatives in the long run. They raised questions regarding Samsung's ability to strike the right note for corporate survival. Nevertheless, Greenpeace International IT analyst Casey Harrell expressed some amount of optimism in Samsung's efforts by saying, "Given the massive energy crisis around the world including caused by depleting & polluting fossil fuel, the next big environmental challenge for consumer electronics companies is to reduce their carbon pollution."[74] He further added, "Companies should work with their suppliers to implement more efficient manufacturing processes and to power the supply chain with renewable energy, not fossil fuels, just as they have successfully done to reduce the toxic materials in electronics."[75]

## ENDNOTES

[1] "Components As Driver for Mobile Innovations: Samsung CES Keynote", http://www.samsungvillage.com/blog/2013/01/samsungblog-components-as-driver-for-mobile-innovations-samsung-ces-keynote.html#more, January 10th 2013

[2] Pogutz Stefano, et al., "Corporate Environmental Sustainability Beyond Organizational Boundaries: Market Growth, Ecosystems Complexity and Supply Chain Structure as Co-Determinants of Environmental Impact", http://www.environmentalmanager.org/wp-content/uploads/2011/09/Article4Winn2.pdf, 2011

[3] ibid.

[4] ibid.

[5] Formally known as the World Commission on Environment and Development (WCED), the Brundtland Commission's mission is to unite countries to pursue sustainable development together.

[6] "Report of the World Commission on Environment and Development: Our Common Future", http://www.un-documents.net/wced-ocf.htm

[7] "Corporate Environmental Sustainability Beyond Organizational Boundaries: Market Growth, Ecosystems Complexity and Supply Chain Structure as Co-Determinants of Environmental Impact", op.cit.

[8] ibid.

[9] "History", http://www.samsung.com/in/aboutsamsung/corporateprofile/history.html

[10] "Our Businesses", http://www.samsung.com/in/aboutsamsung/ourbusinesses/index.html

[11] "Corporate Profile", http://www.samsung.com/in/aboutsamsung/corporateprofile/index.html

[12] "Value & Philosophy", http://www.samsung.com/in/aboutsamsung/corporateprofile/valuesphilosophy.html

[13] "Vision", http://www.samsung.com/in/aboutsamsung/corporateprofile/vision.html

[14] ibid.

[15] "Samsung Profile", http://www.samsung.com/in/aboutsamsung/corporateprofile/ourperformance/samsungprofile.html

[16] "Vision", op.cit.

[17] "Our Sustainability Reports", http://www.samsung.com/in/aboutsamsung/citizenship/oursustainabilityreports.html

[18] "Global Harmony with people, society & environment", http://www.samsung.com/us/aboutsamsung/sustainability/sustainabilityreports/download/2012/2012_sustainability_rpt.pdf, 2012

[19] ibid.

[20] ibid.

[21] "SAMSUNG'S PERFORMANCE IN DETAIL", http://www.greenpeace.org/international/en/Guide-to-Greener-Electronics/18th-Edition/SAMSUNG/, November 2012

[22] "Wipro ranks top by Greenpeace International", http://www.indiainfoline.com/Markets/News/

Wipro-ranks-top-by-Greenpeace-International/5544371063, November 19th 2012

[23] "Global Harmony with people, society & environment", op.cit.

[24] "Environment", http://www.samsung.com/in/aboutsamsung/citizenship/environment.html

[25] "Environment", op.cit.

[26] ibid.

[27] "Global Harmony with people, society & environment", op.cit.

[28] ibid.

[29] ibid.

[30] ibid.

[31] ibid.

[32] ibid.

[33] "Global Harmony with people, society & environment", op.cit.

[34] ibid.

[35] ibid.

[36] ibid.

[37] ibid.

[38] ibid.

[39] "Global Harmony with people, society & environment", op.cit.

[40] ibid.

[41] ibid.

[42] ibid.

[43] ibid.

[44] ibid.

[45] "Global Harmony with people, society & environment", op.cit.

[46] Restriction of Hazardous Substances Directive or RoHS was adopted in February 2003 by the European Union. The directive restricts the use of six hazardous materials in the manufacture of various types of electronic and electrical equipment.

[47] "Global Harmony with people, society & environment", op.cit.

[48] ibid.

[49] ibid.

[50] ibid.

[51] ibid.

[52] ibid.

[53] "Global Harmony with people, society & environment", op.cit.

[54] ibid.

[55] ibid.

[56] Hayley Tsukayama, "Apple report reveals labor, environmental violations", http:// articles.washingtonpost.com/2012-01-13/ business/35438777_l_apple-suppliers-apple-report-shaw-wu, January 13th 2012

[57] Daniele, "Samsung under Public Eye", http://asia-gazette.com/news/south-korea/79, November 1st 2012

[58] ibid.

[59] ibid.

[60] Grossman Elizabeth, "Toxics in the 'Clean Rooms': Are Samsung Workers at Risk?", http://e360.yale.edu/feature/toxics_in_the_clean_rooms_are_samsung_workers_at_risk/2414/, June 9th 2011

[61] ibid.

[62] ibid.

[63] SHARPS is composed of independent labor unions (KCTU), human right groups, occupational safety and health (OSH) groups, progressive political parties, and workers' organizations against Samsung.

[64] "Toxics in the 'Clean Rooms': Are Samsung Workers at Risk?", op.cit.

[65] "Toxics in the 'Clean Rooms': Are Samsung Workers at Risk?", op.cit.

[66] "Samsung under Public Eye", op.cit.

[67] ibid.

[68] ibid.

[69] "Toxics in the 'Clean Rooms': Are Samsung Workers at Risk?", op.cit.

[70] "Samsung under Public Eye", op.cit.

[71] "Wipro ranks top by Greenpeace International", op.cit.

[72] ibid.

[73] ibid.

[74] ibid.

[75] ibid.

# Guide to Case Analysis

*I keep six honest serving men*
*(They taught me all I knew);*
*Their names are What and Why and When;*
*And How and Where and Who.*

*Rudyard Kipling*

In most courses in strategic management, students use cases about actual companies to practice strategic analysis and to gain some experience in the tasks of crafting and implementing strategy. A case sets forth, in a factual manner, the events and organizational circumstances surrounding a particular managerial situation. It puts readers at the scene of the action and familiarizes them with all the relevant circumstances. A case on strategic management can concern a whole industry, a single organization, or some part of an organization; the organization involved can be either profit seeking or not-for-profit. The essence of the student's role in case analysis is to *diagnose* and *size up* the situation described in the case and then to *recommend* appropriate action steps.

# WHY USE CASES TO PRACTICE STRATEGIC MANAGEMENT?

> A student of business with tact
> Absorbed many answers he lacked.
> But acquiring a job,
> He said with a sob,
> "How does one fit answer to fact?"

The foregoing limerick was used some years ago by Professor Charles Gragg to characterize the plight of business students who had no exposure to cases.[1] The facts are that the mere act of listening to lectures and sound advice about managing does little for anyone's management skills and that the accumulated managerial wisdom cannot effectively be passed on by lectures and assigned readings alone. If anything had been learned about the practice of management, it is that a storehouse of ready-made textbook answers does not exist. Each managerial situation has unique aspects, requiring its own diagnosis, judgment, and tailor-made actions. Cases provide would-be managers with a valuable way to practice wrestling with the actual problems of actual managers in actual companies.

The case approach to strategic analysis is, first and foremost, an exercise in learning by doing. Because cases provide you with detailed information about conditions and problems of different industries and companies, your task of analyzing company after company and situation after situation has the twin benefit of boosting your analytical skills and exposing you to the ways companies and managers actually do things. Most college students have

limited managerial backgrounds and only fragmented knowledge about companies and real-life strategic situations. Cases help substitute for on-the-job experience by (1) giving you broader exposure to a variety of industries, organizations, and strategic problems; (2) forcing you to assume a managerial role (as opposed to that of just an onlooker); (3) providing a test of how to apply the tools and techniques of strategic management; and (4) asking you to come up with pragmatic managerial action plans to deal with the issues at hand.

## Objectives of Case Analysis

Using cases to learn about the practice of strategic management is a powerful way for you to accomplish five things:[2]

1. Increase your understanding of what managers should and should not do in guiding a business to success.
2. Build your skills in sizing up company resource strengths and weaknesses and in conducting strategic analysis in a variety of industries and competitive situations.
3. Get valuable practice in identifying strategic issues that need to be addressed, evaluating strategic alternatives, and formulating workable plans of action.
4. Enhance your sense of business judgment, as opposed to uncritically accepting the authoritative crutch of the professor or "back-of-the-book" answers.
5. Gain in-depth exposure to different industries and companies, thereby acquiring something close to actual business experience.

If you understand that these are the objectives of case analysis, you are less likely to be consumed with curiosity about "the answer to the case." Students who have grown comfortable with and accustomed to textbook statements of fact and definitive lecture notes are often frustrated when discussions about a case do not produce concrete answers. Usually, case discussions produce good arguments for more than one course of action. Differences of opinion nearly always exist. Thus, should a class discussion conclude without a strong, unambiguous consensus on what to do, don't grumble too much when you are not told what the answer is or what the company actually did. Just remember that in the business world answers don't come in conclusive black-and-white terms. There are nearly always several feasible courses of action and approaches, each of which may work out satisfactorily. Moreover, in the business world, when one elects a particular course of action, there is no peeking at the back of a book to see if you have chosen the best thing to do and no one to turn to for a provably correct answer. The best test of whether management action is "right" or "wrong" is *results*. If the results of an action turn out to be "good," the decision to take it may be presumed "right." If not, then the action chosen was "wrong" in the sense that it didn't work out.

Hence, the important thing for you to understand about analyzing cases is that the managerial exercise of identifying, diagnosing, and recommending is aimed at building your skills of business judgment. Discovering what the company actually did is no more than frosting on the cake—the actions that company managers actually took may or may not be "right" or best (unless there is accompanying evidence that the results of their actions were highly positive).

The point is this: *The purpose of giving you a case assignment is not to cause you to run to the library or surf the Internet to discover what the company actually did but, rather, to enhance your skills in sizing up situations and developing your managerial judgment about what needs to be done and how to do it.* The aim of case analysis is for you to become actively engaged in diagnosing the business issues and managerial problems posed in the case, to propose workable solutions, and to explain and defend your assessments—this is how cases provide you with meaningful practice at being a manager.

## Preparing a Case for Class Discussion

If this is your first experience with the case method, you may have to reorient your study habits. Unlike lecture courses where you can get by without preparing intensively for each class and where you have latitude to work assigned readings and reviews of lecture notes into your schedule, a case assignment requires conscientious preparation before class. You will not get much out of hearing the class discuss a case you haven't read, and you certainly won't be able to contribute anything yourself to the discussion. What you have got to do to get ready for class discussion of a case is to study the case, reflect carefully on the situation presented, and develop some reasoned thoughts. Your goal in preparing the case should be to end up with what you think is a sound, well-supported analysis of the situation and a sound, defensible set of recommendations about which managerial actions need to be taken.

To prepare a case for class discussion, we suggest the following approach:

1. ***Skim the case rather quickly to get an overview of the situation it presents.*** This quick overview should give you the general flavor of the situation and indicate the kinds of issues and problems that you will need to wrestle with. If your instructor has provided you with study questions for the case, now is the time to read them carefully.

2. ***Read the case thoroughly to digest the facts and circumstances.*** On this reading, try to gain full command of the situation presented in the case. Begin to develop some tentative answers to the study questions your instructor has provided. If your instructor has elected not to give you assignment questions, then start forming your own picture of the overall situation being described.

3. ***Carefully review all the information presented in the exhibits.*** Often, there is an important story in the numbers contained in the exhibits. Expect the information in the case exhibits to be crucial enough to materially affect your diagnosis of the situation.

4. ***Decide what the strategic issues are.*** Until you have identified the strategic issues and problems in the case, you don't know what to analyze, which tools and analytical techniques are called for, or otherwise how to proceed. At times the strategic issues are clear—either being stated in the case or else obvious from reading the case. At other times you will have to dig them out from all the information given; if so, the study questions will guide you.

5. ***Start your analysis of the issues with some number crunching.*** A big majority of strategy cases call for some kind of number crunching—calculating assorted financial ratios to check out the company's financial condition and recent performance, calculating growth rates of sales or profits or unit volume, checking out profit margins and the makeup of the cost structure, and understanding whatever revenue-cost-profit relationships are present. See Table 1 for a summary of key financial ratios, how they are calculated, and what they show.

6. ***Apply the concepts and techniques of strategic analysis you have been studying.*** Strategic analysis is not just a collection of opinions; rather, it entails applying the concepts and analytical tools described in Chapters 1 through 12 to cut beneath the surface and produce sharp insight and understanding. Every case assigned is strategy related and presents you with an opportunity to usefully apply what you have learned. Your instructor is looking for you to demonstrate that you know how and when to use the material presented in the text chapters.

7. ***Check out conflicting opinions and make some judgments about the validity of all the data and information provided.*** Many times cases report views and contradictory opinions (after all, people don't always agree on things, and different people see the same things in different ways). Forcing you to evaluate the data and information presented in the case helps you develop your powers of inference and judgment. Asking you to resolve conflicting information "comes with the territory" because a great many managerial situations entail opposing points of view, conflicting trends, and sketchy information.

8. ***Support your diagnosis and opinions with reasons and evidence.*** The most important things to prepare for are your answers to the question "Why?" For instance, if after studying the case you are of the opinion that the company's managers are doing a poor job, then it is your answer to "Why?" that establishes just how good your analysis of the situation is. If your instructor has provided you with specific study questions for the case, by all means prepare answers that include all the reasons and number-crunching evidence you can muster to support your diagnosis. If you are using study questions provided by the instructor, *generate at least two pages of notes!*

9. ***Develop an appropriate action plan and set of recommendations.*** Diagnosis divorced from corrective action is sterile. The test of a manager is always to convert sound analysis into sound actions—actions that will produce the desired results. Hence, the final and most telling step in preparing a case is to develop an action agenda for management that lays out a set of specific recommendations on what to do. Bear in mind that proposing realistic, workable solutions is far preferable to casually tossing out off-the-top-of-your-head suggestions. Be prepared to argue why your recommendations are more attractive than other courses of action that are open.

As long as you are conscientious in preparing your analysis and recommendations, and have ample reasons, evidence, and arguments to support your views, you shouldn't fret unduly about whether what you've prepared is "the right answer" to the case. In case analysis, there is rarely just one right approach or set of recommendations. Managing companies and crafting and executing strategies are not such exact sciences that there exists a single provably correct analysis and action plan for each strategic situation. Of course, some analyses and action plans are better than others; but, in truth, there's nearly always more than one good way to analyze a situation and more than one good plan of action.

## Participating in Class Discussion of a Case

Classroom discussions of cases are sharply different from attending a lecture class. In a case class, students do most of the talking. The instructor's role is to solicit student participation, keep the discussion on track, ask "Why?" often, offer alternative views, play the devil's advocate (if no students jump in to offer opposing views), and otherwise lead the discussion. The students in the class carry the burden for analyzing the situation and for being prepared to present and defend their diagnoses and recommendations. Expect a classroom environment, therefore, that calls for your size-up of the situation, your analysis, what actions you would take, and why you would take them. Do not be dismayed if, as the class discussion unfolds, some insightful things are said by your fellow classmates that you did not think of. It is normal for views and analyses to differ and for the comments of others in the class to expand your own thinking about the case. As the old adage goes, "Two heads are better than one." So it is to be expected that the class as a whole will do a more penetrating and searching job of case analysis than will any one person working alone. This is the power of group effort, and its virtues are that it will help you see more analytical applications, let you test your analyses and judgments against those of your peers, and force you to wrestle with differences of opinion and approaches.

## TABLE 1   Key Financial Ratios: How to Calculate Them and What They Mean

| Ratio | How Calculated | What It Shows |
|---|---|---|
| **Profitability ratios** | | |
| 1. Gross profit margin | $$\frac{\text{Sales} - \text{Cost of goods sold}}{\text{Sales}}$$ | Shows the percentage of revenues available to cover operating expenses and yield a profit. Higher is better and the trend should be upward. |
| 2. Operating profit margin (or return on sales) | $$\frac{\text{Sales} - \text{Operating expenses}}{\text{Sales}}$$ or $$\frac{\text{Operating income}}{\text{Sales}}$$ | Shows the profitability of current operations without regard to interest charges and income taxes. Higher is better and the trend should be upward. |
| 3. Net profit margin (or net return on sales) | $$\frac{\text{Profits after taxes}}{\text{Sales}}$$ | Shows after-tax profits per dollar of sales. Higher is better and the trend should be upward. |
| 4. Total return on assets | $$\frac{\text{Profits after taxes} + \text{Interest}}{\text{Total assets}}$$ | A measure of the return on total monetary investment in the enterprise. Interest is added to after-tax profits to form the numerator since total assets are financed by creditors as well as by stockholders. Higher is better and the trend should be upward. |
| 5. Net return on total assets (ROA) | $$\frac{\text{Profits after taxes}}{\text{Total assets}}$$ | A measure of the return earned by stockholders on the firm's total assets. Higher is better, and the trend should be upward. |
| 6. Return on stockholder's equity (ROE) | $$\frac{\text{Profits after taxes}}{\text{Total stockholders' equity}}$$ | Shows the return stockholders are earning on their capital investment in the enterprise. A return in the 12–15% range is "average," and the trend should be upward. |
| 7. Return on invested capital (ROIC)—sometimes referred to as return on capital employed (ROCE) | $$\frac{\text{Profits after taxes}}{\text{Long-term debt} + \text{Total stockholders' equity}}$$ | A measure of the return shareholders are earning on the long-term monetary capital invested in the enterprise. A higher return reflects greater bottom-line effectiveness in the use of long-term capital, and the trend should be upward. |
| 8. Earnings per share (EPS) | $$\frac{\text{Profits after taxes}}{\text{Number of shares of common stock outstanding}}$$ | Shows the earnings for each share of common stock outstanding. The trend should be upward, and the bigger the annual percentage gains, the better. |
| **Liquidity ratios** | | |
| 1. Current ratio | $$\frac{\text{Current assets}}{\text{Current liabilities}}$$ | Shows a firm's ability to pay current liabilities using assets that can be converted into cash in the near term. Ratio should definitely be higher than 1.0; ratios of 2 or higher are better still. |
| 2. Working capital | Current assets − Current liabilities | Bigger amounts are better because the company has more internal funds available to (1) pay its current liabilities on a timely basis and (2) finance inventory expansion, additional accounts receivable, and a larger base of operations without resorting to borrowing or raising more equity capital. |
| **Leverage ratios** | | |
| 1. Total debt-to-assets ratio | $$\frac{\text{Total debt}}{\text{Total assets}}$$ | Measures the extent to which borrowed funds have been used to finance the firm's operations. Low fractions or ratios are better—high fractions indicate overuse of debt and greater risk of bankruptcy. |
| 2. Long-term debt-to-capital ratio | $$\frac{\text{Long-term debt}}{\text{Long-term debt} + \text{Total stockholders' equity}}$$ | An important measure of creditworthiness and balance sheet strength. Indicates the percentage of capital investment that has been financed by creditors and bondholders. Fractions or ratios below .25 or 25% are usually quite satisfactory since monies invested |

*(Continued)*

## TABLE 1    (Continued)

| Ratio | How Calculated | What It Shows |
|---|---|---|
| **Leverage ratios** (Continued) | | |
| | | by stockholders account for 75% or more of the company's total capital. The lower the ratio, the greater the capacity to borrow additional funds. Debt-to-capital ratios above 50% and certainly above 75% indicate a heavy and perhaps excessive reliance on debt, lower creditworthiness, and weak balance sheet strength. |
| 3. Debt-to-equity ratio | $\dfrac{\text{Total debt}}{\text{Total stockholders' equity}}$ | Should usually be less than 1.0. High ratios (especially above 1.0) signal excessive debt, lower creditworthiness, and weaker balance sheet strength. |
| 4. Long-term debt-to-equity ratio | $\dfrac{\text{Long-term debt}}{\text{Total stockholders' equity}}$ | Shows the balance between debt and equity in the firm's *long-term* capital structure. Low ratios indicate greater capacity to borrow additional funds if needed. |
| 5. Times-interest-earned (or coverage) ratio | $\dfrac{\text{Operating income}}{\text{Interest expenses}}$ | Measures the ability to pay annual interest charges. Lenders usually insist on a minimum ratio of 2.0, but ratios above 3.0 signal better creditworthiness. |
| **Activity ratios** | | |
| 1. Days of inventory | $\dfrac{\text{Inventory}}{\text{Cost of goods sold} \div 365}$ | Measures inventory management efficiency. Fewer days of inventory are usually better. |
| 2. Inventory turnover | $\dfrac{\text{Cost of goods sold}}{\text{Inventory}}$ | Measures the number of inventory turns per year. Higher is better. |
| 3. Average collection period | $\dfrac{\text{Accounts receivable}}{\text{Total sales revenues} \div 365}$ or $\dfrac{\text{Accounts receivable}}{\text{Average daily sales}}$ | Indicates the average length of time the firm must wait after making a sale to receive cash payment. A shorter collection time is better. |
| **Other important measures of financial performance** | | |
| 1. Dividend yield on common stock | $\dfrac{\text{Annual dividends per share}}{\text{Current market price per share}}$ | A measure of the return that shareholders receive in the form of dividends. A "typical" dividend yield is 2–3%. The dividend yield for fast-growth companies is often below 1% (maybe even 0); the dividend yield for slow-growth companies can run 4–5%. |
| 2. Price-earnings ratio | $\dfrac{\text{Current market price per share}}{\text{Earnings per share}}$ | P-E ratios above 20 indicate strong investor confidence in a firm's outlook and earnings growth; firms whose future earnings are at risk or likely to grow slowly typically have ratios below 12. |
| 3. Dividend payout ratio | $\dfrac{\text{Annual dividends per share}}{\text{Earnings per share}}$ | Indicates the percentage of after-tax profits paid out as dividends. |
| 4. Internal cash flow | After-tax profits + Depreciation | A quick and rough estimate of the cash the business is generating after payment of operating expenses, interest, and taxes. Such amounts can be used for dividend payments or funding capital expenditures. |
| 5. Free cash flow | After-tax profits + Depreciation − Capital expenditures − Dividends | A quick and rough estimate of the cash a company's business is generating after payment of operating expenses, interest, taxes, dividends, and desirable reinvestments in the business. The larger a company's free cash flow, the greater is its ability to internally fund new strategic initiatives, repay debt, make new acquisitions, repurchase shares of stock, or increase dividend payments. |

To orient you to the classroom environment on the days a case discussion is scheduled, we compiled the following list of things to expect:

**1.** Expect the instructor to assume the role of extensive questioner and listener.

**2.** Expect students to do most of the talking. The case method enlists a maximum of individual participation in class discussion. It is not enough to be present as a silent observer; if every student took this approach, there would be no discussion. (Thus, expect a portion of your grade to be based on your participation in case discussions.)

**3.** Be prepared for the instructor to probe for reasons and supporting analysis.

**4.** Expect and tolerate challenges to the views expressed. All students have to be willing to submit their conclusions for scrutiny and rebuttal. Each student needs to learn to state his or her views without fear of disapproval and to overcome the hesitation of speaking out. Learning respect for the views and approaches of others is an integral part of case analysis exercises. But there are times when it is OK to swim against the tide of majority opinion. In the practice of management, there is always room for originality and unorthodox approaches. So while discussion of a case is a group process, there is no compulsion for you or anyone else to cave in and conform to group opinions and group consensus.

**5.** Don't be surprised if you change your mind about some things as the discussion unfolds. Be alert to how these changes affect your analysis and recommendations (in the event you get called on).

**6.** Expect to learn a lot in class as the discussion of a case progresses; furthermore, you will find that the cases build on one another—what you learn in one case helps prepare you for the next case discussion.

There are several things you can do on your own to be good and look good as a participant in class discussions:

• Although you should do your own independent work and independent thinking, don't hesitate before (and after) class to discuss the case with other students. In real life, managers often discuss the company's problems and situation with other people to refine their own thinking.

• In participating in the discussion, make a conscious effort to contribute, rather than just talk.

There is a big difference between saying something that builds the discussion and offering a long-winded, off-the-cuff remark that leaves the class wondering what the point was.

• Avoid the use of "I think," "I believe," and "I feel"; instead, say, "My analysis shows _____" and "The company should do _____ because _____." Always give supporting reasons and evidence for your views; then your instructor won't have to ask you "Why?" every time you make a comment.

• In making your points, assume that everyone has read the case and knows what it says. Avoid reciting and rehashing information in the case—instead, use the data and information to explain your assessment of the situation and to support your position.

• Bring the printouts of the work you've done on Case-Tutor or the notes you've prepared (usually two or three pages' worth) to class and rely on them extensively when you speak. There's no way you can remember everything off the top of your head—especially the results of your number crunching. To reel off the numbers or to present all five reasons why, instead of one, you will need good notes. When you have prepared thoughtful answers to the study questions and use them as the basis for your comments, *everybody* in the room will know you are well prepared, and your contribution to the case discussion will stand out.

## Preparing a Written Case Analysis

Preparing a written case analysis is much like preparing a case for class discussion, except that your analysis must be more complete and put in report form. Unfortunately, though, there is no ironclad procedure for doing a written case analysis. All we can offer are some general guidelines and words of wisdom—this is because company situations and management problems are so diverse that no one mechanical way to approach a written case assignment always works.

Your instructor may assign you a specific topic around which to prepare your written report. Or, alternatively, you may be asked to do a comprehensive written case analysis, where the expectation is that you will (1) *identify* all the pertinent issues that management needs to address, (2) perform whatever *analysis* and *evaluation* is appropriate, and (3) propose an *action plan* and *set of recommendations* addressing the issues you have identified. In going through the exercise of identify, evaluate, and recommend, keep the following pointers in mind.[3]

**Identification**    It is essential early on in your written report that you provide a sharply focused diagnosis of strategic issues and key problems and that you demonstrate a good grasp of the company's present situation. Make sure you can identify the firm's strategy (use the concepts and tools in Chapters 1–8 as diagnostic aids) and that you can pinpoint whatever strategy implementation issues may exist (again, consult the material in Chapters 10–12 for diagnostic help). Consult the key points we have provided at the end of each chapter for further diagnostic suggestions. Consider beginning your report with an overview of the company's situation, its strategy, and the significant problems and issues that confront management. State problems/issues as clearly and precisely as you can. Unless it is necessary to do so for emphasis, avoid recounting facts and history about the company (assume your professor has read the case and is familiar with the organization).

**Analysis and Evaluation**    This is usually the hardest part of the report. Analysis is hard work! Check out the firm's financial ratios, its profit margins and rates of return, and its capital structure, and decide how strong the firm is financially. Table 1 contains a summary of various financial ratios and how they are calculated. Use it to assist in your financial diagnosis. Similarly, look at marketing, production, managerial competence, and other factors underlying the organization's strategic successes and failures. Decide whether the firm has valuable resource strengths and competencies and, if so, whether it is capitalizing on them.

Check to see if the firm's strategy is producing satisfactory results and determine the reasons why or why not. Probe the nature and strength of the competitive forces confronting the company. Decide whether and why the firm's competitive position is getting stronger or weaker. Use the tools and concepts you have learned about to perform whatever analysis and evaluation is appropriate. Work through the case preparation exercise on Case-Tutor if one is available for the case you've been assigned.

In writing your analysis and evaluation, bear in mind four things:

1. You are obliged to offer analysis and evidence to back up your conclusions. Do not rely on unsupported opinions, over-generalizations, and platitudes as a substitute for tight, logical argument backed up with facts and figures.

2. If your analysis involves some important quantitative calculations, use tables and charts to present the calculations clearly and efficiently. Don't just tack the exhibits on at the end of your report and let the reader figure out what they mean and why they were included. Instead, in the body of your report cite some of the key numbers, highlight the conclusions to be drawn from the exhibits, and refer the reader to your charts and exhibits for more details.

3. Demonstrate that you have command of the strategic concepts and analytical tools to which you have been exposed. Use them in your report.

4. Your interpretation of the evidence should be reasonable and objective. Be wary of preparing a one-sided argument that omits all aspects not favorable to your conclusions. Likewise, try not to exaggerate or overdramatize. Endeavor to inject balance into your analysis and to avoid emotional rhetoric. Strike phrases such as "I think," "I feel," and "I believe" when you edit your first draft and write in "My analysis shows" instead.

**Recommendations**    The final section of the written case analysis should consist of a set of definite recommendations and a plan of action. Your set of recommendations should address all of the problems/issues you identified and analyzed. If the recommendations come as a surprise or do not follow logically from the analysis, the effect is to weaken greatly your suggestions of what to do. Obviously, your recommendations for actions should offer a reasonable prospect of success. High-risk, bet-the-company recommendations should be made with caution. State how your recommendations will solve the problems you identified. Be sure the company is financially able to carry out what you recommend; also check to see if your recommendations are workable in terms of acceptance by the persons involved, the organization's competence to implement them, and prevailing market and environmental constraints. Try not to hedge or weasel on the actions you believe should be taken.

By all means state your recommendations in sufficient detail to be meaningful—get down to some definite nitty-gritty specifics. Avoid such unhelpful statements as "the organization should do more planning" or "the company should be more aggressive in marketing its product." For instance, if you determine that "the firm should improve its market position," then you need to set forth exactly how you think this should be done. Offer a definite agenda for action, stipulating a timetable and sequence for initiating actions, indicating priorities, and suggesting who should be responsible for doing what.

In proposing an action plan, remember there is a great deal of difference between, on the one hand, being responsible for a decision that may be costly if it proves in error and, on the other hand, casually suggesting courses of action that might be taken when you do not have to bear the responsibility for any of the consequences.

A good rule to follow in making your recommendations is: *Avoid recommending anything you would not yourself be willing to do if you were in management's shoes.* The importance of learning to develop good managerial judgment is indicated by the fact that, even though the same information and operating data may be available to every manager or executive in an organization, the quality of the judgments about what the information means and which actions need to be taken does vary from person to person.[4]

It goes without saying that your report should be well organized and well written. Great ideas amount to little unless others can be convinced of their merit—this takes tight logic, the presentation of convincing evidence, and persuasively written arguments.

## Preparing an Oral Presentation

During the course of your business career it is very likely that you will be called upon to prepare and give a number of oral presentations. For this reason, it is common in courses of this nature to assign cases for oral presentation to the whole class. Such assignments give you an opportunity to hone your presentation skills.

The preparation of an oral presentation has much in common with that of a written case analysis. Both require identification of the strategic issues and problems confronting the company, analysis of industry conditions and the company's situation, and the development of a thorough, well-thought-out action plan. The substance of your analysis and quality of your recommendations in an oral presentation should be no different than in a written report. As with a written assignment, you'll need to demonstrate command of the relevant strategic concepts and tools of analysis and your recommendations should contain

sufficient detail to provide clear direction for management. The main difference between an oral presentation and a written case is in the delivery format. Oral presentations rely principally on verbalizing your diagnosis, analysis, and recommendations and visually enhancing and supporting your oral discussion with colorful, snappy slides (usually created on Microsoft's PowerPoint software).

Typically, oral presentations involve group assignments. Your instructor will provide the details of the assignment—how work should be delegated among the group members and how the presentation should be conducted. Some instructors prefer that presentations begin with issue identification, followed by analysis of the industry and company situation analysis, and conclude with a recommended action plan to improve company performance. Other instructors prefer that the presenters assume that the class has a good understanding of the external industry environment and the company's competitive position and expect the presentation to be strongly focused on the group's recommended action plan and supporting analysis and arguments. The latter approach requires cutting straight to the heart of the case and supporting each recommendation with detailed analysis and persuasive reasoning. Still other instructors may give you the latitude to structure your presentation however you and your group members see fit.

Regardless of the style preferred by your instructor, you should take great care in preparing for the presentation. A good set of slides with good content and good visual appeal is essential to a first-rate presentation. Take some care to choose a nice slide design, font size and style, and color scheme. We suggest including slides covering each of the following areas:

- An opening slide covering the "title" of the presentation and names of the presenters.
- A slide showing an outline of the presentation (perhaps with presenters' names by each topic).
- One or more slides showing the key problems and strategic issues that management needs to address.
- A series of slides covering your analysis of the company's situation.
- A series of slides containing your recommendations and the supporting arguments and reasoning for each recommendation—one slide for each recommendation and the associated reasoning will give it a lot of merit.

You and your team members should carefully plan and rehearse your slide show to maximize impact and minimize distractions. The slide show should include all of the pizzazz necessary to garner the attention of the audience, but not so much that it distracts from the content of what group members are saying to the class. You should remember that the role of slides is to help you communicate your points to the audience. Too many graphics, images, colors, and transitions may divert the audience's attention from what is being said or disrupt the flow of the presentation. Keep in mind that visually dazzling slides rarely hide a shallow or superficial or otherwise flawed case analysis from a perceptive audience. Most instructors will tell you that first-rate slides will definitely enhance a well-delivered presentation, but that impressive visual aids, if accompanied by weak analysis and poor oral delivery, still add up to a substandard presentation.

## Researching Companies and Industries via the Internet and Online Data Services

Very likely, there will be occasions when you need to get additional information about some of the assignee cases, perhaps because your instructor has asked you to do further research on the industry or company or because you are simply curious about what has happened to the company since the case was written. These days, it is relatively easy to run down recent industry developments and to find out whether a company's strategic and financial situation has improved, deteriorated, or changed little since the conclusion of the case. The amount of information about companies and industries available on the Internet and through online data services is formidable and expanding rapidly.

It is a fairly simple matter to go to company websites, click on the investor information offerings and press release files, and get quickly to useful information. Most company websites allow you to view or print the company's quarterly and annual reports, its 10-K and 10-Q filings with the Securities and Exchange Commission, and various company press releases of interest. Frequently, a company's website will also provide information about its mission and vision statements, values statements, codes of ethics, and strategy information, as well as charts of the company's stock price. The company's recent press releases typically contain reliable information about what of interest has been going on—new product introductions, recent alliances and partnership agreements, recent acquisitions, summaries of the latest financial results, tidbits about the company's strategy, guidance about future revenues and earnings, and other late-breaking company developments. Some company web pages also include links to the home pages of industry trade associations where you can find information about industry size, growth, recent industry news, statistical trends, and future outlook. Thus, an early step in researching a company on the Internet is always to go to its website and see what's available.

**Online Data Services**    LexisNexis, Bloomberg Financial News Services, and other online subscription services available in many university libraries provide access to a wide array of business reference material. For example, the web-based LexisNexis Academic Universe contains business news articles from general news sources, business publications, and industry trade publications. Broadcast transcripts from financial news programs are also available through LexisNexis, as are full-text 10-Ks, 10-Qs, annual reports, and company profiles for more than 11,000 U.S. and international companies. Your business librarian should be able to direct you to the resources available through your library that will aid you in your research.

**Public and Subscription Websites with Good Information**    Plainly, you can use a search engine such as Google or Yahoo! or MSN to find the latest news on a company or articles written by reporters that have appeared in the business media. These can be very valuable in running down information about recent company developments. However, keep in mind that the information retrieved by a search engine is "unfiltered" and may include sources that are not reliable or that contain inaccurate or misleading information. Be wary of information provided by authors who are unaffiliated with reputable organizations or publications and articles that were published in off-beat sources or on websites with an agenda. Be especially careful in relying on the accuracy of information you find posted on various bulletin boards. Articles covering a company or issue should be copyrighted or published by a reputable source. If you are turning in a paper containing information gathered from the Internet, you should cite your sources (providing the Internet address and date visited); it is also wise to print web pages for your research file (some web pages are updated frequently).

*The Wall Street Journal, Bloomberg Businessweek, Forbes, Barron's,* and *Fortune* are all good sources of articles on companies. The online edition of *The Wall Street Journal* contains the same information that is available daily in its print version of the paper, but the WSJ website also maintains a searchable database of all *The Wall Street Journal* articles published during the past few years. *Fortune* and *Bloomberg Businessweek* also make the content of the most current issue available online to subscribers as well as provide archives sections that allow you to search for articles published during the past few years that may be related to a particular keyword.

The following publications and websites are particularly good sources of company and industry information:

> Securities and Exchange Commission EDGAR database (contains company 10-Ks, 10-Qs, etc.)
> > http://www.sec.gov/edgar/searchedgar/companysearch
> Google Finance
> > http://finance.google.com
> CNN Money
> > http://money.cnn.com
> Hoover's Online
> > http://hoovers.com
> *The Wall Street Journal Interactive Edition*
> > www.wsj.com
> *Bloomberg Businessweek*
> > www.businessweek.com and www.bloomberg.com
> *Fortune*
> > www.fortune.com
> MSN Money Central
> > http://moneycentral.msn.com
> Yahoo! Finance
> > http://finance.yahoo.com/

Some of these Internet sources require subscriptions in order to access their entire databases.

You should always explore the investor relations section of every public company's website. In today's world, these websites typically have a wealth of information concerning a company's mission, core values, performance targets, strategy, recent financial performance, and latest developments (as described in company press releases).

**Learning Comes Quickly**    With a modest investment of time, you will learn how to use Internet sources and search engines to run down information on companies and industries quickly and efficiently. And it is a skill that will serve you well into the future. Once you become familiar with the data available at the different websites mentioned above and learn how to use a search engine, you will know where to go to look for the particular information that you want. Search engines nearly always turn up too many information sources that match your request rather than too few. The trick is to learn to zero in on those most relevant to what you are looking for. Like most things, once you get a little experience under your belt on how to do company and industry research on the Internet, you will be able to readily find the information you need.

# The Ten Commandments of Case Analysis

As a way of summarizing our suggestions about how to approach the task of case analysis, we have put together what we like to call "The Ten Commandments of Case Analysis." They are shown in Table 2. If you observe all or even most of these commandments faithfully as you prepare a case either for class discussion or for a written report, your chances of doing a good job on the assigned cases will be much improved. Hang in there, give it your best shot, and have some fun exploring what the real world of strategic management is all about.

## TABLE 2   The Ten Commandments of Case Analysis

| To be observed in written reports and oral presentations, and while participating in class discussions: |
| --- |
| 1. Go through the case twice, once for a quick overview and once to gain full command of the facts. Then take care to explore the information in every one of the case exhibits. |
| 2. Make a complete list of the problems and issues that the company's management needs to address. |
| 3. Be thorough in your analysis of the company's situation (make a minimum of one to two pages of notes detailing your diagnosis). |

*(Continued)*

## TABLE 2 *(Continued)*

4. Look for opportunities to apply the concepts and analytical tools in the text chapters—all of the cases in the book have very definite ties to the material in one or more of the text chapters!!!!

5. Do enough number crunching to discover the story told by the data presented in the case. (To help you comply with this commandment, consult Table 1 in this section to guide your probing of a company's financial condition and financial performance.)

6. Support any and all off-the-cuff opinions with well-reasoned arguments and numerical evidence. Don't stop until you can purge "I think" and "I feel" from your assessment and, instead, are able to rely completely on "My analysis shows."

7. Prioritize your recommendations and make sure they can be carried out in an acceptable time frame with the available resources.

8. Support each recommendation with persuasive argument and reasons as to why it makes sense and should result in improved company performance.

9. Review your recommended action plan to see if it addresses all of the problems and issues you identified. Any set of recommendations that does not address all of the issues and problems you identified is incomplete and insufficient.

10. Avoid recommending any course of action that could have disastrous consequences if it doesn't work out as planned. Therefore, be as alert to the downside risks of your recommendations as you are to their upside potential and appeal.

## ENDNOTES

[1] Charles I. Gragg, "Because Wisdom Can't Be Told," in *The Case Method at the Harvard Business School,* ed. M. P. McNair (New York: McGraw-Hill, 1954), p. 11.
[2] Ibid., pp. 12–14; and D. R. Schoen and Philip A. Sprague, "What Is the Case Method?" in *The Case Method at the Harvard Business School,* ed. M. P. McNair, pp. 78–79.
[3] For some additional ideas and viewpoints, you may wish to consult Thomas J. Raymond, "Written Analysis of Cases," in *The Case Method at the Harvard Business School,* ed. M. P. McNair, pp. 139–63. Raymond's article includes an actual case, a sample analysis of the case, and a sample of a student's written report on the case.
[4] Gragg, "Because Wisdom Can't Be Told," p. 10.

# PHOTO CREDITS

Image research by David Tietz/Editorial Image, LLC.

### CHAPTER 1

Opener: © Greg Hargreaves/Getty Images; p. 6: © McGraw-Hill Education/John Flournoy, photographer; p. 11: © Eric Carr/Alamy.

### CHAPTER 2

Opener: © Fanatic Studio/Getty Images; p. 26: © George Frey/Getty Images; p. 29: © McGraw-Hill Education/Andrew Resek, photographer; p. 39 (top): © Jason Reed/Reuters/Corbis; p. 39 (bottom): © Jay Mallin/Bloomberg via Getty Images.

### CHAPTER 3

Opener: © Bull's Eye/Imagezoo/Getty Images.

### CHAPTER 4

Opener: © Matt Zumbo/Getty Images; p. 101: © Sean Pavone/Alamy.

### CHAPTER 5

Opener: © Digital Vision/Getty Images; p. 123: © McGraw-Hill Education/John Flournoy, photographer; p. 133: © Huntstock/Getty Images; p. 135: © Martin Klimek/Newscom; p. 137: © David Paul Morris/Getty Images.

### CHAPTER 6

Opener: © Bull's Eye/Imagezoo/Getty Images; p. 150: © PRNewsFoto/Gilt GroupeAP Images; p. 153: © David Paul Morris/Getty Images; p. 158: © Jb Reed/Bloomberg via Getty Images; p. 163: © Aerial Archives/Alamy.

### CHAPTER 7

Opener: © Ian McKinnell/Getty Images; p. 188: © Ken James/Bloomberg via Getty Images; p. 194: © John Greim/LightRocket via Getty Images; p. 204: © Kevin Lee/Bloomberg via Getty Images.

### CHAPTER 8

Opener: © Alex Belomlinsky/Getty Images; p. 224: © McGraw-Hill Education/Eclipse Studios; p. 247: © Daniel Acker/Bloomberg via Getty Images.

### CHAPTER 9

Opener: © Fanatic Studio/Getty Images; p. 259: © Helen Sessions/Alamy; p. 266: © PRNewsFoto/Novo Nordisk/AP Images; p. 271: © Jb Reed/Bloomberg via Getty Images; p. 273: © Vivien Killilea/Getty Images.

### CHAPTER 10

Opener: © Ingram Publishing; p. 300: © Lou-Foto/Alamy; p. 303: © Kumar Sriskandan/Alamy.

### CHAPTER 11

Opener: © Bull's Eye/Imagezoo/Getty Images; p. 326: © Imaginechina/AP Images; p. 333: © Corey Lowenstein/Raleigh News & Observer/Getty Images; p. 335: © BananaStock/Jupiterimages.

### CHAPTER 12

Opener: © Fanatic Studio/Getty Images; p. 345: © George Frey/Getty Images; p. 358: © Nacho Doce/Reuters/Corbis.

### CASES

Case 3 (all photos): © Whole Foods Market®; Case 6 (all photos): © Lululemon; Case 10 (all photos): © Chipotle Mexican Grill; Case 15, p. C-212: © A.J. Strickland; Case 18, page C-281: © Vivek Prakash/Bloomberg via Getty Images; Case 25 (all photos): © Southwest Airlines; Case 30 (all photos): © TOMS.

# COMPANY INDEX

# NAME INDEX

# SUBJECT INDEX